The Diaries of a Cabinet Minister

also by Richard Crossman

PLATO TODAY
SOCRATES
GOVERNMENT AND THE GOVERNED
HOW WE ARE GOVERNED
PALESTINE MISSION
THE GOD THAT FAILED (editor)
NEW FABIAN ESSAYS (editor)
THE CHARM OF POLITICS
A NATION REBORN
PLANNING FOR FREEDOM
INSIDE VIEW: Three Lectures on
Prime Ministerial Government
THE DIARIES OF A CABINET MINISTER
(Volume One: Minister of Housing 1964–66)

RICHARD CROSSMAN

THE DIARIES

OF A

CABINET MINISTER

Volume Two

Lord President of the Council
and
Leader of the House of Commons
1966–68

HAMISH HAMILTON
and
JONATHAN CAPE

FIRST PUBLISHED 1976
© BY THE ESTATE OF R. H. S. CROSSMAN 1976

HAMISH HAMILTON LTD 90 GREAT RUSSELL STREET, LONDON WCI
JONATHAN CAPE LTD, 30 BEDFORD SQUARE, LONDON WCI

HAMISH HAMILTON ISBN 0 241 89481 6
JONATHAN CAPE ISBN 0 224 01292 4

BRITISH LIBRARY CATALOGUING IN PUBLICATION DATA

CROSSMAN, RICHARD HOWARD STAFFORD
THE DIARIES OF A CABINET MINISTER
VOL. 2. LORD PRESIDENT OF THE COUNCIL AND
LEADER OF THE HOUSE OF COMMONS, 1966–68
INDEX
ISBN 0–241–89481–6
ISBN 0–224–01292–4
I. TITLE
941.085'6'0925 DA 592
GREAT BRITAIN—HISTORY—20TH CENTURY
GREAT BRITAIN—POLITICS AND GOVERNMENT—1964

SET IN 10 PT. TIMES NEW ROMAN 2 PTS. LEADED
PRINTED IN GREAT BRITAIN
BY EBENEZER BAYLIS AND SON LTD
THE TRINITY PRESS, WORCESTER, AND LONDON

Contents

Illustrations

Editor's Note

This is the second of three volumes of *The Diaries of a Cabinet Minister*. In the Introduction to the first volume Richard Crossman speaks of his ambition to write a book which, like Bagehot's *English Constitution*,[1] would disclose the secret operations of British government. 'It could only be done,' he writes, 'by someone who knew party politics from inside, and that must include council politics, parliamentary politics and if possible the politics of Whitehall and No. 10.'

In October 1964 Crossman became a Cabinet Minister and from then until December 1970 he kept a diary, dictating it every weekend into a tape-recording machine. 'It was not very long,' he says, 'before I realized the interest of a diary which gave a daily picture of how a minister spent his time,' and he decided therefore to publish, not a book based on the diary, but the diary itself.

Crossman died on April 5th, 1974, having seen and approved the proof copy of his first volume. After sustained official objection,[2] Volume I was published in December 1975. It runs from October 1964 to August 1966, the period that he spent as Minister of Housing and Local Government. Volume II, August 1966 to April 1968, deals with his time as Lord President and Leader of the House of Commons. Volume III, April 1968 to June 1970, will describe his years as Secretary of State at the Department of Health and Social Security, and the months leading up to the General Election of June 1970.

These three volumes present a shortened version of the original tape-recorded diary. As Crossman explains in his Introduction to Volume I, since the original was 'dictated very much *ad lib* and often for two or three hours on end ... when transcribed it was hardly readable'. There is much repetition and his practice of dictating at weekly intervals meant that passages do not always fall in strict chronological order. Crossman therefore decided to 're-dictate this whole first transcript in plain intelligible English'. He himself re-arranged and revised the text of Volume I, dictating a new text with, as his criteria, faithfulness, clarity and relevance. He also edited passages that seemed libellous or in bad taste. I then checked this edited text against the

[1] London: Fontana, 1963.
[2] Chronicled in *The Crossman Affair*, Hugo Young (London: Cape, 1976).
1*

original transcription, to ensure that there were no 'improvements' and that the content, mood and balance of the original were accurately preserved.

The text of the second volume was prepared in similar fashion, but because Crossman's illness and death meant that he was unable to tidy up his own revised draft, I have completed this task. For Volume III, the months April to mid-October 1968 were prepared by Crossman; I selected, re-arranged and revised the remainder, following the diarist's own criteria.

In all three volumes I have supplied minor omissions and made stylistic clarifications and small corrections to the revised text. The account, however, is Crossman's own. There are inevitably slips and inaccuracies in a diary, especially one that is kept at weekly intervals, and students of the period may discover inconsistencies between the Crossman *Diaries* and other accounts. I have not sought to correct such discrepancies for several reasons. First of all, Richard Crossman wished his diaries to be published as soon as possible, 'so that controversy could take place while memories are still green' and to provide, quickly, a further mass of material on the basis of which academic controversy could be carried still further. A definitive check of his recollection of every meeting and every encounter would have taken many more years, even if all the documentary evidence were already available. Official papers, including Cabinet Minutes, are closed to historians for a period of thirty years after the events they record. As a former Minister, Crossman was permitted to consult the documents concerning his own period of office and the text of Volume I was checked against Cabinet Minutes, just before his death. Volumes II and III must remain unchecked until the years 1998 and 2000, as the Cabinet Office have not been able to extend this access to his editor.

Secondly, Crossman wanted the *Diaries* to present a direct, unvarnished picture of politics and government as he perceived and reflected on events at the time. Lastly, we agreed that annotation should be kept to a minimum. The asterisked notes are Crossman's; I am responsible for the other footnotes and the bridging passages.

Our method has its drawbacks and, for those who are interested in such methodological problems, the full text of the transcript will be permanently available at Warwick University. The advantage, however, of preparing the *Diaries* as we have done is that it fulfils Richard Crossman's aim of publishing a lucid and intricate account of a Cabinet Minister's daily life, within a reasonable time.

JANET MORGAN

1966

The Labour Government that won the general election on October 15th, 1964, after thirteen years in opposition, scraped into power with only a slim majority: 317 seats to the Conservatives' 303 and the Liberals' 9. It was not this precarious lead, however, but the country's underlying economic difficulties that provided a severe constraint on the programme of social legislation promised in the election manifesto. The incoming Prime Minister was presented with a Treasury memorandum showing an £800 million deficit on overseas payments in 1964, and even after the 'Paris Club' of central bankers agreed, early in November, to make another £142 million loan to Britain, with the prospect of a further £215 million from the I.M.F., the pound continued to weaken.

Devaluation was one possible remedy, but Harold Wilson, the Prime Minister, and James Callaghan, Chancellor of the Exchequer, did not wish to consider this. Sweeping cuts were made in defence commitments and domestic programmes—health, education, housing, social security—but, as sterling weakened, the Government had repeated recourse to foreign bankers, notably the I.M.F., for assistance. Labour's left wing became increasingly disenchanted with the new Government of which they had had such brave hopes, and resentful not only of the Government's dependence on American dollar support for the pound and its consequent pusillanimity in condemning American policy in Vietnam, but also suspicious that the Government was making tacit understandings with European bankers. In the first months of 1965 the Government introduced an Early Warning System obliging the unions to submit proposed wage claims to a Prices and Incomes Board for adjudication and in July 1966 a Prices and Incomes Bill was published, effectively delaying future wage settlements and price increases—a measure which caused the resignation of Frank Cousins, seconded from the General Secretaryship of the T.G.W.U. to the Ministry of Technology. In mid-July 1966 a package of severe deflationary measures was issued with the aim of cutting domestic demand by £600 million and overseas expenditure by £150 million. An unemployment rate of some 1½ to 2 per cent was predicted, a level that might rise during the coming winter.

Even more ominous, however, was the announcement of a six-month standstill on all wage, salary and dividend increases, to be followed by a further six months' 'severe restraint'. Price increases were to be frozen for twelve months. The Government sought voluntary support for these proposals, which were tabled as new clauses in Part IV of the Prices and Incomes Bill, still in its parliamentary Committee stage. This device was received with a great deal of hostility, but nevertheless the Bill passed through all its stages and, on August 12th, became law. Part IV of the Act, however, included a compulsory element, by which the voluntary co-operation of employers and employees could be secured if the standstill was deliberately broken. An Order in Council could be laid before Parliament and those deliberately departing from the provisions of the Act could be fined up to £500. This controversial and unpalatable legislation was to receive its first test in the autumn of 1966. At the T.U.C. Annual Conference at Blackpool in the first week of September the Prime Minister intended to make a speech emphasizing the Government's determination to make the freeze work.

Nor had the Prime Minister been able to rely on the members of his Cabinet for undivided support. At the height of the July 1966 economic crisis there had been rumours of an attempted coup for the premiership, with the Chancellor of the Exchequer designated as the chief conspirator. Since October 1964 there had been persistent tension between the Treasury and the newly created Department of Economic Affairs where from the beginning of the Labour Government's accession to power George Brown had been a vigorous First Secretary. Michael Stewart, who was appointed Secretary of State for Education in 1964, had moved to the Foreign Office in January 1965, where, though dedicated, he had lacked colour. Arthur Bottomley, as the Minister for Commonwealth Relations, had grappled with notable lack of success with the problem of the rebel regime in Rhodesia. To rebuild a stronger Cabinet, to accommodate potential rivals and their differences over the direction of policy, notably on prices and incomes and the state of the pound, on August 11th, 1966, Harold Wilson reshuffled his Cabinet. George Brown became Foreign Secretary as he had long wished, Michael Stewart went to the D.E.A. and James Callaghan remained Chancellor. Arthur Bottomley moved to the Ministry of Overseas Development and Herbert Bowden took his place at the Commonwealth Relations Office. Anthony Greenwood, Minister for Overseas Development, became Minister of Housing and Richard Crossman, who had held that office since October 1964, found himself Lord President of the Council and Leader of the House of Commons with John Silkin as his Chief Whip.[1]

Moving from a large and vigorous Department where (as Volume I of this diary describes) the Minister had enjoyed the challenges of personality and policy, was not easy, but although the Lord President's Office was less conspicuous and had only a slender staff, the job that Crossman was required to master needed great finesse. On April 1st, 1966, the general election had given Labour a comfortable majority of 97 seats, 363 compared with 253 for the Conservatives and 12 for the Liberals, and this state of affairs had led rebellious elements within the Parliamentary Labour Party to lose that cohesive discipline that a tiny majority tends to impose naturally. The traditional Left were unruly. Moreover, the composition of the P.L.P. had also changed in the spring of 1966. Of the seventy-two Labour M.P.s entering Parliament between 1965 and 1966, including the 1966 election, a far higher proportion had a university education and a professional background, compared with the 317 Labour M.P.s elected in 1964. Not only were their political attitudes more questioning and intransigent, but they had high expectations of Parliament's duties and rewards. It was this back-bench mood of disillusion and rebelliousness with which Richard Crossman had to deal.

---

[1] See p. 789 for full Cabinet list.

Wednesday, August 24th

The first day in my new office. More and more nostalgic, more and more aware that I am unlikely ever to be as happy in politics again, more and more uneasy about my new job. That was my mood when I began to settle into this wonderful suite of rooms I've got in the Privy Council Office with its view over Horseguards Parade.

I was told that the P.M. wanted to ring me up from the Scillies and so, sure enough, when John Silkin and I had finished lunch and were settling down to talk, the P.M. came through anxious to know how the Lord President was doing on his first day. 'Well,' I said, 'I've scarcely been here half an hour.' But he obviously wanted to have a long easy talk about things in general and he started by asking me about the morning press—he hadn't seen it in the Scillies. I was able to tell him the announcement that he was due to go to the T.U.C. Conference and try to persuade them to support our incomes and prices policy was the lead story in most of the papers. Then he started gossiping about how George Brown was still in a fury about my appointment and how there was now a ridiculous struggle for the top place in the pecking order between Michael Stewart and James Callaghan. I tried to get him back to something I'd been brooding over for the last two or three days—what we do if, as seems certain, our policy is either defeated at the T.U.C. Conference or carried by such a small majority that it's tantamount to defeat. George Brown and Jim Callaghan intend that if this happens we should clamp on the new Part IV of the Bill and bring it into operation by Order in Council. The Order in Council would lapse within twenty-eight days unless it had been approved by Parliament but we could time the laying of it without recalling Parliament as long as we ensured that the twenty-eighth day fell on the first day of the new Session. That would be after the T.U.C. Conference and before the Labour Party Conference.[1]

I'm very much against this Callaghan–Brown tactic. Even if the policy were defeated at the T.U.C. Conference I think we should try to win and if we are defeated there we must come back to Westminster and get the authorization of the Parliamentary Party on the very first day. What we mustn't do is to ride rough-shod over all our friends. That's my concern. I want to see no little Napoleon threatening the T.U.C. that even if they do vote against him he couldn't care less because he will use the Order in Council. I don't know how much of this I got over to Harold on the phone. We shall see when he gets back. He'll have Bank Holiday Monday at Chequers and next Tuesday I'll come in to see him and to see his draft speech for the T.U.C.

Just when Harold had finished Manny Shinwell looked in, which was very convenient because I wanted to talk to him about the whole problem of managing the Parliamentary Party. John Silkin told him that he wanted to see Standing Orders tidied up. Manny had come with a carefully prepared document containing his proposals for managing the Party. He read it aloud

[1] To be held at Brighton October 3rd–7th.

and it wasn't half bad. But his mistake was that he wanted the liaison committee to poach upon the Chief Whip's prerogative to enforce discipline.[1] I tried to clarify things by saying that wasn't really the question. The members of the liaison committee can tell the Chief Whip that in their view someone should have the whip withdrawn and the Chief Whip can ask the Parliamentary Party to report a person to the Executive.* Normally I should say the Chief Whip must be responsible but of course members of the liaison committee can tell him that in their view he's wrong. And if there's a deadlock the P.M. must be brought in to decide. But the P.L.P. retains sovereignty in matters of discipline. So it was surely a waste of time to discuss who makes the recommendation.

My point was that what really mattered was keeping the Party constantly informed of the Government's policy and I was delighted that Manny saw this straightaway. He agreed that we should have two regular meetings of the Party each week—one will be on Wednesday morning and, even more important, we will restore the old Thursday evening business meeting at six o'clock where the P.L.P. discusses the afternoon's Statement by the Leader of the House of the next week's business. If we can announce that there are going to be two regular weekly meetings and that members will retain the right to call a special meeting I hope we shall be able to start a new relationship with the Parliamentary Party. When Manny left John promised to get on with the job of making his amendments to Manny's document so that we three could agree on a draft next Tuesday and submit it to the other members of the liaison committee.

Another important agreement we achieved was about Honours. Months ago Harold sent me a memo on his proposition that under a Labour Government there should be no Honours for political services—nothing but Honours for public service with the various Government Departments submitting recommendations. Manny and John Silkin entirely agree with this and we can tell Harold that an announcement should be made this autumn in time to influence the recommendations for the New Year Honours. This is something he hadn't been able to agree with Ted Short and Herbert Bowden.

After that John and I went down to the Chief Whip's magnificent office in No. 12 and there we had our first meeting of the liaison committee (the 'small committee') including Transport House people. I hope we shall be able to establish good relations with Transport House fairly quickly. I shall test that tomorrow when I go over to Smith Square to tell Len Williams that John Silkin and I want his help in our new dispensation.

---

* The National Executive Committee of the Labour Party.
[1] The liaison committee was to provide the P.L.P. and the officers of the Party headquarters, in Transport House, with a channel of communication with the Government. The Chief Whip and the Lord President together manage the business of the House of Commons and the parliamentary timetable and the Chief Whip is largely responsible for ensuring that the Government preserves its majority intact.

Monday, August 29th

For days now I've been sitting down at my desk, reading the documents and mugging up the organization and history of Parliament. It's difficult because I know as little about it as I did about housing twenty months ago. Although I've been a back-bencher for nearly twenty years I've really done very little in Parliament. I've taken no interest in procedure and not very much part in debates because I thought Parliament a profoundly unimportant and boring place. But at least, in writing about its ineffectiveness, I have consistently advocated reform. Now, ironically, I've got to see if I can get the case for reform across. After looking at the papers I've a feeling I've got some luck on my side since a package of reforms has been prepared by the Select Committee on Procedure and by my predecessor. It's not very exciting but at least it exists. But of course parliamentary reform will only be a minor part of my job. My main task will be in the organization of the Parliamentary Party and of the relationships between the Government and Transport House, and the P.L.P. and the country outside. Harold has handed over to me the whole Party political aspect of Government and told me to do what I can with it.

So I've been quietly settling into the job. John Silkin and I have been getting to know each other. We like each other very much. Perhaps we like each other too much, get on too well, find life too easy together, because we are both of us anti-disciplinarians from the Left who may well find ourselves having to discipline the Party. John Silkin has now redrafted Manny's paper and we're to discuss it with him tomorrow. What we're trying to define are the roles of the chairman of the Party, the Chief Whip and the Leader of the House. Herbert Bowden never ceased to be Chief Whip when he was made Lord President. He never really became Leader of the House. He left me an office without a Press Officer. It did no work and pretty often he used to go home at night to be with his ill wife. My view is that I've got to be seen as the commander in the field: I've got to be in that House of Commons every working day and spend every evening with the boys, seeing them through the difficulties, spending a large amount of time in personal contact, not so much jollying round the tea room but talking to people individually and so getting a grasp of the Party's reactions. But can I do it? My W.E.A. background is useful but what the job entails is a lot of arduous work in that very boring House of Commons. Nevertheless I think I can settle down and hack my way through.

As for Harold, after my one telephone conversation with him from the Scillies I've left him alone. After all, I mustn't push myself too hard after he's promoted me this far. He says ironically that he has now four heirs-apparent instead of one, the four being of course Stewart, Callaghan, Brown—and Crossman. But I'm beginning to realize that he will expect me to help him in Cabinet. As far as I can see, as Lord President I have access to all Cabinet papers however secret and I can insist on ranging over all the Government's activities, foreign as well as domestic. For instance, this weekend I took down to Prescote[1] all the Rhodesia papers to try and grasp what has been going on there. The situation isn't very different from what I expected. Harold has grossly over-estimated the effect of sanctions and so have the Commonwealth Department. At the Commonwealth Prime Ministers' Conference there'll be tremendous pressure for stronger U.N. sanctions.[2]

What should be our strategy? I can't see any basis for an agreement between Smith and ourselves which will not be regarded as a sell-out by the Africans and, anyway, that would split the Labour Party from top to bottom. But if this is so how can we ever rid ourselves of this appalling liability? There's only one way—to hand Rhodesia on a plate to the U.N. We've got to cut our losses in a way which makes historical sense. And there's one tactical advantage. If we want to make Smith take the idea of a settlement seriously we must present him with a prospect he really fears. I suspect he's really afraid of our leaving him absolutely alone and exposed.

Tuesday, August 30th

In the afternoon I went round to No. 10 to have my first talk with the P.M. since his return from the Scillies. I wanted to give him some ideas for his speech to the T.U.C. Conference but he talked to me almost entirely about Rhodesia. He told me how important it was to find a positive new line; he is convinced that sanctions against Portugal is the way to get out of our difficulties. We can't afford to impose sanctions on both Portugal and South Africa. On the other hand if we can isolate Portugal, knock them on the head, this will stop the main South African leak into Rhodesia along the railway which crosses Portuguese territory. So he is determined to get Cabinet to approve Portuguese sanctions on Thursday and his great hope is that at the Commonwealth Conference he will be able to carry the Prime Ministers with him. 'That,' said Harold, 'is the stick we must now employ.' As for the carrot, he believes we should offer Smith a choice of three constitutional possibilities. These are apparently described in eight Cabinet papers which we are to consider on Thursday. When he had finished I said that in my view the biggest threat we can employ against Smith is to stop shielding him from the U.N. and in fact to begin washing our hands of Rhodesia.

'Well now,' Harold said, 'that's all very well as a threat but we couldn't possibly do it.' And he went on to explain why my idea of doing another Palestine was impossible. It had already been knocked out by the Attorney-

[1] Prescote Manor, at Cropredy near Banbury, was the Crossmans' farm. Their London home was in Vincent Square.

[2] The Commonwealth Prime Ministers' Conference was to be held in London from September 6th to 15th, and, of the twenty-two Heads of State who would attend, some African representatives were already threatening to break off diplomatic relations with Britain (following Tanzania's example) if there was no stiffening of policy towards the Rhodesian regime. The Rhodesian Prime Minister, Ian Smith, had issued a unilateral declaration of independence on November 11th, 1965, but Britain refused to acknowledge the legal independence of Rhodesia before satisfactory constitutional arrangements had been made for African majority rule.

General as legally impracticable.[1] Anyway, he wouldn't consider it even if it were legal, and nor would the rest of my colleagues. So that's the end of my bright idea. But if that is no go then surely the second best would be to settle down to a long haul, sit the whole thing out playing our part in sanctions but by no means taking a lead.

That's the thought I came back with to my office on Tuesday. There I found Shinwell and the Chief Whip who'd arrived in a torrential rainfall. Shinwell was very enthusiastic when I told him I'd already talked to the Prime Minister and made clear that in the considered view of the chairman of the liaison committee, the Leader of the House and the Chief Whip, Cabinet must seek authorization from the Parliamentary Party for putting Part IV of the Prices and Incomes Bill into action. If we are going to have any decent relationships with the Party a clear vote must be taken on this as soon as Parliament resumes. 'I'll tell you now,' Shinwell said to me, 'you wouldn't have had me as chairman of the P.L.P. today unless you had given me that assurance. It's a wonderful relief.' As the meeting went on we found that he was in complete agreement with the draft document John had drawn up. So the concordat between the three of us is really signed and sealed and we can now present it to the P.M. on the one side, and to the other members of the liaison committee on the other.

Wednesday, August 31st

I went to see the Laurence Olivier film of *Othello* with Anne.[2] It was a full house and we had to pay a guinea for our tickets. I've seldom seen a performance which moved me less. There he was playing the part of a negro, acting Othello, and somehow guying the black man in a revolting way. The sets were dull, the oversized figures were unimpressive. We got nothing out of it except that it was mildly interesting to see what we got nothing out of.

Thursday, September 1st

We started Cabinet with Rhodesia. Yesterday's Rhodesia Committee had been extremely bad firstly because the official papers were masses of bumf which didn't present us with any clear-cut choices and secondly because the Committee was dominated by the Prime Minister and there was no one there with a single positive idea to put up to him. At the Committee Harold tried to sell his Portuguese gimmick and failed to get away with it and this was repeated even more sharply at Cabinet itself. He was opposed pretty firmly by the defence people, and even by Bert Bowden. Michael Stewart as ex-Foreign

[1] In 1945 Crossman had been made a member of the Anglo-American Committee of Inquiry appointed to examine the problem of European Jewry and Palestine. With this experience, described in his *Palestine Mission* (London: Hamish Hamilton, 1947), began his life-long affection for Israel. He seemed to favour a similar independent investigation into the Rhodesian question.

[2] Richard Crossman's third wife, Anne McDougall, whom he married in 1954. Patrick, their son, was now aged nine and Virginia, their daughter, seven.

Secretary weighed in against the idea of isolating Portugal. Barbara Castle went to the other extreme and said we ought to go for mandatory U.N. sanctions and break altogether with Smith. I replied to Barbara, saying that instead of taking on any more responsibilities we should play it cool and avoid committing ourselves any further. This might cause a storm of abuse at the Commonwealth Conference but we would have solid support from British public opinion. Why should we plunge any deeper? Portuguese sanctions would certainly bring the risk of an economic blockade of South Africa which we just couldn't afford. When I took this line I certainly got a great deal of support. I can't say Harold was terribly pleased with me afterwards. I assured him he'd be all right at the Commonwealth Conference and he looked at me, grinned and said, 'My God, you've left me with a handful of trouble.'

After Rhodesia we had a kind of interim report from each of the Ministers concerned on how the prices and incomes policy was working. It was surprisingly encouraging. Of course I have to record here that Harold has had a very big effect already by the mere announcement that he is going to face the T.U.C. Conference. In fact he may well have transformed the prospect of defeat into the prospect of victory since the mine-workers seem to have swung to his side.[1] What the Ministers' reports all suggested was that ordinary people were in favour of the freeze and that we would strengthen our popularity by being tough. So the situation was really fairly good. The only danger was that if even a single employer wanting to raise wages decided to take legal action we would be compelled to lay an Order bringing Part IV into operation. I pointed out that the Chief Whip and the chairman of the liaison committee strongly held the view that we must not present the Parliamentary Party with a *fait accompli*. We hadn't had a meeting of the Party at the end of July and I thought that had been a grave mistake (the Prime Minister said 'Hear! hear!' very loudly). So it was all the more important to start the new Session with a Party meeting at which the P.L.P. would be free to make their own decision. Nothing would be worse than to have to give them the news that we'd clapped on an Order. Cabinet couldn't reach any conclusion but at least no one was swallowing the Callaghan–Brown line.

At four that afternoon we had a meeting of Transport House officers.[2] I had asked for this to discuss the speakers at Conference and what policy statements would be required. We decided to have an economic policy statement on the Wednesday and one on foreign affairs and defence on the Thursday. We fixed all the main speakers quite amicably. My job at Conference will be limited to answering a debate in the private session on the future role of the Party. That'll give me the chance to make the kind of speech I want to

[1] The National Union of Mineworkers was, with 413,000 members in 1966, one of the eight largest unions and as such would command a substantial vote at the T.U.C. Conference.

[2] The organizational and research staff of the Labour Party work at Transport House, headquarters of both the Party and the T.U.C. Relations between Transport House officers and politicians were notoriously bad.

make not only on parliamentary reform but also, just as important, on Party reform.

This was quite a pleasant meeting. We sat round the table while Harold chaffed Johnny Boyd of the A.U.E.W. and Dai Davies of the Steelworkers.[1] It was a homely atmosphere and I felt that at last I was now accepted as someone who'd got on to the inside.

Friday, September 2nd
I woke up at six and began to work on the P.M.'s speech for the Trade Union Conference. Gerald Kaufman told me the first draft had been very poor and even the second draft was pretty dreary. There wasn't enough stress on the malaise underlying our society and on the need for self-discipline at a time when democracy is in crisis. I worked away at the speech and then it occurred to me that the point could best be made with a reference to Nye Bevan.[2] So I drafted out a skeleton of this part of the speech and rushed to my office at 9.30 to dictate my notes before I went to No. 10. Ten o'clock Friday morning is morning prayers—the time when the Lord President always visits the P.M. and along with Burke Trend discusses the business for next week.

After forty-five minutes Burke left and I and the P.M. could discuss his speech. Unfortunately the text of my draft only came in bit by bit and Marcia Williams and Gerald were both there. So during this forty-five minutes I discussed the speech in general with him, trying to push and prod him to take up the theme that the prices and incomes policy is not something forced on us in an emergency but a stage in our socialist development—a structure developing logically out of previous structures. I saw the speech later that evening and I think I got all I wanted into it. He seemed fairly pleased with the help I'd given him.

So that's the end of my first week. I seem to have settled in fairly well but I desperately miss the work I was doing in the Ministry. For the weekend I had no red box full of papers, no departmental chores. Of course there is plenty to fill my time. I could spend hours preparing my two big speeches for next Wednesday and Friday when I'm trying to begin my job of selling policy. I could get on with my study of parliamentary reform and reading up the minutes of the Select Committee on Procedure. I suppose what I miss is the kind of work which gave me the excuse for not doing basic reading of this kind. But I mustn't be disappointed. I know the moment people start coming back to Westminster after the recess I shall have a lot more to do and meanwhile I shall not waste time making contact with my Cabinet colleagues.

This afternoon there came to see me a journalist from the *Sunday Times*

[1] John Boyd, a moderate, was the General Secretary of the A.U.E.W. Dai Davies was a senior member of the Executive Committee of the Steelworkers' Union. He was knighted in 1974.
[2] Labour M.P. for Ebbw Vale from 1929 until his death in 1960. Minister of Health 1945–51 and, in 1951, Minister of Labour and National Service.

who'd heard that I intend to keep Peter Brown as my Press Officer,[1] I was also rung up by the *Sunday Telegraph* to ask whether that wasn't something without precedent. I hope I managed to put off the *Telegraph* journalist by reminding him that Herbert Morrison had Leslie as his Press Officer.[2] Nevertheless, this Peter Brown business may cause me a little bit of trouble.

Finally, one general conclusion about the week. There's no doubt the political atmosphere has enormously improved. The Cabinet has settled down much more satisfactorily than I expected and I don't think the P.M.'s anticipation of a major crisis at the Commonwealth Conference is going to be fulfilled. What's more, I'm sure he's going to have a real success when he addresses the Congress in Blackpool. He's going to make an impact and start a tremendous recovery which he'll then have to follow up in succeeding speeches next week.

Monday, September 5th

In the morning I went across to the Chief Whip's office, where there's a television set, to see Harold Wilson deliver his speech to the T.U.C. Tony Wedgwood Benn came in to watch too and Freddie Warren. It was a grim performance, a difficult tight little speech. Harold spoke very fast with no great fervour or drama until right at the end when he lifted them with ten minutes of real stuff. Nevertheless, on reflection I thought it was right for the occasion. If he'd made a brilliant Harold Wilson speech he would have been reminding them of his weakness. This time he was a Prime Minister coming to the Congress to put the fear of God into them, telling them what jolly well had to be done, making them acquiesce, asserting his authority.

That evening I went to a party at the Australian High Commissioner's. I went there partly because in talking to Tony Greenwood that afternoon about whether he could dine with me on Thursday I'd remarked in a very snobbish, silly way that I didn't go to that kind of a party. Sure enough, when I turned up, there was Tony with his wife, and Judith Hart was also there. She came up to me and said, 'Dick, do you believe in the Commonwealth?' 'As a matter of fact, I don't believe in the Commonwealth,' I replied, 'but I also don't think that the Commonwealth ought to break up this week.' Instead of quarrelling I took this opportunity of having a long talk with her; I drew her out and let her give me the Commonwealth Office view about the Commonwealth P.M.s' reactions to Harold. She told me that all they care about is Rhodesia and NIBMAR, which apparently stands for 'No Independence Before Majority Rule'. That was what they'd come to London to get and if we didn't want to get saddled with mandatory sanctions we had better make concessions on NIBMAR in double-quick time. Judith's remarks finally made

---

[1] Crossman's Press Officer at the Ministry of Housing and Local Government. See Vol. I.
[2] During the Second World War, Morrison had engaged Leslie Hunter of the *Daily Herald* as a public relations adviser. After the war, Morrison found that, as Lord President and as chairman of the Cabinet Information Committee, his various journalistic associates were of invaluable use, and, twenty years later, Crossman was to enjoy a similar advantage.

me realize that the kind of isolationist attitude I'd adopted a few days ago is just not practical politics. We've got to let Harold make some concessions to the Commonwealth Prime Ministers while preserving him from commitments on U.N. sanctions, which are too big and dangerous.

Tuesday, September 6th

From bed I rang the P.M. and we had a long talk about his speech at the T.U.C. I always find it difficult chatting with him in the early morning because he can never end a telephone conversation. Normally, busy people have soon had enough of you and say, 'Well, thanks awfully, good-bye,' but with Harold it's always I who have to say, 'Well, thanks awfully, good-bye' and it makes it sound as though I've been bossy to him. Or am I being too sensitive about that?

I spent the morning in my office getting to know Freddie Warren. He's the Chief Executive Officer in charge of the Government Whips' Office. I've heard a great deal about him from George Wigg. Technically he's a Treasury official and he has taken the place of old Sir Charles Harris who for years and years was an absolutely key figure at Westminster,[1] the man who in fact ran the business of Parliament from the Government Chief Whip's Office. Freddie succeeded Sir Charles though he isn't even a Principal by rank, much less the Assistant Secretary he deserves to be. He told me that he'd been called Warren by the Tories and treated as a clerk. I suppose one could fairly describe him as the Staff Sergeant-Major of Whitehall, in a way comparable to George Wigg at Westminster. Already I rely absolutely on him and I suspect all Lord Presidents have relied on Freddie or Sir Charles to do all the detailed working out of parliamentary business. He's a key man because he's a little round ball-bearing which makes the huge joint work that links the Opposition and Government Whips' Offices. I'd imagined that when I became Lord President I would leave behind me the division between the Ministerial and the official level. Now I discover there's an official level here in Parliament just as important as the one in Whitehall. Freddie and the Clerks at the Table between them run the Government's legislative programme for the day, the week and for the whole session. They run the Speaker and also, to some extent, the Opposition. I wonder whether my impression will be confirmed by later experience? I wonder if it's really true that here in the Palace of Westminster business is settled by the officials working together while the politicians come and go.

We worked through the problems I had to tackle. On televising Parliament I found him willing to concede an experiment though he agreed with my criticisms of Driberg's report[2] and thought it an appalling notion to have a

[1] Private Secretary to successive Chief Whips, of various Administrations 1919–24, 1924–9 and from 1931 until his retirement in 1961.

[2] Tom Driberg was M.P. for Maldon, first as an Independent (1942–5) and then for Labour (1945–55) and for Barking from 1959 until 1974, when he left the House of

television Hansard set up inside the House.[1] Next I turned to the problem of morning sittings which I have just been studying in the report of the Select Committee on Procedure. By a majority of one the Labour members of the Committee had very reluctantly accepted the proposal for an experiment in morning sittings that Bert Bowden made when he was Lord President. Reading the evidence shows it's a most half-hearted proposal since it'll merely consist of a collection of bits and pieces of business. Transferring to the morning is supposed to enable M.P.s to get home twice a week at nine instead of at ten. I've always been attracted by the idea that we should start our work at a normal time in the morning like other Parliaments. But Bowden's proposal is a miserable solution. Is it wise for me, though, to turn down what my predecessor got the Select Committee to accept? I think this decision may be one of the most difficult I have to take.

Right at the end Freddie mentioned the problem of Early Day Motions.[2] With the connivance—almost the encouragement—of Short and Bowden, these are now being put down in scores each week. It's a kind of fun for backbenchers. Nobody dreams that these motions will ever be debated but on Thursday afternoon the Leader of the House is cross-examined on them to elicit statements of policy. I have to go through them all, memorize them and think out reasonable answers. Freddie Warren warned me it was a chore I would have to take on and it would require some homework. Alas, I've got plenty of time to do it.

This afternoon I had a visit from the Lord Chancellor who had come to discuss how to end this silly business of Black Rod knocking on the door of the House of Commons with the Commission from Her Majesty for the completion of Bills, often interrupting an important debate.[3] On recent occasions this has been fiercely resented in the Commons and Black Rod himself has been received with a fair amount of noise. One obvious solution would be to have only one visit by Black Rod at the end of the Session, to deal with

---

Commons and, in 1976, took his seat in the Lords, with the title of Lord Bradwell. He was a member of the editorial staff of the *Daily Express* 1928–43 and the first gossip columnist to write as that newspaper's 'William Hickey'. As a successful journalist and author, he had been well suited to act as chairman of the House of Commons Select Committee on Publications and Reports of Debates (1964–5) and of the House of Commons Select Committee on the Broadcasting of Proceedings in Parliament (1965–7), whose interim report Crossman was now considering. Lord Bradwell died in August 1976.

[1] Hansard is the colloquial name given to the official report of the daily proceedings in Parliament, so named after the family of printers and publishers who throughout the nineteenth century dealt with parliamentary papers.

[2] Motions which M.P.s put on the Order Paper for debate on an unspecified 'early day'. Other Members may append their names in support and thus the motion becomes a device to show back-bench attitudes to topical or critical propositions.

[3] The Gentleman-Usher of the Black Rod is that official of the House of Lords with responsibility for services, accommodation and security in the Lords' part of the Palace of Westminster. As Keeper of the Doors he supervises the admission of strangers and he also carries to the Commons the Queen's Commission for Bills to be finally enacted. In 1966 this post was held by Air Chief-Marshal Sir George Mills.

all the Bills at once. But this is impossible because quite a number of the Bills must come into force the moment that they are through. Gardiner had various ingenious ideas for ending this archaism and it looks as though we shall be able to do it.*

Wednesday, September 7th
I worked away on the speech I was to give this evening at Caxton Hall.[1] I thought it was going to be an important occasion since I heard that 580 tickets had been issued by the London Labour Party and there was likely to be a full house for what was the first of the major regional conferences on Party policy. For ten days I had been working with Transport House on the brief which was to be circulated to all M.P.s and candidates on the Government's policy and the background to it and particularly on how to handle prices and incomes. My speech was supposed to be a model of how to use the brief.

In the afternoon the 'small committee'—because the Chief Whip is still on holiday—met in my room. They're all staggered by the magnificence of my palatial apartment. I gave them drinks and after that I went off to Caxton Hall where Bob Mellish was to take me on to the platform. He arrived at 6.30 and the meeting was at 7.30 so we had a drink in a pub outside and went along at 7.25. There was nobody in the hall so we went away and had another drink this time with Keith Kyle, the former *Economist* correspondent.[2] When we returned at 7.45 there were a few people hanging about. However, at 7.50 when we went in we found the hall was then half full; only 210 of the 580 people who'd received tickets had bothered to turn up. I concentrated on prices and incomes, showing that we had not abandoned our policy, but that we had been steadily developing it during the first two years of the Government. However, we'd been relying at first on a voluntary policy which had now broken down. That's why we had now to fashion new social instruments which were necessary for dealing with the problem. They would provide an essential addition to our armoury. In presenting this general theme I laid great emphasis on the limitations of the policy and on its democratic basis.

After the press left we had a terribly sulky meeting. One or two people were friendly and asked practical questions about rent assessment committees or industrialized building,[3] otherwise everyone was narky about the betrayal of socialism. The London organizer told me he'd never had such a

---

* It was ended by a one-clause Bill a few months later.
[1] A large hall near Westminster, used for public meetings.
[2] On the staff of *The Economist* as Washington correspondent 1953–8 and as political and parliamentary correspondent 1958–60. At this time he was working mainly for B.B.C. television.
[3] Two subjects with which Crossman had concerned himself as Minister of Housing. Rent assessment committees were bodies appointed to determine what was a 'fair rent' for property and to settle disputes between tenants and landlords; 'industrialized building' was a method of construction by which buildings were designed, assembled and completed at lower cost.

bad regional conference and I must say the mood was very different from the one I held in a hall in Bloomsbury a few weeks ago. Tam, on the telephone, told me that at a similar meeting in Scotland Peggy Herbison also had a difficult time and that he is finding great depression and scepticism in his own constituency. Obviously the job of raising the morale of our people and making them confident in what we are doing is far bigger than we realize.

Thursday, September 8th
Although I had issued quite a good press release and there were plenty of journalists present, I got practically no coverage for my Caxton Hall speech in this morning's newspapers. I've got to get used to the fact that whereas a departmental Minister with a departmental speech can nearly always get what he wants into the press, the Lord President of the Council making a Party speech distributed through Transport House has the worst possible access. I've been very spoilt as Minister of Housing. Now no television company will look at me because there's no departmental reason why they should ask me to appear. There's always some other Minister entitled to speak on that subject. James Callaghan will get far better press coverage for his regional conference on Friday.

I spent the morning in Coventry at a meeting with the directors of the Standard Motor Works that I'd arranged many months before. I wondered whether to keep this engagement but am glad I did. The directors told me that they are going to put a lot of their men on short time but they are confident that business is expanding and that all the men will be back at work in the spring and this is why they aren't bothering with any redundancy payments.[1] Donald Stokes was careful to say to me that our Government has consulted industry much more than its predecessor and that he and his fellow directors aren't against it.[2] He also told me that he thought the prices and incomes policy pretty sensible since it was essential to wring the inflation out of the economy. After lunch we went back—as I always do with him—to the problem of education. He was at Blundells and sent his son, Michael, there. He agreed that if Michael were Patrick's age now, he wouldn't have gone to a boarding school either. I find I have a pleasant relationship with Stokes though, of course, the impression he gives of being a mild little man is totally misleading.

Anne picked me up by car and we went back to London in order to give dinner to Tony Greenwood and Jill, his wife, before going to the big Commonwealth Conference reception at Lancaster House. Tony was charming.

[1] By the end of the year B.M.C. were to declare 12,500 car workers redundant, and other car firms were to introduce short-time working.
[2] Lord Stokes had joined Leyland Motors Ltd as an apprentice in 1930; in 1968 he became chairman and managing director of the British Leyland Motor Corporation, and, in 1973, its chief executive. He was a member of the North-West Economic Planning Council 1965–70 and of the Industrial Reconstruction Corporation 1966–71. He became a life peer in 1969.

We talked a good deal about the personalities of the Ministry of Housing and I tried to make him realize how powerful the office as a body can be in preventing you having your way. I said at one point how important it was to read all the briefs and Anne told me afterwards that he'd said to her rather pathetically, 'The trouble is your husband reads very fast and I don't. That's going to be my difficulty.'

We all went on to Lancaster House and I'm not sure I behaved very well. I said to too many people how disappointed I was in my new job. That's a bad thing to say too often.

I did have some interesting talks, however, particularly one with Tom Mboya,[1] the key man in Kenya, and I certainly learnt the strength of feeling about NIBMAR. I ran into Judith Hart again. She warned me that I shouldn't throw my weight about too much in the RX Committee (Rhodesia X). The Prime Minister, she said, has been going round saying that just because Dick now has time to read all the papers he thinks he knows all about the subject when in fact he doesn't. Of course he wouldn't have said that if I'd come down on his side in the discussions. I asked her to brief me before Cabinet on Saturday.

Friday, September 9th
I spent the morning preparing a speech I was to give to the Coventry Fabian Society this evening. I realize that so far my efforts to get any publicity for my speeches has totally failed. So I put out Wednesday's press release on prices and incomes again. After lunch I went off to Coventry with Anne.

In Coventry one never knows what is going to happen. In this case we had a really excellent meeting—some thirty-five to forty people, but they were the cream of the cream. There were people like George Hodgkinson,[2] Peter Lister,[3] the staff at the Lanchester Tech., the head of the Art Gallery—a first-rate collection. I gave them a frank, careful, reasoned statement once again on how we hadn't been driven off course and how the new prices and incomes policy was a logical development from the old voluntary policy, a new weapon intrinsic to socialism. It was a reasoned, semi-theoretical speech and it produced an amazingly good response. Maybe they're fond of me and a little impressed by the fact that the Member for Coventry East is now the Lord President of the Council. Certainly there was none of the rage I had expected from the trade unionists present, none of the sulky atmosphere of Caxton Hall.

---

[1] Secretary-General of the Kenyan African National Party from 1960 until his murder in July 1969. He was Kenya's Minister of Justice and Constitutional Affairs 1963–4 and Minister of Economic Planning and Development 1964–9.

[2] An old friend and colleague of Crossman. He was the agent of the Coventry Borough Labour Party 1923–58 and, 1928–67, Councillor and then Alderman of Coventry Council. He was re-elected as an alderman in 1972.

[3] Coventry City Councillor for the Willenhall Ward since 1957.

Saturday, September 10th

I went up from Banbury by the early train in order not to be late for Judith Hart. This ten o'clock Cabinet was a follow-up to two meetings of the RX Committee, one on Wednesday afternoon and the other on Thursday morning, in which the Committee had advised the Prime Minister on the line he should take during the Conference. I'd had a chance to think things over and had come to the conclusion that the best concession Harold could make to the Commonwealth Prime Ministers would be to give them NIBMAR in return for an understanding that they would help him to resist mandatory sanctions. I was also hopeful that we might deter him from carrying on with his Portuguese sanctions gimmick. All this I checked over with Judith. I told her that whenever NIBMAR was discussed at the Committee Harold and Herbert Bowden had simply replied that it would contradict everything they had previously said. I had suspected that this couldn't be proved and she confirmed this. 'To accept NIBMAR,' she said, 'does not require the existing Government policy to be stood on its head.' All it means is putting the same policy with a totally different emphasis. She made me realize that in order to placate the white Rhodesians we had not been emphasizing the fact that a constitution was unacceptable unless it received full black Rhodesian acceptance. Of course that acceptance wouldn't be given to any constitution entrenching the whites' position or providing mere paper safeguards. There would have to be a real transfer of power and it's difficult to see how Smith can be induced to surrender voluntarily his present power and hand over to a constitutional government which will destroy white supremacy. How could he be induced to do this except by something which tricks either him or the Africans? My conclusion from my talk with Judith is that it is this which has created the Commonwealth distrust of Harold Wilson. He seems to be trying to have his cake and eat it, to be all things to all people.

Just as I was finishing my talk with Judith I had an urgent message that I should look in on George Wigg. I found him entirely absorbed in Portuguese sanctions. He busily set about proving to me that the military intelligence at his disposal confirmed the view that petrol moved by rail can only go one way and could be cut off as it passed through Lourenço Marques. Early that morning I had just had time to read the J.I.C. paper. I'd seen the stuff George was talking about but I'd also read the end of the staff paper which said that petrol could also be taken through by road and at a not much greater price. So even if Portugal did cut off supplies it would not be the end of Rhodesia.

I just had time to get down the stairs to the Cabinet room where I found a few people with George Brown, our new Foreign Secretary, and the Lord Chancellor. It had been obvious from what happened at the two RX Committees last week that Harold was still absolutely determined to get his way and get Cabinet consent for sanctions against Portugal and less rigid United Nations sanctions in general. Bowden, as Commonwealth Secretary, started off with a lengthy explanation of the mass of Cabinet bumf with which we had been provided. We had an even lengthier report by the Prime Minister, who plunged into the details of Lourenço Marques and Portuguese sanctions. I thought it was high time he was interrupted and so I broke in when he was quoting all the stuff George Wigg had just been talking to me about. I said, 'Well, this is really all irrelevant because even if the oil does go by that route— by railway—there's an alternative road route at not much greater expense.'

It's the first time I've caught the P.M. out on a technical fact. It may not have been tactful but it stopped the speeches and we then had a serious Cabinet discussion. Dick Marsh weighed in and said the real puzzle for him was why on earth any of us should believe that Smith could be got to put his head in the noose which the P.M. had prepared for him. Why on earth should he allow a constitutional government to be set up in Rhodesia which could destroy his chance of maintaining white supremacy? The P.M. answered at interminable length and then Barbara Castle came in and got on to NIBMAR, whereat Harold Wilson and Bowden both said they were amazed that any member of the Cabinet could ask for this.

I said that there was merely a semantic difference between NIBMAR and the five principles on which Harold based his policy. 'I'm amazed,' said the P.M., 'at your wanting this. I can understand Barbara who wants action quickly but if you want to play for time, Dick, and you're alarmed about the economic consequences, you must realize that conceding NIBMAR would end the chance of negotiations and throw the white Rhodesians into the arms of South Africa.' At this point George Brown suddenly weighed in. 'I must make my views clear,' he said, 'and I must tell you that I'm not speaking for my Department because my Department want no sanctions. On the other hand, I must make it clear to the P.M. that it's really no good his saying that to concede NIBMAR would turn our policy upside down. We only agreed not to mention NIBMAR because it was tactically unwise to do so during our negotiations with Smith. But we never thought that NIBMAR was not the prevailing principle on which our policy was based. We just felt it tactful not to mention it. And that's all we ever agreed to, Prime Minister, and I would be deeply upset if you were to suggest anything else.' George put absolutely clearly the case which I had been trying to think out. What an enormous relief it was to have a real Foreign Secretary at last instead of Michael Stewart. That morning George was much more like a P.M. than the P.M. Harold was prosy and repetitive and unimpressive. George was dynamic, clear and giving leadership. We shall need plenty of friends in the Commonwealth to help us limit U.N. sanctions and if, in order to get their support, we must pay the price of NIBMAR then Harold must be prepared to pay it. So, having demolished Harold, George Brown then supported him. He conceded that if the Prime Minister wanted to try Portuguese sanctions the Foreign Secretary would allow him to do so. At this point Frank Longford said, 'I'd rather resign than tolerate this infamy of imposing sanctions on the weaker Portugal rather than on the stronger

South Africa. It's immoral to do that.' On reflection I feel I ought to have stuck out on this issue of Portuguese sanctions because if you once start sanctions against Portugal you're going to have mandatory sanctions over the whole of the oil sector including South Africa. However, Harold got his way here as on everything else and this means that George Wigg also got his way. The P.M. may not be a very dominant leader but he's certainly very pertinacious. This was my first brush with him since I became Lord President and I had no success. He brushed me aside as easily as he brushed Callaghan aside and the only person who came near halting him in his tracks was George Brown. But then the Foreign Secretary is central to the affair and I am not.

That evening we had to go to Chequers for a singularly dreary Commonwealth Conference dinner. As far as I could see our hosts, Harold and his wife, made absolutely no effort to entertain anybody. We found a few people standing about in the hall, all the ladies huddled together in their usual little chat and the men on the other side. In general conversation I tried out the question of the consequences of our entry to the Common Market. I was struck by the fact that whenever I asked this nobody expressed any doubt that Britain will soon be in and that in our own interests we ought to be there. Of course, when the Commonwealth feels that way about us then the Commonwealth as a power relationship is not going to have a very long life. We are very grateful to Harold for preventing it breaking up this weekend but the little I've seen of the consultations has made me feel that we ought to think about the possibility of eventually entering the Common Market and seeing the Commonwealth fade out as an organization since this is likely to happen in any case. The one thing we shouldn't do is to cut off our long-term interests for the sake of any short-term gain such as strengthening a Commonwealth which is anyway a dying concern.

But I spent nearly all my time talking to Makarios and got on extremely well.[1] We really hit it off when we discovered that we could say openly to each other how much we liked Nasser as a person, how much we were invigorated by his presence, how imaginative and creative we found him.[2] Once we'd said that to each other we could really talk freely. I told him how I couldn't go back to Cyprus because I had given my Cypriot friends the wrong advice when I told them to get their freedom in the way Israel got its freedom. That led us to talk about Jerusalem which I described as one of those ghastly cases where something totally impossible becomes a permanency. Did he think the present constitution of Cyprus was permanent? He smiled and said, 'No, not like Jerusalem.' 'I presume you wouldn't be President if you said anything else?' I replied. 'You're still working for something better than what

---

[1] Archbishop and Ethnarch in Cyprus since 1950, elected President in 1959 and re-elected in 1968 and 1973. Crossman had spent several weeks in Cyprus in the 1950s and was to visit the island again at Easter, 1967.

[2] General Nasser had led the revolt of July 1952 which caused the abdication of King Farouk and the eventual establishment of the Republic of Egypt. From 1958 until his death in 1970 he was President of the United Arab Republic.

you've now got?' and he smiled quietly and said, 'Yes.' He's still under fifty-five and he became Archbishop when he was thirty-seven. He really is a man of great charm.

Sunday, September 11th
It has not been a happy week for me. It's been a week of inner anxiety, frustration and nostalgia. Yesterday on the way back from Leamington, where Anne picked me up on my return from the Cabinet meeting, we motored out to Chesterton to see the lovely Inigo Jones mill which is being repaired by voluntary effort. There we stood on the hill looking down on the plain of Warwickshire and I felt that historic buildings such as this mill were part of *my* job—but my domain has gone to Tony Greenwood, who is scared stiff of being Minister of Housing and would have been delighted to be Lord President.

There's nothing I can do until the Prime Minister has some spare time. All this week he's been seven or eight hours a day in that confounded Commonwealth Conference or at the reception for it in the evening. As P.M. he has to chair it morning, afternoon, evening and he's done that for the whole of the five days of the week. I can hardly blame him for not answering questions about my personal future.

But as a result of the frustration the risk of my dropping a clanger is, I think, quite high. I have no Department, I have no field to work except that I should cover the whole of Government policy. I spent a lot of last week preparing two big speeches and two press releases and got just a few lines in *The Times* on Thursday, a line or two in the *Guardian* and one sentence in the *Mirror*. However I'm not sure whether obscurity is not preferable to the kind of publicity I began to get yesterday. Nora Beloff, political columnist of the *Observer*, rang to ask me about my extremely exciting speech. No, she hadn't seen the text of it: she'd seen it mentioned in the *Guardian* and she'd seen that Russell Kerr, the husband of Anne Kerr, has made a speech this weekend denouncing me for trying to put the trade unions in thrall.[1] That shows the difficulty I'm in as Lord President. Since I haven't got a Department to speak about I'm always trespassing on other people's work and in this case I may have done so. Ironically enough, I may have caused confusion by a speech designed to show M.P.s how to take an educational line with our supporters. It looks as though I set off a minor row inside the Party but at least I taught myself something: I shall have to find methods of co-ordinating my speeches with those of my colleagues if I'm not to tread on all their toes and all their corns in my attempt to sell the policy of the Government to the Party and to the public. After all, it's my colleagues' policy which I'm trying to sell. In this case I thought what I said conformed strictly to what Harold

[1] Labour M.P. for Feltham since 1966, after several unsuccessful electoral contests. He was chairman of the Tribune group of M.P.s 1969–70. Anne Kerr was Labour M.P. for Rochester and Chatham 1964–70. She died in July 1973.

said at Blackpool. Of course I spelt it out a little bit further and added a little more decoration, but basically I made the same policy commitment that when all the legal powers we take under Part IV lapse at the end of the year, we mustn't go back to normal—we must by then have evolved new methods of collaboration in a new prices and incomes policy. Will Ray Gunter and Michael Stewart think I've interfered in their work or will they want me to make this kind of speech? That's the difficulty I face as a political Minister without Portfolio.

What I have to discover is whether Harold Wilson really wants me to be a political Minister of this kind or whether he thinks that I should be content with my ambulance work in the House, being a nurse or a matron to a lot of injured and difficult schoolchildren—the Parliamentary Party. Am I mainly to do just that and have as my only extra assignment parliamentary reform? It's a very limited assignment indeed and I'm not the ideal person for it because I haven't really played any role as a member of the House to justify any claim to know and care about it in the way that a parliamentary reformer should do.

If I'm not to blow up I must get some extra responsibilities. The first possibility is for the P.M. to make me a member of virtually all Cabinet Committees and, in addition, to give me the chairmanship of a number of key Committees. At present I'm not chairman of any important Committee except Future Legislation. But when Douglas Houghton goes Harold could give me his chairmanship of the Home Affairs Committee and the Social Security Committee and then I would have a segment of work where I could have effective control. I could make a real job out of that. If, in addition, I'm a member of all the important exterior Committees like Defence and Rhodesia X and the Nuclear Committee, then I could be what the P.M. calls a half-back—useful as a person to contribute to discussion without departmental briefing.

But I'm hardly encouraged by the role I played in Rhodesia this week. Moreover I don't really like it because I don't like having no power or authority of my own and just throwing ideas into the pool. This is something I've been doing all my life as an assistant editor.[1] It irks me in my old age when I have the chance of really doing something to find myself with my responsibilities taken away—merely advising someone else who is responsible.

Another kind of job Harold could give me would be that of co-ordinating the propaganda and public relations of all the Ministries in Whitehall. If he would let me move forward on that front then I can see a job for Peter Brown as the official in charge of co-ordinating all the Press Officers in each of the Government Departments and checking whether each Ministry is doing its

[1] From 1938 to 1955 Crossman was assistant editor on the *New Statesman and Nation*. He left that periodical when it became clear that he would probably not succeed Kingsley Martin as editor. In 1970, however, Crossman was to become editor in very different circumstances.

job press-wise and television-wise. There's a real job to be done there which, under the Tory Government, was done by Charles Hill and Bill Deedes.[1]

And thirdly, as well as being the Minister in charge of information or propaganda and the Minister in charge of co-ordinating propaganda policy, Harold could also make me the Minister in charge of co-ordination with Transport House itself. A lot will depend on whether I succeed in not treading on too many people's corns and in inspiring confidence in my colleagues. When I'm really hard at work for twenty hours a day I can be relatively tactful to other people. When I'm frustrated I find it much more difficult. Next week I will see from my relations with Michael Stewart at D.E.A. and with Ray Gunter at the Ministry of Labour whether I've committed a clanger with this speech.

Monday, September 12th
Today began the puncturing of all my hopes of building up my job as Lord President, symbolized by the arrival and departure of Peter Brown as my Press Officer. Peter was due back from his leave today and I told him to have a talk in the morning with Trevor Lloyd-Hughes at No. 10 and then to come to lunch with me. So I had a comfortable morning at Prescote and travelled up by the 10.47 to find Peter Brown in my room with Trevelyan and we all walked up to the Garrick. Peter was tremendously optimistic—very full of the strong position I was in to negotiate with the P.M. and to insist on getting functions for myself which would justify keeping a Press Officer. They told me about the morning meeting with Trevor Lloyd-Hughes and we agreed that Trevor had behaved perfectly correctly. They had gone through all the things that Peter Brown could possibly do for me in my position as Lord President and their conclusion added up to this. If I were to be a Lord President like Herbert Bowden there was no work for Peter as my Press Officer. He could only stay with me if Harold expressly assigned me further duties. But what further duties? Peter believed I should insist on being given a general supervision over the home front. I said this was ridiculous. Harold wasn't going to give me general supervision over Callaghan or, indeed, over Michael Stewart. I wasn't even going to get supervision over the supervision exercised by Douglas Houghton in the social services. However, I told Peter that I had drafted a minute ready for sending to the P.M. taking as an example of the lack of co-ordination the position about information on prices and incomes and the failure of the Ministers concerned to put themselves across. We agreed I should send it to the P.M. the same afternoon. But Trevelyan wasn't content. 'That's not nearly enough,' he said. 'You must insist that you need to be appointed Chief Co-ordinator of Information Services

---

[1] Conservative M.P. for Ashford 1950–74. A Parliamentary Under-Secretary at M.H.L.G. and at the Home Office 1955–7. From 1962 to 1964 he served, as Minister without Portfolio, in the capacity which Crossman describes. A journalist, he was appointed editor of the *Daily Telegraph* after leaving Parliament.

2

because unless he gives you that appointment Peter Brown won't be able to stay as your Press Officer.'

After lunch we went back to my room and had a meeting with Trevor Lloyd-Hughes's number two, Henry James.[1] This lasted only fifteen minutes because I simply said: 'The issue is whether or not I get a precise designation of duties from the P.M. That depends on my talks with him and not with any talks at your level.' I then sent the minute across and made the mistake of not marking it 'Personal' to Marcia Williams so that it arrived publicly in No. 10 and alerted the whole Office to what was going on. (However, I sent another covering minute which reached Marcia next morning to tell Harold why I had to have a decision straightaway.) By the end of the afternoon, however, my optimism had worn off. I was beginning to feel very angry and very disturbed by what was obviously going on inside No. 10.

That evening there was another of those eternal Commonwealth Conference cocktail parties—this time at Marlborough House. I ran into Burke Trend and told him that I *must* get a decision since I was virtually unemployed and I could guarantee him that if I got this job it wouldn't be too big for me. After that I took Tommy and Pen Balogh out to Prunier and there I made them nearly mad by lecturing them on how I'd given up a perfectly good job at the Ministry of Housing and was virtually unemployed. Naturally enough Thomas finds this difficult to understand because I am now in the kind of job which he's always had—I'm another of the Prime Minister's advisers though I don't see Harold nearly as often as Thomas or get anywhere near as close to him.

Tuesday, September 13th

My complaints to Burke Trend and to Tommy pretty soon had their effect. Burke certainly doesn't want a Lord President wandering about Whitehall like a rogue elephant blowing his top, while Tommy, by telephoning Marcia, alerted Harold, who acted quickly. When I was in John Silkin's room preparing our programme with him and Freddie Warren, the Chief Whip said that the P.M. wanted me to do the sound broadcast on Thursday evening on prices and incomes and would I make sure to clear the draft with the First Secretary and the Minister of Labour. I know why the P.M. made this offer. He had been warned of the row which my speech at Coventry last Thursday was likely to cause in the Party. *Tribune* this week devoted the whole of its front page to attacking the speech as the most dangerous possible line,[2] and in the *Observer* Nora Beloff had done me as much damage as possible. Harold wanted to show that he hadn't lost confidence in me and to give me a chance

---

[1] A former civil servant and journalist. In 1964, after serving as Press Officer in various ministries, he moved to No. 10, where he became Deputy Press Secretary and Deputy Public Relations Adviser to the Prime Minister.

[2] The weekly newspaper edited and published by the Tribune group on the left wing of the Labour Party. Its editorial staff, of whom Michael Foot was one of the most distinguished, had supported Aneurin Bevan while Labour was in opposition.

of putting myself right. No doubt too he wanted to soothe me down before administering a dose of disappointment this afternoon.

At midday I saw John Grist of the B.B.C.[1] and we discussed the technical problems of televising Parliament. I'm beginning to realize more and more that parliamentary reform and the television experiment are part of a single process. If we can only time it right we may be able to use the television experiment next January and February (which I'm sure the House is going to approve) as a method of enforcing the changes in procedure which we want. Suppose I could make sense of this dreadful proposal for morning sittings by including topical debates suitable for television and Ministerial Statements suitable for regional television! I'm sure the secret of success is to link the television demand with the demand for modernizing the House of Commons. Grist was pleased that I am not the kind of person who believes that what goes on on the Floor of the House will naturally make good broadcasting. The scenes at Prime Minister's Questions in the afternoon which the Select Committee seem to think is so attractive to television companies wouldn't really look so good when televised in the evening.

After a very pleasant lunch with my stepson, Gilbert Baker, I found Peter Brown on the doorstep—in a very different mood. He had come to tell me that he wanted to go back in double-quick time to the Ministry of Housing. I've never seen a bigger or quicker transformation than Peter's between noon Monday and noon Tuesday. He had seen the red light and realized that there was no future for him in my office because Downing Street was determined to down me. Moreover, Fleet Street would down me if Downing Street didn't because Fleet Street doesn't like the idea of the Lord President having a Press Officer—a civil servant paid to do party political work. So there was Peter pleading to go back. Fortunately, I'd got a whiff of this before lunch and could tell him that I'd already told Trevelyan to inform John Delafons,[2] who's still running the Private Office at the Ministry of Housing, what had happened to Peter and how he wanted his job reopened. So the particular scheme which the P.M. had agreed to, that Peter should come with me and that our work should be integrated with No. 10, had all been totally and completely defeated by the officials at No. 10. Trevor Lloyd-Hughes and Henry James had found the idea unacceptable because Peter would be trespassing on their territory, and I suspect Burke Trend didn't like it either. It took them just twenty-four hours to kill it stone dead. Dead in terms of fact, but not in terms of publicity because all the political correspondents were full of the story and there'll be, I'm sure, some malicious comment in the press this week.*

* There was less than I expected. Only the *Guardian* 'Miscellany' was malicious.
[1] Head of the Current Affairs Group of the B.B.C. Television Service 1967–72 and producer and editor of various political programmes, including *Panorama* and *Gallery*. Since 1972 he has been Controller of B.B.C. English Regions.
[2] He had become Crossman's Private Secretary at M.H.L.G. in 1965 and remained in the Private Office until 1966, when he became an Assistant Secretary. Since 1972 he has been an Under-Secretary at the Department of the Environment. See Vol. I.

I was in a foul temper that afternoon, all the fouler because once again I had nothing to do. I filled in time talking to Bernard Floud, the M.P. for Acton who works at Granada TV.[1] Suddenly arrived a message—would I come across to Marlborough House straightaway to see the P.M.

This was very amusing. It was five o'clock when I arrived at Marlborough House and I fought my way through hundreds of press men and Lobby correspondents. Apparently the battle on Rhodesia had eased off for the moment and an attempt was being made to draft an agreed communiqué. I entered by the main door and was taken not to Harold's private office but to the chairman's room, which is a kind of large committee room immediately behind the hall where the plenary session was taking place. Harold and I sat in a corner on little hard chairs while people like George Brown and a number of the Premiers passed into and out of the plenary session. They looked a bit surprised to see us chatting there.

We talked for a solid hour. It was the worst possible moment since the crisis was at its height, with Harold drafting one communiqué and the Afro-Asian caucus a rival communiqué. I gather the Conference was told that the Lord President had come to talk to the Prime Minister about a matter un-related to their business. What would they have thought if they'd realized that he was spending an hour on the tiddling problem of the co-ordination of information services as one of the Lord President's functions? But Harold knew it was vital to keep me quiet. First he told me I would have the broad-cast on Thursday. He was dead tired. His face was parchmenty and flattened out like that of an old tortoise, and his eyes so tired they were scarcely moving. Still, he gave me a running commentary on what was going on and a graphic description of how he'd persuaded Lester Pearson to try his hand at a com-promise communiqué this evening.[2] I had to switch him over to the subject of the Lord President's function by saying I'd brought over the second minute which I'd sent via Marcia but which he hadn't had time to see. He glanced at it but didn't really read it and then he began to talk very fast about the need for an investigation of the Whitehall information services; how I should conduct it with Trevor Lloyd-Hughes, perhaps, as my chief helper and one administrative civil servant; how I should take ten days or a fortnight on it. I said, 'Well, that's fine but what about Peter Brown? I've got to have a decision. I may as well tell you I've already sent him back to the Ministry of Housing.' 'Well,' he said, 'that may be wise because it might have been diffi-

[1] Labour M.P. for Acton from 1964 until his death in October 1967.

[2] Leader of the Opposition in the Canadian Parliament 1958–63 and leader of the Liberal Party and Prime Minister 1963–8. His compromise at the Conference was designed to give the British Government three months, but no longer, for final discussions with Rhodesia, with the undertaking that no agreement would be concluded which did not embody the six principles. If no agreement had been reached by December, the British Government would support mandatory U.N. sanctions and agree to a Statement that without majority rule there would be no legal independence for Rhodesia. See Harold Wilson, *The Labour Government 1964–70, A Personal Record* (London: Weidenfeld & Nicolson and Michael Joseph, 1971) hereafter cited as *Wilson*.

cult to fit him in with Trevor Lloyd-Hughes.' In his own mind he'd already got rid of the awkward promise he'd made me and now he was trying to find some way of patching things up. So we discussed at some length what co-ordination of the information services is required. I said it wasn't much good my just investigating unless I was the co-ordinator. He said, 'Well, that's treading on a lot of people's feet. I would have to make a statement about the Paymaster-General's position.'

Suddenly I remembered that officially it is the Paymaster-General's job to answer questions on co-ordination of the information services. For months the little that had been done was done by me but George Wigg certainly wouldn't like a public pronouncement and I began to suspect that this was one of the causes of my troubles. Here I was barging in saying I should take over co-ordination of services whereas George would rather have no services at all than have me do them.

And, of course, there will be no co-ordination. The job is supposed to be done by Trevor Lloyd-Hughes and his staff at No. 10 but they haven't done it and my little foray has met no success whatsoever. Still I had the satisfaction of making a dog-tired Prime Minister in a crucial moment of the Conference talk to me for an hour and smooth me down.

From Marlborough House I went on to another of those parties, this time an Indian party, where I met Nicky and Clarissa Kaldor along with Tommy Balogh. We all had a very good dinner in Soho where we talked about Europe. This is now one of Tommy's manias. He believes there's a great danger that George Brown and Michael Stewart together will launch an effort to get us quickly into Europe and he was saying this was terrible because we should be deeply humiliated if our application was rejected again. Nicky and I both took a rather different view. We weren't as alarmed as Tommy about the humiliation; what really mattered, we felt, was whether we ought to get in and whether there was a chance of doing so. If we were prepared to devalue the pound could we slip into Europe quickly this year and so escape from our misery? And if we could, would we want to do it? I said I wasn't absolutely sure about anything. But I must say that if it were possible to do it this year we shouldn't turn it down straightaway because I haven't found the twenty months we've spent outside Europe and close to America very attractive, particularly in view of our new subordinate relation to L.B.J.[1] So I think it would be crazy to turn down the possibility of entry. What we ought to do is to discuss it in far greater detail, not only thinking about agriculture but trying to see what would happen to the whole economy if we join.

[1] Lyndon Baines Johnson had become President of the United States after the assassination of John Kennedy in November 1963. In November 1964 he was elected to serve his own full term. On September 13th the Federal Reserve Bank of New York had announced that its reciprocal swap arrangements with the central banks would be increased from $2,800 million to $4,500 million and its arrangement with the Bank of England from $600 million to $1,350 million.

Wednesday, September 14th

The big news this morning was the declaration of 10,000 redundancies at B.M.C.—the dramatic effect of our official Socialist deflation policy. I spent most of the morning preparing my broadcast, trying to deal with this as well as making it a short, sharp directive to our people about their attitude to prices and incomes policy.

When I'd finished the draft I had a meeting with Marcia and Gerald Kaufman from No. 10 and also with Tony Wedgwood Benn. I read the draft aloud and when I got to the piece about the crisis in the Midlands Marcia said she was deeply shocked. I was interested and surprised because I assumed that the right way to handle the news was to be tough and say, 'Yes, we are deliberately creating transitional redundancy in order to prevent mass unemployment.' Indeed, I'd put in a sentence suggesting that we'd raised the terms of hire purchase in order to reduce the home consumption of cars but Tony Wedgwood Benn removed this as being too tough. Having got them to agree on a draft I sent it round that evening to D.E.A., to the Ministry of Labour, to the Ministry of Technology and to No. 10. I learnt a lot from Marcia's and Gerald's detailed criticisms. Because they are close to Harold they are portentously cautious and naturally prefer to say things which are unprovocative, always choosing the soft approach—the soft word which doesn't sharpen thought. I'm inclined to do the opposite and I've no doubt whatsoever that though the redraft lost a great deal it also gained a great deal.

Thursday, September 15th

Trevelyan and David Holmes,[1] poor things, had a terrible morning when we had to work on the draft and put in all the comments we received, including a long personal letter from the Chancellor. The Office was completely bewildered and we had a hell of a rush to get a draft ready and arrive at the B.B.C. at 11 a.m. Percy Clark was there in the usual turmoil but everything came out all right and it was on the tape by 12.15. I got my first propaganda directive out and that was some small consolation for the annihilating defeat I had suffered in the case of Peter Brown and the information services.

After recording the broadcast I took Anne out for a quiet Indian lunch at Veeraswamy's and then went back to my office in the afternoon for a series of conferences. There was an interesting one on the B.B.C. with Sir Edward Fellowes who was really our nicest and best Clerk in the Commons.[2] I went through all my programme with him and to my amazement got quite a lot of support. Trevelyan said to me afterwards, 'Well, you did something I've never seen before, you got Sir Edward Fellowes to be in favour of reform!'

In the evening I gave a dinner at the Garrick for the Chief Whip, Freddie

[1] Crossman's Assistant Private Secretary.
[2] He served as Clerk in the House of Commons from 1954 until his retirement in 1961. He was chairman of the General Advisory Council of the B.B.C. and chairman of the Hansard Society for Parliamentary Government 1962–7. He was knighted in 1955 and died in December 1970.

Warren and a number of the Clerks. As a social occasion it was a great success and I learnt something from it. Some of these officials believe that it's the job of the Lord President, or rather of the Leader of the House, to get his business through as fast as possible. They feel shocked at the mere idea that I am so interested in the right of Parliament to criticize the executive that I might permit business to be slowed down. And if they feel shocked at the idea, other people, including my Cabinet colleagues, would be even more shocked. My chief conclusion from the evening is that I must make sure I don't give the impression that I'm too weak and conciliatory a Leader.

Friday, September 16th

At 9.30 there was a meeting of S.E.P.—the new Committee which I had insisted should be set up in the course of the July crisis[1] so that we could discuss, in a kind of inner Cabinet, serious problems like devaluation. Looking round the table I saw that the Committee was fairly small. It consisted of the Prime Minister, the First Secretary, the Chancellor, the Lord President, the Foreign Secretary, Ministers of Defence and Labour and the President of the Board of Trade. Of course we discussed the Midlands redundancies. We agreed there was so far no cause for alarm and the Chancellor said he wanted 30 per cent redundancy not 40 per cent, and perhaps the effect of the hire-purchase cuts had been a little more drastic than he had expected. We might have to revise our policy fairly soon but there should be no change now. We all agreed but felt if there were a welter of closures among small subsidiary engineering contracting firms then we might have to rebuild business by improved investment allowances and we should have to start reflating.

The second issue was import quotas. Last night Tommy Balogh came to warn me that Michael Stewart was proposing that we should drop the whole plan for introducing quotas when the 10 per cent import surcharge,[2] which we imposed as soon as we came into office, came to an end at the end of 1966. In our July discussions we'd always assumed that we would have to reintroduce these quotas as soon as the surcharge came off to prevent a flood of imports that would make it impossible to achieve a surplus on the balance of trade. But now Michael Stewart was proposing to drop import quotas altogether. At the meeting it was obvious that Stewart was in cahoots with the Treasury; he did all the talking but Callaghan supported him. George Brown and Douglas Jay opposed very well: they wanted the controls prepared. The P.M. took up a middle position. He showed he was glad that we were insisting on continuing preparations for introducing quotas but he said that we didn't

---

[1] It had been announced, on July 14th, 1966, that bank rate would be increased and overseas expenditure reduced and, on July 20th, that there would be a six months' wage freeze to be followed by a further six months' severe restraint and an immediate price freeze of twelve months' duration. See Vol. I, pp. 569–77.

[2] A 15 per cent surcharge had been announced on October 26th, 1964. It was reduced to 10 per cent on April 27th, 1965, and finally abolished on November 30th, 1966. See Vol. I, p. 165.

need to make a firm decision about them until January or February. I'm not at all sure that it is wise to postpone this decision. But under Harold Wilson this isn't the kind of decision which you can get a Government to take.

S.E.P. was followed immediately by a Cabinet meeting in which we had a longish discussion about the recall of Parliament (this was largely a repeat of one of the items of S.E.P.). Should we recall Parliament for two days – one for Rhodesia and the other for Part IV of the Bill – or should we try and spin matters out until Parliament resumes after the Party Conference? My main concern was to make sure that we got the authorization of the Parliamentary Party for introducing Part IV.[1] If the affair can be played out until after Conference and the Order made a week after that it won't be unreasonable to present it to the P.L.P. meeting directly Parliament returns. The rest of Cabinet was devoted to agriculture and Fred Peart asked the Chancellor to tell the banks not to be so bloody-minded about credit to farmers. The Chancellor blithely said that nothing was wrong. I must say from my own practical experience in Banbury I realized that the Chancellor's account of what the banks are doing is completely untrue. But even under pressure from me he wasn't prepared to tell us what the actual terms of his instructions to the banks were. I told him that I had evidence of two banks at least refusing farmers credit on express instructions from the Treasury. Jim Callaghan was anxious to get away and became quite obliging to Fred.

One conclusion I reached as a result of watching Michael Stewart, first in S.E.P. and then in Cabinet, is that he's already become a tool of the Treasury and I foresee the worst possible prospect of complete Treasury domination now that he has taken George Brown's place at D.E.A. In the long run I must get myself out of this damn job and into D.E.A. but if I'm going to do that I've got to do a decent job here and that's something I must settle down to.

Sunday, September 18th

We motored over to Hinton for dinner with Nicholas and Olga Davenport yesterday. There we found Sir Robert Hall, the Treasury adviser,[2] and a nice young man called Bamber Gascoigne, who's the theatre critic of the *Spectator*. It was a very pleasant evening without too much politics. We had a magnificent dinner, really splendidly prepared by Olga's Portuguese staff, and at 11.30 when we were due to go Nicholas took us outside to see how he had floodlit his garden. He's got the lamps two inches underground throwing the light up on to his trees, his boat and a bridge looking like a perfect crescent moon. I couldn't help remembering Chequers just a week ago. At Hinton you

[1] In the autumn the Association of Supervisory Staffs, Executives and Technicians (ASSET), a left-wing union, challenged the employers in the courts for breach of contract in withholding agreed wage increases. On September 29th ASSET were to win a test case, and the Government was obliged to consider whether to invoke the compulsory powers.

[2] Director of the Economic Section of the Cabinet Office 1947–53 and Economic Adviser to the Government 1953–61. He was Principal of Hertford College, Oxford, 1964–7, and in 1969 he became a life peer, taking the title of Lord Roberthall.

really feel you are being entertained in a great house which is being used for a fitting purpose. That's not the feeling I've had at Chequers.

Monday, September 19th

We've been having extraordinary autumn weather. Ever since my Cornish holiday it took a turn for the better and after a dreadful July we've had the most perfect September with the result that Pritchett tells me the farm may have the best year for a decade.[1] We've got all our cereals in, we've got a very decent potato crop and we've also got a crop of timothy-grass seed worth something over £800, a cash crop in which Mr P. is making a rather risky experiment. So there's a good £6,000 profit on the farm and we shall have to consider the tax problem of dividing it up—how much Pritchett should have, how much there should be for the farm and how much for the men.

I travelled up to London from Prescote by the easygoing 10.47 and gave lunch to Michael Stewart (Tommy Balogh's number two economic expert)[2] because the P.M. has graciously permitted me to share the advice of his economic staff. I chose Michael Stewart because he's an able young professional economist and I thought it would be a useful exercise for him as well as for me to make sure I understood the nature of our economic crisis. I've been thinking of a speech in which I could suggest that the thirties' crisis was a Keynesian crisis of demand failure whereas the crisis of the sixties was caused by full employment and the resulting excess demand and inflation. Michael taught me in a severe tutorial that it's politically dangerous to talk about inflation in this way as a disease of the economy. The real contrast, he says, is between the 'demand-pull' failure in consumer demand in the 1930s which could have been solved by Keynesian methods of stimulating expenditure and the new crisis of 'cost-push' and stunted economic growth in the 1960s. If I stress the notion of inflation I'm failing to realize that inflation is not a disease comparable to mass unemployment; indeed inflation has certain advantages as part of a process of economic growth. I got him to write all this down and at the bottom of his third page he concluded that if we don't get our exports to balance our imports we shall be compelled to increase taxation. I immediately said, 'Why should we? Why shouldn't importers go on importing even though exports aren't balancing?' And the real reason is because we want to avoid devaluation. The real justification for the appallingly violent deflation and the amount of redundancy the Government is causing is that we are trying to keep the pound steady.

When I'd clarified this I said to Michael, 'Well, would you please rewrite the end of the paper and tell me what would happen if instead of deflating we

[1] Dennis Pritchett managed the Crossmans' farm.

[2] A Treasury economist until he became an unsuccessful Labour candidate in 1964 and 1966. He worked with Thomas Balogh in the Cabinet Office 1964-7 and in 1969 became Reader in Political Economy at University College, London. His wife, Frances, daughter of Nicholas Kaldor, is also an economist.

2*

decided on economic growth plus devaluation?' 'Oh,' he said, 'I couldn't put that on paper.' 'Come on,' I said, 'you are an economic adviser.' 'No,' he said, 'Tommy and I wouldn't dare do that now since it might get round to Harold.' That very interesting remark shows to what degree Harold is exercising a real intellectual censorship from No. 10. He doesn't want to face the possibility of devaluation despite all the promises he made (to me in particular) during the July crisis. Though S.E.P. has been established there is no sign of any officials working out the promised papers on what would happen under alternative kinds of devaluation. I shall have to go on reminding Harold of his obligations.

This week I had planned to follow up my Coventry speech on prices and incomes with another think-piece on the move forward from Keynesianism. But by the end of the week, thanks to Michael Stewart, most of the profundity, which was bogus profundity, had been knocked out of my draft so I had to set out a very conventional, sensible statement explaining the need for transitional redundancies and saying it is something we can't shirk. I should get a respectable press for it.

That first Coventry speech is reverberating in a most extraordinary way. Both *Tribune* and the *Spectator* devoted their main leaders to the speech this weekend and *The Economist* does too. Of course all three denounce my ideas as wicked, perverse, clever nonsense—a wheeze which I've thought up. *Tribune* is angry because my ideas will split the Left into a pro-Government socialist-planning Left and an anti-Government anarchist Left led by Frank Cousins and Michael Foot. No wonder they are angry. I can also see why the *Spectator* attacks me. They think my proposals are an ingenious device for rallying the Labour movement behind Wilson. But why should *The Economist*, which purports to be a non-party paper genuinely seeking the good of the country, refuse to take seriously my suggestion that we shouldn't just waste twelve months crudely operating Part IV but use the time we have won to work out a voluntary incomes and prices policy to follow it? I suppose the answer is that all of them see a danger that Wilson may be re-invigorated and move forward to a more radical left-wing policy this year if he can really get a grip on incomes and prices and deal with inflation. And of course they are right. From their point of view it would be a terrible thing if Harold pulled himself together and got down to planning the central Socialist control which has been so entirely lacking in the Government up till now.

At tea-time I went to have a general chat with Harold. I was mainly concerned to hear what he had done about the proposal that I should run an investigation into the information services. He said he'd been talking to Burke Trend and Trevor Lloyd-Hughes and I asked whether he wanted an official investigation or a political investigation. 'I want it political,' he said. 'I want you to do it yourself and I'll get Burke Trend to fix it up with the Departments.' I'm still extremely dubious; I can't believe anything will come out of this.

I daresay I carried my depression to the Garrick when I took Barbara Castle to dinner. We agreed that we ought to meet regularly. It's one of my jobs as a senior member of the Government to keep Harold in contact with his left-wingers. Barbara and I worked out a sort of scheme. Of course we can't form a caucus against Harold in the Government or indeed any caucus at all. But I think we shall have to restore the meetings that used to take place between Barbara, Tony Benn, Tommy Balogh, Peter Shore and myself. It shouldn't be too difficult for me to tell Harold that this little group is getting going again and it's one he will know all about and will, I hope, join occasionally. One advantage will be that I can keep them informed of what is going on in the stratosphere when they are sitting in their Departments and feeling left out, as they usually do. That's another job I'll have to try to do as Lord President.*

Tuesday, September 20th
Last night I caught the ten o'clock sleeper to Aberdeen because I was due to have a Privy Council with the Queen at Balmoral this morning.[1] The first thing I noticed was the difference between a trip organized by John Delafons and my Private Office in M.H.L.G. and a trip organized by the Privy Council Office. When we got to Aberdeen at breakfast-time I found no rooms had been booked for us to bath and change in and the hotel was full. I also found that for the return journey we'd been booked on a train without a dining car and we had to change to a later train at 8.30. Though I'm a much more senior Minister now I'm much less well ministered to in my lordly isolation.

We started off from Aberdeen at 10.30 this morning to motor to Balmoral —an absolutely perfect windless autumn day, as we went up the Dee Valley climbing slowly into the mountains. Of course the Grampians are nothing like as beautiful as the west coast. Balmoral was chosen by Prince Albert merely because the weather was drier than in the west. At that time the mountains were almost without trees but now many of them have been beautifully forested. When we arrived we found a typical Scottish baronial house, looking as though it had been built yesterday, with a nice conventional rose garden and by the little church a golf course, which nobody plays on except the staff. As soon as we got there I took a little walk with Michael Adeane[2] by the banks of the Dee and then came back for the Privy Council. As Lord President I had to go and see the Queen first with the papers for the

* Of course nothing came of this.
[1] The Lord President, one of Her Majesty's Privy Councillors, customarily attended the Queen for such formal business as the giving of the Royal Assent to Bills and Orders in Council.
[2] Equerry and Assistant Private Secretary to King George VI 1937–52 and to the Queen 1952–3. Private Secretary to the Queen and Keeper of Her Majesty's Archives 1953–72. In 1972 he became a life peer and has since then served as chairman of the Royal Commission on Historical Monuments.

meeting. We chatted for a few moments, then the others came in and lined up beside me and I read aloud the fifty or sixty Titles of the Orders in Council, pausing after every half a dozen for the Queen to say 'Agreed'. When I'd finished, in just two and a half minutes, I concluded with the words, 'So the business of the Council is concluded.' The Privy Council is the best example of pure mumbo-jumbo you can find. It's interesting to reflect that four Ministers, busy men, all had to take a night and a day off and go up there with Godfrey Agnew to stand for two and a half minutes while the list of Titles was read out. It would be far simpler for the Queen to come down to Buckingham Palace but it's *lèse-majesté* to suggest it.

After the Privy Council we went for a drink in the drawing-room. It has a wonderful long picture painted on slate in which Landseer has a really jolly sketch of the young Princess Royal riding home from a stag hunt with Prince Albert benignly bending over her. What a splendid painter he would have been if he'd just left all his paintings half-finished like this one. During the drinks the Queen was extremely good at keeping things going but I noticed this time even more than last how shy she can be. When we walked back into the drawing-room I was carrying my papers and she was carrying hers. I put mine down on a side table and she held hers tight in her hand. Somebody tried to take them off her and she said, 'No, I must go and get rid of them.' But she stood there for three minutes without a drink, with the papers in her hand and with nothing to say. If one waits for her to begin the conversation nothing happens. One has to start to talk and then suddenly the conversation falters because both are feeling, 'Oh dear, are we boring each other?' She has a lovely laugh. She laughs with her whole face and she just can't assume a mere smile because she's really a very spontaneous person. Godfrey Agnew was right when he said to me that evening that she finds it difficult to suppress her emotion. When she is deeply moved and tries to control it she looks like an angry thunder-cloud. So, very often when she's been deeply touched by the plaudits of the crowd she merely looks terribly bad-tempered.

He also told me an extraordinary story of a Privy Council which went fantastically wrong when Sir Edward Bridges[1] was there with four politician Privy Councillors. Somehow they got themselves kneeling on the wrong side of the room, facing Sir Edward. He waved them away and they crawled across the room on their hands and knees. In the process they knocked a book off the table and it had to be rescued by the Queen, who looked blackly furious. After the Privy Council had gone out Sir Edward crept back into the room and she said something very pleasant to him. He said how terribly sorry he was and she said, 'You know, I nearly laughed.' Then he realized that when she'd looked terribly angry it was merely because she was trying to stop herself laughing.

[1] Secretary to the Cabinet 1938–46 and Permanent Secretary to the Treasury 1945–56. He was made a Baron in 1957 and died in August 1969.

At lunch she talked to Kenneth Robinson about the Commonwealth premiers they had met and I talked to her about the ones I had met, particularly Makarios. He had sat next to her because he's the senior Prime Minister. After lunch we went off for the walk which I had demanded. We were lent a car and motored out with Sir Edward Ford (who was at Harrow when I was at Winchester),[1] Godfrey Agnew and the lady-in-waiting. We made for a lake about fifteen miles up a very lonely road. Near the lake was a largish dull house built in a very gloomy grove. This is where Queen Victoria escaped from the crowded atmosphere of Balmoral for a little solitude; apparently she made Gladstone stay there for a whole week, sleeping in a little room behind hers. Since her time the house has been almost untouched and the others took a look around. I was so anxious to get out for a walk that I didn't stay, but on the walk I heard that the Royal Family have barbecue picnics up there regularly since this is one of the very few lakes in the east Highlands. We walked along the lake and up to a waterfall—it was a perfect afternoon stroll lasting about one and a half hours. Hurrying back, so as not to be late for tea with the Queen, I asked the lady-in-waiting how the Royal Family spent their time and whether they liked Balmoral. 'Oh yes,' she said, 'they like it very much. The Queen feels relaxed up here.' 'Does she like fishing?' I asked. 'No, she doesn't like fishing.' 'Does she like shooting?' 'No, she does a little deer-stalking but she doesn't really like it. Prince Philip, of course, likes the shooting.' 'And how do they spend their time?' I said. 'Oh,' she said, 'they're kept terribly busy. It's a tremendous burden keeping the stags down and culling the grouse. They have to go out every day early in the morning and there's a regular routine of guests arriving for shooting. It's very hard work indeed.' I began to realize how pleasure can become a chore. At Balmoral the elaborate pleasure of grouse-shooting has now become a mechanical routine into which royalty has to fit whether it likes it or not.

As we got back to the house the landrovers had just returned from the grouse-shooting; they had 170 brace. We went in to tea with the Queen while they were disposing of their booty because we wanted to get away at 5.30 and dine at Aberdeen. Just as I was settling down to a quiet talk with the Queen about forestry and whether we should plant conifers, in boomed Philip. He sat down opposite me beside the Queen, took over the conversation and gave me a long lecture on how the Ministry of Land and Natural Resources had been wrongly organized. When I said that we had reabsorbed it some months ago he said, 'Who's we?' I said that I had been the Minister of Housing then. He looked a little disconcerted for a moment but not for long. For over half an hour he simply took over the conversation and then he looked at his watch and said to the Queen, 'Well, they ought to be going now.' And out we went.

[1] Secretary to the Pilgrim Trust since 1967 and Assistant Private Secretary to the Queen 1952–67. He farmed in Northamptonshire, near the Crossmans.

On the way down in the train Sir Godfrey Agnew poured his heart out to me. He's a passionately loyal servant of the Queen.

Wednesday, September 21st

For most of the morning I was with Hugh Greene at Broadcasting House. I had decided to beard the lion in his den and by talking to him quite informally, to establish better relations between the B.B.C. and the Government. I worked very hard but I did find it difficult to keep the conversation going and I'm not sure how much rapport we achieved. It surprised me because after all for nearly two years of the war I worked with him every day and we became pretty intimate friends. But as Director-General of the B.B.C. he is stiff and rigid. However it was worth having the talk to make him feel that with John Silkin and myself in office the new regime would be more reasonable, without the absurd rows between the P.M. and the B.B.C. which marred the first months of the Government. Harold is always complaining that the B.B.C. is prejudiced and biased against him and I've got to try and smooth him out a bit if I can.

I spent the afternoon with Trevelyan and Holmes. Miss Nunn of the Cabinet Secretariat was present as well.[1] She's a very senior and important person in the Burke Trend entourage and she was concerned to see that my Cabinet paper on televising the Commons was properly produced and properly drafted. Obviously there's going to be tremendous opposition in Whitehall against televising Select Committees. However, I got off that subject on to the importance of keeping in step with the House of Lords. What I want is to put up an agreed paper on how we should televise the whole Palace of Westminster—Lords and Commons. Here I did make a little advance. Longford and Listowel[2] tend to agree with me that we should make a single presentation to Cabinet and we might easily make a joint proposition that the eight weeks of the experiment should be divided into four weeks for the Commons and two weeks for the Lords, with a final fortnight for trying to put the whole thing together.

In the afternoon my 'small committee' discussed this all over again. But of course our main subject was still redundancy in the Midlands. I must say that here old Ray Gunter, as Minister of Labour, has been staunchly loyal. He's made speech after speech saying we can't have labour-hoarding, and that transitional redundancy is the only way to save full employment. This is exactly the line we should all take. Still, as he knows very well, it's extremely unlikely that the redundancies we are creating in the motor-car industry have anything to do with scientifically planned redeployment. Nearly

---

[1] Miss Jean Nunn joined the Home Office in 1938. She was an Under-Secretary 1963–6 and Deputy Secretary at the Cabinet Office 1966–70.

[2] The Earl of Listowel succeeded to his father's title in 1931. He had held various offices in post-war Labour Governments. From 1966 he served as Chairman of Committees in the Upper House.

all the quality papers point this out, though Harold Wilson goes on giving it as a great example of economic planning. In the Midlands the redundancies have meant a welcome but unintentional manning-up of such public utilities as the Coventry bus services, but in the development areas the redundancies are affecting the export industries. We are making a mythology which bears little relation to the facts. Nevertheless, as political propaganda the myth has got to be accepted and we have planned a new edition of the TV current-affairs programme *This Week* to prepare the argument for Conference.

Thursday, September 22nd
Cabinet. I was asked to go round to No. 10 a few minutes early for a chat with Harold. He had before him a draft directive for the conduct of my investigation of the information services. I pointed out that it covered all services whereas we ought to exclude the Foreign Office and the Commonwealth Relations Office since this had been a clear-cut decision at the last Cabinet. He accepted this and added, 'Even so, we will probably have great difficulty with our colleagues but I'll do my best for you.' So the meeting started and right at the beginning, before anything else came up, he announced the subject and began to prose on about information services. He prosed and prosed and prosed and when it was over Tony Crosland said, 'Well, an investigation is long overdue.' Suddenly a row broke out about the appalling failure of co-ordination of the information services last week when someone forgot to tell the Ministers concerned about an important decision made by S.E.P. It was an utterly ludicrous example of poor co-ordination of information and it certainly was lucky for me that someone remembered it this morning. After the quarrel had gone on some time Harold said, 'Any other comments?' There was a murmur 'Agreed' and there I was with full Cabinet backing for my investigation and my power conceded 'To conduct an inquiry, to recommend what improvements are required in inter-departmental machinery in the field of home information services in order to ensure the most timely and effective and consistent public presentation of the Government's policies without prejudice to the normal responsibility of individual Ministers for the presentation of their own departmental policies and for the co-ordination in appropriate cases of the policies of related departments.'

This afternoon we had a meeting at No. 10 about political Honours. Harold was in the chair and the only other people there were Tony Greenwood as Minister of Local Government, myself and the Chief Whip. Harold again repeated his determination to get rid of political Honours. I had thought this a good idea at first but after I'd talked to Len Williams at Transport House and heard the reaction of our regional officers and Party agents I realized that excluding political Honours really meant excluding Party agents and regional organizers and virtually no one else. When Harold heard this he replied, 'We'll include them all under public Honours.' But of course once you do this your announcement is merely a gimmick because you *haven't* cut out political Honours. The decision only makes sense if you announce that people who serve a political party are excluded from the Honours list and once you discriminate against professional Party agents in this way it causes a terrible depression and lack of morale in the Party. I've talked this over with Doug Garnett[1] and I'm not sure I shall not have to write another minute to Harold saying that we really can't drift into this unless he can find better reasons for the change.

This evening I had a very sad dinner with Richard Llewelyn-Davies and his wife, Patricia. Tony Greenwood and Jill, and Lord Esher,[2] the architect, and his wife, were the only other guests. I didn't quite know how to behave because Esher showed himself almost heartbroken not only because I had left the Department but because he felt a Government becomes meaningless when this kind of thing happens. He actually said to me, 'How can we make any sense of a left-wing Government which puts a man out of his job just when he's settling down to it? How can this shuffling round of Ministers be justified? It makes the Government look so frivolous.' One has to admit that while Harold's shuffle may have been clever politics and helped him to ward off the danger of a Brown–Callaghan conspiracy against him it made a thoroughly bad impression on the British public because it suggested that politicians don't really know anything about anything and are just shoved round as part of a political game. It was the musical chairs with nobody falling out which made it seem so silly.

The evening was made more painful for me by the fact that Tony Greenwood said first to Anne and then to me how tremendously lucky I was to be Lord President. It's a job which has status, importance and makes me Harold's closest personal friend. All this would obviously have pleased and delighted him and Jill whereas the sheer grind of being Minister of Housing isn't all that attractive to them.

But let's be fair to him. He's extremely good at public relations and already he's made one or two decisions which have put him over very well. It may well be that in terms of the way he presents himself to the public the Government won't suffer any political loss. Where we shall lose is in the reputation of the Government in Whitehall and the power we exert there. Though I may have made many mistakes, the Civil Service knew that I was a Minister who got a grip on his Department. Richard told Anne his impression of the Civil Service attitude towards me. They said, 'Normally we either have a stupid Minister under whom we can get our way or a clever Minister, and if we have a clever Minister then we break him by sheer stamina. But in Dick Crossman we have somebody who is both clever and who beats us in stamina. It's the fact that we can't overwhelm him with work which so much impresses us.' I

---

[1] Labour Party Regional Organizer for East Anglia.
[2] Architect of such major projects as Hatfield New Town and, since 1971, Rector of the Royal College of Art. He was known as Lionel Brett before succeeding to his father's viscountcy in 1963.

think this is true. And it's thoroughly bad for the Government's prestige in Whitehall when the civil servants know that one of the few members of the Government who can really come to grips with his Department has been whipped out just at the moment when he was becoming dangerous.

Friday, September 23rd
Morning prayers with the P.M. and Burke Trend was made pretty useless because George Brown turned up. However, I picked up an interesting fact—Julian Melchett[1] has been selected as chairman of the Steel Board, at a salary of £25,000 a year, double the normal salary for the chairman of a nationalized industry.* I know Julian fairly well since I've often gone to the parties he and his wife, Sonia, give in Chelsea. He impressed me as an agricultural economist and a really charming man but if he wasn't the son of Lord Melchett no one would dream of this appointment. His own background is banking and agriculture. A strange appointment but I suppose it's the result of not finding anybody in the industry itself.

Then the P.M. got talking about Rhodesia and his agreeable surprise at how well Bert Bowden was doing at the talks—the cables had impressed me, too.[2] I'd noticed that all Harold's replies to Bert were based on the assumption that we want to put Smith in the position of having refused every positive idea we put to him. This will give an excuse if the talks fail. I think Harold's really written off the chance of an agreement, at least for the moment. He's now concerned to provide himself with a justification to put him right with the Opposition, the Government and the public at home. If that's true we're in for a very rough time in December when the U.N. impose mandatory sanctions.

Saturday, September 24th
Another beautiful autumn day. I motored along the M1 and right across Essex to Chelmsford, where Doug Garnett had booked me for another regional conference—three hundred people turned up in the town hall. Each time I make this speech it gets better. We had an hour's extremely friendly questions from a number of A.E.U. members, some of them with beards. They'd come to hammer us and afflict me, but one of the things I learnt in the W.E.A. is how to answer lots of questions. At the last moment I ended with a passionate appeal for the Party to participate actively in working out the new prices and incomes policy which must follow Part IV, working it out on the

---

* The story was in *The Times* next morning.
[1] He succeeded to his father's barony in 1949. From 1967 until his death in June 1973 he was chairman of the British Steel Corporation. His family, the Monds, had been among the earliest steelmakers in Britain.
[2] Herbert Bowden, the Commonwealth Secretary, and Sir Elwyn Jones, the Attorney-General, flew to Rhodesia on September 19th for discussions with the Governor, Sir Humphrey Gibbs, and the Chief Justice, Sir Hugh Beadle. They also had several fruitless meetings with Ian Smith before returning on September 28th.

shop-floor level. It's only if the Government works with the Party at all levels, I told them, that we have any chance of achieving a real, workable prices and incomes policy.

All that goes down marvellously with our Party workers but I'm afraid very few members of the Cabinet believe in participation. I learnt the philosophy from Tawney and Lindsay who taught me that social democracy consists of giving people a chance to decide for themselves—that's the essence of it.[1] This philosophy is extremely unpopular, I find, with most members of the Cabinet. They believe in getting power, making decisions and getting people to agree with the decisions after they've been made. They have the routine politician's attitude to public opinion that the politician must take decisions and then get the public to acquiesce. The notion of creating the extra burden of a live and articulate public opinion able to criticize actively and make its own choices is something which most socialist politicians keenly resent. It's not the view of Ray Gunter, for example, or of Michael Stewart, and it hasn't been the view of Harold Wilson up to date.

Sunday, September 25th
This weekend I've been reflecting on what is really wrong with the Government. The basic failing is a complete absence of effective central control. Harold Wilson jumped into panic measures in July. This has given us an opportunity to evolve better instruments for central planning. For instance we've now got our S.E.P. and the chance of a new economic strategy to follow Part IV. But so far this is all just talk. As Thomas Balogh tells me, Bill Nield is now trying to evolve an official committee to provide the papers for S.E.P.'s meetings.[2] Oh, my God. If we're going to have the usual routine of civil servants getting together and servicing us with their conclusions, S.E.P. won't be the strategy board we need. Talking to Harold last week I raised the need for an inner Cabinet as distinct from S.E.P. I walked round the room after him, round and round the table, saying we must get together regularly and discuss strategy. 'Shall we have a buffet lunch, perhaps?' he asked. 'Buffet lunch?' I said. 'Let's sit round this table—an informal group of your Ministers who really are going to think things out along with you.' He didn't turn the idea down because he's uneasily aware that his methods of getting

[1] Professor R. H. Tawney and A. D. Lindsay (Lord Lindsay of Birker). Tawney was Professor of Economic History at the University of London 1931–49 and President of the W.E.A. 1938–44. He died in January 1962. Of his many books perhaps the best-known is *The Acquisitive Society* (London: Bell, 1943). Lindsay was Master of Balliol College, Oxford, 1924–49 and, from 1949 until his death in 1952, Principal of University College of North Staffordshire at Keele. He was made a peer in 1945.

[2] Sir William Nield (K.C.B. 1968) entered the Ministry of Food in 1946 and, apart from two years in the Treasury (1946–9), remained at the Ministry of Agriculture, Fisheries and Food until 1964. He then joined the D.E.A. and became its Permanent Under-Secretary of State in 1966. He was a Deputy Secretary in the Cabinet Office 1966–8, where he became Permanent Secretary in 1969. In 1972 he became Permanent Secretary at the Northern Ireland Office until, in 1973, he became a director of Rolls Royce (1971) Ltd.

round every corner without any strategic thinking aren't working very well, but he didn't give any positive support. As for the prices and incomes policy, I have the gravest doubts from what I hear whether the D.E.A. under Michael Stewart has prepared any machinery for carrying out an effective price control if Part IV is put into operation. This shows the degree to which we lack a central direction. The only central direction this Government has consists of the P.M. surrounded by a few staff—Marcia Williams, George Wigg, Tommy Balogh, and Burke Trend from the Civil Service. But the whole of Whitehall has revolted against this idea of strong Prime Ministerial Government. Central coherent purpose was, after all, the main thing which Harold laid down as the characteristic which distinguished our method of government from the spasmodic drooling of the Tories; now we are drooling in a not very dissimilar way. I've got another personal anxiety. When I think about life now, when I think that here I am, Lord President of the Council, in Harold's Labour Government, I feel no relief. I don't feel I'm part of a Government pledged to fundamental change, with any idea of where it's going. When I'm in Cabinet I'm just sitting with a number of men who are running their Departments. And, strangely enough, just because we won an election, these men now feel that they can relax because they have five years ahead of them as Ministers. Personally, I don't feel very good just being a senior Minister unless I'm a member of a team determined to substitute central purposive direction for the old easy-going muddle-through. Though I'm devoted to Harold I know I'm working with a Prime Minister who has no more purposive direction than Macmillan had—rather less, I suspect—perhaps the same as Douglas-Home.[1] He's enormously skilled and clever but he hasn't an idea how to construct the vital central machine of control. The strange thing is that the Cabinet would be entirely willing to accept central direction from No. 10 because this will make the Cabinet system work and also because my colleagues want to survive and feel that they can't go on muddling through. They shared Harold Wilson's illusion that all that was necessary was for him to get into No. 10 instead of a Tory Prime Minister and then everything would automatically change. But of course since 1964 nothing has really changed. We're still working from hand to mouth trying to overcome the immediate short-term problems. It's true that departmentally in Housing and Education and Social Security things are not going too badly. It's at the centre, where strong strategic purpose is essential, that the failure lies.

Wednesday, September 28th
For the first three days of this week I have been pretty solidly engaged on my investigations of the information services. After today's Cabinet, of which

---

[1] Both were Conservative Prime Ministers, Harold Macmillan from January 10th, 1957, to October 13th, 1963, and Alec Douglas-Home from October 18th, 1963, to October 16th, 1964.

more later, I have still two more Ministers to see, the last being Barbara
Castle with whom I shall travel down to Brighton on Thursday evening for
the Labour Party Conference.

Burke Trend had done his job: Whitehall had been alerted and Ministers
normally turned up along with their chief information officers. The Investigating Committee consisted of myself as chairman along with a man called
Pitchforth[1] from the Treasury and Trevor Lloyd-Hughes. Trevelyan acted as
secretary. We soon got into a rhythm of examination and it became pretty
clear that Harold's decision to wind up what he called the 'Tory Ministry of
Propaganda' had destroyed the central co-ordination of information services
which was working pretty well in the last years of the Macmillan Government.
This meant that under Wilson there has been a great deal of departmental
free-wheeling. Each Ministry has evolved its own monitoring system, its
own advertising campaigns, its own techniques for handling the B.B.C. and
arranging Ministerial interviews. As the investigation goes on it is becoming
clear that all the information officers are convinced that the Tory system was
superior, that it is obviously right that a Minister supported by a small staff
should be in charge of co-ordinating Government propaganda, and that
without someone in this role there comes a great loss of co-ordination, willpower and drive. Nevertheless, I know very well there can be no question of
going back to the bad old days of Toryism. Harold is extremely obstinate.
Once he's committed himself to a public decision that Labour will never
spend Government money on a Ministry of Propaganda he isn't going to
back down on that at all easily.

There has been another complication right from the start. Trevor Lloyd-
Hughes has hated the whole investigation, is scared of losing his independence
and determined to prevent all changes. As a result we have had the extraordinary spectacle of the Treasury representative trying to enlarge the No. 10
staff and Trevor saying he doesn't want it.

Another awkward aspect of the investigation has been that about half the
Ministers and information officers have complained very bitterly about No. 10.
They say that co-ordination is difficult enough between Departments but it is
made infinitely more difficult by the fact that nobody knows which information
coming out of No. 10 is official and which has been leaked. This is something
I don't exactly know about. Of course it's true that Trevor's organization
is still the central agency for disseminating information about the activities
of the Government. But in addition to Trevor there's Gerald Kaufman
in No. 10 who is supposed to provide liaison with the Labour Party but
whom Harold uses from time to time for briefings—if you like it, leaks—
about which Trevor knows nothing. In the background there's the mysterious
George Wigg who, apart from dealing with security and investigating other

[1] Harold Pitchforth had formerly been Director of Establishments and Organization at
the Ministry of Agriculture, Fisheries and Food. From 1965 to 1967 he was Under-Secretary
at the Treasury.

people's leaks, is also entitled by Harold to brief certain press men, such as Ian Waller of the *Sunday Telegraph*.

The suspicion that all this uncoordinated information is coming out of No. 10 is used to justify counter-leaks by various Departments. When I'd established the facts I discussed the problem with many of the Ministers. It has been astonishing how many have said no better system can be created. For instance, Ray Gunter, the Minister of Labour, finds his own Press Officer perfect. He told me he doesn't need anything else. He is his own master — he is happy. I've no doubt he is because the Ministry of Labour is always getting its own way and constantly giving exclusive information to the press which shows it to advantage. Ray has made a tremendous impact as the Minister in charge of Part IV and has made it appear that though he's retiring from the National Executive this year he's concentrating on playing a big role in the Government. This of course infuriates poor Michael Stewart, who went to the D.E.A. last July on the express understanding that the Department was not going to be dismantled and that he was going to be number three in the pecking order and Callaghan number four. Yet when Michael tries to co-ordinate economic policy he finds an extraordinary reluctance not only in the Ministry of Labour but also in the Board of Trade, not to mention the Treasury. By the end of my investigation I couldn't help comparing our Government with the Attlee Government during the Cripps period.[1] At that time there were six or seven home-front Ministers who met every day, knew each other, lunched together, had a common purpose and therefore didn't fight or leak against each other. Owing to the creation of D.E.A. and the permanent rift between Brown and Callaghan, our Government has been riven with dissension and all the other Ministries have become independent and free-wheeling. So the appearance of disorder in Whitehall is a great deal worse than the disorder which exists and which can't be mended without structural alterations in the Cabinet. Nevertheless, most of the people we interrogated have agreed that there should be a Minister who, even if he can't be Minister of Information, is at least able to get hold of his colleagues and suggest that they should get together, issue joint Statements and reduce the amount of chaos in the Government's public relations.

That's the job which the unanimous report of Trevor Lloyd-Hughes, Pitchforth and I will recommend as a task for the Lord President. It's not a real job and involves no real change, but I suppose it's better than nothing. Whether I do it adequately or inadequately will determine very largely whether the P.M. gives me any further responsibility. I'm having to fight for each job whereas I was given the impression that as Lord President everything would be at my feet. Well, nothing is at my feet. I'm not even a member of the Defence Committee yet, though I asked for it straightaway: I'm simply

---

[1] Clement Attlee was Prime Minister from July 26th, 1945, to October 26th, 1951; and from September 29th, 1947, to October 15th, 1950, Sir Stafford Cripps was his Chancellor of the Exchequer.

Leader of the House with a vague responsibility for co-ordinating information as long as I don't upset anybody.

Nevertheless these three days' investigation have been quite an interesting experience. I have enjoyed sitting in that palatial Privy Council Office questioning my colleagues in this particular way.

Thursday, September 29th

At Cabinet we had a report from Bert Bowden and Elwyn Jones, back from Rhodesia. Bert spelt out his mission at great length and was warmly congratulated on what he had done. I couldn't see he'd done anything much— except that he hadn't given anything away. After that we had quite a long discussion on the tactics for the next stage. It seemed to me that Harold and Bert are now thinking again in terms of working up a package which would give Smith yet another last chance. Indeed, I've no doubt that's what they intend to do. In Cabinet I put rather strongly the dilemma as it presented itself to me. We must be clear in our minds whether our main preoccupation in the next stage is to prepare for a break-off or whether to produce a package which Smith can sign. If we think there is any chance of the second, we must be prepared to make some last-minute concessions however alien they may be to African opinion. If, on the other hand, there's no chance of the second, then it isn't worth alienating African opinion. Our whole behaviour from now on must be designed to strengthen our justification when the break occurs at the beginning of December. The evidence of the Bowden mission seemed to me to show that Smith hadn't the remotest intention of permitting any transfer of power from him to another kind of government of which he isn't in full control. All he's prepared to do is to have a formal transfer to the Governor provided he retains all the power in his own hands. And that's exactly what we can't afford. So the Bowden mission seemed to me to prove that deadlock remains absolutely unchanged and there's no real chance of our offering a package he can accept.

We then turned to discuss prices and incomes. That very day the ASSET case against Thorn Electrical Industries was being tried in the county court and it was almost certain that Clive Jenkins would win.[1] So after a longish discussion the Cabinet unanimously decided that Michael Stewart should now start the talks with the C.B.I. and the T.U.C. which would lead towards the implementation of Part IV. Once again there was some discussion about the timetable but we easily agreed to try to play it out through Conference well into Parliament. After that we turned to the reports in the papers about Lord Melchett. Dick Marsh wanted authority to nominate him as the chairman of the Organizing Committee for the steel renationalization. There was a good

---

[1] General Secretary of ASSET 1961–8; since 1968 General Secretary of A.S.T.M.S. The Government hoped that if ASSET won the case, as they did, the employers would consider taking the matter to appeal. Thus the Government would not yet have to decide whether or not to implement the penal element of Part IV.

deal of hostility to this round the Cabinet table and I still find it very extra-ordinary.

In the afternoon I had two important meetings. The first was when John Silkin introduced me to Willie Whitelaw and I found this as exhilarating as I expected. I was completely frank with him and told him all my plans for television; he told me how fiercely he was opposed to morning sittings. I got his tentative agreement to a specialist committee on agriculture in addition to the one on science and technology. After talking to him I really feel there's a hope that we shall get a big advance in parliamentary reform.

After that I had a very big meeting with all the television experts, the B.B.C. and I.T.V. to discuss the Select Committee report on broadcasting the proceedings of the house, and in particular to consider whether their proposal for an eight-week closed-circuit television experiment was practical. The officials were very much against the length because they said it would impose an appalling strain. I then suggested that we should divide the period sensibly with a couple of weeks for the House of Commons and for the House of Lords and some experimental filming of Select Committees and Standing Committees.[1] They seemed to be a bit surprised that the Lord President should have his own ideas and I asked them to report back as soon as possible.

After that I had the last interview of my four-day investigation. The client was Barbara Castle and after it was over we went down by train together to Brighton.

Friday, September 30th
As usual the monthly meeting of the N.E.C. in the week before Conference was transferred from Wednesday to Friday and took place in the Conference hotel. We started it with a farce because we'd only gone to this ghastly Grand Hotel instead of to the excellent Metropole because the Grand Hotel is supposed to have better arrangements for our Conference staffs, and a good room for the Executive to sit and work in. Well, the room we had to work in was impossible. We found after ten minutes that we couldn't hear a word of what anyone said because of the echo so we had to move upstairs to a little balcony where we were able to hear each other but couldn't see each other.

The main business of the morning was to consider the draft statement on economic policy, including prices and incomes, which had been prepared first by Terry Pitt in Transport House and then drastically redrafted by Tommy's Michael Stewart after consultations with Harold and Jim. The

---

[1] Select Committees of the House of Commons (such as the Select Committee on the Nationalized Industries or on Science and Technology, the Public Accounts Committee and the Expenditure Committee) consist of ten to fifteen Members, nominated by a motion in the House, and established either sessionally or by virtue of Standing Order. Their function is either to consider a problem or to hold a watching brief on some matter. Standing Committees have as their principal function the consideration of the Committee Stages of Bills. They consist of between sixteen and fifty Members well versed in the subject at issue, and their size and composition reflects the Party strengths in the House.

main interest was to see what the mood of the Executive would be. Would there be the kind of violent feelings there were in the old Bevanite period?[1] Not at all. There's no kind of deep feeling. Throughout the meeting Government policy had only three opponents—Jack Jones, Tom Driberg and Ian Mikardo. They, like their friend Frank Cousins, were root and branch opponents, but none of the other trade-union members of the Executive made any serious opposition that morning. They were entirely concerned about the problem of redundancy and in particular the impression created by Gunter's public statements that in principle the Government is opposed to work-sharing in the motor-car industry—the redundancies at B.M.C. have dominated the news for the last ten days.[2] Quite rightly, Johnny Boyd of the A.E.U. said, 'Let's be sensible about this', and put a passage into the document to show that where the staff will be fully employed again in the spring, firms are entitled to share the work out during the winter. So the passage was to be carefully written in and everything at the meeting was sweetness and light. It wasn't long before the document was referred to a drafting committee with George Brown in the chair and on which I had to serve.

A really interesting discussion followed on the selection of Executive speakers. I thought the officers' meeting I had staged would have settled the business, but when I looked at the list prepared by Len Williams I noticed that in the big economic debate on Wednesday Jim Callaghan was down to move and Michael Stewart, not Harold Wilson, to wind up. I'd heard rumours that Harold had been persuaded by Michael to make this change and before he went down to Brighton I told him that the Executive just wouldn't wear Michael. He's a very thin-lipped, tight, little man; in last year's Conference he was given permission to open the debate on Foreign Affairs and had caused a good deal of resentment. Now the proposal was that as First Secretary and head of the D.E.A. he should wind up on prices and incomes. Jack Jones said it was an insult to the Executive to suggest that we can't find a member to wind up this debate. 'Indeed,' said Jack, 'I'll propose to wind up myself if no one else will.' Then in came Alice Bacon and a host of others.[3] Of course, Harold Wilson had foreseen the possibility of this and had agreed with me that if Michael failed then Ray Gunter should take his place. Unlike Michael Stewart, who has to speak by permission of the Executive because he is not a member of it, Ray Gunter is a member and chairman of the Organization Sub-Committee and he's also Minister of Labour. The moment his name was put forward everybody agreed. Ray Gunter showed the neces-

---

[1] Michael Foot's *Aneurin Bevan 1945–60* (London: Davis-Poynter, 1972) discusses how, particularly at the annual Party Conference, the supporters of Aneurin Bevan clashed with those of Hugh Gaitskell, who was leader of the Labour Party 1955–63.

[2] B.M.C. had now declared 12,500 car workers redundant, and by November 10th another 100,000 were on short time.

[3] Labour M.P. for Leeds 1945–70, when she became a life peer. A member of the N.E.C. since 1941, she was Minister of State at the Home Office 1964–7, when she moved to the D.E.S., where she remained until 1970.

sary reluctance to be dragged on to the bed of nails but very soon it was fixed.

I may as well say straightaway that I have the gravest doubts about Harold Wilson in this move. He should not limit himself to one speech introducing the report of the Parliamentary Party on Tuesday when the big debate is due to take place on Wednesday. He told me he was convinced he could anticipate the big debate with a big constructive, forward-looking speech. I was very much afraid that he couldn't.*

I spent the afternoon redrafting the document. The meeting was due to start at 3.15. George Brown drifted in twenty minutes late and said he was too busy to attend, so I got hold of Johnny Boyd and we went down into the P.M.'s suite and found a table and secretary. We'd just about finished the job by five o'clock when the Executive resumed its meeting in order to approve the foreign policy document.

As a result of this meeting it was clear that both documents would need a lot more redrafting which I said I would do that evening. After Anne had arrived, in driving rain, I started work again and at 10 o'clock at night I finally got George Brown to look them through. To my surprise he turned out to be a really creative editor. He'd been given a drink by Harold down below and empowered to clear the draft. I saw that in comparison with Harold he has a warm and imaginative mind; in any daytime committee Harold is always a niggler and tries to draft himself. George let me do all the drafting but told me what he wanted in a way that I could carry it out.

But the big issue today was the announcement that the Newspaper Proprietors' Association have decided, after a talk to the unions, to pay their two-shilling increase from the following Monday in open violation of the prices and incomes policy. When we last discussed it we thought only about wages and assumed that the threat of having to impose Part IV had been pushed beyond the Conference. However, the news about the N.P.A. made it perfectly clear that we should have to operate Part IV straightaway. Late this evening I had a talk to Harold and we decided that he would have to call his Ministers together—those who are at Brighton—to decide what Cabinet's response should be.

Saturday, October 1st

This morning I had only two concerns. The first was about the decision the Ministers would take that afternoon about Part IV. On this I had a long talk with John Silkin and also with Manny Shinwell on the phone. My other concern was the speech I was due to make at the big Sunday demonstration. What kind of speech should it be? This morning I went down to Harold and tried out my idea. I said I thought it should be a definition of the role of the socialist party under a socialist government. I thought our people were

---

* On the last day of the Conference he admitted to me that I had been quite right. This is something worth recording because it is not often that Harold will admit he was wrong in a tactical decision.

terribly depressed at the feeling that our Party was of no importance under our Labour Government. But, as he and I agreed, it could have enormous importance; it could sustain the electoral machine and provide the Government with eyes and ears—not merely listening to the master's voice and putting out the master's propaganda but telling the Government how the public was taking its policies. Thirdly, and most important of all, it was the Party and the Party alone which had the job of working out long-term policy for the next election manifesto. I thought the speech should define these three jobs precisely and set them against the background of our belief as democratic socialists in Party democracy and mass participation. Harold immediately thought this was a wonderful idea—just what we needed. When I went back to my room I realized that if the speech was to have any effect there would have to be a long press release. Since there would be no other speech on Sunday night I ought to get a good coverage in the Monday papers. So I started working on the speech.

At 3.30 we had our meeting of Ministers. I made a blob because Harold had said he wanted senior Ministers and I told John Silkin to be there. But it was clear he didn't want people as unimportant as his Chief Whip. In fact the only Ministers present were Michael Stewart, who came down specially from London, Ray Gunter, the Attorney-General and myself. (George Brown was away in London seeing Sophie who is having a gall-bladder operation next week.) But there was very little to discuss because it was clear we should have to operate Part IV. I realized that this might upset the Parliamentary Party because we should have acted without consulting them. On the other hand, thank heavens, the guilty party was not a trade union insisting on a wage increase but an employer and the only person who could be gaoled was Cecil King.

I was also concerned to make sure that when Part IV went into operation we should act as strongly against prices as against wages. On this one or two civil servants from Labour and D.E.A. who were in the room said that the prices front was going so well that there weren't any scandalous price increases to attack. I said rather angrily that they had damn well better find two good examples of unfair price increases. What these remarks show is that the price side of the prices and incomes policy is as much a fraud as the workers suspect. The trouble is that Government policy is the major cause of price increases. First of all it put prices up by using the regulator in the July 20th measure:[1] even worse, huge increases are being caused by S.E.T. which started on September 5th.[2] So there's no way of really pretending that the Government isn't to blame. Nevertheless, it's essential if possible to have a couple of prosecutions against employers who unfairly increase prices.

[1] The Chancellor has the power to vary, by 10 per cent up or down, the rate of purchase tax (now VAT). This device is known as the regulator.

[2] Selective Employment Tax. A payroll tax paid by employers with some rebate for industrial enterprises. See Vol. I, p. 508n.

The Ministers' final conclusions were (a) to operate Part IV from Wednesday of next week; (b) to make the necessary preparations by interviewing the N.P.A. and warning them of the danger they are in; and (c) to use the fortnight's interval for getting a couple of good price cases going at the same time. Just as we were finishing I was reminded by Harold that it would be necessary to alert sufficient Ministers to hold a Privy Council at Balmoral on Wednesday.

They were still talking at 4.15 when I rushed to the compositing meeting at the College of Technology. This is where the delegates who have put down resolutions for debate meet the members of the Conference Arrangements Committee to argue which resolutions will be debated and which dropped. I got there by taxi at 4.20 to find that my resolutions had been dealt with already so I'd wasted my time. As it was a lovely sunny afternoon I walked back to the hotel and then took Anne out for a blowy walk along the front.

Sunday, October 2nd

I'd worked away at the speech late last night and by 11 o'clock this morning it was ready. I took it down to Harold's room and there I found Marcia, Tommy and Peter Shore sitting about and discussing Harold's speech. I read it and found it not my style of speech at all, but I knew that I couldn't do very much to help him with it. At 12.30 Harold came in, immensely excited because at the Sunday service where he and George Brown had been reading the Lessons he had been interrupted by anti-Vietnam demonstrators. He gave a precise imitation of how they'd interrupted him and how he had stood his ground and repeated the last two verses of the lesson which happened to be apposite.* Poor Tommy was furious with him for not showing a proper interest in the revision of his speech. I'm afraid I got Harold off upstairs and made him go through my speech. After he made two or three tiny suggestions I said that perhaps I ought to show it to Len Williams since it was laying down our view of the relationship between the Party and the Government. 'Oh no,' he said, 'I shouldn't bother to do that.' So that was that. No one else had seen my speech but I'd got the Prime Minister's full backing and I was now entitled to make it on behalf of the N.E.C. committing the whole Executive to this precise interpretation of the relation of Party and Government.

I'd better try to explain why Party organization is so important. When Morgan Phillips[1] retired in 1962 there was a real chance of getting a powerful modern General Secretary from outside Transport House. But Hugh Gaitskell,[2] in order to secure his position as leader of the Party, turned these ideas

* He was right to be excited as next morning he made the headlines again and in good form—'P.M. stands up to demonstrators'.

[1] Secretary of the Research Department from 1941 to 1944, when he became General Secretary of the Labour Party. He retired in 1962 and died in 1963.

[2] Labour M.P. for South Leeds from 1945 until his death in January 1963. Minister of Fuel and Power 1947–50, Minister of State for Economic Affairs 1950, Chancellor of the Exchequer 1950–51 and leader of the Labour Party December 1955–January 1963.

down flat though Tony Wedgwood Benn and I both pleaded with him. Instead he appointed George Brown to be Chairman of the Org. Sub. and to run Transport House; George Brown proceeded to appoint Len Williams as Morgan Phillips's successor and Sara Barker to Len Williams's old place. Len and Sara are splendid old war horses but their ideas of organization, finance and general structure are incredibly reactionary. In their six years nothing has been done to reorganize Transport House despite quite a volume of complaints from some of the more intelligent members.

Harold Wilson's penny-farthing report on the scandals of Party organization had come out long before the 1959 election.[1] But nothing whatsoever was done although we had our worst defeat ever in 1959. Harold knows perfectly well that unless we can get the reform of the Party done in the next eighteen months there won't be any improvement in the two years' run-up to the next general election. What we really need, therefore, is for Len and Sara to retire within the next twelve months and for new people to be brought in in time to carry out the reorganization. Len and Sara could possibly retire if they are offered really big jobs outside. But clearly if they are not offered these jobs and don't retire then they must go on up to the election and we must give them loyal support. But will the Executive agree? The critics in Transport House want an independent investigation and there's no doubt that most of the N.E.C. will regard this as an implicit attack on Len and Sara. I suggested to Harold that instead of pressing for an outside investigation we should say that the Executive itself is prepared to undertake a searching inquiry with a view to modernizing the Party, and that my speech on Sunday night will be the public sketch of the kind of Party we are aiming to create. Then on Thursday afternoon I can answer the debate on organization in a reply that won't be published. I begged and pleaded that at the meeting of the Executive this afternoon Harold should back me in this. I was supported by Marcia and Peter, who said, 'You really must intervene this afternoon because otherwise the trade unions will be so unbearable that either Dick will have to make a speech which is completely against his principles or he'll have to withdraw and say he can't speak under these conditions.' Harold listened glumly and said he would do what he could.

At 2.30 the Executive sat down again to the arduous task of going through all the resolutions and the composites. Party organization came right at the end and sure enough there was an outburst. But before it could gather steam, Harold stepped in with a magnificent 10-minute speech saying we had to face the need to modernize the Party. If we are modernizing the trade unions, modernizing Parliament, modernizing industry, we mustn't fail to modernize our own Party too. Naturally, of course, we can't have any suggestion of a vote of censure on the present officials or agree to commissioning an outside investigation, but he felt it essential for the Executive to set up a commission to report in twelve months. Harold had spiked the guns of my enemies but there was still

[1] A report on the Labour Party's 'penny-farthing' approach to electoral organization, presented to the Conference at Margate in October 1955.

a good deal of talk about not being put on the defensive or tolerating any attacks on Len Williams and Sara Barker. 'If attacks are made they must not go unanswered,' said Frank Chapple.[1] In my reply I suggested that the most tactful thing would be for me to be brief and merely to ask for the resolutions to be referred to the Executive. We carried this resolution by 14 to 13. Harold, by the way, voted with the thirteen and said to me afterwards, 'Well, I watched carefully and when I saw you voting one way I thought I ought to vote the other so as to prove there is no collusion.'

The meeting stopped at 6.30 and I had to rush out and get myself ready for the demonstration at the Dome. When I got there it was fairly full—about four or five hundred people. We began with an absolutely unintelligible speech by an Indian socialist. My turn came pretty soon. I spoke from a long written script and I had to deal with a good deal of mild, good-humoured interruption and heckling. I rather shocked some of my colleagues by remarking that Cabinet Ministers couldn't conceivably work out a real socialist manifesto because they were far too busy dealing with short-term current problems to look ahead and show any vision. I came back to the hotel a little depressed and anxious whether tomorrow's press would pick this remark up and get me into trouble.

Monday, October 3rd

I needn't have worried. There was virtually nothing in the press. The *Guardian* had put me bottom of the story and some remarks by the Chairman of the T.U.C. top. Most of them published not a single word though the press release had been issued at six in the evening so that the journalists had hours in which to read it before it was delivered. However there was one report, *The Times*. Before making my speech I had run into David Wood, *The Times*'s political editor and I had asked him to come upstairs and have a chat. In the course of it I explained exactly what the speech was about, how it was linked with my speech to the private session on Thursday, and how I'd concerted with the P.M. that this should be an important declaration on the relationship of the Government to the Party. So today's *Times* had an exclusive story exactly along these lines.

One of the strange things about a Labour Party Conference is that for members of the Executive it's half over before it starts. We had arrived in Brighton on Thursday evening and worked for the whole of Friday, Saturday and Sunday. Today we are nearly half way through and there's only Tuesday, Wednesday and Thursday left, since Friday virtually doesn't count. Nevertheless, when a Conference formally opens on a Monday morning we're always uncertain what the mood is going to be. Moreover, what happens on the first morning is no test. You have the mayor's speech, you have the

---

[1] Assistant General Secretary of the Electrical, Electronic and Telecommunications Union from 1963 until September 1966, when he became General Secretary. A member of the T.U.C. General Council since 1971.

chairman's address, you have the formalities and you always have a flat debate, as I well know since I've replied twice on social security on a Monday morning. This year it was even more trying than usual because we were housed in the new ice-rink, built by Top Rank Entertainment next door to the Grand Hotel. This must be one of the ugliest buildings in the world and it's planked down on the Brighton front. Inside it's tawdry and tinny, with a huge hall specially designed for conferences but where the ceiling crushes you down and the room's so wide you can't see the walls. Despite the excellent acoustics it's going to be very difficult to keep the attention of the audience and arouse the delegates.

This was the day a special train had been hired, at a cost of £750, to bring demonstrators from B.M.C. down to Brighton. From my room in the hotel I saw them beginning to mass outside the Conference Hall. I quickly went downstairs again and picked up our delegates—George Park, the shop steward from Rootes, and David Young[1] and his wife. Meanwhile the shop stewards were outside the hotel booing and shouting. Each member of the Executive had to run this gauntlet after lunch. In the afternoon, while we were sitting in Conference listening to Barbara trying to work the delegates up and not succeeding, Harold made a brilliant stroke. He came out of the front door of the hotel, seized the microphone from one of the demonstrators, asked three of them in and had a couple of hours with them reasoning and hearing their side of the case. Once again he showed what a news sense he has. But there is one little trouble. The headlines are all 'Harold attacked in church', 'Harold attacked outside the hotel by shop stewards'. They're good for the general public but they upset our delegates who feel this is a pretty unhappy Conference. Perhaps this is why the mood of Conference seems to be such a curious blend of unhappiness and good temper. A lot of the delegates, I suspect, are pretty reluctant. They really didn't want to come to this Conference and they feel guilty that they have to support the Government when they really disapprove of what we are doing. Most of them will have to be persuaded, cajoled along the road we want them to go. This is a Conference in which the leadership is heaving the rank and file over the hump. And it's quite a job. The mood today was the worst I ever remember—really disconsolate and listless. One thing I notice is the extraordinary absence of M.P.s and Parliamentary Secretaries. Last year when the Government was successful they were thronging the halls, but M.P.s are fine-weather friends of the Labour Party Conference and this is not going to be the kind of Conference anybody volunteers to attend. Most M.P.s have deliberately absented themselves because of their holidays or delegations abroad.

I had to appear on *Panorama* tonight in a 45-minute programme which I'd been assured would be devoted to explaining how a Party Conference works. They were going to follow through the progress of a Nottingham delegate

---

[1] Chairman of Crossman's constituency Party and, since July 1965, Labour candidate for Banbury (see Vol. I, pp. 279–80). In 1974 he became Labour M.P. for Bolton East.

from his selection right up to the Conference—the climax being a four- or five-minute discussion between a member of the N.E.C. and some typical rank-and-file delegates. Of course things didn't turn out that way. Three of the rank-and-filers were ultra-left-wingers and my part of the programme developed into a futile shouting match. After that I went over to the I.T.N. studio where I was given a model interview for four and a half minutes which appeared on the news.

I had a certain amount to drink at I.T.V. and when I got back to the hotel I was tired and bad-tempered. Tony Crosland and Susan were just off to the B.B.C., who live in the Metropole, and I decided to join them. We went into Oliver Whitley's[1] suite to find that Michael Stewart and George Wigg were already there. We watched the programme and saw Robin Day making one of his characteristic wind-ups predicting acrimony and hostility among the delegates.[2] I said, 'There you are, there's B.B.C. objectivity for you.' We don't mind personalities attacking us but the news should be fair. While I was describing what happened to me on *Panorama* Robin Day came in. We had a tremendous knockabout even though I knew that in my new job I oughtn't to be behaving in this way and sounding as anti-B.B.C. as the rest of the Party leadership. But there it was—I did it till one or two in the morning.

Tuesday, October 4th
I woke up with a hell of a headache and a hangover and tottered down in order to hear the results of the Executive elections. I was fourth this year instead of fifth—I always hover about the middle of the list. Then came Harold's big speech. I found it monumentally dull though of course it had some superb relieving patches. It had been worked and worked over by Peter Shore, Gerald Kaufman and Tommy Balogh until it was a kind of mosaic of Wilsonisms, ideas expressing a curiously anonymous statesmanship. Then right at the end to cheer the delegates up came an astonishing quotation from a prayer by Donald Soper.[3] Considering that Jim Callaghan, Barbara and I who were all sitting beside the P.M. are fervent atheists, it was a little tough to be told by our leader about how the Cabinet was dedicated to God in the Chapel of St Mary-under-Croft in Westminster. At lunch he said to me, 'Well, you even let me put a prayer over on them,' and I discovered that he hadn't put the prayer in his press release or shown it to Peter or Tommy or Gerald. He'd spatchcocked it in at the last moment and I'm sure it was his own carefully worked-out idea.

[1] Chief Assistant to the Director-General of the B.B.C. 1964–8, and Managing Director, External Broadcasting, from 1969 until his retirement in 1972.

[2] A television journalist, formerly a newscaster and parliamentary correspondent with Independent Television News (1955–9). He joined the B.B.C. current-affairs programme *Panorama* in 1959 and rapidly made a reputation for incisive interviewing. He introduced the programme from 1967 to 1972.

[3] Methodist minister and Superintendent of the West London Mission at the Kingsway Hall, since 1936. He was made a life peer in 1965, taking his seat on the Labour benches.

I don't want to be unfair. This was a solid thoughtful speech proving that we are still the radical party and that conservatism is to be found everywhere and must be investigated and hunted out by Labour, which is the irreverent party. All this, of course, is tremendously worth saying as a justification of the new prices and incomes policy but the delegates accepted it glumly with the feeling, no doubt, that perhaps this Government did make some sense and that they should at least suspend their judgment and see whether we could handle the next crisis any better. But the fact of redundancy was what remained in their minds and kept them unconvinced by Harold's speech today.

I had Trevelyan and my dear Janet down for lunch in order to do what little work there was and fix up the details of the Privy Council at Balmoral on Wednesday.[1] One or two journalists have talked to me on the assumption that the Lord President would be going but I'm not going to waste my time on such mumbo-jumbo and I've persuaded the Lord Chancellor to take my place.

This evening we had a full formal Cabinet meeting. It was timed for 7.15 and I got there a quarter of an hour late because Trevelyan managed to send me to the wrong place. The meeting went perfectly smoothly. Indeed, all I remember of it is that right at the end when we were breaking up Dick Marsh remarked *sotto voce*, 'Well, I hope we shall be able soon to have a disavowal of the Crossman line.' There was a hearty peal of laughter and that was that. Nevertheless, the 'Crossman line' has been talked about a great deal in Conference partly because Paul Johnson[2] has written a remarkable article in the *New Statesman* saying that we blundered into socialism and this theory is now attributed to me. What I said was that we had waited too long and that at last we had done something blunt and crude which gave us time for building a real Socialist prices and incomes policy. Dick Marsh was infuriated because in the Conference it was taken that I'd said we should have to retain an element of compulsion in our incomes policy. I'd been careful *not* to say this but of course the general tone of the speech made it clear that I thought we should have to have more state backing than is implied in Part IV of the Prices and Incomes Act. Nevertheless, no one in Cabinet took Dick Marsh's demand seriously. He was asking for the moon in suggesting I should be disowned.

I'd agreed to take Anne out to the Mascot and fortunately I rang up just beforehand to book a table. Then I walked round and found everybody else going there—Tony Crosland and Susan, Tony Benn and his wife, Harold and his wife, Bill Rodgers and his wife—and when we arrived there were Alastair

---

[1] Janet Gates, Crossman's secretary who had joined him at M.H.L.G. and remained with him (as Mrs Newman) throughout his years in Cabinet and, briefly thereafter at the *New Statesman*.

[2] Author and journalist. A member of the editorial staff of the *New Statesman* since 1955 and its editor 1965–70.

Burnet of I.T.N.[1] at one table and Sidney Bernstein of Granada at another.[2] Sure enough, the Lord President was wafted in to a nice table for two whereas all the others had to stand waiting and be shoved in a corner where they had a miserable meal together while Anne and I dined comfortably alone and went off to bed quietly.

Wednesday, October 5th

Patrick's birthday. We telephoned him. Poor boy, he was born on the Friday of the Brighton Conference 1957 and the next time we came to Brighton was for the Conference five years later when Nanny brought the children. Here we are away again on his birthday. It's no fun to be the son of a politician.

This morning came the big debate and Jim Callaghan made a magnificent speech. He raised all the issues which were in the delegates' minds and answered them with magnificent clarity and frankness, making far the best speech of the Conference and pummelling the audience with answers.

In the evening I went to Pam Berry for dinner and found it a bit dull. I usually enjoy her parties enormously but somehow this time the mixture wasn't right. I suspect she'd meant me to dine the previous evening with Hugh Massingham[3] and I thought I couldn't make it. As a result I was in the wrong set.

Thursday, October 6th

In the afternoon came my appearance at the N.E.C. private session. As a result of a change of plan I was now keyed up for a full half-hour reply to an extended debate and had briefed myself with the greatest difficulty by chatting with everybody in Transport House. It was my intention to reply partly by repeating what I said on Sunday, partly by analysing the nature of the problem which faces us in modernizing a socialist party. It was really quite a tricky job because first of all I had to convince my own trade-union colleagues that I was really defending the Executive, including Len Williams and Sara Barker, and secondly I had to convince the Conference that I was committing the Executive to a genuine inquiry and genuine reform. So I got down there soon after lunch and as I might have expected nothing happened. The meeting drooled on and on. Walter Padley is an amiable, boring chairman;[4] his

---

[1] Political editor, Independent Television News 1963–4 and from 1965–74 editor of *The Economist*. He was editor of the *Daily Express* from 1974 until the end of 1975, when he returned to independent television.

[2] Chairman of the Granada Group since 1934, chairman of Granada Television Ltd 1955–71 and of Granada Publishing Ltd 1966–70. He became a life peer in 1969.

[3] The son of H. W. Massingham, editor of the *Nation* (1907–23) and himself a novelist and journalist. He was the *Observer*'s political columnist from the end of the Second World War until 1961, when he moved to the *Sunday Telegraph*, where he remained until his death in December 1971.

[4] Labour M.P. for Ogmore, Glamorganshire, since 1950 and, since 1956, a member of the N.E.C. President of USDAW 1948–64, and Minister of State for Foreign Affairs 1964–7.

3

amiability was to my disadvantage in this private session because he allowed the report on Party activity to be discussed paragraph by paragraph and the hours crept on and on. It was already 4.30 and we only had half an hour to go. It looked as though I wouldn't be given even a minute to speak. Finally, when he had been woken up by Len Williams, Padley told the delegates there was no time for anything more. It was a difficult situation since the delegates too, one from Coventry East and one from South Ayrshire, had prepared their speeches most carefully, expecting a big and important debate. They had to scrap most of what they intended to say and I scrapped the whole of my speech and said what I could in eight minutes. Though I failed to make the speech I intended I said enough to commit the Executive entirely to the inquiry and as a result the newspapers reported that Crossman, now the political boss of the Party, had announced a searching inquiry into Party organization.

After the mayor's reception, the one party a member of the N.E.C. can't miss (Anne and I have not been to any of the evening shows—the Pavilion dance given by the mayor, the agents' dance, etc.), I was talking to Callaghan and he said, 'Of course, Audrey and I don't like dancing but we do walk through as people appreciate seeing us.' Is it a sign of superiority that Anne and I don't feel the necessity even for walking through? I cut right away from the Conference and drove over to Wilton Park to have a delightful dinner with my old friend the Warden, Heinz Koeppler.[1] He arrived as one of the first Jewish academic refugees from the Nazis and lived with me at Oxford in 1933. Now he runs superbly one of the best conference centres in the world. I felt rather bad when I got back to the hotel and saw the others sitting round in their places in the foyer.

Friday, October 7th

All that was left for today was the debate on Rhodesia. It went all right except for a minor disaster when Eirene White, who was winding up for the Executive, lost her nerve, tried to answer the delegates and got the slow handclap.[2]

In the afternoon I found Harold in very relaxed form. I asked him whether he'd received my report on the information services. No, Marcia hadn't shown it to him yet. 'I had my box to read yesterday at four o'clock and I fell asleep—I was very tired.' He certainly has had a tough time. From the beginning of the Commonwealth Conference on he's been working a 20-hour day and he's only going to have two days free next week before Parliament starts.

Anne and I drove back through Sussex, Surrey and the Aldershot suburbs. As we got nearer to home in the Midlands I liked the country more and more.

---

[1] Warden of Wilton Park since 1946 and Warden of the European Discussion Centre since 1972. He too had worked in the Political Warfare Executive during the Second World War.

[2] Labour M.P. for East Flint 1950–70 and a member of the N.E.C. 1947–53 and 1958–72. Parliamentary Secretary at the Colonial Office 1964–6; Minister of State for Foreign Affairs 1966–7 and at the Welsh Office 1967–70. In 1970 she was made a life peer and, since 1972, has been deputy chairman of the Metrication Board.

We got to Prescote at 6.30 and there were the children waiting to see us and we were soon sitting down and reading Rider Haggard's *Alan Quatermain* aloud.

Saturday, October 8th

I spent the day really doing nothing except for going over to Oxford in the afternoon, where Patrick used his birthday book tokens and I bought gramophone records. I've now got a record player and we have a new passion in the evenings which is not to look at the telly but to play music.

That evening we went to dinner with our neighbours the Hartrees and met the new headmaster of Bloxham—the small and not very distinguished public school on the other side of Banbury. A very nice dentist from Boddington also was there and I was made to feel comfy. Pritchett's away for a week's fishing holiday but he'll be back tomorrow and will tell me all the details of the planting which he has completed for next year.

Monday, October 10th

At the end of Conference we were told by the P.M. to have a longish weekend and he promised us that he himself wouldn't be working too hard. In fact he did keep things fairly quiet over the weekend and I decided to take Monday off because poor Patrick always seems to miss a birthday party owing to Conference. But in a family things never quite go as you plan them. First of all Virginia got flu and hadn't recovered by Monday and secondly it rained steadily all day and left us with little to do outside. I took Patrick to the cinema in the afternoon, where we saw an exciting crashing film about motor-car racing.

Though I hope I managed to conceal it, I was really very worried throughout the day. When we motored back from Conference I was already very anxious about what Nora Beloff would be writing in the *Observer* and on Sunday I had noticed that she had a small single article headed something like 'Crossman takes over Transport House'. At the Conference I'd taken the precaution of seeing David Wood of *The Times* and getting a good article out of him, and at his own request I had briefed James Margach in full for the *Sunday Times*. On Thursday, when I had been about to go upstairs with Tam, Nora Beloff came along and interrupted me and forced me to take her up into my sitting-room. I talked to her extremely carefully with Tam present, telling her what the problem was, reminding her I was not in charge of any commission of investigation, and that everything depended on what the Executive would decide at its first October meeting. She kept on pressing me about getting rid of Len Williams and Sara Barker. Her question, I said, was impossible for me to answer; it was clear they must either go early or have their retirement postponed until after the next election but I added that if she mentioned this in the article as my idea she would ruin me and my job at Transport House. She then asked me whether my speech hadn't implied that I was determined to wind up all the existing publicity. I said this was complete nonsense. Indeed, I contradicted her carefully on each of these points. And on each of these points in her brief article she used my denial as a confirmation of her own view. The article could hardly have been more embarrassing to Harold or to me. This afternoon, when it was raining, I dictated over the phone three letters, one to Len Williams, one to Sara Barker and one to Percy Clark describing the article as ridiculous nonsense and I sent copies of the letters to Marcia Williams. I'm not sure the preventive action will be effective. If it isn't, my whole job at Transport House will be ditched.

Tuesday, October 11th

I was due to see Harold at 3 p.m. about the information services report. But as I expected he at once raised Beloff's news story with me. He was not sympathetic because he'd forbidden any of us to talk to her but he said he hoped that the Transport House people had enough confidence in me to forget the whole thing. If they didn't I mightn't be able to do the job at all.

Our talk about the information services was equally chilly. I had sent a message that I must talk to him and Burke Trend alone before we had a general committee on the draft report with Trevor Lloyd-Hughes and Trevelyan in attendance. But I found that Trevor and Henry James were waiting in the anteroom and so the talk I needed didn't take place and never will take place because Harold doesn't want to discuss No. 10 staff with me and Trend alone. He knew I was going to make some critical observations on it because he found them in the report and he simply avoided this scene. Well! If the P.M. decides not to have a talk he doesn't have it—so we had a perfectly business-like meeting. It was decided that I would need one good man in the Lord President's office and Trevor would need one more assistant in his office. On the surface it was a perfectly satisfactory conversation and we agreed to meet once again with a revised draft to be submitted to Cabinet next week.

However, one cheerful thing occurred today. Michael Stewart put in a paper saying that he ought to co-ordinate all economic information. This will strengthen my hand a little since Callaghan won't concede the right of D.E.A. to control any information from the Treasury.

After that we had the week's first meeting of RX. We had to consider a vast mass of bumf including a long policy paper and a draft final Statement of terms. Oh, this Rhodesia X! It's a Committee nearly as big as Cabinet. When Bowden began to discuss the draft I at once interrupted and said that before we considered it we ought to know its purpose. Here I had a great deal of support from Callaghan. We agreed that we must know whether this is a draft of a final Statement designed to improve our position in the rest of the world when negotiations break down or a draft Statement to be presented to Smith in the hope that we might get a settlement. As the discussion went on it became clear that Bowden now feels it is really possible for Smith to settle. He's obviously pleased by the immense impression he's made on Smith and the telegrams make it clear that the two men like each other and I can believe that Smith trusted Bowden in a way he never trusted Arthur Bottomley, or the Prime Minister. Indeed, the telegrams report that the other day Smith said to the Governor that if Bowden had been there from the start none of this would have happened. No wonder that Bowden was hopeful of a settlement and I suppose that in about half his mind the Prime Minister was too because he gave his support to Bowden's description of the purpose of the draft. I said, 'Well, in that case we must be prepared to sacrifice certain attitudes, and even concrete points which might help us, if the negotiations break down.' Then Denis Healey spoke up as Minister of Defence. He said, 'Of course we must be ready to do this because the prospects are so terrible if we don't get an agreement. Shouldn't we really face it that we can't afford to let these negotiations break down? Shouldn't we realize that we must find some alternative course of action which will prevent our drifting into the hopeless situation of mandatory sanctions?' Finally he put it to Harold Wilson quite bluntly. 'If you really think you can get an agreement with Smith at some sacrifice of one or two of the five principles, tell us what those sacrifices would be and let us judge for ourselves.'

This was a challenge which, of course, Harold carefully evaded. He gave us no idea of the price we must pay for an agreement with Smith. Yet I have no doubt that this is the way a Tory Prime Minister would look at it. He would say that we must get the end of U.D.I. at the cheapest possible price.[1] And then he would insist on working out what modifications of the constitution would be required.

But to do this would in fact be an admission of defeat and Harold Wilson never wants to admit he is defeated. So in the course of that afternoon he switched from one extreme to the other. He spent a lot of his time trying to find concessions which Bowden could make to Smith and then spent the rest of it piling up conditions which we must impose on Smith which would remove the remotest chance of success in the negotiations. The major issue of course was 'the British presence', in particular the presence of British troops to guard the Kariba Dam and incidentally also to prevent a Government which had purported to return to constitutionality lapsing from it the moment our back was turned. But Smith won't accept a British presence and we can't force him to. So, if we want a settlement with Smith all this talk is really bluff. When I put this to Harold bluntly and frankly I found myself once again isolated in the Cabinet—apart from Callaghan who was sitting next to me—and extremely unpopular because I was delaying a decision. At 7.30 we had to break off with our meeting unfinished.

Wednesday, October 12th
I had to be in the office at nine punct. because Harry Walston insisted on

[1] Unilateral Declaration of Independence.

seeing me.[1] I found that he wanted to represent the views of Eirene White and Judith Hart, the two other junior Ministers concerned with Rhodesia. All three of them are afraid that Bowden and Wilson are going to pull a fast one and get an agreement with Smith which would mean abandoning some of the five principles. I got him talking about military sanctions and in particular about the idea aired at the Liberal Party Conference[2] that we should send aeroplanes to take out a piece of the railway line that runs into Mozambique. He said he thought there was something in this and I asked him to go and see Eddie Shackleton before he left to make sure that this at least was seriously examined by the military. Since mandatory sanctions will not only be appallingly damaging to us but hopelessly ineffective, we must find other less conventional methods of impressing Smith.

After that I went down the stairs to the anteroom outside the Cabinet room where Callaghan had asked to see me because he was worried by a news story in the *Daily Mail*. Walter Terry[3] had produced a brand-new version of the July plot in which Callaghan is the chief villain:[4] I laughed and said that I thought it really was outrageous. 'As you know, I've never believed in the existence of the July plot, least of all that it had anything to do with you, James. In so far as there was one, it was Roy Jenkins and Tony Crosland and Tony Wedgwood Benn and me who were implicated in it, along with George Brown. Walter Terry seems to have amalgamated two different stories, the real July plot and Harold's row with you as the result of your interview with William Davis of the *Guardian* where you said that you thought you ought to be Foreign Secretary. Harold is still angry about that and believes that at one time you were dreaming of a coalition government because the situation was so desperate and Harold so indecisive.' 'Very well,' he said, 'I must have the Walter Terry story denied.'[*]

We both went in to O.P.D. a few minutes late. I was permitted to be there for one item on the agenda—Malta—on which I had circulated a Cabinet paper protesting against what I thought was an insane proposal of the Minister of Defence.[5] I have no doubt the Prime Minister feels the right time for bringing me into the Committee hasn't come because he still hasn't made up his mind about the size of the Cabinet reconstruction and in particular about the future of Douglas Houghton whose chairmanships, etc., I might take over. Nevertheless I am still very riled and I sat on my dignity, refusing

---

[*] Next day the whole of the front page of the *Sun* was devoted to the denial and an attack on George Wigg for spreading lies.

[1] Lord Walston (who became a life peer in 1961) was at this period Parliamentary Under-Secretary of State at the Foreign Office.

[2] The Liberal Assembly met from September 21st to 24th.

[3] Political editor of the *Daily Mail*.

[4] See Vol. I, pp. 572–9, for an account of the threat to Wilson's premiership while he was away in Moscow in July 1966.

[5] It had been announced in February's Defence White Paper that there would be reductions of British forces in Malta. In return, the British Government were to give £4 million in grants and £500,000 in loans to the island.

to speak and merely listening to the debate. When Bowden pointed out that the proposed defence cuts would mean that we were creating a 25 per cent level of unemployment in Malta as well as going back on our predecessors' defence agreement, Denis replied that one can't take these problems separately. We can't look at the special circumstances of Malta because if we did that in each case there wouldn't be any defence cuts. Actually the trouble is that we are trying to get big defence cuts without a basic change of foreign policy and without withdrawing from our presence in the Far East, our presence in the Middle East or our presence in Germany. Listening to the debate I came to the conclusion that when it comes to a final decision the defence cuts will add up to virtually nothing.

After O.P.D. there was a general shuffle of seats and RX reopened its discussion—this time on the two papers dealing with sanctions and propaganda. I asked whether the Committee might not consider the Liberal proposal to instruct the R.A.F. to take a bit out of the railway line. That would be preferable to sending two brigades in and I wouldn't mind if the fact that we were seriously considering it percolated out to Rhodesia. Indeed, I would regard it as excellent psychological warfare. I made a pretty good fuss but all I got was an agreement that this would be 'looked at seriously' and I spent most of the late afternoon with Bowden at the Commonwealth Office trying to see what could be done.

Before my late afternoon session with Bowden there was yet another Committee at No. 10—this time on broadcasting. This is one of the few items where Cabinet has refused to stomach a Minister's policy. When Ted Short replaced Tony Benn as P.M.G. the Post Office was delighted because they realized they were able to scrap the whole of the elaborate policy Tony had been preparing for a year. Short at once accepted the old Post Office brief proposing that the B.B.C. should close down the pirate radio stations and do a light-programme substitute for them and should also begin some experimental local stations.[1]

But when Ted put this forward in August, Cabinet was hostile and asked him to come back with some concrete proposals for dealing with the central problem of finance. Instead of this, today he simply submitted a paper listing the alternatives. Quite clearly we were back to square one. We could either accept the original Post Office view or accept the Tony Benn view. What was interesting at this meeting was Harold Wilson's attitude. Before the meeting he told me when I asked him whether I would take on Bert Bowden's chairmanship of the Broadcasting Committee that this would not be the case and he would do it himself. This was because he knew that I was on Tony Benn's side on this issue whereas he's a very conventional traditionalist. However he didn't feel like fighting today and when he found that most of Cabinet

[1] Since March 1964 pirate radio stations had been transmitting pop music and advertisements, usually from ships anchored outside territorial waters. The Postmaster-General had been dissuaded from intervening. See Vol. I, p. 167.

didn't think much of the paper he introduced one of his voting occasions. This revealed a clear majority in favour of letting the B.B.C. have a short-term interim music programme and meanwhile making plans à la Benn for a long-term public corporation with advertising which could also sustain Jennie Lee's other great idea, the Open University.[1] The opposition had won —for the moment.

Thursday, October 13th

The first occasion where, as Leader of the House, I had to deal with parliamentary business. I noticed that Quintin Hogg and Sir John Hobson[2] were the Tories selected to open and close the debate on the Second Reading of the Parliamentary Commissioner Bill next Tuesday.[3] When I mentioned this to Cabinet and asked whom they wanted to speak on our side everybody said it was a parliamentary matter and therefore the Lord President's job. I felt it quite a good idea because I shall not often get chances to make speeches and I knew that Harold was trying to get me on my feet in the Chamber. What I didn't know was that poor Douglas Houghton, who's been working on the Bill all the way through, was thinking it would be his big day. I tried to console him afterwards. I've discovered that I shall have to do far more work than I expected.

The next item on the Cabinet agenda was Rhodesia where we discussed the draft Statement. Judith Hart, faithfully representing Walston, said she regarded it as totally unsatisfactory because there was far too mild a commitment to the British presence. Quite a number of changes were made and as we proceeded the terms for the return to constitutionality became more and more peremptory and the chance of Smith agreeing more and more remote. Indeed, by the end of the meeting I was one of the people who was doubtful whether even the Governor would consider these terms because they imposed entirely new responsibilities upon him.

Finally, a short discussion of prices and incomes. I'd always known that Callaghan didn't really believe in the policy of holding down prices. He hardly could since he's Chancellor of the Exchequer but it's disconcerting to find that the head of the D.E.A. is an equally thorough sceptic who has accepted the Treasury view lock, stock and barrel, just as he's accepted the Treasury view on import controls. So we had to listen to Michael Stewart

[1] The Open University was devised to give degree courses by tuition and correspondence with an academic staff who used radio and television as a medium.

[2] Conservative M.P. for Warwick and Leamington from 1957 until his death in 1967. He was Attorney-General 1962–4 and Shadow Attorney-General 1964–7.

[3] Hereafter called (as Crossman referred to it) the Ombudsman Bill. New Zealand and Denmark were two of the countries with an Ombudsman, an official who inquired into cases of maladministration on the part of the civil service. The Bill sought to establish the office of a Parliamentary Commissioner for Administration, appointed by the Sovereign on the advice of the Prime Minister, and empowered to consider complaints referred by M.P.s on behalf of their constituents. He would be given the right to send for departmental papers.

saying that he couldn't find a single case of a price increase which would justify an Order in Council. Meanwhile he's intending to use his powers in the two cases where management has put up wages. This will cause tremendous trouble unless it's rectified. I was so angry that I joined the majority of Cabinet in defeating Michael Stewart when he insisted we should give an instruction to the Coal Board not to increase those prices which hadn't yet been increased. I did so chiefly because I didn't want to let Michael Stewart get away with ordering a nationalized board not to put up its prices when he couldn't find a single private enterprise against which he could file an Order in Council.

After lunch I went round to the Commonwealth Office to discuss psychological warfare in Rhodesia with Bowden and George Wigg. It was difficult because I was being brought in at the last moment while George Wigg had been involved for the past year. Very properly he's concerned himself with the provision of transmitters whereas I am concerned with what is being transmitted. I got it across to them that their first job is to get forty or fifty copies of the text of our new final Statement out this weekend so that the key people in Salisbury will know what Smith is being offered. Then there could be a second stage when a thousand people get the text with a covering letter and finally a barrage of propaganda. I promised to see Hugh Greene and persuaded them to use the B.B.C. to help us in its special Rhodesia programme between now and the end of November.

I was off home by the 8 p.m. train.

Friday, October 14th
I'd promised to open a block of old people's flats at Southam—the Rural District Council over the border in Warwickshire from Prescote—and I had quite an interesting time that morning with all the local R.D.C.s in Warwickshire coming over to see the Lord President of the Council. The Ministry of Housing had said they were very poor flats and indeed they were. We had a very pleasant time together and then I came home to spend the afternoon with my children. We had a lovely walk over the farm to see the flood. There'd been a tremendous downpour of rain on Wednesday and though it stopped raining on Thursday the river had been coming up. It was well across the road and we splashed through it over to the sluice and the island on this brilliant sunshiny afternoon. Afterwards we rushed across to Tring to dine with the Llewelyn-Davies's and meet Madame Vlachos,[1] the very interesting proprietor of a left-wing Greek newspaper.

Saturday, October 15th
Today for once was devoted to the children. We had a splendid time up on the old aerodrome bicycling and playing football on the concrete runways.

[1] Mrs Helen Vlachos published a newspaper, *Kathimerini*. On May 2nd, 1967, she was to suspend its publication in protest against censorship; on October 4th she was placed under house arrest and on December 21st she escaped to England.

3*

In the evening I went across to Coventry to a grand concert in aid of the Pinley Community Centre. Oh dear, these community centres — three of them were given to us by the Americans in 1945 and they have never been a genuine community success. This one is being restarted for the nth time. The people were nice enough but the show they put on was terrible. They called themselves 'The Inimitables' — they'd been in a concert party in 1946. In the last thirty years we don't seem to have advanced in Coventry one iota in terms of the real use of leisure. These community centres remind one of the basic slumminess of so many of the big housing estates in Coventry. If they're not proletarian slums they are very prim estates for skilled engineers earning a lot of money and using it in utterly petit-bourgeois ways. I came back just in time to have a glimpse on television of Heath's final speech at the Tory Conference.[1] If there was ever any risk of a row they avoided it. They've set themselves on the pretty obvious but politically right course — the same as Lord Woolton's in 1946.[2] They're going to be the party of freedom and their slogan once again will be 'Set the Nation free from Socialist Controls'. The slogan will win them the election if we don't succeed in reducing unemployment and getting growth going again.

Monday, October 17th

When I arrived at Paddington this morning I was driven straight to the Privy Council where I had arranged an important meeting between Heath and Whitelaw and John Silkin and myself. By an extraordinary piece of stupidity we had asked Heath to come to the Privy Council Office at the other end of Whitehall instead of my room, which is next door to his, in the House of Commons. He arrived in my palace in a very sulky mood. He has something of Gaitskell's huffiness and much the same cold gleam in his eye. I started him off on specialist committees and said I'd already discussed this with Willie Whitelaw who couldn't have been more helpful.[3] But Heath wasn't going to allow me to appoint a committee on agriculture unless it was expressly stated that it would only be for one experimental year.

Next I got on to television and he at once objected to the whole idea of Standing Committees and Select Committees upstairs being televised. 'If that happened the TV would show the Government supporters writing their letters,' he pointed out, 'and where should we be then?' He was thick and resistant and prickly and difficult and I had to remind myself that he wasn't any more reactionary than Herbert Bowden would have been.

Next I turned to morning sittings and explained what I wanted. 'I know you're opposed to this,' I said, 'but I want you to understand the social

[1] The Conservative Party Conference at Blackpool had opened on October 12th.

[2] Lord President of the Council in the 1945 post-war Caretaker Government, and chairman of the Conservative Party Organization 1946–55.

[3] Crossman hoped to establish specialist Select Committees of ten to fifteen M.P.s who would examine some aspects of a Department's work, meeting weekly, usually in public, summoning witnesses and producing reports.

reasons why we have to try the experiment. We really must help our people to get more early nights at home and I hope you'll collaborate in this.' But he wasn't going to play at all. He didn't believe in morning sittings: he regarded them as absolute nonsense. What he wanted was a really radical reform of Standing Order 9 in order to get the proper number of topical debates.[1] I tried to explain my idea of moving the Standing Order 9 debates on to the next morning sitting. He wouldn't have anything of it and pointed out that the new Speaker[2] was hopeless and the situation was now totally different to when the Tories were in Government and Standing Order 9 debates were a regular occurrence.* Finally I looked at him and said, 'If you want me to help you get really radical revision of Standing Order 9 you ought to help me a bit about my morning sittings.' At this point our Chief Whip chipped in. 'What will you do,' he asked, 'if despite your objections the House accepts the proposal for morning sittings? Won't you help me then?' Heath said, 'No, we shall not help you at all. The proposal ought to fail.' I could see Willie Whitelaw blanching a bit at his behaviour and the psychological hammering he was giving us.

One lesson of this meeting with Heath was that when the House is sitting my headquarters must be not the Palace in Whitehall but the miserable room provided for the Leader of the House in the Palace of Westminster. The House of Commons resumes this week and just when I'm getting used to my palatial room in the Privy Council I have to move across to the Leader's room behind the Speaker's chair in the House of Commons. I've worked quite hard at my Privy Council palace. I've switched the three armchairs and the settee round to give a kind of club atmosphere looking out at the Horse-guards Parade. Then behind my own writing table I've put the tables together as a single long table round which we can hold a meeting. Most important of all, I've persuaded Philip Hendy,[3] who runs the National Gallery, to let me choose four pictures from the National Gallery store to hang on my walls and make the room really worth seeing. Now when I've just begun to like it I have to move into those ghastly rooms in St Stephen's.

All I have is two very modest rooms. Into the outside little anteroom are crowded all my staff—that's Trevelyan, David Holmes and my dear Janet. Anne Ridoutt has been left behind to live upstairs and in the old place.[4]

---

* I couldn't correct him at the time but Freddie Warren has provided a list for me to send him which shows that in twenty years since 1945 there have been fifteen Standing Order 9 debates successfully moved so it's no good Mr Heath saying that there's been any change since the change of Speaker.

[1] Under Standing Order No. 9, M.P.s could seek to raise at very short notice debates on matters of urgent public importance, for discussion either on the following day or even at a later hour on the same evening. A wealth of precedent had permitted successive Speakers to restrict this opportunity and it was only when the S.O. was redrafted in 1967 that M.P.s could make full use of its possibilities.

[2] Dr Horace King.

[3] Slade Professor of Fine Arts at the University of Oxford 1936–46 and Director of the National Gallery, London, 1946–67. He was knighted in 1950.

[4] Mrs Anne Ridoutt, an Assistant Principal.

Beyond the anteroom is my room, which could be quite nice but is jammed full of the ugliest furniture which I'm trying to get sorted out. At present there's hardly room for two visitors and I've had to wait and wait because they had decided to redecorate it and to paint the very dark panelling white. All that was intended and still hasn't been done and yet I've got to live there. The single success I've had has been to pressure the Ministry of Works into supplying me with a television set. It took weeks to get it and I was told time after time that this is something which no previous Leader of the House asked for or even wanted. I knew perfectly well that if Herbert Morrison had been Leader in the period of television he would certainly have had one. If I'm to lead the Party in the Commons I must keep contact with what's going on—I must see the topical programmes and debates. Anyway, I have to spend so many hours there in the evening that I will want some relaxation. So I've got my way, but it's significant of the way the Civil Service rate the members of the Government that though I've got my set the Chief Whip has been refused one although the case for his having one is even stronger than mine.* The only other change I've made in this dark dismal room is to open up one of the cupboards and put some drinks in it so that I can at least entertain those who come to chat to me. In addition I've put a bed in one corner since I've got to be with the troops whenever there's a late night, however boring it may be. Of course I can go out to dinner provided I'm back in time for the winding-up speeches at nine o'clock and provided I hang about after ten until the final division has taken place and the adjournment is on.

Tuesday, October 18th

My main job was to move the Second Reading of the Ombudsman Bill. I had worked very hard at it over the weekend, and the more I learned the less impressed I was by the powers we had given the so-called Parliamentary Commissioner. But I had to make the best of it and found that the Treasury had produced three complete drafts of the speech. Young Mr Couzens was there to help.[1] He was the extremely clever chap who helped me with mortgages last July. Switched to deal with the ombudsman, he only knew what he had mugged up. I managed to reshape one of the drafts to show that the ombudsman will not be taking over the constituency work of M.P.s but would be at their service. I also decided to emphasize something I hadn't realized before —the enormous investigatory powers he will possess. We propose that he should be given access to all the files in Whitehall, permitted to disregard Crown privilege and entitled to cross-examine everyone concerned in the case from the Minister down to the lowest clerk.[2]

* He got one a month or two later.
[1] Kenneth Couzens joined the Inland Revenue in 1949, moving to the Treasury in 1951, where he remained until 1968. After two years in the Civil Service Department he returned to the Treasury as an Under-Secretary in 1970, and, in 1973, became a Deputy Secretary. See Vol. I, p. 474.
[2] Not only was the ombudsman to depend upon M.P.s alone to refer complaints to him

When the debate started at 3.30 I got up very nervous and raced through my speech in fifty-five minutes. If I had delivered it properly it would have been quite good, but fortunately I was interrupted enough to keep the interest alive. In the debate Hogg and all the other Tories poured cold water on the whole scheme on the grounds that people with real grievances would be excluded as it wouldn't cover local government, the Health Service or Civil Service grievances. On our own side a number of people showed how little they knew about the Bill by expressing alarm that their constituents would go direct to the ombudsman—something they *won't* be entitled to do. Apparently no effort had been made to sell the Bill either to the House or to the public.

Throughout the debate Sir Edmund Compton himself was sitting under the gallery at the Members' end of the House. I caught him in the act of trying to slip into the officials' gallery at the other end. As I was making a great fuss in my speech of his being not a Government stooge but an independent character I made him move. I took him out for dinner and he said one thing which struck me very much. I had mentioned that on planning appeals, though the ombudsman couldn't deal with the content of a planning decision, the damage caused by delay would be his concern. 'Delay,' he said, 'is a major scandal in Whitehall. Given the chance I could deal with cases in every Department, and I intend to do so.'

The debate was far too quiet to get any press publicity. Anyway the Home Secretary had captured the headlines when he announced a free pardon for the dead body of Timothy Evans, who had been executed in 1950 for the murder of his daughter sixteen years ago.[1]

Wednesday, October 19th

I started with morning prayers at 9.30. This is normally on Friday but I was told late on Tuesday night that the P.M. wanted to see us on Wednesday morning. There we sat alone with him—while all the O.P.D. people muttered outside the door. The Chief gave him a report on the state of the Party with regard to the two big debates next Monday and Tuesday. We had been planning very carefully to make sure that the Party would accept the Part IV Order as easily as possible. But our plans had been complicated by the fact that the Tories had a supply day on the Monday and had chosen unemployment for the topic.[2] This is to be followed on Tuesday by the Part IV Order.

---

but his investigatory powers were to be restricted. The Act excluded from his concerns matters affecting the armed forces, the police, hospitals, local authorities and the nationalized industries, as well as matters for which a tribunal or a remedy at law already existed. His authority to make recommendations was to be a narrow one. (In 1973, Sir Edmund Compton's successor, Sir Alan Marre, was empowered to investigate certain complaints against the working of the National Health Service.)

[1] The Brabin inquiry reported, however, that while he probably did not murder his daughter, he may have killed his wife.

[2] On twenty-nine days in each Session the House of Commons debates the supply of

The Chief told Harold that fortunately the Left is divided and there are a number who think they ought to acquiesce on this occasion, but Frank Cousins and about twenty are determined to oppose. After a quiet talk for a quarter of an hour about this we went out and let the O.P.D. phalanx pour in. Once again Malta was on the agenda and I came back for this single item and got nowhere.

This afternoon I had my first six Questions to answer as Lord President. One of them was about parliamentary reform and I replied that I thought we should have the debate on the report on broadcasting proceedings first and the debate on the report on procedure a few weeks later. Thereupon George Strauss thought up a point I wasn't prepared for.[1] 'Will the matter be left to a free vote?' he asked, and I said, 'Yes.' The moment I'd said it I realized it was almost certainly wrong and that evening after a quiet talk with the Chief we realized I would have to make a personal Statement. Fortunately I've got my business Statement tomorrow and I shall have to slip this apology in. Meanwhile this evening I've been to see Strauss and told him that I'm sorry, I'd have to withdraw. I hope it isn't too delicate an operation.

Directly after Question Time I had a crucial meeting with the Chief and Bert Bowden. Bert now, like Ted Short, is a happy departmental Minister. He's got an important job, he's negotiating with Smith and he adores having a clear-cut responsibility instead of the nerve-fraying assignment which Silkin and I have inherited. Nevertheless it was absolutely vital for me to persuade him to support my proposals on television and procedure first in the Ministerial Committee and then in Cabinet. So we sat down together and it didn't take us long to get his backing for all our proposals.

After that came the first meeting of the liaison committee while the House is sitting. Manny Shinwell was in the chair, with John Silkin, myself and Freddie Warren in regular attendance from the Government, and Malcolm MacPherson and Willie Hamilton as the two elected representatives of the back-benchers.[2] We discussed at some length the tactics we should use in the meeting of the Parliamentary Party next Monday evening where I'm due to wind up for the Government (just as I'm due to wind up for the Government in the House on Tuesday when nobody else in the Cabinet wants to take on the rough assignment of defending Part IV). How should the Parliamentary Party be handled? Manny was for not having a vote on Part IV and trying

---

money to the Crown, i.e. the Government, to cover its estimates for civil and defence expenditure. The voting of supply is now formal and regular and a supply debate is customarily used by the Opposition to put down a motion criticizing Government policy and administration or a neutral 'adjournment motion', on which to base a discussion of Government action, with or without a vote.

[1] Labour M.P. for Lambeth since 1929, a Minister in the 1929–31 Government and Minister of Supply 1947–51.

[2] Malcolm MacPherson, Labour M.P. for Stirling and Falkirk 1948–74, vice-chairman of the P.L.P. 1964–7. William Hamilton, Labour M.P. for West Fife since 1950, noted for his republican opinions.

to slip it through. I said we've got to have formal approval and after a longish discussion got my way. Then I turned to my other proposition—for a business meeting every Thursday at six o'clock—and, to my surprise, heard Malcolm MacPherson, who's supposed to represent the back-benchers, saying it would merely give 'them' a chance of talking. By 'them', of course, he meant the left-wing extremists. Again I insisted on having my way. I hope our first meeting was reasonably successful.

Thursday, October 20th
This was my really big day—at 3.30 my first appearance to handle business Questions. I was extremely nervous and I had very little time since I seemed to have a mass of other business to arrange with Harold; I was trotting in and out of his room at the House of Commons and from his to mine and tidying things up with Marcia for the rest of the morning before and after Cabinet.

Cabinet was a curious meeting. It began as usual with parliamentary business and I had to report on the very hostile response which Heath had made to our proposals for parliamentary reform. John also reported on the state of morale on our back benches and then we discussed the spokesman on Part IV once again. As I feared, I found myself selected not only to wind up the Party meeting on Monday but also to wind up Tuesday's debate in the Commons.

With parliamentary business behind us we were off on a whole series of characteristic Cabinet items. For a time we discussed import quotas on apples, with one of those bickers between Fred Peart and Douglas Jay which Fred with his charm always wins. The only item which interested me was broadcasting. Harold, who had chaired the Committee, had to report that by a narrow majority Ministers had been in favour of a short-term pop music programme on B.B.C. radio followed by a long-term proposal to set up a sound radio corporation, financed in part by advertising. When I was dining with Hugh Greene, the Director-General of the B.B.C., the other day, I warned him against being too bloody-minded. He sort of dared me to do our worst, and that was one of the things which made me so determined to win in the Cabinet Committee. Now the same debate was repeated in Cabinet and once again Harold asked each member to vote and lost comfortably. One reason for his defeat, I'm afraid, is that the Lord President nipped in after the P.M.G. had put his case and remarked that we really had to face the problem of B.B.C. finance and the impossibility of constantly raising the licence fee. As he'd insisted on taking a vote on the apple quota as well as on the B.B.C. I felt very depressed about his method of handling Cabinet business and arranged to go round and talk to him that evening. But now it was time to rush back to my room, get hold of Freddie Warren and Silkin, get my notes together and go down to the Commons in time to hear Harold conduct a superbly confident and efficient Question Time, scoring off Ted Heath on Rhodesia and on the Scottish economic situation. I watched him in admiration and then there was I on my feet dealing with the business and Anne watching me from the Speaker's Gallery. I think it went fairly well. I managed to get my retraction out with an 'Ooh' from the House but quite a friendly ooh. The only place where I nearly came unstuck was on hanging. I'd noticed at the Tory Party Conference that Quintin Hogg had made a remarkable speech in which he persuaded the Conference not to pass a resolution insisting on bringing the death penalty back for the murder of police or prison officers and he'd done this against the pleas of Duncan Sandys.[1] Now Duncan Sandys in revenge had got an Early Day Motion signed by 175 Members. When I was asked about it I thought this was an easy one and tried rather facetiously to snub Duncan Sandys. Clearly this offended the House. When a Tory got up and said I'd been frivolous there was some support and I had to clamber back to safety. Fortunately I had read the answer that had been supplied me from the Home Office that I saw no reason to change when the House had so recently passed a decision by a large majority on a free vote. With an enormous sense of relief I read those words aloud and got away with it but I'd received a warning of how quickly the House can move from sympathy with its Leader to hostility. It was very exhausting and nerve-wracking but exhilarating. I knew I'd done fairly well—but I can still fail at the Party meeting on Monday, I can fail next day in the wind-up on Part IV. I am living a dangerous life now. But still, we did carry it off this afternoon.

This evening, after my first quite successful conference with the Lobby journalists, I went round to No. 10 where Harold had asked me to have a chat. I found George Brown and Burke Trend there and George at once burst out about the way Harold had handled Cabinet this morning. I'm afraid I joined in and we both pummelled him on the subject of those votes. At one point George Brown said, 'Of course you can keep a list, but you should know that other people round that table are keeping their lists and taking them away for use in their memoirs. It undermines the whole idea of collective Cabinet responsibility. You ought to take the voices, Prime Minister, and then make up your own mind.' Harold looked down rather sheepish and difficult but he slipped away after the meeting without saying a word. However, he can't feel too badly about me because when I got home that evening I found a little note in my red box which read, 'I was delighted with your maiden effort today —the most enjoyable since the Morrison–Churchill days. On top the whole time, apparently effortlessly so: conciliatory, servant of the House, yet scoring political points the whole way by being mainly non-political. Above all, a lofty intellectual or mock-intellectual superiority which made their would-be intellectuals look very silly. All our people were delighted. Con-

---

[1] Conservative M.P. for Lambeth 1943–5 and for Streatham 1950–74. He was Minister of Supply 1951–4, Minister of Housing and Local Government 1954–7, Minister of Defence 1957–9, Minister of Aviation 1959–60, Secretary of State for Commonwealth Relations 1960–64 and for the Colonies 1962–4. He was to sponsor a Private Members' Bill on November 23rd, 1966, calling for the restoration of capital punishment for the murder of police officers and prison warders. It was defeated by 292 votes to 170.

gratulations.'[1] I had got home to bed and opened my red box, read this note and turned to my other papers when I fell asleep. I woke up at 12.30 a.m. with the telephone ringing and Harold Wilson saying, 'I hope you're still awake. I tried to get you. I was talking to George again last night. You are a member of the inner club—the O.P.D.—I just wanted to ring you up and tell you.' I was slightly bewildered by this as I sank back into sleep after a long and exhausting day.

Friday, October 21st

After going into the office and tidying things up I took the train to Birmingham where I'd agreed to a 10-minute interview as a Midlands M.P. It took the whole day to get there, to have a miserable lunch in the Birmingham studio, to have the 10-minute interview and to motor home. When I got there I had a little walk with the children and then found the interview was put on at 11.50 p.m., when nobody could possibly listen. That is an object lesson in how not to spend a day. My only excuse was that I'd done the interview on the express advice of Downing Street.

From 1961 to 1963 Britain had explored in negotiation with the six countries of the E.E.C. (France, Germany, Italy, the Netherlands, Belgium and Luxembourg) whether and on what terms to join the Common Market. In 1963 General de Gaulle had vetoed Britain's entry, a decision that had shocked those who felt that Britain's future outside Europe could only be as an etiolated little England. Some were relieved for they discerned an insistent supra-national philosophy in the Treaty of Rome and in addition some critics did not wish to jeopardize Britain's existing Commonwealth ties.

By 1966, however, attitudes were changing. General de Gaulle's determination to pursue an independent French foreign policy and the deterioration of the Commonwealth as a politically effective body undermined these earlier objections. Moreover, membership of the E.E.C. seemed to offer some remedy for Britain's own enfeebled economy. Before any announcement could be made to the British people or an application offered to the European Community, however, the Cabinet had to decide where the Government stood on delicate matters of economic, defence and foreign policy. One of the most urgent questions was that of the Anglo-American special nuclear relationship. Another was to consider how Britain's EFTA partners would view our application to join the E.E.C.

Saturday, October 22nd

Well, now we come to the great Chequers meeting on Europe—that well-advertised secret conference for which each of us had received a mass of papers provided by the officials, including an introduction by George Brown

---

[1] Winston Churchill had been leader of the Opposition from 1945 to 1951 while Herbert Morrison was Lord President and Leader of the House of Commons.

and Michael Stewart which tried to justify entry as the only way to make sure that Britain kept a place at the top table. There was a curious passage about Little England, suggesting that this would be perfectly all right if we were prepared not to count in the councils of the world. So I was clear before I got to Chequers that George and Michael now wanted full backing from the Cabinet for a new European initiative and it was also clear that ideally they would have liked a declaration of intent to sign the treaty.

The morning was an experimental one. Instead of meeting alone the Cabinet met with a large number of officials taking part in the discussion—officials from the F.O., from the D.E.A., and from the Treasury, plus the economic advisers, including Nicky Kaldor and Tommy Balogh. Of the twenty-three members of the Cabinet seventeen were present. The morning was supposed to be the time when the officials and the experts gave their opinions and subjected themselves to questioning. William Armstrong started in the absence of his Minister, since Callaghan couldn't get there on time.[1] To my great surprise he admitted under questioning that entry in 1968 (which all the papers took as a working assumption) was now a bit too early in view of the time it would take to restore the economy to a state healthy enough for entry. This remarkable confession stimulated a long discussion of the timetable. Some of the officials suggested it would take two years of the slow growth we must now expect before we got the economy right and then another two years to prove that when growth started we wouldn't have an inflation. I could see George Brown getting angrier and angrier at this point. The trouble about the morning session was that the Ministers present were determined to use the officials mainly to supply information confirming their own personal points of view. The questioners, including Tony Crosland, started, 'Now I just want to ask a pure question of information,' and then the question turned out to be an effort to try to get the statement from the official which would push the Minister's point of view. That is the obvious difficulty when you try and have a joint meeting between Ministers and officials. This, I suppose, was a moderately successful one but considering the number of officials massed behind us what we got out of them was very little, either little formal statements which were just repeats of the briefs we'd already read or the wriggling efforts of officials trying to avoid being used in a battle between Ministers.

After lunch Cabinet sat alone and we had a series of statements with very little discussion. George Brown made an initial statement that what he wanted was a declaration of intent. 'The probing,' he said, 'really hadn't got anywhere, since nobody in Europe will take it seriously until it is clear that we are determined to join.' Michael Stewart backed him up in all this. They were

[1] Sir William Armstrong (K.C.B. 1963) had spent the greater part of his career in the Treasury, becoming its Joint Permanent Secretary in 1962. From 1968 until his retirement he was the official Head of the Home Civil Service and the Permanent Secretary of the Civil Service Department. In 1975 he became Chairman of the Midland Bank and accepted a life peerage, taking the title of Lord Armstrong of Sanderstead.

then cross-examined about the timetable and in particular about the suggestion of waiting four years. George said that four years was far too long. He wanted to start straightaway with a new round of investigations. He wanted to push hard because he was convinced the door was open and we could get in. At this point the P.M. revealed his passionate interest in an article in this week's *Economist*, which I hadn't read but which had apparently charmed him. I read it this evening and found it gimmicky and of no particular significance.

As the afternoon went on it was clear that while George Brown and Michael Stewart were already committed to a new initiative, most of us were agreed that there were at least two points on which it was vital to secure further information before a decision. This was what Harold Wilson had brought out at the beginning of the session. The first of these was whether the abolition of exchange controls when we entered meant that we would have to devalue straightaway. Harold didn't like his colleagues using these words but the issue couldn't be burked. The second question was whether the Commission in Brussels would really deprive us not only of some of our sovereignty but of some of our power to plan the economy. Would investment grants be allowable or not? Would we still be able to see that new factories are put in Scotland rather than in South-East England? Of course Fred Peart and Douglas Jay pushed their objection to the common agricultural policy. But most of us, I think – and here Tommy is absolutely right – felt that agriculture is really an ancillary argument. If we try to go in when the economy is weak and we have to suffer deflation and unemployment then the increased agricultural prices will be a heavy burden on top of that. But if we go in when our economy is booming and our industry growing then the agricultural prices will be something we can sustain.

The meeting this afternoon, at which there were no officials, was not a formal Cabinet and Harold said we should talk to each other using our Christian names. The result was that the discussion got much rougher than he intended. After Callaghan had made a very judicious and tentative speech supporting George Brown I said there was something I wanted to talk about frankly and that was whether Little England was the alternative to the Common Market. I didn't think so. I regard Little England as the precondition for any successful socialist planning whether inside or outside the Common Market. Whatever happens, we need to cut back our overseas commitments and withdraw our troops from the Far East and the Middle East. 'Again, take devaluation,' I said. 'This is also a pre-condition of our recovery whether we're inside or outside the Market,' and I maintained that what Sir William Armstrong had said confirmed my point of view. This produced a really furious row, with half the Cabinet in disagreement about what Sir William had or had not said in the morning when Callaghan wasn't there. I'm sorry that I deeply upset Harold by talking so openly about devaluation as a pre-condition of our success but it really had to be said. I suppose it was because we weren't an official Cabinet that that discussion got so knock-about. I was on the receiving end for once and Harold, despite finding it acutely embarrassing, had to restrain my colleagues in order to enable me to say my say. So I got back on to Little England and told them they shouldn't go into Europe in order to remain great. On this I got a great deal of support from Dick Marsh, Barbara Castle and Tony Wedgwood Benn. It became clear that there is a pretty even split between the Europeans, who feel we must now try to get in virtually as fast as possible on the best terms we can get, and the rest of us, who are fundamentally uninterested in entry. The Europeans are headed by George Brown and Michael Stewart but they have strong support from the Lord Chancellor and also from James Callaghan, who has reluctantly come off the fence in favour of a new approach to Europe. In addition there is George Thomson at the F.O. supporting them. On our side there is Douglas Jay and Fred Peart one hundred per cent anti-Europe, and there are people like Barbara, Dick Marsh and myself all saying that the net result of the morning talk with the officials was to show how dubious the economic advantages of going into Europe are. Towards the end Tony Wedgwood Benn made an extremely good speech asking what was European about us and what was American and whether the Anglo-American relationship isn't worth a great deal more than entry into Europe. Some of us tried very hard, including the P.M., to get Tommy Balogh's paper on the North Atlantic Free Trade Area considered seriously.[1] But the trouble was we all know this is a non-starter because the Americans aren't prepared to take it seriously. The real choice is between staying out and seeing what we can do to get in. A very good point was made by Denis Healey, whose point of view I found rather close to mine. He said that at least we must have a proper calculation about what would happen on certain assumptions. For instance, if we have to stay out how will we work our passage outside Europe? He himself is convinced that de Gaulle is going to veto our entry anyway and we shall have to survive outside.

Finally came our Harold. I suppose I was a bit dumb to be surprised by what he said. He started with an elaborate declaration about how he felt more committed than other people there and how everything he said would probably meet with disagreement from everybody else. Then, having screwed himself up in this way, he said that what he proposed was a tour round Europe by George Brown and himself to visit the chief capitals and try to clarify the doubtful issues, their probing centring on the two points we had discussed at such length. He said that if the two of them went it would allay suspicions. His presence would allay the suspicion of the anti-Europeans that their point of view wasn't being fully considered. But his presence would also

---

[1] The proposal for NAFTA envisaged a free trade area of the EFTA countries, Canada and the United States, possibly embracing Australia and New Zealand as well. It foundered on the rocks of American protectionism and the instinct for self-preservation of Australian manufacturers. Another alternative was GITA: 'Going It Alone'.

allay the fears of the pro-Europeans who remember the P.M.'s famous Bristol speech in which he accused Heath of fawning on the Europeans like a spaniel.[1] I admit I was both disconcerted and surprised by this announcement. In order to over-trump George Brown, Harold had in fact conceded him far more than he'd asked for. All George and Michael Stewart came to Chequers asking for was a declaration of intent to sign the Treaty of Rome. But now Harold had conceded a tour round Europe by George and himself which was bound to commit us far further towards entry than any paper declaration of intent. Towards the end of the meeting I begged him to have second thoughts. I said I would trust George Brown to go round on his own but what I didn't want to see was our Prime Minister being committed in this way. Nor did I really see why either of them should go. Why shouldn't the probing on these two main points be conducted through diplomatic channels and the whole job completed on a professional plane? If one is really probing and investigating it shouldn't be done in the gimmicky way of a tour by the Prime Minister and the Foreign Secretary. But as always Harold had made up his mind. There was no going back. He switched to a discussion about publicity. 'There must be no leaks,' he said. 'It would be fatal to have any suggestion which would commit us either for or against entry. All of us must show absolute discretion about this.'

It was now six o'clock and we'd had three hours of really solid argument after those three hours in the morning with the officials. It was time to break off.

The select few who were to discuss defence stayed to dinner. I begged the P.M. to have the discussion about defence over dinner since we were so tired but George Brown had drunk a little too much and he'd also been cheered up because Sophie's gallstone operation is over and quite suddenly he got drunk. So we had an uproarious dinner and then afterwards, upstairs in the long gallery, we settled down to our discussion. George still wasn't quite fit to take part in it but there we were—the seven of us. Denis Healey started by saying that he had now reconsidered the defence budget and thought it was possible to get it down next year to something below £1,850 million. This would mean cutting between £250 million and £400 million by halving our expenditure East of Suez, cutting our costs in Germany by a third and winding up our Middle East commitment altogether. He said in rather a superior voice that intellectually it might seem to be easier to do this by cutting the East of Suez commitment altogether but our allies would never allow that. All through Denis's exposition George Brown kept on shouting, 'But you just said something different to me last time, Denis. What do you really mean? Is there no cut in commitments? How can you make such an enormous cut without demanding something of me as Foreign Secretary?' Denis replied quietly that

---

[1] During the general election campaign in March 1966, Harold Wilson had said of Edward Heath that at 'one encouraging gesture from the French Government ... he was on his back like a spaniel'.

no change was required in foreign policy. We would still have the forces to maintain it. What came out of a very long discussion is that the defence policy Healey proposes would mean leaving token forces in the Far East quite unable to fulfil any of the precise obligations we've undertaken in SEATO. And there may well be token forces in the Middle East unable to fulfil the obligations we've undertaken under CENTO. I made this point and said, 'But surely it's far better first to make a major change in foreign policy and follow Ernest Bevin's example? You remember when he totally withdrew from Greece and Turkey and forced the Truman Doctrine on the Americans.[1] Now isn't that the kind of thing we should now do? We should make a proper basic foreign policy change and not merely whittle away our defences while maintaining our commitments.' Again Denis said that intellectually that might be true but practically it was impossible.

Harold tried to stop me and I realized straightaway that I was alone among the seven. I'm really completely out of sympathy with the whole atmosphere of this Government's attitude to foreign policy and defence—they want to maintain our commitments while cutting away the forces with which we sustain them. What George Wigg and I have argued for years and years is precisely that the one thing a Labour Government must not do is to assume huge responsibilities and then deny our troops the weapons necessary to sustain them. Just think of it. The first Defence Review isn't yet twelve months old. Already, in July, it's been cut by £100 million. Now Denis is saying he can cut it in six months' time by another £300 million while we still retain all our commitments in the Far East, in the Middle East and in Germany. Both before the meeting and at the end I was reminded in the presence of the others that I was a new member of the club and must mind my tongue especially because I couldn't yet fully understand what was involved. I'm afraid I do understand only too well. But I never suspected that when I got inside O.P.D. and discovered what was actually being done by these colleagues it would be so crude, so unskilful—a futile attempt to remain Great Britain, one of the three world powers, while slicing away our defences.

While our talks were going on someone rushed in to say that George Blake had just climbed over the wall of Wormwood Scrubs and made his escape.[2] George Brown woke up and said we must give instructions to alert all the ports. The P.M. asked what statement we should give to the press. I asked why we should make any statement to the press. We've presumably got capable people running the prison and really we're not much good, as Ministers, in trying to catch a prisoner who's run away. This was thought to be in

---

[1] In March 1947, when Britain found herself unable to meet her obligations to resist Communism in Greece, Ernest Bevin, Foreign Secretary from July 1945 to March 1951, encouraged President Truman to declare that America had the duty to oppose the threat of Communism in any country.

[2] In 1961 George Blake had been convicted of espionage and was serving a sentence of forty-two years in Wormwood Scrubs.

rather poor taste. However George Brown went off to bed and I was left in the end talking alone with Harold.

This was quite a solemn occasion. 'I brought you into this club—the one you attended this evening,' he said. 'Do you still want to be a member? Because if you do, you know, your behaviour has got to be very different. You mustn't go on talking to Barbara, least of all about the things we discuss here. You mustn't even let her know what is going on in RX. You've got to be a member of this club—an insider—along with us. Otherwise it won't work.' I said I was pretty security-minded after five years at SHAEF. 'No,' he said, 'it's not only a matter of military security; it's a matter of your relationship with your colleagues. You've got to have a new style of relationship with the other members of this inner group now that I've brought you right in.' He said this time after time and I did get the impression that he's trying to tie me tighter and tighter to himself. Why? He got me in, knowing in advance that I'm a Little Englander, knowing in advance my view that we have to change our foreign policy before we cut the defence forces. Then why take the risk of bringing me in as a jarring element? Perhaps he's doing it for the same reason he has Tommy Balogh as his chief economic adviser and George Wigg there in the background. He feels a need to have unconventional people close to him because he knows his own extremely conventional nature.

During our private talk Roy Jenkins rang up in a great stew about George Blake. When Harold put down the receiver he turned to me and said, 'That will do our Home Secretary a great deal of good. He was getting too complacent and he needs taking down a peg.' Then we got back to our talk and I tried once again to deflect him from this half-baked idea of the European tour. I told him there was bound to be a great deal of resistance in the Foreign Office and also I thought from Burke Trend, Douglas Jay and Denis Healey. I will do everything I can to reduce its importance. 'Why not leave matters at this stage to the professionals?' I said. 'Leave it to the diplomats.' 'I am a professional,' he replied. '*I am* professional, Dick.' He said it in a strange voice which made me realize that he already regards himself as an expert on foreign affairs and a statesman able to achieve what no professional diplomat can achieve. Well, perhaps he is a statesman but I'd been trying to tell him that it wasn't the right moment for the politician to intervene—at this stage we should leave it to the professionals since we didn't want to get the Prime Minister committed too early, as he had been on Rhodesia. I'd much prefer to see the probing carried out by professionals and the British position worked out in detail and tested by professionals before the politicians intervene. But here you come up against a real difficulty in our system of government. If the officials are allowed to do everything first you've got to accept incredibly slow progress. Whitehall is appallingly sluggardly in the way it gets to work on its own—as a result a politician like Harold or George suddenly wrenches free and does something on his own, and then it's probably half-baked. This is basically due to the fact that we haven't got a proper relationship between Ministerial decision-making and official decision-making.

Sunday, October 23rd

I'll just wind up my account of Chequers. Now that I've had more time to reflect about yesterday I realize that the meeting with the officials in the morning was enormously useful because those of them who wanted were able to register the warning which is strongly felt outside the Foreign Office that there are grave economic dangers about getting into Europe. And Sir William Armstrong put across unforgettably the idea that entry would certainly mean devaluation. What was the value of that long wrangle in the afternoon? Well I suppose we clarified the difference between the Europeans, who are really committed to getting in as soon as they can, and the much less united antis, who were able to exploit the officials' arguments very successfully. Then there was the third point, which I think I managed to get across, that withdrawal from our East of Suez commitments is essential whether we enter the Market or not. It is an illusion that we could remain Great Britain by becoming a member of the E.E.C.

There's one other very important thing I must add about the Chequers weekend. It was interrupted by more than one big external event. As well as the escape of George Blake from Wormwood Scrubs on Friday night there was the disaster at Aberfan, the Welsh valley where a huge coal tip broke away and ran over a school killing hundreds of children.[1] Harold Wilson had gone straight down there by helicopter and stayed there and Callaghan has gone over by motor-car. Everybody has been rushing to get into it and I feel the whole thing has been emotionally exploited by the B.B.C. in the most terrible and extravagant way. But I have no doubt whatsoever that Harold Wilson was profoundly moved. The tragedy gave a macabre background to the weekend.

Monday, October 24th

Yesterday we had my American publisher, Mike Bessie, and his future wife, Cornelia, staying with us so instead of going up as I should have by the last train I caught one this morning and was twenty minutes late for S.E.P. But in plenty of time, thank heavens, for the important discussion of reflation. It's obvious that the anxiety about the crisis of business confidence has greatly increased in the last fortnight. In July Callaghan said he wouldn't allow people to increase their overdrafts in order to pay the new S.E.T. in September. Now today he's giving that concession and adding that we must consider investment grants and other reflationary actions. I got the impression that in his view private investment is the key. If we can't get private investment moving upwards we're in for a long period of deflation without any economic

---

[1] On October 21st, at Aberfan, Glamorgan, a slag-tip slid away, taking a school and houses in its path and killing 116 children and 28 adults.

growth. Not that there's grave anxiety about the level of unemployment this winter. It may rise above the half million mark but not above the 750,000 mark.[1] It's next winter we have to concern ourselves with and that's why it's so vital to keep investment going. What more can we do to prevent deflation? One of our weapons has already been knocked out of our hands by the decision to send George and Harold round Europe. We couldn't consider putting on import controls while they're on their tour. The surcharge ends this December so really import controls should go on at once but it looks as though they are out. Tommy Balogh consoles me by saying we shan't need them because imports are now being controlled by the lack of business confidence and the failure of businessmen to buy so much abroad. The more I think about those Chequers talks the more I am convinced that we shall genuinely try to get into Europe and I think you'll find that when we do we shall be prepared to loosen our special relationships with America. Indeed, we may well find America will begin to push Britain politely but gently to a less intimate relationship and into a more intimate relationship with Europe, and this would mean that we could throw off all those world commitments we now have and cease to regard ourselves as a power with world duties in Africa and Asia. Those are all advantages to be added to the most important one, namely that a determination to get into Europe might create confidence in business and might give us that marginal difference in business investment which should be so important in preventing an inflation.

I spent some time after lunch getting briefed by Michael Stewart's officials for tomorrow's debate on Part IV. One thing I asked is that they should give me the Statements of Conservative Ministers so that we should know what they said about incomes policy. One of the civil servants replied, 'I should know because I drafted their speeches as well as those of the present Minister.' He said this in the presence of Michael Stewart who smiled and when I got hold of the briefs I found that many of the words and sentences were almost identical. So it's broadly true that for five years now the civil servants have been dictating to Ministers in successive Governments the same kind of briefs irrespective of party.

Next we went to the House to hear the Secretary for Wales make a Statement on Aberfan[2] and then to watch poor Roy Jenkins in some trouble about the escape of George Blake. He was pressed very hard by Heath to make a really severe investigation into Blake's escape and replied cautiously that he wanted a general investigation of the reason for escapes throughout the prison system. Heath came back very hard and Jenkins's reply seemed obstinate and a little stupid. Talking it over with Burke Trend later that day I discovered it wasn't mere thickheadedness on the part of Jenkins. He realized that what Heath was trying to elicit was an admission or a suggestion that

[1] Unemployment rose to 541,585 in November and to 564,083 in December.
[2] The Government announced the appointment of a judicial inquiry under the chairmanship of Lord Justice Edmund Davies.

Blake's escape was the result of some inner treason, some collusion between the prison and Russians outside. They were fishing for another security scandal. Burke tells me the trouble is that though there's no reason to think there was any Russian intervention here, we literally don't know. If I'd been Home Secretary I'd have been tempted to give in on this and have a special investigation of the Blake affair, but Roy stuck to his guns and so Mountbatten will conduct an inquiry into the safety of prisons in general.[1]

In the afternoon we had the first meeting of the new PESC.[2] This time I'm a robber converted into a cop—one of the five just men whose job it is to sit in judgment on the expenditure of the spending Departments and decide who should be cut back. It was interesting to see the cuts proposed by the Treasury. They wanted to see school-meal prices doubled to transfer most of the cost to the customer; a charge for each visit to the doctor of two shillings and six-pence; and, thirdly, a very considerable postponement of the decision to relate the level of old-age pensions either to the cost of living or to average earnings. There was also to be a 10 per cent cut in less essential local govern-ment expenditure and some further reduction of road building. As we sat informally round the table looking at the figures I started a discussion by pointing out that even after these cuts we would have a 43 per cent increase in road building this year and a 30 per cent increase in school building. This was because we had inherited Tory programmes and were carrying them on. Callaghan replied rather crossly, 'We don't consider a revision of Tory priorities at this stage. We're merely seeing what reasonable cuts we can enforce in the crisis.'

I then pointed out that there is something sadly wrong because these pro-posed cuts—by increasing school-meal prices, for instance—were not being considered in relation to possible tax concessions. It was important to see this because a Chancellor simply won't be able to get Cabinet to agree to cuts in the school-meal subsidy unless simultaneously he announces an increase in family allowances, possibly linked with a drastic change in the income tax child's allowances such as Brian Abel-Smith[3] and Nicky Kaldor have been working on for a long time. Callaghan simply replied that in order to keep within his 4 per cent limit these cuts have to be made and there was a com-plete failure to resolve this problem round the table.

I just had time to get upstairs for the big meeting of the Parliamentary

[1] Lord Mountbatten's inquiry into prison administration reported on December 22nd, and recommended more careful grading of prisoners with a special escape-proof prison on the Isle of Wight in which the highly dangerous could be segregated; improvements in all aspects of security and of the prison service were also advised. On December 12th, Frank Mitchell, who had been serving a life sentence for murder, escaped from Dartmoor.

[2] The Public Expenditure Survey Committee of Ministers, which scrutinized the long-range expenditure plans prepared by all Departments of State with assistance from the Treasury.

[3] Professor of Social Administration, University of London, since 1965. Consultant and adviser to innumerable bodies and committees, he was also to serve as Crossman's Senior Adviser at D.H.S.S. 1968–70.

Party to consider Part IV of the Prices and Incomes Bill. John Silkin and I had insisted on this meeting on the ground that the Party must be consulted and take its decision before the debate. Everything went very quietly. Michael Stewart made a thin, dry, precise but correct approach and then we had a very sober debate. I wound up very briefly and the vote went 204 to 37.

When that was over I went down to the Chamber to see what was happening in the redeployment debate.[1] It was completely flat and only half full for the winding-up speeches by Nicholas Ridley[2] and Shirley Williams.

Tuesday, October 25th

This was my big day because I had to wind up the debate on Part IV. I'd been given the job because nobody else wanted it. Douglas Jay and Fred Peart were most unwilling, George Brown was now Foreign Secretary, and Austen Albu[3] and Bill Rodgers weren't considered up to it so it fell to me. The trouble was that I was busy the whole morning. First I had Legislation Committee of which I was chairman. After that I got back to my office and did a bit of the central section of the speech which I discussed with Tommy. But then I had to rush to RX where we had the report from Morrice James, now back from Rhodesia.[4] He made it clearer than ever that there is no chance of an agreement on the constitutional issues and as for the return to legality it wasn't even considered during his talks because they're thought to be so remote from reality by the Rhodesians. Right at the end Denis Healey said that since there was no chance of agreement we really must revise our strategy for the new phase ahead. We have to accept it as a fact that mandatory sanctions will have virtually no effect on Rhodesia—even if they include oil sanctions—whereas they may have an appalling effect on us and if we get involved in an economic war with South Africa we may either split the Commonwealth or commit economic suicide. Denis and I, faced with this prospect, both pressed very hard that the Committee must now consider the possibility of pulling out—whether by handing Rhodesia on a plate to the United Nations according to Ernie Bevin's Palestine formula or by just letting it go in with South Africa. I think our colleagues at last thought they were really up against it. But on the other hand we didn't make any headway with our argument.

This Committee took most of the morning and I had lunch in my room while I worked on my speech and got a little more done. But before I knew where I was I was due on the Floor of the House to sit by Harold Wilson when he answered his Questions.

[1] The Government survived a vote of censure by 328 votes to 234.

[2] Conservative M.P. for Cirencester and Tewkesbury since October 1959, P.P.S. to the Minister of Education 1962–4; Parliamentary Secretary at the Ministry of Technology June–October 1970 and Parliamentary Under-Secretary of State at the Department of Trade and Industry 1970–71.

[3] Labour M.P. for Edmonton until 1974. He was Minister of State at the D.E.A. 1965–7.

[4] Sir Morrice James, at this point Deputy Under-Secretary of State at the Commonwealth Office.

After a disastrous reply by Fred Lee to a Private Notice Question on Gibraltar,[1] Michael Stewart rose to open the debate on Part IV—he was longer, more precise and even duller than he was in the Party meeting yesterday. Following him came Iain Macleod who's in two minds what to do. The Opposition had clearly not decided their view on incomes policy which made his attack somewhat ineffective.

I then sat through the rest of the debate. Perhaps I ought to have gone out and prepared my own speech at my desk but I sat on that front bench, listening, taking desultory notes and getting more and more bored because the Speaker called a series of absolute nonentities and held back the big left-wing speakers, like Frank Cousins, to whom I would have to reply. The debate lagged and sagged and I got more and more jumpy and uneasy. I got the outline of the speech prepared and a last peroration and I planned for the middle an attack on the Opposition showing the discrepancy between Maudling's view and Enoch Powell's view and challenging them to say where they really stood. Looking back now I can see the tactic was right enough but I failed to foresee one misfortune. The debate had dragged on until there wasn't adequate time for Frank Cousins before nine o'clock, when Mrs Thatcher was due to get up.[2] So the Whips did a deal under which she started a quarter of an hour late. She made a good, professional, tough speech and sat down just after 9.45 instead of at 9.30.

I suppose very few people can realize what devastation such a little procedural change can bring about. Everybody comes into the Chamber on a three-line whip expecting to vote promptly at ten and they soon get very impatient if the speeches go on after that moment. I got up at eleven minutes to ten and I was doing quite well when ten struck. I had got to the central point of Tommy's argument when I looked at the clock and realized that whatever I said the audience would get bored and I wouldn't be able to hold their attention. I should have spoken on till about 10.25 but I lost my nerve and decided to leave out my attack on the Tories and sit down with a very brief peroration. This I did.

As I sat down Harold beside me said, 'Have you finished, Dick? Or are you giving way to Frank Cousins?' I said (perhaps this was the second mistake), 'Giving way,' because the Chief Whip hadn't got up and moved the

[1] On October 5th the Spanish Government closed the frontier at La Linea to all but pedestrian traffic, and the Governor of Gibraltar had announced that the colony would face an indefinite period of severe restrictions. Although the Foreign Secretary had offered to refer the issue to the International Court of Justice at The Hague for a ruling on Britain's sovereignty over the Rock, the Spanish Government persistently declined to go to the international court. The people of Gibraltar remained loyal to Britain, but on October 25th Mr Lee, the Colonial Secretary, gave only an ambiguous reply to the House of Commons, which did nothing to reassure the islanders of the British Government's support.
[2] Conservative M.P. for Finchley since 1959. She was Joint Parliamentary Secretary at the Ministry of Pensions and National Insurance 1961–4 and Secretary of State for Education and Science 1970–74. In 1975 she succeeded Edward Heath as Leader of the Conservative Party.

adjournment. So I had to lumber to my feet again to answer Frank Cousins. Then, of course, Edward Heath joined in and I was caught, getting up, sitting down, trying to get into my speech again until it dragged on into a complete anti-climax. There were no cheers from our side and there were plenty of shouts of 'resign' from the other.

Then we had the division—307 to 239, with 28 abstentions. John Silkin had expected between sixteen and seventeen. I don't think any of them were in the faintest degree influenced by anything I did say or didn't say or by what Frank Cousins had said in the speech before mine.

After the result was announced I went through into the Members' lobby and ran into George Wigg. He looked at me severely and said, 'Well you got through that all right but now we shall have to take action. Unless you enforce discipline I can't guarantee the consequences. I've been trying to hold the boys back but they're thirsting for blood.' I knew very well that he had not been trying to hold the boys back but had been whipping them up and inciting them to a bloodbath and so had Manny Shinwell. It was obvious that John Silkin and Dick Crossman's new deal would soon be put to its first test.

I went home rather shattered.

Wednesday, October 26th

After a haircut at nine in the morning I was at morning prayers with Harold at 9.45. He was cool and collected, and remarked cheerfully, 'That's probably the worst debate we shall have to go through in this Parliament: we survived it fairly well.' He told us we'd been right to hold the Party meeting the day before and get an overwhelming vote in support for the action he'd taken. Of my performance he said, 'Don't be worried about it. It was perfectly all right,' and he soothed me down as only Harold can.

After that I rushed across to Smith Square where I expected nothing to happen at the monthly meeting of the N.E.C. because nothing usually does. But this time we were all caught unprepared. George Brown and Harold stayed away on the day when the trade unions decided to play it rough.

Quite soon they got on to the subject of the proposed Committee of Inquiry into the Party Organization. Dai Davies of the Steelworkers' made a bitter speech about the leaks in the capitalist press and the rumours that a politician was taking over Transport House. All the work I'd done by writing to Sara, Len and Percy Clark was undermined that morning by the bitterness of Dai and the other trade-union M.P.s whose attacks were entirely based on Nora Beloff's article. In their rage they insisted on selecting the five members of the investigating commission. When the result was announced Simpson,[1] Gormley[2] and Jack Jones each had got twenty, I got eighteen, Alice Bacon

---

[1] Will Simpson, a member of the National Executive Committee of the A.E.U.W. 1955–67 and, since 1967, its General Secretary. A member of the N.E.C. since 1962.

[2] Joe Gormley, since 1958 a member of the National Executive Committee of the N.U.M. and, since 1971, its President. Elected to the N.E.C. in 1963.

fourteen, and Wedgy Benn ten. So I was on the committee but I had been deliberately insulted by the trade-union members. We shall see what happens now the committee's been elected. Perhaps I shall be chosen as chairman but I don't think they will do this. Of course all this had blown sky high Harold's elaborate plan to leave the decision about the committee's membership until after the new chairman of Org. Sub. had been elected and I had got the place. No chance now of any of that being achieved. It was a baddish morning and I personally had a baddish time.

Back to the House of Lords where we were having a Ministerial Committee on Lords' reform under the chairmanship of the Lord Chancellor.[1] This was a very rum show. The Cabinet had already decided that there should be no change in the composition of the Lords but that its powers, in particular the power of delaying legislation and controlling delegated legislation, should be drastically curbed. We were worried that they could exercise a veto on legislation during the last year of a Labour Government. Normally this kind of proposal would have been worked out in a lengthy considered paper. But there was nothing of the sort. The Lord Chancellor, who is the most extraordinary mixture of simpleton and brilliant lawyer as well as being a quite determined, artful and thrusting man, was trying to get his decisions without a paper. As nearly always happens if anyone tries to cut a corner in this Cabinet system, he was defeated on every point and the meeting was soon being described as merely a trial run before a serious Ministerial meeting. Callaghan and I made it clear that the Home Office, not the Lord Chancellor's Office, would have to take responsibility for the Bill. It also became clear to me as the discussion went on that if we were going to have any reform I must be concerned to make sure that they made the House of Lords more useful to us in the Commons. I've already realized that it's jolly useful to have a second chamber; in reducing its powers we mustn't reduce its utility. Indeed, I'm sure we ought to try to push off into the Lords quite a lot of work which now is done by the Commons—the control of Affirmative Orders, for example, could be left to the Lords provided their delaying powers were removed.[2] Quite a useful reform may come out of this Ministerial Committee but there'll have to be a lot more investigation than we got in this haphazard meeting.

[1] Under the terms of the 1949 Parliament Act, the Lords were in 1966 able to delay legislation passed by the Commons with which the Upper House disagreed. The period of delay was effectively one of less than thirteen months, for the Act cut from three to two the number of Sessions in which a Bill must be passed by the Commons. But even such short delay could kill legislation in the last year of a Parliament's life. Furthermore, the Lords not only enjoyed more time to discuss delegated legislation (that which Ministers were statutorily empowered to lay before Parliament as Orders rather than Bills), but in this sphere they were able to reject measures outright. With its majority of Conservative peers, it seemed that this gave the Upper House powers which a Labour Government feared.

[2] Affirmative Orders are those which must be laid before Parliament for positive approval before the delegated legislation may be implemented. (Negative Orders must be laid before the House but are effected if no objection [or Prayer] has been voiced and carried within a specified number of days.)

I had to have the liaison committee in my room and I knew we would have a fierce debate with strong proposals to sack the twenty-eight M.P.s who had defied the Party whip and abstained from voting for Part IV. Sure enough Manny Shinwell, Willie Hamilton and Malcolm MacPherson, the three elected members of the liaison committee, all demanded that we should withdraw the whip. But since it wasn't practical to apply this to all twenty-eight defaulters it was suggested that we should pick off the ringleaders. Four was the number first suggested and then came a later suggestion of seven or eight. At this point John Silkin stepped in and said, 'This is not your decision.' He had written down his view very carefully on paper and it was in strict accord with the concordat which Manny had signed. In that concordat it was laid down that while the decision rested of course with the Parliamentary Party the initiative for recommending discipline remained with the Chief Whip. It's up to him whether he merely reprimands people or recommends the Party to withdraw the whip. He said, 'In this case I do not intend to recommend any expulsions.' Manny exploded and Willie Hamilton threatened to resign. John Silkin turned on them and outlined his whole liberal philosophy, which centred on the view that once you concede a conscience clause to members you can't deny that for Frank Cousins or for Michael Foot Part IV is an issue of conscience. I supported John. 'If you withdraw the whip from four lesser ringleaders and leave out Michael Foot and Frank Cousins they will resign within twenty-four hours. The whole thing will play into the hands of the Tories and we shall be in tremendous difficulties with the constituency parties if we split the Party at this moment. If we have seven, eight or ten of them thrown out then they will have the tremendous advantage of being an independent party with their own whips and the Speaker will give them the right to speak in all major debates. We mustn't do that at all costs.'

John's behaviour was absolutely magnificent at this meeting. He had told me beforehand that he was determined to have a special meeting and move the two traditional resolutions,[1] but it was only as the argument went on that I realized how completely we both accepted the liberal philosophy as the only way to run a modern left-wing party. This is based on the assumption that every member of the Party may well on occasion have to abstain conscientiously; conscientious abstention won't in future be limited to pacifists and teetotallers but will be recognized as a right of every member. And in particular we would have to realize that when a Government suddenly does things which are not in the Party manifesto and which are profoundly controversial, then members have the right to challenge that Government and in the last resort to abstain conscientiously. This is what had happened on Part IV, and instead of demanding blood and slaughter the liaison committee ought to be very relieved that we got the Party to support Part IV with only twenty-eight abstentions and not a single vote against. But of course this idea would sound wildly revolutionary to many members of the Party which

[1] Deploring 'fraternal feuding' and the existence of 'a party within a party'.

has been run on totalitarian lines ever since Standing Orders had been reintroduced in order to defeat the Bevanite group. It would have to be explained
very carefully and it would only work if there were far more consultation
between the Government and the rank and file. Ministers must consult the
Labour members serving on their Standing Committees, as I had done on the
Rent Bill and as Dick Marsh is doing on the Iron and Steel Bill,[1] and Cabinet
must collectively consult the Party as a whole at regular weekly meetings.
We have got to get all this over to the rank and file next week. What really
excited me was the discovery that John and I felt ourselves dedicated
liberalizers.

That evening I had to give dinner to a French journalist who had been
palmed off on me by the F.O. Afterwards I went into the smoking-room
where I found the Left gathered in Nye Bevan's corner. Among them were
Michael Foot, John Mendelson[2] and Eric Heffer from Liverpool as well as
Russ Kerr. The Land Commission Bill was being debated in the Chamber so
I had time to have two full hours with them and staged a regular teach-in. I
made it clear that I was going to assert the rule of conscience in full. On the
other hand I was not going to tolerate a party within a party and I knew
quite a lot about how that kind of opposition is organized. Conscience must
be individual, not collective, not organized. We don't want cliques and coteries
and apartheid under the new deal John and I are preparing.

After the group had broken up I went back into the Chamber where the
Land Commission Report Stage finished at four in the morning.

Thursday, October 27th

I had to be at No. 11 at 9.30 to talk to Callaghan and the Chief Whip about
our proposal to take the Committee Stage of the Finance Bill upstairs and
not on the Floor of the House.[3] The more we reflected on the timetable the
clearer it became that we can't get people home at a reasonable time in the
evening unless we make this reform. Callaghan's reaction was entirely in
terms of his own convenience and that of the Treasury staff. He couldn't
have been more narrow-minded and it's clear we shall have to defeat him in
the Ministerial Committee.

By now it was time for Cabinet and directly proceedings started I was on to
parliamentary business. I warned my colleagues about the Party meeting
on Wednesday and said I hoped they would all attend and then I began to

[1] On the Rent Bill, see Vol. I, pp. 192–264.
[2] Labour M.P. for Penistone since 1959.
[3] The Finance Bill contains the taxation proposals which the Chancellor has introduced
in his budget, and until 1968 all its Commons stages were taken on the Floor of the House,
with the Committee Stage taken in Committee of the whole House. After the 1965 Finance
Bill, an exceptionally complicated one which required sixteen days of scarce parliamentary
time, there was support for the 1968 experiment to take the Finance Bill Committee Stage
upstairs. After 1969 a compromise situation was devised by which those clauses dealing
with taxes of wide application are taken on the Floor and the rest sent to a Standing
Committee.

discuss the principles of our great libertarian reform. The P.M. interrupted me very firmly and said, 'No, not now. Perhaps another time.'

This shows how autocratic the powers of the Prime Minister, the Lord President and the Chief Whip are. We three can make our own decisions on Party discipline without consulting the Cabinet who are brought in later and simply told what we have decided. And the strange thing is that someone like George Brown, though his brother Ron is a Whip who is opposed to everything John and I are doing,[1] absolutely accepts this situation. So Cabinet will not be allowed to discuss it and my colleagues will have to attend the Party meeting and vote there alongside rank-and-filers.

It was a dull day in Cabinet apart from one other item—homosexuality. Earlier in the week, Roy Jenkins had come to me and asked whether I could get him half a day for the Second Reading of Lord Arran's Sexual Offences Bill, which has twice passed the House of Lords and which now has passed its first stages in the Commons because Leo Abse presented it as a Ten-Minute Rule Bill and it was not objected to.[2] This is really a staggering result and Roy was able to make a persuasive case. I didn't make any comment and listened to Callaghan, the Prime Minister, George Brown and others asking why any time should be given at all to such a Bill and why we should abandon the neutrality which the Labour Cabinet had always shown to such controversial issues as homosexuality, abortion, divorce and Sunday opening of cinemas. I was able to point out that we couldn't really be completely neutral in this case because both Houses had already expressed a clear will for legislation. In that case it was clearly better to let the House of Commons debate the matter freely now and to provide time for this rather than let the subject drag on until nearer the election. With this highly tactical argument we persuaded the P.M. to drag the rest of his colleagues with him.

After a number of other minor items there was a discussion about Aberfan. The terms of the tribunal of inquiry submitted by the Attorney-General seemed perfectly sensible and so did the choice of Lord Justice Edmund Davies as the chairman. When all this was agreed Elwyn Jones added that he thought we really must stop the newspapers and television carrying out inquiries of their own and bullying witnesses. Cabinet gave its general approval to this and it was so late in the day that I felt unwilling to get into another argument. Of course I should have known better because this was to lead to a lot of trouble.

My business Questions on Thursday afternoon are becoming almost a

[1] Labour M.P. for Shoreditch and Finsbury since 1964 and an Assistant Government Whip 1966–7.

[2] In May 1965 the Earl of Arran had introduced a Sexual Offences Bill, legalizing homosexual acts between consenting adults in private, and in October 1965 it was passed by 93 to 31 votes, although it lapsed at the end of the session. He reintroduced it in May 1966 and it passed the Lords in June but was defeated in the Commons. However it was introduced in the Commons as the Sexual Offences (No. 2) Bill by Leo Abse, M.P. for Pontypool since 1958, under the Ten-Minute Rule, and the Commons business managers decided to give it support. It became law in July 1967.

4

routine. Directly I'd finished I slipped out to go to my press conference, leaving the Attorney-General to make his Statement about Aberfan without bothering to read it through.[1] When I got to the press conference I found myself flooded with complaints about what the A.-G. had said. I was asked whether we were not trying to terrorize and bully the press and I was at the grave disadvantage of not being able to remember clearly exactly what he had written. However, I managed to cool them off a bit.

That evening I was dining with George Weidenfeld, who has now married an enormously rich and very tall American girl. It was one of those dinner parties with everybody in the world of semi-politics there, from Cecil King to the Melchetts. I didn't feel particularly interested and got back to my room at 10.30. When I'd finished my box I went into the tea-room knowing that as Wednesday had been spent with the left-wingers I must spend Thursday night on a teach-in with the right wing of the Party. Actually I found the teach-in in progress. John Silkin was trying to explain his philosophy to some thirty or forty people crowded round him. I joined him and it was clear that a good many of those present—Jim Wellbeloved[2] and Ron Brown, for example—were appalled and amazed at the idea of interpreting the conscience clause as giving every member the right to abstain on any political issue if he felt conscientiously opposed to it. 'If you do this,' said Jim Wellbeloved, 'how can you ever ensure that the Government has a majority? You can be quite sure that if you announce this concession to the Left, we on the Right will start having consciences.' What he really meant was that he was appalled that he would no longer have the excuse of the Whips' categoric imperative for blindly voting the way the Government wanted on a three-line whip. The teach-in went on till half past three and for the second night running I got home desperately late to poor Anne.

Friday, October 28th

I had to be in my room at 9.15 to talk to Burke Trend about my Cabinet Committees. I have got everything and more than I asked for. He told me that there is no Committee from which I can be excluded, and in addition I have my regular morning prayers with the Chief Whip on Thursdays and with Burke Trend and George Brown on Fridays. So my first objective is at last attained. Let me try to list the others and see what's happened. On my second main objective, getting myself a job equivalent to that of a Tory Minister of Information, I'm still not sure whether anything has been achieved. Harold will put to Cabinet next week his very moderate proposal that I should become the senior Minister dealing with Transport House. I

---

[1] The Attorney-General had warned the press against inducing witnesses to make statements about the disaster in television interviews. It was for the tribunal to hear evidence in appropriate, neutral circumstances.

[2] Labour M.P. for Erith and Crayford since November 1965. P.P.S. to the Minister of Defence 1967–9 and to the Secretary of State for Commonwealth Affairs 1969–70, and an Opposition Whip 1972–4.

think I'd better face that we'll have virtually no success. Yes, I have a place on the commission of inquiry but only after maximum resistance all round. I'm not wanted in Transport House. As Leader of the House in the Commons I've now survived two hot business sessions—the first went very well, and the second was a respectable holding operation. I've done one uninspired but competent Second Reading speech on the Ombudsman Bill and I came pretty well unstuck on Tuesday's debate on Part IV. I did so badly in fact that I produced a devastating article by Matthew Coady in the *New Statesman* with headlines about Crossman taking a dive. All I can say so far is that though I've not come unstuck entirely I'm by no means established yet as a successful Leader.

Finally what about my personal frame of mind? Alas, the enormous sense of exhilaration and belief, and sleeping easy which I had as a Minister of Housing with a real job has all evaporated. Now I've got a hair-raising job which produces all the anxieties and the morning panic of my life before 1964—a job in which there's constant uncertainty and harassment and this has a considerable effect on my physical health. It will certainly wear me out quicker and I hope to God I don't have to do more than a term of a year or eighteen months since it might wear me down altogether.

Monday, October 31st
I left Prescote on a day with the clouds hanging drooping round us. What a contrast to last weekend, but a foul day was still lovely in Prescote's own style—the place is drawing and attracting me more and more.

At S.E.P. this morning we continued the discussion of reflation. Once again the Chancellor made a further concession. The Bank of England, he told us, would instruct the banks that they can now lend up to the full amount to all priority creditors.[1] We had an amusing discussion about how this concession should be described in the Statement. Callaghan said it wasn't reflationary and we came to the conclusion that it was only anti-deflationary. This sounds like semantic nonsense but I think the result was that he got a much better Statement published than on previous occasions.

We then turned to PESC. The five grand old men among us had of course discussed it at length already. We found ourselves repeating the argument. We all agreed that since we are deliberately slowing down the growth of the economy we must have a corresponding slow-down in the growth of public expenditure. No doubt Callaghan would prefer to get most of the cuts out of overseas military commitments but because it is impossible this year he has been driven to propose what is tantamount to a savage attack on the social services. Once again I made it quite clear that we can't agree to these cuts unless we can be assured that they are balanced by a reorganization of family allowances and personal and child income-tax allowance along the lines of the plans which Brian Abel-Smith and Nicky Kaldor, for example, have been

[1] Exporters, and for financing agriculture and bridging loans for house purchase.

talking about for years. I added that we'd been very proud about our claim that our deflation differs from Tory deflation because it doesn't affect our social-service programme. But Callaghan's new cuts would obviously affect those programmes. When I'd said this he replied, 'Well, I'm not going to discuss the budget at this Committee today. I can't afford any breach of budget secrecy.' To this I replied that I had already complained after his last budget that S.E.T. had made a caricature of Cabinet government.[1] I can see that we are moving towards some very awkward arguments in Cabinet when this issue comes up in two or three weeks' time.

I went into the House at 7 p.m. to hear Quintin Hogg launch the vote of censure on Roy Jenkins for the escape of George Blake from Wormwood Scrubs and for Roy's refusal to set up a special inquiry.[2] Quintin was in his most florid, rumbustious form and at the beginning made a deplorable impression. However, he worked his way through his demagogy and was quite effective in presenting his central theme—that Henry Brooke[3] had taken special precautions to prevent Blake escaping and that these precautions had not been enforced by Roy Jenkins. Having heard Quintin I went out and had dinner with the Chief Whip. Once again we talked over our tactics for the Party meeting on Wednesday, where we shall try to introduce our new Standing Orders. Then we went back to hear Roy Jenkins wind up with a tremendous annihilating attack which completely destroyed the Opposition. Before he got up he sat there next to me rubbing his hands and looking as nervous as hell but the moment he started one realized that he'd prepared that speech with tremendous care. He demolished Quintin's case and demonstrated that no special precautions had been taken by Henry Brooke. The demolition job was so total that when the vote came many of the Tories just weren't there. It was a tremendous reversal achieved by sheer debating skill—the first really good evening the Party has had since we came back from the recess. It did a lot to change the atmosphere.

Tuesday, November 1st

One of my jobs which my predecessors have regarded of first-rate importance is the chairmanship of the Legislation Committee where every Bill has to be considered before it can be finally printed. Under Dilhorne,[4] I am told, the most searing cross-examination of lay-ministers was undertaken both by the

[1] It had come as a surprise to Cabinet in the pre-budget meeting on May 2nd. See Vol. I, pp. 510–11.

[2] There had been some 520 escapes from prison in 1965 and, up to June 11th, 1966, some 200 more. The Home Secretary survived the vote of censure by 331 votes to 230.

[3] Conservative M.P. for West Lewisham 1938–45 and for Hampstead 1950–66. He had been Financial Secretary to the Treasury 1956–7, Minister of Housing and Local Government 1957–61, Chief Secretary to the Treasury 1961–2 and Home Secretary 1962–4. He became a life peer in 1966, taking the title of Lord Brooke of Cumnor.

[4] Reginald Manningham-Buller, Conservative M.P. for Daventry 1943–50 and for South Northants. 1950–62. He was Solicitor-General 1951–4, Attorney-General October 1954–July 1962 and Lord Chancellor 1962–4. In 1964 he was made a peer and took the title of Viscount Dilhorne. Since 1969 he has been a Lord of Appeal.

Lord Chancellor himself and by the law officers. I find the whole of this ridiculous and I've decided to keep the Committee meetings as short as possible. I managed to push Douglas Jay's Companies Bill through in record time.

We went straight down to Cabinet where the main issue was Europe. The debate started with George Brown remarking that we really must get on and take decisions quickly. We couldn't stand still without drifting backwards and there would be no business confidence in the country until we'd made our declaration of intent or the visit to the capitals had started. All the ideas then put forward had already been put forward at Chequers. Finally, after a rather scrappy discussion, Douglas Houghton made a suggestion which enormously pleased the anti-Marketeers. Before George and Harold went round Europe, he said, there must be an EFTA meeting and our EFTA colleagues should be told about our intentions.[1] All the anti-Marketeers lifted their voices to say that this was a splendid idea. The item is again on the agenda for Thursday.

After this discussion was over the P.M. suddenly raised the issue of the press attack over the weekend on the Attorney-General for his Statement about Aberfan. The attack had been very savage indeed and the serious papers had played a prominent part in describing him as a totalitarian who was trying to muzzle a free press. Apparently over the weekend he had almost broken down. Harold Wilson told me that when Elwyn came to see him he burst into tears and said he couldn't stand it because the people at Aberfan were his people and how could he be accused of totalitarianism in dealing with their tragedy. The P.M., I think, was genuinely moved and while he was labouring under this emotion George Wigg got hold of him and told him he had a great chance to hit back because of the precedents. I persuaded Harold to let the rest of Cabinet depart and then I sat down with him and did my best to dissuade him from drafting a Statement. The Attorney-General, who'd been to see me that morning, wanted to make the Statement himself and put things right and I'm sure that is what ought to have happened. But from the best of motives Harold was determined to take a hand. He likes Elwyn very much and I think another factor was that George Wigg had convinced him he had a chance of liquidating Heath on this topic as effectively as Roy had liquidated Quintin. I was extremely doubtful whether this would work and anyway I knew that since this was a question in which the press were deeply involved they wouldn't treat even a successful liquidation of Heath very sympathetically. I struggled with him from 12.30 to 1.30. I went back again at three o'clock when the draft was nearly ready and at least I got a sentence into it admitting that most of the press had been perfectly responsible—a sentence which, characteristically, had been left out of the original draft. But I didn't get the Statement into the shape I wanted. Sure enough, when the confrontation came that afternoon the P.M. didn't crush Heath, though he

[1] This was to be held in London on December 5th and the visit to the capitals began with an expedition to Rome on January 15th, 1967.

was able to score off him. The honours were not more than even on that particular day. I was due to go to the PESC Committee that afternoon but I was so sick of it all that I walked into it and then walked out again, leaving the rest to cross-examine Tony Greenwood on housing, Kenneth Robinson on hospitals and Peggy Herbison on social security.

That evening I'd agreed to sit and listen to Lord Esher's second presidential address at the R.I.B.A. (he was in his second year), and to move a vote of thanks. Well, it was a nostalgic evening. When I got there I saw in front of me the wife of Lord Esher alongside Colin Buchanan's wife.[1] Hugh Wilson and Jimmy James were there,[2] and a host of people from the Ministry. I was at home. Esher made a charming and thoughtful presidential address. I'd pencilled a few notes of reply when suddenly I saw Matthew Stevenson down there.[3] In the reply I started by congratulating Esher on emphasizing the gap between political ideas and culture. A politician, I said, must never think himself too close to the culture of architecture and it was probably time I was moved after twenty months because I was beginning to get a feeling that I knew something about the subject. But what I really could and did learn about was the Ministry and the civil servants and I was off on one of my old satirical descriptions of the British Civil Service—their remoteness from reality, their timelessness, the way they collect and hoard information like squirrels. It was amusing and the architects were delighted. Matthew Stevenson wasn't.

Afterwards J. D. Jones[4] came up to me looking very stormy and Jimmy James looking very pleased. At dinner I sat between Lord and Lady Esher, and found her a most attractive woman. She has six children because she had to produce five boys before she got a girl as the sixth. Four of the boys have gone to Eton and the last one to Bryanston. She told me they have just given up their big house below the Chiltern escarpment to their eldest son and are building themselves a tower in the beechwoods. 'A tower,' I said, 'W. B. Yeats.' 'How did you know that?' she asked, and I realized that she belonged to the same generation as me—the young people for whom *The Tower* changed their whole thinking and provided them with new values.

It was a lovely evening but it opened all the wounds.

[1] Professor of Transport at Imperial College, London, since 1963 and author of the celebrated report 'Traffic in Towns' (1963). He was knighted in 1972.

[2] Sir Hugh Wilson, architect and town planner and, 1965–7, Technical Adviser on Urban Development to M.H.L.G. Since 1973 he has been a part-time director of the Property Services Agency. He was to follow Lord Esher as President of R.I.B.A. in 1967. John Richings James joined the Ministry of Town and Country Planning in 1946, becoming Deputy Chief Planner in the Ministry (now M.H.L.G.) in 1958 and Chief Planner in 1961. He held this post until 1967, when he moved to the University of Sheffield as Professor of Town and Regional Planning. Since 1970 he has been Pro-Vice-Chancellor of that university.

[3] Matthew Stevenson (K.C.B. 1966) was at this point Permanent Secretary at M.H.L.G.

[4] James Duncan Jones (K.C.B. 1972) joined the Ministry of Town and Country Planning in 1946 and served there and in M.H.L.G. until 1966, becoming Deputy Secretary in 1963. In 1972 he became Permanent Secretary of the newly-created Department of the Environment.

Wednesday, November 2nd

This was the second meeting of a brand new Cabinet Committee on Science and Technology which Harold had founded. He had suggested I should take over the chairmanship from him in due course. I'd found the first meeting pretty awful and the second was worse. He must see that I shall be no good at this Committee because I can't stand collecting numbers of important, valuable people round a table for no good purpose.

The first item was *Black Arrow*, a communications launcher rocket.[1] This has been up to Cabinet four times and it'll be there for a fifth time soon. There is nothing new to be said about it. The Ministry of Defence has stated it has no scientific value; D.E.A. has said it has no economic value. The Foreign Office regards it as vital for its European policy and therefore refuses to take no for an answer. I said bluntly this was a political decision. If we wanted to convince the Europeans of the seriousness of our intentions we probably couldn't afford to cut it off. If we were going to go it alone this was exactly the kind of ruthless cut we would need. This was thought to be a remark in bad taste.

I rushed across to the Party meeting in Westminster where Fred Peart was winding up the first day's debate on prices and incomes. Then the debate on discipline began. John and I were trying to get the Party to accept our new code of discipline. This involved us reintroducing the ban on fraternal feuding which Clem Attlee had introduced, and the ban on the party within a party. This had also been introduced by Clem Attlee in 1952, in an effort to suppress the Bevanites; obviously, Harold Wilson and I were then both against it. I've made some effort to persuade Michael Foot and the other left-wingers to understand what we were doing about the conscience clause and that we were trying to achieve a real breakthrough to a modern liberalized discipline. If I was to have any chance of making the right wing concede on this I had to reimpose these two old disciplinary conditions. Michael was not convinced. Manny Shinwell had agreed that he would open the debate formally and that John should make the speech. But Manny's a crafty, ratty man and of course he didn't like what we were doing because he himself wanted to expel the ringleaders as a penalty for what they did after the Part IV debate. So instead of calling John straightaway he called Konni Zilliacus.[2] Then he got into a quarrel and began to lay down the law about what the new discipline meant. We had half an hour of very bad-tempered debate between the two before Jim Wellbeloved said, 'What's the good of those two debating before we hear the Chief Whip?'

So at last John was called and he made a deeply moving, simple speech

[1] Part of the European Launcher Development Organization (ELDO) programme. See Vol. I, pp. 530, 537.

[2] M.P. for Gateshead 1945–50 and for Gorton, Manchester, from 1955 until his death in July 1967. From 1945 to 1949 he was a member of the Labour Party, but stood as an Independent after his expulsion from the Party in May 1949 for persistent opposition to the Party's foreign policy. After February 1952 he received the Labour whip once more.

on how conscience couldn't be limited to temperance or pacifism, how it applied to all political issues and must be an individual matter. He emphasized that he wasn't going to allow collective group decisions to be called decisions of conscience and then he made another telling point by defining an organized group as a number of people whose intention to abstain was known to the press before the Whips knew it. There was a sardonic laugh because everyone knew he was referring to the fact that the *Daily Telegraph* had been able to publish the correct number of abstainers when the Whips had got it quite wrong. That showed that the group was in active contact with the press.

After John, Michael Foot got up and made a passionate speech in which he reminded us that Harold and I had led the attack on this motion when it was first moved in 1952. He was not going to give up his principles, he said. He was going to continue fighting just as before. Of course, it was the kind of speech which the right expected and for that reason it was impossible. The debate wasn't too bad. Jim Wellbeloved made the point that he didn't see how there could be any discipline if this new concession were made, and there were then a number of quite sensible questions. Finally, I made a short speech which was not improved by a lot of suggestions on bits of paper which were being pushed to me by Harold throughout my speech. On one of the bits of paper he had written that I should say the Bevanites accepted the decision of 1952. I was a bit doubtful but I said it, whereupon I was immediately asked what had happened. I said it was a damned nuisance because we had to meet informally, and there was a roar of applause—it was thought that I had cast a brick through my own glasshouse. The number of people who bothered to attend this meeting was modest. John and I got 120 votes and those opposed to our new code got 49. There were probably twenty or thirty abstentions. I doubt whether thirty of the hundred members of the Government were there. People stayed away because they hated the idea but knew some discipline was necessary.

Thursday, November 3rd

Most of the papers this morning said that the Silkin–Crossman reforms got a lukewarm reception. That was true enough, but what we were putting over was rather a lukewarm plan. Anyway there was no heart in the attack the Left made upon us since they knew very well we were shielding them from expulsion. Probably the lukewarm mood was what we needed but it didn't make it a cheerful occasion.

Cabinet started this morning with Harold's delayed announcement about information services. There was virtually no discussion. When one or two questions had been asked the Prime Minister said, 'Well, I'll circulate a notice in Cabinet minutes,' and that was that.

Next we plunged again into the debate on Europe. Today's meeting started with a paper from George Brown specifically giving us the choice of either a formal declaration of intent followed by probing at diplomatic level or a speech at Strasbourg[1] on our intentions followed by the tour of the capitals. He said he slightly preferred the tour of the capitals but he knew that others thought it was too hazardous or difficult. In that case he would accept the declaration of intent. The Prime Minister then at once came in and said that he thought we would have to have the EFTA meeting at the beginning. This put George back a bit but the Prime Minister went on to say that it might be timed simultaneously with the announcement of the tour round the capitals. The choice was then debated. At this meeting Michael Stewart and Callaghan switched their support to the declaration of intent as less dangerous than going round the capitals without any declared policy. This was my view and I'd come to Cabinet to say it, but it was much more effectively said by them. At this point the anti-Marketeers joined in expressing their alarm at the prospect of seeing Harold and George touring Europe as suppliants and trying to clarify the issue before the British Government had really made up its mind.

At the end of a one-and-a-half hour discussion Harold came up with a six-point plan which was very characteristic since it entirely consisted of points of procedure—when exactly to have the first consultation with EFTA, whether there was going to be an address by him in Strasbourg before the round of the capitals, etc. I suggested he'd got the cart before the horse. Before we discussed how to do the tour we had first to consider the policy decisions the Government needed to take in order to brief the Prime Minister and Foreign Secretary for the tour. How far would they be allowed to go? What reservations would they be bound to make?

But if I try and insist on policy decisions, which way will they go? I've come to the conclusion that any policy decisions the Cabinet reaches must be virtually what George Brown wants. We must show a readiness to sign the Treaty and take protocols.

Harold talks vaguely of the Javits alternative as a fall-back.[2] I was talking to Walter Lippman[3] the other day and he asked what the Javits alternative was like. When I told him he said, 'Well, that's a non-starter. You can't talk about that now as an alternative to Europe.' But Harold is still keeping his options open. I shall go to see him this week and say, 'Take your courage in both hands. Have this out with the Cabinet and I'll try and bring the Party round. I'm pretty sure we'd have a clear majority for you if you decided genuinely that you wanted to try to go into Europe and that you wanted to accept the Treaty and get in. If you say that clearly then we as a Government will have a strategic directive which will hold this Party together. At present we're falling apart because we haven't got any central purpose in life.' And if

---

[1] Headquarters of the Council of Europe.

[2] Senator Javits, Congressman for New York from 1946 until 1957, when he became Senior Senator for New York. His alternative was the NAFTA plan.

[3] Born in 1889. Writer and journalist, from 1931 to 1962 for the New York Herald Tribune Syndicate. He died in December 1974.

4*

I succeed in getting that far I hope to add, 'If we fail to get in then we shall fall back on my go-it-alone programme. And all the things we've done in order to get into Europe will be not unhelpful in going-it-alone. We shall, I hope, have given up our East of Suez posture: we shall have introduced a working national incomes policy: we shall have got our balance of payments in order. All these things which are necessary if we want to go into Europe are equally necessary if we have to live as an offshore island.'

I can't leave this Cabinet meeting without describing the line-up. George Brown was supported by Michael Stewart, Jim Callaghan and me, saying that it was preferable to have a clear declaration of intent followed by probings. It was also obvious that the Foreign Office and the D.E.A. would prefer this. But the Prime Minister was determined to have his tour round the capitals. Roy Jenkins and Tony Crosland's other bother was to make sure that if they couldn't get a declaration of intent they got the talks. Denis Healey and I were concerned that whatever happens we should set ourselves down to the jobs we have to do whether we enter the Common Market or not. I think Denis and I may well win on this and force on Cabinet the issue which Harold has been so anxious to avoid. If we do we may be able to save him from the kind of débâcle he looks like having on Rhodesia as a result of avoiding some unpleasant decisions early on.

Waiting on the front bench for my business Statement this afternoon I saw an extraordinary scene when Harold Wilson coolly and deliberately decided to knock Heath out on the Common Market issue. Mind you, he'd earned a nasty knock because he was very offensive. Nevertheless, the P.M. showed a malicious, concentrated pleasure in scoring off him and I couldn't help disliking him for it and feeling it was a pity that he ever sank to this level. The row certainly went on for far too long. Having said this I must add that a P.M. who, on a Thursday afternoon, busts the leader of the Opposition in that style has done a great deal for his own side. The leader of the Opposition had suffered a major defeat and if Harold made himself a little unpopular in élite circles, well 'let them hate provided they fear' is still true. I got away with my business Statement and with my lobby only too easily.

Then I was off to Cambridge to debate incomes policy with Enoch Powell. When I had been asked to do this they had suggested as the subject a planned prices and wages policy and I had said no, I would only agree to a debate on a national incomes and wages policy. Enoch agreed provided he had the last word; I didn't appreciate then what advantage that would bring him. The motion as I had redrafted it was one which Maudling, Heath and Macleod would all have had to accept. I was very careful not to have another fiasco like the one in the House and so I carefully prepared a speech indicating what a national incomes and wages policy was, why it was needed and what the alternatives were. For the final part of my speech I had dug out all the statements Powell himself had made when he was a member of the Macmillan Government and had spoken strongly in favour of an incomes policy, including a wage-freeze on nurses' pay. He had only begun to oppose it, I explained, when he left the Government.

It was a pretty effective debating speech (say B+) but it was followed by a tremendous oration. Without the faintest inhibition Powell turned the whole audience against the concept of any kind of incomes and prices policy, demonstrated that it was complete intellectual nonsense and concluded it was an insult to the intelligence of the Cambridge Union to ask them to support it. He got a standing ovation, which made me grind my teeth a little. I should have realized that in the Cambridge Union, unlike the House of Commons, the Tories and Liberals will cheer a great speech even though it makes nonsense of their support for their Party leaders.

I offered him a lift back to London in my car and on the way had a most interesting talk. I asked him what Heath would think about the speech and he said, 'Oh, it's only Reggie Maudling who's the problem and Reggie is so busy with his business affairs that he's hardly ever with us. If it wasn't for him I think Iain Macleod would go along with us.' Enoch is obviously running a campaign up and down the country against Heath and the incomes and prices policy. I then said to him, 'I doubt if you'll ever make your view acceptable to the country,' and he replied, 'Well, I think you're likely to be there for a long time.' He obviously sees us in for our four full years and possibly winning the next election too. Meanwhile his life will be spent fighting it out inside the Tory Opposition in a war to the knife for a real Tory policy.

Since the beginning of 1966 the Federation of Nigeria had been jeopardized by a fundamental breakdown of relationships between the various regions of the country. In late July Southern politicians demanded that the Northern region be subdivided. General Gowon, a Northerner, assumed the powers of Head of State and abolished the decree of unification, offering to open negotiations with Lieutenant-Colonel Ojukwu, the Eastern Regional Governor. A National Constitutional Congress was held in Lagos on September 12th but no solution either of confederation or of looser regional ties could be found. The Conference was to be reconvened on October 12th, but as the Eastern delegates by then refused to attend it was adjourned.

In the Statement on defence that Denis Healey had published on July 18th, Britain had announced the forthcoming withdrawal of British troops from Singapore by the mid-1970s, but the Government stated that aid would be given to soften the economic hardship that evacuation would cause. In July a system of selective national service was begun in Singapore and in October the Prime Minister, Lee Kuan Yew, had visited the United States and emphasized the need for the Americans to guard resolutely against the Communist challenge in Asia. Meanwhile, Malaysia, Singapore, Thailand, the Philippines and Indonesia were drawing together and at a meeting in Bangkok in August 1966 the Association of South East Asian Nations (ASEAN) was formally established.

The O.P.D. Cabinet Committee found that the problems of British with-
drawal from overseas bases were exacerbated by the worsening economic situa-
tion at home as demands for compensation escalated. To the running sores of the
Vietnam war and the Rhodesian crisis and, for good measure, Spain's intran-
sigence over Gibraltar were added implacable demands by Singapore and
Malta, trouble in Aden and the prospect of civil war in Nigeria.

Friday, November 4th

I had motored back the evening before through the fog because I had morning
prayers and O.P.D. early this morning. At Vincent Square I had just time to
read the *Guardian* report of our Cambridge Union debate and the quality of
it put me in good heart. At morning prayers Burke Trend was listing the
enormous number of subjects Cabinet had to deal with. When he'd finished
Harold took me aside. He was deeply concerned to find that the morning
papers were all blaming him for the blazing row with Heath at 3.30 yesterday
and talking about his being rude and cruel and a bully. 'Was it really very
harsh?' he asked me. 'Can you do anything about putting it right in the Sunday papers? Are you going to see any of them?' I told him I'd arranged to see
Ian Waller of the *Telegraph* and Jimmy Margach of the *Sunday Times*. 'Brief
them very carefully about that row with Heath,' he said. That's the second
time he's asked me to do a job with the press and I spent part of the afternoon
doing it. He had told me at Chequers that he is going to give up his Lobbies
altogether and only see a group of journalists on Sunday evening. Everything
else is to be left to my weekly Lobby on Thursdays. We'll see whether he
really wants to hand over this much responsibility to his Lord President.

Meanwhile our Friday morning O.P.D. is becoming a regularity. Last
week we had dealt at length with Gibraltar and Nigeria. In both cases the
official papers were extremely cautious. It was shown that any kind of forward
policy in Gibraltar would only be to the advantage of Spain. As for Nigeria,
where apparently whole areas are going back to tribalism and the central
Government looks like breaking up, the paper was most carefully written to
advise us against any kind of military intervention. This week we were dealing
with Singapore and Sarawak. Apparently there had been a fantastic proposal
that the Singapore Government should be allowed to build up a huge army,
navy and air force of its own. Once again the official papers were extremely
cautious and temperate, strongly advising us to do as little as possible. But
this is surely a futile defence policy. If we take each item separately—Gibraltar, Nigeria, Malta, Sarawak—and accept a policy of restraint and cut-back,
there comes a point where the whole policy collapses for lack of resources.
What we need is the major foreign-policy decision and because Harold,
George, etc. failed to take it two years ago we are now faced with the possibility of cutting back our social programme in order to make ends meet. I
suppose the value of my sitting here at O.P.D. is that at these meetings I shall
be provided with the ammunition which I can use at the critical moment

when the great foreign-policy decision is no longer avoidable. Then one at least of the inner Cabinet will come out in favour of a policy of total withdrawal.

After that I went across to the Cabinet Committee on Prices and Incomes which was dealing with the draft White Paper. I'm afraid I haven't been attending this Committee regularly. It's an enormous public meeting with endless Parliamentary Secretaries reading aloud the briefs from their Departments. Right at the top of the table were sitting Michael Stewart, the President of the Board of Trade, the Chancellor and now myself. We were the prefects. The rest were the schoolboys. The draft was anaemic and bureaucratic to a degree. As an attempt to present the new dynamic policy of a socialist Government to the people of Britain it was really intolerable. Indeed, I thought I saw how right Enoch Powell was to say that he finds it easy to make hay of prices and incomes. He will have a splendid time with this White Paper when it is published because it combines the innocuousness and the intellectual dishonesty of Whitehall.

In the afternoon when I was briefing the *Sunday Times* man, Trevelyan, who was sitting in the anteroom, pushed a note in which I didn't see but which I found in my box this evening. It reminded me that in February 1965 a Cabinet instruction had been issued that Ministers should never give press interviews without one at least of their staff being present. Of course this means that Trevelyan will report me to someone or other, but how on earth was I to explain to him that I was doing the briefing on the Prime Minister's express instructions.

I spent this evening at Loughton, next door to where I was brought up at Buckhurst Hill. I'd been asked to be guest of honour at the annual dinner of the Chigwell and Loughton and Ongar Labour Party and had a delightful time with them. A really vigorous Party, very few industrial workers but an excellent cross-section of a suburban population. I got back to London too late to go down to Prescote.

Saturday, November 5th

I caught the early train to Banbury. At Prescote we've had terrible deluges of rain and wild storms. This evening we are having our November 5th bonfire and fireworks and I hope the rain will hold off for it. Today Pritchett has gone off shooting and I have spent the whole of the morning on this diary. Of course the diary is playing an important part in my political life as well as in my domestic life. Helga Greene, my agent, has nearly completed the contract now with Hamish Hamilton and the *Sunday Times*. I shall have enough to see me through three or four years after I've retired from politics. But there's no doubt that politically too my ability to write a major book and the existence of Prescote combine to give me an increasing detachment from the Cabinet.

Sunday, November 6th

With Pritchett away I have a morning in which to look back on my new job. All last week I had a continuation of my doubts and uncertainties about it, the sort of uncertainties which I used to have when I was a working journalist and was plagued with the fear that I'd done something desperately wrong in my column. I got rid of these panics entirely at the Ministry of Housing, but they're back again. I suppose I must bore the poor Chief Whip with all my doubts and worries about whether I'm making a decent impression in the Cabinet, in the Party and in the Commons. The fact that I worry suggests the job doesn't suit me. It's been a doubtful week for the Government too. We started of course with Jenkins's tremendous success against Hogg and we got some lukewarm support for our new code of discipline, but the atmosphere in the Parliamentary Party is uncertain and the strength of the Left is quite formidable now. Inside the Cabinet the most striking feature undoubtedly is the sag in morale and energy which has occurred as a result of our tremendous election victory. Before the election we were all tense and excited and defending our majority of one, and there was a correspondingly high morale in the Parliamentary Party. The moment the election was won there came this sag. The Parliamentary Party felt it could indulge itself now in a way it couldn't before and Ministers settled down in Cabinet for a five years' term. There is a strange relaxation not only of tension but of energy. Ministers don't feel the necessity to decide things, to push and drive, and this is just when they require leadership from the centre of the kind Harold isn't giving. Yes, the P.M.'s tactically immensely resourceful, but he doesn't have any clear sense of direction. He feels, I think, that he wants to be pushed into trying to get into Europe and that's why he's not going to take any positive lead.

What about the rest of the Cabinet? Well, George Brown, thank heavens, has become a real Foreign Secretary straightaway. Whether you agree with him or not, there is one fact about George which makes him a good colleague. Whatever Ministry he's in at the moment is a booming zooming Ministry. He created D.E.A. in his own image as the Prices and Incomes Ministry. Now he's making the Foreign Office in his own image as the Ministry of Europe.

Callaghan started off very badly after the election because of the rumours about his part in the imaginary July plot. This has left him sullen and uneasy. As Chancellor, he's also deeply committed to a huge cut-back not only of consumption but also of public expenditure, on the social services in particular. And, of course, he's got a powerful case because this year he can't get the defence budget down to a reasonable level.

What about Michael Stewart, our new number three? He's becoming a bit of a nightmare. He's very honourable but he's also bureaucratic, vain and enormously sensitive about his own status. He's no good as a replacement for George Brown in D.E.A. because although he has got himself a place in the pecking order one above the Chancellor of the Exchequer he has no drive.

What is needed at D.E.A. is someone who can get the C.B.I. and the T.U.C. to believe that this Government has a real prices and incomes policy which it is going to carry out and that they must help us to do so. In fact he's doing nothing of the kind. On the economic side things are falling apart, and what is left of the prices and incomes policy is disintegrating before my eyes.

I suppose I come next, and I'm certainly in a very dubious position. I've been taken out of the Ministry where I was doing extremely well and have already been compelled to undertake a number of very unpleasant jobs such as winding up the debate on Part IV and, despite my Bevanite background, imposing discipline on the Party. In the Cabinet I think I am recognized as one of the few people who stands up to the P.M. and dares to tell him to his face of the problems he's trying to avoid. To that extent I'm being useful.

Douglas Jay? A competent Minister, God knows, but still so reactionary and narrow, and rigid even on Europe. His mind just doesn't assimilate new ideas.

Barbara Castle is the coming person. She's doing extremely well as Minister of Transport—she got a standing ovation at a conference she was holding last week for her statement on planning. She was being praised very highly at the R.I.B.A. last Tuesday night. As a result of her success the centre of balance in planning has been transferred from the Ministry of Housing to the Ministry of Transport in a way which shows you what a difference Ministers can make in their Departments.

Tony Crosland and Roy Jenkins are our two leading Europeans. Roy keeps himself to himself with extreme care. He's the most conspiratorial member of the Cabinet. I watch him as he sits opposite me. He speaks very little but when he does it's always terse and to the point, as though he had kept a lot in reserve. Tony Crosland is proving himself a jolly good departmental Minister, but in Cabinet he's curiously lightweight. Tony Wedgwood Benn, one of our two bright young men, is a complete flop. So far he hardly ever speaks and when he does he doesn't carry very much weight. It's just the same with Dick Marsh, the other person brought in to represent youth. He seems to me to be brash, erratic and unnecessarily rude, and he's hardly strengthened his position. I don't know anything about Cledwyn Hughes, the new Welsh Minister. He is a pure cypher.

That leaves me to deal with the terrible collection of old lags who should be got rid of. Fred Lee is now a sheer embarrassment. So is Arthur Bottomley, and so in quite a different sense is Frank Longford, who's become a farcical figure. A very different case is Douglas Houghton, who's the oldest member of the Cabinet and due to retire but who carries real weight and often comes up with the compromise the P.M. wants. He's one of the half dozen people whose contributions matter. Looking round the table, who have I left out? There's the Lord Chancellor, priggish, weak, ineffective, totally out of touch and nearly always doing what the P.M. wants. Fred Peart, who remains a nice, competent Minister of Agriculture; Willie Ross, a narrow-minded politician but again a competent Secretary of State for Scotland; Tony Greenwood at Housing about whom I'll say nothing. There is also Denis Healey. He's very much one of the members of the inner Cabinet to whom all top secrets are open. In Cabinet he talks quite a lot and is always alert, thrusting and absolutely relevant. I find myself agreeing with him more often than not. What sets him apart is that he always behaves as though Defence were outside the Cabinet and he had come there to represent it, and was not otherwise a member of Cabinet at all. But so far this has stood him in good stead. By standing outside and having his own private relations with Harold he has prevented the axe falling too heavily.

And how do they sit round the table? In the middle Harold with, on his right, Burke Trend and, beyond him, Fred Lee, Tony Greenwood and Cledwyn Hughes. Now we've reached the top end of the table and there we find Dick Marsh, Tony Crosland and Douglas Houghton with their backs to Horseguards Parade. Then comes the Lord Chancellor and next to him Denis Healey, George Brown, Michael Stewart, Roy Jenkins, Arthur Bottomley, Fred Peart, Barbara Castle, the Chief Whip. Then round to our side of the table, where we face Horseguards Parade, Douglas Jay, Willie Ross, myself and the Chancellor.

How long will this Cabinet last without another reshuffle? It certainly desperately needs a change. I asked Trevelyan the other day what was the chief criticism of the Government in Whitehall and I was surprised and interested to hear him say that it was Wilson's failure to clean up his Cabinet. It's certainly true that there's a lot of dead wood in it but I'm not sure there'd be all that difference if it were cut out. If Fred Lee is thrown out he would be replaced by Gordon Walker to whom Harold has promised a place in the Cabinet; at his age and with his temperament Gordon Walker wouldn't add to our strength or vitality. But suppose that instead of Gordon Walker he promoted Kenneth Robinson, Peggy Herbison and Fred Mulley, who are the three obvious choices just outside the Cabinet. It wouldn't make the faintest difference to our vitality. One would have to jump right over the Ministers of State and down to the Parliamentary Secretaries in order to discover some personalities who would really wake this Cabinet up.

Monday, November 7th
My first appointment was the first meeting of the Cabinet Committee which was to consider the package I was putting forward on parliamentary reform: the television experiment, some minor reforms in the Finance Bill, morning sittings and two new specialist committees—one on the Ministry of Agriculture and the other on science and technology. Things seemed to be going quite well when suddenly in came Fred Peart furiously angry, threw a newspaper on the table and said, 'How on earth did this leak occur?' I had read the Sunday papers but I hadn't noticed at the bottom of a page in the *Sunday Times* a little piece in which their political correspondent summarized my

package (I had briefed him last Friday) mentioning the specialist committee on the Ministry of Agriculture and attaching to it the names of Fred Peart and Willie Ross. To make things worse, neither of them had received the letter I had written asking them to allow me to select the Ministry of Agriculture for this first experiment.

I was caught red-handed. Fred said he wouldn't do it, he wasn't going to be the test-tube for this experiment, whereupon other Ministers who'd been so keen last week—Tony Crosland at Education and Roy Jenkins from the Home Office—all politely opted out as well. I found myself with no volunteer ready to be the first Minister who would have a specialist committee attached to his Department. It was a nasty atmosphere and there was a great deal of objection to morning sittings as well. In fact the first meeting with my fellow Ministers couldn't have gone worse.

On the way up in the train I had decided that I must get Harold to capture the European initiative this week from George Brown. He must really make up his mind and go all out for entering Europe. I got hold of the Chief after the Cabinet Committee on Monday and we had a long talk. John is an anti-European. No doubt he was made Chief Whip partly for that reason, but he realized straightaway how vital it was to get Harold into a positive frame of mind. He agreed that we would raise it with the Prime Minister this afternoon. We started by briefing Harold on the mood of the Party. We were able to tell him that even if he announced that he wanted to make a declaration of intent to sign the Treaty of Rome he needn't expect more than sixty abstentions and not a single resignation from the Cabinet—though of course two or three people would be extremely angry.[1] With no fear of serious resistance in either the Parliamentary Party or Cabinet he was completely free to run this operation as he wished. 'The announcement you make this week,' we told him, 'must end this awful sense that the Labour Government can't make up its mind; it must be a wholly positive announcement.' Harold hummed and hawed and said that he was quite prepared to consider the possibility but that we oughtn't to try to go into Europe unless . . . and he began to make a long speech about conditions. We both interrupted him, we pressed him and we pushed him, and we told him this was a great moment in his life. 'You can take charge of this,' we said, 'and if you don't, it will look as though George Brown is running the show.' This caught his attention. 'Yes,' he said, 'I don't at all like the way George's paper is written. It's much too personalized, and I rather resent that.' That gave us our chance. The conversation started with us sitting at the table but now we began chasing Harold round it saying, 'Act now. Take it on yourself. Show statesmanship. Only you can do it.' I can remember at one point saying, 'Once you've accepted this course, once

---

[1] On March 25th, 1957, Germany, France, Italy, Holland, Belgium and Luxembourg signed two treaties, to set up a European Economic Community and to establish a European Atomic Energy Community. It was to the first of these that Britain agreed to adhere on January 22nd, 1972.

you're in harness, you will be the best negotiator in the world. You will understand exactly how to mobilize enthusiasm and you will do the job magnificently. All we need is to commit you to it this week.' It was the first time John and I had really tried to use our influence upon Harold and when we left I felt we might have done something effective.

I went straight from Harold's room to a meeting of PESC where we were interviewing Barbara Castle. She was straightforward and convincing. She demonstrated that by postponing £200 million of road contracts she could save £25 million but it would upset the whole of the five-year programme which she had inherited from the Tories. We knew it was impossible to ask her to do this and that we should be forced to find our economies in the housing programme and in local authority expenditure. Callaghan then came into the meeting and we had a further discussion on how PESC would work. I agreed to back him in a squeeze of local authority expenditure which I know will be unpopular with the authorities but popular with the public— though I suppose it's something I should have resisted as Minister of Housing. I then repeated that I was not prepared to move an inch on school meals unless he was willing to move on family endowment. This time he made it clear that he was against the whole Nicky Kaldor–Brian Abel-Smith idea of revamping income tax allowances to relate them to family allowances. In this respect Jim has become a pure Treasury man, determined to hold us through this period of deflation at a fairly high level of unemployment and with massive cuts in public expenditure.

Tuesday, November 8th
Another of those interminable RX meetings at No. 10, with nearly all the Committee now convinced that there is no point in negotiating further with Smith, and Harold still trying to find ways of keeping the dialogue going. It was clear that he would have liked Herbert Bowden to go back for another round of talks and so I know would George Wigg, but Herbert Bowden point-blank refused and the meeting after that was concerned with the questions which could be put to Smith to fill in time until December. This was one of the most heated and bad-tempered Cabinet Committees I've ever attended. Harold got quite testy at one point and talked about the defeatism of Denis Healey and myself. 'Things looked worse in England in 1940,' he observed. 'If a paper had been circulated on the situation and if any of you had been in a position to read it you would have all thought there was no chance of victory. Things are no worse now despite what the papers which have been circulated tell us about the effect of sanctions.' At this point Denis Healey rather rudely said, 'That's a strange and irrelevant comparison, Prime Minister.'

The trouble is that for Harold this is his Dunkirk or his Cuba, or whatever it may be. He's terribly alarmed to see us drifting towards mandatory sanctions and the open admission of failure. I've no doubt he doesn't like the prospect that on Friday of this week, November 11th, Smith will be able to celebrate Remembrance Day and combine it with a celebration of the first anniversary of U.D.I. and to claim that Rhodesia is in a far stronger position than it was a year ago. In his frustration he more than once accused me of being prepared to surrender to Smith. I responded that there was no question of surrendering to Smith. The question was whether we should take upon ourselves more and more obligations such as mandatory sanctions which might involve us in a disastrous economic war against South Africa. I wanted to avoid this by finding a way of disengaging from the issue less dishonourably than by outright surrender. To say that any form of disengagement would be surrender is utter defeatism. As I say, I got some support from Denis Healey. Callaghan, who I thought was supporting me, suddenly switched round and began to back Harold. Herbert Bowden sat in as a kind of bureaucrat in charge of the Commonwealth Office and made virtually no contribution. George Brown? Well he was very concerned about the U.N. attitude and as clear as I that we must try to disengage. He saw the transfer to the U.N. as the only possible solution and therefore broadly we were in line. But the trouble is that we were trying to persuade the Prime Minister to face the fact that his policy had utterly failed. Who can really blame him for refusing to do that?

Lunch with Cecil King. We had it alone in his room on the fourteenth floor of the *Daily Mirror* building looking out over the City of London. There was an antique table and a butler. He gave me a little drink—he himself doesn't drink or eat much. Suddenly he said to me, 'Well, this Government is not going to last, you know, more than a year.' 'No,' I said, 'I think this Government will hold out for four years before the election.' 'No, I didn't mean the Government,' he said, 'I meant the Prime Minister. He's not going to last. He's failed. We need younger men.' I looked up and saw the glint in his eye and remembered he was the nephew of Northcliffe.[1] There opposite me was Cecil King seeing himself as the kingmaker, the man who put Harold in and would pull him out. We then had a long argument about failure and Cecil said to me, 'What can you think of a man who when I attack him for cowardice thanks me warmly for my help? And on two later occasions thanks me again and again for helping him when I really attacked him? What do you make of a character of that kind? Look at his indecision about Europe, about Rhodesia, about everything. It's hopeless. He's a man who cannot act and cannot administer. He must go.' I went away after I'd made it clear that I couldn't accept this. I said Harold would in fact stay because there was no possible alternative Prime Minister and I told him that the young men Cecil King so much admires are really no good—Dick Marsh, for instance. 'Dick Marsh is first-rate,' he said. (Apparently Marsh has just put Cecil King on

<hr>

[1] The press lord. Cecil King's own account of the lunch suggests that he found the Lord President reluctant, or unable, to offer any solutions. See Cecil King, pp. 94–5. *The Cecil King Diary, 1965–70* (London: Jonathan Cape, 1972).

the National Coal Board.) I've no doubt that what Cecil was really getting at was the old idea of replacing Harold Wilson by Roy Jenkins, and to that extent he's emotionally in sympathy with the so-called July plot. I shan't tell Harold about this conversation but I'll describe it at length to Gerald Kaufman.

That afternoon I had a meeting with the chairmen of the Labour Party groups along with Manny Shinwell and John Silkin. They seemed really keen to help and quite enthusiastic about our new regime.

Dinner with Alec Spearman this evening.[1] I found that my fellow guest was Michael Adeane from the Palace. I had a chat with him about the Balmoral incident. Apparently the Queen had strongly objected to my absence from the Privy Council which took place during Conference. We agreed that the whole thing was a mistake. In retrospect either she should have come to London or I should have gone up, and we agreed amiably about that.

Wednesday, November 9th

This was the day of the Cabinet decision about our approach to Europe. We were presented with a very big official paper. It contained a recapitulation of Harold's plan of procedure and attached to it a draft annexe showing the policy to be included in the Statement or alternatively in the brief. This included the key sentences about the Treaty of Rome and our attitude to it.

Cabinet began in the most extraordinary desultory way. George Brown moved his paper, did a little bit and hummed and hawed. Harold did a little bit and hummed and hawed. The Europeans were holding back. Roy Jenkins never says much in Cabinet but he knew that we all regarded him as deeply committed and he didn't see why he should say anything. There was a mild altercation between Tony Crosland and Fred Peart and a little sparring by Barbara Castle, but mostly people were talking about the details of the procedure and the timetable. Even Callaghan, who came in late and said he supported the paper, talked in a rather half-hearted way. I followed Callaghan with a carefully calculated speech. It's the first 'speech' I've ever made in Cabinet in the proper sense of the word. I started by saying that I should make my own position clear. I was not a Common Marketeer. I was one of the minority who believe in Britain's future as an offshore island, cutting down all our overseas commitments, getting ourselves an economic position as favourable as that of Japan in the Far East and living on our own as an independent socialist community. I understood that this was an unpopular view and unlikely to be realized in the near future. Certainly nobody would be prepared to take the decision to accept our position as an offshore island until a genuine effort had been made to enter Europe. And it was no good suggesting there is any real alternative. The so-called Javits plan—the North Atlantic Free Trade Area—is a non-starter because the Americans won't move. The only choice at the moment is between a half-

[1] Sir Alexander Spearman, Conservative M.P. for Whitby 1941–66.

hearted effort to enter Europe and a whole-hearted effort to enter Europe. What we needed today was a Cabinet decision giving a dramatic indication that we are going all-out for entry. If that effort fails I shan't be particularly upset because then we can consider the possibility of the offshore island. But if we try at all, I'm in favour of a whole-hearted approach. We should have the Statement tomorrow in accordance with George Brown's paper and if possible the P.M. should make it his theme at the big Guildhall speech next week. After I'd said all this, Callaghan decided to speak again. 'That's that,' he said, 'and I must add something else in favour of what the Lord President has said. One reason for going into Europe is that it's the only way to give hope to private business and to end the crisis of confidence in industry which is preventing the growth of essential private capital investment which we need to get over the winter slump. Dick's quite right but I must add something else. We are now faced with a commitment in Africa which will almost certainly lead to mandatory sanctions and that will produce grave stresses and strains on sterling. If we are going to face those problems in Rhodesia without any effort to enter Europe I can't give any guarantee about the future of the pound.' That really finished it. Barbara added her own left-wing comment. 'Of course,' she said, 'a strong Rhodesian policy would make it much easier to sell the approach to the Common Market to the Parliamentary Party.' And that was the kind of deal which was struck round the table that morning. It was the knowledge of the appalling dangers which faced us in Rhodesia that prevented any serious opposition to the new approach.

This afternoon in the House I was caught by Gerald Kaufman and asked to go straightaway to Harold's room. There I found Marcia, and the Prime Minister showed me in writing (I was the only person to see it) the draft Statement he was due to make with the key sentence that we meant business. 'That's fine,' I said and ran for my train to Cambridge which I just caught at Liverpool Street. Actually I was off to waste my time. An attractive reactionary called Maurice Cowling[1] had asked me to address his political science group on the workings of Cabinet government. When I got there I found that he'd forgotten to call the group together and he'd had to substitute an advertised mass meeting. It was a fair waste of time.

Thursday, November 10th
This was a tidying-up Cabinet after the big decision. The draft Statement was presented to us and the proposed amendments were only part of a defensive move by the anti-Marketeers to try to water down any commitment. I made my own view clear that if we want to give the impression of a serious attempt we shouldn't niggle about the words. But the amending took most of the morning.

Right at the end of Cabinet came an item in which I was vitally interested — my paper on the television experiment. I had hoped that if it came so late in

[1] Fellow and Director of Studies in History, Peterhouse College, Cambridge, since 1961.

the morning I should have an easy time; I'd already got Callaghan to send me a letter saying that he was keenly in favour of the experiment, though we might have to raise the question of costs, and I'd also got Bert Bowden to agree. Surely the rest of Cabinet would go along? I emphasized, in introducing it, that this was merely a trial run. All seemed to be going very well when Harold was suddenly struck by the problem of television magazine programmes. If the B.B.C. and the programme companies all had full video transcripts of every day's proceedings, would they be able to cut the videotape up and take a little bit of a speech and introduce it into a magazine programme? 'Certainly,' I said, 'that was the intention.' Harold said that couldn't possibly be allowed. They could only be allowed to do straight direct reporting of what happened in Parliament. I replied that if we insisted on this I.T.N. wouldn't think it worthwhile. And then I tried to soothe him by saying that of course there were a lot of these technical difficulties but surely they were the kind of things we ought to work on in the course of the eight-week experiment. Then suddenly Callaghan said, 'Well anyway, I don't think we ought to have it this spring. It's too expensive and we can't have a supplementary estimate of £150,000 this February.' At this point there was a general clamour, making clear that nobody wanted the television experiment. They didn't want a change of this sort in the Palace of Westminster. Harold saw his chance and took the votes round the table. There were not more than five in favour of having the experiment this spring. So I was left with my whole programme for Parliamentary reform in ruins. What's worse, the Conservatives have already consented to the experiment and I have to go back to Willie Whitelaw and confess to him that Cabinet wants it postponed. It was a terrible blow.

Now for the big occasion in the House. I was sitting there in my usual corner seat with Harold two places beyond me and in came George and squeezed between us; Tony Crosland was on the far side. Harold did his Question Time as skilfully as ever. The Opposition is obviously still in disarray and extremely ineffective. Now it was 3.30 and he read his Statement aloud.[1] It produced a kind of flabbergasted atmosphere on the Labour back benches. There was no pro cheer for Harold during the whole length of it because they didn't know whether to praise it, and when the anti-Common Marketeer Manny Shinwell managed to get up there was a very feeble cheer for him. On the Opposition side Duncan Sandys had the sense to welcome the Statement. That's what Heath should have done. He should have killed Harold with kindness but instead he tried to nark. Altogether it was a disappointing great occasion. There was no sense of history partly because the Statement may have been difficult to assess at first hearing, especially when

---

[1] ' ... the Government are approaching the discussions I have foreshadowed with the clear intention and determination to enter the E.E.C., if, as we hope, our essential British and Commonwealth interests can be safeguarded. We mean business.' *House of Commons Debates*, vol. 735, cols 1539–51.

people know that Mr Wilson is a crafty little man, and partly because it sounded so curiously *ad hoc*. George Brown would have made it historic but Harold didn't want to make history that afternoon. And one of his reasons is very interesting indeed. When he got on to the bench beside me he started whispering. 'I've had to make one big change owing to the Bank of England. They said they needed it in order to prevent a run on the pound.' Apparently there was originally a section about the pound riding high but over lunch the Bank of England and Callaghan had made him climb down and take out the phrase, even though this meant sending a telegram to all the embassies instructing them to change the words about parity. This intervention of the Bank of England and the Chancellor just before the Statement may have knocked Harold off his confident poise.

Then came my business Statement. As I'd reckoned, there wasn't much to it after what had gone before. Nor was there much for me in the press conference upstairs with the Lobby. Harold spoke to them for nearly an hour and I saw how brilliantly he handles the Lobby. He's a kind of further education lecturer and they eat out of his hand when he explains everything very sensibly, rather pedestrianly, in a style with which they feel at home. I would never have dared take so much of their time but he does it in a complacent easy fashion.

From the Lobby I had to go straight to our Thursday evening business meeting of the Parliamentary Party, which is now accepted as a regular show. Naturally the Party was pretty bewildered by what they had heard at 3.30 and anxious to argue it out in private. Harold, who was in the chair, started straightaway by explaining that he wanted John and me to run a series of Party meetings to discuss the entry into Europe. This took the wind out of the left-wing sails. Stanley Orme and Norman Atkinson could hardly believe their ears.[1] At the end of the meeting Norman came up and said to me, 'My God, you ought to tell all this to the press. This is a real change. You are really treating us democratically.'

I must say the reintroduction of the business meeting has been a tremendous success. If this Thursday we hadn't had Harold there the place would have been seeping with suspicion, there would have been groups and counter-groups, and Early Day Motions would have been clapped on the Order Paper. Instead we explained how the Party meetings and the consultations with the Party outside were going to be arranged. To start with, next Tuesday morning Harold will come to listen to the back-benchers before the big debate on the Floor. This led to an argument about whether we should have a big debate next week or whether we should postpone it for some weeks until the Party has come to a decision. I agreed with those who said we can't wait, and anyway the constituency Parties have the right to hear us. 'But that means

---

[1] Stanley Orme, Labour M.P. for Salford West since 1964 and, since 1974, Minister of State at the Northern Ireland Office. Norman Atkinson, Labour M.P. for Tottenham since 1964.

having a disagreement on the Floor,' someone said, to which I agreed. 'Certainly we shall have different views aired on the Floor, but they won't be attacks on the Government but the expression of different views within the Labour Party and the Conservative Party as well.' I managed to take the wind out of Manny Shinwell's sails because he'd been very difficult in private. He'd already threatened me at the liaison committee that he might have to resign from the P.L.P. chairmanship to challenge the new attitude to the Common Market.

Friday, November 11th
Our morning prayers developed into a long discussion because I found the Prime Minister obsessed with the problem of leaks. He was very upset by a leak which appeared in the *Sun* about the Common Market discussions in the Cabinet, and Burke Trend tells me there was a leak which was much nearer the commercial, profitable zone, about North Sea Gas, in the *Daily Mail*. Before coming over for morning prayers I myself had noticed in this morning's *Daily Express* a front-page story stating that George Wigg was handing control of the information services over to Dick Crossman whose job it was to clean up the Party image. I'm afraid I assumed that George himself put it in and now that I've made some inquiries I am still suspicious because both Gerald Kaufman and Tam Dalyell saw him talking at length to the *Daily Express* man who wrote the story. Of course, when I put it to George he indignantly denied responsibility. In the course of our discussion I mentioned this leak to Harold as an example of the problem we face. Harold himself is constantly briefing the press and encouraging me to do a great deal of briefing too. I now have my own Lobby and my own regular individual contacts and I feed them regularly and, of course, I'm aware that other Ministers are feeding and guiding their regular contacts, including George Wigg. I suggested that if we were to discuss it in Cabinet there would merely be a lot of accusation and counter-accusation and nothing would be achieved. I also told him that one way to reduce the number of leaks is to reduce the membership of the Cabinet from twenty-three to sixteen or seventeen. But as long as Harold himself feels that anything he tells a journalist is briefing and anything any other Minister does is leaking, we're not going to have a very constructive discussion.

We didn't get very far during morning prayers partly because I was obviously in Harold's bad books, and I must assume that George Wigg had accused me of talking to the *Daily Express*. However, Harold didn't seem to hold it against me because he told me that he had sent for Fred Peart and put all the pressure he could on him to let the Ministry of Agriculture be the Department to conduct the experiment with the new specialist committee. In this way Scotland is out and Willie Ross's objections answered. I only hope Harold can do it because otherwise I shall be in a very weak position on Tuesday.

I said I had talked to John Silkin and we thought the way out would be to postpone the experiment but to televise the State Opening of Parliament, with a closed-circuit experiment immediately afterwards. I was about to check with the B.B.C. to see if this was practicable. Harold seemed quite pleased with this idea. So I went back to my room, saw the B.B.C. and I.T.N. and they agreed that they could arrange everything to their contentment if we postponed until November. Indeed, they said that November was a good month if we really wanted to do it then and it gave them plenty of time to prepare.

Finally off to the Palace for a Privy Council. I made a little explanation and a half-apology about the misunderstandings between the Party and the Court about the last Privy Council at Balmoral. She didn't relent, she just listened, and I thought that was that.

Saturday, November 12th

I had agreed to go over to Coventry to report back to the Party on Conference along with David Young, the chairman, who was their representative this year. He came over to fetch me and we had lunch at his nice house on a private-enterprise estate near Binley; on the other side of the road I saw those ghastly new tenements looking like Government hutments which Coventry Council describes as its new industrialized housing. They're particularly ugly because of their grey slaggish colour—the design is appalling too.

I hoped to be able to give a general report on Conference and on the political situation but David, who was in an obstinate mood, insisted it ought to be mainly about Party organization and in particular about a resolution which Coventry East tried to move at the private session of Conference and which the chairman refused to accept. I had to let him have his way. He started off with a longish speech, I replied briefly and then we had a long hour discussing various Party problems. To try to make things more interesting, I raised the issue of Party discipline and explained what John Silkin and I were doing in the Parliamentary Party. The Coventry Labour Group is a great believer in monolithic discipline and my ideas caused complete consternation. After a bit of tea we got on to the motor-car industry and that discussion lasted for two or three hours. In answer to a question, I began to discuss the whole idea of two-way traffic between the constituencies and Government, the constituencies acting as the eyes and ears of a Labour Government. To this Peter Lister replied that that couldn't work since there wasn't a single M.P. who kept real contact with the rank and file. On the other hand George Park, the chief convener at Rootes, was pretty cool and collected but also very depressing. The chaps in the works, he said, were all fairly patient but they all assumed that we'd be swept away if an election were held now. The kinder of them sympathize with us as 'poor things having a hell of a time'. What he said about the chaps in the factories applied just as much to the delegates at the meeting. They were terribly worried by what they felt was the failure of the Government. But alas, they haven't given me a chance of really rallying them because they didn't allow me to make a full report before they started asking questions, and they really do know terribly little.

Peter Lister took me home. He told me about the appalling problems at Nuneaton next door, where Frank Cousins has just resigned in order to go back to his union.[1] David Young hopes to become the candidate as a member sponsored by the Co-operative movement. But Peter Lister's also in the fight and he is far abler and a leading councillor. They're fighting each other for this and probably neither will get it. He then told me quite frankly that behind my back they are all complaining that I'm not in the constituency enough. I replied that I'm always ready to go whenever I'm invited but it's no good unless they have organized a meeting for me to speak. I told Peter frankly that the constituency doesn't want to see me and that they prefer to complain about me behind my back. It was a painful discussion. He felt embittered because the whole of the Labour movement was going downhill in Coventry and indeed throughout the Midlands. Why didn't I realize, he asked, that I had a duty to my own constituency instead of doing so many meetings away from home? I told him not to be too depressed. In the twenty years since I was elected in 1945 there's been a fairly steady decline in the activity of the Labour movement in Coventry. It's been running down all the time and trade-union participation in the Coventry Labour Party has been getting steadily weaker. Is that because the old-fashioned political parties' function has somehow been rendered out of date or is there something peculiarly wrong with Coventry? Or is there something wrong with the Coventry M.P.s and, in particular, the Member for Coventry East? And what do they actually want me to do? So we sparred all the way back from Coventry to Prescote. It was useful to me because it showed how desperately unhappy the Party is. In the Midlands it has taken a hell of a knock as a result of the July crisis and the redundancies. When we won the election we seemed so secure, but now people feel they're in a tunnel with no end to it and the few party workers who still turn up are facing the municipal elections next spring with dread in their hearts that they'll be swept away by a landslide. All this is something which as Harold's Lord President of the Council I have to answer for.

Sunday, November 13th
I woke up this morning feeling a little gloomy and grey about everything because I think there's worse to come this winter. We seem to me to be lurching from a moderate Government-induced deflation into a much worse deflation produced by a crisis of confidence and a failure of industry to expand its investment.

Meanwhile, all I can say is that during this week I have at least helped to resolve the chronic indecision about our attitude to Europe. We've had a

---

[1] He was succeeded by a young lecturer in economics, Leslie Huckfield, who has held the seat since March 1967. See p. 272.

magnificent press and Harold has got everything I predicted out of his bold clear Statement. Now we have two years before us when he'll be busy trying to get into Europe and that will give us a clear strategy. The only drawback is that Harold has managed once again to commit us against devaluation. As a result of his last-minute change to the Statement he's now committed not to devalue the pound before entering Europe, yet I'm not sure that we can keep parity throughout the coming winter without so much deflation that we may split the Party. Devaluation is after all the only way to get our exports up quickly and so become economically strong and healthy. Indeed, I believe that a devaluation deliberately planned and timed for next spring or summer would be the best preparation for entering Europe. Yet, characteristically, just before he made his Statement Harold was persuaded by the Bank of England to forbid himself the one economic change which would be necessary to create the conditions for any satisfactory entry into Europe in the foreseeable future.

Monday, November 14th

S.E.P. is beginning to fulfil its proper role as a strategic steering committee. Each week we meet to watch how the situation is developing and what actions we shall need to prevent deflation going too far. This week's discussion started on the sharp rise in the unemployment figures to be announced next Thursday (it will bring unemployment well above 2 per cent)[1] and the simultaneous sag in the production figures. There's no doubt about it: the crisis in business confidence is beginning to sap the whole economy and make the chance of a quick climb out of this deflation far more difficult.

What's to be done to stop the rot? There's now an almost open conflict between the Chancellor and the rest of us. The Chancellor has decided he needs an unemployment level of between 2·2 and 2·5 per cent as a regular brake on inflation and he doesn't want anything done to prevent the figures rising to that level. He's also prepared to be the iron Chancellor who keeps production down so that for 1968 as well as for 1967 we shall have to accept a very low level of production. That's his policy now. Who is opposed to this? George Brown, who's an expansionist, is now terribly busy on foreign affairs, and Michael Stewart, who replaced him at D.E.A., can't yet make up his mind on which side he stands. The P.M. himself wants something done to prevent the depression going any further but agrees with Callaghan that we mustn't relax the cuts in consumption. The next most important figure is Douglas Jay. To my surprise he's an expansionist; he has put in a paper urging that we should deliberately relax the terms of hire purchase on motor-cars in order to create business confidence. These were the rival solutions we discussed. The P.M., not liking the hire-purchase concessions, talked a great deal about tax incentives and launched the idea of a brand new initial incentive grant. Round that table there was no one, as far as I could see, who

[1] Now 541,585.

thought that such a new tax allowance, even if we could introduce it, would do a particle of good. The trouble isn't shortage of cash but shortage of confidence. Tax allowances are nice things to have if you have decided to invest but they don't stimulate people to start investing and their absence doesn't deter people from starting investing. So the initial incentive allowance was out. But there was equal opposition, Douglas Jay and myself apart, to hire-purchase concessions. It came from the Prime Minister in particular. He had told me the other day that they would make nonsense of our economic policy and he staunchly supported his Chancellor to that effect.

After the meeting I talked to the P.M. in private. He is certainly aware that Callaghan is pushing his deflationary ideas very hard and now that Michael Stewart is at the D.E.A. resistance to the Chancellor has been greatly reduced. I think we shall pay very heavily this year for the Cabinet reshuffle which put Michael in this key position.

In the afternoon I went across to Question Time and there was George Wigg, our Paymaster-General, answering the standard Question on why he replies for the information services. Of course he'd already seen the paper which gives me responsibility for co-ordinating all information services at the Ministerial level. He was conscious of this decision when in his usual tone he answered the Tories, virtually accusing all co-ordinators of being more or less corrupt, and making it as difficult as possible to announce the transfer of the job to me.[1] Odd things are happening in my relations with George. It may well be that he didn't leak the news about me to the press. It may have come from Terry Pitt at Transport House, but however that may be a wide gulf now divides us. I also get the impression that he's a good deal less important in No. 10 than he was at one time and he thinks that is something to do with my change of job.

At the liaison committee this evening Manny Shinwell was being very awkward and I had a tough time getting all the groups alerted to get on with the job of appraising the proposals to enter the Common Market. Manny, of course, is passionately opposed to the Common Market and he's also passionately opposed to all the new ideas of discipline which John and I have put forward and which have begun to create a much better atmosphere in the Parliamentary Party as well as getting some surprising praise in this week's *New Statesman*. However, if the price of this improved atmosphere is an irritable Mr Shinwell, it's the price John Silkin and I can easily pay.

Back home to change for the Lord Mayor's dinner. We set off at 6.30 with Molly driving us to the Guildhall. We entered a vast tent-like place full of officers with drawn swords, and then proceeded through a series of tents rather like a Hollywood version of an oriental durbar since it was full of men dressed as Yeomen of the Guard with helmets and leather jerkins—all a bit tatty, as Anne observed. Past the tents we proceeded into the library, where

[1] 'It was a corrupt operation of the previous Administration to have two Ministers paid from public funds doing a party job.' *House of Commons Debates*, vol. 736, col. 28.

a large audience was sitting. As each guest of honour goes up to be introduced to the Lord Mayor he is given either a titter, or formal applause or a round of hearty applause. I was interested to notice that James Callaghan and I got exactly the same titter as Harold, whereas the Archbishop of Canterbury was applauded from the heart when he came in. From the cloakrooms we proceeded into the Guildhall itself, where I had dined a few weeks ago with the G.L.C. officers. We found ourselves at the top table. I was sitting opposite the Bishop of London and next to the wife of a City alderman. The food was really very good and not too much of it—wonderful beef and quite decent pheasant. The drink was excellent too—just right and not too much. So we came in the end to the speeches and Harold made his big declaration about the Common Market. After S.E.P. this morning I'd been in and found Thomas Balogh there with the draft of the speech. I'd read it through and thought it awful. But this evening in the Guildhall I think it was infinitely better than anything I could do under these conditions.

This Lord Mayor's dinner was the first top-level invitation which Anne and I have accepted since I was a Minister. We've always refused the Guildhall and Buckingham Palace in the past and the only reason we went there this evening was because, having under Harold's pressure agreed to go to a banquet at Buckingham Palace last Thursday and then cancelling because of a television debate, which in turn was postponed for the Common Market debate, we found ourselves with a brand new forty-guinea dress which Anne had bought and looked like never wearing. So I said, 'If you can't wear it on Thursday at Buckingham Palace, wear it on Monday at the Guildhall,' and I got myself back on the Guildhall list. Once I was on it I said to Harold I would go in a dinner jacket. He said he would do the same and we found that not only were he and I in dinner jackets but because the rumour had spread so were the Lord Chancellor and two or three of the other socialists. But I saw Denis Healey in his white tie and of course Bert Bowden, who's a professional diner out. It was quite an interesting occasion but I can't say I want to see it again. It would jolly soon become a bore.

Tuesday, November 15th
These days I have to start very early in the morning because my colleagues need to see me before Cabinet to ask what help I can give them. Today I had Peggy Herbison on social services and Fred Mulley about the debate on aviation. Cabinet started with the first part of our PESC exercise in cutting public expenditure. We shall do it again on Thursday and once again on the following Tuesday. The two big items we dealt with were *Black Arrow* and housing. I predicted the other day that *Black Arrow* would come back to Cabinet and here it was once again with a new paper by Solly Zuckerman,[1]

[1] Lord Zuckerman, Fellow of University College, London, and Professor at Large, University of East Anglia. A distinguished zoologist, who had served as the deputy chairman of the Advisory Council on Scientific Policy 1948–64, he was Scientific Adviser to the

who has a great influence on Harold as a scientific adviser and whose paper had encouraged the P.M. to refuse to sanction the cut which the Science and Technology Committee had almost unanimously agreed. The discussion showed how little any of us politicians can really understand these enormously expensive space enterprises. I was in favour of cutting it on the clear evidence of both the Defence Department and D.E.A. Now Solly comes up with a paper giving a totally different account of what *Black Arrow* is. How can Cabinet come to a sensible decision when none of us have the vaguest idea what these things really are?

Then we moved on to housing where we had a very strange situation because, after agreeing to the cuts PESC demanded, the Minister of Housing made an extraordinary Ministerial announcement virtually saying that the target of 500,000 houses a year had been abandoned. This infuriated Harold, who very nearly rebuked Tony openly in Cabinet. The net result of the morning was *Black Arrow* postponed: housing postponed.

I lunched at the Garrick with Harman Grisewood,[1] the old head of the B.B.C. Third Programme, and Sir Robert Lusty,[2] the managing director of Hutchinsons publishing company and one of the leading Governors of the B.B.C. The topic of discussion was the bad relations between the B.B.C. and the Government and how they could be improved. As a result I've agreed to have an evening with Normanbrook to try to explain how the Government feel.[3] Obviously a great deal hinges on the personality of Hugh Greene.

That afternoon we had the first meeting of the Org. Sub. of the N.E.C., which shows how the best laid plans can gang agley. When Harold and Marcia and I were discussing the future of the Party at Brighton we had hopes that he could arrange to have me elected as chairman of Org. Sub. so that indirectly I should be able to play a leading part in the investigation of the Party. Alas, the Commission had got itself established and at the first meeting of the Org. Sub. the trade unionists had immediately proposed to vote Joe Gormley into the chair. For the Commission of Inquiry I had proposed Willie Simpson as the chairman so as to keep Alice Bacon out of the chair. One of the results of the appalling relations between the Government and the trade-union leaders is that the trade-union members of the N.E.C. are determined to hog all the chairmanships for themselves.

At six o'clock this evening we had the first big Party meeting on Europe.

Government 1964–71 and the Chief Scientific Adviser to the Secretary of State for Defence 1960–66. He became a life peer in 1971.

[1] Controller of the Third Programme 1948–52, and Chief Assistant to the Director-General 1955–64.

[2] He joined the Hutchinson Publishing Group Ltd as managing director in 1956, and retired in 1973. A Governor of the B.B.C. 1960–68, he was vice-chairman of the Governors 1966–8.

[3] Norman Brook (created Lord Normanbrook in 1963), Secretary of the Cabinet 1947–52, Joint Secretary of the Treasury and Head of the Home Civil Service 1956–62 and chairman of the Governors of the B.B.C. from 1964 until his death in June 1967.

I've been in some difficulty about it because at the liaison committee on Monday Manny had made a tremendous fuss and insisted it should start with a full-length statement of Government policy. I said it was absurd to demand this: it would be far better if the Ministers were there to listen to the Party before the big debate in the House on Wednesday and Thursday. I suggested that if George Brown must speak first he should be asked to limit himself to ten or fifteen minutes and to discuss only the reasons why he is taking the initiative now. To my surprise George Brown took this fairly well. He spent a lot of this morning in Cabinet throwing pieces of paper across the table to me pointing out how embarrassing it was to be committed to a statement of this length and dealing only with these two ticklish themes. But, as often happens when you put a person up against it, George did admirably. He got the discussion off in an uncontroversial mood and half an hour later it was obvious that the Common Market was not going to divide the Parliamentary Party. Very few were enthusiastic for entry but the majority seemed to regard the effort we are now making as inevitable and are willing to discuss carefully and thoughtfully the terms we should accept or those we should resist. In the present mood the Government would have a relatively easy time if, next spring, after the tour of the capitals, we have very few conditions to make about going in.

I left before the end of that meeting because I had to go to the Women's Press Club—a rather tatty organization at the back of the old *Daily Mirror* building—which had invited Anne and me (when I was Minister of Housing) to come and chat with them informally. I found myself discussing parliamentary reform with a group of women either working in the Mirror/I.P.C. Group or in public relations. I came to the conclusion that women journalists and public relations officers are not attractive when viewed in the mass.

Wednesday, November 16th
At 9 in the morning to a meeting with the Lord Chancellor and Niall MacDermot on an odd side-issue of the Ombudsman Bill. Niall, who isn't very experienced in handling back-benchers, has got himself into trouble with the left-wingers on the Standing Committee. One of the mildly worrying features of the Bill we had drafted was that it excluded peers from bringing cases to the Parliamentary Commissioner. In our Bill he wasn't a Parliamentary Commissioner at all but a House of Commons Commissioner. The Tories had given notice that they would raise the issue in Committee Stage. The point had already been discussed in Cabinet when the draft Bill was presented to us. I found myself in the minority who said it was unreasonable to forbid peers to make use of a Parliamentary Commissioner. We are now told that if this clause arrives unamended in the House of Lords our back-benchers there might well rebel since most of them are new life peers and feel that if there's going to be any meaning for the House of Lords then at least in this area peers should have rights like Members of the House of Commons.

The meeting had been called to resolve this point and, in addition to the Lord Chancellor, Niall and myself, Frank Longford and the Lords' Chief Whip, Shepherd, were present. I found that there were really quite sound practical reasons for keeping it a House of Commons affair but I realized the genuine grievance Labour back-bench peers might feel and I was perfectly prepared to settle for a compromise when Frank, that great stalwart of the House of Lords, caved in. He reckoned, he told us, that he could keep some thirty of the Labour peers voting with the Government and if it was sent back to the Commons he could hardly expect us to capitulate to a Lords' amendment on this point. So Frank had sold the pass for his colleagues and I didn't have to bother to compromise.

In the afternoon I had an important meeting with Fred Peart, who had been so infuriated by a leak that he had almost broken up the Cabinet Committee on parliamentary reform by refusing to let his Department be the first to be subjected to a Specialist Committee. Subsequent inquiries have shown that though he had a genuine technical grievance he was in fact guilty of rather sharp practice in rebuking me because my official request had not been received before he read the leak. I found that I had cleared it with him personally many weeks ago. It had been cleared once again by Freddie Warren with Fred's Private Office a month before and we'd then gone to the Tories with the confidence that he would let us do it. The letter he failed to get was merely a formality. I asked myself therefore why he had got so rough. I concluded that he'd been got at not only by his own civil servants, who of course disliked the idea, but by Willie Ross, the Secretary of State for Scotland, because agriculture is common to two Ministries—Fred's Ministry of Agriculture and the Scottish Office. I had to work hard with Fred. Finally I said to him, 'Look, you'll be able to select all the subjects they look at. You'll be able to select your chairman and all the team on the Labour side.' I think I sent him away a bit influenced by a pledge which I hope I shall be able to keep.

In the House of Commons Michael Foot was moving a Ten-minute Rule Bill asking leave to bring in a Bill establishing an inquiry into the Suez adventure.[1] This is a point on which I had responded to him in the adjourn-

[1] Under the terms of the 1954 Anglo-Egyptian Treaty Britain had agreed to evacuate the Suez Canal Zone and to close her military base there while in return Colonel Nasser had recognized the right of the Suez Canal Company to operate the canal until the concession expired in 1968. In July 1956 the Americans withdrew their part of a substantial loan to Egypt; Nasser abruptly nationalized the Suez Canal. In October Israel invaded Egypt and in November a Franco-British force landed at Port Said. The U.N. Security Council condemned this aggressive act and on November 8th the Franco-British force withdrew and was replaced by a U.N. Emergency Force. Although Anthony Eden, the British Prime Minister, denied that there was collusion between Britain, France and Israel to provoke the Israeli-Egyptian war and give the Anglo-French forces a reason for moving in, later revelations in *No End of a Lesson: The Story of Suez* (London: Constable, 1967) by Mr Anthony Nutting, who had resigned his post as Minister of State at the Foreign Office over this issue, suggested that the charge of collusion was justified.

ment debate on the very first day I was made Lord President. At that time I thought there was everything to be said for the idea. Since then I've had a wholly negative reply from George Brown drafted in terms of the departmental requirements of the Foreign Office. Perhaps more important, I've had some long talks with Tam about the attitude of the Labour backbenchers. Suez is already ten years old this week. Yet only 55 per cent of our Labour M.P.s were here at the time of Suez. That shows you the speed of turnover. Half the Members have less than ten years' experience. So the Leader of the House has to remember that Suez is ancient history for most of our own Parliamentary Party just as it is for the Tories and the public outside. To establish a Select Committee in order to rake over the ashes might make us liable to the charge of diverting attention from the modern scene to ancient history. I came to the conclusion that what we want to do is to keep the threat of the inquiry hanging over the Tories and that is what Michael Foot accomplished with conspicuous skill.

This evening Anne and I went out to dinner with Peter Lederer[1] and his wife, Jean. We hadn't seen them since he left the Ministry. We went to the Empress, an extremely expensive restaurant in Berkeley Street run by the owners of the Caprice. God knows what it cost, but it confirmed my suspicion that Costains, where Peter is one of the chief brains, is doing well. When I was Minister Peter had been very critical of my behaviour; he thought I was too offensive and too rough. I learnt over dinner that he'd been in contact with the Ministry quite a lot since I left and he's now more impressed by what I was doing and the effect of my leaving than he had been before.

Thursday, November 17th
Cabinet. Before we got back to our PESC discussion the Prime Minister had decided to take my procedure package of parliamentary reform. Actually it took nearly two hours and was a ghastly discussion. How ghastly you certainly wouldn't get an idea from the Cabinet minutes. Discussing how to handle our colleagues, John and I had decided that the order of presentation was extremely important and I would start with morning sittings, then deal with Standing Order No. 9 and finally discuss the Specialist Committees. The Cabinet minutes merely attribute to me the brief which I took with me of which I didn't read a single word because I knew it was unsuitable. The official minutes even change the order of the items on the agenda so that they agree with the brief. According to the minutes Specialist Committees come first and then morning sittings. I record this because it's important to remember how little historians can trust Cabinet minutes to tell what really went on. What they do tell is what went on according to the officials and the official briefs.

I put the case as well as I could knowing it was unpopular. I reminded them

---

[1] A construction expert from Costains Ltd who had joined Crossman in M.H.L.G. to push ahead a programme of industrialized building. See Vol. I, pp. 31–2, 131.

that I'd inherited this package from my predecessor and that the Party was deeply committed to it at the general election. The moment I'd finished George Brown said, 'Well, it's asking a terrible lot of us, Prime Minister. We're busy men. What you're asking is that busy Ministers should have morning sittings as well.' I explained that the aim was to get the back-benchers home early two nights a week. I couldn't guarantee that we should achieve this aim and I had put the topical debates in to spice things up in the mornings. Now, however, I realized that a topical debate was something which might take the time of a Foreign Office spokesman and that is the way in which George Brown considered it. He was followed by Minister after Minister round the table simply saying how busy they were, how they were harassed by all these Cabinet Committees, and how they simply couldn't be burdened with any more work by the House of Commons.

Barbara was the only person with any political sense. She said, 'I'm as bothered as anybody about the extra work but frankly, you know, if what's being said here was reported to the Parliamentary Party we would be blown to smithereens.' She was specifically referring to the remarks of the First Secretary. Michael Stewart had said to the Cabinet that these new Members on whose initiative morning sittings had been proposed really must be told that they'd got it all wrong—that a back-bench M.P. has a perfectly satis-factory full-time job to do and there's no reason to create work for him to keep him happy. Indeed, our back-benchers should be thankful that as a socialist government we want to keep the Executive strong, not to strengthen parliamentary control. Michael's remarks had been applauded by many people round the table. When I heard them I remembered that he'd hardly been a back-bencher at any time in his twenty years in the House of Commons. He's always been either a junior Minister or a Shadow Minister on the front bench. I've had nineteen years as a back-bencher and I know what they are talking about so I was tickled when Jim Callaghan joined in and said, 'We've got to be careful of our Lord President now he has trans-ferred his attention from boosting housing to boosting the House of Commons. Just as he knew nothing about housing before he went to the Ministry this fellow was never there when he was a back-bencher. Now he's boosting the Commons with all the strength and power he gave to his housing programme and we've got to resist him in the same way.'

Most of these Ministers were individually as well as collectively committed to parliamentary reform. Yet after two years they've become Whitehall figures who've lost contact with Parliament. And of course what they're saying is pure nonsense. Ministers aren't bothered by Parliament, indeed they're hardly ever there. A departmental Minister has many other major worries what with boxes, Ministerial committees, visits outside London. But the amount of time a Minister spends on the front bench or in his room in St Stephen's is very small. The Executive rides supreme in Britain and has minimum trouble from the legislature. Perhaps it's because Parliament is so entirely subordinate to the Executive that my colleagues were saying, 'We can't allow this Parliamentary Party to bother us.'

In summing up, the P.M. to some extent rebuked Cabinet but he gave way on the crucial point of having Standing Order 9 debates in the morning. On Specialist Committees he helped me a great deal with Fred Peart and it looks as if I got my two Committees through as part of the package.[1] I shall have to submit the draft Statement to Cabinet next week.

The PESC debate which followed was very important but I was too tired and angry to notice it. However I did observe one rather significant little scene when the Home Office budget was discussed. In the prices and incomes policy Roy had got a special policemen's wage increase. Now he argued that the Home Office budget couldn't even be cut by £600,000 in £20 million. He hadn't bothered to go to PESC to make his point but he'd been allowed to make it direct to Cabinet. When he had finished, Cabinet remained absolutely silent—I'd never known it happen before. The P.M. asked, 'Well, why is nobody talking?' so I piped up. 'Frankly,' I said, 'they're all silent because if Roy Jenkins gets his £600,000 for the Home Office each of the others will have an enormously strengthened case for remitting his PESC cut too, and there in a nutshell is all that is wrong with this ridiculous way of cutting the Estimates. It's all a question of grabbing what you can get for yourself.' We didn't settle it.

Over lunch a minor harouche had blown up about telephone tapping. The *Daily Express* had been working this up with the help of four back-bench Labour M.P.s headed by Russ Kerr. They told the *Express* that they knew their telephones were being tapped and wanted Questions asked of the Home Secretary. Harold had arranged to have the Questions transferred to him and dealt with them superbly. 'He had inherited,' he said, 'the rules about telephone tapping recommended by a Privy Council report,' and he had only made one change. He had eliminated the special reference in the report to M.P.s being treated like other people. He had given an instruction that this was not correct and that there should be no tapping of M.P.s under any conditions. There was a clear implication that under previous Governments it was permitted to tap M.P.s' telephones but of course he didn't actually say this.[2]

Immediately afterwards in my press conference upstairs I had the job of parrying further questions about this and then trying to explain the background of the Rhodesia problem. As a result of Harold's encouragement I'm

[1] On Agriculture and on Science and Technology.

[2] The Report of the Committee of Privy Councillors appointed to Inquire into the Interception of Communications was published in October 1957. In his answer to the House, Mr Wilson reminded M.P.s that, although the Report said that M.P.s should not be treated separately from other members of the public, he had decided in 1964 that a Prime Ministerial instruction should be given that there was to be no tapping of M.P.s' telephones. As Mr Wilson explained, any tapping that 'becomes necessary by any Crown servant concerned with the things covered in that Report' can be done only with the authority of the Home Secretary, under very strict conditions (*H.C. Debs.* vol. 736, cols 634–41).

now beginning to turn my weekly press conference into the kind of Lobby he used to conduct every week at No. 10. As Lord President I'm quietly taking over that particular activity more and more.

Friday, November 18th

At morning prayers the P.M. was very nervy. He's becoming extremely aware of the danger that the deflation is getting out of control and that the D.E.A. under Michael Stewart doesn't provide the counter-balance to the deflationary activities of the Treasury which George Brown used to. He was quite open about this with Burke and me and George. We also discussed the disastrous situation in Rhodesia without coming to any conclusions.

Outside, as usual, O.P.D. was waiting to come in. We had a series of quite interesting subjects. First of all there was a paper on the overseas information services, which Callaghan proposed to cut back even more severely. I'd already protested in July against a cut of £4 million for the B.B.C. foreign information services, etc. Now he wants another £4 million cut which requires whole services to be dropped from the B.B.C. overseas broadcasting. I couldn't help reminding myself that he's doing this at the same time as he's agreeing to spend £10 million a year on some damn communication satellite which we're borrowing from the Americans at colossal cost. However, I was obstinate and I may possibly have prevailed.

I caught the 1.10 to Banbury because I wanted to be able at least to go out and walk part of the fields in our annual shoot, which had started at ten that morning. After sunset our neighbours came back as usual for supper and stayed till after nine. I let them have a real political 'go' at me and they're really quite good. It was a wonderful relief from London.

Saturday, November 19th

After a regional conference at Sheffield I went down to Brian O'Malley,[1] who has his constituency at Rotherham, six miles away. Rotherham is in the same valley as Sheffield and to the outsider they all look part of one single steel complex. I was soon told how totally different life in Rotherham was. Rotherham is a real community—people work together—whereas Sheffield people are narrow and individualistic. And there was a Rotherham Labour Party which had been in control of the Council for the last fourteen years and which had organized a 15,000 majority for Brian. He is a strange young man. Local Secretary of the Musicians' Union, he won his seat in competition with a local steelworker and a local mineworker. His selection for a by-election four years ago caused consternation in Transport House. But Brian has made a first-class M.P. and now he's resigned from the Whips' Office in order to build up his independent position. He has a charming wife who has much in

---

[1] Labour M.P. for Rotherham since March 1963, an Assistant Government Whip 1964–6, Deputy Chief Whip 1967–9, Parliamentary Under-Secretary of State at D.H.S.S. 1969–70 and Minister of State for Health and Social Security from 1974 until his death in April 1976.

common with me since she's had phlebitis and thrombosis. I had a most splendid evening with them.

Sunday, November 20th

I caught an early train this morning and spent the whole morning trundling to Birmingham, where there was an official car to meet me. On my way to Prescote I decided to visit the Chesterton windmill to see how it's getting on. When I first visited it some years ago it was in ruins and the roof was coming off. I'd just been made Minister of Housing and set about rescuing it when suddenly it was saved by a group of engineers from Leamington who decided to put it in order by voluntary effort. They managed to collect £3,000 and I was able to add £80 the other day — a cheque I couldn't accept myself for an interview I did for Midland Television. Having to give it to a charity, I chose Chesterton Mill. So it's nice to go over and stand there looking out over the plain towards Warwick and to hear that next October we shall be opening the mill with the sails sailing round in the rotating roof.

In November unemployment rose to 541,585 and in December it was to reach 564,083. Although the November export figures were to stand at £474 million, giving a surplus on the balance of trade of £78 million, imports were to rise steeply the following month when the import surcharge ended, and in December the trade deficit was to be some £24 million. The pound was still uncertain but with the help of loans that the I.M.F. and the B.I.S. at Basle had given in the autumn sterling held its own against the dollar. On November 22nd, however, the First Secretary announced that the incomes policy would be continued with a further six months' severe restraint following the six months that were due to end on January 20th, 1967. Until July 1967, apart from certain exceptions approved by the Government there would be a 'zero norm' for wage increases, and the freeze on incomes, prices and dividends would continue until July 1967. The T.U.C. was still adamantly against state intervention in wage negotiations but to some extent the voluntary principle seemed to be working. On November 22nd the T.U.C. vetted fifty-one wage claims submitted by individual unions, and referred twenty-one of these back to the unions concerned for reconsideration in the light of the Government's exhortation to look to the wider national and social interest. In real terms national production for 1966 was only 1 per cent to 1·5 per cent higher than that of 1965, and the Government were justifiably anxious.

Monday, November 21st

At S.E.P. this morning things looked blacker than ever, since we had advance knowledge of the ghastly unemployment figures to be announced on Thursday. After two years of Labour Government the increase of production had been practically flattened out and there is a sharply rising rate of unemployment and no prospect of any improvement in living standards.

We're about as fantastic and sensational a failure as any government could be. The situation is so bad that I'd warned the Prime Minister that I'd have to raise the subject of devaluation. He didn't wait for me to do so but threw a note across and said himself that he realized the problem of parity would have to be considered. He then reminded the Committee—as I had reminded him—that last July some of us were only dissuaded from demanding devaluation by the promise that if things still remained difficult in the winter and if the July measures weren't getting us out of the trough then the case for devaluation should be reconsidered since there would be some slack in the economy to be taken up. I said straightaway that we should have a paper on it in a week's time. 'No paper,' he said. 'There's too much risk of a leak,' and he was strongly supported by Callaghan, Jay and Stewart. Denis Healey and I said it was absurd to be told that we couldn't distribute an official paper, at which we were told that the officials couldn't be trusted. But there may be something in it. As we walked out of the room after the meeting Michael Stewart told me that there really isn't an official in Whitehall today who doesn't want devaluation and think it inevitable. It's not only Tommy Balogh and Nicky Kaldor. The Treasury and D.E.A. are both convinced and only Harold and James, who are somehow personally committed, are holding it up. Only three months after the July measures we can see that they were not strong enough to get us out of the crisis. They deflated the economy and flattened out the growth in production but if we were to reflate now we should just go back into inflation. On the other hand if we wait until the officials tell us it's wise to reflate, the results won't show for years ahead and we'd have no prospect of winning the election. Devaluation is the only way out.

Tuesday, November 22nd
Michael Stewart's White Paper on Prices and Incomes for the period of severe restraint was published today and got an appalling press. To rub it in Michael Stewart came to Cabinet this morning and said he was very sorry but the trade unions had refused to endorse the White Paper and were criticizing it. Just imagine that happening? He had made two major concessions to get the trade unions' support—including refusing a comparability clause to public servants—but despite these concessions to the T.U.C. they were now fiercely attacking the White Paper and blaming him for the very thing he put into the draft in order to please them. That's not what would have happened when George Brown was at D.E.A.

Meanwhile I'd got myself into a row with the Chancellor of the Exchequer about a speech I made at Sheffield last weekend. I had drafted the hand-out with the greatest care and submitted it to the Treasury as well as to the P.M. and got approval from both of them. It's a good thing I did because yesterday's *Guardian* and *Financial Times* financial correspondents had headlines about the Crossman speech embarrassing Ministers and upsetting the Chancellor. Apparently James discovered that the speech was so much disliked in the Treasury that he wanted to disown it. However, the P.M. has been splendid and when challenged in the House will say he read it in advance and found it excellent. All I said, by the way, was that the deflation might have gone too far. This was something we had to watch very carefully since there were two dangers—if there was a danger of reflating too soon there was also a danger of letting deflation carry us down too far. Success would be measured by our avoidance of both extremes. It sounds harmless but it was enough to upset the Treasury.

Wednesday, November 23rd
I had to give the final lecture of the autumn Fabian series in the Caxton Hall this evening. Two of the previous lectures had been given by Brian Abel-Smith and Peter Townsend,[1] who had launched a tremendous attack on the Government for its failure to abolish poverty. I'd spent four hours last night sweating away digesting their lectures and preparing a really rumbustious reply. I delivered this to a packed audience. Titmuss,[2] along with Abel-Smith and Townsend, was sitting just in front of me and the audience was pretty strongly on their side and obviously agreed with their accusation that the Government was losing its sense of direction and betraying its principles. I replied by telling them some of the real difficulties we had to face and asking them how they could say their own Government had failed when it had only been there for two years. I gave the reply with great gusto and I think it may have done a power of good because I've noticed that many members of the Fabian Society had been deeply disheartened by the attack on our Government by our own socialist professors and the enormous press coverage it got.

Thursday, November 24th
This was the day for debate on televising the House. As usual I didn't have much time for preparation. I've already described the appalling Cabinet reaction to the proposals which had compelled me to postpone the experiment for a year and indicated that I had very little support from my colleagues.[3]

This had made the speech very difficult to prepare. A further difficulty was my increasing doubt the more I studied the Select Committee's own recommendations. They wanted a video-tape to be made of every word said in the House of Commons and the House of Lords—a tape which would be issued to the broadcasting companies to be used as they liked. I found this

[1] Lecturer in Social Administration, L.S.E., from 1957 to 1963, when he became Professor of Sociology at the University of Essex.
[2] Richard Titmuss, Professor of Social Administration at the London School of Economics from 1950 until his death in 1973, and the author of numerous books and articles. He was deputy chairman of the Supplementary Benefits Commission 1968–73. Crossman refers subsequently to the advice and recommendations of the Titmuss group, a working party preparing papers on social policy.
[3] See p. 117.

expensive and impracticable. My own personal belief is that if we have the House televised it should be done much more simply by having the facilities there and using them occasionally for live broadcasts of debates, as a number of European countries do.

I had Cabinet on Rhodesia all morning and in the afternoon I had a very rough time answering business Questions because I was harried on whether I could keep my promise to have a Rhodesian debate before the sanctions motion tabled in the U.N. Then all my colleagues scurried out of the Chamber and I was left completely alone on the Government front bench to introduce the television debate. Since I have no Parliamentary Secretary and no real staff the speech really was my own. After it and during the whole of the rest of the day no one came to speak to me on the front bench or to give me a word of encouragement—except of course John Silkin, who was splendidly helpful throughout. I felt it was rather a good speech—thoughtful and critical of the Select Committee's report but urging an experiment which was a genuine trial to see whether television would work technically or not. I didn't ask the House to give uncritical or enthusiastic support to the Select Committee's particular recommendation but urged that *experiment* was a good thing. I was followed by Paul Bryan, the Tory front-bench spokesman,[1] who supported it in his own way, but after him I soon discovered, to quote Yeats, 'that the best lacked all conviction and the worst were full of passionate sincerity'. Speech after speech from Charlie Pannell, Quintin Hogg and the rest denounced the whole idea as false to the tradition of the House of Commons and rejected even an experiment. Things got worse and worse and I realized I'd completely misjudged the whole atmosphere in preparing my own speech for the beginning of the debate. I had assumed the motion would be carried comfortably but, as Geoffrey Rhodes, my P.P.S.,[2] warned me, the enthusiasm of the House was turned against the experiment. Right at the end I got up to reply and made a much better, tougher and shorter speech. But it was too late to save the situation. We lost by a single vote.[3] In the lobby I found I was the only Cabinet Minister voting for the proposal.

Afterwards I sat in the smoking-room, which I don't often do these days, drinking gin, which I've now given up, and feeling absolutely sick of life and furiously angry with my colleagues for letting me down.

Friday, November 25th
I must admit I was so angry I lay sulking in bed and almost refused to go to

[1] Sir Paul Bryan, Conservative M.P. for the Howden Division of Yorkshire since 1955. Assistant Government Whip 1956–8 and Whip 1958–61, he was Minister of State at the Department of Employment 1970–72.

[2] Labour M.P. for East Newcastle from 1964 until his death, at the age of forty-six, in 1974. He was Crossman's P.P.S. for fifteen months, taking the place of Tam Dalyell. After a visit to 'Confrontation against Indonesia' in Borneo Tam Dalyell had criticized the government's East of Suez policy in this area and, in view of Crossman's own controversial background in defence policy, he thought it best to resign as his P.P.S.

[3] The vote was 130 to 131.

the office. Instead I rang up John Silkin and told him what a miserable life it was and how I hated the job and hated my colleagues. I don't think I've quite got over it yet. That was the second real schemozzle I've had in the House since I became Lord President and I am beginning to realize that it is a thankless job.

There's been one compensation, however. I see a great deal more of Harold than I expected—not only in morning prayers and the regular meetings but I'm in and out of No. 10 incessantly. He doesn't yet talk to me quite as often as he talks to John Silkin because he still feels John is a more reliable person. I am much more independent. But he is beginning to use me more and he does regard me now as a member of his inside team. On my side I now understand that I mustn't say things in public which are far away from his wishes because every one of my remarks is attributed to him. I have to try to change my nature to be a member of this alliance. I have to remember that from his point of view the technical leadership of the House, the responsibility for parliamentary reform and television, are secondary considerations. Why he wants me close to him is for the battle for power inside the Cabinet and the reorganization of the Parliamentary Party, which so far John and I have carried through with enormous success. The Party is delighted with our revived business meeting on Thursday evenings and is getting used to our new liberal discipline. On the other hand, though to Harold my job as Leader of the House is of secondary importance, it is what I'm going to be judged by, not only at Westminster but outside. So far I'm not a popular Leader and I've not had the real success I need; it's certainly going to be proved against me that no one, however keen he is, can reform the House of Commons if the House of Commons doesn't want to reform itself.

In the afternoon I had to go down to Cambridge and give the Labour Club a report on the first two years of the Labour Government. It went very well. From there I had to motor back home getting there at half past midnight.

On December 2nd and 3rd, in an attempt to end the Rhodesian crisis which had now dragged on for a year, the Prime Minister and Ian Smith met in the Mediterranean on the British cruiser Tiger *which had been paying a goodwill visit to Casablanca. At the meeting the British Government understood that the Rhodesian Government had given their Prime Minister plenipotentiary powers, and the hope was that Ian Smith could return to Rhodesia with a signed agreement on a new constitution and a return to a legal relationship with Britain. Though the basis of such an agreement was worked out on board the cruiser, Mr Smith maintained that he would need the approval of his own Cabinet for signing the document, and he undertook to obtain such endorsement by 10.0 a.m. on December 5th. At 4.0 p.m. that day Mr Smith announced that the arrangements which had been devised on board the* Tiger *(to be published on December 20th as Cmnd. 3171) were after all unacceptable to his Cabinet. He declared that it was the proposals for the restoration of legal government*

5*

rather than the proposed constitution with its timetable for eventual African majority rule to which his Cabinet objected.

Sunday, November 27th

Yesterday I went to Fleet in Hampshire for my niece, Gay's, wedding. After that Anne and the children came up with me to Vincent Square for the week-end and I got a little rest.

I've had to alter my diary arrangements partly because the family spent the weekend in London and partly because events in Rhodesia have come with such a rush and I can only deal with them at the end of the week. So I've had to get Jennie to lug the tape-recorder from which she types the manuscript down here so that I can dictate the diary at my ease. It's now just midnight and I've been preparing what I want to say.

The strange thing is, now I am used to my tape-recorder, how I'm settling down to talking to it. One of the awkward things about a machine is how inhibiting it is, how difficult to dictate to compared with a secretary. You are much less considerate to a secretary than to these damned wheels turning in front of you. But gradually I'm getting over my inhibitions and talking to it more and more naturally and I was amused last week to find that our children are getting used to it too. For months they've come in to me and said that they wanted to talk to the recorder and then when I've put it on for them they've just squeaked and giggled and been unable to say anything coherent. But last Sunday they came into the study and said, 'We want to experiment with the mike,' and finally they got used to it.

Let's get the Rhodesia story told. Harold had laid it down at the Commonwealth Conference that Smith should be given till the beginning of December to come to an agreement. If he didn't, all the offers which had been made to him would be cancelled and NIBMAR would be imposed upon him. Well, November 28th is creeping nearer and nearer and we've been making our preparations for the final break—a Statement by the Prime Minister on the fateful Monday and then on Wednesday and Thursday this week, a two-day debate. This is the plan we finally agreed on last Monday at RX. We were all worried and Harold has been becoming terribly worried the more he studies the future after November 28th, when mandatory sanctions become inevitable. We have to face the fact that the threat we make to break with Smith will be far more damaging to us than to him.

It was a great surprise to me when last Tuesday morning I went late to a meeting of RX and found Harold discussing whether to send Bert Bowden to Salisbury all over again. What had brought him to it was a message from the Governor threatening to resign unless Bert Bowden came out, and urging that there was a reasonable chance now for a settlement. At first I was all against it. I thought it was just a device the Rhodesians were using for persuading us to overrun the date we'd fixed with the Commonwealth. Bowden was even more opposed than I was and threatening to refuse to go. But the

Committee was against us and later that morning I had time to read the cables from the Governor and to see what a disadvantage it would be if he resigned on the ground that we hadn't genuinely tried to reach a settlement. The next thing to do was to get a White Paper prepared in detail and that was done by Thursday morning when Cabinet met. Of course they were angry that they hadn't been consulted but they agreed the White Paper and off went Bowden that same day. Sure enough, by yesterday evening it was clear that Smith had begun to talk. I'd always rather dreaded that he would. But there the evidence was. This morning I rang up Harold and he said, 'Yes, it's true. The messages show that for the first time there's a chance of a settlement.' Later today I talked to Harold at length on the phone. 'As you know, I've been against you on this,' I said. 'I've been for handing the whole affair over to the U.N. and getting out from under when they declare a republic. That's been Callaghan's view too but now, if there's a reasonable chance of your getting an agreement by talks with Smith I think you ought to take it.' He replied, 'Others have said the same. George Brown and Michael Stewart take the same view.' So we were all really suddenly pressing him and saying, 'Get a settlement if you possibly can.' In terms of overt attitudes it was a great switchround but basically for months each of us has been aware of the ghastly consequences to this country and especially to this Government of the Rhodesia crisis dragging on at ever greater expense.

Though it sounds terribly trivial my concern has mainly been with the timetable of the House of Commons. Week after week I've been having to say on Thursday when I'm asked about Rhodesia that I must have another postponement, giving the assurance that there will be a debate as soon as we have anything definite to say. So I'm pledged up to the hilt that there will be a Commons' debate before final decisions are taken. The difficulty is that we are now running right up against the deadline. We really can't postpone for very much longer the tabling of the motion in the Security Council for mandatory sanctions and we have to fit in the Commons' debate somewhere.

But what are the chances of a settlement? I think these deliberate delays of Harold's and the last effort of sending out Bowden have produced some result. Harold is now saying he thinks Smith's bluff must be called. I'm not so sure and at the moment I'm chiefly concerned to ensure that he and Bert have plenipotentiary powers of negotiation. If there are going to be talks we ought to be ready to make sufficient concessions to get success and I fear Harold may be inhibited by Barbara and people like her who'll exert moral blackmail on him. John Silkin and I have been telling him he has nothing to fear in Britain. Among his back-benchers he would have at most fifty abstentions and he would have the whole Tory Party solidly behind him and the whole country as well. Our troubles would not be here at home but in the United Nations and of course in black Africa.

Monday, November 28th

RX met at 2.30. It's an enormous Committee which includes the First
Secretary, the Chancellor, the President of the Board of Trade, the Commonwealth Secretary, the Minister for Overseas Development, the Secretary
of State for Defence, the Lord President, the Lord Privy Seal and in addition
to them always three or four people from the Commonwealth Office—a
gigantic group incapable of decision. But at this meeting it was clear that we
were all in favour of Harold meeting Smith. Smith will be told on Thursday
and the meeting will take place at the weekend. But we recognize that we are
clutching at a straw.

This afternoon I had to attend another meeting of our Labour Party
Commission of Inquiry. It's now clear that it's a complete flop. Willie
Simpson, who was chosen by Jack Jones and me as a chairman, is a very nice
man but they're just going to sit round and chat and they won't investigate
what's wrong at Transport House because they're going to have Len Williams
sitting there as a member, not as a witness.

I've been getting more and more exasperated by sitting about in the House
of Commons because the place seems sillier and sillier. But I did have a
pleasant evening on Monday when my new P.P.S., Geoffrey Rhodes, got me
six of the new young M.P.s and we sat and drank and discussed problems in
my room. I shall get less depressed if I talk more with these young people.

Tuesday, November 29th

All through Monday the RX and the officials have been working away at the
mechanics and the timetable of the talks. The next stage came at Cabinet
this morning. The P.M. introduced the subject and did so in a way totally
different from anything RX had agreed the day before. Yesterday we'd been
all agreeing that we must have genuine negotiations and that we must insist
on flexibility for our two negotiators to really give a chance of agreement.
But at today's Cabinet the P.M. worked himself up, describing Smith as a
frightened worried man, talking about our skill in pushing him up to the
brink to make him break, and assuring us that now we would be able to force
him to accept our terms. At the end of this harangue the P.M. paused and
said he thought he had faithfully reflected the views of RX; was there any
comment from any member? There was a dead silence and I remarked that
I only had one comment. My impression of the Committee was not of an
intention to deliver an ultimatum or drive Smith into a corner. What we had
urged was the need for Smith to be a real plenipotentiary of his Government
and for Harold Wilson and Herbert Bowden to be real plenipotentiaries of
the British Government with maximum room for manoeuvre and negotiation.
It wasn't to be a confrontation, I imagined, but a negotiation, even if it was
with rebels.

Straightaway Barbara Castle weighed in, saying she wouldn't concede
any kind of flexibility since any concessions would split the Commonwealth.

She wanted to see every detail of the British position written into the brief we would prepare for Bert and Harold. As the discussion went on it soon became clear that Barbara was odd woman out. To be fair, she was standing on the position which Cabinet had almost unanimously adopted at the time of the Commonwealth Conference, when it insisted on mandating Harold to announce NIBMAR if he thought it necessary. But now the situation had changed in all our minds except Barbara's and to some extent that of the Attorney-General. The rest of us, even Dick Marsh, who was a bit equivocal, all knew that we had to go for an agreement and some let Barbara flounder by herself in a private dialogue with the P.M. After a time the P.M. turned to the Foreign Secretary, who gave a very sensible account of the reasons why he felt it essential to negotiate. If we didn't we should be destroyed by British public opinion. That's why Barbara was being unfair. Afterwards Harold went round the table requiring a short statement from each Minister in turn. He got virtual unanimity.

During the afternoon the detailed plans were made. Harold will start tomorrow, getting there on Friday morning, and they will therefore really have only two days to negotiate because he has to be back to receive the EFTA P.M.s at Chequers on Sunday afternoon.[1] Of course everything is still totally secret but more and more people suspect that there are going to be talks in the imminent future.

Wednesday, November 30th
George Weidenfeld came in this morning and again this evening and we had two excellent talks; as a result I can see him as my consultant on propaganda about our approach to the Market. I really don't think the F.O. is very skilled at this side of public relations and George Brown's made a fair balls-up so far of the debate. We shall get from George Weidenfeld infinitely superior advice on how to handle the problems of presentation. I shall do it all the more easily because next Monday Trevelyan goes back to the Home Office and Freddy Ward, the Assistant Secretary at the Ministry of Housing (who came up to Blackpool and helped me to prepare my speech)[2] is coming over to be my Assistant Secretary and head the Private Office with a Principal under him. That's a big advance and the circular about my new job as co-ordinator of information is out today and announces next Monday as the date when the job begins.

This morning at our business meeting, with Burke present, I expressed my surprise to Harold that he'd talked to the Cabinet as though he was imposing an ultimatum on Smith when really we wanted to negotiate a settlement with him. He looked at me and said, 'I was trying to drive Barbara into a corner: we got her isolated pretty well.' This is a good sign. He's limbering up for the

---

[1] The P.M. was to tell the other countries of the European Free Trade Association of Britain's exploratory talks in the E.E.C. capitals.
[2] An Under-Secretary at the Department of the Environment since 1968.

talks he adores and getting rid of his compunction and inhibitions. I was afraid he was going to stick and be unable to move away from his prepared position. I was also cheered when he said, 'It's either a victory or a draw: I can't lose as a result of these two days. This is the game of musical box when someone plays a record and the box is passed round and the person who's holding it when the record stops loses. I shall have handed the box back to Smith and shaken off the blame on myself. I can't lose.' I think he's right about this and it's had a big effect on his morale, which was pretty low.

I went across to the Party meeting which was discussing unemployment, and as I came in Callaghan was in full spate. I noticed that he referred to Rhodesia and said rather brutally that as Chancellor we couldn't afford sanctions. I heard later that this was a statement he had made in a more thoughtful form to the Party's economic group the day before with seventy or eighty people present.

So many things were piled on each other that I hardly noticed the meeting of the Cabinet Home Affairs Committee which I attended this afternoon. What made me furious was the discovery that the little Secretary of State for Wales wanted to publish his own White Paper on local government reform and even to legislate on it for Wales in this Parliament before our Royal Commission in England and Scotland had reported. That seemed to me absolute nonsense and I said so with considerable brutality. The result, as I might have predicted, was only to create sympathy for Cledwyn. I shouldn't bully Ministers about a subject where I was once responsible as a departmental Minister. It looked as though I was not only being rude to Cledwyn but teaching Tony Greenwood his own job. If I'd only not bothered to attend the meeting I'd have been a great deal better off.

RX met yet again this evening in preparation for Cabinet. We were able to see the draft brief for Harold and Herbert and in particular to study the concessions they could make on the constitution and the military presence. I think we all knew that it wasn't much good trying to lay down rules and we had to leave them to stick within the six principles but move as far as possible. The P.M. was really getting warmed up. He's terrible when he's undecided and casting around in his devious way but once one can get him off the launching pad into the air he really is a tremendous projectile. All that RX could do was to give him even more of the confidence which he requires for this job and which John Silkin and I have been pumping into him at all our private meetings. He told me that he'd been up till three this morning, partly because he was having young M.P.s to see him in his room and trying out his Rhodesian ideas on them and partly because he was waiting for the reply from Smith without knowing how to answer it.

Thursday, December 1st
Yet another RX at 9.45, when we completed consideration of the brief and discussed again the business arrangements for Thursday of next week.

Then in streamed the Cabinet, which was a mere formality. Barbara Castle was opening something in Paris and Judith Hart, who had not been at RX, wasn't at this meeting either. Nor were Arthur Bottomley and Fred Lee. All Harold's Commonwealth experts were just absent. And the Cabinet didn't even see the brief which we had been studying or the list of breaking points RX had prepared. They were told by George Brown to wish the P.M. good luck and they did so. Heaven knows, RX included nearly half the Cabinet but if I'd been one of the excluded members I'd have felt sore. But there were lots of other matters to discuss, including decimal coinage and the White Paper on option mortgages,[1] and Cabinet went on till nearly lunchtime.

I stayed behind to check the details with Harold and prepare for things at the House. He had not only his Questions but a Party meeting before he left. I told him he oughtn't to have any real discussion at the Party meeting but try to get the biggest cheer after his Statement. However he had taken the precaution of getting John to list the eight people most likely to cause trouble on the Floor of the House when he made the announcement. They included Jimmy Johnson, Alex Lyon, Ben Whitaker, Andrew Faulds and Joan Lestor —mostly left-wingers.[2] They were all brought in at 2.30 that afternoon and sat down on the other side of the table along with the Chief Whip and myself while Harold briefed them and answered their questions more fully than I had dared answer those of the press. It worked like magic. They all shook hands and wished him well and remained silent in the House. This was important because the reaction was not very encouraging—a round of cheers from the Tories but silence from our side, and those eight could have created a riot. I might add here that throughout the Rhodesia affair Marcia Williams was strongly opposed to the meeting with Smith whereas George Wigg was for it. Not that this made George Wigg any friendlier to me, as I learnt from his behaviour in the television debate last week. He won't forgive me because next Monday I'm taking over his co-ordination of the information services.

So the P.M. was off and meanwhile the two-day censure debate on economic affairs on which the Tories had been pinning their hopes was due to come to its climax. Harold is a devil on such occasions. Heath was due to make his big speech at 3.30 but the Prime Minister's Statement on Rhodesia dwarfed it straightaway. Moreover, by putting down a vote of no confidence in the Government's economic policy the Tory whips had made it certain that every

[1] In October 1966 Crossman had announced a scheme providing for subsidies on mortgages, whatever the ruling interest rate, if mortgagees would forgo tax relief at the standard rate. See Vol. I, p. 321.

[2] James Johnson, Labour M.P. for Kingston upon Hull since 1964. Alex Lyon, Labour M.P. for York since 1966 and, from 1974-6, Minister of State at the Home Office. Ben Whitaker, Labour M.P. for Hampstead 1966-70 and a Parliamentary Secretary at the Ministry of Overseas Development 1969-70; since 1971 he has been Director of the Minority Rights Group. Andrew Faulds, an actor, since 1966 Labour M.P. for Smethwick. Joan Lestor, Labour M.P. for Eton and Slough since 1966, Parliamentary Under-Secretary at the Department of Education and Science October 1969-June 1970 and Parliamentary Under-Secretary of State Foreign Affairs from 1974 to 1976.

one of our left-wingers would vote with the Government later in the evening.*

By a coincidence that evening I was due to dine with the Speaker. His wife had died six months ago and I went in expecting to go upstairs to his house and have a dinner served by a butler. But I saw a little man getting up at the end of the big library and there he stood up by his chair and beside him was a little table with some hot plates which had been brought in from our House of Commons restaurant. There was also a bottle of wine. He liked me being there because I too had experienced the sudden death of a much-loved wife.[1] His wife had been a very fine woman in Southampton local government, and the loss to him had been tremendous. But it did rather disconcert me when he said he'd got his housekeeper coming to live with him and he'd be marrying her next June.[2] Apart from that we discussed the television problem. Of course he's opposed and he was careful to tell me how skilful my speech was. No doubt he thought it had nicely got the project defeated. Nevertheless we worked out a sensible programme together. I pointed out that I'd been careful to leave open the suggestion that sound broadcasting had not been excluded by the defeat of the week before. I believe we should consider this on its merits during the next twelve months and we might also consider putting a first-rate television studio right inside the Palace of Westminster so that M.P.s could go there straight from the Chamber instead of rushing off to Lime Grove or standing out in the rain being interviewed in Parliament Square. On all this he seemed perfectly co-operative.

Friday, December 2nd
I started the morning with a business meeting attended by the Chief Whip, Freddie Warren and Dennis Trevelyan on his last day. We were going over the details of our big procedure package in preparation for its being taken in Cabinet. I'm still alarmed at my lack of a really efficient Department, however small. Freddie Warren is a tremendously skilled operator who runs the business of both sides of the House but he does it all off his own bat without any papers or briefing. He's got no idea about such things as parliamentary procedure in the broadest sense because his sole concern is to save Government time and reduce the amount of time wasted in debating whereas one of my major concerns is to restore some authority to the House and some of its old control of the Executive. In fact Freddie is a perfect civil servant for working with the Whips but not a very helpful collaborator for a reforming Lord President. Trevelyan was never really interested in this side of my job and from Monday I shall have Freddy Ward, who knows a great deal about getting a Bill through Parliament but is completely inexperienced in the procedure of the House. It's this absence of skilled experts which makes me nervous about our next big debate.

* They duly did and gave us a majority of 83.
[1] Crossman's second wife Zita.
[2] He did indeed marry Mrs Una Porter in 1967.

To O.P.D. at ten, where the big issue was the provision of married quarters for our troops if we bring a division or two back from Germany. The previous week we had a very strange episode where an offer by President Johnson virtually to give us thirty-five million dollars had been hedged around with political conditions including our remaining in the Far East, which I keenly resented. I was very much opposed to accepting the cash. But we did accept it and we wrote in a number of the conditions on which I insisted. But now we were faced with the problem that we still had made no preparation for housing our troops who are known to be coming back from the Far East and may well come back from Germany in large numbers.

Bob Mellish had produced a jolly good paper saying that we ought to buy private-enterprise housing this winter. At this point I was able to add something useful. I agreed with Bob but said that we couldn't expect the Ministry of Housing or the Ministry of Defence to buy just like that. We should set up some sort of purchasing organization, perhaps a housing corporation, to buy up private houses within twenty miles of the twelve specified barracks, with the intention of re-selling them again when the need had passed.

I had Sir William Haley[1] to lunch at the Garrick and we talked about the outrageous paragraph in *The Times* gossip column which had quoted me as the source for the revival of the press stories of the July plot. Sir William told me what had happened. At the Blackpool Conservative Party Conference a number of journalists had pooled all their knowledge of the July plot. One of them happened to be the *Newsweek* man, who had been at a lunch given by the *Washington Post* at which I had—strictly off-the-record—briefed Matt Meyer.[2] Having said the plot was non-existent and that I didn't believe in it, I added that there were some grounds for Harold's suspicions and I explained what those grounds were. At Blackpool the *Newsweek* man had given my name to these journalists, whereupon David Wood had written a paragraph and *The Times* had popped it into its gossip column.

I didn't let Haley apologize straightaway. We had an excellent lunch, discussing the B.B.C. and the complete breakdown of the Government plans for setting up a public corporation relying partly on advertising and doing some regional broadcasting. The Government had been utterly defeated by the B.B.C. and Haley was pleased. I found him extremely likeable and it was useful to hear his reactions.

Saturday, December 3rd
Last night I went to Oxford to a great conference at All Souls'. Richard Wilberforce and Justice Salmon had about forty lawyers there with some

---

[1] He was Director of Reuters 1939–43, editor-in-chief B.B.C. 1943–4, Director-General of the B.B.C. 1944–52, editor of *The Times* 1952–66, chairman of Times Newspapers 1967, editor-in-chief *Encyclopaedia Britannica* 1968–9 and, since 1973, has been chairman of Barclay Trust International.

[2] President of the *New York World-Telegram and Sun.*

civil servants, including Lady Sharp, to discuss administrative law.[1] Some professor suggested introducing the French system of administrative law and fortunately everybody said it was nonsense.

I was motored home to Prescote at one in the morning so today I've been having a real day off before the farm party. I took the children and Sukie, Virginia's poodle, out for a lovely walk round the fields on a bitterly cold day after all the showers and hailstorms.

Sunday, December 4th

It was about 9.30 this morning that Trevelyan rang me up to say that Cabinet had been summoned for 2.30. That meant catching the 10.55 from Banbury because no later train could get me there on time. We had our farm party last night and it had gone on till 12.30 in the morning when I went outside and found a thin powdering of snow covering the cars, the moon lying on its back with white clouds chasing over it and tremendously brilliant white moonlight on the first snow of the winter—very lightly powdered but making the roads a bit treacherous. This morning it was brilliant again with the bluest of blue skies. We'd woken late and hadn't rushed ourselves but before I knew what was what I'd cancelled my arrangements and was on the train to London. With the lines being repaired as usual on a Sunday I got to Paddington forty minutes late and got myself motored to Vincent Square where I tried to do some lists of Christmas presents before walking across to Downing Street where quite a number of people had collected to watch us go in. It wasn't long before Harold came. He hadn't been back for more than an hour but we all streamed in and everybody was there, as far as I could see, except Willie Ross. While the copies were being made of the document which had been signed by Smith and Wilson the Prime Minister filled us in on the events on the *Tiger*.

On the way up I'd been pondering what could have happened. I was quite hopeful that an agreement must have been reached and that Harold was reckoning that he could get the whole thing lined up and approved before going down tonight to Chequers for his dinner with the EFTA P.M.s at 7.30. But I was by no means right. Nothing had been lined up. The document Smith and Harold had signed was merely a working document for which authorization was required by both Cabinets. Harold wanted us to give it by 2.30 this afternoon so that it could be known as soon as possible that the British Cabinet was fully behind him. I thought of his talk about the game of

---

[1] Lord Wilberforce, a Fellow of All Souls College, Oxford, since 1932 and High Steward of Oxford University since 1967, was a Judge of the High Court of Justice 1961–4. In 1964 he became a life peer and has since served as a Lord of Appeal in Ordinary. Mr Justice Salmon, a Judge of the High Court of Justice 1957–64 and a Lord Justice of Appeal 1964–72, became a life peer in 1972 and since then has served as a Lord of Appeal in Ordinary. Baroness Sharp (Dame Evelyn Sharp) had been a distinguished public servant, serving from 1955 to 1966 as Permanent Secretary to successive Ministers of Housing, of whom Crossman was the last. She became a life peer in 1966. See Vol. I.

musical boxes. This time the box has been left in the hands of the Rhodesian Government—this was my first conclusion. But I wasn't quite right. In fact our Prime Minister was still reckoning on an agreement and he was wanting an early decision in order to impress the Rhodesians. All Cabinet could do was to accept or reject the document entire and Harold said to me grinning, 'This is the way we deal with a prayer against an Order in Council in the House of Commons. You can either accept it or reject the order; you can't amend it. Well, Cabinet has the same choices about this working document.' So you might have supposed that we wouldn't have gone through that document in the greatest detail. But for some reason we did. I don't know whether he wanted to but we started at the beginning and went through it clause by clause. On the clauses dealing with the constitution it became only too clear that not even Harold or the Attorney-General understood very exactly what the document meant. But it didn't really matter. There hadn't been any great difficulty in bridging the gap on the written constitution. The whole difficulty was about the return to legality and our insistence that the rebel regime must be wound up and replaced by a new broadly-based regime in which we could have confidence. A second big difficulty was our insistence on a British military presence, the ending of censorship and the release of detainees—requirements which Smith had simply brushed aside in all previous negotiations.

I came to the conclusion that if Smith could be made to accept the British military presence and the other symbols of that kind, in return we ought to be easy about the nature of the new broadened government. However, Barbara Castle finally said that when she looked at the return to legality she was glad Harold had said it was a choice of evils. If the choice was between accepting mandatory sanctions or accepting this document she thought he had made the wrong choice since a compromise along these lines was the greater evil. To this Harold made a remarkable reply. 'Let's not forget we aren't like General MacArthur on the battleship *Appotomax* accepting the unconditional surrender of the Japanese. This isn't like the French surrendering to the Germans at Compiègne.[1] This is a British Government which has failed to achieve its objectives, painfully accepting the best agreed terms they could get for the voluntary winding-up of the rebellion by the rebels themselves and since that is the case we can't quite expect the terms we would have imposed if we'd won.' I had never heard Harold say this before and he said it very clearly. Then, almost in the same breath, he began a vicious complaint about the suggestion that we'd been driven into these negotiations by financial weakness. 'It was quite wrong and malicious to say that the British Government was so scared at the prospect of mandatory sanctions that we'd funked them. That,'

[1] The first reference, attributed to the Prime Minister, confuses the Japanese surrender, on board the *Missouri*, at the end of the Second World War with the surrender of General Robert E. Lee to General Ulysses S. Grant in April 1865, during the American Civil War. The second refers to the armistice signed by the French, on June 22nd, 1940, after the fall of France.

he said, 'was outrageous.' Of course I knew that he was still worrying about certain remarks made by Callaghan. But the *Financial Times* and the *Guardian* had interpreted them as an admission by the Government that it is because of its own economic weakness, because of its fear of its inability to stand up to sanctions that the P.M. started these talks with Smith. 'This,' Harold said, 'has greatly weakened us.' And it certainly has. These statements by Callaghan — or rather the way these statements have been treated in the press — have made the prospect of a refusal by Smith to stand by the working document infinitely greater than they would have been. Indeed, we have to face it that if tomorrow morning Smith refuses our terms then there may well be an immediate run on the pound. That will launch a terrible row between Brown at the Foreign Office and Callaghan at the Treasury which will somehow have to be reconciled. Callaghan will straightaway want to say we have no intention of confrontation with South Africa. Brown will want, for a few days at least, to stand by our principles even at the risk of confrontation with South Africa. Callaghan throughout this period has been opposed to any further concessions to the U.N. He was also against the whole dubious device of saying we would keep the Commonwealth together by a compromise which might well merely lead us to the threat of economic war with South Africa. In all this I don't blame the Chancellor. But it's certainly true that his statement at the Economic Committee, repeated at the Party meeting, and then leaked to the press was extraordinarily ill-judged. And it's certainly made Harold extremely vicious in Cabinet, though of course he never mentioned Callaghan's name.

At one point Jim whispered to me, 'When I said these things I didn't say them in order to let the public know the reason for Harold's talks with Smith. Actually at the Party meeting, as you well know, Dick, I was not intending to speak. I was only brought in half way through the debate.' Now that happens to be a fact. Callaghan, I remember, came in to that meeting thinking he was going to listen to the debate, not knowing that he'd been announced as opening it. So he got to his feet impromptu. I'm sure it wasn't a planned operation. Yet he did repeat what he said at the Economic Committee and he allowed the papers to suggest that he was playing the role of Harold Macmillan saving the country from Anthony Eden's folly at Suez.[1] I'm sure there was no plot but he's got a character like that. And tonight after the EFTA meeting at Chequers the three of them will have to argue out what is to be done tomorrow in the event of failure.

But will there be a failure? I must say I was very optimistic at one time. Though we've had to yield a lot, especially on the return to legality, Smith too has made tremendous concessions. Indeed, as the Chief pointed out to me when we were trying to tidy up the parliamentary business after Cabinet, it is Smith who has given way on seventeen of the twenty-two clauses and not

[1] In 1957, some months' decent interval after the Suez adventure, Eden resigned as P.M. and leader of the Conservative Party and Harold Macmillan took his place.

Harold. By these concessions he has obtained from Harold a real compromise which concedes that there shall not be any real difference between his rebel government which we refuse to recognize and the new broadly-based government under the Governor-General. But he may have given way so much that he's unable to hold his own people. It's just touch and go. If he does by any chance turn us down then the pound is in for a drubbing tomorrow and we shall have the worst of all worlds at the United Nations. But if he agrees Harold will have scored a tremendous success. In fact he'll have created the basis upon which we can take the next step of freeing the pound by letting it float next spring and saving the economic situation at home. Yes, if Harold resolves this Rhodesia crisis the Government will have a tremendous opportunity to stage a big come-back on the economic front as well.

Well, that's my picture of what happened today at Cabinet. There wasn't much discussion. It was the Prime Minister talking at great length with the Commonwealth Secretary chipping in very little and the Attorney-General very little indeed. At one point Dick Marsh rebuked Barbara Castle by telling her that we gave the two plenipotentiary powers and that we were wasting time on details. But the curious thing is that though Harold could have got everything through in half an hour we spent a solid afternoon on it. Right at the end I had to take over the job of publicity. We had decided to put out a communiqué—something we don't often do about Cabinet meetings. Then John and I waited and worked out with him the kind of presentation he wants to make in the Commons tomorrow. We must be sure he prepares for both alternatives—success or failure. Two alternative White Papers must be produced by the Government printers today and all through the night so that we shall be able to have the right one ready for simultaneous release with the P.M.'s Statement at 7.15 tomorrow evening.

Monday, December 5th
My first interview was with Solly Zuckerman, Wedgwood Benn, the Minister of Technology, and Tony Crosland, the Secretary of State for Education, about the terms of reference of the specialist Select Committee on Science and Technology. I'd fondly imagined this had all been fixed in a talk with Heath and Willie Whitelaw months ago. Little did I know what endless finagling there would be in Whitehall. I'd agreed with the Opposition leaders that the Agricultural Research Council should be the first subject of study which this new Specialist Committee would undertake and this had been settled by the two Ministers with their Departments. Then Solly was given his new Cabinet job as Scientific Adviser to the P.M. with his own special Science and Technology Committee, a body which I think is a pretty good waste of time. The moment he heard of our activities he came barging in to me in my office and said, 'Your Select Committee on Science and Technology can't do an investigation of the Agricultural Research Council. I've already started one.' And there he was this morning with the two Ministers laying down the law and saying

the Select Committee couldn't start its work on this topic because it would interfere with his work. I pointed out that we'd come to our decision before he'd even been appointed and I wasn't prepared to go back on my agreement with the Opposition leaders. Then he said rather impatiently, 'Well, what are these specialist Select Committees really? What are they for?' After the meeting I sent him the excellent book by David Coombes, which explains what the Select Committee on Nationalized Industries does, so that he could try to understand what goes on in these bodies.[1] But at the meeting he did reveal what the attitude of the Whitehall warriors is to my parliamentary reform. Even the two Ministers were a bit flabbergasted.

Later on this morning I had a meeting at the Ministerial Committee on Procedure to discuss the proposal to appoint a special Select Committee to supervise the work of the ombudsman and his relations with Parliament. Niall MacDermot happened to be away with a bad back and I was left to present what were really his proposals. It was a very good turn-out with nearly all the Ministers there, headed by Roy Jenkins, Willie Ross and Tony Benn. From the chair I said that I wanted the Committee to realize how important this decision was. I wondered whether all of them fully realized what the powers of the ombudsman would be and once again I outlined his powers of investigation, his right to open up all the secret files in a Department, his right to discover which civil servant was precisely responsible for what, his right to pick out and put blame on individual civil servants—in fact, his capacity to get well behind the façade of Ministerial responsibility to Parliament to see how decisions are really taken in a Department.

It didn't take my colleagues very long to admit that a Select Committee was necessary. But as the discussion went on they began to wonder whether this Bill should be allowed to become law. At one point Roy Jenkins said, 'But this alters the whole constitution by destroying the doctrine of Ministerial responsibility. If you're right, in many cases the ombudsman will be able to find out that a particular civil servant has taken a decision without the Minister being consulted.' 'Yes,' I said, 'that's what I explained in the Second Reading debate.' 'Well how far has the Bill gone?' said Roy. 'Can't we hold it back?' So there in Solly Zuckerman and Roy Jenkins we have two lively examples of the extraordinary attitude of the politicians and the senior civil servants in Whitehall to the whole idea of permitting Parliament, through its agent, to control the detailed working of the Executive. Both these highly intelligent friends of mine seem to want to keep Parliament as weak as possible so their own Ministerial functions will be undisturbed.

The third thing I did today was to let Dick Marsh come and talk to me about North Sea gas.[2] For weeks I've been worried about North Sea gas

[1] *The Member of Parliament and the Administration* (London: Allen & Unwin, 1966).
[2] During 1966 there had been twelve commercial discoveries of natural gas in the North Sea. Only British Petroleum made a contract (minimum 50,000,000 cubic feet a day, 5d. a

because, as Burke Trend goes on pointing out to me, there had been very serious leaks about the price dispute which could be of great commercial value. Broadly speaking, I gather that the Gas Council wants to pay a very low price (under 2*d*. a therm) whereas the oil companies claim that they must be compensated for the cost of their investigations by charging a higher price, say fourpence or fivepence a therm. This issue had been discussed at length in a paper which went before the relevant Cabinet Committee and it was the leaks from that Committee which Dick wanted to discuss.

He soon came to the point and told me that he suspected Tommy Balogh was leaking. And he pointed out, as though this were evidence, that Tommy had deliberately placed his friend Michael Posner[1] in the Ministry of Power— were these two men really reliable, he asked me? This worried me because I've always known from Tommy himself that he regards himself as the leader of the anti-oil lobby in the battle for cheap gas and for this purpose he's using his position as a member of the official committee which briefs the Cabinet Committee. We tried to sort all this out and I explained to Marsh what the position of Tommy and Posner was. These leaks, as Burke always tells me, are extremely dangerous because if the oil companies think they have been unjustly treated by the Government they can make a stink and insist on a Tribunal of Investigation into the actions leading up to the Government decision.*

Later this afternoon John and I were getting ready for tonight's Statement by the Prime Minister. We'd so arranged business for Monday that he could make a Statement between seven and eight. It's not as easy as you might imagine to permit anyone, even the Prime Minister, to break into Commons business. You have to wait until one piece of business has ended and then spatchcock his Statement in before the next starts. This is what we had planned to do. We'd arranged for the London Government Bill Committee Stage to end punctually with a vote at 7 p.m.[2] Then Harold would make his Statement before the next three Bills. At six o'clock we began to get strong rumours that Harold would not be ready. I went in to see the end of the London Government Bill and they were already on Amendment 12 and

therm) with the Gas Council. After several years' campaigning, notably by Lord Balogh, the arrangement for licensing the exploitation of the North Sea gas and oil fields was to be substantially revised.

* On the very next day, Tuesday, December 6th, there was a malicious paragraph in the Peterborough gossip column of the *Daily Telegraph* saying that Tommy was a leading member of the Committee which was trying to keep the price of gas down. However, this little crisis petered out when later in the week it was discovered that the leak Dick Marsh had complained about came from the Gas Council.

[1] Fellow and Director of Studies in Economics, Pembroke College, Cambridge, since 1960. He was Director of Economics at the Ministry of Power 1966–7, Economic Adviser to the Treasury 1967–9 and Economic Consultant to the Treasury 1969–71. In 1974 he returned to Whitehall as an Economic Adviser.

[2] The Commons were discussing the postponement of the borough elections and the reorganization of secondary education in London.

the whole House was sitting about not listening to what was being said but waiting for the P.M. Well, Amendment 17 came to an end and the vote was taken and we were forced to go on to the next Bill—some little Foreign Office Bill and another on Tribunals and Inquiries, which went whirling through. We were in danger of running out of business so I went out to talk to Heath at about 7.45. I said that I hoped he would appreciate it wasn't the Prime Minister's fault—he was waiting for Smith to give his answer. Meanwhile John Silkin had been busy making sure that when he wound up the Attorney-General would talk things out on the last Bill. Finally, at 8.45, the P.M. arrived to make his Statement. Despite his promise to me that he had prepared two alternative versions of his Statement it looks as though the P.M. had staked everything on achieving agreement. Indeed, he spent the morning and afternoon with the EFTA Ministers. The time-limit was up at 10 a.m. and Smith hadn't asked for any extension. He simply took one, and hour after hour went by while Smith was known to be out to lunch and to have come back from lunch. But no answer came and gradually as the afternoon wore on Harold had to accept that he had failed.

At this point another factor intervened—Callaghan and the financial crisis. The *Tiger* talks had dramatized the importance of Harold's peacemaking to the whole world—and particularly to the City of London. It was not until he was certain Smith was going to refuse that Harold suddenly began to consider how to make this admission while avoiding a run on the pound. This brought him into the expected argument with George Brown and James Callaghan. Sunday's Cabinet had left it to these three to work out the text of the passage of his Statement referring to mandatory sanctions and saying we wouldn't extend them to South Africa. These sentences were felt to be essential to save the pound but apparently an hour was spent by the three wrangling about them and that was another cause of the delay.

However, when the Statement finally came he read it very well and answered Questions quite well and then he was out and back to Downing Street. The Chief and I heaved a sigh of relief and kept the House going discussing one of those prayers against an Order in Council arising out of Part IV of the Prices and Incomes Act. On any other day it would have been an important event but now nobody took any notice of it.

Tuesday, December 6th
Cabinet was in a difficult and unpleasant mood because we had to consider the consequences of the Rhodesian failure. Of course all the plans for our strategy at the U.N. had been laid down in advance and George Brown was due to leave for New York this evening. The difficulty we were discussing was not what to do but how to present what had happened on the *Tiger*.

Harold Wilson's main concern was the picture of Smith we should give to the British public. Should we name the list of the Cabinet Ministers in Salisbury, who had been named by Smith and Harold as members of his new enlarged government? Should we name the Cabinet Ministers he was going to dismiss and the thirty members of the Rhodesia Front Party he wanted to get rid of? Should we publish all the dirt about him which had come out on the *Tiger* and so try to destroy him, or should we regard him as something worth preserving? I soon discovered that Harold Wilson wasn't really interested in planning psychological warfare because he hadn't made up his mind what he wanted to happen in Salisbury. What he was doing was to work himself up for his swing from his attempt to appease Smith on the *Tiger* to an attempt this coming Thursday to appease his anti-Smith back-benchers in the House of Commons. To this end he was beginning to feel a deep indignation against Smith and to treat him as an absolutely contemptible character, a crook and a waverer. How idiotic it was, he said at one moment, that Smith should be going for this figment, this will-o'-the-wisp of independence. At this point I interjected and said, 'For heaven's sake, let's keep some grip on reality. It's quite probable that what the P.M. calls the will-o'-the-wisp of Rhodesian independence will be a fact long after the Labour Government is thrown out of office.'

That afternoon after Harold had answered his Questions and I'd replied to quite a rough attack on my business Statement from Heath, George Brown opened the big foreign affairs debate with thirty-four people in the House of whom sixteen were Tories. This nearly always happens. For weeks at Questions back-benchers ask for a foreign affairs debate and then no one turns up. My mind that afternoon was entirely preoccupied with the prospect —as I then thought it was—that on the following Monday I would have to move the resolution for guillotining the Iron and Steel Bill. John Silkin hates guillotines. He had succeeded in getting the Prices and Incomes Bill through in July without one and now he was determined to get Steel through without a guillotine. But in Committee upstairs, instead of Harold Lever, a brilliant chairman, he had poor dear deaf Legge-Bourke,[1] and instead of George Brown, who is pretty adaptable, he had as his Ministerial team Richard Marsh, quite inexperienced, and Jeremy Bray who, I gather, was dreadful.[2] As a result of their inability to handle the Committee Stage it has gone through all-night sitting after all-night sitting and it really looked this afternoon as though we should have to clap on a guillotine next week.

Well, fortunately the threat was eliminated later that evening. Quite suddenly the Tories came to an agreement and we shall get the Committee Stage finished by Christmas.

---

[1] Sir Harry Legge-Bourke, Conservative M.P. for the Isle of Ely from 1945 until his death in May 1973.

[2] Labour M.P. for Middlesbrough West from 1962 until his resignation in 1970, and for Motherwell since 1974. Parliamentary Secretary at the Ministry of Power 1966–7 and Joint Parliamentary Secretary at the Ministry of Technology 1967–9.

Thursday, December 8th[1]

At Cabinet this morning Harold was chiefly concerned with his big speech but we had a not uninteresting discussion on broadcasting in which he scored a complete triumph over his modernizing adversaries. Ted Short simply reported that the scheme for a public corporation partly dependent on advertising was impracticable and all the modernizers—including Tony Benn, Tony Crosland and myself—gave up. So the idea which Tony Benn rejected when he was Postmaster-General had prevailed and the White Paper will be published tomorrow committing us to a completely impracticable method of financing the B.B.C.[2]

Unfortunately, at the business Statement this afternoon I was caught unprepared. The issue was on my refusal to lift the whip for all the votes during the debate on my procedure reforms. People objected but if I'd only known it there are endless precedents for whipping on procedure votes and I could have cited these. But alas, I'd only had Freddy Ward in my office for three days and Freddie Warren is wonderful at fixing things between the Whips but he is not very wonderful at providing the Leader of the House with a brief.

Then came the big Rhodesia debate. It started with a perfectly decent light-weight speech from Douglas-Home. Then Harold began. As I suspected from his attitude on Tuesday morning he had swung right back. Having come to the edge of an agreement with Smith for which he had paid with very heavy concessions, he had now swung back to the other extreme and made an ultra-moralist speech addressed in particular to the forty or fifty left-wingers who'd have refused him their vote if he'd got his agreement with Smith. The central theme was that this was a great moral issue, that anybody who was against Wilson was for Smith, that the Tories were the allies of the rebels in Rhodesia, and he ended with a peroration quoting Abraham Lincoln addressed to the workers of Lancashire[3] and which worked up the Labour Members to such a passion that when he sat down they gave him a standing ovation waving their Order Papers. I found the Chief Whip was standing beside me and I also rose though I couldn't bring myself to wave my Order Paper. But there's no doubt about it, Harold had roused the Party which is a moralistic party and which disliked the idea of any settlement and is delighted to cheer when they are told that no settlement is possible.

That was the high point of the debate but we were all waiting to see what Heath would do. Sure enough when he got up at nine o'clock he made a

---

[1] There is no record of the events of Wednesday, December 7th.

[2] The White Paper on Broadcasting Finance (Cmnd. 3169) that was published in December 1966 followed six months of discussion of a proposal floated by Mr Wedgwood Benn, the then Postmaster-General, to establish a new public corporation with one wavelength financed by advertising revenue. Mr Short's White Paper declared that the B.B.C. would continue in its present form, as a public corporation deriving its revenue from the licence fees, paid by the public to the Post Office and voted, as a matching sum, by Parliament.

[3] Asking them to accept privations for their principles.

very powerful speech. 'All this moralism,' he said, 'is a piece of hypocrisy. The Prime Minister talks about fighting a moral battle and raises the banner of morality but actually he's been doing everything to avoid a confrontation in Africa, thank heavens, and he will accept a settlement if he possibly can.' Heath was doing fine when he mentioned Aneurin Bevan's remark that the British Tories were lower than vermin. Suddenly there rose a woman in white samite, mystic, wonderful, in the third row back of our benches. It was Jennie Lee denouncing Heath for maligning her dead husband. She so upset Heath that he ran on until 9.38 and left little time for Judith Hart. Judith had been appalled to hear how near we had come to a settlement and she proved again that she's so soaked in the subject that she's able to raise real emotions in the House. She at least had time to give the news from New York for which everyone was waiting—that mandatory sanctions were on.

Then came the vote and we found that we'd won by a comfortable majority since the Liberals were on our side. This was one of the few big occasions in my memory where the events matched the occasion. Both Ted and Harold had made fine speeches, Bowden and Douglas-Home had done very competently and Judith had made her mark. The debate in fact had mattered.

Friday, December 9th

Morning prayers with the P.M. He was wild with fury at the badness of the press. 'The press are contemptible and corrupt. Unbearable! Look at what they have done to my speech.' 'True,' I said, 'but if you lambast the Tory leader you mustn't expect the Tory press to be wildly enthusiastic. And then you have also got to notice that Reg Paget has made the headlines by resigning the Party Whip.[1] I knew it was a mistake to let him resign.' 'What?' he said. 'Yes,' I said. 'I knew Reg Paget wanted to vote against us and John told him he should resign first. I think we shouldn't have let him resign but kept him in, let him vote and then expelled him. Then we wouldn't have had the headlines against you which we've got today.'

After this we got down to discussing business and I noticed that both the P.M. and Burke are very anxious to hear no more either of RX or of S.E.P. Both these Committees have been trying to be strategic-planning boards and they've caused the P.M. and the Secretary to the Cabinet increasing frustration. It is clear they want to get rid of them both.

O.P.D. this morning was extremely important. We were considering a joint paper from the Foreign Secretary and the Minister of Defence proposing cuts of up to one half in Far Eastern Command and about a third in the Middle East and in Europe. This was the idea which was first broached in the after-dinner talk at Chequers when I was brought into the inner group (I'm not at all sure I'm still there, by the way). In this paper it was worked out in detail—and it was totally and completely unconvincing. It seemed obvious that if you were to make these gigantic cuts in defence costs then they made

[1] Labour M.P. for Northampton 1945–74.

the previous Defence Review utterly senseless. Alternatively, what you are doing is to make major changes in foreign policy under the veil of cutting defence—and of course the second alternative is nearly true.

Callaghan started straightaway by making this point very clearly indeed. I weighed in on the same side. I added that I noticed there were certain differences. In the case of the Middle East there was an instruction in the paper that a special study should be undertaken on the political assumption of a total withdrawal. But a total withdrawal from the Far East was not even to be made the subject of a study. On the contrary, the whole assumption was that we are there for ever because it is necessary to keep a British military presence in the Far East to sustain our membership of the four-power agreement with Australia, New Zealand and the U.S.A. As a result of my intervention it was agreed that there should be a study of total withdrawal from Malaya. But the intervention of Callaghan and myself occasioned a considerable speech from Denis Healey. He said, 'One mustn't be afraid of the idea of penny-packages throughout the world. There is a lot to commend them: a penny-package can make an immense difference as we found the other day when a battalion of our troops in Kenya prevented a revolution. A single ship in Hong Kong could make all the difference. One can't dismiss the validity of a strategy based on penny-packages.'

I couldn't help recalling all the lessons I'd received from George Wigg on the fatal effect of the policy of scattering penny-packages round the world during the 1920s and the 1930s since each of these packages involved a large commitment that we might have to honour. And we can't honour the commitment entered into as a result of the penny-package without maintaining a vast strategic reserve. Yet here was George Wigg actually supporting Denis Healey. I realized that the whole weight of the Prime Minister's enormous influence would be on the side of preserving the British military presence in the Far East. I have no doubt, for example, that the Prime Minister has already made a number of personal commitments on the subject to L.B.J. in Washington. At one point, indeed, Callaghan mentioned them by saying, 'I don't want to refer to or argue about any specific commitments, Prime Minister, you have made to L.B.J.' It is the personal commitments in Washington of Harold Wilson, of George Brown and of Michael Stewart which are holding us down in Malaya. They're making it as difficult for us to withdraw there as it is to get out of Aden and there we shall find that our own people will create a situation which will require nothing less than a war in order to achieve a withdrawal.

I lunched with Philip Hendy and discussed the National Gallery pictures he's promised to get me. Going round the store under the Gallery with him I had chosen a huge Teniers of a bowling match with a tremendous thunderstorm coming up, two Dutch seascapes and a nice school of El Greco for over the mantelpiece. He tells me this last painting is thought too valuable. The Teniers I'd originally chosen was also too valuable but the bowling-match picture has been allowed. I also got the two seascapes. My room in the Privy Council is going to look quite nice with these splendid pictures from the National Gallery on the walls to balance some of the finest silver in the whole of Britain which adorns my table.

Saturday, December 10th

When I caught the train to Banbury, Fred Peart and his wife were on the platform. He was coming to stay at Prescote and address the Banbury Farmers' Club. The speech was quite an interesting occasion as I've never seen Fred in action with the farmers. He brought one of his Secretaries with him and he was met at Banbury Station by two of his regional men; the three looked after his speech and went round with him. It's obvious he's tremendously well tended by his Ministry on such occasions—no better than I was at Housing, by the way. The dinner went all right. The farmers were friendly to Fred and they also greeted me very heartily and very civilly, which obviously surprised him. After the dinner we got to the speeches. I'd read Fred's beforehand. It was a fairly empty after-dinner speech, full of political sagacity in the sense of not saying anything very definite and shying away from a precise commitment but full of goodwill for the farmers. It didn't deserve high praise but it certainly didn't deserve the surly treatment it got from the farmer who moved the vote of thanks extraordinarily offensively. Fred sat there looking as though his breath had been blown out of him and I got up and whispered over his shoulder, 'Don't answer back. Just offer to answer questions.' And that is what he did. The questions were thrown into a hat and were read aloud and he answered them rapidly and competently. Fred's a schoolmaster and he's always pleased with his facility for answering questions, he did it extremely well.

Sunday, December 11th

At least everyone at the dinner last night got the impression that their Minister of Agriculture was an extremely competent politician. But I doubt whether many of them believed he had any understanding of farming and I must admit that feeling was greatly confirmed this morning when I took him up to Pritchett's and we went round the farm. It was a horrible morning of heavy rain and in any case at this time of year there wasn't much to see outside. I took him into Mr Pritchett's office and we let him see how Mr P. works out the profit and loss account on the herd's milk, and how each animal is costed. I got the impression that he didn't understand accounts very much. Or perhaps I was wrong—perhaps he wasn't interested in them. Then we rushed him down to the village hall, which has been built by the energy of Len Edwards, our remarkable local inventor of laundry machinery, and Mr Pritchett and half a dozen newcomers. This small group had got together and collected the money and a lot of the actual work of construction had been done by Prescote staff. It was a splendid turnout and Fred did his job to everybody's contentment. After drinks, back to Prescote for lunch, and then he was off with his wife to Stratford for a Labour Party regional conference. I had a quiet afternoon before we fetched Janet Newman, my pretty secretary, from the station and Janet and I spent most of this afternoon preparing my big speech on procedure for the debate next week.

This evening I stopped work on the speech for a bit and looked back over the last fortnight of the Rhodesian crisis. I've been watching Harold swinging between extremes. I've seen him at his best and at his worst. First John and I helped him off the launching pad as the man willing to negotiate with Smith and to defy the fifty left-wing back-benchers. I saw him plunging out into the venture on the *Tiger*, cutting loose from the Party and determined to get an agreement even if it meant a couple of resignations from Cabinet. Next I saw him back from the *Tiger* extraordinarily confident that he'd got an agreement in his pocket. (This is something Mary Wilson remarked on at a moment when I spotted her and walked her down the lobby.) Now that I've read the *Tiger* minutes verbatim, I see that optimism as wholly unjustified. Nevertheless, he came back full of this optimism and at the Cabinet meeting on Sunday afternoon persuaded us to give him one hundred per cent support for his plan even though it contains major concessions to Smith. Then on Monday morning he expected Smith's reply at ten a.m. and didn't get it. He busied himself with EFTA to keep his mind off the subject and waited all through the day desperately anxiously. He was hopelessly cast down when he was gradually forced to the conclusion that no reply is a negative reply and finally, at 8.45, he made a Statement on the failure of the talks. For that he had to use a corrected version of the Statement on the success of the talks because he hadn't, as he promised he would, prepared alternative drafts. All he could do as last-minute preparation was to put some corrections into the Statement he drafted on how the talks succeeded. Next morning we saw him at Cabinet discussing our long-term plans rather vaguely but by then he was wholly concerned with the speech he was going to make and spent a lot of thought in Cabinet drafting Thursday's resolution. Already he'd determined that his main objective was to demolish Heath in that debate and this he did. We had a tremendous scene with Harold, the moralist, rallying his left-wing back-benchers against Heath, the criminal collaborationist, and completely burning his bridges by swinging from a mood of extreme appeasement to a mood of no concession to treason. That's what we saw on Thursday. I had to admit that during those four days Harold didn't consult me and as far as I know he didn't consult anybody outside his No. 10 circle. In that period I had no influence on him. I think the only people he talked to were George Wigg and Marcia Williams. But I saw him again on Friday morning entirely concerned about the effect his speech produced, and planning to demolish the RX Committee, with which he now feels he has had to waste so many weary hours while they tried to run his Rhodesian strategy for him.

After Thursday's Cabinet I walked to the front door of No. 10 with Roy

Jenkins, who's a cautious, conspiring kind of man and plays little role in Cabinet. 'Heavens,' I said to him, 'I wish we could have been given a clearer vision of his long-term policy in Rhodesia.' He replied, 'I'd give anything for evidence that we have a long-term plan for any part of this Government's policy, thank you very much, Dick,' and he walked on.

I was reflecting on all this and talking to Thomas Balogh, who's the only friend with whom I can talk freely these days. I find I share Roy Jenkins's depression. Because I've watched Harold from close at hand, I've seen him during this crisis as exactly what his enemies accuse him of being—a tough politician who jumps from position to position, always brilliantly energetic and opportunist, always moving in zigzags, darting with no sense of direction but making the best of each position he adopts. But it's far too simple to say he's a simple opportunist: he does have a number of long-term thoughts and he does give a great deal of long-term consideration to certain policies, principles and promises. We've promised to build 500,000 houses by 1970, that's an election promise he takes very seriously indeed and here he is prepared to think long term. He sees the objective and he is determined to take steps to ensure we achieve it.

I expect I could list a number of other long-term convictions. In addition to getting house-building up he's determined to keep our military presence in the Far East, even if it involves keeping penny-packets of British troops scattered over the world. He's also got a long-term conviction that we must keep our special relation with the U.S.A. and that Britain will remain great if we do. But in this Rhodesian affair his main concern is to prove himself right: to prove that he can win this as Kennedy won his Cuba.[1] It's winning that matters here, whether by settlement or by defeating Smith. He can't make up his mind, but he's going to go on hammering, manœuvring, intruding, evading to prove himself right.

When we turn to the economy we are on much more insecure ground. What are Harold's long-term economic objectives in this country? Does he really want to go into Europe, or doesn't he? I don't think he knows himself. Does he want to devalue? He certainly doesn't want to but is he going to after all? He knew the answer a few months ago; he's not so sure of it now. And what about the long-term future of the Labour Party? Does he see it as a real socialist party or does he, like the Gaitskellites, aim to turn it into an American Democratic Party or a German Social Democratic Party? I see him more than most people and he probably talks to me about these subjects more than he does to anybody else. But he certainly doesn't confide in me any profound thoughts about the future of the Labour Party and I'm prepared to say as of today that I don't think he has them. He has a number of moral

---

[1] In October 1962 John F. Kennedy (United States President from 1960 until his assassination in November 1963), officially acting without the overt support of America's allies on the U.N. Security Council, successfully called the bluff of the Soviet Government which had established and were furnishing long-range missile sites in Cuba.

convictions: he's a perfectly sincere Sunday Methodist; he's against the legal reforms to deal with homosexuality or abortion. He has a conventional respect for the B.B.C. as a public corporation and won't allow advertising. He likes playing golf with ordinary businessmen; he's devoted to the Queen and is very proud that she likes his visits to her. He's really fond of Burke Trend and sees him as a close personal friend and confidant. In all these ways his moral values are extremely conventional. Yet, on the other hand, he tenaciously keeps hold of Marcia Williams, George Wigg, Tommy Balogh, Dick Crossman—a most extraordinary unconventional collection of personal advisers whom he plays off one against the other and prefers to use individually and not as a group but still retains despite the strenuous advice of most of the people round him. That's the picture of Harold Wilson I've got after this *Tiger* crisis. I'm more convinced than ever that he'll stay as Prime Minister but I'm also more doubtful than ever whether he's going to lead us anywhere, whether he has any real vision of a future for this country which we in the Labour Party can achieve.

His main aim is to stay in office. That's the real thing and for that purpose he will use almost any trick or gimmick if he can only do it. But I haven't completed the picture unless I add something about another side of him. His natural modesty has remained unchanged. So have his modest tastes, his simple liking of high tea, his completely unaffected petit-bourgeois habits, his determination to avoid any unpleasant scene with his friends or, indeed, with his enemies. All these are another side to him which exists alongside his opportunism and which help to make him a most disappointing leader for a radical left-wing movement. There are plenty of sensible things he wants to do, plenty of reforms he'll be convinced we should carry out, but radical changes are not in his temperament. He will simply shy away from them because he dislikes them.

Monday, December 12th

The day started with a Cabinet Committee on Housing. This is the Committee Harold started when he wasn't content with my housing policy last summer. It's the first he's had for a long time and I looked forward with tremendous interest to see what would happen. I took a look at the papers for it—one on the housing report, one on speeding up public-sector housing and one on the comparative costs of public- and private-sector housing. There was nothing much there but as soon as the meeting got going it was clear the policy I had pursued was going to be changed. My aim had been to increase public-sector housing and to strike a balance of roughly fifty-fifty between public and private in the total target of 500,000. But whenever the private sector sagged, as it had last summer, I had felt myself entitled to fill in by more public-sector housing. Now, though Bob Mellish was faithfully asking for the extra 15,000 to make up for the failure of private building, the P.M. was urging that we must get the private sector on its feet again, get the building

1 Richard Crossman leaving No. 10 with Harold Wilson, on their way to the
House of Commons, November 1966

2 (*above, left*) Signing the consent to nomination form in his Coventry East constituency, March 1966

3 (*below, left*) Handing in his nomination papers, March 1966

4 (*above, right*) At the Labour Party Conference at Brighton, October 1966

5 (*below, right*) Discussion with Harold Wilson at the Conference at Brighton, October 1966

6 With the Soviet Premier, Alexei Kosygin, and Lord Longford, looking round the Houses of Parliament, February 1967

societies campaigning for it and, if necessary, give the builders the bridging finance I had been forced to refuse them. The Chancellor, who was present, was prepared to be generous to them so it was obvious that the two of them had been discussing it beforehand. Between them they made the reason for the change pretty obvious. The Treasury has worked out that under present conditions it's cheaper to have private-sector houses built than public. And, anyway, an increase in house-building will do something to counter deflation and unemployment.[1] It looks as though with Harold's permission Jim will now stimulate the private sector all he can and do nothing to help the public sector. He reckons that in Cabinet he'll be popular and that Barbara Castle and Tony Crosland will rally to his side when he tells them council housing will get less money.

This afternoon I was working quietly in my room at the House when I looked up and saw that it was 3.30 and perhaps I ought to go in. There was nothing much on in the House and I didn't bother. I should have glanced at my printed list to see that a Statement was being made on support costs for British forces in Germany. Actually it caused a minor riot when George Thomson announced the agreement I so much disliked under which the Americans will let us have the equivalent of thirty-five million dollars before 1967 as a substitute for German support costs provided we don't move any troops out until June of next year. Unfortunately, before George Thomson got up Harold and Jim apparently strolled out of the Chamber and gave the impression that they wanted to dissociate themselves from this Statement of our acceptance of aid with strings. I don't think that was their intention at all. George Thomson had insisted on making the Statement because he had negotiated the deal. Nevertheless this was the impression they gave our back-benchers and I heard a great deal about it from Tam a few hours later in the evening.

I had to change for dinner because I was the guest speaker at the annual banquet of the Haifa Technion—one of the four places of higher education in Israel of which the others are the Hebrew University, the Tel Aviv University and Weizmann Institute. I'd been dragged into this by Bob Maxwell, but where was it? Oh yes, at the big new synagogue behind the Cumberland Hotel. Not a very full house but a very grand dinner and I felt I knew very little about the Technion. A miserable brief had been provided by the Foreign Office although the B.B.C. was recording my speech. Fortunately I'd rung up Solly Zuckerman that morning and he'd suggested I talk about desalinization —something the British are very good at. So I got a bit out of him, a bit out of Tony Wedgwood Benn and the rest out of my head and I must admit I got a standing ovation, which showed that my hand had lost none of its cunning as a fund-raiser though I probably hadn't made a Zionist fund-raising speech since 1950.

[1] By the end of the year unemployment had reached 2·4 per cent (564,000) compared with 1·4 per cent in December 1965.

6

Tuesday, December 13th

Cabinet again with Rhodesia the sole item on the agenda. This was a great surprise to me because in our business meeting with Burke on Friday Harold had said he didn't want to have long-term Rhodesia problems discussed. I suppose Bert Bowden insisted. Bert has been against any compromise throughout. He didn't want to go out again and resume talks with the Government. He had been very much against Harold's escapade on the *Tiger*. Now, to judge from his paper, he wanted to break off negotiations and maintain an absolutely uncompromising attitude to Smith. Bert, no doubt, wanted to make sure of full Cabinet support for this no-compromise line. But why did Harold let the meeting be called? Did he really mean to burn all our bridges, or was he still hankering for another round of negotiations? When I put this to him he was very snappy. 'There's no suggestion here,' he said, 'of our demanding unconditional surrender. Of course there's a possibility of a settlement but it must be along the lines of the 1961 constitution.'

The other problem of course is how to implement sanctions. The elaborate plan which George Brown had taken to New York had worked pretty well and the agreement with the Commonwealth leaders had been faithfully kept—so far.[1] Sanctions were being implemented along the moderate line we agreed. But when would our NIBMAR promise to the Commonwealth come into effect? The no-compromisers were prepared to see this through. But Harold was reserving his position and I came to the conclusion that once again he was moving to keep his options open.

After Questions this afternoon Roy Jenkins had to give an explanation about the escape of Frank Mitchell from Dartmoor yesterday.[2] Poor man, he'd spent the previous evening on moving the Criminal Justice Bill and hearing a series of tributes to his grand reformist measure right up till midnight. But providence had suddenly stepped in with the terrible news of the mad axeman's escape and all the stories about how he'd been going out to have drinks in pubs while in working parties. Hogg's Questions weren't easy to answer.

At the Ministerial Committee on Procedure this evening I won a small battle against the Chancellor. It concerned my proposal for taking the Finance Bill upstairs in Committee and relieving the House of the twelve whole days for which, on average, it sits in Committee taking the Bill clause by clause. Jim, like all his predecessors, is against the change, so I got the Committee to ask him to submit in writing the evidence which he wishes to give to the Select Committee on Procedure when it considers the matter. That evidence was before us this evening. It was a ghastly paper made even more reactionary

---

[1] George Brown had flown to New York on December 6th to ask the U.N. for mandatory sanctions against the illegal regime.

[2] Frank Mitchell had escaped from Dartmoor where he was serving a life sentence for murder.

by a covering note saying that the demand was anyway not very serious since
it came from only a few Members who were speaking in ignorance. I was in
the chair and let Tony Crosland and Tony Benn express their sense of outrage. Roy Jenkins would have been there as well if he hadn't had his own
troubles. The Committee gave hell to poor John Diamond who tried to
present the paper. He was told that the evidence, if it is to be given at all,
must be official Treasury evidence for which Ministers take no kind of
responsibility. So this reform, which would make an enormous difference
to the life of the Commons each summer, is still a possibility. I still have a
few friends who believe in parliamentary reform.

I gave dinner that evening to John Gunter and his beautiful wife, Jane.[1]
I'd been terribly shocked two or three days before to see him in the lobby—
old, with his flesh falling in like an old bull who's lost his fatness and whose
skin is wrinkling round his neck. And at dinner I found the old boy, who'd
once had such a superb memory, failing to follow a political story. It was
painful and the presence of Bob Maxwell made it more so.

I was just going home to get a decent night before my big procedure debate
when John Silkin came to me with the appalling story that there'd been a
wave of feeling going through the tea-room against morning sittings. He
gathered it was stimulated by people like Ted Short and Manny Shinwell
who were saying that morning sittings on a Monday were an outrage that
must be voted down. I became really alarmed that in tomorrow's vote we
would have the same situation as we had on televising proceedings and that
would finish me as Leader of the House. But John reassured me. He told me
all the Whips were out at work and it was a very different situation. 'I can
guarantee you a majority not more than twenty.' My God, I thought, a
majority of twenty with the Whips on. That's almost equivalent to defeat.
I insisted on seeing Harold. 'Harold,' he said, 'has got a lot of those young
people there with him.' So we went into his room to try to get him to talk
to us and there I found a group of young back-benchers sitting round him,
among them Joan Lestor and Alex Lyon. They'd been having a long discussion with the P.M.—one of the regular long discussions Harold is holding
with back-benchers—over brandy and whisky. I soon found it was no good
talking about procedure because they'd started with that and had told the
Prime Minister they were all against morning sittings and that they were
inclined to abstain on the vote next day. So I had to sit there from 11.30 to
1 a.m. watching Harold handle his weekly meeting with newcomers. He did
it very well indeed. There was a long talk about the difference between the
parliamentary vintages—the intake of 1964, for example, and 1966. At one
point Harold told them, 'Well, the really big difference is that for you the
moral issues are all-important and that's why you were all so terribly anxious

[1] John Gunter wrote for the *Chicago Daily News* 1922–36, until he resigned to devote
himself to writing books, notably the *Inside* series, of which perhaps the best known is
Inside Europe Today (London: Hamish Hamilton, 1962).

about Rhodesia. You all see it as a moral issue.' And I thought to myself, my God, I suppose they do and that's what differentiates them from me, because I see Rhodesia not as a simple moral issue but as a choice between a greater and a lesser evil.

After that I tottered home and fell into bed.

Wednesday, December 14th

I woke up early with a sudden realization that the whole of the last section of my procedure speech was quite wrong. I had made it an argument that morning sittings were indeed the thin end of the wedge of a major, modernized reform leading to a brand new House of Commons. Douglas Houghton had warned me that there'd be protests about this and I suddenly realized it was a tremendous bloomer. So early this morning in bed I recast the whole thing. Then I rang up Harold and said I hadn't been able to talk to him last night. I had cold feet about a majority of twenty. 'Well, for God's sake, let's get the Chief Whip to muster the Government troops,' he said. And after that John really got to work and each of the hundred members of the Government got two separate messages—one from his P.P.S. and one from his Private Office telling him to ring back and personally confirm that he would be there to vote for the Cabinet decisions on procedure. Sure enough, this evening we'd never had such a turn out of the political bigwigs—they were all there and our majority was eighty-seven, largely due to Harold's last-minute orders.[1]

I'd hoped to have the morning to finalize the speech and get the new peroration on paper. But this morning Harold kept me from 9.45 to 10.30 with a long fascinating gossip. First of all it's quite clear now that the possibility of devaluation this spring has altogether disappeared as the result of the improvement in the trade and unemployment figures. He's now convinced that the export drive is coming without the devaluation which Tommy had assured him was the only basis for improvement, and this has cheered him up. Then he had a long frank discussion with me about the reshuffle. I said there were two of his old friends who would have to go. He replied, 'It's not so easy. I can't trust the rest of the Cabinet and those two provide me with two important votes.' I said, 'But on really important issues you take the voices and not the votes. You only make us vote on unimportant issues and usually these two are in Fiji or somewhere on the other side of the world.' But then Harold went back to last July and said that when he was away in Moscow he had the Right against him and very nearly the Left as well. I replied, 'If you mean there are occasions when the whole Cabinet tells you not to do something or to do something—last July was an example—you can't avoid that by any Cabinet reshuffle.' It was interesting but we didn't get very far. Anyway my speech still has to be finished.

I left his room when I was summoned suddenly to the Party meeting, where

[1] The vote was 264 to 177.

I found Michael Foot in the middle of a great philippic denouncing the Government for signing an unconditional surrender to the Americans about keeping our troops in Germany. I had to sit listening to this for an hour and a half. Afterwards I protested to Manny and found that he had put the item on the agenda without consulting anybody and that when I was away with Harold Manny had got up and abused the Ministers for not being present; when the Chief had tried to protest he had slapped him down as well. This is serious. For some weeks I've been having trouble with Manny. He's suddenly grown old and very difficult. Of course it's true that John and I have been running the Party meetings and John has been running the Party, and Manny hasn't liked it. On this occasion he just took the law into his own hands because he deliberately wanted a good row about Germany. It will get us a terrible press tomorrow about another Labour Party revolt.

It was now one o'clock and I'd missed my two hours' of preparation. I had a desperate time sorting out my speech and getting it typed before I had to go and answer Questions and sit through a Statement on civil defence by Roy Jenkins and a Ten-Minute Rule Bill on Slagheaps. Then I was up and making my big speech. It was carefully calculated. In the long first part I described the utter futility of the modern House, which had lost its main function of controlling the Executive and which must reshape itself and redefine its functions if it ever wanted to be anything again. After that there was a deliberate anti-climax when I put forward my mousy little proposals for Specialist Committees, morning meetings, Standing Order No. 9, etc. Selwyn Lloyd, who followed me, was extremely amusing and didn't do any irreparable harm. Then we had George Strauss and Irvine and Michael English from our side beating about the great traditions of Parliament and also doing not much harm.[1] I had to go out to the liaison committee where there was a flaming row between Manny, John Silkin and me about the morning's events, particularly about Manny's attack on me for not being there. Then I gave Anne, who'd been listening to the debate, a quick dinner and got back in time for the winding-up speeches. Thank heavens, Douglas Houghton was magnificent. He had to speak for exactly twenty-five minutes because we couldn't have the closure on procedural recommendations and he had to sit down exactly at ten for the Speaker to put our ten resolutions. Everything went well. The majority was eighty-seven and I felt we'd had a thoroughly successful day. But I also had an uneasy feeling that Harold Wilson hadn't liked it. He'd sat beside me while I made my speech and when it was over he had gone out. This feeling was confirmed by Tony Crosland. He leant across and said, 'Well, before anybody else tells you something different, that was a magnificent speech.' I was sure it was one of the best speeches I'd made and I also knew it was a great shock to Harold Wilson.

[1] Sir Arthur Irvine, Labour M.P. for Edgehill since 1947; he was Solicitor-General 1967–70. Michael English, Labour M.P. for Nottingham since 1964.

Thursday, December 15th

My birthday opened cheerfully. I found that *The Times* political correspondent had written an amusing and complimentary description of Dr
Crossman and his diagnosis of the parliamentary disease. Despite everything
I got pretty good reviews in the papers for what was obviously a remarkable
speech. As for missing any chance of appearing on *24 Hours* or any other
television programmes the night before—well that's something you've got to
accept as Lord President because you have no Press Officer to organize it
and no departmental pressure to apply.

By the time I saw the P.M. at 11.45 the row with Manny was really boiling
up. George Wigg was clearly working with Manny and he had talked at
length with the Chief Whip and then with the Prime Minister for more than
an hour. Manny had sent Harold a long letter. The Chief was standing
absolutely firm and refused to have any nonsense from Manny. He made it
clear that he wants to get rid of him and he probably will. When I went in,
the P.M. looked up and said to me, 'A great many people think you made a
very good speech indeed yesterday, Dick.' I knew what this meant. Despite
the fact that personally he'd been shocked he recognized that I'd taken a big
risk and for the second time I had brought it off. I'd repeated the success of
my speech on local government reform at Torquay when I told the A.M.C.
that the local authorities were antediluvian monsters.[1] This risk had come off
since the speech, though revolutionary, had been approved. Now my revolutionary reform speech had been accepted by the House so the degree of
radical change I thought possible would now be acceptable to Harold. So
at once I poured out my ideas and described to the P.M. how I wanted to
link House of Commons' reform with Lords' reform. What we wanted was an
overall reform of the whole of Parliament. Then we got on to the question
of what would be the right Ministerial Committee. Harold suggested the
Lord Chancellor, the Lord President, two Chief Whips, Roy Jenkins and
Tony Crosland, and I told him we must get the right official committee as
well. Then he warmed to it and said, 'Burke Trend must have a unit under
Miss Nunne if a proper job is to be done,' and I said that would fit in very
well. This was the most constructive meeting I've ever had with Harold.
I got it because I'd won the night before.

Back in my office I dictated a memo to Burke Trend recording my discussion with the P.M. and planning a meeting for tomorrow. I had lunch
—my birthday lunch with Anne—at Prunier. There we found Frankie and
Jack Donaldson lunching with Harold Hobson of the *Sunday Times* in
preparation for the first night of the revival of *On Approval*, her father's
famous play.[2] I had to be back in time for the P.M.'s Questions. While I was

[1] In August 1966. See Vol. I, p. 622.

[2] Lady Donaldson, daughter of the playwright Frederick Lonsdale, and herself author of
The Marconi Scandal (London: Hart-Davis, 1962) and *Edward VIII* (London: Weidenfeld
& Nicolson, 1973). Her husband, Lord Donaldson of Kingsbridge, a former farmer, had
been made a life peer in 1967.

sitting beside him I tried to pop a question about George Weidenfeld, who'd been terribly anxious to have his appointment announced. I whispered to Harold that I wanted to tell the press that he was now my publicity adviser. I hoped he would just slip me an easy answer, but immediately he stiffened. 'No,' he said, 'we mustn't do that.' 'Make it easy for me,' I said. 'No, no. Let's get some solid homework out of him first.' So that was that.

We had our last P.L.P. meeting before Christmas. I had lost my voice by then so I just announced the post-Christmas campaign where I wanted M.P.s to volunteer to work in constituencies. The P.M. turned up, as he always does at these Party meetings, and he sat there quietly until I whispered that he should say a word. Whereupon he not only said a word of Christmas greeting but made a longish speech clearly revealing to anyone who understood that the shadow of devaluation had lifted from him and that he could look forward to 1970. I left him and rushed home to change into a dinner jacket to go to Covent Garden for *Benvenuto Cellini*. My cold had been coming on and by eight o'clock it was terrible. I was so somnolent that I fear Anne is right and I did snore through a large part of the performance before I tottered to bed.

Friday, December 16th
I had to go down to Wood Green to take part in a big B.B.C. programme on the future of Parliament, which they will show in January. Selwyn Lloyd and Jo Grimond[1] were the other two.

I took Janet down with me and while Grimond was doing his piece I was able to dictate two extracts from my speech for press release on Saturday and Sunday. Afterwards we had lunch with Selwyn Lloyd who told me how he ceased to be a Liberal in 1931 and switched over to the Conservative side, joined Monty's[2] headquarters and became a Tory—not all that convinced a Tory—by 1945.

He has got a new lease of life. He's now happy, light-hearted, enjoying life on the back benches and, I would say, having a healthy influence there as well. I said, 'How you have changed, Selwyn!' He said, 'Well, there is nothing like being kicked out of your job (especially if you get a job too early, as I did in the Foreign Office) to make a man of you.'[3]

In the afternoon Burke Trend came into my office to discuss the note I had sent him about my talk with Harold. He agreed to build up a unit in the Cabinet Office. He likes my idea for planning legislation over the next four years, he also likes the idea of a constitutional reform for the whole of Parliament and he sees that it is going to strengthen the Executive as well as strengthening the Specialist Committees. He's a strange character—a nanny-

[1] Jo Grimond, Liberal M.P. for Orkney and Shetland since 1950, leader of the Liberal Party 1956-67 and temporarily for part of 1976.
[2] Field-Marshal Viscount Montgomery of Alamein.
[3] He became a Minister of State at the Foreign Office in October 1951, four years after entering Parliament.

like, very able, very sweet, very shy man. He strengthens Harold in all his most establishment tentativeness, making him on the whole less abrasive and less radical. On most things he's the opposite extreme to me in his influence on Harold.

Saturday, December 17th

I had planned to have two days of intense Party activity on the north-east coast and got to Sunderland on Friday evening. Instead of putting me in a hotel on their beautiful riviera—a lovely piece of sea coast—I was stuck on the other side of the bay right behind the shipyards in a very dim hotel. After breakfast I took a walk down through an enormous new housing estate —a mixture of tower blocks and low-rise housing—and got my feet terribly dirty walking on the mud on the front by the Gulf petrol tanks. It was a beautiful sunny morning with a fresh breeze and I was just thinking how ghastly the place was when a man came rushing up and said, 'It is you, Mr Crossman? I saw you coming and it would make my morning to be able to speak to you. How are you?' I greeted him and asked him almost without thinking, 'How do you feel living here?' 'Oh, marvellous, Mr Crossman. I and my friends find this perfect after where we were living before.' This taught me a lesson about my superiority. No doubt for the people in Sunderland this new housing estate I found so ghastly is wonderful. And yet at dinner on the night before I'd felt very critical of Karl Cohen, the Leader of the Labour Group. I thought him uninspired and condemned him for putting up thousands of boxes called houses. People may well like it—that's something I have to bear in mind.

Monday, December 19th

Today started with an enormously important early morning for me— Legislation and Future Legislation Committees. Here was my first chance as Leader of the House to tell my colleagues some of my ideas about planning and organizing the legislative timetable. I'd discovered by now that the method of filling the legislative programme was hopelessly unsatisfactory. It just gets itself filled up by Departments listing the things they want to do and fighting to get the maximum time for each. There is no Government plan for a balanced policy. I had to try to introduce one. So there I was in the Cabinet Committee Room in the chair with the Lord Chancellor sitting on my left, grouped round me a few senior Ministers like Roy Jenkins or Barbara Castle who really had something to fight for that morning and then a host of junior Ministers who'd been sent there to join the queue and make the right noise at the right moment. My carefully prepared plans were knocked to pieces in the first moment when I heard that the Prime Minister had a crucial meeting in half an hour's time and that therefore various Ministers had to leave at 9.40. I started off by reviewing the Session's legislative programme. It had already been announced that the Home Secretary would have a second major Bill this Session which was to deal with the extraordinary consequences of Rab Butler's measures for legalizing gambling.[1] This has turned London into the gambling headquarters of the world and Roy insists that we must act to control the activities of this vast and dangerous new industry. There were noises of protest round the table as the Home Office had only just had the major Criminal Justice Bill, but I told them that the Government decision had been announced weeks ago and so the Committee's decision was a mere formality.

Next came the Minister of Aviation, Mr Mulley, who had put in a request for urgent legislation on sonic bangs. His excuse was that the Attorney-General had ruled that without legislation we wouldn't be allowed to test the sonic-bang effect of Concorde over Hull as we had intended to.[2] He said this with great solemnity and emphasized the risks if his request was turned down. I told him I was prepared to take this risk and that there was not time for his Bill. That was that.*

One Bill I was concerned to push forward was Leasehold Reform. The Chief and I had been constantly asking what had happened to this measure and I was amazed to hear from Tony Greenwood that it couldn't be ready for the date we had already booked for its Second Reading—February 7th. 'What is the lastest news?' I asked, and I heard that the Minister would like it squeezed in at the end of March just before the Easter recess. 'Impossible,' I replied. 'There's the Defence White Paper then and all the days are booked with defence business. You must keep to our timetable or lose your Bill.' I then harangued the Committee and tried to make them realize that I was going to get the House up at the end of July and not let it drag on into August and upset the holiday plans of the younger Members. The only concession I made was to Fred Mulley. Having smashed down his sonic bangs I said that Cabinet might be able to find time for his Bill to enable the Government to take equity shares in a new airframe firm. That was the only addition I allowed to the programme.

I then began to outline my new approach to further legislation right up to the election in 1969/70. I suggested that we should all do our homework in a rather different way. Instead of each Minister trying to get as many of his Bills into the Session ahead, we should work backwards from the election. The first question to be asked in planning the programme is what we want to see in the election manifesto, i.e. what promises we want to make. The second question is what measures would be suitable for White Papers or

* A day or two later I mentioned it to the Attorney-General and he looked a bit surprised. It was simply an invention by the Minister of Aviation. He said that according to the Lord Chancellor, 'what they really want is a Bill to say that the Government will not be responsible for broken window-panes!'

[1] R. A. Butler, Conservative M.P. for Saffron Walden from 1929 until 1965, when he became a life peer and Master of Trinity College, Cambridge. He was Home Secretary 1957–62.

[2] The supersonic aircraft being built in a joint project by Britain and France.

6*

even for draft Bills to be published in the year before the election but which wouldn't become law. And then having got this part of our election programme prepared we should ask ourselves the third question: what measures do we have to put on the statute book because they must go into operation straightaway? At least this succeeded in silencing the usual time-wasting listing of demands by each Minister present. They promised to go away and submit papers along the lines I suggested.

This afternoon there was an important meeting of O.P.D. Though the story is complicated, the situation was so piquant that it's worth telling. As a late-comer to O.P.D. I came into this half-way through. The P-1127 was a plane the Tories had scrapped but which Healey had resurrected last February. And Cabinet had agreed that its cost should be carried outside the normal defence budget because it was a particularly good plane and because it was impossible to go on developing planes and cancelling them half-way through as we had done with the TSR2.[1] Now Healey came to tell us that we were in a dilemma. Either we had to accept the P-1127 firmly, in which case it couldn't be contained within the defence budget in 1968, 1969 or 1970 without cutting items of much higher priority, or it ought to be scrapped straightaway. He himself recommended immediate cancellation.

Now, of course, he was supported very strongly—on purely economic grounds—by the First Secretary and also by the Chancellor. They both said that if the Minister of Defence himself didn't want the plane for military reasons they couldn't see any good economic reason for keeping it outside the defence budget or for preventing us from getting the defence budget down below the agreed ceiling. I took the same view and the argument went on and on until the P.M. said, 'Do you want this to go to Cabinet?' and made it clear that if it went to Cabinet he would back Mulley, Jenkins, George Wigg and Jay who wanted to keep the plane.

I think Harold's motives were mainly political. He himself had publicly praised the plane very highly indeed and Healey had quite gratuitously pledged in the House that we were not going to cancel it. So cancellation would require both the P.M. and the Minister of Defence to eat a lot of humble pie. Harold didn't feel inclined to do so. But why was Healey taking this extraordinary line? I suspect that it was a carefully calculated device. Having advocated cancellation, what he wanted was to get himself overruled by O.P.D. or, as a last resort, by Cabinet. In that way he would be able to go on carrying the plane at a cost of £130 million over ten years *above* his proper defence budget.

I moved from committee to committee today. A few minutes later I was back on the other side of the House of Commons chairing the Services

[1] Denis Healey had announced in the February Defence White Paper that the projected aircraft carrier CVA-01 was to be abandoned, that fifty F-111 aircraft were to be purchased from the U.S.A. and that the British P-1154 strike aircraft had been dropped in favour of a combination of the American Phantom and the British VTOL P-1127. The TSR2 was scrapped in April 1965. See Vol. I, pp. 191–4.

Committee. We'd received a really searing report from the Treasury O & M on the inefficiency of our kitchens. Already in 1961 an outside consultant had listed all the things that were wrong. But now, five years later, nothing had been done. Nothing apparently was properly costed—indeed it was possible that the splendid banquets on Friday evening, which are supposed to make so much money, are really running at a loss. I proposed that we should have a special meeting in January to decide what action to take. We also had a report from our sub-committee on the new parliamentary building which it was proposed to put on the other side of Bridge Street. In the sub-committee's view this is a hopeless place to put it. If it was just an office for office staff it would be quite all right. But what was proposed was to transfer not only the Members' work-rooms but the restaurants to the other side of the street to leave more room for library facilities in the heart of the building. So we might well have a division where four hundred M.P.s were dining over the other side of Bridge Street and trying to fight their way down in the lifts back into the Chamber. The sub-committee, I think quite rightly, had come to the conclusion that, the Chamber being the heart of Parliament, Members' real lives can't be led on the other side of the road. What can be moved to the other side is administration, which is not an essential part of the parliamentary organism. So they recommended that we should now look at one other possibility—finding space for the office accommodation each Member must have either within the present Palace of Westminster or possibly in a building between the Victoria Tower and Lambeth Bridge. Of course that would mean invading the House of Lords, but I promised that I would spend a morning in the first fortnight of January looking round the geography and discussing the problem with Lord Gardiner and Lord Shepherd.

By now I was late for the Christmas party in my Privy Council Office for our Party officials in the Commons, for all our Whips in both Houses and the four Treasury officials who sit about in the inner lobby and do the job of marking up our records, keeping our pairs, etc. All these in addition, of course, to Freddie Warren and his staff and Freddy Ward. It was a new kind of gathering and the thirty or forty people quite enjoyed meeting each other. I think I'm just beginning to thaw out the Whips' suspicion of me.

Back in a hurry to the Chamber because the Second Reading of the Sexual Offences (No. 2) Bill was going to take place with a two-hour extension. Some of our Whips, headed by George Lawson and Walter Harrison,[1] were determined not to miss the chance of being violently partisan. Like a lot of our northern Members Lawson is passionately opposed to this Bill, much more so than those of us who come from the Midlands and the South. He and several other Whips objected fiercely that it was turning our

[1] George Lawson, Labour M.P. for Motherwell April 1954–74, was a Government Whip 1964–6 and Deputy Chief Government Whip 1966–7. Walter Harrison, Labour M.P. for Wakefield since 1964, was an Assistant Whip 1966–70, Deputy Chief Opposition Whip 1970–74 and, since 1974, has been a Government Whip.

own working-class support against us. I kept poking my nose into the Chamber throughout the evening. John and I, who strongly favour the Bill, had given the two extra hours in order to see that the vote was taken at midnight because we assumed that the people who stayed would be people in favour and not against. Every time I looked in I realized what a stalemate we had reached in the argument. It was quite clear that nobody could think of anything new to say after two debates in the Lords and another in the Commons. Indeed I was asked whether the free vote shouldn't be taken early. I said, 'No, we've got the Ministers whipped to come in to this free vote at 11.30. We should try and keep the debate running till then.' I was sitting in my room when I suddenly looked up and saw on the announcer that we were on the adjournment. The Bill had really run out of speakers by 11 o'clock whereupon an amendment on the application of the Bill to the Merchant Marine had been called and because the Home Secretary had satisfied the movers on this particular point the amendment was not opposed, whereupon the main Bill went through on a technicality. John Silkin pointed out that since nobody had voted against the Bill, when the Standing Committee is formed it should have nobody on it but those in favour. However, that won't actually happen.

Tuesday, December 20th
Cabinet. The most interesting item on the agenda was the future of *The Times*. The Government had already considered the proposal that *The Times* should be bought up by the *Sunday Times* and that one single managing director should control both. Because it gives the Thomson Press astonishing powers this proposal has been submitted to the Monopolies Commission and this morning Douglas Jay was to report to Cabinet. He told us that the Monopolies Commission was going to recommend acceptance.[1] Only Brian Davidson[2] is saying he wants more explicit assurances from the Thomson Press that they would respect the independence of *The Times* and above all that they would not integrate it in any way with the *Sunday Times*. Here was an interesting example of how Cabinet Government works. The future of *The Times* is a major issue of free speech yet we never discussed the issue in principle. It went automatically to the President of the Board of Trade who automatically sent it to the Monopolies Commission and then made his personal report to Cabinet. Government has really played no part whatsoever.

The next item was the pay of service doctors and dentists. There are only a few hundred of them but Denis Healey insisted that he must give his service doctors and dentists an $18\frac{1}{2}$ per cent increase straightaway whereas the rest

---

[1] Lord Thomson, a seventy-two-year-old Canadian newspaper and television proprietor, who had been made a life peer in 1964, had bought *The Times*, subject to the approval of the Monopolies Commission, on September 30th. The *Sunday Times* now had a circulation of $1\frac{1}{3}$ million.

[2] A solicitor (since 1969 with the Gas Council) and a member of the Monopolies Commission 1954–68.

of the Prices and Incomes Ministerial Committee said this would make nonsense of the whole policy and the most they should get was 10 per cent. Denis of course knew he couldn't possibly win and I've no doubt his intention was to be able to tell the services that he'd tried hard and been overruled. But it seemed I wasn't the only Minister who thought this was an abuse of Cabinet government. Why should we waste our time formally overriding the Minister of Defence just because he wants to popularize himself with the services? I'm glad that the P.M.'s now given an instruction that no Cabinet Minister can have an item put on the agenda unless the Minister personally vouches for the need to have it discussed in full Cabinet.

At last we came to the main issue of the morning, and a major issue of social policy—family endowment. The problem started months ago when the Chancellor proposed to PESC a whole series of savage cuts in the social services. Some of us had replied that we couldn't consider the proposal for cutting free milk and doubling the cost of school meals unless it was put forward in connection with proposals for revising our policies on family endowment, i.e. for increasing family allowances and changing our tax allowances for children. At first Jim said he would not be dictated to and that budget secrecy forbade him from even discussing the issue with his colleagues. But week by week he's gradually been withdrawing and he now admits the need for considering the two together. Indeed, he himself has proposed that a means-tested scheme of allowances should be introduced next spring for the 165,000 families in acutest need. This aroused passionate opposition from Douglas Houghton, Peggy Herbison and myself. We pointed out that the Callaghan scheme would be tantamount to subsidizing the lowest wages out of the taxpayers' money. With the Cabinet so divided it was finally decided that Douglas Houghton, as overlord of the social services, and the Chancellor should produce a joint paper. It was this joint paper we were considering at Cabinet. It was a typical production whose preparation I had watched through the eyes of Tommy Balogh, who had acted as the adviser from Harold's Office throughout the negotiations.

Jim introduced it with a very powerful speech, passionately in favour of the means-tested scheme and of concentrating our limited resources on those in need. So he has wholly adopted the Conservative policy of selective social security outlined by Heath before the 1966 election. His only really effective argument against the claw-back proposals of Titmuss and Nicky Kaldor is that it would involve taxing men in order to pay more to their wives and taxing better-off people with families in order to pay for worse-off people with families. That was an *ad hominem* argument which obviously impressed some of my colleagues. Peggy Herbison made a dignified reply. She'd done an excellent special paper for this meeting and was allowed into the Cabinet Room just for this single item on the agenda. I saw her look desperately round the table and then notice a seat just by the window but behind the Cabinet circle. It was only when I insisted that she should be brought to the table that she got there. What a terrible disadvantage it is to be a non-Cabinet Minister. You sit outside the door for an hour or two and then the rest just go on talking while you are seated outside the charmed circle. Still, she did extremely well.

In the discussion which followed most of the Cabinet supported Peggy. The Chancellor's only votes were gained from those who shared his male views and in particular objected to taking away money from middle-class families by tampering with their children's tax allowances. Of course on this Douglas Jay was speaking for his wife, Peggy,[1] who'd already told me what a scandal the Kaldor–Titmuss proposals were. If you are going to pay for improved family allowances out of the reduced tax allowances of the middle classes, she says, you are doing something not only unpopular but unfair. I was not surprised that this was picked up by the First Secretary. But I was amazed to hear the Prime Minister say that he hadn't realized the point involved. Tommy Balogh and I had certainly put it to him. The whole idea of the claw-back scheme was to finance an increase of family allowances largely out of general taxation but partly out of a device which made sure that those who paid income tax at the full scale got no benefit from it. The debate petered out at this point. A great majority of Cabinet had committed themselves to the Kaldor–Titmuss ideas and that was a great achievement. We agreed we should have a White Paper but only after a firm Cabinet decision had been taken in the New Year.

In the Commons this afternoon I expected to have a busy and anxious time since we had put down the motion for the Christmas adjournment of the House to take place at 3.30. What we hadn't foreseen when we did it was that at 3.30 the P.M. would make a momentous announcement on Rhodesia. Since the U.N. had finally approved sanctions we had to implement the Commonwealth Conference communiqué, withdraw all previous offers from Smith—including the *Tiger* offer—and announce that from now on our policy was No Independence before Majority Rule. Harold got up and was in his best form. His declaration was clear-cut and dramatic and it should have produced a storm from the Opposition as well as a prolonged debate on the adjournment. Indeed, Harold was so certain this would happen that in Cabinet this morning he proposed that Bert Bowden should be ready to speak in reply to Heath's attack. I said this was wrong and that if Heath spoke the Lord President should reply to his comments on Rhodesia just as he would have to reply to the comments on Vietnam bombing, German occupation costs and all the other subjects which would be raised on the adjournment. I got my way on this point because I was right on procedure, but Harold didn't like it. When it came to the point nothing happened. There was no blaze-up at Question Time and our Christmas adjournment debate was as much of a formality as ever I remember. I was greatly relieved

---

[1] A Labour councillor on Camden borough council; her marriage to Douglas Jay was dissolved in 1972.

since it would have been quite a responsibility to wind up that debate if the Tories had made it into a great occasion.

So with that fire unexpectedly extinguished I was able to go to the Christmas party given by the Labour peers. As I walked in I saw, sitting on the left, the ghastly living corpse of Attlee, now virtually stone deaf and almost inarticulate.[1] Patricia Llewelyn-Davies said to me, 'Do go and talk to the old man. He wants company.' I had to say to her, 'I'm sorry, I can't face it. He has always hated me and I now hate him.' I'm afraid I walked the other way. The peers are an interesting lot of people, a much more attractive gathering these days than the Labour commoners, and I shan't be the least sorry if I'm made a Labour peer on retirement because the House of Lords is the best club in Europe whereas the House of Commons is one of the worst.

I came back from the Lords and stayed on in the Commons until business was finished at two in the morning. Most of the time I was in the tea-room with John Silkin. The Secretary of State for Scotland and various Whips and other personalities came in and there was some satisfaction in their knowing that the new Lord President had kept his word that he would always be there to the end of every debate. So far I have been.

Wednesday, December 21st
The last morning prayers before the recess. This mostly consisted of Harold thanking John and me for what we'd done for him in the Parliamentary Party. I think he's genuinely appreciative of our efforts to change the atmosphere and to destroy the old war between the trade-union praetorian guard and the left-wing rebels. I think he feels that we have transformed the atmosphere and averted what could have been a catastrophic split on prices and incomes policy.

Next, to Buckingham Palace for a Privy Council. In my private audience beforehand I talked to the Queen about her royal television appearances and the proposal which the I.T.V. and B.B.C. have made to the Postmaster-General that they should alternate in future in presenting her Christmas broadcasts and the Opening of Parliament. This was a very good thing to put to her but I'm afraid I rather fluffed it at the beginning by talking about simultaneous cameras. She said she didn't want simultaneous cameras. I then said, 'Well, do you want the B.B.C. and I.T.V. to alternate?' She answered, 'It would be selfish of me not to allow this.' Plucking up my courage, I said 'It's not a question of selfishness, Ma'am; you must do exactly what you want. That's what we would like you to do.' At this point she revealed that she would much prefer to keep the B.B.C. camera team she had got to know so well. She didn't want to face a new team from I.T.V. Then she mentioned a live broadcast which was said to be being prepared for

---

[1] Clement Attlee, leader of the Labour Party from 1935 to 1955, when he retired to the House of Lords with an earldom. He was Prime Minister 1945–51 and Leader of the Opposition 1951–5. He died in 1967.

the States. 'I don't know why I should broadcast live to the States,' she said to me. 'The Prime Minister was telling me the other day how he fluffed something and it was only all right because he was doing it at rehearsal before the live show.' And I said again, 'For heaven's sake, don't do anything you don't want. You must do exactly what you feel like. That's what the B.B.C. and I.T.V. want you to do.' Though I'd not been very clear, I felt for the first time that I might be doing something useful for her. We had a most pleasant time for a minute or two while the Ministers outside were wondering what on earth was going on because the private audience lasted for six minutes. When I came out I told Michael Adeane and drafted a note for Godfrey Agnew and I expect that's the last we shall hear of that proposal from I.T.V.

This afternoon Solly Zuckerman put his head round the door and said he must have a word. In he came and warned me that I really must take a sensible view about the P-1127. I told him I was perfectly content that it should be kept in the programme provided the ceiling was kept down to the agreed figure. It was up to the defence people to decide what they spent their budget on. What I was determined to prevent was the P-1127 being paid for as an addition to the maximum defence programme which I thought we could afford. Of course, Solly had been sent from No. 10 to try to seduce me, which proves once again that Harold's choice of people is sometimes very extraordinary.

I had promised Marcia that I would pick up Harold and take him to the Transport House party. When I arrived at No. 10 I was wafted upstairs and taken to the far side of the house where Harold was eating celery and cheese and biscuits and tidying up with Marcia in a frantic last-minute session. I almost physically pulled him out. We drove round to Smith Square in my car. In the big room where the party was being held we found a few junior officials and their wives but all the seniors seemed to be out—not even Percy Clark or Terry Pitt was there, let alone Len Williams. So we did our duty, spent fifteen minutes drifting round and Harold agreed it was a good thing we'd clocked in. Then I dropped him back at No. 10. He was flustered and hurried and I was flustered and hurried. I suspected he dreaded my coming in and trying to lobby him about the Cabinet shuffle which is bound to come after Christmas. So we said goodbye and that was that.

Thursday, December 22nd
One more Cabinet at 9.30 to deal with only two issues—the P-1127 and a new top-secret crisis in the motor-car industry. I was curious about the P-1127 because on the way to Transport House Harold had said to me, 'It will be all settled. I've done a deal with the Chancellor. Healey's going to get his £130 million cut.' Later that evening I'd run into Callaghan and he said, 'Yes, he's an artful bugger. Of course I've got no solid assurances out of him but there'll be no fight tomorrow.'

And there wasn't. The proceedings started with Denis Healey, who'd obviously been brainwashed by Harold, making the astonishing statement that as Minister of Defence he had brought the issue to Cabinet and as a member of Cabinet he now advised us not to accept the advice of the Minister of Defence. This confirmed my suspicions that he had recommended cancellation not because he wanted the aircraft cancelled but in order to be instructed to produce it without paying for it. So we went through all the formalities once more: Wedgy Benn in support, Michael Stewart against, Callaghan against, and I said again, 'I'm not against the P-1127: I'd rather have it than six battalions of troops in Malaya. But I'm not going to see defence spending pushed above the ceiling.' After all this, Cabinet agreed that the cancellation would not take place and that it was still an extra outside the defence budget. As usual Harold had got his way.

We then turned to the secret item which explained why some Ministers had been ripped out of my Legislation Committee on Monday. Rootes had been losing a million pounds a year and Chrysler had now announced that it was willing to buy the firm lock, stock and barrel. An effort had been made by B.M.C. and Leyland to get together and make a counter-bid but it was not forthcoming and Cabinet was told that the Chrysler offer had to be accepted. The thing was all tied up and it was left to Cabinet to congratulate Wedgy Benn on imposing such powerful terms on Chrysler.[1]

My last job today was to talk with Tony Greenwood and Peter Brown about the publicity of the housing Ministries—the first action I've taken in my new job of co-ordinating the information services. Peter Brown couldn't have been more helpful and I took him off after the talks to lunch with me and Freddy Ward. We ate and drank well, remembering old and happier times and from there I went back to the Privy Council Office at No. 70 Whitehall, tidied up, got my Christmas cards off, had my hair cut, got back to No. 70 in time to have a drink at the office party and caught the 7.10 home to Banbury. The Christmas holidays had begun.

[1] In July the British Motor Corporation had merged with Jaguar to form British Motor Holdings, with three major divisions, B.M.C., Jaguar and Pressed-Steel Fisher. Chrysler was an American company that already owned a large share of Rootes.

1967

1961

Sunday, January 1st

This is the first proper day of my holiday because up till now there have been Christmas festivities to organize and I have had to take my share. It's been a pretty full time and a great success for the children. We have had some beautiful cloudless brilliant days and starry moony nights and some rain and mist muddled up with it. But now at last it's early in the morning and I've got nothing to do before this evening when we have Upper Prescote and the vicarage to supper. I've got the whole day from breakfast through lunch till after tea to reflect and relax. I've started too late—there's the bell for breakfast. I will come back when breakfast is over.

As always happens in life at Prescote one says one is just going to do something after breakfast and one doesn't. We've had another perfect day of brilliant sunshine, white clouds and a nip in the air. I had a splendid walk after breakfast with Pritchett up to White Barn and over the farm. Then I came back to give lunch to the schoolmistress, Miss Samuels, and then I took a walk down to the village to take her back to the schoolhouse. It's now nearly tea-time and the children are looking at Billy Smart's Circus on television and I can get back to the reflections I want to make about the year 1966.

I start with the weeklies. One of them, reflecting on 1966, called it Harold Wilson's 'make-or-break year'. I don't find that misleading. I believe it was a make-or-break year and that the July measures were 'make' measures. I'm convinced that the total squeeze and freeze has even been a success with the general public because it's the first thing we've done that has really been understood. If only we carry on and create a permanent prices and incomes policy for the period after Part IV our success may start from here.

Apart from the July measures I can't deny the Government has settled down into a very conventional rut. We are indeed a very dull Government. Our most deeply conventional aspect is the Bevinite character of the foreign policy which Harold Wilson, Michael Stewart, James Callaghan and George Brown between them have worked out during the last two years. I suppose the personal reliance on L.B.J. could be described as a peculiarly Wilsonian touch and I very much fear that he and James Callaghan between them have committed us more deeply than any of their predecessors to the Americans. I'm fairly close to Harold now yet I have no idea how far he has committed the Government. I'm pretty sure that when he was Shadow Foreign Secretary he made his first pledges to Kennedy about our policy East of Suez. I've every reason to believe that since he's been P.M. the assurance that we shall not pull out of Singapore and that we are determined to remain a major power and play our role in world affairs has been a most important element in obtaining assistance from the Americans. It has enabled Harold Wilson not to send troops to Vietnam because he's been able to argue that our role in Singapore is more important than merely sending a brigade to Saigon. But it looks as though the decision not to devalue the pound and the East of

Suez policy are very closely united. When he made the decision in November 1964 he relied entirely on American help and he got it by all his talk about staying a great power. And then later on there followed the second decision — to stay in the Middle East as well and to try cutting defence spending while retaining the basic foreign policy.

Our foreign policy is virtually the same as that of the Tories. Perhaps on Rhodesia we've gone a little further in carrying out U.N. wishes than Heath and Douglas-Home would have done. Nevertheless, Harold has been scrupulously careful to continue the African policy which Douglas-Home and Macleod developed. We have even taken over the Tory determination to get into the Common Market and we've done it for the same reason — not in order to get rid of sterling as a world currency or to have an excuse for cutting our obligations East of Suez but in order to keep Great Britain great. And to this day George and Harold continue to assert that entry into the Common Market won't upset our special relations with the U.S.A. or reduce our role as a world power. It's my view that this determination to cling to parity and keep Britain great has been the basic reason for all our economic troubles and our difficulties at home.

I held this view long before I was transferred from the Ministry of Housing to this new job. Everything I have seen as a member of O.P.D. in the last six months has strengthened my conviction that we ought, quite simply, to announce our decision to cancel our commitments East of Suez and to wind up our presence within a reasonable time limit.

I said, by the way, that Harold's policy is a Bevinite policy. But I must in fairness to Ernest Bevin recall that in 1947 he suddenly told the Americans he was going to withdraw British troops from Greece and Turkey and forced Truman to announce the Truman Doctrine. And, indeed, he was a member of the Government which withdrew from India, despite the fact that it cost a million lives. So we made two major withdrawals under the Attlee Government but under this Government, so far from withdrawing from the limited commitments we still have, we have promised to maintain them although our economic position is infinitely weaker. It is often said that cancelling these commitments would be impossible because the electorate wouldn't swallow it. That's what Nye Bevan used to say time after time in the smoking-room. 'It's all right, Dick, you being a Little Englander: that's a thing an intellectual can afford. But remember no Labour Foreign Secretary can afford to be accused of being a Little Englander. We have to believe in Great Britain even more than the Tories if we are not going to hand over the emotional leadership of the country to the fascists who would destroy us and sweep us away.' That's how Nye Bevan excused himself on nuclear policy. But I am inclined to think that now things have changed and the danger of fascism is very small. In my view the vast majority of the electorate will be perfectly content to accept the end of our imperial pretensions and to cut-back the mumbo-jumbo and humbug and will welcome the kind of realistic foreign policy I want. I must add that in terms of the Parliamentary Party there would be every advantage in converting Harold to my views. There's a lot of trouble ahead if we don't look out. Our back-benchers not only detest our support for the Americans in Vietnam—they also resent the weight of the defence burden and they've been wanting something socialist which Harold, George and Michael have refused to give them.

Now let me reflect on my first five months as Lord President. How have I fared? 1. In relation to the Party outside I was to be the member of the Government who bridged the gulf which separates the Cabinet from Transport House and the rank and file. 2. In relation to the Parliamentary Party I was to work with John Silkin at introducing a new liberalized discipline which would satisfy the new intakes of 1964 and 1966. 3. In Whitehall I was to become the co-ordinator of information services *de facto* while avoiding any appearance of being a Minister of Information. 4. Finally, and in the eyes of the public most important, I must be Leader of the House and as such manage the business and introduce as much parliamentary reform as Members will take.

Well, the first of these jobs has turned out to be a complete flop. I am a member of the Commission of Inquiry into Party Organization but I don't run it and it's going to be utterly futile. As Harold's right-hand man, far from integrating the Government and Transport House, I am resented and suspected by everyone there.

On the other hand my job in the Parliamentary Party has gone fairly well. Of course, I always have to remember that John Silkin as Chief Whip with all his detailed thinking and knowledge of personal relations in the Party is responsible for detailed management and he keeps me pretty severely out of that. The Chief Whip has his own elaborate machinery and his own way of handling the Party and he doesn't expect me to dash in. I'm expected to limit myself to policy matters and leave administration to him, in particular the detailed discipline and reporting to Harold. I think we're working well together because I recognize this distinction between me as the Leader and policy-formulator and him as the administrator and disciplinarian. Together we've achieved the liberalization of Party discipline which we planned without any of the disastrous consequences predicted by the old guard.

There has recently been one very awkward consequence—the breach with Manny Shinwell. As chairman of the Party he was always a difficult cuss and he's never really liked me. We started off well by signing the concordat with him in August and things went smoothly when John and I began to impose the new liberal discipline although he didn't approve of it. But now he is being really difficult. I've described in this diary the last and worst row we had about his mismanagement of the Party meeting on German support costs. George Wigg is now working very closely with him; so far Harold has backed John and me against Manny and George. I can only hope and pray, though I don't expect it, that George Wigg will be out of the

Government in the reshuffle next week and that Manny can be levered out of the chairmanship.

The third job—co-ordination of information services—was very nearly totally destroyed right at the beginning by Trevor Lloyd-Hughes's intrigues. I still look back with a shudder to the moment when Peter Brown got back from his holiday and within twenty-four hours was summarily sent back to the Ministry of Housing with his tail between his legs. Since then I have signed a concordat with Trevor under which he remains complete chief on the official level and my activities are strictly limited to the Ministerial level and this concordat has now been issued to Whitehall as a Cabinet document. It has also been announced in the House that Questions on co-ordination have been transferred from George Wigg to me, an announcement that was received without any murmur of interest in the press. Moreover Freddy Ward has now come into the Office and he's slowly getting his small unit together. I'm pretty sure that on the organizing of official briefs for Ministers' speeches my office will be able to be mildly useful. But I'm also clear that Trevor Lloyd-Hughes will limit my effectiveness as co-ordinator and will also poison my relations with Harold Wilson. Like Manny he really has become an enemy. He sees me as a threat to his position, he sits in on all my press conferences and reports adversely on them to Harold and I think he's going to make sure that I can do relatively little co-ordinating.

As for my fourth job, the management of the business of the House and the introduction of parliamentary reform, I was very slow at the beginning to take it over because I was so mentally and emotionally out of touch. I'm only just beginning to see what can be done in terms of planning the legislative programme but I'm much more hopeful than I ever expected. So that leaves parliamentary reform. Here I have made some real progress, largely thanks to my speech in the procedure debate. The fact that I got away with my demonstration of the ineffectiveness of the present House of Commons is in itself quite remarkable. I got everybody to say that the reforms I suggested were not too drastic but mousy and inadequate and more was needed to give back to the House its proper powers. So there is a reasonable chance of creating a political climate for a major parliamentary reform in 1967/8, including a reform of the House of Lords as well as of the House of Commons and linked with the rebuilding of the Palace of Westminster. I'm now quite hopeful that I may pull this off. I've spent a little time this holiday reading the history of procedure. A. J. Balfour's reforms were the last before mine.[1] I think there's now a real chance because those like Willie Whitelaw and Jo Grimond whose views I take seriously recognize that we must have a complete timetabling of all the legislation so that we can plan the debates for

---

[1] Arthur Balfour was Leader of the Commons and First Lord of the Treasury 1891–2 and 1895–1902; leader of the Conservative Party 1902–11 and Prime Minister 1902–5. Much of the procedural reform at the turn of the nineteenth century was devised to deal with the troublesome group of Irish Members in the House of Commons.

the whole year and create a reasonable framework to give everybody a far better chance of discussing Bills without endless all-night sittings. I can see a big change here and when I link it with the reform of the House of Lords and the transfer to the Lords of a lot of our boring but necessary duties I get a sense that I could leave something behind me when I retire from the Leadership.

I suppose the other thing I should look at in this survey is the amount I've achieved in my role as a senior member of the Cabinet without a Department and therefore with time to read all the Cabinet papers.

I can't say my successes have been very great. I did have an early success on Rhodesia when I persuaded Cabinet to forbid Harold Wilson the mandatory sanctions he wanted to concede to the Commonwealth Conference. But Harold then had me reversed on this and of course went the whole hog with NIBMAR and all the rest of it. So I first succeeded and then failed. Since then there have been one or two cases where I got Cabinet to accept a cut and then had Harold overrule me, on P-1127, for example. It doesn't pay to stick your neck out and be defeated too often. On foreign policy and withdrawing from East of Suez I have had temporary successes and each time Harold has quietly managed a reversal. He has had his way and beaten down opposition. As for devaluation, I can say that I was having some success a few weeks ago. But now all that has disappeared because our exports are improving.

So I fear the conclusion is clear. I have been kicked upstairs. Harold found a powerful Minister of Housing using his position to interfere in general Cabinet policy. He nipped that interference in the bud and has given me a new job which is politically terribly vulnerable and gives me far less power and influence than I had five months ago.

Nevertheless what I can do is wait and watch. I can write my diary, I can read the papers much more carefully than before, I can advise him whenever I want. John and I see him more than any other Ministers and are often sitting alone with him while Cabinet Committees fret outside. I suppose most people think that we influence him enormously—I doubt whether we do. We shall see next week when we come to the Cabinet reshuffle.

Wednesday, January 4th
I've hardly been doing any work this week. The family's been up in London and yesterday we went to a Walt Disney film and today to *Treasure Island*, and we've been out to dinner in a restaurant. The only important thing I did was to see Burke Trend this morning to report to him that Freddy Ward and his assistant, who was brought in specially from the Treasury to help Trevor Lloyd-Hughes co-ordinate information at No. 10, are reporting complete failure. Indeed Trevor has gone to Harold Wilson and said that the assistant is supernumerary and should be sent back where he belongs. So I explained all this to Burke Trend and we agreed that I should start having a daily meeting next week to see how that works.

After this I had another interesting meeting with the Cabinet Secretariat. Burke brought Miss Nunn, now back from long trouble with arthritis, and we went over my plans for an integrated reform of Parliament linked with the physical replanning of the building. Burke said that he thought they'd better set up the right kind of official committee and added, 'We'll get one of the parliamentary draftsmen; we might get Barney Cocks, the Clerk to the Commons, as well as David Stephens, the Clerk of the Parliaments.'[1] When he paused I asked him, 'But aren't these people going to be there to *prevent* a radical reform? Aren't they all pledged on your side to serve the convenience of the Executive and on the other side to remain strictly non-political?' It was quite a moment. They quickly agreed that I should expand my idea in a draft directive.

I also made the tour of the House of Lords which I had promised the Services Committee I would undertake during the recess. This was to see whether instead of building a huge new building for Members of Parliament on the other side of Bridge Street we mightn't look again at the idea of keeping everything in the Palace of Westminster and building out into Millbank Gardens. Of course when the sub-committee made this report the mere rumour created a hostile reaction on the Conservative side, particularly in the Lords. Willie Whitelaw had told me before the recess that it was hopeless even to discuss it so I wasn't surprised at what happened on my tour. Gerald Gardiner was very frosty. 'I want to walk fast,' he said. He's an enormous man with long legs and he started off at eight miles an hour down the passages, being chased by Billy Listowel and myself, with a poor little chap from the Clerk's Department clinging on. However, I did see quite a lot. I saw that the whole of the Lord Chancellor's Department, including his Permanent Secretary, are stationed quite unnecessarily in the Palace of Westminster. I saw that there were vast areas not properly used. Then I went down to the kitchens. The Lords' kitchens adjoin ours with a wall between them; separate staffs, separate equipment. As for the two huge libraries, the Lords aren't prepared to have theirs touched.

And of course they have some justification. With the influx of life peers the quality of life in the Lords is changing and the number who attend regularly is increasing. They've trebled their average attendance in ten years, which is more than we can say for ourselves in the Commons. So they're likely to need their library and dining-room space. I thought that was a very fair point. When we'd finished our tour Gerald Gardiner asked me to sit down and rest and said, 'Every three months somebody in the Commons has the bright idea of taking our space; last time I took that walk it was with Barbara Castle.' I said, 'You seem to be under some misapprehension. I'm only concerned to see that we don't start an enormously expensive rebuilding

---

[1] Sir Barnett Cocks, Clerk of the House of Commons from 1962 until his retirement in 1973, and Sir David Stephens, Clerk of the Parliaments, House of Lords, from 1963 until his retirement in 1974.

of the Palace of Westminster before we've defined the functions of the two
Houses of a reformed Parliament.'

Thursday, January 5th

I gave a big dinner at the Garrick for the parliamentary reform group with no
less than three professors of politics present and two of the best clerks, Ryle and
Menhennet. Norman Chester came from Nuffield and Bernard Crick from
Sheffield, and the inimitable Freddie Warren was there.[1] They listened politely
when I sketched out my plan. But the most interesting thing happened when I
mentioned how difficult I found it to envisage how the House of Commons
functioned prior to the Balfour reforms and told them how I'd been reading
Robert Blake's *Disraeli*[2] over Christmas and could get no idea of what he
did as Leader of the House. One of the professors said, 'We are not historians,
Lord President.' Another went on, 'And even if we were, no one can really
understand what happened as recently as the 1930s simply by reading books
on procedure and the constitution. One has to read the political journalism
of the period.' Nevertheless I hanker after some genuine comparison and got
Barney Cocks and his wife to come to dinner. He is our Chief Clerk in the
House—a tall fellow, who's been there thirty-five years and who's cagey and
careful. He has a wife—I suspect a second wife—who was described to me as
a great left-winger, perhaps because she talks a little about Vietnam. But she's
a really gay, cheeky woman and we had a fine time together, though I hope he
didn't rebuke her too much when they went away. At one point I spoke in
favour of the ombudsman and had a very sharp retort from Lady Cocks.
Why on earth did I choose a civil servant who wasn't going to do a damned
thing which would cause trouble to the Civil Service? I said I thought he
was going to be first-rate. What about the job he'd done in Public Accounts?
I found myself explaining the whole background of the affair—how we
needed to get Bruce Fraser into the job of Comptroller and Auditor-
General and that was why Compton had to be catapulted into the Parliamentary Commissioner's job.[3] 'That's interesting,' said Barney 'because at
one point I was offered Bruce Fraser as a kind of extra here.'

Talking of the Civil Service, the Labour Party's evidence to the Fulton

---

[1] Michael Ryle, now (1974) a Deputy Principal Clerk in the House of Commons. David
Menhennet, now (1974) Deputy Librarian of the House of Commons. Sir Norman Chester,
Warden of Nuffield College, Oxford, since 1954; his writings include *Questions in Parliament*
(London: O.U.P., 1962). Professor Bernard Crick, Professor of Political Theory and
Institutions at the University of Sheffield 1965–71 and, since 1971, Professor of Politics at
Birkbeck College, London; among his books is the classic *The Reform of Parliament*
(London: Weidenfeld & Nicolson, 1964).

[2] London: Eyre & Spottiswoode, 1966.

[3] Sir Bruce Fraser (K.C.B. 1961), Permanent Secretary at the Ministry of Health 1960–64
and Joint Permanent Under-Secretary at the Department of Education 1964–5. He became
Permanent Secretary at the Ministry of Land and Natural Resources in 1965 and in 1966
Comptroller and Auditor-General, holding that office until his retirement in 1971. See
Vol. I.

Committee was published last weekend and made headlines because it accused the Civil Service of concealing facts from Ministers and revived the old proposal that we should bring three or four active outside collaborators into a Department.[1] This seems to be regarded by most of the press as proof that the Lord President at least, if not the Prime Minister or the Foreign Secretary, has had a hand in preparing the evidence. I mentioned this to Harold who said he hadn't read it, nor had George Brown. So the fact is that none of us had read it because we didn't want to be accused by the Executive of being anti-Party. We laughed a good deal and I then said, 'We're in a hopeless situation over there.' He agreed it was no good even trying to handle Transport House. But this is a decision which will cost us dear in the election. I repeated, 'You know, the important thing is to get Len Williams a job and a peerage and to put in a first-rate General Secretary. That could transform the whole situation.' I've got to plug away at this because we can't leave Transport House as hopeless as it is and merely appease them by letting them publish evidence to the Fulton Committee.

Friday, January 6th

Today I had a meeting at the Privy Council for George Weidenfeld and his group of publicity experts. I have got the room looking absolutely lovely because three new pictures from the National Gallery finally turned up. One of them is the enormous Teniers, which eight men had to lift into place on the wall. I should think that for the first time it's in a big enough room to set it off. Then on the other wall there are the Van de Velde and Van de Cappelle seascapes with, between them, room for a third picture which will be a good portrait from the National Portrait Gallery.

Among the people George brought were Richard Mayne, who used to write for the *New Statesman*, John Vaizey from Oxford and Hugh Thomas, who wrote the book about the Spanish civil war.[2] Tommy and I briefed them on the realities inside the Cabinet and the fact that we have a few keen Europeans and keen anti-Europeans and a large number of non-Europeans. I explained my personal wish that we should become an offshore island and my view that Atlantic union was not a real alternative. We all agreed that

[1] The Commission on the Civil Service had been established in 1966 under the chairmanship of Lord Fulton, the Vice-Chancellor of the University of Sussex (1959–67) and, since 1966, a life peer. The Commission was to produce its report in 1968.

[2] Richard Mayne, a former Rome correspondent of the *New Statesman*, worked in the office of Jean Monnet at the European Commission in Brussels 1963–6; he is the author of *The Recovery of Europe: From Devastation to Unity* (London: Weidenfeld & Nicolson, 1970) and *The Europeans. Who are we?* (London: Weidenfeld & Nicolson, 1972). John Vaizey, Fellow and Tutor in Economics at Worcester College, Oxford, 1962–6, became Professor of Economics at Brunel University in 1966; his books include *The Costs of Education* (London: George Allen & Unwin, 1958) and *The Control of Education* (London: Faber, 1963). He was made a life peer in 1976. Hugh Thomas, Professor of History since 1968 and, since 1973, chairman of the Graduate School of Contemporary European Studies at the University of Reading, is author of *The Spanish Civil War* (London: Eyre & Spottiswoode, 1961) and *Cuba* (London: Eyre & Spottiswoode, 1970).

during the period of the six visits by the P.M. and George Brown nothing should be said by other Ministers and we also decided it would be a good thing to arrange an exclusive interview between André Fontaine of *Le Monde* and the P.M. as a preface to his visit to Paris.

Most of the changes made in the Government reshuffle of January 6th were at the low level of Ministers of State. The size of the Cabinet itself was reduced from twenty-three to twenty-one. Fred Lee's office of Secretary of State for the Colonies was abolished and his duties absorbed by the Secretary of State for Commonwealth Affairs, while Mr Lee became Chancellor of the Duchy of Lancaster with responsibility for concentrating on the wages and prices policy. Arthur Bottomley remained Minister for Overseas Development but left the Cabinet. Patrick Gordon Walker returned to the Cabinet, assuming the place of Douglas Houghton as Minister without Portfolio and taking over the long-term review of the social services. John Stonehouse replaced Fred Mulley as Minister for Aviation, Lord Shackleton became Minister without Portfolio and George Thomson was appointed a Minister of State for Foreign Affairs with special responsibility for relations with Europe and negotiations for entry to the E.E.C. under the overall co-ordination of the Foreign Secretary.

Sunday, January 8th

The Cabinet shuffle at last. Let's see what effect John Silkin and I had by our series of talks with the P.M. We suggested he should replace Longford with Shackleton and drop Bottomley and Lee from the Cabinet. Well, he's gone some way on the first point by bringing Eddie forward to be Deputy Leader to Longford. On the second, Bottomley and Lee are out but they've both been given other jobs: Fred Lee a good one. He's always been an inveterate believer in the wages policy and he's now a Minister of State in the D.E.A. to strengthen the hand of Michael Stewart. That's a good idea. I'm only sorry that in moving Peter Shore also to D.E.A. he hasn't promoted him, but merely put him alongside Harold Lever, another new appointment, as Parliamentary Secretary.

The P.M. has allowed George Brown to shake up the Foreign Office by getting rid of Walter Padley and Eirene White, as I hoped he would. Now we have a new team in there—Fred Mulley and Bill Rodgers. That should do a great deal of good, and even the removal of Harry Walston won't do any harm. George Brown should be allowed to have his own team.

But he's hardly strengthened the Cabinet by substituting Gordon Walker for Douglas Houghton. This seems to me a feeble thing to do. Tommy Balogh tells me that Gordon Walker possesses a promise in writing of a Cabinet job. At least Harold has brought him in at the bottom of the Cabinet as a Minister without Portfolio. Moreover all the papers say that he won't inherit Douglas Houghton's supervision of social security so it looks as though, in response to my request, he's seen to it that that shall be taken over by the Lord President.

The press are already complaining that this is merely yet another Wilsonian shuffle. Once again you have the endless crablike musical chairs—the transfer of people at the same level and for no apparent good reason. More serious I think (certainly it's going to worry the Chief Whip) are the appointments from the back benches. Harold Lever is a good promotion but isn't exactly an encouragement to young men. Of the three young men appointed Roy Hattersley is a solid right-winger but Reg Freeson and Norman Buchan are notorious left-wingers and no Whip has been promoted to help John keep up morale in the office.[1] I think he's going to find the loyalists even more difficult when Parliament resumes. In fact the whole Parliamentary Party will be disappointed, because this reshuffle shows a complete failure to recognize the need for pushing youth on. It's fair to point out that the Harold Wilson who was Cabinet Minister at thirty-one would not have stood such a good chance under a Wilson Government.

I've been doing this diary looking out at our first fall of snow. Prescote is magnificent now the grey skies have blown off. I'm sitting here in comfort and am therefore bound to wonder whether that fierce old Tory, my brother Geoffrey, is reasonable when he says that I can't be a socialist and have a farm which makes good profits. I tell him the two are compatible provided that as a member of the Government I'm ready to vote for a socialist policy to take those profits away and even, in the last resort, to confiscate the property. Nevertheless that isn't a complete answer. Having Prescote deeply affects my life. It's not merely that I'm more detached than my colleagues, able to judge things more dispassionately and to look forward to retirement, it's also more crudely that I'm comfortably off now and have no worries about money. I can eat, drink and buy what I like as well as adding 170 acres to Prescote Manor Farm. Anne and I have a facility of freedom and an amplitude of life here which cuts us off from the vast mass of people and in particular from ordinary people in Coventry. I am remote from Coventry now. I feel it and they feel it too.

But does Prescote reduce my belief in left-wing socialism? Part of the answer to that question is that my radical passions have never been based on a moral or egalitarian philosophy. It's been really an expression of my bump of irreverence, based on my conviction that governments and establishments are fools and that participation by the people will probably improve

---

[1] Roy Hattersley, Labour M.P. for Birmingham (Sparkbrook) since 1964, was Joint Parliamentary Secretary at the Ministry of Labour 1967–9, Minister of Defence for Administration 1969–70 and, since 1974, has been Minister of State for Foreign Affairs. Reginald Freeson, Labour M.P. for Willesden since 1964, was Parliamentary Secretary at the Ministry of Power 1967–9 and at M.H.L.G. 1969–70 and, since 1974, has been Minister for Housing and Construction. Norman Buchan, Labour M.P. for Renfrewshire since 1964, was Parliamentary Secretary at the Scottish Office 1967–70 and, for some months in 1974, was Minister of Agriculture, Fisheries and Food.

government in this country. Can I hope that if irreverence is my main socialist quality and not moral indignation, it won't necessarily be blunted by the marvellous kind of life we're able to live here at Prescote?

Monday, January 9th

We had only one item on the S.E.P. this week—the enormous briefs which have been prepared in Whitehall under the editorship of Bill Nield for the P.M. and George Brown's tour of the six European capitals.[1] I've been trying to get hold of them ever since I got back to London after Christmas. Douglas Jay, however, had got his earlier from his Permanent Secretary and had found time to fire in a powerful paper making his anti-Common Market position clear. I got mine last Friday afternoon and on Tommy's advice read those on defence, politics, and economics. Each topic was provided with an enormously verbose brief for an actual speech and then notes on the brief. If either Harold or George had taken them seriously it would have become a *tour de farce* because they consisted simply of Civil Service evasions. When I put this to Harold before the meeting he said, 'I haven't read it myself, I can assure you. I never bother with these briefs before a conference and take my own line when it comes to negotiations.'

The only value of the meeting was watching Harold's mind at work. He was quite polite about Douglas Jay's paper and gave him the assurance that he was prepared to abide absolutely scrupulously by the agreement Cabinet reached last November defining our attitude to Europe. He has certainly swung a long way back from the dynamic optimism he displayed at the Lord Mayor's banquet. I am glad I had read the brief on defence because the discussion revealed his attitude to General de Gaulle. It seemed to exclude any discussion of a possible withdrawal from East of Suez and even any discussion of European nuclear policy as well as of our special relations with America. I asked whether this kind of wholly negative approach was an essential part of his brief from Cabinet. He then began to talk about the way he thought one should deal with General de Gaulle. 'In a sense one should free-wheel,' he said. When someone remarked that that in itself was a political brief he replied, 'It will be a purely political occasion. I shall not be concerned with the substance of defence but with the politics of how to handle the General.'

Whether one can handle the General in this way is another question. But Harold's clearly very confident. He feels he can woo him politically without giving way any vital position. Gordon Walker, in his first contribution to a Cabinet discussion, suggested that in dealing with the French we had to be prepared to do a certain amount of strategic deception. After half an hour or so Harold showed that this is exactly what he is going to do. So all we can

[1] They were to visit Rome January 15th–17th, Strasbourg January 23rd, Paris January 24th–25th, Brussels January 31st, Bonn February 14th–16th, The Hague February 26th–27th and Luxemburg March 7th–8th.

be sure of is that he isn't going to budge from what we agreed—to reserve our position—last November.

The only point on which he was tough was when somebody (Denis Healey, I think) urged that S.E.P., possibly Cabinet, should be given a verbatim report on each of his meetings and that we should then have a discussion before the next one. On this I must say I held up my hands in horror. 'Look,' I said, 'for heaven's sake give them room for manœuvre.' The Chancellor and the First Secretary also pressed Cabinet not to tie them down tightly. The idea was dropped. I said there must be a sign of forward movement and the fact that we three said this without dissent has, I suppose, made a certain difference though it has not been minuted.

I had lunch with Ronald Butt, the *Financial Times* political columnist, who has just spent a year at Nuffield writing a book on Parliament.[1] He's the only person who's written a well-informed critical attack upon my procedure speech. He thinks I over-exaggerate the ineffectiveness of the modern House of Commons. So we met at Wheeler's and had a most enjoyable discussion. This is the sort of intellectual gossip I really enjoy.

After that I made my way to Coventry where I had to see the Labour Group on the City Council. Many weeks ago Peter Lister came over to Prescote and complained I wasn't playing my proper role in Coventry and that I wasn't seeing the Group nearly enough. I replied that I went and saw them whenever they invited me and this invitation was the result.

When I got there I found they'd drawn up their own agenda and put Arthur Waugh in the chair with me next to him. The agenda consisted of a number of things they wanted me to do—to try to get them a medical school for Warwick University and a motor research unit, and to help them with the problem of the miners' village at Binley. Warwick University was dealt with easily enough but the miners' village was more difficult since the Council has acquired a job lot of terrible company houses which will cost a mint of money to put in order. Some of the tenants have long wanted to buy their houses and have been refused by the Coal Board. They had come to me and I had said it was reasonable for the Council to consider selling some of these old properties to the present tenants. However, the Labour Group strongly objected to my saying this publicly and letting the *Coventry Evening Telegraph* print it. When they protested too much I couldn't resist saying that I remembered the occasions when as Minister of Housing I found the Council Group publicly disagreeing with the Labour Minister's policy. If they could do that, why could I not imitate them on this minor constituency issue? We had quite a good discussion and then suddenly Arthur said, 'We're going to stop now.' To my surprise there were drinks and sandwiches and Anne sitting next door. We had a most pleasant evening.

---

[1] *The Power of Parliament* (London: Constable, 1967).

Tuesday, January 10th

This time PESC turned out to be a mass meeting. In order to consider the Chancellor's reply to his critics in S.E.P. the Prime Minister had arranged that every Minister concerned with public expenditure should attend in Cabinet Room A. There were, I think, twelve Cabinet Ministers plus Kenneth Robinson and Peggy Herbison.

The first part of the paper was a reply by the Chancellor to a very gloomy official forecast which Treasury experts had prepared last autumn predicting a rate of unemployment over 2 per cent, no growth for two and a half years, and no real expansion till 1970. At the time Tommy and I had suspected that this was an attempt by the mendacious to push Harold into devaluation. But Callaghan's paper was designed to show that we could achieve everything without devaluation. His proposals for dealing with the problem of the balance of payments was to cut in half the surplus we planned to achieve, i.e. to reduce it from £300 million to £150 million. Once he'd explained his case George Brown, Michael Stewart, Denis Healey and I all quietly reserved our position instead of getting involved in an argument. We said that we didn't think it was for this mass meeting to discuss the desirability of devaluation: that was a matter for S.E.P. After the four of us—all sitting at one corner of the table—had made this declaration no one else dared to say a word on the subject.

The second half of the paper dealt with the Chancellor's revised proposals for cutting public expenditure over the next four years. He proposed a cut of £500 million during this period, concentrating on housing and health. The main reason for the cut was that social services had to be paid for by increased taxation and increased taxation stifled growth. Tony Greenwood then cut short the discussion by stating that since Housing was being considered at a special Cabinet Committee it couldn't be discussed here. Indeed the only subject on which we had any intelligent discussion was pensions, where the Chancellor's paper seemed to commit us to a far lower rate of increase than that achieved by the Tories before 1964 and therefore to leave us open to a searing attack by the Titmuss group. I was then able to put forward my case that the shape of public spending would look quite different if National Insurance contributions were rated as savings and if we regarded Government tax concessions to private pension schemes as decreases of taxation. Since Douglas Houghton was away and Gordon Walker had taken his place without any knowledge of the subject I was able to get my way and have this considered.

But I was mainly worried about my own personal position. From the press reports I had assumed that when Douglas Houghton was sacked social services were to be transferred to the Lord President. But on Monday I heard a rumour that this was not the case and this evening I went to see Burke to put my cards on the table. 'I hear a rumour,' I said, 'that it isn't coming to me.' Burke replied, 'I know it isn't. It's perfectly clear that Gordon

Walker gets exactly the responsibility which Houghton had and those statements in the Sunday press were unauthorized. No, I'm afraid, Dick, there's nothing for you and I'll confirm it to you tomorrow.' I went straight away to talk to Marcia and said she'd really got to fight for me, alongside Tommy.

Wednesday, January 11th

I spent the day at Sandringham. When I got to Liverpool Street for the 8.30 train I found we were quite a party: Cledwyn Hughes, Ted Short, Fred Lee, George Thomson, and myself. There were five Ministers instead of the usual three. The explanation was that poor Godfrey had got three of us to go before he found that the old Chancellor of the Duchy, George Thomson, and the new Chancellor, Fred Lee, could only exchange their seals in the presence of the Queen, so they had been added to the list. I had arranged beforehand that at King's Lynn we would all get out and make a tour of the city as it's one of the five towns I'd chosen for model schemes to preserve the city centre.[1] My colleagues were not enthusiastic. After that we drove out to Sandringham where we found ourselves facing an extremely dull, Edwardian baronial house. We stood about in the main hall, looking at the Queen's jigsaw and a superb photograph of Queen Victoria. After half an hour in go the new and the old Chancellors of the Duchy to exchange their seals. Next I go in for my interview and I tell the Queen that Ted Short has brought along copies of the new stamps which I think she'll like better than the awful Wedgwood Benn series. She said she would be pleased and she was.

Then we had the Council. It lasted thirty seconds. When it was over we'd finished our job. The more I think about this mumbo-jumbo the more intolerable it is, the more I would like to get it changed. Why shouldn't I talk to the Queen myself about the possibility of having it all done by signature?

At lunch she was very relaxed. 'At Sandringham,' she told me, 'I feel a great deal more remote from London than at Balmoral.' They all love this place because it was Edward VII's hideout and has become a family hideout where they feel more like ordinary human beings. It struck me that it would be nice if one could arrange for the Queen to commute from Sandringham in future and to use Buckingham Palace merely as an office. Then she changed the subject and said, 'I see the Labour Party is beginning to admit that civil servants sometimes conceal things from politicians and are difficult to manage. I should have thought they always did what they were told.' (She's been reading the newspaper reports of the Labour Party's evidence to the Fulton Committee.) I said, 'I'm afraid that's not true.' And she then said, 'How do you know?' 'Well, Evelyn Sharp was my Permanent Secretary,' I said.

After our afternoon walk round the huge gardens I found her doing an

[1] See Vol. I, p. 517. The others were Bath, Chester, Chichester and York.

enormous, incredibly difficult jigsaw. Her lady-in-waiting had told me she was jolly good at jigsaws and sure enough while she was standing there talking to the company at large, her fingers were straying and she was quietly fitting in the pieces while apparently not looking round.

As we left I felt this time it had been a great deal easier. I suppose the truth is that she really likes people she knows and every time you see her she tends to like you better simply because she's got more used to you. I remember once asking Godfrey Agnew whether she preferred the Tories to us because they were our social superiors and he said, 'I don't think so. The Queen doesn't make fine distinctions between politicians of different parties. They all roughly belong to the same social category in her view.' I think that's true.

This evening, to a dinner party at George Weidenfeld's. Pam Berry's lunches and George's dinners are the only really slap-up political-social occasions which I attend. Pam's have all the brilliance of intimate political gossip. George's are much larger and we all eat at small round tables and are then pushed out to the sitting-room which is full of those not asked to dinner but only after-dinner. That night at George's there was a Mrs Heinz, with whom I got into conversation and I nearly asked her whether she owned the '57 varieties'. It was a good thing I didn't because she did.

Thursday, January 12th

I went round to No. 10 at 9.30 to see the Chief Whip. He's just come back from Cyprus where he's been staying at Famagusta in a lovely new air-conditioned hotel which interests me as a possibility for a family holiday this summer. I checked through everything with him and then he told me about his deep disappointment at the Prime Minister's selection of back-benchers for promotion. He thought he'd had a clear understanding that one of the Whips would get a job and, even more depressing, he had thought that Harold wouldn't have a reshuffle while he was on holiday. Yet it had taken place in his absence without his knowing the full details in advance. The Chief Whip should be big enough in standing and status to make it impossible for the P.M. to behave like this. What worries me is that Harold is treating John as a lieutenant and not as a powerful satrap.

At Cabinet we had two extremely interesting items that had come up from Cabinet Committee level. First was the wage demand of workers who make wooden legs for limbless people. They'd been going slow because they didn't get their wage agreement last autumn. Clive Jenkins has been pushing the employers and they've now decided to give a very big increase in violation of the prices and incomes policy. For obvious reasons Ray Gunter wanted us to let it through and then to say we'd let it happen because we couldn't let the limbless suffer. He was opposed by Michael Stewart and it was really a contest between Stewart and Gunter. Harold sided sharply with Stewart and on these occasions he automatically gets the support of his predecessor,

George Brown, and, of course, Jim Callaghan. So he won easily. I think I was the only person who supported Gunter. We shall get a lot of odium for this decision.

The second item concerned the future of the Pye Electric Company. Should it be taken over by Philips, which is basically a Dutch firm, or by Thorn, which is a brand new, one-man show created by Julius Thorn? In the Cabinet Committee the P.M. and Wedgy wanted to back Thorn and keep Philips out, even in a sense unfairly. The Chancellor, Douglas Jay and Stewart all thought there was no need to do so, because Philips is virtually an English firm and European, and we can't behave in this way when we say we want to go into Europe. I suspect the P.M.'s major motive was the Chrysler decision. Having recently given permission for Chrysler to take over Rootes he felt he couldn't allow a second foreign invasion. In this case Cabinet was against him and we clearly overrode the Prime Minister and the Minister of Technology.

Back to Coventry again this afternoon in order to lecture at Warwick University. What two years ago had been a ploughed field is now an enormous £3 million building and there were some five hundred people in the lecture hall to hear the Lord President and Member for Coventry East discussing parliamentary reform. It went well and I had a pleasant evening with the Vice-Chancellor, Jack Butterworth.[1]

Friday, January 13th
S.E.P. was the most important Cabinet Committee meeting I've attended since last July. It started quietly with the usual survey of the situation and Douglas Jay's regular request that we should make an h.p. concession to the motor manufacturers. As usual the rest of us said we couldn't afford to do it yet. We are all waiting for Callaghan's budgetary concessions.

After this we returned to the first half of the Chancellor's paper which we had refused to discuss in PESC. The Chancellor repeated all his usual arguments and this time he was supported by Patrick Gordon Walker as well as Douglas Jay. Denis Healey was the first person to challenge him. 'We shall be living on a knife-edge,' he said, 'with a trade surplus of only £150 million,' to which Callaghan made the great mistake of replying, 'Well, that's the normal way one has to live in the modern world.' Michael Stewart, who had already put in a paper, then gently supported Denis but he made no difference. Next was my turn. I said that the gamble was far too great. It looked as though the Chancellor had learnt nothing from the last two years and was accepting the likelihood of an annual July crisis. This brought quite a protest from Jim but I forged ahead and said, 'If you keep as narrow a margin as that you can be knocked off it by another seamen's strike or bad luck of some kind. I think there's something to be said for the Committee looking at several different models. Let me suggest one. Look at a model based on the

[1] A Fellow of New College, Oxford, from 1946 to 1963, when he became Vice-Chancellor of the University of Warwick.

assumption of devaluation and winding up all our commitments East of Suez and then compare that with the model on which you are now working.' Nobody else had dared to mention devaluation directly. George Brown came in next and fully supported me. So the line-up was important. There were four of us—Denis Healey, Michael Stewart, George Brown and myself— who wanted to take a look at the devaluation anti-East of Suez model. There were three against us—the Chancellor, Douglas Jay and Gordon Walker—and the P.M. sitting in the chair betwixt and between. But I'm afraid he's not on our side and I'm pretty sure that Burke is one hundred per cent against us. However I had got the item on to the agenda.

When the meeting was over the P.M. took me aside and said that after great consideration he wanted me to take over responsibility for social security. 'I don't suppose you want to do all the social services,' he said, 'but I think you should do social security.' He said this to me very carefully— almost pushing Burke aside. Tommy and Marcia apparently had waged war for me valiantly and so he'd gone back to the original intention. However, I'm canny enough not to move hand or foot until Gordon Walker has been told exactly what has happened. I see tremendous chances because pensions and pension investments are a major part of our economic wealth. Here I shall really be impinging on the central planning of government. There's power here which I've lacked since I became Lord President. Now I've got to get hold of the Titmuss group and Tommy's Michael Stewart and Nicky Kaldor and get a working party together.

After than Burke rejoined the conversation and we discussed Trevor Lloyd-Hughes. Harold said we should try to settle this and that afternoon at 3.30 Burke and I and Trevor Lloyd-Hughes and Freddy Ward solemnly sat down together in my room. Nothing happened. Trevor Hughes was firmly determined and as long as Harold Wilson doesn't discipline him he'll win all along the line. I was so angry I walked out and left Burke to pick up the pieces.

I was able to catch the 6.10 and get to Prescote this evening so I shall have the whole of Saturday at home. On Sunday I have to be in Coundon Road at a day-school on Government policy I promised them ages ago.[1]

Sunday, January 15th
Politics is hotting up. All the papers this morning had full stories from Conservative headquarters about the decision to destroy the image of Harold Wilson and to crucify him as a promise-breaker and a crook. There was also a highly-publicized exposure of George Brown in the *Observer* which turned out to be a complete anti-climax. However, it certainly increased George's standing with the general public. By and large we're a Government of pygmies compared not only with the giants of the past but even with the Attlee Government of 1945. That great big straw figure Jim Callaghan,

[1] At the headquarters of the Coventry East Party.

who becomes bigger and hollower and more sanctimonious every week; dynamic George; little eager-beaver, india-rubber Harold—as a troika they are not much. But George Brown has dimensions—though he's illiterate and volatile he has spunk and imagination which make him stand apart from dreary acidulated figures like Michael Stewart. Could I stand up to personal attacks like those to which he's subjected? I shall know more about it in a week's time when the *Sunday Telegraph* publishes my profile. We heard a long time ago in the Private Office that their reporters were roaming round collecting material about me. Then Tam rang up Anne saying that this young chap was going to Scotland to get Tam's inside knowledge of my private life and he'd already been to some twenty people in the Ministry of Housing—from Dame Evelyn right down to the bottom—to talk about my behaviour as a Minister. Finally he turned up in my room when I had Freddy Ward there. He started by saying, 'I'm the man who's due to do a hatchet job on you. It's nearly finished and I thought I'd try some of the stuff out. My job is to show you're no good as Leader of the House and of course we do that by seeing what went wrong when you were Minister of Housing. What do you think of the following comments made upon you by the civil servants who worked under you, including Dame Evelyn?' I can't resist that kind of thing and I talked to him very freely off-the-record and got him to talk to Tam, who also extracted some more information about his assignment. Suddenly it occurred to me—why not write to Michael Berry asking whether it was his usual practice to send a young man off to do a hatchet story on a leading politician? I was careful to say, of course, that the young man may have got it wrong and the directive may never have been given. David Holmes duly took the letter round by hand and back came the reply that the directive had never been given and that the profile would portray me as a rough diamond 'with emphasis both on rough and diamond,' whatever that may mean.

Monday, January 16th
Barbara Castle, now busily drafting an enormous Transport Bill, came along to the Home Affairs Committee to get clearance for her proposal to create an independent freight authority. I know very little about transport but I'm getting quite experienced now as a Cabinet half-back, a Minister without a Department whose duty it is to read the papers and stop possible dangers. It was obvious, reading her papers, that the creation of this independent freight authority would split the railways up and infuriate not only the head of British Rail but also the staff. The case against her was made by Gunter who was an official of the old union of railway clerks, now called the T.S.S.A. He had obviously had one brief from the union and another from the management and gave her a long lecture on how terrible the fissure would be. But he never stands up to anything and she replied that she'd heard all that before and she'd made up her mind. 'But we can't give you authority to do this,'

he riposted, 'until you have got the approval of the unions.' Having finished
with him, she turned to the rest of the Committee. There were fifteen people
there but once again they sat round with their departmental briefs and not
one of them discussed the major policy decision. As a result she was given
clearance provided only that the proposals were accepted by the unions. So
much for Cabinet control of major policy decisions.

By coincidence a few hours later another Cabinet Committee was discussing Anthony Greenwood's proposal that the new planning appeal policy
recommended by the P.A.G. Committee should be implemented in a great
Bill next session. As Minister of Housing I'd had a great deal to do with
P.A.G. and approved of its work. But I couldn't swallow the Greenwood
recommendation. He wanted the new Planning Bill to be put on the statute
book but its implementation postponed for most local authorities until after
the Local Government Boundary Commission has reported and the new
local government scheme is in operation, i.e. possibly five or six years. Meanwhile five or six selected authorities should be experimenting with the new
procedure. This seemed to me politically impossible and I came to the
meeting determined to say so. I'd arranged with the chairman, Patrick Gordon
Walker, that it should be early on the agenda and when he had said a word or
two and Tony Greenwood had launched it with a few very inadequate words,
there was a complete silence. Once again the fourteen or fifteen people round
the table had nothing to say on the general principle of the policy. They were
mostly Parliamentary Secretaries with small departmental points. So I had
to do the demolition work and I admit I did it a bit roughly. That afternoon
Tony rang me up and said, 'Am I being listened to by your Private Office?'
I said, 'Yes, you are,' and then put him on my one private line. He was
furious at my violation of Cabinet propriety. 'It was appalling,' he said, 'to
see two Cabinet Ministers arguing with each other.' 'Then what the devil
are these Cabinet Committees for,' I said, 'except for argument?' When he
went on to say that I should have warned him in advance, I said to him, 'I
may have sinned in not telling you what I would do but what about your own
sin of omission in not coming near your predecessor at Housing who had been
largely responsible for the shape of the P.A.G. report? If you really wanted
my advice I would have given it to you straightaway. From the start my
advice would have been that you can certainly pass legislation to enable the
vast majority of planning appeals to be decided by inspectors. But what you
can't do is to add on as well an enormous and highly controversial planning
reform—and expect me to sit silent.'

Anyway it's a good job I did kill the proposal. It's gone back with a deadly
report from the Cabinet Committee and now I shall really have to try and
pick up the pieces after the smash.

This evening I was dining with Heinz Koeppler, up from Wilton Park, at
the Athenaeum. I wanted to see the *Panorama* programme so we went down
to the servants' quarters—we found them very spacious, by the way—where

there was a television. It was a 45-minute programme on poverty, based very largely on the campaign of the Titmuss group against the Labour Government for its maltreatment of lower-paid workers with large families.

For thirty-five minutes we were given a picture of unfortunate families with seven or eight children living in ghastly poverty. One had six children, one eight and one twelve. The trouble was that most of the mothers looked mentally deficient and one felt bound to ask whether free family-planning might not be the solution. But nevertheless it is part of the social security campaign we have to face.

Tuesday, January 17th

I had to give evidence to the Fulton Committee—an appointment I'd been postponing week after week—so I went round to the Treasury and found them sitting around one of those huge bare office tables. There was John Fulton himself, Edward Boyle, Sheldon from the Labour Party, and two Permanent Secretaries—Ned Dunnett and Philip Allen.[1] I fired off a considered broadside which started with the declaration that before I became a Minister I had found Tommy Balogh's chapter on the Establishment the most important statement on the Civil Service.[2] Now I had some experience I was even more impressed by it. Then I gave a description of the mandarins, of the circulation of Permanent Secretaries at the top, and I blurted out the whole story of how the whole Government's working had been held in suspense in order to find Sir Bruce Fraser a job. I then went on to Treasury domination, how the Treasury spies on Ministers through ex-Treasury men in each Department, how difficult civil servants find it not to feel a greater loyalty to the Treasury than to their Minister, and I then described the difficulty of the Minister faced with the agreed solutions of official committees. To cheer them up I concluded with the description of the excellence of the Private Office system and how I'd been converted to the view that one shouldn't substitute a *chef de cabinet* system for the Private Office system.[3] Sheldon came up to me afterwards and said that I was the first Minister who'd faced them with a really serious piece of evidence.

---

[1] Edward Boyle, Conservative M.P. for Birmingham (Handsworth) from 1950 until 1970, when he became a life peer and Vice-Chancellor of the University of Leeds; he was Financial Secretary to the Treasury 1959–July 1962, Minister of Education 1962–4 and since 1971 has been chairman of the Top Salaries Review Body. Robert Sheldon, Labour M.P. for Ashton-under-Lyne since 1964, has been Minister of State at the Civil Service Department since 1974. James Dunnett (K.C.B. 1960) was Permanent Secretary at the Ministry of Transport 1959–62, at the Ministry of Labour 1962–6 and, from 1966 until his retirement in 1974, at the Ministry of Defence. Philip Allen (K.C.B. 1964) was Second Secretary to the Treasury 1963–6 and, from 1966 until his retirement in 1972, Permanent Under-Secretary at the Home Office. He became a life peer in 1976.

[2] In Hugh Thomas (ed.), *Crisis in the Civil Service* (London: Blond, 1968).

[3] A French Minister's *cabinet* consists of personal appointees who, unlike the staff in the Private Office, are not always drawn from within the public sector. Many departments have no Permanent Secretary so that the Minister and his personal advisers are directly responsible for policy-making.

This afternoon Tony Wedgwood Benn made a Statement on the Chrysler take-over of Rootes.[1] He'd done his homework well, preparing all his supplementaries with subheadings—each on a separate bit of paper—with red ink at the top so that he could find it rapidly. He completely foxed the House and there wasn't any really serious opposition. Admirably done. I was sorry that, despite this, Maurice Edelman, my neighbour in Coventry, was able to get six Labour M.P.s to sign a protest about the take-over. Rootes's number one factory is in my constituency and as I know very well from last Sunday's day-school in Coventry everybody there feels grateful for the take-over because otherwise the whole place might have been closed down.

When I went to see Tommy he told me that Marcia, who works on the floor below him, was desperately upset so I went downstairs and burst into the room. There was not only Marcia but Gerald Kaufman and Harold as well. Marcia, whom I'm beginning to get to know, has got more influence with Harold now than any single man. There's no doubt that my appointment to Housing and now to the Leadership of the House was largely her doing. But she not only influences him on Government appointments, she has strong views on politics. I should describe her as solid Labour—a little left of centre, an able but typically conventional Ward Secretary. She was in tears because of a disgusting article about her which had appeared in the *Evening Standard*. I tried to cheer her up by telling her how miserable Anne had been when the *Daily Express* published all that dirt about our slum cottages at Prescote.[2] But Harold had to soothe her till eleven o'clock this evening and as a result he couldn't get much work done on his speech for Strasbourg.

Meanwhile the Agriculture Bill was ploughing on in the House. Near twelve I went and saw John Silkin who told me it would probably be an all-night sitting, that the Tories had some people there and the Tory Whips' Office had been shut up already. So it wasn't a serious event. I was allowed to stay away on the assumption that I would have to stay late the rest of the week on Iron and Steel.

Wednesday, January 18th

I woke up to hear on the wireless that the Agriculture Bill was still drooling on (the Report Stage finished at 10 a.m.) and went across to see Harold at morning prayers. The Chief was still in bed and I was therefore able to tell Harold of his shock at the deplorable effect which the back-bench promotions had had in the Whips' Office. Of the three appointments from the 1964 intake there were two notorious left-wingers and not a single Whip. Just when I

[1] The Chrysler Corporation of America had asked the Government in December 1966 what their attitude would be to an application for Treasury consent under the 1947 Exchange Control Act to enable them to inject more capital into and to obtain control of Rootes Motors Ltd. Chrysler had first made a substantial investment in Rootes in 1964. The Board of Trade decided that no investigation of the transaction need be made by the Monopolies Commission and the necessary Treasury consent had been given. See p. 177.

[2] See Vol. I, pp. 224–5, 226 n.

7*

was going I reminded him that he still hadn't solved the problem of Trevor Lloyd-Hughes and asked him whether he'd told Gordon Walker that I was to have social security. When he said he hadn't I waited and watched while he actually told Michael Halls[1] to give the order for Gordon Walker to come to No. 10.

Next I saw Roy Jenkins for a quiet talk about his legislative programme. We also discussed the Parliamentary Boundary Commission and agreed that the right line to take is to let them complete their recommendations and then say that it is absurd to implement all of them pending the local government reform. They should be asked to propose a list of twenty to thirty constituencies which have become grossly disproportionate and we should limit the changes to these urgent cases.[2]

This afternoon Shinwell deliberately absented himself from the liaison committee. This is quite funny. When John and I first saw him in August and made our great concordat one of the things he complained about was that Herbert Bowden had insulted the liaison committee by making them meet in a committee room downstairs instead of inviting them into the Leader's room. So of course I invited the committee to my own room. Now Shinwell has said that he can't really feel on equal terms with the Leader if he has to be 'on sufferance' in the Leader's room and he has insisted that we meet in a committee room in order that the committee shall not be put in a position of inferiority. Having got us into the committee room he then absented himself, which meant we got through our business pretty quickly. We decided to hold the meeting at which Callaghan has promised to give his reply on German support costs.[3] This should be our first meeting of the New Year though the Party, I was warned, would certainly prefer a meeting on Vietnam. Indeed they've already stuck down a motion for debate. My aim is to postpone it for at least a week until just before Kosygin's arrival on February 6th.[4] If we have it then there'll be no difficulty in getting the Party to avoid a vote which would embarrass the Russians.

This afternoon the Report Stage of the Iron and Steel Bill began. Within

[1] An old friend of Harold Wilson, whom he knew from their days as civil servants in the Board of Trade. He became the Prime Minister's Private Secretary in No. 10 in April 1966 and served until his sudden death in April 1970. See Vol. I.

[2] The Home Secretary was statutorily responsible for laying before Parliament Orders implementing the recommendations made by this Commission for redrawing constituency boundaries to take account of demographic shifts. It had become plain that if the next general election were to be fought with the new boundaries, Labour might lose as many as twenty seats. A tactical compromise might be to delay implementation of the recommendations until the Maud Commission on Local Government in England reported (possibly as far ahead as 1969). The matter was to become a constitutional *cause célèbre* in 1970. See Vol. I, pp. 64–5.

[3] The Statement on Defence Estimates 1967 (Cmnd. 3203), issued on February 16th, announced that the Government intended to bring back some 25,000 men and 6,000 service families from stations outside Europe by April 1st, 1968. This and other cuts in military expenditure would enable savings of some £47½ million to be made.

[4] The Soviet Prime Minister was to pay an official visit to London February 9th–13th.

a few hours Willie Whitelaw was round with John Silkin to discuss a deal. John immediately offered him an extra day. Willie was taken aback and virtually accepted the offer that there was to be an early night both on Wednesday and Thursday, and possibly an all-night sitting on Monday and they would then give us the Bill on the following Thursday. This was the deal John and Willie hatched. Before I went out (to give dinner to Rudolf Augstein, the owner and editor of *Der Spiegel*) I had seen it fully agreed. This was a tremendous achievement for John Silkin because there had been a great build-up in the press about the Tories' determination to fight the Bill tooth and nail when it came back to the Floor of the House. Why did they suddenly succumb? The main reason, I think, was the Agriculture Bill. After the all-night sitting on Monday, Willie realized that if he had two more all-night sittings this week the Tory back-benchers would refuse to stay late.

Thursday, January 19th

A very short Cabinet meeting at which Harold gave a lecture on leaks and infuriated me by giving as an example the story in last Monday's *Times* about the prices and incomes legislation. When David Wood came to see me I had briefed him carefully and told him that the only new Bill we were likely to have was a Prices and Incomes Bill but Cabinet hadn't decided this yet. Out of this David Wood had deduced a major Cabinet row and of course described it graphically. When the others had left the room I said to Harold, 'For God's sake, don't attack me in Cabinet in that way without telling me first. You must have known that David Wood had been briefed.' 'I didn't know it was you who had done the briefing,' he said. 'I thought David had picked it up from several people.' That shows the difficulty of trying to share press relations between the Leader of the House and the Prime Minister. I'm prepared to tell him everything I do but often he doesn't want to hear it. Yet if I don't tell him and then I do a briefing he draws the oddest conclusions. He is getting more and more leak-obsessed, regarding as a leak what everyone else does and regarding as briefing what he and Trevor Lloyd-Hughes do in No. 10. So he and I are not getting on very well in this particular line of business.

I had lunch with Arthur Gavshon of Associated Press, one of the P.M.'s special boys and also a friend of George Wigg. Through him I heard something of George, who has become an increasingly grave problem to me ever since the announcement that I had taken over the co-ordination of information. Indeed I haven't spoken to George since the beginning of December and everything I hear suggests he's become a ferocious enemy. One special reason I want to see him is a visit I had from Alun Chalfont last Monday morning, who came to tell me of his alarm at a decision on nuclear weapons which has been taken not at O.P.D., where I sit, but at a secret committee from which I am excluded. (This shows, by the way, that the invitation Harold gave at Chequers for me to join the inner group on defence has been tacitly withdrawn, as I suspected.) Alun obviously wanted me to treat him as an ally in the battle against the creation of an independent British deterrent. I had told him of course to go and consult George Wigg. Now I would like to do the same, particularly because (if I could persuade him to favour withdrawal from East of Suez) he might use his influence on Harold. But can I afford to resume contact? It may be dangerous for me to consort with him now.

This afternoon in the House was really exciting since Jo Grimond's resignation as Liberal leader had been announced and Jeremy Thorpe was to make his first appearance. The Liberal Party had virtually degenerated into a personality cult of Grimond. Jeremy is charming and young but I doubt if he'll carry the weight to unite the Liberals.

After Jeremy had asked his four Questions, Harold greeted him warmly and then made a little joke at Heath's expense which set the House roaring for a couple of minutes. When it is printed in Hansard nobody will be able to see there's anything funny about it. However it nonplussed Heath, who on that very morning had read in the papers that the rating of the Tory leader had sunk lower than at any time for thirty years.

Then came my business Questions. I've been a bit worried about them for a week or two because there have been one or two comments in the press that I wasn't as well prepared as R. A. Butler and others of my predecessors. So I took special trouble on this occasion. I noticed that the P.M. waited beside me to see how I was doing. He never misses a press comment and he knew that my capacities were in doubt. I had a nasty problem about the galleries upstairs to handle. Apparently owing to shortage of staff we shall have to keep the public galleries closed during Monday morning sittings. However I seemed to get away with it.

Upstairs with the press I kept my word to Harold and dealt exclusively with the Tory assassination campaign and particularly the decision to go for the Prime Minister personally. I had some luck there, I gather, since at the meeting of the 1922 Committee[1] an hour or two later there were a number of protests made by people who regarded this campaign as a disaster for the Tory Party.

When the Party met that evening in our usual committee room, No. 14, Manny turned up and took the chair. George Brown and Harold were there to hear the back-benchers demand a Vietnam debate and insist on a vote on a motion. I had been pleading with a number of young people who came to see me last night on this very point. 'Motions,' I said, 'merely stiffen resistance and make the leadership harsher.' But I found the back-benchers obstinate and the real reason for their obstinacy is that they are utterly fed up with the reshuffle.

The meeting was thoroughly useful because it gave them a chance to blow off steam. It was far better to have the grousing there with George and

[1] The back-bench committee of the Conservative Party.

Harold present than in the corridors or to the Lobby correspondents. One other thing which helped me in the course of the meeting was Manny's behaviour. He was deliberately rude all the way through and tried to snub me and the more he snubbed me the more the Party liked me. They are obviously looking forward to the time when this silly old man is got out of the chair and we put someone like Willie Hamilton in his place.

Friday, January 20th

We were due to have our business meeting at 9.45. George Brown and I were both punctual and while we stood outside waiting, George told me how badly the Party had reacted to the P.M.'s promotions. He himself had warned him about the unwisdom of the three back-bench promotions.[1] There ought to have been six and they ought to have been chosen quite differently. At this point we were ushered into the room to discuss the business with Burke as usual.

At the Cabinet Committee on Housing which followed I watched Harold once again trying to sweeten the Chancellor. This time his proposal was that the local authorities should be instructed to build houses for sale because a council house for sale doesn't rate as public expenditure as a council house to let does. He seemed to be unaware of the fact that such an instruction would create the most frightful difficulty with the builders.

I stayed behind with Burke to try once again to solve the problem of Trevor Lloyd-Hughes and information co-ordination. We got nowhere. Having announced that I am to do this job the P.M. is fighting shy of the consequences in No. 10 and letting Trevor behave outrageously. As I heard from Gordon Walker today when I ran into him, he hadn't even been told that I was to take over social security. I took the precaution of ensuring that his files are transferred to my office.

After this I had to prepare a speech for a Labour Party dinner at St Albans tonight. I decided once again to rub salt into the wounds caused by the Tories' leadership fiasco. When I arrived at the station I was met by a nice man and driven up to a magnificent hall in the middle of a vast estate where an imitation of Big Ben is to be found over the stable because Barry who built it built Big Ben as well. It's now a great golf club bought by the Council in 1938 and run at a loss but with a very good restaurant. Here the local Labour Party was holding its annual dinner, price 32s. 6d. a head without drinks. Outside a double line of cars had drawn up because the Labour Party there seems to be composed either of aircraft workers from De Havilland and Handley Page or of prosperous London commuters. However it was an excellent lively vigorous party which seemed pleased to be told how well we were doing.

By the way, I forgot to mention that just before I left my Privy Council

[1] Dr Dickson Mabon (Minister of State, Scottish Office); Mrs Shirley Williams (Minister of State, D.E.S.); Gerry Reynolds (Minister of Defence for Administration).

office I was rung up by David Astor[1] who told me cheerfully that he hoped I wouldn't be too upset because they were having a little amusing piece in Pendennis's Diary on the back page of the *Observer* about the fact that I've got a very good contract from Thomson's for my diaries. I said that the diaries weren't going to be published and I'm still under contract to my own publisher, Hamish Hamilton.[2] All that's happened has been that Hamish Hamilton has been taken over by Thomson who would now be able to offer me much more favourable serial rights since they own *The Times* and the *Sunday Times*. Anyway the contract is for two *books*—my memoirs and a book on the British constitution. My diaries, I said, would never be published. 'Ah,' he said, 'that's interesting. By the way, Barbara Castle is having the same treatment as you, and George Wigg and George Brown have also been approached.' It will be interesting to see what will be in the *Observer* on Sunday about the diaries and in the *Sunday Telegraph* when they publish my profile.

Monday, January 23rd

A quiet day until the Committee which deals with party political broadcasts met in the evening. This is a really high-powered show where the Leader of the House and the Chief Whip speak for the Government, with the Leader of the Opposition and his Chief Whip for the Conservatives. There's one official from each party headquarters and the Leader of the Liberal Party and his Chief Whip. We are faced by Hugh Greene and Whitley from the B.B.C. and from commercial television by Bob Fraser[3] and Bernstein. This meeting should have been over quickly because, after long negotiations through the usual channels, the B.B.C. were proposing virtually no change in television and only one minor shift in radio. They only wanted to shift the party political broadcast from its present position after the evening news at 10.10 to 10.30 when the whole programme was over. Pretty tactlessly Greene said this would reduce the unpopularity politicians incur by being spatch-cocked into the news programme. Ted Heath said huffily that this was quite unacceptable and so did Jeremy Thorpe, who was representing the Liberals for the first time. I saw what an awkward cuss Hugh is. There he was stiffening and rigidifying and I remarked, 'Well, who knows. You may be right about the unpopularity of our party politicals but we can review that question in due course along with other big issues. Meanwhile, Hugh, let's keep things as they are.' Then I really went for him and said, 'You are revealing exactly why we have to have party politicals. It's because the B.B.C. thinks it knows so much better than we do how we should run our own propaganda.' But

[1] The Hon. David Astor, son of the second Viscount Astor, editor of the *Observer* from 1948 until the end of 1975.
[2] Crossman eventually decided that his diaries should be published jointly by Hamish Hamilton and Jonathan Cape.
[3] Sir Robert Fraser, Director-General of I.T.A. 1954–70 and chairman of Independent Television News since 1971.

Hugh was stubborn and finally said, 'All right. As an alternative I'm prepared to substitute several five-minute programmes in the Light Programme for the ten-minute slots you are now getting on the Home.' Heath jumped in straight away and said he would vastly prefer that. Whitley, the B.B.C. administrator, looked embarrassed and rapidly agreed that all this should be considered in the big discussion later on. I think Hugh is a wonderful Director-General but he's certainly no negotiator. On Monday he united the opposition against him.

The Tories had announced to the world that tonight they would show their power to keep the House up until daylight on the Iron and Steel Bill. However it was a complete flop. They had divisions at eleven and 11.30 and I stayed on to see what would happen. After that I listened to an interesting debate by the Labour Left in which they discussed industrial democracy with Dick Marsh. Most of the Tories had gone home and I got into bed at three for quite a decent night's sleep.

Tuesday, January 24th
Lunch with David Astor of the *Observer*. He asked to see me a quarter of an hour early—God knows why because he didn't have anything to tell me. Then we went upstairs and found a lot of young men and women talking very fiercely about the situation in the Party and about the new liberal discipline John Silkin and I were seeking to introduce. I then flew a big kite—an idea I'd got by studying Balfour's reforms, namely the complete compulsory time-tabling of all Government legislation. I've discussed this more than once with Willie Whitelaw and I've had a private talk with Rudolf Klein.[1] I've every hope I shall get the front page of the *Observer* next week.

At the Services Committee this afternoon I had to deal with the awkward row about the manning of the public gallery for Monday morning sittings. My main problem is the attitude of the Serjeant-at-Arms—a well-born naval gent called Gordon-Lennox.[2] He said that the public galleries had to be closed because he hadn't the staff to man them. I now discover there wouldn't be enough Commons' door-keepers but the custodians — who are not his but Ministry of Works officials — actually get less work to do with morning sittings because they won't be able to take visitors round the House and so they would be available for employment manning the galleries. I'm sure it's one solution which needs looking into. At this meeting I had the usual help from Willie Whitelaw and Selwyn Lloyd who are proving themselves extremely sensible and reliable colleagues on this awkward Committee.

That evening I moved a little bit nearer to the Speaker once again. I'm now looking in on him pretty regularly in his enormous lonely house. We've

[1] The *Observer* home affairs editor 1971–2. In 1972 he did research on the organization of medical care and has since been Senior Fellow at the Centre for Studies in Social Policy.

[2] Rear-Admiral Sir Alexander Gordon-Lennox, President of the Royal Naval College, Greenwich, from 1961 to 1962, when he became Serjeant-at-Arms of the House of Commons. He retired in 1976.

got him out of his huge library, which is now part of the Commons' library, to a most beautiful room where he sits in a corner at his desk: underneath there is a cupboard and out of the cupboard he pulls his bottle of sherry and asks me to share a drink with him. And then he pours his heart out about the Serjeant-at-Arms and the battle he is waging. It's worth winning Horace over on parliamentary reform because things go more easily in the Chamber when he's friendly. Indeed, in dealing with morning sittings I have to admit that though he's strenuously against me he has loyally supported me.

That evening was the Report and Third Reading of that worrisome Ombudsman Bill. Perhaps unwisely I've left Niall MacDermot to handle it in Committee and now I hear a great deal of complaint that the only amendment allowed has made the Bill even narrower and even more impotent. The debate went on from seven, when the Iron and Steel Bill was finished, until midnight, with Quintin Hogg very skilfully leading the Tory back-benchers in constant assertions that this was nothing but a swindle. He has certainly created the impression outside Westminster that our Ministers have tied the ombudsman up with so much legal red tape that he won't be able to do a genuine job and he won't even be a threat to maladministration. I see that this week's *Economist*, for instance, has a leading article saying that the House of Lords, of all people, ought to throw the Bill out and produce a decent one. Towards midnight there was one amendment I knew would be troublesome—to put the Health Service under the ombudsman. I noticed the House was quietly filling up as some thirty of our back-benchers came in to make a protest. I told Niall, who had irritated the House by his long and legalistic replies, that I would be the first Government speaker. I spoke for just two minutes in order to enable the back-benchers to have a long go. He would have spoken for twenty minutes. And then, right at the end, I kept him down again and gave the House the assurance that we would look at the problem very seriously. We avoided a division and an endless debate.

Afterwards I asked Niall to bring his staff into my room for a drink. We were drinking cheerfully when up came that phrase Quintin Hogg is always using: 'Really, it's only a swizz.' Out of the blue Niall MacDermot said, 'I'm not sure Hogg isn't right,' and his Treasury official, Couzens, added, 'Nor am I. Perhaps it is. We shall see.'

I went home, my bowels turning with anger because all my worst suspicions had been confirmed. In handling this Bill all the way through Niall MacDermot has been working for the Treasury and the Treasury has been seeking to do what Quintin Hogg accused it of—stripping the ombudsman of any effective powers so that we would be spending vast sums of money providing him with a staff which won't be able to do anything.

Wednesday, January 25th
We had N.E.C. in the morning but since nothing much was doing I went across to the Party meeting on German support costs. There weren't many

people there and it was going quite quietly. Right at the end a vote was forced by Jack Mendelson and someone challenged the peers' right to vote. At once Manny Shinwell ruled that peers could not vote on this issue. He was clearly wrong since a decision had been taken months ago that in the Party meeting peers were allowed to vote on policies common between the two Houses but not on matters affecting only the Commons. I knew perfectly well that within a few hours there'd be a row blowing up. And it's true that during the course of the afternoon we had letters in from peers and from George Strauss. When the liaison committee met, John and I decided that this was the moment when we must counter-attack Manny for what he had done to us before Christmas in his sabotage of the Party meeting. So we got the other members of the liaison committee to tell him unanimously that his ruling was wrong and that this must be announced at the business meeting tomorrow. At first he said he wouldn't do this and he wasn't going to be told to admit a mistake or to apologize. I said there was no need to apologize. We would have a statement drafted and read aloud by Frank Barlow[1] just announcing the decision of the liaison committee. This was the first occasion when Manny and I were openly at loggerheads. He said he wouldn't be treated like this by me. I said I was very sorry. He couldn't make a completely wrong decision to exclude the peers and get away with it as chairman of the liaison committee.

I was just going home when I ran into Barbara Castle, who said to me, 'Have you seen this message from the P.M. on the problem of the publication of Cabinet minutes and books by Cabinet Ministers? Apparently it's going to be raised tomorrow morning.' I went back into my room, opened my red box and there was a note from Burke Trend saying that George Brown was going to raise the issue and another from the Prime Minister to the same effect. I went home that evening somewhat disturbed.

The Prime Minister, Burke Trend and George Brown are all over in Paris for their crucial talks with de Gaulle. Presumably one of them spotted the paragraph in the *Observer* and thought it so important that they telephoned London to insist that it should be discussed on Thursday morning. Strange that Harold didn't give me any notice.

Thursday, January 26th
In my anxiety I woke up too early but the more I reflected the less I could see any chink in my armament. Harold's always known I'm going to write these two books and so have most of my colleagues. I've never concealed from any of them that I keep a diary which covers Cabinet meetings as well, and provided I don't violate the Official Secrets Act I can publish anything I like. The more I thought the less I could see anything wrong.

When we got to Cabinet the subject was raised right away before I could even get down to parliamentary business. Harold Wilson raised his head and said, 'There's something the Foreign Secretary wishes to raise.' Then George

[1] Deputy Secretary of the P.L.P.

Brown in a distinctly modest tone said he wanted to raise something which had been published in the papers. Apparently colleagues were now actually signing contracts for books based on Cabinet secrets which would destroy the sense of collaboration without which effective Cabinet government is impossible. He had felt it was something he had to raise straightaway. George only took about three or four minutes and then the Prime Minister made a speech from a written brief which was thirteen or fourteen minutes long. I have no doubt the brief was prepared in Burke's office. By the end he'd managed to weave a web of hostility and surround me with it. Throughout, of course, he kept repeating that he wasn't discussing individual cases and that no names would be mentioned. But he added that he and George thought the present situation very undesirable and that a Committee to make recommendations should therefore be set up with the Lord Chancellor at its head.

At this point he stopped and Barbara Castle then raised the side issue of whether under Harold's proposals former Cabinet Ministers in opposition would still be entitled to have access to their Cabinet papers, not only for writing books but for an occasional speech. Harold admitted that the present Opposition was exerting its rights and that ex-Cabinet Ministers are publishing more and more Cabinet secrets in their memoirs. The only value of this part of the discussion was that Harold admitted that there could be no objection to Cabinet Ministers keeping diaries or indeed making use of them.[1] What was serious—as Harold put it—was that if a Cabinet Minister signed a contract with a publisher it might mean that the publisher would have an undue hold over him.

Obviously it was Harold's tactic—having got his Committee appointed and woven his web of suspicion—to close this discussion without a single name being mentioned. I thought, 'That won't do. There's nothing for it.' I therefore said 'Before you move on to the next business, Prime Minister,' because he was just going to move on, 'there is something I want to say to you.' Then I made a speech which I wish to God had been taped because it was one of those few speeches which changes things. By the end everybody round the

[1] In August 1975 Lord Widgery, the Lord Chief Justice of England, heard in the High Court of Justice an application by Her Majesty's Attorney-General (Samuel Silkin) for an injunction against the publication of Volume One of Crossman's *Diaries of a Cabinet Minister*, and of extracts from the diary, by Times Newspapers Ltd and by the publishers, Jonathan Cape and Hamish Hamilton. After nine days of hearings, during which evidence was heard from the Cabinet Secretary and affidavits read out from Crossman's former colleagues, judgment was deferred until October 1st, 1975. The Lord Chief Justice then declared that he could see no ground in law which would entitle the Court to restrain publication of these matters and that he had not been satisfied that publication would in any way inhibit free and open discussion in Cabinet hereafter ([1975] 3 W.L.R. 606; [1975] 3 All E.R. 484). Volume One was published on December 8th, 1975. A Committee of Privy Councillors, with Lord Radcliffe as chairman, had earlier been established to examine the whole question of Ministerial publications and they produced their report (Cmnd. 6386) in January 1976, proposing that a period of fifteen years should elapse before an author could regard himself free of 'approved rules and procedures governing Confidential Relationships'.

table was roaring with laughter, relaxed, relieved and feeling they were having a really enjoyable time and the atmosphere of hatred and suspicion was dissipated to the winds. I started by saying that for years I'd been determined to write a book which would blow sky high Herbert Morrison's outrageous book *Government and Parliament*.[1] Indeed, when I thought I had no political future under Hugh Gaitskell I had started giving lectures at Nuffield College on this subject. I had signed a contract with Hamish Hamilton for a theoretical book replying to Herbert Morrison and also for my political memoirs in which all the evidence would be found. Then my life changed: in 1963 Hugh died, Harold came in and I knew I would have a chance of being in the Cabinet. When I got into Cabinet I obviously wasn't going to cancel that contract. On the contrary. By sitting there and keeping my diaries in full I was getting invaluable information which would greatly improve my book. In fact what had happened recently had been that Hamish Hamilton, my publisher, had been taken over by Thomson and new contracts had to be negotiated. Since my books were obviously so much more valuable now I was a Cabinet Minister, they were prepared to offer me more. That is why I needed the new contract. However, I saw the danger of leaks from a diary and that's why I had kept it on tape and, as a security measure, hadn't let the tapes be transcribed. I also pointed out that the contract I had signed provided me with a large capital sum directly I ceased to be a Minister on which I would be able to draw for five years without publishing a line so I would be able to avoid the disadvantage of having to earn money directly after the Labour Government fell by receiving, say, £1,000 an article for malicious attacks on my colleagues. In all this I'd made no concealment whatsoever and I wondered what had happened suddenly to change the view of the Prime Minister and the Foreign Secretary. I concluded by saying that if the Prime Minister felt that keeping a diary was incompatible with collective Cabinet responsibility I would be the first of many to get out of the Cabinet and I would do so eagerly because it meant I should be able to start work on the books sooner. It was quite all right by me if I had to resign but I just wanted to know where I was.

I must say I managed to make it lively and amusing and Callaghan led the shouts of laughing applause when I stopped. The P.M., rather podgy and puffy, tried to join in the amusement. I could see what was going on in his mind. He had decided to say to George and Burke afterwards, 'I always told you my Dick would have some good reply to you which we hadn't thought of.'

There wasn't very much more after that. The Lord Chancellor's Committee was set up though he himself showed no enthusiasm for it, and said that nothing could come out of it. And of course nothing will.*

* I was wrong about one thing—namely that I expected this item would not be recorded in the Cabinet minutes. But it is there including a report of what I said, which is very unusual in Cabinet minutes unless the Minister is introducing a paper. Here is what the

[1] London: O.U.P., 1954.

This evening I ran into Fred Peart. 'My God,' he said, 'I enjoyed myself listening to you. Of course everybody round that table keeps a diary. I do, and Harold was trying to scare us all. You blew it sky high.' Barbara's attitude was careful. She has kept a full diary for years and intends to base a book upon it. Roy was his usual retiring self. He intervened only when Dick Marsh said that he was bewildered and couldn't imagine how it was possible for a colleague to be sitting there and recording what was on in his private diary for later publication. Roy added rather dryly, 'It may be better to have publication based on what is remembered and put down next day than on what is put down some thirty years later.' The truth is that most of my colleagues are preparing to write their memoirs because it's their only way of looking after themselves in old age. But I was the only one who actually blew up the P.M.

Of course it isn't a wise thing to blow up the P.M. I'm now in pitched battle with him and even more with Burke who I'm sure organized the whole operation. I hear that Burke sent telegrams back from Paris to the Cabinet Office giving all the instructions and Harold's brief was certainly prepared by him.

After this the report on the discussions with de Gaulle came as a curiously gay and irresponsible anticlimax. However it became clear that George and Harold both thought that they had begun the major job of charming the General. On the other hand, they admitted that he resented the notion of British entry because it would change the whole character of the Community. But it's my impression that whereas George is unchanged Harold comes back from Paris for the first time determined to enter the Market. Something has happened to him to make him get off the fence and most of his terms for entry are disappearing. Agriculture went some weeks ago, movement of capital has probably gone by now. Something seems to have happened during that de Gaulle interview which has made him work unreservedly for entry.

Cabinet then broke up and I talked very breezily to the P.M. who wasn't

---

Cabinet minutes say about my remarks. 'The Lord President said that in so far as the press reports related to himself they had no other foundation than the fact that before he became a member of the present administration he had signed a contract for the publication after his retirement from political life of a book of personal memoirs together with a study of Government and Parliament. It was intended to be a serious and responsible contribution to informed discussion of these institutions. He had carried the project no further since becoming a Minister apart from negotiating the necessary readjustment of the relevant dates of contract.' The last sentence is quite untrue. It was not the dates of contract but the capital sum of advanced royalties which had been changed and this I had very carefully and candidly explained. I had told the Cabinet that a book by an ex-Cabinet Minister on how the Cabinet works would be worth far more and sell far better than a book by a back-bencher. Yet not one word of all this is put into my mouth. I do not think this is a deliberate falsehood. Cabinet draftsmen are so used to putting in the Cabinet minutes what Ministers ought to say instead of what they actually say that they only half listen to our remarks. On this occasion the Cabinet Secretariat expected me to accept my rebuke in silence. They got the minutes all wrong because I was not silent as they expected.

quite so breezy with me, before going back to my room to get ready for the business Statement this afternoon.

I have to be ridiculously efficient with the business Statement these days, briefed to the last because of all the press criticism that I am not master of my job. So I cancelled a lunch with I.T.V., had a quick meal at Vincent Square and then went to the House at 2.30 to master an enormously complicated brief full of summaries of Early Day Motions and answers to all the small questions which might possibly be raised. It all went smoothly and I was in fine fettle when John and I strolled down to the Party meeting. We suspected that Manny might welch on us but we thought he couldn't get away with it. That Party meeting was a colossal blow-up and the political sensation of the week. It started quite quietly. I announced the business and explained that it wasn't really illogical for us to have the first morning sitting on Wednesday and then that night have an all-night sitting on the Consolidated Fund Bill, because that Bill was a back-bencher's paradise which had nothing to do with Government business.[1] Then Manny got up and made his statement about the Labour peers' rights to vote at our meeting. He added that he didn't agree with it and would like to see the matter discussed in due course. At this point one or two people got up to try to speak, in particular Carol Johnson[2] whom the Chief and I had stopped from going to Brussels because he had been the Secretary of the Party for fourteen years and he could provide the evidence that peers have always been entitled to vote. Manny twice refused to call him whereat I nudged him and said, 'There's Carol Johnson sitting over there.' He was allowed to make his point.

Stanley Orme then raised the issue of an invitation which he had had to attend an Albert Hall meeting on the Common Market at which George Brown was speaking. Stanley asked whether this invitation had gone to all M.P.s and whether they should attend. I haven't had the invitation or heard about it. But Manny knew about it and probably intended Roy Roebuck,[3] a solid right-winger who was sitting on the other side of the room, to start the discussion. If he had been scored off on the issue of the Lords he would get his own back by causing George Brown to blow his top about the Albert Hall meeting. George Brown certainly blew his top and Manny then said the affair should be reported to the P.M. George said he would be reported to the P.M. There was chaos and then shouts of, 'Next business.' Finally I got up beside Manny and said, 'Next business has been called.' This forced him to put next business to the vote and when the vote was taken four-fifths of the

[1] The Consolidated Fund is the Exchequer's account, kept at the Bank of England, into which all revenue is paid. Consolidated Fund Bills, passed in January, March and July of each year, authorize the grant of 'supply' to the civil and defence Departments. The July Bill also sets out in detail the amount and purpose of the appropriation allocated to each Department. Spring supplementary estimates, for the current year, are laid before the House in February and March, before the end of the financial year in April; the summer supplementary estimates for the new financial year are laid in the following June and July.

[2] Labour M.P. for Lewisham South 1959–74 and Secretary of the P.L.P. 1943–59.

[3] Labour M.P. for Harrow East 1966–70.

Party were against him. Then he shouted at me and I walked out straight through the lobby to the P.M.'s room. 'Harold,' I said, 'this can't be allowed to go on. John Silkin agrees.' Harold said that George Wigg was down in Stoke-on-Trent but would have to be got at in order to control Manny. Meanwhile John Silkin was told to brief the press on what had happened at the Party meeting.

That evening I got a great deal more sympathy than I'd ever had before. For once I was the innocent victim of aggression.

Friday, January 27th

When I looked at the sensation the morning papers have made of our Party meeting I was not so hopeful as I was last night. I thought perhaps I should check with Harold and found that he is due to go to Huddersfield by the nine o'clock train. I rang him at 8.20 but of course George Wigg was on the phone.

Last night I'd been in the Chief's room when he was talking to George Wigg in Stoke-on-Trent and trying to persuade him to give his help in getting Manny out of the chair. I'd listened in to the conversation and wasn't convinced that all was well. Yes, he would help, said George, but he was saying it in a crafty way. This morning George occupied the P.M.'s telephone line from 8.20 to 8.45 when the girl rang me back saying he was off the line and the P.M. was now in the bath. I said, 'I must speak to him.' Just after nine he rang back, telling me nothing could be done. I said, 'That won't do. John and I can't take this. Our prestige is at stake. You have either to get rid of Manny or of us.' 'No,' he said, 'we've got to let this thing blow over,' and there was a real altercation between us. Finally I said, 'O.K. Go off to Huddersfield now.' But I couldn't help resenting the fact that he'd had two long talks with George Wigg and not found time to have a chat with John or myself. After talking to the Chief I realized how impotent we were. We couldn't call a meeting of the liaison committee before Monday and we haven't yet persuaded the P.M. to take any action against Manny.

Saturday, January 28th

Down at Prescote I have a moment to reflect on this exciting dangerous week. On Friday there was a great deal of press briefing and other activity and as a result Manny staged a tremendous comeback in popular sympathy. I'm accused of handling Manny tactlessly, of behaving like an arrogant bully and there's a powerful profile in tomorrow's *Sunday Telegraph* providing evidence to show what a bully I really can be. However, to judge by this morning's newspapers, what was a mere fracas in the Parliamentary Party is now being transformed into a Common Market row. When I rang up Harold and finally got a long talk with him, even he had to admit that this was so. He had read the papers, he told me, and had further long talks with George Wigg and Tommy Balogh and they all now feel that it was George Brown who did the wrong thing and was to blame. And the P.M. added, 'I've had a

Cabinet Minister threatening to resign if Manny goes.'[1] I replied that as long as it was a mere Party fracas John and I were trying to manage it ourselves but if it turns into a policy row about the Common Market then the P.M. can't stand on the sidelines. That made him slightly bad-tempered so I went to the point that, even if George Brown was wrong in accepting the invitation, any competent chairman could have prevented the thing blowing up into a row. The question that had been put was whether if George Brown was to speak at this meeting an anti-Common Market member of the Cabinet could speak at an anti-Common Market meeting. The obvious answer the chairman should have given was yes—provided that, like George Brown, he cleaves religiously to the Government line. But Manny had deliberately blown up the whole affair. Harold let me make my point but I knew very well that he was still determined not to intervene in the hope that it would blow over.

Monday, January 30th
We started the week with O.P.D., which lasted three hours, on the Defence White Paper.[2] I'd already been warned by my talk with Lord Chalfont about what might be found in the White Paper this year. The second part of it, as usual, was a mass of figures and details. What really matters is always the first chapter, which only arrived on Friday evening. It contained a flaming apologia for Britain's role in NATO as the chief apostle of a return to massive nuclear retaliation. When I'd finished it I thought to myself: Oh God, have I got to go and have another row with Harold on Monday? Have I got to be the only one to raise this in O.P.D.?

It so happened that I didn't have to because George Brown arrived in time to say exactly what I'd intended to say. He told the Committee that he didn't want to challenge the doctrine or the strategy but he did ask himself why on earth we should have to put it forward in this form this year. Would it not profoundly shock the Germans, not to mention Kosygin, who arrives this week? Would it not be the cause of a frightful row in the Party? Something which Healey had included in his initial remarks suggested that his officials had not wanted this first chapter and that he'd written it himself. George Brown ended with a bitter complaint that he'd only received this on Friday afternoon and that Thomson and Chalfont, his two Ministers of State, saw it for the first time on Sunday. Surely we had a rule about O.P.D. being given decent time to discuss something as important as this? Healey made no effort to answer this question though he did not in any way deny that he himself had written the offending first chapter. Nor do I know whether Healey had warned the P.M. about the character of this chapter. I rather fancy from Harold's behaviour that he wasn't given much warning and that Healey was once again acting as a lone wolf pushing his own ideas in his own

[1] Probably Ross, who was to speak in Shinwell's support at Cabinet on January 31st.
[2] Cmnd. 3203.

peculiar style. George Brown was supported by George Wigg and then by me from rather different points of view and, of course, by the Chancellor. The Committee was virtually unanimous that this chapter of the White Paper was a quite unnecessary provocation.

In addition to our objections to the exposition of nuclear strategy I pointed out that there was another reason why the chapter should be wholly deleted. It gave advance notice of further major cuts. But surely it was unwise to commit ourselves to these now. Harold replied that what was much more serious was that if we didn't announce the cuts now and then made them in July, we would be accused of surrendering to our own left-wingers. On the other hand George Brown, from the Foreign Office, and Judith Hart, from the Commonwealth Office, said that such announcements would have a demoralizing effect throughout the Commonwealth in view of the things we were doing in Malta. Finally it was agreed that Healey should bring the Paper back to a special meeting of the O.P.D. on Thursday and we should have a special Cabinet on Friday to pass the revised draft White Paper.

I lunched that day with Alan Watkins of the *Spectator*; he is an old friend of mine and one of the best political commentators now writing. He was still anxious to talk about the Manny row. I understood why as yesterday's and today's newspapers are still crammed with pro-Shinwell propaganda listing all my misbehaviours and even accusing me of insisting that meetings of the liaison committee should take place in my room against Shinwell's wish. I was also accused of having tried to shove him out of the chair at Thursday's meeting and of generally behaving in a bullying way. I tried to tell Alan what had really happened and then said that I strongly suspected that my old friend George Wigg was the man behind the scenes.*

This afternoon Peggy Herbison came to see me about her future plans for legislation on social security. However, what she really wanted to talk about was the outrageous fashion in which she'd been treated. She feels that at the Cabinet before Christmas (Douglas Houghton's last Cabinet) it was firmly decided that both sides in the dispute about family allowances should put in papers and that they should be considered at a special Cabinet before a White Paper was issued. The final major reform would then be incorporated in the 1968 budget and meanwhile there might well be an interim concession this year. Well, that was the agreement and she had duly put her paper in before Christmas. No acknowledgment. Week after week the Treasury had delayed until now it is too late for any interim concessions. She told me she was going to see Harold that evening and threaten resignation. I tipped off Marcia and I gathered late in the evening that Peggy had been persuaded not to resign and had got an assurance that her legislation would be pushed forward in a satisfactory way.

* A comparison of the article in the *Spectator* by Alan Watkins with that in the *New Statesman* by Matthew Coady shows up the normal pro-Shinwell and anti-Crossman line of political commentators.

Tuesday, January 31st

A special Cabinet was called at 9.30 ostensibly on Malta. But before we got to that the Cabinet spent an hour discussing the Shinwell affair. Officials were present but it was decided that no minute should be taken. Still, we had a long discussion. Harold stated that Shinwell had behaved outrageously and then added that perhaps George Brown had been unwise. George agreed that he shouldn't have accepted the invitation to address the huge Albert Hall meeting and then we discussed whether the eight Ministers whose names were associated with it should have them taken off the list. Quite clearly no one there was prepared even to consider Shinwell's resignation: they wanted the affair patched up and the Party to allow it to blow over. The Chief Whip and I remained completely silent during this wearisome hour. Right at the end I said we would carry on and that was all.

Cabinet then turned to Malta, which we had discussed briefly at O.P.D. and which I'd thought about very carefully since. We are behaving abominably and Bert Bowden (who was away with 'flu when the decision on the cuts was taken) had agreed on that point. Yet if we concede the Maltese demand that we should maintain employment in the harbour, what answer shall we give in Aden, where I'm told 30,000 people have work related to the British presence, or in Singapore, where there are 40,000? I regret it but we shall have to stand firm and face the fact that we create unemployment when we make our major withdrawals.

This afternoon I had a formal meeting with Kenneth Robinson and Peggy Herbison about the legislative programme and when it was over I asked Kenneth to stay behind and talk to me about the ombudsman. I told him how depressed I was by Quintin Hogg's success in creating the impression that the Bill is a swindle. I told him I had made a pledge to the House and I now must seriously consider the possibility of putting the administrative section of the Health Service under the ombudsman.[1] Kenneth blankly disagreed. He didn't mind the narrowness of the ombudsman's function because he was convinced that his own system of dealing with complaints in the Health Service makes such an appointment unnecessary. Indeed he said that if he conceded on this the implication would be that there was something wrong with the N.H.S. After some time I said to him, 'But Kenneth, all your arguments are not really about the Health Service. They're against the whole idea of having a Parliamentary Commissioner at all.' He didn't bother to deny this. In the course of these two years he's become a very nice, very competent non-political administrator.

After this I saw Aubrey Jones[2] because I was desperately anxious to discuss the prices and incomes policy where Tommy Balogh has been begging for

---

[1] This was, in some measure, done in 1973.
[2] Conservative M.P. for Birmingham (Hall Green) 1950–55. He was Minister of Fuel and Power 1955–7 and of Supply 1957–9, and was the first chairman of the National Board for Prices and Incomes 1965–70. See Vol. I, p. 198.

my help. For the last ten days there have been appearing in the *Financial Times* and also in the *Guardian* an almost daily series of revelations of exactly what is going on inside the Cabinet Committee on Prices and Incomes. The general impression given by these articles is that the committee has come to the conclusion that the Government can't afford new legislation. That is why Aubrey Jones came to see me. He told me that he had submitted an extremely powerful paper giving not only the case for legislation but his suggestions about how the Prices and Incomes Board should be reconstructed. By this evening he was extremely gloomy because he thought Michael Stewart was going to do nothing to help and Gunter would win easily. Gunter has argued that the Government must trust the unions to implement a sane voluntary incomes policy. We should only have Part II in reserve and clap it on if voluntary restraints fail. Aubrey Jones gave me the figures of the wage claims that have piled up and showed me what disastrous pressure would occur if Part IV lapses without any substitute legislation.

I went to bed very gloomy. In my red box I found a long paper by Michael Stewart—an agonized last-minute reappraisal which comes reluctantly to the conclusion that it isn't sufficient to activate Part II or to rely on the voluntary efforts of the unions: we must have new legislation before Part IV lapses. I rang Aubrey Jones up straightaway and said to him over the phone, 'Before you see Stewart tomorrow you'd better realize that he's moved a long way in your direction.'

Wednesday, February 1st

This was the first day of morning sittings and the Chief and I had made our preparations as carefully as we could. I was in a weak position because I'd been brought in a novice while John has a great reputation. So he didn't have much difficulty in convincing me against some of the Whips' advice that the right thing to do was to take the Consolidated Fund Bill as the business of the House on the first day of morning sittings. After all, this is always a back-bencher's occasion and the debates go on through the night until the last victor in the ballot has had his say. John calculated that if he put any Government business on that day he would have to keep one hundred people for the closure if the Tories decided to prolong the proceedings. On the Consolidated Fund Bill, however, all he needed was forty people present to keep the House if a count were called.

I went in to see the beginning of the morning sittings. It was a successful start with sixty people there and a sensible discussion on the Ministry of Aviation Dissolution Order.[1] We knew the Tories would talk it out that morning and we were planning to give it another hour one evening and so get it through. Everything seemed to be going quite well. Our only concern was the fact that the House had been counted out the night before and as a result the Opposition had been denied their full debate on a prayer which they

---

[1] The Ministry of Technology was to take over responsibility for the aircraft industry.

had put down against the Prices and Incomes Order.[1] When I had heard this on the B.B.C. at breakfast-time I had been very disturbed and the Chief and I went out of the morning sitting to talk it over in his room. Apparently John himself had for once gone home a bit early and left George Lawson in charge. As bad luck would have it the Liberals then irresponsibly called a count and George, for a reason we can't understand, told our people to stay away and let the debate be counted out. Of course he shouldn't have done this and there was a real risk of vengeance by the Tories on the first possible opportunity.

At lunch-time I went in to see the Speaker about the form the debate on the Consolidated Fund Bill should take. He confirmed that because it was a debate on supplementary estimates there couldn't be the Consolidated Fund broad debates we usually have each March and July and back-benchers could only raise items which occurred in the estimates. The Speaker was obviously very tired and made it clear to me that he would like a closure that evening. He'd had the first day of morning sittings and he wanted to be in bed before midnight. This put me in great difficulty. I knew that John didn't want to have one hundred pepole there on the first night of morning sittings and I had to explain this to the Speaker who was obviously irritated.

The liaison committee met this afternoon. Shinwell had seen Wilson and we all behaved with strict propriety.

Then I went out to dinner with Tommy Balogh to meet Chalfont and discuss the redraft of the Defence White Paper. We went through it very carefully and all felt very gloomy about the disastrous decision on nuclear weapons, which has been made secretly without even members of the Defence Committee knowing. I thought I would go back to the House on the way to Vincent Square at about midnight. Everything was going quietly. There were few people there: virtually only back-benchers who wanted to speak. I sat on the front bench a little and chatted to John, who seemed quite cheerful. At one o'clock I strolled home because I was told I wasn't needed.

Thursday, February 2nd

As soon as I woke up I telephoned and heard that the House had finished at three a.m. That seemed quite all right until, on the radio, I learnt the news that for the second night running the House had been counted out. At once I knew we were in real trouble. It took me most of the day to discover precisely what had happened. Apparently as the first item of the morning sitting our Eddie Milne from Northumberland had moved a little ten-minute

[1] Any Member may call for a count of Members present in the Chamber and if there are fewer than the quorum of forty, the House must adjourn. The procedure was abolished on November 16th, 1971, and now if fewer than forty are present, no decision is taken on that item of business and the House moves on to the next business. During a debate any Member may rise and claim to move 'that the question be now put'. If the Speaker believes that representatives of all sides of opinion have been able to put their case he may order the House to vote at once, but there must be a majority of 100 Members in support of the motion for the closure to be given and a debate brought to a sudden end.

Bill.[1] Kenneth Lewis, a Tory M.P.,[2] at the end demanded a vote and, according to our new Standing Orders, this was postponed until the end of the sitting—which of course might well be early in the morning. As the night went on Lewis, who's quite an indefatigable fellow, went round the lobbies to look for Eddie Milne and discovered he wasn't there. This angered him and to make sure that he'd gone away Lewis had the idea of calling a count, even though it meant denying the last two Tory speakers their time for debate. Presumably he assumed that the Government would have its forty members present and the count would soon be forgotten. Actually, to the fury of his own side it ended the proceedings. The fury was shared by the two Chief Whips. Soon after midnight when I was still there I was told that the Speaker had complained that he wasn't feeling well and wanted to be relieved. He asked whether we couldn't shorten proceedings. I mentioned this to John and the two sides got together and agreed to cut speeches down though, having agreed, we couldn't of course then demand a closure. So there was complete consternation in both the Whips' offices when Lewis moved the closure because it broke an agreement between the two Chiefs. The one bright spot was that while the count was on, John's deputy, George Lawson, had saved the situation by running to the Table and putting in a motion to have the Consolidated Fund Bill reinserted in the business for this Thursday. I felt quite elated when I learnt this from John in his office, where we had a hurried meeting with Freddie Warren before O.P.D. at 9.30. Freddie hoped everything would be all right and that the Speaker would rule that the Consolidated Fund Bill could be taken at 3.30 on Thursday and disposed of with a closure in a very few minutes. He did mention, however, that this interpretation might well be challenged by the Clerks.

Feeling considerably relieved, I went in to O.P.D. where we were presented with the new draft of Chapter 1 of the Defence White Paper. Again I pleaded that the whole chapter should be excised and was quite strongly supported by George Brown. George Wigg, whom I'd rung up this morning, failed to turn up. The Prime Minister said that the Committee must never again be given so little time for appraisal but it was clear that Healey had once again got away with it. He is a very ruthless operator.

As soon as the soldiers had gone out the Cabinet came in and we had our meeting on prices and incomes. Before the discussion started John Silkin reported briefly on how he had saved the situation last night and got a round of applause for his Deputy's quickness of mind and brilliant success. I reported that morning sittings had started fairly well though we might have a good deal of trouble from the Opposition.

So we come to the crucial debate on Michael Stewart's paper arguing the case for new prices and incomes legislation, in order to prevent the wages

[1] Labour M.P. for Blyth from November 1960 until 1974, when he fought the general election without the support of his Party as an Independent, losing narrowly by 78 votes.
[2] Conservative M.P. for Rutland and Stamford since 1959.

dam being broken in three or four months' time. He made a very good speech and Ray Gunter made his usual reply and then came the significant moment — George Brown spoke in favour of Gunter. He said that he and the Prime Minister were bound by the pledges they'd given to the unions when he was trying to get his original Bill through. This revelation made the rest of the Cabinet very wonky and only Barbara Castle spoke up for poor Michael. Even the Chancellor of the Exchequer, who was the person chiefly concerned and mainly responsible for a prices and incomes policy, was very half-hearted. It was a terrible meeting. All one can say is that the situation wasn't absolutely lost because we are meeting again next week.

Over lunch in my room I prepared for the business statement this afternoon. I knew I was likely to be in real trouble and I briefed myself as far as I could on the rulings about the situation arising from the counting out of the Consolidated Fund Bill. It was going to be a difficult business Statement followed by an even more difficult time when the leader of the Opposition would challenge our decision to put the Bill back on the Order Paper. Looking at the mass of paper I was disconcerted to discover that in fact there was only one precedent which applied to us. In 1952 the Tory Government was counted out on the Second Reading of the Iron and Steel de-nationalization Bill. Next day the Speaker advised the Tory Leader of the House that it would not be appropriate to resume debate on that day because it was a contentious measure. The Speaker had agreed that it could be put back but he had advised the Government not to do so. When I looked at this I felt that to call the Consolidated Fund Bill a contentious measure really was unreasonable and I would hope that the Speaker would give us the benefit of the doubt.[1]

While I was making my preparations John came in and told me that it was essential that I should explain to the House in one of my Supplementaries what had really happened on the night before and make it clear that a Tory had prevented the last of his own side from speaking. John felt that if we did this our own people could be got to understand that the outrage of the night had been committed by the other side.

The business Questions went quite well though they were long and tedious. I sat down feeling rather surprised that the Tories hadn't touched it, but finally Heath got up on a point of order and raised the issue of the return of the Consolidated Fund Bill to the Order Paper. He made the case that it was a contentious measure and quoted the only precedent. To my complete consternation the Speaker got up and ruled in his favour. I was nonplussed

[1] On November 26th, 1952, the House was unexpectedly counted out on the Second Reading of the Iron and Steel Bill. The Conservatives wished to take the business again on the following day, even before the customary twenty-four hours had elapsed, and they were at first advised, by a procedural 'fudge', that they could do so. However, the matter was sufficiently contentious for the Speaker to advise the Government not to press the point. It is interesting that in 1967 Crossman seized on the point that the measure was contentious rather than that the procedure was incorrect

because I had assumed that the Speaker was going to rule for us and I hadn't taken into account the possibility that he would simply back the Opposition. However, I had learnt from my brief that the decision was mine. The Speaker was only advising me. This encouraged me to start reasoning with him but I soon discovered that most of the House thought I was challenging his ruling and soon I was being howled down, not only by the Tories but by some of our own people, who were already moving upstairs for the Vietnam Party meeting.

Looking back there's no doubt I went on arguing too long in my determination even at that late moment to get the facts on record. Of course the record didn't have the faintest effect because nobody cares what really happened. I was now in the dock for unsportingly challenging the rules when I'd lost a round in the parliamentary game.

After that I had my usual Lobby conference and I knew we were in for a terrible press because they would talk about nothing else. Ironically enough the sketch-writers in the gallery had given me lunch two days before—a very pleasant affair. When I'd recovered from what I realized was a disastrous performance I went upstairs for the Party meeting where the Vietnam debate was going on. Harold had been confident that he could prevent a vote by pleading that Kosygin was coming. I was much more doubtful and in fact there was a division with 68 voting against the leadership and 144 in favour. There were also a lot of abstentions. It was a very bad meeting indeed and the Party is obviously out of tune. It started with the Cabinet reshuffle. The row between Manny and me unsettled it and this afternoon's mess in the House had certainly done us no good. We have a really bad situation on our hands.

After giving Anne dinner in the House I went home early.

Friday, February 3rd
I woke up to a terrible press—the worst I've ever had. The news stories about me were long, prominent, detailed and humiliating. I was made to look a fool. And my arrogant refusal to accept the Speaker's ruling was presented as the climax of a long series of clangers. First there was my ill-tempered row with Manny Shinwell at the Party meeting. Then I'd allowed the House to be counted out on two nights running. And finally I'd argued interminably with the Speaker instead of sportingly accepting my defeat. That was the picture of myself I read in the morning papers. It wouldn't have looked so bad if any of the Tory papers had told the story from the other point of view and treated this as a brilliantly successful Tory manoeuvre for spiking our guns on morning sittings. On reflection I think this is really what it was. I've been trying to bring in morning sittings against the strong conviction of the Opposition, against the wish of the officials, against the Speaker, against even the journalists who have to go and report them. And our own side is divided on the subject. To make matters worse it's a half measure which I would never

have dreamt of introducing if I hadn't inherited it as something Herbert Bowden had willed on the Select Committee on Commons' Procedure and the Select Committee had recommended to us in its report. But though I see morning sittings as the cause of my downfall no one else in the country will after this morning's press. I draw the conclusion that I must stop playing the role of the great parliamentary reformer and try to save the situation by just quietly running the business of the House in a wholly uncharacteristic, self-effacing style.

At No. 10 the special Cabinet on the Defence White Paper was an insulting formality. Poor Barbara made her protest that she'd only had a draft the previous afternoon and the document itself didn't contain many of the appendices. But nothing could be done about it. The timetable was fixed and it was railroaded through the Cabinet. The P.M. got rid of it and pushed it aside.

I went along to the Chief's room at No. 12 to discuss what he and I should do. We decided to see the Speaker that afternoon. We were pretty crestfallen. John looked tired and harassed, and no wonder. After all, he knew that the balls-up had started owing to his Deputy Chief Whip, George Lawson, behaving intolerably on Monday night and the second cause of it was the gamble he took on having only forty people there and refusing to have a closure earlier on. Of course he also thinks, quite rightly, that I mucked up the front-bench presentation of his case so that we share the blame. Still, we got down to planning action and at two o'clock we went to see the Speaker. I told him I was sore that he'd given the House the impression that I was challenging a ruling. He denied this until I was able to show him the passage in Hansard where he'd used the word 'ruling'. He said he was very sorry it had happened to me but really he had wanted the closure earlier. Indeed, it's obvious that our refusal to let him go to sleep before midnight on Wednesday had turned him against us and I had paid a very heavy price for it when he got up to give his advice yesterday afternoon. However, we got one very important thing out of him—if he keeps his word. He has promised us that when we put the Bill back on next Tuesday we shall be able to get the closure after an hour and a half. So we shall actually only waste one and a half hours of Government time on this and if we can keep out of the limelight this week John and I will be devoutly grateful.

There was one more scare before I got away. This afternoon John came up to me grave and grim and said, 'My God, the Tories are going to defeat us on the closure at four o'clock today on the Pensions Bill which Robert Carr is moving.'[1] True enough we found a Tory conspiracy against us. They were trying to collect one hundred people to move the closure and we would have nothing like that number there. With his usual vigour John collected Ministers

[1] Conservative M.P. for Mitcham from 1950 to 1974 and for Carshalton from 1974 to 1976, when he became a life peer. He was Secretary of State for Employment 1970–72, Lord President of the Council April–November 1972 and Home Secretary 1972–4.

from all round the place so that we got 105 votes. If we'd failed to get that number and suffered yet another defeat in this disaster week our political careers might really have been over.[1]

I stayed and voted before driving down the M1 with Anne in beautiful weather.

Sunday, February 5th

We've had the most exquisite weekend. Yesterday we were over on the Burton Hills with the children and I spent the morning at the Managers' meeting in the village school discussing the new building, which is going up with tremendous speed as the result of weather which has been unheard of in January. Today we've got Robert Blake coming over with his wife to discuss Disraeli and the workings of Parliament.[2]

Looking back over the last fortnight it would be an exaggeration to say that it has destroyed me as President of the Council and Leader of the House. But I shall have quite a job to live down this series of fiascos, particularly if the press goes on with its campaign against me. In today's papers they're still getting at me with the same indictment.

One of the last things I did on Friday was to send for John Mackintosh and give him a dressing down.[3] John is a really brilliant professor of politics who wrote the first book on Prime Ministerial government and who now sits for the Berwick constituency. He's tremendously keen on Specialist Committees and has been one of the most ardent members of our parliamentary reform group. So I was furious when I noticed that he had put down on the Order Paper a motion objecting to the absence of a Scottish member from my new agricultural specialist group. Of course the reason for this is that on Willie Ross's request Scotland is expressly excluded from the terms of reference. I was feeling depressed and rightly or wrongly I gave John Mackintosh hell and told him that if he had any objection to what I was doing the right place to make it was not on the floor of the House but in my room with me. What I hadn't reckoned was that he would go straight upstairs to the journalists and give them a really juicy news story about yet another example of the arrogant bullying behaviour of Labour's Lord President. It is all over the papers this morning.

This evening I was so miserable that I did something I hardly ever do—I rang up Harold Wilson at home because I knew he too would have read it all in the press and I wanted to talk to him about it. Over the telephone he

---

[1] The Conservatives lost the vote on the Public Service and Armed Forces Pensions Commission Bill, Second Reading, by 96 votes to 105.

[2] Lord Blake, Provost of Queen's College, Oxford, since 1968. He became a life peer in 1971.

[3] Labour M.P. for Berwick and East Lothian 1966–February 1974 and since October 1974. Professor of Politics at the University of Strathclyde 1965–6 and, since 1972, Visiting Professor at Birkbeck College, London. His books include *The British Cabinet* (London: Methuen, 1968).

poured out a flood of 'don't worry' talk. 'It's never entered into my mind,' he said, 'to worry about this minor little incident.' And the more he consoled me the more I became aware that there was something to worry about. I think it was that conversation with Harold which alerted me for the first time to the full extent of the damage which has been done.

But most of it is exterior damage. Inside myself, though I wouldn't admit it ever publicly, I am convinced the affair is not my fault. It was Manny who caused the row in the Party meeting. It was John Silkin who was entirely responsible for the House being counted out on Monday and Tuesday. The only fiasco for which I was personally and entirely responsible was my argument with the Speaker on Thursday afternoon, and even there I was at a disadvantage because I hadn't been adequately briefed and warned by Freddie Warren. So I feel no sense of guilt or real blame. On the other hand, I realize that the job of the Leader of the House is to be vulnerable, to be attacked, to take it, to be a St Sebastian. I have been the victim of circumstance during the last fortnight and have got to make the best of it. It was interesting to find that as the P.M. talked to me his only rebuke was for the Mackintosh affair. 'You shouldn't do that kind of thing,' he said. 'You are the chairman of the governors of the school. You should leave the castigation of pupils to the headmaster. Keep yourself completely out of that.' That is sensible advice and I shall certainly do so in future. Secondly, I must regain my imperturbability on the floor of the House and make sure I never even seem to bully anyone. Thirdly, and this is very important, I must be careful in my relations with John Silkin. John is an extremely Jewish Jew, very much the son of his father,[1] and he has an enormous confidence in his own skill at personal relations. That's why he always says to me, 'You're the man who does the policy. I am the man who does the personal relations.' Now that is a very sensible arrangement and I ought to keep to it on my side as he keeps to it on his. This applies even to relations with the P.M. He sees him much more than I do and as Chief Whip he has a more intimate relationship with him. In fact, he's a henchman and one hundred per cent devoted to Harold and politically dependent on him. He's there to run the machine for the P.M. and if I get into trouble on his behalf, as I well may, he will probably survive me. He's much more likely to be still Chief Whip after I cease to be Lord President. I get on with him extremely well though I'm not sure I get on with his wife so well.[2] He is very good at handling me, very flattering, very comfortable, but he's reserved and watches me and is really more of a business associate than a personal friend. I have to retain that relationship while looking after myself since John won't wholly look after me.

For instance, this week I have to see Matthew Coady of the *New Statesman* and Alan Watkins of the *Spectator* to give them the full story for their

---

[1] Lewis Silkin, who was made a peer in 1950 and, from 1945 to 1950, had been Minister of Town and County Planning.

[2] John Silkin's wife was Rosamund John, the actress.

periodicals, even though this will mean that their accounts put me in a greatly more favourable light. But then John had been wonderfully screened from criticism by the press concentration on my failings.

And I have to add something else. All the schemes for parliamentary reform are mine, not Silkin's. He goes along with them, he hasn't criticized them but he has never been enthusiastic about them. As Chief Whip he has an illiberal attitude which is in many ways supported by Freddie Warren. It comes into conflict with some of my ideas for restoring parliamentary authority. For example, John's notion of handling Specialist Committees is to select the members so as to prevent the Committees from being the tough inquisitors I really want them to be. When I think about it, the row I had with John Mackintosh (who is a firm friend of my parliamentary reforms) is due to the Chief Whip's method of manning the Select Committees. I was a fool and a nitwit to get dragged into that. I hope I've learnt my lesson.

Monday, February 6th
I went straight from the train to the morning sitting and found nothing to disturb me. True, at 11.50 the Opposition spokesman got up and therefore succeeded in talking out the Ministry of Aviation dissolution Order because our Minister wasn't quick enough on his feet. Still, that doesn't upset the Chief or me too much. I spent part of the time talking to our ombudsman and doing the job I promised of trying to get the Ministry of Health back to his area of jurisdiction even if he's excluded from the clinical side. I'd been warned by Niall MacDermot that though Compton had wanted it to start with he didn't want it any more. However I thought I'd have a try. Niall was quite correct. Compton told me that he wouldn't want to do it for purely practical reasons. He had built up sufficient staff for the number of cases he calculated he would have. As for hospitals, he was already responsible for three central hospitals—Broadmoor and the other two criminal lunatic asylums. Here he would be able to test whether he could make the distinction between medical and administrative problems. Of course, if he was ordered to take on Health he wouldn't object but he would have to ask for more staff.

It wasn't quite what Niall had told me but it was a negative which made it useless to quote the ombudsman's support when the matter comes up in Cabinet. On the other hand Gerald Gardiner turned out to be an enthusiastic ally for my project for a Ministerial broadcast on the day the service starts operation. The Bill, by the way, is now in the House of Lords and this week they'll be dealing with details in Committee Stage.

But, of course, this morning what chiefly concerned the Chief and myself was the business Statement I had to make at 3.30. I found that my luck had turned. The first lucky accident was that the Foreign Secretary preceded my business Statement with an exciting report on the problem of a guardsman

Gabriel who'd been condemned to death in Aden by a civil court because he'd gone out and murdered an Arab while drunk but off duty. This case had been raised by Sydney Silverman,[1] who fell into the trap of entangling himself in an extremely complex problem of jurisdiction—that took the edge off Question Time. When we came to my business Statement and Edward Heath barged in it was obvious he was there for the kill. There on the other side sat the Lord President unpopular and discredited. The Leader of the Opposition was going to rub him out and he started a long attack on my competence. He was very offensive but I kept my temper and that saved me. If I'd lost my nerve and fluffed it or got angry I'd have been in real trouble within seconds. But when I got myself off that front bench I realized after a few minutes that I'd done all right and that I was beginning to rally a little support among my own people. The Tories had already put down a vote of censure on the Leader of the House. This evening Michael Foot put down a counter-amendment which has collected a good number of names. Michael really has been a stalwart friend through the most difficult crisis of my life, supporting me in *Tribune*, and helping me on the Floor in a way that no other Labour back-bencher has done. One of the troubles about the new entrants is that they only have the haziest notion of what this row is all about. Alan Watkins told me he'd tested public opinion by asking four Labour back-benchers and four Tories to describe the row and not one of them had really the faintest idea of who had done what. They had condemned me because of the deadly poison the sketch-writers in the gallery had printed in their papers.

I had dinner with Tom Driberg, just back from a delegation to Malta, who pleaded with me to make concessions to the island. I said that once we'd started on a big defence cut we couldn't go back without disastrous consequences in the rest of the world. I wasn't aware when I told him that this was only a few hours before Healey had begun to stage a retreat from his extreme position. I might have guessed it from the telegrams. For weeks the Malta High Commissioner's office has been sending us bromidic telegrams with no indication that there was any danger involved in a massive cut of the defence programme. Now suddenly we received a paralysed panic paper on the disaster that total evacuation would mean and on the need to understand the Maltese position.

Tuesday, February 7th
The day started with another long discussion of sonic bangs at Gordon Walker's Home Affairs Committee. I have already described how I managed to prevent Mulley rushing through a Cabinet decision that sonic bangs required immediate legislation this year. Fred had looked like winning in Cabinet because he had not only the defence interests but the Foreign Office

[1] Labour M.P. for Nelson and Colne from 1935 until his death in February 1968. See p. 675.

and above all the Chancellor of the Exchequer urging him on. For once people were open to rational argument. It was Niall MacDermot who first asked whether legislation really was necessary. The Americans haven't got any, the French haven't got any: they've merely allowed their planes to fly over the country making bangs and then examined the effect. That is the line we should take. But suppose we actually decided on legislation. What is the legislation for? Apparently the intention is to seek legal authority for sonic bangs. Public endurance will be taken to breaking point and there will be maximum public opposition. The only part of the British public which will complain will be the opponents of supersonic planes and we shall create a violent anti-Concorde atmosphere. When the Attorney-General was asked what he thought he very cannily replied that the instruction he had been given was that the Government intended to test public opinion up to breaking point and so he had replied that this required legislation. If we don't have a test of this kind, legislation may not be necessary. This was a really constructive meeting because we changed our minds as a result of thinking down to the bottom of the problem.

This afternoon at 3.30 came my crucial moment. I'd nothing to say but I had to sit there and see whether our resolution on the Order Paper to restore the Consolidated Fund Bill was acceptable to the Speaker. I had been canny on Monday and refused to give anything away although Freddie Warren and John both wanted me to try this tactic. They wanted me to answer a carefully planted Question asking for my opinion on whether the Bill would be restored intact or whether the debate would be resumed where it left off. I saw a danger in doing that and a great advantage in not doing it. Greatly daring, I defied my experts and said nothing at all about it leaving it all to the Speaker. Sure enough, I'd avoided a deadly pitfall. All the squabbles today were between Ted Heath and the Speaker. And Ted had another real grievance. The Speaker had told John and me on Friday that he would closure the debate after an hour and a half, but I think he had concealed his purpose from the Opposition by putting out a list of fourteen subjects which strongly suggested that the Bill could get another ten hours or so. As a result, when John moved the closure after an hour and a half at 6.33 there was a frightful row from the Tory side. For an extra half hour Heath led the attack on the Speaker's decision. Having come down on their side last week the Speaker was leaning to me this week. Indeed he said to me afterwards, 'I leant their way 45 degrees and your way 45 degrees this afternoon.' I can't say I admire a Speaker of this kind but on this occasion I was grateful for his equidistant neutrality. The worst crisis of my life was over—but only of course until Manny picks another quarrel, as he certainly will.

The effect of these events was miraculous. John had put a tremendous pile of business on the agenda and the House had to complete the Land and Natural Resources Order, then complete the Hartlepool Order, then do a lot of Scottish business. No wonder Heath had accused us of incompetence for trying to do all this. But we achieved it quite easily. At 8.10 we closured the Ministry of Aviation Order after an hour's debate. The Land debate then started and ended just after eleven and the Hartlepool Bill then went through by 11.30 and the Scottish business was over by one in the morning. We'd got it. We'd broken through. Our business was back on keel and for the rest of the week we've got easy debates ahead of us.*

That evening I went to the Kosygin dinner at No. 10. Oh dear, it was a boring affair. Enormous amounts must have been spent on the food and the drink. The drink was all right, the food only so-so and I found myself sitting at the end of a long table with Edna Healey on one side and no Russian anywhere near me. As soon as I could I slipped back to the House to be sure that nothing was amiss and to wait until the Scottish business was finished before going to bed.

Wednesday, February 8th

At morning prayers I had to tell the P.M. that the Chief couldn't be there and then to report to him how marvellously we had got through yesterday's business. He could hardly believe it. But the important thing which sprang out of this talk with the P.M. was my discovery that I took a completely different position towards prices and incomes from John. John belongs to the Gunter–Callaghan anti-intellectual opposition which says that whatever the logical case for new legislation may be we just can't introduce it. He was advising the P.M. of the danger of a split in the Party and I was not. My worries were about the presentation of the Defence White Paper to a Party that is anyway in an extremely bad mood. To see what they were really feeling I trotted across at 11.30 when the Parliamentary Party was debating unemployment and social security. Some sixty people turned up at the beginning but there were only twenty-five people there when Peggy Herbison wound up. The real weakness of the Party now is not left-wing militancy but sheer lethargy.

I lunched with Anne and then, at 3.35 when the Consolidated Fund Bill was safely on the Order Paper again and my crisis over, Douglas Jay rose to begin a debate on the Press. The subject had been coming up a good deal in Cabinet as a result of the Thomson takeover of *The Times*. Throughout Harold officially took a strictly non-interventionist view and supported Douglas Jay. But he had also asked Arnold Goodman and me to see if there weren't any practical proposals for preventing, say, the *Guardian* or the *Mail* from folding up. We had looked very hard for some weeks and found nothing practical. That is what Douglas Jay had to report at the beginning of the debate and it is something he could do very well. However Sir William

---

* The papers began to show me a little sympathy. The Tories had been forced to put out a press release saying they didn't intend to prosecute a personal attack on the Leader of the House – not for his sake but because they cared about the dignity of the place. Of course they knew they'd overreached themselves and had better pull back.

Haley, when he read that there was going to be a debate, thought it was so important that he insisted on coming to lunch yesterday in order to make sure that I was speaking and would say the right thing. I told him I didn't take part in debates which ended in no decision. (See what Bagehot says about that kind of debate.[1]) Then, as our conversation went on it became clear that Haley too favoured a policy of complete non-intervention. When I asked him what the Government should do if it was faced with the certainty of the disappearance of the *Guardian* he replied quite roughly, 'If that happened it would be the *Guardian*'s fault and the Government should do nothing'. I've never met such a smug fellow as Haley. Imagine him urging us to let the *Guardian* disappear because he and *The Times* were safely washed up on the coast of the Thomson press.

After that to the Soviet Embassy with masses of plain Soviet ladies on display. I found myself sitting between the present Soviet Ambassador and the old Soviet Ambassador. Anne was on his right and Michael Stewart on her right. This was an ideal little corner where we really could talk freely and we had some excellent caviar and wonderful blinis before the terrible main course. I found myself testing out Soldatin, the ex-Ambassador, telling him about the trying things in my own life and asking him what was trying in his. When I said, 'Come on, fair exchange, fair play. I've told you mine,' he raised his hands in horror and I realized I had gone just too far for a Soviet Ambassador. Meanwhile there are the usual press leaks about George Brown's drunken behaviour at a Downing Street dinner last night and rumours that he's repeated the performance this evening. Let me add that I'm quite convinced by reading our official papers and by the atmosphere of those two meals that this Soviet visit is a flop.

Thursday, February 9th

I went to the first meeting of the Cabinet Committee which deals with the Farm Price Review and then we came back to No. 10 for the big Cabinet discussion of prices and incomes. It was soon clear that a split was developing between working-class trade unionists and middle-class intellectuals. The supporters of Michael Stewart's paper were Crossman, Crosland, Gordon Walker, Barbara Castle and one trade unionist, Fred Lee. But the Chief was clearly on the other side. Dick Marsh, as a young trade unionist, came out categorically against any kind of statutory policy and said he stood for the C.B.I. and the T.U.C. being left to do the job voluntarily. Of course there were some who tried to throw bridges between us. A lot of time was spent by Callaghan airing a compromise proposal and by Barbara, who also produced an ingenious solution to take the powers but only use them if the C.B.I. and T.U.C. failed to achieve voluntary control. Wedgy Benn made a good remark right at the end. 'If the Cabinet is going to put forward a perma-

[1] W. Bagehot, *The English Constitution* (London: Fontana, 1963), for which Crossman wrote the introduction.

nent solution,' he said, 'I would gladly vote for it.' I am pretty sure this has got to happen because at the moment it looks as though the Cabinet will try to patch up a twelve-month solution good enough to last for part of next year and then to play it by ear year after year till the election.

Back to my office for lunch and to get my business Statement ready for 3.30. I've discovered the secret is to master the detail so completely that you can answer any question without having to cast your eyes down at your written brief. And as you're being fired at from all directions, left, right and centre, front and behind, it's a great strain when it lasts—as it often does— for thirty-five minutes. There's another annoying feature of this weekly performance. If nothing goes wrong not one word is printed in the press, not one single word, no matter how important my announcement is. So although the Lord President can do no right in public he can do endless wrong. On the other hand, efficiency and success does have an effect in the House of Commons. Next I went along the passage to the House of Lords where I had to join in introducing Kosygin to the meeting of both Houses he was going to address. Some eight hundred peers and M.P.s were gathered —an amazing number since it was obvious he was going to say nothing of importance. His speech lasted about half an hour in translation and much of it consisted of lambasting British policy, particularly in Vietnam. Tam came up to me that evening and said, 'I must tell you that on this Vietnam issue most of us back-benchers are much more on the side of the Russian P.M. than on that of the British.' I blew my top and said, 'What on earth can you mean? You can't be on Kosygin's side. He's a totalitarian *apparatchik* and his aim is to divide Britain and to cause trouble. Apart from that he's not going to give us a single inch. He will only gain from the propaganda storm he makes because it will undermine Party resistance and extract a softer line from Harold and George.'

Just as the five days of Kosygin's visit look like being an absolute waste of time the journeys round Europe begin to look equally futile, as some of us predicted at the Chequers meeting. The trouble is the time it wastes. Here we have Harold and George who should be concentrating on vital domestic problems like prices and incomes gallivanting round Europe and occupying the time of very important officials. We don't get their attention on Party matters because their minds are floating in the stratosphere of diplomacy.

When Kosygin had finished his statement I got back to the press gallery in time for the Lobby conference. Last week's Lobby had been all about my fiasco. This week not a single question on it. As Walter Terry said with a smile, 'This is Ted Heath's bad week, not Dick's.'

I found I had a completely free evening with nothing to do and so I wandered into our dining-room and sat down opposite Tony Crosland. As I hoped, we discussed the problems of book-writing and diary-writing as well as the situation in Malta and incomes and prices. He told me that of course he keeps his diary like everyone else, including Fred Peart and Barbara Castle.

Even more surprising, when Anne sat next door to Michael Stewart at the Russian Embassy, she got into conversation with Mr Soldatin. She had the sense to recommend the study of Pepys's diary to the Russians in order to understand what life in Whitehall was like in the seventeenth century. When she'd explained all this to the Russian, she turned to the Foreign Secretary and said, 'Do you keep a diary?' He said, 'Yes, when I can. I keep it in long-hand but I find it very difficult to be regular because of all those red boxes. I hear that Dick keeps his on tape. How does he manage that?' Anne told him that I do it on Saturday evening and Sunday morning and Michael said, 'Ah, Sunday morning. That would be a good deal easier. I must think of that.'

All this talk about how to keep diaries has made me wonder once or twice whether I shouldn't have dictated mine every day of the week. As it is I spend two or three hours on Saturday evening organizing my thoughts and putting in order the official papers the office has sent down—the actual diary of each day of my life, all my official appointments, all the Cabinet minutes and the Cabinet Committee minutes, and all the press-cuttings which my Office collects, not to mention Hansard. With all this as background I check through the main events of the week and remind myself of the key things which happened. To deal with the Commons I usually read the P.M.'s answers to Questions and look through the topics of debate in Hansard just to remind myself what subjects the House finds interesting. Then by going through each day I select the incidents which seem to me memorable, write them down, and attach to the list the pages of my source material which refer to them. Of course this means that I'm giving my reflections after a whole week and not my views at the end of a single day. This also means that the diary isn't a compendium of anecdotes. I'm not naturally good at anecdotes and don't tend to remember even the funniest of them. I can never tell a funny story. But because my memory is a practical one I do remember key anec-dotes and key bits of conversation at such moments decisions are taken.

So my diary is that of a practitioner, not of an observer. That's why it couldn't be more different from Harold Nicolson's or Pepys's.[1] What I'm writing at the moment is not a vivid anecdote about a conversation I had with Tony Crosland but a kind of narrative summary of a political opinion. My talk with Robert Blake on Sunday confirmed to the full that the kind of diary I am now keeping has never been kept before by a British Cabinet Minister—far less published. It carries you along because it is the narrative of a practical Cabinet Minister trying to get his way. Of course this Cabinet Minister is most unusually an academic student of British politics and therefore writes the diary with a special interest in how decisions are taken.

---

[1] Sir Harold Nicolson, author and critic, was a member of the Diplomatic Service 1909–29 and National Labour M.P. for West Leicester 1935–45. His *Diaries and Letters* (3 vols, London: Collins, 1966–8) were edited by his son, Nigel Nicolson.

Friday, February 10th

I had my weekly meeting with the P.M. along with Burke Trend and George Brown. I started off with a tremendous effort to clear up the muddle about family endowment and to express Peggy Herbison's hurt feelings. It had been decided just before Christmas that Cabinet should make up its mind finally and publish a White Paper after receiving two papers on family allowances and taxes, one from Herbison, the other from the Chancellor. Poor Peggy put her paper in on January 13th and so far nothing had happened. The Chancellor simply kept her waiting and I suspect his plan is to issue the paper on the Friday before Cabinet, just as Healey issued the Defence White Paper when no one had time to read through it. Peggy had come to me in a terrible state to ask me whether I couldn't at least get her the right of reply to the Chancellor. So I had rung up Burke and made a stink and finally I managed to get the debate postponed for a week. But today I *still* haven't got the Chancellor's paper.

The other thing I raised was S.E.P. I pointed out that when we had our last meeting well before Christmas many members had not accepted the Chancellor's optimistic view that we could get through with a £150 million margin on our balance of payments. I had asked for a discussion of this and I had suggested that we should have various models put before us, including one dealing with the possibility of devaluation. Harold said at once that we would have to make time for such a discussion and Burke suggested we could have it on April 5th when we start the budget discussions. I thought about this and it seemed to be O.K. But of course Harold, in his Micawberish way, has succeeded in pushing off the discussion for another fortnight. He's going to coast along on this inadequate margin of surplus on the balance of payments and introduce no really effective prices and incomes policy. By next Christmas we shall be facing another July crisis.

This afternoon we had a meeting of O.P.D. postponed till 3.30 because of the lunch with the Russians. George Brown turned up with a very red face and so did Harold, and we didn't get very far with yet another discussion of the priority to be accorded to home defence costs against foreign affairs costs. The problem has never been presented quite in this way but I was able to show that if we're determined to go right into Europe it's futile to have a bleeding row with the Germans in order to extract a small cut in our soldiers' support costs. It would be sensible to realize that we shall always have to have half our troops on the European continent and we should be preparing to make the really big cuts East of Suez and in Malta. I wasn't very popular for putting this forward and I didn't try very hard.

I slipped off to Leicester where I was due to dine with the Oadby Labour Party. Oadby was once a pleasant village in the country and is now a commuters' paradise but it has an excellent local Labour Party, who gave me a warm-hearted reception—partly, no doubt, because I failed to tell them how grim the situation is.

Saturday, February 11th

Well, there's the week and I see the sun is coming out once again after a muggy cloudy morning. I've got today pretty well free for the children. When I look back it's been a bad week for the Government and not too bad a week for the Lord President of the Council.

Monday, February 13th

The first thing I did when I got back to London was to have a talk with David Piper of the National Portrait Gallery.[1] My four National Gallery acquisitions from Philip Hendy look splendid on my walls and I want to add a couple of portraits. At lunch time I strolled round to his gallery and he offered me two or three pictures but it was clear that the one he thought suitable for me was a rather sinister picture of Halifax. When I pressed him he said that he thought that in character Halifax resembled me more than anyone else. Well, with him hanging over the mantelpiece the room will look magnificent. I use it now more and more for working and, though it's impossibly inconvenient to get at my staff in the House, I love giving parties in it, particularly giving people a drink here before lunch. In fact it's the only departmental asset I've got.

At the Economic Committee Barbara was once again her vigorous self. She has discovered that the London Passenger Transport Board is going to demand a big fare increase (possibly 50 per cent at the bottom end) in the next three or four weeks. Since all the argy-bargy would take place in the three or four weeks before the G.L.C. elections this would be politically disastrous and she proposed that we should allow the G.L.C. to take the L.P.T.B. over and in the course of the transfer the Chancellor should pay the extra subsidies for any losses incurred. A Bill in the next Session would do it. Well, the Chancellor wasn't prepared to go in for that as his contribution to the G.L.C. election campaign. But to my surprise he came that morning prepared to have the fare increase postponed for three or four months during discussions between the two bodies. That's all that the politicians required.

What a contrast there was today between Barbara Castle and Tony Greenwood as Ministers. I discovered last week that Tony had already accepted a recommendation made in a secret meeting between his officials and the local authorities that of the £130 million which the Government would make available for local authority mortgages this year the G.L.C. should only get £26 million, against the £50 million it got last year, and he had also agreed that the announcement should take place on April 13th. Bob Mellish and I tried to work out some gimmick but the Minister refused to budge. He had given his word to Callaghan and he wasn't going to play politics. He had to consider the rights of the authorities outside London to

[1] Director, Keeper and Secretary of the National Portrait Gallery 1964–7, Director of the Fitzwilliam Museum, Cambridge, from 1967 until 1973, when he became Director of the Ashmolean Museum, Oxford.

their fair share of mortgage money. Of course in all this he was following his departmental brief.

This evening the influential parliamentary reform group of back-benchers headed by David Kerr,[1] George Strauss and Donald Chapman[2] came to discuss how we are getting on. It was good to have some frank expressions of opinion after the morning-sittings fiasco and that side was quite easy to deal with. What disconcerted me was the continued sense of frustration. A lot of the people there were back-benchers of the 1964 vintage and their main complaints were about their lack of occupation—couldn't the back-benchers have discussions with the Government before Bills were passed, I was asked? Why should a Government discuss everything with vested interests outside Parliament and not with them? The more I heard the more convinced I became that their reforming zeal was the result not of a real interest in parliamentary procedure but of the frustration produced by our present system of two-party machine politics. Already a lot of people who were reformers six months ago are settling down to jobs outside Parliament and I told these people honestly that I myself would never have dreamt of being a back-bencher without a job outside because there isn't a real job to be done here in Parliament from the back benches except by a very few political guerillas. That's what made it so very difficult to decide what we should do about morning sittings. Should we go in for the really big reform and have the sittings starting every day with Question Time at 9.30 a.m., making the House a completely whole-time business? If we do that the Tories are going to be a hundred per cent against us and at least 75 per cent of our own people will, I suspect, be in favour of the *status quo*.

But they did raise two genuinely important subjects. The first was how the new Specialist Committees were selected. David Kerr said to me, 'They are packed by the Whips and have no genuine independence. Why shouldn't a Committee elect itself?' I showed that this was impractical in a British Parliament. But I am beginning to realize that the complete control which the Chief Whip keeps on the selection of members and the assumption which he and each Minister has that they will in future be able to control the business and forbid the Committee to do anything of which they disapprove is really unconstitutional. Of course we can't swing over to American lines where they have the seniority system, thereby ensuring that people grow in power by their long membership of specialist committees and are really enabled to challenge the Executive. But if we are going to give our Specialist Committees any effective authority the Whips have got to take a very different attitude.

The second problem was very closely related. They complained to me that the Chief Whip was interfering far too much in the Agriculture Committee.

[1] Dr David Kerr, Labour M.P. for Wandsworth Central 1964–70.
[2] Labour M.P. for Birmingham (Northfield) 1951–70 and chairman of the House of Commons Select Committee on Procedure which issued the 1966 Report. He was created Baron Northfield in 1976.

Now I knew something about this because last week Michael Noble, the Opposition front-bench spokesman from Scotland, came to me wild with anger about the behaviour of this Committee.[1] We had excluded Scotland on the request of our Secretary of State, Willie Ross, and therefore had excluded all Scottish M.P.s. But if the Committee is now going to study what sort of statistical intelligence the Ministry can provide as a background to E.E.C. entry then the Scottish Members have an absolute right to be present. That was the case Michael Noble put to me and of course it's the case which John Silkin and I had discussed at some length. It's already clear that the assurances we gave poor old Fred Peart that the Committee would be hand-picked and would eat out of his hand are going to be falsified by facts. I must secretly whisper 'a good thing too'.

After dinner I gave drinks in my big room to some twenty junior Ministers, an experiment I undertook because they are always complaining they are outside Cabinet and have no contact with Government policy. All they know about is the work of their Departments. So I got together these twenty, who included Stephen Swingler, John Morris, Jennie Lee and Arthur Skeffington.[2] We started by discussing the lack of contact and I soon discovered an amazing variety in the amount of information they had about Government policy. Swingler and John Morris have all the Cabinet minutes from Barbara, whereas Arthur Skeffington has nothing from Tony Greenwood. They soon got down to asking me about prices and incomes, complaining they knew nothing about the new policy. I could hardly tell them that we did not know anything either.

This was successful and it looks as though I shall be holding a monthly meeting of this kind. I know it's a ticklish thing to do because I shall be briefing junior Ministers about what goes on in Cabinet and obviously if I interpret a crisis wrongly or in a way that a particular Minister thinks unfair it will go straight back to him and I shall be the loser. Still, I've got so little to lose these days, I'll take the risk.

During Mr Kosygin's official visit to Britain from February 6th to 13th, he and the Prime Minister apparently held lengthy discussions on the Vietnam war. At the very beginning of 1967 the British Foreign Secretary, George Brown,

[1] Conservative M.P. for Argyllshire 1958–74. He was Secretary of State for Scotland 1962–3, President of the Board of Trade June–October 1970 and Minister for Trade at the Department of Trade and Industry October 1970–November 1972.

[2] Stephen Swingler, Labour M.P. for Stafford 1945–50 and for Newcastle under Lyme from 1951 until his death in February 1969, was Joint Parliamentary Secretary at the Ministry of Transport 1964–7 and Minister of Transport 1967–8; from 1968 to early 1969 he was one of Crossman's Ministers of State at D.H.S.S. John Morris, Labour M.P. for Aberavon since October 1959, was Parliamentary Secretary at the Ministry of Power 1964–6, Joint Parliamentary Secretary at the Ministry of Transport 1966–8, Minister of Defence for Equipment 1968–70; since 1974 he has been Secretary of State for Wales. Arthur Skeffington, Labour M.P. for Lewisham West 1945–50 and for Hayes and Harlington from March 1953 until his death in February 1971, was Joint Parliamentary Secretary at M.L.N.R. 1964–7 and at M.H.L.G. 1967–70.

had called upon the Americans and the North Vietnamese to arrange a cease-fire, but the initiative had been rejected by Hanoi and China and scathingly received by the Russians. However a four-day Lunar New Year truce was called on February 8th, and the Americans ceased bombing north of the seventeenth parallel. President Johnson emphasized that only if the Vietcong were to end their infiltration into South Vietnam would the American bombing stop altogether, but as an encouragement to the Wilson–Kosygin discussions, the truce was briefly extended beyond February 12th.

The British Prime Minister gave the impression that he and the Russian Premier might have been able to act as intermediaries between the Americans and the North Vietnamese; however their private talks at Chequers and a call that the Prime Minister and the Foreign Secretary made at Mr Kosygin's hotel at 1 a.m. on February 13th produced nothing more than a communiqué calling for a speedy end to the war. Some observers deduced that the accord shared by the two leaders had been exaggerated; others that the Russian leader was reluctant to appear to be backing the West against Russia's Chinese rivals and their allies.

Tuesday, February 14th

Cabinet today was extremely interesting. Harold started with a long report on the Kosygin week, which I think I've described as though it was a mere series of dinners with nothing really going on. This is quite wrong. There was something on. They'd obviously used the opportunity for a British attempt to get in on the peace negotiations in Vietnam.

Harold was in his more elevated form, telling us how he had 'the absolute confidence of L.B.J.' and now had 'won the absolute confidence' of Kosygin. Then he told us graphically how on two occasions—first on Friday and then on Saturday—they'd been on the very edge of success and how it had been dashed away and how disappointed they were. But, he added, one must be fair to both sides—we must not be anti-American. On the other hand we must not be anti-North Vietnam. What we should rejoice at is that the mechanism for peace negotiations has now been established and in the coming months they would succeed.

At this point he paused and I popped in two questions. 'Look, if you really were on the edge of peace on Friday and then again on Saturday didn't the bombing start again rather rapidly on Monday? Wasn't the explanation that the Americans thought peace might be breaking out?' He was very sharp in denying this so I pressed him. 'But look, so *very* soon afterwards?' Then he began to backpedal a little on 'being so near to peace' and it came out that no actual contact with Vietnam had been established during the five days. The only evidence they got that they were near peace was the impression given by Kosygin. It's worth seeing how the Cabinet minutes report the P.M.: 'We had taken advantage of the opportunity to try to ascertain whether some contact could be established between the United States and the North

Vietnamese Governments. There had appeared to be some prospect of success in this attempt at one stage but in the end it had failed and the United States' bombing of North Vietnam had now started again.'

What a contrast there is between those words and what Harold actually said in Cabinet. I vividly remember the P.M.'s claiming that he was twice on the edge of peace—by which he meant prolonging the bombing truce. The cautious record smooths out the exaggerations. As we left the room Callaghan said to me, 'You have an irresistible temptation to say what people don't like to hear. You certainly satisfied it by your behaviour at Cabinet.' I suppose I did. It's perfectly true that in putting that kind of question on that kind of occasion one upsets him most of all. Tommy never does it, yet as Callaghan notices, I can't resist doing it.

The main item was prices and incomes. Michael Stewart was allowed to make his claim for authority to go to the T.U.C. and explain that we wanted them to run a voluntary system, that we wanted to try it without state interference but that we must have reserve powers in case the T.U.C. failed. He spelt all this out beautifully and then Harold remarked, 'We need to have a hawk-like attitude now and then become more dove-like after March 2nd.' At this moment I thought he'd persuaded the Cabinet to accept the whole package since there'd been no resistance except from Ray Gunter and Dick Marsh. But then he began to talk about his other favourite idea of substituting a national dividend, expressed in money terms, for the norm expressed in percentage terms. That woke up George Brown who began to have doubts and then Callaghan had doubts and before we knew what we had a long second round of discussion in which a number of people revealed their attitudes for the first time. Fred Peart came right out in favour of Ray Gunter, so did Willie Ross and Cledwyn Hughes. The split between the proletarians and the socialists was clearer than ever. And Harold wanted to have it out in the open. Otherwise, if he'd taken the vote after the first round, he could easily have got away with it.

Finally we discussed the Farm Price Review which was presented by Gordon Walker as the new chairman of the Agricultural Committee. There was a completely characteristic official compromise. The Minister was asking for 2d. a gallon extra on milk, but the Treasury had been willing to concede only three-farthings, which had been gradually increased to 1½d. Jack Diamond made a long detailed bitter Treasury attack on all agriculture and then all the agricultural Ministers made their long attacks on the Treasury. There were no other contributions except mine—and I'm a farmer.

Last weekend I had talked to Pritchett who had told me that he thought 1½d. was very good if only the farmers could get it, so I realized that this was not a minimum by any means, and that Fred was demanding a great big bonus. All I said was that the selective expansion programme might be endangered unless farmers were really encouraged. At this Harold Wilson intervened. 'Why don't we just let through the compromise which Gordon

Walker has so admirably provided?' he asked, and sure enough Cabinet assented. No one knew that the compromise was a very generous concession to the farming industry.

At Question Time that afternoon Harold talked about Kosygin and made the best of it. Then he rushed to the Party meeting but, as I knew, he made no progress there. They met for half an hour and he pleaded with them not to vote because we were on the edge of peace. Now he is off to Bonn. The end result was that one hundred names were added to the Early Day Motion that evening after he left. I felt very sick and tired at this.

However, I went off to the Garrick to give dinner to Dame Evelyn, now Lady Sharp. I'd originally asked her because I was infuriated that in my *Daily Telegraph* profile she had permitted herself to be quoted in a number of extremely offensive anecdotes about me. However we soon got over that because I couldn't really keep a grievance against her for too long. We talked about the Local Government Boundary Commission. She explained how our Chief Planner, Jimmy James, had done the job on the big city regions and how she thought that it was a poor document because others below him hadn't done their work and she was now very worried lest the units were too large. Only forty units of local government! Would people tolerate that? I said they probably were a bit too large and that under the pressure of politics they might be expanded up to a hundred. She discussed very frankly what was happening in the Ministry and talked about the relationship between Greenwood and his Permanent Secretary, Stevenson. She ended by saying that those she liked as Ministers were those who were worth fighting against.

Wednesday, February 15th

After I'd had an official talk with Callaghan about his Department's legislative plans up to 1970 he asked me to go back to his room. When we got inside he said, 'I've decided to stand for Treasurer of the Labour Party and I've got the T & G on my side. What do you think of it? If I do this all my constituency votes will come to you. I've been advised by Len Williams that though I won't be defeated this year, next year I shall be in danger and I thought it was time for a move.'[1] 'Well,' I said, 'I'm thinking of resigning myself this year because there are too many Ministers on the Executive so your votes won't be any help to me.' But what I was really thinking was that this was a pretty suspicious manoeuvre. To think that as the Chancellor of the Exchequer in a Labour Government operating a prices and incomes policy the unions detest he has already got Frank Cousins's vote in his pocket!

We talked about Europe and I said that on the whole I was prepared for the great leap forward and I thought we ought to say we were prepared to sign the Treaty of Rome and negotiate afterwards. What did he think? He

---

[1] Some members of the N.E.C. were elected by the representatives of the trade unions, others by the constituency section.

said he agreed. 'What about devaluation?' 'Well,' he said, 'Harold and I have discussed this and of course we would accept a 10 to 15 per cent devaluation as a condition of entry. Yes, that's all clear in Whitehall, that's what we face as a precondition for entry.'

We also discussed my position and how it had weakened. He said, 'You ought to be about more, in the tea-room listening to what people say and chatting as I do. Why can't you just be friendly with the chaps?' I said, 'Well, if I go slumming in the tea-room I shall probably talk shop in much the same way as I do in my own room. I have to behave in my own style—I can't change now.' He said how much he thought Harold was upset by what I'd said about the Kosygin meeting and finally he concluded as I got to the door, 'Of course, I know we're all material for your book.'

Lunch with Hugh Cudlipp.[1] He tells me how furiously Cecil King is now anti-Wilson. He himself is not anti-Wilson. Indeed, he agrees with me that Wilson is the best man and that in order to help Wilson he and I must see each other regularly.

This afternoon an important meeting in the Lord Chancellor's room about the Ombudsman Bill, which has now reached its Committee Stage in the Lords. The Financial Secretary, who turns out to have acted as a pure Treasury agent, had assured me that a new clause 'on discretion' he was introducing 'really made no difference'. The Lord Chancellor, who should know as much as Niall about law, thinks it would make a great deal of difference and that it has to be got rid of. A Liberal Lords' amendment may help us to stem the violent press campaign. But MacDermot fought like a tiger.

When I got back to my room in came Tom Swain, the Member for Derbyshire, in great dismay.[2] He'd heard that the prayer protesting against the Sheffield boundary Order was going to take place on the following Monday. 'That's impossible,' he said. 'I've arranged a special train to bring seven hundred of my people down next Thursday and that'll be three days after the decision has been taken.' 'All right,' I said. 'I'll move the prayer to the day your people arrive.' 'That's fine,' he said. 'Of course I know it'll be carried all right but we just want to make sure the people can all come down.'

That tells you something about Parliamentary democracy—a special protest meeting, the whole lobby packed with people, but all a mere formality so that Tom can tell his Parish Councils how he fought against the wicked plans which extended Sheffield's boundaries into Derbyshire.

The Statement on the Defence Estimates (Cmnd. 3203) *announced that some twenty-five thousand men and six thousand service families would be recalled*

[1] Sir Hugh Cudlipp, former editor of the *Daily Mirror* and the *Sunday Pictorial*, deputy chairman of I.P.C. 1964–8 and chairman Daily Mirror Newspapers Ltd 1963–8. He succeeded Cecil King as chairman of I.P.C. in 1968 and served until 1973. He became a life peer in 1974.

[2] Labour M.P. for Derbyshire North-East since October 1959.

*to the United Kingdom from stations outside Europe by April 1st, 1968, permitting
a further £47·5 million saving in defence expenditure. Off-set agreements and
sales of defence equipment by British firms promised to earn some £100 million
in the current financial year, balancing the £21 million to be provided in military
aid to overseas countries, and the £74 million estimate for purchases of military
equipment abroad. By the end of the 1967–8 financial year savings on defence
expenditure should reach some £75 million.*

Thursday, February 16th

I woke to hear two items of news on the radio. First Ted Heath's Gallup
Poll rating has fallen a stage further and the Labour Party has risen to an
11½ per cent lead. Good. Each day sees the Opposition more torn by uncertainty. Just because the Government is grappling with the economic crisis,
with the prices and incomes policy, the Opposition doesn't know what to do.
They are not prepared to oppose us outright or support us outright. The
second item of news wasn't so good. It said that Douglas Jay had been
addressing the Economic and Financial Group of the Party and had mounted
a very powerful case against the Common Market. When I went into the
lobby I ran into Joel Barnett, the chairman of the Group.[1] He told me that
Douglas had invited himself there and had come along without stating a
subject. He then said, 'I might as well talk about the Common Market,' had
taken out a sheaf of notes, and read them aloud. It was quite clear they were
intended for publication in the press. Poor Harold had arrived in Bonn at
four and was trying to cope with the news there.

After this a Home Affairs Committee—another creative idea from Barbara
Castle. She wants to evolve a new technique for preventing evasion of payment for motor-car licences. This requires the transfer of various powers.
When we cross-examined her we discovered that in certain important in-
stances the burden of proving the case was to be transferred from the accuser
—the Government—to the accused. For example, if someone had bought an
old car he would be liable to be fined if he couldn't prove that during the
period between past and new ownership the car had not been used. Well, of
course this won't do under English law. Barbara argued it departmentally.
True, there would be a great deal of money in a Bill of this kind. But the Lord
Chancellor and the other lawyers saw the difficulties and I backed them.
Finally I said from the chair, 'If we railroad this, you can put it through. But
you really must wait your time. If you want to get a Bill quickly, give way to
the lawyers and the Chancellor, and I'll see it goes into this year's Finance
Bill.' She was left with these two choices.

Since there was no Cabinet I had time to get on with the written version of
the Fabian lecture in which I reply to the Titmuss gang's attack and for
adequate preparation for the business Statement. I don't find it gets any

---

[1] Labour M.P. for Heywood, Lancashire, since 1964, and Chief Secretary to the Treasury
since 1974.

easier. This week I had some four hundred Early Day Motions on which I could be challenged, though strictly speaking only the last hundred are in order. Then I had to deal with the problem of Jennie Lee. We have suddenly discovered that at a time of severe restraint she had got a rise of salary by becoming Minister of State. The Tories are also likely to be troublesome about the disclosure that our Whips had openly shouted 'object' and blocked Private Members' Bills last Friday.

Harold just got back from Bonn in time to answer his Questions and then we had long discussion on various Statements. I waited and waited to make the business Statement and when I finally got up of course all my colleagues walked out. I got through pretty well until I was pressed and threatened by the Tories on the Whips' blocking of Bills on Friday. I knew this would be difficult but I didn't know how difficult. In itself it's an interesting problem. When the Bill which is first on the list on Friday has been discussed and voted on then a whole number of other Private Members' Bills in the queue are read aloud and they can go forward to Committee without a Second Reading unless they are objected to. An objection can be made by any single back-bencher and it's been traditional for Governments to look carefully at these Bills and get them stopped but not to admit that the Whips are active here. Last week, for a reason I don't quite understand, John admitted that one of his Whips had said 'object'. I was really harassed and in great difficulty about this because John hadn't briefed me fully on what he was up to. However I recovered myself and got away with an assurance that I would inquire into it and reply next week.

Afterwards John cheerfully said to me, 'Oh, we may as well be open about it and say that we at least are honest about it and that when the Government objects our Whips say "object".' When I heard him I wondered whether I could pull this off in my present weak position or whether I lack the authority to do it. I felt a bit nettled because I had been pushed into my last fiasco without preparation and had had to fight without an adequate brief. I didn't want to have it happening again. The Speaker had allowed my questioning to go on for forty minutes and I was really quite hot and bothered when I had this talk with John behind the Speaker's Chair. But then I went straight up to the Lobby where I was right in guessing that the main topic of interest would be not this but the vote on account which had been published that afternoon.[1] I briefed them fully and then went down to the Party Meeting, which was in a much more amenable mood and willing to discuss morning sittings quite sensibly. Immediately afterwards at the Prime Minister's weekly meeting a tiff broke out with Burke Trend about the treatment of Peggy Herbison's family endowment plans. I said it was a scandal that the

[1] The vote on account for the civil service, a lump sum guaranteed by the House to finance the civil Departments until the House has voted on all the Estimates in July at the end of the Session, is laid before the Commons in January. The vote on account for the defence Departments is laid in February.

Cabinet Office had held her paper back and that the Treasury's reply was being postponed until three days before Cabinet. Burke then said that he thought there were no less than eleven papers on this question and he might well sum the matter up for Cabinet in a single brief paper. I didn't react at that moment and only realized later in the evening how dangerous this is and how essential it is to stop it.

After this we chatted about Callaghan's decision to go for the Treasurership of the Party. I confirmed that it had been taken without telling Harold; and George Brown then said, 'Well it means that old Callaghan is coming over to our side now. Now he won't have to pay attention to his constituency Party.' Harold is wild because this means that Callaghan will be trimming his policies in order to win trade-union votes at Conference and this will determine his attitude on prices and incomes. The more I think about the Chancellor doing this the more reprehensible I find it.

That evening I took Anne to *Volpone* and found myself greatly enjoying an Elizabethan masque with a wonderful mass of verbiage—not a serious play but exhilarating.

Friday, February 17th

I had Wedgy Benn in to discuss his legislative plan—a really useful meeting because I found that in the next Session he wants five Bills for his new Department. Since this is impossible I asked him whether he couldn't have a general enabling Bill. 'No, we're not allowed to do that,' he said. I'd forgotten that Otto Clarke, that old Treasury pundit, is now his Permanent Secretary.[1] 'Well,' I said, 'for God's sake work out with your Permanent Secretary a streamlined enabling Bill where only an Affirmative Order would be required for each policy. It would suit me far better to push this through and have a good row with the Tories about it than to get a constant stream of legislation from your Department.'[2] He went away determined to help.

He was followed by Miss Nunn, who'd come to discuss the progress of the reform of the House of Lords. I started by asking her about Burke's remark that there were eleven papers on the problem of family allowances. Of course I didn't tell her that this had been Burke's claim and she confirmed that in fact the only papers are one from the Minister and two from the Chancellor—everything else is mere background stuff. So there's no need whatsoever for Burke to come in and sum the matter up in a paper from the Cabinet Office and this makes it certain that he wants the paper in order to back Callaghan and Gordon Walker against Peggy. Indeed I feel that

---

[1] Sir Richard Clarke (K.C.B. 1964) served in various Ministries before going, in 1945, to the Treasury, where he remained until 1966. He then became Permanent Secretary at the Ministry of Aviation and later at the Ministry of Technology, where he served until his retirement in 1970. He died in 1974.

[2] Parliament can approve legislation by passing an Act, by positively authorizing items of delegated legislation (the Affirmative Order procedure) or by refraining from expressing disapproval (the Negative Order procedure).

Whitehall is working up tremendous pressure in favour of the Chancellor's proposal for means-tested family allowances.

I put this to Harold when I went to see him and he said rather peevishly, 'The Chancellor and Gordon Walker are always trying to lobby me about their proposals. I refuse to be lobbied before a Cabinet.' In fact, of course, he permits himself to be lobbied – in the right direction! I must try to see him before Thursday and brief him in full because there's a great deal at stake in next week's Cabinet.

We had Anne's cousin, Arthur Haslett, and his wife to lunch. They came up to my palace in Whitehall and I then took them across to the House. He was in College at Winchester with me and for years has been the top *Times* science writer and I was interested to ask him what he thought of the new *Times*. In the last three weeks the paper has been completely transformed by Rees-Mogg and Denis Hamilton.[1] Indeed they've done more in three weeks than has been done in the previous fifteen years and it's now an exciting rival to the *Guardian*. When I said this to Arthur he replied, 'I'm afraid I don't feel that way. I suppose I'm one of the old guard, fighting for a dying cause.'

Back home via Oxford with Anne in our new car – a Ford Executive. I had a Labour Party meeting in the town hall on the campaign against poverty and was just settling down to answering questions when in streamed a crowd of undergraduates who had been booing Michael Stewart and had been themselves excluded from his meeting. They rowed until I too withdrew.

Sunday, February 19th
Last night I went to South Oxfordshire Labour Party for their annual dinner and had a splendid time. Barbara Castle made the main speech and after she had warmed their hearts I was able to talk to them in the way I really want. It was a wonderful meeting.

Now it's pouring with rain but we've got Tam coming for the day and that's something I'm really looking forward to. Meanwhile I've been working at this diary and looking at my engagement list for last week. It makes me realize that I've got a lot more free time than I had as Minister of Housing. For example, I was able to spend a whole morning preparing the written version of my Fabian reply to the Titmuss attack on the Government's failure to deal with poverty. I insisted it should be published in a book along with their lectures and not as a separate pamphlet and I'm having to spend a lot of time on making sure this is as good as it can be. The fact that I have more time for this kind of thing as Lord President than I did as Minister of Housing is I suppose the justification for the existence of a Minister without Portfolio. Gordon Walker and I are there to think about general policy more

---

[1] William Rees-Mogg, who had previously been on the *Sunday Times* (he was deputy editor 1963–7), became editor of *The Times* in 1967. Denis Hamilton, who was editorial director of Thomson Newspapers 1950–67 and editor of the *Sunday Times* 1961–7, has been editor-in-chief of Times Newspapers since 1967 and was Chief Executive 1967–70; he was knighted in 1976.

than departmental Ministers can. I should be able to do this since I only have one box a night and it often takes less than half an hour or forty-five minutes. In the daytime I have nothing like the pressure of departmental work. It isn't only a question of physical time but also of the energy I expend. I now have much more energy left for reading Cabinet papers and spotting difficulties. I even do a little book-reading at weekends. I'm reading, this weekend, for example Lord Moran's account of Churchill, which seems to me a pretty convincing picture of a feeble old man who should never have tried to be Prime Minister after the war.[1]

Monday, February 20th

The first meeting I had was with the Lord Chancellor to discuss the Ombudsman Bill and the trouble caused by the amendment Niall MacDermot had put in during the Commons' Report Stage. This particular amendment excluded a whole range of cases—all those involving Ministerial discretion—from the ombudsman's competence. For instance, he wouldn't be able to investigate the merits of a planning decision like that of the Oxford Meadow Road,[2] only maladministration or a decision that was 'an abuse of Ministerial discretion' where perhaps a factor had been totally neglected or a vested interest had had undue influence. But the whole thing was highly ambiguous and the lawyers had raged around it for days. I have a feeling Niall MacDermot was pulling a fast one and that despite his assurances the amendment was designed to cut down the number of cases the ombudsman could deal with. The net result of our meeting was that when the Bill goes to the Lords this week they will put in a new clause as an antidote.

There's also the business of setting up the Select Committee to which the ombudsman will report. This has been an appalling story. When we discussed it originally we decided that the chairman should be a member of the Opposition, on a parallel with the chairman of the P.A.C. This would be a risk to the Government, which is always vulnerable to mistakes and repercussions of episodes of the Crichel Down type,[3] but it would be best not to be seen to be packing the Committee and to be seen to be being fair. So it was minuted that we'd give the chairmanship to the Opposition and Niall MacDermot quietly said so in the Committee Stage of the Bill. A few weeks later we had the reshuffle and Douglas Houghton was dropped. I immediately said to the Chief Whip, 'What a pity. But he'd be the very man for this job.' So John approached Willie Whitelaw and asked if he'd have any objection to Douglas as chairman of the Select Committee. Then I thought, 'I must be

---

[1] Charles Moran (who became a peer in 1943) was Winston Churchill's doctor and published *Winston Churchill: The Struggle for Survival* (London: Constable, 1966).

[2] See Vol. I, p. 279 and n. for details of this prolonged controversy over the possible placing of a ring-road through Christ Church Meadow, Oxford.

[3] A celebrated case of 1954, where land compulsorily purchased by the Air Ministry and later transferred to the Ministry of Agriculture had not been offered to the original owner when it was put back on the market. The Minister, Sir Thomas Dugdale, resigned.

fair,' and reminded Willie Whitelaw of the pledge to have an Opposition chairman and said to him, 'It's no good your giving us your assurance unless you can be certain of carrying your Shadow Cabinet.' He came back two or three days later and said, 'I'm sorry. You were quite right to mention it. The Shadow Cabinet won't budge and they claim this is a job we ought to have.' Meanwhile, unfortunately, John Silkin and Patrick Gordon Walker had apparently approached Douglas Houghton with a kind of offer and that had to be withdrawn. Last week I got a letter from Charlie Pannell saying this was an outrage and that the original offer to the Opposition had been an off-the-cuff decision of mine that the Party now wanted to discuss. So I've now got that to look forward to.

After a session examining the research, international and press Heads of the departments at Transport House—Terry Pitt, Gwyn Morgan[1] and Percy Clark—I gave lunch to Lady Spencer-Churchill[2] and Selwyn Lloyd. I'd asked her to the House of Commons to see the new room we'd set aside for M.P.s' wives and relatives. It's in the inner lobby, round the corner to the left and we'd ejected the trade-union M.P.s who used to use it, to their great grief. When we looked in there was Hugh Jenkins's wife[3] and Eric Heffer's wife, using the room almost as a secretarial office and rather resenting the incursion of Members' wives up from the provinces. Whatever I do in this job upsets someone. Anyhow, Clemmy and I found a place for Oswald Birley's portrait of Churchill and we decided to try to get some of Churchill's own paintings to hang there. Walking along the passage, we talked about the first volume of Churchill's life and I said what a wonderful job Randolph had done. She agreed and said, 'Wasn't the early part moving with the letters?' 'Yes,' I said, 'those letters about how terribly his father and mother had treated him.' Drawing a bow at a venture, I added, 'Did Winston ever discuss that with you, Lady Churchill?' and she looked at me and said 'No, not really.' This is what I suspected, that he was always a public figure and even in private with his wife he'd never discussed that terrible background. At lunch she was extraordinarily candid. For example, she said she'd never liked Birkenhead and had thought him a thoroughly bad influence on Winston in a way that Lloyd George had never been.

After lunch I saw the Chief and the two Freddies about the blocking of Private Members' Bills on Fridays. I had thought it over and discussed it with Tam. I was very careful because I want to avoid any accusations of stifling the House and any more rows and catcalls. I made absolutely sure there is a

[1] Head of the Overseas Department of the Labour Party 1965–9 and Assistant General Secretary 1969–72. He then became *chef de cabinet* to George Thomson at the E.E.C. Commission in Brussels and in 1975 Head of the Welsh Information Office of the E.E.C.

[2] Clementine Spencer-Churchill, widow of Sir Winston Churchill (whom she married in 1908), was made a life peer in 1965. Her son Randolph had been writing his father's biography: *Winston S. Churchill: Youth 1874–1900* (London: Heinemann, 1966) and *Young Statesman 1901–14* (London: Heinemann, 1967).

[3] Hugh Jenkins, Labour M.P. for Putney since 1967, and from 1974 to 1976 Parliamentary Under-Secretary of State for Education and Science, with responsibility for the Arts.

case for blocking Bills—and there is. We aren't 'blocking', we're merely preventing a Bill from getting through without having a Second Reading discussion or, sometimes, without even any debate at Committee Stage. And, what would be even worse, if such a Bill were allowed to get through it would be taking precedence over other Bills. So there was an overwhelming case for shouting 'object'; the only question was whether the Whips should do it openly.[1] We decided to draft a Statement and to enlist the support of our own back-benchers. I am getting the Chief to write a letter to Whitelaw to give the Opposition full warning of our intentions. We shall see what the result will be.

I took the night off to go to the National Sporting Club with the mysterious Desmond Hirshfield[2] and watch boxing. The boxing was moderate but there was a jolly good dinner at which I found myself sitting between a fat and rather smooth U.S.D.A.W. official and Harry Nicholas—Frank Cousins's number two at the T & G.[3] In the course of the evening I picked up something interesting from Harry. He knew all about the Callaghan/Herbison struggle on family allowances and he assured me that he was doing all he could with the T.U.C. Economic Council to see that Jim was defeated on this. 'That's a bit surprising,' I said, 'in view of what Jim told me last week about the support the T & G are going to give him when he stands for Treasurer.' Harry said, 'Not my support. I've heard rumours of this and he may have talked to Frank but I dislike it intensely. I don't think we want any more of these confounded politicians barging their way into Transport House.'

Our Mr Callaghan is doing himself no good by forcing himself on the trade unions and simultaneously undermining his integrity as Chancellor. He's not going to have quite such an easy time as he thought.

I didn't go back to the Commons, where the debate drooled on till four in the morning. The Conservatives' tactic now is to ensure that after every morning sitting we have a long night. They prolong the debate and then they ask business Questions about how morning sittings are saving time.

Tuesday, February 21st

First I had Legislation Committee at 9.30 with a meeting on leasehold reform. I dislike this measure intensely and so does the Lord Chancellor. It's

---

[1] Private Members may put down Bills for debate on Fridays and, as each one is disposed of, by passage or collapse, the next is taken. At 4 p.m. the Clerk reads over the remaining Titles and, if no Member takes objection, the Bill can get a Second Reading 'on the nod', and go forward to Committee Stage. It has even been known for a Bill (the Sunday Entertainments Bill) to be taken through all its Commons' stages in this way. The Government are sometimes happy to use this procedure for non-contentious Bills.

[2] Senior partner in a firm of chartered accounts; since 1961 founder and chairman of Trades Union Unit Trust Managers Ltd, and since 1962 of the Foundation on Automation and Human Development. He was made a life peer in 1967.

[3] Sir Harry Nicholas, Assistant General Secretary of the T.G.W.U. 1956–68 (and Acting General Secretary 1964–July 1966 while Frank Cousins was in the Cabinet). He was a member of the T.U.C. General Council 1964–7, General Secretary of the Labour Party 1968–72 and has been a member of the N.E.C. 1956–64 and since 1967. He was knighted in 1970.

going to make a lot of landlords unhappy and a lot of tenants unhappy when they don't get all they're expecting. It doesn't really redistribute income according to social need because its application is completely arbitrary and it only matters in half a dozen places – Jim Callaghan's constituency in Cardiff, in Swansea and in Cardiganshire and, perhaps to a lesser extent, in Oxford and in Birmingham. But it's been forced on us by fantastic political pressure inside the Labour Party and now there's the administrative pressure from the Ministry of Land and Natural Resources which has had nothing else to do except the Land Commission Bill.

The Law Officers, the Lord Chancellor and I and everybody who has had anything to do with it apart from Mr Willey[1] have tried to delay this Bill in the hope of modifying it. But here it was and I thought the only thing to do was to get it through. I'd arranged to publish the Bill this Thursday so that we could have the Second Reading ten days later, with an interval to digest it. As I didn't want a row in Legislation Committee, my carefully-laid plan was to railroad the Bill through with the minimum discussion. I had postponed a consideration of the draft till today, two days before publication.

When I explained the programme, Niall MacDermot said this was intolerable. I then said (and this shows the power of the chairman of a Cabinet Committee), 'I'm very sorry but it's a choice between evils: either we take longer or we get the Bill through. The next ten days are for consultations with the Attorney-General and the Solicitor-General. I know there are one or two points of difference we can raise now but let's see how we get on.' Sure enough, we started off on Clause 1 with the F.O. and M.O.D. objecting to the fact that diplomats living abroad won't benefit under the Bill. I was able to answer that and say it could always be dealt with at Committee Stage. Then we had the Solicitor-General saying that landlords with outstanding mortgages will find themselves treated unjustly. I said this objection clearly undermined the whole principle of the Bill but that we'd consider it. The whole thing was pushed through in half an hour without any serious detriment and the Minister of Housing was duly grateful.

But the truth is that at this point what the devil can Legislation Committee do anyway when the Bill's finally been prepared? You can't discuss the policy because that has been fixed in Home Affairs Committee or at Cabinet. You can only discuss legal points and really it is hopeless for lawyers to chatter away with fifteen or sixteen departmental people there. If there is some departmental grievance all we do is sit and chat and I am against Cabinet Committees that are all talk and no action. In this respect I am the most ruthless and efficient Cabinet chairman – if by that you mean a chairman who only allows discussion if it leads to action.

I expected to have to go across to O.P.D. at ten o'clock but it was called

---

[1] Fred Willey, Labour M.P. for Sunderland since 1945. In 1964 he became Minister of Land and Natural Resources; in 1967 his office was transferred to that of Minister of State at M.H.L.G.

8*

off. I presumed that was because Gordon Walker had only just got back from Malta, but in fact the decision on a Malta climb-down had already been fixed.[1] The whole venture has been a classic example of mismanagement—first to propose a phased withdrawal, taking a tough line with the Maltese and being unnecessarily brutal, then to backpedal halfway through, cutting the economies by £5 million and slowing down the withdrawal from four years to five. We have been grossly inconsiderate and now that our bluff has been called it is obviously going to cost us dear in the end.

After a rather bewildering lunch with the French Ambassador, who seemed rather apologetic about the negative attitude of the French to our E.E.C. entry, I had a little talk with the Speaker and the Chief Whip about short speeches. This was an idea the Chief had mentioned that would give the Speaker discretion to say at the beginning of a debate where a lot of people wanted to speak that the first eight or so mustn't take more than two hours— no speech to be longer than fifteen minutes, this to be decided on the merits of each debate. The Speaker was pleased and I hope he'll let me make the proposal next week. Then I complained rather bitterly about these endless altercations on the business Statement and at Question Time. 'Oh, you just want to shut them up,' he replied.

The Chief and I went on to No. 10 to see the P.M. about tomorrow morning when the P.L.P. are going to discuss defence before the defence debate next Monday and Tuesday. I was glad to find that he'd asked along George Brown and Denis Healey. Denis was full of ideas for his speech. Perhaps I was unduly alarmed about disturbance in the Party but I told him, 'It's not your speech that matters, it's the motions in the House.' This was quite new to him. George Brown saw the point and suggested that we draft a resolution referring to 'continuous cuts', so enabling the doubting brethren to rally to the Government. The Chief calculated that we shouldn't have more than forty-five abstentions but by this device we hope to reduce the number to thirty-five or so. It was an invaluable meeting and it allowed the P.M. to get his mind off Europe and on to practical issues for a while.

Wednesday, February 22nd

Morning prayers were cancelled and I had no chance to talk to the P.M. about Emrys Hughes's Abolition of Titles Bill.[2] This is quite amusing. I had quietly talked to the Queen about it and received her advice. Yesterday evening I found a note in my red box telling me that Roy Jenkins had written to her and had given her exactly the same recommendations as I had—that Emrys Hughes is regarded only as a jester and that he should be allowed to proceed with his Bill because it would only be misunderstood if we stopped it.

---

[1] Patrick Gordon Walker had flown to Malta on February 19th and after a visit to London on February 26th by the Maltese Prime Minister, Dr Borg Olivier, a settlement was reached.

[2] Emrys Hughes was Labour M.P. for South Ayrshire from 1946 until his death in October 1969.

However, Michael Adeane had caught on to this and the Court had obviously felt rather differently about it. Adeane had gone to the P.M., the P.M. wanted it stopped, the Lord Chancellor had been apprised, the Chief Whip had been apprised. Ha, ha, there it was. I shall have to arrange it. This is a good example of the P.M. and the Queen hobnobbing together, the kind of stuffiness I don't take seriously. But for all my talk about my bump of irreverence, it doesn't go as far as the Palace. I went off to the Privy Council later this morning and saw the Queen upstairs in a dim, horrible little room with a picture of her corgi over her writing table. She and I had a little chat about stomach upsets but we didn't touch on the matter of Emrys Hughes's Bill because I had agreed not to raise the matter with her.

I slipped into the House to hear Fred Peart's Statement on foot-and-mouth disease and I saw what a definite improvement it is to put Statements on in the morning when there is much better publicity and a keener House.[1] Then I went upstairs to the Party meeting where Healey made an excellent start and Manny handled the Party with great skill, even avoiding a vote at the end. So we've settled down, Shinwell and John and I, after all the commotion. Our relations are still strictly aloof but he's our Old Man of the Sea and we can't get rid of him.

Off to lunch with Alec Spearman and some of his fellow directors. Rab Butler was there and he remarked (about the only remark he made) that he thought my Introduction to Bagehot was good but that it underrated the influence and power of Parliament. He said in the end the House of Commons always gets its way. 'I was Leader for six years,' he reminded me. Of course this is a characteristic theory for a Leader of the House and one that's important for him to believe. My weakness is that I don't believe it—and events this week, Malta and defence, for instance, have proved that I'm right.

Over lunch we discussed prices and incomes and I was interested to hear Gordon Richardson[2]—a very distinguished banker from Schroders—taking the line that we shouldn't need prices and incomes legislation anyway because with unemployment up and profits down employers would be tough and there wouldn't be a burst of wage increases in the autumn. Of course the City want to break down the incomes policy and get back to a high level of unemployment but they didn't convince me. I briefed them on the Government's plan for preventing the policy from collapsing.

The Home Secretary caught me this afternoon about his troubles with the legislative programme. He's just had the Criminal Justice Bill and now he wants a Gaming Bill and a Dangerous Drugs Bill. The Drugs Bill would be a much smaller and less contentious measure and I did try to get agreement to

---

[1] The disease had now broken out on thirty-two farms in Northumberland. Between July and September 1966 some 5,753 cattle had been killed and by the end of 1967 over 352,290 cattle had been slaughtered in the attempt to stamp out a severe epidemic in Cheshire, Shropshire and neighbouring counties.

[2] He was chairman of Schroders Ltd from 1966 until 1973, when he became Governor of the Bank of England.

get it through with Second Reading procedure but the Conservatives turned that down.[1] When I told Jenkins he wanted another try, this time with a meeting *à cinq* of himself, Quintin Hogg, the two Chief Whips and the Lord President. But Freddie Warren and the Chief tipped off Whitelaw, who said he wasn't prepared to consider it. I gave Roy the message but he's very quick off the mark. He caught me again and said, 'Well now, look, if I lose the Gaming Bill can I have a little Commons' time for the Bill about the Registration of Clubs which is just going through the Lords?' It's a minor Bill and I think we can just fit it in but he is certainly an intrepid pusher and shover and we have to push and shove back to get the programme right.

Brian Abel-Smith and Titmuss came to dinner at Vincent Square to discuss the new work on pensions legislation. Weeks and weeks ago Harold made me chairman of the Committee on this but nothing has happened and every time I ask for the papers I am fobbed off by the officials. I know that they've been beavering around since last August but they've been delaying a further Ministerial meeting on the grounds that they haven't completed their plans. Finally I got sick of waiting and last week I asked Tommy Balogh, who's fortunately on the official side, to send me copies of his papers. Then I asked Miss Nunn for a set of my own but she told me I could only have them when the work was complete and that I couldn't have minutes of meetings where I hadn't been present. I said, 'I'm not going to deal with stuff cooked in advance. I'm the cook and I want to get into the kitchen.' I still didn't get any papers from her but I did get them from Peggy Herbison, my stalwart supporter. So at last I can meet the Committee with a commanding view of the position. I suspect that the officials' plan isn't on the lines I want and I explained to Brian Abel-Smith that I want to set up a working party to go through the whole principle of the legislation again, a brains trust with people like Nicholas Davenport, Peter Shore and Harold Lever. Our dinner was like old times and we agreed that we couldn't possibly get to work on this unless we win on the family endowment issue and beat Callaghan in Cabinet tomorrow.

Thursday, February 23rd

An absolutely key Cabinet, the most important, I think, since the July crisis. We started with a report on Malta and none of us raised a bleat about the incompetence of our disastrous surrender. Thank God we didn't congratulate Patrick Gordon Walker on his success, as the *Guardian* has been doing.

Then we came to prices and incomes. The situation now is that the T.U.C. General Council have unanimously rejected the proposals put forward by Michael Stewart and Ray Gunter after our last Cabinet. They won't have any new legislation and they simply want a return to the voluntary system. Michael Stewart was asking for another meeting with the T.U.C. Executive

---

[1] Non-contentious Bills may sometimes be referred to a Standing Committee for their Second Reading.

on March 2nd. Ray Gunter weighed in against taking a firm line and he was backed very strongly by Dick Marsh, a T.U. man, by Fred Peart and George Brown. Unfortunately they were supported by Callaghan as well, the man who as Chancellor had insisted on the freeze but who now—influenced, I am afraid, by his candidature for the Treasurership—is watering it down into a wishy-washy policy. He was saying that the economic situation isn't nearly as bad as some people suggest and there is no reason whatsoever to be afraid of a disaster. My point was that economic *facts* are against us and Barbara Castle, despite all the pressure from Frank Cousins, emphasized that without an effective incomes policy we won't have a basis for a rapid increase in production or for a reduction in unemployment. The only possible alternative to an incomes policy, she said, is perhaps devaluation. Here she got a very cold shoulder from the P.M.

I can't blame Harold for letting us get into this appalling battle between the T.U. proletariat and the socialist intellectuals. He has been away for weeks and has let the initiative slip. And of course he has a traitor within the walls in the shape of Ray Gunter who has been a kind of T.U.C. agent. Well, Harold didn't get out of it too badly. He's agreed to see the T.U.C. next week and try to come to some terms with them.

We next turned to social security and here there was great tension and excitement because Peggy Herbison and the Chancellor were presenting their rival proposals. Since January the Chancellor had postponed this week after week in order to ensure that nothing can be done in 1967; meanwhile he has been putting tremendous pressure on members of the Cabinet who know that if there is a big increase in family allowances their own Departments will suffer. He had persuaded Tony Crosland to come across, Roy Jenkins, Denis Healey, Douglas Jay, Dick Marsh, his own man (Jack Diamond), Cledwyn Hughes—shamefully—and Kenneth Robinson—shamefully. Above all he had got Patrick Gordon Walker, who has replaced Douglas Houghton and is now a henchman of the Chancellor, for the proposal to stop the whole notion of universal family allowances and go in for means-testing. The general view beforehand was that the Chancellor had packed the Cabinet and achieved a victory but I knew that Harold much resented the pressure that the Chancellor and Patrick Gordon Walker were putting on him. He was also resisting Burke Trend who had put in a private brief to the P.M. that came out wholly for Callaghan and against Peggy.

Moreover, our side had had one stroke of luck. As I've reported already the T.U.C. delegation had seen Miss Herbison and as a result the General Council had met yesterday and gone on record as opposing means-tested family allowances. Peggy was able to end her speech with this statement. Then came Callaghan's reply. He was pretty vulgar and the speech was dreadful, with the fatal mistake of frankly stating that he was against the whole principle of universality. When he had finished, Gordon Walker came in feebly, toeing the line, and then Dick Marsh immediately weighed in strongly in his favour. He is a brash young man, against the incomes policy, for means-testing. It became clear that there was quite a strong force behind Callaghan. On our side we had Peggy Herbison, supported by Stewart, Gunter, Cross-man, Barbara Castle, the Chief Whip, by Willie Ross doubtfully, by the Lord Chancellor, the Lord Privy Seal, Fred Peart—thank heavens—and by Tony Greenwood and Tony Wedgwood Benn. George Brown had left the meeting but had given Harold a sort of middle-of-the-road note. Herbert Bowden was away. I dare say that if those two had been there we should have had a much more difficult situation.

In reply to the Chancellor I immediately picked up this point and said that he was right, the issue was universality and this episode was the watershed, the great divide. In March Ted Heath had made a speech saying that the Con-servatives wanted more selectivity and what the Chancellor was saying was verbatim what the Tories were saying. None the worse for that, but all right, at least we knew where we were. I hadn't come into the Cabinet to do this kind of thing. Barbara was valiantly on our side and the Chief Whip quietly said that the Party couldn't possibly accept means-testing, but other people didn't add much to the discussion. In fact all of them were concerned only to save their departmental budgets under threat from the Chancellor. It was getting to one o'clock and Harold finally collected our opinions from round the table, including those who hadn't said anything in the discussion. There was a small but decisive majority in favour of the Minister of Social Security whereupon Callaghan said, 'Well, I'm sorry. In that case I can only be in favour of increased allowances but we can't have this particular scheme because here the Cabinet is determining my budget. These tax issues involve the issue of budget secrecy.'

I had been waiting for this so I leapt in and said, 'Since the Chancellor has raised this issue, Prime Minister, I must remind the Cabinet that just after the S.E.T. budget I put in a paper to you insisting that Cabinet responsibility had been undermined by budget secrecy over S.E.T. If the Chancellor is raising this now I would be delighted to have a whole Cabinet on this issue because if Cabinet can't discuss how to relate the tax concessions to middle-class families to family allowances and grants then the Cabinet has packed it in.' The P.M. then said, 'The Chancellor must reserve his position,' and the meeting broke up. As we got up Callaghan said to me, 'You've done a dangerous thing. You've raised a profound constitutional issue which may ruin the constitution and I shan't stay in a Cabinet which does that to me.' 'Well,' I said, 'I wouldn't have stayed in a Cabinet if it had done the opposite, my dear James. There is a great principle at stake.' And he stormed out in a fury.

Ironically one of the results was that the last item on the agenda got through with ten seconds' consideration. This was the proposal that the Lords should be allowed to spend £18,000 on a television experiment and it was on the Chancellor's insistence, after I had got agreement from the

Cabinet Committee and the P.M., that it had come to Cabinet. So the Chancellor was defeated in ten seconds flat.

While I prepared the business Statement for this afternoon, at the back of my mind was an anxiety about my announcement that our Whips were overtly blocking Bills. In fact I got away with that perfectly easily and the thing which caught me unawares was decimalization.[1] When I was asked I replied that the decision had already been taken and that a Bill would be brought forward in the near future. Macleod then got up and said that there was a great deal of non-party feeling on this and that the House would like a debate. When I said that we could have a debate if there was time for it he answered that the Opposition would give time, so that I found myself being engineered into agreeing to have a debate with a free vote. I carefully avoided this and it was left open. But of course this has infuriated the Chancellor who is saying, not unreasonably, that since Cabinet has made up its mind, come to a decision and issued a White Paper, we can't change it now. On the other hand we have to remember that it was only when the White Paper appeared that the public debate began and as the discussion has gone on it has become clearer and clearer that we came to the wrong decision. We should have had a ten-shilling unit, not a pound unit and I'm sure that if Cabinet took it again we would decide the other way. However, the Chancellor is determined to have a Bill and he has been urging me to put it on the agenda for a Legislation Committee meeting on Tuesday. I'm saying, 'No. I fix the time.' I've got to be fair to the House of Commons, annoyingly fair sometimes, and that's that.

This evening we had our weekly meeting with the P.M. on future business. He was obviously rather uneasy about a Question that had come up this afternoon on D-Notices and his remarks suggested that the F.O. had been intervening, through George Brown, and that there might be trouble.[2] Last Tuesday he had referred rather abruptly and savagely to a Question about the *Daily Express* and D-Notices and Chapman Pincher had replied with a denial in the *Express*.[3] The Opposition had weighed in and today Ted Heath had asked for a Committee of three Privy Councillors to go into the matter. Harold had refused this and referred it to a committee from which the Editor of the *Daily Mirror* has now resigned, rather than handle it, and so the P.M.

---

[1] The Decimal Currency Act was to provide for the introduction of decimal currency in 1971. The Government decided that there would be a basic unit of a pound, the equivalent of 100 new pence. The old shilling (twelve old pennies) would be equal to five new pence. As the public suspected, inflation and decimalization together quickly drove from everyday circulation the new half-penny piece, made the new one-penny piece worth very little, with the new two-penny piece the most common small coin.

[2] The Joint Services, Press and Broadcasting Committee can issue a 'D-Notice' request to journalists not to publish an item affecting national security.

[3] Chapman Pincher, defence correspondent of the *Daily Express*, had reported that the practice of vetting overseas cables had increased under the Labour Government. It was alleged that the *Daily Express* had ignored a D-Notice request not to publish this story. A Committee of Inquiry was established, with Lord Radcliffe at its head.

has had to give in and concede the Committee of Privy Councillors. I am wondering what our old pal George Wigg has had to do with this.

When we'd talked about this I mentioned that we must soon deal with family endowment on the basis of today's Cabinet decision. Burke Trend said, 'Well, I'm not sure that we'll find it at all easy, Prime Minister, to formulate the decision because apparently all Cabinet agreed on was that there should be an increase of family allowances.' 'Not at all,' I said. 'Cabinet decided in favour of Peggy Herbison's scheme and against the Chancellor's.' 'Oh no,' said Burke Trend. 'Certainly not.' But the P.M. ruled that we had and firmly took my side. So even after our triumph we would have lost if I hadn't been present to see that the minutes were written the right way. So ended a very important day.

Friday, February 24th

I had the usual meetings in the morning followed by a talk with two *Sunday Times* correspondents about Arnold Goodman whose profile they want to write. Then off to Coventry to address the annual meeting of the Coventry Church Housing Association. This was the first speech I've made on housing since I became Lord President and I took the occasion to do a general talk on the relationship between voluntary effort and housing associations and local councils. Afterwards we went off to the Bishop's Palace for whisky with the Bishop and his secretary, with his fawning ladies around him. I tottered home, to find the documents on the new pensions legislation waiting for me to go through at the weekend.

Monday, February 27th

I drove straight from Paddington to the House to see how the battle of the Sheffield Boundaries Order was going. Here was a ding-dong struggle between two Labour authorities – Derbyshire County Council defending its outlying areas and Sheffield County Borough trying to acquire them for a huge new housing unit. Rather reluctantly I'd given my judgment in favour of Sheffield[1] and there I was sitting on the front bench with the Derbyshire M.P.s attacking me from behind and six hundred Derbyshire people due to arrive at lunch-time to lobby after the debate was over (but not, thank heavens, after a vote had been taken because in a morning sitting all votes are postponed until the end of the morning's business). When the vote *was* taken there was quite a mix-up because forty Labour people went into the Derbyshire lobby whereas the official Party line was to support Sheffield.[2] Seeing Labour Tellers at both doors they preferred the look of Derbyshire to Sheffield. I couldn't blame them since it was only the fact that Dame Evelyn had committed me in advance which made me give the decision in favour of Sheffield.

After that John and I had a meeting with the Chancellor about decimal

[1] In April 1966. See Vol. I, p. 497.
[2] Ayes 39; Noes 156.

currency. I was not surprised to find that he was violently angry with me. When I was questioned in business last week I had given way a little to the Opposition about the possibility of a debate on the White Paper before the debate on the Second Reading of the Bill. I suppose I did this because my own personal view is that we're making a terrible mistake in having a pound unit instead of a ten-shilling unit and public opinion is now moving against us. Nevertheless I shouldn't have given anything away because I'd assured James in writing that if he could get his Bill ready in time the Second Reading could take place before Easter and it should go through Committee Stage before the Finance Bill operates. As I'd promised all this and there was a clear Cabinet decision in favour of the £ unit the sooner we got the debate over the better. All a preliminary debate on the White Paper would do would be to arouse our own people so that when we came to Second Reading we should have even greater difficulties. In view of all this I gave him the assurance that we wouldn't, on any account, have two debates and as a sign of goodwill I promised to get the Bill through the Legislation Committee so that we can publish this week and have the debate on March 23rd.

When I got back to my Whitehall palace I found that my old friend Sir Philip Hendy had come to see the National Gallery pictures. He was delighted by how the enormous Teniers looked on the embossed wall. He agreed that he'd never seen a Teniers better hung. He also liked the two little Dutch sea paintings on the wall opposite the window and I then said something about the central heating. 'Those walls aren't heated,' he said in grave alarm, and when I admitted they were he went white as a sheet, poor man. Apparently there's a special directive from the Ministry of Works that no pictures can be hung on walls which have heating in them so I've had to have the heating turned off on that wall and now the Lord President's room, though its pictures are beautiful, has lost half its heating as a sacrifice to art.

This afternoon Denis Healey introduced his defence debate. He had told me last week that he had a strong and immensely powerful speech to deliver which really would convince the back-benchers and I'd made the mistake of suggesting this to the press at my Lobby conference. Well, he certainly hadn't. I dare say what he said would please the students of international affairs and perhaps members of the Institute of Strategic Studies. But it seemed to be addressed to McNamara[1] and it left our back-benchers sitting solemn, listless and bored.

Later that evening I had half a dozen back-benchers in to discuss morning sittings. But I found we were discussing decimals and defence and I got extremely alarmed by their mood. I have been feeling increasingly uneasy during the last ten days but the Chief has been completely resolute and has given an absolute assurance to the P.M. and to George that he knows there

[1] Robert McNamara, President of the Ford Motor Co., which he joined in 1946, from 1960 to 1961, American Secretary of Defense 1961–8, and since 1968 President of the International Bank for Reconstruction and Development.

are only forty-five people who might abstain. I think it is more like sixty and Tam Dalyell has kept on saying seventy or eighty. Certainly the mood as I went round the lobbies today was not good. People were saying if we don't do it this time how can we ever oppose this bloody defence policy? And on the other side there were loyalists asking why the Leader of the House was allowing the bloody left-wingers to abstain and relying on the right to provide the majority? That was the mood tonight.

Tuesday, February 28th
At Legislation Committee I pushed through the Decimal Currency Bill ready for publication on Thursday. In the afternoon George Brown was due to speak on defence. He made an excellent speech—courageous—and especially good about Germany. But after that the debate was a disaster from our point of view—not that the speeches really mattered. It was the malaise in the Party that was mounting up and I felt in my bones that we were going to get a far bigger abstention than John anticipated. I dined with Joel Barnett and Robert Sheldon—the joint leaders of our back-bench Economic and Financial Group; left-of-centre people, thoroughly sensible and responsible. But they are taking the lead and insisting on abstention and I felt angry and told them how outrageous it was.

After dinner I came across to Tom Steele[1] in the lobby—an ultra-right-winger—and he said, 'I'm bloody well going to abstain just to teach you a lesson, just to show you what we think of the new discipline we've got from you.' It was a disconcerting moment.

In his wind-up Denis talked about the split on the Tory side but he was hopelessly out of touch with his own people. Ironically enough the House of Commons' Services Committee had just arranged that the press would be able to get the full division records with all the names within fifteen minutes of the vote being taken. So as chairman of that Committee I'd managed to organize that the extent of our abstention would be advertised more than any previous Government abstention! At ten o'clock it was clear the fat was in the fire. There were sixty-two abstentions by any normal reckoning, and John could only obstinately calculate that his forty-eight prediction was correct because the others were unofficial pairs.[2]

Wednesday, March 1st
At first the morning wasn't so bad. I had my hair cut as usual at the shop where Ted Heath has his cut too and asked Mr Large, my hairdresser, what he thought. 'We think the M.P.s are better for showing a little independence,' he said. 'No, we don't think worse of you at all for the news this morning.' I was cheered and that morning I came to the conclusion we hadn't done ourselves any great damage. The Gallup Poll last week has shown that

---

[1] Labour M.P. for Lanark 1945–50 and for West Dunbartonshire 1950–70.
[2] The vote on the defence account was 270 in favour and 231 against.

people in the country are very much in favour of defence cuts and I couldn't feel they'd mind their feeling being registered in the Commons. If only the Labour Party had kept calm I think the vote would not have weakened our position in any way.

After my haircut I went straight back to No. 10 for morning prayers. John argued very strongly that his calculations were right and then we all agreed there should be no inquest and no action before the by-elections next Thursday at Pollok and Rhondda. The P.M. didn't seem unduly shaken by the larger figure of sixty-two and it was agreed that we would carry on as quietly as possible in the Party meeting and clamp down the right-wing critics who we knew would be furious. John reported fully on the growing bitterness between Left and Right inside the Party and said it must be relieved if we were to have a reasonable chance in the by-elections.

At 11.30 I had a very satisfactory meeting with the Lord Chancellor about the ombudsman. We finally prepared the amendments in the Lords to ensure that the Bill would be effective and thereby defeated the machinations of the Treasury acting through Niall MacDermot. That was one good job done.

Back in my own office I found Trevor Lloyd-Hughes waiting for me with his new girl and we sat down with Freddy Ward to discuss the co-ordination of the information services which we'd agreed on so many months ago. The new girl is to sit in a nice office in the Privy Council and work with Freddy Ward and she is to go to Trevor's press conference and keep us in contact with what's going on. Not a very good week to start having improved information co-ordination when all the information is bad and the Lord President seems to be doing nothing but losing votes by his behaviour. However these things happen.

This afternoon in the House we had a Statement by George Brown on Aden; it was much better than the last one because he didn't quarrel with the Tories.[1] Then we went on to the Navy Estimates. At the usual time John and I went down to the liaison committee where we suggested that at the Party meeting no discussion should be allowed of the vote on the Defence Estimates. The best thing would be for the Prime Minister to make a short statement which would not be debated. When we put this to the meeting Manny Shinwell immediately said that discipline had broken down and asked what we were going to do about it. 'Are you going to take the whip away from the rebels?' he said to me. Reasonably and quietly John said, 'No, I am not.' He was supported by Malcolm MacPherson. At once Manny made it perfectly clear that he would get out of the chair in order to make his view clear that we need a discipline which works. It was this remark which alerted me to a major crisis. John went straight back to the Prime Minister in

[1] At the very end of 1966 the National Liberation Front (N.L.F.) in Aden had seceded from the Front for the Liberation of South Yemen (FLOSY). The disturbances that ensued created even more difficulties for Britain's attempt to leave a stable government in Aden after withdrawal. On March 17th, George Thomson, Minister of State at the Foreign Office, was sent to discuss a plan for independence in November.

No. 10 and told him that Manny was out for trouble. No doubt George Wigg alerted him too and made him realize that he would have to intervene himself and make a considered statement at the Party meeting on Thursday.

While John was busy that evening there was another fiasco on the Floor of the House at the end of the Navy Estimates debate. Denis Healey consulted George Lawson, the Deputy Chief Whip, and decided to talk the debate out for fear that a hostile amendment might be called. The result was disastrous, of course, and the management of the Party was accused of being panicked into a cowardly withdrawal. Poor John. George Lawson is fiercely against the new regime and he has been a great pain in the neck to the Chief ever since that occasion at the beginning when he allowed our members to abstain on the count.

However, this all happened while I was away. In the evening Mrs Meake (who cleans for us at Vincent Square) brought in her daughter Heather on her way to Australia to say goodbye. Then Anne and I slipped off to an excellent film called *Accident*, a wonderful study of the relationship between dons' families, with beautiful photography of the country round Oxford.

Thursday, March 2nd
The day started with a most pleasant meeting with Arnold Goodman, who has ideas for a Bill to enable authors to get some return on the books which are borrowed from libraries. It's an old idea that an author should have the same right to make a living out of his book as a composer does out of his gramophone records. Arnold is still deliciously vague and cross-benchy and had no idea how to go into action. I advised him to get on to Jennie Lee at the Ministry of Education because if she took charge of the Bill she would get the benevolent blessing of Roy Jenkins and the Prime Minister. I had just time to meet Roy before Cabinet and get the thing tied up.[1]

In between I had a rapid meeting with the Chief and Freddie Warren to sort out the Navy Estimates muddle and to arrange to have it put straight. When we got into Cabinet we found that the officials had all been ordered out and without telling me or John the Prime Minister said he would now have a discussion of what happened last night. This made me suspicious because it showed that he'd been got at beforehand. Callaghan, Cledwyn Hughes and Willie Ross (to name only three) had all gone to him and said that discipline had completely broken down and that something drastic must be done. Harold started with a long statement accusing us all of being out of touch with the back-benchers in the tea-room. He also accused Ministers of being disloyal to each other, telling back-benchers things against each other and leaking to the press. It was a long gloomy speech about the causes of the bitterness in the Party. Then he suddenly stopped and asked for views. I

[1] In December 1974, Roy Jenkins, as Home Secretary, was to announce that, although the practical details of a public lending right scheme had not yet been worked out, a Bill would be published in the coming year.

noticed he didn't ask either me or the Chief Whip to give a report at this point
so Callaghan weighed in as chief complainant. He asked for a re-imposition
of discipline since the new liberal system simply wasn't working. There
followed a desultory discussion in which only Barbara Castle staunchly came
out on our side. None of the other people who believed in liberalization said a
word. All the comments came from those who said the situation was impossible
and that something really must be done about it. Naturally enough there was
no discussion of the P.M.'s rebuke to Ministers for attacking each other;
all the speeches were full of discontent against John Silkin and myself. After
the discussion had run for more than an hour the P.M. said, 'I think we'll close
that now and turn to our proper business.' At once I said, 'But surely before
we close it, we should hear an estimate of the situation from the Chief Whip
since we've had such a lot of friendly advice from our colleagues?' The P.M.
looked annoyed and said, 'Of course.' So John gave a short careful estimate
of the situation heard in silence and I then added a few words. 'I know that a
number of members of the Cabinet are deeply opposed to the liberalization
which John and I are trying. It would make it easier if you didn't reveal your
opposition but gave us a fair chance by at least tacitly supporting us in public.
It's intolerable to have Ministers attacking us in the *Daily Telegraph*.' (I said
this because in the *Telegraph* this morning there was a statement 'by a senior
Minister' which had clearly been supplied by George Wigg or Callaghan.)

The only thing which emerged from this discussion was a general agreement
that the crisis would require a statement by the P.M. to the Party meeting.
This was something I very much wanted provided Manny could be got to see
that no debate must follow the statement. The Prime Minister should simply
read the riot act to the Party.

So we moved on to the single item on the agenda—the salaries for members
of the Steel Board. George Brown had gone out before this and Michael
Stewart was in Stockholm so the two key people were away. I knew how
strong George's view was on this subject—the scale had been approved by
Cabinet and submitted to Melchett but George thought it too high and had
threatened resignation. However, I thought Dick Marsh was quite right to say
that there was no alternative to accepting this scale. If we're going to have
comparability of salaries, something like £25,000 will have to be paid to the
members of the Steel Board.[1] Indeed, as Barbara Castle rightly said, this
affects not only the Steel Board but all the nationalized industries where we
are recruiting third-rate personnel because of the miserable salaries we pay.
Harold went round the table and found no one who could object. It was
intolerable, most of them felt, but it had to be done. When the votes had been
taken I added a thought. 'Right,' I said, 'I'd now like to say something referring
to the previous item. Ministers are constantly making extremely brave

[1] The annual salaries of members of the Steel Board were eventually to be settled at
£20,000–£24,000 for the deputy chairmen, £15,000–£19,000 for full-time and £1,000 for the
part-time members. Lord Melchett, the chairman, agreed to serve for £16,000.

decisions here round the Cabinet table and then, outside. they leave it to me to take the blame when that decision is announced and the Party protests against it. This is what happened, for example, on judges' salaries. Now you have decided on this highly unpopular decision, we must *all* fight for it—not only for the sake of the Steel Board but in order to give the public sector a fair chance. We must deal with this as a major issue of Party policy.' I think I made my point—at least it was minuted.

As we went out I was uneasily aware that the P.M. hadn't warned John and me that he would be raising the issue of discipline—that his mood had clearly changed between Wednesday and Thursday and that he was now under tremendous pressure from the Wigg–Manny lobby. However one could at least say that he was still keeping his options open between the disciplinarians and the liberalizers.

After Cabinet the Chief went into No. 11 for another terrible row with Callaghan about discipline while I went back to my office to prepare for the business Statement. My whole mind was on getting the Navy Estimates muddle right and nobody warned me there was any possibility of trouble from our side about decimal currency.

There was nothing particularly interesting in the Prime Minister's Questions and we got on very quickly to the business Statement. It was very soon clear that the real threat was not from the Tories on the Navy Estimates but from my own side on decimals. As a result of the Cabinet decision which had been reinforced that morning, I had no room for manoeuvre at all. I had to refuse a preliminary debate on the White Paper and, as for the proposal for a free vote, I should have said this was something for the Chief Whip to deal with. Looking back now I can see that unfortunately I'd let the two questions seem a single issue and that this suited my critics. There were plenty of nice good people behind me who tried to help by changing the subject and I tried too. But whenever we did so one of the right-wingers dragged us back to decimals and played into the hands of the Tories by attacking me from behind and turning the afternoon into a major demonstration against the Leader of the House. I pleaded with them that this was something which ought to be discussed outside in the Party meeting, not on the Floor, but they wouldn't listen and it went on and on. In retrospect I think it's true that Bert Bowden would have got away with it much better by being negative, narrow and bureaucratic. It's my more expansive personality which makes me say more about a subject and got me into trouble this afternoon.

After this terrible scene I went up to the Lobby conference where I found all the journalists fanatical about decimalization. As the P.M. said to the Party, 'There isn't a vote in decimals in the country.' But there is a genuine interest among Lobby correspondents and M.P.s and for three or four weeks it will be a really fashionable subject. Anyway, the Lobby found it outrageous that I should assert that decimalization was a subject which the House could not discuss freely with a free vote.

When I'd finished the Lobby I went downstairs and into the P.M.'s room to see what was going on. There I found that he had finished his speech for the Party meeting and it was too late even to show it to me, though there was no sign that he ever wanted to.[1] He was infatuated with its toughness—nobody had ever talked like this to the Party before, he said. He gave me a drink and we had a chat for ten minutes before he went upstairs to deliver his speech.

It was a tough speech and extremely well done in its way. It silenced the critics by smashing them. But no one could say it wasn't a brow-beating speech. And while I sat listening to it I realized that by giving leadership in this sense of the word Harold Wilson was creating a completely new situation which put me in an almost impossible position because it meant the end of the liberal regime. The speech he made was a George Wigg anti-liberal speech and the fact that he made it passionately on my behalf didn't make any real difference to that.

After the meeting I went back to my room and had a talk with Jimmy Margach. I was tired and devastated and I found myself talking about resigning. He took me up. 'You've no intention of resigning now?' 'No,' I said, 'not now but in three or four years.' He said 'You've got fifteen ahead of you —you're ideally suited to your job.' He couldn't have been nicer to me and I was a bit surprised in view of the very offensive attack he'd written on me three weeks ago about the problems of discipline.

Friday, March 3rd

I woke up to a terrible press. True enough, the P.M.'s action had taken some of the heat off me: if it hadn't been for that I would have been pilloried in every paper. As it was I was only the second lead story—another fiasco for Crossman, more and more indications that his position as Leader of the House is becoming untenable.

I was due at No. 10 at 9.45 for our weekly meeting on business. George Brown wasn't there—only Burke Trend. On the way I'd already talked to the Chief and told him that after the P.M.'s speech we would have to fight the decimalization issue through at a P.L.P. meeting. We wouldn't like it but we should have to allow the Chancellor to address the troops, insist on a vote and carry on with a two-line whip. If people chose to have conscientious scruples about decimals rebellion would be the reason for expulsion. It seemed to me that Harold felt that decimalization was an ideal issue on which to discipline the Party. We were just about finishing our discussion when in rushed Mr Callaghan to insist on what we'd already decided, that we must fight on his side. What I hadn't told Harold was my own feeling that my position had become quite impossible as a result of his conducting a more reactionary leadership than anyone had ever previously dared to do.

---

[1] See *Wilson*, pp. 337–8, for his description of his remark, 'very much in a throwaway reference', that every dog is allowed one bite but that, if biting becomes a habit, owners tend to have doubts about renewing the licence.

After that there was a little meeting in No. 10 on the abolition of titles—Emrys Hughes's Bill which I've mentioned before. I had talked to the Queen about this at my last Privy Council but one. At the most recent one I was going to give her our advice formally when I was suddenly told to stop by Harold Wilson and now we were to discuss it together with Roy as Home Secretary who has an official status in the matter. Roy's advice had been exactly the same as mine—namely that we must let it be known that no steps would be taken by the Government to stop this Bill. If he wasn't a court jester, Emrys Jones was a Commons' jester. Harold Wilson soon made it clear in an elusive sort of way that the Queen didn't agree and that he didn't agree either. However when Roy and I stood firm he suddenly changed and said that on reflection he realized the Bill ought to be debated. So on this he gave way to Roy and me.

I spent the rest of the morning preparing a few paragraphs on the discipline crisis which I would deliver at Warwick University this evening where I was addressing the students. I made sure that it was obvious that the tone of voice I was adopting—cool and reasoned—was at variance with the P.M.'s truculent and vulgar declaration. Then off down the M1 to Coventry where I read the discipline paragraph aloud to quite a nice gathering of Labour students before Anne drove me home.

Saturday, March 4th

I took a long walk over the farm to think things out and I finally decided that I must write a letter to Harold offering him my resignation. What had finally convinced me was the tone of the press on Friday and my own realization of the complete contrast between his attitude to the Party rank and file on Thursday and the Silkin–Crossman liberal regime—that our regime should be saved by a speech of that kind is intolerable. I also became more and more aware as I walked that the position of the Leader of the House is nothing more than a public posture. That's all there is to it and if your public posture is bad and unsuccessful the sooner you get out the better.

Sunday, March 5th

I've just finished drafting a letter to Harold which I will have delivered via Marcia on Monday morning. It runs as follows:

Dear Harold,

I would not be surprised if over this weekend you are beginning to wonder if, or perhaps when, you will require a new Leader of the House. I have been thinking this over carefully. We may get through without the need of a sacrificial victim. But the chances are we shall not. I am sure of two things. (1) If the change is made it should be done in the Easter recess. (2) It should be the result of a resignation, not a shuffle. To have its full tonic effect, the Party must feel that the man responsible for the failure has paid the price.

Not of course that I'm vain or stupid enough to claim that my actions were a main factor. But my personality was a big factor. On the Friday morning after my row in the Party meeting with Manny I rang up and told you that if he survived the weekend as chairman my position would be gravely undermined. You gave excellent reasons for letting the storm blow itself out. It did, but the confidence the new regime had been building up and its authority were shattered in the critical weeks before the defence budget. The traditionalists were able to reawaken all the old suspicions — especially of me — particularly since it was well known that Manny had been helped in his press relations by George Wigg.

Of course I may be over-gloomy. I doubt it. In the B.B.C. programme *The Week at Westminster*, Manny was interviewed by a stooge and discussed the breakdown of the new liberal regime. The fact that he and George now feel that they can, with impunity, conduct their vendetta in the open explains why the open counter-protest was launched against me last Thursday afternoon. And of course you realize that the toleration of Manny's original blow-off has enabled him to build up his popularity week by week while my authority has declined.

It's quite an interesting example of the ups and downs of politics that I should be reading this letter into my diary just seven days after the Sunday when I had such a happy, confident sense that we'd turned the corner. What happened of course was a series of catastrophes. It's been a disastrous week for Harold as well as for me though I should add that by Friday some compunction was being felt in the Parliamentary Party and one or two people who had felt outraged by the events of Thursday afternoon expressed some sympathy with me. Having drafted this letter let me try and guess what the result will be. Harold will of course seek to avoid the choice I'm forcing on him. What he's most likely to do is urge me to accept a switch and to make Patrick Gordon Walker Leader of the House while I take over all the Committees of which Patrick is chairman. He would hope that this will patch things up and leave the options open again as well as preserving John Silkin as Chief Whip.

John's position is the other thing I have to consider in this situation. I've been talking to him a lot on the phone this weekend and I think he's disconcerted by what I am trying to do because it's going to be difficult for him to stay as Chief Whip if I resign on the ground of the failure of the liberal regime we tried to introduce. And if he were to resign too that would be a decisive victory for the Right and also a decisive incentive for the Left to sharpen the conflict and split the Party. I'm not surprised that John wants me to stand and fight. But then I look at my own future and I say to myself that resignation on this issue would be an honourable action and it's much better to get out rather than to be reshuffled. If I get out I should be able to see the children, live here, get to work on my books and above all I would be anticipating and resigning before the series of economic disasters which I'm afraid are now coming upon us.

Well, there it is. It's the worst week I've had in politics. Not the worst week in the sense of inner unhappiness—strangely enough I haven't been unhappy this week at all—but I've been reflecting, seeing that we are coming near the real crunch, where the options which were kept open are closing in and where a decision just has to be taken.

Monday, March 6th
Directly I got to London I went to see the Chief and showed him my letter to Harold and promised not to deliver it until I had talked to him again.

Then I had a meeting with Dick Marsh and a couple of Parliamentary Secretaries from D.E.A. and the Ministry of Power to settle the question of the salaries to be paid to the members of the Steel Board. After last week's Cabinet decision to pay salaries at the high levels recommended by Marsh and required by Melchett and the Board, we had now to decide how to put this over. I suggested that it had better be done, not in a Written Answer but in a morning Statement and that we must now come right out and say we were taking this line because we weren't going to allow our nationalized industries to be penalized by an inability to get the top leadership they require.

Next I went through to No. 10 for S.E.P. where we were discussing the great new idea which has emerged from Nicky Kaldor's fertile mind. He calls it the Regional Employment Premium and it is another development of his S.E.T. The idea is a perfectly simple one. Whereas employers in Coventry or London would only get back 7s. 6d. per worker from the Government, employers in the development areas would get back 30s. 0d. R.E.P. in fact would be a subsidy designed to encourage employers in development areas to take on labour. We all thought the idea first-rate and soon began to discuss how to present it. After the mess we got into with decimals with a White Paper committing ourselves to a particular solution, we were anxious to present this new R.E.P. in such a way that the C.B.I. and the T.U.C. could react to it over the summer and we could then finally formulate the legislation in the winter.[1] The discussion turned out to be interesting and I believe extremely important. Michael Stewart led and argued the case that in his philosophy of democracy there was a need to evolve a new method of presenting a policy which wasn't a Government White Paper and wasn't just the vague personal commitment of a speech. What we were looking for was something halfway between the *fait accompli* of a White Paper and the mere flying of a balloon. We realized that Whitehall wouldn't like this at all but we agreed that Michael Stewart should present a paper to a meeting of the N.E.D.C. which could then be published as an idea

___

[1] The Regional Employment Premium became effective on September 4th, 1967.
9*

the Government believed in but where it wanted to have industry's reactions before it was finally committed in practice.*

After S.E.P. I went out to lunch with Alan Watkins and came back in a furious temper. I turned up at No. 11 and blew my top to John about the impossible situation and how I wanted to get out of politics altogether. Dear old Charlie Grey was present and looked a bit embarrassed and disturbed.[1] I asked John to give me back my letter and told him that anyway I was bound to put it in. John insisted on one change, the addition of four words at the end making it clear that the alternative to my going would be to get rid of Manny. Indeed, after this amendment the theme of the letter was 'You must choose between Manny and me'.

In the House that night the corridors were full of rumours. I heard and the Chief heard too that a full-scale attack was now being prepared by Manny and George behind the scenes. They were putting the heat on the Prime Minister and simultaneously ordering the Chief Whip to repudiate our new discipline. John told me he is absolutely firm and I believe him. Unless Manny has been got rid of by the end of the month I shall resign. That talk with John was very important. He put some spirit into me, made me make that vital addition to my letter to Harold and encouraged me to fight back. I delivered the letter to Marcia and that same evening I briefed Coady of the *New Statesman* on how John and I were going to fight back and win.

Tuesday, March 7th
We had a mildly interesting O.P.D. on what was to happen to the little bits and pieces of colonies too small for independence—the Falkland Islands and Gibraltar, for example. As soon as it was finished Michael Foot came to see me. I briefed him on what George and Manny were up to and told him how I must fight back and was determined not to give an inch on the liberalization of Party discipline. My mood was quite different from Monday—largely owing to what the Chief had done to me during our talk. Over the weekend I'd been a bit self-pitying and not merely defeatist but defeated. I had some reason for this because I'd had a terrible press and was faced by Harold with a terrible situation. Even Tam Dalyell had guessed I was thinking of resigning and getting back to my family and writing my book, but by the time of that talk with Michael my mood was very different. And so I felt at Vincent Square this afternoon when Eric Heffer and his wife came to lunch. They're the two working-class people I like best in the Parliamentary Party. I think they were pleased to be invited and I realized, in entertaining them, how we miss in the Labour Party the social relations of the Conservative and Liberal Parties. It's easy enough to say that I should entertain people like Eric regularly but if I did I would be accused of throwing my wealth about in order

---

* This meeting was the origin of the so-called Green Paper, which has now become an established Government procedure.

[1] A miner and Independent Methodist minister. Labour M.P. for Durham 1945–70 and a Government Whip 1964–9.

to buy up back-benchers. Undoubtedly he had come to the conclusion that the Harold Wilson speech was the end of the liberal regime. I don't, by the way, think that this was what Harold intended when he talked about the dog licence. Nevertheless that was the feeling which was abroad and I managed to dissipate it in Eric Heffer's mind that afternoon. I made him realize that John and I were really on the side of the back-benchers and that the implicit threat of the dog-licence speech wasn't going to be carried out because Harold hasn't carried Silkin and Crossman with him.

When I went into Question Time this afternoon I found that Callaghan was laying about him in a very helpful way. He'd made a blunt tough Statement that Governments can't go floundering about wasting their time — they have to make decisions, etc., etc. In fact he'd unhooked me and put himself on the decimal currency hook very much to my convenience.

I was in there really to listen to Barbara make a Statement about her tremendous triumph in persuading the N.U.R. to agree to the opening of the freightliner terminals for container trains. She'd got this after three days of almost continuous negotiation during which — as I heard from Jennie Hall and her husband Chris, who is Barbara's Press Officer[1] — she used techniques and methods which would have shocked her to the core if used by anybody else; she had finally threatened to cut off all further payment to the railways unless they agreed. Well, she got her way and she earned the applause at that Question Time.

The main business this afternoon was the Second Reading of Fred Willey's Leasehold Reform Bill. I am passionately opposed to this Bill and I think it will bring us appalling difficulties. Nevertheless I must frankly admit that it's had a wonderful press and it's been an enormous success. The Land Commission and Leasehold Reform have given our Government the kind of radical note which my Rent Act, for example, completely lacked. We need measures like these which affect millions of ordinary people by giving security to leaseholders and Fred Willey went over jolly well this afternoon.

However, I soon had to go out to the Services Committee where I had to get agreement on a draft report on how we should meet the £60,000 deficit on the Kitchen Account. We just dare not publish the report of the accountants or the Treasury O & M until we have a concrete policy. What we finally decided was to bring Bob Maxwell on to the Committee and put him in the chair. When I first heard the idea I was shocked but John Silkin swallowed it and persuaded Bob Maxwell to accept and to my amazement the Tories on the Committee accepted him too, in particular Willie Whitelaw and Selwyn Lloyd. I think they realized that one has to get a businessman of

[1] Christopher Hall, a journalist, had joined the Ministry of Overseas Development in 1965 as public relations adviser to Barbara Castle. From there he moved to the Ministry of Transport as Chief Information Officer. In 1969 he became Secretary General of the Ramblers' Association and in 1973 the Director of the C.P.R.E. His wife, Jennie, had been Crossman's indispensable personal secretary since 1962 and worked in his Private Office at M.H.L.G. 1964–6. She worked in the Private Office of Harold Wilson 1973–4.

experience and courage and that Bob is the only businessman in the House who will be prepared, out of sheer vanity and ambition, to spend a couple of years saving the House of Commons' kitchen from corruption and bankruptcy.

I might add that I am not at all an unsuccessful chairman of this Committee which is doing a lot behind the scenes to clean up the House of Commons. I suppose I say this because last week *The Times* had a leading article about the row saying that Manny was wrong to whip the Party back to the old discipline but he was right about me since I was possibly the worst Leader of the House for generations. I fancy there would be quite a number of people who would agree with that judgment: indeed there's a great danger still of my failing in this spectacular way. But the condemnation isn't as definite and universal as *The Times* suggests; indeed, I think a number of Tories rather like the abrasive tone of my Leadership. They realize that I'm a reforming Leader who's getting things done on the Services Committee, getting our Specialist Committees to work, getting our morning sittings to function and, by the way, getting legislation through at a faster rate than any Leader since the war. It's my own Party who really suspect and dislike me.

Anne came to dinner this evening and John brought his Rosamund and the four of us sat together. It's enormously important that we should get along and that his wife should like me and Anne. I'm not sure Rosie does. As for John he's very Jewish and he gives nothing away but he's enormously professional in his personal relations—even with me. I know, even from this week, that he has intimate relations with the P.M. of which he doesn't tell me anything. Indeed, he really tells me nothing of what he does in his room or whom he sees amongst the press—all that he keeps to himself. I'm much more open with John than he is with me. Nevertheless the central fact is that he is committed to fight and win this battle for the liberal regime even more than I am and his faith in it is even simpler and more ingenuous and more direct. All that is fine. The difficulty is that he insists on having his own extremely peculiar personal relationship with Harold and also has a peculiar feeling that he must get on with George Wigg and Manny Shinwell; in these ways he's more of a compromiser than I am. I suspect he finds me abrasive, awkward and impatient and regards himself as wiser, shrewder and more practical. There are times when I can't accept this judgment as absolutely fair.

Wednesday, March 8th

I spent the whole morning at a Cabinet Committee on power-station construction. Dick Marsh at the Ministry of Power had planned the erection of one coal-fired station and one new nuclear station but D.E.A. had recommended that we should cut out the former. The last time we discussed this the Committee had finally decided that we simply didn't know enough to make a decision and had instructed the officials to come back with absolutely clear facts and figures about both the nature of the power stations and about the state of the electricity supply in the 1970s.

Now, three weeks later, the officials had come up with a completely different view and, even more sinister, with quite different figures. Three weeks ago it was suggested we didn't need the new coal-firing station. Now we are given figures that demonstrate that we need both. I was so angry that I insisted that the minutes of the meeting should record our displeasure at this contradiction in the evidence. I was amused when the minutes turned up to read the following: 'It was further suggested that it would have been helpful to the Committee at their previous discussion if the implications of cancelling Drax for the adequacy of generating capacity in 1973 had been brought out more clearly.' They had been brought out perfectly clearly but with different figures and in fact D.E.A. had concluded that the coal-firing station was unnecessary. Our civil servants always win when it's a matter of covering up a gross inefficiency.[1]

After that I went back to my room at the Privy Council and rapidly knocked off a speech for that evening. To my annoyance I had found that morning that I was due to speak in a G.L.C. election meeting in Merton and Morden, right down in Surrey.[2] Well, I thought, I'll try once again to get my ideas across because my speech at Warwick on the previous Friday had been printed nowhere and only a couple of lines extracted by the B.B.C. I suppose I was a bit peeved that nobody had thought it worth publishing. Now I knocked off another similar piece and sharpened it by saying that so long as the Chief and I were there, there would be no question of going back on the liberal discipline we had introduced. I made it as sharp as this because of what Manny had said in his interview in *The Week in Westminster* last Saturday where he had directly announced the collapse of the Crossman–Silkin regime.

After finishing the draft I had lunch with Peregrine Worsthorne.* After that I had to get back to the front bench to hear another excellent Statement by Barbara Castle. Then back to my office to tidy up the draft of my own speech which had to be issued by Transport House. I had just finished when the Chief looked in. He glanced at the draft and said that it was O.K. I said, 'Right, I must send it straightaway across to the Press Office in Transport House,' and as I discovered later in the evening it was issued at 5.20 having been cleared by the Chief at 4.45—though I knew that he hadn't had time to read it properly.

After that we went down to the liaison committee. We had discussed our tactics there and against my advice John had decided to present to the committee his long and excellent—but, I thought, untimely—report on discipline in which he described, for example, how he had written to Jim Wellbeloved and Roebuck asking for apologies for their personal attacks on the Leader. (I must say, they didn't seem to me personal attacks in the

---

* The result was, once again, a good article in the *Sunday Telegraph*.
[1] The White Paper *Fuel Policy* (Cmnd. 3438) was to be published on November 14th, 1967.
[2] The G.L.C. elections were to be held on April 13th.

normal sense of the word.) When John had finished there was very little discussion but Manny Shinwell said that over the weekend he had consulted with the P.M. and had put to him a form of words which he thought should be put to the whole Party. Then he read aloud, very fast, a form of words which I can't exactly remember but which basically said we should revert to the old conscience clause. This would mean that whenever the Party came to a decision and a three-line whip was imposed Members would have to vote the Party line unless it contradicted pacifist or temperance principles. I'd been forewarned by John about this because George Wigg had rung him up and dictated a similar formula and tried to make him agree it as something the P.M. had already consented to. Once these two presentations were made there wasn't much more to be said and I wanted to get away from the committee and off to my meeting at Merton and Morden.

It was a filthy night and we drove through drenching rain. I sat beside Molly in a thoroughly bad temper and couldn't find my way, knew I was going to be late and was feeling embarrassed at the thought of having to read this damned piece of paper aloud to people who were really concerned with the G.L.C. election. I certainly had no idea as I sat in the car that I was going to achieve a dramatic transformation of the situation.

When I got there there were 120 people in a school hall and I thought I'd better start by reading aloud my press release. I was surprised to find how interested they were in problems of discipline and I then had a perfectly good routine meeting on G.L.C. topics.

When I got back to the House I found that the ticker in the lobby was surrounded by eager M.P.s who were all reading an enormous report of my speech that evening. In addition, apparently, there had been tacked on to it a statement from the P.M.'s office explaining that this speech was not an attack on Harold Wilson but something he fully approved of. Something was certainly up. People who met me in the lobby stopped to talk to me about my wonderful speech. Along came Tom Driberg and took me into the smoking-room and said, 'George Wigg has been here for an hour running you down and attacking you but I think your speech was wonderful.' Then Gerald Kaufman got hold of me and said, 'I've had endless trouble because David Wood of *The Times* interpreted your speech as an attack on Harold and the P.M. sent me to interpret it to him in the correct way and I got most of the mistakes removed from David Wood's article. By the way, it's the lead story.' At midnight when I slipped out the Housing Subsidies Bill was over and I knew that what I'd done as a rather routine contribution to the G.L.C. election campaign was likely to hit the headlines next day.

Thursday, March 9th
Right enough, in *The Times* and the *Telegraph* my speech was the lead story and the *Guardian* made it an important back-page story. The fact that the Leader of the House had staked his career on the Crossman–Silkin liberal

discipline meant that I had seized the initiative and was fighting for my life. This is what I woke up to this morning.

The attitude of my colleagues at Cabinet showed that they had also been impressed by the news. But we started with parliamentary business and at once plunged into a discussion about decimalization. Callaghan gruffly said it was all nonsense about the Party opposition and we'd better go ahead. Then the Chief gave a warning about the very strong feeling of support in the Party for the ten-shilling against the £ unit. Callaghan replied that it was only because they'd never heard the case against the ten-shilling unit and I said, 'Well, it's really a question of the image you want to present to the country. If you want to give a picture of strength and directness in Government then we push this thing through and I think we could probably get it approved for you next Wednesday at the Party meeting. If we want to popularize ourselves as respecters of Parliament then of course we can insert the offer of a second debate or a free vote.' There's no doubt what the Cabinet wanted. They decisively wished that Callaghan should both speak and wind up in the Second Reading debate and that there should be a straight vote at the Party meeting on the issue, after the Government had stated the reason why it wasn't prepared to concede a free vote.

After an inordinately long oration by Harold about the timetable for the European discussion we turned to Malta, where the crisis still goes on. Amazingly enough the talks still continue, largely because of my concern with parliamentary business. Last Tuesday I heard that they decided to break off the talks on Wednesday morning so I went to see Gordon Walker and said, 'For God's sake, don't do that because they will move the adjournment of the House under Standing Order No. 9 on Wednesday afternoon and that means that the Housing Subsidies Bill will go on till four in the morning. Can't you carry on at least over Wednesday till Thursday, which will be quite a good day on which to have the adjournment moved because the Tories have got a Bill they want to get through?' Patrick said, 'All right, I don't mind continuing the talks,' and they duly were going on while Cabinet was discussing Malta on Thursday.

All through Cabinet, however, I was brooding about the business Statement this afternoon and I concentrated on it once again over lunch. I was determined not to be dragged into any statement on Party discipline: I was determined that decimalization should not be mentioned because it wasn't in the business for this week. The Chief Whip told me he'd arranged to have twenty or thirty on our side getting up to ask about Eric Heffer's Bill to abolish live hare coursing and this should make life easy for me.

Harold's Question Time at 3.15 went quietly enough and then came my critical moment. I got up, Hansard records, to a round of applause. Could it be true? A great warm cheer from behind me? Was it out of a sense of shame? No, these people were cheering the speech I had made the night before. They were cheering the Leader of the House who they'd been booing and jeering last Thursday; they were giving him an ovation for standing up for the rights of the back-benchers and making the right noises compared with Harold Wilson's dog-licence speech. That ovation was about the most surprising thing which has happened to me since my speech on National Superannuation at the 1957 Labour Party Conference when I received an ovation having expected to be thrown off the Executive that Tuesday morning.

After that the business Statement went perfectly easily. I was neat and concise and precise and none of the Questions on hare coursing materialized because our own people, having heard the ovation, knew the crisis was over and went out. Of course I realized that Shinwell would be infuriated. He went and blew his top to George Wigg and George was busy that evening feeding the press with long stories about my outrageous behaviour at the liaison committee and Manny's threatened resignation. Apparently I should have given him advance notice of my Merton and Morden speech although he hadn't bothered to tell me anything about the interview he gave on Saturday's B.B.C. review.

This evening three members of the Specialist Committee on the Ministry of Agriculture came to see me. I'd heard stories about this Committee going wrong—trying to study the impact of the Common Market on British agriculture although this has nothing to do with its terms of reference which confine it to studying the English department. Now three loyalists came to see me headed by a very weak chairman, Tudor Watkins,[1] in order to reveal that Derek Page,[2] one of the Labour members, had taken the bit between his teeth and is determined to take the Committee out to Brussels to study the Common Market on the spot. They all seemed a bit flabbergasted and I had to put some backbone into them and tell the chairman to run the Committee properly.

Late in the evening I went over to the House of Commons to sit in the television room with Tam Dalyell and watch the results of the by-elections at Rhondda West, Pollok and Nuneaton.[3] I knew we would do badly in Nuneaton because a ghastly young man with a beard had been selected to replace Frank Cousins.* The result was about as bad as I thought. Then came Rhondda West and that really was a shock. Twenty-seven per cent of the Labour vote had switched to the Welsh Nationalist. We had to wait till one in the morning for Pollok and at least we were number two which was not too bad.

---

* I could not have been wronger. The young man with the beard turned out to be a first-rate constituency Member, Leslie Huckfield.

[1] Labour M.P. for Brecon and Radnor 1945–70 and P.P.S. to the Secretary of State for Wales 1964–8. He became a life peer in 1972.

[2] Labour M.P. for King's Lynn 1964–70.

[3] The Glasgow Pollok by-election was caused by the death of Alexander Garrow in December 1966. Labour lost to Professor Esmond Wright, a Conservative, largely as a result of the intervention of an S.N.P. candidate who polled 10,884 votes out of a total of 38,652. At the Rhondda West by-election, caused by the death of Iowerth Thomas, Labour's majority of nearly 17,000 at the general election was reduced to 2,306. A Plaid Cymru candidate came second. Labour held Nuneaton, but the majority of 11,403 was cut to 4,054.

Friday, March 10th

The press were clearly determined to make the most of the bad by-election results and rubbed the lesson in with huge stories about Manny Shinwell's threatened resignation with every kind of dirt thrown at me. There's no doubt that this press campaign had been organized by George and Manny and I at once rang Harold in a white fury. 'It's no good my coming round before O.P.D.,' I said, 'I want more time than that. I will be with you after O.P.D. is over.' At that meeting I had my first bleeding row with Harold. I told him his behaviour was totally impossible. I had delivered to him an important letter on Monday and he had hardly acknowledged it—merely remarking to me at a committee meeting, 'I got your letter. It's daft.' Then he had gone off to look for Burke. I made my speech mainly because he had completely disregarded me. I felt I had to do it in my own interest because George and Manny were conspiring to destroy me and I knew that throughout Harold had been in contact with them. 'Well,' said Harold, 'I spent hours with George and had him on the phone and he's threatened resignation four or five times this week.' 'Why the hell didn't you accept it?' I said. 'Because of the D-Notice affair,' he said. 'We must keep Manny whatever happens until he has done his job on the D-Notice Committee to which he's been appointed as a Privy Councillor.' I had to admit that Harold couldn't have a row with Manny until that Committee had done its job. But I repeated that the situation was impossible because he had let me down so badly. 'No,' he said. 'What you say about George is always an exaggeration.' 'Shut up,' I said. 'It isn't. As you know perfectly well George has been poisoning the press against me. Look at the *Sunday Telegraph*, for example.' 'No,' Harold said, 'he assures me he didn't write that.' He was pleading with me and rattled and I was for the first time really angry with him. 'I hate this job,' I said. 'It's an abysmal job and I'll get out.' Nevertheless we patched it up and I promised not to do anything over the weekend. In particular I promised not to make any reply to the outrageous attacks upon me which Manny and George had organized in the press.

Then I was off to my room where I found Nora Beloff waiting for me. I knew how dangerous this was so I sent for Gerald Kaufman and the interview took place in his presence. A good thing too because she didn't use a single thing I told her and wrote a particularly bitchy article in the *Observer* about the general situation.

I only just caught my train at Liverpool Street for Norwich, where I had to open the ten thousandth council house on an estate which I had seen started two years earlier when I visited Norwich as Minister of Housing. Once again it was a lovely afternoon with brilliant sunshine and I was out in the open air with a keen wind—I knew the right thing to say and said it and got on with the Norwich Housing Committee. Oh dear, how much I enjoyed it. Thence I was motored to Anglia Television where I was pressed on the subject of discipline. Then off to a Labour Party meeting near Cromer, where six buses brought three hundred people to the local cinema and I had a splendid agricultural audience.

Saturday, March 11th

I got up to find the press once again full of Shinwell's blasting attacks on me as an impossible Leader. I rang up John Silkin who cooled me off by saying very sensibly, 'We're winning, old boy.' Certainly the three paragraphs of my Merton and Morden speech had worked wonders. But we were winning at a terrible price to the Party. This morning I had one of those area conferences in Norwich and, my God, the delegates—headed by Arthur South, the leader of the Norwich Council and an East Anglian big shot—blew their tops. They weren't so much concerned about the liberal regime as about the newspaper stories of disagreement in the Party. The right-wingers, of course, blamed Michael Foot, but the centre and the Left were blaming Harold Wilson, who was certainly discredited by the dog-licence speech. I talked to them briefly and cogently with the press present and it took some skill not to say anything quotable. Then off to Bury St Edmunds for a magnificent lunch in the new Labour Party Headquarters and a series of afternoon and evening meetings arranged by Doug Garnett, the regional organizer, who motored me back through lovely country and lovely weather to Prescote which we reached at eight o'clock this evening. Six engagements for the Party. A useful job of work but I'd also learnt a lot about the state of Party morale. It is shocked and appalled by what has been happening at Westminster in the last fortnight. The G.L.C. people, Doug tells me, are shaken to the core by the harm we have been doing to their election chances. John and I have to fight on for the liberalization of discipline but we have to make the new discipline work. The M.P.s when liberalized must be got to take their responsibilities sensibly and that's what I have to concentrate on next week.

Sunday, March 12th

It's strange to think that just a week ago I was drafting my resignation letter and feeling absolutely desperate. Today the situation has been completely reversed as a result of my Wednesday speech. I'm now temporarily a hero, at least for the left and left-of-centre back-benchers, and regarded as their patron and protector against Harold. As for Manny's counter-attacks on me on Friday and Saturday they must lead, as far as I can see, to his resignation. It's only now that I can look back a week and see the low level I'd reached last Sunday. My position seemed to be irreparably confused by Harold's dog-licence speech. I'd been made to appear an upholder of orthodoxy and discipline against freedom. I'd been hopelessly compromised by Harold's efforts on my behalf. What happened during this week was first that Callaghan self-assertively came out on Wednesday at Question Time and made it clear that it was he and the Cabinet who had insisted on the decimalization decision, not the Leader of the House. Then on Thursday morning came the account in the newspapers of my own speech which created a completely new atmosphere when I made my business Statement and earned my ovation. All today I've been waiting for the P.M. to ring me up. When I left him on Friday he said he was going to Chequers and would communicate with me on Sunday. He hasn't done so and I haven't communicated with him because I really have nothing to say to him now. To judge from the Sunday papers he has ordered the Shinwell–Wigg attack on me to be stopped. I'm pretty sure he'll want me and John to make friends with George and Manny and work together with them and I suppose we shall be driven to do so. The one good thing is that he hasn't contacted me. I think he knows now that he's got to do something positive for me before he sees me next. Will he stop Manny and George bitching my liberal regime? If he won't I'm out.

Monday, March 13th
In the morning three interesting meetings. First I had to collect all the Ministers who are liable to give evidence to the new Specialist Committees and also to the Select Committee on the Nationalized Industries, of which Ian Mikardo is chairman. The existence of these Committees is now producing some of the constitutional changes I hoped. Ian Mikardo's Committee, for example, is going to do a detailed study of the relationship between a Minister and whichever nationalized industry he's responsible for.[1] Barbara Castle is keen to give evidence. Dick Marsh is firmly against it. But Jack Diamond from the Treasury had to warn Ministers that in his view they couldn't say 'no' to a Select Committee whether they wanted to or not. Everyone agreed that if Ministers are to give evidence—particularly in public—there must be much better co-ordination of briefs and departmental policies than ever before and we've got to provide a kind of code of conduct for Ministers and senior civil servants interrogated by the new Specialist Committees.

In the second meeting I found myself in the chair when E.D.C. was discussing the transformation of the Post Office from a Government Department into a nationalized industry. At the previous meeting the Lord President was the only person who had had time to read the huge draft White Paper which described how all the powers of this vast monopoly were to be handed over lock stock and barrel to the new Post Office Corporation with only the vaguest policy direction left in the Postmaster-General's hands.[2] I pointed out that this will make ours the only post office not owned and controlled by the state and I wondered whether this was wise. But I could get no support from any of the departmental Ministers because of the old trouble that unless the Department's interests are concerned they don't like interfering in the reorganization of another Department. As a result the decision has been taken in principle without any general discussion of its desirability and now

[1] Their report, published in 1967, recommended that there should be a Minister for the nationalized industries.

[2] The Post Office became a public corporation in 1969.

we have a detailed White Paper pushed through without the Cabinet ever seeing it until the last moment. The fact is that so-called Cabinet decisions are nearly always made today by a departmental initiative without any adequate check from outside.

The third meeting was the Home Affairs Committee and was concerned with a beauty spot in Cornwall. For four years the Ministry of Defence has been negotiating with the private owner about selling back to him some of the land they took in the war. Now suddenly the Ministry discovers that part of the land they were due to hand back is wanted for Post Office radar in Cornwall. So the Postmaster-General coolly proposes that he should be allowed to go back on the four years of negotiations and claim that this is the only site in the whole of Cornwall suitable for the radar station. Some of us challenged this. How did he know it was the only site? What steps had he taken to find somewhere else? What evidence was there for the allegation in his paper that the owners were just out for the money? This was a case where bad departmental initiative was stopped by the alertness of Ministers—perhaps because they remembered the political trouble caused by Crichel Down.

At lunch-time I heard that I'm summoned to a special meeting in the P.M.'s room in the House and that everything else must be cancelled. When the Chief and I got there we discovered that George Wigg and Manny were the only others in attendance. Harold Wilson had apparently spent the weekend preparing an ultimatum to us all—a five-page foolscap document laying down the precise behaviours we should adopt to each other. I read it through and as far as I can see it gives one hundred per cent support to John and myself. It excludes George Wigg altogether from any interference with us and it ties Manny Shinwell tightly down and expressly forbids him and George Wigg to brief the press any more against me. The only important concession he makes to the Party is that in future the Chief shall discuss with the liaison committee any discipline he proposes to impose before taking action. Otherwise it's a paper on how to enforce the liberal regime of John Silkin and Dick Crossman through the liaison committee and proposes an enlargement of the committee by two more elected members.

It was read through paragraph by paragraph for any comments and at the end of five pages there were no comments. All accepted it in total silence. Then there was some discussion. Manny said he was going to resign by the end of the month. He is out. George was silent all the way through. Manny and George withdrew, clearly licked, and John and I stayed behind to have drinks with Harold and Marcia as though they'd been solidly backing us all the way through. It was an easy atmosphere and we began to discuss how to get through the next three or four weeks without disaster. Before John and I left, the P.M. took the document back from my hands saying he didn't want anybody to have it. But I suspect that he didn't really want me to have it for my diary and will keep it for his book.

Looking at this in terms of my relationship with Harold, I think I can say that the scene we had last Friday morning produced action on Monday afternoon. He did make the document an ultimatum in which he finally backed John and me against Manny and George and when that happened the fight was over. On the other hand, though I have won, I've won with considerable damage to myself and I'm now accident-prone as Leader of the House. Harold knows I've been injured and terribly hurt inside, which make me insecure.

After this I went off to Haringey for another G.L.C. election meeting.

Tuesday, March 14th
Cabinet today consisted of the third round of the battle on family endowment. For this meeting Callaghan had merely circulated a paper repeating the argument that the decision of the previous meeting[1] pre-empted his next budget and on Monday, with Tommy's help, I had circulated an explosive anti-Chancellor paper pointing out that he was cheating in the way he was estimating the amount pre-empted and asking the Cabinet to stand by its decision. It was a kind of declaration of war between the Chancellor and myself and Cabinet met quite tense and alarmed at what was going to happen. I need hardly say nothing happened except for a long argument in which the two sides remained, as far as I could see, exactly the same. We had on our side Michael Stewart, George Brown, Barbara Castle, Dick Crossman, Tony Wedgwood Benn, Tony Greenwood, Ray Gunter, Frank Pakenham and the Lord Chancellor. Callaghan had on his side Roy Jenkins, Tony Crosland, Cledwyn Hughes, Kenneth Robinson and Fred Peart. I think the score was 10–8. Harold was obviously even less enthusiastic in helping us than he had been in the second round. Announcing it was clear we were deadlocked, he put forward his compromise proposal that we should concede next October some £40 million of increased family allowance without accepting either the Chancellor's means-tested or Peggy's claw-back scheme. Immediately Patrick Gordon Walker supported this strongly. I said it was totally unworkable and was simply wasting millions of the taxpayers' money. Peggy Herbison was also able to show all the impossibilities of the scheme. It was clear that this was a Burke Trend compromise — a characteristic Civil Service device. By giving a small increase in comprehensive family allowances Whitehall hoped to kill our claw-back scheme and give the Chancellor a chance of persuading the Cabinet to accept his means-test scheme. The Cabinet clearly was not willing to accept the compromise and then Tony Crosland asked why we had to decide it now. How long could we leave it? Could we wait until July? So characteristically we agreed to postpone it till July on condition that administrative preparations for the Herbison claw-back scheme went on being made so that we could introduce it next year ready for 1968. Peggy Herbison was terribly depressed when she had to

[1] See p. 252.

withdraw from the Cabinet and the Chancellor rushed back and said he had won. Actually we lost nothing this morning, except possibly half the support which Harold Wilson had half-heartedly given us in the previous meeting.

At the Services Committee this afternoon we were still labouring with the losses of the Catering Department. Ever since 1956 it's been going downhill and losing thousands through utter incompetence. This was the first meeting with Bob Maxwell as chairman of the Catering Committee and we had to decide what to do with the reports from the accountants and the Treasury O & M. It was suggested that I should publish them whereupon Willie Whitelaw said, 'This isn't something our chairman should take responsibility for. This is a report to the Catering Committee and I propose that it be sent to them. Our chairman's got quite enough on his plate already.' That was a pretty handsome action of Willie's because if I'd had to make this Statement to the House I would have been on the defensive and the whole Tory Party would have been attacking the Catering Committee through me. Willie pushed that aside.

Wednesday, March 15th
In morning prayers the Chief Whip and I were alone with Harold. After Monday's ultimatum had been delivered there was very little to do. We discussed mainly the details of the code of honour the Chief Whip is now preparing in consultation with the P.M. We also had to decide how today's Party Meeting on the decimal problem should be conducted now that Manny has told us he will announce his resignation this morning.

The members of O.P.D. were waiting outside when we'd finished. It was a very important meeting since the paper we were discussing recorded the decision to go ahead with the purchase of fifty F-111 at nearly £2·7 million each. It was clear to me that this should be postponed until our big July discussions on public expenditure when we can consider it in relation to other factors. Taken early in this way it prejudged the whole of our East of Suez policy as well as our home priorities. George Brown mildly supported me. But obviously the P.M. and the Defence Secretary had fixed this between them. I tried to have my disagreement recorded in the minutes but I know very well that this is never done. I then urged that it should go to Cabinet but I was told that technically there is nothing for Cabinet to decide since the policy decision has already been taken. I was glad to see that Gerald Gardiner and Frank Pakenham were pretty upset when they heard the Prime Minister state this. After all, it means that by far the biggest decision on defence expenditure has been taken months before the July Defence Review which shows once again that Denis Healey is a lone wolf who runs very close with Harold Wilson and that Harold and he think they know what they are up to.[1]

---

[1] The order was to be cancelled in the January 1968 cuts in civil and defence expenditure, thereby saving some £400 million.

We had to get across straightaway to the Party meeting on decimalization which Jim Callaghan had insisted on. He was confident he could carry the Party and he was quite right. Everybody knew you can't pretend that decimalization is an issue of conscience. Moreover, there hadn't been a word of complaint until weeks after the Chancellor had committed himself against the ten-shilling unit. His speech was unanswerable. Then there came fifteen speakers of whom the ten well-informed were all passionately for the ten-shilling unit. So when Jim came to wind up he had to make the practical plea that we are committed already and we can't afford a free vote on our side when there won't be a free vote on the Tory side.

The result of the vote was ninety for the pound and sixty for the ten-shilling unit with some eighty abstentions. It was about the best result we could hope to get and it showed that the liberal discipline was at least making some sense.

After that Manny said he would announce his resignation, and did so. Then Harold Wilson made a charming, skilled little speech praising Manny for his wonderful service while we had a majority of three and very carefully saying nothing about what he had been doing in the new Parliament. With that out of the way I went off to lunch in the press gallery.

This afternoon in the House Fred Peart announced his price review which had been accepted by the farmers with a tremendously favourable press describing it as the most generous review since 1948.[1] I wasn't surprised that some of my Cabinet colleagues were shocked and thought that there'd been some sharp practice by Fred and me in getting it through, particularly the increase in the price of milk. But of course it was really Patrick Gordon Walker who, as chairman of the Committee, surrendered the pass. We got more for the farmers than many of the farmers expected and we were absolutely right to get it in terms of the selective expansion programme.

I was due this evening to speak to the socialists at London University. However L.S.E. was in the throes of a tremendous crisis with student sit-ins, strikes and riots.[2] Owing to this the socialists at the University decided to cancel my meeting and I was able to spend the evening having dinner with the back-benchers and talking of the new discipline and trying to understand the new intake. Most of them are on the side of the Silkin–Crossman discipline but mainly because they don't really understand it.

Thursday, March 16th
At Cabinet the main subject was Aden. I had cross-examined George Brown more than once at O.P.D. about his real intentions and convinced myself that he is determined to get us out fast but with the minimum of dishonour. He put this very well to Cabinet and got it through successfully. But Cabinet

[1] The guaranteed cattle price was to be increased by 5s. a cwt and the guaranteed milk price by 1½d. a gallon. The net effect was that the value of the guarantees was increased by £25 million.

[2] From March 13th to 21st there was a boycott of lectures and a 'sit-in' by students at the L.S.E. who were protesting at disciplinary measures against two students.

was not told a word about the F-111 decision because it was felt that this
was something which could be slipped through.

We then turned to consider the airbus and at the end of an hour we're
committed to another £130 million aviation project, which is bound to lose
money, as a kind of entry card into Europe.[1]

Finally we had to approve the Prices and Incomes White Paper which
makes it only too clear that we've abandoned the chance of doing something
really creative which we won for ourselves by the July freeze. There will be no
effective substitutes for Part IV when it lapses next summer and all the
Government will have is the power to impose four months' delay. So on this
major issue the Cabinet had failed and we are having to coast along without
any incomes policy and so without any alternative to unemployment as the
method of deflation next time. I said to Harold later, 'Well, you've lost the
incomes policy, haven't you?' And he said, 'Yes, but you know we must
now hope we shall get through without it.'

Then the usual Thursday routine. Back to the Privy Council, talk to
Trevor Lloyd-Hughes and his girl, talk to Freddie Warren, talk to Freddy
Ward, prepare business Statement, lunch in the House, then over to hear
Harold's Questions. I then got to the business Statement and was told by the
Tories they have no Questions to ask. This didn't trick me: I thought it
seemed the lull before the storm. Sure enough, bang, snap, up got Heath to
say he wanted an explanation of what happened yesterday morning when
Dick Marsh made the announcement about salaries for the members of the
Steel Board. The Tories' outcry was that I had broken my pledge — that we
were not to have controversial or important Statements during morning
sittings. I tried to argue that this was nothing to do with business for next
week but the Speaker didn't help me and so we plunged into a bitter altercation, in which at one point I leaned across and asked the Chief how we'd
classified this item. He told me the Departments had not claimed it was
important and I then said so. This roused the Tories to howls of rage but by
now I was all right because our own side thought this was a put-up job and
that Ted Heath was trying to destroy their Leader of the House. I remained
strictly courteous and sensible and the one thing I didn't do which perhaps
I should have done was to counter-attack the Leader of the Opposition.*

At the Party meeting in the evening Malcolm MacPherson was in the chair
and handled proceedings very skilfully. There was the tricky issue of the
promised debate on discipline which had to be resolved. Malcolm said that the
liaison committee thought it was unnecessary but if the Party insisted we could
have one next week. There was a moment's silence, then Jack Mendelson said
it was unnecessary and I knew we had won. The great discipline issue had

---

* Or to attack the Speaker, as Barney Cocks was to recommend to me over an excellent
dinner that night.

[1] On July 25th, 1967, France, Britain and West Germany agreed to build a 250–300 seat
'airbus', with France and Britain each contributing 37·5 per cent of the estimated £190
million cost and West Germany 25 per cent. Britain was to lead the engine design team.

been shoved to one side and frankly the Party doesn't want to talk about it any more. Anyway, if we're going to have a new chairman elected, we must wait for him to settle in before we discuss discipline and the new code of honour.

That evening I'd been invited to dinner by the Chief Clerk, Sir Barnett Cocks. His rooms are difficult to find — right on top of the roof where it feels like being on top of a liner. It was a very pleasant evening we had with them and when we were drinking our port Barney settled down to give me some advice. He told me in a very firm way that I ought from time to time to judiciously attack the Speaker and complained that I was being exposed and exploited by him. The Speaker only responded to a Leader of the House who challenged him from time to time about his fairness. 'Wait for your moment,' he said. 'Wait till you've got your own people strongly behind you and then challenge the Speaker in this way. The one thing he's really afraid of is a vote of censure.' It's good advice but it'll be many months before I shall dare to think of carrying it out.

Friday, March 17th

At our weekly meeting with Burke and the P.M. I noted that Harold was trying to avoid talking to me about a number of awkward topics I wanted to raise. One of them was George Brown's refusal to let me be the Minister representing us in Israel at the Balfour Declaration celebrations on November 4th, 1967. I'd sent Harold a memorandum describing what had happened about this invitation. The Israeli Foreign Office had invited the P.M. to attend and said that if he couldn't go they wanted me. Harold had passed this letter to George and the Foreign Office had quickly got in a proposal that Ted Short should be the man. I said this was very tart because they had asked specifically for me. George then minuted me that he objected very strongly to a speech I had made to a Zionist organization in London. To this I replied by letter asking him to send the text of the offending passage. To this I got the following reply:

Your letter of 7 March about the Balfour Declaration celebrations was waiting for me on my return. I should like you to understand my principal objection is not the reports of what you are alleged to have said, though from the point of view of Arab reaction it doesn't much matter whether they are accurate or not. The real trouble is that the presence of a Cabinet Minister of your seniority would make difficulties for us in the Arab world. Goodness knows, we have enough of these already. I realize your personal disappointment about this and I wish I could give you a different answer.

On this I minuted the P.M.:

I am sorry to worry you with this but the attached minute from the Foreign Secretary compels me to do so. He states he cannot permit me or any other senior Minister to celebrate the Balfour Declaration in Israel for fear of repercussions in the Arab world. If it is true that our relations with the Arabs depend on appeasing them to this extent the situation is depressing indeed since I doubt whether in the worst days of the Bevin regime it was as bad as that. But frankly I believe the Foreign Secretary is doing himself and his Department an injustice by suggesting that our relations with Israel have to be conducted within these extraordinarily narrow confines in order to sustain our Arab policy. Perhaps we could have a word about it?

I got the following reply from Marcia Williams: 'You sent the P.M. a minute about the Balfour Declaration celebrations in Israel. He feels you should sort this out with George or raise it at Cabinet.' I was tempted to discuss this this morning with Harold and Burke. But I didn't. I realized that if I wanted to stay in the Government I'd got to accept it.

Once again the members of O.P.D. poured in when we had finished in order to have a discussion of offset costs in Germany. As usual the Chancellor and the Foreign Secretary got into an interminable bicker, which I found very boring so I pushed my chair back and went into a coma. The P.M always notices when I do this since I'm sitting beside him. At the end of the meeting he said, 'I hope you're getting away for a holiday?' I doubt if he really believed I need one but he was trying to re-establish some kind of personal relations with me since that searing row we had on the Friday before last. I suppose the fact that he's forced Manny to resign is something of a triumph but I don't feel at all happy or secure because my own natural congenital disadvantages as Leader of the House have been exposed over these weeks and there really is a question whether I'm the right man for the job. If Harold really wants abrasive reform to be driven through then I'm his man. But let's see whether Harold really wants it. If he doesn't I shall find myself out or being shifted round by the autumn.

Monday, March 20th

I was going up early in order to talk to Miss Nunn about the legislative programme but the train broke down at Bicester and we had to get a new engine. I was grateful to have an hour and a half to read the European document produced by Harold and George. Harold has spoken more than once about its enormous length and how unreadable it is. Actually it took me just two and a half hours to read it because there were five versions of George Brown's speech on agriculture which he had delivered in five different capitals and the number of new things we had to read carefully were concentrated in the account of the talks with General de Gaulle and the Germans and, to a greatly lesser extent, with the Dutch.[1] I was able to assimilate most of this before we arrived in London and Molly rushed me in late to yet another S.E.P. on Nicky Kaldor's idea of a Regional Employment Premium.

This afternoon in the House I had to answer some Questions about morning sittings. I'm afraid it's now clear we haven't succeeded in our main objective. As many hours are being worked after ten o'clock this year as last year — if not slightly more. The Opposition has set itself to the task of bitching morning sittings, and have made sure that the penalty exacted from us is a late night for each morning sitting. But of course we are doing a lot more business because we have so many more hours each week. I defended the experiment quietly but have to face the fact that as long as the Opposition objects it will not achieve its purpose.

The series of debates on the Consolidated Fund Bill started this afternoon with a discussion on Aden.* This was the time George Brown had chosen since he was confident that by then we would have reached agreement on our final departure. Unfortunately, however, the locals had spotted what we were up to. If it paid us to advance the time of independence and get out first and off the land, they were bound to spot this and cause trouble. Poor George Thomson, who had been sent there to finish off the talks, was kept for two days on- and off-shore trying to get them to agree, and on Monday afternoon there was no Statement to make. I sat and watched George Brown deliberately rough it up with Duncan Sandys in the absence of Ted Heath, who is at Harvard where he's doing the Godkin Lectures. It was a very skilled operation.[2]

When the debate turned to quieter subjects Willie Whitelaw signalled me out and asked me whether I'd got a letter from him (which I hadn't received) about the problem of taking visitors round the House during morning sittings when entry to the Chamber is closed. I had suggested we should stop all parties taken by professional guides and that M.P.s should take their own parties round. This, Willie said, was objectionable to his Party. They preferred to ration the conducted tours just as we ration tickets for the Gallery. I said I would put this to our party and then took the opportunity to chat to him about the Finance Bill. It is an excellent thing that the Procedure Committee have come out with a unanimous report fully supported by Selwyn

* They ran through to the morning closure at 10 a.m. on Tuesday.

[1] When the visits to the six capitals were over, the Prime Minister had told the Commons on March 9th that, after Easter, the Government would give a full Statement of their intentions. Meanwhile there was some restlessness in Labour ranks on the whole E.E.C. issue and, on February 21st, 108 Labour M.P.s signed a motion that indicated their underlying suspicion of a venture to join.

[2] At George Thomson's discussions of a plan to grant independence in November, the Federal Ministers were not satisfied with the flimsy defence arrangements Britain proposed. On March 20th, therefore, George Brown was unable to announce a date for independence. A U.N. mission was sent to Aden on April 2nd, but FLOSY refused to meet the delegates and called for a general strike. On April 7th the mission withdrew and on April 12th the Foreign Secretary sent out Lord Shackleton with an open brief.

Lloyd. Willie said his Party would accept an experiment of voluntary time-tabling this year. I replied that this was not quite good enough. Since we'd got a unanimous report I thought it should be debated by the House and accepted. The difference between us, though subtle, is extremely important. The Committee on Procedure has realized that a voluntary timetable on the Finance Bill will not work unless it is backed by the sanction of Government powers. It has unanimously recommended that the Government should take powers under the Standing Orders to operate a compulsory guillotine after two hours of debate. I was astonished that Selwyn had agreed this and I'm certainly keen to get it into operation. But will the Tories throw Selwyn over?

I then turned to a subject I very much wanted to discuss with him—the behaviour of the Opposition during business questions in the previous week. John Silkin had already written protesting against Ted Heath's statement last Thursday that he had made a formal written complaint to me about timing contentious Ministerial Statements in the morning. In fact nothing came through the usual channels and the Heath attack on me was unprovoked and a complete surprise. Willie Whitelaw immediately agreed and said that he shouldn't have behaved in that way and his own people shouldn't try to destroy me with a trick of that kind. I replied that I didn't particularly mind it but said, 'I warn you, Willie, that as a result any hope you had of getting rid of morning sittings is clean out because you've now made it a Party issue. Lots of my people aren't keen on morning sittings and I'm certainly not committed to the kind of morning sittings we have now got. But as a result of Ted's behaviour my prestige is at stake. Every time you attack me in that way and obviously stage a demonstration against me because you object to morning sittings you doom yourselves to another three months of them. So please do think over the possibility of agreeing that we should do Private Members' Bills in the morning because that's what I've decided to do eventually.'

When he got up to leave my room I remarked that I'd had a pretty awful eight weeks. 'We've had our own difficulties,' he said. 'I've had an even worse eight weeks than you have—the worst in my whole life with all the ructions inside my Party.' This was a surprising remark in view of the results of the recent by-elections and the expectations of a big success on the G.L.C. But that isn't helping Willie in the internal struggle at Westminster, where Heath is still an unsuccessful leader and where there is no agreement on the Opposition front bench on incomes policy or defence or Rhodesia. It's nice to feel that he's had the worst eight weeks at the same time that I have.

This evening the P.M. had a party for Commonwealth guests at No. 10. I went over to it and found him cheerful and amiable. It was the first time I'd seen him close since our rows in the previous week and I was just getting down to a chat when I was told that Willie Ross wanted me on the phone and I had to leave the room. When I came back I found it empty but for the

P.M., Harold Davies[1] and George Wigg. It's difficult to cut somebody dead when there are only three people present without having a row but George and I both succeeded in doing so. We are still not on speaking terms and I doubt if we ever will be again.

Then I was off to George Weidenfeld's dinner. I stayed there until 11.30 and then went home to bed, leaving John Silkin to supervise the all-night sitting in the House. He had to stay because on the last Consolidated Fund Bill he'd been counted out so notoriously. Also, he was getting rid of George Lawson as his Deputy and Will Howie[2] as his pairing Whip and having a complete reorganization of the office for which he had to do a series of ghastly interviews which should occupy him most of the night.

Tuesday, March 21st
Cabinet. This was a special meeting at which we were to discuss the Wilson–Brown report on their tour of Europe.

When they'd made their introductions Denis Healey and Barbara at once launched their attack on the account of the meetings with General de Gaulle. Both of them complained that George and Harold had made too much of their success in these talks, in which, they claimed, they had made an immense impression on the General, who hadn't been nearly as adamant as they expected. Denis added that the record they had given us provided no reason to believe there was the remotest chance of getting in. I'm sure Denis was right but I also have a strong feeling that Harold and George want to make an immediate effort to enter and if they do the only way is to get inside first without negotiation and negotiate afterwards. Their idea is to get in by 1969. It would certainly be an enormous advantage if we could be there for that crucial agricultural review. But there would certainly have to be one devaluation if not two and we would be in real economic danger since we would be entering with the economy flat on its back, our growth rate low, our capital oozing out into Europe, and our factories being moved there because it's more profitable. On the other hand, would that matter politically? We would have completely outbid the Tories and we would be able to hold an election to confirm our success in 1969 before there was any hard evidence of the hardships we were due to suffer as the result of the devaluation.

This morning Harold was obviously testing Cabinet out. What he learnt was that only Douglas Jay is one hundred per cent against entry. Fred Peart didn't commit himself against trying, nor did Barbara, nor did Denis. I still think he will face only one resignation if he makes a dash to get in before 1969.

This afternoon the Chief and I had excellent staff talks about the results of

---

[1] Labour M.P. for Leek 1945–70. He was Joint Parliamentary Secretary, Ministry of Pensions 1965–7. In 1970 he became a life peer.

[2] Labour M.P. for Luton 1963–70. He was an Assistant Whip 1964–6, a Whip 1967–8 and vice-chairman of the P.L.P. 1968–70.

all my meetings with individual Ministers on the legislative programme. Then I was off to another G.L.C. election meeting, right down in Hornchurch, where I was speaking on the same platform as Bill Fiske, the leader of the Labour Party on the G.L.C.[1] Oh dear, about forty people being addressed by Fiske and myself in a hopelessly lethargic atmosphere. Yet for me it was suddenly a beautiful sight when I spotted in the second row Anne Ridoutt from my Private Office who had brought her husband over plus my dear Janet Gates. There they were sitting and grinning, and apparently they greatly enjoyed it and are all solid Labour people. I had no idea before that meeting.

We got back to the House rather earlier than we expected and I did something really bad. I let myself be driven on to Harold Lever's to a delicious party where I sat and enjoyed myself with Victor Rothschild[2] and Tommy Balogh and Harold Lever, just discussing taxation. But I *should* have let myself be dropped at the House since there was an incomes and prices prayer which drooled on till 12.45 with all the people cursing the Lord President for the failure of his morning sittings to get them home early.

This is something I mustn't do – absent myself two nights running. Now I'm established as Leader of the House I must not fall into the mistakes which Herbert Bowden fell into.

Wednesday, March 22nd
I woke up at four when Tam came in and told me how peeved people were last night. They were right to be peeved. But fortunately for me there was enough goodwill in the House to forgive me on this occasion.

As soon as I got into that ghastly room at the top of Transport House for the monthly N.E.C. meeting I realized there was a terribly surly atmosphere and we were in for trouble. I had to leave at 11.30 to take the chair at the first meeting of the new Cabinet Committee on Pensions and when I left one of the T.U. members was attacking the arrogance of Ministers and their remoteness from policy in trying to impose a statutory prices and incomes policy.

The Pensions meeting went exactly as I had planned it with Peggy Herbison and the officials last week. I told them the first thing to do was to put in to S.E.P. a paper on the economics of pensioneering which I would prepare and that meanwhile the officials should get on with some of the new work on the technical side. At the end of the meeting I got it agreed that officials from the D.E.A. and the Treasury as well as from the Ministry of Social Security and any experts I might choose to select would in future attend all our meetings. I was jolly pleased at bringing this off since I still have a passionate belief that Ministers and officials should sit down together in the same Committee.

[1] Lord Fiske, leader of the G.L.C. from 1964 until 1967, when he became a life peer. He served as chairman of the Decimal Currency Board 1966–71. He died in January 1974.

[2] Lord Rothschild, a distinguished zoologist, was until 1970 chairman of Shell Research. He then became Director-General of the Central Policy Review Staff, established in the Cabinet Office, and remained there for four years.

When this was over I thought it was worth looking in at No. 10 for the O.P.D. which was discussing Aden. But when I put my nose in the Cabinet Room nobody was there and I found Harold Wilson pacing up and down in what was for him real dismay. I've never seen him so rattled before and Michael Halls said to me, 'He really needs your help. I'm glad you're here.' What happened was this. The night before he had gone to see the trade-union group of back-benchers and addressed them in an interminable 45-minute speech which most of the members couldn't understand. This caused an outcry even from the ultra-right-wingers who threatened to break away if there was any question of a prices and incomes policy with reserve powers. The whole meeting had been absolutely opposed to statutory prices and incomes. Then, this morning, at N.E.C. there had been an equally violent demonstration against prices and incomes with Jack Jones threatening to disaffiliate the Transport Workers.

For the first time he was realizing what the ruin of statutory prices and incomes meant. Walking up and down, he threw out to me the idea of forming a Labour Party independent of the unions, like the American Democratic Party, but then added, 'But we shan't be like the Americans, we shall be like that miserable French socialist party.' I said I thought we'd missed our chance in October and November of last year. He should never have left the D.E.A. to Michael Stewart and the only way we could have swung the unions would have been if he'd taken over the job and run it himself. No one else could have helped. 'Ah,' he said, 'Barbara Castle could have done it.' That interested me as much as it surprised me. I then told him that I thought the only course he could take would be to prepare for accepting a virtually voluntary system while warning the public in advance that if it doesn't work the Government will have to take other measures. But the one thing he couldn't do was to go back to Part IV and impose a wage freeze over again. 'No,' he said 'that's quite impossible. What we should have to do is to cut public expenditure. If they take too much in real wages we shall have to cut their schools, their hospitals and housing. This is what we've got to tell them.' 'If that's what you want to tell them,' I said 'the great thing is to get it out in the open now, as soon as possible.'

Then I walked out because I had to prepare for Michael Stewart's Statement in the House on a Prices and Incomes White Paper at 3.30 that afternoon.[1] I had planned to counteract its bad effect by following it with a most dramatic Statement by John Stonehouse, Minister of Aviation, on the news that the Bristol-Siddeley aircraft company was paying back £4 million of overpayment to the Government. I hoped it would take the headlines next day

[1] The White Paper explained that, although Part IV of the Prices and Incomes Act was due to expire on August 11th, 1967 and that it was the Government's objective to return to full reliance on a voluntary policy, nevertheless the Government felt it appropriate that for twelve months after July 1st any proposed wage or price increases should be justifiable only against the restrictive criteria of the 1965 White Paper. Thus the 'positive norm' for wage increases would be annually, 3–3·5 per cent.

and I also sent a message to Tony Wedgwood Benn saying that he ought to get six back-benchers up to join in the attack on the Tories because this was a scandal, something like the Ferranti scandal.[1] However I got no response from him and no encouragement from Stonehouse. Indeed, when the Statements were made Michael Stewart was dry but harmless and Stonehouse was obviously playing the whole story down. This deeply alarmed me because I suspect it means that we haven't cleaned things up inside the Ministry of Aviation and Tony and John both feel that we've so much to conceal that we can't afford to have the story headlined. But it will be headlines whether they like it or not.

The Statements were followed by the long-awaited Second Reading of the Decimal Currency Bill. James Callaghan made a brilliant speech and when the division was called we had a majority of ninety. Even Mr Cant,[2] that greatest of decimalists, found himself voting in the Government lobby in a fairly good temper, because Harold had told them that decimalization was a three weeks' wonder. It's quite likely that the whole excitement in the country will as quickly subside. But I'm not absolutely certain. We have thrust the £ unit through against the ten-shilling unit without a free vote and without leaving proper time for consultation with the public. Will this be something which costs us dear because in practice people will go on preferring the ten shillings? I don't know.

I spent the whole of this evening trying to clear up the furious row about the behaviour of the Specialist Committee on Agriculture. At the Ministerial Committee earlier in the week Fred Mulley from the Foreign Office had blown his top about their proposal to go to Brussels to collect evidence. He says it must be stopped. I warned him that we had no right to decide the behaviour of a select Committee and I was sure the Clerk would keep them within their terms of reference. Our only right was of course to advise our Labour Members. Meanwhile I suggested Mulley should offer to give evidence and I would get from Barnett Cocks an exact account of the powers the Committee possessed. So this evening I saw Barney who told me that everything they did was perfectly in order and this was repeated to me by the Clerk. I also saw Derek Page, who is the ringleader and who is trying to organize the Brussels expedition, and told him to come and talk to me whenever he liked. I made it perfectly clear I wasn't intervening in any way

---

[1] In 1964 it was disclosed that Ferranti Ltd had made excessive profits from a production contract for an advanced guided-missile system. The House of Commons Public Accounts Committee made a study of Government contracts with private industry. On this later occasion the Minister announced that Bristol-Siddeley Engines Ltd had repaid to the Ministry of Technology a sum of £3,960,000 to reduce the profits which the firm made on sales at fixed prices totalling some £16½ million under a number of contracts for the overhaul of certain types of aero-engine between 1959 and 1963. On some contracts double payment had been made in error. It later appeared that there had been some confusion in the firm and the Ministry about the exact arrangements by which allowance was made for overheads in costing contracts.

[2] Robert Cant, Labour M.P. for Stoke-on-Trent since 1966.

and that all I had suggested was that the Committee should listen to Mulley's evidence. What I wanted to avoid were press revelations of a row between the Government and the Committee.

Thursday, March 23rd

I was in No. 11 by nine o'clock with the Chief preparing for our last Cabinet before the adjournment. He was pretty nearly all in with physical exhaustion and sciatica and suddenly looked up at me with blinking eyes and said, 'These have been the worst eight weeks of my life.' I remembered what Willie Whitelaw had said and replied, 'Yes, they were the worst eight weeks of our lives, Chief, but they were the worst eight weeks for the Cabinet too – and the Shadow Cabinet as well. And there's one difference, we two have won through and neither the Government nor the Opposition has done that.'

We then took a look at the morning papers and saw that the Bristol-Siddeley affair had taken the headlines and the Chief revealed to me that he'd been pressured by Wedgwood Benn to give the matter no particular publicity.

At Cabinet we were expected to talk at length about the Kennedy Round but it's one of those subjects a Labour Cabinet can't discuss – especially when Douglas Jay is in charge.[1] Anyway the P.M. was anxious to talk about the great new subject of the moment – the *Torrey Canyon* – the huge tanker grounded off the Scillies.[2] The moment the news came the P.M. was in action because of the effect on the Scilly beaches but also I think because he adores being in action – acting as the great commander organizing his forces. All the Ministers concerned adored rushing down to Plymouth and taking command of the Navy and issuing orders. This is the kind of politics politicians enjoy. They don't like sweating it out with papers and working out blueprints behind the scenes. They like being ostentatiously in command and being seen taking great decisions. So Cabinet had a fine time discussing the *Torrey Canyon* and setting up an emergency committee which would supervise operations over the Easter recess. I sat there laughing to myself because frankly I don't believe the politicians can do very much. Indeed it's possible, as the *Guardian* says, that what Harold has done by pouring all the detergent into the water on top of the oil has been to destroy the fish. But at least he has taken a big decision and I felt a bit psychologically out of it as I always do on these occasions.

[1] The final Act of the Kennedy Round, signed on June 30th, 1967, provided for tariff cuts averaging over 30 per cent on industrial trade between some fifty countries and for reductions in agricultural tariffs. The cuts were to be made in stages, beginning in 1968 and ending in January 1972.

[2] On March 18th an oil tanker bearing a Liberian registration ran aground off the Seven Stones rocks near Land's End, spilling a cargo of 100,000 tons of crude oil. The tanker broke up on March 26th and on March 28th the Government authorized the bombing of the wreck until, after two days, it was burnt out.

10

As this was the last day of the Session the House was meeting in the morning and Cabinet had to work in Harold's Commons' room. Waiting to make my business Statement I listened to Willie Ross dealing with an extremely awkward problem. He had to remove one key figure on the Scottish Highlands and Islands Development Board for some trouble about petrol.[1] The affair smelt badly and looking at the Statement before it was made I thought he wouldn't get away with it. But he did. There was no row and no sensation. I reflected that he showed considerable skill. Indeed most of my colleagues show great skill in taking evasive action and most of their Statements to the House are designed to evade awkward issues, whereas I'm always inclined to meet troubles head-on.

After lunch I had to attend a crisis meeting of the Prices and Incomes Cabinet Committee which I usually miss. The issue was the sudden decision by Dick Marsh to put up electricity charges in a way which would increase the consumers' bills by 15 to 20 per cent. He was strongly supported by John Diamond, representing the Treasury, and none of the other Ministers present had anything to say against it. I was left to point out that if the increase was made before April 13th, G.L.C. election day, we should never be forgiven. Once this was said it was easy to find a way of postponing the increase but what struck me was the fact that everyone else round the table was keeping to his departmental brief and I was the only person who was allowed to think about political considerations.

I went to see Burke who was panicking about the Specialist Committees. He told me that the whole of Whitehall was alerted and shocked by the activities of the Agriculture Committee and I said I thought it was time Whitehall settled down to the existence of Specialist Committees. And he said, 'Well, we must stop them travelling all over the world.' 'Of course, it's a new precedent,' I said. 'Certainly we don't want them just gallivanting round but we can't have any suggestion that we're trying to stop their inquiries. In fact European select committees wander round constantly discussing what's going on in other countries without anybody being upset, so don't let's be too disconcerted, let's keep our heads.' But clearly Burke was representing Whitehall's fears and indignation. They feared the worst and they were getting the worst in this case.

After this I drove down to Windsor for a Privy Council. The Easter crowds were just starting out on the roads in lovely weather. In my usual private audience with the Queen I found myself discussing the future of the Royal Africa Society, and I'd been forewarned that I should agree that it should be given a charter. Then I said to her something about Emrys Hughes's little Bill for the abolition of titles. The debate had taken place on the previous

---

[1] Mr Frank Thomson, a part-time member of the Board, was also chairman of Invergordon Chemical Enterprises Ltd; and since there was a likelihood of petro-chemical and associated development in the Invergordon area, to avoid any possible misunderstanding he had offered his resignation to the Secretary of State.

Friday and Emrys couldn't even sustain it for an hour. I told the Queen there'd been not more than three or four people in the Chamber and it was interesting that a debate which even twenty years ago would have packed the members in was no longer a sensation and nobody took it seriously at all. The Queen said that she'd looked through all the papers on Saturday rather anxiously and found nothing there. I told her there were actually two reports—one in the *Guardian* and one in *The Times*—which said what a flop it had been. I couldn't resist adding that I was glad Roy and I were correct in our guess that if the Government took no action it would pass without notice. It was a mistake to say this since she didn't reply. Instead we turned to our Privy Council business which consisted of pricking the list of Sheriffs with a bodkin—a bodkin because Queen Elizabeth did it with a bodkin and the tradition has been carried on. Then I had to read aloud all these names and the Queen had to give us a drink. Jeremy Thorpe was there for his first Privy Council looking gallant and romantic. The Queen told me almost straightaway that she wanted to go and see her children and actually she only talked to Anne and myself about a new weedkiller called Paraquat, pointing out of the window to a field where it was being used. Right at the end she asked me how morning sittings were going and I looked at her in surprise. 'Oh, I'm sorry,' she said, 'I wasn't really criticizing.' And I realized how sensitive she is and that my face must have revealed my irritation.

And then off to Prescote in time to find the children in their pyjamas just finishing supper. Tomorrow we are all going to the cinema to see *Thunderbirds*—a cartoon film about a killer whale—and now we're settling down to our week of really enjoyable time off with nothing to do except to get ready for Easter Saturday, when Paul Johnson and Marigold are coming over for the day with their children.

Sunday, March 26th
Easter. A cold cloudy day with a piercing wind. Nevertheless Prescote has been more beautiful and the farm has looked neater and more handsome this winter than ever I remember. I've never known so much sunshine, so many clear blue skies with sailing white clouds, so many magnificent sunsets with the evening star coming out over the poplars. I've had a day and a half here most weekends and it's this winter weather which has kept me going during these ghastly eight weeks of failure, frustration and fiasco up in London. So there is Prescote solidly behind me as I settle down to my week's holiday in which I can reflect upon my life in politics.

At the end of last week I felt that, though I was through the worst, my own personal position had still not recovered. By today my personal position has substantially recovered. When we started up again last Monday the mood which John and I met in the lobbies was a great deal better than we had any right to expect. Even the Tories felt a bit ashamed of themselves for their behaviour last week and they were shrewd enough to see that it didn't pay them because it made our own people rally behind me. So last week they were extremely quiet and *piano*. The business Statement got through on Thursday morning without any kind of a row.

And in our own Party the mood has been one of growing confidence in John and me. It's been an extraordinary period during which feelings have swung from one extreme to the other. I've been described in *The Times* as possibly the worst Leader of the House for a generation and then, six days later in Ian Trethowan's column, as 'probably the best Leader of the House since Herbert Morrison'.[1] And I went away for the Easter recess after an Early Day Motion had been signed by an extremely representative group of back-benchers congratulating me on my courtesy, firmness and fight for reform. Whereas the Government's stock has gone down steadily and Harold's stock has sunk, the only people whose stock has risen in this period are the Chief Whip and myself.

In my long talk with John last Thursday morning I said it was vital to try to foresee the future clearly; certainly I had to carry on till next October before I was replaced. But I rather felt that this replacement might be impossible now he and I had won through this stage and we would have to complete the process of reforming the Party and reforming Parliament. That, I said, would mean staying for at least eighteen months. 'That's just what the Prime Minister is thinking,' he replied. 'He wants you to get these reforms done and then we can permit some cypher like Tony Greenwood to take over.' But I'm still a bit doubtful whether I'm the man for the job. Somebody said to me the other day, 'What you want to do is to read through all the things which Butler said during the questions on the next week's business. You have to learn from him to say nothing politely.' Willie Whitelaw has also told me that I lack the small-talk a Leader of the House requires. That's true. I'm inclined to reply clearly and precisely; I find it very difficult to be dull and I find it even more difficult just to fill in with words and smooth the House down. So I lack the two things really required for the job which Herbert Morrison had—first the power to still the House with emollient fluff and secondly the power when necessary to pick a quarrel with the Opposition or occasionally with the Speaker. I shall never be able to combine Morrison's small-talk with his deliberate moments of pugnacity when for tactical reasons he knew how to pick a quarrel. I'm a bit of a snob in this way—like Stafford Cripps, who was such a disaster as Leader of the House[2]. I resent the idea of being boring—fluffing along, vulgarly picking a quarrel. Yet I must learn to do these things and if I can learn there's no reason why John Silkin and I should not get our reforms through in the next eighteen months.

[1] Ian Trethowan, a former editor of Independent Television News, joined the B.B.C. as their political commentator in 1963. He wrote for *The Economist* 1953–8 and 1965–7 and for *The Times* 1967–8. Since 1969 he has been managing director of B.B.C. Radio.

[2] Sir Stafford Cripps was Leader of the House of Commons in 1942.

And there's one other responsibility I now have to face. Now that George Brown has pushed off into Foreign Affairs and with Michael Stewart a dehydrated rabbit in the D.E.A., there is no one else to lead the Left in the Cabinet against Callaghan and against the City of London. The job is falling to me and I've begun to do it, for instance, on family endowment. I shall have to do it on East of Suez. And in a way this Cabinet job is linked with my job in the House because there I'm relying on the centre and the Left of the Party.

As for the other jobs Harold promised me when he made the change, they've collapsed. At Transport House I've been completely squeezed out by the anti-politician trade union drive. As for co-ordination of the information services, I now see I shall never get very far since Harold will do nothing to Trevor Lloyd-Hughes. After all my trouble getting Sheena Jeffries, his girl, across to my office as a liaison she is not allowed to attend his Lobby conferences so I'm back where I was. What I'm left with is the management of the legislative programme, the conduct of parliamentary business, the reform of both Houses of Parliament and the remoralization of the Parliamentary Labour Party by giving it a lead from the Left.

Monday, March 27th
Why am I at it again so soon? Well, I've got a week's holiday and I must admit my diary is becoming an addiction; I must take care lest I do too much of it. Nevertheless I want to write down some comments which have arisen in my mind as a result of reading through the transcript of the first part, from October 1964 to the end of February 1965. The main impression of those early months is the extraordinary sense of happiness and exhilaration. During the first fifty-seven years of my life I had always been denied the power of decision. I've been number two — assistant editor of the *New Statesman*, Assistant Director of Psychological Warfare, and then for nineteen long years a back-bencher who controlled nothing whatsoever. Now at last I was a Minister in charge of an important Department and I could take decisions, lay down the law, handle people as I wanted. The relief was enormous and it's quite true, as I write so often in those early months, that all my anxiety and my morning panics disappeared. What a difference there is between the life of the man who operates from a powerful Ministry and the man without a Portfolio who has to operate without one. Take my Private Office today, compared with what I had under John Delafons. I've slowly built it up. I got Freddy Ward, one of the less able but nicer Assistant Secretaries in the Ministry of Housing — quite competent and very loyal. He's in charge. In addition there is Anne Ridoutt, the good-looking girl who does my engagements, and Janet Gates, my stenographer, who is developing into an absolutely first-rate private secretary. These few are backed by Molly, my driver. So I have this huge office in Whitehall which does practically nothing compared with my Private Office in the Ministry of Housing. But I feel most of all that my Private Office here in the Privy Council

does not provide me with the check on my activities which the Private Office in a big Ministry imposes on the boss. In the Ministry of Housing, though it was exasperating, it was a relief to know that every letter I wrote, every document I drafted, every telephone conversation I had, was subjected by the Private Office to the most searching investigation and test before anything was sent out. These checks applied to my speeches as well as my letters. But here I can write any speech I like, any letter I like, any memo I like, and there is no Department to keep a check on me. I am completely on my own and therefore I'm inclined to make my own mistakes and be the victim of my own folly because I have no one to correct my weaknesses. And of course I have no one to help me with the media. I have no Peter Brown, no Press Officer. When I prepare a press release I can't put it out through the press department of my Ministry, I can't even put it out through No. 10. I have to put everything out through Transport House as though everything I did was Party politics. I miss Peter Brown desperately. There's no one looking after the press at the weekend or smoothing down Sunday feature writers who attack me.

The lack of a Press Officer is really extraordinary. In this job my press relations are even more important than they were in the Ministry of Housing because my life is a life of public posture and therefore I need a Press Officer more than any other member of the Government; the fact that I haven't got one is perhaps my gravest disadvantage. Of course Harold promised that I could have Peter Brown here. But that would only have been possible if he'd made me the Minister in charge of co-ordinating all press relations of the Government. Since he refused to do that I couldn't have Peter as my Press Officer and I'm totally excluded from No. 10 again despite all the promises and despite the presence in my office of Sheena, who was to be my link with No. 10.

The one thing which keeps me going has been my relationship with the Chief Whip. True, we have officials who are bitterly suspicious of each other. Freddie Warren and his little staff in No. 12 resent a dynamic Leader of the House and so do the officials in the Chief Whip's office in the Commons. They are very much his private staff and they want to hear nothing of me. These officials know that I'm turning my job as Leader of the House into something totally different from what Herbert Bowden did and some of the time they enjoy it. Freddie Warren has said to me more than once that in terms of parliamentary reform more has happened in the last six months than in the previous ten years. But I still think he would prefer a normal Lord President who keeps things ticking, keeps the House of Commons quiet, is willing to fluff issues and to make things easy. I don't do that because I've been appointed as the reformer of the House of Commons and of the discipline of the Parliamentary Party. That means I'm exposed to attack from all sides and my only ally is the Chief Whip. I certainly haven't any reliable allies in the Cabinet. The Chief and I stand or fall together.

Now a word about the Cabinet structure of power. The 1964–6 Cabinet was a Cabinet run by Wilson, working through his Ministers. Before George took over the F.O. the Prime Minister was able to run it through his menials – Gordon Walker and Stewart – as he ran the Commonwealth Office through Bottomley and now runs it through Bowden. George has already made the Foreign Office as independent, vigorous and self-assertive as he made the D.E.A. during the time he was there. He has the power to create a dynamic in any Department he takes over. Now this has meant that the departure of George to D.E.A. has suddenly dehydrated that vital planning Department. Michael Stewart is a clever little man but he undynamizes any Department he takes over. In the case of the Foreign Office it didn't matter much because the P.M. maintained his control. But in the case of the D.E.A. it mattered terribly when the P.M. suddenly decided to spend last autumn and winter touring Europe and left the whole future of the prices and incomes policy to the First Secretary. The D.E.A. dried up at the critical moment when the new substitute for Part IV should have been developed and should have been sold to the trade unions. The result was that Michael Stewart was easily defeated in Cabinet by Ray Gunter and the other trade-union opponents of a statutory incomes policy.

Moreover, by letting the D.E.A. run down, Harold has given Callaghan the opportunity to reassert the Treasury rule which had been challenged in 1964 by the creation of the D.E.A. Here is the other big change. Not that Jim is now capable of taking big decisions. He never will be. But whatever we think about him, he is a big man and a bit of a bully these days and in Cabinet he collects a lot of support whenever he needs it. Roy Jenkins and Tony Crosland recognize their master in big Jim. He is the leader of the right wing in the Cabinet and with George Brown absent that has shifted the whole balance of Cabinet policy to the right. Who has taken on the leadership of the Left? The only person who can try to do this is the Lord President. Despite the disastrous eight weeks when I was nearly tumbled out of my job I've not been unsuccessful inside Cabinet. Indeed, though I can't claim to have entered the inner Cabinet – because there isn't one—I'm now a member of the inner circle and live in the inner stratosphere. I'm something of a power in my own right.

Finally, what do I learn from reading these old diaries about the development of Harold as Prime Minister? It looks to me that the biggest change is in the relationship between him and Burke Trend. This has grown steadily closer during these two and a half years and Burke is now far the most powerful of the Prime Minister's confidants, and has got Harold tightly integrated into the Whitehall set-up. Harold as an old civil servant is at home in Whitehall though he still retains his unconventional friends – Balogh, Crossman and, to a lesser extent, Wigg (the decline of Wigg is a new factor in the situation). But he hasn't developed any new unconventional friends. On the whole he's moved away from the Left and he's more anchored right in the centre with only vestiges of the vague leftism which he brought with him to the job. In this change in his state of mind Burke has played a very big part. Indeed if I had to describe the essence of this Government I should say that whereas the first Wilson Government was a troika, this one is a Wilson–Burke Trend axis.

Friday, March 31st

Since the holiday's nearly at an end I'd better describe the one piece of politics where I did try to intervene from Prescote. It wasn't of course the *Torrey Canyon*, although I was rung up on the first Friday and asked if I wanted to go to the Emergency Committee on Saturday morning. I said 'no' rather indignantly because I suspected that no decisions would be taken in London. But there was one affair where as the Minister in charge of co-ordinating information I thought I had the right to intervene during the recess. I've described how on the last Wednesday of the Session I tried unsuccessfully to interest John Stonehouse and Tony Wedgwood Benn in the political potentialities of the Bristol-Siddeley scandal. The press next day headlined the affair but not in a way which was favourable to us. So this week I rang up Tony and urged him to get as much of the story published as he possibly could before we went back to Westminster. He told me he preferred to wait and make a Statement in Parliament. I told him that within the first week it will be difficult to get much attention for a Statement on Bristol-Siddeley with all the excitement about the *Torrey Canyon*. Anyway it's too complicated a story to deal with in a single Statement. Since then I've been bombarded with telephone calls from John Stonehouse, who brought the whole problem with him from the Ministry of Aviation to the Ministry of Technology and who's blotted his copy book by the unfortunate Statement he made in a Supplementary last Wednesday that throughout the owners behaved perfectly correctly. All the evidence shows that they behaved scandalously. It was two years before they finally agreed to let the Government see the books and when the secret had been revealed they simply signed the cheque as quickly as possible. It's the delay in revealing the secret to the Government which is surely the story of misbehaviour by a big aviation firm.

However Stonehouse tells me there are two sides to the affair. There had been great dilatoriness in the Ministry and Stonehouse was infuriated at the statement which the Department has issued last Saturday using his name but not showing him the draft. He said that the civil servants were determined to put the blame on the Ministers to keep themselves in the clear. There are a lot of questions here to clear up and I'm beginning to see the danger of trying to intervene in an affair like this. I'm extremely doubtful if up till now I've done any good whatsoever by my intervention. It looks as though in the two and a half years that we've been in office we have completely failed to put right the Ministry control of contracts and the Ministry's relations with private firms – we have neglected precisely the sort of factors that produced the Ferranti scandal. We ought to have a much better record than we have, and of course one of the men to blame is John Stonehouse, who was Minister of Aviation.

Well, that's all there is to write in my political diary on this the 31st March—another of these perfect mornings of a perfect winter. This is a brilliant sunshiny day with plenty of water in the sky to give us a bit of colour and a nip in the air yet plenty of hot brilliant sunshine. I have three more days before returning to the fray and feel like a senior prefect returning to school after a very bad term. I shall go back to Westminster with some pretty dark forebodings repressed inside me.

Monday, April 3rd

I was still very gloomy as I travelled up to London but when John Silkin and I looked in on the Prime Minister at midday we found him in full bouncing beaming form, delighted with the *Torrey Canyon* affair, delighted in particular with the prospect of challenging Heath to a vote of censure and if he didn't put one down taunting him with his failure to do so.

On this occasion the P.M. was unusually frank about his luck. 'Yes of course we had luck,' he said. 'If the wind hadn't changed the oil would all have gone on the coast and we'd have been for it.' He was also extremely sharp about the behaviour of Roy Jenkins and John Harris, Roy's public relations officer. This came up when I put forward the suggestion that we should devote next Monday to the *Torrey Canyon* and John had agreed to offer a debate to the Tories—either a full day or a half day. I then said I thought the obvious thing was that Harold shouldn't speak unless Heath spoke and so the speakers would probably be Roy Jenkins and Tony Greenwood on our side. Harold said, 'Yes, Tony should have his chance now. He's done very well: he's impressed me. But Roy? I don't like to give him a big speech after what he did. The moment he took over on that Sunday afternoon he tried to create the impression that he found everything in a shemozzle and that no decisions were taken until he, the decisive Roy Jenkins, took command. That's an impression I resent,' he said, warming to it. 'He's rigged the whole Sunday press as well.'

There was a good deal in that complaint about the Sunday papers. Moreover I must add that having looked at the Cabinet minutes it is clear that no big decisions were taken the moment Roy took over. Indeed, I have a strong suspicion that it didn't make very much difference which of them was in command. Anyway the episode has caused a positive hatred in Harold of Roy Jenkins and of the readiness of John Harris to put the P.M. in the wrong and his man in the right throughout the episode.

The next item was the Bristol-Siddeley affair and I gave Harold a report on my talks with Stonehouse and Tony Benn. He then showed me the ferocious minute he had sent to Wedgy—a real censure minute demanding an explanation of this outrageous mess-up. He also told me he'd decided to set up a Committee of Investigation and that this would give us a way out of the very awkward scene in the House of Commons which we would otherwise face.

It was only after we'd dealt with these two matters that I was able to get on to the main issue which was whether he would back John and me on a full-scale programme of reform of both Houses of Parliament. I began to explain to him how far we had got in reaching agreement on a Bill to limit the power of the House of Lords. When I'd finished he said, 'That would be a very dull Bill. The press will say it's a bore.' 'Of course,' I said. 'But if it was a Bill which modernized the House of Lords as part of the modernization of Parliament and integrated the work of the two chambers, it wouldn't be dull at all. I can see a way of taking a lot of dull stuff off the Floor of the House of Commons, but if we're going to do this we must deal with composition. The simplest way of doing so is with a Bill to make all the existing peers who are active in the House become life peers and introduce a formula providing the Government of the day with a built-in majority. I know Frank Longford has sent you a memo,' I said. 'Yes, that interminable stuff I got from Frank Longford.' 'Well, disregard that memo. Listen to John and me and Malcolm Shepherd, John's opposite number in the Lords. We think we've got a practical plan for a really serviceable and progressive parliamentary reform provided we're allowed to deal with the composition of the Lords.' 'But there's a Cabinet decision against dealing with composition,' said the P.M., 'an absolutely clear and overwhelming Cabinet decision. You'd have to upset that.' 'Yes,' I said. 'But now we've got so far forward in parliamentary reform we can see that this reduction in the power of the Lords is really unnecessary since Lord Carrington himself has stated that the Lords can only use their powers once more without being abolished. The Tories also see the need for a different kind of House of Lords.' At this point, when I was just going to explain more about my plan, he jumped in and said, 'In those five minutes you've persuaded me, Dick. I'll back you if you put it to Cabinet.' 'No,' I said, 'I won't put it to Cabinet unless I'm sure of success and first I want to get the Ministerial Committee established. We've got to have the Lord Chancellor on it and Roy Jenkins and the Chief Whips from both Houses and perhaps the Scottish Secretary as well as me and Gordon Walker. We've got to work out a clear agreed scheme and put that to Cabinet, perhaps orally in the first case, as the big surprise measure for next session.' 'Well,' he said, 'I'll back you if you can do that.' And so we got out of his room, just at one o'clock after a full hour, with a real sense of achievement. It was, this time, my achievement. The Chief Whip demands my support for his discipline and he's willing to support me on this kind of thing although he's not particularly keen on it. I was able to go back to my Private Office and tell Freddy Ward that things were moving.

At Home Affairs Committee in the afternoon I had to report on Laurie Pavitt's Hearing Aids Bill.[1] Before he was an M.P., Laurie worked in the

[1] Labour M.P. for Willesden October 1959–74 and, since 1974, for Brent.

Health Service and is himself stone deaf in one ear. He's been pestering us for his Private Member's Bill but I find it is detested by the Board of Trade, by the Ministry of Health and even by the Privy Council. We don't feel prepared to support a Bill which gives so much help to a rather undesirable industry which is producing hearing aids. I promised the Committee that I would see it was knocked out at Legislation Committee next morning and then wrote to Harold telling him what I had done.

This evening there was a dinner-party at No. 10 for Hubert Humphrey, the Vice-President of the U.S.A., who was over for the usual kind of official visit. I thought it was going to be another Kosygin dinner and indeed to some extent it was. I found myself sitting between the wife of a Minnesota business-man who travels round with Humphrey and Phil Kaiser, the pleasant Minister at the American Embassy.[1] After dinner, in the drawing-room, I was put at one of the little tables next to Humphrey who gave us a long talk about Vietnam: he's a real liberal but he's also a dedicated containment man, very like Dean Acheson.[2]

I spent about half an hour listening to the words pouring out of his mouth and then I'd had enough. When I got up I ran into Burke Trend, and very unwisely began to complain about the way the Cabinet Office was treating my Granada lecture. Each year Granada select someone of distinction to talk on a subject related to the media and this year their choice had fallen on me. I realized that as a Cabinet Minister I couldn't take the fees but in the course of a chat with Iain Macleod he had suggested that even if one couldn't accept one could give them to a charity of one's own choice. This is what I had decided to do and I had chosen to contribute to the restoration of the Inigo Jones Mill which stands on an escarpment looking out towards Warwick and Leamington and which has been falling to pieces since the lead was stripped off the roof by robbers. The scandal was first revealed when I was Minister of Housing but the local authority refused to help and the dilapidation was going on until a group of engineers in Leamington decided to undertake the job themselves as a spare-time hobby (they're kind of professional-amateur mill-menders). They wrote asking me for help and I thought this was an ideal place to put my £750. When I received the invitation from Granada I sent it over to the P.M. to get his consent and the P.M. had submitted it to Burke because of the issue of the fee. Burke at first pretended that the whole affair had been dealt with in his office and he hardly knew anything about it. Then I asked him what the precedents were. 'There are no precedents,' he replied, 'because no Tory was silly enough to ask us.' 'Well, I'm the kind of person who would ask,' I said, 'because I don't like hypocrisy.' 'I know,' he said, 'I think that's just what you are—the kind of person who asks that kind of

---

[1] Philip Kaiser was Minister at the American Embassy, London, 1964–9. He was chairman and managing director of Encyclopaedia Britannica International Ltd, London, and since 1975 has been director of Guinness Mahon Holdings Ltd.

[2] United States Secretary of State 1949–53. He first served in the State Department in 1941.

question.' I could see that he felt that Ministers shouldn't stir up this kind of trouble and if they do stir it up by asking the wrong questions then they'll be told that they're forbidden to do something, whereas if they didn't ask and went ahead it would be quite O.K.

As we were getting our coats I ran into Wedgy Benn and Anne and I went home with him and Caroline and were joined by Peter and Liz Shore, Tommy Balogh and Pen and we had a tremendous gossip. Suddenly Peter said, 'Why can't we do a regular Wednesday meeting? Why can't we meet and plan future policy with Marcia there as we used to? What's gone wrong with us since the election?' 'We can't do that,' I said, 'Harold wouldn't like it. He would be suspicious. No, it wouldn't work at all.' As soon as I'd poured cold water on the idea I began to feel I was wrong and went on until one in the morning talking and chatting and feeling what a splendid thing it would be if we of the Left could get together as I'm sure Jenkins and Crosland and their gang get together. Our trouble is that before the election we had an excuse for a regular meeting because we'd been selected by Harold to make secret preparations for the election manifesto. Now, as Barbara Castle often points out to me, we would have to tell Harold what we were up to and Harold just wouldn't like it. He is profoundly suspicious of Roy Jenkins and he's even more suspicious of Callaghan, who was recently described by James Margach as the crown-prince Chancellor. He's not suspicious of us but the reason for that is not merely that we *don't* intrigue against him but that he *believes* we don't intrigue against him. Alas, he is the kind of man who can only too easily believe that his colleagues are conspiring when no kind of conspiracy really exists.

Tuesday, April 4th
After a brief Legislation Committee, at which I announced that the Pavitt Hearing Aids Bill had been canned, we went on to Cabinet where we had another of the interminable discussions on prices and incomes. This was an unusually painful meeting, at which Michael Stewart admitted that the essential reserve powers required for any effective policy couldn't be legislated. He had to make the admission after John Silkin bluntly stated that our majority would sink to less than twenty and that on the issue of retrospective legislation we might have forty voting against us. On this occasion the Chancellor of the Exchequer, who last July was assuring us that an effective prices and incomes policy was essential in order to persuade the American Treasury to help us, was now clearly on the other side. I can't help remembering that he's seeking to be elected Treasurer of the Party and needs Frank Cousins's vote. But he went even further this time. 'A statutory policy,' he argued, 'doesn't respond to the real needs of human nature. We must face it that George Woodcock was right.[1] If a voluntary policy failed then we would

[1] Assistant General Secretary of the T.U.C. 1947–60 and General Secretary 1960–69. He was chairman of the Commission on Industrial Relations 1969–71.

have to have cuts in public expenditure and a higher rate of unemployment.'
In fact he seemed to be triumphantly welcoming the end of the prices and
incomes policy and reversion to unplanned *laissez-faire*. It was too much for
people like Roy Jenkins, who said he was staggered by the Chancellor's talk.

Michael Stewart looked sicker and sicker until he finally caved in, and
allowed the Cabinet to kill any effective policy. In the circumstances it was
inevitable but I have no doubt that Harold could have got those reserve
powers written in if he'd put his whole energy to this issue through October
and November instead of going off on his European tour. The permanent
alternative to Part IV had to be evolved and sold to the Parliamentary Party
and T.U.C. during the six months' period of total freeze, not during the
period of severe restraint when the policy was getting more and more unpopular. Once the complete wage freeze was over the momentum began to
move against the policy and we'd missed our chance.

I rushed off from Cabinet because the children are in London this week on
holiday and I'd promised to take them to lunch at the top of the huge new
Post Office Tower up the Tottenham Court Road. We decided to go and see
what we could of the tower at 1.15 and had reserved our table for 2.15.
Actually there's nothing to see until you get into the restaurant, which
revolves in roughly forty minutes round a hard inner core so that one can put
one foot on the revolving part and one foot on the stable part. That was the
one thing the children enjoyed. As for the meal — it was one of the most expensive I've eaten in London — eight guineas for the four of us and very modest.
But it was a good day for seeing the view and the place was absolutely packed
with what looked like businessmen on expense accounts.

I got back to the House at 3.15 in time to hear Harold Wilson answering
Ted Heath's questions about the *Torrey Canyon*. It was a supremely skilful
performance. Harold played Heath around for three or four questions and
then slashed him with his own questions. 'When is the vote of censure coming?'
I've never seen a more total disappearance of an Opposition Leader. He never
dared to rise again and for the rest of the forty minutes about *Torrey Canyon*
the P.M. gave a supreme exhibition of the parliamentary gamesmanship of
which he is master. With the White Paper published that afternoon the
Government had done well and we had started off after the Easter recess with
a bang.[1]

Wednesday, April 5th
I spent some of the morning with the children and then we had morning
prayers at eleven. Harold was just back from Windsor where he had been
attending the Queen's dinner for the American Vice-President. Anything can
happen at morning prayers and on this occasion he was at his most decisive.

---

[1] The White Paper (Cmnd. 3246) set out a record of the events, the decisions that were
taken and recommendations for national and international action if such an accident
occurred again.

He announced that I should hold the inquiry into the Bristol-Siddeley affair
and report to him on exactly what had occurred inside the Department.
Next he dictated a minute to Michael Stewart about the method of launching
the new prices and incomes policy. Finally we came to the *Torrey Canyon*.
In the House Heath had demanded a Select Committee because he wanted a
post-mortem. How to prevent this was the problem. After a lot of thought
we had the idea of referring the *Torrey Canyon* to the new Specialist Committee on Science and Technology. That's a very smart idea because we
certainly want to show our belief in our new Specialist Committees and at
the same time we want to avoid an inquiry which merely concentrates on
discovering exactly what took place in Cornwall during that week.

This afternoon—the second day of Parliament—we had a big display at
the end of Question Time. First Michael Stewart presented his new Green
Paper on the Regional Employment Premium. Then Wedgy Benn presented
his remedies for the bankruptcy of a dock on Clydeside.[1] Next John Stonehouse
defended himself in the Bristol-Siddeley affair and finally complaint of a
breach of privilege was raised by Gerry Fitt, the Northern Irish Member.[2]
This went on for an hour and ten minutes after 3.30. I had spent many hours
trying to get all these Statements in order. I'm now just beginning to see what
the job of the Leader of the House really is; when he's functioning well
he's a stage manager. I sat there not saying a word until right at the end when
I knew that the Speaker was going to agree that a *prima facie* breach of
privilege had occurred and I would have to move the reference to the Committee of Privileges on which I would have my first case as chairman.

The whole occasion went very well. Michael Stewart's Green Paper
interested the House and can really be seen as a new advance in parliamentary
democracy. Wedgy Benn got over a nasty crisis in Scotland by saying quickly
and decisively that he was taking the whole dock over. John Stonehouse's
stonewalling was embarrassing to me but the Opposition front bench was just
as embarrassed by the Bristol-Siddeley affair because the original contract
had been made when they were in office.

While I was sitting on the front bench Harold told me there was something
of the greatest urgency he had to discuss so I followed him into his room and
he revealed that he was terribly het up about Laurie Pavitt's Bill. His own
father is eighty years old and very deaf. He's therefore deeply concerned to
see that something should be done for deaf people who are now so grievously
exploited and he wants Laurie's Bill to be given a chance. As I left the room

[1] The Firth of Clyde Dry Dock Company.
[2] S.D.L.P. M.P. (formerly Republican Labour) for Belfast West since 1966. He was Eire
Labour M.P. for Belfast in the Parliament of Northern Ireland 1962–72, S.D.L.P. Member
for North Belfast in the Northern Ireland Assembly 1973–5, Deputy Chairman of the
Northern Ireland Executive 1974, and S.D.L.P. Member for North Belfast in the Northern
Ireland Constitutional Convention May 1975–6. His complaint concerned an article in the
Belfast Telegraph on March 24th, 1967, and an article calling him an 'arch-traitor' in the
Protestant Telegraph of April 1st, 1967.

he handed me a long detailed minute which he himself had prepared. I shall have to eat the bold words I spoke at the Legislation Committee and I decided that the quicker I did this the better. So this evening I saw George Darling[1] of the Board of Trade and we're now preparing to work out another Bill for Laurie Pavitt to provide consumer protection for hearing-aid users.

As I was leaving the liaison committee this afternoon I suddenly felt very faint and a singing began in my ears. I got out to the lobby and I couldn't walk. I tottered up to the bench at the side, sat down and put my head in my hands and felt, 'Oh God, have I got another perforated ulcer? Have I got a major haemorrhage inside?' I got back to my room and then had to go upstairs to Barnett Cocks's apartment where Anne had brought Patrick to play with young Matthew Cocks. I rested there and felt much better. I got myself home but was feeling desperately anxious and went to the lavatory straightaway to see what colour my urine was. It was perfectly normal so I went to bed.[2]

Thursday, April 6th

I woke up at seven feeling absolutely all right. I suppose I was just mentally and emotionally exhausted although I'd had a full week's holiday. Yet during those first two days of Parliament I was so anxious about failing on the front bench, so worried about the Party that pure emotional exhaustion had tired me out. All I needed was a good night's sleep.

At Cabinet we had our second big discussion of the Common Market, this time on the topics of the movement of capital and regional development. Douglas Jay put the case about regional planning extremely well. Entry to the Market would remove both the carrot and the stick with which we now get our industrialists to put a new factory in Scotland or West Wales rather than in Coventry or London. Hard pressed, Harold came out with a defence which captivated me. He didn't deny the dangers to which Douglas pointed but he said that what regional policy really gave us was a general expansion of capital investment and that's what we must get in the Common Market. Once it's known we are going into the Common Market the industrialists who are holding back now will put in an extra 20 or 30 per cent of investment. That will get the growth rate up. It's the lift we require to restore growth that will help the development areas more than any artificial scheme a British Government could think up. And Harold got so warmed and carried away that he made it absolutely clear that he's now a completely converted Common Marketeer.

We had another good day in the Commons this afternoon. Harold's

---

[1] George Darling was Labour M.P. for Hillsborough (Sheffield) 1950–74 and served as Minister of State at the Board of Trade 1964–8.

[2] Despite his immense energy Crossman had had occasional serious illnesses and the Diaries refer to the attacks of fatigue he suffered from time to time. He was gravely ill in 1970 and in April 1973 he died of cancer.

answers to Questions were as skilled as ever and when my business Statement came I was actually able to make a joke or two and bring it off. As I went out everybody said, 'Back on your form, old boy.'

I had to go to Harold's room for an urgent discussion on Tommy Balogh's future. For some time now Tommy, Pen and I have been discussing how long he should stay with Harold and when he should go back to Oxford and this has got mixed up with a terrible struggle between Tommy and Burke for the ear of the P.M. Burke has compiled a formidable dossier against Thomas, who of course works in No. 10 and not in the Cabinet Office. He accuses him of being a terrible snooper. He accuses him of going into the Cabinet offices and reading documents. In particular, he says, that Thomas makes a practice of looking into the box prepared for the Prime Minister late at night and seeing what briefing Burke Trend has provided so that he, Thomas, can insert a memorandum giving the reply to it. Harold didn't show me the memorandum but he talked to me at length and said that the situation was now impossible. 'But Thomas is invaluable to you,' I said. 'How will you replace him?' and Harold said he would be content with the other Michael Stewart who is Thomas's number two. I said it would be good for Tommy too since he would see more of Penny and also do rather less of the work which was killing him. Although there was a long queue waiting outside we talked for more than half an hour, and finally Harold said that he would see Pen as soon as possible. Actually he spent two further hours that evening talking to Thomas and trying to steer him round. The fact is Harold can't stand people being hurt.[1]

I was busy this evening in my office preparing the final draft of my Ministerial broadcast on the ombudsman. This had been made quite important by a leader in *The Times* this morning pointing out that the broadcast was carefully timed to coincide with the G.L.C. elections. This is perfectly true. Ministerial broadcasts are an anomaly but we are using them skilfully and I don't think you can deny the Government the right to present to the people of this country the meaning of an important measure like the Parliamentary Commissioner Act. On the other hand one has to play fair and not put any of the propaganda in which would justify an Opposition reply. What I have done is to explain why we have introduced not a Danish ombudsman to whom the people can go to direct but a Parliamentary Commissioner approached by the constituency M.P. It is a good text and we just managed to get it on the tape within the two hours permitted, then we went upstairs to supper with the B.B.C. where we watched it, saw the David Frost programme and got home in reasonable time. What a sigh of relief—I'd had my third successive successful day in Parliament and I was still on the crest of the wave. I had put behind me that accident-proneness which had been growing on me

[1] Fourteen months after the date of this entry, Balogh was informed by the University Authorities that he would have to resume his full time duties or resign his Readership. He then returned from No. 10 to Oxford.

and making me so liable to morning panic. I rate Thursday as being a very happy evening in my life.

It was also an evening in which I had seen a great deal of the Harold I like best. What impresses me is his equanimity and his humanity, the time and trouble he takes on Tommy's personal problems or on Laurie Pavitt's Hearing Aid Bill. As a result of Harold I've had to spend a lot of time on small problems relating to ordinary human beings — and a good thing too.

Friday, April 7th

I had my first private talk with the Lord Chancellor about the reform of the House of Lords. He explained to me that he is the kind of socialist who wants to abolish all peerages, not to entrench some of them. However I think I'd moved him a little before we walked downstairs to a meeting of the Home Affairs Committee on that eternal subject, sonic bangs. Yes, John Stonehouse from Technology and Merlyn Rees from the Defence Ministry[1] were back once again demanding the Bill we had twice rejected already. I wondered whether we could knock out the vested interests on the third occasion. Quite simply the issue was whether we needed special legislation which permitted the Government to subject the civil population to sonic bangs in order to see where the breaking point came or whether this kind of study was best done as in France by letting the R.A.F. fly over the country. At this meeting the new argument propounded by the Defence Ministry was that in the latter case the wrath would fall on the wrong person and the R.A.F. would become unpopular. I made mincemeat of this argument but our position was weakened because Niall MacDermot who'd supported us last time had been brought into line and told to keep to his Treasury brief, which of course supported Concorde. But after forty-five minutes Roy Jenkins — one of the relatively impartial Ministers — suddenly said he'd been converted by our arguments and we sent the paper back again with the instructions that the R.A.F. should work out a plan which met our objections.

I went back to my office to find Yigal Allon (the Israeli Minister of Labour) and Aharon Remez (the Israeli Ambassador) waiting for me. They immediately broached the subject of why I couldn't come to the Balfour Declaration celebration on November 4th. I said, 'George Brown and the F.O. don't want me,' and explained that I couldn't raise a finger on my own behalf but if they wanted to plead with Harold on my behalf they could do so next day at Chequers.*

This evening I had a talk with Tommy and Pen; they seemed fairly pleased. They took their Tessa off to see the *Barber of Seville* at Covent Garden while I took our children to see *Dr Zhivago*. It's not as good as *Lawrence of Arabia*

* They did, and Harold consented to their having a senior Minister. But it made no difference. In the end Ted Short went as George had wished.

[1] Labour M.P. for South Leeds since 1963. Parliamentary Under-Secretary of State at the Ministry of Defence 1965–6 (Army) and 1966–8 (R.A.F.) and at the Home Office 1968–70. Since 1974 he has been Secretary of State for Northern Ireland.

but there's a wonderful train journey across Russia to the Urals before the ghastly sentimental end.

Saturday, April 8th

I spent the day motorcading round the North London suburbs to help the G.L.C. I did the round in a big car with Bill Fiske, starting off from his own constituency—30,000 people living on a G.L.C. housing estate. I soon found what the form was. Each time we stopped for twenty minutes, there was a five-minute speech by me, a five-minute speech by Bill, a few questions and handshakes with important people. Minimum words, minimum argument—mainly a matter of being photographed. That's what I did from 8.45 to six in the evening, when I ended up in a twilight Pakistani area in Willesden.

I tried to get out of this day of public electioneering since I thought someone better at it, Barbara Castle for example, should do it. But perhaps having the Leader of the House of Commons in the same car with the leader of the G.L.C. was quite effective. Anyway I got myself delivered to Hampstead and Tommy and Pen drove me down to Prescote. We got there at 8.30, in time for supper and for playing my new volume of Beethoven's later string quartets until midnight. Pen had seen Harold for an hour and had reached the agreement that Thomas should go back to Oxford half-time in January and simultaneously become a peer. I think this will make him happy. From Thomas's point of view, and even possibly from Harold's point of view, three years is enough.

Sunday, April 9th

I spent the afternoon canvassing in Cropredy village taking round the election address for our Labour candidate for the County Council seat. I doubt whether I influenced anybody but the atmosphere was much nicer than last year when I went round with Richard Hartree. If the candidate benefited it was from the children—Tessa Balogh, and Virginia and Patrick rushing to and fro like dogs but being very polite when they got to the door. Then a pleasant supper before Thomas was driven off to Chequers. It's been a good week. I only hope the improvement can be maintained.

Monday, April 10th

I went up to London very worried because of a talk I'd had with Ian Aitken of the *Guardian* on the phone yesterday. He'd rung me up to ask about Harold's attitude to the Common Market. I told him that Harold was enjoying all his elaborate system of Cabinet and Parliamentary Party consultations but in fact knew perfectly well that both the Cabinet and the Party are already converted to the new approach. '*Perhaps,*' I added (and this is where I went wrong), 'this is because he wants to conceal that the real crisis he faces is on prices and incomes, where he's been defeated by the trade-union group and our policy has been largely destroyed.' Instead of treating this as background information, Ian has printed it in full and stated that it came from a senior Minister. It was therefore labelled as a leak and pretty obviously a leak by me. This worried me a great deal and I record it in this diary because in my job I'm now doing a great deal of press briefing and I oughtn't to fall into this kind of failure. No doubt Ian Aitken had let me down badly but in this game it was my fault, not his.

The morning was spent in a crashingly boring Cabinet meeting on the budget. What is one to do at Cabinet when one hears the Chancellor's decisions and it's too late? What's the good of crying over spilt milk? The only comment I made was that I couldn't see why the surtax surcharge imposed in July had been dropped whereas all the other increased taxes had been sustained.[1] Barbara and I tried to get that changed but of course without any success.

This evening I gave a dinner to Donald Chapman, the chairman of the Procedure Committee, Sir Barnett Cocks and John Silkin to discuss future plans and in particular the problem of timetabling all Government Bills. This was a useful step towards the next big procedure report which is being prepared for us.

In the early months of 1967 the T.U.C. General Council and its affiliated unions affirmed their support for the Government's wage freeze and their intention of operating a voluntary wages policy after the period of severe restraint ended in July. Confidence in sterling remained sufficiently high and trade buoyant enough for bank rate to be reduced from 7 to 6½ per cent on January 26th and to 6 per cent on March 16th. There was even some hope that in 1967 the 1966 balance of payments deficit could be turned into a surplus, and by the end of March some £463 million had been repaid to the U.S. Treasury and Federal Reserve, and to other central banks. Gold and dollar reserves continued to rise in April but nevertheless the Chancellor's budget Statement was cautious. There were only slight tax concessions—for working widows and on dependent relatives' allowances—and the 'steady as she goes' budget was welcomed by foreign bankers.

Tuesday, April 11th
Our normal Cabinet. Right at the beginning I had two papers, one on four reports from the Procedure Committee and the other on Ministerial appearances before Select Committees. The first one went easily apart from my proposal that in order to shorten speeches the Speaker should be given discretion to limit their length in certain debates. Cabinet objected strongly to this for fear that he would use these new powers to cut their speeches short but finally they suggested (I quote Cabinet minutes) 'A limited period between six and nine during which the Speaker would be able to impose limitations on length of speeches for a period of an hour or two.' So the speeches of back-

[1] In July 1966 a surcharge of 10 per cent on surtax had been imposed for one year.

benchers are to be shortened while front-bench speeches are to be left as long as the Minister likes—a delicious disregard of back-bench opinion. This was even more striking when we started to discuss my second paper. I soon found that the majority were really against Ministers appearing at all before Specialist Committees which deal with policy issues. James Callaghan called the proposal an outrage. Michael Stewart, who's usually on the side of the angels, said he couldn't understand how any socialist could propose to limit the powers of the Government by creating Specialist Committees to poach on their preserves. My proposal would split colleagues and disrupt the unity of the Government and make Parliament inefficient. Then George Brown came in supporting him strongly and Dick Marsh even more violently. Apart from the Chief I had on my side Fred Peart, Barbara, Wedgy, Tony Crosland and Roy Jenkins. But they were countered by Ray Gunter and Willie Ross. Patrick Gordon Walker was no help and Tony Greenwood was silent. The attitude of my opponents was summed up in the Cabinet minutes as follows: 'It should be advantageous to members of the Opposition but it was doubtful whether it was compatible with good government particularly with the purposive style of government to which the present administration was committed or with the maintenance of the principle of collective responsibility.'

When they'd exhausted themselves I merely replied that Cabinet was not this morning considering the principle of Ministerial appearances since that had been accepted months ago. We were not discussing whether we should appear before the Specialist Committee but the best way of organizing our appearances. Of course I was technically right and after this morning's performance I realized that the main obstacle in the way of the reforming Leader of the House is the resistance of his colleagues in the Cabinet who resent or fear any change.

There was one other item of interest this morning. A brief discussion on the defence expenditure studies which had recently been presented, as the result of O.P.D.'s decisions to cut back commitments in the Far East. A number of my colleagues were smart enough to see that they oughtn't to give George Brown complete freedom when he goes out to Singapore unless they had further information. So a little debate did take place after which the P.M. tested the Cabinet. Six members felt we should maintain our military presence in the Far East and shouldn't make any drastic cuts or try to get off the mainland by 1975. Everybody else felt equally strongly that the cuts were not radical enough. This view was best expressed by Roy Jenkins, who put the Foreign Secretary in a very difficult position. As George pointed out, he would now be going to Washington to negotiate knowing that a majority of the Cabinet wanted no military presence in the Far East at all and were determined not only to get off the mainland but to withdraw our naval and air forces from anywhere East of Suez. How was he to negotiate with our allies, he plaintively asked, in terms of a slow orderly process of withdrawal when most of Cabinet wanted a drastic revision of policy next July?

This afternoon we had the budget Statement. I went in well beforehand, sat with the Chief Whip and watched the House filling. Although he had virtually nothing to say, the Chancellor made the appalling mistake of speaking for one hour and forty-five minutes and trying to blow up his minor into major concessions.

My reflections on hearing that budget were that the Chancellor had deliberately used the occasion to promulgate his new doctrine that we should abandon an artificial prices and incomes policy and revert to a higher rate of unemployment and higher cuts in public expenditure. But does Harold hold this view? I'm not so sure and I wouldn't be a bit surprised if he were planning a change at the Treasury fairly soon. He may really have left the Chancellor to kill himself by listening only to city advice and launching a deeply reactionary budget. But all this may be far too clever. I made a point of going to my room and watching the Chancellor do his television interview this evening. It was a superb performance. Nevertheless I had to remember that Jim himself had chosen to have the budget just before the G.L.C. elections in order to give us the maximum aid. Having done this he must take responsibility for the defeat which he has helped to produce and which we shall suffer on Thursday.

This evening a most important dinner-party with Malcolm Shepherd, the Chief Whip in the House of Lords, Eddie Shackleton, the Deputy Leader, and John Silkin. Unfortunately last Friday that idiot George Brown suddenly took it upon himself to order Eddie Shackleton to become temporary resident Minister in Aden during the end of the British presence. This is a disaster because he's a key figure in our reform group and we can't spare him. What was to be done? We knew we are to have the first crucial meeting of the Ministerial Committee next Friday so we decided over dinner to stage a deadlock between the Chief Whips about the methods of curbing the power of the Lords. This should give us time to think out a tactic.

Wednesday, April 12th
The press reaction to Callaghan's budget was dreadful. In a leading article in its new Business Supplement *The Times* pointed out that the Chancellor had now accepted the Paish doctrine that the cure for our ills is a higher level of unemployment and a lower production target of 3 per cent instead of the 4 per cent we so proudly announced.[1]

At morning prayers this morning we discussed at length our preparations for the loss of the G.L.C. majority. We all foresaw defeat on Thursday, and agreed that the Prime Minister should deal with the significance of it either at Fulham on Saturday night or at Huyton on the Friday. The theme should be Nye Bevan's last speech about the test of democracy being whether it can take the unpopular decisions necessary to its survival.

[1] Frank Paish was Professor of Economics at L.S.E. 1949–65 and is now Professor Emeritus, University of London.

Having settled this the P.M. launched into a discussion of Callaghan. He said that the budget lacked imagination and that Callaghan had never shown him any draft or asked for any advice until it was too late. He was particularly angry because he was convinced that it was Callaghan who was responsible for the articles in the weekend press about himself as the crown prince and about his future policies for lending. Apparently he thought his great budget would make him even more of a crown prince but he'd come unstuck and Harold was being quite cheerful about it.

We then moved across to the Party meeting on the budget. When we got there there were only twenty people and even by 12.30 when the debate ended there were only sixty or seventy sleepy, tired colleagues at the meeting. Callaghan made a boring speech and Harold beside me kept on whispering *sotto voce* throughout. One of the things he said to me was 'I wonder whether he'll want to resign after this or want to stay on and take credit for the reflation when it comes?' And a little later he said, 'I wouldn't mind seeing him go. I wouldn't mind at all seeing him go this summer.'

After lunch I began my investigation into the Bristol-Siddeley case by interrogating John Stonehouse for one and a half hours. Then the Estimates Committee had asked to see me—about the shortage of staff and my future intentions. I found them extremely helpful and I'd got Barnett Cocks to attend the meeting. We discussed the problem of recruiting more Clerks and heard that Barney would like a college of Clerks—more like an Oxford college—and insists we must give them the same chance of promotion as civil servants without making them civil servants. When the Committee went away I got down, with Freddy Ward, to getting the six motions ready for the procedure debate after which we had a quiet little liaison committee—the last before Douglas Houghton's election to the P.L.P. chairmanship was duly announced at 5.15.

Then off to Lancaster House with Anne for a reception for Willy Brandt[1] and from there on to what we had chosen for Anne's birthday party—the film of the play *A Man For All Seasons*. We had greatly enjoyed the play with Paul Scofield as Sir Thomas More and it was a lovely little film, but though Anne liked it—and I heard her sniffing—I was completely untouched and sometimes fell asleep. Why was it she was so stirred by Thomas More, the martyr, when I wasn't stirred at all? The trouble was that I was really on Henry VIII's side. This quiet little man who sticks to the oath and doesn't let any practical reason come in his way irritated me exactly as Michael Stewart irritates me in Cabinet. Anne's character on the other side is much closer to Thomas More, though I don't think she'd like to be married to him. So the film taught us a lot about each other and after it off we went to Prunier to have our regular birthday dinner with still champagne.

[1] Then Foreign Minister of the Federal Republic of Germany.

Thursday, April 13th

Our third Cabinet on Europe. Harold started by outlining his timetable and at last announced that we must get our decision taken before the Whitsun recess. Then we got back to the question about the next Chequers meeting and whether officials should once again be present. I said I was strongly in favour and immediately there was a tremendous row. Callaghan observed that he thought we'd agreed not to have officials since they ruined the whole thing last time and George Brown strongly supported him, along with Cledwyn Hughes and Dick Marsh. On the other hand Tony Wedgwood Benn, Tony Crosland, Roy Jenkins and I all wanted officials present and on this point Harold made it clear that he was on our side. This difference is almost a class difference. I remember the talk I had with Andrew Cohen the other day at Nicholas Davenport's dinner when he asked me about the Fulton Committee.[1] I said the most important thing was that they should insist on officials sitting on a level with Ministers right from the top down and he agreed this would make the biggest difference in the world but added 'You'll never get it past your colleagues.' He was quite right about this Labour Government. I tried hard but all I got recorded in the Cabinet minutes was the following: 'However it was suggested that any requirement for factual advice could be reconciled with constitutional precedent and propriety in appropriate cases. Each Minister so concerned would be accompanied for this purpose by an official to whom he might himself wish to refer as he thought fit.'

That of course is not what I wanted but all that George Brown and Jim Callaghan would tolerate. The fact is that university people feel quite differently from working-class people who haven't been to university about the Civil Service. We feel they would add an enormous lot to any discussion of policy whereas our working-class colleagues fear they would undermine their position unless they were kept severely in control.

All through Cabinet I'd been worried about my business Statement because I had a terrible feeling that the Prime Minister might suddenly tell us that a week had been cut off the Whitsun recess. That would matter to me personally because we've got a family fortnight in Cyprus booked and paid for and this is the one time Anne and I can get away. But this problem of holidays affects the whole House. So Gerald Nabarro got up and asked whether I could give an absolute confirmation of the date of the Whitsun recess.[2] Since John Silkin keeps his whip private from me as well as the rest of the Party until it is published on Thursday evening, I didn't know that he had inserted in it a firm confirmation backed by both Parties that the Whitsun recess would last three weeks. So instead of giving the assurance and ending the discussion I

[1] Sir Andrew Cohen (K.C.M.G. 1952), Governor-General of Uganda 1952–7 and Director-General of the Department of Technical Co-operation 1961–4. He became Barbara Castle's first Permanent Secretary at the Ministry of Overseas Development. He died in June 1968.

[2] Sir Gerald Nabarro, Conservative M.P. for Kidderminster 1950–64 and for Worcestershire South from 1966 until his death in 1974.

said I hoped but couldn't commit myself, and when he pressed and pressed I repeated that I couldn't give him an assurance and added that there were specially important reasons why I couldn't. I was thinking of the Common Market, where Harold is determined we shall have the announcement before the recess. A lot of people understood this and there was a sort of gasp from the two Chief Whips when I sat down. However, I did recover myself because kind Evan Luard got up and asked politely whether I recollected my promise for a debate on foreign affairs.[1] This gave me a chance of correcting my bloomer within half a minute of making it. Of course if I had made that correction three weeks ago there would have been a major row, with both Heath and my own people attacking my incompetence and complaining that I didn't know my job and tomorrow there'd have been an irate press. Suddenly the House was friendly and let me off and, as I discovered when I went upstairs to my Lobby conference, the press was friendly too. Now I am in a patch of good weather; then I was in a patch of bad weather. In good weather you can make a mistake and it's regarded as a pleasant idiosyncrasy of the Leader of the House, but bad weather turns the tiniest slip into a clanger.

Later this evening Tam and I saw the G.L.C. election results on television and felt pretty devastated by the sight of poor old Bill Fiske, the leader of the Labour group, accepting defeat.[2]

Friday, April 14th
The Tory papers were exultant and happy. I distracted my attention from the defeat by preparing for our crucial Ministerial Committee on the House of Lords which began at 9.30. We played it exactly as we'd planned our tactics at the dinner with the two Chief Whips. They very deliberately got into conflict after which Roy Jenkins expressed his interest in composition and I said it was excluded by our terms of reference. Then Frank Pakenham, as we all feared, barged his way in as the patron of House of Lords reform. However, the two Chief Whips and I quite skilfully managed to bring about a situation in the Committee where the chairman (that's me) was told to draft a paper on functions not excluding composition.[3] Since Eddie Shackleton's away, I'm not going to worry about this.

[1] Labour M.P. for Oxford 1966–70 and since 1970. He was Parliamentary Under-Secretary of State at the Foreign and Commonwealth Office 1969–70 and returned to that office in April 1976.

[2] On April 13th the Conservatives won 46 seats in the G.L.C. elections, giving them 82 seats to Labour's 18. It was the first time since 1934, when they had gained control of the L.C.C., that the Conservatives had taken London. Altogether the county council elections were a disaster for the Government, as Labour lost heavily throughout the country and retained control of only three county authorities: Durham, Glamorgan and Monmouthshire. The borough elections on May 11th were to show a similar trend, for not only did the Conservatives gain 535 seats and Labour lose 596, but Liberals and Independents also made inroads into the Labour vote.

[3] The composition of the Upper House, which was made up of a minority of life peers and a preponderance of hereditary peers, had always made the House vulnerable to criticism, not least because there had always tended to be a majority of Conservative members and because a large proportion of those entitled to a seat came only infrequently, if at all.

However, too much delay is made more difficult by the fact that the House of Lords devoted a whole day to discussing its own reform last Wednesday. Apparently Lord Longford, after replying for the Government, went to see David Wood of *The Times* and gave him a background briefing hinting that the Government was now thinking of reforming the composition as well as the power of the Lords and discussing the possibility of inter-Party consultations. When I complained about this leak, Roy Jenkins coolly replied that radical reform was in the air and there was no need to conceal the fact. I replied that it was essential to conceal it because if it comes out too soon the Cabinet will nip it in the bud.

The rest of the morning was spent at O.P.D. where we discussed the deplorable paper produced by the officials on the political and economic implications of reducing Far Eastern defence costs. I pointed out that the essential strategic problems are all burked in these official papers. We never get a clear view of the power relations in the Far East, the strength of the Americans or the value of our role. None of the essential facts is properly collected. They're all mushed up in order to lead the mind to a typical officials' half-way house. It's obvious that what Whitehall wants is what George Brown, Denis Healey and Harold Wilson want. They're all going for a compromise under which we slowly get off the mainland and out of Singapore in the next ten years to build up a military presence in Australia. It's a barmy compromise. We ought to stay on the mainland or to withdraw from East of Suez altogether. But any clear-cut choice by the Cabinet is going to be made almost impossible by George's tour of the Far East. He is being sent to negotiate a withdrawal from the mainland and in the course of doing so he's certain to commit himself to an effective military presence in Australia and we shall be told in July that we can't repudiate him.

Together with the Chief and Freddy Ward I gave a lunch at the Garrick to four of the leading Lobby correspondents. We had a splendid meal as we always do at the Garrick and we're establishing a much better relationship with the Lobby. We began to discuss the proper way to handle the press gallery's catering and how to remedy their grievance about access to the Terrace. Here I do feel something is happening under my leadership.

Back at the Privy Council I just had time for Otto Clarke – Tony Wedgwood Benn's Permanent Secretary and the second of my witnesses in the Bristol-Siddeley inquiry. Then into the new electrified train roaring to Coventry in one hour and ten minutes, and interviews in Coventry before getting back late to Prescote.

Saturday, April 15th
Today is Anne's birthday and it's been a wonderful day which started with presents and the children, who had arranged with Nanny that they bought their presents themselves, duly came into our bedroom. Anne's present from me, a dress from Fortnum & Mason, was under the bed and we gave her

breakfast in bed as well. We've been out this afternoon to the Cotswolds buying plants and visiting a wonderful mysterious wood in which a great house and a castle of the Camperdowne family used to be. They're now ruins and we had an adventurous afternoon exploring them.

Sunday, April 16th

A week ago I certainly wasn't conscious of the impact our cataclysmic defeat in the G.L.C. and the landslide pro-Tory vote in the other local elections would make on the country. In my head I knew that we were heading for a disaster but it just hadn't registered on me as an important event until I watched the results on Thursday. However, as Harold cheerfully remarked to me, it has no immediate importance because we've still got three or four years in which to recover. The results in fact are far more important as a fillip to the Tories and a strengthener for Heath's leadership than as damage for us. If the Tories had not captured London I think it would have been difficult for Heath to retain his leadership. He's now in an assured position and the Tories will go into action against us far more vigorously. That will have its reflection at Westminster as well. The defeat could only affect us if we ourselves made it do so. From what I've seen of Harold since the election he won't allow this to happen. He's remarkably cocker about the whole affair and almost sounds glad that Callaghan got what he deserved from the electorate as vengeance for his empty budget. I'm inclined to agree with him that the utter emptiness of this third Callaghan budget transformed a heavy defeat into a landslide Tory victory.

But I also agree with Tommy that Harold can't blame Callaghan for that. In Callaghan's first two budgets Harold took an enormous interest from January onwards—advising him and pressing him and sometimes ordering him to be more adventurous. This year, so Tommy tells me, there was hardly a budget file at No. 10 throughout January. By the time Jim consulted the P.M. it was too late to make changes and so it's the first genuine Callaghan budget.

Nevertheless, now that they're over, I don't think these elections will make any difference to us except perhaps that the Parliamentary Party may be less difficult to deal with. This week for the first time for months I've been bothering about the Party and not about my own position which has gone on steadily improving. It has also been strengthened by the easy election of Douglas Houghton to replace Manny Shinwell as chairman. He's a liberalizer who, I hope, will stand fairly well with John and myself though I don't underestimate how erratic his temperament can be.

So it's been a good week from my point of view. I've started once again enjoying my life at home without being emotionally agonized by life in the House of Commons.

Monday, April 17th

I read the papers as I travelled up in the train and found that the whole press was talking about the devastating impact of the Greater London and the county council election defeats on the relations of the Government to its back-benchers. And since we had a ticklish meeting of the Parliamentary Party this evening it was predicted that we should have a hellish post mortem with all the back-benchers blowing off steam.

When I lunched with Alan Watkins of the *Spectator* he made the same point. 'Unlike the Tories,' he said, 'in whom disaster always produces a sense of solidarity, this will produce fissure and division in the ranks.' I told him I wasn't so sure.

This afternoon I discussed the presentation of his prices and incomes Statement with Michael Stewart before going into the Chamber to listen to George Brown answering Questions. He got through with the greatest of ease since most of the Questions were tame ones from our own side. At the end Lord Balniel got up and complained that the Questions had been rigged and it was a scandal that the Foreign Secretary should protect himself in this way.[1] George dismissed the suggestion as outrageous but afterwards I found out that steps had been taken by his P.P.S. to protect the Foreign Secretary by arranging easy Questions for him from our own side.[2]

Despite all my forebodings, Michael Stewart's Statement went very well, largely because he's a self-righteous little man who will never be prepared to admit that he has been defeated. The impression he gave was that he was carrying on with an excellent and effective prices and incomes policy. He got away with it because it was in no one's interest to say that he had sold out to the unions. Neither our left-wingers nor the Tories, nor Fleet Street want to accuse him of that. And maybe in the short term he has gained something. There was a fascinating interview in *The Times* with George Woodcock who showed a sudden willingness to be reasonable and to reach agreements with us. Perhaps this is the price the T.U.C. is willing to pay for the complete surrender of our policy.

In the afternoon I had my first experience of conducting a meeting of the Privileges Committee. When I went into the room I was immediately moved into the chair by the father of the House, Robin Turton.[3] I had the Clerk to the Committee on my left and beyond him were Ted Heath, John Boyd-

---

[1] Son of the Earl of Crawford, and Conservative M.P. for Hertford 1955–74. He was Minister of State at the Ministry of Defence 1970–72 and at the Commonwealth Office 1972–4.

[2] In December 1971 Julian Amery, as Minister for Housing and Construction at the Department of the Environment, was to admit that back-benchers had been encouraged to ask Questions (devised with official help) casting a favourable light on his Department's activities.

[3] Sir Robert Turton, Conservative M.P. for Thirsk and Malton from 1929 (and thus the longest serving Member of the House) until 1974. He became a life peer in 1974.

Carpenter,[1] George Strauss, Nigel Birch,[2] and then two very weak brethren
of ours—John Hynd and Arthur Woodburn.[3] The Attorney-General sat on
my immediate right. The Tories on the Privileges Committee are a much more
distinguished group than our people. The complaint we had to consider had
been made by Gerry Fitt, who is not a Labour Party M.P. but a Catholic
Republican from Belfast. Directly the discussion started it was obvious that
the Tories wanted to dismiss this as a piece of scurrilous abuse which wasn't a
real breach of privilege. But the Attorney-General and I had already decided
it was a gross breach of privilege and a gross contempt of the House, and the
Committee soon accepted this view and began to discuss what should be
done.[4] Here Arthur Woodburn and George Strauss, before the Tories could
get a word in, said that we should do nothing and that we should make ourselves absurd if we took it seriously. Obviously they were as anxious as the
Tories because they knew that the guilty man was none other than the
Reverend Paisley—the notorious wild man of the ultra-Protestant right wing.[5]
He is the owner of the paper and author of the article. Ted Heath agreed with
Woodburn and Strauss that it would be disastrous for us to try to enforce
our will on Mr Paisley. He certainly wasn't prepared to apologize and if we
condemned him to a term of imprisonment he would gladly go as a martyr.
Nevertheless I couldn't let the Committee dismiss the whole incident as
completely unimportant. After all, Gerry Fitt is an M.P. and he has the right
to the protection afforded by privilege as much as any other M.P. Paisley's
threat to suppress the republican clubs in Belfast is a very real one. After a
good deal of chatter it was finally agreed that the Lord President and the
Attorney-General should draft a form of words which condemned the breach
of privilege but made it clear we were going to deny the author of the breach
the notoriety he desired. That's quite a difficult assignment. It also showed the
amazing change which has taken place in the last ten years in the attitude of

[1] Conservative M.P. for Kingston-upon-Thames from 1945 until 1972, when he took a
life peerage and became chairman of the Civil Aviation Authority.

[2] Conservative M.P. for Flint from 1945 until 1970, when he was made a life peer, taking
the title of Lord Rhyl. He had held several offices in post-war Conservative Governments,
including that of Economic Secretary to the Treasury from 1957 until his resignation in
1958.

[3] John Hynd was Labour M.P. for Sheffield 1944–70. Arthur Woodburn was Labour
M.P. for Clackmannon 1939–70.

[4] 'Freedom from arrest and freedom of speech are the chief of the Commons' ancient and
undoubted rights and privileges', claimed by the Speaker on behalf of Parliament at the
beginning of each new Parliament. The Privileges Committee of each House protects its
privileges and punishes their violation. They also judge cases of contempt of Parliament,
when the actions, words and behaviour of Members have been criticized, whether justifiably or not.

[5] Ian Paisley, Protestant Unionist M.P. for North Antrim 1970–74 and Democratic
Unionist M.P. for that constituency since 1974. He was a Protestant Unionist M.P. for
Barnside, Co. Antrim, in the Northern Ireland Parliament 1970–72, Democratic Unionist
Member for North Antrim in the Northern Ireland Assembly 1973–5, and United Ulster
Unionist Coalition Member in the Northern Ireland Constitutional Convention May
1975–6. He began to publish the *Protestant Telegraph* in 1966.

the House to privilege. Ten years ago we were summoning John Junor, editor of the *Sunday Express*, to the Bar and publicly rebuking him for the most minor breach of privilege. Now the House sees that this kind of behaviour makes it ridiculous and we've actually got a Committee sitting to reform the law. But at present we have to operate on the old rules.

The meeting went on so long that I was very late for the Parliamentary Party. I gather the mood was quiet and quite definitely sobered. The only person who made a sour speech was Hugh Jenkins and he got a very poor response. Indeed the relations of the Government with the Party have been made slightly easier by the sense that we now must sink or swim together.

Talking to one or two of the Tory members of the Privileges Committee I gathered that they too are not going to gain much from their G.L.C. election successes. They can hardly attack Jim Callaghan's budget because there is not a trace of radicalism in it and indeed it is terribly conventional and conservative. And if they complain that it lacks imagination, there is the simple reply that we are now prepared for a period of temporary unpopularity in order to achieve the necessary degree of deflation. They also foresee the difficulties they will have now that they're taking over in County Hall. They are responsible for the level of the rates, for housing and transport, and all the other things they were attacking up till now. Pretty soon we can expect a lot of tension between the Tories in County Hall and the Tories in Westminster.

Tuesday, April 18th
Cabinet was due to continue the discussion of the Common Market. In fact we spent most of our time discussing the future of the Royal Mint. It has been decided to move it and its 1,400 skilled workers out of London and the choice has narrowed to Llantrisant at the end of the Rhondda Valley, Washington New Town in the North-East, and Cumbernauld near Glasgow. Not unnaturally the Cabinet Committee was completely split. The Chancellor and the Treasury officials said there was no doubt the people in the Mint themselves would prefer South Wales if they had to move at all. But the Chancellor's credibility was somewhat undermined by the fact that he represents a Cardiff constituency. Michael Stewart for the D.E.A. said that on the whole in terms of dispersal policy the strongest case for was the North-East, and Willie Ross, as Secretary of State for Scotland, insisted on Cumbernauld. Poor Willie Ross, who sits next to me in Cabinet, was very depressed. Harold Wilson tells me he's talking of resignation because he's so miserably unhappy at the 10 per cent unemployment rate in Scotland and his failure to achieve any effective regional policy. What makes matters worse is that recently all the dispersal decisions have favoured Wales. Barbara Castle has put a great new section of her Ministry in Swansea and the Defence Department is moving a lot to South Wales. All that Scotland has recently acquired is the GIRO part of Post Office. Willie Ross spoke with great bitterness and sounded like a man who knew he was defeated before the debate

began. After an hour and a half the P.M. counted heads and finally said that Wales had it. He's created quite a crisis for himself and for the Secretary of State for Scotland.

When we turned to the Common Market, agriculture was the chosen topic of the day and Fred Peart started with a sensible speech which is fairly recorded in the Cabinet minutes. Of course the main objection to entering the Market is the reactionary character of the Common Agricultural Policy but in Cabinet there was virtually no discussion about this because apart from Fred Peart and myself no one is interested in agriculture. Before very long the P.M. made a very important intervention which no doubt shortened the discussion. It had been suggested, he said, that we should seek for transitional arrangements only but it was clear that if we accepted the C.A.P. as it stands we should be compelled to pay an outrageously big proportion of the levies. So we couldn't just discuss transitional arrangements in any negotiation. We had to get some firm understanding about the long-term policy. As stated in the Cabinet minutes, this is a very important reservation which runs, 'We should reserve our freedom to seek adjustments in agriculture going beyond transitional arrangements.'

This afternoon we had the first confrontation between Heath and Wilson since our election defeats. The leader of the Opposition sat there looking uneasy and more and more like Gaitskell; I thought, 'He's not up to much.' Then a Tory back-bencher put a Question about the Royal Commission on Local Government and Heath lunged. The lunge was successful and caught the Prime Minister on a very sensitive point—whether he was going to use the delay of the Local Government Boundary Commission's report as an excuse to delay the statutory revision of parliamentary constituency boundaries. Of course we intend to do so and that indeed was one of the arguments I used in persuading the Cabinet to accept a Royal Commission.[1] The P.M. had no adequate reply and this was a score by Heath, but it's the only score he had in his victory week.

I spent most of the evening preparing my speech for the procedure debate.

Wednesday, April 19th
The day of the procedure debate. The day started, however, with morning prayers at 9.30. The P.M. made it quite clear that he wanted disciplinary action to be taken if anybody voted for the Private Member's Motion on Vietnam which was being moved on Friday. This was a motion designed specifically to repudiate the Party's decision to support the Government about the resumption of American bombing. It was clear from the discussion that the P.M. is now keeping a very careful and close control of the Chief Whip in all matters of discipline. Next he made a complaint about the number of M.P.s who are helping in the Brierley Hill by-election. It was clear that we were in for trouble because George Wigg sits next door for Dudley and he has been

[1] See Vol. I, p. 439.

rampaging round the House telling everybody that the Party is failing to do its job and insisting that members should be brought down in squads to canvass and knock up.[1] I found this out because Tam Dalyell came to see me yesterday saying he couldn't attend the procedure debate as I wanted him to do because he and Will Hamling[2] have been pressganged to pay for their own rail tickets to Birmingham for that day. I said I could understand why the Midland M.P.s who had free passes should go but not Tam and Will. I can't think that their presence would make much difference to the result at Brierley Hill. But the P.M. was not satisfied. Clearly John and I are no longer in his good books.

The procedure debate this afternoon was a bit of a mess. The Chief and I worked out an ambitious plan. We wanted the House to accept several motions of mine, including a general motion approving the First, Second, Third and Fourth Reports of the Procedure Committee, a motion shortening the time of divisions, a motion on the Finance Bill and another on Specialist Committees. I had to move them all in a single speech at the beginning. I had worked it out very carefully with Freddy Ward, whose help had been invaluable. Right at the beginning I came unstuck because the Speaker seemed to want me to move a motion slightly different from that on the Order Paper. However I got going after about ten minutes' interruption and sat down in under half an hour. As the debate went on it seemed clear that we would get our motions approved with reasonable luck. But owing to the rules of procedure I had one very awkward hurdle to get over. I had to sit down just in time for the Speaker to get up and read the motion aloud before 9.30 — otherwise all the motions could fall if the word 'object' were spoken by any Member of the House. Of course, this meant that the two front benches had to collaborate through the usual channels and collaboration had duly been planned. Willie Whitelaw had agreed to fix this with us on condition that we made reasonable concessions to any strong objections registered in the course of the debate. It soon became clear, for instance, that I would have to sacrifice the resolution about short speeches, and probably also the first resolution about the time spent on divisions. Both these concessions I made while the debate was going on.

All day I sat alone on the front bench. I had no Parliamentary Secretary to help me and only Geoffrey Rhodes behind me as my P.P.S. Apart from the Chief Whip I carried the whole responsibility and the Chief was busy and only turned up right at the end to deal with the problems of the vote. After a time it was clear that the mood had changed and a spontaneous Tory rebellion was taking place. They had been given a free vote while we had our whips on. This meant that their wild men could object to anything—in particular to our

[1] On April 27th Fergus Montgomery increased the Conservative majority from 1,567 to 10,220.
[2] Labour M.P. for Woolwich 1964–74 and for Greenwich since 1974. He was an Assistant Government Whip 1969–70.

crucial motion about the Finance Bill. Finally I got up and made my most satisfactory—or least unsatisfactory—speech as Leader of the House, speaking from notes only, and I filled in nicely and sat down exactly at the right time for the Speaker. But at this point three Tories, headed by Douglas Glover,[1] jumped up and the Chief was forced to move the closure, which was carried by an enormous majority.[2] But then it was long after 9.30 and the Tories shouted 'object' to every one of the motions. So our procedure debate had ended in sterility.

Thursday, April 20th

It was pretty exasperating to read the morning papers telling me how I'd mucked up procedure once again. True *The Times* and the B.B.C. were not too bad but the *Guardian* and the *Telegraph* were extremely offensive and damaging. I felt very depressed and angry, but more angry than depressed since this time I didn't think it was my fault. After all, I'm not a great procedure man and I'd left it to John Silkin and Freddie Warren to work out the details of putting down the motions and arranging how we should carry them. I had asked them why we didn't move the suspension of Standing Orders and so give ourselves time to discuss each motion. The reply had been that this would mean an all-night sitting with an unlimited debate on each of the seven resolutions. This could have gone on right up to two or three in the morning. It was preferable therefore to get them through fast, and by agreement through the usual channels. The trouble was that the usual channels didn't work on this occasion.

At Cabinet this morning I got a very quick reaction. As I went past the P.M.'s chair to my own place he turned round and said, 'Your procedure advisers weren't in very good form last night.' I thought straightaway, 'That's George Wigg's work.' Sure enough he had rung up Harold the night before and again that morning telling him what a balls-up John and I had made of the debate. The P.M. was still angry with us about Brierley Hill and was obviously taking George's view of the matter.

After that another Common Market discussion—this time on GITA (Go It Alone) and NAFTA (North Atlantic Union). Two Green Papers had been prepared by the officials with an extraordinary covering note by Burke Trend speaking for the Permanent Secretaries and saying that neither Green Paper was nearly severe enough in showing the disastrous disadvantages of staying out. In their view there was no future whatsoever for a Britain which failed to get in. A number of people, particularly Barbara Castle, said this was purely defeatist. I added that the essential thing was to realize that we must try all out to get in but if that failed we mustn't be caught like Harold Macmillan saying there's no future for this country. We must have our alternative policy ready. We must have a dynamism of rejection as well as a

---

[1] Conservative M.P. for Ormskirk 1953–70.
[2] There were 240 Ayes and 101 Noes.

dynamism of entry. When I'd finished the P.M. leant over and said, 'That's the best contribution which has yet been made to the debate in any of our meetings.' He was delighted because he felt I'd given him his options back. Most people afterwards agreed this was the first realistic discussion we'd had because at last we were recognizing the fact that this Government was bound to try to enter the Common Market but also needed to have a clear alternative policy if we were rejected, as we probably shall be. Even Barbara, as the P.M. noted to me afterwards, now seemed to accept that we must try to get in and that what we should do is to consider the terms on which we would be prepared to enter and also the policies we should have to apply if we remained outside.

What Cabinet did reject, thank heavens, was the proposal in the Burke Trend paper that if we failed to get in we should stand on the threshold in a stance of eager expectation. That I got my colleagues to repudiate totally. Only Douglas Jay objected. After the meeting he told me he wants postponement since this is the wrong time to apply for entry. I said that he didn't seem to realize what a change there had been in these six months since Harold and George decided to tour Europe. I was against that exploration. But once it was started the momentum was bound to take us further forward. My impression is that most of the Cabinet now realize that whether we like the idea or not we must make a serious effort to get in as fast as possible.

Before the business Questions this afternoon I sat down to think out my tactics with Henry James and Freddy Ward. The business Statement was pretty provocative since I'd put back the motion on the Finance Bill next Wednesday morning and followed it by Eric Heffer's Live Hare Coursing (Abolition) Bill the following Monday. Sure enough, after some mild questions the Tories attacked me for breaking my promise to have noncontroversial morning sittings. I stood up to them strongly and got my own supporters cheering behind me. It was a good Thursday afternoon which proved that I'd lost nothing by the fiasco of last week's procedure debate.

The Party meeting this evening was crucial for John Silkin since he had to put over the decision to withdraw the whip from anyone who voted for the Vietnam resolution in the Private Members' debate on Friday. Douglas Houghton, who was in the chair for the first time, had prepared the tactics in advance very carefully with him. John was extremely skilful. He very quietly gave the impression of firm action without an actual threat and when challenged about the closure he just left them to wonder what would happen if they moved it. As a libertarian he was having to stand firm and assert that though abstention is a right on any great issue, no Labour M.P. should vote against the Government. We were arguing that even though it was Private Members' time on Friday a vote for the resolution was a vote against the Government. Listening to him and watching the Party I had the feeling he was carrying people with him. It was clear, whatever they said, that the rebels were in fact challenging a vote on official Party policy and were attempting to show the strength of their rebellion by forcing a division. There's no doubt that the local election defeats were helpful in getting most of our middle-of-the-roaders to swing into line.

In the evening I had one of my informal gatherings of Junior Ministers. I learnt quite a lot. First of all I tried to persuade them to give more of their weekends to work for the Party. There was a good deal of resistance, partly because they said that people wanted senior Ministers not junior Ministers as speakers. So I turned to the problem of Specialist Committees and aired, for the first time, Harold's idea of a Committee on forthcoming legislation, on decimalization for example, before we drafted the Bill. I expected something like enthusiasm for this but I got none. Peter Shore, for example, was strongly against it. He wanted new ideas discussed in the Party groups, not in Specialist Committees. This made me realize that junior Ministers are very much part of the Government, concerned to get their Department's policies through and to keep in touch with the Party. Like the rest of the Government they've lost any sense for parliamentary reform.

Friday, April 21st
Instead of our normal business meeting with George Brown and Burke the P.M. said he would like to see me alone. This gave me time to think of the points I wanted to raise. First I asked him when, during the big Common Market weekend, we should discuss devaluation—would it be on Saturday morning with the officials present? 'No,' he said, 'that should be on Sunday.' And he plunged into a detailed account of how he and the Chancellor had made the most elaborate arrangements to discuss devaluation at the last meeting of S.E.P.—when I didn't raise it. My next point was the Brierley Hill by-election. I told him that the Chief had been very much upset by his complaints and rebukes. 'Ah, the Chief has no follow-through,' he replied. 'He's failed to get the M.P.s up there and is relying on you to placate me. He has no follow-through.' In that sentence I traced Wigg's influence at work. Obviously I was going to get no change so I dropped the subject and asked him about my decision not to stand for the National Executive this year. There are far too many ageing Ministers on the N.E.C. and last year I wanted to set an example for the simple reason that if some of us don't retire we shall be flung off in the kind of landslide which had flung Harold and me on to the Executive in 1952. Harold wouldn't let me because his plan then was to make me the Minister responsible for Transport House and give me the job of chairman of the Organization Sub-Committee. But everything has gone wrong. I'm not chairman of Org. Sub. and with the trade unionists in complete charge I'm completely excluded from any power. Nevertheless, I was surprised when he said that he thought it was really quite sensible for me to retire because he was going to reappoint a special campaign committee and as Leader of the House I would automatically be one of the officers on it. It was this campaign committee where all the serious work would be done.

Right at the end we just touched on the Common Market. Was he content with progress, I asked him? He said how pleased he was with the role I had played in the discussions and how he felt that the deliberate filibustering was now over. 'But what are our chances of getting in?' I asked. 'Well,' he said, 'perhaps in the last resort I shall have to see General de Gaulle alone and spell out to him the real alternatives. Either we come right in, I must say, or we are hostile members of an American bloc.' Then, as I was going out of the door, he added, 'I shall be seeing de Gaulle on Tuesday.' (He's going to Bonn to the funeral of Adenauer who died this week.)

Harold's illusions of grandeur in foreign policy scare me stiff. If he tries to talk to de Gaulle in this particular way it won't come off any better than his 'straight talks' with L.B.J. when he thought he was speaking on equal terms.

I went across to the House to see how the crucial debate was going on Vietnam and U Thant's proposals to the U.N. for a peaceful settlement. It had been opened by Norman Atkinson and when I got there Orr-Ewing, the Tory,[1] was speaking with about six Conservatives on his side and six Labour people on ours. Then back to the Privy Council where I had my third witness in the Bristol-Siddeley inquiry—the Permanent Secretary who had been in charge.[2]

After that I should have gone to a memorial service for Cassandra of the *Daily Mirror* at St Paul's Cathedral.[3] It was a tremendous service, with Harold Wilson reading the lesson. Why wasn't I there? It half occurred to me to go, but I'm feeling out of politics and I don't like being present at these official great occasions. But clearly I ought to have been there—as an ex-*Mirror* man, as the Lord President, and also as a friend of Cassandra. Was it slackness on my part? Yes, a bit of slackness, a bit of inverted snobbery, a bit of my new mood of retirement.

I got back to Prescote on the 6.10 and found the children waiting on the platform for me to get me home for a good two and a quarter days.

Sunday, April 23rd
There wasn't much in my red boxes and I haven't a speech to write or anything special to prepare so I've really had two days off. Drusilla Shulman[4] with her two girls and her boy, Jason, spent the day with us and we spent the afternoon fishing for our aquarium. Drusilla kept on sympathizing with me for the ghastly job I've been given. Everybody looks at me now with embarrassment. They don't so much think that I'm doing badly as that it's bad luck for me to be moved away from Housing. None of them understands a thing about procedure in Parliament and it's going to be very difficult to build up any

---

[1] Sir Ian Orr-Ewing, Conservative M.P. for North Hendon 1950–70. In 1971 he became a life peer.

[2] Sir Ronald Melville.

[3] Sir William Connor had written for the *Daily Mirror* from 1935 until his death in 1967, publishing a famous column under the name of Cassandra. He was knighted in 1966.

[4] Drusilla Beyfus, wife of Milton Shulman, the journalist and critic.

kind of reputation for myself so long as I'm Leader of the House. Drusilla
didn't seem the least upset by the fact that I was obviously more interested in
my children than in my job. Do I care too much about them? Do I spend too
much thought on them? At the moment I think I do. I'm prepared to sacrifice
my work for my family in a way I wouldn't have dreamt of doing twenty
years ago. Then I was automatically sacrificing family for work and making
Zita's life intolerable. Now I've switched the other way round. The family and
Prescote are number one—the diary is number two and my job as Lord
President is number three.*

Nevertheless, I'm interested enough in politics this weekend to put down
some reflections about the problem of leaks from the Cabinet. These have
now become an important fact in our Cabinet behaviour. Harold often says
he can't discuss things in Cabinet because of the leaks. When he does so, four
members out of five in the Cabinet would reply that 'the leaks are chiefly the
result of your setting the example'. Certainly in his early days in No. 10
Harold set a new standard of press relations—talking and feeding out to the
press and discussing his new ideas with them. When I became Lord President
he'd cut himself off from the press. He held no Lobby conferences but only
had selected pressmen occasionally down to Chequers. Now he does a lot
more. He still has Trevor Lloyd-Hughes running his Prime Ministerial press
service from No. 10, he still has Gerald Kaufman, and he still has George
Wigg operating in the background. In addition he now has me running my
weekly press conference on Thursday and doing quite a number of jobs for
him as well.

This is keenly felt by the rest of Cabinet and I'm sure that many Ministers
talk to the press in order to counter the influence of No. 10. Sometimes they
do it to counter the influence of another Ministry. Recently, for example, we
have had weeks on end when the press has been full of leaks and counter-leaks
from the Ministry of Labour and the D.E.A. about the prices and incomes
policy which was being discussed in a Cabinet Committee. This has given
Harold the excuse for keeping vital issues out of Cabinet and that brings me
to the fight about devaluation. Devaluation had never been discussed in
Cabinet since last July. In order to have some discussion of the subject, at
least by the inner Cabinet, S.E.P. was created but we've never discussed
devaluation in S.E.P. We were due to discuss it time after time but it's always
been postponed. Harold actually told me when I was talking to him on Friday
that I had been expected to raise the issue at the last S.E.P. and that he and
the Chancellor had agreed that if I did so Jim would take a sealed envelope
out of his pocket in order to discuss it with me. In fact I had no idea of what I
was expected to do so I didn't raise the issue and he didn't need his sealed
envelope. This shows how careful and calculating Harold is in avoiding un-

---

* I may have imagined this in the spring of 1967 but neither Anne nor the children would
have accepted it for one moment as a realistic picture. They found me entirely absorbed in
my work.

palatable discussions. He only revealed all this when on Friday I'd asked him about how devaluation could best be raised at the Chequers' conference on the Common Market. He told me to raise it when the officials were not present on the Sunday and then went on to tell me that he and the Chancellor had looked at the problem very carefully and at the moment there wasn't any necessity. On the other hand, there may well have to be a degree of devaluation before we go in and there was a certain risk that even the announcement of our intended entry would produce a run on the pound. He made it perfectly clear that these are things he felt perfectly entitled to keep from Cabinet and discuss with the Chancellor alone.

Another issue he has certainly avoided discussing with me is nuclear weapons. Despite that famous first evening at Chequers I've been kept off the vital Committee and all I know is the result of approaches by Chalfont and Solly Zuckerman. They both wanted to brief me to ask awkward questions at O.P.D. which would make the Prime Minister deny that we are contemplating a new generation of nuclear weapons and through the denial make it more likely that we'll use *Poseidon*.

But is there much else which is being kept from me and from most other members of the Cabinet? What about Foreign Office and Defence telegrams for instance? Is there an 'eyes only' classification to which Harold, George and Denis alone have access? I'm not sure. Just this week I said that one of the things we should certainly want to know more than anything else is the assessment of the situation in Europe made by our Ambassadors in the various capitals. Should we not recall them for a special meeting with the Cabinet? This raised the alarm and I was told that it would be quite impossible since it would alert the general public. I had asked for the meeting because I'd been reading the telegrams from Paris and Bonn very carefully and I've noticed that for weeks there's been nothing in them about either the European reaction to our entry or the Ambassadors' assessment of our chances. I now gather that a special instruction was sent out cutting off the confidential telegrams on this subject for four or five weeks. I have tried to insist that everything relevant should be collected and presented to us before next Saturday's Common Market meeting but I know that it won't be.

I sometimes feel that one of my most useful jobs in this Government is to provide a one-man check on the efforts of the Civil Service to blinker the politicians who are supposed to be in charge. Maybe Thomas Balogh and I are obsessed by the feeling that vital information is being suppressed. But certainly I'm still amazed at the violence with which the P.M. reacted when the Labour Party in its evidence to the Fulton Committee suggested that Ministers were the victims of suppression of vital information. In everything he says about Government he fiercely denies this and suggests that if the politician isn't well informed it's his own fault.

Monday, April 24th

My first job was to see the last and the most important of the Civil Service witnesses in my Bristol-Siddeley inquiry. This was Mr Haynes, who was Head of the Contracts Department in the Ministry of Aviation.[1] When I'd finished with Haynes I set out on my journey to No. 10 to S.E.P. This involves me in the first place in summoning somebody from my Private Office to proceed along the corridor with me and unlock the door out of the Privy Council Office. Then, as I pass through the Cabinet Office, I have to summon someone else to unlock the door into No. 10. This occurs every time I want to move. I have to pierce two perimeter defences—the defence of the Cabinet Secretariat from the Privy Council and the defence of No. 10 from the Cabinet Secretariat. Each time an important official has to get up and unlock the door for me.

At S.E.P. I learnt that we had now fixed that each employer in the regions should be paid a Regional Employment Premium of 30s. for each worker he employs. I also learnt that the beginning of the reflation is timed not, as I thought, for next October but for early July. It is now thought that by then it will be time to relax the h.p. restrictions and I begin to see that July is a time when we must bring out the social service package. We must have our family endowment plan ready for announcement, along with an increase of old-age pensions, cuts in defence and some concession on school milk and school meals. Instead of July being the month of desperate emergency measures to avert disaster, in 1967 it should mark the first stage in the march towards reflation.

My next meeting was the Procedure Committee, where we had to consider the question of instructions to Ministers giving evidence to Select Committees which had been referred back to us by Cabinet. The point at issue was the narrow one—at what point in the process of getting legislation ready should the Minister be barred from giving evidence? Cabinet had agreed that the Minister should be forbidden when it's actually being discussed in the House and Cabinet wanted to make the veto come into effect when the relevant Cabinet Committee began to consider the policy. I was surprised to find some fourteen people in the bigger Ministerial conference room and thought I could get it through quite easily by accepting the Cabinet recommendation. Then, once again, the old trouble started. Niall MacDermot from the Treasury began to challenge the whole issue of whether Ministers should be allowed to give evidence on policy to the new Committees. I realized that I was fighting not a junior Minister but the Treasury speaking for the whole Whitehall machine and protesting against the danger to the Civil Service presented by these Specialist Committees. Fortunately my friends were strong on the ground, particularly Harold Lever and Roy Jenkins. They knew as

---

[1] Edwin Haynes, Under-Secretary at the Ministry of Aviation 1964–8 and at the Department of Trade and Industry (formerly Ministry of Technology) 1968–71.

well as I that I was supported by earlier Cabinet decisions so I managed to get my way.

From Procedure I had to move straight to the Privileges Committee, where I'm Chairman too. As I went into the room Jo Grimond, who'd been absent at the first meeting on Gerry Fitt's complaint against Paisley, came up to me and said, 'I don't like this draft very much. It is a breach of privilege and we can't just laugh it off.' The Attorney-General and I had struggled to reconcile our contradictory instructions and I was not surprised to find that not a single member of the Committee liked what we had done. It was disliked by Jo Grimond and one or two others who thought Mr Fitt was genuinely in need of protection. It was equally disliked by the Tories, who wanted nothing to do with an attack on Ulster M.P.s and the Ulster establishment. Finally, with the help of Selwyn Lloyd and Ted Heath, I managed to dig a form of words out of the precedents of the past which achieved the approval of the Committee. Our aim was to avoid being noticed and if noticed, being forced to a debate.*

This was a long day because I moved from there to a meeting of the Labour Party Parliamentary Reform Group where we discussed the question of Specialist Committees with the Chief Whip. The case they presented was simple and answerable. The House 'ought to select the members of our Committees', their spokesman said to me. 'It's intolerable that the Chief Whip should have the right to name us and, if we offend him by our independence, to leave us out in the next Session.' The Chief was patient but unrelenting. He said this raised an important issue of constitutional principle. Traditionally the control of patronage is shared by the Chief Whip and the Prime Minister. They have to be able to impose discipline by giving people jobs and by taking them away and he simply can't understand why if members of the Party behave awkwardly on a Select Committee he shouldn't remove them. Yet I want to see these Specialist Committees develop as a really effective control over the Executive. For this purpose they need to have a core of members who grow old and hoary in their service, not unlike the cadres of the American Congressional Committees, which of course are independent of the Executive and organized on the seniority system. How can our Committees grow powerful and influential if my friend the Chief Whip and his opposite number in the Opposition have the power at the end of a Session to behave like the Greek tyrant Polycrates, who cut down the highest ears of corn? Though I sympathized with my young parliamentary reformers I couldn't support them. Then the Chief Whip said in reply that the only solution is to have a Chief Whip who is trusted, who is liberal-minded, and uses his enormous powers with discretion. I very well knew that as long as the Whips have their power Parliament has no effective control of the Executive.

* I'm glad to say we were successful. A week later when the report came out it was buried in the back pages of the papers.

Back in my room I had to brief Sir Barnett Cocks on the job which our Committee had set him with regard to the reform of the House of Lords. I had been told to take his advice on the allocation of functions in a reformed Parliament. After Freddie Warren and I had explained our problem Barney looked at me from under his eyebrows and said, 'You want to make me make a takeover bid for the House of Lords.' I said, 'Yes, I want you to tell us how, if we integrate them to our convenience, we can use them best. If we had a reconstituted Lords with a built-in Government majority, how could we best use them as a second chamber?' 'First and foremost,' he said, 'in dealing with Private Bills.' 'Give them control of all those Private Bills.'[1] 'That's a start,' I said. 'Now work out in a fortnight the rest of the solution.'

Tuesday, April 25th

For a change we had quite a big issue to decide at the Legislation Committee. Ages ago—in August 1965—Harold Wilson had persuaded the Cabinet to accept in principle the reduction of the fifty-year limitation on the publication of state documents to thirty years. Whitehall didn't like this and has resorted to the usual delaying tactics. Finally, I got a letter this week from the Chancellor himself which I read with interest and compared with the Cabinet minutes of 1965. There was no doubt about it, the Foreign Office had launched a counter-attack and was going to have even more material classified so that after the reduction to thirty years there would be even less material actually available. I sent a stinking minute back to Harold, with copies to Gordon Walker and the Lord Chancellor, arguing that it was no good passing a law reducing the limit to thirty years if there were so many exceptions that the thirty-year rule was really a hypocrisy. I had taken good care to issue this minute in a form which made sure it would be circulated around Whitehall and have maximum effect. The result was quite impressive. The moment I presented the Bill to the Legislation Committee George Thomson for the Foreign Office explained at length how they didn't want to hold back any documents and were only going to have the same reservations as they'd had under the fifty-year rule. The Lord Chancellor spoke in the same way and I managed to see that all these assurances were written into the Bill. I very much doubt if they would have been given if it had not been for the circulation of my minute.

Anne's aunt May Cowper was up for the day, and I had a little party for her in the Privy Council before she lunched with me in the House of Commons. I very often have parties now in my room; it looks magnificent with its view over Horse Guards Parade and the splendid pictures: my two Dutch sea pictures, the portraits of Lord Halifax and Prince Frederick

---

[1] Private Bills seek special provisions or powers outside the general law for corporate bodies or, occasionally, for individuals. Local authorities often use this type of legislation. Standing Orders oblige the promoters of a Private Bill to notify its provisions to any body or individual likely to be affected by its terms and during Committee Stage in each House petitions can be lodged against the Bill.

behind the sofa, and my great Teniers on the huge damask wall on the right. And now I have got a new piece of furniture—a cupboard in the alcove for drinks and glasses. There were May and Anne and my Anne Ridoutt and Sheena Jeffries, the new number two brought over from No. 10, and it was a very pleasant party.

After I'd had a long meeting of the Services Committee I had to give evidence for an hour and a half to the Select Committee on Procedure about my long-term plans. It was quite a job and I sat for another one and a half hours as Chairman so that by the end of it I'd had three hours on end in committee before I went off to the theatre to see an all-star cast in Bernard Shaw's *Getting Married.* Well, I only just didn't fall asleep chiefly because the cast was brilliant and the setting very nice. The trouble is that the play is entirely static and morally cowardly—nothing really happens, there is no development and really no logic. In some of his better plays Shaw does have development but here he daren't move from his initial position and the effect is like a rather arid string quartet in which the voices of the actors are the different instruments.

After that we took May home for a delicious supper. We really had given her a jolly nice day.

Wednesday, April 26th
This was the second appearance of my vital motion on the Finance Bill which had been thrown out after the procedure debate. It was due to be objected to by Boyd-Carpenter and we would then vote it through. It was already clear that there was a split in the Tory Party with Iain Macleod, Boyd-Carpenter and Enoch Powell all saying that Selwyn Lloyd had sold them out by agreeing to the plan of the Labour members of the Select Committee. Poor old Selwyn Lloyd. (This was the very same week in which Anthony Nutting's devastating disclosures about Suez were being serialized in *The Times.*) In a sense I agreed with Selwyn's critics. I'd been amazed to see this unanimous report—amazed that Tory members of a Select Committee could concede to the Labour Government the ultimate reserve power of a guillotine obtained in two hours if the voluntary timetable on the Finance Bill broke down. I could hardly blame Enoch Powell and Iain Macleod for seeing the cloven hoof of Crossman in all this. Actually I'd had nothing to do with it. It had all been done by the Select Committee. In moving the report I pointed out that the Government had accepted the unanimous recommendation of the Select Committee and that if the Tories were to turn this down we would have to reserve our position and revert to our previous decision to send the Bill upstairs. After Boyd-Carpenter had accused the Committee of extremism Selwyn Lloyd got up and admitted that the Labour members had wanted to go much further and he had stopped them by accepting this compromise. It was the kind of nice easy-going sensible speech which reveals the kind of man he was even as Foreign

Secretary where he had obligingly carried out Eden's policy. I was thinking of this when the P.M. sent for me at three o'clock this afternoon. He was just back from Adenauer's funeral in Bonn where he'd had a short chat with the General, an hour with President Johnson and a talk with Kiesinger to whom he had frankly admitted that there are economic disadvantages in entering the Common Market but they are being overlooked by the British Government because we see the tremendous political advantages.[1] Then he turned to the Nutting revelations and explained to me how Burke Trend had tried to keep the job of censoring the book in his own non-political hands whereas Harold regarded it as a political matter and wanted to consult me and George Brown on how to handle it.

Of course Nutting has written an odious little book which has come out in the same week as Hugh Thomas's serious examination of the Suez fiasco.[2] Nutting puts Selwyn in a terrible light and shows quite clearly that he's been waiting for ten years to take his chance of vengeance. It's true he's driven a railroad through the whole idea of Cabinet confidentiality. But it's also true that the double-crossing and lying to the House which he reveals is something which anyone who cares about Parliament has got to take seriously.

In the evening I had Roy Hattersley to see me. He is the new young ambitious Parliamentary Secretary to the Ministry of Labour—a working-class boy who's made good and is now an eager Birmingham M.P. He took Shirley Williams's place under Gunter when she was promoted to Education. For some reason he's very unpopular but he's one of Harold's favourite choices—perhaps because he's extremely able and efficient. He must have defended more than a dozen Orders in Council against which the Tories have prayed, all dealing with Part IV of the Prices and Incomes Bill, and each one has to be taken between 9.30 and midnight. He came to complain about the appalling relationships between the Ministry of Labour and the D.E.A.—where of course the Departments have been at war. Ray Gunter as the spokesman of the T.U.C. has wrecked the new Prices and Incomes Bill and the two Departments have leaked and counter-leaked for weeks on end. Poor Hattersley has then to go to the House and to the detestation of our back-benchers defend all these Orders. All he wanted to do was to tell me about his difficulties and the inflexibility of the D.E.A. I listened very cautiously because with a young man like Roy it is better only to listen when he states his case.

Since the beginning of the year there had been political turmoil, rioting and rumours of an impending abdication by King Constantine II of Greece. A left-wing group of army officers and some prominent politicians were accused

---

[1] Dr Adenauer died on April 19th. He had been Chancellor of West Germany from 1949 until his retirement in 1963. Dr Kurt Georg Kiesinger was the present Chancellor.
[2] *The Suez Affair* (London: Weidenfeld & Nicolson, 1967).

*of military conspiracy and in mid-March eighteen accused officers were
convicted. The King found it difficult to establish a government that commanded
the confidence of the people, and, amid this uncertainty, on April 21st a group
of army officers seized power in a bloodless coup. A decree appointing the
officers appeared over the King's name, but according to some his signature
was obtained by force or even forged. The 'Colonels'.' regime finally collapsed
in the spring of 1974, and in November of that year general elections were
held and the Greeks returned to a parliamentary democratic form of government.*

Thursday, April 27th

At Cabinet the P.M. started straightaway by discussing the terrible dangers
to confidentiality created by the publication of Nutting's book. He assured
the Cabinet that the Lord Chancellor's Committee was working on the
problem of diary writers and publishers of books and I was referred to very
genially by colleague after colleague but always with a sense of moral horror.
Apparently the P.M. was content with this expression of collective feeling
because he asked for no action at all.

George Brown then reported on the military coup in Greece and told us
he was anxious to carry on without formally recognizing the new regime,
which he could do because the King had maintained a continuity of the
system. Dick Marsh, who hardly ever plunges into foreign affairs, suddenly
asked why we should carry on relations with a lot of damn dictators who
have destroyed Greek democracy. George assured him it was perfectly
normal—we were not concerned with the morality of these regimes but
with our *de facto* relations.

I said, 'Wait a second. That's not true. We can give *de facto* recognition
to this government but we don't have to give *de jure* recognition as well.' And
George Brown said, 'Why make fine distinctions? The King has maintained
continuity of the regime and made it a constitutional regime and we don't
have to make difficulties about it.' Of course I recognized the old Foreign
Office arguments; Dick Marsh and I cross-examined George for about
twenty minutes as to the rights and wrongs and all he did was to read aloud
the Foreign Office brief.

Then we turned back to the Common Market and the P.M. complained
of a terrible leak in the *Guardian*. Ian Aitken had announced the names
of eight Ministers who had met together to concert their opposition. I
suspect Harold was the only person there who really believed the Aitken
story—a ridiculous, ludicrous story. But the P.M. is the greatest reader of
the press in the Government and therefore the greatest believer in leaks.
In this case he really got a hilarious response from the rest of us because
we all knew there had been no meeting. The real trouble about the Wilson
Cabinet is that it is a set of absolutely separate individuals who *don't* meet
together and co-ordinate their work. Harold is the only conspirator.

This evening was the great Party meeting when the P.M. was to make the well-publicized statement which was to be released to the press.[1] Actually he was winding up and Manny Shinwell, to whom he was responding, had therefore released his speech to the *Evening Standard* before we heard it. Towards the end of it the Tories cleverly staged a division which made us all stream down to the Chamber and put Harold off. He spoke for rather too long, I felt, perhaps because I was waiting to get away to dine with the new correspondent of the *New York Times*, Anthony Lewis.

Friday, April 28th

I woke up to see in the papers the news of the Brierley Hill by-election. The Conservative majority of 10,000 was what we expected: indeed after his visit Tam had expected a lot worse. It only shows how deep a trough we're in after the G.L.C. defeat. Nevertheless this was only a 7 per cent swing compared to the 12 per cent of the G.L.C. I realized that since I was speaking at a Labour regional rally in Essex tonight I had to say the right thing about these defeats and I managed to prepare a decent tough speech explaining quite simply that we could have prevented all these defeats by staging a premature reflation. Instead we'd had the courage to accept our unpopularity. When I had tidied up at the office I was off with Molly driving down to Grays, which was once a village near Pelbury and is now an enormous working-class suburb. I was amazed that 323 people turned up and fortunately the press release I'd prepared was quite effective and the speech which followed it cheered them up.

Saturday, April 29th

Common Market Cabinet—day one. We were due to have two days on the Common Market—the first session in the morning at No. 10 and the second and third sessions being for a whole day at Chequers. Starting time was 10.30. I had to sit about at Vincent Square and read the papers and a piece from young Michael Stewart on devaluation, which wasn't much good, and be rung up by Nicky Kaldor, who for some extraordinary reason begged me not to raise the issue of devaluation that morning, and by then it was time to go. When I got to No. 10 I found all the officials sitting round the room. As we had agreed, each Minister brought one official with him and permitted him to intervene where he thought necessary. Of course it was a complete flop and made a hypocrisy of the whole morning session—at least until the officials withdrew. Then we started a discussion on the balance of payments with a very short statement by the Chancellor, followed by Michael Stewart. The first important speech came from Douglas Jay, who

---

[1] At the P.L.P. meeting the P.M. told back-benchers that an announcement would soon be made on the question of Britain's application to join the E.E.C. The following day, April 28th, the Council of EFTA Ministers were to meet in London and, at the weekend, Ministers were to assemble at Chequers for a two-day seminar on the subject.

launched out on his massive unanswerable demonstration that entry to the
Market would produce a balance-of-payments crisis in this country. By
the time we stopped at one o'clock one thing at least was clear. Whatever the
political and long-term economic advantages of the Common Market, entry
was going to produce a quantifiable balance-of-payments crisis and one
devaluation if not two. I suppose a morning which achieved that was a
morning well spent. And with that clear in my head I rushed out and caught
the 1.45 train to Banbury.

There was a little problem on the 1.45. I'd been compelled to travel in a
reserved compartment because the security authorities have laid it down
that a Minister can't open his red box and study his documents unless he
is in a reserved compartment which he has to himself. Now suddenly British
Railways have twigged what is up and stopped charging only for my one
first-class seat. Since I insist on having the whole compartment they now
want to charge me for six first-class seats; that means that each journey to
Banbury would cost £17. I said I wouldn't dream of seeing that bill paid
and on this occasion I sat in the buffet car and read my Cabinet minutes
there. No doubt we shall soon discover how security reacts to my solution.

On Banbury station I found the children waiting for me and we all
motored off to Fawsley. Here there is a mysterious ruined house, a series
of lakes, a wonderful park and a huge home pasture with a little chapel
in the middle of it. We had a splendid time up behind the lakes tracking
the stream and then we got back to Prescote in time for the children's
television programme.

In the evening Anne and I went off to High Wycombe for the first annual
dinner of the Chiltern Society. It's run by Christopher Hall and Jennie, his
wife, who had to give up work for me and who is now working for Chris
on the news-sheet of the Chiltern Society. I found it a tremendously dynamic,
lively gathering—a wholly middle-class society full of old friends from the
time I lived at Town End Farm,[1] and even older friends from the time I
ran my three-year W.E.A. tutorial class at Princes Risborough and at
Slough. At the top table we found those nice people the Eshers with whom
I had dinner at the R.I.B.A. on the night when I upset Matthew Stevenson.
I made a racy speech about the dynamic of planning and how we must
have pressure from below to make it effective. It was a lovely evening and
we spent the night with my step-daughter Venice and Christopher Barry
at their home at Stokenchurch.

Sunday, April 30th
At 9.30 Barbara picked me up in her ministerial car and swept me off to
Chequers. The morning sitting which started at 10.30 was supposed to be
a second reading session. That meant that a lot of people made long policy

---

[1] Richard Crossman and his second wife, Zita, bought Town End Cottage, Radnage,
just before the war and kept it as a weekend cottage until Zita's death in 1952.

declarations. Apart from Tony Wedgwood Benn, who is Minister of Technology and who has now been converted for technological reasons into an ardent Common Marketeer, no one seemed to have changed his mind.

I sat next to Harold at lunch and throughout the meal he kept on talking about the press and ribbing me for being too kind a Christian to the journalists and giving them far too much. I felt awkward because in fact I now don't see many journalists. I see Alan Watkins of the *Spectator* regularly but nobody else. Indeed, I doubt if I see more than one journalist a week apart, of course, from my official briefing of the Lobby on Thursdays. But Harold believes that I do and holds me responsible for any number of leaks and in all this George Wigg plays a great role. When he'd finished attacking me he launched a great attack on the journalists themselves and told us all that we should never talk to them or trust them—except the few who were good. I pricked up my ears and said, 'Tell us, who are the good ones?' And he said, 'Well, *The Economist* is quite good now.' 'What about *The Times*?' I said. And he replied that Ian Trethowan and David Wood are utterly hopeless and nobody should talk to anybody from *The Times* at all. 'What about the *Guardian*?' I asked and he answered that Francis Boyd is now wholly hostile and shouldn't be talked to. One I didn't ask about was Jimmy Margach of the *Sunday Times*. In this week's issue there's a really very embittered account, obviously given by an insider, of my ignominious failure to take over as Minister in charge of Transport House and of how I am now generally detested there. It hasn't come directly from Harold but it's certainly come from one of his contact men—either George (with his wonderful anti-leak machine), Gerald Kaufman or No. 10. However, I had the sense to seal my lips and let him go on talking now about a particularly scandalous leak in the *Daily Mail* which has revealed the full details of our decision to withdraw from the mainland in Malaya. 'That was dastardly,' said Harold 'and I know where it came from.' 'So do I,' I said. The main difficulty about it is that he wants to be omnipotent and feels very jealous of anybody else having contacts in Fleet Street, particularly anybody he considers as a rival.

When the afternoon session was over Harold turned to Burke Trend and me and remarked, 'In what other country in the world could the Cabinet sustain a debate for four hours at that level?' I thought the discussion had been pretty good in the relaxed atmosphere of Chequers but that seemed to me a high-flying claim. In fact nobody said anything new except Harold himself, who wound up very briefly by saying that this was an informal discussion and that therefore no vote would be taken and no formal conclusions minuted. Formal decisions would be postponed until next Tuesday when he would present a draft Statement in the same way as he had last November. Having said this he added that there would be a cold collation downstairs and no doubt people would want to get off fairly soon.

Obviously his only concern this evening was to see that no decision and nothing approaching a decision was taken which could be reported in Monday morning's newspapers.

The Chief and I thought, 'Well, well, that's that,' and we drove up to London together and had an excellent dinner in Chelsea to discuss our impressions. First of all what changes had occurred since last November? Certainly the biggest change was the attitude of the Prime Minister. After the last Chequers conference he had told me that he would be going round Europe with George Brown to make sure that he didn't commit us to anything and to make sure that the tour was nothing more than a probe. Well, he certainly converted himself during those visits to the six capitals and at Chequers this time he was as enthusiastic as George Brown. Indeed, apart from Wedgy Benn he's the only convert.

But although there have been very few conversions there's been a very big shift in opinion in two respects. In the first place the economic advantages which Common Marketeers used to point out are now seen to be acute economic difficulties in the short run. Not even the most ardent marketeer now denies that entry in our present economic plight will expose the pound to the gravest dangers and that there'll have to be one devaluation if not two. It would also expose us to even greater deflationary pressure unless we can get growth going before we go in. So we all see now that the Common Market in the short run is far less economically attractive and even Roy Jenkins admits that in the first three or four years we shall lose but not gain—it's only after we're in, after our economy has been reorganized, that there's a chance of profiting from membership.

The other shift in opinion relates to our own economy. Those who are in charge—Michael Stewart, George Brown, Harold Wilson, Jim Callaghan —all now feel that the attempt to have a socialist national plan for the British Isles keeps us balanced on such a terribly tight rope that it really has got to be abandoned and that of course is the main reason why they favour entry into the Market. Today Barbara made a tremendous speech saying that entry would transform our socialism and make us abandon all our plans. In a sense she's completely right. If anybody wanted, apart from myself, Britain to be a socialist offshore island, entry to the Market would mean the abandonment of that ideal. Up to the July freeze it was still possible to believe that we in the Wilson Government would strip ourselves of the sterling area, withdraw from East of Suez, and take the Swedish line of socialism. We could have done that a year ago but now it is felt by almost everyone that it's too late. The thing I shall remember most from this Chequers conference was Jim Callaghan's admission at yesterday morning's debate in our talk about devaluation. In reply to my challenge he said that if we devalue now it's the Tories who will benefit in three or four years' time. (Of course the reply to this is that if we'd done it in 1964 we should have been benefiting before the next election.) But now it's too late. The socialist insular offshore island solution which we could still have had after the 1966 election is now desperately dangerous even to attempt.

Barbara has been the most interesting person at this conference. When she drove me across to Chequers this morning she had decided to attack Harold for four or five hours and then having attacked him to let him have his negotiations but on the stiffest possible condition. By lunch-time she was furious with me and asked me why I wasn't helping. I told her quite truthfully that I had decided to spend the morning extracting from the Chancellor his real views about the future of sterling and about parity with the dollar. In this I was successful. For example, I got out of him the astonishing statement that as long as he was Chancellor there wouldn't be a devaluation and that he had made personal promises of such a sort that he would have to leave the Treasury before there could be any question of altering parity. That seems to me pretty important and I don't think it embarrasses Harold Wilson at all since he shares Jim's view about devaluation and is just as opposed to it. All this I put to Barbara in self-defence and I ended by saying, 'As for your last-ditch resistance before you gave way—which all of us knew you were going to do—that wasn't for me to take part in.' I'm afraid John Silkin didn't say very much at dinner that evening—it consisted mostly of me dashing off my impressions. But there's one of his impressions which I mustn't forget. In the discussion he had given a carefully considered calculation of the amount of resistance Harold would have to expect in the Parliamentary Party which he didn't think would exceed more than fifty or so. At dinner he told me that he was convinced that Harold had learnt everything he needed from the meeting. He knew exactly the strength of the Opposition and he knew that he now had an overwhelming majority ready to permit him not merely to seek to enter the Market but to make a genuine bid to get in as soon as possible.

Monday, May 1st
Lying in bed this morning I read a characteristic piece by Ian Aitken in the *Guardian*. He claims he knows exactly how the Cabinet is divided. *Yes:* Crossman, Brown, Jenkins, Longford, Cledwyn Hughes, Gunter. *Yes if:* Wilson, Benn, Gordon Walker, Stewart. *Maybe:* Callaghan. *No unless:* Gardiner, Crosland, Marsh, Bowden. *No:* Greenwood, Ross, Castle, Peart, Healey, Jay. I find this a characteristically inaccurate piece of mixed leak and guesswork. The division seems to me to be: *Yes without qualification:* Wilson, Brown, Stewart, Jenkins, Crosland, Gardiner, Jones, Benn, Gunter, Longford. *No without qualification:* Jay, Peart, Healey, Castle, Ross, Marsh, Bowden. *Maybe:* Callaghan, Crossman, Gordon Walker, Greenwood, Silkin, Cledwyn Hughes. That makes ten unqualified supporters. Seven unqualified opponents, and six in the middle. But if one is to be realistic one has to add that this greatly exaggerates Harold's difficulties, since the six of us who are in the middle are nearly all convinced that if any approach

is to be made it should be made quickly with a will. This means that on the issue immediately before him Harold has sixteen on his side and only seven against. Lying in bed and reflecting on this list I felt bound to ring up Harold—a thing I don't often do these days. 'I don't often give you advice,' I said, 'but on this occasion I will. Your danger now is not too much dis-agreement but too much agreement—that you'll get no resignation on Tuesday morning. I just want to say that you must on no account tone down the draft in any way in order to win anybody over. Your sole concern should be to make a Statement which will have the best possible effect in Europe, not to make a Statement in order to placate any of your colleagues.' Harold replied, 'I think I agree with you.' But he's still not quite sure whether Douglas will resign. 'He's been talking to me as though he would,' he said. 'Well,' I said, 'don't worry about that. It would make quite a difference and you should want him to do it.'

Before I left Vincent Square the Prime Minister had rung me back and asked me to look in and see the draft Statement. 'You and George Brown are the only two who will see it,' he said. I checked that evening and he was right. So I went in to see the draft, which I thought much too long and cumbersome. I got it shortened at various points, but mostly he resisted, and wherever I could I took out any kind of weakening words which implied we were writing conditions into the Statement. He seemed quite pleased and almost grateful for the help.

At ten o'clock this morning Eric Heffer brought in his Live Hare Coursing (Abolition) Bill. We've had great difficulty to know what to put into morning sittings. One soon runs out of prayers and completely non-controversial minor measures and we're limited by the fact that we can't afford more than one division in any one morning. The reason we gave Eric Heffer the right to start his Bill there is because the P.M. was keen and it will fill two whole morning sittings, but the chances of it getting very far after the Second Reading are very small.

Across to the Cabinet Office, where there was a fascinating meeting of the Cabinet Economic Committee on Barbara's paper on concessionary fares. However, I'll deal with this on Thursday when the paper has reached Cabinet.

This afternoon the debate in the House was on the F–111–V contract with Denis Healey mounting a powerful counter-attack against Enoch Powell. I got in to hear the Minister and his number two, John Stonehouse, being attacked from behind by Maurice Edelman with some singularly insulting and difficult questions simply designed to floor them. It made me realize how many people we have now on the back benches who are motivated primarily by resentment. Maurice's attitude is almost entirely due to the fact that he didn't get the job he obviously deserved—like John Cronin for whom I shall be speaking at Loughborough on Friday.[1] Both

[1] Dr John Cronin, Labour M.P. for Loughborough since 1955.

of them came into politics more or less at the same time and they can't help feeling exasperated that they've been denied the chance of making their mark. I wonder if the Prime Minister realizes the danger of creating enemies by all his shuffling and reshuffling?

Later this evening we came back to the motion on the Finance Bill which we'd discussed already in the procedure debate and again in a morning sitting. Now we were due to finish it and the Tories knew we would get a closure soon after eleven.

There were only two really striking speeches, one by Ramsden, who used to be the Under-Secretary of State for War,[1] and the other from Douglas Glover, who doubted whether I knew what I was talking about. 'What makes me suspicious,' he said, 'is that the Rt. Hon. Gentleman the Leader of the House, during thirteen years of opposition was conspicuously absent from a detailed discussion of Bills. He came here on many significant occasions, thrilled the House with his oratory, then went away to some other activity. He was rarely present in the early hours of the morning for detailed Committee Stages. With the greatest respect to him—I think that he is learning—but he does not understand how the House of Commons works not even with some of his own procedures.'

That was a damaging attack and I had to reply at the end when our people were getting impatient for the vote. This reply was a real test as to whether I'd recovered my authority as Leader of the House. I just about managed to do it. When I dealt with Glover they tried to shout me down and knock me off. It was the roughest House I've had as Lord President (apart from the business Statement) and a bit scaring. When we came to the division Enoch Powell and Iain Macleod were both on the front bench leading their back-bench rebels into the lobby. There were some sixty of them, whereas the rest followed Selwyn Lloyd's advice and remained silent.[2] Of course this revolt undermined all the work which the Tory Chief Whip and Selwyn Lloyd had done to work out a method of moving forward to a major agreed reform of procedure. But they'd also enormously strengthened my hand in the next Session when I shall be able to impose on the House by a three-line whip the proposal to put the Finance Bill upstairs.

After the debate I found Selwyn mooning along the lobby. He looks pretty broken now, I must say, and it's all because of Nutting's book. Coming out ten years after the Suez affair, it shows that Nutting has forgotten none of the ill-feeling and a basinful of dirt is poured on the unfortunate Selwyn, who's made to look a complete jackass. Selwyn said to me, 'Of course I'll never forgive him. When he tried to get back into the House and got a constituency at Oldham he asked me to speak for him! Now he does this to me.' Then he looked at me and said, 'What

---

[1] James Ramsden, Conservative M.P. for Harrogate 1954–74. He was Secretary of State for War 1963–4.

[2] The vote on the main Question was 194 in favour and 50 against.

about the debate?' 'I shan't hurry back, my dear Selwyn,' I said. 'Anyway there are two quite separate issues—the issue of the responsibility of the Eden Government to Parliament when it invaded Egypt and the issue of Nutting's behaviour in breaching Cabinet confidentiality. I don't see how we shall avoid a debate but I shall just make a short Statement.' 'I shall walk out,' he said and stalked off down the passage. I've got to know him very well in these weeks because he really cares about reform and he's an extremely loyal and decent member of the Services Committee. He's hurt by Nutting's behaviour because he finds it unintelligible and intolerable that he should be the man who is the prime sufferer as the result of the Suez fiasco.

Tuesday, May 2nd

Cabinet was called solely to approve the draft of the Statement Harold was to make this afternoon. There was no sign of resignation or protest: everybody worked very happily together, trying to improve it by minor amendments but nobody dared to move it an inch away from the form in which it had been drafted. I was tickled by the P.M. who started by apologizing that the draft had not been circulated the night before as expected or even this morning. The reason was that he had been writing it in longhand, he said, late into the night. When I heard this I must admit that I assumed it would look very different from what I had seen on Monday afternoon. But in fact it was the same draft and nothing had been done to it since then except to make the smallest possible changes. When Harold lies he does so with a good conscience. No doubt he had done some minor tinkering in longhand which gave him the excuse for this apology.

We then had a long discussion about the timing of the three-day debate. Should it be next Monday, Tuesday, Wednesday or Tuesday, Wednesday, Thursday? The Chief wanted the latter because the Opposition had asked for it and also because his wife was very keen to attend the great dinner in the Painted Hall at Greenwich for King Feisal on Wednesday evening.[1] I said that the Chief's proposal was quite impossible because of the borough elections on Thursday. If we were to order our people to turn up for a three-line whip on Thursday evening we should never be forgiven by any provincial Member. The provincial M.P. reckons that one part of the stint he does for the local authority is to appear on that last day, walking round, knocking up, doing a bit of loudspeakering and turning up at the count. Occasionally one isn't asked to do this. Coventry, for instance, this year decided not to have any of their M.P.s in Coventry at all because we are so unpopular and they do not want to be associated with us. But still, we must be available—we must ring up. I, for instance, rang up the Party Secretary, Albert Rose, and my Party agent, Winnie Lakin, and made it clear that I would come over at a moment's notice. They said they would much prefer

[1] King Feisal of Saudi Arabia was to arrive on May 9th for an eight-day State visit.

me not to put in an appearance. But I think in this case the Coventry Labour Group is being unusually beastly and also unusually cowardly. They would do far better if they dared to stick up for the Government.

The great Statement on the E.E.C. this afternoon went very quietly.[1] What stood out was Shinwell's threat of relentless opposition and Heffer's courageous reply calling him an ancient Briton. All the conflict and tension in fact was on our side of the House. But the P.M. didn't put a foot wrong and I was able to say to him afterwards in his room, 'Well, that's a perfectly conducted operation.' But I didn't feel it was in any way a historic moment, mainly because I don't see that anything has changed in France and I'm certain the French will play us along and keep us standing in humiliation on the doorstep. The real question we have to answer is at what point we shall break off this attempt to get in and turn aside to the new policy of devaluation+ which we shall have to impose and which will include a total withdrawal from East of Suez and a dose of old-fashioned insular socialism. Or will it?

This evening I had a surprise. The P.M. asked a group of us to keep eight o'clock free. I got there a bit early with Tommy and there Harold was with some rather soggy sandwiches on a table in front of him and drinks at the side which he was providing for Tony Wedgwood Benn, Peter Shore, Marcia, Gerald Kaufman, Tommy and myself. It was the old gang brought together at last. As we were all leaving two hours later, after a perfectly sensible discussion, Wedgy said to me that when he's summoned to a meeting of the old gang he feels there must be something seriously wrong with Party morale. That's a bit cynical but it's also true. Harold called his old friends in because he's alarmed by the devastating losses in the G.L.C. and fears more devastating losses on Thursday. I tried out on him the idea of getting a new broom into Transport House. There was a long discussion of whom we could put in instead of Len Williams and he suggested Vic Feather: 'He's only got three or four years to run at the T.U.C. but he's number two to George Woodcock and thoroughly sick of being number two.'[2] It's true enough. If Len were given a life peerage and Vic put in his place next January it might do a lot for the Party.

Wednesday, May 3rd

Before morning prayers I filled in the Chief on the most important things which have happened at the old gang meeting. In particular we had discussed Harold's idea for a speech on the great leap forward which had occurred in the last twelve months and we had all told him there hadn't been a great

[1] 'Her Majesty's Government have today decided to make an application under Article 237 of the Treaty of Rome for membership of the European Economic Community, and parallel applications for membership of the European Coal and Steel Community and Euratom.'

[2] Vic Feather joined the T.U.C. staff in 1937 and served as Assistant General Secretary 1960–69 and General Secretary 1969–73. He became a life peer in 1974. He died in 1976.

leap forward. But at morning prayers we concentrated on how to conduct the Party meeting and what should happen about the vote on the E.E.C. We knew already that the Tories were going to have a three-line whip because Heath had insisted on this at the 1922 Committee. This made our choice a great deal easier. My own inclination was for a free vote and I know Douglas Houghton wanted it too. As I told the P.M., 'We should summon all the M.P.s with a three-line whip so as to get a big attendance and then give them freedom to vote according to their conscience.' But the Chief was very much against this idea, which he said is not in our tradition. 'Well,' I said, 'that's the way the Tories will work it. They'll get a big House but they won't do anything to the people who are anti.'

On this point the Chief was very strongly supported by the P.M., who insisted that there would have to be discipline if anyone voted against the three-line whip. I pointed out that this would be awkward with Shinwell and Michael Foot as the two chief rebel leaders in the Opposition lobby. We decided that we would have a Wednesday morning meeting of the Party where the line should be laid down and the Party informed that abstention was allowed but not a hostile vote.

I lunched with Geoffrey Rhodes, who told me that the Ministry of Housing had just announced the Minister's decision on Newcastle. Greenwood is not going to proceed with the Crossman plan for a single one-tier authority for Greater Tyneside.[1] Tony had come to see me a fortnight ago with Ted Short and two other Newcastle M.P.s and told me that he felt he couldn't do it. I said I felt this was a great failure of willpower and was not surprised to find that Ted Short and his colleagues were wholly on my side. Of course it would have needed fighting through, but in a Greater Tyneside we'd have secured a Labour majority and held it.

This afternoon the Tory Chief Whip came in to see me. After we'd talked about some minor procedural matters I warned him about Nutting's book and told him the two big issues the Cabinet was considering. I emphasized that confidentiality was considered by Harold to be quite separate from the merits of the Suez adventure.

This talk made me late for the meeting of the Cabinet Pensions Committee of which I am chairman. This brought me a tremendous disappointment. I had hoped that it would be decided to get the Bill on the statute book and the new graded contributions being paid before the election. I was told that this is out of the question and that Peggy Herbison's very slow timetable is the best we can manage. My difficulty is that both the Ministry officials and the Chancellor don't want to have the scheme working before the election. So I can't get a move on. It's a dreadful pity.

At seven o'clock I went home to dinner with Anne in order to tidy up my diary. Then back for the 9.30 vote and a couple of hours of chats round the lobby and the tea-room. I know now that I'm bound to stay in this job for

[1] See Vol. I, pp. 347–8.

a year or more and I've got to get to know back-bench M.P.s without being accused of being an intellectual slumming in the tea-room. It's a pleasant relaxing way of spending one's time, though it doesn't stretch me intellectually or administratively. But I'm getting the habit of it and feel more content.

Thursday, May 4th

The main item at Cabinet was a paper from Peggy Herbison proposing an increase in the O.A.P. of ten shillings which was opposed by the Chancellor who was insisting on cutting it to eight. I was in a fix because I would have voted for eight shillings if I could have been sure that the extra two shillings would have gone to family endowment. Then the Chancellor proposed a nine shilling compromise. But the majority of the Cabinet voted for ten, mostly out of sheer sentimentality.

By far the most interesting item on the agenda was Barbara Castle's plan for concessionary fares. The first law we ever passed in 1964 gave munici-palities the right to give concessionary fares on their transport services and this has been shoved through owing to the desire of our Chief Whip, Ted Short, whose favourite Private Member's Bill it was. As so often happens, this single concession had created a huge number of anomalies, particularly as it did not apply to those bus services which were not municipalized. So here was Barbara trying to tidy the whole thing up and it was quite clear from her paper that she was creating a lot more anomalies especially as she couldn't deal with London and had to leave out children's concessions. Moreover, if the concessions were fully taken up it would have cost some £9 million a year. Last week this was all argued out at length in the Cabinet Committee under Gordon Walker's chairmanship. He said Barbara couldn't pre-empt £9 million before the big July get-together when the case for her concessionary fares could have been measured against school milk, etc. I strongly supported Patrick Gordon Walker and the conclusion in the official minutes of the meeting runs, 'The Minister without Portfolio concluded his summing up by saying "If the Minister wishes to pursue the matter further in advance of the review he would be glad to discuss it with her. But in accordance with the Prime Minister's request to the Cabinet she should not seek to raise the matter in the Cabinet in advance of the review except in agreement with himself or the P.M." ' Patrick tells me that he got an assurance that Barbara wouldn't go to the P.M. But she couldn't resist the temptation to exploit the goodwill she enjoys with Harold because she knew how keen he was on concessionary fares. And the P.M. had put it on the Cabinet agenda.

In this case Prime Ministerial government did not work. Harold came in early on with an extraordinary speech. He rebuked the Home Affairs Committee for showing no understanding of the issue involved and said we were committed to it by our election programme. I got more and more irritated and broke in to say that it was absurd to accuse us of showing any misunderstanding. Barbara had no right to pre-empt the money before the July review. At this point Harold began to outline his own personal proposals, which were duly torn to shreds. I don't think there was a single person round that table—because Ted Short wasn't there—who had much sympathy with Barbara. She was behaving pretty badly, though I must add that she was behaving in a way which I had often adopted as Minister of Housing, trying to force her way through the Cabinet with the help of the P.M. But in this case the Cabinet was absolutely solid against her and we managed to stop the P.M. despite his lengthy account to us of the problems of Huyton where people in Liverpool overspill houses on one side of the road had no concessionary fares and people in Huyton council houses managed to get them. But it was no good. He was forced to withdraw.

When making the business Statement this afternoon I found myself faced with an awkward problem. For once an Early Day Motion had become of real significance.[1] Two hundred and seventy-five members had signed one claiming that twelve British officers should not have been denied their share of the £1 million hand-out from the German Government to the victims of the Nazis since they had been prisoners of war in Sachsenhausen concentration camp. The Foreign Secretary has gone into this at length and George had convinced Harold that these officers are really quite well-off people. But Airey Neave[2] (an ex-P.O.W. himself) is an extremely adroit lobbyist and he has mobilized David Ginsburg[3] and John Mendelson, who both are Jews, as his supporters. I felt the House was against me when I firmly refused a debate and tried to push it off on to the new Parliamentary Commissioner. But otherwise my Questions went well—for the third time running.

At my press conference with the Lobby upstairs I dealt with the Nutting book. This morning I had got Cabinet to accept my view that we should go slow and keep the issue of confidentiality separate from the issue of collusion. In the afternoon I filled the Lobby in at considerable length and I'm expecting quite a successful reaction, at least in the quality press.

This evening at my business meeting with the P.M. Burke raised the matter and made it perfectly clear that he and he alone had taken the decision about Nutting's book because the Prime Minister, like any other Labour Minister, must be denied access to the minutes of the other side and doesn't therefore know whether Nutting's account of the Suez Cabinets is correct or not. So the Secretary to the Cabinet becomes the independent

[1] Early Day Motion No. 518.
[2] Conservative M.P. for Abingdon since July 1953. He was Joint Parliamentary Secretary at the Ministry of Transport and Civil Aviation 1957–9 and Parliamentary Under-Secretary of State for Air 1959. He has been a member of the Commons' Select Committee on Science and Technology since 1967 and its chairman 1970–74.
[3] Labour M.P. for Dewsbury since 1959.

arbiter in such affairs and in this respect he's played a role as important as
that of the monarch a hundred years ago.

Friday, May 5th

At my office I gave the O.K. to the final draft of the Bristol-Siddeley report.
Freddy Ward had done an excellent job which I'd worked over and redictated. It will be presented for recess reading to the P.M. at the end of
next week.

I was just in time for an important meeting of the Home Affairs Committee
on Welsh local government. I've recorded in this diary the disastrous
occasion months ago when I lost my temper at the prospect of the Welsh
going ahead and reorganizing their local government in an incredibly
reactionary way in advance of the English. Well, the Secretary of State is
back with a draft White Paper and I realized I couldn't make the same
mistake twice. While I was sitting in the Committee a simple solution struck
me. Cledwyn Hughes complained that he'd had to water down the proposal
for a Welsh regional council and I thought, 'That's terrible. They're going
to get the worst of both worlds—an antiquated local government reform
and a futile Welsh national council.' Why not accept this local government
reorganization as a political necessity and then go for a really ambitious
plan for a Welsh Council or Parliament? The P.M. has several times said
that the question of decentralization and regional government—Welsh
nationalism, Scottish nationalism—might become the most explosive issue
at the next election.

Now this is where Cabinet Committees can be important. I was on my
own. Everybody else had a departmental brief and they made no real
objections. It was virtually agreed—and then I put forward my idea. If,
as I think we have to, we agree to local government reform, then we ought
to hold up the recommendations on the Welsh Council and think of something more drastic—we must see this in terms of the great constitutional
issue of the day, decentralization. I got it referred to the Environmental
Planning Committee on the one side and a small committee of Ministers
on the other, and I sent in a report to Harold Wilson.

This is the kind of thing which Lord Presidents and Ministers without
Portfolio are supposed to do. Anyway, I felt pleased.

Back in my office I found the new Director of the National Portrait
Gallery waiting to see me.[1] He'd come to see how I'd hung the two pictures
he'd offered me, Halifax and Prince Frederick. He was so overwhelmed by
the magnificent sight of their hanging in that room against the magnificent
wallpaper that after a drink he allowed them both to stay and in return I
invited him to attend the Trooping of the Colour.

---

[1] Dr Roy Strong, Director, Keeper and Secretary of the National Portrait Gallery,
where he succeeded Sir Philip Hendy in 1967, until 1974, when he became Director of
the Victoria and Albert Museum.

At the Garrick lunch for the journalists I found there was a great deal of discontent with the P.M. I tried to explain why he wasn't going to have the Lobby back and told them that they must get used to having me.

After that I caught a train to Birmingham, where I had a splendid rough meeting with the Birmingham University Socialist Students—two hours of argument. Then home by train to Leamington, where Anne met me and brought me to Prescote.

The White Paper (Cmnd. 3269) *announced the Government's intention to apply for entry to the E.E.C., and both Mr Heath and Mr Wilson refused to allow their Parties a free vote on this proposal. Labour and Conservative back-benchers had tabled motions of amendment withholding approval from the decision, but in the event the Government's motion was carried by 488 votes to 62. Fifty-one Labour back-benchers abstained and into the No lobby went 34 Labour M.P.s and 2 tellers, 26 Conservatives, 1 Liberal and the Welsh Nationalist. A similar Government motion was approved in the House of Lords on May 9th without a division.*

Monday, May 8th

The first day of the big E.E.C. debate.[1] The Prime Minister has told me several times that he'd prepared a speech of Gladstonian length and consistency. Well, it was certainly long but it was also good and concise.[2] There we were all lined up on the front bench and we sat there from 3.30 until five or thereabouts. I found it difficult to listen to simply because I'd heard it so often before during those eight interminable Cabinet meetings. Every argument had been chewed over and over and the P.M.'s own formulations as they came out were already familiar. I left the debate at five to attend the Labour Party inquiry committee. This has been going on regularly week after week but I am not there very much because I recognize that it's completely ineffective. At this meeting, for example, we were discussing the re-shaping of the National Executive and the paper proposed that we should only have a couple of sub-committees and things should really be run by a very powerful General Secretary. I share the malaise of the rest of the Committee and I'm still wondering whether to stand for the Executive or not. Once or twice recently I've been asked by the press whether I've made up my mind. Well I have made up my mind but now in this appallingly critical year I'm wondering whether I can walk out. Partly it would be decided by what the Coventry East Labour Party thinks. We're going to have a meeting at Prescote one day this summer and talk it over.

---

[1] The debate on membership of the E.E.C. was held on May 8th, 9th and 10th.
[2] He rose at 3.31 and sat down at 4.56.

Tuesday, May 9th

The main item at Cabinet was Stansted Airport.[1] It was the second occasion on which we had discussed this problem. At the first all sorts of Ministers who hadn't been briefed, including George Brown and Jim Callaghan, rushed in to say we couldn't afford it or they didn't like it. Well, it had now been brought back to Cabinet but this time everybody had been adequately briefed by their Departments; it's sometimes amusing to see the change when this happens. I don't know who briefed George Brown but he laid off his attack altogether and the Chancellor remained virtually silent as well. As for the P.M. he'd obviously been convinced there was no alternative.

The man who made the most effective contribution was Wedgy Benn, who's coming out more and more as a strong character. He made the sensible observation that if you're going to live in a modern technological age you've got to have a modern airport somewhere near London. I supported him, saying that this was one of the occasions when delay had determined the decision. Stansted was now the only place because we'd been waiting nine or ten years for the final decision and everyone, particularly the Air Ministry, had made a whole series of decisions based on that assumption. For example, that was the reason why Silverstone has been excluded, though it would otherwise have been suitable. My difficulty was that the man who is in charge of the Stansted project is Douglas Jay and when he combines with Tony Greenwood at Housing one gets the worst representation possible, particularly when they're opposed by such highly capable people as Roy, ex-Minister of Aviation, who has always been opposed to Stansted, and Tony Crosland. Roy reminded Cabinet that it was I who had set up the public inquiry which had not favoured Stansted. At that inquiry, as I pointed out, the Inspector was not allowed to consider whether there were real alternatives and just before I left the Ministry I set up an interdepartmental inquiry to make recommendations on this issue and they had come back to Stansted as the only site for an airport in the early future. The decision had been taken very reluctantly.

At this point the P.M. suddenly began to talk about Specialist Committees, which were not on the agenda, and I noticed he had in front of him a little note from George Brown. I heard that George had been upset when he

---

[1] It had been decided in 1954 that, in principle, the third London airport should be sited at Stansted in Essex. There was a public outcry against the proposal, which would not only invade valuable agricultural land but would also ruin acres of hitherto unspoilt countryside. A public inquiry was held between December 1965 and February 1966 (see Vol. I, p. 624) and the Inspector recommended that, although Stansted was possible from an air-traffic point of view, it would be disastrous for the neighbourhood, and that the Government should undertake a further review of the whole problem. The Government consulted other experts and in a White Paper in May (Cmnd. 3259) announced the decision to put the airport at Stansted. When Anthony Crosland succeeded Douglas Jay at the Board of Trade in August 1967 a further inquiry was held into the Stansted site. There was continued opposition and, in May 1969, yet another inquiry drew up a short-list of four sites, ruling out Stansted altogether.

heard that the Science and Technology Committee wants to study Euratom, which he thinks might upset his negotiations, and that the Committee is also proposing to visit New York. At once other Ministers started complaining, and I had to defend the Specialist Committees impromptu as best I could; I realized I would spend most of my time this week trying to mend fences. But there's no doubt their importance is growing. This was shown yesterday morning when Wedgy Benn was the first Minister to appear in a public session before a Committee and submit himself to cross-examination. However, he was rebuked for absenting himself from Cabinet. It's obvious that Whitehall is putting great pressure on Harold and that he's now in two minds. When he's alone with me he's always in favour of Specialist Committees but in Cabinet he's always accepting Ministerial objections.

After this Harold allowed the Cabinet to discuss whether there should be a free vote after the Common Market debate or whether we should impose a three-line whip. Roy Jenkins and Herbert Bowden claimed that it was for Cabinet to decide. Sheer nonsense, of course, since it's the Chief Whip and the Parliamentary Party who have the right. Nevertheless, Cabinet did minute that there shouldn't be a free vote though it had no power to do so. When the division takes place this will face John Silkin with a terrible dilemma which would have been avoided if we had only conceded a free vote on the grounds that this was a unique unprecedented occasion.

Day two of the great debate on the Common Market began with a speech from the Leader of the Opposition. Poor man. Though the Labour Party has collapsed in the Gallup Poll and the P.M.'s position has fallen by ten points, Ted Heath has made no progress at all. We were all curious to see how he would do. It was quite an able contribution, neat and precise, if rather pedantic. Then at the end he made a great effort to raise the morale of the Conservative Party by expressing his belief in the European nuclear deterrent. But all he achieved by this was to give Harold a chance to shake him by some questioning, an opportunity Harold duly took.[1]

After this Harold and I went out to discuss the situation with Douglas Houghton and the Chief. I watched Douglas being swung away from his preference for the free vote and being forced to admit that there must be a three-line whip where discipline would be enforced if anyone voted against but where the right of abstention was preserved. I had invited all the chairmen of Select Committees to have dinner with me and the Chief Whip as well as the chairman of the Party. Willie Hamilton, chairman of Estimates, Donald Chapman, chairman of Procedure, Ian Mikardo, chairman of Nationalized Industries, and Palmer, chairman of Science and Technology,[2]

[1] See *Wilson*, pp. 389–90.
[2] Arthur Palmer, Labour M.P. for Wimbledon 1945–50, for Cleveland, Yorkshire, October 1952 to September 1959, for Bristol Central 1964–74 and for Bristol North-East since 1974. Chairman of the Commons' Select Committee on Science and Technology 1966–70, he has held that office again since 1974.

all turned up. The only absentee was Tudor Watkins, chairman of Agriculture. In the light of the harassment I'd suffered at Cabinet that morning this meeting was absolutely invaluable and we had a most sensible discussion before we went into the Chamber to hear Fred Peart wind up for the Government. It was a perfectly correct speech on agriculture but owing to the skill of our back-benchers in cheering all the passages which were critical of the Market it was made to look a thoroughly prejudiced attack by an anti-Marketeer. I went home convinced we were in for trouble in tomorrow's division.

When I was chatting with the Prime Minister there was a little incident I would like to record. We were just checking over on the routine for the Party meeting that morning when I told him how all the papers had the story that Tommy Balogh was due to go back to Oxford and I added that all these experts seemed to be petering out. 'Then Michael Stewart is off to Nairobi, I heard, and Robert Neild to Stockholm. I'm told they're all disillusioned because the Government isn't doing well.'[1] The P.M., puffing his pipe, looked at me and with a broad smile said, 'Well the fact is we're not doing very well, are we?' And he said it so coolly and with such realism. Sometimes he faces reality with extraordinary intellectual courage and equanimity, yet at other times he's a tremendous escapist who shirks the problem. We are doing very badly, we're in a tough patch—he faces that perfectly clearly and knows we're going to have a disaster when the borough election results appear in Friday's newspapers.

I was anxious as we went across to the Party meeting but actually it was one of the best I've ever been to. The debate was a serious sustained discussion of the basis of discipline. The anti-Marketeers all pleaded that this was an exceptional occasion and that a free vote should be allowed. But they were answered by a number of extremely capable speeches, the first by, of all people, Arthur Woodburn. As he got up the Chief and I thought, 'My God, the whole Party's in favour of a free vote and Arthur Woodburn will strengthen the feeling.' But actually he spoke very well. Then the Chief got up and made a tremendous oration. John Silkin lives on his nerves and he's been under a tremendous strain this week. Afterwards I agreed with the Prime Minister when he said that his speech was one which neither of us could conceivably have made. 'He's shown himself a real Chief Whip,' said Harold and I felt just the same. That is a man who has political leadership in him.

I specially went into the House to hear Manny Shinwell. Everybody around was calling it a most powerful speech. I thought he was a ham old actor hamming his way through his part. Then Anne and I were off to the Painted Hall in Greenwich where King Feisal was being entertained. I'd

[1] Michael Stewart served as economic adviser to the Kenya Treasury 1967–9. Robert Neild, who had been an economic adviser to the Treasury since 1964, in 1967 became director of the International Peace Research Institute in Stockholm.

always wanted to see the Painted Hall by artificial light and I got Anne to come and to wear her new evening dress for the second time. It was a beautiful evening as we motored down and as there was no traffic we got there far too early and went up to the top of the meridian. Back in the anteroom of the Painted Hall we stood about for ages waiting for the King and his retinue. When they arrived I behaved rather badly. Frank Longford had come up to me and complained that we weren't all to be presented to His Majesty. I replied angrily that I didn't want to be presented to him. There was George Brown trying to ingratiate himself with the Saudi Arabians by talking about our common religious background. I found the whole thing pretty odious so as soon as we'd had dinner and admired the hall I got back to the Commons, where Michael Stewart was making his winding-up speech. There was a steady hum of conversation which went on even after the Speaker's rebuke. Everybody was waiting for the votes. When they came it showed that there were some twenty-six Tories and thirty of our own people in the Opposition lobby.[1] A lot of our abstainers had skulked out. I noticed the Whips were working closely together. Willie and John know each other intimately and like each other, and it's far more convenient when the two machines are working together than when they're working against each other. On these occasions you see what a great cahoots there is between the two big Parties. I watched the abstainers slipping out and I saw a few proud rebels striding into the no-division lobby and I didn't feel any great elation. I felt gloom and depression and knew that we had trouble ahead.

Lord Shackleton had now been in Aden since mid-April pursuing the delicate negotiations between FLOSY and the N.L.F., and on May 11th the Foreign Secretary told the Commons that the British High Commissioner in Aden, Sir Richard Turnbull, was being replaced by Sir Humphrey Trevelyan, former British Ambassador to Cairo, who had wide experience in the affairs of the Arab world. Sir Humphrey was to make arrangements for an orderly and speedy British withdrawal. On June 19th George Brown was able to announce that Independence Day would be on January 9th, 1968.

Thursday, May 11th
In Cabinet we were supposed to discuss the South Arabian policy and the Aden crisis but as we sat down the P.M. began to talk about the press and we had a full hour of desultory discussion about press relations. Once again Harold started with his old complaint about colleagues who would go on talking to columnists and commentators who were hostile to us. Ian Trethowan and David Wood were quoted as the kind of person one shouldn't speak to. This started off a discussion in which Ministers really began to answer back. I was glad of this because the one thing I find obsessional in

[1] The vote was 488 Ayes and 62 Noes.

Harold is his attitude to the press. After all, no one was more successful at handling the press than he in his first period as Prime Minister. Now he sees a few selected journalists on Sunday evenings at Chequers, condemns the press in general and suspects his colleagues of leaking. He's a voracious newspaper reader and each morning he's busy guessing which of us has given the particular piece of poison to which he takes objection and George Wigg feeds him in his hatred.

In addition there's a continuous row with the B.B.C. which he always compares unfavourably to I.T.N., with its friendly editor, Geoffrey Cox.[1] Yet last Monday evening I stayed behind in the Commons specially to see Harold give a superb 45-minute performance on B.B.C.'s *Panorama*. He thinks he got this by being unpleasant to the B.B.C. Actually it was because he provided a superlatively good show. After the diatribe had finished Tony Crosland replied. 'Look here, P.M., isn't that a recipe for disaster? If you tell us not to speak to the press at all or only to the correspondents you like, are we going to get the press we need?' He was followed by Patrick Gordon Walker who pointed out that in America L.B.J. was getting a terrible press because his attitude is exactly the same as the one Harold was recommending to us. Barbara then took up the discussion and said that he'd made accusations about members of Cabinet briefing the press against each other and it was high time he gave some concrete examples. I went on to say that I thought it was a mistake that he'd given up his press conferences. It seems to me essential he should hold at least one press conference a week in order to restore his relations. I hope the discussion did some good because we shall need it if we're to recover.

This afternoon I'd hoped to do some shopping but I was forced to stay in the office to receive Wedgy Benn and Stonehouse. I'd sent them my draft report on the Bristol-Siddeley affair and Stonehouse came roaring back that it was all unjust and unfair and I had misunderstood the whole thing. Though he didn't realize it, I learnt a great deal from his violent complaint and made a second drastic revision of the report, which I've left behind for Harold to read. Meeting Stonehouse's objections makes it fairer, I think, than it was. But it doesn't alter the basic lesson I draw—that where you have no confidence between a Press Officer and a Minister, where the Minister just doesn't trust the Press Officer, nothing can possibly come right, particularly when you also have a weak Permanent Secretary.

After that I had a most interesting meeting with the editors of Hansard. We're in a terrible fix about morning sittings. If we're going to make them permanent Hansard must have an enormously increased staff, not because of the morning sittings, but because they run simultaneously with the Standing Committees of the House. We sit normally on Tuesdays and

[1] Editor and chief executive Independent Television News 1956–68, deputy chairman of Yorkshire TV 1968–71 and, since 1971, chairman of Tyne Tees Television. He was knighted in 1966.

Thursdays. So the problem of manning Hansard will force me to make up my mind either to abandon the morning sittings or to make them permanent. I'm by no means irrevocably committed to making them permanent.

This afternoon I had to sit there and listen to the sessional adjournment debate and reply to it. It was the usual series of complaints about Stansted, Greece, etc., which I managed to close at six o'clock. I didn't make as much of my reply as I should have because I'd talked too fast and the press simply can't take it down. I didn't very much mind because I didn't want my remarks printed. I went downstairs to the liaison committee where we were discussing what action to take against those who had disregarded the three-line whip. John had one of his gimmicky ideas and proposed a suspended verdict, but no one else liked it very much. I left the committee before the end but I gather that all that will happen will be a severe rebuke and then we'll be in a position to pick off one or two of the most bloody-minded Members.

I gave Anne dinner in the House, where we were virtually the only people left because everybody else had gone off to the borough elections. There was a terrible last-minute atmosphere on this the hottest of summer days. Just as we got back to Vincent Square Albert Rose rang up from Coventry to say we had lost eight seats at least and with it the control we've had for thirty years, since the Tories will use their majority of councillors to throw out our Labour aldermen, including George Hodgkinson. I knew in my heart that this must have happened all over England. The Party's been massacred in a way it can ill-sustain.[1] In Coventry, as Albert Rose agreed, there's been a combination of two factors—a decline over the last fifteen years in the quality and effectiveness of the Council Group and a tremendous anti-Government swing, which was rendered even more acute by the local Party's determination to have nothing to do with their M.P.s or their Government. Albert tells me this wasn't just a case of our people abstaining. In some wards there were very big votes and there really was a swing against us.

Friday, May 12th
Just before flying out to Cyprus with Anne for our holiday I rang up Harold Wilson to confirm my impression of the local election results. I found him not unduly disturbed at the losses. Indeed, he was saying that there was some advantage for us in seeing the Tories made responsible for local government for the next three years. It would give the Tories a number of unpopular responsibilities and it would also give us areas in which our local parties could fight back and regain their losses so that we shall be on an ascending electoral tide in 1970. All this jarred with my mood and made me realize the difference between a socialist who had his first experience in

[1] The Conservatives had a net gain of 535 seats and Labour a net loss of 596. Labour now controlled fewer cities than at any time since the war.

local government, as I did, and another socialist who went straight from the
civil service into the Commons.

I've no doubt my depression was partly due to the vote on the Common
Market on Wednesday night. John Silkin had done marvellously at the
Party meeting and his Whips had made a tremendous effort but after all
this there remained a Left of ninety people—thirty-six voting against and
forty or fifty abstaining—who were militantly and stridently opposed to
the Government. Moreover, even apart from Manny and Michael, most of
the people whose names one knows on the back benches were against us.

But this isn't all due to the Common Market. There is a swing against
us because of the prices and incomes policy. Prices are now rising faster
than incomes because deflation is working and we now look ahead this
year to a miserable rate of growth and to even higher unemployment figures
this winter—difficulties which will be intensified if we were to succeed in
getting into the Common Market. What I can't see as I look ahead is anything which will give us the lift that is necessary to take the Party out of
this trough. We're led by an enormously resourceful man who is still cool
and determined. I suspect he is preparing as a result of our July measures
for a crisis with the Chancellor out of which we may get really big defence
cuts East of Suez and even devaluation as well. But we know from what
Jim Callaghan said at Chequers that if the Prime Minister wants a devaluation next year he must have his shuffle next autumn and choose a new
Chancellor.

Those are some of my last thoughts before my fortnight's holiday in
Cyprus.

*On May 19th the U.N. Secretary General, U Thant, agreed to Colonel
Nasser's demand on the previous day for the withdrawal of 3,400 U.N. troops
who had patrolled the Ghaza strip and the Israel–Egyptian border since the
1956 Suez crisis. On May 24th George Thomson was to fly to Washington
for Anglo–American discussions, the U.N. Security Council met, and British
ships and those of the U.S. fleet were put on alert.*

*In a statement on May 24th the Prime Minister repeated the British
Government's policy of regarding the Strait of Tiran, which Egypt had
threatened to close, as an international waterway. If necessary the British
Government would support international action to ensure free navigation in
the area. On May 31st Mr Wilson had talks with Lester Pearson, the Canadian
Prime Minister, and on June 2nd he visited Washington with the intention of
securing a declaration from all maritime nations to support free passage in
the Gulf of Aqaba. On June 5th, however, fighting broke out between Israel
and Egypt, and in the ensuing Six-Day War Israel routed Egyptian and
Jordanian forces and secured control of the whole of Jerusalem and the land
between the east bank of the Suez Canal and the Israeli frontier. On June 5th
Britain had declared her own neutrality, and the Foreign Secretary called for*

*an immediate cease fire, but on June 6th President Nasser accused Britain
and the U.S.A. of intervention in Israel's support. Iraq and Kuwait were
persuaded to cut off oil supplies to Britain and America, and until September
Britain suffered from a total Arab oil embargo. Richard Crossman returned
from his holiday in the early days of the crisis.*

Monday, May 29th
Today is Bank Holiday—the new kind, a secular holiday, not related to
the date of Whit Sunday, which was a fortnight ago. Here at Prescote it's
a beautiful morning after devastatingly rainy weather. I came down early
to listen to the seven o'clock news—a thing I don't often do—and to ring
my Private Office to find out whether Harold has called the Cabinet meeting
for Monday instead of for Tuesday. Meanwhile I may as well put down in
this diary some of my reflections on my holiday.

We finished our own work in the House on the morning of May 12th
with Douglas Jay's Statement that the Government would go ahead with
Stansted and by the evening I was flying away with Anne to Cyprus. At
Heathrow there was the usual muddle. I was supposed to be put in the
V.I.P. lounge but since it was an Olympic, not a B.E.A. flight I was shunted
into a little windowless room and finally brought out and shoved into a
car with a very solemn elderly gentleman who turned out to be the Greek
Ambassador in London. He'd just been sent for by the six young colonels
who had set themselves up as military dictators in Athens last week. I
gathered later that he was against the regime and was being permitted to
resign respectably. If it hadn't been for the currency problem Anne and
I would have gone to Crete since we don't have particularly happy memories of Cyprus ten years ago when I behaved rather badly and egged on
the Greeks to stir up their Enosis campaign. Nevertheless, Cyprus is now
very impressive. Whereas it and Crete were level ten years ago, Cyprus
is now a hundred years ahead. Agriculture has been mechanized and
expanded. I saw any number of tractors and combines, and elaborate
cultivators and spraying machines for the vines. We were in Famagusta
for the potato season and in the country around I saw the beautiful new
potatoes being picked and sorted and I read in the paper that 30,000 tons
reached England by ship during the second week I was there. This enormous
injection of British capital is of course due to one fact only—the existence
of the British bases. We spent an afternoon motoring round Dikhelia just
outside Larnaca, seeing the huge British hospital at the top of the hill and
every kind of facility—football grounds, libraries, churches, women's
institutes—which it's possible to conceive. We also spent a day at Episkopi,
the other great base, with the tunnel through the mountain to get down to
its own private beaches. To the capital from Britain has now been added
an enormous annual dollar subvention as the result of the arrival of the
U.N.O. troops who are there to police the peace settlement between the

12

Greeks and Turks. I've never seen anything like the seaside colony which has grown up outside Famagusta—a mile and a half of huge new hotels all along the beaches—and wherever we went on the island, both towns and villages, we found the standard of housing and living going up. We then went to Paralimni, which was once a poor little village but which is now set among orchards and horticulture and grows potatoes. One of the Englishmen who knew it well before was an officer called MacDonald whom we met in the hotel. He described to me how he'd had forty ambushes in Paralimni when he was trying to get supplies through to his troops camped out towards Cap Greco. Now the village is oozing with prosperity. Nevertheless, Cyprus is still on the edge of civil war because the Turks have been driven into their ghettos and they are blockaded by the Greeks and forbidden such essentials as concrete and petrol. And each side spends a great deal of its time building fortifications around the other. In addition to the Greek militia there is a Turkish militia, a Turkish police, and a huge new national army under General Grivas and a huge new Turkish army under Turkish command. But we didn't think much of this political background during our first week, lying on the beach and bathing at Famagusta and Salamis. Our second week we started by spending a night at Paphos in order to see the southern coast and bathe at the spot where Venus Anadyomene came out of the sea. Then we went on across the island via the Troödos mountains to spend five nights at Kyrenia with its magnificent sand beaches. We bathed three or four times a day in the buoyant lovely water which was really not too hot at that time of year, and when the air was too hot we drove up into the mountains and along forest paths cut for the woodcutters. It was a wonderful holiday and I left the last day for Nicosia where I'd agreed to see the High Commissioner, the Archbishop and the Turkish representative. The High Commissioner filled me in on the big crisis between Israel and Egypt. I hadn't even heard of it because I hadn't read the newspapers.

Directly I'd arrived in Cyprus I'd decided not to buy one and I found it each day easier and easier to concentrate on reading very slowly the *Antigone* in Greek and rather faster the *Iliad*, and also finishing Elizabeth Longford's enormous book on Queen Victoria[1] and a lengthy novel about life during the crusades. This all worked fairly well until this meeting with the High Commissioner before we went to visit Archbishop Makarios.

I had seen him last during the Commonwealth Conference and he was still as cautious and crafty as ever.[2] He began by telling me of a great new peace initiative he was going to launch which, as I confirmed from the High Commissioner afterwards, was not new at all. He genuinely wants an agreement with the Turks. One thing he didn't discuss with me was the Middle East crisis. But immediately after he'd seen me he gave out a press

[1] *Victoria R.I.* (London: Weidenfeld & Nicolson, 1964).
[2] See p. 30.

release in which he stated as President of the Republic that the British bases were on no account to be used for any anti-Arab action. I climbed into the aeroplane and spent the hours on the way to London catching up with the newspapers on what had happened in the previous fortnight.

Apart from the Middle East crisis the major event has of course been General de Gaulle's press conference and the snub he administered to Britain—as near a veto as anybody could possibly get.[1] I wasn't unduly surprised but it does look as though Harold Wilson and George Brown have been whistling to keep up their courage.

As for other prospects, things have got no better during my holiday. It is clearer than ever that unemployment will rise this year and that our export drive is now tending to flatten out and the improvement in our balance of trade has disappeared. In fact we're in for a lousy summer. We shall be faced in July with the problem how to reflate or rather whether we can reflate this summer just at the time when the prices and incomes policy is coming virtually to a full stop. Won't the resulting lack of confidence in the pound put us back into another July crisis like that in 1966?

But of course all this is overshadowed by the Middle East crisis which blew up during my last week in Cyprus as a result of Colonel Nasser peremptorily demanding that U Thant should withdraw the U.N. security force from the Gaza Strip and Sharm el Sheikh and peremptorily stating that the Tiran Strait was Egyptian territorial waters and that he was going to assert his right to mine them and prevent all ships entering Eilat. Once again Nasser has seized the initiative and he obviously has had full Russian backing.

I gather that during this last week there were two Cabinet meetings. George Brown was due to go to Russia and there was a long discussion whether he should go and if so what he should say. He went off hoping to persuade the Russians to help us in acting as mediators but before he got back they had denounced us as imperialists playing along with Israeli aggression. So it looks as though he achieved nothing. By the way, it also looks as if the whole of George Brown's pro-Nasser policy, on which he's been spending weeks and months, has collapsed overnight. Instead George and Harold have suddenly done a complete volte-face and are now wholly pro-Israel, seeking to persuade the Americans that we and they must send ships to call Nasser's bluff and break the blockade without the Israelis having to make war.[2] What will my view be? I'm pro-Israel and my first reaction is that we can't stand aside and let Israel be strangled by Nasser in the Strait of Tiran. When I rang up Roy today he asked me which side I'd have been on in the two big debates. I said I would have been hopelessly torn

---

[1] On May 16th, General de Gaulle told a press conference in Paris that there would be 'formidable obstacles' to Britain's becoming a member of the E.E.C. It might lead to 'destructive upheavals' in the Market itself. This was interpreted as a 'velvet veto'

[2] See *Wilson*, p. 401

in mind. I'm a pro-Israeli but I'm also a great getter-outer. 'Well,' he said,
'I'm just as big a getter-outer as you but frankly I was on the Israeli side.
I want to see us standing up for Israel and I'm glad it came out last week
as it did.' Since he said this to me I've read the minutes of the two Cabinets
and feel more divided in mind than ever. For once part of me is on the side
of military action but another instinct says we shouldn't take part. We
should stand aside and let the Americans take the rap, to which my reason
replies that if we stand aside the Americans will let the Israelis down, in
which case the Israelis will be forced to fight a war on their own and be
dubbed an aggressor by the U.N. We would have another Suez on our
hands with a Labour Government this time colluding with the aggressor.
What an irony to remember that in the Whitsun adjournment debate the
issue of collusion at Suez was raised and I made a carefully considered
Government Statement that we were looking forward to a debate in July.
I've no doubt that whatever this crisis has done it has entirely removed this
particular embarrassment from the Tories. Indeed, Selwyn Lloyd will now
be able to say that this proves how right he was.

The other strange by-product of the crisis is that maybe I shall now be
allowed to make the big speech at the Balfour Declaration celebrations next
November. I found a note in my box from Marcia saying that I was to raise
the issue again and telling me there is a request that I should be the main
speaker at a big rally at the Albert Hall next week. George Brown thinks
this would be fine. I'm not particularly happy when I reflect on the reasons
why George Brown now supports me. It's because he's pro-armaments,
pro-Great Britain, pro all the things I want to cut.

Finally I must add that reading the Cabinet minutes and comparing them
with the accounts Roy and Barbara have given me of the meetings has made
me realize once again how misleading the official record can be. What
happened over those two days was that first George and Harold passionately
advocated intervention to aid Israel and they were to some extent supported
by Denis Healey. Later on Denis had to back-track and warn Cabinet that
after further conversations with the Chiefs of Staff it was clear that the
forces were simply not available to carry out the policies George and Harold
wanted. Of course, once this had been said by the Minister of Defence a
number of other people, including Jim Callaghan and Barbara and even
Roy, began to realize how dangerous it was to call Nasser's bluff without
sufficient military backing and with what would be an almost wholly British
expedition. The discussion was passionate and extremely stirring yet when
it had been boiled down and dehydrated by the Cabinet Secretariat very
little of it remained. In fact the account which they circulated was trimmed
down to suit the conclusions the P.M. wanted to have recorded.

Tuesday, May 30th
Going up in the train for the Cabinet meeting on the Middle East crisis,

I had breakfast and throughout digested a short paper from the Foreign Secretary and an enormously long official paper of sixty pages from the Foreign Office. The proposal it made had obviously been watered down since last week's exuberant ideas. It was that we should seek to get a declaration of the maritime powers in the United Nations while continuing contingency plans for what should be done in the event that the declaration was ineffective. The most striking feature of the F.O. document was its passionately anti-Russian and anti-Nasserite tone. The case for action was entirely in terms of the Russian threat to the Middle East. The line was broadly to do a Suez but without the mistakes involved in the actual Suez campaign.

At Cabinet we started with lengthy orations by George and Harold. Harold, just off to Washington, said he was seeking Cabinet authority to go ahead and discuss with L.B.J. full British participation in an Anglo-American initiative.[1] The first thing would be to get the declaration in the United Nations. But if that failed we and the Americans would organize a joint maritime force for action, designed to hold back the Israeli army. Indeed, throughout their speeches George and Harold were constantly urging that we had to do something to stop an Israeli attack. George threw in the news that in talking to the Israeli Ambassador about Israel's possible go-it-alone policy, he had used the most violent language and put the heat on with the strongest force he could. I must say I found this line of talk singularly inane. If you prevent the Israeli soldiers taking the action they think necessary and say that if they go to war we shan't help them, then of course you assume responsibility for action yourself. Harold mentioned that in their talks with Eban[2] the Americans had used the phrase, 'The only danger of your being left alone is if you go it alone.' He seemed quite unaware of the implication which is that the Americans will fully back the Israelis if they seek by military force to maintain the freedom of the Gulf of Aqaba.

The first person to reply to the P.M. and the Foreign Secretary was Denis Healey, who made a speech with every word of which I warmly agreed. He emphasized that everything now depended on our posture. On no account must we seem to be concerting with the Americans an Anglo-American military adventure designed to re-assert Western suzerainty in the Middle East. If we did so we would line up the whole Afro-Asian block in the United Nations against us. Moreover we hadn't got the military force to do it. He added finally that if we went in for such a gamble the Americans would give us titular support and then let us down. There might be one or two mine-sweepers from Denmark and Canada but by and large it would be an exclusively British military effort with nothing better than American

[1] See *Wilson*, pp. 398–402.
[2] Abba Eban, Deputy Prime Minister of Israel 1963–6 and Minister of Foreign Affairs from 1966 to 1974.

backing from a distance. After that people lined up very much as they had done in the previous week. There was great relief among those who had opposed extreme policies that we were now only concerned with a U.N. statement and contingency planning for the failure of that statement. I felt a number of people were waiting to hear what I had to say since I had been away in the previous week and I'm fairly knowledgeable about the Middle East. I started by saying that I thought the talk about an Israeli military attack was exaggerated. 'The immediate military crisis is over. The danger now is that the Israelis will bide their time and the hawks will then find another opportunity in, say, six or eight months to launch a pre-emptive strike and restore the situation.' What we had to fear was an ignominious diplomatic defeat in the sense that we wouldn't achieve very much for the Israelis by our intervention. I then said that we had to face it that Nasser's action had achieved a considerable victory for the Arabs and the Russians and shifted the balance of power. The only gains they'd been able to retain after the Sinai war were the opening of the Strait of Tiran and of Sharm el Sheikh. With the Russian aid Nasser has torn this back twenty-four hours. I didn't see how we and the Americans could eject the Egyptians and the Russians by military force and we certainly weren't going to negotiate them out of their new positions. I concluded that though I was passionately pro-Israeli I agreed with Denis Healey about the danger of being isolated and classed as a Western imperialist trying vainly to reassert our suzerainty when we hadn't the military force to do so.

My remarks deeply shocked Bowden and Gunter, who turned out to be the two totally committed Zionists in the Cabinet, prepared to take unilateral British action to force the Strait of Tiran. They were the hawks who were trying to push Harold and George into stronger action. I saw Tony Greenwood, just as fanatical a Zionist and a wonderful speech-maker at Zionist gatherings, cave in when it came to the point and he was asked his opinion. He supported me. In the previous Cabinets the opposition had been led by Barbara Castle and Roy Jenkins—on this occasion they were led by Denis Healey and myself. Wedgy Benn was wholly on our side. So were Roy Jenkins and Tony Crosland and, more cautiously, Jim Callaghan and Michael Stewart. This was a case where Prime Ministerial government certainly didn't work. Faced by this resistance the P.M. drew in his horns. He accepted Cabinet's instructions that he should try to extract support from L.B.J. for the declaration by the maritime powers, first in the U.N. and, if not there, outside. Apart from that there should be some contingency probing—some attempt to find out who would contribute to an international force, what the force should consist of and how it would work. It was made clear that until it was certain there was an effective force we would not be committed to any international action and that if it turned out to be merely an Anglo-American force Britain should not take part.

Legislation Committee had been postponed until the afternoon. The most important item was the Abortion Bill which had twice been approved by the Lords and which was now stuck in the Commons.[1] It had got an easy Second Reading with a majority of two hundred but since then, owing to the mismanagement of the Bill and the attempt to insert much more drastic proposals, it had mobilized opposition from both the Catholic and the Anglican hierarchy. I proposed that Cabinet should provide some Government time so that the House of Commons should be given an opportunity to make up its mind—of course on a free vote. The only opponent was Frank Longford. He made the most menacing speech and when I pointed out that Cabinet was neutral he shouted, 'Neutral be blowed. You have all the hierarchy against you. I warn you of it.' It's clear he'll appeal to Cabinet.

This evening I was dining with Patricia Llewelyn-Davies and Victor Rothschild was there. I tried to explain to him, though not very convincingly, the position I'd adopted in the Middle East crisis this morning. He then revealed that Leskov, the previous Israeli Chief of Staff, was passing through London next day and that he would be giving him lunch at his sister-in-law's house in St James's Place. I virtually asked myself to lunch as well.

Wednesday, May 31st
At morning prayers the P.M. rather sardonically welcomed the Chief and me back from our holidays. 'I only got seven rounds of golf,' he noted. But of course he's thriven on the crisis. He enjoys this kind of moment and it makes him relaxed and good-tempered. I wondered how he would feel about my intervention in Cabinet. Instead of supporting the strong line he and George had been taking I'd strengthened his critics by throwing my whole Israeli loyalty in to back up Denis, Roy and Barbara—the doves. He didn't answer at once but later on when we were sitting there around the Cabinet table he remarked, 'I find Tony Greenwood absolutely unbearable. That really was treason. He was listening to Barbara because he was solely concerned about the vote in the National Executive elections at the next Conference.' 'But what about me?' I said. 'Haven't I been just as much of a traitor?' 'Ah,' he said, 'you're rather more robust, Dick. It's very different with you.' I found that remark illuminating. Harold really needs and knows he needs robust critics round him who say what they really think. The one thing he can't forgive a friend for is not robust criticism but voting the wrong way for cowardly reasons.

I then asked him if he'd had time to read my report on Bristol-Siddeley. 'Oh,' he said, 'haven't you seen my minute?' And when I got back to my office I found it there congratulating me on a brilliant document and attaching a copy of the very severe minute he sent to Wedgy Benn as a result of what I'd done.

---

[1] The Medical Termination of Pregnancy Bill (hereafter cited as the Abortion Bill) which Lord Silkin had taken through the Lords, had been introduced in the Commons by the Liberal David Steel.

Lunch today was given by Mrs James Rothschild (who'd once entertained us at her bijou palace in Buckinghamshire and driven us over to Waddesdon Manor to see that astonishing collection). Leskov, a thoughtful chap with spectacles, had a few hours and talked the whole time. These are my impressions.

First of all he clearly shared the view of Dayan[1] that a tremendous mistake had been made in not reacting immediately to the withdrawal of the United Nations' forces from Gaza. He thinks Israel missed their opportunity for a pre-emptive strike on that occasion. In the second place I was surprised and relieved to find that he expects nothing of this country. The British public expects to see its Government taking big risks and acting toughly in order to help the Israeli. But I don't think Leskov does because he knows who the British are. He confirmed that the French were providing all the planes and equipment they wanted without demanding payment for them and added, 'You should do the same.' (I mentioned this to the P.M. the same evening and he replied, 'But we are doing so. We're piling it in.' Half an hour later I ran into George Thomson, who's really in the know, and I asked him the same question. 'No,' he said, 'we're not doing anything. We're merely letting them have some ammunition but it's not comparable to the French.') 'Let me get things clear,' I finally said. 'What exactly do you want Britain to do?' 'Help us on the Security Council,' he said, 'if we launch our pre-emptive strike. If necessary use the veto, then help us by providing all the equipment we ask for and that's all we need.' He wasn't the least keen on an Anglo-American maritime force and he was completely sceptical about a declaration of any kind. He just felt that the Israelis should be left alone to deal with the Arabs and with confidence they could do it.

Right at the end of lunch an interesting point came up. When Marcus Sieff[2] had rung me I had been inclined to accept the invitation to speak at the demonstration a week from now at the Albert Hall—and George Brown wanted me to do so. But by the end of Tuesday morning I didn't know what the hell I could say. Now it was lunch-time on Wednesday and Leskov as well as Victor Rothschild said, 'Don't do it. A man in your position can say nothing to compete with Quintin Hogg, who will make a passionate speech in favour of the Jews. Don't disappoint yourself by disappointing your audience at the Albert Hall.' With that thought I left and walked across the park to the Commons.

This was the afternoon of the big debate on the Middle East and it went off like so many of these great occasions. George Brown made a dull statesman-like speech, which kept strictly to the brief. He was followed by

[1] General Moshe Dayan, Israeli Chief of Staff 1953–8 and Minister of Agriculture 1959–64. He was Minister of Defence, an office hitherto held by the Prime Minister, 1967–74.

[2] The Hon. Sir Marcus Sieff, chairman of Marks and Spencer Ltd since 1972 and vice-president of the Joint Palestine Appeal.

Ted Heath, who was equally respectable, and it developed into one of those solid occasions when everybody was playing consensus politics from the front bench. Stanley Orme and Will Griffiths[1]—left-wing Nasserites just back from Egypt—made passionate speeches but the House was overwhelmingly pro-Israel. However in demanding action it was already uneasily aware of the dangers. Cabinet had taken the guts out of the speech Harold Wilson had hoped to make. After this he was off to Washington leaving George Brown to chair the Cabinet tomorrow.

Thursday, June 1st

At Cabinet this morning I had a very awkward problem to deal with. The Standing Committee on Fred Willey's Leasehold Enfranchisement Bill had voted by 18 to 1 to abolish the limits of rateable value which the Bill had laid down. If the rateable value was above the top limit set in the Rent Act, the property would not be able to be enfranchised. This had been settled after a long and bitter discussion in Cabinet Committee. The lawyers have never liked the Bill because they regard this enfranchisement as clearly arbitrary and they argue (and here they are right) that on the big estates the capital gain will be immense. In order to placate them therefore we had set the limit of rateable value and this had been destroyed with the support, unfortunately, of Sam Silkin[2] and the Minister himself.

I talked at length with Fred, Sam and the other Labour Members who all point-blank refused to restore the limits on the Report Stage and after a great deal of thought I'd put up three proposals for the Cabinet to decide between. At one point I unwisely remarked, 'Nobody thinks we could actually restore the limits,' whereupon the Lord Chancellor said, 'I do,' and the Attorney-General chimed in too. Then Callaghan woke up, found his brief from Niall MacDermot and said he also thought they should be restored. Of course the only leases he's concerned with in Cardiff are those of poor houses and he didn't see why we should allow windfalls to the rich in London and Birmingham.

Then the leading question came up as to how on earth it had happened, how could the vote have been 18 to 1? Now I had always imagined that the one was Willey but then, as the Chief Whip said to me, what about the Whip? What about the other Minister?

Whereupon Fred Willey explained that the motion had been moved by Sam Silkin and that when it had been discussed he had tried to withdraw it. But the Tories had objected and they had all voted for it. Poor Willey, he's been caught out in his deviousness by Callaghan. There was a real sense of outrage round that table and Barbara behaved like a headmistress with a child up before her for breaking the school rules. 'Pop, pop, pop.

[1] Labour M.P. for Manchester Exchange 1950–70.
[2] The second son of Lewis Silkin, he has been Labour M.P. for Dulwich since 1964. He became Attorney-General in 1974.

12*

The rateable value must be restored and that's that.' I never heard a Minister crushed so thoroughly. He went out degutted.

The other thing which came up this morning was Stansted. A tremendous opposition is building up led by the new *Sun* newspaper. Of course no word in defence of the Government's position is spoken by either Douglas Jay or Tony Greenwood. I think it's a bad decision but as it was forced upon us by five years of delay and evasion it's no good thinking we could get a better decision through just now. What's wrong with us is that we haven't fought hard for the second best which is the only thing available.

Cabinet over, I had my own job back in my office preparing for business Questions and this time there were a number of very tricky ones—abortion, homosexuality, Sachsenhausen. However, it all went very easily. We had George Brown answering for the Prime Minister with a kind of knockabout frivolity which slightly upset me. But I had an easy time because early on I was asked about abortion and gave the correct answer. That took the tension out of the Supplementaries, and the business Questions didn't last very long.

After that we had the Party meeting. Douglas Houghton rose to make the liaison committee's proposal for the chairman to hold a full-scale press conference after each meeting. It had gone down extremely well when George Brown suddenly got up and came across the platform towards me. 'Have you consulted the P.M. and myself on this?' he asked me *sotto voce*. 'No,' I said, 'this is one of our assignments.' And before I knew what, George Brown was on his feet protesting that he hadn't been consulted about this idiotic idea. He hasn't got a leg to stand on. The Prime Minister has devolved upon the Lord President and the Chief Whip the job with the liaison committee of running the Parliamentary Party. The liaison committee had unanimously accepted this proposal as an experiment. Now as a result of his intervention we shall have headlines in all the papers about another ruction in the Party.

Late this evening I saw Fred Willey and Tony Greenwood in order to discuss the disasters which had fallen upon them at the Cabinet meeting. I said I would do all I could do to get a compromise on leasehold enfranchisement and that I hadn't yet seen the Cabinet minutes, but I very much doubted whether anything can be achieved without a reference back to Cabinet and I was pretty sure that the result would be the same.

Friday, June 2nd

I spent most of the morning trying to prepare a press release for my speech to the West Midlands regional rally in Coventry on Sunday. I have never felt so reluctant to open my mouth in public. What on earth am I to say? We've had disastrous borough elections. Unemployment is going up, imports are far too high, the growth rate is miserable. We have nothing to tell the Party, no light at the end of the tunnel.

I was in a mood of depression when I went up to Manchester to submit myself on television to cross-examination from six teenagers, three boys and three girls. Everything went well. Bill Grundy, who used to do the *Who Goes Home?* programme in which Malcolm Muggeridge and I appeared week after week, was in attendance and at once picked a quarrel with me.[1] I blew up and had a frantic row with him, which of course paid off because the Granada people got cold feet and let me go in and talk to the young people for twenty minutes before the programme started. This softened them up and in terms of public relations I'd done quite a decent job before I was brought home that night by a Mercedes which did the 120 miles from Manchester to Prescote in two hours and five minutes. My depression of the morning had been spirited away.

Sunday, June 4th
Yesterday we took the children over to Oving, bathed in Pam Berry's swimming bath and had a splendid time with her and her daughters, Eleanor and Anne. Oh dear, how enjoyable it was. Patricia Llewelyn-Davies and Pam Berry are the nicest women friends we have, mainly, I suppose, because they like our children.

This morning I had to go over to Coventry to face the music. Actually things weren't so difficult because the atmosphere had been transformed by the Chancellor's extremely optimistic Saturday night speech about the way he was mastering inflation. This enabled me to be much more positive in describing the Government's attitude to social security, housing and our other campaigns. I had three or four questions but they weren't so very hostile.

After that I took Peter Lister, Albert Rose and George Hodgkinson out to lunch at the Bridge Restaurant. We had a long talk about the future of the Coventry Labour Party. The loss of the majority on the Council has left them completely stunned. Of course it means for a lot of people like George that their lives are suddenly wound up now they've been shoved off the aldermanic bench by the Tories. They're going to fight the five by-elections very strenuously but I'm afraid there's no hope of any kind of success there. What we shall now have to do is to see that their opposition policies on the local council fit with our Government policies in Westminster, otherwise on issues like rate rebates there may be a complete contradiction. The discussion went better than I expected. After it Albert Rose motored me home.

[1] Bill Grundy, a former producer of Granada Television current-affairs programmes, is now a press columnist and presenter of *Today* for Thames Television. Malcolm Muggeridge, author, journalist and broadcaster, was editor of *Punch* January 1953–October 1957. In his argument with Grundy over dinner Crossman refused to accept the opinion that no politician was sufficiently honest to admit his mistakes in public. In eventual refutation Crossman later sent Grundy a copy of his *Socialism and Affluence* (London: Fabian Society, 1967).

Monday, June 5th

The first thing I saw in London was the early edition of the evening paper announcing that the war in Israel had started. So the statement yesterday by Moshe Dayan that the tension was now relaxed and some of the Israeli reservists had been sent back to work was just a cover. The pre-emptive strike had started after all. I felt a dullish kind of shock.

However, I went into the House of Lords for a meeting of the House of Lords Reform Committee, which was chaired by the Lord Chancellor. Gerald Gardiner insisted on going ahead with the decisions necessary to lay a Bill before Cabinet to limit the power of the House of Lords although everybody else there was convinced that such a Bill would not only be futile but positively harmful since if we sought to cut back the power of the Lords without dealing with composition the Tories would immediately amend our Bill to improve the composition and expose us to ridicule.

A good deal of fencing took place. Malcolm Shepherd, Patrick Gordon Walker, Roy Jenkins and I were all trying to persuade the Lord Chancellor that he was running the meeting the wrong way and he was saying to us, 'I must keep to our terms of reference.' Finally I said to him that I had discussed this with the Prime Minister and he was ready to see the Committee go as far as possible in working out an alternative before telling the Cabinet and having our terms of reference changed. It was finally agreed that Gerald and I should clear things up with the Prime Minister but I suspect that this will mean a great deal of delay since if your chairman is Gerald Gardiner and he dislikes the project you're trying to push through he's a tremendously skilful saboteur.

I spent most of today feeling desperate and distraught because of the war news. In the House George Brown made his first Statement on the situation and it was absolutely first-rate. He declared that Britain must remain completely neutral and it was clear that as the week went on there would be more and more rowing on the back benches. There was, I gather, a foretaste of this on tonight's *Panorama* programme where the viewers were shown Christopher Mayhew[1] interviewing Colonel Nasser in the friendliest possible way and Manny Shinwell staging a ferocious row on behalf of the Israelis. Considering that he, as Minister of War, supported all Ernest Bevin's worst excesses in Palestine it's staggering to listen to speeches he now makes.

Back from the Chamber in my room I was delighted to have a visit from Remez, the Israeli Ambassador, who had asked to see me. He gave me a very full and accurate briefing on how hostilities started. I asked him about Israeli intentions towards Jordan and he replied that they intended to occupy the hills of Samaria but gave me an assurance that they would not

[1] Labour M.P. for Woolwich East from June 1951 until 1974 when, having joined the Liberal Party, he failed to be elected for the Bath constituency. He was Minister of Defence (R.N.) from 1964 until his resignation in 1966. See Vol. I.

occupy the whole West Bank because they want King Hussein of Jordan to survive. 'Can't you get a message through to him?' he asked. 'He should not commit all his eight brigades because he will need them to defend his country against our enemy, Nasser.' I said, 'Do you really mean that about the West Bank?' 'Yes,' he said, 'we don't want to get 600,000 Arabs inside Israel. All we need is the triangle and the Samaria hills.'*

Remez raised my morale because I have been upset to read in the *Financial Times* and in the *Guardian* an outrageous description of myself and Tony Greenwood as appeasers on a level with Neville Chamberlain. Of course I realized that this was the danger of the line I took in arguing in Cabinet, particularly with Bowden and Gunter present and completely unforgiving of what I said. But it was nice to put the record straight with Remez, especially as I did so in the presence of John Silkin, who of course is a Jew and at this moment a fanatical pro-Israeli. It's interesting because his father is completely anti-Zionist and has brought up his sons without any Jewish religion or Jewish sense of nationhood as pukkah Englishmen.

After an hour Remez left and Sam Silkin came in with half a dozen Labour members of the Standing Committee on the Leasehold Enfranchisement Bill. They said they'd heard rumours that Cabinet was intending to restore the rateable value limits and this couldn't be permitted. I said it wasn't a matter of rumours but of fact that Cabinet had come to this firm decision. I explained that the original Clause had been based on a very careful balance between the viewpoints of those who resented all forms of confiscation and those who wanted no limits to enfranchisement. When the Committee knocked this clause out it was not surprising that Cabinet should have unanimously resolved to restore the limits. I said I would prefer to find some compromise which would make their position tolerable but the prospects were very bleak. What surprised me was the shock this revelation gave them. They had taken it for granted that they had won a great victory and that their Mr Willey and Silkin would be able to persuade Cabinet to be sensible. None of them seemed to have any concept of how Ministers react to Labour majorities which upset Cabinet decisions on a Standing Committee.

I had dinner with the Pharmaceutical Society, whose beautiful Nash house I've been trying to save from destruction by David Eccles and William Hayter—they are trustees for the British Museum and want the site for new bookstacks.[1] Then I returned to the House, where the Finance Bill was ploughing through. I had a long talk with Ben Whitaker, the new M.P. for

---

* By the end of the week the Jews had occupied both the West Bank and East Jerusalem.
[1] David Eccles, Conservative M.P. for Chippenham 1943–62, was, among various other offices, Minister of Education 1954–7 and October 1959–July 1962 and President of the Board of Trade 1957–9; he was made a Viscount in 1964, and was chairman of the Board of Trustees of the British Museum 1968–70. Sir William Hayter had been Ambassador to the U.S.S.R. 1953–7, Deputy Under-Secretary of State at the Foreign Office from 1957 to 1958, Warden of New College, Oxford from 1958 to 1976.

Hampstead, who is a very elegant left-winger. In fact he's the kind of left-winger Tom Driberg likes; I couldn't make much of him so went off to bed.

Tuesday, June 6th

In the chair at Legislation Committee I had to steel myself to resist the endearments of colleagues who wanted me to accept a whole number of small Bills. At this point in the session we face three main concerns. First we have the morning sittings, which enable us to get through on the quiet a great many secondary, non-contentious Bills. Secondly we have quite a number of controversial but progressive Private Members' Bills to which we are giving Government time. And in the third place we have our own enormous legislative programme. We're pushing along the Abortion Bill, the Sexual Offences Bill, the Employment Agency Bill and I would have liked to have had the Sunday Entertainments Bill too. The skill of the job is to keep them running and pack in a few extras when you can, but not to get overloaded. In fact, the Chief and I do very little because really the whole of this is done by Freddie Warren in his office. The Chief doesn't spend much attention or time on the parliamentary timetable. Neither did his predecessor, Ted Short, nor my predecessor, Bert Bowden. They were completely in the hands of Freddie Warren as their predecessors were in the hands of Charles Harris. Partly this is inevitable and healthy because the goodwill of the Opposition is required and this is most easily attained when they spend their time talking to a non-political, non-partisan civil servant like Freddie Warren.

At Cabinet we had a desultory discussion on the Egyptian–Israeli war, where it was already clear who was winning. No one had a word now to say against the neutral line. Indeed, the moment war came it was absolutely clear that neutrality was essential because if we hadn't been neutral our oil would have been stopped and a large part of our sterling balances would have been withdrawn. In fact most of the gains we made by the July measures would have been upset by an unneutral policy. This being so, it was surely unwise last week for George and Harold to barge in and talk about putting warships through the Strait of Tiran. But at Cabinet today that kind of talk had entirely disappeared. Instead we started with Harold's account of his Washington visit, where it was clear that L.B.J. was not in the least inclined to do anything positive to help Israel. George then reported on the war and told us that the Israelis had already blocked the Suez Canal. This made those who had objected to the Wilson–Brown–Bowden–Gunter line feel very self-satisfied. They were able to say how wise it was to leave the Israeli alone, not to bully them but to let them have their one chance.

Unfortunately the atmosphere in Cabinet was poisoned by another portentous Wilson explosion about leaks. What had particularly infuriated Harold and indeed the rest of the Cabinet was the *Guardian* story about the doves and the hawks which had done me such damage. But now I was obviously Harold's suspect as the chief leaker when he called on the Lord Chancellor to put into operation the procedure for leak detection.

I went straight from there to the Connaught Hotel, where I was lunching with Ian Trethowan. He's an extremely charming man and wanted to talk about parliamentary reform which I did at great length. But I also decided to talk to him about my own view of the war because I detested being called an appeaser. I had said much the same to David Wood yesterday evening in the lobby and I was to say it again to Alan Watkins this evening. So much for the Lord Chancellor's investigation. If I'm attacked in this way I have to see that somebody puts my point of view.

That evening John Silkin had given me an evening off since it was the defence debate and I took Anne to see the film *Ulysses*. Though I admit it made me snooze once or twice, what I saw of it seemed to me extremely beautiful. Molly Bloom's long and famous speech scene sounded totally without obscenity.

However, I had to return to the House after all because I'd received an extremely worried message that the Chancellor of the Exchequer was on the warpath and had instructed Freddie Warren to prepare a draft guillotine Order which he could apply to the Finance Bill. When we had made the proposal for the change in Standing Orders allowing us to take certain parts in Committee upstairs the Chancellor couldn't have been more obstructive or difficult.[1] Now here he was suddenly wanting to use the Order in a way which would have made nonsense of all the safeguards I had promised. I had said the whole point of this Order was that we shouldn't abuse it and that it should only be a reserve power. I went back and found the Chancellor safely under the control of the Chief and Freddie Warren. But what is interesting is that though the guillotine wasn't used that night the Chancellor has become a complete convert. He has got a taste for the reserve powers it gives him and feels he can threaten the Opposition with them. This disconcerted me because it's exactly the argument the Tories used against passing the Standing Order. It gives him a sense of power and he is not the kind of man who uses that sort of power very well.

[1] In 1965 a report from the Select Committee on Procedure suggested that part of the Finance Bill be taken upstairs but the Government rejected this. The Chief Secretary to the Treasury proposed an ingenious compromise for keeping the Committee Stage on the Floor of the whole House with a voluntary timetable. If no voluntary timetable could be agreed, or if the timetable failed to work, the Government had the 'reserve power' to impose a compulsory timetable with a guillotine to end debate. The Government proposed that an all-party Business Committee should consider and recommend the compulsory timetable and that the matter should receive two hours' debate. On April 26th and May 1st, 1967, this proposal for a sessional experiment was discussed in the Commons and, after a division, agreed. The procedure was not used until 1968. On June 6th, 1967, Standing Order No. 40 was changed to allow certain parts of the Finance Bill to be taken upstairs after the Conservatives had objected to the use of the guillotine to end debate.

Wednesday, June 7th

We had to face the prospect of two important and possibly rowdy Party meetings. We started the morning with a meeting on procedure where I presented the problem of morning sittings. Some seventy people turned up at 10.30 when I began to put my case. I told them we had four possibilities. (1) We would carry on as now. (2) We could cancel morning sittings and go back to the old time schedule. (3) We could take morning sittings to a much further stage by rolling the whole House of Commons' business forward and starting Question Time at 10 a.m. (4) We could do as the Chief and I wanted, which was to have two morning sittings a week on Tuesdays and Wednesdays, which we use mainly for Private Members' motions and Private Members' Bills, and then on Friday we would retain part of the time for the Report Stage of Private Members' Bills, Lords' amendments, etc., but have the rest of the time for Government business. I put this proposal forward as sensibly as I could but got virtually no support. Willie Hamilton as a member of the liaison committee denounced me and complained that if we put Government business on the Friday then the privilege of most Members of going away on Thursday night would be lost. In his reply John said almost as a joke that although we had increased M.P.s' salaries to £3,000 a year he noticed that the suggestion that anybody should be here on Friday is already resented. Was he to conclude that the M.P.'s whole-time job starts on Monday afternoon and ends on Thursday evening? The moment he said it I'm sure he nearly bit his tongue out for he wasn't forgiven precisely because it is true. Having got their salaries up to £3,000 a year most provincial Members have no intention of staying longer. They're determined to get home by the Thursday night train.

The debate went on but it was notable only for a tremendous attack on John and me by George Lawson, the ex-Deputy Chief Whip, who said in a lather that the whole thing was entirely unrealistic. After an hour of this it was clear we wouldn't finish and all I could do was to get up and adjourn the meeting until next Wednesday morning. I think that then John and I will seek a compromise along the lines suggested by Donald Chapman for only a couple of morning sittings a week, as adjourned sittings of the night before, one for Private Members' and one for Government business.

At morning prayers with Harold I started by telling him that whatever the Lord Chancellor's Committee reported he really must forbid Ministers to have their own private public relations officers. I was thinking of course of John Harris who works for Roy Jenkins; there's no doubt about it that this has poisoned Roy's relations with Harold. I've no doubt that John does a lot to obtain pro-Jenkins articles in the press describing what a wonderful fellow he is and urging that he ought to be Chancellor of the Exchequer or leader of the Party.

It was now time for the second Party meeting—this time on prices and incomes. On Monday night the trade-union group had been addressed by

George Woodcock, who told them that the Government wanted legislation on prices and incomes as a mere bauble, a plaything, and that in his view the Prices and Incomes Bill was a silly, puerile thing which really nobody should fuss about. Now, of course, it is not very dignified for a Labour Government to have its Prices and Incomes Bill treated in this way, but on the other hand it did remove the last-ditchers' justification for a major mutiny by back-benchers saying they must fight against a totalitarian intervention into collective bargaining. George Woodcock had therefore undermined the resistance and apparently he had done it so effectively that Ness Edwards, who had started the meeting by saying that they were all against the Bill, said by the end of it that the whole position had changed.[1]

So this evening we were all waiting to see the reaction to the Woodcock line. John and I had carefully arranged to put Ray Gunter in as the first speaker and together with the Prime Minister we had taken great trouble to ensure that Michael Stewart wouldn't be nettled. One of the difficulties we had was that Gunter had given the impression, sustained by a whole series of outrageously detailed leaks, that as the Bill was being hammered out in Cabinet Committee the Minister of Labour was against it, and that it was wholly Michael Stewart's Bill. We wanted Gunter to speak first so that the trade-union Members would connect him with the Bill.

Sure enough he started a long and emotional speech by saying that the Party should be assured that if the Bill was any kind of threat to the trade unions he'd have nothing to do with it. He delivered the goods. He made the impact and I think he has removed any serious danger. But even Ray didn't reveal the whole truth, namely that Michael Stewart had been forced to make a whole series of concessions to meet the particular demands put by the T.U.C. in his secret meetings with them.

This evening the Lord Chancellor had asked to see me about the leak. I told him what I knew, mainly that I had spoken to Ian Aitken, who had rung me up on Sunday, and given him a briefing on the Prices and Incomes Bill, as well as telling him that I wholly approved of the Government's Middle East policy. It was this remark which he had transformed into a sensation by classifying me as an appeasing dove. He then said that he thought this leak must have been from somebody in the Ministry of Labour. As I was going away he looked up, smiled and said, 'I have never understood how one could even hope to discover any information about the source of any leak but maybe it will be different on this occasion.'

Thursday, June 8th

I got to John Silkin at 9.30 in order to have a word before Cabinet and tell him how I was dealing with Sachsenhausen. I've checked with Edmund Compton and he says that as ombudsman he thinks it's within his jurisdiction and that he would love to make a good job of the case. This is very

[1] William Edwards, Labour M.P. for Merioneth 1966–70.

good news, particularly since some 360 Members have now signed the motion. It's quite likely that despite all George and Harold say the ombudsman will discover some irregularity or some facts which have not been adequately considered. Anyway, since the Early Day Motion only asks for an independent investigation it seems sensible to me to submit it to our new professional independent investigator. But I'm aware there's a very strong feeling, particularly among Tory back-benchers, that this is merely an escape route which the Government is using to avoid a debate in which they would have to reveal their hand.

At Cabinet under parliamentary business I had to make a slightly comic explanation about the grave leasehold enfranchisement crisis we had discussed last week. Quite suddenly we'd received a message from Willie Whitelaw through Freddie Warren that if we didn't put the clause back the Opposition front bench would. So with the two Whips in cahoots there's no danger left.

The discussion of the war was desultory because it was clear by this morning that Israel was already the victor and that all that mattered was getting the oil embargo lifted and negotiations going. However, the Government's position had been greatly strengthened. George Brown's daily Statements in the House were better and better each day. His line was that whatever our personal sympathies Britain must remain neutral and be seen to make peace between the two sides. By now, of course, the pro-Israel feeling in the country is absolutely overwhelming and there is a great sense of triumph and victory. No one worried about the Israeli pre-emptive strike being an act of aggression. Their army has brought off the biggest military victory in our lifetime against President Nasser. What next? George and Harold made it clear that they doubt the utility of the U.N. Truce Commission and want four-power talks in order to prevent a two-party fix between the Americans and the Russians.

Another item we discussed was the prejudice displayed by the B.B.C. broadcasts, in particular Party members had been infuriated that the sole Labour representative on Monday night was that fanatical pro-Arab, Christopher Mayhew. The Chief Whip had now been instructed to write a letter which will bring this row to a head by pointing out that we've had practically no quarrels with I.T.V. but endless quarrels with the B.B.C. about political prejudice. I'm wondering at what stage we will get a response to the letter.

Our routine business was dealt with so fast that the P.M. said we now had plenty of time to discuss what we should do at the Chequers conference on Sunday. He explained that this had been fixed up in February with the National Executive and that it was entirely designed in order to let the trade-union members blow their tops. It was the job of the Cabinet to sit quiet while they did so. But what does that mean? Who will actually speak? He told us that he would intervene at one point, Michael Stewart — who was not a member of the N.E.C.—at another, and Denis Healey and George Brown as well. It was pretty clear that the rest of us were going to have a deadly boring day and I pleaded that he should provide another cold collation so as to get us back to our homes and into bed early.

But he hadn't finished. Leaning back in his chair and putting his fingers together he began to talk aloud about the economic situation. We'd all got used to the Galbraithian theory of private affluence and public squalor,[1] and under Macmillan and Maudling there had been a switch to public expenditure on a very large scale. Now that had been sustained by us and as we had always expanded public spending—housing, schools, hospitals, roads—we ought to ask ourselves whether we weren't in danger of swinging the pendulum too far over towards public expenditure and cutting back the increase in private consumption to a figure so low that public opinion won't take it. He said he wanted to air this view; it was an interesting and important thought that needed consideration. I immediately pricked up my ears at this because it is exactly the line that Callaghan had been taking. It's my strong suspicion that the P.M. and Callaghan have come to an understanding. It looks as if Harold has decided against devaluation. The only way of getting our growth rate up and our exports up suddenly and dramatically would be devaluation this summer, preparatory to going into the Common Market, and if we don't devalue we have to accept a 3 per cent growth rate, even though the R.E.P. will to some degree mitigate it in the development areas. What we must look forward to is an artificially high rate of unemployment in the south and in the Midlands and an artificially low rate in some of the regions and in order to get the money for these subsidies to the regions we shall have to cut back public expenditure still more if we want to leave more for incomes. If the P.M. repeats this argument at Chequers on Sunday I shall be sure I'm right.

I had to rush off to a Privy Council where a new New Zealand Minister was being admitted. Talking afterwards to Godfrey Agnew I realized for the first time that of forty Privy Councils which have taken place since I've been Lord President I've only attended seven. I don't really like them very much and for that reason I'm not a very good Privy Councillor, as the Queen must observe.

At my business Questions this afternoon I had a good deal of trouble about Sachsenhausen. From behind me Mr Leadbitter attacked me for refusing to consider the interests of the House.[2] On the other hand I thought I traced a little more support on the Opposition front bench, with Ted Heath's attitude being slightly more hopeful.

In my Lobby conference just afterwards I was asked about the Government package this July and almost without thinking I said, 'I've been looking

[1] Elaborated in *The Affluent Society* (London: Hamish Hamilton, 1958) by John Kenneth Galbraith, Professor of Economics at the University of Harvard since 1949.
[2] Ted Leadbitter, Labour M.P. for Hartlepool since 1964.

carefully at the Bills we've got ready and I can tell you we should now expect a pension up-rating Bill to be published within the next fortnight.' The journalists all pricked up their ears and asked when it was due. 'The up-rating will take place in November,' I said, 'as part of the normal routine. Every two years we up-rate pensions in order to see that they don't lose their purchasing power.' My remarks fitted quite well because only the day before Douglas Jay had announced generous concessions on hire purchase—though of course the news had been entirely eclipsed by the Israeli victory. But I was aware that there was something wrong and as I went out of the room one of them said, 'You've told us everything except the amount.' Downstairs Trevor Lloyd-Hughes said nothing, Henry James said nothing, Gerald Kaufman said nothing but in the corridor I had an urgent message from the P.M. I went in and he asked me whether I had told Peggy Herbison that I was announcing her Bill. He was in a terrible flummox because, as he put it, I'd revealed to the press the closely-guarded secret that we were up-grading pensions.

But Harold's real concern was that Peggy's going to resign, and at the moment that I was making the announcement she was making preparations for her resignation. This was complete news to me. I thought her resignation had been withdrawn but no, owing to the amount being nine shillings rather than ten she had decided to resign and that was that. And so I had to ring up Peggy and apologize. Fortunately she thinks me a very good friend and couldn't have been nicer. But there was Trevor Lloyd-Hughes rushing round saying the Lord President had ballsed it up again, there was Gerald Kaufman trying to defend me, there was the P.M. absolutely nerve-racked about Peggy and an anxious confusion about who was right. At one point James Callaghan strolled in and when he heard the news remarked that he couldn't conceive how I could do such an outrageous thing because we had worked out months ago at S.E.P. a rough timetable of the reflation announcements throughout the summer. Of course there's no reference to this in the Cabinet minutes though I do vaguely remember the conversation.

Anyhow it was a tremendous flurry and it indicated very clearly how many people there are who are wanting to pounce on me when anything goes the slightest wrong. So I had to spend a lot of time this afternoon while the Finance Bill was trundling along in the Chamber trying to clear up the mess before rushing to the weekly meeting at No. 10.

Thence back to the Speaker for rather an awkward interview. As Leader of the House I had to see him on behalf of the Services Committee because he had insisted that his Secretary should get a rise although the Staff Board was against it and said he didn't deserve one because his work was less responsible than that of the Secretary to the Chairman of Committees. But because he was the Speaker the Services Committee felt they couldn't say no. So I had got the rise from the Treasury but I promised that I would go and see the Speaker and tell him it mustn't happen again. So with some embarrassment I explained to the old boy that those of us who were in a position of great influence ought to avoid upsetting the Staff Board and the arrangements for salaries by asking for what were virtually favours for individuals. It was a difficult thing to say to him, especially when he asked whether Barnett Cocks had approved the rise and I said no—I thought that Barney Cocks thought, as I did, that it wasn't quite the right thing to do.

Later this evening Tony Crosland came in to see me and we talked about Roy. I said I thought that Roy was doing himself damage with the activities of John Harris and asked if Tony couldn't say a word to him. 'Well,' he told me, 'I hardly see Roy now, I'm hardly in a position to. I entirely agree with you but he and I have ceased to know each other at all intimately and I think he is behaving in a very funny and remote and ambitious way.' So I learnt that Tony is completely on his own and Roy is running his drive for power completely on his own.

Friday, June 9th
I was determined to attend the Home Affairs Committee because I was keen on the Sunday Entertainments Bill, the fourth of the Private Members' Bills I was hoping to get through by providing Government time. Though it's finished in the Lords it hasn't had the Second Reading yet in the Commons and I was hoping to slip it through without controversy because it had gone so quietly in the other place. However, yesterday evening I'd received a round robin from ten Welsh M.P.s saying that such a Bill was a volatile proposal to waste Government time. Sure enough, when I got to the Cabinet Committee room there was Charlie Grey, the Deputy Chief Whip, who's nearly as religious as some of the Welsh, and he and the Secretary of State for Wales were saying that the least they could ask for was local option for Wales if we brought the issue up. Now I've got to see a delegation of Welsh M.P.s and discover whether I can persuade them to accept local option. This is a good indication of what a very small group of M.P.s can achieve. Overwhelmingly the English M.P.s and the English people want the Sunday Entertainments Bill, which will liberate the holiday for sport. Overwhelmingly the Welsh who play or watch games feel the same. But the Bill will be stopped all right.

That day I had one of my journalist lunches at the Garrick and among my guests were David Wood of *The Times* and Francis Boyd of the *Guardian*. It was a gay and pleasant affair. One of the sad things I have to admit is that it was delightfully productive. I can't deny that it was as a result of my entertainment that a charming paragraph appeared in the gossip column of *The Times* about the wonderful work of John Silkin and myself. And Ian Trethowan's piece is also amiable. It certainly does pay to be nice to journalists.

This evening the children came up to town and we got ready for the Trooping of the Colour tomorrow. All Ministers are provided with excellent tickets for this occasion if they want them. I never would have bothered except that my room looks out over the Horse Guards Parade and has a very good view. So we had decided to have a little party. I've invited Sir Philip Hendy and Roy Strong, who had lent me my pictures. Then there are to be the civil servants, Freddy Ward and Jimmy James and his wife and family and John Delafons from the Ministry of Housing and his wife and children, and one or two others. All the people from my Private Office have seen much more of the show than they wanted during the rehearsals and are delighted to have the day off at home.

Saturday, June 10th

After breakfast Patrick and I walked across the Park to get a haircut in Duke Street, St. James's, before walking back through Trafalgar Square. The crowds were already piling up. It was a beautiful sunny day with white clouds in the sky and just a little moisture in the air—wonderful colour. The view from my office is not perfect because you can't see the saluting stand and you can't see quite all that's going on. So Godfrey Agnew and his Privy Council staff do slightly better round the corner. Nevertheless we could see more than enough. It is interesting that Virginia watched far more carefully than Patrick, who played about with young Matthew Cocks (yes, Barney and his wife were there too). There were a number of other boys who would glance up from time to time but who really like drinking unlimited Coca Cola and rushing around. It did seem to go on much too long.

Then we motored down to Prescote and a little later John Silkin and his wife arrived because tomorrow he is going to take me over to Chequers.

Despite the Chancellor's optimistic words in the April budget, the economic measures of July 1966 had not succeeded in repairing Britain's balance-of-payments deficit or in restoring confidence in the pound. The trade figures for June were to show a trade gap of some £39 million and pressure on sterling had increased. The Chancellor and the Prime Minister, however, remained adamantly opposed to devaluation.

The twelve-month freeze on wages, prices and incomes was due to end on July 1st, and although the Government continued to rely on the unions to exercise voluntary restraint in making wage claims, the Cabinet none the less decided to retain their reserve power to delay wage increases, extending the operation of that part of the Prices and Incomes Bill until August 12th, 1967. The Order enacting the delaying power was to be put before the House of Commons for passage on July 17th.

Sunday, June 11th

John and I motored over on a perfect Sunday morning, pretty angry that we had to spend the whole day inside that not very exciting room with all the beautiful weather outside. He's got a very nice fast Triumph and we were there just in time to find the meeting starting with Johnny Boyd of the A.E.U. in the chair and Len Williams, Sara Barker, George Brown and Harold Wilson at the top table. The rest of us sat like a mass meeting in lines on chairs.

If the aim of the meeting was to permit the trade-union members to blow off steam they certainly blew it all right this morning. In the course of doing so they show that there are as many divisions between the trade-union leaders on the Executive as there are among the Ministers and M.P.s. Jack Jones alone took the extreme position anti prices and incomes. In a very tough speech he said it was endangering the success of the T.U.C.'s voluntary policy. As for the T.U.C., it had been playing the role of stooge for the Government and its position was being undermined. His first suggestion was that the Government should announce a date after which all legislation restricting wage movements would be completely ended. Then he said that the voluntary T.U.C. policy musn't be restrictive. It must be a strategic co-ordination for trade-union advance to higher living standards. His second constructive point was to discuss the industrial democracy which was the main subject of a N.E.C. report which his committee had just produced. He wanted the modernization of arbitration and then attacked Dick Marsh for his cautious attitude to industrial democracy. This was far the biggest speech of the day. But a number of his colleagues denounced him as an extremist and Bill Andrews, one of the new members, said he was advocating anarchy by making a demand for a return to unrestricted collective bargaining.[1] Dear old Gormley blathered about how we must have ammunition as well as faith and then Dai Davies made a speech supporting Andrews against Jack Jones. Bradley of the T.S.S.A., who is also P.P.S. to Roy Jenkins, was another of Jack Jones's critics but then went on to demand discipline of the Parliamentary Party and he managed to turn the criticism against the new Silkin–Crossman liberal discipline in the House of Commons.[2] At the end of the morning Michael Stewart made a characteristic rational reply which convinced no one. He said that the reason for the electoral defeats was not Government legislation about prices and incomes. In the spring of 1966 wages were going up faster than prices though we won. In the spring of 1967 prices went up faster than wages so we lost the G.L.C. and the municipals. Then he went on to talk very ineffectively about prices. All he could say was that without the legislation there would have been a runaway rise in prices when actually it was limited to sixpence in the pound. Finally he talked about the statutory powers necessary to hold the situation and made one good point. 'What would you do,' he asked the trade unionists, 'with all the millions of workers who are not members of unions if you revert to a completely voluntary system?'

[1] William Andrews, Assistant General Secretary of the Union of Post Office Workers.
[2] Tom Bradley, Labour M.P. for Leicester North-East since July 1962.

In the afternoon Ministers replied to the points which had been made. Dick Marsh was quite effective, and there was an annihilating attack on Walter Padley's speech about defence from Denis Healey. It was clear that whenever any Minister got up there was no answer available from the other side.

After tea George Brown started by lecturing the N.E.C. on their attitude. 'Its members must learn to defend Government decisions,' he said, 'even if they themselves would have decided differently. There must be an end to the public belly-aching. Of course the Cabinet would try to consult the Executive before all important decisions but such consultation could not be guaranteed. That is why we should have an annual get-together like this one early in each year.'

Ian Mikardo made a serious attack, saying that N.E.C. members and back-benchers are like workers excluded from managerial decision, and they feel excluded because they have no opportunity to share decision-taking. There's a feeling that the Government doesn't care about their views and just wants to tell them what to do. An annual staff outing to Chequers just isn't enough. Then he talked about the minor irritants—the appointment of the steel magnates, the regional hospital boards all packed with Tories— and said there had been a dangerous run-down of the Party's advisory group which makes it difficult to do any long-term work. You can't get people to go to these advisory groups because they feel that what they produce makes no difference.

Ian was followed by Joe Gormley, who made a tremendous attack on lack of discipline among M.P.s. 'It's M.P.s and their bloody conscience votes that are wrong,' he shouted. He wasn't going to try and discipline the unfortunate members of the constituency Parties unless the M.P.s had some discipline too. One or two other trade unionists took this line but John and I very sensibly decided not to be baited into reply.

In his final summing-up Harold Wilson said there are two sovereign points, the N.E.C. and the Cabinet. Each has its jurisdiction and theoretically of course they're totally independent. But if each insists upon its independence the constitution can't be made to work and this causes total bewilderment outside. Here he was laying down the bi-focal theory as he has often done before and he did it very well. 'As for consultation,' he said, 'we must improve it but it's often impossible,' and he cited the Six-Day War in Israel. But he was quite concrete about the joint studies we must undertake on docks and workers' participation, and the role of the nationalized industries and private enterprise in a mixed economy. Finally, as I expected, he switched to the theme he had outlined in Cabinet and suggested we had gone too far in social welfare and must now switch back to more private affluence and less private squalor. After that John Silkin and I drove away as fast as possible to take a walk over Prescote farm on a lovely evening.

So that was Chequers and now I must have my bath and get off to catch the train to London. I have nothing to add about that meeting with the National Executive except to emphasize the humiliation of its necessity— the inadequacy of Transport House and in particular of Len Williams and Sara Barker. However Harold thought it was a tremendous success since it called the bluff of the trade-union members without causing offence.

Monday, June 12th

Looking at the morning press in the train on the way up I was relieved to find there were no leaks from Chequers. But maybe this was mainly because the front pages were dominated by the account of Charlie Hill of the I.T.A. doling out new contracts and making a number of people millionaires. This is an extraordinary part of our so-called free enterprise— the feudal deal in T.V. franchises which has been given to I.T.A. I think *The Times* in its new form has done some splendid work in exposing it. I wish our Labour Government had done something about it, but we didn't. Anyway it's pushed the Chequers' stories off the map.

The first meeting I had this morning was a Cabinet Committee of which for once I am not a member—Environmental Planning or E.P. I was asked for the first item because it dealt with the problem of the Welsh Regional Council or Parliament for Wales. As I've recorded before there are a number of Welsh M.P.s—headed by the present Secretary of State, Cledwyn Hughes —who regard the threat of Welsh nationalism as very serious and would like to meet it by moving towards something very like Welsh self-government. They of course are opposed by most of the South Wales M.P.s such as Ness Edwards since the miners don't in the least want a Welsh Parliament and think any surrender to the nationalists is an act of cowardly appeasement. Their conviction that Wales does better economically as part of Britain is almost certainly true. But so too is the conviction of the M.P.s from North Wales that Welsh nationalism is a force to be reckoned with.

Of course in terms of regional structure what Wales probably needs is two city regional units—one in the north and the other in the south. That's what it would get if it were a part of Britain and our Royal Commission does its job and recommends city regions. But administratively there seems to me no difficulty in treating Wales as a single unit and, with the reform of local government, giving to its Parliament slightly more authority than we shall be giving to our new city regions. Now here was Cledwyn Hughes back again with his miserable form of local government combined with an equally miserable recommendation for a co-opted Welsh Council, which as far as I could see would do nothing but supervise tourism. Barbara Castle, I'm glad to say, supported me when I said that it was no good attacking Cledwyn since he was faced with a very real political difficulty. He had to move forward far enough to hold his position. Anyhow Cledwyn will be allowed to put his compromise to Parliament.

I went straight on to an important meeting of O.P.D. about the package for Southern Arabia, and the kind of military support we will provide for the independent regime we leave behind. It's going to cost us £55 million in aid and we're going to have to keep Vulcan bombers somewhere in the Persian Gulf as a kind of ultimate deterrent.[1] No wonder George Brown and Eddie Shackleton and our new man there, Humphrey Trevelyan,[2] are all nervous lest the methods we choose for withdrawing may commit us to staying.

George had also set me something of a problem in the Commons. Off his own bat he'd promised a full debate on Aden and said that he would make a full Statement before it. Then, again, off his own bat he had a series of private exchanges with the other side and I gather he offered to show his policy Statement to Alec Douglas-Home so that he would have time to consider it. This would require the Statement to be made on a Monday with the debate two days later, on a Wednesday. In view of the concessions George had already made the Chief and I felt inclined to make this concession to the Opposition. But after the Chequers' meeting the Chief saw the P.M. and George Brown alone and Harold said that this was just the kind of demand we would make in opposition and there's no reason why the Government should concede it. It looks as though I shall have a difficult time on Thursday.

I gave lunch to Lady Wilson whom I used to know quite well as the beer-drinking left-wing industrial correspondent of the *News Chronicle*.[3] She wanted me to give her my impressions of Frank Cousins as a Minister because she is writing a book about him. My impression of Frank as a Minister is that he never learnt the art. He had endless hours alone with the P.M. and tremendous concessions were made to him. But he never came off in Cabinet or in committee and I suspect he was no success in his Department—though this was partly because he was given Charles Snow[4] as his Parliamentary Secretary and Maurice Dean as his Permanent Under-Secretary. He was also hopeless as a front-bench spokesman. The odd thing about him was that he began to be an effective Member as soon as he resigned. In fairness one must also add that all his warnings about the unworkability of a statutory prices and incomes policy and the rows with the trade unions were fully justified by the event.

At Question Time there was, as I expected, a tremendous row about Aden. George Brown blew the gaff on our Monday and Wednesday idea by saying he's jolly well going to have it the way he wants it and so undermining any friendly negotiations the Chief and I are having for him.

[1] On Masirah Island.

[2] Sir Humphrey Trevelyan, Ambassador to the U.S.S.R. 1962–5 and, from 1967 until his retirement in 1968, High Commissioner in South Arabia. In 1968 he became a life peer.

[3] Margaret Stewart, former industrial correspondent on the *News Chronicle*. Sir Stewart Wilson was her third husband.

[4] Lord Snow, writer and Extraordinary Fellow of Churchill College, Cambridge. He was Parliamentary Secretary at the Ministry of Technology 1964–5 and became a life peer in 1965.

This evening the Chief, Donald Chapman and I sat down to discuss Donald's draft of his final paper for the Procedure Committee on the time-tabling of legislation. I thought the Chief and I had agreed at the previous meeting that the setting up of a steering committee to plot the timetable of each Bill was a good and hopeful sign. But now, under Freddie Warren's influence, John was saying that steering committees were dangerous things because they would hand over control to back-benchers and so weaken the co-operation of the Chief Whips on each side. This argument for preserving the power of the Whips and conceding nothing to the committees is a complete contradiction to my idea of parliamentary reform and it shows how differently our functions make John and me think. As Leader of the House, I genuinely want to strengthen Parliament against the Whips' machine but, as Chief Whip, John wants to retain his machine and is naturally drawn to anything which keeps him close to Willie Whitelaw. So here was Freddie Warren, who runs both the Whips' offices, intervening at the last moment to save our Chief Whip from conceding to Parliament the control of the timetable which he and Willie hold tight in their hands.

Before we'd finished John and I had to go over to see the P.M. We were expecting him to discuss the debate on D-Notices next week but he wasn't prepared to do so. He told me that we should get a White Paper as well as the Radcliffe Report before the Cabinet which was taking place tomorrow.[1] But he refused to give me an advance copy. He was still obviously anxious whether the Cabinet would repudiate him and I assured him that from what he described there would be no difficulty in getting Cabinet backing for both documents. All the Chief and I knew this evening was that we were being completely excluded from this key issue. Instead of taking our advice on that he wanted to talk about the balls-up of which I was accused in my previous business Statement and my so-called leak of the announcement of the up-rating report. I argued the case quite toughly with him and finally I said, 'Look here, you've put me in charge of the co-ordination of the information services. I made the announcement and I got an excellent press. What are you complaining about?' 'Ah,' he said, 'that was luck.' To that I replied (I think not ineffectively), 'Harold, you've had your share of luck and taken credit for it too.'

But yet another disclosure came out of this conversation. It was revealed that without telling anyone the Chancellor had gone to Peggy Herbison at Chequers and asked her whether she would withdraw her resignation if he would concede her ten shillings instead of the nine shillings Cabinet had

---

[1] The Report (Cmnd. 3309) concluded that the Secretary of the Services, Press and Broadcasting Committee, Colonel Lohan, had not made it clear to the *Daily Express* columnist that the cable-vetting story was a matter for which a D-Notice should be applied. The Government issued a White Paper (Cmnd. 3312) accepting the Committee's findings on the wording and future of the D-Notice system but dissociating itself from the conclusions on this particular issue. In the face of this implicit censure Colonel Lohan suddenly resigned and Admiral Denning took his place. See *Wilson*, pp. 415–18.

agreed. Very wisely she had just listened and gone away leaving Callaghan on the hook. I said it would be ridiculous if she resigned now and that I would go and see her that very evening.

Actually I was still in the Chief's room when she walked in, and soon made it clear that we weren't going to stop her resigning unless she got what she wanted for the old-age pensioners. On the other hand, I realized there was only one way of getting that shilling agreed by Cabinet and that was that nobody knew it was the price of Peggy's remaining Minister. If a word of that deal came out Cabinet wouldn't agree. On Thursday the Chancellor himself must say he's changed his mind and make the case for increasing the nine shillings to ten. Peggy hates the Chancellor just as she hates Douglas Houghton. She thinks she's being done by everybody except perhaps by me but even for me she wasn't going to take her teeth out of the Chancellor now she has got them right into his flesh. She's a remarkable woman; she's done nothing except slave away in that Ministry. She adores the staff there and they adore her. She adores the old-age pensioners and works and slaves for them. She feels she has to get every penny she can out of that nauseating Chancellor and she's done it this evening. I went away feeling a great respect for her.

Tuesday, June 13th

I started reading the D-Notice documents at 5.30 in the morning. I found the Radcliffe Report a fascinating exposition of Civil Service stoogery and idiocy. Evelyn Waugh at his most fantastic could not have invented it. When I had digested the Report and read through the White Paper I realized two things. First that there was a mass of material in both to show the total lackadaisicalness of the Civil Service and secondly that the White Paper as a piece of apologetics is extremely unconvincing and will do Harold untold harm.

When Cabinet got to this item on the agenda Harold started by saying that he had to have a White Paper because he was so profoundly concerned about D-Notices. It was clear that he wanted to get the business through with the minimum of discussion. Neither Denis Healey nor George Brown, the two other Ministers concerned, spoke a word. Harold simply asked us to accept the White Paper.

This was the first occasion when I can remember him taking the strictly presidential line. First of all he'd arranged the timing of that Cabinet so that we should get a vast amount of reading material late the night before. Secondly he'd arranged that the White Paper should be published at four this afternoon so there was no chance of Cabinet amending it. Thirdly he'd arranged that we should discuss Rhodesia and the Middle East, before we came to the D-Notices, for half an hour and that his next engagement should be at 10.45. So we had only half an hour to discuss the D-Notices. In this way he'd made it virtually impossible for the Cabinet to refuse him sanction. Nor had we any inclination to do so since it was entirely the P.M.'s affair and his honour which was at stake. Nevertheless when he'd finished and George and Denis had failed to say anything, Dick Marsh observed the danger that Colonel Lohan would be regarded as a victim, the fall-guy who'd been sacrificed in order to defend the senior civil servants. Harold said he saw the danger of this and I suggested that if he was to take the line in the White Paper it wasn't merely Lohan who should be blamed but the people who had appointed him and kept him at his job. At this point it came out that no one was quite sure whether he'd been positively vetted or not and I observed, 'Well, there are three Permanent Secretaries concerned as well as the Secretary to the Cabinet and they all bear strong collateral responsibility for the mess.' Of course the P.M. was authorized to publish the White Paper but I shouldn't think there was a single person there who thought that it was a good thing to publish a White Paper instead of accepting the Radcliffe Report.

As we were walking out I said to Burke Trend, 'You've got a lot to answer for. That quixotic Prime Minister is going out to do battle for your Civil Service against the forces of evil.' He replied, 'I have pleaded with him to accept the Radcliffe Report and I actually drafted a Statement to show how he could do it.'

I lunched that day with Alan Watkins because I didn't want to see him joining the attack on the Prime Minister this week if I could avoid it. I pointed out that there was big news that morning: Michael Foot was to stand for the Treasurership against Jim Callaghan, thus following faithfully in the Nye Bevan tradition but very characteristically doing it so late that there was no chance of winning this year. I talked to Alan about it but I doubt if I succeeded.*

After the Home Affairs Committee, where we all agreed to a permanent summertime with only the Scots dissenting, I went down to hear the P.M.'s Questions. Everything was pretty dull until we came to his Statement on the D-Notices. Then Heath absolutely immediately jumped on to the point that Harold had refused to accept the Radcliffe Report which had acquitted Chapman Pincher. The effect was as devastating as I expected.

Fortunately attention was diverted by yet another Statement about the Middle East—this time by George Thomson, who does the job quite well. But these occasions are getting more and more embarrassing because the House of Commons lives in a world of wish-fulfilment and illusion, discussing how Great Britain should shape the future of the Middle East. They don't seem to realize that the net effect of this tremendous Israeli victory has been to expose British impotence. We were forbidden by the locals to use our Cypriot bases. We were forbidden to use Malta and our so-called power in the Persian Gulf merely makes us obsequiously anxious to please the Arabs. Already we are mending our fences and paying a heavy price to the

* I didn't. Most of the *Spectator* was devoted to lambasting the Prime Minister.

Arabs for those heady days when Harold and George wanted to re-open the Strait of Tiran. But despite all this the House of Commons wants to believe, as does the Government, that we are still a decisive factor in the Middle East.

This evening I had to attend a meeting of the Welsh group to discuss the Sunday Entertainments Bill. There in front of me was the split between the north, passionately in favour of Sunday observance, and the South Wales miners wanting their sport on Sunday. It was clear that local option was the only possible solution and since we are faced with a grave pressure of business we agreed to postpone the Bill until next session. To my amazement I found myself very popular with the North Welsh M.P.s by the time we went home to bed.

Wednesday, June 14th

I found I hadn't got an engagement until eleven so I popped off to the Army and Navy Stores just round the corner and collected three new records —the Brahms Piano Concerto No. 2, a Mozart piano concerto for Anne, and Burl Ives for the children. Already I'd had a look at the press and it's clear that every newspaper has been turned against Harold by his White Paper. Despite my hopes the *Guardian* wasn't the least friendly. They all talked as though he were drunk with power.

The P.M. will be very upset. A sign of his worry was his attitude to the vote on the Prices and Incomes Bill which took place last night.[1] He told John he wouldn't mind forty abstentions because it would blanket the news of the D-Notice debate on June 22nd. Actually we had only thirty-one and no newspaper found room for the news on its front page.

My main job this morning was the resumed Party meeting on morning sittings. This time everything was sweetness and light. We got our compromise and we were even able to get unanimous Party support for the experiment of a press conference at the end of each meeting, which George Brown had so idiotically opposed a fortnight before.

Judith Hart rushed in just before lunch on what she described as desperately important business. I gave her a drink and she told me that she'd been asked by the P.M. to take Peggy Herbison's job. What was my advice? 'I hope Peggy won't resign,' I said, 'but don't for heaven's sake be crazy enough to take her place and let her attack you from outside for failing to carry on her tradition.'

After that I went back to the Privy Council where John Pope-Hennessy of the Victoria and Albert was waiting to discuss what kind of clock he should lend me to go on my mantelpiece.[2]

At the liaison committee this afternoon we had to discuss how to handle

---

[1] The Second Reading was carried by 288 to 235.

[2] Sir John Pope-Hennessy, Director and Secretary of the Victoria and Albert Museum from 1967 until 1974, Director of the British Museum from 1974 to 1976.

Stansted at Westminster. I've described how we got a snap decision in Cabinet just before the recess. Since then Douglas Jay and Greenwood, the two Ministers responsible, haven't moved hand or foot to sell the Government's proposal to the electorate. When I saw them they both told me they were waiting for a debate in the House.

Meanwhile the opponents have got together and two very vigorous local M.P.s, Stan Newens and Peter Kirk, have achieved a real snowball movement of local opposition with the press, led by the *Sun*, joining in.[1] Every paper is now campaigning against us and the air lobby is our only ally. Already this week 236 M.P.s are ready to sign their names to an Early Day Motion and Peter and Stan are holding a great briefing meeting on Tuesday evening. We agreed to hold a special Party meeting on Wednesday where Jay and Greenwood will present the Government's case. Douglas Jay sees his job as limited to speaking in a parliamentary debate and Tony Greenwood is unwilling to lift up his head and speak at all, whereas inside the Cabinet we have Roy Jenkins in almost open opposition and the P.M. extremely unsympathetic. Furthermore the Chief Whip in the Lords thinks it will be defeated there. The last thing I want is to see a split in the Cabinet and in the Party revealed before the recess. Fortunately there are really serious legal problems and the usual channels have agreed to postpone the debate. We will put it off till October if we can.

This evening the Chief and I asked Harold Wilson to see us again. He agreed to do so at 9.30. The reason was his failure to ask our advice about the D-Notices; George Wigg has been his chief adviser. We didn't want to complain but just to make sure that he wasn't suspecting us of turning into enemies. So we consciously went there and sat telling him how we'd begun to collect the back-benchers to speak up for him in the debate and we were glad to tell him that people like Charlie Pannell were spontaneously rallying to fight for the P.M. against the *Daily Express*. I think we succeeded in making him feel that we were solid behind him and not questioning him or querying his decisions. 'You're always at your best in this kind of crisis,' I said to him. He looked at me rather bleakly and replied, 'I'm not sure I shall be on this occasion.' He was full of insecurity and wanted our help.

Thursday, June 15th
Cheerful news in the *Daily Mail*. The National Opinion Poll shows signs of some improvement in the Government's and in Harold's position. The Gallup Poll didn't show it as much but the P.M. is so sensitive to these polls that I'm sure it cheered him up. Now that Israel has got us off the hook we should be doing better with the general public. Indeed with this marvellous weather I think the worst should be over for this summer.

[1] Stan Newens was Labour M.P. for Epping 1964–70. Peter Kirk, Conservative M.P. for Gravesend 1955–64 and for Saffron Walden since 1965, has led the British delegation to the European Parliament at Strasbourg since 1973. He was knighted in 1976.

So we were quite cheerful when we walked into O.P.D. to continue the discussion about Aden, and Eddie Shackleton and Humphrey Trevelyan gave us some very sensible advice.

The main thing at Cabinet this morning was the awkward matter of the extra shilling on the pension. I've never heard Callaghan more uncomfortable. He explained how, since he'd made the calculations, the cost of living had gone up rather more than he'd anticipated (this was quick work in a fortnight) and it looked as though ten shillings would be fairer to the old people. Poor Gordon Walker, who had opposed the increase to nine shillings on the last occasion, was out on a limb. The rest of the Cabinet looked feebly round. Peggy seemed quite happy. The Chancellor got away with it by saying it would all go on the employers' contribution. So Peggy will not resign. End of story.

The other item was the report of the Further Legislation Committee on next year's legislation. As chairman I had agreed this with every Minister individually and then in Committee, and the whole thing went through in a few minutes, with pleasant compliments from Bert Bowden, for once, and from Harold. He handsomely complimented John and me on the volume and speed of the legislative programme this Session, but frankly this is more to do with Freddie Warren and with the extra time morning sittings have given us.

It's always difficult to predict what will happen on Thursday afternoon at the business Statement. When the Prime Minister's Questions turned out to be dull I whispered to John, 'I'll get all the bad temper now. They'll blame me for Aden.' Actually I had quite an easy time about Sachsenhausen and on Aden I was positively embarrassed by the sympathy of Alec Douglas-Home for having George Brown as my colleague. Of course I repudiated it indignantly, but it remains true that George has been appallingly uncertain of himself about the Aden policy and it has shown in his handling of it. The person who caught the Tory bad temper was poor Bill Rodgers, who was answering Questions about four British ships which had been caught in a convoy going through the Suez Canal and were now anchored in the Bitter Lakes. Poor boy, he answered the Questions perfectly competently but then they began to extend them and to ask him things he couldn't possibly know. They wouldn't have tried bullying George Brown or George Thomson in this rather unpleasant way.

At my meeting with the P.M. and Burke this evening I was appalled to discover that while George was in New York—and Harold too might have to go there to meet Kosygin—Harold intended us to have the D-Notices debate next Thursday after a big Cabinet that morning and a big S.E.P. meeting the day before. In fact, he wanted the whole economic crisis to be dealt with next week as well as D-Notices and General de Gaulle. I said, 'You can't do this. It must be postponed,' and we are postponing it. Burke and I sat back, relaxed and happy, having got this nightmare out of

7 In office as Lord Privy Seal, 1967

8 Making a point, 1967

9 Answering questions from council house tenants in Coventry, September 1967

10 At Prescote with his wife and the Labour Party agent for Banbury, John Hodgkin, October 1967

11 With Barbara Castle and Tom Driberg (Lord Bradwell) at the Labour Party
   Conference, Scarborough, October 1967

12 Relaxing at home, 1967

13 On the farm at Prescote, 1967

the way. All that's left is the D-Notice debate on Thursday and I think, 'To hell, we'd better get the damned thing over as soon as we possibly can.' But the P.M.'s mind was moving on to the possibility of a four-power conference in New York about Israel.

This evening Anne and I went to the Queen's Birthday dinner, given traditionally by the Foreign Secretary and the Commonwealth Secretary at Lancaster House to all the Ambassadors and High Commissioners. George Brown had told me it was a splendid affair, and we'd never been invited to dine at Lancaster House before. I found myself host at a little round table with Harold Caccia[1] and his wife, the Malta High Commissioner and his wife, the Panamanian Ambassador and the Liberian and Tunisian Ambassadors. There was also a fellow called Johnson, whom I didn't know and who sat next to Anne. It was a miserable affair, the food consisting of paltry bits of cold meat on the table and the occasion was enlivened only by the brilliant speech of the Swedish Ambassador on the subject of Palmerston, whose portrait George Brown now has over his fireplace. After that there was the spectacle of George grimacing and bowing to people and making up to the ladies. He has a streak of genius but on these occasions he's utterly impossible. I met Con O'Neill as we came in and we had a long talk.[2] I asked him what he thought about the Middle East and he said, 'Why can't we keep our heads down? It's all the fault of parliamentary Questions. My Ministers have to make Statements every day because Parliament demands to be made to feel important.' He took exactly the view that I did of that ridiculous exploit in the Gulf of Aqaba.

Friday, June 16th
At Home Affairs this morning there was an interesting little item on Epping Forest which might have led to a major row. The Corporation of the City of London have got a Private Bill through the Select Committee of the House of Lords with a clause giving them special power to deny wayleaves or any planning rights to anybody either in Epping Forest or in Burnham Beeches. Three Departments—Transport, Power and Post Office—all briefed their Ministers to come together and protest that this would be an obstacle to their work. The Post Office would be embarrassed in laying cables and the Ministry of Defence in putting up defence installations in Epping Forest. All of them wanted to challenge the House of Lords. Roy Jenkins and I pointed out that we were having quite enough trouble at Stansted without having a row on Epping Forest and Burnham Beeches. To this the Departments replied that if the precedent were permitted then the National Trust would do the same

[1] Head of the Diplomatic Service 1964–5 and, since 1965, Provost of Eton. He was made a life peer in 1965.

[2] Sir Con O'Neill, Deputy Under-Secretary of State at the Foreign and Commonwealth Office 1965–72 and British Ambassador to the E.E.C. 1963–5. On his return to London he was regarded as a forceful proponent of European entry. He resigned, disenchanted, in 1968, but returned to the F.C.O. in 1969 (see Vol. I, p. 442 and n.).

13

thing with their property and then where would the Government Departments be when they wanted to do something which was objected to by the planners? I was in some difficulty when it occurred to me to inquire what had happened in the House of Lords Select Committee. None of the Departments had bothered to discover or put anything in their Minister's brief. So we were able to send the paper back. You can just imagine the row if the Government were to give the impression that it wants to put defence installations in Epping Forest.

In the evening I found Marcus Sieff waiting to brief me on a few days he has just spent in Israel after the war. He corrected all the nonsense (of which I had been pretty sceptical) about Israeli misbehaviour on the West Bank. Indeed, what alarmed me was the impression he had that George Brown and Harold Wilson were going to take a neutral or slightly pro-Israeli line. I had to warn him that in fact the Government were having to pay heavily for the pro-Israel noises made in the first two days to look after the sterling balances and our oil interests. Alas, it looks as though Harold and George have been talking one language to the Jews outside and another language to us inside Cabinet.

Very reluctantly I stayed up in London to be the guest of honour at the Labour lawyers' annual dinner. I went there feeling very uninspired. But things went fairly well; I made some jokes about myself and my father and why I was hostile to lawyers and then gave them a serious account of our parliamentary reforms.

We were off in our car by 10.15 and drew up at Prescote just after 12, a drive of an hour and forty-five minutes in brilliant moonlight.

Sunday, June 18th
It's now 7.40 in the morning and a wonderful day. We have got this burst of summer which has lasted all the week and come in the nick of time for silage and hay-making. We spent a wonderful afternoon yesterday exploring Weston Park again and the cavern we spotted last time we went there. We discovered it was a huge ice-house some fifteen feet deep in the ground. The Campernownes must have had plenty of ice throughout the winter. Climbing into it through a narrow hole was the making of our expedition.

Today we are going out to dinner with our neighbours, John Makepeace and his wife. John is a wonderful furniture-maker and Ann designs fabrics. We are hoping that he is going to design and make a great new central table and possibly the armchairs and sofas for our drawing-room.

At dinner I was just thinking what a relief it was to get away from politics when I found myself quarrelling with my fellow guest, Terry Frost, a very successful modern artist who is in the Fine Arts department at Reading University. I felt thoroughly ashamed of myself for becoming an old bore, so I shut up and relaxed.

The Makepeaces have constructed a wonderful new house out of a ruined barn, just below Farnborough village, with wheatfields all round them and their workshops next door. Motoring back through the moonlight Anne and I both felt that life at Prescote is the kind of life we really enjoy.

Had I been particularly depressed last week? Not at all. Though it has been a terrible week for the Prime Minister as a result of the D-Notice débâcle, it has been a pretty good week for me. I don't at all feel that I am getting nearer retirement. On the contrary, in the next six weeks we are going to go through a period of high crisis in Cabinet in which I will play an important inside role. At present I don't feel any incipient doom hanging over me.

Monday, June 19th
Once again I travelled up in the restaurant car, not in a reserved compartment; but this time without my red box open since I was busy reading the newspapers. The main feature was the tremendous build-up of a D-Notice press campaign against the poor Prime Minister. I am afraid, however, I was more interested in one article by David Wood on Transport House. It gave a very accurate account of the relationship between the Government and the Party machine and then went on to explain the complete flop of the attempt to make me the liaison between No. 10 and Transport House. I was pleased because I had seen David on Friday and briefed him very fully. What he turned out was a completely objective picture, and thereby confirmed me in disregarding Harold's veto on any of his colleagues ever speaking again to those wicked agents of *The Times*, David Wood and Ian Trethowan. In speaking to them in recent weeks I have got three very fair stories.

My first meeting was in the Lord Chancellor's room and I went there rather gloomily because of his absolutely obstructive attitude to Lords reform. However, he is quite unpredictable. He started straightaway on composition, which he had previously forbidden us to discuss, and laid down two principles. One, we should make a clean break with the hereditary principle; and, two, that we should abandon the idea of giving any Government a built-in majority in a reformed House of Lords since this should make it purely a machine of patronage controlled by the P.M. On the first point we were soon able to assure him the Committee was unanimous. The second Chamber must consist of a new kind of person—peers of Parliament—they would all be life peers and the hereditary peers would only become members of the second Chamber if they were appointed peers of Parliament as well. Of course, the Queen would have the right to go on creating dukes and marquesses and any other title she wanted. We were not concerned with the royal prerogative but with the composition of a reformed second Chamber.

When we turned to the second point we found there was a neat division in the Committee between members of the Lords and members of the Commons. The peers did not want a built-in-majority and said we must trust our reformed House of Lords to back the Government. We from the Commons insisted on a built-in majority because, of course, they are making a real bid to take over the

Lords. In the course of discussion Roy Jenkins said that he had entirely changed his mind since last year about composition and saw a new composition was an essential part of any reform for reducing the Lords' powers. Anyhow, Malcolm Shepherd and John Silkin are going to draft a paper to see if we can resolve the differences.

This afternoon in the House there was the big debate on Aden.[1] George Brown had sent his draft speech down to me on Sunday by dispatch rider as a kind of sweetener. I found it a perfectly honest account and sent it back with the one comment that he should delete a couple of paragraphs which seemed to me too apologetic in tone. I had to be out in committee during most of his speech but when I got back in the late afternoon it was clear that he had produced an extraordinary effect. The Tories had interpreted it as a last-minute conversion of George Brown to their views and were absolutely delighted by it. The more the Tories cheered George as the Foreign Secretary determined to stay on in Aden after independence, the more wild the disarray on our own back benches. Actually, as I convinced myself at O.P.D., George is genuinely and passionately determined to get out of Aden at all costs and the package is solely designed as a cover for this operation. But the Tories were so pleased that there was no vote at ten o'clock. However, we had to pay for that. When the Aden Independence Bill[2] came on they dragged their feet and it took two hours. By this time we had too few people to get the closure for the Gas Industry Order which was not finished until four in the morning.

Tuesday, June 20th

With Harold away in Paris talking to General de Gaulle, Michael Stewart took the chair at Cabinet. We started with permanent summer time, which Roy Jenkins had got through the Home Affairs Committee very easily indeed. Roy Jenkins said we should shift to Western European time and give up Greenwich Mean Time altogether. This should give the school children an extra hour for games in the afternoon throughout the winter. The only person who objected was the Secretary of State for Scotland, who reserved his position and pointed out that up north this meant getting up, having breakfast and getting into the office many hours before daylight. No one else supported his view but Tony Crosland said that since we were often accused of being dictatorial in Government we might offer to try the experiment for five years. Roy, however, said this would cost a fortune and that once it had been accepted the advantage would be so great that there would be an immediate change in public opinion.[3]

[1] On June 19th the Foreign Secretary announced that Aden would become independent on January 9th, 1968, with a new constitution providing for an independent South Arabian State to which £60 million of civil and military aid would be channelled and British naval and air backing given to ensure its territorial integrity.

[2] The Aden, Perim and Kuria Muria Islands Bill.

[3] British Standard Time was eventually introduced on February 18th, 1968, one hour

Then we had Tony Greenwood's paper on planning, which he has now revised after consultation with me and greatly improved. We did agree however that one new paragraph should be inserted to deal with the weakness in the planning system revealed by the Stansted affair. This is an idea the Chancellor and I put to him at the Cabinet Committee, but he had only inserted a very ineffective and weak sentence. It just isn't good enough to have a local inquiry in which the inspector is only permitted to consider the merits of the proposal put up to him. There should be another kind of public inquiry on issues like airports where all the alternative possibilities are also considered. Otherwise all you get is a series of local inquiries in which local opinion is worked up and one after the other each possible site is turned down. We should look at all possibilities and assess them together.

Cabinet ended relatively early and as I was going across to the Chief's office I ran into David Wood. I thanked him for his excellent story on Monday and then he asked me what I thought of the back-bench reaction to George Brown's speech on Aden yesterday afternoon. 'The fact is,' I said, warming to the theme, 'there's no change of policy here, no somersault. Don't think there's any shift of line. All this is a smokescreen for getting out.' I thought he might write something about George Brown standing firm and on the mistake the Tories were making. That was all I intended.

At Question Time this afternoon the Prime Minister, back from Paris, gave quite an optimistic account of his talks with de Gaulle, trying to make the best of what had obviously been a dull, ineffective meeting. I sat beside him on the front bench and he told me that he was going to do the most wonderful television programme that afternoon. Before I could ask him a question he had rushed away. I stayed put for the Report Stage of the Leasehold Reform Bill expecting an appalling mess when we got to the point where we had to put back the clause imposing rateable value limits for enfranchisement. I told the story of how the committee voted 18 to 1 to abolish the limits and how the Minister was snubbed by the Cabinet when he asked it to give its consent. But the whole of the Report Stage went perfectly easily, partly no doubt because the Tories had kept us up till four in the morning on the Gas Order. It's a curious fact that if the Opposition keeps you up one night they are reluctant to try it twenty-four hours later.

At 8.30 the D-Notice took place in No. 10. We'd been summoned to approve the draft motion for Thursday's debate and when I got there a number of people were waiting outside the door. There was George Wigg, the Chief, myself, Elwyn Jones and Denis Healey. George Brown, of course, was still away in New York. In addition there were masses of officials. To my

---

ahead of Greenwich Mean Time. British clocks were advanced one hour and this agreed with Central European Time. The Home Secretary announced that the measure would be reviewed at the end of 1971, but it proved unpopular and an interim review was announced on December 1st, 1968. The experiment was abandoned after two years.

astonishment the draft motion welcomed not only the White Paper but the Radcliffe Report. It tried to show that the Government was in favour of everything. Denis got quite a laugh when he pointed out that we would make a mockery of ourselves if, after writing a White Paper to say that Lord Radcliffe was wrong in acquitting the *Daily Express*, we moved a motion welcoming his Report. We should merely take note of the White Paper. At this George Wigg threatened to resign but the P.M. pushed him aside and after half an hour or so the Chief and I were able to get back to the House, having got the motion drastically redrafted.

This was the first time I had spoken to George Wigg since December. He has appeared occasionally at O.P.D. but usually we sat on opposite sides of the table. On this occasion he attacked me bitterly for each drafting change which I moved. But Denis Healey, the Chief and I held together and I noticed Sir James Dunnett, heading the Ministry of Defence, nodding eagerly and Burke making it clear that he knew we were saying the right thing.

After we left I gather the briefing of the P.M. went on till 10.30 and that George Wigg had still not left by midnight. His hold on the P.M. has been strengthened by this schemozzle.

I was walking through the central lobby later this evening when Wilfred Sendall of the *Daily Express* sent a message that he wanted me urgently on the phone. He told me that he had just seen the first edition of *The Times* and asked whether it was true that I had rung up George Brown in New York because I disagreed with his Aden policy and wanted it reinterpreted. I said this was absolute tripe, but a few minutes later Gerald Kaufman came into my office with the same story. So David Wood, on the day I congratulated him, had completely let me down and confirmed the P.M.'s warning about the dangers of talking to the wicked *Times*' men. After talking to the Chief I asked David to come down to my room and to my amazement he came carrying with him the offending front page. I sat down with him and got whole slices of it taken out.*

Wednesday, June 21st
When I got to No. 10 this morning I found the P.M. delighted. 'Perhaps that will teach you a lesson,' he said. 'You had your pleasure on Monday. Now, this morning you get what you deserve for trusting David Wood.' I felt we were going to have a real row particularly in view of my attitude on D-Notices. But all he said was, 'Well, write a letter to the B.B.C. demanding an immediate apology.' This I did and back by return messenger came a note from Oliver Whitley admitting the mistake and apologizing. But of course they didn't do anything about it on their news bulletins.

At S.E.P., this morning, we were discussing Paper 105, a brilliant demo-

---

* Indeed, he rewrote the story in my presence in a relatively harmless form which was demoted to the bottom of the page next morning after the first edition. However, the B.B.C. bulletin was carrying the original version at both 8 and 9 a.m.

lition of the theology of PESC. At present, PESC is just crudely adding up all
public expenditure and assuming that it has an identical effect on the balance
of payments or on growth. But as the paper pointed out, local-authority
mortgage loans have a different effect from local-authority expenditure on
council houses. Overseas military aid has a very different effect from overseas
economic aid. It was interesting to see the different reactions to this brilliant
report from the officials. Callaghan treated the paper as a piece of intellectual
virtuosity and emphasized that it would take years to develop the crude PESC
technique into a serious policy and one shouldn't take the paper too seriously.
Michael Stewart, on the other hand, said that he felt it was a positive act of
self-indulgence to read a report which gave such keen intellectual pleasure,
and I shared this view. Frank Longford was looking through it desperately
and saying it was all nonsense; and Denis Healey was only concerned that
one of its main conclusions was hostile to his Department. I don't know what
will happen but I should like to feel that after this paper we can't go on just
relying on the old PESC theology.

From that we all went across to the Party meeting on Stansted. I had suggested this but I was a little apprehensive because some eighty people had signed
a motion opposing the third airport or demanding further investigation. I
wondered what would happen. In fact Douglas Jay gave a thorough, rather
dull speech and then Stan Newens, our Member for Epping, a nice, left-wing
proletarian back-bencher, made a constituency speech, no kind of answer to
Douglas. Stan was annihilated by Terry Boston,[1] who pointed out that all the
arguments Stan had used against Stansted could be used against placing the
airport anywhere, particularly Sheppey where there are about 30,000 caravan
dwellers who'd have to be moved. He warned Stan that he was being made
the agent of a conservative middle-class lobby, and there was a bit of truth
in this. The debate went on—with the Scots saying they wanted the airport
at Prestwick—and it really did show those who were there the danger of being
governed by a Tory bandwagon. I may be wrong, but I felt that we could
afford to go ahead on Stansted and we could prevent our own people from
feeling it necessary to abstain in large numbers. But of course the difficulty is
that only 80 Labour M.P.s out of 350 were there.

The debate this afternoon went very well. Despite all the furore outside
we pushed the Decimal Currency Bill through with only some 60 abstentions.
This shows that the discipline and morale of the Party are fairly good.

Back in my room I found Chalfont waiting to see me about the determination of the Agriculture Specialist Committee to go to Brussels. George had
put him in charge of this affair instead of Mulley and Chalfont had pleaded
vainly with them. I told him he could take a fairly strong line about the in-
convenience it would cause the Government, but he must be careful not to
say that the Government opposed their going or indeed had the right to stop
them going. This affair is really only the first of many which we shall

[1] Labour M.P. for Faversham 1961–70.

encounter before we smooth out the relationship between Ministers and these new Committees. The Departments are making every kind of difficulty and if a Committee is as rough and silly as this one it plays into the hands of the Ministers who are their opponents. I haven't heard the last of this trouble.

Anne was up today and we decided to have a little meeting at Vincent Square with Barbara Castle, Wedgy Benn, Peter Shore and Tommy Balogh. I mentioned to Barbara Tommy's feeling that we should invite Marcia too because otherwise Harold would be suspicious. Barbara blew up. 'He pushes his friends to one side,' she said. 'He takes us for granted and appeases our enemies. The only way to impress Harold is to make him fearful. We ought to let him know we are sitting together and discussing what to do.'

Actually only Wedgy and Barbara could come, apart from the Chief and myself, and although I was able to brief them pretty fully about the discussions at S.E.P. and in particular about Paper 105, neither of them could really pretend to be interested. I could remember the time when I couldn't lift my eyes above my departmental interest and I came to the conclusion that Harold was in no danger from anything which Barbara and Wedgy could plot against him at our dinner.

When the Chief and I had strolled back to the House we found a crowd round the tape, studying another speech by George Brown at the U.N. attacking the Israelis, telling them they had to get out of the territories they had occupied and that they could not be allowed to have Jerusalem.[1] When he read this John walked down to the library with me and told me that if that was our policy he would have to resign. I rang Harold at once and told him that this was really intolerable for the Chief and that there was bound to be a bleeding row in Cabinet next morning.

Thursday, June 22nd
We started Cabinet with Harold's report on his talks with de Gaulle. The main impression he gave me was that he found de Gaulle old and tired and that he had felt the terrible snub Kosygin gave him on his way through Paris to New York.[2] When he had finished Denis Healey said that he supposed now there wasn't the remotest chance of getting into Europe, 'No,' said Harold, 'the chances have improved as the result of my talks.' Denis pressed him to tell us what happened which made him feel the situation had improved. Harold tried hard but he really couldn't provide any substantive reasons for his impression.

It was only after this that we got round to Israel and George Thomson was

[1] The Foreign Secretary warned Israel that, although as a result of the war its frontiers might be revised, there should be 'no territorial aggrandisement'.
[2] On his way to and from New York to address the U.N. Kosygin met President de Gaulle; and not only did the U.S.S.R. reject the President's proposal for four-power talks in the Middle East situation, but de Gaulle felt that the Soviet leader attached more importance to his forthcoming meeting with L.B.J. (at Glassboro', New Jersey), on June 23rd and 25th.

asked to make the weekly report on foreign affairs. He started by referring to the Foreign Secretary's speech, saying that we naturally had to concern ourselves with the sterling balances and with oil, and indicating that the speech had not done much more than that.

However, this didn't quite do because in the *Guardian* this morning there was a very full account of what George had actually said and many of us were asking why the deuce he was making great speeches just now and whether we shouldn't keep our heads down and be quiet—as Con O'Neill had suggested to me at the Lancaster House dinner. The whole Cabinet of course was aware that in the fortnight before the war George had been flaunting himself as the friend of Israel, ready to open the Gulf of Aqaba and offering to get the minesweepers in. Then when the Israelis struck he had been totally neutral and now they have won the war he is becoming violently anti-Israeli. Opinion has swung from one extreme to the other in the course of six weeks. I said that it was intolerable to order the Israelis back to their frontiers. The one thing one could safely say was that the 1967 frontiers of Israel were impossible peace frontiers. When peace was made there would certainly have to be a new frontier land in Samaria and on the Golan Heights and probably in the Gaza Strip. I asked whether we couldn't get George to disown the distortions of his speech that afternoon.

Well, sometimes God is on one's side. Questions ran very fast and a later Question of Manny Shinwell's was reached to everybody's surprise. On this occasion Harold made what I think is the most brilliantly evasive action I've ever seen. He extricated George from some quite unambiguous commitments. He interpreted his speech to say not that there should be no territorial aggrandisement but that there should be no automatic annexation of occupied military territories. His answers were absolutely brilliant and he mastered what could have been a really dangerous situation.

Later this evening when the D-Notice debate was over, Harold said to me, 'You know, I probably did a bigger job with those answers on Israel than I did on D-Notices.' How much I agreed with him though I couldn't say how much without upsetting him.

But I must go back a bit to my own business Statement at 3.30. Once again I was taken by surprise when I was asked about the time the Government had given to the Abortion Bill. I studied my brief and said it was Thursday evening from 10 p.m. onwards. Immediately shouts of anger exploded all round. It was only afterwards that I discovered that David Steel had circulated his supporters telling them that they had been given Monday next from 7 p.m. right through to 1 p.m. next day.[1] They certainly had not got this information from either the Chief or myself. Apparently it had been given them by Tom Bradley, Roy Jenkins's P.P.S. If this is true, I must have a chat with Roy, who has been throwing his weight around a bit and trying to decide the alloca-

[1] Liberal M.P. for Roxburgh, Selkirk and Peebles since 1965 and Party Leader 1976. Sponsor of the Private Member's Bill on the Medical Termination of Pregnancy.

13*

tion of parliamentary time. I had a very rough time for ten minutes or so as the result of his interference.

This evening I got Marcia around to see me. I was upset at the thought that I had given dinner the night before without inviting her. When she arrived I found she was utterly miserable about the D-Notice debate which was then going on. She was not being consulted and she felt that George Wigg was in complete control. As for Burke Trend, she was convinced that his concern was not to protect Harold but to cover up the Civil Service. Like me, she was appalled when Harold refused to accept the Radcliffe Report, and wanted to see Harold surrounded by his true friends once again.

All this time the D-Notice debate was going on. It had been started by the Attorney-General because Harold changed his mind at the last moment, with the idea I suppose of deflating the occasion. If that was the idea it certainly succeeded. Elwyn was followed by Anthony Barber, a clever young Tory who is Deputy Shadow Leader of the House and who made a vicious but quite effective speech.[1] After that we had speeches from Manny Shinwell and Ray Fletcher,[2] who had obviously been briefed by George Wigg, trying to divert the attack off Harold on to the unfortunate Colonel Lohan, though the one thing we had all agreed in Cabinet when Harold had asked our advice was that Lohan must not be made the fall-guy, and the Government mustn't look as though it were throwing him to the wolves in order to protect the higher civil servants. But this is exactly the impression which Shinwell and Fletcher created by their speeches. And Bill Deedes picked it up and at once began to defend the unfortunate Colonel. I was back on the front bench in time to listen to Heath, who seemed to me never to have got off the launching-pad. Harold, winding up, started very well indeed and gave us the feeling of a Prime Minister really concerned with security. But suddenly, right towards the end, he was stopped by a Question and started making a series of charges against Lohan. It was a fatal mistake, since it almost certainly means that the press campaign will continue and the D-Notice case will not be closed, as I hoped it would be, by this debate.

When I asked Harold afterwards he told me he hadn't intended to mention Lohan and it was only after Bill Deedes's speech that he rewrote his last paragraph and included all these imputations.

Friday, June 23rd
After morning prayers I stayed behind and Harold talked to me at length about George Brown. I told Harold that I was thinking of writing him a reasoned minute about Israel and sending a copy to George, but Harold said, 'Don't do that or he'll think you wrote the story in the *Daily Mail* this morn-

---

[1] Conservative M.P. for Altrincham from 1965 until 1974, when he became a life peer. He was chairman of the Conservative Party Organization 1967–70 and, among other offices, Chancellor of the Exchequer 1970–74.
[2] Labour M.P. for Ilkeston since 1964.

ing. I know you didn't. I expect Walter Terry got it from the usual source.
By the way, I gave Walter Terry the full briefing for Wednesday's *Mail*
piece on de Gaulle and I didn't give him a word of this.' Mmmm. I wonder.
It's poisonous stuff and it will cause a major explosion. Harold is very
upset that George is in a bad patch again, misbehaving at the Lancaster
House dinner last week, now getting out of control in New York. I think it's
true that, gifted and brilliant creature though George is, he's too dangerous a
liability now and I wouldn't be surprised if Harold isn't making another
effort to get him out of the F.O. altogether. His behaviour during the Israeli
crisis has been so unstable, so erratic. And the trouble is, as Harold said,
that he can in fact give orders to the Ministry. I said, 'Yes, instant statesmanship. Each order is atomic and bears no relation to the next.' And Harold
agreed that this was precisely the problem, his power to say to the F.O. what
Michael Stewart couldn't. We talked on until the Lord Chancellor arrived
for the House of Lords reform discussion. The question was: how the matter
should be presented to the Cabinet. Gerald proposed our Committee should
draft a report and then ask for a remit to suggest a change in composition.
I said this wouldn't do. We should explain to the Cabinet that we can't reduce
the powers of the Lords without dealing with composition as well. Finally the
P.M. achieved a compromise. We should report to the Cabinet in September
against the proposal to have a Bill dealing exclusively with powers and then
perhaps, ten days later, we should present the new package to them.

This afternoon I had to catch the 1.15 to Coventry, where I was due to talk
to the boys at Caludon Castle, the first of our comprehensive schools. I found
my audience were the more stupid fifth-formers and the more I talked to
them about Parliament the less interested they were. They had just finished
their exams and were due to leave. But right at the end one of them asked me
about pirate radio and the whole place sat up. What they really care about is
that the Government isn't allowing them the kind of radio they like.

From there I motored over to Warwick University, where I spent five
most enjoyable hours. First we had a meeting of the Labour students, a little
buffet supper and after that an informal discussion, which the B.B.C. recorded for use in my profile. Actually they recorded forty-five minutes and
the producer was wildly excited. But if I know them, they will use a minute
and a half.

Saturday, June 24th
This was the day when we were to have the Coventry East General Management Committee at Prescote. We planned to have it ages ago, on the terrace.
But the weather had broken and there was a huge thunderstorm yesterday
which went on throughout today. Moreover, only fifteen people turned up
because most of them had taken umbrage and said it was an insult to have
to go to Prescote in order to hold their G.M.C. We had quite an excellent
afternoon, nevertheless. But it was in the middle of a great deal of television

since Robin Day and the *Panorama* team were photographing the farm and Pritchett with the children and me reading aloud on the terrace. Finally I persuaded them to film a little scene of myself in my study talking to the officers of the Party, and then we settled down to our session. I must say it did reveal that these fifteen people at least are friendly and faithful. But what shocks the Party has been submitted to. It needs faith and guts and drive to remain loyal and to be determined to do the rebuilding if necessary.

The only clear decision of the afternoon was a surprising one. They felt unanimously that I should stand for re-election this year. Since they feel so strongly I must certainly do it. And frankly there is not nearly as strong a reason this year as last for my trying to set an example by showing that one Minister at least is prepared to resign and give way to younger people from outside Parliament. That means that I must postpone standing down for twelve months, at least.

Monday, June 26th

I knew that S.E.P. was going to be really important so I got Thomas Balogh to meet me at Paddington and brief me in the car on the way. What we were discussing was the middle-term Public Expenditure Survey, which was presented by the First Secretary with a very sharp introduction but which has been treated by the Chancellor as a satisfactory basis for all our planning. It assumes a 3 per cent maximum rate of growth, unemployment running at 2 per cent and ultimately going down to 1·75 per cent and a much smaller margin in the balance of payments than had previously been thought necessary. So, if there's to be anything left for an increase of private spending there will obviously have to be savage cuts in expenditure. As soon as the meeting started it was clear the P.M. and Callaghan had both accepted this survey beforehand. Indeed, that's why the P.M. told the trade-union leaders at Chequers that the pendulum had swung too far towards public expenditure and we must now make sure that private spending has its fair share of the national cake. Michael Stewart was obviously dissatisfied. So was Douglas Jay. Then I weighed in and said that I was also alarmed because to accept these assumptions without question was to put our whole political future in jeopardy. If this was the basis for the expansion of the economy in the next three years we hadn't a chance of winning the general election. Indeed we couldn't hold the Parliamentary Party for the next twelve months if they had a suspicion that we were planning on such a high rate of unemployment next winter. 'If this is the best which can be done on the present model,' I said, 'then we must try another model with a different set of assumptions about such items as imports and parity.' At this point Callaghan interrupted and said, 'We can't go on for ever discussing devaluation, because that is what the Lord President is really doing in his usual diplomatic way. We discussed it only a few weeks ago at Chequers. We can't have it up every time.' Then someone said, 'We had hardly any discussion of devaluation at Chequers—

just a statement by the Chancellor.' We've never had a statement of the case for a change in parity put carefully and with papers because the P.M. forbids it on the grounds of security. This is perfectly true except, in fact, that he forbids it because all his economic advisers are in favour of devaluation.

At this meeting I was once again the only person who spoke out. I had no support from the other Ministers without Portfolio—Lord Longford, for example, or Gordon Walker. I was in fact a one-man team.

When the meeting was over Harold took me aside and said, 'Now look, it isn't excluded and I must talk to you privately.' 'Well,' I said, 'if you want to talk to me privately talk to the Chief and me. We two must be given your complete confidence.' He replied, 'I hear Jim's been talking to you privately. I must have a talk to you privately as well.' Of course I'll try to keep him to his word but will it actually come off?*

This afternoon George Brown, back from New York, made his Statement in the House on the talks on the Middle East crisis and answered Questions for forty minutes.[1] At the end I thought he had been a flop and that this mixture of candour, gawkiness and sincerity wasn't coming off. But it did. It impressed the House: and the press. In fairness I must add that the mood in which it was received was only possible after last Thursday, when Harold Wilson explained away George's inconsistency, completely against the evidence.

This afternoon we had a long O.P.D. on a new position paper prepared by the officials at enormous length with a summary at the end clearly designed so that Ministers needn't bother to read anything except the summary. The job of a Minister in my position is to read everything and I'd gone through the whole document on the way up in the train and realized it was the most appalling guff, not a serious strategic analysis but a leading article no better than what you could read in the *New Statesman*. I now feel sure that the officials don't reveal any of the important facts to a Committee as big as O.P.D. The general argument of the paper was that we should phase our withdrawal over a long period, up to 1975–6, cutting back our forces, but only gradually and offering a defence capability in exchange. Everybody else seemed to feel that it was too late to do anything about the policy and I'm afraid the meeting degenerated into a cross-examination of Denis by me. When I'd been doing this for an hour and a half and had got half way through the paper George complained that it was sheer waste of time and kept on at me. At one point he said, 'Of course I've only read the summary. Unlike some of these other Ministers I haven't had time to read the whole text of official papers.' I thought I'd infuriated Harold but Tommy tells me he said this evening that Dick had been doing his work for him. Maybe he now realizes that we've simply got to accelerate the process of withdrawal if we're to go into Europe.

* It didn't.
[1] The Foreign Secretary had spent five days talking at the U.N. with other statesmen.

I was out to dinner at Harold Lever's and found myself sitting in the drawing-room with an extremely grave, good-looking, middle-aged woman who told me at the beginning of the conversation that she hadn't read a novel until she was twenty-three. When I asked her what she had read she said mostly theology. It took me some time to discover that this is Keith Joseph's wife — a rich American. We then got into a serious discussion on children's health and I began to realize something of why Keith Joseph, my predecessor at the Ministry of Housing, was such a difficult tense man.[1] He certainly has a difficult tense wife.

Tuesday, June 27th

The Cabinet meeting at which the conclusions of the S.E.P. meeting were put to the rest of our colleagues with a precise proposal that public expenditure should be cut by £500 million in order to meet the requirements of the middle-term survey. Most of us PESC members stayed quiet so that those who had not been present could express their views. This gave Tony Crosland the chance to make a most remarkable speech in which he presented the economists' carefully reasoned case against a £500 million cut — apart from military defence cuts abroad. I had specially briefed Barbara and she was careful not to speak only on the needs of her own Ministry. By the end it looked as though Callaghan's figure of £500 million would be cut down to £350 million, of which £200 million would be defence. In that case the cuts in the rest of public expenditure could be tolerable.

It was quite a successful meeting. We seemed to have crushed the PESC exercise — the idea of a group of Ministers sitting in judgment on other Ministers. Callaghan had probably assumed that if he asked for £500 million he would get £350 million and the exercise had therefore degenerated into a normal haggle.

After Cabinet the Chief and I stayed behind to tell the P.M. that we'd been gravely alarmed by what we had heard from Marcia Williams. She told us he had got ready an appalling draft answer to a Question this afternoon on D-Notices. So instead of trying to end the affair he intended to trail his coat and make a whole set of further charges. We told him this really must stop and that he had to adopt a posture of magnanimity and to show that he really wanted to end the affair by a final settlement with Heath. He'd obviously prepared for our coming because he said, 'What about the passages in square brackets in the Statement?' We hadn't seen the Statement actually so we didn't know what he meant but I had to bluff and I said, 'Delete them without question. Those are the sentences which will cause the trouble.' He went on arguing a bit and finally I said to him, 'Harold, look, what do you imagine it's like to be Leader of the House? I can never answer back. I have to be controlled and create an impression of magnanimity and confidence. As

---

[1] Sir Keith Joseph, Conservative M.P. for Leeds North-East since February 1956. He was at M.H.L.G. 1962–4.

P.M. you ought to behave more as you expect the Leader of the House to behave—restrain yourself from brilliant repartee and destructive polemics. Be as ineffective and quiet as I am.' He smiled and said, 'I'll have a go.'

This afternoon, by providential good luck, we reached the Question at 3.29. He did show control, he did make the offer to Heath and he created a totally different atmosphere in the House. It was far too late to restrain the press however, particularly the *Daily Mirror*.

After that we had a Prime Minister's dinner-party for the Italian official visit where the food was quite good but the company was boring.[1] I was sitting near the Italian Ambassador and the wife of some dignitary. Harold sent across to me at dinner a piece of the tape as well as the letter from Heath and on the back of it I scrawled a message of thanks and appreciation. After the Italians had gone we went up to his room with Tommy and Marcia and tried to make him feel that his friends are proud of what he is doing.

Wednesday, June 28th

At morning prayers Harold was still concerned with the D-Notices and upset by a furious *Daily Mirror* attack on him. He could think of very little else. Soon we went along to the N.E.C. which was quite quiet, obviously as a result of the Chequers conference. It actually finished early and I went back to the House, where the Liberals were having their first quasi-supply day. Despite the protests of some of my colleagues I had given them some Government time because they were an official opposition party without time. They were using it for a discussion of I.T.V.

Just before lunch I had to go to Buckingham Palace for a Privy Council. The Queen was just off to Ottawa[2] and I said politely that I supposed it would be quite fun though the exhibitions are terrible. She said, 'I'm too small to see them,' and suddenly I saw a picture of the tiny little woman looking upwards and only seeing the soles of the feet of the statues above her as she was traipsed miles and miles around on the red carpet.

This afternoon in the House I had a long talk with the Prime Minister of Singapore, who had asked to see me.[3] I had Tam Dalyell there as well as my P.P.S., Geoffrey Rhodes (who, I have come to the conclusion, is completely ineffective). Harry Lee got a double first at Cambridge and he's the man who charms Harold, George and Herbert Bowden and runs rings round them. I'd always known that it is he who has largely persuaded them that we must stay much longer in Singapore than we would naturally do and that our withdrawal must be extended over a decade. I'm always told that he's the only social democratic Prime Minister East of Suez and so we can't let him down. When he had talked a little in this style I said to him, 'The speeches you've

---

[1] Signor Moro, the Italian Prime Minister, and Signor Fanfani, the Foreign Minister, visited London on June 27th and 28th to discuss Britain's application to join the E.E.C.

[2] To visit Expo '67, the World Fair.

[3] Lee Kuan Yew, Prime Minister of Singapore since 1959.

made to my colleagues have made an immense impression on them. I personally am concerned to resist your moral blackmail and look after the concerns of this country. It is in the interest of Great Britain to get out of the Far East as fast as we possibly can. Our presence may be useful to you but it isn't useful to us. We mustn't have a strategy beyond our economic strength.' All I did was to outline the views I'd been preaching in O.P.D., ever since I got there. He looked appalled and thunderstruck. 'How can you talk like that?' he said. 'How can you create that kind of damage in our part of the world?' I then said to him, 'What's the minimum time we need to get out?' He said the absolute minimum would be five years. 'Thank you,' I said, 'that's what I wanted to learn from you—your view on our withdrawal.' I could see he'd rather have bitten his tongue off than tell me this and that he thought I'd tricked him into it. At this point the division bell rang and when I came back from the division I found he'd said he had to go out to the lavatory because he was so upset.

Our conversation continued with my saying that of course we should try to avoid hurting our friends abroad, but that what we really needed was a rapid ruthless withdrawal. I quoted Attlee in India and Bevin in Greece and Turkey. The big withdrawals that were abrupt and sudden were the only ones which really worked. And I found one point of contact with him because he kept on saying, 'Well, at least you oughtn't to announce the date.' I said, 'Yes. But in that case we ought to leave much quicker, not much slower.'

He was dining this evening with Tam, who found him extremely sobered by his realization that there were one or two people in our Cabinet who weren't as soft and squeezable as Harold and George.

This evening we had a long meeting of the Cabinet Housing Committee, at which the only interesting thing I picked up was that the new objective inquiry I had laid on as Minister had revealed that by any reasonable test we've got two million, not one million, slum houses to deal with.

After that at the liaison committee we spent an interminable time trying to draft a motion for the Stansted debate to satisfy those Ministers who want a clear mandate for going ahead without offending Douglas Houghton, who is anti-Stansted. Douglas finally consented to what Jay and Greenwood wanted.

Thursday, June 29th

At 9.30 I sat down with the Chief to see how on earth we could get through our business in the next week and incidentally recess on July 28th. We've got some troubles to face. Tonight we are due for an all-night sitting on Abortion with a filibuster organized by Norman St John Stevas.[1] Unfortunately we were compelled to propose another all-night sitting on Monday for the

---

[1] Conservative M.P. for Chelmsford since 1964, he was Parliamentary Under-Secretary of State at the D.E.S. from November 1972 to 1974. Author, barrister and journalist, he had edited the collected works of Walter Bagehot.

Sexual Offences Bill. This means that the 120 to 150 Labour people who are progressives will have two all-night sittings to face very close together. They wanted Monday's postponed for a week but we daren't risk it for fear of losing the Bill in the House of Lords. The only thing which cheered us was the news that Willie Whitelaw and the Opposition are determined to get away on the 28th come what may so he'll give us some of his time for the debate on the new Defence White Paper and the debate on foreign policy and the Coal Industry Order. He will see to it that we only have to use half a day on the Second Reading of the National Insurance Bill. So we're okay unless there's a blow-up by the back-benchers on either side. We certainly are dependent on the goodwill of the Tories. We've got a new petrol rationing Bill[1] that we might have to get through and we've got the order implementing Part II of the Prices and Incomes Bill also as an extra.

At Cabinet before we could get down to the proper agenda we had to have another of those interminable discussions about leaks. This time Denis Healey raised the issue because of all the attacks on George Brown and in particular an article by Walter Terry in the *Mail* which said the Foreign Secretary was due for the high-jump because of his misbehaviour at the Lancaster House dinner. Curiously enough, this story about his misbehaviour at the dinner had been retailed to me by the P.M. because though I was there I hadn't seen anything. Then we got on to the subject of the Foreign Secretary's pronouncements on Israel. This was more interesting because George felt himself completely justified. However I suspect that he may have learnt his lesson.

Then we came to something much more important. George proposes to go to a meeting of the W.E.U. next Tuesday and wants to make an important declaration there on Europe. Apparently the French refusal to start negotiations with us has rallied five of the other countries to the idea of turning this meeting of the W.E.U. into a presentation of the British case. After a long discussion of timing we are to have a special Cabinet meeting on Monday to consider George's draft.

After Cabinet had approved the miserable little White Paper on Welsh local government reform which I've discussed so endlessly and approved so reluctantly, we'd finished and I rushed over to the Foreign Office to have a word alone with George Brown about the problems of the Agriculture Specialist Committee's visit to Brussels. True to form, they had reached a deadlock, first with Mulley and then with Chalfont. When I saw the Committee yesterday they were in white anger because Chalfont had told them there was a Cabinet veto on their expedition; I had to have a very long and tactful discussion with them. Directly I got into George's room I showed him a draft letter which I proposed that Chalfont should send to the Committee. Once he saw the letter George said there would be no difficulty whatsoever and complained that he had got the impression that I was going to ask the

[1] Bill for the Control of Liquid Fuel.

impossible of him. What the letter proposed was that during our negotiations the full Committee should not go to Brussels, but if a chairman and a sub-committee would like to go that would be quite O.K. This was a case where the officials had been deliberately making trouble between George and me.

Back in my office I found waiting for me a dramatic letter from the Speaker which had been lying there since yesterday evening. It revealed the fact that during the all-night sitting on the Abortion Bill the side galleries would have to be closed because otherwise there would be no door-keepers. The Speaker was far too polite to say so, but what the letter meant was that we were threatened with a strike by a section of our staff. I then summoned the Serjeant-at-Arms—a distinguished gentleman who doesn't like me, doesn't like all-night sittings, doesn't like morning sittings and, above all, doesn't like sittings on abortion and homosexuality—and I said that in view of a threat of a strike I would accept the necessity for keeping the side galleries closed. He said there was no threat of a strike. 'Well,' I said, 'in that case, let's have the galleries open tonight.' 'Then you'll have no door-keepers on Friday,' he said. I got Willie Whitelaw round at 2.30 and when he heard what had happened he said, 'My God, there'll be a blazing row when you announce the side galleries will be closed.' I went into the business Statement certain I was in for another crucifixion. But everything went miraculously well thanks to Cyril Osborne who hates my guts and began to attack me for lack of con-sideration to the door-keepers.[1] Now that I'm getting experienced I imme-diately recognized that he'd offered me an escape route. I said that I was aware of the door-keepers' grievances and that it was in view of these grievances that I'd made the arrangements for the night to keep the side galleries closed. How could the House blame me for looking after the door-keepers? So I got away with it, partly because I'm now more skilful but mainly thanks to Cyril Osborne's dislike of my personality.

As I left the front bench Douglas Jay was starting the Stansted debate,[2] of which I didn't hear a single word. Upstairs in my Lobby conference I had an equally easy time. My main difficulty with the journalists was that I had just learnt that Callaghan had vetoed any package Statement this July on domestic cuts. Since I had confidently told the Lobby more than once about this Statement I had quickly to begin to ease my way out of it without seeming to admit any change of plan.

The whole of that evening was the anticlimax John had planned, and our abstentions—about sixty—were exactly what he had predicted. Afterwards I dropped into Lady Pam's in Cowley Street. Roy Jenkins was deep in con-versation with Kay Graham, proprietress of the *Washington Post*. I saw Hugh Cudlipp, who told me that the *Mirror* had virtually declared war on Harold, which explained the outrageous article on D-Notices on Wednesday morning. If only he'd accepted the Radcliffe Report. If only he'd made the

---

[1] Sir Cyril Osborne, Conservative M.P. for Louth from 1945 until his death in 1969.
[2] On national airport policy.

kind of Statement ten days ago which we'd finally persuaded him to make last
Tuesday!

Immediately after the Stansted vote the abortion debate had begun and the
Chief Whip and I slipped away, but the reason we disappeared was because
we're both convinced abortionists. If we'd stayed we'd have voted throughout with the abortion lobby and most of the Ministers were in that lobby. If
the Chief and I as neutral managers of the House had voted the way we
wanted I foresaw great difficulties in keeping my management above suspicion. So at midnight I walked home to bed.

Friday, June 30th
At 2.30 in the morning I woke up and felt I really ought to be in the House.
However I lay there for a couple of hours, then I got up at five and worked
for two hours and finally I strolled in at seven and was there till ten during
the last stages of the debate.

Then the Chief and I walked across to morning prayers at ten o'clock.
Harold's mind, of course, was still on the D-Notices and I told him that at
Pam's party I had run into Hugh Cudlipp, who had given me the explanation
of the outrageous article on Wednesday. Harold replied that this was entirely
owing to Cecil King and asked me whether I knew about the cause of their
quarrel. When I said 'no' he explained that when he offered Cecil a life
peerage, he had insisted that he wanted a real peerage or nothing at all and
that is how the rift between them started. This is an interesting story and I've
no doubt it is true.

This morning in my office I drafted a short Cabinet paper on the Defence
White Paper and submitted it to Harold and Tommy in draft. There are three
points: (1) the fatal effect of trying to extend withdrawal over a period of ten
years; (2) the absurdity of trying to have a presence in Australia after we get
off the mainland of Asia; (3) the appalling implications of conceding economic aid throughout the ten-year period. These seem to me to be the issues we
must have argued out first in O.P.D. and then in the Cabinet.

This evening at Coventry, where I had gone for interviews, I found myself
invited out to dinner. This happens very rarely to me. It was a dinner in the
Cathedral, at which the Provost was entertaining the Prior of Ottobeuren in
Bavaria—the tremendous baroque basilica, which I have seen. It was a
tremendous example of Coventry's ecumenical anglo-catholicism. I had not
been at a civic event since the Tories took power and I had a quiet talk to
their leader on the Council. I had travelled down by chance with the Town
Clerk who told me it's virtually a one-man show and the leader is developing
a highly-centralized system with only Tories on the policy committee. As for
all the other committees, they're being remodelled so as to hand most of the
work over to the officials. It all sounded first rate and it needed to be done.
Incidentally, I also heard that the Labour Group have now elected George
Park as their leader and Peter Lister as their vice-leader. They're by far the

two best of the younger generation of councillors and so the defeat may be doing Labour good.

Sunday, July 2nd

In the village this is the biggest weekend of the year. Yesterday and today we held our annual fête and managed to persuade the traction engines to share it with us. The first day is a joint show, the profits of which we share evenly, whereas today the traction engines have had it to themselves. Because there is nowhere else big enough we had to let them have our top field on the farm. The whole house—and indeed the whole village—has been working for weeks for the day. The weather was marvellous on Friday but yesterday it was cloudy, despite all the forecasts, and we had a few drops of rain in the evening.

Elizabeth Longford came down to open the fête on Saturday and Frank— her husband—to bless the steam engines on Sunday. As the result we've been having not merely a hard-working village weekend but a politically entertaining weekend as well. Yesterday evening, for example, lying full length on a chaise-longue on the terrace Frank began to discuss that eternal problem of leaks. He told me he'd been cross-examined by Gerald Gardiner and was so outraged that he had written to the P.M. telling him that Cabinet Ministers should not be ordered to examine each other and that he proposed to raise the issue once again. His view is that every member of the Cabinet has got to be his own public relations officer and prepared to do his share of talking to the press; if you talk to the press a certain number of accidents will occur and a certain number of malicious stories will get into circulation and that all this is something which ought to be accepted in public life. I find this perfectly tenable. He also feels, quite rightly, that no investigation of the Lord Chancellor's will ever find the source of the kind of gossipy leaks that most offend the Cabinet. Indeed, the Lord Chancellor's investigation should only be for more serious security leaks or leaks of actual documents.

Like me, Frank is a compulsive addict of conversation and chat. He's a likeable person, with this enormously attractive wife. She's quieter now, not nearly as gay and vivacious as she was, and he seems to carry most of the conversation. After we'd finished our drinks we took Elizabeth and Frank out to dine at the Craven Arms at Southam where we had a long discussion about life peerages and House of Lords reform.

Apart from poor Pritchett, who's been trying to manage a couple of thousand cars which have turned up to see the traction engines, today has been a quieter day for us. It's also given me time to reflect on what was a remarkable week. When I was leaving on Friday Harold said to me, 'Only five weeks left. All we have to do now is to hold out until the recess.' It was a highly uncharacteristic remark, but it shows the strain to which he has been subjected and I think it shows his recognition that his Leader of the House has also been under pretty heavy emotional tension at this period when everybody at Westminster is short of temper at the end of such a long two-year session.

What about those confounded D-Notices? Well, I may be optimistic but I have a feeling that the reply we persuaded Harold to make last Tuesday may have ended the affair. Now that Heath has been invited to read all the correspondence and will therefore be able to see the case there is against Lohan, he will realize that the criticism—if it lies anywhere—lies with the civil servants who allowed Lohan to go on doing a job which was quite beyond him. It also lies with Burke Trend, who wrote a letter recommending that nothing should be done, and with James Dunnett for letting all this fester on. I hope that now Heath has been given this offer this is the last we shall hear of D-Notices.

Our other big achievement this week was to survive the Stansted debate without any damage. Although over a hundred M.P.s had signed the Early Day Motion they obeyed the three-line whip and not a single one voted against the Bill. This did the Government—and, in particular, the Chief and myself—a power of good.

Finally, there's the eternal problem of George Brown. After all the campaign against him this weekend the counter-offensive has begun with a fine article in *The Economist*. The Sunday papers also are rallying to George and saying that the Government can't do without him.

The supplementary Statement on Defence Policy (Cmnd. 3357) to be published on July 18th estimated that by 1970–71 the defence budget would be cut to £2,200 million and by the mid-seventies to £2,100 million. The armed forces were to be reduced by some 75,000 by the mid-seventies, a new Army Strategic Command would be formed and by 1970 seventeen major units abolished. The R.A.F.'s present Fighter and Bomber Command would be merged into a new Strike Command with aircraft largely concentrated at home. British forces would be completely withdrawn from Malaysia and Singapore by the mid-seventies and Britain's main commitments in the future would be to NATO and in Europe.

But before the Commons debate on the White Paper on July 27th another aspect of the Government's defence policy was to come under attack. On July 5th Denis Healey announced the cancellation of the Anglo-French swing-wing strike plane by the French Government. This was to have replaced the V Bomber force in the 1970s and the Secretary of State was accused of jeopardizing British security and the future of the R.A.F. on an unsuccessful gamble.

Monday, July 3rd

Late yesterday evening Mr P. came in to report on the fête. We'd had more than 2,000 cars at one time parked in our top field, he told us. The village seems to have netted £750 profit this year out of the first day. The traction people took all the proceeds on the second day when there was perfect weather. What about Prescote? Well, we had a crop of clover pretty well ruined and we had the gates and hedges bashed about and the piped-water system broken down. I wasn't in the least surprised that Mr P. said firmly, 'Never again.' The interesting thing is that the village spent only £80 on advertising. What brings 10,000 cars to a remote village over two days? The answer of course is that on a fine weekend people must have somewhere to go in their cars and therefore a traction engine display brings them from hundreds of miles away despite the narrowness of the roads. Going round the entries quietly in the late evening I found them quite charming—wonderful brasswork, wonderfully maintained. Many of the owners are people of substance who have servicers for their vehicles, chauffeurs so to speak, who look after them as a whole-time occupation; taking them round the country and displaying them at the weekend has become a kind of hobby. As we set out to catch the train this morning there were still some of them out on the field.

The main item this morning was of course the Cabinet meeting on the draft E.E.C. declaration. It had been sent down to Prescote and I'd read it through and discussed it with Frank Longford. The detailed part at the end was quite all right but there was a 14-page ideological introduction which I found vague and dangerous. There was one particular phrase to which I objected, where it said that we wanted to see a European personality develop which would express itself not only in commerce but also in defence.

Directly Cabinet started there was a great outcry from Barbara about the way the pendulum had swung from economics to politics and there was also a fair degree of protest from Fred Peart and Douglas Jay. But after the initial roar everyone, including the outright opponents, settled down to help in the redraft and George Brown was allowed to get away with his first fourteen pages although I got rid of the word 'personality'. I myself am still perfectly confident that we could stay outside if we completely cut back our overseas military commitment, ceased to be the banker of the sterling area, and face the need for devaluation. If we did all this I can see no great difficulty in the short run in achieving a better standard of living, and in the long run as well. But this is not the view of Harold and George Brown or indeed of the Cabinet as a whole, and so we are committed to getting in for political reasons and in so doing we are disregarding in the most reckless way the portentous short-term economic cost of entry. They've recently experienced the difficulties of trying to introduce socialist planning in our economy outside a great bloc, and they're determined to escape from these difficulties by getting inside. Even if we can't get in I think we shall be committed to a treaty of transition.

Immediately after Question Time we had yet another O.P.D. in order to conclude consideration of the Defence White Paper. It's a terrible document but there's no readiness to change it at all. However, two important points arose. One was the question of the sophisticated weapons we're committing ourselves to supply to our allies in the Far East. The White Paper assumes that when we withdraw from the mainland we shall commit ourselves to this policy and I pointed out the enormous expense involved. Even George Wigg had to admit it was quite impracticable. The second issue was the amount and extent of the economic aid we should provide. Looking to the figures in the document it's clear that aid will increase during the eight- to ten-year period of evacuation from small beginnings to major contributions. I asked on what principle the aid was fixed and whether it was related to the damage to the economy our withdrawal would cause. Bottomley, who'd remained silent up till then, replied that it was decided by the Foreign Aid Committee we'd sent out to make a report. 'But what instructions did you give them about the basis on which the aid would be fixed?' I asked. It gradually became clear that Bottomley's only concern was to make sure that all the aid provided by the Overseas Aid Department would go on flowing into the countries and that this aid would be additional to it. As for the Committee, it had just plumped for a figure which meant that the longer we went on with the withdrawal the bigger our subsidies would be. Harold was shocked enough to insist on this being referred back.

This evening at ten prompt we started the all-night sitting on the Report Stage of the Sexual Offences Bill and at two in the morning it looked as if it was going to last thirty hours. But the Opposition conked out. Neither Cyril Osborne nor Cyril Black,[1] the leaders, could get there. The speech-making was left to Rees-Davies,[2] and three or four other Tory back-benchers of that ilk. The Chief and I spent the night going round the lobbies and encouraging the troops. This was necessary since though we had 116 to start with there were only ninety-nine left when the Third Reading vote came.[3] But of course they were down to fourteen on the other side as well.

Walking back to Vincent Square with Tam on a lovely clear morning, we discussed the effect of getting the 'Buggers' Bill' through. Frankly it's an extremely unpleasant Bill and I myself didn't like it. It may well be twenty years ahead of public opinion; certainly working-class people in the north jeer at their Members at the weekend and ask them why they're looking after the buggers at Westminster instead of looking after the unemployed at home. It has gone down very badly that the Labour Party should be associated with such a Bill. On the other hand we agreed that this had a boomerang effect in creating a positive demand for the Abortion Bill and it's clearer and clearer that this will be a pretty popular measure, especially among working-class women.

Tuesday, July 4th

We spent the whole morning at S.E.P. discussing the strategy of PESC. By now Jim had his list of specific cuts and we looked at each one separately.

---

[1] Sir Cyril Black, Conservative M.P. for Wimbledon 1950–70.
[2] William Rees-Davies, Conservative M.P. for Thanet since March 1953.
[3] On the Third Reading the vote was 99 to 14.

Once again the Treasury had slashed in a most uninspired way. For instance, Harold Wilson had wanted to see whether a special licence on heavy vehicles on main roads should not be imposed in order to make them pay their share of wear and tear, but Jim was not interested. All he wanted was the cash, which he got by cutting the estimates.

When we came to education Harold said he thought we should achieve our cut by postponing the raising of the school-leaving age from fifteen to sixteen. There's no doubt that most schoolteachers would find the postponement a great relief since they don't know how to handle the crowd of reluctant students they will get and they've no idea how best to use the extra year. There aren't enough teachers or classrooms for it. Of course, socially it's true that this means giving a continuing advantage to the child whose parents decide that he should stay on voluntarily. Nevertheless on balance I supported Harold. He was opposed by the educationalists, led by Michael Stewart and also by Jim Callaghan and George Brown. We left it that the Minister of Education should make his own decision how to make his contribution to the cuts.

This afternoon I had to confront the Serjeant-at-Arms at the Services Committee. Before he came in I told my colleagues how furious I was with his behaviour at the time of the door-keepers' 'strike'. Willie Whitelaw, who's a shrewd operator, put a very different point of view. 'Why on earth should the Leader of the House be held responsible for the exact way the galleries are kept open? Why shouldn't this be left to our officials since they want to control policy?' he asked. I replied that the difficulty had been that the Speaker had refused to make a Statement and that's why I'd had to do it at business time. After that we had the Serjeant in and told him to keep the galleries open in the best way he could and made it clear that he wasn't to present us with any more *faits accomplis* or ultimata. When he had withdrawn I realized how shrewd Willie had been. If I'd had my way there'd have been a bleeding row which would have got out into the press. As it was they handled him firmly but without any publicity.

This evening John Silkin and I sat down to a serious discussion on what to do about the Abortion Bill. We assumed that we couldn't get it in under two or three days and that amount of time wasn't available if we were to recess on the 28th. Yet how could we go away on the 28th and leave such an important social measure unfinished? We decided that we must make a contingency plan for an extra week, which would carry us into August. This would give us time to finish Hugh Jenkins's Employment Agencies Bill as well. So, contrary to the feelings of Harold and George Brown last week that there was no time for the Abortion Bill, by this evening it was pretty clear that there was a majority in the Party which was prepared to have an extra week in order to complete it. I don't believe the motive was chiefly or mainly enthusiasm for abortion, though that's genuine and strong. There was also a deep sense that Private Members' time was for the first time being used constructively and that big decisions were being prevented by the St John Stevas filibuster. Fortunately, by the way, he'd absented himself on Monday night; if he'd been there and supporting the Sexual Offences Bill we might have had the greatest difficulty in getting a hundred of our people to stay. The truth is that at the moment many more of our back-benchers are enthusiastic for the social measures contained in the Private Members' Bill than they are for the Government's own legislation like leasehold reform and steel nationalization. All that, they feel, belongs to the Government up there whereas homosexuality and abortion are issues on which back-benchers can enforce their own discipline and where they are free to vote according to their own consciences. The couple of hundred people who stay all night feel contempt for their fellow Members who've slept comfortably in bed and they now form a most formidable pressure group. I was very much alarmed that if on Thursday afternoon at business Questions I get up to say that the Government can give no more time for the Abortion Bill I will be knifed in the back by 160 daggers within seconds. Yet constitutionally the argument would be perfectly respectable. I could point out that there must come a point when the Government can't afford to give more time for a Private Member's Bill because there is no prospect of the House reaching a decision. But if I try that argument the decimal-currency row would have been nothing to what I would get. I was going to avoid this at all costs so the Chief and I prepared our contingency plans for the first week in August and made sure that the rumour about it was current in the lobbies. As we hoped, the Tories were horrified since they have been working all out for July 28th. As we didn't want to get unnecessarily committed to an extra week what we finally decided in our own minds was to start the Abortion Bill again on Thursday of next week and then let it run through Friday's, Saturday's and Sunday's business if necessary in order to force it through at a single go. But this threat of three all-night sittings should not be made Cabinet policy and should not be known until next week.

Wednesday, July 5th

All the papers made George Brown's speech at The Hague[1] their lead story but they also gave prominence to a public speech last night by Michael English,[2] who is Douglas Jay's P.P.S., in which he remarked that George 'is the best spaniel outside Crufts'. I had to waste a lot of time summoning

[1] On June 4th the Foreign Secretary had opened a debate on the European economy at the meeting of the Council of Ministers of the W.E.U. at The Hague. George Brown later spoke of the speech as the only one he ever made 'as a Minister where every word was vetted by the full Cabinet beforehand'. The first forty-nine paragraphs give Britain's reasons for wanting to become a member of the E.E.C.; the fiftieth contained the text of the formal conveyance of Britain's application 'before the French realized what was happening'. See Lord George-Brown, *In My Way* (London: Gollancz, 1971), pp. 221–2.

[2] Labour M.P. for Nottingham West since 1964. His reference was to the annual dog show in London.

Michael English and telling him to apologize if he didn't want to be reported to the liaison committee. But before this we'd had morning prayers with Harold and broken it to him that we must have more time for the Abortion Bill. Despite what he'd said last Friday, he couldn't have been easier. He's uncomfortable about abortion because he has a large number of Catholic voters in Huyton and is a close friend of Archbishop Heenan.[1] But on the other hand he accepted the argument that if we didn't get the Abortion Bill through during this Session it would be brought up again in every Session of this Parliament.

After lunch the Chief and I sat down to work out our new plans. We abandoned the idea of an extra week beyond the 28th. With full-scale co-operation from the Opposition we can cram everything into a fortnight provided we finish off the Abortion Bill next week. We were just finishing when we received an urgent message to go round to the P.M.'s room since he'd just received a reply from Ted Heath and Douglas-Home about the D-Notices. Apparently they were not content and were insisting on yet another inquiry at which Lohan could rehabilitate himself. We were brought in because Marcia was alarmed. Apparently George Wigg was taking the view that Heath didn't want to go on with this war and we could afford to concede to his demand for an inquiry with all the evidence published. Marcia was so furiously anti-Wigg that she wanted the inquiry turned down altogether. We advised that of course this was impossible. Certainly there must be an inquiry but we emphasized it should be a Civil Service inquiry held in private and that the only thing to be published was whether Lohan was suitable or not for his post. Harold's main point was that he wanted to appoint Helsby, the ex-Head of the Civil Service, because he knew in advance what his report on Lohan would be.[2] Partly because I'd had no sleep I felt bad-tempered this afternoon and wasn't very helpful, and I kept on saying that Ted Heath will want to bury it now. Harold was also desperately trying to prepare for the House of Lords' debate on D-Notices, briefing Arnold Goodman, briefing Chalfont, briefing Gerald Gardiner. I suspected this was useless because Radcliffe would take all the headlines with his speech. They wouldn't listen to Dilhorne on the one side or Gardiner on the other and as for bringing Francis-Williams in I doubted if he'd be any help to us at all.[3] 'Oh God,' I thought.

Back in my office I found Freddie Warren, Anne and Jennie Hall waiting to have a drink with me. It turned into a gay dinner-party before I had another of my groups of back-benchers for a discussion which finished at ten, when

[1] Cardinal Heenan, Roman Catholic Archbishop of Westminster from 1963 until his death in 1975. He was Archbishop of Liverpool 1957–63.

[2] Sir Laurence Helsby (K.B.E. 1955), Joint Permanent Secretary to the Treasury and Head of the Home Civil Service from 1963 until his retirement in 1968, when he became a life peer.

[3] Francis Williams, editor of the Daily Herald 1936–40 and then Controller of News and Censorship at the Ministry of Information. He was the Prime Minister's Adviser on public relations 1941–5 and 1945–7 and, subsequently, Attlee's biographer. In 1962 he became a life peer as Lord Francis-Williams. He died in June 1970.

John and I had to go back to Downing Street to run through the tactics for Thursday and Friday night. The P.M. was perfectly obliging but we knew that all he wanted was to talk about his D-Notices. We had waited twenty-five minutes outside his room before he was ready. John and I were sitting in one corner with George Wigg walking past us unlocking a door, going into a little side room and then coming out without speaking. Gerald Gardiner was also pacing to and fro—each group separately waiting for its cue for entrance and then the P.M. finally coming along the corridor late from dinner. We were pushed in and pushed out and got rid of ourselves and that was that.

But I still had one more job this evening. Just before midnight I saw Michael English. He'd been waiting half an hour for me and I let him in, gave him a drink and gave him hell. 'Now you've refused to sign an apology, you're for it and no one will lament because you will provide a shining ex-ample of how our new liberal discipline works,' I said. After a minute or two Michael, who thought we really were going to expel him from the Party, said he would sign the letter.

Thursday, July 6th
When I went into the Chief's office before Cabinet there was the letter duly signed by Michael English. Thank God we got through without a with-drawal of the whip. Our bluff had worked.

At Cabinet the first item was the Abortion Bill. There was never really any doubt that we should get our way since our only two strong opponents were Willie Ross and Frank Longford. There were some very strong sup-porters headed by the Home Secretary, with Tony Crosland, Barbara Castle, Wedgy Benn and Gerald Gardiner. Harold was dubious but Callaghan came right out and said extremely sensibly that it is a Bill the back-benchers want and that the House of Commons has to get rid of this Bill. He couldn't have been more helpful. George Brown and Michael Stewart were already on our side. I was mainly concerned not to reveal our tactics for endless all-night sittings from Thursday to Monday and I obtained the sanction that the Chief and I should use our discretion. That enabled me to get through the business Statement in the afternoon without committing the Cabinet to sup-port abortion. Nevertheless, what we shall be doing next week has pulled us off our neutrality fence. The Government will be pushing the Bill through and will get the credit or discredit for it.

Then we turned to the main item—the Defence White Paper—which we considered alongside the brief paper I'd put in as Lord President. My paper fell absolutely flat. I got support from Barbara and Wedgy and I would have got it from Roy if he'd been there. Six of us wanted a far more drastic policy, but the rest flaccidly accepted the paper with only minor changes. I think I know why the discussion was so flat. Wedgy Benn may have been right when he said that even though it talks about a ten-year period of withdrawal this

White Paper is the death knell of the British Empire east of Suez, the abandonment of all that Harold and Herbert Bowden and George Brown and
Denis Healey were saying only a year ago. So it ends a myth and because of
that it seems my colleagues were reluctant to have a fight this morning. Indeed,
four of them seemed to regard the White Paper as a useful smokescreen under
which the withdrawal could take place.

In preparation for the business Statement this afternoon I saw David
Steel at two o'clock. I told him of our decision and asked him for heaven's
sake to support the Thursday evening sitting. I then had Norman St John
Stevas at 2.30 and told him equally politely that the Government have now
decided to give enough time to let the Bill through come what may and that
he should draw any conclusion he wanted from that statement. He was very
dignified and said, 'I fancy we shall find that the Opposition will modify itself
somewhat on Thursday night next week.' The Whips did a lot of preliminary
work around the lobbies that afternoon and when I rose to make my Statement I had a resounding cheer from our side organized by Douglas Houghton
as a response to the announcement of the all-night sitting. It was no good
Quintin Hogg saying that the evening is the wrong time for the Bill when I
could point out that the majority of the House wanted it this way.

It was a pretty successful business Statement and, as I walked behind the
P.M. after I'd finished, Jim Callaghan said, 'Not a foot wrong this time:
you're really learning that job pretty skilfully.' And all my colleagues who
for weeks have been looking at me and praying that I would get it right
seemed to feel a bit better about me too. But of course it involves a lot of
hard work, particularly memorizing work. In bed that Thursday morning I
gave Anne the business Statement to read and all the briefs and she said,
'How can you remember all this?' But it's no good just memorizing it. It has
to become part of your system so that you not only know all the Bills by
heart, you live with them and are solely concerned with how they are doing.
In this way you begin to get control of the business of the House. But the
House does need a lot of living in too.

Upstairs at my Lobby conference there were some very shrewd questions.
Francis Boyd, who's not always very smart these days, remarked to me, 'Last
time as Leader of the House you were careful to say the Abortion Bill would
have to be stopped in order not to overrun the Finance Bill. But this time
you've said nothing about Government business on Friday. Is that right?'
and I said, 'Yes.' And on that basis he wrote a correct story about the tactic
we intend if the Thursday all-night session doesn't work.

The Party meeting this evening was also good-humoured. When it was
over I found Barney Cocks waiting for me in my room. Because he's been a
pure House of Commons man for forty years he's as remote as any ineffectual
don and entirely immersed in his battle against the Speaker's Department,
the Serjeant-at-Arms and the Lord Great Chamberlain. His trouble this
evening was the Clerks' new salary scale. The Services Committee had left it

to the Staff Board, headed by Lidderdale, to negotiate with the Treasury.[1]
And when the Treasury complained that the Board wouldn't negotiate I
dropped a note to Lidderdale asking him to be flexible and start talks. In
reply I got an enormous memo from Barney saying there could be no question
of negotiation. He wasn't a civil servant who put forward treble what he
expected to get. He recommended what was right and he was coming to see
me to say the Clerks wouldn't negotiate. See me he did, but I had the sense to
avoid a row. Instead I prepared Barney for a meeting next Tuesday after
which I shall go to see the Chancellor myself because we've got to get money
for the door-keepers and the Clerks if the House isn't to break down in the
next Session.

This was my evening off and I went home and had a delicious time. We sat
and quietly drank our Chambéry and then we walked slowly in this beautiful
summer weather to Lockets, the new restaurant in Marsham Court, just
round the corner. There we had a delightful dinner and our first evening off
together for many a day and it was lovely.

Friday, July 7th
At the P.M.'s business meeting this morning George Brown raised the
problem of oil, which is alarming us all and for which no adequate preparations are being made. Dick Marsh was trying to buy up expensive Venezuelan
oil and Callaghan was saying we ought to have rationing to save our foreign
exchange.[2] What we needed but didn't get, I pointed out, was an Emergency
Committee with the power to overlook the whole subject and take decisions.
The trouble is that this D-Notice affair has distracted the P.M.'s attention
from much more important problems.

When I stayed behind to talk business I found that all the P.M. could
discuss were the reports in the press of the House of Lords debate on D-
Notices. The only great speech—Arnold Goodman's—he'd said to me, is
hardly mentioned and Chalfont's is suppressed. Of course the papers have
published Radcliffe's attack which, as expected, was annihilating and unanswerable. I was just going to get down to business when he said, 'Well, I
haven't any time now. The Paymaster must come in,' and he spent the rest
of the morning with George Wigg and Helsby on D-Notices. 'Oh God!' I
thought, 'Harold's in such a rattled state, with Wigg on one side and poor
Marcia and Gerald on the other.' I don't think the Chief and I were much
help, frankly, because all we could do was to beg him not to write a great
riposte to Heath but curtly to give him his Civil Service inquiry with the condition that it shouldn't be published. But I left feeling that I had done badly

[1] David Lidderdale, Clerk-Assistant to the House of Commons 1964–74 and from 1974
to 1976 Sir Barnett Cocks's successor as Clerk.
[2] The closure of the Suez Canal made it necessary to buy oil elsewhere. On June 30th
petrol prices had been increased by 2*d*. a gallon.

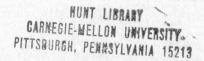

by Harold by being testy and bad-tempered, and driving him back into the arms of George Wigg, Helsby and Burke.

After another of my Garrick press lunches I had one more job—to hand over the George Weidenfeld group to Chalfont. We'd had three or four quite good meetings, but George's first two projects had come unstuck and the group was rather fading out. I hoped that with Chalfont having a house in Brussels and moving out there in September this group could work direct with him in Europe. Listening to him I found him an extremely skilled public relations officer but curiously empty. No doubt he intended to tell them nothing and he did it with the greatest accomplishment. Whether he's the right man to give these people, who are very gifted, a sense of serious purpose I doubt. But I've decided this isn't my job, so I handed them over and took the train back to Banbury, where we are having wonderful weather.

Saturday, July 8th
This has been a fairly easy week for me. Now that the Six-Day War is over we're beginning to realize just how expensive it's been to this country in terms of our balance of payments and in terms of our economic stability as a whole.[1] The other day Jim Callaghan observed that it's heartbreaking to see all the results of last July's measures being frittered away so that soon we may find ourselves without a balance-of-payments surplus this year. We've also had the threat of oil rationing hanging over us all this week.

On the other hand, inside Cabinet it's been a really good week because we've got through a number of difficult decisions. The Defence White Paper is now agreed and due to be published on Tuesday week, and this confounded PESC exercise has been almost completed without any major sense of crisis. Nevertheless, we most of us still feel that we must be prepared for further measures, including devaluation. At long last Harold is prepared to talk to the Chief and me and we're going to have our talk on Monday, he tells us, i.e. the day after tomorrow.

John and I have also had a good week in the House with the Sexual Offences Bill through and the Cabinet accepting our tactics on abortion. Indeed, the only disastrous aspect was the Radcliffe speech in the House of Lords on Thursday. I've now had time to read it. The man chosen by the P.M. to act as an impartial adjudicator can't be expected to be impartial when his Report is rejected in a White Paper. I suppose this was the most effective quiet rebuke of a P.M. by a public servant of modern time.

Tomorrow the whole family are off on an expedition somewhere north of Shrewsbury, where I'm addressing a Labour Party Regional Conference, and we're going to have a picnic.

---

[1] It was estimated that the cost of the war to Britain's balance of payments was some £200 million a year.

Monday, July 10th

I'd better start with yesterday. We motored up to Shrewsbury via Stratford and Alcester, round through Worcestershire and up into Shropshire and had our picnic lunch at a medieval monastery in the Severn Valley some ten miles south of Shrewsbury. When I got to the meeting place—a small Victorian hall in the middle of the town—I must admit I hadn't had much time to prepare the speech, partly because both the children had been sick on the way and I'd been reading *Sir Nigel* to them to keep them quiet and partly because I had left behind the document upon which I intended to base most of my argument. It was an excellent document prepared by the Treasury on the achievements of the Labour Government and it celebrates our thousandth day in power with a comparison between our achievements in the first three years and those of the Tory Government in the last three years, measured in terms of houses and hospitals built, old peoples' homes opened as well as levels of social security and education. I'd meant to base a press release on it but didn't have time on Friday. But knowing that a conference of the Shropshire Labour Parties wouldn't be all that important I was quite content to deliver the speech I'd made seven or eight times already, starting with wages and incomes and relating the policy to the balance of payments, then going on to describe my work as a parliamentary reformer and culminating in the Government's social achievements.

It was a very hot day when we got to this little old hall, but there was an excellent turnout from four Labour Parties. Before I began I noticed there were two pressmen at a table at the back. Since everything turns on the exact words I used I must now be careful what I say. I'm sure I made an absolutely clear and straightforward explanation of how under George Brown we tried a voluntary incomes and prices policy; how in 1966 we'd been forced to impose the wage freeze and the brutal severity of Part IV; how we were now relaxing Part IV which was only justified by the breathing space it gave us to negotiate a new relationship between Government and industry based on the voluntary principle; how many of us had thought we ought to retain more reserve powers but had sacrificed this to achieve the co-operation of the trade unions. And it was here I issued the warning that if the voluntary system breaks down then we will be back at square one. We shall have all the troubles we had last July and we will have to accept our medicine. Then I went on to our other two subjects, had an excellent question period and motored back home.

It was a long sultry evening and we didn't get in too early. When we did we got the children to bed and didn't bother to listen to the wireless either that evening or next morning. But when I got into my reserved compartment this morning and took a look at the front page of the *Daily Telegraph*, it woke me up. Nearly the whole of it was devoted to a sensational story that on Sunday Richard Crossman had warned his audience of the Government's intention to reintroduce a compulsory wage freeze if the country got into economic difficulties. Turning to *The Times*, I found the story printed prominently but only on page 3, and so too with the *Guardian*. But comparing the three stories it was clear that they all came from a common source, which must have been one of the two local men at my meeting acting as a legman for the Press Association. This was obvious because each story began with the general claim that I had announced the Government's intention to revert to a compulsory wages policy and only substantiated it with two or three sentences, not very much in quotes. Indeed, the only evidence for the claim that I had advocated a return to a compulsory policy was the use of the words 'the same medicine as last time'.

Opposite me in my reserved compartment was Neil Marten,[1] my local Member, and when he'd read the story he agreed straightaway that the *Telegraph* had seized on this because we were debating the critical Report Stage of the Prices and Incomes Bill that afternoon. The one thing which terrifies our Labour M.P.s is the fear of any return to statutory restraint. Hence the endless references by Government spokesmen to the voluntary principle and the explanation that the Bill is only being extended for another twelve months to give that principle a chance. True enough, the First Secretary has been very careful not to rule out explicitly and absolutely the taking of greater powers. But he has all the way through expressed the intention not to take them and to make the voluntary principle work. So the statement I was purported to have made at Shrewsbury may have seemed common sense to many outsiders, but in fact went right back on the informal compact we reached in the Cabinet, where those of us who wanted to keep reserve powers agreed to try to make the voluntary principle work and to avoid talking about any reversion to statutory powers. I knew that the moment Ray Gunter and Michael Stewart saw the *Telegraph* they would think I had made an appalling clanger and all the back-benchers who have put down amendments would be getting ready for a tremendous row in the House that afternoon. So going up in the train I roughed out a Statement saying that at no point in my speech had I either directly or by implication stated the Government's intention to return to a compulsory wages policy.

I was due at a meeting on Lords reform and when I got to my office I only had time to shove my bit of paper into Freddy Ward's hands, ask him to get it typed and to put it out. It happened that that day I was due to attend no less than six important committees as well as preparing for a difficult business Statement. Somehow I would have to deal with what I knew was a major personal crisis in the intervals between.

At the previous meeting we had asked John Silkin and Malcolm Shepherd to put forward a paper trying to reconcile the conflicting views of the two Whips' offices. They came down heavily in favour of a two-tier system in which voting peers will be nominated for each Session of Parliament and paid a lot extra. The voting peers would be selected in proportion to the

[1] Conservative M.P. for Banbury since 1959.

numerical strength of the parties in the House of Commons, since this was a
sure way of providing an in-built Government majority. The rest of the House
would consist of speaking peers who would not be able to vote. I knew that
one or two peers were keen on this scheme and I had tried it out at dinner
one evening on some of the more intelligent members of our Parliamentary
Reform Group. Everybody was shocked. 'You're not really saying,' said one
of them, 'that we should pay peers more for voting your way?' This had been
my instinctive reaction and it was Anne's as well. Of course it would be
highly convenient for the Whips to have a built-in majority in the Lords. But
neither the Lords nor the Commons, nor the public outside, would tolerate
such an abuse of patronage. Every single member of the Committee was
against poor John Silkin, including Frank Longford, who has his own pet
variety of the two-tier system and would be ready in the first instance to make
all existing peers who are life peers and peers of first creation into peers
with voting rights. It was soon clear that even if we could agree to turn John
Silkin's plan down there was agreement on little else. So we decided that
Gordon Walker, Shackleton and the Home Secretary should get together
and work out an alternative plan.

Directly we finished this long meeting at 12.30 I rushed back to my Office
and asked what they had done. The answer is that my press release had been
typed out and that Freddy Ward had absolutely refused to issue it. 'None of
us can touch this stuff,' he said. 'It's all about a Party regional conference and
has nothing to do with the Government. Any press release must be put out by
Percy Clark in Transport House.' I couldn't deny that in saying this he was
cleaving to the strict Civil Service interpretation. It was clear I was going to
get no help whatsoever today from Freddy or any of the other officials in my
Private Office. Freddy's objection was all the better founded because he told
me that he was certain I'd made the offending remark and was merely trying
to wriggle out of it and he was greatly against my doing that. Right to the
end of the crisis he stuck to the view that I would have done far better to
brazen it out since the general public would be convinced that I was right.
He seemed to be completely unaware of my obligations, particularly to
Michael Stewart and Ray Gunter—not to mention the back-benchers. But
what about help from my colleagues? I had instructed Freddy to ring up the
Private Office of the First Secretary and the Minister of Labour. From
neither did I get any response. As usual I was isolated and would fight this
through completely alone. So I gave instructions that the press release should
be taken round to Transport House where it was duly issued at lunch-time.

My next meeting was at three with the Chancellor, Patrick Gordon
Walker and Peggy Herbison to find a way of breaking the deadlock on
family allowances. I had just twenty minutes to read the Chancellor's long
paper in which he proposed to have an interim increase of family allowances
in October and then next year to substitute a new housing allowance. I
thought this idea was a good one provided you started from scratch. But to

14

introduce the idea of a housing allowance in the middle of a long Cabinet dispute was ridiculous. Moreover I discovered he'd had no preliminary discussions with either Peggy Herbison or even with the Minister of Housing, who was chiefly affected. It was obvious that all Jim was up to was producing another obstacle with which to prevent the Titmuss claw-back scheme from being approved by Cabinet.

I moved straight from there to a long meeting of the Home Affairs Committee. First Tony Crosland raised the issue of whether the Public Accounts Committee could investigate the accounts of the University Grants Committee and secondly Barbara Castle discussed a complex problem of speed limits. I couldn't pay very much attention because throughout the meeting Freddy Ward was sending messages into me, including a copy of the tape which showed that my Statement had been issued in full and had stimulated the Press Association to publish what they claimed to be the full text of what their man had written down, not merely the version he'd sent to London but his complete notes. Reading this full text I felt greatly relieved because it strongly suggested that I had used the word 'medicine' not about a wages policy but about the higher level of unemployment that a Government would have to permit if a voluntary wages policy fails. I would have liked to put out another Statement but there was no time since I was now due at No. 10 for the meeting on devaluation which Harold had promised John and me.

Directly I got there Marcia rushed in to say that Percy Clark was very upset and I must hold a press conference. This is a very bad thing for a Leader of the House. He has off-the-record discussions with the Lobby but he normally never holds an ordinary on-the-record press conference. However, off the cuff I said, 'All right. Let the press come down to my room at six this evening —anybody who wants to ask me about this speech. It won't be a Lobby, it will be a press conference.' Until Marcia left the room Harold remained completely silent and refused to interest himself in my affairs. Then he put his feet on the table and said, 'Well, what do you want to talk to me about?' I replied that we had not come to see him—he had invited us to a special private meeting when I was trying to get devaluation discussed at S.E.P. So he proceeded to talk about the economic situation and said nothing new. He assured us he hadn't excluded the possibility of devaluation but the floating of the pound would probably be more difficult than fixing a new rate. Moreover the chance of our devaluation being followed at once by that of the French and the Germans was now much greater than it had been and he himself was looking more to import controls and such devices than to devaluation.

John and I also felt very aggrieved because he had failed to consult us before the purely political decision whether to reject the Radcliffe Committee's report. Surely that was a point on which the Leader of the House and the Chief should be consulted because it was bound to affect the parliamentary position? He didn't dispute this. Instead he said the real mistake was made by not having a lawyer to advise him in drawing up the terms of reference of the Radcliffe

Committee. That was a fatal mistake. I saw he was slipping out of our clutches and took him back to the danger of his isolation from his friends, and reminded him that in his decision on the Radcliffe Report he had disregarded the advice of everyone except George Wigg. 'George Wigg,' he said with a show of surprise. 'Don't imagine I always take his advice. He does an awful lot of dogsbody work for me.' 'But surely you won't deny,' I said, 'that it was on his advice that you made the initial attack on the *Express*?' 'No,' he said, 'that's quite untrue. I did it on the advice of Burke Trend.' This astonished me.

At this point Marcia came rushing in to say the journalists were wild and Transport House in despair and I must go back to my room and answer questions. I found some sixty or seventy journalists milling in the lobby and I had to hold a totally unprepared press conference. Of course it wasn't my normal Lord President's press conference but the kind of mass meeting an afflicted M.P. might be expected to hold. Without too much preparation I dictated a statement of what I had actually said at Shrewsbury. I added I wasn't challenging the press report and I accepted everything they attributed to me but what they had selected was about a tenth of what I actually said and they had left out all the passages referring to the voluntary principle. I said the full text of the journalist's notes made it clear that the medicine I referred to was unemployment.

I suspect most of this crowd thought me crazy to make this correction because what I'd been accused of saying was just what most of them thought. By the time I got rid of them my two next guests were very impatient. They were senior officials from the Ministry of Technology who had come to protest because they had read the text of the report I had submitted to Harold on the Bristol-Siddeley scandal. After they'd gone on for a bit I made it clear that whatever they said I wouldn't change a word of the report or speak to the P.M. about it. 'If you wish to complain to your chief, Helsby, that you've been wrongly treated by me that's your affair. But the report is over and it's best forgotten by all,' I told them.

By now my last meeting was long overdue. I was exhausted but I spent more than an hour discussing an esoteric point of procedure with the Chairmen of Committees in the Lords and the Commons. I was well aware that throughout the afternoon the row had been raging in the Commons. The Whips asked me on no account to go into the Chamber because that would make it worse, so I stayed in my room and reflected on how furious the whole Parliamentary Labour Party now was about the way I'd ballsed the whole thing up. I was only too well aware that nothing Michael Stewart said from the front bench relieved the pressure on me and the same was even more true of Ray Gunter. However, I did what I was told until ten o'clock, when I'd agreed to go on the ten o'clock news to be cross-examined. I did extremely well. Indeed, by the end of the day I was pretty sure I had established my version of the facts. But was I right not to go into the House and accept a charge of cowardice? Absolutely. Before I saw my fellow M.P.s I had to see that my explanation had been made and largely accepted because otherwise I would be disowned by Michael and Ray from the front bench. I had done it first with the press conference and then with television by becoming the first item on the I.T.N. news programme. At one in the morning I thought the time had come to go and sit at my place behind the dispatch box while Macleod was moving progress on the Prices and Incomes (No. 2) Bill in order to continue the attack on me. So I sat there while I was booed at and shouted at by the back-benchers on both sides and derided by Macleod. After an hour I decided to go to bed in my room and slept a bit on the couch in Room 4. When I went out to vote John told me that he'd agreed to stop the debate at six because the Tory obstruction was being successful. Of course I knew this was the admission of defeat. Since we'd given in we'd have to find a second day and accept another all-night sitting. John tried to ease the blow for me by pretending that the Tories had been plotting this last week, but I knew very well that I had provided them with an ideal excuse for spinning out an all-night sitting. Without my Shrewsbury speech the Report Stage of the Bill could have been got through in one night and we could have avoided two all-night sittings running.

Tuesday, July 11th

When I got home I went to bed but not to sleep. As soon as the newspapers arrived I went downstairs and found I was now the main news in the popular press as well, but I was relieved that at least I had got my point across. Unemployment was the medicine of which I warned, not the wages policy. From that moment I didn't feel much fear about the consequences of the speech. The trouble is once we have compulsory sanctions it means that conceivably a trade-union leader could be punished for industrial action during this interim period. All way through the development of a prices and incomes policy Frank Cousins has been against the whole idea of sanctions and has therefore been leading the opposition to the whole Bill. The situation in Cabinet has been very mysterious because George Brown has also made it clear he isn't terribly keen on the legislation and that he's doing it in deference to pressure from Callaghan. Indeed, I get the impression—though it's never actually been said—that this is one of the assurances Callaghan must have given to the American Treasury.

In the afternoon I had to go down and make a fairly humiliating business Statement announcing that we've put the Prices and Incomes (No. 2) Bill back on the Commons agenda for Tuesday. I told the House I was determined to get the second half of the Report Stage, the Third Reading plus the motion on the Order for the commencement of Part II and sat down having scored a defensive victory.*

---

* This was recorded in Wednesday's papers only by one journalist, Norman Shrapnel of the *Guardian*, who is usually no friend of mine. The rest hardly mentioned it, though they'd given headlines and mountains of space to the trouble I had the day before.

I went straight from the Chamber to the Services Committee, which in its quiet way gave me a great deal of consolation. One of these days I'll write at length in this diary about how the Services Committee is quietly reorganizing the House of Commons. Charlie Pannell thought he'd nationalized that institution but my God he hasn't. He had merely done the most formal take-over, leaving the Serjeant-at-Arms' Department, the Speaker's Department, the Clerk's Department and the Catering Department all separate, all at loggerheads, all pretty inefficient. Now the Services Committee has been placed on top, but we have no executive authority since there are four other sub-committees advising the Speaker on how to organize the Palace. Selwyn Lloyd and Willie Whitelaw quietly supported me in all the proposals I put to the Committee and then we three went along the passage to the Speaker's annual tea-party. I found a number of Labour M.P.s standing around and Lena Jeger,[1] an old left-wing opponent, said to me, 'Did you hear Woodrow Wyatt[2] on the wireless today singing your praises? It was nauseating, horrible stuff.' To which I replied, 'I dare say it was. But it would be nice, Lena, if one day you would sing the praises of your Leader of the House if you think you're a friend of mine.' She looked at me as though she knew I'd made a point. One of the unattractive features of the Labour Party is the profound reluctance of colleagues in the Cabinet, in the Parliamentary Party or in the constituency to help each other in adversity, especially if they belong to the Left. The main activity of the Left is sniping and being anti and they find it very difficult to support even their own Party.

This evening I was busy mending fences in the corridors and in the tea-room until ten o'clock came and the all-night session on the Report Stage of the Bill was resumed. After my Statement I felt I could afford to go into the Chamber and there I sat for a number of hours. When I was challenged I made it quite clear that it would be out of order for me to deal with the speech in that debate and so I sat quietly talking to people.

At ten o'clock we had an excellent turn-out for the vote on the suspension of the closure. But by 1.32, when we had two highly technical procedural divisions, people had drifted away and there were only twenty votes left between us and extinction.[3] Harold and I had been chatting away together and after the Division he summoned the Chief Whip and for the first time I saw him really lacerate John. Harold had undoubtedly been drinking a little too much whisky[4] after his dinner with Peter Shore, and he really gave the Chief orders and treated him like dirt. 'You're at the end of the liberal experiment. What's happening to these people? Why aren't they here? Summon them all. Pull them out of bed.'

So the Chief got out of the room and began the job of waking everybody

[1] Labour M.P. for Holborn and St Pancras November 1953–September 1959 and since 1964.
[2] Labour M.P. for Aston (Birmingham) 1945–55 and for Bosworth 1959–70.
[3] The vote was 141 to 121.
[4] Other sources suggest it was brandy.

up. For two and a half hours he rang round, brought poor Gordon Walker back from his bed and the aged Alice Cullen[1] from her hotel room. He really was rattled. One of our troubles was that late that night nearly all the amendments we had to deal with were moved not by the Tories but by our own people. Probably wrongly John had allowed them to table amendments provided they didn't go into the division lobby against us. And there they were—nine or ten of these damn' abstentionists—putting us through hell. I had to keep the P.M. out of the Chief's hair and began to discuss the reshuffle. I found that he'd talked to Peter Shore that day about the possibility of his taking Jay's place at the Board of Trade and he'd also mentioned to Barbara the possibility of D.E.A. This was an idea I'd thrown out as a joke some months before but that joke had become a sober possibility. As for his relations with me, throughout the night he never referred to the mess I had made. He had watched me putting myself right and relied on me to get myself out of my own mess. He seemed to be mildly amused by the press reaction to my efforts. I had no way of knowing whether, like Freddy Ward, he thought that I was lying when I made the contradiction. He was really a terrible nuisance and at three o'clock we managed to persuade him to go to bed and let us deal with our own problems. At six came Macleod's offer. He would let us have the Bill in reasonable time if in exchange we took the Order later. We agreed and within two and a half hours we got the whole Report Stage, which would otherwise have taken twenty hours.

Wednesday, July 12th
I got home at 8.30, washed, cooked myself breakfast and went back to Cabinet, which was still discussing PESC. I'd been up two nights, the second without any sleep and the first with only an hour. This was a great strain though the second was easier than the first but sitting there during the PESC discussions I couldn't keep my eyes open, particularly since I knew that they would come to nothing. Harold is working only for a consensus in Cabinet for a few cutbacks in our planned spending on education, transport, housing and local authority expenditure—the usual cutbacks we take in our stride— and for the postponement of the school-leaving age.

It was all done with the greatest skill. A long speech from Callaghan, a long speech from Harold. But the big issue, the school-leaving age, simply wasn't argued out. At least three people—Patrick Gordon Walker, Roy Jenkins and me—had been for postponement, but Tony Crosland was against it for purely political reasons, and I don't blame him, as Minister of Education. I daresay if I hadn't been up two nights running I'd have argued it, but this time I decided discretion was the better part of valour. So once again Harold's process of endless boring talk dulled us into acceptance of the shape the cuts would take.

[1] Labour M.P. for the Gorbals from 1948 until her **death at the age** of seventy-seven in May 1969.

From Cabinet I went round to lunch with Lady Pam at Cowley Street where I found Arthur J. Schlesinger,[1] Tom Driberg, Chalfont and Perry Worsthorne. Of course D-Notices came up time after time and we gave Arthur an inside picture.

This afternoon John and I sat down to review our plans once again. Was it still possible to get through the business by July 28th? We'd lost the Coal Order and various other things last night but what could we salvage from the mess? I admit that yesterday I thought we'd have to give it another week, giving way to the Tories and blaming them for it. But by this morning John, Freddie Warren and I thought that if the Tories would play we could get through by July 28th. The Opposition are as tired as we are and their Whips find their people as difficult to manage as we do ours. So there is tremendous underground work between the usual channels. But of course in the last resort the decision is not with the Government and the Opposition but with the back-benchers who are handling the Abortion Bill. Were our people so totally exhausted by all-night sittings on Monday and Tuesday that they couldn't be expected to do another one on Thursday, which might run into Friday as well? The position wasn't nearly as bad as it seemed because when John worked through the division lists he found that only fifty-four Labour M.P.s had stayed all through both nights and thirty of them were Whips or Ministers who damn well had to do so. So really only twenty-four had stayed voluntarily and they seemed keen enough to keep it up.

My other concern was, of course, with the staff of the House. After these all-night sittings what would the door-keepers do if we had an endless sitting for Thursday, Friday and Saturday? With all these threats of strikes were we going to be able to carry on without a total breakdown of machinery? What makes things worse is the hot, stuffy, sticky, cloudy, sweltering weather which makes everyone bad-tempered. It is a typical July crisis, I keep telling John. We're having no more late sittings than many of our predecessors because we haven't a single one on the Finance Bill. So we thought that things would be O.K. and this afternoon he went off to the garden party at Buckingham Palace.

At this point I had to represent him at the liaison committee. When I came in Douglas Houghton looked at me rather quizzically and made one or two snide references to my Sunday speech, but nevertheless he was passionately friendly to me—and with good reason. He had sent me a personal letter of thanks for all I'd done for the Abortion Bill; certainly he and his wife, who are virtually the progenitors of the Bill, wouldn't have stood a chance without John and me.[2] Thank God I've won a loyal friend there. It's pretty important

[1] Son of a famous historian and himself a distinguished historian and writer. He was Professor of History at Harvard University 1954–61, Special Assistant to Presidents Kennedy and Johnson 1961–4 and, since 1966, Schweitzer Professor of the Humanities at the City University of New York.

[2] Douglas Houghton's wife, Vera, had been a prime mover of the Abortion Law Reform Association.

that the chairman of the liaison committee should be solidly on my side this week.

At ten o'clock this evening I went up to see how the Companies Bill was going. What a relief it is to see a Bill being really well managed. Whatever you think of George Darling's politics and whatever age he is, he does know how to handle a mass of amendments efficiently. He has them properly grouped and discussed with the Opposition Whips and he reaches some agreement. Blow me if at 11 p.m. we got to exactly the point in the Bill that they'd planned to reach and we were able to go home for some sleep.

Thursday, July 13th

The Chief and I got together at 9.30, before our third Cabinet this week. The news is that Sir Arthur Harvey,[1] the chairman of the 1922 Committee, and all the other members of the Executive have tabled a motion of censure on the Leader of the House and got it signed by ninety-six Tories. This was done late last night but at 10.30 Judd and Bob Brown of Newcastle began to take round an anti-motion expressing confidence in the Leader.[2] John tells me that by my business Statement this afternoon we shall have more than ninety-six names on our motion. Freddie Warren also had a bright idea this morning that we should scotch the Tories by getting from the Serjeant-at-Arms, the door-keepers, the police and the Clerks' opinions on whether life would be easier for them if we ran into August. The reason for this inquiry is that the Tory censure motion accuses me of exhausting the staff of the Commons. Of course we knew what the answer was going to be. Overwhelmingly the staff want to shut up shop on July 28th and they'll take almost anything in order to be off on that date.

In Cabinet we started with leaks—as usual. But this time it is I who had put up Barbara to protest about the *Financial Times* where a bitter attack on me as Leader had obviously been inspired by senior colleagues. The P.M. remarked, 'Everybody in the press gallery knows who it is.' I said straightaway that I didn't want any further investigation. Tony Crosland is quite right. This endless discussion of leaks is doing us no good and things are made worse by the Lord Chancellor's ineffective investigations. The truth is that as long as there's a Wilson Cabinet there will be a Wilsonian number of leaks.

Then we went on to the road-hauliers and Barbara's proposal that we should introduce quantity control of C licences, the very control which was dropped from the Nationalization Bill of the Attlee Government in 1947.[3]

[1] Conservative M.P. for Macclesfield from 1945 until 1971, when he became a life peer with the title of Lord Harvey of Prestbury. He was chairman of the 1922 Committee 1966–70.

[2] Frank Judd, Labour M.P. for Portsmouth West since 1966 and Robert Brown, Labour M.P. for Newcastle-upon-Tyne West since 1966.

[3] Since the early 1930s road-hauliers had been obliged to obtain a 'C' licence entitling them to carry their own goods. Such licences had always been issued, for a small fee, without proof of need. The 1968 Transport Act abolished them.

To put it back would be a really bold step since it would provoke a ferocious reaction from private enterprise. This was what the Chancellor was hinting at when he led the opposition to Barbara. Of course he agreed with it in principle but he warned us that it was the wrong time to do it. Jim was supported by his usual clique—Gordon Walker, Tony Crosland, Cledwyn Hughes and Bert Bowden. Barbara had the Left, headed by Wedgy Benn, on her side, but she also had Michael Stewart and Roy Jenkins and the Prime Minister to some extent, as well as myself. The P.M. cleverly placated the minority by saying that she should take powers to do it but give ourselves a year to see if we really can take over the road-hauliers.

The next item was family allowances and this must have been the sixth or seventh Cabinet discussion of it. This time we had the new paper from the Chancellor (as I've mentioned already) suddenly proposing a housing allowance instead of his means-tested benefit. This had provoked a furious paper from the Minister of Housing who had not been consulted, and it was clear that the idea was still half-baked. There was much the same line-up as usual—Roy Jenkins and Tony Crosland both supporting the Chancellor with some embarrassment and Michael Stewart and Denis Healey maintaining a discreet silence, though still on our side. The Prime Minister was still apparently in enormous confusion. At one point he said that the issue between us was not whether we should have family allowances but whether we should have a means test or not. And I had to reply, 'No, Prime Minister, there is no dispute about selectivity. The difference is that the selectivity the Chancellor wants will apply at the bottom to those in need and the selectivity I want will apply to those who are well off and pay the full rate of income tax and surtax. He wants to make sure that he doesn't pay too much to the poor. I want to make sure that the rich pay back every penny of benefit they get from the increased family allowances.' Well, in the end the P.M. had to sum up and we've been left with the decision that the Chancellor and I will meet on Friday to draft a Statement that doesn't tie the Chancellor's hands too tightly. Of course the real issue now is budget secrecy and whether the Chancellor can insist that tax concessions and tax variations cannot be considered in relation to social security payments. In fact it is impossible to make the payments fair without considering the tax system.

I was so busy preparing for my business Statement that I had no time to lunch before I went down to listen to Harold answering Questions. He'd been asked a series of Questions about a speech which I made at Coventry and one which he made at Coventry and therefore he was able to make a very characteristic comment. 'If my Rt Honourable friend here had the misfortune to be misinterpreted last week, it was far more cruel to the leader of the Opposition who was correctly reported.'* This blew the whole House into one tremendous laugh and it was really the end of my Shrewsbury speech crisis.

* Heath had issued a 30-page hand-out of a speech on economic policy which had been a complete flop.

14*

The balloon had been burst by a gay turn of phrase at the end of a very successful Question Time.

When it came to my Question Time life was infinitely easier than it would have been without Harold's success. In due course I was asked about the Tory vote of censure and made a reply pressed on me by Freddie Warren and John Silkin rather against my inclination. 'I've been studying the list of names on the Early Day Motion,' I said, 'and the list of names of those who took part in the prices and incomes debate. Of the ninety-six only six managed to survive the full two days.' Of course the criticism of me was that I had fatigued the officials by all-night sittings and I felt it a shame that I could score the Tories off in this way. But there's no doubt it was a triumph and thereafter the whole vote of censure subsided. In twenty minutes I was finished with Questions.

We had also prepared very carefully for the Party meeting. Right at the beginning I told the Party the truth about Monday and Tuesday—how the Tories had forced the pace and how they were really responsible for the two all-night sittings and what hypocrisy it was for them to blame the Leader of the House when last week they had planned coolly and deliberately to keep the House up. When I'd finished I got a quiet reception and within seconds the back-benchers were quarrelling about who had failed to stick it out on Tuesday night. So the Chief says he will publish the division records and the meeting ends amicably.

The Abortion Bill started punctually at ten when we moved a suspension of the rule and there were 170 people there in the first division. I'd had dinner this evening with the Chief and I'd had an hour with my own staff drinking with them and making them see that I'm surviving pretty well despite their failing to help me. And finally I'd been to the B.B.C. for the ten o'clock programme and breezily said to the audience, 'This is just a light fever; it will all be over soon.' Afterwards I went to bed in my room; I must say I slept soundly until two in the morning when I went into the lobby and did my turn. Then, thank heavens, Willie Hamilton—seeing I was tired—sent me home and asked me to be back at breakfast-time. This was the third all-night sitting and one really can't take it at the age of fifty-nine. But I was back by eight o'clock and I was sitting there when we finished the Third Reading at 11.45.

John tells me that St John Stevas caved in at 6 a.m. It was the threat of the open-ended sitting which really worked. By using it as a threat without letting Cabinet know we got the Bill through. If I'd gone to Cabinet and taken them into my confidence they would never have given me consent.

Friday, July 14th
By sheer coincidence I went to the City to lunch with Alec Spearman, my stockbroker ex-pair friend, to meet the famous Paish with whose views, since the headline on Tuesday, I'm said to show some sympathy. I found him

charming, talkative, loquacious, academic—a kind of thermometer, because you can put Paish into a situation and his analysis will always be entirely predictable. Alec had collected for lunch a director of Courtaulds, a director of a merchant banking firm, and his stockbroker partners; all the talk was about import controls. I pricked up my ears and thought about leaks because we are talking about import controls very secretly at No. 10. But these people had no special information. It was sheer common sense which drove them to the view that a Government which tries to avoid self-destruction when the imports are pouring in but which refuses to devalue must consider controls. And of course they were discussing this the day after some extremely bad trade figures had been published. I suspect that my experience at lunch is often repeated in Fleet Street and that many news stories which Harold believes are due to leaks are due to innate common sense.

When I got to Banbury station I was met by Anne and the children and as soon as I got home I heard that Freddy Ward had rung me up in great dismay. He was concerned about my *Panorama* profile, which the B.B.C. has suddenly decided to project next Monday. Actually all I know about it are the films they've taken of me but I hear rumours that they've got a number of hostile critics, including Manny Shinwell and Quintin Hogg, expressing their opinion. I've been filmed here at Prescote, with the students at Warwick, in the Privy Council and in the Whips' office, where I had half an hour of business discussion with the Chief. It was absolutely natural because it was unrehearsed and because it had been made clear that not one word of it could be used except with my editorial approval. I'd made the same conditions about my talk with the students and also my conversation at Prescote. I told Freddy to go to Lime Grove and find out what they were up to and he rang back in the evening to say that the Office were greatly worried as they've chosen the piece in which I remarked that the Transport and General Workers were responsible for our election defeat in Coventry as well as a longish piece where I describe myself as an offshore islander who doesn't like the Common Market.

Saturday, July 15th
John Grist, the boss of the show, was on the telephone to me today. Yes, he'd seen the film for himself and he gathered from the producer that I'd given my approval. I was sharp with him. 'You know perfectly well,' I replied, 'that it was done under the express condition that the script would be submitted to me. I didn't insist on seeing the video tape but I said I must O.K. the words I used.' He agreed finally that he and the producer would come down to supper on Sunday and go through the script with me. What upset me was that the B.B.C. thought that they could cut this corner and get away with it because I wouldn't be smart enough to react. They do this constantly to people they interview. Unless you're on the alert they will get that little bit extra out of you which they hope to get away with.

Sunday, July 16th

John Grist and the producer, who had filmed me at Warwick University, arrived at 6.30 this evening and we sat on the terrace playing back forty minutes of the Warwick conversation. I said at once they couldn't possibly use the passage about the Transport and General Workers and when they told me that they'd already got a statement from Frank Cousins I said they ought to be thoroughly ashamed of themselves. As for the offshore islander passage, I allowed it to go through and I think it will do me nothing but good. There was no apology for their misbehaviour but they didn't argue with me and accepted all my demands.

Apart from this it has been a lovely day. We've been walking and lying on the terrace, and Patrick has been collecting waterlilies from the river for our new aquarium while I talked to Thomas Balogh on and off about how we can organize next Saturday's meeting at Chequers, where the P.M. is asking his old friends to spend a day with him. As for my own position, the Sunday press is not too bad. The times have turned—the starlings, I called them once in *Encounter*, who have all been sitting on the anti-Crossman tree have now flown across to the pro-Crossman line of telegraph wires and are chirping my praises in unison. It's an uncanny situation and it's luck for the B.B.C. to have my profile tomorrow at 8 p.m. John Grist keeps on saying it's so complimentary it'll have no news value, but I'll believe that when I see it.

Monday, July 17th

Going back to London in my reserved compartment I now have the pleasure of paying for my guests, including Neil Marten, because the Ministry has to buy every seat. That's the new arrangement and it arises because, after I'd sat in the restaurant car for a fortnight, a complaint came to Burke Trend from the Security Service that a Cabinet Minister had been seen with his red box open in a restaurant car. So now Burke has got to give sanction for the payment.

Today's papers were still all about Tony Crosland's Norwich speech. One or two of the Sundays had headlined it as a great dynamic speech and there was still a good follow-up this morning. Partly, of course, this is because Tony is a really interesting person. He, Roy and I are the only serious socialist intellectuals in the Government, and he's written the only thorough and thoughtful book on modern British socialism. So when he came out with a plea for the social services and a challenge to Heath which all the papers interpreted as a challenge to Jim Callaghan everybody took up the idea that there was a Cabinet crisis. In fact, Tony was careful not to make his speech until he was certain there was going to be no serious cut in his education estimates and the Cabinet would turn down the proposal for postponing the raising of the school-leaving age. So there is no truth whatsoever in the story of the Cabinet crisis—which is mildly interesting because these kinds of press reports in the quality newspapers make it difficult for the future historian to extract the truth.

My first meeting was of the Pensions Committee, where I'm in the chair. My basic feeling is that we can't wait, as the Ministry wants us to wait, until 1972 or 1973 before starting national superannuation. The civil servants (and they're backed by Peggy Herbison) propose that we should get the scheme on to the statute book in 1969 or 1970, have the first contributions paid in 1972 or 1973 and the first benefits in 1974. It was in 1957 that we first evolved the scheme and we've been in Government since 1964, making an intolerable ten-year gestation period. Moreover, every year longer that we wait we undermine even more the effectiveness of the scheme because we have to up-grade the present flat-rate benefits and contributions, impose more and more injustice and waste more and more money on flat-rate benefits. I should like to achieve a breakthrough by introducing graded contributions much earlier and using part of the extra money they produce to pay for decent up-grading of our present pensioners. But I get no support from Peggy. She's a darling and she fights for the old-age pensioners, but she's wholly in the hands of her officials. If she resigns, what I should like is to have someone like Peter Shore to take her place.

After this unsatisfactory and untidy meeting, which took the whole morning, I rushed over to the Commons to give lunch to Len Williams, with whom I've now agreed to eat regularly in order to pacify the N.E.C. Of course nothing will come out of it. He is amiable, sly, deaf, stupid and totally ineffective. That's the man George Brown put in charge of Transport House with the loyal but narrow Sara Barker as his number two. We exchanged views today and I don't think it did any harm.

Back in my room at the House I found Remez, the Israeli Ambassador, waiting for me and once again tried to spell out to him the realities of British Middle Eastern policy. I had to make it clear that those of us in the Cabinet who were pro-Israel couldn't possibly have hoped to get any policy favourable to Israel out of the Foreign Secretary. He replied, 'We don't want you to be pro-Israel. All we need is that you don't give positive assistance to our enemies.' But that's precisely what none of us can guarantee.

This evening I had been invited to dine at the Middle Temple by one of our socialist barristers. It was a sweltering hot evening when I changed into evening dress and I half regretted that I hadn't cancelled my acceptance. The main reason why I didn't cancel was because the *Panorama* profile of me was being shown and I didn't want to admit to myself that I was so anxious to see it that I'd rather stay at home. So off I go and found myself sitting opposite John Davies, the king-pin of the C.B.I.[1] I asked him whether he thought it

[1] Director-General of the C.B.I. 1965–9, and since 1970 Conservative M.P. for Knutsford. He was immediately brought into the Cabinet as Minister of Technology (July–October 1970). He was Secretary of State for Trade and Industry 1970–72 and Chancellor of the Duchy of Lancaster with special responsibility for E.E.C. affairs November 1972–February 1974.

would help or harm our economic prospects for the Government to announce our withdrawal from the Middle East. 'It would help enormously,' he said. 'It would give a sense that the Government was becoming realistic.' 'But suppose,' I said, 'that the Government decided not to make another military plane but to switch all the R and D to peaceful uses?' 'Ah,' he said, 'it would depend what you switch it to but in principle we wouldn't object.' So the idea that British industry resists so-called left-wing foreign policy is an over-simplification. They're quite prepared to see us slash back defence, accept our new status in the world and knock out the futile millions spent on military aircraft.

I had to go back to the House in the evening to vote on the Prices and Incomes Order, which had been postponed from last week. In the lobby I soon found that the *Panorama* profile had been a success. It wasn't only John Silkin who said, 'How much did you pay the B.B.C. for that?' Many of my colleagues seemed somehow gratified that I had been described as one of the most brilliant and incalculable politicians alive and by the fact that so much time had been devoted to me on television. Yes, it had gone over pretty well.

Tuesday, July 18th

I started with yet another meeting on Lords reform. This one was fascinating because Gerald Gardiner had clicked back into his old posture of total opposition. He insisted that we should discuss in detail a paper by the officials on how to reduce the Lords' powers on statutory instruments. I told him it was sheer waste of time because most of us would be prepared to take all the Lords' powers away and give them to the Commons unless we can achieve a change in composition. Indeed, it's our view that by curbing their powers and leaving the composition untouched we will make them much more dangerous than they are at present. But Gerald was mutinous: he was determined to get that Bill drafted in complete detail. Finally I said it was grossly out of order for us to draft that Bill now. 'Our instructions are to go to the Cabinet and tell them why we're not going to draft it and why we're going to propose a change of composition.' In the end he was finally frustrated. The Lord Chancellor is one of the most curious combinations of good-hearted idealist liberalism and blind obstinate reaction and personal mulishness.

This evening I went off to the big annual party Alma and Ellis Birk always hold in a marquee at the back of their house.[1] I had to go there early because I was due to dine with the Speaker and found myself almost alone with Cecil King. Hugh Cudlipp had already told me that King had decided to make war upon the Labour Government and I had read his onslaught in his address as chairman of I.P.C. As soon as he saw me he said, 'I can't think of any time in British history when the whole press was united in condemning the Prime Minister in the way that we have condemned your Mr Wilson.' I said, 'The

[1] Ellis Birk was the legal adviser to the Daily Mirror Group. His wife, Alma, the Associate Editor of *Nova* 1965–9, had become a life peer in 1967.

last time I remember a press as hostile as you was when Roosevelt was launching the New Deal and won two elections running without a single paper on his side. Maybe the P.M. did the wrong thing about D-Notices but I'm not afraid of unanimous condemnation by the press lords. You can't bully me in that way, my dear Cecil.' As I said this in the presence of Phil Kaiser, the American Minister who I knew would report me in full, I got a great deal of pleasure out of it.

This was the evening of the long-postponed dinner the Speaker was giving to John Silkin and me on our side and Willie Whitelaw and Selwyn Lloyd on the other. It's surprising, in view of the importance of good channels of communication, that this is the first time since I've been Leader of the House that the Speaker has invited me to dinner. He did suggest once that he should give a dinner with Harold Wilson and Heath there but I pointed out that this would be an absolute waste of time because when those two men were there no candid exchanges could take place. On this occasion however quite a lot did take place. First we all agreed that next Session we should arrange that the closure should be moved by one of the Speaker's deputies. It's intolerable that he should be brought back to the Chair each time we move the closure. When John suggested that we might have a third deputy chairman the Speaker replied, 'We wouldn't need that if only the present ones did their work.' He's always talking about his overwork but I'm not sure he doesn't first of all insist on doing everything himself and then complain that others don't share the burden of work fairly.

Then we turned to the crisis with the staff. The Chancellor has been sitting on their wage claim for six weeks. They are all on the edge of revolt because their wages are far too low and their hours too long. It was finally agreed that Selwyn and I should go to the Chancellor as the Speaker's plenipotentiaries and that if we couldn't get any satisfaction from him we would be compelled in the last week of the Session to stage a procedure debate at which I would report that I couldn't guarantee our Standing Committees being manned because of the Chancellor's refusal to get us extra staff. It was a thoroughly useful meeting before we went back into the Chamber to vote.

After ten o'clock we had an all-night sitting on the Coal Industry Order, specially arranged for the miners' group of M.P.s. It was their idea that Dick Marsh's long Statement on pit closures should be made after ten o'clock so that they could debate it for as long as they liked throughout the night. I thought it was a perverse idea but I discovered they were quite right because by the end of the night there were only two or three Tories present and miners' M.P.s were able to have the whole House of Commons to themselves for the protest which they wanted to make before accepting their fate. The Marsh Statement was really devastating, since it meant that literally scores of pits would be closed down in a year of high recession and unemployment. I listened to most of the debate, which ran till 8.30 in the morning, and heard some excellent speeches. It was a cosy occasion but pathetic because it was clear that provided they could make their protest these miners felt that they were bound to support the Government in an action which really meant the destruction of the mining industry. What these miners' M.P.s showed was a not very edifying loyalty, because people should not be as loyal as that to a Government which is causing the total ruin of their industry. As the night went on I was pleased that they were so pleased to have me there but I was also shocked by their pathetic lack of fight.

Wednesday, July 19th
I got back to Vincent Square and into my bath just in time to hear the B.B.C. nine o'clock news recording nothing of the eleven-hour debate except the speeches at the beginning in which I was attacked by Manny Shinwell and Nabarro for incompetence in having an all-night sitting and for being a skulking absentee at the very end.

At No. 10 I found John Silkin already with the P.M. looking bright and energetic because I had let him go home on condition that I was allowed Wednesday night off in turn. Our main discussion was about the big censure debate on Monday. We agreed that on this occasion we couldn't allow even abstention. Members would have to vote for the Government on a vote of confidence for there are rare occasions when we do require total loyalty; this we thought was the essential to our liberal regime.

Cabinet was dealing once again with family endowment and it was one of the most bitter and unpleasant meetings I've ever attended. This is not surprising since this row has been going on since Christmas last year. As usual the P.M. started by saying we were all agreed on an across-the-board increase of family endowment. As usual, I replied that I was sorry but he was wrong. We all agreed there should be selectivity: the argument was whether it should be applied at the top or at the bottom. The Chancellor was proposing an inadequate increase of the universal flat rate. We were proposing an adequate increase financed by a claw-back from the children's allowances of the full income-tax payer. With the Chancellor standing pat for five shillings and Peggy Herbison insisting on ten shillings, it was obvious that the point would come when the Prime Minister said, 'Shall we agree on seven shillings?' 'No,' said Jim, 'I insist on five.' 'All right,' I said, 'I insist on ten, which is the right amount and which we can afford with the claw-back.' Then there was a flaming row and the P.M. finally called us to order. The majority was undoubtedly on our side but it was a majority most of whom were unwilling to fight.

Finally I got so sick of the miserable solution we were being offered that I stalked out and I don't know what happened for the rest of the time. I went across to the Party meeting, where Denis Healey was explaining the Defence White Paper and it was already clear that it had been overwhelmingly accepted. Of course he had Woodrow Wyatt getting up and saying it was an appalling White Paper but he also had Eric Heffer countering by saying, 'My

God, we've won. Let's admit we've won.' So the debate on the Floor would be harmless. Our Party would be united behind Harold and the Tories behind Heath, who has suppressed the view of Powell, his Shadow Defence Minister, whose ideas are very like our own.[1]

After lunch, despite my bloody row with Jim, I had to go to the Treasury at 2.30 for a most important meeting. That was the time that had been fixed for Selwyn Lloyd and me to discuss the salaries of our parliamentary Clerks, door-keepers, catering staff, etc. Fortunately Selwyn proved an ideal emollient. In the last discussion about the Clerks' salaries he had been the Chancellor sitting on the other side of the table. So he was able on this occasion to keep the peace. After ten minutes or so the Chancellor looked up and said, 'Why shouldn't we get our own men talking to each other?' Fortunately our man was sitting there beside us and we had forty-five minutes of well-informed sensible discussion during which we got Callaghan to agree to the extra team of Hansard staff, to the wiring of the House and even to the idea of taking over the debts of the Catering Committee. As for the door-keepers, he also promised to help. So a great deal was achieved.

At the Home Affairs Committee, which had already started, I found Roy Jenkins making his case for a new Race Relations Bill next Session. He got his way easily and then turned to the problem of theatre censorship. A Select Committee has reported in favour of abolishing censorship by the Lord Chamberlain and Roy wanted authority to bring in a Bill straightaway. I said this couldn't be done because the Home Secretary couldn't add a Bill like this to his departmental programme next Session without making somebody else sacrifice. Roy Jenkins is getting more imperious every day and he's not always very well briefed.

Straight after that I had to go to No. 10 for one of Mary Wilson's tea-parties for the ladies. This year I was asked as well as Anne – the intention was to provide a few honourable guests for the ladies to meet. I went out of the sweltering hot afternoon to a delightful room upstairs, open from end to end, with flowers and all the ladies in their summer dresses and hats. Frankly they were all jolly good-looking and I would have enjoyed it but for the fact that 170 M.P.s' wives were all saying to me, 'Of course you know who I am?' or, 'Of course you don't know who I am?' How does one remember? This year they didn't have labels giving their names. Oh dear, I didn't even recognize Bob Maxwell's wife. However it was a nice occasion.

Back from there to a discussion with the Chief of the business for the final week. Not much to discuss now, merely sorting out the bits and pieces and seeing how they fit in. Then I had a little dinner at St Stephens restaurant for Marcia, Tommy and Peter. We had an excellent informal talk about how to

[1] The Defence White Paper (Cmnd. 3357), which had been published on July 18th, failed to satisfy Labour's left-wing supporters, for whom the reduction of some £2,200 million in the 1970–71 defence budget and, by the mid-1970s a further £2,100 million, was insufficient. The Opposition objected that the reduction in the strength of the armed forces and the further withdrawal from the Far East diminished Britain's world influence.

handle Harold, how much more of his life we should share and how we must make ourselves more available for him to relax with. This dinner was very important mainly for making Marcia feel we were available to help her in this particular way.

It was my turn to miss the all-night sitting so, though the Companies Bill was ploughing its way through the House, I slipped off at eleven.

Thursday, July 20th

I woke up at 5.30 with a terrible conscience and rang up John Silkin who told me the Companies Bill would be through by six. The last time the Tories had called for a count a hundred of our people had come in but only ten of theirs and he reckoned that they had only three people there in the final stages. A great deal of nonsense is talked about the strain night sittings impose on Members. The strain of these two all-nights on the Tory Party was felt by at most twenty to twenty-five people after midnight. The problem on the Government side is to keep 100 or 120 people there each night, though we carefully keep them in relays and there's no great strain. The people who really have a lot to bear are the officials, the door-keepers, the Speaker, and the Chairmen of Committees. The strain on them is almost intolerable.

At Cabinet this morning we at last finally and irrevocably disposed of PESC and the cuts. We've spent week after week cutting back the public-sector programmes of the next four years in order to bring them into line with the expected growth of 3 per cent. Now we are reviewing the results of all our work. Barbara at Transport got away with a £25 million cut in her £894 million programme. Education lost £9 million instead of £45 million because we failed to agree on postponing the extension of the school-leaving age. Health lost nothing at all and so we went on round the table until we came to social security. Here the cuts were serious. The Chancellor was proposing that in each up-grading we should only give half the increase in average national earnings instead of the whole increase to which we pledged ourselves in 1964. No wonder Peggy is going to resign. The cuts achieved seemed minimal when compared with the amount of labour they had imposed. Indeed the whole process seemed to me ineffective—a very primitive way of organizing our socialist priorities.

Because I was tired I was extremely anxious about my business Statement this afternoon. Would I be jeered and assaulted for not being present last night? Would I have a huge attack on morning sittings? Would they continue to raise their Early Day vote of censure? I needn't have worried. The issue of Crossman's clangers had burnt itself out. *Panorama* on Monday evening had had its effect and people knew we were getting near the end of this sitting. There was so little life that suddenly the Speaker got up and stopped the business Questions after a few minutes.

The Party meeting was equally easy. When John Silkin told them there could be no question of abstaining on a vote of censure, there was silence. I think he's made an arrangement with the left-wing that they should be allowed to put down an amendment which won't be called. Finally Douglas Houghton got them to accept the increase in the size of the liaison committee and the introduction of the new disciplinary code when we return in October. I was never much impressed by Douglas as a Cabinet Minister and found him a rather ineffective Chairman of Committees, though he could be a good old Nestor in the Cabinet itself. But he's developed into a marvellous chairman of the Party and his press conferences afterwards became at once an enormous success and one of our most successful experiments in public relations.

John Silkin and I had both received messages that we were wanted at No. 10 and should go across quietly without our movements being detected. What on earth were we wanted for? As we went across we both predicted that it must be a Cabinet reshuffle and Callaghan must be on his way out. But in fact the P.M. wanted to talk to us about Rhodesia. There's a Rhodesia X Committee on Friday and he intends to propose sending a Royal Commission to Salisbury in exchange for Smith lifting censorship and making one or two other concessions on civil rights. I thought it fairly sensible. But when that was over the P.M. relaxed and we sat there from ten to twelve drinking whisky while he talked. I told him about Peggy Herbison coming over this evening to tell me once again she was going to resign. This time I thought she was serious and I urged him to let me have Peter Shore in her place and Harold seemed to like the idea very much. He then discussed once again the possibility of replacing Michael Stewart at D.E.A. with Barbara Castle. Once again I said to him that I thought it might be beyond her strength. However, he was firm on that and I think his idea is to make Michael a Minister without Portfolio because he suddenly asked me whether I would mind losing my Lord Presidency. 'Certainly I'd mind losing it,' I said, 'I've just got my pictures from the National Gallery beautifully hung. I can't lose that room, it's the only consolation I get for a job I don't like.' It was a fairly light-hearted chat and then John and I got out into Whitehall and saw the light still on over Big Ben, went into the House and found that Emrys Hughes had been filibustering on a Civil Defence Bill. Within minutes of our getting there we were counted out by an angry Tory. I went home a little uncertain whether we hadn't bitched it again and that the press tomorrow morning wouldn't be full of it.

Friday, July 21st

I needn't have worried. There wasn't even a mention, perhaps because the papers were full of the thousandth day of the Labour Government. We couldn't have chosen a worse day because we had to announce terrible unemployment figures.[1] I saw this in the newspapers as I lay in bed. I had drunk too much of Harold's whisky and I felt very tired and only dragged myself to my office.

[1] In July unemployment stood at 496,572, the highest July figure since 1940.

Soon Barney Cocks and Hugh Farmer, the Clerk to the Services Committee, came in and we discussed the deal that Farmer had made with the Treasury officials. Soon we clinched it and I agreed to tell Callaghan. Barney thanked me profusely and I said, 'All the credit goes to your man Farmer.' It was a tremendous relief to have got this out of the way.

At the Garrick I had the last of my press lunches this Session. This time I chose overseas correspondents—a Canadian, an Australian, a Frenchman and an Italian. The Italian talked the whole time. It was a fairly wasted lunch.

Back in the office I tied up the agreement about the Clerks' salaries, wrote my letters and then went off to the RX Committee at 5.30. It didn't take long. George Brown took against the Royal Commission straightaway and Malcolm MacDonald,[1] who happened to be there, drove the final nail into the coffin by saying this would turn the whole of Africa against us. I tried to support Harold and was rebuked by George Brown. I left before the end knowing the thing was pretty well finished to catch the train to Brighton since I was due at Wilton Park to talk to Heinz Koeppler's conference about parliamentary reform.

After dinner Heinz Koeppler told me that he had been running Wilton Park for twenty years as a place where foreigners talk about the English way of life and through that period the influence and strength of Britain had been steadily declining. At first he had to spend all his time saying to the foreigners, 'Don't over-estimate us. We aren't as big as that nor as powerful. We simply can't do all these things.' Now none of his visitors over-estimate us, or indeed rate us high at all. They think us incompetent and ineffective and he has therefore experienced personally this disastrous decline in British prestige. We've lost one image and we certainly haven't found a new one.

Saturday, July 22nd

I had to be at Chequers at four o'clock for Harold's session with his friends. Anne and I had the most delicious drive right through the back of the Chilterns. I hadn't motored up that way from Henley and along through Nettlebed and Christmas Common for many years. It's still absolutely unspoilt, with the odd houses in little openings in the beech woods.

At Chequers the first meeting was for me and the Chief alone. We had asked for it and it lasted from 4.30 till six. We got Harold's agreement for the draft code of discipline and then we spent the rest of the time on parliamentary plans for the autumn. What should we do about morning sittings? I told him of my anxieties and admitted frankly that the Tories had been successful in defeating us. We were winning no advantage for the back-benchers and imposing a great deal of extra work on officials as well as on the Speaker.

---

[1] Labour M.P. for Bassetlaw 1931–5 and for Ross and Cromarty 1936–45; he is the son of the former Prime Minister J. Ramsay MacDonald. He was British High Commissioner in Kenya 1964–5, Special Representative of H.M. Government in Africa 1966–9, Special Envoy to Somalia in December 1967 and to the Sudan in November 1969. Since 1970 he has been Chancellor of the University of Durham.

We must either abandon them or go right forward to a Parliament which really begins its business in the morning and finishes before dinner. Harold at once said we couldn't possibly abandon them and spent the rest of the time discussing the possibility of a four-day Parliament starting at ten in the morning.

By now the others were turning up. They came into the little room where we had found Harold with his wireless, his red box, his cigar and his pipes. The room was crammed and there was a heavy thunderstorm outside. In rushed Marcia. 'Oh,' she said, 'the terrible fug. You can cut it with a knife,' and had all the windows opened by the Wrens. The first session was appallingly scrappy. The only thing I picked up was what happened at the Durham Miners' Gala last week. The Chancellor, the Foreign Secretary and the P.M. were the main guests and made their speeches to a solemn unenthusiastic audience. Afterwards they had a meeting with Alf Robens,[1] Paynter,[2] and other key people in the Union and the Coal Board, in which they were told the real facts about the disaster which the Government's closure policy was precipitating. James Callaghan got cold feet when he was told that the closures this winter would create 15,000 unemployed men at a time when unemployment is due to rise to 750,000. Another fact of life the Chancellor learnt was the appalling shock caused by the recent announcement that our atomic power station is to be built right in the centre of the coalfield at Seaton Carew. Though he retold these stories against Jim, I couldn't make out what the P.M.'s own attitude to the closure policy was.

After dinner the talk was just as unsatisfactory until suddenly Harold pulled himself together and said, 'Well, we can't let this meeting finish without a discussion of devaluation.' He said this just as he came back through the door, as though he'd gone outside to brace himself. Actually it turned out the best discussion we've ever had. Thomas Balogh was instructed to give the pros and cons, and did so very thoroughly. Then it was discussed in relation to other medium-term measures—import controls, Tony Benn's new enabling Bill, the Regional Employment Premium, etc. At one point he turned to me and said, 'You see, they all agree. Devaluation is too risky.' 'If you don't do it,' I replied, 'the catastrophes are not risks but certainties. Without devaluation how can you get the boost to our exports and the growth we need without creating too much consumer demand at home?' This was a good discussion since I think it enabled him to think more clearly and that, after all, was the purpose of his friends being there. We were able to go away feeling that for at least one hour there had been serious discussion of the problem.

I mention the rain because when we broke off it was clear that Barbara would need transport. She'd been brought by Ted in their car and had no one

[1] Labour M.P. for Wansbeck 1945–50 and for Blyth 1950–60. He served as Minister of Labour from April to October 1951, and in 1961 became chairman of the National Coal Board and a life peer. Since 1971 he has been chairman of Vickers Ltd.

[2] Will Paynter, Secretary of the N.U.M. 1959–68 and, since 1975, a member of the Conciliation Board of the T.U.C. and C.B.I.

to take her back to her cottage in the Chilterns.[1] At once Tony and John offered to take her. 'No,' Harold says, 'I'll get my son Giles to take her back.' I couldn't help wondering why on earth poor Giles should be got up in the middle of the night and I asked myself whether a British Prime Minister should really find it so extraordinarily difficult to provide transport for one of his senior Ministers after a long session.

Of course this shows Harold's curious modesty. He adores Chequers but he's still the visiting stranger who is neither accepted nor acceptable. His whole life is still simple and unassuming. As a good middle-class socialist I had my own official car and the driver delivered me to Prescote at 2 a.m.

Monday, July 24th

Yesterday we had Chris and Jennie Hall with their boy, Gil, over to Prescote and it was still lovely weather. We spent most of the day on the terrace mucking about getting water for my new aquarium, playing with the children in this superb summer which has gone on throughout July and which is breaking today for the time being. The Sunday papers showed that at least there had been no leaks about our visit to Chequers.

This morning as I went up in the train I found there was another column about me by Ian Trethowan in *The Times* saying that despite my tactlessness I really had begun to get the House moving on the way to reform. The fact that Trethowan and David Wood have been on my side has undoubtedly made a very great difference. Not a difference outside Westminster among the general public, of course, but in the House of Commons, the place which really matters to me—the place where I've got on my side both Selwyn Lloyd and Willie Whitelaw as well. Here at Westminster it's the tone which matters. Suddenly it's become fashionable to say, 'Despite everything Dick's doing quite a good job.' Six weeks ago it was fashionable to say that I was a hopeless blundering arrogant intellectual. The change has been helped a great deal by articles in the quality press as well as by the *Panorama* profile.

I was going up for an urgent special meeting of S.E.P. We'd had a message that a big document would be circulated at the last moment and when I got to No. 10 I found a number of my colleagues standing about trying to read an enormous mass of bumf which had been typed by three or four different typewriters. It was pretty obvious that the P.M. had dictated this statement on Sunday afternoon and a glance through it confirmed that it was a résumé of the ideas which had come out of our Saturday discussions. I recognized many of them—bulk machine-tool orders by the Government, selective import controls including newsprint rationing, etc. The document's conclusion was that while Callaghan's speech would have the required effect of stopping devaluation, it was necessary to consider controlled reflation, which would mean relaxing hire purchase on consumer durables and motor-cars pretty

---

[1] Ted Castle, a former journalist, was a G.L.C. alderman 1964–70 and has been an Islington alderman since 1970. He was made a life peer in 1974.

quickly. This document was handed to us in addition to several other papers. And before the meeting had really got under way the P.M. had half apologized for it and said that he just wanted to give us his ideas and it should not be regarded as a paper for this particular meeting. The Chancellor at once said he was relieved because he found the document extremely dangerous, particularly in the passage which suggested that his speech was a cover for reflation. So, after a rather desultory talk this new document which Harold must have meant to form the basis of a new strategy got pushed aside and was never discussed. Really there is very little to record about this meeting except my sense of its incoherence: and the failure of the P.M., after dictating his memo the night before, either to get it accepted as a basis for discussion or to push it across. I must add also my sense of the Committee's failure to come up to scratch in discussion. Once again most of the people there remained totally silent when challenged to give their views on the crisis, leaving the field to the Chancellor, who obviously felt he was winning and that the P.M. was in his pocket. The only person who spoke up was Douglas Jay, who proposed some reflation of consumer durables and made it clear he also had proposals for the motor-car industry and the use of the regulator. In fact, here we were with twelve Ministers present beginning to consider a mini-budget for the autumn. Straightaway under pressure from Callaghan Harold said this could not be allowed: such decisions must be left to the Prime Minister, the First Secretary, the Chancellor of the Exchequer and the President of the Board of Trade.

The Rhodesia meeting which followed was just as futile. The proposal for a Royal Commission, which had been knocked by Malcolm MacDonald, was now finally buried. It was overruled by the Foreign Office and the Commonwealth Office. John Silkin and I were the only people who were prepared to say, 'Well, if none of you can think of anything else to do, why not give it a chance?'

Before the big censure debate on economic affairs this afternoon we had arranged for Gordon Walker to make our miserable announcement on family allowances. I was curious what the reaction would be. We were saved by the Opposition spokesman, Mervyn Pike, who got up and made such a routine Tory propaganda attack that she rallied our own supporters to Gordon Walker's side and we had virtually no criticism from our back-benchers.[1] The Opposition were very badly briefed and failed to elicit from him the fatal admission that only half the poorest families would get any improvement as a result of this announcement.

Then came the big economic censure debate, with Callaghan starting and Douglas Jay winding up. The P.M. decided, rightly, not to intervene. Callaghan made one of his brutal save-the-pound speeches openly justifying the rise of unemployment, and our back-benchers were not in the least

[1] Miss Mervyn Pike, Conservative M.P. for Merton from December 1956 until 1974, when she became Chairman of the Women's Royal Voluntary Service.

impressed. Nevertheless, when it came to the vote the new liberal discipline
worked. Ian Mikardo had been permitted to put down a bitterly hostile
amendment to our motion provided he didn't move it. The Speaker whispered
to me during the debate that he nearly rebuked him when he got up and
attacked me for not allowing him to have his motion. I knew perfectly well
that he'd only put it down because he was certain it wouldn't be called. So
this undercover collaboration between the Chief Whip and the Left gave us
the unanimous vote we required and the largest majority this Government
has ever had.[1]

If it was a triumph of our liberal regime it was also a triumph of professional whippery. In the inner lobby the Chief was rushing to and fro, pro-
claiming the result, pleased himself and enormously exciting me.

Tuesday, July 25th

The morning papers didn't give us much credit for our famous vote of confidence. But I didn't mind because they at least printed our excellent housing
figures and the launching of the option-mortgage scheme. I'd almost forgotten
all about the plan which Dame Evelyn and I had launched together. Now I
see it as removing the last justification of the Chancellor's insistence that we
can't relate social security policy to tax allowances. That is exactly what the
option mortgage does.

At Cabinet this morning we started with Aberfan. I'd had a row with the
P.M. about this on Saturday when he told me he intended to release a statement before the publication of the Report, which is immensely damaging.[2]
The Government, I said, could only decide its attitude and announce it after
the public had heard the appalling facts. The authors of the Report indict the
Coal Board by name as morally, though not legally, responsible for the
complete failure to provide any precautionary measures to safeguard coal-
tips. When Cledwyn came to me yesterday to discuss publication I suggested
that he shouldn't hurry it but let the preparation run on, with maps and
diagrams until, say, the middle of August. I would just announce this in our
adjournment debate. Cabinet agreed that I should make the announcement
this afternoon and meanwhile appointed Gordon Walker chairman of a
Committee of Ministers to consider the implications of the Report.

Then we turned, as usual, to transport. Barbara, who's got her enormous
Transport Bill in preparation, always has one or two items for Cabinet now
and she nearly always gets her way from sheer energy and drive. By the way,

[1] The vote was 240 to 333 on the Conservatives' censure motion.
[2] The report of the inquiry which Lord Justice Edmund Davies had held was published
on August 3rd. The National Coal Board was criticized and the chairman of the Board,
Lord Robens, severely censured for his attitude to the inquiry and his denial that the Board
had any responsibility for the disaster. On August 7th Lord Robens offered his resignation
to the Minister of Power but was asked to stay on for the time being. The mineworkers
supported Lord Robens, who had been battling on their behalf at a time of great difficulty
for a declining coal industry, and on September 15th the Minister of Power asked Lord
Robens to continue in his post.

last night on the B.B.C. there was a curious item—a one-hour study by Nicholas Tomalin, Reporter of the Year and now the *New Statesman* literary editor (an astonishing mis-choice I should think).[1] His subject was how people in power positions take decisions, and he had chosen four decision-takers—Sir John Hackett,[2] now Commander-in-Chief of Berlin, Arthur South, the Labour boss of Norwich, Henry Brooke, the ex-Home Secretary, and Barbara Castle. Despite all the presentational flippery which so delights the B.B.C. producers, she came across as the person who by nature took decisions easily and well. But will she become the new First Secretary and head of the D.E.A.? In such a desperate period I'm beginning to wonder whether it shouldn't be allowed to happen.

When I got back to my office Godfrey Agnew suddenly revealed to me that a new Minister was to be sworn in at the Privy Council on Friday and he had been told that it was Judith Hart who was taking the place of Peggy Herbison. That was the first I knew of this decision. As Judith informed me, she had stayed at Chequers on the Saturday night and on the Sunday morning the offer was made to her. My advice had been asked but not taken.

This afternoon I had to sit on the front bench for the summer adjournment debate just twelve months after my appointment as Leader of the House when my first job was to answer this self-same debate. This time it seemed more futile than ever. This is the kind of inferior Oxford Union debating which some Members of the House enjoy. It lasted from 3.45 until 6.30. Strictly speaking, each speaker can only give reasons why the House should postpone its recess or alternatively why the recess should be shorter or prolonged, but they constantly go beyond this and argue the merits of the case. On Tuesday the striking difference from a year ago was that there was no mention of Vietnam. Foreign policy was out. Most people were complaining about the mismanagement of morning sittings or home-front problems. There was no front-bench participation and no tension. It was just not important—which was quite O.K. by me.

This evening the children came up to London for a stay. But when we'd put them to bed I went back to the House for the Consolidated Fund Bill. Why on earth was I staying all night? Because of that desperate occasion in the spring when our absence in the Consolidated Fund Bill had started all our afflictions.[3] I wasn't going to let there be the remotest chance of a repetition of these troubles. Anyway I wanted to be with the troops and so John and I decided to stay the night. I had two nice periods of sleep—from 12.30 to 2.00 and again from 3.30 to 5.00. Apart from that, I was round the tea-room and the smoking-room and the lobbies and really enjoyed it.

[1] Nicholas Tomalin was killed in Israel in 1973 while reporting on the Yom Kippur War. In 1974 his widow, Claire Tomalin, became literary editor of the *New Statesman*.

[2] General Sir John Hackett, Commander-in-Chief B.A.O.R. 1964–6 and Commander of the Northern Army Group 1966–8. He was from 1968 to July 1975 Principal of King's College, London.

[3] See pp. 219–20.

Wednesday, July 26th

At seven o'clock I went home and had a bath and got the children and then we all went over to see a closure moved. Throughout the night we'd had some sixty-five to seventy people there and for the closure we'd called back members of the Government and our numbers had gone up to 160 by eight in the morning. Patrick and Virginia went up into the gallery where they sat in the centre—the only occupants. The Speaker grinned at them. Wedgy Benn grinned at them. Everybody grinned at them. Only Mr Kenneth Robinson went on talking about drugs to two Tories who were waiting to speak on the same subject. So my two blond beasts up in the gallery beamed down at the Speaker and the Speaker beamed up at them. It was a pleasant scene with the Lord President's children there in the gallery and the sun streaming in and the end of an easy-going pleasant Consolidated Fund Bill debate.

I walked back home to another breakfast in Vincent Square before going over to Downing Street for morning prayers. The only subject the P.M. wanted to talk about was theatre censorship. There had just been published a report from a very representative committee which unanimously recommended the abolition of the functions of the Lord Chamberlain as censor of the living drama. This Roy Jenkins had very much wanted to accept but the P.M. told John and me this would be a terrible mistake and he also let us know that he'd sent George Wigg to the Home Affairs Committee to warn them against accepting it. I had had to leave the Committee just when George Wigg was starting to speak and hadn't realized that he was the P.M.'s emissary: indeed, I thought he'd gone there with a brief from Arnold Goodman, who was a member of the original departmental committee. Harold's explanation was very elaborate, I think because he was a little embarrassed. 'I've received representations from the Palace,' he said. 'They don't want to ban all plays about live persons but they want to make sure that there's somebody who'd stop the kind of play about Prince Philip which would be painful to the Queen. Of course,' he hurriedly added, 'they're not denying that there should be freedom to write satirical plays, take-offs, caricatures: what they want to be able to ban are plays devoted to character assassination and they mention, as an example, "Mrs Wilson's Diary".'

I pricked up my ears. 'Mrs Wilson's Diary' is, of course, one of the most popular features of *Private Eye* and there were ideas about putting it on the stage.[1] When I asked him, Harold told me that he had been shown the text of the play, which made him out a complete mugwump and gave a picture of George Brown's drinking and swearing and using four-letter words. My first reaction was to tell him that he could hardly keep censorship of the live theatre and leave television and radio free. He had a quick reply. 'That'll all be lined up now,' he said, 'because Charlie Hill has already cleaned up I.T.V.

---

[1] The series was to be adapted for the stage by Joan Littlewood. It opened at the Theatre Royal, Stratford East, in September 1967 and was transferred to the Criterion Theatre, where it ran for nine months.

and he'll do the same to B.B.C. now I'm appointing him chairman.' It was obvious from the way he talked that he wanted the censorship as much as the Queen. Indeed he wanted it so much that he'd put it on Thursday's Cabinet agenda.

I had to leave John with Harold and go off to the Economic Committee because I didn't want to miss the first item which was how to dispose of the accommodation made surplus by the winding-up of the Territorial Army. In literally hundreds of towns there are ugly but spacious drill halls and buildings of this kind used by the Territorials, which the Ministry of Defence wanted to sell off quick. They were supported in this by D.E.A. and the Treasury. I had to point out that these buildings could be invaluable to our community services and local authorities at least must have the chance of buying them before Defence disposes of them. I got the Committee on my side but I'm doubtful whether we shall get our way because the local authorities will need £2 million extra to save this accommodation just at the moment when their funds for this kind of purchase are being slashed by the Chancellor.

There was another equally interesting item — forestry — where Douglas Jay and I found ourselves ranged once again against the Treasury and the D.E.A., which wanted to wind up forestry as a totally uneconomic activity. I learnt about forestry from Hugh Dalton who, as Chancellor,[1] did a tremendous lot for the Commission and often used to take me for walks in order to see new plantations. With the help of the Secretary of State for Scotland, Douglas and I had quite a victory. We got a small increase for forestry in Scotland and a new inquiry into forestry in England.* I had to leave before the two important discussions — one on pit closures and the other on subsidies for shipyards. I had to meet Anne and the children, drive them in the official car to Olympia where with Venice and her children we were to see the Royal Military Tournament. On the way we had to buy Venice's birthday present and give her lunch. For the Military Tournament, thanks to Denis Healey, we sat in the Chairman's box just below the Royal Box. It seemed to me just as good as when I last saw it in 1914 and the best turn was still the naval guns being hauled across the imaginary rivers.

I had to get back to the House at seven for a Party meeting which had been called to discuss social problems. The talking point was Peggy Herbison's resignation, which had been announced on the front page of every newspaper this morning.[2] I got there a little late and saw Peggy sitting down below and

* But when the report was published the new inquiry came down on the side of the Treasury. Jay and I were wrong. Forestry under modern conditions in Britain is uneconomic and it is of very little amenity value because of its concentration on soft wood.

[1] Chancellor of the Exchequer 1945–7.

[2] On July 24th Patrick Gordon Walker had announced increased family allowances and higher charges for school meals and milk. Peggy Herbison, adamantly opposed to any move towards 'selectivity' in welfare benefits, resigned on July 25th and Judith Hart took her place.

Callaghan from the platform rallying the boys. He made an immensely demagogic speech saying that we'd spent more on social services than the Tories in their last three years, denying there was any question of social-service cuts, and altogether in my view protesting too much.

Of course his real concern was what Peggy would say after he'd finished. But in fact she said nothing whatsoever. I would have thought that the only point of resigning is when you're convinced that you can conduct your campaign more effectively outside the Government. But Peggy is the kind of loyalist who resigns rather as Anthony Eden resigned in 1938[1]—because she can't let herself be associated any more with an attitude of which she disapproves: but on the other hand she can't let herself oppose her colleagues in public because she does not want to be accused of disloyalty. I have very little sympathy with this kind of resignation. To resign without explaining what it is you're protesting against is to get the worst of every world.

When I went through the morning papers this morning I noticed that only one of them—the *Daily Mail*—gave an accurate account of her resignation. Walter Terry was able to state exactly the three reasons why she resigned of which far the most important was her upset at the breach of our 1964 promise that we would make pensions dynamic, i.e. we would make sure that they would go up every year as fast as average male wages increased. All Callaghan had allowed Peggy was an increase which is somewhere between that required in order to keep up with the cost of living and that related to earnings. Most of the newspapers suggested she'd quarrelled with Gordon Walker but in fact she got on with him rather better than with Douglas Houghton. Nor was there anything in Peter Townsend's suggestion in a letter to *The Times* that she was discontented with the speed at which the pension scheme was being prepared.

Knowing that her resignation was due this week, I had tried to brief Ian Waller of the *Sunday Telegraph* on the issues involved and to emphasize to him that the choice was not between selectivity and universality but between two kinds of selectivity. Though I'd briefed him extremely carefully, he just didn't believe me and put out the same old story once again.

The P.M. was giving a special party for the press and when I went along I found there were two topics of conversation. The Lords had just passed an amendment to our Abortion Bill which knocked out a central clause. On this I made rather a fool of myself because I'd been assured by the Chief Whip that the Parliament Act doesn't apply to Private Members' Bills whereas alas in fact it does.[2] So the Lord President was talking nonsense. Fortunately the pressmen were much more interested in the second topic—the appointment of Charlie Hill to be chairman of the Governors of the B.B.C.[3] Harold's

[1] From the Foreign Office.
[2] The 1947 Parliament Act set out the extent of the Lords' delaying powers, see p. 94.
[3] Lord Normanbrook had died on June 15th. The appointment of the former I.T.A. chairman to be the new chairman of the B.B.C. caused some anguish.

words this morning had been the first I'd heard of what seems to me the most characteristic piece of Wilsonian gimmickry that he's yet achieved. Charlie Hill has very much run the I.T.V. to suit the convenience of the politicians and in particular he has made sure that their treatment of news and current affairs and discussions does not offend the establishment, including the leaders of the two big Parties. He has carefully avoided all the irritating things the B.B.C. do. Of course, as a public service the B.B.C. is determined to show itself independent and sometimes unaccommodating and this tendency has been strengthened by Hugh Greene's new style directorship and the desire to compete with I.T.V. and to be newsier, edgier, and more exciting. And this has all paid off in terms of the audience ratings where the B.B.C. has been doing well in the last six months, winning the battle for the audience by its with-itness.

So Harold has coolly switched Hill to the B.B.C. to discipline it and bring it to book and, above all, to deal with Hugh Greene. And in Charlie's place he is going to pop an absolutely safe politician—Herbert Bowden. A bureaucrat, an establishment man if ever there was one, who has always done what Harold required. Even at the Commonwealth Office he's remained a Chief Whip. His appointment as Charlie Hill's successor hasn't been announced but all the press is carrying inspired stories about it. I'd assumed that Bowden would be resigning but now I see that Harold's intention is to move him out of the Commonwealth Secretary's job and have a reshuffle at the beginning of September.[1]

After the party Anne and I went home for a little supper and I went back to the House to see how the Criminal Justice Bill was going. But I fell asleep and came home again.

Thursday, July 27th

Cabinet once again—three Cabinets running in a week. Theatre censorship, as Harold promised, was the first item on the agenda. Despite George Wigg, the Home Affairs Committee had recommended acceptance of the committee's report. One of its main arguments was that one could hardly forbid the portrayal of living persons in the live theatre when it was not prohibited on television. Here Harold had equipped himself with an effective reply, namely an assurance from Charlie Hill that the powers vested in the Governors of the B.B.C. were quite adequate to ensure that character assassination was altogether forbidden.

I had been expecting a great confrontation between Harold and the man he detests and whose influence he really hates in the Cabinet. Faced with the P.M.'s unexpected coup Roy was quite firm, cool and collected. He said of course he would consider this and the matter must certainly go back to Home Affairs for reconsideration. But he added that it would be extremely

[1] Herbert Bowden became a life peer, taking the title of Lord Aylestone.

difficult to evolve any way of controlling the live theatre which didn't mean
the reintroduction of censorship and more discrimination against it in comparison with television and radio. The Prime Minister seemed content with
this and when I intervened to suggest that we needn't rush the Bill he indicated
that it should be given high priority and he hoped that Roy would be able to
satisfy him on this point. The agreement reached, as recorded in the Cabinet
minutes, runs: 'In neither medium would ordinary political satire be forbidden but there should be safeguards against the theatre being used deliberately to discredit or create political hostility towards public political
figures.'

But the main item was prices and incomes, not this time legislation or the
principles of the Bill but how it works out in practice. In the spring the
Treasury and the D.E.A. were both insisting that electricity prices must be
raised and I had managed to have the increase postponed till after the G.L.C.
election. Then they were insistent and, against Dick Marsh's protest, the
prices went up. Now we had a paper from D.E.A. completely reversing their
argument and saying that in view of the effect on prices and incomes policy
gas prices, which must logically follow electricity prices, should be kept down.
Simultaneously Dick and Barbara, who a few months ago had been ordered
to increase charges to cut the railway deficit by £30 million, were told to keep
the price of tickets down. The fact is we've been panicked as badly on these
nationalized industry prices as we have been on pit closures, which have also
been a subject of discussion several times this week.

Ironically, the very people who had been destroying all the statutory
sanctions of prices and incomes were now trying to use the policy for effective
price control. The fact is that this winter we may well face rising unemployment, rising prices and an attempt to raise wages at the same time—without
any effective statutory control of incomes. It was surely the most unsatisfactory Cabinet debate we've ever had. Finally Tony Crosland, who's becoming quite a statesman these days, asked why we had to rush this thing—
why not wait till September? This was the one decision we were capable of
making this morning.

My business Statement went smoothly today. There weren't many questions
because the Speaker now stops them, and I was soon up in the lobby answering questions about Charles Hill's successor at I.T.V. The press were already
busily talking about Herbert Bowden but they also put forward the name of
Vivian Bowden,[1] who's head of the Manchester College of Technology, and
so it was Bowden versus Bowden. It was an easy lobby because at the moment
I stand well with them.

At the Services Committee I was able to report on the successful deal
Selwyn Lloyd had made with the Chancellor about the Clerks' salaries and

[1] Principal of the University of Manchester Institute of Science and Technology since
1964. He became a life peer in 1963 and served as Minister of State at the D.E.S. 1964–5.
See Vol. I.

we received a rather terrifying account from Bob Maxwell of his tough campaign in the Catering Department. But at least we've got the Chancellor to concede that he should be able to clear the deficit with a grant in aid.

We also had a report on the delicious old indicators up on the walls all over the House that tell us the name of the man who at that moment is speaking in the Chamber. The problem is one of staffing; we are told it would save staff to introduce internal television—some 80 big ones and 240 small ones for M.P.s' rooms. It's proposed to buy them in bulk and dump them in each room on a table or cupboard. I gaily tried to persuade the Committee that just as in the time of the great Barry who designed the new Houses of Parliament (every clock and every piece of furniture was specially designed) so today we should try to get our new furniture designed to suit our House. The fact that this seemed quite a novel concept shows how barbaric we've become these days.

I had to go straight from the Services Committee to the Speaker on a very delicate mission. Charles Pannell had noticed in a Wednesday local paper that the Speaker had agreed to open the illuminations at Blackpool this year. This had deeply upset him and I must say it upset the Chief Whip and me just as much. I felt it was an undignified thing to do, especially because he was taking the place of Ken Dodd, the comedian. I had a word with Willie Whitelaw and also with Ted Heath, who entirely agreed. I gave my message quite briefly and then went away without giving him time to reply. Back on the front bench I found Harold and told him what I'd just been doing. 'Ah,' he said, 'if he'd been going to Ascot that would have been O.K. Because he's doing something popular he's stopped. I certainly shouldn't stop him at all.' I thought this an interesting episode with which to end this two-year Session.

Anne and I were giving dinner this evening to my stepson Gilbert Baker and his wife. It turned out a terrible fuss because the big defence debate was on so that I had to be on the front bench for Harold Wilson's speech at nine. Moreover when we had got to our table in the Strangers' dining-room I was summoned at eight to approve the draft Statement on Aberfan. It only took five minutes to see that this was the kind of draft I never would agree to and at 8.30 I stalked out in dudgeon.

When it came to the big speeches at nine the debate was flat, as it often is on great occasions. Reg Maudling was followed by the P.M., who made a perfectly adequate knockabout speech which he hadn't had time to prepare. However, it was serviceable and so was the vote. Only nineteen actual abstentions while twelve other people didn't turn up. I think the Chief probably concealed an abstention of about forty-five by this device.[1] He's quite an able and shrewd customer in these ways.

[1] The vote on the supplementary Statement on Defence Policy 1967 (Cmnd. 3357) was 321 to 231.

I stayed to see the business finished before I walked across to Kingsley's flat where he'd invited me to join in his seventieth birthday celebrations.[1] I fortunately came late when almost everybody had gone. Indeed, the only people left there were Gerald Barry, Sagittarius (the old poetess of Kingsley's days), and Kingsley's sister. It was pleasant to sit with him and find him so gay and happy. He's been very nice to me recently—speaking up for the Leader of the House on the *Panorama* programme. I couldn't help wondering what would have happened if he'd allowed me to become editor of the *Statesman*. I think I would have been happy there but it would have meant that I missed this chance of seeing Government from close to, and I would never have been able to be sure that I understood its workings. Now I am beginning to understand it a good deal more.

Friday, July 28th

I had a Privy Council where we had to deal with the marriage of the Earl of Harewood to Miss Tuckwell, for whom he has left his nice musician wife.[2] Harold brought it up in Cabinet and told us that the Queen expressly wanted to be advised by us. Since he's eighteenth in succession to the throne, the Royal Marriages Act of 1772 requires her to do so. It was my duty, therefore, formally to give her the Cabinet's advice which of course she was duty-bound to take.

This morning at O.P.D. there were two items I particularly didn't want to miss. I got back just in time for the discussion on Aldabra—an island somewhere in the Indian Ocean where the Minister of Defence in consultation with the Americans wants to create a huge staging-post. O.P.D. was asked to authorize the expenditure of £30 million for this purpose. As I entered the room forty-five minutes late, James Callaghan looked up and said, 'My God, I feel like Wellington when Blücher arrived just in time for the Battle of Waterloo.' 'We aren't going to win this battle,' I said. But I was wrong. If we didn't actually win it we drew it. Callaghan had made the Treasury case already. I joined in to say that if we are going to cut our Far Eastern commitment down to a mere capability as distinct from a presence, then staging-posts like Aldabra must not be built. This is where expenditure ought to stop. George Brown also came out with much the same view, and so did Frank Longford. Indeed, the only friends of the idea were the Prime Minister, Herbert Bowden and Denis Healey, who was beautifully half-hearted as usual, saying that it was a marginal case which he didn't really believe in. But it didn't make any difference. This was the first occasion when I've heard the P.M. after collecting the voices and finding he'd lost simply say, 'There's a

[1] Kingsley Martin, editor of the *New Statesman and Nation* 1930–60. He died in February 1969.
[2] It had been announced on January 2nd that the Earl of Harewood was to be sued for divorce on grounds of adultery with Miss Tuckwell. His divorce had been approved on April 6th and on July 31st he married Miss Tuckwell.

majority on my side,' and so we were committed to Aldabra. At first Callaghan
boldly said he would take it to Cabinet. The P.M. said, 'No. It's not a question of policy but a case.' So it's not going to Cabinet and this huge item has
been successfully forced through, presumably because either he or Healey
committed themselves to it with firm personal pledges.

We then turned to an astonishing paper on Cyprus, a copy of which I had
discovered among the huge mass of bumf which was provided for this meeting
of the Committee. This paper advised that if on the instructions of the Greek
Government the Greek army in Cyprus staged a coup against Makarios in
order to achieve Enosis, we should dissent from it but prevent our troops
getting engaged in any hostilities. Denis Healey and I were the only two
people there who had noticed this extraordinary proposal. A Commonwealth
country is attacked by a fascist dictatorship which tries to upset its constitutional government and although we have 15,000 armed men there we stand
aside. We both thought this was totally intolerable and the passage was
deleted.

What made it even more astonishing was that this proposal was part of a
huge paper recommending that we should make our presence in Cyprus
virtually permanent. I suppose it's explained by the fact that authority is
divided between the Foreign Office and the Commonwealth Office, but when
I asked the Foreign Secretary afterwards he said, 'After all, the Cypriots
have got a very bad record of voting with the Russians in all U.N. matters'—
as though that settled the issue. As Foreign Secretary, he saw it in terms of
the United Nations whereas the Commonwealth Secretary, who ought to
have seen the big issues involved, was so feeble that he said nothing. When I
saw Burke and Harold afterwards, they said, 'That's what comes of one
member of the Committee reading the papers.'

Although this was the last day of the Session I didn't bother to go to the
House but went straight from No. 10 to an enormously enjoyable lunch at
the Gay Hussar given by some of the Lobby to John and me in exchange for
the hospitality we've given to the journalists. I rushed home to find Thomas
Balogh waiting for a gloomy discussion. He was deeply disheartened by the
events of the week. All one can say is that Harold is dead tired and I am dead
tired and everybody is dead tired, and we've got to hope that by the end of
August we shall have enough energy and ability to pull this Government
together.

Saturday, July 29th
Poor David Young, the chairman of my constituency Labour Party, came
over to Prescote on an embarrassing mission. Albert Rose had rung up and
Anne had taken the message which said there had been another meeting of
their G.M.C. at which George Park had put forward the view that I should,
after all, stand down from the N.E.C. this year because there were too many
Ministers on it. Apparently there was a great deal of muddle about what

15

actually happened but there's no doubt there were only fourteen people there whereas they need a quorum of fifteen. But that didn't interest me. The moment I heard the news I felt it would be much more convenient to resign this year than next. On the whole the time has come for the creation of two vacancies on the Executive, one by my retiring and one by Callaghan's becoming Treasurer. It would be good for the party to be able to choose between Cabinet Ministers and others for their representatives. It's partly because I'm sick to death of the way the Executive has treated me and the absolutely fruitless tension between the Org. Sub. and the rest. On the other hand it's equally relevant that I don't want to be on the N.E.C. during the period after this Labour Government because I want then to be writing my book. And so it does seem to me that it's a genuine advantage to get out this year and I must be grateful to George Park for behaving so unconstitutionally.

Sunday, July 30th
So the famous July 28th for which I've been longing for six long weeks has come and gone. Parliament's adjourned until October 23rd and the weather has broken. At long last it's raining; cold, very wet rain and I'm worn out. Slowly I'm beginning to recover from the most exhausting year of my three years as Cabinet Minister.

I must admit that the physical recovery is going to take place in a period of extreme political depression. This isn't due to my own political position because John and I got through the week all right and we ended the Session with quite a lot of honour and goodwill in the Party. But though we're all right, the Government certainly isn't. I've recorded in this diary before now how the morale of the Cabinet has sagged because it's caught in a dead end and how the resourcefulness and resilience of the Leader has bounced us out of our depression. I don't think this happened last week and I suspect that the closer one is to Harold the less one feels it happened. It's true he was able to stand up to Heath on Thursday and give as good as he got. It's true that he's pulled off one of his most characteristic tricks by appointing Charlie Hill to be chairman of the B.B.C. He's got through the resignation of Peggy Herbison without the slightest embarrassment. But looking at him from very close I get the impression that this time the situation is getting on top of him: he's unable to break through, throw it off and burst forward out of the fix he is in. He's in a dead end about Rhodesia, about the Common Market and about the Suez Canal, which seems to be closed indefinitely. All over the world we're having trouble with people assaulting and insulting us and it's natural enough because we're rapidly going downhill. But it's on the home front that Harold's failure is most striking because, after all, his profession is economics and economics is the area in which he promised there would be the most difference from the Macmillan regime. It's his absolute failure to get economic growth going and the desperate expedients he's now lifting and sifting which alarm me. And what depresses me most is that one set of expedients—import quotas followed by devaluation, which I think the only possible remedy—is something he's still sedulously trying to avoid.

Monday, July 31st
I went up early this morning because I specially wanted to attend the Cabinet Committee on pit closures. As I've reported in this diary, Jim Callaghan and Harold came back from the Durham Miners' Gala so shaken that they proposed—first in S.E.P. and then in Cabinet—that we should postpone the pit closures this winter in order to cut the number of unemployed by about 15,000. There were two papers. First an analysis of the situation and then a summary of the proposals. The analysis made it clear that we already have 30 million tons of surplus coal for this winter and it will grow to 50 million tons if we postpone the closures and start the closure campaign next year. It's in view of this surplus that Cabinet took its decision on fuel policy which cut back a long way further the amount of coal to be produced, marketed and sold in the years immediately ahead. The total cutback is therefore fixed. On the other hand, exactly which pits will be closed and how many of them is not nearly so clear and the Minister couldn't even give us the list for this winter. Eirene White, who sat next to him, remarked that the latest list showed five collieries in South Wales which had always been reckoned as the most modern and on which vast sums had been spent which were now due for closure. Dick Marsh replied that once we agreed to the new total cutback we agreed to these South Wales closures. I said this was absurd. Cabinet could agree with an economic analysis but before it agreed the closures it would have to consider the social impact. I then turned to Marsh and said, 'Where is your paper on the social impact of the closures?' There isn't one of course. What he has tried to do is a deal with the Treasury under which he makes the closures and then placates the miners by obtaining £140 million for redundancy pay if they retire after the age of fifty-five. No doubt this was thought sufficient when it was assumed that there would be a fully employed economy. But now we're going to have 750,000 unemployed this winter and next and the closures come in an atmosphere not of full employment but of unemployment. No one in the Ministry seems to have taken this into consideration. We then asked him whether it would be possible to carry out the Callaghan–Wilson idea and either postpone this winter's closures or revise the list downwards. Marsh replied that of the 15,000 men thrown out this winter only 3,500 would be redundant and he asserted roundly that it would be impossible to hold up any of the closures without losing millions of pounds on surplus coal. He then showed us the letter he'd written to Callaghan, which is about the most snubbing negative I've seen. The fact that he can send it indicates the weakness of central control in this Government. Indeed, the lesson of this meeting was the appalling fact that after three years the Labour Government had evolved neither an instrument for assessing the social impact of its actions nor an instrument for ameliorating that impact

upon the community. The only concrete result of this long meeting was that Marsh was instructed to report to S.E.P. at our first meeting after we come back from our holiday on September 6th.

Later this morning in the Lord Chancellor's room I discussed Lords reform and within five minutes we were in our old deadlock, since he insisted on preparing a paper on the reduction of powers only. As I was getting nowhere I mentioned to him my surprise that Frank Beswick has been suddenly promoted to be the Lords' Chief Whip in place of Malcolm Shepherd, who's become Minister of State at the Commonwealth Office.[1] I can conceive few people more suitable to be a Chief Whip than Frank Beswick, who's a thoroughly good fellow but with a terrible chip on his shoulder. Yet Harold has plonked him with this without consulting either John Silkin or me or, I gather, even Gerald Gardiner. What made it even more odd was when I suggested to Gerald that Beswick must now join our Committee. 'Oh no,' he said, 'he doesn't know a damn thing about it. We don't want him on the Committee.' I had to insist that even if we kept Malcolm on it we should have to include Frank as well.

This afternoon I went to see the P.M. first and foremost about my Coventry problems. I wasn't absolutely sure about his attitude to me and therefore I asked him straightaway whether I could include in a letter for publication that I was writing to my constituency a statement that I wanted next year to concentrate on my work at Westminster. 'Can I safely say that one of the reasons I'm going off the Executive,' I asked him, 'is because I want to concentrate on Westminster? You know that implies that I shall be Leader for the next year.' 'Oh, you can certainly do that,' he said. 'That'll baffle them and put them off the scent a bit more.' I must say the reply baffled me as well. Nevertheless, I had no doubt that he sees the tremendous programme for our second year of reform in both Houses and is assuming that John and I will carry it through together. As for my place on the Executive, it was quite clear that Harold now doesn't see any point in my staying on. He's given up any hope of reorganizing the Party and he also no doubt feels that if two places are left for the constituency parties to fill with their choice this might be quite a safety valve. As for myself I feel more strongly than ever that this is a resignation with no return. I've never walked out on anything in quite this fading-out style. I shall never want to go back to the N.E.C. and they'll never want me back. And it's also an acceptance of the failure of Harold's idea that I should combine the Leadership of the House with Party liaison as well as an acceptance of a new idea of myself—not as a failing politician but as a politician who's reached his zenith and must now stay on this level or gently move towards retirement.

Even though I am a book-writer this sense of fading out is something one

[1] Lord Beswick, Labour M.P. for Uxbridge from 1945 to October 1959, became a life peer in 1964 and served as Government Chief Whip in the Lords 1967–70. From 1970 to 1974, when he became Minister of State for Industry, he was Opposition Chief Whip.

accepts with a bit of reluctance, particularly since Tommy is so passionately against it. If Harold showed any interest I shouldn't dream of leaving the Executive. But was I right just to accept Harold's view of my future? Yes, I think I was right because I am Harold's henchman—the person who has no ambitions beyond Harold, who sees himself finishing as a politician in this Government and then retiring to write his book. And the sooner I make that decision an irrevocable one the better.

Tuesday, August 1st

There was a big meeting about the presentation of the Aberfan Report, which I had expected to handle myself unless the P.M. gave it to Patrick Gordon Walker. However, he decided to take the chair and have it at No. 10 and he called a lot of people to it. Patrick Gordon Walker had felt we should accept Alf Robens's resignation or even force it on him but without apparently realizing that we should then have all the problem of the pit closures being sabotaged by Alf from outside. On the other hand it was equally dangerous to say, as Dick Marsh did, that we must on no account let him resign. I finally said to the P.M., 'We ought to spend three weeks playing it out and request a report from the National Coal Board before we decide whether any resignations are accepted or not.' And this is roughly the line of the communiqué which was issued after this long desultory meeting. Of course, the result of Harold's sitting in the chair was that he got all the publicity he was trying to avoid.*

I gave lunch to Judith Hart in order to try to clear up the confusion about pensions. I at once agreed to postpone the meeting of the Cabinet Pensions Committee on Thursday and to give her at least four weeks to put her house in order and also to do the homework on national superannuation. She told me she'd had a talk with her Permanent Secretary, Jarrett,[1] who said how much they'd all loved Peggy and how they were giving a dinner for the most wonderful Minister they'd had. He said all this without inviting poor Judith to attend. And she was careful, she told me next day, not to be available when Jarrett wanted to see her. She will certainly have a struggle and I shall be fascinated to see what ideas she comes up with.

I went down this afternoon to Beatrice and Sidney Webb's old house at Passfield Corner, where the Labour Party summer school takes place each year. I was due to speak on parliamentary reform and was the N.E.C. big-wig selected for the big speech that week. One thing I learnt from my brief visit was how well-informed the Transport House staff are about internal Cabinet affairs and how they seep with anti-Government gossip—how disloyal to the Government, for example, Terry Pitt is and how loyal to his idea of Transport

---

* Wednesday's papers were full of stories about the meeting, gave the names of all those who attended it, and contained a lot of speculation about Robens's future.

[1] Sir Clifford Jarrett, Permanent Under-Secretary at the Ministry of Pensions (to become D.H.S.S.) 1964–70, where he was to work closely with Crossman.

House interests. They all in their different ways hate the Government as well as mostly hating each other.

Wednesday, August 2nd

Burke came round to my office specially to ask me whether I was content about information control. I contained my anger and said that in the course of the year we'd got quite a decent briefing system for Ministers going under Freddy Ward. As for the general co-ordination of Government propaganda and of departmental information services, I had achieved absolutely nothing and would continue to achieve nothing as long as on the official side it lay in the hands of Trevor Lloyd-Hughes. He would continue to keep it all at No. 10 and exclude me until the P.M. was willing to give orders—and he never would be.

When I'd finished my statement Burke said, 'But are you content?' 'Yes,' I said. 'By now I'm quite busy as Leader of the House and I've got quite a programme of parliamentary reform.'

I lunched with Pam Berry at her house in Cowley Street to see Joe Alsop[1] again along with Tommy Balogh and Eddie Shackleton. The last time Joe was with Pam he'd given us an awe-inspiring account of the American decision to launch a major war in Vietnam and build up their forces to half a million. Everything came true except his confident anticipation of communist defeat. This time we gave Joe the lecture. I described to him the decision to wind up our military commitments in the Middle East as soon as possible and said this was something which the whole Cabinet, including George Brown and Harold Wilson, were agreed on. In the Far East, however, things were far more open and there was still a division of opinion. Though an increasing number of us believed in total withdrawal, this view was not shared by Harold Wilson and George Brown. He showed complete scepticism when I said all this until Eddie Shackleton, just back from Aden and hardly a left-winger, completely confirmed my view. I wonder whether a word of this will ever appear in the Joe Alsop column?

Thursday, August 3rd

On and off during the week John Silkin and I have been discussing our programme for the next session of parliamentary reform. Our biggest change in the Commons will be to send the Finance Bill upstairs despite the opposition not only of the Chancellor but of his two subordinates—John Diamond and Niall MacDermot. But what about morning sittings? This week we have been trying to make practical sense of the idea for which the P.M. was so enthusiastic that day at Chequers that our normal parliamentary day should run from eleven in the morning until seven in the evening, like any other business. The more we thought about it the more impossible it seemed in

---

[1] The American syndicated columnist who had been writing about political and foreign affairs since the 1930s. See Vol. I, p. 250.

practice. One objection is that the House would be sitting in the mornings simultaneously with the Standing Committees and this is something which back-benchers would never accept. But suppose one put the Standing Committees in the afternoon? That's the very time the back-benchers want to be in the debates on the Floor of the House. Moreover, I was pretty sure that the House wasn't ready for Question Time at 10.30 a.m. As I remarked at one meeting with Harold, 'If we did this and produced a new timetable next October, one of my successors in the not too far distant future would reveal a brilliant reform which consisted of putting Standing Committees back in the morning and starting the main business of the House at 2.30.'

On the other hand, we simply can't keep the present system of morning sittings, which is a complete failure. What we're now working on is the idea that instead of using a threat of an all-night sitting we should reverse things and use the threat of a morning sitting to deter all-night sittings. What we need for this is a Standing Order which enables the Leader of the House to suspend the sitting at any time he likes. There are of course real practical difficulties about any scheme which requires a sudden decision to restart the sitting next morning at 10 a.m. but we were hard at work all this week trying to solve them.

We also had an important meeting of E.N. with Wedgy Benn's enabling Bill as first item on the agenda. I've recorded in this diary how the first idea of this Bill emerged when he asked me for time for four or five separate Bills for his Department and I said I'd much prefer to give him the power to deal with these things by Order in Council. Tony won the first round in Cabinet, which committed us to the White Paper he wanted in August. But then he had a meeting with the First Secretary and the C.B.I. where it could not be denied that the C.B.I. was utterly opposed to this kind of Government action. If we were to get the Bill past them we should have to make clear that it was for assistance to private industry and not an enabling act for the extension of socialism. Since the C.B.I. would have broken off collaboration with the Government on any other terms, this surrender was duly made. We're going to have the enabling Bill in the Queen's Speech but it isn't the one Wedgy and I intended.[1]

In the Cabinet reshuffle on August 28th, the Prime Minister announced that he intended to supervise the D.E.A. himself with Peter Shore as Minister of State, replacing Michael Stewart, who remained in the Cabinet as First Secretary with oversight of the Government's social policy. Douglas Jay, formerly President of the Board of Trade and an implacable anti-marketeer, left the Cabinet to be succeeded by Anthony Crosland, whose place at the D.E.S. was taken by Patrick Gordon Walker. George Thomson moved from the Foreign Office to replace Herbert Bowden (now at the I.T.A.) and Arthur Bottomley and Fred Willey resigned from the Cabinet.

[1] It became the Industrial Expansion Bill.

Friday, August 4th

So there's the week. It's really only been a mopping-up operation. The letter
to the constituency Party had finally been approved and David Young and
Albert Rose have received their copies. The draft had to be cleared not only
with Harold but also with Barbara Castle and Anthony Greenwood, who
have both been passionately opposed to my resignation and who directly they
saw the draft rang up urging me to rely exclusively on purely personal reasons
for my retirement since any other reason for withdrawing would imply a
criticism of them! I made some minor modifications just to humour them but
I can't for their convenience suppress my view and the view of the Coventry
East constituency that there are far too many Ministers and far too many
elderly people on the Executive and it's high time some young vigorous
constituency people replaced them. It was amusing how strongly the two of
them felt about this letter of mine. By the way, they are not on speaking
terms with each other—Barbara regards Tony as a bit of a wet and Tony
regards Barbara as a bit of a bitch, and as always they're competing for the
top place in the Executive vote at Conference this year. However, the letter's
been sent and Albert and David will present it to the Coventry East Executive
on August 14th and make my announcement in the *Coventry Evening
Telegraph*.

I've been relaxing a little during this tidying-up week in London and I've
been by myself at Vincent Square with our Mr and Mrs Meake staying at the
top since their furniture has gone to Scotland and they're waiting to move
there at the end of August. I came down this morning on the 10.35 and lay on
the terrace reading Gore Vidal's novel about Washington, D.C.[1] Now we
shall settle down to packing before we set off on our holiday—first a fortnight
in Cornwall and then on from there to France, where we shall motor south
from Cherbourg to Provence to stay with the Baloghs. It's a whole month
clean away before we get back for that first Cabinet meeting on Wednesday,
September 6th.

Monday, September 4th

Back in London from the first full month of holiday I've had since becoming
a Minister. It felt even longer than that because on this occasion I really did
cut myself off entirely from my work. In Cornwall I had no daily papers and
only saw one Sunday paper. Then when we crossed over to France I really
was so much cut off that I only heard about the Government reshuffle from
somebody who brought in a copy of *The Times* while we were having a drink
in a friend's house.

Far more important than the papers are the books we have read aloud.
First *Huckleberry Finn*. Then I went on to *Moon Fleet* which I think at least
as good as *Treasure Island* and far better than *Kidnapped*. Over in France we
naturally tried the *White Company*, since it's about the area we were travelling

[1] *Washington, D.C.* (London: Heinemann, 1967).

through, and found it greatly inferior to *Sir Nigel*. We were better pleased by *Mistress Masham's Repose*, which I think is far the best of T. H. White's books. A good many people listened to part of it and were spellbound, not only the Baloghs but also Jock Campbell, who has come to live on the hill just above them in the Dordogne.[1]

As to the holiday itself, we started by motoring to Polzeath in north Cornwall, where we were staying for the third year running, and stopped off on the first morning at Dauntsey in Wiltshire, where I wanted to see the Danvers tombs in the church and the Danvers house next door. The John Danvers who married the rich lady of Dauntsey and made his fortune was of course an ancestor of the John Danvers who built the two splendid rooms on to Prescote in 1695. The Dauntsey church is quite unspoilt and though the house is in a poor state its position by the river is lovely. From there we went on to stay with Anne's aunt, May Cowper, in Bath, where the rain deluged down. Nevertheless, we decided to make one excursion on the way to Polzeath —to Camelot where excavations were being carried out by Leslie Alcock of Cardiff[2] and a huge team of amateurs who'd been largely stimulated by some powerful promotion in the *Observer*. They all collected there to help the Professor discover whether there was any archaeological evidence that our King Arthur had anything to do with that hill at South Cadbury which is supposed to be Camelot. We found it very difficult to pick out the hill because it's surrounded by trees. But we parked ourselves in a very expensive modern car park in a tiny village south of Wincanton and then down there came through the trees a Land Rover driven by a chap with beard and sandals and we drove back through the woods. Suddenly we were on top of an enormous open plateau with lots of tents and hundreds of young people either washing bits of pottery in tubs of water or sitting busily scratching the soil with tiny mortars. There was something comic about Alcock's enterprise. He had raised money to excavate Camelot but what they were actually excavating was a neolithic site where only at one point was there anything which could possibly come from the sixth century in which Arthur is supposed to have lived. Being very modern, Alcock had preceded his dig by a careful study of the site with geiger counters which had provided evidence of solid walls under the ground. However, when the digging started they found what was in fact probably a First World War trench dug by volunteers to learn the art of trench-digging. He had also erected some enormous wooden two-storey structures on top of which his foremen stood making sure their slaves before them worked. Poor Alcock patiently walked round with us and then let us slide down the immense steep embattled hillside at the top of which were the remains of a gateway which could be Roman or possibly a gateway nearer

[1] Created Lord Campbell of Eskan in 1966. As chairman of the Statesman and Nation Publishing Company he was to play an important part in Crossman's later career.

[2] Reader in Archaeology at University College, Cardiff, 1966–73, and Professor of Archaeology at Glasgow University since 1973.

15*

the times of King Arthur. Newspaper-promoted archaeology, I came to realize, has its complications; I hope that our children also got an impression of how boring actual work on a site may be.

When we got to Cornwall we had a couple of decent days and then the weather broke and we had ten days of really bad Cornish weather and that's some of the worst weather you can have in a bad English summer. This year Anne had brought nobody with us to help with the children so we all had to do the washing up. Anne did all the cooking and the household chores, which were intensified by having two very nice boys with us as well. Nevertheless, because we are hardened surf bathers and can stand the Cornish sea water we enjoyed ourselves and we found that by having the children in the same place as last year we could measure their achievements. They were swimming that much better, walking further along the cliffs, standing up to the big waves so much better. We had our big annual expedition once again to Fowey to visit the Trinnicks, the family of a delightful young man who works for the National Trust, who spend their summer in the remotest coast-guard cottage on the cliff. With Trinnick I had some interesting talk, as I always do, about the National Trust and was very much struck by his disappointment when I told him that I hadn't persuaded the Prime Minister to order an independent inquiry into the National Trust. As a Trust official he feels it's essential.

The other big event of our Cornish life was our encounter with the seal. The next house to ours was occupied by a Winchester housemaster—a very characteristic Wykehamist who, once he heard who I was, asked me in 'to have a noggin' one evening. There he was with his wife and daughters and a son (at Haileybury), very distinguished and elegant, and tremendously Wykehamical. And while we were there they told Patrick that the only way to see a seal on Pentire Head was to go and stand in that dip between the rumps and sing hymns. A day or two later Patrick and I went out for an evening walk purporting to take a look at the excavations they were doing on the rocks but actually wondering about the seal; when we got to the dip we sat down rather self-consciously and sang Parry's 'Jerusalem' to the seal. No effect. Then Patrick started up in his piping, tuneless, toneless voice some Methodist hymn which Nanny had taught him and when we got to the end of the first line of the second verse he suddenly put his arms round me and said, 'There's the seal. It's come.' And there the seal was, an enormous grey seal immediately below us, swimming round slowly and steadily as though it had come directly in answer to his hymn. But my Patrick is growing up a rationalist. As we were walking back and reflecting on this experience he said, 'You know, Pop, it wasn't in answer to the hymn. I think the seal came because the seagulls had told him we were there.'

On the last day of our holiday the weather changed and we had an exquisite day motoring through Devonshire and the south part of Wiltshire and Dorset. When we got to Shaftesbury I decided that I would like to take the family for a picnic on Wingreen, the highest spot on those downs, three or four miles from Ashmore where we used to spend our holidays in the First World War. It's now a National Trust property and I regret to say that the Trust have made a track along which people are allowed to drive their cars right up to the top of the down where the trees stand. So much for conservation. From there it wasn't far to Southampton, where we shipped on *Viking II* for Cherbourg. We were used to old car-ferries and we thought we'd stay on board and have a leisurely breakfast while our car was unloaded on to the quayside. But on the new *Viking* car-ferries you drive your own car on and off and we found ourselves at 5.45 a.m. already off the ship and outside Cherbourg. This was tough on grown-ups but just to the children's taste. They'd had half an hour of sea at each end: half an hour travelling down the Solent seeing a bright red moon rise over the sea and then half an hour coming into Cherbourg, formally going through customs and setting off through a very French French town.

At Avranches, where we had a magnificent French breakfast (café-au-lait in bowls and croissants), we met our first Frenchmen who addressed the children in French. We were off to the Balogh's villa in the Dordogne, a longish trip, and I was hoping that on the way we could do some sightseeing. But a morning at Mont Saint-Michel made me realize how bored children get with travel. They only have one desire when they're in a car and that is to get on and get out. They were a little more interested in the tiny medieval walled town where we stayed our first night. I was relieved to find that we could have a good dinner, bed and breakfast for £2 a head.

On the next night we stayed at a town with a Roman arena and cathedral crypt. But again the children were mainly interested in a magnificent *brasserie* where we had a five-course meal with wine for £1. Here we ran into three young men who were learning publicity at Hennessy's place in Cognac. Next morning we drove out there and they took us round the works and we saw that the secret of making cognac is simply to put the distilled wine into casks made of a special oakwood that has the peculiar acid which provides the cognac taste.

It wasn't long after leaving Cognac that we found ourselves driving through Le Bugue, a little town just preparing for its saint's day celebration, and on up a lovely wooded valley to the village of Campagne. Further up the valley we looked out for the two white posts and there behind them we saw Tommy waving his arms and jumping up and down on the top floor of his tower. Chez Balogh is really an old barn which they've converted, standing in a little wooded valley.

We spent a wonderful week bathing in the Dordogne (which I expect is the latrine for the whole of that part of France but has water which glides brown and peaty over the rocks), caving and also wooding in the forests round the Balogh's villa. The Dordogne is being rapidly occupied by foreigners. First the Dutch and the Belgians came; now the English are pouring in, followed by the Scandinavians. This is partly due to the new agricultural situation in France where rationalization under the Common Agricultural Policy is enormously reducing the number of small farms and the number of people who live on the land. The Dordogne is the most lovely fertile country. But we saw nothing but mass evacuation and everywhere you walk over the countryside there are half-deserted villages and isolated homesteads falling down. So there are enormous possibilities for the speculator who buys up the land and resells the ruined houses and farm buildings to the foreigners who want to modernize them as holiday homes. Sure enough, around the Balogh home were living a pair of dons—the man a lecturer in history and the wife an eminent psychologist, just above Tommy there was Jock Campbell, the chairman of the *New Statesman* board and his darling wife, Phyllis. There was also Anthony Sampson, author of the *Anatomy of Britain*,[1] and a remarkable artist who runs one of the county council art schools.

It was this artist who came into a party brandishing a copy of *The Times* and said, 'Here's the latest Cabinet reshuffle.' I felt a sudden twinge of physical anxiety pierce my stomach, took one glance at it and saw that Peter Shore had gone to D.E.A. and Tony Crosland to the Board of Trade. Then I went on with my conversation. Of course this was a tiny bit of affectation but it was true, I really couldn't face studying the details because I was too deeply immersed in life out there. However, that evening I realized that I didn't know who had succeeded Bert Bowden at the Commonwealth Office and discovered it was George Thomson.

I might have guessed about the shuffle because two days before a telephone message had come from London summoning Tommy back. But we had both assumed that this was something to do with the preparation of economic plans to present to S.E.P. on September 6th. With Tommy away I saw even more of Jock Campbell and his wife. I got really fond of both of them. He's the ex-chairman of Booker Brothers and has taken on the chairmanship of Milton Keynes New Town only to find that under Tony Greenwood and Matthew Stevenson what was planned as the biggest-ever New Town is being cribbed and confined inside the PESC limitations. Already he tells me that he has been told that over half the houses must be owner-occupied and he must hand over half the land to the big firms of Wates and Costains whereas he was hoping to have a properly planned publicly-owned New Town like the others. In talking to him I was reminded that in the Labour Party the greatest idealists are sometimes the most remote from the movement. Here is Jock, a big businessman, who is also a very idealistic socialist who really believed that the job of this Wilson Government was to introduce new socialist planning and who is beginning to be bitterly disillusioned. How could I pretend to disagree with his view that there was very little left of the socialist impetus which brought us into power in 1964?

[1] London: Macmillan, 1967.

Even after Thomas went back to London I couldn't reattach myself to real life. Day after day I stayed on like the hero of *Death in Venice*. I would wake each morning at six, looking out and seeing the lemon-coloured sky and then the sun rising over the wooded mountain in front, and I would go out on the terrace and watch it rise and feel the earth grow warm. And in the evening I would watch the moon rise and hear the crickets outside while we dined under our little tree. In the last days I also took up wooding in a rather haphazard way with an old axe and a saw. But I soon found myself carving out a church aisle in that dense little forest and bathing myself in sweat. This Dordogne holiday suited me better than Cornwall and we were really sorry when we had to pack up and motor slowly back to Le Touquet where we were due to fly across. We reached Normandy in driving torrential rain and drove through it to the town of Le Touquet, which we found empty and where we could stay quite cheaply. We bought our little presents in this ghastly modern Pompeii—Brighton is far too grand a comparison since Brighton has lovely housing and prospects. From there we flew over with the car and found ourselves sitting in a tiny plane with Lord and Lady Cobbold.[1] I couldn't think who he was when he first came in. He began to talk to me, of course, about the Select Committee's proposal to abolish censorship of the theatre and to tell me how important it was that we should have some control of plays relating to live persons, and referring once again to Hochhuth's play about Churchill and to 'Mrs Wilson's Diary'.

It was the children's first aeroplane trip. It couldn't have been more exciting since vast thunder clouds were piled up all round us, the sky and the sea were a brilliant blue and the cliffs of Dover were white on one side and shadowed on the other—the sand-dunes of Le Touquet seen at the same time looked quite perfect. Within a matter of minutes we had arrived at Lydd. We were waved through customs and we were soon across the Romney Marsh and motoring through lovely crumbling Winchelsea, then down from there to the beach and the crashing breakers, on through Battle, and so to London in time for a quiet evening.

Tuesday, September 5th
My first work day started at Vincent Square with Thomas coming round about 9.45 to brief me on Harold's mood. He was extremely useful. 'Don't put any pressure on about devaluation,' he said. 'He's now in a mood of complete euphoria. He thinks he's produced the greatest coup ever by putting Peter in D.E.A. and taking charge himself. Congratulate him on all this. You've got to play it very quiet now.'

Yesterday evening after the children went to bed I'd spent three hours going through the press cuttings. Harold had got quite a good press for Tony Crosland moving to the Board of Trade and Bert Bowden going to the I.T.V.

---

[1] Lord Cobbold was Governor of the Bank of England 1949–61 and Lord Chamberlain of H.M. Household 1963–71. He was made a peer in 1960.

but the press had been thoroughly hostile to the idea of appointing Peter Shore, Secretary of State at the D.E.A. but with the P.M. taking personal responsibility for the Ministry. So his central theme that he was now taking personal control failed to get across mainly because the press refused to believe that he hasn't been in control before now.

This morning I walked across the park to No. 10, turned up the passage, went into the anteroom and there we all were, eyeing each other rather sorrily and hardly saying a word. We Labour Ministers don't look a very friendly gang when we get together after a month's holiday.

We started O.P.D. with a discussion on Aden. George Brown says the Foreign Office now wants to negotiate with the extreme nationalists, the F.L.N., because FLOSY, the moderate party they'd previously backed, hardly exists now. At once George Wigg was up in arms. This meant betraying everyone in Aden who had promised to support us. George Brown says that there is no alternative and doesn't deny that the F.O. has swung in a few months from one extreme to the other. I reinforced George Wigg's argument that we shall certainly undermine the Federalists in Aden and this will be noticed by the sheikhs in Kuwait and elsewhere. But I agree with George Brown that it can't be helped. 'Anyway,' says George, 'we want to be out of the whole Middle East as far and fast as we possibly can.' It's possible that the whole very expensive military commitment, including bombers and protective screening for the independent Aden Government, may now go by the board because that Government won't be there. George Wigg thinks it a disaster. I think it first rate and most of the Committee share my view.

We then turned to the other great crisis—Nigeria—where a huge civil war is now raging between the Federal Government and a western [sic] element which wants to break away.[1] We are told that the Russians have been supplying jet planes to the Government but we are still determined to adopt a discreet position of neutrality for the time being.

I stayed behind to talk to Harold and true enough he *is* in a state of complete euphoria. 'Last July,' he said to me, 'I managed to increase my crown princes from two[2] to six. That was the point of my reshuffle and for making you Leader of the House. Now I've got seven potential Chancellors and I've knocked out the situation where Jenkins was the only alternative to Callaghan. You know,' he concluded, 'this is one of the most successful political operations that's ever been conducted. I come back from my holiday and take all the negotiations myself and complete them almost before the press gets wind of it. I've completely foxed them all,' he said, 'and I've got the reorganization of the Government done.'

[1] On May 30th Lieutenant-Colonel Ojukwu declared the eastern region's independence as the Republic of Biafra. The Federal Military Government blockaded the region, attempting to compel the separatists to renounce Ojukwu and re-enter the Federation of twelve states announced by General Gowon in mid-May. By July civil war was being waged in earnest.

[2] Jenkins and Callaghan.

He confirmed what I knew already that he intended to have Gordon Walker at the Commonwealth Office but was scared off this by George Brown who said there'd certainly be memories of Patrick's appalling behaviour when he was last at that Ministry. So he had to put Gordon Walker at Education and Peter Shore, whom he'd intended for the Board of Trade, at D.E.A. I'd awfully like to know whom he originally meant to have at D.E.A. At one point it was Barbara, but did he really want to keep Michael there or was it Healey, in which case it would have been a much more extensive reshuffle?

I let him tell me all this before I raised the problem of the back-benchers. In his previous July reshuffle he had incurred enormous unpopularity by selecting for favour Reg Freeson and Roy Hattersley. He's repeated it again this time by selecting Gerry Fowler, the Oxford ancient-history don, to put into technology and Gwyneth Dunwoody (Morgan Phillips' daughter) at the Board of Trade.[1] These are the only two promotions from the back benches. My main complaint was that once again he'd done all this without bothering to consult the Chief Whip. I knew that John had been in Italy and that he wasn't easy to get hold of but I do object to these big changes taking place without any consultation with the Chief. After all, his job is to manage Party morale, and in our new liberalized regime where we've reduced the amount of stick poor John must increase the amount of carrot he employs. Nobody can suggest that the appointment of Fowler and Dunwoody will provide any sweetness to the back benches. Harold would not reply—instead he talked about Dick Marsh, who had been out in Yugoslavia attending a wine festival when the area boards suddenly announced enormous increases of electricity prices. Harold had first asked him and then ordered him home and he'd behaved with extraordinary rudeness.

But Harold was always coming back to his central theme that he was now in charge of the Government in a sense that he wasn't before the shuffle. 'I was held responsible,' he said, 'but I wasn't actually taking the decisions. I was writing minutes and letters to you colleagues and getting no action out of them. Now I'm exerting the power which people always thought I possessed but I didn't possess.' I told him that he was getting the wrong idea. 'Even if your responsibility has only increased,' I said, 'from 80 per cent to 100 per cent, the risks have also increased if anything goes wrong.' 'Ah,' he said, smiling, 'but the chances of success have increased from 50 per cent to 130 per cent. If I can't run the economy well through D.E.A. I'm no good. I was trained for this job and I've now taken the powers to run the economy.'

He gave me a sharp twinge with his last remark. Two by-elections are

---

[1] Gerald Fowler, Labour M.P. for the Wrekin 1966–70 and since 1974, was Joint Parliamentary Secretary at the Ministry of Technology 1967–9, Minister of State at the D.E.S. 1969–June 1970 and has served in the same office since 1974. Gwyneth Dunwoody, Labour M.P. for Exeter 1966–70 and for Crewe from 1974, was Parliamentary Secretary at the Board of Trade 1967–70.

coming on at a terrible time, on which Sara Barker has insisted, he told me.[1] 'She's fixed the date without really informing me at all. This could be disastrous.'

This afternoon I'd arranged meetings with Tony Crosland and George Brown. Tony Crosland was supposed to discuss a Specialist Committee on education but all he would now talk about was his new job at the Board of Trade. It had always been his nightmare that he might be pushed into this ghastly Ministry which was nobody's business and where any reorganization would take an appallingly dreary amount of time to do. Nevertheless, he added, he had no choice. He'd been got at when he was holidaying alone in Cyprus and over the phone he had just had to come into line. In order to cheer him up I could only remind him that his new job put him at least on a level with Roy in his chances of becoming the next Chancellor. And I quoted to him Harold's remark about the seven potential Chancellors which included himself.

At the Foreign Office I found George Brown fresh, young and charming and, to my great surprise, eager to ask my advice about the reorganization of the Foreign Office. I found this very puzzling until he went on to reveal that six or seven of the leading people in the Foreign Office are all due for retirement in 1969 and there must be new appointments. To replace Gore-Booth as Permanent Under-Secretary the F.O. as such wants Denis Allen — a very conventional fellow.[2] George, on the other hand, wants a man called Greenhill, chiefly I gather because he was the son of a railway clerk and a man of the people with a really first-rate unspoilt mind.[3] I've never seen Greenhill and all I know of him comes from the Radcliffe Report on D-Notices from which he emerges in a very peculiar light. Nevertheless, the fact that George Brown is determined on this battle with the F.O. establishment shows that he's still a radical at heart. Right at the end of our talk I asked him about two controversial problems of my own. Will it be regarded as a defeat if we were to use morning sittings as a threat to reduce the risks of all-night sittings? I found he was delighted with this proposal and didn't for a moment regard it as a climbdown but as part of a jolly good package deal if we could also get the Finance Bill upstairs and Standing Order 9 in its new form. On the House of Lords, however, he was much more difficult. No, he didn't like it. He'd assumed I would be on his side on this and was

---

[1] At Cambridge and Walthamstow West, caused by the deaths of Robert Davis and Ted Redhead. They had been fixed for September 21st.

[2] Lord Gore-Booth was Permanent Under-Secretary of State at the Foreign Office 1956–9 and Head of the Diplomatic Service from 1968 to 1969, when he became a life peer. Sir Denis Allen joined the Diplomatic Service in 1934. He was Deputy Commissioner General for S. E. Asia 1959–62, Ambassador to Turkey 1963–7 and Deputy Under-Secretary at the Foreign Office from 1967 until his retirement in 1969.

[3] Sir Denis Greenhill joined the Foreign Service in 1946 and was Deputy Under-Secretary of State 1966–9. In 1969 he became Permanent Under-Secretary of State and Head of the Diplomatic Service. On his retirement in 1973 he was appointed Government director on the board of B.P. Co. Ltd. He became a life peer in 1974.

disturbed that I wasn't. It will be far better to leave things completely un-changed than to tamper with composition.

Then I mentioned our Specialist Committees and he said, 'You will be surprised to hear that personally I would like to see a Specialist Committee on foreign policy. Not on the Foreign Office but on foreign policy. It should obviously be public and it should give the House of Commons the feeling that it could cross-examine the three Ministers. I would have the right to refuse to answer a question if I wanted, but I believe this could be invaluable and it could also bring the young Foreign Office people, who are so out of touch, into closer relations with Westminster.'

He couldn't have been more sensible. I was excited. I asked him what Harold's reaction would be. He replied, 'Last year when Harold came over to foreign affairs he lost control of the home front. He came over to do the Common Market, and frankly I could have achieved exactly what we have done without Harold's help.' I didn't add, 'But at the time when Harold offered to help and to do the tour round Europe he was there to keep a check on *you*, George. It was only halfway through the tour that he became a convinced European.'

From the F.O. I went through the back door to Downing Street and into No. 12, where I found the Chief just back from his Italian holiday looking very brown and fresh. I told him the bad news about the P.M.'s obstinate attitude to morning sittings and he agreed we must be firm.

I only just had time to get to Vincent Square, where I had invited Tommy, Wedgy and Peter Shore to dinner. Peter is excited by his new job but also a bit overawed. It was clear to Wedgy that the P.M. is now going to rely on him and Peter along with Tommy a very great deal. Of course Thomas is now chief adviser to Peter and Wedgy as well as to Harold. It's his idea that these lieutenants—Tony and Peter—should work with the P.M. as a triumvirate running the economy. 'What about Callaghan?' I asked. 'Well,' said Tommy, 'we have to evolve a kind of dyarchy with him. Harold seems to have made a deal with the Chancellor, though I don't know what the terms are.'

Wednesday, September 6th

At S.E.P. we had to deal with the increase in nationalized industry prices which had been postponed for purely political reasons in July.[1] Callaghan made it clear that he wanted the prices put up so as to reduce the burden on the tax-payer. Harold was at his most fertile and ingenious and talked an enormous lot. 'But a private firm,' he said at one point, 'would never increase its prices at a period of slump: it would keep the prices down and cut its profits and we must organize a comparable performance on our side of the line.' And he then went on to talk a great deal about the efficiency audit which

[1] See p. 446.

he was suggesting. He wanted all the nationwide prices to be referred, including natural gas, to an audit of this kind. I took no part in the debate and watched with interest how he got each of the Ministers concerned to accept the deal on which he had decided. He was being as good as his word — he was actually taking personal charge.

I went off to a long-delayed lunch with my old Ministry of Housing Press Officer, Peter Brown. He invited me to Prunier and wanted to tell me his great idea of how, when I was appointed First Secretary, he could become my Press Officer and help me to reform D.E.A. I had to disillusion him, whereupon he turned to a description of the terrible time he'd been having at the Ministry of Housing. All his previous Ministers, he said, had been able to stand up for themselves. This was the first who had fallen completely below that level.

Back to No. 10 for a meeting with Harold about procedure — in particular morning sittings. He's a funny man. A few hours before he'd been really obstinate. Now, when John and I explained the difficulties, he acceded to us at once. He also went through the problems of the Lords once again and found himself in considerable agreement with us. The only point where he jibbed was when I mentioned the Foreign Secretary's personal willingness to consider a Foreign Policy Committee. I saw Burke purse his lips and Harold open his mouth and I realize that it's extremely unlikely that this will ever happen.

Back in my own office I found Judith Hart waiting for me. She's also relaxed after a month's holiday and more settled in at her Ministry. When I told her that it was essential to get the contributions raised as soon as possible and spend them to improve the state of the existing pensions she agreed entirely. I was disappointed however that she hasn't yet consulted her own officials.

Thursday, September 7th
The first meeting of the new Cabinet and I'm struck by the difference from the old one. With power suddenly shifted to Shore and Crosland, the change on the economic side is enormous. But if you want to see a symptom of what has happened you should look at item three of the conclusions. 'The Committee [i.e. S.E.P.] had taken a number of decisions on which the Cabinet would wish to be informed.' And it then lists the decisions of the S.E.P. This was the first time that I can really say there has been hard evidence that Harold was introducing what I've often described as Prime Ministerial government. Up till then he'd acted in a chairmanly, not a dictatorial, way, co-ordinating everything and leaving all the initiatives to his Ministers. He'd also relied on the creative friction between the Treasury and the D.E.A. Now that phase is over and he is taking the lead himself, laying down the policy in S.E.P. and then telling the full Cabinet of the decisions. I notice also an interesting change in his relationship with Callaghan. It is obviously

very intimate. Throughout Cabinet they were chatting to each other, heads together, and there was no sign of anything but prior agreement between the two. Tommy's convinced there's been a sell-out by the P.M. I'm not so sure. I believe he still reserves his position and still thinks that he has the capacity to introduce a new Chancellor and devalue if it were really necessary. Callaghan, of course, thinks the opposite. He believes he has made himself effectively number two on the home front, equal in power with George Brown, the number two on the foreign front.

The only item which concerned me this morning was the House of Lords. The paper the Chancellor had prepared was excellent and everything went perfectly well, as the official minutes record. The only vital fact the Cabinet Secretariat omitted was that both the Foreign Secretary and the Chancellor expressed the gravest doubts about a change of composition. George Brown was unusually powerful, and I felt that people like Fred Peart, Willie Ross and Cledwyn Hughes would naturally join with him if he started a movement against Lords reform. This was confirmed this afternoon when Roy Jenkins looked in to see me about something else and expressed doubt whether, in view of the Cabinet attitude, it was possible to deal with composition. Roy always has a very good nose for changes in public opinion.

The last Committee meeting today was Home Affairs and the main item was whether we should sign the U.N. Convention on Human Rights. Michael Stewart was back in the chair after his move. The F.O. proposals were put forward by that sinuous Welshman Goronwy Roberts,[1] who urged that we should sign first and make a number of reservations before final ratification. Michael Stewart didn't make his position any easier by then going through the details and listing endless reservations which would be required. The more I heard the more doubtful I was. Only eight countries had signed it, and of these Italy was the only European country of any size. Why should Britain take the lead? I suspect because George Brown wanted to make a big speech at U.N. that month. I argued that if we signed and then made a mass of reservations we should get blamed for the reservations and get no credit for the signing. It was agreed that the matter needed more consideration. However, George Brown certainly wants it and he will try to force it through Cabinet or else put up a better case than his adjutant at the Home Affairs Committee.

I had asked Roy to see me in my office because I wanted to talk to him about the problems of censorship and to tell him of my meeting with Cobbold. As Harold's henchman I felt bound to put to him the P.M.'s point of view and say how strongly this was felt not only by him but by all the Royal Family and by the court as well. When I'd finished he said, 'As a

---

[1] Labour M.P. for Caernarvonshire 1945–50 and for Caernarvon 1950–74. He was Minister of State at the Welsh Office 1964–6, at D.E.S. 1966–7, at the F.C.O. 1967–9 and at the Board of Trade 1969–70. In 1974 he became a life peer and since then has been a Minister of State at the Foriegn Office.

matter of fact I don't think anything can be done. I propose to leave the
Bill unchanged.' 'You'll be in trouble there, Roy,' I said. 'But I've got a
majority of the Parliamentary Party on my side,' he replied. 'Perhaps. But
you may not have a majority in the Cabinet and you've certainly got the
P.M. opposed.' 'Well,' he said, almost petulantly, 'I'm not prepared as a
radical and liberal Home Secretary to have my image ruined by being
ordered to impose worse conditions on the live theatre than they are getting
now under the Lord Chamberlain.' And he made it quite clear that he was
thinking of the threat of resignation in order to get his way.

After dealing with Roy in this mood, I had two hours with the Chief trying
to make the new Lords' Chief Whip, Frank Beswick, see sense on Lords
reform. Frank's attitude is like that of Gerald Gardiner. They've only been
there a few years but they are already in love with the House of Lords and
only want to see the mildest changes. Certainly they're going to oppose any
built-in Government majority. I wish Harold had consulted us before he
appointed this man.

By now it was eight o'clock and I was due for my weekly meeting with the
P.M. Fortunately when I got there I found that he too was running behind
schedule because he'd been having his selective press conference with such
people as Francis Boyd, Walter Terry and Victor Knight. I noticed a little
fellow there called Max Weber, who had once been Swiss Finance Minister.
Like me he was waiting to see the P.M. and when Harold put his nose out he
asked both of us to come in. This gave me a chance of listening to how he
talked to foreigners. Max Weber started by saying that things look very
black. 'No,' said Harold, 'we're probably turning the corner. There's a new
whiff in industry. The reports show our investment for the first six months of
this year at an all-time record. The unemployment figures aren't rising as
fast as they were before.' And he went on to rehearse the speech he's going
to make at Newport on Friday—a speech which Tommy and I have seen and
both think wildly optimistic. At last the Swiss withdrew and we got down to
the weekly meeting with Burke. What I learnt at that meeting confirmed
something Tommy told me. Burke's had a knock. This latest Cabinet reshuffle following the mess about D-Notices where, to his cost, Harold took
Burke's advice, has weakened his position a great deal. The P.M.'s not taking
the Chief's advice, or my advice or George Wigg's advice. He's certainly not
taking Burke's advice either. I think Burke and I both felt very much in the
role of the P.M.'s assistants in discussing the business of the week.

By this time I was terribly late for a dinner with Meyer Weisgal at the
Dorchester.[1] However I got there by 9.30 and there he and his wife were
sitting waiting for Topol, the famous Jewish actor from *Fiddler on the Roof*
at Her Majesty's Theatre. We had a delicious dinner during which Meyer
made it very clear that my reputation has been seriously damaged by the
stories in the press about my being soft on Israel just before the Six-Day War.

[1] President of the Weizmann Institute of Science, Israel, 1966–70.

Friday, September 8th

I began with a crucial meeting of my Cabinet Committee on Procedure where I put up to them the first half of my sessional programme of reform, my proposals for Specialist Committees for the Finance Bill, etc., etc. The Committee agreed even on the proposal to send the Finance Bill upstairs. I had heard a rumour that Jack Diamond and Niall MacDermot have between them got the Treasury and the Chancellor to give a reluctant yes to my proposals. What I hadn't heard at that time was that Harold Lever had been moved into the Treasury as Financial Secretary and Niall MacDermot had gone to Housing. Throughout that Committee I sat with bated breath. What line would Harold Lever take? When he said that the Chancellor couldn't give more than reluctant acquiescence but he himself must add that he thought it would greatly improve the debates, John and I knew we were safely past the danger point.

I lunched with Trethowan in order to fill him in on parliamentary reform. I also talked to him about Harold's new and more commanding role in the Cabinet. We then talked about the P.M. and the press and I emphasized how the P.M. seemed to have got over his obsessive dislike of holding press conferences. I mentioned the discriminating press conference he was now committed to and to my surprise Trethowan (unlike David Wood, who bitterly attacked it) remarked that he was perfectly entitled to select any journalists he wanted to talk to. 'All Prime Ministers do that,' he added, and he mentioned Harold Macmillan and Alec Douglas-Home as two examples.

This evening George Wigg delivered a speech to a newspaper dinner which got enormous publicity in the Saturday morning papers. I read it with pleasure and amazement. It was an attack on the press and publicity officers but it was also perfectly fair and balanced. I must find out from Harold whether George asked his advice before composing it.

Well, there we have the first week back after the summer recess—an enjoyable week because Parliament is not sitting and we have had just enough pleasant adequate work for a person of my age and energy. I can do the work and feel like mastering it. It's when Parliament is thrown in on top that one feels overwhelmed. In the second place, Harold's reform of his Cabinet, his shaping up of a Prime Ministerial system, is quite impressive. Indeed, I think he may have improved our chances of survival whatever he has failed to do below Cabinet level. But I'm still racked by the same old anxiety because of his bogus optimism. However, it's early days yet and we'll see how we go.

Monday, September 11th

I must start by winding up one or two little tag ends of last week. This morning I got a minute from the Prime Minister which states that he thinks it would be wrong for me to sit on the E.N. Committee under such a junior chairman as Peter Shore. Of course this really means that he wants all the problems to be brought direct to him by Peter. I shall mention, however, if I get the chance, that if he doesn't have senior Ministers without Portfolio on this Committee the result will be that all the junior Ministers will merely stick to their departmental briefs and no adequate decisions will be taken.

Another Committee in which I've been interested is of course the old RX— the famous Rhodesia Committee. This Session I am excluded along with the First Secretary. I can't say I'm surprised.

Finally I've now got hold of a full text of George Wigg's weekend speech. It was delivered at Keele University, which was of course founded by the Master of Balliol, A. D. Lindsay, who is one of George's heroes. The theme of the speech is the decency of the common man and the importance in democracy of belief in the common man. George suggests that Lindsay and Bartholomew, the old sodden editor of the *Daily Mirror*, were linked by this common faith.[1] I think it's a fairly absurd theory but it's thoughtfully worked out and it seems to me that the speech should have an excellent effect. It will stimulate a new kind of dialogue between the Government and the press.

Lunching with Eddie Shackleton at the Athenaeum I discovered to my horror that I hadn't seen an important paper which he had produced for the Chequers meeting this week about Lords reform. After lunch we went back to my office, dug it out and went through it carefully. It's a really first-rate account of the kind of two-tier structure we need to put forward, which differs a great deal from that of Frank Longford. Eddie told me that it wasn't on the original agenda proposed by the Lord Chancellor and had only been inserted by him. I've never doubted Eddie's energy but I must say I am surprised by the sheer ability with which the scheme was drafted. Perhaps Wheeler-Booth had a hand in it.[2]

I was looking forward to the unprecedented meeting of the Home Policy Committee that morning. During our Chequers meeting with the National Executive the trade-union members had insisted on having proper statements from Ministers and in response to this Harold had suggested that the Home Policy Committee should meet them. With the help of Ministers quite good briefs had been provided by the Departments and by Terry Pitt. The meeting was due to start at 4 p.m. By this time Peggy Herbison from the N.E.C. and I were both present and George Brown had just come in. A little later we were joined by Judith Hart and Peter Shore. But not a single trade-union member of the N.E.C. turned up—not even Jack Jones, who had insisted on the meeting. It does reveal the strangeness of the attitude of the trade-union

[1] Guy Bartholomew was editorial director of the Daily Mirror Newspaper Ltd from 1934 until 1944, when he became chairman. He resigned in 1951 and was replaced by Cecil King. He died in 1962.

[2] Michael Wheeler-Booth, Private Secretary to the Leader of the House of Lords and, subsequently, Clerk of the Journals. In 1974 he took charge of the Overseas Office.

members of the N.E.C. to a Labour Government. They'd called for a special meeting of a Cabinet Committee, they required a great deal of advance work to be done and then not one of them turned up.

However, the meeting had its uses. We were able to discuss one of the minor sensations of the recess—Ray Gunter's speech in August, in which he said we must be realistic and brave and face up to the need for selectivity and the means test. This speech apparently had raised a tremendous flurry and it wasn't surprising that Gunter got a total rebuke from the Trade Union Congress when he went to listen to their debate on social security.

Judith and I defined the position and explained that you have to distinguish between the means test that is a kind of cross-examination before you get state charity, that causes a certain stigma, and what we mean by selectivity, the very reasonable testing of your income to see if you are entitled to an income-tax concession or benefit. Since George Brown didn't seem fully to understand it, it's possible that Gunter didn't either.

Later this evening I went round to No. 10 for an impromptu emergency meeting about the Cunard crisis. The Q4 was due to be launched by the Queen on September 20th when it was suddenly realized that Cunard was in danger of going into liquidation just before the ceremony.[1] It was felt, therefore, that urgent measures were required and that was why the P.M. had called the meeting. Tony Crosland had been alerted at the Board of Trade and Harold Lever, in his new position at the Treasury. Tony at first held out firmly and said that he didn't see why we should spend a lot of money putting Cunard to rights. Let them go bankrupt and afterwards the Government could buy up the remains cheaply. However, others felt that this would be unfortunate for the Queen; and Harold Lever had come up with an ingenious new scheme. He is obviously the latest wonder boy of this Cabinet and I see some dangers because he's not a socialist intellectual but a brilliant bridge player, who made vast sums of money, married a rich banker's daughter and is a kind of intellectual *flâneur*. In so far as he has economic convictions, they're fairly right-wing.

What was really disconcerting on this occasion was that the plan he proposed only dealt with the passenger side of the business. But what really matters to the Government in terms of the shipping policy we developed last July is of course the cargo side and especially the containers. We were relying on Cunard to buy two container ships from the British shipyards and under Lever's plan all this would have gone by the board. So the one thing achieved at this emergency meeting was the modification of the original plan to make

---

[1] The Cunard Steamship Company announced early in 1967 that they had decided to sell the passenger liners *Queen Mary* and *Queen Elizabeth*. On October 31st the *Queen Mary* left Southampton for Long Beach, California, to become a floating museum. On September 20th the Q4 was launched at Clydeside and named *Queen Elizabeth 2*. During the ten-day trial sailing at the end of December the liner developed serious turbine trouble and Cunard refused to accept her from Upper Clyde Shipbuilders on the scheduled date. Her introduction to service, planned for January 1969, was postponed.

it clear that they wouldn't get any money from us unless they looked after the containers as well.

Anne had come up by car this afternoon and we gave a dinner-party for Tommy Balogh, Wedgy Benn, Judith Hart and Peter Shore, as well as Brian Abel-Smith, who had come in to discuss pensions from the Titmuss group. Tommy and Wedgy were a bit shaken by the P.M.'s astonishing reliance on Harold Lever to cook up a brilliant solution for Cunard and more amused to hear how he failed to remember the container side of the business. But the main thing we discussed was the pension plan, on which Judith outlined the ideas that she'd thought up. She believes that we should introduce a graded social security tax well before the election and use it not only for dynamizing flat-rate pensions but for paying out all sorts of family benefits which would show we were really helping the poor. As for national superannuation, we shouldn't try and bring it forward but phase it in in 1975, when a large number of existing pensioners will be dying off. The idea is very ingenious but in practice I wonder how far you can go in undermining the contributory element of the pension scheme by making it liable to pay for all kinds of disabilities and benefits which have nothing to do with social insurance. I doubt whether many of her ideas will survive when her paper is submitted to detailed examination in her own Ministry.

Tuesday, September 12th
The whole of today I spent at Chequers for the first day of the session on Lords reform, though it was only by the evening that I discovered that Gerald Gardiner was not only the formal host but had to pay the bill for all the food and drink and everything else. Since there wasn't room for seventeen or eighteen people, including our civil servants, I decided that along with Wheeler-Booth and Freddie Warren I would go out and stay at the King's Head in Aylesbury. When Burke discovered this there was a terrible fuss. 'That's impossible,' he said, 'because if the Lord President is seen in Aylesbury with officials from the House of Lords the journalists will realize you are holding a secret meeting and conclude you're discussing House of Lords reform.' This reveals the way the Trend mind works on security problems. We stayed very comfortably at the old coaching pub and spent quite a time in the bar without anybody suspecting who we were.

My driver, Molly, said that to get to the meeting in time I would have to start at 8.30. That seemed much too early for my taste. We started at 9.10 and drew into the front door at 10.29. At 10.30 I found them all sitting upstairs rather tight-lipped and uneasy. The Home Secretary came in a few minutes after me. From the start Gerald was in his most adamant obstinate mood. 'I've decided,' he said, 'that the best way to deal with this problem is to take the two schemes—the one-tier scheme and the two-tier scheme—and go through each, point by point. I shall record our decisions point by point. We start now with the one-tier scheme and I ask you, Lord President, the first question. What is the total number of peers required in the single House for a one-tier scheme?' My mild protest against the difficulties of operating in this way was pushed aside. So, rapidly collecting my thoughts and grateful for what I'd learnt at lunch with Eddie, I replied that the Chancellor would find in Lord Shackleton's paper my own view on this point. There was a protest from each of us as he went round the table asking his questions. But we spent a full hour and a half on this procrustean bed of his devising. As Jenkins put it to me afterwards, 'This is a typical lawyer's solution.' A lawyer starts with the details of the two plans and having dealt with them *seriatim* he turns to look at the two plans as a whole. A politician, an economist or a philosopher, on the other hand, will deal with the principles or general ideas first and then ask whether he's got the right means to achieve his aim. As the discussion went on somebody remarked in desperation that we really ought to be asking ourselves what the aim and object of the operation was. What were we trying to achieve by Lords reform? I jumped in and said we were trying to achieve co-ordination of the two Chambers and that the principle we must work on is that in future there would be only one source of authority—the Chamber elected by popular vote. Once you abolish the hereditary principle there can be no other authority than the House of Commons, and the Lords must derive its authority from the lower Chamber. That's why I personally wouldn't be afraid of a reformed House of Lords where the balance of power between the Government and the Opposition reflected the results of the last general election.

After lunch Gerald got control of us again and we seemed to spend hours discussing how many bishops and law lords we should have. But at least it was decided that the two-tier scheme should be considered after tea. There we weren't taking any chances. I gave a very brief introduction and then Eddie explained his model at length. At once he was backed by Shepherd, the ex-Chief Whip of the House of Lords, by John Silkin and, to a limited extent, by Gordon Walker. The scheme is based on two principles. First, the immediate abolition of the hereditary principle and, secondly, the creation of a top-tier of voting peers and a lower tier of hereditary peers permitted to speak. From the point of view of the Party managers this is clearly a workable scheme but it is not at all easy to explain and Roy Jenkins, who'd been quiet up till then, launched into a major attack. I've never heard him before either in Cabinet or in Cabinet Committee commit himself so firmly. He accused the two-tier scheme of rigidity and said that it required far more patronage than we could permit. It was this undue reliance on patronage which made it inferior to the one-tier scheme. This brought him into a confrontation with me which lasted for some twenty minutes with the Lord Chancellor an interested spectator.

It made me wonder whether there isn't a certain amount of paper tiger about Roy. He didn't seem to have done his homework thoroughly enough and having got himself out on a limb he was unable to withdraw. I think most people there became uneasily aware that our great Home Secretary hadn't done too well and that the Lord Chancellor hadn't been greatly assisted by his support. Indeed, there was a great contrast between his behaviour and that of Gordon Walker, who showed himself on this occasion competent, quick and active, all the qualities normally attributed to Jenkins. But, of course, as well as this Patrick is elderly and accident-prone.

Suddenly the Lord Chancellor intervened and said, 'Well, we had better come to our decisions. It's clear now we shall have to present a paper to Cabinet propounding the two solutions and asking Cabinet to decide between them.' I replied that this would be fatal. 'Rather than have a divided report from this Committee I would much rather accept the advice of George Brown and Jim Callaghan and postpone the whole issue for a year. Unless we can get an agreement on this Committee I want to see no action recommended.'

This was really the turning point of the conference because suddenly the Lord Chancellor collapsed and said, 'Oh, we can't wait a year: we must have action now in view of what the Tories might do between now and the election. Of course I'll accept the two-tier system under certain conditions rather than face this postponement.' Jenkins quickly added that he too would make concessions rather than face a collapse of the conference.

During dinner a solution suddenly came into my head. I saw a way of getting out of this deadly conflict between two-tier and one-tier. Why shouldn't we announce our decision to legislate on the reform of the Lords in the Queen's Speech but also announce our intention to negotiate with the Conservatives and the Liberals? Then, rather than putting forward the two-tier system as our own plan, we could propound it at the end of the negotiations if we thought there was a chance of it being accepted. This was suggested after dinner and the Committee quickly reached an agreement that we should put a firm commitment into the Queen's Speech to abolish the hereditary element and that we should treat the two-tier scheme not as acceptable on its merits but as a scheme to be accepted only if the opposition parties agree. If they didn't agree we could then be much more radical in a really thorough one-tier scheme. Well, to my amazement, all this was agreed. And Freddie Warren, Freddy Ward, Wheeler-Booth and I went off to the King's Head to celebrate in drinks.

Wednesday, September 13th
This morning we got down to work on a fearful draft presented by one of our officials. We had to work very hard on it but the job was done by twelve o'clock and to the draft was annexed all the appendixes on powers, composition, etc. After we'd finished the Chief and I slipped off to drive back to London in appalling rainstorms that had been drenching down ever since the night before.

That Chequers conference staggered me. I had gone down there extremely gloomy, thinking there was no possible chance of reconciliation between Gardiner and myself and knowing that in the atmosphere created by George Brown and Jim Callaghan I would have no chance of getting agreement to our proposals. Yet now we were able to go back and present a unanimous paper.

I got back late for the meeting of the National Executive at Transport House which was considering the interim report of the Committee of Inquiry into the Labour Party's organization. I think I've mentioned in this diary already how utterly futile this Committee of Inquiry is since it is dominated by Len Williams, the man into whose activities we need to inquire. Anyway I had been excluded from the only important working party on the National Agency Scheme[1] and was not surprised to see that the proposals on political education were just as futile. However, the huge document had come out much better than I expected because at least it concluded a recommendation in favour of earnings-related contributions to the Party following the model of the S.P.D. in Germany, and secondly a completely new concept of the General Secretary's task which would make him a leading political figure. These were the two controversial recommendations my colleagues had been bullied to accept from me. I don't know what people expected when this enormous document was presented to the Executive. It's not in the least surprising that after a long and desultory discussion George Brown proposed that it shouldn't be published at all. Others suggested that it should be published omitting the section on the General Secretary, which would be interpreted as an attack on Len Williams. After they'd finished I pointed out that the Annual Conference would not like to feel the report had been suppressed and that it would be far wiser to publish it in full and have it debated at Conference. On this at least I got my way. Mind you, most of it had already been leaked to the press before we began to discuss it today.

I was curious how members of the Executive would react to my presence now that my decision to retire has been announced in the press and also the reason for it—the fact that there are far too many Ministers on the N.E.C. Of course nobody said a word to me direct, though I was told that most of the trade unionists seemed to think that I'd performed a very clever trick which had made me the most popular member of the N.E.C. Well, I may be popular at the moment but I'm still feeling extremely sore. I've served on this Executive for fifteen years, done as much hard work as any other member and never been made a chairman of anything. Despite Harold's express wishes the Executive refused to make me either the chairman of the inquiry or of Org. Sub. That in itself is a good enough reason to withdraw but I also have a growing conviction that it's now too late to reform the Labour Party except

---

[1] A working party of six were examining a National Agency Scheme whereby the N.E.C. and constituency Parties might jointly pay for a Party agent in every constituency. A scheme was devised but for marginal constituencies only.

by appointing a brand new General Secretary. Once appointed, the right man could reorganize the whole thing. But in that case sitting on the Executive wouldn't be all that important since the key problem during the next election will be the relation of the Party not to Transport House but to No. 10. A party in power can win an election from Whitehall and neglect its organization outside.

This means I will be sensible to concentrate my work in Whitehall. I know all the difficulties but frankly there's more chance of getting something done in Whitehall than there is of getting something done in Transport House. So Harold may be right in thinking that my resignation won't do any harm.

We finished the Executive business a great deal earlier than I expected and I was able therefore to get off in good time to Cambridge where I was to speak at the by-election. I got Molly to take me down but I found that she'd been instructed by my Private Office to drive straight to the school where the meeting was being held. That would have been a fatal mistake since I'm not supposed to use my ministerial car for a purely Party occasion and on this occasion the only excuse was the danger of a railway strike. So the black saloon drew up some distance from the Party office and from there I went in a Party car to the small school hall crammed with people where the candidate was making an address on leisure and culture to a packed audience. I'd been told that he was an extremely bad candidate—arty, with a beard, owning a high-class shop where he'd made a pile. But when he'd finished his speech I found him really splendid, particularly in answering questions at question time. Judging from the Party members I met afterwards he's really inspiring them in this campaign and certainly if they have the remotest chance of victory it will be largely due to the candidate.

I motored back to London that night to be in time for tomorrow's Cabinet.

Thursday, September 14th

An emergency meeting of O.P.D. on South Africa had been inserted before Cabinet. Here the minutes are worth looking at since they give a totally misleading picture. This is what really happened. The Prime Minister was presented with a formidable official line-up of the three main parties concerned with the problem of selling arms to South Africa. The Foreign Office, the Ministry of Defence and the Commonwealth Office were obviously in agreement that a major shift of policy was essential. George Brown began the attack saying that though he realized it was very painful one couldn't really go on being so unrealistic about the sale of arms. He was then supported by Denis Healey, who said one must surely make a distinction between arms which could be used for suppressing insurrection (such as *Crusader* tanks or *Saracen* cars) and strategic arms—that is to say, the Air Force and the Navy which are needed for our own Commonwealth interests. He said we need the Simonstown base to be kept going by South Africa in our own interest and therefore we should sell South Africa maritime arms but not arms for domestic use. In this sense he felt we should have to repudiate the Prime Minister's Statement of November 1964 when he said that all defence contracts would stop. Both George and Denis emphasized that this was a major switch of policy which couldn't possibly be concealed. When they had finished the Prime Minister intervened to say that this switch was quite impossible. He reckoned that no less than six members of the Government, junior Ministers mostly, would resign; the effect in the Parliamentary Party would be even worse. After the P.M. had finished the First Secretary supported him very strongly, saying that the greatest issue of world politics in the future was race. We were opting out of that great issue if we accepted George's proposal and submitting ourselves to policies of pure expediency and opportunism. Michael Stewart was very strongly supported by Frank Longford. He was followed by Tony Crosland, who made a balanced statement saying he wasn't quite sure that the disasters anticipated were rightly calculated. Then came the last of the spokesmen of the interested Ministries. As might be expected, George Thomson, making his first contribution as Commonwealth Secretary, lined up with the other Departments and read his official brief. I then interrupted to make the point which I'd mentioned to the P.M. on the phone that morning that you couldn't separate South Africa from Rhodesia. How idiotic we would look appeasing the racialists in South Africa while we were standing pat in Rhodesia! If the South Africans would help us to settle with Smith I would consider a concession on South African arms trade tolerable.

George Brown then dismissed this as totally impracticable, but the P.M. clutched at it. He may possibly be right that what I proposed is really impracticable. The way to do this practically is probably to sell out first in one and then in the other. But you have to start somewhere. My own view is that Rhodesia and South Africa between them are costing us an enormous amount in our balance of payments. We are completely immobilized because of the moral blackmail exerted by the left-wing of the Party and Harold Wilson's personal commitments. It's a miserable situation and this first move by the three Departments was highly significant. I must add, however, that I didn't disclose to the P.M. my private views on the subject. He was so miserable and unhappy and divided in his mind about it that my main concern was to remain close to him and to say nothing without consulting him in advance.

After the Cabinet meeting which immediately followed, the Chancellor, the First Secretary, the Chief Whip and I stayed behind to report to the P.M. about the Chequers conference. We had sent him a copy of our agreed paper to study beforehand. This morning he just looked at us and said, 'Well, that's all right.' He was surprised but I think he'd accepted it and he didn't ask a single question. We'd only spent two minutes with him when he obviously wanted us to go but that wouldn't have been decent. So I then raised the issue of the extension of patronage implied in our proposals and went on to discuss the Queen's prerogative, at which he slightly warmed up. Nevertheless he remained coolly acquiescent, accepting our proposals and telling us he would support them. It was a very curious attitude.

This evening I had a talk with Tam, who agreed to become my P.P.S. again since Geoffrey Rhodes doesn't suit me. We agreed I should make Geoffrey Rhodes the chairman of the Specialist Committee on education—if we get it as we now may from the new Secretary of State. And the Chief agreed to support that proposal. The change will be very important to me since a good P.P.S. makes an astonishing difference even to a Minister without Portfolio.

Friday, September 15th

The Gallup Poll was depressing as hell. It gives a thoroughly black picture of Harold's declining popularity and also of the Labour Party's long-term trend. It does seem that almost within weeks of the general election the long-term trend has set against the Government and I've been feeling throughout this week that we're going to have a shock in the by-elections and could easily lose Walthamstow as well as Cambridge.

The only thing which holds the situation for us is the failure of Heath to build up any popularity—a failure which has been greatly intensified this week by the mess he has made of getting rid of du Cann.[1] Ted has been on tour in Scotland trying to work up his personal popularity. He was obviously making a tremendous effort one evening in a cross-examination by the *Daily Express* journalist; when asked whether there was a row blowing up between him and du Cann he replied that this was a damned lot of lies. That was all very well but a very short time afterwards he did sack du Cann and put Barber in his place. Of course I can see what happened. He had been extremely pleased that he had persuaded du Cann to go without a row and when the *Express* man asked his question he lost his temper. Though one can explain it, nevertheless his behaviour has caused him a great deal of damage just at a time when his Gallup Poll index is sinking to a new low.

At morning prayers this morning George Brown was present and we got talking informally about the South African arms dispute in O.P.D. George Brown said that the F.O. had wanted to pretend there was no change of policy. And then he went on, 'You know, Prime Minister, I have come to all kinds of personal understandings about this change of policy, as you agreed I should do some months ago. It will be pretty awkward to go back on those personal understandings just now.' Harold sat silent and embarrassed but George went on. 'I didn't want to make too much fuss of this at O.P.D. or to emphasize the change of policy. I would have preferred to suggest we were just gradually extending it. It was Denis Healey who insisted

---

[1] Edward du Cann, Conservative M.P. for Taunton since 1956. He was replaced as chairman of the Conservative Party Organization in 1967. From 1971 he was chairman of the House of Commons Select Committee on Public Expenditure and, since 1974, he has been chairman of the 1922 Committee.

that we must accept the important policy shift.' All this came as complete news to me. I strongly suspect what George was saying was basically true.

The discussion then switched to Lords reform. A lot of argument took place and we finally decided not to take it to Cabinet but to have a meeting of the big five — as Harold called it — consisting of himself, George Brown, Michael Stewart, the Lord Chancellor and myself. Actually the Chancellor also had to be included, making it six. 'If the six agree,' said the P.M., 'we needn't have a Cabinet for weeks. And if we don't agree there is no point in having a Cabinet.' So we six shall be meeting next Monday at five o'clock.

All this talk had kept the members of S.E.P. waiting outside the door. At this meeting we were supposed to agree our strategy and to approve the short-term measures for dealing with winter unemployment and pit closures. Harold again repeated the long list of proposals he'd made in July and then, turning to the paper in which they were analysed, said what wonderful work had been done. Actually this was a third-rate paper and it mostly consisted of puncturing the P.M.'s bright ideas. As for winter unemployment, the proposals for dealing with it will not produce more than 20,000 jobs. The most controversial proposal was that we should postpone the closure of twenty-six of the thirty-one pits on the condemned list. Marsh wanted only sixteen postponed and, with the P.M.'s help, got his way against Shore. Peter struggled a bit, which only made him look ridiculous since the Secretary of State has the right to insist that all thirty-one be considered. But this morning he was treated like an office-boy. Otherwise the meeting was uncreative.

I rushed out to lunch with Arthur Gavshon of A.P. and then back to see Evan Luard, the Oxford M.P. The children were in London this evening and we took them to see the film of *Oklahoma!*

Saturday, September 16th
Gilbert Baker had persuaded me to open the local Party bazaar at Carshalton and he specially wanted me to get a mention in the press. The gathering was chaired by the leader of the Labour Group on the Surrey County Council who's just been made a life peer. Arthur Garnsworthy is a great comprehensive pundit and I was specially asked to talk about the comprehensive school.[1] To please Gilbert I talked to the P.A. man and dictated a press release to him. At the last moment, remembering what happened to me at Shrewsbury, I removed a conclusion which stated, 'we shall complete our plans whatever the difficulties are and whatever means are required'. It was the words 'whatever means are required' that I deleted. And thank God I did. Otherwise it might have looked as though I was supporting Gordon Walker's appalling disaster at Enfield.[2] This is the last thing I must mention

---

[1] Six times an unsuccessful Labour candidate for Reigate and, from 1966 to 1974, a Surrey alderman. He became a life peer (of Reigate) in 1967.

[2] In August eight ratepayers and a parents' association had applied for an injunction restraining the borough council from amalgamating a number of boys' schools and from

this week. Though he'd expected to go back to the Commonwealth Department, Patrick was thrilled to get Education. The first problem put on his plate was the deal with Enfield School, where Iain Macleod is a governor and Edward Boyle has a very keen interest. Despite the G.L.C. majority, there is still a Labour borough council, which is trying to turn a grammar school into a comprehensive. The courts had told them that they ought not to do this without leaving the parents proper time to protest and they had finally ruled against Enfield last weekend. Then Patrick suddenly intervened and changed the constitution of the school leaving the governors only five days to protest against this move. This was bad enough but what no one expected was that on this very Saturday morning John Donaldson would rule against the Minister, with costs, and tell him he has to give the governors a full month. That's the biggest smack in the eye a Minister could get and Heath is not exaggerating when he demanded Patrick's resignation and called this an intolerable action. If I'd been seen at Carshalton to be approving Patrick's behaviour by saying we must overcome our difficulties by 'whatever means are required' the fat would really have been in the fire. It was a very near shave.

Monday, September 18th

I woke up with violent gastric flu, which went on all day and I just managed to hold out till evening. Apparently there's an epidemic now in London. Flu makes one depressed. An extra cause of my depression is returning to work as Lord President when all the other Ministers are back and getting down to their Departments and I am only half employed.

Today there were huge gaps in my time. There was nothing fixed for me to do—no work apart from House of Lords reform and parliamentary procedure, both completed. I can't spend all my time chatting with John Silkin.

This sense of emptiness is greatly intensified this autumn by the P.M.'s reorganization of the Cabinet Committees and drastic reduction in their membership. What was the big E.N. Committee has now been split into an Industrial Committee, a Foreign Trade Committee, and an Environmental Planning Committee with only S.E.P. above them in strategic control. I'm not allowed to be a member of any of these lower Committees because I've

---

changing Enfield Grammar School to a non-selective school. Under the terms of the 1944 Education Act a local authority had to give public notice if it intended to 'establish a new school' or to 'cease to maintain' an existing one. The Secretary of State for Education had advised the council that in this case such notice was not required but the Courts of Appeal had ruled otherwise. The council then put forward a revised scheme but a governor of the school challenged the council's power to do this and an injunction was granted by Mr Justice Donaldson. The school governors were told by the Secretary of State that any representations they wished to make concerning an amendment to the school's articles of government must be made within five days, a period which Mr Justice Donaldson judged unreasonable.

been elevated to the stratosphere. Yet what I like best is tackling the concrete problems which you meet in the lower level of Committees. I have a hunch that on defence we shall find there is now an overall O.P.D. and an inner group which does everything important and has all the secret information and works under the personal control of the Prime Minister. This re-organization means that what the P.M. calls his half-backs (his Ministers without Portfolio) can only play a role in the remote stratosphere and this has greatly decreased our value since we don't play any part in the concrete decisions further down.

My only important meeting was of the big six at 5.15. The P.M. had called it to discuss Lords reform because George Brown is due to leave London this week for the United Nations in New York and Callaghan off for Rio de Janeiro.

The P.M. started very briefly by expressing his surprise that the Committee had reached unanimity. Then the Chancellor explained the political reasons why we had made our recommendation in the way we had and George Brown and Callaghan were asked their opinions. George was completely unchanged. Any tinkering with Lords reform would be regarded as trying to distract attention from the real issue of unemployment. It would also upset our own socialists and the press would deride us for doing it. Callaghan said he didn't feel quite as strongly as that but he did feel that this was a kind of bread-and-circuses stunt—or at least would be regarded as such. However, if the P.M., the Lord Chancellor, the Lord President and the First Secretary all thought Lords reform important he would go along with it.

We then discussed the two alternative solutions—one-tier and two-tier—and George Brown immediately barged in with a total opposition to the two-tier idea. But I got the impression that his main objection was psycho-logical. He was deeply affronted that the Deputy Prime Minister had not been consulted and that all these consultations had been going on behind his back.

At last the supporters of the plan got their turn and I explained the tactical reasons for going ahead and inserting in the Queen's Speech a pledge to reform the House of Lords with an offer to negotiate with the other Parties. I emphasized that if we did nothing this wouldn't stop the Tories or the Liberals from putting forward proposals for reform of composition. There's no doubt that the strength of argument was on our side. But I went away from that meeting feeling pretty depressed. Having postponed the Cabinet meeting, we would now have it after the Party Conference[1] in very unfavourable circumstances.

By now my cold was almost unbearable and I went home to try to nurse it through the night.

---

[1] To be held at Scarborough from October 2nd to 6th.

Tuesday, September 19th

I spent the morning quietly at home and then went out to buy some gramophone records at the Army and Navy Stores before going on to the P.M. at 12 o'clock for a top secret meeting on the Parliamentary Boundary Commission. I had suggested to Harold that we must have a meeting with the new Minister of Housing and Local Government and the Home Secretary to see that we were still absolutely O.K. about the line we would take when the Commission produced its report. We went through the arguments all over again; Roy was still completely reliable but Tony Greenwood added nothing. Apparently the publication dates of the Parliamentary Commission and the Royal Commission on Local Government will not be so very far apart. When both reports have come out we must make it clear that we are postponing the operation of the Parliamentary report until the new boundaries of the new local authorities come into effect. All that we would have before the next general election was an interim measure dealing with the twenty or thirty largest constituencies.

I then raised the point about the Speaker's Conference, which I just discovered had turned down the proposal that where it was desired the voting slip should in future contain under the candidate's name the name of the Party to which he belongs. It's my view that Party labels on voting slips would help us more than the Tories because more of our supporters are semi-literate. What angered me is that when this was opposed at the Speaker's Conference Sara Barker had written to one of our M.P.s to advise him to oppose it and I asked Harold how on earth she had acquired the authority to do that. Harold promised to have the affair looked into and then asked the Chief and me to stay behind. I'm glad to say that he told me straightaway that he wasn't unduly concerned about yesterday's meeting on Lords reform. George was probably acting out of pique and he himself was sure we had ten Ministers already committed to support us. Unfortunately this is the kind of statement he is inclined to make with a great show of inside knowledge but I went away doubting if he knew very much about it.

I had lunch with Gerald Gardiner in order to meet Sir Leslie Scarman, the chairman of the Law Commission.[1] I found it most interesting because he told us that the Law Commission is publishing a report on how to make the law more intelligible. In fact it's taking up one of my oldest complaints, which is that the parliamentary draftsmen re-write plain instructions in intelligible English into unintelligible legal lingo. I talked to Scarman at length about this on one previous occasion and I was enormously excited that he had taken the idea seriously. We might get a real piece of Benthamite legislation knocking some of the mumbo-jumbo out of the law.

By the end of lunch the gastric flu was coming on again and I wasn't

---

[1] A Lord Justice of Appeal since 1973, he was chairman of the Law Commission from 1965 to 1973, when he became chairman of the Council of Legal Education.

feeling too good so I retired to Vincent Square for a few hours to try and get myself fit to make my speech at the Walthamstow by-election.

At 6.15 in the evening I tottered out of bed, got myself a cup of tea and was just ready at 6.45 for the Walthamstow agent who had promised to pick me up in his car. He turned up punctually and I gave him a glass of sherry. He is an accountant by profession — brown-eyed, fattish, youngish, bouncing, self-confident — and a comrade who hadn't been in the Party very long and had only just taken over the secretary-agent's job a year before. His name is Jack Manning and he lives in Walthamstow and has just bought himself a nice new little house, three up, two down, by the side of the reservoir near the bird sanctuary. When I got to his home I met his very good-looking wife and an exquisitely beautiful daughter, who said she had flu and wouldn't come with us. Jack is a great admirer of the old Member, Ted Redhead, who was the uncrowned king of West Walthamstow.[1] When I first got into the House in 1945 the old boy, McEntee,[2] was the Walthamstow Member and Ted had been his agent. When McEntee died in 1950 he was replaced by Clem Attlee although the whole constituency had wanted Redhead to have the seat. But they took their orders from Transport House and Attlee was imposed upon them. Redhead served as Attlee's agent until Attlee went to the House of Lords in 1955 and Ted himself became the M.P., running his own election as his own agent right up to the end, when he suddenly died on the Saturday after the G.L.C. election. Taking Ted Redhead out of West Walthamstow was like taking the mainspring out of a watch. Jack Manning told me about their terrible council group — a lot of little tinpot dictators who had just put up council rents by 25 per cent without trying to explain it to their voters. Jack is convinced they are going to be overwhelmingly defeated at the borough elections next spring. He also warned me that all the work in the election was being done by agents imported from the eastern region who had been slaving away to prevent another Leyton.[3] Leyton, by the way, is next door to Walthamstow.

In the course of the campaign they had visited every house at least once and were doing a great deal of revisiting. What they were finding was not merely apathy but a refusal by some of our strongest and staunchest supporters to go to the poll. The trouble is that there's no Party in Walthamstow since Redhead had done the whole job himself for more than twenty years.

After tea we went to the meeting which was in a kind of concert hall in the middle of a park. There we found some eighty or ninety people scattered in a hall which would hold 400 with Arthur Bottomley slogging away. He was

---

[1] Labour M.P. for Walthamstow West since 1956 and a Minister of State at the D.E.S. 1965–70.

[2] Labour M.P. for Walthamstow 1922–4 and 1929–50.

[3] In January 1965 the Foreign Secretary, Patrick Gordon Walker, defended a majority of 8,000 in the Leyton by-election but lost the seat. See Vol. I, pp. 134–50.

followed by Eric Deakins, the candidate—earnest, a bit of a lecturer, but he made quite a decent speech—and then I wound up in my usual style.[1]

Jack Manning drove me back to London and on the way I checked over my impressions with him because, I told him, I wanted to put them down in my diary. All the agents brought in from outside were working well and the canvass was going on quite efficiently. But it was clear that we were going to face a mass abstention entirely because of the prices and incomes policy and the increase of unemployment. Manning hoped for a 2,000 majority but I came back pretty well convinced that we were quite likely to lose Walthamstow this time. An old-fashioned Labour electorate was sick of its Labour council and utterly disillusioned with this Labour Government. They would vote for us in a general election but they just weren't going to vote for us in this by-election. Walthamstow in fact is much worse than Cambridge, where the candidate and the Party are working together far better and the mood is not so utterly disillusioned.

Wednesday, September 20th

First thing in the morning we had a meeting of the Queen's Speech Committee which consists mostly of senior Ministers and is something of a formality. However, both Michael Stewart and I noticed that towards the beginning the draft ran, 'The primary objective of the Government's policy is to achieve a balance of payments surplus.' Of course, if that was the primary objective we would accept mass unemployment in order to achieve it. When we pointed this out we were told that the original Treasury draft had run 'A primary objective' etc. This was bad enough but it had been changed to 'The primary objective' in the Cabinet Office.

This took some time and afterwards John Silkin and I had our weekly meeting with the P.M. Harold was full of the employment figures.[2] He told us in great secrecy that tomorrow there would be the announcement of an actual reduction of a few hundreds in the total number of unemployed, the first check to the increase in four months, and even better, that for the first time vacancies were on the up. 'This confirms my feeling,' he said, 'that there's a new industrial atmosphere and we've turned the tide. We have a housing boom, a motor-car boom, and now a reduction in unemployment.' I then reported my impression of the two by-elections and said that I thought Walthamstow was much worse than Cambridge. Maybe we would scrape home with a majority of 2,000 but the situation in the constituency was terrible, and all because of the unpopularity of our prices and incomes policy.

---

[1] In 1970 Eric Deakins was eventually elected Labour M.P. for this constituency, and in 1974 he became Parliamentary Under-Secretary for Trade.

[2] Unemployment had reached a peak of 2·4 per cent in August but at the beginning of September it had begun to fall very slightly, dropping by some 20,000 to give an average of 2·3 per cent in the last quarter of 1967.

I then went on to ask why he shouldn't set up a Strategic Committee, as Tommy and I had proposed months ago, for putting over the prices and incomes policy. 'Do you want me to do anything about this in my old role as co-ordinator?' I ended. To which he replied, 'I think that Peter and I must do the day-to-day work with the help of Trevor Lloyd-Hughes. I don't think we could let that go. We do it best ourselves.' 'All right,' I said, 'if you don't want any help that's that.'

Thursday, September 21st

Before Cabinet I had an urgent talk with Peter Shore. I had to see him first about the redraft of the Queen's Speech, in which he has been extremely helpful. Then I was due to mention to him something which I'd raised with the P.M. during our talk the day before. I had suggested that we might now refer to the Prices and Incomes Board two or three of the really bad Tory councils' rent increases. The idea had come to me when one of the Labour Party ward secretaries in Coventry wrote about their rent increase of 50 per cent all round. It suddenly occurred to me that we should refer these Coventry rent increases to Aubrey Jones. It was ridiculous to say that we believed in a prices policy and then make no effort to control council rents. If we can refer the prices of gas and electricity to the P.I.B. we can refer these rents as well. We hadn't done it previously because so many of the councils had Labour majorities which would have taken umbrage, but now the Tories have taken over there seemed to me everything in favour of getting the policies referred. When I put this to Peter he picked up the idea very quickly indeed and seemed delighted.

Cabinet today started with a severe Prime Ministerial rebuke administered to poor Gordon Walker for the mess he'd made in Enfield. He was rebuked for not taking legal advice from the Attorney-General. I talked to him afterwards and found out that his departmental lawyers were certain he would win and that before they entered the court the Solicitor-General expressed the same view. Gordon Walker believes that if the A.-G. had been consulted he would have said the same. However, what he didn't seem to realize was that, quite apart from the lawyers he ought, as the politician in charge, to have seen the political insanity of this behaviour.

The second item was the report of the leaks committee which the P.M. had put into operation months ago. As everyone predicted, the Lord Chancellor came up with absolutely nothing. His conclusion in the Cabinet minutes ran, 'The Lord Chancellor recalled that he had been invited by the Prime Minister to investigate the sources of certain apparent leaks in information relating to Cabinet Ministers. He was satisfied that there had been no deliberate leakage of such information.' In the discussion which followed Willie Ross made a very sensible remark. He pointed out that we have very few leaks when Parliament is not sitting and, he said, 'To me this seems to indicate that the leaks come through Parliamentary Secretaries, P.P.S.s etc.'

Then we came to the Lord Chancellor's report on publications, i.e. on the problem George Brown had raised about my keeping a diary. We had seen the Cabinet paper in advance, which revealed a difference of opinion. The three non-legal members of the Committee (Roy Jenkins, Gordon Walker and Frank Longford) were in favour of Ministers taking the advice of the Secretary of the Cabinet. The two lawyer members of the Committee (Gerald Gardiner and the Attorney-General) wanted Ministers to be made to sign in advance a document promising to abide by the decision of the Secretary of the Cabinet on whatever books they wanted to publish. When Gerald and Elwyn had briefly introduced the paper, Roy Jenkins spoke up. He accepted that they should try to work together but he couldn't swallow the recommendation that the last word should belong to a civil servant. He also made the very sensible point that even if Ministers did sign this promise they would make a secret reservation in their minds between theory and actual practice, particularly since the person who would make the decision might be an unknown civil servant twenty years later on. Quite unexpectedly the Prime Minister turned to me. I was unprepared but I remarked that it's absolutely astonishing to propose that in the book I intend to write on the relationship between the politicians and the Civil Service a civil servant should be made a complete censor of my work. What was even more outrageous, I went on, was that if this report was accepted there would be censorship of all books written by Ministers about their political experiences but not about newspaper articles, which could be far more damaging and malicious. One advantage of a long-term contract for a book is that a Minister would not be tempted by an acute shortage of money just after a lost election to earn £10,000 from the *News of the World* or the *Sunday Express* for spicy anecdotes. That's what the papers really want to print and that is what destroys collective responsibility. The P.M. then rapidly intervened to say that there could be no question of Burke Trend or his successor having the final word on anything except defence security. Shouldn't we as reasonable men agree that where the Secretary of the Cabinet told us that a passage had to be omitted for reasons of national security we were bound to omit it? But Roy Jenkins and Frank Longford even objected to this, saying that we ought naturally to take his advice but there was no reason to tie ourselves in advance.

Having had no luck here the P.M. then said that he thought the real issue is 'collective responsibility to each other and to the Party', and he evolved the theory out of his head that the leader of the Party (he might be leader of the Opposition then) should informally read all manuscripts written by members of his ex-Cabinet before publication. I'm afraid he was made to look a complete jackass, not only by Roy Jenkins and Tony Crosland, but also by Gordon Walker. One of them asked him whether he would really have been willing to accept Hugh Gaitskell's censorship of his own autobiography. And another question was whether it would be wise to compel the unfortunate leader of the Opposition to make himself unpopular with his colleagues by vetting their manuscripts. If he didn't remove an offensive passage it would have been said to have been printed with his approval and if he did remove it there would be a terrible row.

This whole discussion lasted for a full two hours. It was one of the most futile I've ever heard. But I should recall that the opponents didn't have it all their own way. Dick Marsh supported the Lord Chancellor, saying how appalling it was that these professional writers should be preparing their diaries in order to do him down. He didn't mind an odd dirty newspaper article by an ordinary colleague; what he minded was the prospect of serious weighty attacks by professional writers equipped with all the advantages of a detailed diary. How could he reply to that? Tony Greenwood also made one of his rare interventions, saying he was deeply disturbed about the security of these diaries—what would happen if the diarist's home was broken into?

Having been chivvied all round the place Harold finally said that he would draft a new memorandum, at which I burst out quite spontaneously with the remark, 'Oh heavens, don't let's have this again. We've had this discussion twice already. All this talk about the books we shall write after the Government has fallen is ghoulish and makes me feel that the Government is falling.' What I remembered was that it was the day of the by-elections and we were faced with an imminent political débâcle and all we could talk about was leaks and publications.

By this time it was 12.30 and when we turned to my solid paper on parliamentary reform I said I thought it was better not to take it today but to leave room for a decision on the Beagle company. This was a firm making light aircraft which the Ministry of Technology had acquired. Peter Shore and the Treasury were for cutting our losses but Tony Benn was for going ahead. He pointed out that closure would mean sacking one thousand people and winding up just when a new managing director had been appointed. I've no doubt Peter and the Treasury were right in thinking it a thoroughly bad bet. Nevertheless, facing this particular winter most of us felt that it was a baddish issue for the new Secretary of State at D.E.A. to bring to Cabinet from his Committee.

After lunch Shackleton came to see me. He has now decided to set up a working party and get down to the detailed work on House of Lords reform. This is all the more important because it is clear that George Brown's and Callaghan's opposition was partly due to the total inadequacy of the appendix in which we outlined the two-tier plan. Shackleton is now going to redraft Annexe 2 as a really solid, detailed job of work. What a good man he is. He's got drive and energy and he actually offers to do something himself. When he was out in Aden he suffered a great deal under George Brown because he doesn't allow this kind of private initiative. But he's a pretty good friend of mine.

My next visitors were Tony Greenwood and Bruce Millan,[1] representing Scotland, who came to persuade me to give them time for a big Bill on the compulsory improvement of old houses. I told them that the Bill is essential provided it's big enough. If they can get the Treasury to agree a really generous formula for compensating owner-occupiers of slum-clearance property the Bill will be a winner. If they can't get that I won't give it time.

When this was over Tony stayed behind to ask me for another Bill to deal with gypsies. I told him this was minor legislation which might stand a chance if he was prepared to start it in the House of Lords. After that I talked to him about the reference of council-house rents to the Prices and Incomes Board. His reply was characteristic. 'Politically I can see there's a lot to be said for taking this risk but I have to think of it as a Minister.' There he was shivering at the prospect of taking a departmental risk which would help the whole Labour Government on the same day when he'd just come back from the A.M.C. where he'd been telling them about his record number of houses under construction.

This evening I had Tony Crosland and Tommy Balogh to dinner and when we'd discussed the January prospects I said I was going home to see the by-election results on my own filthy little television with Tam Dalyell. Tommy said he would ring up Marcia and as a result I found myself watching the results with Marcia and the P.M. 'I hate the television taking one inside so that one is present at the count,' he said, and it was clear that he was very jumpy. In came Gerald Kaufman to tell us there was a recount at Waltham-stow so we knew the worst—we were in for another Leyton over again. So when the final result came it wasn't really such a blow.[2] We just talked and chatted trivialities while we waited for Cambridge.[3] Of course, that result was an enormous help because in Cambridge the swing was 9 per cent whereas it was 18 per cent in Walthamstow. That steadied the P.M., whose mind was fixed on the failure of Heath and who kept on assuring himself that this was merely a Labour protest against the prices and incomes and that there was no swing to the Tories. I went away soon afterwards and found Tam still up, and agreed with him how good Wedgy Benn had been during that fill-in part of the show where he and Iain Macleod and Bob Mackenzie[4] and a Liberal called Pardoe[5] had been asked their opinions. Tony is a wonderful

---

[1] Labour M.P. for Craigton (Glasgow) since 1959. He was Parliamentary Under-Secretary of State for Defence (R.A.F.) 1964–6 and for Scotland 1966–7; in 1974 he became a Minister of State at the Scottish Office.

[2] Labour's majority of 8,725 at the general election was turned into a majority of 62 for Frederick Silvester who kept the seat for the Conservatives until 1970.

[3] At Cambridge, Labour's majority of 991 was turned into a 5,978 majority for the Conservative also, David Lane, who held the seat from 1974 until he resigned in 1976.

[4] Professor of Sociology at L.S.E. since 1964, broadcaster and author of, notably, *British Political Parties* (London: Heinemann, 1953, revised 1964).

[5] John Pardoe, Liberal M.P. for Cornwall North since 1964.

public relations man and he reacted perfectly to those defeats. Watching that television performance, one saw poor Iain Macleod, who was celebrating a great by-election victory, being driven by a kind of pincer movement by Bob Mackenzie and Wedgwood Benn on to the defensive. The explanation of course was that Macleod isn't all that pro-Heath himself and he had no alternative to the Government's policy. He wasn't in favour of devaluation or of scrapping the prices and incomes policy and I think this is something we can cling to as the signpost to the way out of our troubles. It was a good idea to go to sleep on.

Friday, September 22nd

How should the P.M. be handled on the morrow of defeat? I had long talks that morning with John Silkin and Tommy Balogh on that subject. Out of the Leyton catastrophe we had got from him the small committee which linked Transport House and the Government. Out of this catastrophe we all agreed that we should try to get an inner group which would guide propaganda policy.

At ten o'clock I popped off to my weekly meeting where—Burke Trend being in Canada on holiday—Bill Nield was in charge and we found there was very little work for Cabinet on Thursday. When the business was over I asked the P.M. to see me alone and put the proposal to him. His first reaction was that I was inventing a device which would enable me to push devaluation and such things. 'No,' I said, 'It's not that. I want to use this, with Peter Shore and Tony Crosland, for getting the prices and incomes policy sold in a way you have never done so far. That will be the first job. Maybe we shall have other suggestions about action to take, for instance referring rents to the Prices and Incomes Board, for the Alcan project for smelting aluminium and saving imports of so many million a year. Maybe we shall have ideas about regionalism.' Then he began to say, 'Yes, but let's think about what I ought to put into my Conference speech.' And I knew I had to stop.

I then went back to my office and there I had a talk to Agnew which is well worth retelling in full. Ever since I came back from the Dordogne I've been told by him that we would have to have a Privy Council with not less than four Ministers present before October 11th: otherwise the Legislature of the Seychelles Islands would automatically lapse. After some beating about I suggested that we could manage the last Friday of the Labour Party Conference. I could catch the sleeper to Aberdeen on the Thursday night with Eddie Shackleton and one or two others and we would all go up together, have the Council on the Friday morning, lunch there with the Queen, have a walk in the afternoon and come back by the night train on Friday. This had then been checked with Michael Adeane at the Palace and had been found suitable, though there had been a great difficulty in collecting my four Ministers. Suddenly, however, last Wednesday Agnew told me that it had been put to the Queen and the Queen had said, 'I'm so sorry I have a private engagement—it just can't be done.' I was annoyed that when an arrangement had been found suitable and convenient by her own Palace staff, by the Privy Council and by the four Ministers, she should simply say that she had a private arrangement. We set to trying to find another date and Agnew began to insist that we must have it on the Monday after the Conference—that is, on the 9th if the Seychelles Legislature were to be safe. I said that would be almost impossible. All the Ministers would have been ten days away from their offices in London and would certainly not like to go up on the Sunday night and come back on the Monday. Despite Agnew's protest I insisted that we should have it on Tuesday. When I got into the office this morning he told me he'd received another note from the Palace that the Queen had consented to it happening on Tuesday, though she has another private engagement and wouldn't be able to give the Ministers lunch that day. I felt pretty angry. 'All right,' I said, 'if we don't have lunch with her I don't really mind. We can have it in the servants' quarters. There will be plenty of her staff having their lunch and she can have her private entertainment in another part of the house. But I do insist that we should be given a meal after the Council and before we leave.' Poor Godfrey Agnew got to work again and this evening, just before I left, he came up to me and said, 'It has all been fixed up. She's going to be able to entertain you to lunch on Tuesday.'

It's an interesting story because it illustrates the relationship between the Queen and her Ministers. First of all it's striking that when the Government is at work in London and the Privy Council is called, she doesn't come down from Balmoral to the Palace but the Ministers have to go to her private home in the north of Scotland. If this is necessary to the magic of monarchy, I accept it as fair enough. But surely there must be a limit to which busy Ministers are compelled to sacrifice their time to suit royal private engagements. This I think is unchivalrous. It's only fair to add, however, that I am pretty certain that the Queen herself knows nothing about all this and it's all a matter between endless courtiers.

Saturday, September 23rd

I spent a good many hours yesterday preparing a draft inquest on Walthamstow with proposals for policy changes which I want to discuss with Peter, Tommy and Wedgy on Monday evening when Harold will be having his big *Panorama* interview. The point is to have our ideas clear before the big S.E.P. meeting on Tuesday morning which discusses the economic situation and the measures for dealing with unemployment this winter. I think it's worth putting down a summary of my reflections on Walthamstow which form the first part of this paper. First of all I observe that it's really staggering if you go through the year of N.O.P. poll background reports how wide the gap is between the amazingly bad results of the G.L.C. elections and the by-elections and the figures shown by the Gallup Poll. The only explanation of that gap is that in the Gallup Poll people are asked which way they would vote in a general election whereas in a council election or a by-election they are not voting in a general election. So from this we can draw the conclusion that as long as that gap continued the by-election votes were mainly protest votes.

However my second point is that since mid-summer this year there had been a dramatic and dangerous change. The Government has taken a header and what Walthamstow shows is that the sense of protest is beginning to be dangerous to our general election prospects. It's now affecting confidence in the whole Government and in particular in the Prime Minister. He had 90 per cent approval as late as June, but now it has dropped below 80 per cent. There's been a sudden collapse of confidence, almost entirely due to the prices and incomes policy and unemployment, with Vietnam as a secondary cause. If this analysis is correct the practical conclusion is that we must concentrate on putting over the prices and incomes policy and the economic analysis on which it is based.

However, to counter-balance this depressing picture there is one encouraging feature in the situation. Neither the polls nor the by-elections reveal any real evidence of a positive belief among voters that the Tories are fit for Government again or that Heath is fit to be Prime Minister. This is almost the biggest advantage we possess. It enables us to say that if we work vigorously we can regain the position of a few months ago. I myself think we've got to carry on along the present lines for at least two months but that then there will have to be a convulsive major change of policy. Almost certainly we shall have to have import controls and devaluation. This convulsion is required in order to produce the dynamic required to increase the rate of growth and reduce unemployment to a tolerable level. One lesson we can draw from our present plight is that two winters of unemployment at over 2 per cent is something the Labour movement won't stand.

Sunday, September 24th

I had been looking forward to an appalling Sunday press explaining Walthamstow as a second and even more devastating Leyton. But even a glance shows that the papers have given the by-elections remarkably little attention. Apparently there isn't any feeling in Fleet Street that Walthamstow was a presage of doom. I suspect the editors know that the Government can comfortably run its course and that it will also be able to tolerate a whole series of disastrous by-elections like this. Walthamstow really settled nothing and the reason why it didn't was because of the failure of the Conservative opposition to provide a serious alternative government. That perhaps is why today, in the *World at One*, Gerald Nabarro gave a characteristically snide interview attacking his leader.

In the evening I was rung up by Harold Lever who told me he'd been asked to appear on the *World at One* on Monday in order to represent the Civil

Service and defend the Treasury against the attack on it which Max Nicholson launched in his new book, *The System*.[1] Max, of course, is an old friend from P.E.P. days in the 1930s and I saw something of him when he was Permanent Secretary to Herbert Morrison who, as Lord President of the Council, was in charge of such things as Science and the Research Councils. *The System*, which I read in the Dordogne, is a tremendous onslaught on the Civil Service and in particular on the mandarin mind. This, he thinks, is the product of mods and greats at Oxford which teaches one abstract philosophy and ancient history and which is based on the assumption that a mind trained in such abstract and remote subjects can apply itself to every modern problem with assurance of success. *The System* got a tremendous write-up in the Sunday papers, which gave me a good deal of pleasure since it is nice to see someone else being blamed for our problems apart from the Labour Government. So when Harold Lever rang me up I said, 'Why on earth are you going to speak?' 'Well,' he said, 'I'm the Financial Secretary to the Treasury and therefore it's my job to look after the Civil Service. I've been asked to do this by Sir Laurence Helsby.' 'That's all right,' I said, 'but for heaven's sake don't start attacking Max Nicholson, because he provides invaluable propaganda for the Government. What you should do is to refer to the Fulton Commission on the Reform of the Civil Service and say that it's doing a radical job of work, and somehow indicate that we know in advance the things which Nicholson suggests are wrong.'[2] He didn't sound very convinced when he said goodbye.

Monday, September 25th

I had no engagements and I intended to stay at home. Heaven knows, when I woke up with a streaming cold I wanted to. But over Sunday I'd decided I must go back in order to do two major bits of writing. First, I was determined to complete the paper on the lessons of Walthamstow and get it distributed to Peter, Tony, Harold and Marcia before we met tonight. Secondly, I had to do an article for the *Jerusalem Post*'s special number on the fiftieth anniversary of the Balfour Declaration. This had been wished on me by Meyer Weisgal on his last visit to London by the simple device of telling me about the filthy stories which were circulating in Israel revealing all the terrible things I'd done in Cabinet just before the Six-Day War. You can clean it all up by a good article, he'd told me, and so I had to do it.

I spent most of the day sweating and streaming from the nose while I dictated the two articles. I missed Harold Lever's radio talk because I took

[1] London: Hodder & Stoughton, 1967. Max Nicholson was Secretary of the Office of the Lord President of the Council 1945–52 and a member of the Advisory Council on Science Policy 1948–64. From 1952 to 1966 he was Director-General of the Nature Conservancy and, since 1963, has been convener of the Conservation Section of the International Biological Programme.

[2] The Commission on the Civil Service, of which Lord Fulton was chairman, was to report in 1968.

Gordon Walker out to lunch at the Athenaeum and gave him grouse and a bottle of wine. This put him in the humour to tell me more about his Enfield schemozzle. He confirmed that he had taken all the lawyers' advice and then I asked him when the Prime Minister first sent for him. 'He never sent for me.' 'When did he first speak to you?' 'He never spoke to me. The first time I spoke to him about the Enfield catastrophe was at Cabinet when I was sitting opposite you on the other side of the table, being rebuked for not taking legal advice.'

This is characteristic of how Harold Wilson runs his Cabinet. All of us are on a loose rein and the rein suddenly gets looser when a Minister puts his foot in it.

This evening Harold was due to give his important television interview and I had arranged to have a quick dinner beforehand with the group. At six o'clock Marcia rang to say that we could all come and look at the television in her room downstairs at No. 10 and then go up to the 'white boudoir' to see the P.M. He might be a bit late coming back from the B.B.C. but he would like to see us because he had been taken by my suggestion that we should give him ideas about his speech for Conference. Tommy and I went across a few minutes after the programme had started and found that the interview was preceded by a film, which lasted at least twenty minutes, about unemployment in West Cumberland. From time to time there was a cut-on which showed Harold looking at it and when at last the end came he could hardly be blamed if he was a bit slow on the uptake and a bit sluggish. Indeed, the whole thing was sluggish until Robin Day suddenly broke off and said, 'Let's consider the result of those by-elections,' and Harold was launched on the genuine interview for which he had come. They were a funny team of inter-viewers—Robin Day, the foreign correspondent of the *Christian Science Monitor*, and James Mossman. They didn't have anything in common. To start with Harold displayed the loquacity which enables him to talk himself out of the most awkward question. As Anne remarked when I rang her up, 'He is not unflappable but he is untrippable.' Nevertheless, as the pro-gramme went on he did get across his major theme that though his policy was unpopular he stood by it and although he foresaw a really rough winter he wasn't going to be panicked into abandoning it. Towards the end he got out of the Vietnam problem by saying that he cared desperately about the war but he wasn't one of those people who would merely stand on the sideline and protest; he was going to try to stop it. Then he did another equally routine piece on Rhodesia and that was that.

We went upstairs to the 'white boudoir' agreeing that he had done pretty well and after rather more than an hour he came back from the B.B.C. to tell us that he'd been talking to Charlie Hill and complaining that the programme was scandalously organized. It did seem to me very tough to interview the Prime Minister after a gloomy 20-minute film on unemployment which cer-tainly lost him a large part of his audience. Soon he went out to see his doctor and get the anti-cold injection which he regularly has before each Annual Conference. When he came back and sat down on the sofa I sat beside him and took my chance. 'I want a Ministerial Committee on publicity,' I said, 'along the lines we discussed last Friday. Tell me, Harold, am I going to get it?' 'What membership do you want?' he said. 'Not departmental Ministers: co-ordinating Ministers—Peter Shore, Michael Stewart, the Chief Whip, Wedgy Benn. That's five and that's enough for the Committee.' 'All right, that's fine,' he said. 'A Ministerial Committee and of course working as an official committee as well.'

It's nearly a year since I was appointed the Minister to co-ordinate publicity and at last I'm being allowed some part of the machinery necessary to do it. How important will this Committee be? At election times it could be extremely important. Meanwhile its main jobs will be co-ordinating advertising campaigns and policies of information officers, and such things as the monitoring of television. In addition, I hope, it will allow us to foresee and prevent a number of disasters and also to take a number of opportunities on television which we're now missing.

When I'd finished I mentioned Harold Lever's radio broadcast. 'Why on earth is he getting himself into that?' asked Harold. And when I told him that Helsby had drafted him in Harold remarked, 'For heaven's sake, I hope he hasn't just been anti-Nicholson, considering the assistance Nicholson's giving to us.'

Tuesday, September 26th

In my red box I found a text of the Lever broadcast. It was a complete whitewash of the Civil Service and a violent attack on Nicholson, so I rang up Harold and said he would get a medal for his wonderful work. 'Oh, do you think so?' he said. 'I hope I didn't overdo it.' I said that he certainly had and told him of my talk with Harold Wilson the night before. He was a bit shaken by this and asked whether the P.M. was upset. 'Oh no,' I said, 'he's not upset but it shows how nice people like you can be taken over as soon as they get into a Department like the Treasury.' He insisted that he had not been taken over, but that he was so keen to make his radical reforms in taxation that he wanted to win the confidence of the Treasury by helping them with this broadcast and so endearing himself to them. He almost certainly did.

My cold was getting steadily worse but I dragged myself out of bed in time for a Defence Committee at ten and the big S.E.P. at 11.15. We started S.E.P. with some comments on the situation and I got the clear impression that Harold is now closer than ever to Jim, more optimistic than ever and more determined than ever to get through without devaluation. In the coming months it's going to be more and more difficult to justify devaluation and even more difficult for the P.M. and the Chancellor to remain at their jobs if a devaluation is forced upon them. Every time they make speeches—for instance, that *Panorama* interview last night—they commit themselves a shade further against devaluation taking place as long as they are in office. By the time Conference is over they will have committed themselves a long way further. So, though I think we need it in the coming months, I reckon that the chances of it coming are very small indeed.

When we turned to pit closures it was clear the P.M. had once again got his way. They have all been postponed until December 1st and even then they will be open to review. But are they too palpably a piece of pre-Conference appeasement of the N.U.M.? It's supposed to show humanity and kindness but somehow I feel it hasn't gone down very well.

On the next item, references to the Prices and Incomes Board, Peter Shore put forward the proposal that we should include council-house rents. Tony Greenwood read his departmental brief in reply, saying how embarrassing it would be for him as Minister of Housing. I hit back by saying it isn't a question of Ministers but of the Cabinet. We shan't have a prices and incomes policy at all if we funk this issue. With Denis Healey in strong support we managed to get a clear S.E.P. majority for the reference.

Then we plunged through the rest of that enormous 200-page paper which was the result of the P.M.'s July inspiration—all the ideas he'd collected for dealing with the crisis. He himself admitted ruefully that most of them had been knocked out or proved non-starters and there was damn little left to look at except industrial training. Here our great trade unionist, Ray Gunter, put forward his usual narrow curmudgeonly views. When Peter urged a much more ambitious training programme Gunter said that it was possible for intellectuals to talk in this way but trade-union leaders don't believe in industrial training and none of them practise what they preach. 'I know the possibilities, you don't, my dear Minister of Economics. You're an intellectual.' And that was that. Harold did not support Peter against Gunter that morning.

We spent the rest of the time on the famous Industrial Expansion Bill which had caused such a row between Wedgy and the rest of the economic Ministers. Michael Stewart has tried to stop it, the Chancellor of the Exchequer has tried to stop it, and the President of the Board of Trade too. But Wedgy has the Prime Minister's solid support and they are going to shove it on to the Statute Book despite the C.B.I.'s outright opposition. The Prime Minister wants it to demonstrate that we're active interventionist socialist planners. In discussing the draft White Paper that morning it was interesting to see that an effort was made to have a reference to the market economy in order to please the C.B.I. Wedgy Benn said, 'I can't allow that because I'm not going to be committed to a market economy—I'm an interventionist.' A new tension is now growing up in S.E.P. between interventionists—Harold, Tony and Peter—and non-interventionists, headed by the Chancellor and Tony Crosland.

This afternoon Gerald Gardiner brought forward at Home Affairs a Divorce Bill to implement the reforms recommended by the Law

Commission.[1] He said rather airily that he thought that this had been so widely accepted not only by the Law Commission but by the Archbishop's committee that it was bound to get through without any controversy. This was greeted with a hearty roar of laughter by the Secretaries of State for Wales and Scotland who said there'd be plenty of disagreement. That brought us to a longish discussion about how to handle it. The Lord Chancellor said that it ought to be a Government measure with a free vote. I had to point out that it was an impossible operation from the point of view of the Whips. The only sensible thing was to give it to a Private Member and then provide Government time, using the technique we'd evolved for abortion and homosexuality. That requires Cabinet agreement. Personally I think this is an extremely sensible and skilful way of getting out of our difficulties in dealing with social reforms of this sort. But there are members of the Cabinet who don't and that's why it will come up to Cabinet next week.

I ought to mention one other item which was the recommendation by Patrick Gordon Walker that we should abandon the project for a huge new extension of the British Museum library on a Bloomsbury site of some seven acres.[2] Clearing the site would involve rehousing some 900 people and destroying a large number of hotels and hostels as well as seven listed buildings — including the whole of one side of Bloomsbury Square, which has the Pharmaceutical Society at one end and two more Nash buildings at the other. Patrick was strongly supported by Tony Greenwood. Directly I read the paper I was uneasy because I remembered that I had begun to deal with this as Minister of Housing. The whole Basil Spence[3] concept of this new skyscraper-cum-piazza had seemed to me disgusting and I had sent for Jimmy James and our chief architect and said I wanted to stop it. I said, 'Yes, it is a horrible project but it will also cause tremendous opposition by the number of homes it will destroy and I gather that Camden Borough Council will lead this movement against it. There are sound conservationist reasons for not doing it. There are sound housing and town-planning reasons and finally there are sound aesthetic reasons.' When they saw that I was in earnest they warned me that this project had been going on since 1951 and that the Ministry of Works had already spent £2 million on it. They wondered whether I could really upset a long-standing plan of the Trustees of the British Museum.

I was moved from the Ministry before I came to any final decision. It surprised me that Greenwood and Gordon Walker should now have got departmental backing for stopping the plans. I was even more surprised to

[1] On July 29th the Archbishop's Group had recommended, in a report entitled *Putting Asunder*, that breakdown of marriage should replace matrimonial offences as the sole ground for divorce. The Law Commission had also produced a report (see *House of Commons Debates*, November 23rd, 1966), *Reform of the Grounds of Divorce* (Cmnd. 3123).

[2] The scheme proposed by the architect Sir Leslie Martin was to be abandoned in October 1967 (see p. 537). In 1975 it was decided to put the library at Somers Town near Euston on the site of a disused railway yard.

[3] Sir Basil Spence, Professor of Architecture at the Royal Academy 1961–8, President R.I.B.A. 1959–66 and a member of the Royal Fine Art Commission 1956–70.

hear it said that the library must be moved to another central London site, possibly Covent Garden. After a long discussion I said that it was impossible to upset a plan which had been seventeen years in the making without an outside opinion. And I hoped that this recommendation would be carried out.

The discussion lasted much longer than I expected and I got back to my office to find a queue of people. But I just had time to squeeze in a meeting with the Treasury people about sending the Finance Bill upstairs. Harold Lever and his staff were in attendance because Jim had flu and Harold couldn't oppose me on anything because of his guilty conscience about the anti-Nicholson broadcast.

Wednesday, September 27th
Today my streaming cold was confirmed as flu but I had to be out the whole day in Coventry—not the thing one wants to do with flu. But it was quite a useful expedition. I spent the morning with the old A.E.U. members who have A.E.U. pensions. There are hundreds of them but some forty bothered to turn up to hear the Member for Coventry East and the Lord President talking about pensions. They were very grousy mainly because they allege that immigrants were getting more national assistance than they got in pension benefit. It was useful meeting them because it reminded me of the large number of our old people who are just too well off to draw supplementary benefit.

Then, after lunch with just the editor and one of the directors at the new *Coventry Evening Telegraph* building, I went back to Coundon Road to see a delegation from Bristol-Siddeley led by Philip Higgs; I warned them about the problems of the aircraft industry and told them it might really be closed down. I also told them about the local difficulties they are going to face. They were attentive and friendly and I think anxious for information.

Then I drove a mile or two north to the 72-acre area of desolation which used to be the municipal gas concern and is now part of the West Midlands Gas Board. Since the coke-making has stopped a huge dump has been put down on one corner, and it was deeply upsetting to the residents into whose gardens the dust was blowing. There was 20,000 tons of rubbish there and a burning apparatus that still wasn't in use. I asked how such gross neglect of the needs of the local inhabitants could occur and was told the new production manager had been brought in but that the councillor concerned hadn't yet appeared.

Back to Coundon Road to meet delegations from Stoke and from Willenhall. The Stoke delegation was led by a near-communist and the wife of a local parson. They asked me to state what I was prepared to do to help them stop the Tory rent increase. As it happens there is a council by-election on Thursday and I said to them that if they wanted to change council policy the best thing for them to do was to vote Labour in the by-election. There was nothing the Labour Government could do, I said, to force the Tories on the Coventry Council to change the level of the rents they'd fixed. 'The only way you can change them is by changing the councillors,' I concluded. At this point the leader of the group got up and said, 'I'm not going to be addressed in this political way. I shall walk out since we are a non-political organization.' Pretty cool for a communist.

Of course when Peter Lister and Betty Healey brought in the Willenhall tenants they didn't behave so stupidly. But most of the rank-and-file members of the delegation were just as deeply convinced that it's the Government in Whitehall which takes decisions and the Government which can change the rents in Coventry. Of course this idea is fed out by the Coventry Tory Council as well and they've been clever enough to quote a Labour White Paper to indicate that they are carrying out Government wishes. It's also true that the Labour councillors in Coventry hadn't been too anxious to say that we in London are not to blame. As a result these people felt deeply insulted when I finally said to them, 'You've got a Conservative Party in power which has decided to increase rents and rents therefore will be increased. I can't stop it. Indeed it's not my job to stop it.' I found myself extremely unpopular after this discussion. Even council tenants feel that Governments decide everything and local councils don't really matter. No wonder they use their votes to protest in municipal elections.

I went back to London feeling like hell and dropped into Eddie Shackleton's party in his flat right up on top of the Admiralty. There I met Max Nicholson and was able to tell him the story of Harold Lever's radio broadcast. Then off I went to bed.

Thursday, September 28th
Cabinet at ten and I could feel that my temperature was now pretty high and I just wasn't fit to travel to Scarborough that night.

At Cabinet we had a good round of foreign affairs with George Brown reporting first on his impressions of the United Nations and then on Vietnam, which he said was terribly depressing because there was no prospect of peace. Then questions were asked for and when there were no questions I said I would like to ask a few because I observed that this was a problem where an overwhelming majority of Labour Party members were opposed to the Government and wanted us to stop giving support to the Americans. Were we supporting them for reasons of expediency or did he really feel the Vietnam War was a just war? He said of course they were right because the communists attacked first and we were bound to support them in this war, whereat Barbara came back with a great spiel about how we were losing the support of all Asia by supporting the Americans. I said that what worried me was that most of our Labour Party supporters felt that there really was a moral issue here and that we were acting immorally in supporting an unjust war. At this point the Prime Minister said that these moral postures were all very well; what mattered was whether we had been able to do any genuine peace-making. He then asserted that there were no less than thirty-seven occasions on which we had tried to intervene, never with success, but we still retained our mediating position and that was the key to our policy and the reason why we were accepting all the unpopularity by not denouncing the Americans. This was all very well, I said, but as he could see if he had bothered to read Iris Murdoch's article on the front page of this week's *Listener*,[1] serious people were convinced that this war was unjust. To my surprise Roy Jenkins came in to say that to introduce such crude ideas as a just war was very unlike the Lord President and no serious politician could judge things by these standards.

I got the impression from this long discussion that most of my colleagues disliked the issue being pressed in an argument of this kind. This explains why never before this debate have we discussed the principles involved in our support for the Americans in Vietnam. We failed to because the Cabinet aren't ready to face up to the awkward issues involved. How well I remember my wrath, when the Attlee Government was introducing its Palestine policy, that Aneurin Bevan hadn't made sure that Cabinet faced up to the issues of principle involved! Now I realize how rarely great issues are discussed in Cabinet as issues of principle and how one moves normally through a series of *ad hoc* decisions on narrow issues which don't seem to raise the great moral principles. I'm afraid this has been just as true of the Wilson Cabinet; it has failed to insist on serious discussion of foreign policy. I was glad when Barbara insisted that we should at least be given a paper laying down the Government's position on Vietnam in some detail.

It was getting late when this debate was finally wound up and the Prime Minister said, 'We must let the Lord President have a word about Parliamentary procedure.' But sometimes it's a good thing to come in at the end of a lengthy debate. My long, detailed paper was disposed of in forty minutes. Nothing was challenged except the proposal to send the Finance Bill upstairs. Since Jim was away in Rio de Janeiro Jack Diamond represented him and told the Cabinet that the Chancellor was acquiescing reluctantly in my plans but wondered whether it would not be wiser to postpone them for a year. It wasn't difficult to show that this was a ridiculous suggestion—each year is the right moment to postpone for another year. Jack Diamond's argument got me a quick firm Cabinet decision to act at once.

After the meeting Jack said to me, 'Of course I had to try the old trick but personally I knew there shouldn't be any delay. I'm glad you got what you want and so is Harold Lever.'

To show how successful I was I even got Cabinet to grant the wish of the Clerks at the Table to have their wigs abolished—despite the Prime Minister's proposal that they should wear them during Question Time and take them off at 3.30!

This afternoon Niall MacDermot, who has now replaced Fred Willey as

[1] The novelist and philosopher. She has been a Fellow of St Anne's College, Oxford, since 1948.

the number two at the Ministry of Housing, came to discuss the new Planning Bill with me. We plunged into technical details and when it was over I asked him what he was doing apart from this. He told me he was dealing with the Land Commission where things had reached a complete standstill. It had already been in operation for three or four months but not a single acre of land had yet been purchased, and the whole of its purchasing policy was in virtual abeyance. Niall wanted the local regional L.C. offices—which were full of quite eager, vigorous people—to be allowed to go ahead, but he had apparently discovered that the chairman, Henry Wells, was centralizing the whole of land-purchasing policy and refusing to have anything done without his personal sanction.[1] The trouble was that land purchase always involved a row between the urban areas trying to spread out and the counties trying to prevent building in their green belt and, as he didn't want to get his Land Commission involved in a row between the county boroughs and the counties, his personal sanction was rarely given.

None of this surprised me. From the start I'd regarded the proposal as half-baked and reputable people, like Arnold Goodman, who were on the committee that worked it out have since claimed that they weren't responsible for the final solution which was placed on the statute book by Fred Willey when he was Minister of Land and Natural Resources. Most of the objects for which we established the Land Commission could have been achieved by minor changes in the Planning Acts and a vast increase in the local authorities' powers of compulsory purchase. There was no need to produce the monstrous white elephant we've now got.

After this Judith Hart came along with all her officials to try to get clearance from me to go ahead with drafting national superannuation. The main thing, they told me, was that in their view it was quite impossible to introduce the earnings-related contribution first before we launched the whole scheme. In order to substitute earnings-related contributions for flat-rate contributions vast new computers will have to be built and it will be three years before they are ready. So my main proposal for getting things moving on the pension front has collapsed ignominiously.

Sunday, October 1st
Although the Conference demonstration takes place tonight and I should have been at the N.E.C. meetings on Friday and Saturday I'm still at Prescote. The reason of course is the flu. I came back with the family on Friday and I've been upstairs sweating it out in bed ever since—listening to the wireless half asleep, watching the television we've got in our bedroom and having a very pleasant time reading Pepys. Do I really mind? No, I don't at all. After all I'm resigning from the Executive this year and so it doesn't make all that much difference whether I miss the agitations of this year's Conference or not.

[1] Sir Henry Wells was deputy chairman 1961–4 and chairman 1964–70 of the Commission for New Towns. From 1967 to 1970 he was chairman of the Land Commission.

Monday, October 2nd

After I had taken yesterday off to convalesce today we motored quietly up to Scarborough, first pausing to see the marvellous minster at Beverley and arriving at five o'clock when the first day's session was just concluding.

As soon as we'd got ourselves unpacked in our room at the Royal Hotel I went downstairs to have tea and meet people. It was clear at once that on this first day when one takes the temperature of the delegates things had gone well from the N.E.C. point of view. I also learnt from Wedgy and John Silkin that at the weekend, when the Executive prepares for the Conference, nothing very much happened. Last year we took nearly five hours on the Sunday afternoon to deal with all the composite resolutions. This year it was finished in just over an hour and the draft Executive statement on the Common Market was passed without discussion and with mere formal opposition by Jack Jones, Ian Mikardo and Driberg. Wedgy said there was an air of desultoriness during the Executive sittings. People wanted to get on with things quickly and there'd been very few scenes. The most amusing and interesting scene must have been when Len Williams read aloud the list of speakers and allocated the reply on the motor-car industry to Andy Cunningham, the Municipal and General Workers' delegate representative from Durham, while he gave Tony Benn some aspect of foreign trade. Tony mildly suggested that as he was the Minister responsible for the motor-car industry and not for foreign trade it should be all right for the two of them to switch. Whereupon Cunningham said, 'No, I'll do the motor-car industry,' and that was that.

The rule on the N.E.C. is that only members of the N.E.C. can reply for the Executive and that a politician replies not as Minister or Member of Parliament but as the member of the Executive selected by his colleagues. The trade unions are sensitive about this because they think it essential to mark the difference between the Parliamentary Party and the Party outside, which is represented at Conference. Anyway the net result was that Tony will be denied a chance of giving a very fine account of the achievements of the Government with regard to the motor-car industry.

As for today's business, I gather that in the morning Alice Bacon was able to win both her card votes on education with a good majority, that Tony Greenwood had a spot of bother about the sale of council houses, and that Barbara—who wound up the last debate today—got a tremendous ovation for her report on transport.

Whatever the delegates were feeling in the other hotels we in the Royal, where the Executive is all together, felt rather complacent at tea-time today, all the more so because of the gigantic press build-up about the revolt of the delegates which would take place. Fleet Street had apparently concluded that what happened at the T.U.C. Conference at Brighton must be repeated in the Labour Party Conference. There had been a large majority against any support for the Government's prices and incomes policy. They'd snubbed the

Government decisively. Now that much the same people were meeting a few weeks later at Scarborough, weren't they bound to do the same thing? And wouldn't there also be a great left-wing revolt on Vietnam? I'd always thought these expectations a mistake and I'd rightly guessed that Walthamstow and Cambridge would put the delegates from the constituencies up against the difficulty that to attack the Government would be suicidal. I thought it would be an uneasy, unhappy Conference, but not impossible, and that we would get away with most of the votes, though perhaps not on prices and incomes. Everything that happened this first day confirmed it.

Hearing that the new draft of the Prime Minister's speech was nearly ready I went downstairs to his room. Just as I was being greeted by Marcia he came in in his shirtsleeves—rather podgy in his grey flannels and white shirt—and told me that this speech would be the best that he'd ever delivered. He would like me to come back and see the finished draft. Actually I went to bed early and though I got my copy of the draft from Marcia I didn't read it until next morning.

Tuesday, October 3rd

We started with the N.E.C. election results and, as I usually do, I found myself sitting next to Barbara on the platform and she was certainly expecting to come out top. But no, this time Ian Mikardo and Tom Driberg were made number one and number two, clearly as a minor anti-Ministerial demonstration. Barbara came number three, Tony Benn number four, then Frank Allaun[1]—one of the newly-elected people—and after Tony Greenwood the second newly-elected, Joan Lestor. James Callaghan had transferred to the Treasurership where he was not in danger. The retirement of James Callaghan and myself had probably saved the life of Tony Greenwood and had brought on to the Executive two new people, neither of whom will be a tremendous force. Allaun is amiable but ineffective. Joan is a great big fine-looking girl who is not on any slate or list but is quite a left-winger and is popular because of her activities in nursery schools. So we could have had worse replacements and though in a way I was sorry to be going I wasn't racked with agonizing regrets because it didn't seem to me to be something to be agonized about.

Then we got down to an appallingly dreary debate. While it went on and on and on I began to work on Harold's speech. The draft that had been brought to me was far too long and Marcia had said Harold should cut out a fifth of it. During the debate I did some hard work subbing and editing. It wasn't a noteworthy debate though Fred Lee made a valiant contribution, by far the best speech apart from Callaghan's itself, but I didn't hear much of the anti side from Danny McGarvey[2] or Clive Jenkins. It was clear they weren't try-

---

[1] Labour M.P. for Salford East since 1955.

[2] President of the Amalgamated Society of Boilermakers, Shipwrights, Blacksmiths and Structural Workers and a member of the T.U.C. General Council since 1965.

ing to kill or even wound us, but were making a formal indictment, much more modest, flatter in key than the controversy at Blackpool last year. Conference was saying to itself, 'I wish to God, I hope to God we shall be allowed to believe in this Government.'

By the end of the morning I felt that the slow job of educating the Party rank and file and the unions to a prices and incomes policy as an essential part of any Labour Government's administration had made some progress since last year.

After lunch I talked to Harold about his speech. When I left after more than an hour I felt it had been enormously successful. He seemed to have adopted so many of my suggestions. At one point Michael Halls came in to say that George Brown was very upset because he believed that what he'd read about himself in the morning papers had come from the P.M.'s camp. Harold looked up and said sharply, 'There aren't any camps, Michael, and George ought to know it.' Apparently what had happened was that yesterday George had seen a passage in the E.E.C. Commission report in which our financial situation is extremely damagingly analysed by a Frenchman. George had taken tremendous umbrage and ordered all his Foreign Office experts to fly up to Scarborough at once. The press had reported this, along with an account of his behaviour at the agents' dance last night. Harold tried to brush it all aside and told me that George was being more crazy than usual.

This afternoon Callaghan replied to the economic debate and made the speech of the Conference. From the first moment he displayed an extraordinary assuredness as though he was completely at home with this couple of thousand people. He was able to jibe at the chairman of the National Farmers' Union for negotiating the wrong way—and to get away with it. He was able to make the Conference laugh at itself. He knew exactly how to combine good-humoured raillery, emotion and an appearance of serious statesmanship while carefully avoiding the main issues. He never discussed devaluation, he never mentioned the permanent pool of unemployment, he didn't put over a very powerful case for a prices and incomes policy but described instead a voluntary incomes policy exercised by the trade unions with some mild Government action. Conference was wanting to believe in the Labour Government and here was Callaghan giving them an excuse for believing and for getting back their faith after the inhibitions of Walthamstow. Some people say that when there's a Labour Government Conference is a hopeless sounding board. This was not true today. The confrontation of the Government with the rank and file was real but so was the delegates' desire to support us. Probably the vote would have been almost the same—the miners' vote was very largely obtained beforehand by the pit closure concessions—and the Government got just the majority they wanted and a bit more. But Jim's importance was that he asked for a vote of confidence and got it by showing himself to be completely *en rapport* with the rank and file.

This evening while I was waiting to see the final draft of the Prime Minister's speech Gerald Kaufman was telling me how successful my talk with him had been. Meanwhile I had dinner with Thomas and the old gang. In due course I was told I was wanted and found myself sitting round with Peter Shore, Marcia, Gerald Kaufman, Michael Halls and Tommy Balogh. Well, we were there from 10.30 till two in the morning and it was an interesting experience though I don't think I did the faintest good. Whereas I had cut it by a fifth at lunch-time the speech had blown itself up again since then and got longer than ever. Even worse, many of the sentences had got more complex and opaque and difficult to say. I realized that Peter and Marcia are in a special position. Peter really is allowed to write long drafts of the speech itself right at the beginning and throughout the whole process of speech construction Marcia is permitted to be perfectly beastly to him whenever she feels like it. The most valuable contribution the rest of us could make at this particular point was to boost his morale and give him pleasure as we went over it page by page. Then I slipped off to bed and said to myself that one hour and twenty minutes is far too long for a Conference speech and it would need wonderful delivery and punch to put it over.

Wednesday, October 4th

The P.M.'s speech came as the first big event after the fraternal greetings from the T.U.C. As I sat there listening I was spellbound to hear a speech on which I'd worked so hard actually delivered. What struck me was the sheer punch of the delivery. Harold looked young and cheerful and vigorous and, my God, he put it across. As he went along he added many additional little touches and there was a great use of hand and expression. I would say he added 30 per cent at least to the quality of the speech we had worked at. I think he deserved more than the minute's ovation he got. After all, Jim Callaghan had been replying to a debate and that is what Conference likes and that is what it's relatively easy for an N.E.C. member to do. But Harold had to make an oration cold without any previous debate and that was an astonishing achievement. There was no doubt that these two speeches have absolutely transformed the Government's relations with the Party. Whether they've had the same impact on the country outside is slightly more doubtful but I shall be surprised if they haven't.

After that came foreign affairs—a messy debate with hardly any discussion of Vietnam or Greece. George Brown had time for a very short reply and he was not at his best, but I must say I thought that on Vietnam he would lose by a far bigger majority. The Government were lucky to get away with it as well as they did here. But a hostile vote at Conference could have been a great advantage inside the Cabinet.

After lunch I stayed in the hotel to work away at my own speech. I was only doing a short reply on social security tomorrow afternoon. But if you're an old Conference hand a speech you have to deliver dominates your thinking and also your emotions. Of course it was tricky because I had to speak with Judith, the new Minister, on the one side, and on the other Peggy Herbison, who as an ex-Minister would be ready to attack me from the floor. Peggy came to lunch with me today and she had obviously heard rumours from the Ministry of the idea Judith and I had discussed for extending national insurance cover to such things as physical disability or a broken home. At one point in the discussion she blankly said, 'I hope you won't do that. If you do I shall attack you.' After she'd left I had another long talk with Judith and then I sat down to prepare the speech almost paragraph by paragraph. I couldn't, of course, describe any details of national superannuation because they weren't worked out. What I had to do was to bring it back right into the centre of politics and to knock out any idea of a means test so as to help in the battle against the Chancellor on family allowances.

This evening at the Royal I had to switch my mind to Lords reform. On and off throughout the day I'd been telephoning and discussing with Freddy Ward in London the new Annex 2 to be attached to our Cabinet Paper with a model of the proposed two-tier scheme. A hopeless draft had arrived yesterday and I'd wasted a lot of time trying to redictate it over the phone. Today Eddie Shackleton arrived with a completely new redraft and we gathered in Frank Longford's room. There were the Lord Chancellor, the Lord Privy Seal, the Home Secretary, the Secretary of State for Education, Eddie Shackleton, myself and Freddy Ward. Only a glance was needed to see that Eddie had delivered the goods. It was a decent paper. The first half I had redictated had made some difference but the real job had been done by Eddie and Freddy, who was squeaking and protesting with a bad cold. We didn't take long to get it in a form for the Lord Chancellor and the Lord Privy Seal to take back to London and get ready for circulation.

Thursday, October 5th
I got cold feet about my speech and began to work away desperately. I also got Judith over and for the first half of the Common Market debate we were wasting our time trying to improve it. I had now heard that there might be five composite motions[1] and so instead of a general debate there would be a string of movers and seconders. I got down to the Common Market debate in time to hear Eric Heffer make a jolly good speech and George Brown reply in an unexciting but sensible way. The vote for the Government was rather bigger than we expected with a two to one mandate for its attitude to the Market.

Back to a quick lunch because I had to be down at two o'clock for the start of the debate on social security. There was nobody there but by ten past two the moving of the composites had started and, with Peggy and Judith sitting beside me, I listened to what in the circumstances was really a jolly

---

[1] Motions amalgamating similar resolutions proposed by various trade unions or constituency Labour Parties.

good debate. My only difficulty was that I was told we had to stop punctually at 3.15 not at 3.30, to leave fifteen minutes to clear the hall, so I had five minutes less than the twenty I had asked for. This was probably a good thing since it forced me to speak pretty well impromptu but within the structure I'd laid down. It was a competent speech, vigorous, self-assured, intellectually stimulating but no more than that. I was pleased when I got such a warm round of applause. When I heard it, Callaghan, who was sitting next to me, said, 'That's not because of your speech but because it's you after fifteen years. It was a little tribute to a resigning member.' Of course he was right. I felt at that moment that there were very few people on the Executive who could put a complex policy across and to that extent I'm a loss to them. But it's also a loss to me because the Executive was a sphere where I was able to increase my dimensions as a Cabinet Minister. If I'd had a long political career ahead of me I should have been an utter fool to resign.

In the evening we had Pam Berry's dinner-party for our friend Dingle Foot[1] and his wife and for Tom Driberg. It was announced yesterday that Dingle is flying out to conciliate Nasser. Of course, I am not in favour of this attempt of George Brown to woo Colonel Nasser. I don't think we are in any position to do it, and I would have thought myself that our main job now would be to get out of Aden as quickly as we can and to cut our military commitments in the Persian Gulf and cease to be a Middle East power.

I tried to talk to Pam about Balmoral and the problems of the monarchy but what interested her was Harold and Marcia. She has an obsession about that; she'd had a dinner-party with Harold there for two hours at which Marcia had come in for a short time. How is one to explain the Marcia–Mary–Harold triangle to a person like Pam? Though she looks very distinguished and has lovely hairdos and dresses nicely, Marcia remains the chairman of a Labour Party ward party, just left of centre, very loyal, disliking the kind of free discussion I indulge in very often and intensely critical of anyone who criticizes Harold. Her importance to Harold is that she constantly represents the rank-and-file Party member in his discussions. The relationship between Marcia and Mary is extremely good. The whole thing is a stable relationship in which Marcia has most of the suffering. Mary, I think, has ceased to suffer. Mary really quite enjoys herself now; she quite enjoys going round, quite enjoys her success and her fame. Mrs Wilson of 'Mrs Wilson's Diary' is a great character. It is Marcia who has all the snide references, all the accusations, and who is terribly neurotic and upset, and Harold has to spend more and more hours calming and cooling her when these references are made. I tried very hard to make Pam see this and we went on talking there until we were alone in the Gourmet Dining-Room and everybody else had gone up to the I.T.N. drinks party.

[1] Sir Dingle Foot, Q.C., brother of Michael Foot and Lord Caradon (Hugh Foot), was Labour M.P. for Ipswich October 1957–70. He was Solicitor-General 1964–7 and received his knighthood in 1964.

Friday, October 6th

We had intended to get up fairly early and drive straight down to Prescote, where the Chief and his wife were to stay the night with us. It was a filthy morning and very early I was rung up to ask whether I would do a radio programme at 2.30 for the main B.B.C. Conference programme that night. I said I couldn't be bothered because I was off. Then I ran into Harold in the hall and he said that he very much wanted me to do this programme because it's a new idea, an informal discussion for reflections on the Conference. I was suitably impressed and so we changed our plans. This was quite a good thing because as an outgoing member I went down to the last debate and took part in singing the 'Red Flag' and 'Auld Lang Syne' and then had a quick lunch with Tam Dalyell before I started the recording. They treated it very much as my swansong and kept on asking me why I was resigning, and it was a long time before we got on to the questions I wanted to raise about the morale of the Party and why it was losing its soul.

I only hope I did a decent job before we got into the car and drove down through York and across from the A1 to the M1 and reached Prescote at seven in the evening to find those enormous great children standing outside the door waiting for us at dusk and jumping into the car, where Patrick got his birthday present of a wrist-watch and his *Sherlock Holmes* while Anne unpacked his punchball inside. It was all very nice indeed. It was also nice to have John and Rosamund Silkin but at dinner this evening I had a row with him about lawyers, one of my worst subjects. I must stop myself ever talking to Elizabeth Young about nuclear warfare.[1] I must stop myself ever talking again about lawyers to the Chief Whip.

Sunday, October 8th

John and Rosamund went off early yesterday and I had an afternoon's wooding. Now the bell has gone for breakfast. We must dedicate today to organizing Patrick's postponed birthday party for fourteen boys.

Monday, October 9th

I had insisted on Tuesday for my Balmoral trip because I'd assumed that the Monday after Conference would be crammed full of Cabinet business. Actually today was the day when the Prime Minister was taking the chair at N.E.D.C. as part of his new job of running D.E.A. The Committees were all postponed till Tuesday. I decided to get hold of Burke Trend, back from his holiday in Montreal, and establish the new Ministerial Committee on publicity. I saw him just before lunch and he told me everything was in order as he had checked with the Prime Minister and the official notice appointing the Committee would go out later this week. Chairman—Lord President.

---

[1] Wife of Lord Kennett (Wayland Young) and joint author, with her husband, of several books on nuclear warfare and disarmament.

Members—First Secretary, Economic Secretary, Chief Whip and attached to it the normal official committee. All in charge of the co-ordination of home publicity. Now that I've got this after more than a year's struggle against Harold and Trevor Lloyd-Hughes, what can be achieved by it? Certainly we can co-ordinate the advertising campaigns of the Departments, we can look at the provision for a monitoring survey of television, we can prepare a campaign to put over the prices and incomes policy as Peter Shore is demanding. Whether we can go beyond this and I can use my position as I did during the war in order to influence policy is very doubtful. The membership of the Committee is favourable but everything really depends on the Prime Minister's attitude. I know I would not have got this Committee unless I'd struck while the iron was hot in the aftermath of Walthamstow.

One thing I picked up from Burke was that Roy Jenkins will be in America next Thursday when the Cabinet has its crucial meeting on Lords reform. This afternoon I got terribly scared. I rang up Barbara but she had a cold and couldn't see me and then I began to work round on various people, including Fred Peart, and made sure that Eddie was talking again to his old friend Denis Healey.

After that I went to see Eirene White about Alfred Gollin—an American historian who I think is enormously gifted and who wrote a wonderful book on the relationship between Garvin of the *Observer* and the Conservative Opposition during the battleship controversy of the early 1900s.[1] He'd written to me saying that for his next study he wanted access to Tom Jones's diaries, and as T.J.'s daughter and executor, Eirene is the person who decides such things.[2] Because we neither of us were in a hurry she gave me a great deal of fascinating information. Her father had kept a diary throughout the period of his service in the Cabinet Secretariat and as Secretary to a succession of Prime Ministers. It was all typewritten in twelve volumes and apparently he used to dictate it to his devoted secretary or else to give her short notes from which she expanded. When the Second World War was imminent T.J. had taken these twelve volumes over to Switzerland where he found a printer at St Gallen who printed a special edition of six copies. This was done in order to secure their immortality. The least interesting part of the diary, covering the period after he left Whitehall in 1936, has already been published. Now a historian at Sussex called Middlemas has been hired by Eirene to cover the 1920s. She told me he's having great trouble with Burke who has so far refused to let him publish any of the vivid descriptions of Cabinet meetings which occur throughout the diary. Burke obviously strongly disapproves of the very idea that T.J. should have kept a diary. (It's now forbidden to civil

[1] Professor of History at the University of California since 1967 and the Official Historian of the *Observer* 1952–9. The book to which Crossman refers is *The Observer and J. L. Garvin, 1908–1914* (London: O.U.P., 1960).

[2] Tom Jones's diaries, edited by Keith Middlemas, were published as *Whitehall Diary: 1916–25* and *1926–30* (London: O.U.P., 1969); and *Ireland: 1918–25* (London: O.U.P., 1971).

servants.) He regards publication of such secrets as a disgrace to the Civil
Service.

After this the Chief and I went to make an official call on the Speaker who's
filled his vacation with official tours in Rome and other places. He seemed
much younger, less flyblown than he was before, no doubt as a result of his
marriage. We went carefully through our reform package with him. He was
obviously delighted that in future the Deputy Speaker would have the power
to give the closure on Report Stage of Bills. He was obviously reluctant to see
the Clerks get rid of their wigs. He liked our idea for the new type of morning
sitting as really helping him and the officials of the House. He did raise one
or two difficulties about having the Finance Bill upstairs, which John Silkin
promised to look at and which made me wonder a little uneasily whether
Freddie Warren is such a perfect civil servant as we all assume him to be.

Then it was time to go to King's Cross for the night train to Aberdeen. I
dined on it with Leigh, who is Agnew's number two and who turned out to
have been in code-breaking at Bletchley where my Anne spent the war.[1] He's
an amiable, silly man from whose company I soon retired to read the
new volume of Macmillan's autobiography, which I'd agreed to review for
Encounter.[2]

Tuesday, October 10th

One arrives at Aberdeen at the comfortable hour of seven o'clock and I had
a long bath at the hotel before going down to breakfast. Then Elwyn Jones
and Eddie Shackleton came in from a later train. It was a morning as lovely
as on my last visit to Balmoral a year ago. This time, forewarned, I'd taken
tremendous trouble with Martin Charteris, the Queen's Assistant Secretary,
who has promised to spend the afternoon walking me round the estate. And
we'd real luck for that walk, because it had been a drenching day yesterday
and now there was a pale blue sky with clouds moving across constantly,
seeming to thicken and then spreading out again. A perfect autumn day.

The driver of our car was a young Welshman with whom Elwyn Jones
conversed a bit in their native language. When we got near to Balmoral we
all said we wanted to write postcards to our children whereupon Leigh told
us we couldn't do that because we had to get there by 11.15. Under pressure
however he admitted that the Council was at 12.30. Since the Lord President
wasn't just going to sit down in the equerry's quarters and wait we got out
and picked our postcards, wrote them and sent them off before proceeding
further.

Martin Charteris was at the front of the house waiting to take us round to
the equerry's entrance at the side and there he and I had an extremely pleasant
talk about Palestine, where he was Chief of Army Intelligence to General
Macmillan when I was a member of the Anglo-American Commission, in

---

[1] Neville Leigh, Deputy Clerk of the Privy Council 1965–74 and, since 1974, Clerk.
[2] *The Blast of War* (London: Macmillan, 1967).

1946.[1] Then he told us what he'd laid on for the afternoon and showed us the geography of the house before taking us out for a little walk in the garden to see the autumn flowers. We learnt that there are twelve London policemen up there as well as a whole section of the London Post Office.

This week the Queen is alone, since the children are at school and the Duke is away on business. Apparently she enjoys this since what she really likes is riding. Indeed she was out riding when we arrived and we saw her return by the back entrance.

Yesterday I'd checked with No. 10 and learnt that on his recent visit Harold had discussed the Lords reform with her so I was entitled to mention that Cabinet was discussing it on Thursday. This I did in our normal talk before the Privy Council. I said I didn't quite know which way the Cabinet would react. She wanted to know why. And I said that some members of the Cabinet, like George Brown, think that socialists shouldn't handle this type of thing but I believed we could do it by agreement with the other Parties. 'Agreement,' she said. 'That will be a great feather in your cap, won't it?' And I said, 'Yes, it would be an extremely good thing.' Then she pressed the button and that was the end of my talk. In came the rest of the Privy Council and four busy men stood there for a couple of minutes while I read aloud the usual collection of bits and pieces, including the prolongation of the Seychelles Legislature. Then we moved into the next room for drinks and here she explained (she didn't of course apologize) why she was twelve minutes late for the Council. When she was furthest from the house her horse had got a stone in its foot. 'One always carries one of those penknives, doesn't one, as an instrument for taking out stones, but today was the one day I didn't have it.' Then she mentioned that the horse she was riding was a Russian horse which Bulganin gave her on his visit. 'These Russian horses,' she said, 'are very obstinate. Some weeks ago Margaret took this horse out and had gone over six bridges and at the seventh bridge it had refused, although it was exactly like the others. It just wouldn't budge.' Hours later the rest of the family had gone out and found Margaret and the horse standing by the bridge with the horse still mutinous.

Over lunch I started to discuss the Philby story, which had dominated all the Sunday papers, and asked whether she has read it. She said, 'No, she didn't read that kind of thing.' I was suddenly aware that this was not a subject which we ought to discuss.[2]

When we finished lunch she shook my hand, she was off and that was that, and we were left to have our afternoon tea with the equerries.

The afternoon was absolutely lovely. Martin Charteris had planned a

[1] Sir Martin Charteris, Assistant Private Secretary to the Queen 1952–72 and, since 1972, Private Secretary and Keeper of Her Majesty's Archives.

[2] Kim Philby, a former Foreign Office man who had warned the two agents Guy Burgess and Donald Maclean that they were about to be arrested in 1951, had himself fled to Moscow in 1963. This had been the subject of two articles which revealed that for many years he had himself been a Soviet agent, recruited before the war. See p. 546.

magnificent ride around the estate in the Queen's great big estate car. We climbed up through the deer forest at the back to a waterfall with a little bridge built over it by Queen Victoria. The paths there, we were told, had been kept up by three whole-time gardeners, but they were getting a bit decrepit now. How we climbed towards the River Dee! I observed the usual problem. It's difficult to combine a deer forest for stalking with serious tree planting since the deer eat all the young trees unless they're enclosed with enormously expensive fences. And of course the erection of the fences takes all the profit out of the trees.

After a quick tea we were off on the afternoon flight from Aberdeen airport since I had changed my mind that morning and decided to go back to London early by air. I had to have a talk with Frank Longford and Eddie about the preparations for Thursday's Cabinet meeting. The plane took off at 6.35 and we were in La Rève—a little resturant in the King's Road, Chelsea, which Frank likes—by 8.45, which is pretty good going. It was really an excellent evening. Eddie was being driven frantic by his working party, which is far too full of officials who want nothing to be done. He also has to contend with his Chief Whip, Frank Beswick, who, as I had suspected, was proving a man with a chip on his shoulder, all the time worrying about his new status and being thoroughly difficult about reform.

We decided that the first thing to do was to get the Prime Minister to agree to the size and composition of the delegation to negotiate with the other Parties and work out our plan. It should consist of three from the House of Lords (Gerald Gardiner, Frank Longford and Eddie Shackleton) and two from the House of Commons (myself and Roy Jenkins, or alternatively Michael Stewart, if Harold insisted on that). Alas, we should have to keep John Silkin out in order to keep Frank Beswick out. As soon as this delegation had been set up Harold should give instructions to wind up the Ministerial Committee and the official committee so that we could start again and get the work done by a selected team of politicians and officials. When all this had been agreed Frank said that he thought that I should lead the delegation. I must say this was very good of him because as Leader of the House he would naturally like to lead it himself. Considering how passionate he is about this and how much he knows and how little I know, he has shown an astonishing power to put his personal feelings behind him and a real care for the cause we all have at heart.

Frank and Eddie went on to a party at Lord Melchett's. I went back to lie in bed and reflect on Balmoral. And I thought more and more about one strange episode in the car as we drove back to the airport. It had been such a nice day that Elwyn Jones said to Leigh, 'I should like to write the Queen a bread-and-butter letter.' Leigh said, 'Well, of course, she doesn't like you to write just to the Private Secretary and ask him to tell her how much you enjoyed it. If you write she likes you to write personally to her.' 'That's just what I want to do,' said Elwyn Jones. 'But how do I address her?' Leigh said, 'It's so complicated I'll have to write it down.' This is what he wrote down. I have the bit of paper beside me. 'Letter to the Queen. This should begin "Madam, with my humble duty", continue with what you wish to say. And end "I am, Madam, your Majesty's most humble and obedient subject". The envelope should be addressed to the Queen at Buckingham Palace and bear your initials at the bottom right-hand corner.'

When Elwyn read this he said, 'I can't write a decent bread-and-butter letter enclosed in those appalling formalities. Do I really have to?' 'Of course,' said Leigh. 'You couldn't write anything different from that. That's what she has to get from anybody who writes to her, however personally, including one of her Ministers.' I also reflected on the absurd waste of time to which we had been subjected that day. If I were staying on for a further year (which I sincerely hope I'm not) I would make every effort to do away with it. She could have the pleasant old-fashioned Privy Council once or twice a year as an informal occasion with drinks served afterwards and then for the rest she and the Lord President could sign things together or there could be some other formal method of approval.

Wednesday, October 11th

All the papers are dominated by a remarkable report on the brain-drain, which has been produced by a group of scientists for the Ministry of Technology. Of course Fleet Street has used it to add to the general depression about Britain being the kind of terrible place one ought to emigrate from. As a nation we do revel in our gloom. Only one paper, the *Financial Times*, pointed out that the brain-drain from Switzerland and indeed from the whole of Western Europe was at least as great as ours. Whereas we can compensate for our brain-drain to America by the brain-drain to England from Australia, New Zealand and Canada, there is no such compensation for countries like Switzerland, France and Germany. Perhaps when we get our new Publicity Committee going we can do something about this one-sided treatment which just adds to the general depression.

At Cabinet we started with an hour's discussion on the E.E.C. Commission's report—which stated so harshly that our financial position made us unsuitable for membership of the Common Market. George Brown, before his appalling outbursts at Conference, had jumped to the assumption that this passage had been written and inspired by the French. But Denis Healey and Tony Crosland both pointed out how dangerous this assumption was. It's not only the French, they said, who hold this view about the weakness of the British economy. Most of the Six feel just in the same way. The Prime Minister did everything to protect George from criticism and it's clear that the two of them were covering up and trying to conceal something from the rest of us. What was that something? Chalfont has been active in Brussels, making a number of speeches saying that we don't claim to have any special relationship with America and certainly wouldn't do so if we got into the

Market. Are Harold and George still desperately trying to curry favour and get in at any price or are they, as Tommy Balogh believes, willing to accept a period of association when we're on trial? I've seen no evidence of this but I record Tommy's view for what it's worth. Anyway, Barbara pressed them, Fred Peart pressed them, Denis pressed them, I pressed them, but they were dumb about their intentions.

We then turned to the Middle East and George Brown made a short statement. The P.M. repeated what he'd said the week before about the unusual influence certain members of the Cabinet exert in Israel. He urged those of us who could do so to use our influence in persuading the Israelis to withdraw 25 miles north from the Canal. He told us that we should remind the Israelis that, as the result of what she'd tried to do for Israel, Britain had lost tremendously. We're in fact losing £20 million a month. The Israelis should remember what price we were now paying for standing by them.

I didn't know that at O.P.D. on Tuesday, when I was at Balmoral, the speeches which Ted Short and I were to deliver at the celebrations of the Balfour Declaration had been raised and discussed at great length, and I replied to Harold rather abruptly. 'I'm afraid, Prime Minister, there's nothing the Israelis have to be grateful to us for. Frankly, I can't see any connection between the things we discussed about the opening of the Strait of Tiran and the Israelis withdrawing 25 miles from the Canal. I'm not prepared to say that the Israelis ought to do this as a return to us for our help to them. They don't feel we've done anything for them. Everything they've gained they've got by winning wars, breaking treaties and affronting the United Nations. It's terribly dangerous but it's their way of life.' George Brown interrupted to say that he hoped I didn't advocate this kind of thing in my talks with the Israelis. 'Of course I don't,' I said. 'I'm a dove not a hawk, but it's a fact about their history which largely determines their policy. They have so far won three wars. In the first they fought against us and the armies we armed. In the second war we encumbered them by our presence and afterwards bitched them by a double-cross. As soon as the third war broke out we got ourselves out of the way and didn't do actual harm. The only possible reason the Israelis should leave the Canal is in their own interest. There's nothing we can give them in return for leaving the Canal—except of course direct negotiations with the Arab states. Until they get that I predict they will stay at the Canal.'

I realized that the only thing I achieved by talking like this was to make Harold as angry with me about Israel as George was himself. However that can't be avoided—more particularly since the speech I'm to deliver at Drury Lane on the Balfour Declaration has now been made much more important than the speech Ted Short is going to deliver in Israel as head of the delegation. This has been achieved by the Israelis adopting the simple device of arranging for Abba Eban, their main speaker, to speak with me in London and not with Ted Short in Tel Aviv.

The morning was mainly over when we got to the basic item on the agenda

17

—the Prorogation Speech and the Queen's Speech. That was done and when the others left I stayed behind to put to Harold the proposals on the Lords' Reform Committee Frank Pakenham, John Silkin and I had agreed the night before. Harold agreed to everything including having Roy, not Michael Stewart, as the fifth member of the delegation. Then he said, 'I hope we shall be all right tomorrow. I'm not sure we shall be with so many people away,' and he told me that Tony Crosland was off to America straight after Cabinet and I had missed him. I rushed back to my office, mobilized Freddy Ward and just caught Tony on the phone at the airport. I got him to declare himself in favour of the Bill in principle and to leave a message for the Prime Minister at No. 10. As for Barbara, who had been evading me, I went across and saw her in her room this afternoon. 'I'll support you, Barbara, on everything to do with your Transport Bill,' I said, 'if you will support me on this. This is my job in life and I can't do without it. You honestly haven't had time to read the papers but I assure you it makes sense so let's do a deal.' It worked and, as she always does, she kept her word. I also got hold of Denis Healey, who at once said, 'All right, Dick, Eddie has nobbled me already.' With those votes in my pocket I felt greatly relieved.

I felt so sure of myself that I went off that evening with Anne to see a Cuban play at the Aldwych. It was called *Criminals* and was really a successor to *Marat Sade* and produced by the same man. In a sense it was also a successor to *Waiting for Godot*. It was about three people locked up in a room, all mad, or alternatively all sane, either murderers of their parents or alternatively not murderers of their parents. Yes, it was one of those long loony plays and surprisingly I enjoyed it a great deal and didn't fall asleep once. Of course it was marvellously acted and produced but, unlike *Marat Sade*, there was more to it than sheer production.

Thursday, October 12th
This was the great Cabinet day for me. We started at 9.30, in time for Harold to go to Attlee's funeral. I don't think I mentioned that Attlee died on the Saturday after Conference and Harold insisted that he must go to the actual funeral while the rest of us would attend the memorial service in Westminster Abbey next week.[1]

The first thing to say about this Cabinet is that very few people attended. There were quite a number away—not only Tony Crosland and Roy Jenkins but also Tony Greenwood, Dick Marsh and Cledwyn Hughes. Four people, including Barbara, came in late. General Gardiner and I put the case pretty concisely and immediately George Brown and Jim Callaghan joined battle with us. Both of them struck me as extremely excited, incoherent and surprisingly ill-informed.

George made a long speech saying that our scheme was ill thought-out, and that for instance the thing that would happen would be that all these life

---

[1] He died on October 8th at the age of 84.

peers would come and vote at P.L.P. meetings, and as they had no discipline we would have undisciplined voting. He didn't seem to know that there was a Whip in the House of Lords.

Jim was equally incoherent and complained that our proposals would give the peers control of Statutory Instruments. He was apparently unaware that this is a power they now have but that we would remove.

Listening to their speeches, strong and emphatic as usual, I suddenly realized that this was the first time I had ever heard George Brown or Jim Callaghan speaking without a departmental brief. For once they were floundering in an area where they had no knowledge.

The key speeches on our side were from Peter Shore and Barbara. I had mentioned that the younger generation of Labour M.P.s were strong supporters of Lords reform and Peter underlined the point. Barbara took much the same line but was a good deal shrewder and got on to the question whether the two-tier system we were proposing was in our eyes an interim solution before we got to a wholly nominated House without any speaking peers at all or whether we regarded it as permanent, with a great extension of patronage. She'd spotted that. We had Ray Gunter and Fred Peart sharply but firmly supporting reform as inevitable, so I was quite wrong to anticipate that the proletarians would line up behind George. Indeed, it was striking that only George Thomson, though he supported us in principle but made a number of objections, lined up behind George. Tony Wedgwood Benn helped us a very great deal though he was unhappy about it and, knowing all about the Lords himself, wanted to limit our scheme. What Dick Marsh would have done I don't know but he would probably have been against it. So there it was. We had won. It was an overwhelming victory and afterwards the P.M. said to me that he was relieved we didn't win with seven or eight votes against us.

Why were George Brown and Jim Callaghan so excited? I should say their predominant motive was resentment at not being consulted. This is the only major Cabinet decision since 1964 from which they have been excluded until the last moment. We'd been working on this for six months and they hadn't known anything whatsoever. Indeed this has been one of the few Cabinet secrets which has been successfully kept. I think it might have been much wiser of Harold to bring in George Brown much earlier on.

Now that it's been before Cabinet I shall be interested to see whether the leaks start. Enormous trouble was taken to prevent leaks before this meeting. The relevant sentence has not been included in the draft Queen's Speech. We didn't circulate any papers till the day before and they were removed immediately after the meeting. No minutes will be circulated.

There was another important item this morning—the confounded Industrial Expansion Bill—which had started when Wedgy and I discussed ways and means of cutting down the number of separate Bills he wanted to present. Now the whole issue has become tremendously political because of the quarrel with the C.B.I. who were anxious that the Government will pour money into some firms and allow them to compete unfairly with others. It is an obvious objection, and if we back one firm and leave out others in the same market we shall be accused of favouritism. So we have to work out how to do it.

This morning a new difficulty emerged when Wedgy Benn said there could be no top limit for expenditure because if there were it would have to be high enough to include aircraft and with aircraft excluded the whole point of the Bill would be removed. The question of the upper limit of assistance and indeed of parliamentary control was left in the air. After the meeting Harold said to me, 'We'll have to keep watch on Wedgy. He's always letting me down.' I notice that he's extraordinarily ambivalent about a man who is one of his favourites.

Finally we got everything we wanted on the Lord Chancellor's Divorce Bill. The full details of the draft Bill are to be prepared in Gerald Gardiner's office and handed to a back-bencher to take responsibility for it. We shall apparently provide Government time whether the back-bencher wins in the ballot or not. It's moving a stage further with our new device for putting controversial legislation to the House provided that, on a free vote, the House really wants it.

I was late for a very pleasant lunch with Nicholas Davenport and Anne, at which we discussed the future of Prescote and what she should do with the very few equity holdings she still possesses.

Burke and I were alone with Harold at our weekly business meeting this afternoon. The P.M. was white with anger: having just had one libel action against a pop-singer group for circulating a fake picture of him he now learns that the *Washington Post* correspondent had published in the *International Herald Tribune* another scandalous attack on his private life.

We talked about Rhodesia and Harold suddenly said, 'There is pressure on me to settle. They're building up pressure on it. I shall have to stick it out.' I regard this as an indication that George Brown, George Thomson and Callaghan are once again trying to get us to move from our absolutely immobile position, but I very much doubt whether they will succeed with Harold in his present mood.

Friday, October 13th
I had to act quickly in order to get Lords reform moving after the Cabinet decisions. What I needed was a memorandum circulated in Whitehall. Burke, who can be very helpful when he wants, rang me up to give me the three essential points. One, that the five people who do the negotiating for the Government must also prepare the Bill; two, that the staff required, whether they are of the Home Office or of the House of Lords, must be selected by him; and three, that in any case the officials we should ask for should be Wheeler-Booth from the House of Lords and Moriarty from the Home

Office. I went through this with Gerald and the memorandum was prepared in his office. This is an interesting sample of how Whitehall works when the officials want to make it work.

At Home Affairs Committee we had a long and acid discussion about the rebuilding of Whitehall and Westminster. Bob Mellish put up the proposal from the Ministry of Works that they should be empowered to demolish the Shaw building next door to Scotland Yard, which under Leslie Martin's original plan had been left as the only building in that area to be preserved.[1] This was not very warmly received by the rest of us. We are already committed to pulling down two remarkable buildings, the Foreign Office and Richmond Terrace.[2] Before we commit ourselves to any more demolition, it seems sensible to review the whole scheme in the light of modern conditions. Leslie Martin proposes that there should be a tunnel under the House of Commons to carry a new road which would link with Horseferry Road. This seems to be as out of date as the proposal to build vast office buildings on this site which pack in like sardines the number of civil servants in the area.

Now, as in a previous committee we had knocked out the new British Museum Library scheme which had been cooking since 1951, I didn't see why we shouldn't hold this up as well and finally we got our way for two or three months' delay—but it took some doing.

After the meeting, off I went to Sussex University for a charming meeting to discuss foreign policy with the students, and then back to London ready to come down to Prescote on Saturday morning.

Sunday, October 15th

It has been a splendid weekend here. Yesterday there was a tremendous gale and bouts of drenching rain. I got soaked to the skin wooding on the island— my new occupation to try to keep my muscles a bit alive and my fat down. I sweated like a pig and came in dripping wet while the children were watching television, had my bath and read *Kidnapped* to them. Then Anne and I had a lovely evening with gramophone records.

Today the gale is over. The air is absolutely still and clear blue. And Prescote is looking at its most beautiful. It's been a successful week for me since we got Lords reform through Cabinet. On the other hand it's been a week when for the first time I've been able to appreciate the effects of the reshuffle Harold carried out when I was in the Dordogne. I'm afraid it's clear that so far from giving himself a commanding position from which he can control the whole economy he has merely assumed departmental responsibilities which ruin Peter Shore's chances of success and distract his own attention from the strategic problems.

---

[1] Sir Leslie Martin, Professor of Architecture at Cambridge University 1956–72 and a member of the Royal Fine Art Commission 1958–72.

[2] They were both eventually preserved.

This week, for example, he took the chair at N.E.D.C. and got into a row with the C.B.I. about the new Industrial Expansion Bill. Then off he went to the North-East because he is now taking an active interest in the regions. He thinks it's good publicity, but I think it's pretty bad public relations because it lowers him from Prime Ministerial to departmental level and puts him into dyarchy with Jim.

There's no doubt that Jim has come out of Conference a very big man and in the Sunday papers and the *New Statesman* this week we were back with the old theory of Jim the Crown Prince. If Harold died suddenly, Jim would succeed him because he's far above George Brown and Michael Stewart. Indeed, I think I can say that the person who could conceivably stop Jim getting right to the top would not be George Brown or Michael Stewart or Roy Jenkins or Tony Benn. If Harold died there would be a mighty anti-Jim movement and the person who might be pushed temporarily into the leadership would be myself. That is, if I wanted it in any way. But I certainly wouldn't want it. I would prefer to stay out and let Jim be P.M. if I could get to be Foreign Secretary, but that's beyond the realm of surmise.

But it's not only Harold's position that has weakened. The Government is not doing too well either because of a sudden renewal of uncertainty about sterling. The trade figures published on Thursday were extremely bad and produced the inevitable run on the pound, since they seem to confirm the E.E.C. Commission report on Britain's economic instability. This is all the more disappointing because we had such an excellent Conference. It couldn't have been better and Harold and Jim's success was overwhelming. Yet it's wearing off remarkably fast.

This afternoon our solicitor, Leslie Paisner, has been down here from London and the accountants from Banbury and Dennis Pritchett from Upper Prescote came over for a tremendous session on the future of the farm and the land. The problem is quite a simple one. When Anne's father handed it over to her on our return from our honeymoon he had failed to sell it over a period of five years for £27,000. The latest estimate shows that it's now worth at least £150,000. If Anne were to die we should have to sell half the farm to cover death duties because all the insurance is out of date. We must now decide what trusts to organize, how much we should hand over to the children and whether to go on running the farm as a private company in view of the ruinous changes in the taxation of private companies introduced by Callaghan and Kaldor.

This year we find we pay 40 per cent corporation tax and then, with income tax and surtax as well on what is distributed, we pay 80 or 90 per cent, so we have to give the whole of the profit to Pritchett because there's no other way of doing it. I often reflect on the difference it makes to me that we are now people of substance with no worries about money and this constantly accumulating capital. It certainly makes me more detached and makes me a freer agent in politics—but it also makes me enormously better acquainted with the facts of life. You may laugh, but from this farm responsibility I have learnt about growth, about investment and about tax. It's a business with a £30,000 turnover, and I have learned a tremendous lot about business management.

After a long discussion we have now come upon a brand new idea for dividing the property fairly between Anne and the children. During the course of the discussions today I realized more than ever that she and I are concerned not so much with our own economic interests as with Prescote as an entity: the unity of the house and these five hundred acres, and how to preserve it. Here we do feel a sense of obligation. I don't think it's a very powerful sense because neither of us thinks it probable that the world will go on with the same values and laws for the next twenty or thirty years so that all the plans we now work out will come true. Neither of us has really thought we deserved to own Prescote and we have felt obliged to continue to manage it on lines which Anne's father would have liked. But what's changed the situation has been the enormous increase in the value of the property. I would have had no notion in my old radical socialist days that the kind of motive would operate among property owners and wealthy people which prompted our decisions this afternoon. I must add in fairness that it has a profound effect upon my attitude to the Government. I'm now very doubtful whether the fiscal changes introduced by Jim Callaghan with the assistance of Nicky Kaldor have not been clumsy, academic interventions in the economy. I'm becoming more and more uneasy about the fact that people like Harold are so confident they can intervene in the economy by means of investment allowances and be sure that this will stimulate private investment. The evidence at Prescote gives no support for this view. I'm still very doubtful about the new Industrial Expansion Bill which Wedgy is working out with Harold because I feel that such a Bill will enable him to take decisions which neither he nor his civil servants are really capable of taking. As someone who helps to run a small farming business, I can see rather more clearly the dangers of the kind of intervention by amateurs advised by civil servants which Harold believes in so much.

I must finish the diary here because this evening we are having one of our rare outings—motoring across to Oxford to see the film of *Dr Faustus* at the cinema and dining afterwards with Robert Maxwell at a party with Richard Burton and Elizabeth Taylor.

The Steering Committee on Economic Policy that met on Monday 16th had two immediate problems to face. One was the threat by the railwaymen's leaders to call a strike provoked by the introduction of new labour-saving equipment, and by disputes between the N.U.R. and ASLEF. *On December 3rd* ASLEF *did call for a work to rule but it was settled after a few days. Not so the other threat, a long unofficial strike by the dockers in London's Royal group of docks and in Liverpool. Their strike action, lasting six weeks altogether, added to the*

October trade deficit, which reached £162 million. At least £100 million of exports were delayed, and the raising of bank rate from 5½ to 6 per cent on October 19th and on November 9th to 6½ per cent was a symptom of sterling's profound weakness.

Monday, October 16th

I'll start with what happened at Oxford last night. When we got to the cinema we ran into the Lord Mayor, Frank Pickstock, the old W.E.A. organizer, and his wife, and were pushed up into the gallery, which was almost completely empty, and there we saw Peggy Jay and Douglas seated at the other end. We sat there for a full hour waiting for Quintin Hogg and his wife, who had been invited to the reception for the Duchess of Kent and Richard Burton and his wife. I can't help feeling a bit peeved at the contrast between the treatment accorded to the present Labour Lord President and the Conservative ex-Lord President of the Council. The film itself was quite appalling. Afterwards came the supper, where we ran into Bob Maxwell. He was terribly upset because he hadn't got a ticket for his wife but only for himself. However, it didn't deter him from fighting valiantly on our behalf. He fought his way through the crowd, got in almost first and found a table for us all. There I was sitting beside Senator Scott of Pennsylvania,[1] who is over here lecturing on the American political experience, and on the other side of me I had Peggy Jay. It was enough of a victory to have got ourselves into the dining-room and to be sitting down in front of a dinner. Soon Anne and I slipped off back home, she taking great care about the new breathalyser law which has started this week.[2]

This, by the way, has been an enormous success and a great triumph for Barbara Castle. It is producing consternation and the takings at country pubs are down by a third, more at the weekend, which only proves that people were drinking too much and so endangering their driving. This is something Barbara's put over with her own unique verve and energy. It's something really radical and she has done extremely well by us.

Back in London this morning I started with S.E.P. where we were given a report on unemployment and trade which both indicate that though there's a slight upswing we are still on a miserable tightrope. Then we were given a report on the danger of a dock strike coinciding with the railway strike and there were some signs that there would be pressure on Cabinet to be soft on the railwaymen. I believe, on the contrary, that we must be in favour of the

---

[1] Hugh Scott, Senator from Pennsylvania since 1959.

[2] On October 9th it became an offence, under the 1966 Road Traffic Act, to drive with more than a specified quantity of alcohol in the blood stream, even if the driver's capabilities were unimpaired. The police were able to request motorists involved in accidents or suspected of a motoring offence, to take a 'breathalyser' test. If crystals in a plastic bag into which motorists blew changed colour, the driver was then required to take a blood or urine test. Penalties were severe and the effect was immediate as road accidents fell significantly.

Board and absolutely tough. It is really heartbreaking that this strike comes
at a time when Barbara is prepared to give real help to the railways by imposing C-licences on road transport and making the road-hauliers prove that
they move freight more efficiently before they are given a licence. But we
were all agreed that if we're going to help the railways in this way the reliability of the service they provide must be made credible over a test period.
The guards have already stopped the wonderful new line from Euston to
Liverpool, Manchester and Birmingham and the strike is absolutely disastrous. The new Midland services were just setting a new standard for the railways and beginning to win back some of the passengers from the airlines and
some of the freight from the roads. All this goodwill is being dissipated by the
bloody-minded behaviour of the guards and their attempt to threaten us
despite our attempt at arbitration. I supported Barbara when she said there
could be no question of conceding.

I spent the evening watching Ted Heath on *Panorama*. He was treated
just as abominably as Harold Wilson. He was shown a 20-minute film of
people saying how frightful he was and then asked to react to it. Of course
this was so outrageous that it could be regarded as grossly unfair to him and
it will have won him a great deal of goodwill from the *Panorama* audience
who had read in their *Sunday Times* lead story that only 38 per cent of the
voters still approve of the leader of the Opposition. He couldn't have wanted
a better lead-up to the Conservative Party Conference this week since this
kind of attack will compel the delegates to express their loyalty in a most
exuberant way.[1]

When the programme was over it was a pouring wet night and I decided
to have a spot of dinner at Lockets. So I walked out into Vincent Square
to find I had left my keys in my red box in the study. It was terribly wet and
I trotted up Marsham Court and sat in Lockets not too upset because I knew
that Tam was coming down by the night plane. I stayed there eating an
excellent meal and reading until 11.15, when I went back home and found
that Tam wasn't there and I was still locked out in the driving rain. This has
happened to me before so I went next door to No. 10 thinking I would have
to walk along the terrace and break the glass into my bedroom. I couldn't
get any response when I rang the bell and I kicked the door whereupon it
opened. I walked in and found on the ground floor two comfy rooms, beautifully furnished, with the bedlights on and bedclothes folded back but nobody
there. I walked upstairs and found two more rooms in the same well-furnished
condition. Then I opened the window on to the terrace, turned right and
walked along, pressed my french window, found it wasn't latched and walked
into my bedroom—only to find that the door handle had come off on the far
side and I couldn't get out for twenty minutes. It was such a nice story that
I enjoyed experiencing it.

[1] The Conservative Party Conference was to be at Brighton from October 18th to 21st.
17*

Tuesday, October 17th

Gardiner, Shackleton, Silkin and I had agreed that we must tackle Roy Jenkins, who was just back from a week's tour in America studying drug addiction. Directly we'd finished a brief Legislation Committee, we walked round to the Home Office and found him obviously happy to see us. We got down to briefing him on what had happened at Cabinet and the arrangements we were setting up. He pointed out that we'd overlooked one thing—the possible effects of the Abortion Bill on the relations between Lords and Commons. We are now in the autumn over-spill and at the end of next week we shall finish the Session. But we may find ourselves in a Lords–Commons crisis if the peers don't pass the amendments we require on the very last day. Then we would have to threaten to use the Parliament Act. Of course he was quite right that at all costs we must avoid this happening. In order to do this we must tell the leader of the Opposition and of the Liberal Party of our plan to have all-party talks. We had planned to tell them the news on the day before the Queen's Speech but, as Roy pointed out, we must now tell them two days earlier because Wednesday evening will bring the crucial abortion debate and we don't want a lot of speeches from the Opposition. So we've agreed to brief them earlier and to brief the press.

Roy also agreed that Moriarty, who'd just come back to the Home Office from four years in the Cabinet Office, should be seconded to work with Wheeler-Booth on Lords reform.

That evening I had to go north to the Gorton by-election, which was caused by the death of Konni Zilliacus. Gorton is not unlike Walthamstow and we were all afraid that it might provide us with another similar débâcle in Manchester. In 1964 Zilli's majority had shrunk to 4,430 and now our candidate was being opposed by young Winston Churchill.[1] I was relieved to hear that he was a tough local schoolmaster and not Gerald Kaufman, who had got his name on to the short list.[2] Before I left I'd had a row with my Private Office when I discovered I was due to fly back that night. I said I preferred taking the midnight sleeper in order to see something of the local people after my speech. When I got there I found, as I feared, that the agent was furious that I wasn't staying and that in order to catch the aeroplane I'd have to go off in the middle of the meeting. However I'd heard enough to be very impressed by the local candidate, a reliable headmaster of a local school, an urban district councillor—indeed the only kind of chap who could regain the confidence which had been largely lost by Zilliacus. But he was having a tough time, not only because of young Winston but because a Liberal and a Communist are also against him. I made my speech in one of those huge working-men's clubs which dominate the suburbs of Manchester. The people

---

[1] Winston Churchill was eventually elected Conservative M.P. for Stretford, Lancashire, in 1970.

[2] Kenneth Marks held the seat at Gorton (Manchester) but Labour's majority was cut from 8,308 to 577. He was re-elected in 1974.

who thought the electorate were lethargic were quite wrong. The moment I'd finished people were leaping up saying they wanted to ask questions of the Minister. I managed to answer quite a number but then I had to go and catch my plane. It was quite clear it was futile allowing Ministers to arrive and depart in this way because it doesn't help the candidate at all. I should say that Gorton will be touch and go and it'll be fine if we can hold it. If we do, it's because we've got the ideal candidate.

Wednesday, October 18th

Another S.E.P. to consider two enormous White Papers—one on the railways and the other on fuel policy.[1] True, on the second issue we had already agreed on the main policy, including pit closures, but the presentation of the policy with an enormous background of figures and statistics in order to justify the priority given to gas and nuclear energy was of the greatest importance to our relations with the miners. So was the section which tried to justify our only having a twopence a gallon tax on oil—not nearly enough to please the miners. But the subject of the second White Paper—the pricing policy of the nationalized industries—was also a key issue. And yet when we got down to it even the Prime Minister hadn't read them through carefully —though he'd been briefed by Burke—and, if Harold hadn't, nobody had except the Lord President. As Tony Crosland said to me that afternoon when he sat next to me, 'Well, Dick, you're the only person who'd read the papers and you didn't get much thanks for it.' Once again one sees the difficulties of modern government.

What had happened in both cases was that the officials of all the Departments concerned had agreed on the texts, the Ministers had been told that the officials had agreed on the texts and the Ministers were therefore bound by the official agreement. Therefore the White Papers were written totally by officials, and no Minister had taken any active part in their drafting. And bluntly obvious it was.

So the strategy of the Government in the public sector is being dictated now by the lowest common denominator of official opinion, not by the Minister taking charge of the Department and shaping the White Paper for himself. I asked why the Ministry had both fixed on the twopence a gallon oil tax and even so promised to reduce it and I was told that the reason for this couldn't be published in a White Paper. Apparently, the calculation is based on the assumption that all Middle Eastern oil will be nationalized and 75 per cent added to the price. Even so oil will be two or three times cheaper than coal. So the twopence a gallon is no longer a penalty on oil to help the coal industry. It is merely £70 million a year of revenue that the Chancellor is getting.

I finally managed to get the passage which mentions the desirability of

---

[1] *Railway Policy* (Cmnd. 3439) and *Fuel Policy* (Cmnd. 3438), published on November 14th.

reducing the twopence a gallon tax removed from the White Paper. I did this by the device of telling the Chancellor that he's supposed not to like being committed in advance to his budget. How then could he agree in advance to be committed to a reduction in the fuel tax? I also tried to persuade the Minister that he really should emphasize when he's quoting all these highly tentative statistics that the calculations aren't all that hard, and may be complete nonsense within eighteen months.

The paper on the nationalized industries was far more disconcerting. This is a paper which the Chancellor has been struggling to produce, really revising the 1961 decision that the nationalized industries should be run strictly commercially, and defining where prices were to be fixed by purely financial targets and where they were to be socially costed. We had exactly twenty minutes to consider it. Having rung Harold beforehand and prepared a number of amendments with Tommy I insisted on tabling them, much to the annoyance of my colleagues. As I got up from the table I said to Callaghan, 'This is a very poor paper.' 'What does it matter?' he said. 'It's only read by a few dons and experts.' 'Well I'm one don,' I said, and he replied, 'You're a don who knows nothing about the subject. Personally as Chancellor I couldn't care less. I take no responsibility and I took no part in composing it.' Here was a key issue of socialist strategy and the Chancellor of the Exchequer washes his hands of it. I suspect that the number of Ministers who take a formative role in drafting important documents and White Papers in Conservative Governments is quite considerable. I would have hoped that a Labour Government would have even more and yet on the evidence after three years we have far less influence.

I'd invited to lunch a fellow called George Jones from L.S.E.,[1] who'd been looking into the Hansard Society, which was founded by Stephen King-Hall[2] in 1944 to popularize Parliament and which, thanks to his personality, had collected sufficient funds from big industrialists to keep the Society going and to finance its quarterly, *Parliamentary Affairs*, for which the editor receives some £2,500 a year. It seems to me a thoroughly worthy organization and the quarterly isn't half bad. But now that Stephen King-Hall has died it's been running downhill and Jones came to tell me that various people wanted to take it over and turn it into a research organization. Suddenly it became clear to me that this was something we in the House of Commons could use. We have no public relations officer for the Commons. Here is a society which we could take over and finance and whose journal we could edit and we could

[1] Lecturer and, subsequently, Reader in Political Science at the L.S.E. He was joint author, with Bernard Donoughue, of *Herbert Morrison: Portrait of a Politician* (London: Weidenfeld & Nicolson, 1973).

[2] Commander Stephen King-Hall (knighted 1954) had been Independent Labour M.P. for Ormskirk, Lancashire, 1939–44. In 1936 he had founded the *King-Hall Newsletter*, a broadsheet of current events and world affairs, and in 1944 he founded the Hansard Society for Parliamentary Government. He was chairman of the Society's Council 1944–62 and president from 1963 until his death in June 1966, the year in which he was made a life peer.

use the whole thing as our public relations department, putting it on a par with the Commonwealth Parliamentary Association. This seems to me an idea well worth taking seriously.[1]

The afternoon was consumed by an enormous meeting of O.P.D. on Rhodesia. In advance we'd received a great wad of paper in our red boxes — the combined work, I suppose, of the officials in the Home Office, the Commonwealth Office, the Foreign Office, the Board of Trade and the Ministry of Overseas Development. Together they had produced an official paper listing five alternative possibilities and in characteristic official style indicating that all of them were hopeless. On top of this vast document we received a 2-page paper by George Brown and George Thomson simply saying they accepted the official paper and recommending a mild intensification of sanctions. Then right at the end, in almost the last paragraph, they added that they thought it might be worth looking again at the possibility of handing over our responsibility to the U.N.

Eighteen people were present and a lot of people had been specially called in, including the President of the Board of Trade, the Lord Chancellor, the Lord Privy Seal, the Paymaster-General, etc. After the two Georges had said virtually nothing the Prime Minister went round the table and, as nobody dared to speak, he himself made a longish speech saying that there must be no surrender but that one had to look for ways forward. He then resurrected the idea of a Royal Commission. When still nobody had anything to say he turned to the Lord President. I said, 'I'm in a minority here. I think we should stop intensifying sanctions if we think they can't have any effect. We should cut our losses and insist on looking seriously for the first time at how to hand responsibility over to the U.N. I've read some vague allusions to it in official papers but nobody's bothered to do a job on this as a practical proposal.'

Surprisingly there was quite a lot of support for this, whereupon Harold immediately called George Thomas, who'd been specially brought there as number two at the Commonwealth Office.[2] He told us that he'd just been round the African states (actually he'd been to South Africa and to the three Protectorates, which are hardly representative). His impression was that there was no great desire to intensify sanctions and therefore he wanted to support the P.M.'s proposal for a Royal Commission. I suppose it was to George Thomas that the P.M. was referring last week when he told me he was going to be under great pressure to moderate his policy. Well, it wasn't much of a pressure and there wasn't much moderation demanded. George Thomas had been deliberately brought in to say this and immediately George Wigg spoke up and said there was no question of a Royal Commission. It came in for a great deal of criticism, from the Foreign Secretary, from Denis

---

[1] See p. 729.

[2] Labour M.P. for Cardiff since 1945. He was Joint Parliamentary Under-Secretary of State at the Home Office 1964–6, Minister of State at the Welsh Office 1966–7 and at the Commonwealth Office 1967–8. From 1968 to 1970 he was Secretary of State for Wales, from 1974 to 1976 deputy chairman of Ways and Means and, since 1976, Speaker.

Healey and from me. As Denis Healey said, a Royal Commission merely gets the worst of both worlds. I had to go after this but I gather they then considered the P.M.'s attempt to increase sanctions against Portuguese oil, his oldest idea, on which he was defeated. So actually nothing was achieved.

What on earth was the point of staging this mass meeting and presenting us with all that bumf? I have the feeling that Harold wanted to present himself as desiring to intensify sanctions and then to be over-persuaded by us that he shouldn't do it.

This evening we took Tommy and Pen round to Lockets for a meal where we ran into Jeremy Thorpe and Kenneth Rose, the gossip-writer for the *Sunday Telegraph* who also writes political biography.[1] Jeremy invited us to go up to his eighth-floor flat where we had a very interesting evening. Jeremy was scintillating with his brilliant imitations and Rose was dry and calculating as they tried to exchange tittle-tattle about appointments.

Thursday, October 19th

No Cabinet because Harold has to go to Scotland on one of his D.E.A. expeditions. It was a crucial day when the Cabinet should have met. The dock strike was coming to a most ferocious hopeless climax and there seemed to be very little chance of a settlement. Simultaneously the railway strike was getting hotter.

However, there was one item of great interest at Home Affairs—the problem of the Kenya Asians.[2] Soon after we got back from the recess Roy Jenkins had come to see me in my Privy Council Office to tell me that he might urgently need a slot for legislation to deal with the problem of Kenya Asians with British passports. There are some 200,000 of them who are now threatened as a result of the black-Africa policy. This morning he put this problem to the Home Affairs Committee in a very indecisive way. I couldn't blame him for that. It's quite clear we couldn't allow some 50,000 Asians from Kenya to pour into Britain each year. On the other hand it's doubtful whether we have any legal or constitutional right to deny entry to these people from Kenya since they have British passports. This is the kind of problem which Labour Ministers discuss rationally and well. We finally agreed that Roy must of course face the possibility of this threat developing into reality and that he must work out appropriate policies and consider the practicability of legislation.

After this we had a meeting of the Emergency Committee, again under Roy's chairmanship. It was quite clear that Cabinet was prepared to go to the limit both in the docks and in the railways. If necessary we would put the soldiers in.

[1] For example, *Superior Person: A Portrait of Curzon and His Circle in Late Victorian England* (London: Weidenfeld & Nicolson, 1969).

[2] Some 500 Asians a week had been leaving Kenya for Britain after the introduction in August of new legislation making it more difficult for them to obtain work permits at home.

I then went across the river to lunch with the Archbishop[1] and the Church Commissioners at Lambeth Palace. I found a great roomful of people and one or two other politicians—Elwyn Jones, A. J. Irvine, Mallalieu.[2] But fortunately I found myself sitting near to the Archbishop and he gave us an excellent lunch—good white wine, good red wine and paté. Yes, the Church does itself well when it lunches with its Commissioners. Finally, afterwards, I had a quiet talk with him about Lords reform. 'Supposing we were to reform the Lords, Archbishop, how would you like to see it?' I asked him. We talked round it for some time and then I popped a direct question. 'I want to know about the future of the Bishops in the Lords.' 'Well, the kind of cleric in a future House of Lords would be Donald Soper, the Methodist minister, selected on his merits as a life peer. That's the way I'd like to see clerics chosen in the future.'[3] 'So you don't want a block reserved for the Church of England Bishops?' I said, to which he replied that their pastoral duties make it impossible for them to attend regularly and if they do so it may not be desirable. (I believe by this remark he meant the Bishop of Southwark, who attends regularly and is too political.)[4] I was interested by this since I hadn't thought of the line we would take.

Back in my office there was a large and futile meeting of the old Ministerial Committee on Lords reform followed by yet another meeting of our inner group. After this I had to go out to an official dinner at the Institute of Mechanical Engineers. Godfrey Agnew is always telling me that as Lord President I ought to attend public functions. On this occasion I found myself sitting between Christopher Hartley, and William Penney.[5] It was an agreeable dinner and I was all right because I hadn't got to make a speech. I got out quickly, got home and began to prepare my papers for tomorrow.

Friday, October 20th
I started with half an hour with Judith before a meeting of our Pensions Committee at which I was in the Chair. I had told Michael Stewart I wasn't prepared to resign the chairmanship, but that he could put it to the Prime

---

[1] The Rt. Rev. and Rt. Hon. Michael Ramsey, Archbishop of Canterbury 1962–74. He became a life peer on his retirement.

[2] Arthur Irvine, Labour M.P. for Edge Hill (Liverpool) since 1947 and Solicitor-General 1967–70. J. P. Mallalieu, Labour M.P. for Huddersfield since 1945. He was Under-Secretary of State for Defence (R.N.) 1964–6 and Minister 1966–7. He was Minister of State at the Board of Trade 1967–8 and at the Ministry of Technology 1968–9.

[3] Donald Soper had been superintendent of the West London Mission, Kingsway Hall, since 1936 and president of the Methodist Conference since 1953. He became a life peer in 1965.

[4] Mervyn Stockwood, Bishop of Southwark since 1959.

[5] Air Marshal Sir Christopher Hartley was Controller of Aircraft, Ministry of Aviation and Ministry of Technology from 1966 to 1971, when he retired. Since 1970 he has been Deputy Chairman of the British Hovercraft Corporation. Sir William Penney was deputy chairman of the Atomic Energy Authority 1961–4 and its chairman 1964–7. He became a life peer in 1967 and from 1967 to 1973 was Rector of the Imperial College of Science and Technology.

Minister, to which Michael had quietly written to me saying that he didn't intend to do so. This taught me a lesson. Whenever Ministers ask one to do things the best effective negative is to refer them to the P.M. A few weeks ago Roy Jenkins wrote me a long minute to say that he couldn't permit a pre-legislation committee on privacy because it would involve telephone bugging, a subject he didn't want discussed. I said he could raise it with the Prime Minister and got a rapid disavowal of Roy. In our Cabinet system decisions are decisions are decisions. Once the decision has been recorded in the Cabinet minutes Ministers may try to make you change your mind, but if you're firm they're very reluctant to appeal to the P.M.

At the Pensions Committee there was an interesting little scene when the officials said they were now ready to ask me to authorize technical discussions on the appallingly intricate subject of contracting-out. Under the old Tory scheme it was relatively easy to arrange that employers who were prepared to provide an improved pension themselves could contract out of the Government scheme. But we are introducing an enormously improved Government scheme which will require an enormous improvement in any private pension scheme except for a very few very good ones. So this is an absolutely crucial question between the Minister and the insurance industry. I began to question the officials, therefore, on the nature of these technical discussions. Would they, for example, be concerned with the ceiling to which the pensions would be permitted to rise? They said yes, they would. And after a brief examination I found that my officials had made up their minds that contracting out was impossible and that they wanted a scheme which didn't include it. So they were going to talk to the industry along lines which would make them break off negotiations. Now this is the kind of thing which good officials (and I think Clifford Jarrett, the Permanent Secretary of the Ministry of Social Security, is a good official) are often tempted to do. A Department makes up its departmental mind and then it decides how to bring the Cabinet Committee to accept a decision it's already decided for itself. That's what the officials were doing that morning. As chairman my job was to stop them. So I asked them only one more question. How long will these technical conversations last? And when they'd replied six months I said that we can't possibly hold things up for six months. We must carry on with the scheme and start our Ministerial negotiations.

Back in my room I found Eddie Shackleton and Burke Trend waiting to discuss practical arrangements for the meetings of our Lords Reform Committee. So far we've got agreement that a unit consisting of two men, Moriarty and Wheeler-Booth, should work inside the Home Office. But the Minister who is going to be in charge of them and do all the detailed work with them is not Roy Jenkins but Eddie Shackleton. How can we get Eddie Shackleton officially involved? Suddenly I had a bright idea. 'Let's get the Prime Minister to appoint Eddie Shackleton,' I said, 'Minister of State for this one Bill responsible to the Home Secretary.' Within a few minutes Burke had worked out the formula and I was able to rush off to catch Jenkins and his Permanent Secretary, Philip Allen, to confirm the arrangement with them.[1] After lunch I went round to the Lord Chancellor and got his signature as well. So Eddie and I had achieved a set-up which may possibly work. It's only after three years as a Minister working in Whitehall that I'm beginning to realize of what tremendous importance these procedural devices are.

The Emergency Committee late this morning was enormously important but decided nothing which hadn't been decided before. By this time we were all waiting for the Royal Proclamation and I had made arrangements for a Privy Council at 12.30 on Monday for a proclamation that the troops were going into the docks and on to the railways. Today nobody raised a peep against it. Poor Barbara, who looked pale and drawn, knows that her chances of getting a fair deal for the railways depend on stopping the madness of the men pretty soon. Ray Gunter was instructed to make no kind of concession when he saw the N.U.R. on Saturday morning.

This evening I'd agreed to speak at Keele University and arranged for Molly to take me to Coventry and for Anne to pick me up there and take me on to Stoke. It was a beautiful afternoon and I went down reading my papers. When Anne and I reached Keele we found 500 young men in the main university hall and I gave them a talk rather similar to the one that I gave at Sussex University a fortnight ago—partly on the role of Britain as a declining post-imperial power and how a socialist should behave in this period, and partly on prices and incomes as the central problem. I provoked a hornets' nest of questions and right in the middle I was nearly caught out because someone had heard the news that Ray Gunter had announced the Royal Proclamation and the troops were in. 'Was that fair to the dockers?' was the question put to me. Fortunately I had the sense to say that I hadn't heard the news and managed to get out of it that way.

Sunday, October 22nd
Well, this has been quite a week. At one time it seemed as though we were being blown completely off course once again. Indeed as the week went on and it seemed almost impossible to avoid a simultaneous dock and railway strike those of us who knew about the state of the balance of payments felt pretty terrible. On Friday afternoon Thomas Balogh said to me, 'It's gone beyond repair. We're finished. There's no more to be done.' It's the kind of thing Thomas says every now and then but I must admit that on this occasion, with the Government gummed up and Harold immersed in the details of D.E.A. and therefore unable to put the blame on anyone else, things look grimmer than I have known them since July 1966. Yet yesterday afternoon

[1] Sir Philip Allen (K.C.B. 1964), Second Secretary at the Treasury 1963–6 and Permanent Under-Secretary at the Home Office 1966–72. Since 1973 he has been chairman of the Occupational Pensions Board, a member of the Security Commission and of the Royal Commission on Civil Liability and Compensation for Personal Injury. He became a life peer in 1976.

the threat of a railway strike was off and I had to see Gunter congratulating himself on his cleverness on the television. Meanwhile poor old Harold spent all night struggling in his hotel at Liverpool alongside Jack Jones and Jack Scamp but by this morning he hadn't yet got the dockers back.[1] Every day of this kind of industrial insecurity increases the danger to the pound.

I should like to throw in one other thought about last week. In America there has been an enormous demonstration of 10,000 Americans marching and protesting against the Vietnam War at Oak Ridge and then outside the Pentagon. The Vietnam War is becoming more and more a great moral issue on which depends the whole future of American leadership in the Western world. I am quite sure that in the coming months George Brown and Harold Wilson will find it more and more difficult to keep to their policy of remaining America's staunch and loyal ally and supporting the American line, against the growing moral protest of their own rank and file.

Monday, October 23rd

A special Cabinet had been called with only Rhodesia on the agenda. Harold has odd ways. O.P.D., which is two-thirds of the Cabinet, has already met and given him authority to send George Thomson out to Salisbury provided there is no change of policy. But this isn't enough: he must have Cabinet sanction as well. The discussion is nothing like as free and frank as in O.P.D. Indeed, all that really happened is that everybody sat silent while Harold made a very long speech and Barbara made an impassioned Barbara Castle reply. 'No retreat,' she cried. 'Keep hotting the sanctions up and go even further. Consider cutting off the television programmes, removing their passports, really make yourself unpleasant to these Rhodesians.' Of course there's no evidence that this kind of pin-pricking sanction will do anything but strengthen Smith's hold on Rhodesian public opinion. And after her speech I was provoked into saying so. I added that surely we were to discuss all the points she raised after George Thomson got back and that up to that point we could expect no change in policy. George Thomson has his brief; he is to have what will be almost formal talks with Smith since each side is completely without manoeuvre.

Of course it was the strike situation that was dominating our thoughts at that meeting. The railwaymen's grievances had been settled but the dockers' strike was still going on and it was by no means certain that they would go back to work on Wednesday. Gunter had had all the luck and was warmly praised. Harold had been unlucky because the chairman of the strike committee had put the recommended solution wrongly to the dockers and had failed to get their agreement. But as the strike threatened to continue we dis-

---

[1] Sir Jack Scamp, a former personnel director and known as a persuasive 'trouble-shooter'. He was seconded to the D.E.A. as Industrial Adviser 1965–6, was a director of Fairfields Shipyard in Glasgow 1967–8 and of A.E.I. 1967–72. Since 1970 he has been Associate Professor of Industrial Relations at the University of Warwick.

cussed the possibility of bringing the troops in and found it unlikely that we should ever be driven to do so.

When everybody was getting up from their seats Harold announced that he'd set up a Publicity Committee with me as chairman and three other Ministers without Portfolio as members. No one took any notice.

In the Commons this was the first day of the overspill after the summer holiday and I went and listened to Question Time to get the feel of the House —there were very few people there. It's curious how the House just starts again as though you turned on the engine of a car. Suddenly it's moving as though it had never stopped. It isn't like an organism suddenly jumping into life again but like a machine. If there were few people there it was as if they had always been there, as if the press had always been sitting up above in the gallery. I slipped out before the end of Question Time because I didn't want to stay for the Attlee commemorative speeches. I'm told they were pretty dismal and Harold was as dull as he was in his broadcast.

After this I was off to Leicester by a fast train from St Pancras. The by-election was quite a shock to me.[1] The agent there is a splendid chap called Dick Delafield, who used to be at Lincoln and who now runs the four constituencies at Leicester. Like Coventry, Leicester is a Midland city which has to be fought as a whole: it's wealthy, prosperous, and now that it's switched from its old concentration on shoes and textiles it has a very high wage standard. In fact it's an enormously active working-class city and here we face a most awkward by-election because when Herbert Bowden accepted Charles Hill's job at I.T.V. he just forgot to ask his Party's advice so that they only read the announcement in the papers. The result was fury in the Party, particularly when the by-election was fixed for November when there is virtually no Party organization in Leicester as for that matter there isn't in Coventry. But the limit was passed when the Selection Committee chose a young lawyer, Neville Sandelson,[2] because the two local worthies had fallen out of the contest. Sandelson is a very decent socialist barrister who's already fought six hopeless by-elections in different parts of the country.

As soon as I got down there Dick took me to a pub for a drink and for a frank fill-in on the situation, which he thought was as bad as at Walthamstow. Their canvassers were finding plenty of Labour voters but nearly all of them were saying they weren't coming out this time. They disliked the treatment they'd got from Herbert Bowden, now Lord Aylestone, and they also had a profound distaste for a Labour Government which seemed to be against the working man. One of the biggest blows in the by-election has been the introduction of Barbara's breathalyser. I thought it was a brilliant move but in Leicester it was regarded as an extremely unpleasant attack on working-

[1] The seat for Leicester South-West had been vacated when Herbert Bowden had gone to the Lords as Lord Aylestone. In the by-election on November 2nd Tom Boardman transformed a former Labour majority of 5,554 to a Conservative lead of 3,939.

[2] Labour M.P. for Hayes and Harlington 1971–4 and, since 1974, for Hillingdon, Hayes and Harlington. He contested eight elections and by-elections before coming to the House.

class drinkers. We are in danger of becoming known as the Government which stops what the working classes really want. The Government which introduces the breathalyser is as unpopular with motor-car drivers as the Government which stops pirate radio stations is with the younger generation who listen to pop music. Today they had another grouse about the Government—the announcement that we were going to stop coupons in cigarette cartons. When this proposal was urged by Kenneth Robinson at Home Affairs Committee I had pleaded that we should hold it back for at least twelve months after the breathalyser was introduced. But no, the Minister of Health had to make his policy announcement and he chose to do so this morning, thereby battering the poor old Leicester Labour Party with another blow.

By now it was time to go for the meeting. When we got to the huge council housing estate where it was to be held it was almost impossible to find the school and when we found that we couldn't find the entrance. We had to walk across the courtyard and through a long passage until we found a classroom with about thirty electors in it and a good many press men. To be accurate, the audience was four when I got there and when I left there were just over thirty. I had to address the four for fifty-five minutes because the candidate was out canvassing. He then spoke for forty minutes and then there was ten minutes of very ineffective questioning before we packed it in.

I drove back from Leicester aware that everybody there feared we would lose the seat and that Transport House had written it off, despite its 8,000 Labour majority. Sara Barker had decided that they must concentrate their energies on holding Gorton. I got back in time to be told the good news that tonight the House of Lords had behaved well on abortion and the crisis had disappeared.

Tuesday, October 24th
This morning came the virtual French veto on our entry to the Common Market. They declared that we couldn't be considered for membership until the pound had ceased to be the second international currency and we had got the problem of parity under control.

But immediately I'd had to think more about the Abortion Bill because all our plans had run away as the result of the Lords' behaviour last night. I had arranged to brief the Opposition leaders about our intention to reform the House of Lords to give them fair warning not to try to fight the abortion issue. But now I discovered that Heath and Whitelaw refused to meet us before the Queen's Speech. The reason was simple and I should have foreseen it. They'd obviously been informed of every detail by Carrington and Jellicoe[1] because Frank Longford can't resist talking to them out of office

---

[1] Lord Jellicoe succeeded to his father's earldom in 1935 and after some years in the Foreign Service became a Conservative Whip in the House of Lords in 1961. He was deputy leader of the Opposition in the House of Lords 1967–70 and Leader of the House from 1970 until his resignation in 1973.

hours. I don't blame them for their decision. But today, without saying anything to me, Longford proceeded to talk in even greater detail to Carrington and Jellicoe and the news began to percolate down the corridors into the House of Commons.

This afternoon a large delegation of Coventry tenants arrived to see their three M.P.s About eighty of them turned up with ten children. It was the usual kind of Coventry spree to London—they'd all come in a couple of charabancs and were greatly enjoying the expedition. Bill Wilson,[1] Maurice Edelman and I had to see them for a very long time after 2.30. What happened was a repetition of the troubles I had with the two previous delegations. Bill Wilson, as a back-bench M.P., got quite a decent hearing. Basically I didn't say anything different from him, but the tenants made it perfectly clear that they had chucked out their Conservative councillors because the rates were too high and now they would chuck out the Government if we didn't bring the rents down. It was no good telling them that fixing rents was a matter for the council, not for the Government. The Government, in their view, had to do something about it and these were Labour supporters determined to tell the Labour Government just that. They were savage and fairly rude but I managed to be fairly good-tempered.

These tenants showed me another side of the problem I'd been meeting at Leicester. Even when a Conservative council is elected after thirty-five years and raises the rents by 50 per cent a majority of them will blame the Government in Whitehall for what the local Conservative councillors have done. This is the extent of the crisis of confidence I had to face.

At the Services Committee we were still struggling with the proposals for the new Parliament building. The latest plans are to add a floor on top of the tea-room building, but this would block out all the windows in the corridors and make life virtually impossible. I managed to persuade the Committee to postpone the whole thing. I want to have the problem of the new building seen in conjunction with the reform of the Lords and the creation of a single parliamentary unit with the Upper House as a mere additional complement to a dominant House of Commons. In such a case we should have the whole building designed in a different way. As an excuse for this delay I was able to quote the decision of the Home Affairs Committee to have a two-month period in which to review the whole problem of the area on the other side of Bridge Street.

Waiting for me in my room was the Minister of Health, anxious to talk to me about his Bill to ban cigarette coupons. I should have told him about the disastrous effect of his Monday Statement in the Leicester by-election. But the Chief was there and I knew I had to be polite so we discussed the possibility of a Private Member's Bill and I said nothing when he talked about the importance of getting it. I'm sure we were wrong to give him this concession and I think we ought to take it away at the first opportunity.

[1] Labour M.P. for Coventry South 1964–70 and for Coventry South-East since 1974.

By far the most interesting episode of this day however was my meeting with Michael Adeane—at the Palace to discuss my attendance at the State Opening of Parliament. Let me explain. Weeks ago I received a programme from the College of Heraldry telling me of a rehearsal which as Lord President I had to attend. Without very much thought I wrote back saying that I didn't want to attend the State Opening so I would just like to have a diplomatic illness. For a fortnight or so we heard nothing. Then Harold told me that he had received a letter from the Duke of Norfolk[1] saying that he heard I objected to attending the State Opening owing to my anti-monarchical sentiments. This letter was actually shown to me by Michael Halls and it certainly indicates some amount of malice among the court officials. I was delighted when Michael Halls drafted a reply from the Prime Minister saying that he was amazed to receive this extraordinary epistle from the Duke. 'The truth is the Lord President is keenly distressed because he suffers from a phobia about public occasions of this sort which make him unable to attend.' I thought this letter would be the end of the business and I heaved a sigh of relief because I really was dreading the idea of having to go to Moss Bros and hire morning dress, which I've never in my life worn before, and parade up and down in the Royal Gallery. I was looking forward to doing a quiet morning's work during the State Opening of Parliament as I did during the Attlee memorial service. However I underestimated the court. Last Tuesday I received a letter at Vincent Square from the Duke of Norfolk stating that he was deeply alarmed and disturbed by what I had said about not going to the State Opening and that only the Queen could relieve me of the obligation to go. Harold by now was a bit flustered by the affair and I rang up Michael Adeane and he asked to see me at 7.45 tonight before I went off to dinner at the German Embassy. When we had driven in to Buckingham Palace it was pitch dark and I found some difficulty in discovering the door into his little office. He told me that Harold Wilson had just come in to discuss the Queen's Speech with the Queen and said that I'd mucked things up terribly by writing to the Heralds and the Duke of Norfolk. 'Why didn't you come to me?' he said straightaway. 'I could have cleared it with the Queen and I can clear it now if you really want not to go. Indeed, all you need to do is to write a letter to her asking to be excused without stating any reason why.' He then went on to add, 'Of course, the Queen has as strong a feeling of dislike of public ceremonies as you do. I don't disguise from you the fact that it will certainly occur to her to ask herself why you should be excused when she has to go, since you're both officials.' I sat down this evening and wrote a letter to Michael Adeane saying that I would attend. His handling of the affair had been as masterly as that of the Duke of Norfolk had been clumsy.

But before I wrote that letter I'd been at a dinner-party at the German Embassy for Kiesinger, the Chancellor. From our side there was Harold

---

[1] Bernard Marmaduke Fitzalan-Howard, 16th Duke of Norfolk, Earl Marshal and Hereditary Marshal and Chief Butler of England.

Wilson, George Brown, Shirley Williams and myself and on their side there was Kiesinger and Blankenhorn.[1] Blankenhorn's an old friend of mine. I met him first when he was sent over to spy out the ground for Adenauer to try to get some kind of British recognition. He was, I think, the first professional diplomatist to arrive in Britain after the war. The interest of the evening was of course that this was the day of the French bombshell. Kiesinger looked enormously complacent and when I watched him talking to Harold and George he reminded me of a headmaster patting his two young prefects on the back and being kind to them and telling them not to be disheartened. I had a word with Con O'Neill afterwards (he was another guest) and I asked him what would happen if we did devalue in order to carry out the instructions the French had given us on what to do before joining the Common Market. 'Ah,' said Con, 'in that case they would have a final reason for refusing us admission—that we had devalued and shown our currency was worthless.' I laughed and said, 'They always get it both ways.'

Wednesday, October 25th
I had to go over to Downing Street to tell the P.M. that as a result of Frank Longford's talks with Jellicoe and Carrington it had been revealed that Carrington was deeply upset by the text of the Queen's Speech because it didn't specifically refer to all-party consultation. So we added the necessary words and by 10.30 the draft was corrected and ready. After this I suggested to Harold that he or I should have a Lobby conference on Thursday as usual and then Frank could have his on Friday. But he was adamant. He wanted to announce nothing because he was proud that security has been so well kept.

I spent the rest of the morning working away at my Balfour Declaration speech. Fortunately I hear that with Abba Eban coming I shall only need to do twenty minutes and I'm leaving Monday evening to finish it off. Lola Hahn, the sister-in-law of Kurt Hahn,[2] who lives near to us at home, has written me a passionate letter begging me not to pull my punches and saying that everyone has been waiting for my speech in expectation. That doesn't make it any easier.

This afternoon Patricia Llewelyn-Davies had asked Anne and me to come to lunch with her before she was introduced as a life peer, escorted by her husband whom Harold nominated two or three years ago. I found myself sitting next to Dame Peggy Ashcroft, the actress, and enormously enjoyed her company. Then into the Chamber to see this ridiculous ceremony for Ifor Evans,[3] and for Patricia. For the first time I exercised my privilege as Lord President and sat on the steps of the Throne to watch the ceremony.

[1] Herbert Blankenhorn, West German Ambassador to London 1965–70.
[2] Born in Berlin in 1886. He was co-founder in 1920 of Salem Co-educational College and, after his emigration to Britain, founder in 1934 of Gordonstoun School and in 1962, of the United World College of the Atlantic in Wales.
[3] Provost of University College London 1951–66. He took his seat as Lord Evans of Hungershall.

This afternoon we had another meeting of the Broadcasting Committee. The Chief and I represented the Government and Ted Heath arrived with his Chief Whip and Jeremy Thorpe with his.[1] We had the usual senior officials from I.T.N. and the B.B.C. It was quite lively because Heath had decided to stage a great demonstration. He proposed in a very rapidly delivered speech that we should first of all depart from the rule that party broadcasts should be simultaneous on all channels so losing the captive audience, and secondly, in exchange, that we should allow the broadcasting time available to each Party to be divided up into as many five-minute intervals as we could get in. He thinks this would endear us to the public and he also thinks we could then pay much more attention to regional interests. These proposals were slapped down immediately by Hugh Greene and the other officials as technically impossible. The Chief and I were pretty wholly on the side of the B.B.C. I want to keep the captive audience, keep simultaneity and though I want shorter programmes I don't want us to degrade ourselves with endless short snappy advertising captions.

Ted has come back the hero of his Party Conference but this afternoon he seemed nervy and almost violent. At one point he said, 'I've just spent five years going round England and I can tell you how they all hate central government. Regionalism is the great thing. We've got to concede this to people if we want to endear ourselves to them.' Willie Whitelaw looked rather embarrassed.

We gave dinner this evening to Mike Bessie, my American publisher, and Helga Greene, now Connolly, my literary agent. The House conked out early since the Abortion Bill was finished at six o'clock and that left Tam Dalyell time to make a 58-minute speech on Aldabra. This is one of Tam's most effective back-bench campaigns. For weeks he's been asking questions about the ghastly air-base which we're trying to plank on an island that is of enormous value to ecologists and ornithologists. As I've reported in this diary, we're not enthusiastic about it in O.P.D. and if he goes on as well as he did in this adjournment debate he may well succeed in killing the scheme.

Thursday, October 26th

As I feared the leaks about Lords reform are beginning to appear. There's one in the *Guardian* and another in the *Express*. If we're going to keep our intentions secret till next week we must give the Lobby some more news about the Commons and since I can't have my own Lobby conference I'm going to see a number of individual journalists—for example, from the *Financial Times*, the *Guardian* and the B.B.C.—and brief them about our plans for morning sittings.

At Cabinet I slipped in my amendment to the paragraph of the Queen's

---

[1] The Liberal Chief Whip was Eric Lubbock, M.P. for Orpington 1962–70 when he lost the seat. He succeeded to the Earldom of Avebury later that year.

Speech about House of Lords reform and got it through without comment. Soon we were in the midst of another furious argument about the Middle East which took the form of a long, slow but fiercely repressed argument between George Brown and myself on the subject of Israel with the P.M. intervening from time to time. I asked the Foreign Secretary whether his desire to resume relations with Egypt would be affected by the news of the blowing-up of the Israeli destroyer. (Last Sunday the big news was that the second largest ship of the Israeli navy had been destroyed forty miles off Port Said by a U.A.R. naval unit. The Israeli reprisal was to shell the oil refinery at Suez and totally destroy Egypt's indigenous oil supply.)[1] George said the news made no difference at all. Since we broke off relations with Egypt over Rhodesia I asked if it was normal to resume them without getting any satisfaction from the Egyptians. The Prime Minister intervened to say that the one thing which matters to us is the reopening of the Suez Canal, about which Israel is being terribly difficult, and surely it was a good thing to have an Ambassador in Cairo so we could try to play a positive role. 'Yes,' said George, 'and if we had someone there at the time the Israeli–Egyptian war broke out we might have made a decisive difference.' They were at it again, showing their passion to play a role on the world stage and pretend we are still a great power. The fact is that a British Ambassador in Cairo couldn't have made the faintest difference to the Israeli pre-emptive strike. At last the P.M. ended the dispute by saying that George should prepare a paper for Cabinet about the resumption of negotiations. So we'd won a point.

Next, Cabinet considered the two White Papers which had already been discussed in S.E.P. Once again there was no adequate discussion and we quickly reached the last item—the Industrial Expansion Bill. Each week it seems to be getting into ever greater difficulties. Now the I.R.C. and the C.B.I. are both furious about it and a row is raging between the Treasury and the D.E.A. on one side and the Ministry of Technology on the other. The Prime Minister is personally deeply committed to it and the sooner we get it out of Cabinet the better. I found the White Paper dreadfully feeble and the truth is that the Bill is little more than a parliamentary gimmick. When Tony Benn and I first thought of it we saw the convenience it would be to save legislative time by having one Bill instead of five and doing everything by Affirmative Order. But now we have to pretend that it's a Bill for actively intervening and helping industry and that it certainly isn't.

At Question Time this afternoon the Foreign Secretary dealt effectively though unimpressively with the French bombshell. Then we had a Statement from Gordon Walker on the British Museum library which showed only too clearly how this Government suffers from so many self-inflicted wounds. He just announced his decision to Parliament without bothering to consult the

[1] On October 21st the Israeli destroyer *Eilat* had been sunk off Sinai. On October 24th the Suez oil refineries were destroyed in retaliation.

Trustees although they include such friends as Noel Annan, the ex-principal of Kings, William Hayter of New College, and David Eccles.[1]

This evening George Strauss and Douglas Houghton came in to see me about the age of majority. They've been serving for the last two years on the Speaker's Conference and have now reached the major issue of whether we should reduce the voting age from twenty-one to eighteen and indeed in general make eighteen the age of majority. I told them that the Lord Chancellor and the Cabinet have already agreed to support the proposals but there won't be a Bill in this Session's legislation. Instead we're to have a debate in both Houses on the Latey Commission's report.[2]

After that the Chief, Brian O'Malley, his Deputy, and I got together for a long chatty dinner in the far corner of the Strangers' dining-room—a splendid dinner at my expense. The Chief is passionately keen that the code of discipline he has worked out with Douglas Houghton should not be introduced in this Session at all if we can get on without it. I must say I'm doubtful about this. I would like to have it passed and held in reserve, as Herbert Morrison held the Standing Orders in reserve during the 1945 Parliament. But I see the difficulty. In order to get the code through we need at least four Party meetings and that might blunt the good relations between the Chief and the Parliamentary Party. We shall have to sort this out at the liaison committee.

Friday, October 27th

All the press had the news about the abolition of morning sittings, which is a relief. At O.P.D. George Brown started a discussion on Aden by apologizing for having to tell us that we'll be out in November instead of January.[3] The rest of the Committee couldn't be more pleased. Really we've been miraculously lucky in Aden—cancelling all our obligations and getting out without a British soldier being killed. But George feels desperate because it's different from what he promised. We spent an hour trying to encourage him and we shall have to go through the same process in Cabinet on Monday.

Then the P.M. and I went across to the House for the Prorogation ceremony. I've never seen this before. First we sit in our House and then we march into the Lords and the Lord Chancellor reads out at dreary length all the Bills that have been passed. Then there is a Prorogation Speech repeating the whole thing, then we march back to the House of Commons where the Speaker is found sitting below his chair at the Committee Table and he reads the whole damn thing all over again. Then I was off after wasting a whole hour.

We settled down to our weekly business meeting. Tommy, Nicky and Tony

---

[1] The Government announced its decision not to proceed with the scheme and to set up an inquiry into national library facilities.

[2] On July 20th a Commission chaired by Mr Justice Latey had published a Report (Cmnd. 3342) recommending that the age of majority should now be lowered from twenty-one to eighteen, thus giving young people the right to marry without parental consent, to own land, make contracts, obtain mortgages and bring or defend legal actions.

[3] Aden became independent on November 29th.

Crosland had been emphasizing to me the enormous importance of getting the right timing for the crucial S.E.P. meeting when Tony is to put forward his ideas on import controls and devaluation. Burke wanted it fairly soon. I said it must wait until after the Queen's Speech and since Jim Callaghan and I will be making big speeches on Tuesday, Wednesday is the earliest possible day. So Wednesday it will be. This is one of the real privileges of the Lord President. Through his regular business meetings with the P.M. and Burke, he can have a big say in the timetable of the Cabinet.

Afterwards the P.M. began to discuss his Cambridge visit. He was going there this afternoon for a Labour Party regional meeting at the town hall and it's well known there'll be a violent hostile demonstration organized against him. I said that he shouldn't have accepted at all and he agreed it was a mistake and promised me it'll be the last one he will do for a time. Sure enough, wherever he goes now there are demonstrations and it's bad for his prestige.

Sunday, October 29th

I drove back to Prescote on Friday night and then on to Cambridge yesterday to inspect a geriatric hospital where by chance there was a dear old lady I know.[1] She is eighty-four and she used, when a girl, to have tea with Lenin because her husband was Russian Minister of Transport in 1918 before they moved to Canada. I found her cool and collected and dominating the ward.

Yesterday we had to go over to a village near Bedford in order to attend the marriage of my sister Bridget's daughter, Sue Bardsley. Oh dear, weddings have become very formal and well-dressed these days. All the men were in tailcoats, grey waistcoats and top hats; all the women were dressed up to the nines, there was a marquee and I was the only person who had got an ordinary suit on. But even I had been forced to go to Moss Bros on Friday to order a damned morning coat for the State Opening of Parliament. I had to make a speech toasting the bride and bridegroom (about the only thing I do for my family) before we drove back to Prescote.

Sunday reflections. Well, we are through another strenuous week. A long Session has ended and we've prorogued Parliament. We've prevented not only the railway strike but also stopped the Liverpool dock strike—though the London one is still going on. In Parliament we've got the Abortion Bill through in the House of Lords without a crisis—rather to my disappointment. On the other hand the Government still teeters along indecisively with Harold Wilson immersed in his new Ministerial responsibilities at D.E.A. and not gaining much authority as a result. It's also clear that the Parliamentary Party has come back to Westminster unhappy, critical, waiting desperately for a lead but without much confidence that things are coming out right. Personally I now feel at the bottom of my heart that a change has got to come and it won't be import controls; it will have to be floating of the pound or devaluation and there will be a pretty good row whichever of them it is. The

[1] Raissa Lomonossiff, an old friend of Anne Crossman's family.

change may come much faster than we expected thanks to the French bomb-shell announced this week. Perhaps that is what has finally tipped me over into the conviction that we can't get out of our problems now without a major change and that the whole issue is how that change is to be conducted.

At such a time there's always such a lot of backstairs gossip. Thomas came to me full of the story that Jim Callaghan and others—by which he probably means Harold Lever—are not so much against devaluation as they were because the crisis it would cause might make Jim Prime Minister. I rebuked Thomas and said this was absolute nonsense. I don't believe a word of it. If we're going to devalue, this Chancellor has got to do it and then hang on for three or four months afterwards to give credibility to it and stability to the pound. Indeed what we need from Jim before devaluation is a good deal of actual prompting of Harold because it's Harold who may prove most difficult in the end.

I also had Marcia in this week and she seemed to be telling me that Harold too is facing up to the necessity for a major move and that he is only waiting for the right time to do it. I have deliberately kept out of Harold's way on these subjects and busied myself on Commons business and Lords reform, not least because if I even mention devaluation to him he assumes that I'm speaking with my master's voice, i.e. quoting Tommy Balogh. Because I'm not an economist Harold refuses to take me seriously on these subjects.

There was one other major event of the week. Heath has been established as the leader of the Tory Party. Once again he had a tremendously successful Conference, largely owing to the newspapers and the B.B.C. announcing that his personality was an utter failure and that his leadership would be the critical issue of the Conference. This campaign virtually compelled the Party to give him a great vote of confidence and the longest applause ever heard at the end of a speech. But there's no harm in this for us because he will never be a very successful leader.

Anyway what will decide the fate of the Government is not the popularity of the Tories but our own failures and consequent unpopularity. I can't help remembering how only three years before victory we were ruled out completely by all the serious observers as an alternative government. We didn't begin to move up in the polls because we had changed but because people had lost faith in the Tories. So too with Heath today. He will automatically look more convincing the moment the public seriously wants an alternative to this Labour Government and I think for the first time this winter there's the beginning of a serious anti-Labour shift which is illustrated by the mood of the Party in the by-elections now going on at Gorton and Leicester. The mere fact that these two safe Labour seats are in danger shows us that we are faced with a leadership crisis which can only be overcome by a new initiative at the centre—a new breakthrough. Unless Harold can achieve this we may linger on for another two or three years but shall be doomed to defeat at the end.

Monday, October 30th

The special Cabinet to authorize George Brown's decision to withdraw from Aden a month earlier than planned went according to form. Once again he spent his time apologizing for what all his colleagues considered a wonderfully lucky and fortunate result. That the regime he backed should have been overthrown by terrorists and has forced our speedy withdrawal is nothing but good fortune. It now looks as though we shall get out of Aden without losing a British soldier, chaos will rule soon after we've gone, and there'll be one major commitment cut—thank God.

There was one other item on the agenda—the fourth of Barbara's Transport White Papers, which looked very dull indeed. The discussion suddenly developed into a bleeding row between her and Ray Gunter. The week before she had sacked Stanley Raymond, the chairman of the British Railways Board, owing to a policy disagreement—or, rather, she had asked him to move to the chairmanship of the new Freight Corporation in order to give his present chairmanship to a new man.[1] As soon as she'd finished explaining her White Paper Gunter began to describe the terrible treatment of his old friend, Stanley Raymond, a loyal Labour supporter whom nobody could have treated more vilely than this. Barbara counter-attacked with spirit and revealed that she had heard the news that this afternoon the exact story of his sacking would be published in the *Daily Mail* and that somebody in the room this morning had leaked the story to the press. And so we were plunged into a typical Cabinet row between two Departments—the main cause of the leaks which flow from this Labour Cabinet.

I lunched in the restaurant at the top of the new Hilton with Louis Fischer whom I first got to know when I edited *The God That Failed*[2] and got him to contribute one of the least distinguished essays. He's a great big burly Russian Jew—more Russian than Jewish, handsome, gentle and one-time fervent communist, now derevolutionized and living happily in the famous Princeton Research Institute lecturing on the Russian revolution and writing enormous unreadable books on Russian history. He loves me because when Hamish Hamilton was reluctant to publish his enormous life of Stalin I helped to persuade him to do so. America suits him perfectly because it has an academic world rich enough to keep him at a very good standard of living which enables him to give me a very good lunch at the Hilton.

This afternoon came the rehearsal for the State Opening of Parliament. I wandered down the corridor towards the House of Lords and in the Royal Gallery I found a woman with a bogus train wandering about surrounded by

[1] Sir Stanley Raymond, former chairman of the Western Railway Board and general manager of the Western Region, was chairman of the British Railways Board 1965–7. In 1968 he became chairman of the Gaming Board and in 1972 of the Horse-race Betting Levy Board.

[2] *The God That Failed: Six Studies in Communism*, by Arthur Koestler, Ignazio Silone, André Gide (presented by Enid Starkie), Richard Wright, Louis Fischer and Stephen Spender, with an introduction by Crossman (London: Hamish Hamilton, 1950).

a lot of men. One of them I recognized as the Duke of Norfolk and in due course we were marshalled by our Earl Marshal and made to walk up and down. It was one of those wonderfully incompetent English performances where no one is really in charge. There were Monty and Eddie Shackleton standing together because one will hold the Sword of State and the other the Cap of Maintenance tomorrow and march in front of us. Then comes the Lord President and the Lord Privy Seal (the only two civilians in civilian costume), then the Lord Chancellor, then all those Heralds Pursuivant, and that's about the size of the procession before you come to the soldiers—the dragoons and the horseguards. This rehearsal was only for officials and dignitaries. I was anxiously thanked by the Earl Marshal for coming and Frank Longford seemed surprised at my being there.

After this I did a little party political broadcast on pensions which made me late for the Prime Minister's annual eve-of-session party at No. 10 where the Queen's Speech is revealed to all the members of the Government. I missed his speech including his defence of Chalfont and I also missed the murmur of applause which greeted the announcement of the only thing they really liked—the reform of the House of Lords. I saw Chalfont and tried for a moment to give him a cheerful look. He's in appalling trouble because of the way he talked to journalists after the E.F.T.A. Conference at Lausanne last week.[1] Then I went across to the Privy Council office where Janet was waiting for me and I knocked out a draft of my Balfour anniversary speech.

Tuesday, October 31st
The Chalfont story is still booming on. I was rung up by Arthur Gavshon, my contact in Associated Press, who said he'd been at the F.O. last night when George Brown moved across from the P.M.'s party to talk to journalists there. He had gone right through the Chalfont story treating Chalfont in a hostile way which is after all natural since Chalfont is a Wilson man who has been put into the Foreign Office by the Prime Minister as a check on the erratic George Brown.

I had been convinced when I read the *Sunday Times* and on Monday *The Times* that Chalfont had been more sinned against than sinning. He hadn't really meant to make a statement but had been merely thinking aloud and had given the journalists the wrong impression. Apparently he talked to the journalists before, during and after the buffet supper for the E.F.T.A. Ministers and there had been, as I noticed at the Kiesinger dinner last week, a little bit of vague rumbling by George and Harold that 'we must have a fallback position, we can't stand for ever here. We must be prepared to let

[1] On May 23rd Lord Chalfont had been appointed Chief British Negotiator for Britain's application for entry to the E.E.C. His words on this occasion had been interpreted as a threat that Britain would be obliged to reassess her European policy, especially where defence was concerned, if General de Gaulle should block her application. Lord Chalfont, who had supposed his remarks to be off the record, offered the Prime Minister his resignation but it was refused.

the E.E.C. feel that our being kept out would be very damaging to them.' So of course the thoughtful press was saying that they found it incredible that Chalfont would have loquobrated in this way, have launched these kites without some encouragement, possibly from Mr Wilson. Harold assured me on Friday that he hadn't seen Chalfont except at the briefing which was given to him before he left London for the E.F.T.A. meeting. So in Harold's view Chalfont acted completely on his own and that means that we have the choice between taking the view that he's a very simple and incredibly inexperienced journalist turned politician or that someone isn't telling the truth.

Although this was the day for the State Opening of Parliament I put on my ordinary suit and went along to my room in the House of Commons. From there I found my way to Eddie Shackleton's room where champagne was already being served. In the Lords there was a great sense of party—almost like Derby Day. The State Opening is a festive occasion. Eddie got into his uniform and his robes and I sheepishly got into my morning suit and actually found it perfectly comfortable. I could wear my ordinary white shirt and didn't have the separate hard collar for which I'd carefully gone out and bought the collar studs for 1s. 3d.

In due course Frank Longford and I stroll through the anteroom of the Lords and there we are suddenly in the Royal Gallery—usually a huge empty corridor with the vast picture of the battle of Waterloo on the one side and that of the battle of Trafalgar on the other. Now there are boxes on each side, packed with people who've been standing there for hours. They've done this just to see the Queen emerge from the Robing Room and walk with her procession behind her into the House of Lords. Then they won't see anything more until she has read the Queen's Speech and walked back down the Royal Gallery again. That's all that this distinguished crowd of waiting people will see. Gradually the boxes begin to fill up and the space where we are standing fills up with chaps wearing swords. Frank and I are told we should be stationed behind the Lord Chancellor on the stairs leading down to the Norman Porch, where the Queen enters. These stairs are also packed with troops on both sides and when we stand there it is very difficult not to get knocked by the trooper behind you when he presents swords, which he seems to be doing on and off for twenty minutes or so. Above us in the Royal Gallery are Field-Marshal Montgomery and Eddie getting ready for their function, surrounded by Air Marshals and Generals. But I am down on one of the lower stairs and suddenly looking up I see a bloated caricature, whose eyes you can hardly see because he is covered by a helmet with white plumes flying at the edge. It is Frank Bowles, walking very gingerly down the stairs so as not to trip over his golden spurs because if he did he could never get up.[1] And then I see Frank Beswick looking almost as idiotic in his costume

---

[1] Labour M.P. for Nuneaton from 1942 to 1964, when he made way for Frank Cousins. He became a life peer in 1964 and from 1965 until 1970 served as Captain of the Yeoman of the Guard (which accounts for his appearance on this occasion). He died in December 1970.

of Captain of the Gentlemen-at-Arms. In all this fancy dress Frank Longford and I stand out because we're the only people in ordinary civilian clothes — yes, my morning coat felt quite ordinary in that assembly. We are able to stroll about and talk to our friends and quite to enjoy ourselves.

What do I think? I think it's like the *Prisoner of Zenda* but not nearly as smart or well done as it would be at Hollywood. It's more what a real Ruritania would look like — far more comic, more untidy, more homely, less grand. The only grand things I saw were the Crown dazzling with jewels on its cushion and the Queen herself, with the royal princes and princesses. However, even there one could see that Snowdon's top hat had fallen off before he could get out of his car. The older royals are the best — particularly the Dowager Duchess of Kent, but not the goofy Duke of Gloucester, looking terrible with his very dull wife. Well, they come piling in one after another, the Cap of Maintenance comes, the Sword comes, the Crown comes and then down comes the Lord Chancellor in his magnificent robes and stands just in front of Frank and me — I on the right and Frank on the left. And suddenly I notice that the lace under his chin is trembling. The whole Lord Chancellor — though he adores these ceremonies, he tells me, because he always wanted to be a great actor — is trembling. Is it emotion or fear or tension? I don't know, but for more than half an hour he stands there trembling before the Queen arrives. And, of course, we never get more than a glimpse of her because as she arrives we have to turn and march smartly ahead of her up the stairs whereupon she turns left into the Robing Room while we form up and wait inside the Royal Gallery and then in due course process in front of her into the House of Lords.

On this state occasion the House of Lords is really magnificent — all the Law Lords, the Bishops, then the diplomats and their ladies with all their jewels, and behind them lines and lines of peers and peeresses, and above all of them the gallery and enormous arc lights for the televising of the Queen.

I come in at the right-hand door and stand just by the throne next to the Lord Chancellor and the Duke of Norfolk. And I have to watch her reading the appalling Speech for which I am responsible. It is certainly not designed for reading aloud in the House of Lords. Next time I must take some trouble to get a speech that sounds good when it's read aloud because this one sounds difficult and Harold Wilson's sentences about inflation are impossible to enunciate. But I did notice that when she read the sentence about curbing the power of the Lords she made a little pause and read it with just a *frisson* and the whole House had just a *frisson* too. The moment she has withdrawn I have to dart out behind her with Frank Longford and we process back along the Royal Gallery and she disappears into the Robing Room. And then the Earl Marshal comes up to me and says, 'I suppose you're anxious to be off as soon as possible? If you go back the way you came you'll get out straight away.' So I walk slowly back through the Royal Gallery chatting to Frank as we go with everyone looking at us and within seconds we're back in his room drinking a glass of champagne. Then a quick change and back to Room 14 for the Party meeting.

This was completely uneventful. Afterwards I took a quick lunch because I felt I ought to be on the front bench at 2.30 for the opening Speeches on the Address. I've never attended this kind of ceremonial and I thought the House would be packed and even the front bench full. But when I got there the House was only half full at most and there were four people on our front bench. I understood why when I had to listen to the long series of ridiculous announcements by the Speaker about the Amnesty Act and so on. It was twenty minutes or so before Hugh Delargy got up to move the Loyal Address in an excellent constituency speech full of humour, with Jack Ashley second-ing—not quite as good but a very good pair taken together.[1] And then we were ready for the first combat of the Session between Wilson and Heath.

Heath's speech reads much better than it sounded. It was delivered with a tension and nervous tautness which made it very unconvincing. At no point did he relax, or wave an arm or do anything to make you feel that he was a live person. The P.M. replied for over an hour, just about twice too long, but there was plenty of joke and vitality in it, particularly towards the end.

I realized later that I must have fallen asleep because I didn't hear what he said about Chalfont. When he sat down he turned to me and said, 'I nearly cut the end, it was so long.' 'Thank God you didn't,' I said, 'because it cheered our people up,' and he can of course run rings round Heath. If only he could resist piling all the stuff into it on these occasions, particularly all the stuff about D.E.A. and the regions. This comes of his being a departmental P.M.

I went straight up to my Lobby conference. The P.M. had forbidden me to hold one last week and I did today's jointly with Frank Longford and Eddie Shackleton. I had thought out my initial statement and my answers pretty carefully. The only difficulty was that Frank Longford kept on making additions all the way through about his own personal two-tier reform scheme for the Lords. We have told him time after time that Cabinet is not committed to a two-tier scheme or indeed to any scheme at all, and that we want to negotiate with the other Parties on equal terms. Whenever I was asked about details of the scheme and reserved my position, Frank would rush in and say, 'I personally feel … ' and give another long answer. However, I don't think it really did much harm. What was clear by now was that the anticipations of Callaghan and Brown were completely falsified. In the House of Commons the only loud cheer on our side had come when the P.M. mentioned the reform of the Lords. Provided we make it a good reform they are going to like it.

---

[1] Hugh Delargy, Labour M.P. for Platting (Manchester) 1945–50 and for Thurrock from 1950 until his death in 1976, and Jack Ashley, Labour M.P. for Stoke-on-Trent since 1966.

18

Wednesday, November 1st

Lying in bed and thumbing through the morning papers I knew that our press conference had been a great success. But then I switched on the eight o'clock news and after it heard the recording of George Brown's astonishing scene at the Savoy, where he really misbehaved himself in public.[1]

This is intolerable, I felt, and I took up the phone and rang up Harold and told him what had happened. He'd read something in the press but he hadn't heard the radio and he said quickly, 'Don't say any more. I'll act on this. This is it but don't say a damn thing to anybody.' And he rang off.

At the Party meeting this morning I made a full-length statement on the reforms we were introducing in the Commons. It went quite well. When I had first told the P.M. that John and I had decided to drop morning sittings because the Opposition had succeeded in frustrating us, he had said we couldn't possibly do it because we would never live down the defeat. Well, on this occasion I frankly told the Party that morning sittings had failed and the Tories had done what they intended to do to them and we therefore wouldn't go on with them. The statement was received in silence with obvious relief. Indeed, when I sat down after explaining the whole package I got the nearest thing to an ovation which I've had since I became Leader of the House—a continuous round of applause for what they obviously thought was highly satisfactory, including of course the reference at the beginning to the Lords reform.

I lunched with Donald Stokes to talk about the possibility of an Institute of Motor-Car Engineering at Warwick University. But of course the conversation turned to George Brown and when I strenuously objected to his behaviour Donald observed, 'I don't take it so seriously, Dick. I happened to be at that dinner last night and we didn't know what was going on. It sounded a bit odd but we know our George now. We manufacturers can never forget what that man did for us. He launched the prices and incomes policy and as long as he was there we believed in it and we believed in the Labour Government. He made all that difference to you. If I were you I should never turn against George however badly he behaves.' It was clear this afternoon that Stokes's view was very widely held inside the Parliamentary Party. Of course there were a number of people who like me felt that he'd gone beyond the limit of misbehaviour. But indeed I have always felt schizophrenic about George. He's a good thing and yet he's a bloody disaster. I've been expecting him to go pretty soon and I had certainly not foreseen what an enormous hold he would get on the country and the Party and how long he would teeter on the tightrope and cause Harold all these agonies.

I had to be on the front bench at 2.30 to move the motion on Private Members' time which after a brief debate was carried with seventy-nine

---

[1] George Brown had clashed with Lord Thomson, proprietor of the *Sunday Times* newspaper, in which one of the articles about Kim Philby, the Foreign Office official and Russian spy, had appeared.

Tories voting against. I could have avoided the vote but the Speaker cut the debate short and irritated the back-benchers. After that Michael Stewart and Geoffrey Rippon[1] restarted the debate on the Queen's Speeches—Michael competent, efficient but a little grey, Geoffrey Rippon vulgar and superficially rhetorical. A half-empty House, no spirit and no discussions.

I went off to the Lords for one of our regular meetings of the new management Committee on reform and there was a real row between Roy Jenkins and Frank Longford. At Chequers we had only reached agreement because Jenkins and Gordon Walker, the advocates of the one-tier system, had agreed to come along with us on condition that the two-tier scheme was not regarded as an end-all but as something we were prepared to concede if necessary at the end of negotiations. Frank had never accepted this and had been talking to the Tories as though his personal two-tier scheme was Labour policy. Well, Roy Jenkins blew his top. I watched with interest while he was being deliberately bloody in a way which I reckon on this occasion was sensible and correct since it certainly cleared the air. As a result Eddie Shackleton was able to get on with our work much more easily.

Back in my office I had to brief two key journalists—David Watt, now political editor of the *Financial Times*,[2] and Jimmy Margach of the *Sunday Times*. This was important because I was aware that none of the dailies would deal with serious matters after the excitement of Chalfont, George Brown and the by-elections. This evening we gave dinner for Barbara, Wedgy and Tommy and Peter Shore and his wife, Liz, came later on. There is no disagreement among us. We all know there's got to be devaluation and that Harold ought to try to get it while Jim is Chancellor. We all know we should float the pound and not devalue to a fixed point. We all agree that import controls will be quite ineffective. We are just waiting for devaluation but we don't know how and when.

Listening to Wedgy and Peter I became a little bit worried about the future of the Party. Wedgy is brilliant at public relations and has enormous drive and ambition and even imagination but he refuses to face the real difficulties because he has a second-rate intellect. Peter is infinitely more intelligent but he completely lacks Wedgy's power to put himself across. He has made a very poor appearance on the front bench this week, reading aloud a dull script dully and getting a bad response from our back-benchers, poor man. I doubt if he's achieving much in his Department either, with Harold breathing down his neck. He's been given an impossible job but as private friends we must give him time and work closely with him.

[1] Conservative M.P. for Norwich South 1955–64 and for Hexham since 1966. He was Minister of Public Building and Works 1962–4, Minister of Technology 1970, Chancellor of the Duchy of Lancaster 1970–72 and Secretary of State for the Environment 1972–4.
[2] He had just returned from America, where he had been Washington correspondent since 1964.

Thursday, November 2nd

Bill Rodgers came to see me about the redrafting of the departmental reply to the Specialist Committee on Agriculture's criticism of the Foreign Office. This is an old affair which has been running for weeks. The Committee has been managed by one or two people who want to be a nuisance and their attempt to have a session in Brussels was bound to create Foreign Office opposition. I spent many weary hours trying to heal the breach—with a little success—but now of course the Committee has published a long and detailed report charging the Foreign Office with sabotaging what they regard as their completely legitimate attempt to visit Brussels to study the impact of the European Common Market on British agriculture in order to elicit whether we are adequately briefed for the forthcoming negotiations. We had received the F.O. draft some weeks ago and I had sent it to Barnett Cocks so that the Clerks to the House of Commons could consider the F.O. contention that all negotiations and contacts with foreign governments must be channelled through the F.O. and that therefore the Committee was acting *ultra vires*. Barnett's reply to me was that the Government would make itself a laughing stock if it permitted the F.O. to publish this document. For many years now some contacts with European governments have been channelled through officials of the House of Commons as well as through the Commonwealth Parliamentary Association. There is a vast interchange going on of which the F.O. seems to be totally unaware. The F.O. document has stimulated the Clerks to compose two papers which are eye-opening exposures of F.O. ignorance. I gave the papers to Rodgers and told him to go away and read them aloud to the F.O. officials.

It was now time for Cabinet. Once again we were discussing diplomatic relations with Egypt on the basis of the paper I had demanded of George Brown when I opposed him.

George put in a very convincing paper proposing the resumption of diplomatic relations with Egypt in mid-December. But, thank God, I had read the telegrams and discovered one in which it was reported that yesterday General Moshe Dayan of Israel had said there was nothing wrong in Britain's recognizing Egypt, and that indeed it might be a very good thing for Israel if we did. I assumed that Burke would have shown this to the Prime Minister when he prepared the P.M.'s brief last night. When I looked carefully I thought I could see the cable hidden in his brief. He obviously intended to call on me after George and then to annihilate me by reading Moshe Dayan's aloud. However, once I knew the facts it was easy to evade the net. I said that I now accepted the need to resume relations with Egypt and wanted to ask a couple of questions and indeed extracted a couple of assurances. Everyone looked relieved and wondered why I had been so mild. But I had learned caution.

The second item was the Latey Commission which had reported in favour of reducing the age of majority from twenty-one to eighteen. Alas, I had already heard the Lord Chancellor's speech twice. When he's got a piece clear in his mind he repeats it identically and metallically with every joke and inflection exactly the same. There were only two issues. Douglas Houghton and George Strauss had reported to me that the Speaker's Conference after two years were now about to discuss the issue of votes at eighteen and wanted to hear the Commission's findings. The Cabinet agreed that we should advise them to postpone their discussion until they'd heard the debates in the House of Lords and the Commons. At present, I gathered, the Speaker's Conference were in favour of reducing the age from twenty-one to twenty. The only new feature was that our youngest member, Dick Marsh, came out resolutely against votes at eighteen. I thought there'd be more support for him, but even Willie Ross stayed silent. Right at the end when Cabinet was getting up the P.M. slipped in my proposal that it should sanction a B.B.C. experiment for live radio broadcasts of extracts from the House of Commons debate. It slipped through almost unnoticed.

This afternoon at Question Time the House was seething with excitement about George Brown. Would Alec Douglas-Home as Opposition spokesman take the occasion to attack and destroy him? I sat next to the P.M., who said he thought that Alec would launch the attack. I replied, 'I'm certain he won't. First of all he's a gentleman and second he's too clever a politician to get you off the hook. To attack George would be to make him safe from dismissal.' 'You're probably right,' said the P.M.

Upstairs at my Lobby conference I ran into unexpected trouble about Stansted. I knew of course that Tony Crosland, now in control of the Board of Trade and in disagreement with Douglas Jay, was intending to raise the matter again in Cabinet. But the issue the journalists were raising concerned a statutory instrument. They had got wind of the fact that we were preparing to put forward an important Order for realigning the runway. 'Why hadn't the Order been published?' I was asked. 'Would it be published? When would it be debated?'

In giving a truthful answer I couldn't possibly prevent them from concluding that in fact we were having second thoughts about Stansted. This is the kind of case where either you lie to a press conference, which I wasn't prepared to do, or you give something away however hard you try. To try to placate them I gave the journalists the story of the radio experiment and also of the package of House of Commons reform which we had held over until then. However, I got a very bad press for this because all they worried about was the comic story of the Clerks wanting to take off their wigs, and this was an excuse for avoiding a serious story.

This evening I dined with Crosland. We talked a little about the British Museum, where we're in agreement, and Stansted, where we're not. Then we got down to our main subject—the line to be taken at the key S.E.P. meeting where import controls and devaluation will be discussed. We both agreed on the danger of leaks from Nicky Kaldor, though Nicky is immensely useful as an adviser. But we also agreed we couldn't press the Chancellor too hard. I find Crosland pretty helpful these days and he's become a definite addition to the Cabinet because he has a mind of his own. His only weakness is that up till now he hasn't been a very strong or vigorous Minister. Though I backed Stansted as the third airport, I was highly disconcerted to hear him say that all he intended was to recommend yet another inquiry. 'But surely,' I said, 'now that you've read all the papers you know there's no point in an inquiry. What we want is a decision.' 'I didn't have time to read all the papers,' he said. 'I just felt it was time to have another inquiry because I don't like the decision.'

After dinner I got down to work with Janet in my office and, thank God, the Balfour Declaration speech suddenly came and was completed by 11.30. I switched on the television and found the by-election results hadn't come through so I decided to go back to Vincent Square and see them there.

The outcome had been pretty clear this morning because the Gallup Poll had shown an enormous Tory lead in Leicester and Gorton. Long before, I had written off Leicester, where everything was against us—the breathalyser, cigarette coupons and Sandelson, the young travelling lawyer. The result was the inevitable mass Labour abstention. But though I didn't underestimate the magnetism of a young Winston Churchill I was very much hoping that we'd an excellent local candidate who could hold Gorton and thus show the difference between an election fought in the wrong atmosphere and one fought in the right atmosphere. It's when a man like Herbert Bowden accepts a job at a high salary with a peerage to boot and doesn't bother to tell his constituency that we get into real difficulties. So Leicester wasn't a surprise and Gorton was a great relief when it came. But the Hamilton result which came last of all was a shock. True, Tam Dalyell had predicted this to me very strongly. Indeed he'd told me that the Scot. Nat. woman might win and the Tories would certainly lose their deposit.[1] Tam had been working there a great deal and he said that the way Tom Fraser, like Bowden, went off to a highly-paid job had caused great resentment among the miners and a boost for the Scot. Nat. movement.[2] This, of course, follows the Scot. Nat. success in Pollok, more Welsh nationalist success in Rhondda and absolute success in Carmarthen. I was reminded of how Ted Heath had said last week at the

[1] The rise of the Scottish Nationalist Party in Scotland and Plaid Cymru in Wales was particularly worrying to the Government, who foresaw wholesale defections by disenchanted Labour supporters. At Hamilton, for example, Mrs Winifred Ewing, the Scottish Nationalist candidate transformed Labour's former majority of 16,576 into an S.N.P. majority of 1,799. In 1970 the seat returned to the Labour candidate, Alexander Wilson, who retained it in 1974. In 1974 Mrs Ewing returned to Parliament to represent the S.N.P. as Member for Moray and Nairn.

[2] Tom Fraser was Labour M.P. for Lanarkshire 1944–67. He was Joint Parliamentary Under-Secretary of State at the Scottish Office 1945–51, Minister of Transport 1964–5, a member of the Highlands and Islands Development Board 1967–70, chairman of the North of Scotland Hydro-electric Board 1967–73, and has been chairman of the Scottish Local Government Staff Commission since 1973.

Broadcasting Committee meeting that nationalism is the biggest single factor in our politics today.

Friday, November 3rd

The bashing, crashing news of defeats dominated the morning papers. What a week. The Chalfont scandal, the Brown scandal, the by-election defeats—all one after the other. I rang up Harold and said, 'Look, I was going off today but I'd like to see you. Can I look in this morning?' 'No, but I'm there all the afternoon.' 'I've got to go to Dulwich, may I come in afterwards?' 'Yes.'

Then I was off to the Home Affairs Committee where we had a lively discussion on planning. Cabinet had decided that in view of the Stansted mess-up we really must work out a form of planning inquiry where alternatives can be discussed. The officials had thought hard and had cooked up the idea of a special professional committee of inquiry which would do the whole job in special selected cases. But this, as was pointed out, meant altogether removing the final decision from the Minister and handing it over to a committee responsible to no one. So now the Ministry have come back with another proposal that the commission would work in two stages—first collecting information and then acting as inspectors conducting a public inquiry. This seemed to me just as unsatisfactory and I had some support from Dick Marsh. But it was no good because everyone else round the table was briefed not to oppose the Ministry's proposals. So the poor First Secretary in the chair got more and more bored because he thought the later items on his agenda more important and it was obvious that I was getting nowhere since I was only a Minister without Portfolio. I wanted the whole policy to be looked at and I didn't want to limit the change to a special commission for a few big cases because there are a number of quite small cases where the present system leads to endless delay—the Meadow Road at Oxford, for instance. So the Ministry will have its way and shove through a Bill which is not very good. Yet another bad departmental decision will be pushed through because there are no inter-departmental reasons for officials advising their Ministers to exert a veto.

I went out to Dulwich College to talk to the sixth form and got back at five in time for my appointment, which I assumed would enable me to catch the 6.10 to Banbury. But though the P.M. was punctual he kept me there longer than I thought possible and I had one of the most interesting talks I've ever had. I told him I'd come there simply to talk as a friend about the by-election results. 'In Transport House,' I pointed out, 'there wasn't a single person capable of considering the strategy of our propaganda, the effects of the by-elections and drawing conclusions from them. This kind of work simply isn't going on either in Transport House or in Whitehall.' 'You want an inner Cabinet,' he said at once. 'Yourself, Michael Stewart, Jim Callaghan, Roy Jenkins—yes, I'd have him in now but notice I don't bring in George Brown,' I said I'd noticed that and he added, 'Well, he's got to go, but not straightaway.' 'Nobody realizes,' he went on, 'what an awful time I've had with him.' And he told me a number of stories of George's behaviour and how Harold has had to cut the phone off because of what George was shouting down the line. Suddenly he said, 'I want you to do something—see Jimmy Margach today and tell him that Cabinet is against George.' 'Have you got that information from Cabinet?' I asked and he looked at me with those great grey eyes and said, 'Well, they told Burke Trend.'

In addition, he asked me to talk to the press about Chalfont having not got a glimmer of information from No. 10. 'I don't like asking you to do these things often,' he said, 'but in this case do it quickly. Some action must be taken.' Then he began to talk about his reshuffle. He said there were many choices and I pointed out that he couldn't move Jim Callaghan to the F.O. unless as Chancellor Jim had already carried out the devaluation. That was a bold thing to say to the P.M. in his present mood. 'Of course my mind is open on that,' he replied. 'It's Jim who has a closed mind on devaluation.' 'It may be closed,' I said, 'but you and I have got to make him do it. And he's got to have done the job before he can get the Foreign Office as his reward.' 'But the issue,' he replied, 'is the floating pound. I agree with Thomas, I'm for the floating pound but the fixed pound is what the other side want.' I said I thought he would find Tony Crosland on his side about this and he said, 'Mind you, my mind is open, we shall have to discuss all this at S.E.P. on Wednesday.' And then he came back to his idea of an inner Cabinet. 'I'm not sure you need an inner Cabinet,' I said, 'but you certainly need political staff and civil servants here in No. 10 to help you to work out a policy.' 'Then we must use Marcia,' he said. 'We must have our meetings once a week.' 'That's what I suspected,' I said. 'It's an enlarged kitchen Cabinet you want, not a new inner Cabinet. Well, let's try to get it done and to have John Silkin in as well.'

The new fact to emerge from this conversation was his reference to Roy. He's now determined to bring Roy into the inner circle and to have George out. He now thinks highly of Tony Crosland and regards him as wholly reliable. Tony looks to me like the man booked for the Treasury. Just when we were finishing Harold suddenly looked at me and said, 'Is it time for you to go back to a Department?' 'Yes,' I said. 'Provided I've got through these reforms in the Commons and the House of Lords reform's well launched I'd like to go back to a Department, but it rather depends what Department it is.' And I'm still wondering what it might be.

After that I went back to the Privy Council and got Foreign Office clearance for the text of my Balfour speech and then we had to make arrangements to issue it through the C.O.I and clear it personally with George Brown in his country mansion.[1] When all this was done, I finally caught the 7.30 and got down to Prescote to find Anne's friend, Lucy Curry, back from Australia and the rain settling in.

[1] Dorneywood, a house provided for the use of the Foreign Secretary.

Sunday, November 5th

Guy Fawkes was rained out yesterday and now it's been raining for a second day. This was the day of my big Balfour Declaration speech. It's quite true I've spent more trouble drafting this speech than I've ever spent on any speech in my whole life. I was determined to make it an act of faith in Zionism and in Israel which every Israeli could recognize and yet to keep it compatible with Labour Government policy. And, this weekend, I believed I had succeeded in doing this because I had obtained official clearance. Nevertheless this morning, despite the clearances, I received a message from Freddy Ward that the F.O. wouldn't put the speech out and that it would be put out through the C.O.I. because they wanted it to be known that George Brown thought the speech was extremely offensive in its Zionist tone though he couldn't fault its policy. In answer to this message from Freddy I made the one concession of putting into the speech the remark that 'it is based on personal experience'. What I didn't know was that in the *Observer* this morning there was a longish piece stating that I was insisting on making this personal statement and that the Foreign Office was permitting me to do so. If I'd known this I would have been wild with anger whereas I had no idea that half the audience at Drury Lane that night thought I was making a purely personal statement.

It had been raining all day when Anne and I packed Lucy into the back of our car and went up the ninety miles of the M1 in two hours, easy-going in driving rain the whole way, and then had just time to wash and change at Vincent Square before arriving at Drury Lane. There we found ourselves in one of those first-floor royal boxes on the right with Barnett Janner and Ian Winterbottom on one side and Bob Boothby and his young wife on the other.[1] In the box on the other side of the theatre I could see Abba Eban and his lovely wife. There was a gigantic audience and every seat was taken. They told me they'd had 8,000 applications. The evening started in a relaxed atmosphere for us because we were able to sit there quietly listening to the brilliant young Jewish pianist Daniel Barenboim conducting and at the same time playing the solo part in Beethoven's First Piano Concerto. After that we were ordered on to the stage and found ourselves in the usual Jewish celebrity crowd. I am sitting to the left of the chairman and Abba to the right. Beyond me is Julian Amery[2] and then Barnett Janner. The speakers, apart

---

[1] Sir Barnett Janner was Liberal M.P. for Whitechapel from 1931 to 1935, when he joined the Labour Party, sitting as Member for Leicester West 1945–50 and Leicester North-West 1950–70. In 1970 he became a life peer. Ian Winterbottom was Labour M.P. for Nottingham Central 1950–55. In 1965 he became a life peer and served as Parliamentary Under-Secretary of State for the Royal Navy 1966–7, at the Ministry of Public Buildings and Works 1967–8 and for the R.A.F. 1968–70. Robert Boothby, President of the Anglo-Israel Association, was Conservative M.P. for East Aberdeen 1924–58 and P.P.S. to Winston Churchill 1926–9. He became a life peer in 1958.

[2] Conservative M.P. for Preston 1950–66 and, since 1969, for Brighton Pavilion. He was Minister of Aviation 1962–4, Minister of Public Buildings and Works June–October 1970

18*

from myself, are Bob, Julian Amery and Abba. The President read his speech through and then Barnett Janner was as pontifically boring as usual. Next the chairman managed to introduce me not as Lord President but as Lord Privy Seal and that gave me an initial crack, which went down quite well. I had at the last moment to cut out the first third of the speech because Barnett of course overran interminably and I didn't want to speak for longer than twenty minutes. So out went the early part about Zionism and I concentrated on the central piece about Israel's relations with her neighbours, and the fact that the three wars had brought the Israelis nearer to peace by destroying one by one the layers of foreign interference and during the last war by destroying forever the insane armistice lines. It was an implicit attack on the United Nations and an overt plea for direct negotiations between Jew and Arab exactly in line with what Abba Eban was going to say. I think the audience was quite shattered and elated to hear a member of the British Government say what I said which didn't bear much relation to what they had been told by the Foreign Office. It was clear that they were teetering on the edge of staging an anti-Government demonstration unless they got from the Government spokesman what they thought they couldn't possibly get. Bob Boothby, who'd obviously prepared a rather different speech, had to follow in my tracks and ask for direct negotiations and then he got a great cheer by saying that we oughtn't to have any relations with Nasser at all.

Monday, November 6th

When I woke up I found Anne speechless with such flu and a bronchial chest that she had to stay in bed. We took a glance at the papers and as I had predicted last night my speech wasn't mentioned except for a sentence in the *Financial Times* and one paragraph in the *Guardian* saying it was a personal statement and not Government policy. I got the doctor round to see Anne and then went off to the office to prepare tomorrow's wind-up speech which traditionally ends the debate on the Queen's Speech.

I had just time to go in for ten minutes to see the P.M. before the Turkish President arrived.[1] I cleared with him my ideas for my Tuesday speech and then as I went out ran into George Brown, who had just finished his talk with Abba Eban. 'Did you deliver that speech yesterday?' he asked me. 'I couldn't find it in any paper.' Of course I realize he was saying the F.O. press department made sure that Fleet Street was told that it wasn't worth bothering to publish you. So was the B.B.C. since in the account of the event it only quoted a sentence from Eban and didn't mention that I had spoken. Never-

---

and Minister for Housing and Construction at the Department of the Environment 1970–72. He is author of volumes 4, 5 and 6 of *The Life of Joseph Chamberlain* (London: Macmillan, 1932), of which the first three volumes are by J. L. Garvin.

[1] President Sunay of Turkey had arrived in London on November 1st for a week's State visit.

theless I was pretty sure that the speech had made its impact and that there would be some repercussions.

At lunch with the Zionists I talked to the Ambassador and to Abba and told them that I had my speech cleared as official Government policy. Abba said he'd already seen George Brown this morning and had asked him whether my speech was a personal statement or whether it was Government policy. George had said to him, 'I worked over it with him word by word. Indeed there was nothing left for Dick to do but to deliver it. Did he deliver it well?' So to the Jews he took full credit for the speech but I needn't have thought for a moment that I'd changed Government policy. Later I learnt that a telegram had been sent out to interpret my speech as no change of policy and at the U.N. in New York Caradon duly disowned it.[1] A Minister cannot make foreign policy merely by intervening with a speech. What I had done was to make an impact so considerable that the F.O. had to swallow its pride and pretend one thing to the Jews and to the Arabs another. Of course the Jewish press are printing me in full and the *Jewish Observer* has already called it 'Crossman's Declaration'.

This afternoon in the House I had to answer Questions on behalf of the Services Committee. When a session ends all the Select Committees end too and have to be reappointed so this week there is no chairman of catering, etc., and only the Lord President can answer for all the sub-committees. I had one very delicate question about tipping. The Office bluntly committed me to replying that there was a $7\frac{1}{2}$ per cent surcharge but actually 5 per cent of this goes to increased wages and $2\frac{1}{2}$ per cent to a pool of tips. I dare say this may be common practice in hotels but it seems to me something which we can't possibly tolerate as Honourable Members of the House of Commons. If we have only $2\frac{1}{2}$ per cent deducted for tips we should tell the Members so. One of the troubles, I gathered, is that only about forty of the total catering staff get any tips, mostly those in the Strangers' dining-room. The men and the girls in the other room never see a tip and never reckon on them. So if you have a tips pool and divide it equally among the whole staff those in the Strangers' dining-room lose enormously and everybody else gains slightly. That, I gather, is the real grievance which has got to be dealt with. However I was careful this afternoon, and told the House that the new Committee was in the middle of its negotiations and I couldn't make a Statement until they were completed. I didn't let out a single word of what I had learnt about the actual division of the surcharge.

After my Questions we had a whole series of Statements from Ministers which lasted no less than forty minutes. The last was by Kenneth Robinson. I had tried to persuade him to postpone his Statement till Wednesday but he insisted on using today for a long official announcement on an inquiry

---

[1] Lord Caradon (Hugh Foot) was Minister of State for Foreign and Commonwealth Affairs and Permanent U.K. Representative at the U.N. 1964–70. He had been made a life peer in 1964.

into the structure of the National Health Service. He's become quite a problem to me recently. I used to know him as one of the few M.P.s who regularly went to Covent Garden and incidentally he also started having children as late in life as I did. But mainly I thought of him as an entirely progressive left-wing M.P., but he's turned out the most rigid departmental Minister in Whitehall and I've already recorded the troubles he caused us by insisting on making his Statement about cigarette gift tokens just before the voting in the by-elections. John has just had a small poll taken among the eighty M.P.s who went canvassing in those by-elections and fifty complained of Barbara's breathalyser and Kenneth Robinson's Statement.

I stayed on the front bench to hear Peter Walker[1] launching his attack on Barbara Castle's Transport Bill. It's monumental, 200 pages long and has caused me endless trouble. But at least it's a serious effort to reorganize transport in this country as nobody has dared to do before. If we were a Government with a reasonably good record in other ways, this Bill would be a tremendous gain. A Government which is succeeding in its central economic theme benefits by such extras but if a Government is failing centrally then such bold innovations become unpopular; you can win respect for an unpopular thing if you're doing well but if you are doing badly it only adds to your unpopularity.

While Barbara was trouncing Peter Walker (something she did with the greatest of ease) I was in my room having an extraordinary talk to Barnett Cocks. I had asked him to come and see me about the problem of Select Committees seeing confidential documents, because the Minister of Power was having a row with the Select Committee on Science and Technology, to whom he had sent a copy of a document marked 'confidential' only to be told that it was entirely up to the Committee to decide whether or not they respected confidentiality in their final report. This is intolerable and I said so. To this he replied, 'Look at the Public Accounts and Estimates Committees. This has been the convention there and there's never been an occasion when the chairman hasn't carried out the pledge that although they claim the right to publish they will respect the confidentiality the Minister asks for.' 'But in the case of these new Specialist Committees,' I replied, 'the Minister himself will be expected to give evidence in public and the Committees will be discussing policy, and not merely past events. With new situations arising we have to have new rules.' He then said he couldn't give way a single inch and insisted that the final word on publication of any document, however it is marked, must rest with the Select Committee. I pointed out the obvious fact that in that case my new Specialist Committees wouldn't get any confidential documents. 'You'll be cutting off your nose to spite your face,' I concluded. All he could reply was that a Select Committee can't give way on this because

[1] Conservative M.P. for Worcester since March 1961. He was Minister of Housing and Local Government June–October 1970, Secretary of State for the Environment 1970–72 and Secretary of State for Trade and Industry 1972–4.

it's vital to its existence. 'Would you rather have no documents?' I challenged him. And of course his honest answer should have been yes. I discovered that Barnett Cocks isn't the least interested in encouraging the House to set up investigatory committees and he intensely dislikes the idea of the Committees sitting in public and interrogating Ministers. He's in fact a traditionalist who wants these Select Committees to go on in their old, cosy, minor role—getting on well with the Government and persuading the Government that because they never breach confidentiality or say anything too unpleasant in their reports the Government can afford to give them some information. After a lot more discussion I said laughing, 'Well, would you agree to meet Burke Trend? Can I bring the Pope and Patriarch together?' He immediately agreed.

The rest of the day until 1 a.m. was taken up with preparing my speech. I was determined not to repeat the fiasco which I'd suffered in trying to reply to Part IV of the Prices and Incomes Bill. During the morning I'd been glancing through the Treasury brief and noticed seven points which Iain Macleod had given to the Brighton Tory Conference. It suddenly occurred to me that I could make the House laugh by taking his seven points and showing the hollowness of the Tory alternative. A wind-up speech is always a difficult thing to prepare because you start at exactly half an hour before the vote is taken and you've to sit down a few seconds before it strikes ten. You've got to look at the clock all the time and have your speech carefully divided up into sections with a final two-minute section which you begin at exactly two minutes to the hour. I knew that my two-minute section and, indeed, my last seven or eight minutes must be about the record of the Labour Government, but I was going to make my demolition of Macleod the centre of the speech. In preparing it I had to remember that I was winding up an eight-day debate which was mostly about economic problems. That's a real difficulty for a Lord President who isn't an economist. If you try to ape the Chancellor or the President of the Board of Trade you're howled down. If you talk ordinary Party propaganda the Opposition in its post-prandial mood tries to drown you with quiet conversation. The man who knew how to behave on those occasions was Harry Crookshank and he was the model which I had to imitate.[1] It must be the kind of clever near-Oxford Union speech, hard-hitting, light, humorous and yet with a bite. This is what we worked on this evening until finally Molly, who was waiting, motored my secretary home to her place in Dulwich and then took Freddie on to his place at Leatherhead while I walked home.

Tuesday, November 7th
At Legislation Committee I had to play my traditional role as controller of the legislative timetable and haul the Ministers over the coals. Each of them

[1] Conservative M.P. for Gainsborough 1924–6 and 1951–5, and Leader of the House of Commons 1951–5. He became a viscount in 1956 and died in October 1961.

had promised me six months ago that if I gave their Bill a place in the programme it would be ready to go to Second Reading before Christmas yet
now we come to the end of the Queen's Speech and there are fewer Bills
ready than ever before. All the big Bills are teetering over and it looks as
though they won't start till after the Christmas recess. I told the Committee
that their Bills would be lost if they weren't ready by the end of the Session.

The debate this afternoon was delayed by a long series of points of order
on the amendments put down by back-benchers to the Queen's Speech.
James Dickens, who's a solemn and very intelligent back-bencher,[1] had put
down a long detailed amendment not thinking that it had the remotest chance
of being called. Nevertheless, being a good back-bencher he found it necessary
to get up and make a long and reasoned protest to the Speaker calling his
attention to the precedent in 1946 when no less than two amendments were
moved by back-bench spokesmen, mine on foreign policy and Victor Yates's
on conscription.[2] I noted this as a useful point for the start of my speech.
At last Iain Macleod got up. He didn't make the expected thundering
attack on the Government. Instead he delivered a very careful, thoughtful
oration discussing with great learning the unemployment figures, and
expounding their real significance. I suspect he didn't attack the Government's
policy because basically he knew that if he were Chancellor of the Exchequer
he would be doing much the same as Jim. But I didn't care about the details of
his speech. What caught my attention was an odd remark he made at the end
of this long and detailed analysis of the movement of unemployment figures
during the last ten years. At this point he remarked, 'We can all make our
points on by-election platforms and I am as good at selective quotation as
anybody else. But nobody can seriously argue that when the performance of
both Governments …' The moment I heard this I knew I had got him because
he had frankly admitted the difference between the kind of nonsense one talks
outside and the serious speech one makes in the House of Commons. With
that remark and with James Dickens's reference to the precedent of 1946 I
had my two points to add to the structure of the speech I had prepared.

Then we came to poor old Jim Callaghan. He was tired and overwrought
and he made the mistake of being offensive to our back-benchers. 'Now I
come to the question,' he remarked, 'of the Governor of the Bank of England,
who made the speech — which I very much doubt many honourable Members
have read …' (Dickens had undoubtedly read it and felt offended.)[3] Callaghan
then made things worse by quoting the Governor of the Bank. 'He said: "It

[1] Labour M.P. for West Lewisham from 1966 to 1970, when he became Assistant
Director of Manpower Planning for the National Freight Corporation.

[2] Labour M.P. for Ladywood (Birmingham) from 1945 until his death in January 1969.

[3] In a speech in Argentina on October 5th, the Governor of the Bank of England, Sir
Leslie O'Brien, had said that the Government's economic policy was based on retaining
a margin of unused capacity in the economy. It seemed that the Governor's remarks were
made with official approval and Labour M.P.s attacked this suggestion that there was a
deliberate pool of unemployment. The Chancellor had refused to repudiate the speech and
some seventy Labour M.P.s put down a motion of censure.

is impossible to manage a large industrial economy with the very small margin of unused manpower resources that characterized the British economy in the 1940s and 1950s." That is true ... We must have a somewhat larger margin of unused capacity than we used to try to keep. That is the truth of the matter.' If you read it in Hansard[1] you realize how terrible it was for a Labour Chancellor to say such a thing, particularly if he profoundly believed it, and was suspected of believing it by his back-benchers. Immediately Callaghan sat down Michael Foot and Mendelson rose and made fighting speeches against the Labour Chancellor who was insisting that we needed a higher level of unemployment.

After they'd finished there was a powerful speech by Dickens, followed by two of our moderates — Sheldon and Barnett — who are chairman and secretary of the Economic Group but who attacked Callaghan on this particular occasion. It was a disastrous speech and it hung an albatross round Jim's neck.*

The Tory wind-up was provided by Reg Maudling. I'd had a cup of coffee with him and Quintin Hogg after lunch and he'd told me that this kind of rough and tumble on the last day didn't suit him. I said it didn't suit me either. He got through his speech perfectly respectably and then came my turn. I knew I had won the House over when I looked across the table and said to Macleod, 'You've told us you have one style of serious discussion for us here and something very different for the boobs in Brighton.' This brought the House down and then I was able to take him through his Brighton programme point by point and tear it to farcical smithereens. The Tories laughed themselves out of their discomfort and the back-benchers behind me roared. At two minutes to ten I began my little carefully rehearsed wind-up and as Big Ben started striking I sat down to a deluge of applause. That hadn't happened to me for a very long time — everybody coming up to me in the lobby and wanting to shake my hand. Everybody was voting for the Government with a good conscience. Of course they'd have voted for the Government anyway that evening but they'd have gone into the lobby surlily regretting they were not abstaining whereas on this occasion they went with gaiety in their hearts. I'm afraid that many of them were talking about the contrast between poor Jim and me and next day a vote of censure was put down not on the Lord President as it was a few months ago but on the Chancellor of the Exchequer.

After the division I asked Jim whether he had planned to make those remarks about unemployment. 'No, no,' he said. 'It was that fellow Mendelson with his awful *sotto voce* interjections in my speech. They made me so angry that I lashed out and attacked them much more than I intended. I should have put it the other way round — the way Harold puts it.' That often happens in life. What you don't intend to say is what you really mean. What he'd

* It stayed there for a long time.
[1] *House of Commons Debates*, Vol. 753, cols. 874-5.

said that afternoon were the true sentiments he shared with the Governor of the Bank of England about the pool of unemployment.

Later this evening I wandered into Harold's room to hear his congratulations. I found Bob Maxwell there talking about a homosexual circle which George Wigg had just exposed and somehow I soon found myself in a furious argument about tipping. I don't know how it came up but I was explaining to Harold the difficulties I got into in my answers to Questions on the previous afternoon, how outrageous the $7\frac{1}{2}$ per cent surcharge was and how it must be dealt with. Harold then said to me, 'But you never tip, do you?' I replied that I nearly always did in the Strangers' dining-room where tipping is normal. He seemed shocked and surprised and wholly sided with Bob Maxwell, who said that what mattered was increasing the wages. Is tipping one of my Tory weaknesses? It was an amusing end to what was for me a successful day.

Wednesday, November 8th
Of course, I got no press at all for my very successful speech. It was just mentioned in a line or two in one of the quality papers but everybody else virtually ignored it because the big parliamentary story for them was under the headline 'Callaghan rows with his back-benchers'. They had got their story conveniently early and they weren't going to change it merely because of what I said at 9.30 p.m. If I'd repeated my previous fiasco? Yes, they would have written that in—and so added another catastrophe for the Government. Jim would still have led the story but I would have been a useful tailpiece. I didn't care too much and nor did John Silkin because it was the morale of the Party which concerned us. The Party really had responded to me and it was our parliamentary leadership that seemed important.

This morning we had a meeting of the Cabinet Social Services Committee to reconsider next April's package for increased family allowances with supplementary allowances and children's tax allowances, the price of school meals, the price of welfare milk all considered together. At the very first meeting of my new Home Publicity Committee we had discovered that each Department was already preparing the publicity plans about the change it was introducing. Two of them already had designed their own posters. When I discovered this I had asked for a special meeting of Social Services and here, as I expected, it was revealed not only that the propaganda was separate but that the policy decisions had been made in complete isolation. The Treasury and the Ministry of Social Security had negotiated about the family allowance package, but the Ministry of Education and the Ministry of Housing were working completely on their own. Finally I suggested that we must stop the publicity altogether until we have got the policy issues sorted out.

I then moved on to the long-awaited S.E.P. meeting on imports and devaluation.[1] It started with a speech by Tony Crosland, very skilful and cautious, and strictly along the lines he had discussed with me. His main aim was to show that import quotas were no substitute for devaluation — a subject he skirted around until the Prime Minister himself brought it right out in the open and said we must discuss the pros and cons. At once the Chancellor made it clear that he was still against devaluation and believed we must soldier on. Floating of the pound was, he said, a delusion. If we were forced off that was that: it would be a disaster but there could be no question of freely deciding to go off. The P.M. was keeping his options open. 'I am politically open on this subject. I am prepared to think there could be some merit in a free decision, and in that case we must of course decide whether we float or devalue by a certain amount. My mind isn't closed,' he said. Long before this it had become clear in the general discussion that no one objected in principle to devaluation except the Chancellor. Jim was absolutely isolated, with the possible exception of Ray Gunter, and Harold had got what he once told me he wanted. He had smoked the Chancellor out, and proved he was alone in his objection, while at least three of us — Tony Crosland, Michael Stewart and I — were convinced we should do it as soon as was practically possible. Each of us begged Harold not to wait until he was forced off.

Out of this came a second statement by Callaghan. He was just not prepared to reconsider the issue for several months. But, he added, there was a serious chance of our being forced off in the immediate future — in a matter of days, the next ten days or so. This he said more than once and Cabinet decided to leave that to him and the Prime Minister to handle. Up till now Crosland had made all the running but at this point I interjected that I felt we couldn't possibly leave things as they were and urged that we must have another meeting because most of us were convinced we must now devalue as soon as possible. To this Jim replied that we must not underestimate the catastrophe of devaluation. It would be a political catastrophe as well as an economic one. I couldn't resist telling him that he mustn't underestimate the catastrophe of our present policy. 'We are in the middle of a political catastrophe now,' I said, 'and there's no prospect of getting out of it until there's a new breakthrough which we can only get by devaluation.' But it was also true, I concluded, that we could only get it if the Prime Minister and the Chancellor of the Exchequer carried it out themselves. These two are essential to the credibility of a Labour Government which devalues. I simply want them to do it as soon as they can. Harold insisted there should be no minutes of this part of Cabinet and assured us that he and Jim would hold on and see what possibilities there were of rallying support from our allies in the Six, in Basle and in New York.

I was told later in the day that the Prime Minister was pleased by what he had achieved at the meeting. I was pretty worried because I could see that

[1] For the Prime Minister's account of this meeting see *Wilson*, pp. 449–51.

he and Callaghan are determined not to devalue until they're forced off and I wouldn't be a bit surprised if they borrowed another £300 or £400 million and led us into debt over the £2,000 million point in order to avoid making a decision.

I went back to Vincent Square and had a bit of lunch with Anne, who was still in bed but her temperature was down, thank heaven. I got back to the House just in time to hear Tam get up and complain to the Speaker that he had been denied two Questions about Aldabra. When it was revealed that he'd already tabled fifty Questions on the subject and the Speaker had added that he thought there must be a top limit, the House smiled but Tam is clever. As he said to me afterwards, 'The publicity about the top limit brought the subject up again.' His one-man campaign on Aldabra is going well. Already he knows more about it than anyone except Denis Healey. When I sent him to Eddie Shackleton the other day he admitted to me afterwards that Tam ran rings round him. I think he's going to win.

In the evening—Anne was much better now—I had to put on a dinner jacket and take her to a strange dinner with Ronnie Grierson, who had just resigned from the I.R.C.[1] He had invited the Chalfonts and the Melchetts as well and I'd only accepted when I heard the Melchetts would be there since I wanted to see something of him. I sat next to Sonia Melchett and she gave me a very interesting picture of Dick Marsh, the attractiveness of his youth and vigorous intelligence which enabled him, despite his brashness, to get on well with her husband. As we went on talking I got a very pleasant picture of their relationship but it also revealed the terrific danger for men of Dick Marsh's youth and lack of experience who are suddenly plunged into this world of tremendous wealth. The Griersons were by no means the wealthiest people there but their house is terrific and their dinner was terrific, with wonderful food and drink and any number of waiters. This financial society is one I don't usually see. I keep to the Weidenfeld or to the Pamela Berry table.

Thursday, November 9th
Bank rate went up by another half per cent[2] and very obviously there is another sterling crisis. But of course it was not mentioned in Cabinet today. Instead we discussed Stansted, which is now developing into a big political issue; the story of this will be quite worth studying by anyone who writes the history of this Government. This morning for the first time we had Tony Crosland dealing with it instead of Douglas Jay. Like Roy Jenkins he had been against the original decision to go ahead and, now that he'd taken over from Jay and taken a good look, he insisted that a proper cost analysis must

---

[1] He was deputy chairman and managing director of the I.R.C. 1966–7, chairman of the Orion Bank 1971–3 and Director-General for Industrial and Technological Affairs at the E.E.C. Commission from 1973 until he resigned and returned to banking in 1974.

[2] From 6 to 6½ per cent.

be made before we reach any final conclusion. However, he weakened this argument by admitting that it was almost certain that Stansted was the only practical place for a third airport and if it wasn't Stansted it would be Nuthampstead, which happens to be seven miles nearer Cambridge. This seemed to me a *reductio ad absurdum*. He said that the last inquiry had been so unsatisfactory and the public sense of outrage was now so strong that a further inquiry was fully justified and after all it wouldn't lose us too much time and might put ourselves right with public opinion.

Tony Greenwood was against him, chiefly because a few weeks before he had made a speech listing all the arguments against delay and saying that we must stick by the decision. What we should tell the House, he added, is that we could realign the runways and thereby greatly reduce the noise at Bishop's Stortford and this change would justify the two or three months' delay in tabling the Order. There was a good deal of support for Crosland from the Lord Chancellor, Barbara Castle and others. Roy Jenkins said we shouldn't turn this issue into a battle as futile and costly as Passchendaele had been. To this I replied that if he wanted to talk about battles and generals he should think of the Grand Old Duke of York and remember that one can't march one's troops up the hill and then down again without ruining their morale. We've already ordered the two hundred people who wanted an inquiry to vote against an inquiry. How could we now force them to vote for an inquiry? We should be the laughing stock of the world. I agreed with Greenwood that we must use the excuse of airport realignment for delay. This argument seemed to influence the Cabinet. If we had been strong and vigorous and on the crest of a wave, the Government might have been able to concede another inquiry on Stansted. But at this particular juncture, with our back-benchers in a state of confusion and fury, another reversal of this kind would just about have finished us.

At lunch-time I first heard the rumours that George Wigg was to go to the Lords and become the head of the Horse-race Betting Levy Board. Later I got the facts from Harold.

This afternoon at my Lobby after the business Statement I briefed the journalists fully on Stansted because the Ministers involved refused to make any Statement. I told them they were bloody fools not to and as I thought it right to do it I gave the press a full and thorough fill-in, which I've no doubt they will use.

Fortunately they didn't ask me about George Wigg, though they pestered me about Callaghan's row with the back-benchers and Party discipline. I managed to send them off fairly happily. I remarked, 'I'm used to being the unpopular man who makes the abrasive comment and causes the disturbance which is then smoothed down by Callaghan. Now Callaghan is being abrasive and I'm smoothing the disturbance down.'

The Party meeting this evening lasted a full forty minutes and the P.M., John and I had the job of keeping our colleagues quiet. They were full of indignation, wanting to get at Callaghan and attack George and we had to expend a lot of our fund of goodwill to soothe them.

On the way to No. 10 I had a word with the Chief about the result of the ballot for Private Members' Bills this afternoon. Bill Wilson had got into the top eight and I said to him that he's exactly the man we want to do the Divorce Bill for the Lord Chancellor. The Chief was very snubbing. 'It's for me and only for me to consider the names of people for Private Members' Bills,' he observed. However, I smoothed him down and later that evening went round to the Lord Chancellor and smoothed him down and now there's a reasonable chance of Bill Wilson having his first parliamentary opportunity, and of something being achieved on the divorce front.

I left John at No. 12 and went through to my business meeting with the P.M. I found him alone with Burke; George came in later. The three of them then had a long and fascinating discussion about Vietnam. They felt that the Government must now move from its present position of close association with L.B.J. but not too far away. This, they all agreed, was a delicate operation and it must be reflected in the paper they were preparing for Cabinet. I listened quietly and learnt a great deal about the delusions of grandeur which are the fatal defects of George and Harold and which are constantly stimulated by Burke Trend. They believe that as acknowledged actors on the world political stage they can perform these manoeuvres, moving a little bit away from L.B.J., and influencing him from a distance. They all seem unaware that they are figures of fun as long as Britain is on the edge of economic ruin. They should accept their lot, concentrate on home affairs and stop trying to obtain opportunities for appearances on the world stage. This is my basic disagreement with them.

After they'd gone I had a word with the P.M. about George Wigg. He explained to me that Antony Head had been offered and had refused the job.[1] This gave George his chance and if he didn't take it now he would miss it for ever. 'Anyway, I think it's the right time for him to move on.' This confirmed the impression I'd got that afternoon from Trevor Lloyd-Hughes that George didn't really want to go and had to be pushed, but in a nice favourable way. The Prime Minister confirmed that this would require a by-election at Dudley and when I said, 'Oh hell,' he replied, 'Well, we could hold it over until next June when it ought to be all right. George's going will be a great relief, you know,' he added. 'He was becoming a great early morning pressure on my telephone, as you very well know.'

Physically as well as mentally Harold's beginning to show some strain in conversation. I don't like the fact but he now sits at the Cabinet table sipping whisky instead of water. Callaghan hasn't got much nerve left and George

---

[1] Conservative M.P. for Carshalton 1945–60. He was Secretary of State for War 1951–56 and Minister of Defence 1956–January 1957. In 1960 he became a viscount and first High Commissioner to the Federation of Nigeria. From 1963–66 he was High Commissioner to the new Federation of Malaysia.

Brown is on the way out. There's a real danger that our people at the centre of things are cracking from sheer exhaustion.

Friday, November 10th

Burke came to see me in my room. He understands the strain under which the P.M. is working and is very worried about it. After speaking of this he told me that the S.E.P. next Monday morning had been cancelled because neither the Chancellor nor the Prime Minister wanted to see us that day. I rang up Harold straightaway and asked him why this had happened. 'I can understand your not wanting a big S.E.P. but surely you want to consult your inner circle of friends?' I said. 'At least I want to make sure that nothing will be decided before S.E.P. meets again if it isn't to meet on Monday. This can't just be fixed by you and Callaghan.' I had never talked to him quite like that before. I could hear him gulp a bit and then I said, 'Well, that's all I want to say. I am sorry to have bothered you.' He said, 'I don't want any panic measures by people who are *parti pris*.' Of course, by that he means anyone in favour of devaluing or floating the pound.

At lunch today Arthur Gavshon told me a curious fact about my Balfour speech last Sunday. Apparently he had rung up my Private Office and asked for a copy of the final text and in the text he was given someone had written in the phrase in longhand 'this is a purely personal statement' instead of what I had dictated, 'this is based on personal experience'. Presumably this was the work of Freddy Ward and only shows how the Civil Service operate together when they think it important to do so.

This afternoon I went down to Oxford to speak to the Democratic Socialist Club. Days ago I'd been warned that the old Labour Club, which is now the home of the roistering anarchists and Marxists, had decided to arrange a demonstration which would stop me speaking in the same way the Prime Minister was attacked a fortnight ago at Cambridge. If the Marxists were going to repeat this with knobs on at Oxford I was in for a lively time. The chairman of the Democratic Socialists had rung me up on Thursday saying that the police would be there and he'd arranged that only members of the Society would be allowed to come in. Would I rather cancel the meeting? I said, 'Certainly not. My wife won't come but I will.' Little did I know what it was going to be like.

When I reached Oxford station I found two young men there to meet me and a number of policemen, who immediately surrounded me. The head of the police then came up and asked me where I was staying the night and I said that was my affair. He said, 'I hear you're going to Holywell Lodge. I shall have a police car to take you there.' I said I wasn't going to Holywell Lodge and he said, 'I must look after your security.' To this I replied that I didn't want any looking after in Oxford.

However, by then the stairs leading to the Union dining-room had apparently been filled with demonstrators who were going to throw themselves in my path, and already they were beginning to gather outside in St Michael's Street, with their banners and their chants of 'Up—down' or something of that kind. It was a horrible atmosphere because the people who were entertaining me were nervous and scared.

We went up to dinner through the kitchen and when we had sat down I found conversation a bit difficult. 'I suppose you feel yourselves rather a gallant last stand of Labour people supporting this Government,' I remarked. And the chairman said, 'Oh, we're not supporting the Government. I don't think there's any Government policy I agree with.' 'Is it our pensions policy or our housing, or our general economic policy that you think so wrong?' I asked. 'No, no,' he said, 'not domestic policy. It's Rhodesia and Vietnam.' 'Then why aren't you demonstrating in St Michael's Street,' I asked, 'with the Labour Club?' 'Oh,' he said, 'our demonstration is tomorrow night. We wanted you to come and speak first and we could demonstrate afterwards.'

Surrounded by police, I was taken down the back stairs and across the gardens, hoping that once I got inside the Union debating hall there would be an exciting meeting. But when I entered the meeting consisted of a tiny knot of people—about 150 or 160 though the hall holds 800 or 900—sitting cold, bleak and silent along the inner rows. The Democratic Socialists had forbidden anyone except their own members to hear me and the police had stopped even them going in. However I spoke to them in a glacial atmosphere on the selected subject, parliamentary reform, and answered questions for about an hour. When I got outside the door I found I'd lost the chairman and was surrounded again by police who tried to shepherd me to a police car. I said I wasn't going and walked back into the hall, found the chairman and asked him to walk with me to Balliol. But the police protested that this wouldn't be safe. I told them that I was going whatever they thought and when we got to the Cornmarket from St Michael's Street about fifty yards to the right I could see the crowd of demonstrators chanting outside the other entrance to the Union. Quite safely I moved along with these young men round me, black beards, strange atmosphere and suddenly I remembered that this was the atmosphere of a Weimar Republic meeting when you had to be shepherded by the police, when your own supporters inside the hall were frightened and when, outside, there was the threatening force of the popular will. It shook me mainly because it all happened at Oxford. In the 1960s the mass of the student Left is behaving in the way which we used to say the fascists behaved in the 1930s.

Inside Balliol I found that the dons were having one of their ladies' nights and I was taken into their common room and given a drink by Christopher Hill, the Master.[1] After that I sat down by Tommy's wife, Pen, and told her what had happened to me. She replied, 'I rather sympathize with those young men. After all, you can't blame them for protesting at what the Government's done in Vietnam.' I very nearly hit her. If these Oxford socialists had had the

[1] Historian and Master of Balliol College, Oxford since 1965.

guts to come to the meeting and howl me down I wouldn't have minded but to try and break the meeting up by making a disturbance outside and scaring those who wanted to hear me seems pretty awful.

Saturday, November 11th

I spent the night with the Baloghs and next morning walked across the Parks — an exquisitely beautiful day, lovely beech trees and copper beeches beaming in the sun. I was going to see my sister Mary and her husband, Charles Woodhouse, who told me they would motor me out to Prescote. But directly I got inside their house I was told that No. 10 wanted me on the phone. They'd rung Prescote and found I wasn't there and now they were ringing me here. It was Harold. 'I'd like to have a good long talk to you. Can't talk on the phone, come up tomorrow any time.' I said I would come on the last train from Banbury so that during the day he could write his speech for the Guildhall while I wrote my speech on parliamentary reform. I would be there at 10.30 p.m. He told me to make sure that everyone knew I was only coming to see him about parliamentary reform. I said I would take care that this was rumoured. So now I'm due to see him alone tomorrow evening when the whole world is aware that we're going to devalue, and when Jim and he are palpitating, resistant, uncertain, unable to cope.

When I got to Prescote I had the day to myself and the family — time for a few reflections on a terrible week for the Government. When a government gets into a run of bad luck or rather unsuccess, then what would have been quite easy to carry in normal times becomes an insupportable burden. One ill-fortune creates another and turns what would have been accidents into pieces of ineptitude. The Chalfont crisis is followed by the Brown crisis, the Brown crisis is followed by Callaghan's row with the back-benchers, and that in turn, has been followed this week by the Robens crisis, Robens rowing with Dick Marsh and making deliberate political capital out of the pit closures.

But ironically enough this disastrous week for the Government has been one of the most successful weeks of my political career. My Balfour Declaration speech on Sunday night was a classic oration which disappointed none of the Jews and yet conformed with the Government's foreign policy. Then on Tuesday I wound up the Queen's Speech debate with half an hour which reminded the *Daily Telegraph* of Crookshank at the top of his form in the early 1950s. Though they were scarcely reported, these two events had a tremendous effect on my position in Westminster and if the week ended with my being shouted down at Oxford that doesn't change the fact that as a leading politician during the Government's discomfiture I have improved my position inside the Cabinet and in the Parliamentary Party. I'm told that tomorrow Jimmy Margach in the *Sunday Times* and Terry Lancaster in the *People* are talking about me as a successful Minister whose future looks good. That's the kiss of death all right. It also shows the frivolity of the political commentators. Six months ago I was a miserable, arrogant, impossible failure. I've not changed in any way. It's just the luck of the toss in how things go. By sheer chance Crossman's stock goes up in the same week that the Government's stock plummets down.

Sunday, November 12th

I was just going to get started on this diary when I was interrupted by the sight of a deluge of water coming down outside my window. I rushed upstairs and found it was Patrick siphoning water from his bath in order to water the flowers on the terrace. He's now in an experimental scientific phase and when Charles and Mary brought me over from Oxford to lunch yesterday they found him at his most communicative. He's growing into a very big boy but his mind is also growing and he's being allowed a freedom for reading and roving in his thoughts which he certainly wouldn't have got at his prep school. Up till now Charles, although he's a master at Dragon prep school in Oxford, feels we haven't lost by keeping him at the village school.

Talking of education, we had an interesting incident last night when we dined with Harry Judge, the headmaster of what is to be our local comprehensive school, and there met Miss Moorhouse, the woman who for years has been in charge of primary education in Oxfordshire.[1] We started with the usual arguments about how to handle clever children but very soon we were down to what is the bitterest subject of disagreement in our village school, italic script. The headmistress tries one thing, tries another but always in the end puts them on to italic script. I complained about this and Harry Judge, rather frivolously, said, 'If you do get the children to write in good italic script with proper pens at their primary school then when they come to secondary school they won't find the italic pens provided and all the work will be wasted.' Miss Moorhouse then asked him whether this happened at Banbury comprehensive and he replied lightheartedly that he was afraid it sometimes did. I then showed some impatience and complained that writing isn't as some teachers believe a question of calligraphy, making a beautiful pattern on a page. It's a useful method of taking notes or communicating and all I want for my children is that they are able to do it competently and clearly before they learn to type. Since then I've got a solemn letter from Miss Moorhouse saying she was distressed at the tension between the headmistress and ourselves on this subject: couldn't we really provide the children with italic pens for their homework? We've never been asked to do this because the headmistress at our school doesn't approve of homework. What I really object to is the obvious lack of adequate liaison between those who run secondary and primary education in Oxfordshire.

I went up to London on the last train and clocked in at No. 10. Harold is

---

[1] Harry Judge was principal of Banbury school from 1967 to 1973, when he became Director of the Oxford University Department of Educational Studies. Miss Edith Moorhouse was Senior Organizer for Primary Schools in Oxfordshire.

there waiting in the big room downstairs and we settle down for two hours from 10.45 to 12.45. And it's fencing all the time. He chooses to keep the argument on the technical problem of devaluation and I keep on saying, 'I'm not an economist,' to which he replies, 'What about those thousands of hours you spend with Thomas? Of course you're a trained economist.' And then I say, 'But you can always defeat me in argument on economics,' and he tells me I'm misguided and that devaluation will be a disaster. I wonder what on earth the point of it all is and finally I say to him, 'I think you have the choice, Harold, between doing it freely and being driven to it miserably. What matters here is the posture you adopt.' I then rub in a second point which I've agreed beforehand with Thomas. 'We must have this inner Cabinet,' I say, and at once we turn to a longish discussion about the membership. He says he's ready for it this time and he's talked to George and he's talked to Jim, and they quite like the idea. Michael Stewart? They thought it wasn't worth having him because he didn't count. He would have liked to have Gunter but he leaks too much. I asked about Roy, but there's no enthusiasm for Roy. He's off Roy for the time being.

So there we are. He's going to have his inner Cabinet. But I finally remind him that though he has cancelled the S.E.P. meeting tomorrow there must be consultation. We can't permit another of those packages slip-slapped on the Cabinet table at no notice. The inner group must have a reasonable discussion of the social policies to be pursued. He says 'Yes'—and I have a feeling he doesn't really mean it.

I slipped off to Vincent Square thoroughly frustrated because I know I've achieved nothing at all by all that talk.

Monday, November 13th
I ran into Jim on his way to the Chief from No. 10 and he took me into his room. 'Well, we are for it,' he said, 'unless we get the right answers this morning. This time the bankers' terms will be unacceptable.' He then gave me a great deal of detailed information about the American and German attitudes and finally, in utter dejection, added 'The only point of devaluing would be the package we could lay down.' I said, 'What do you mean? Why should we lay down a package?' and he replied, 'Because it'll be a chance to teach the people of this country what a fools' paradise they've been living in.' Poor Jim, he's Treasury-minded now and the only pleasure left him is to anticipate what people in this country will suffer before they learn what bloody fools they've been.

This talk so shocked me that I went straight back to my office and composed a careful letter to Harold Wilson in which I again told him that he can argue rings round me about devaluation but what really matters now is his posture when it comes. That, I told him, is the only thing on which he now has to decide. It's like the outbreak of war in 1939 when Chamberlain said, 'My life is all in ruins.' But Churchill felt all the better and relieved that it had started. 'I want you to be Churchillian, to feel better for the devaluation when it occurs while Jim is feeling his life is in ruins. Jim must be the Chamberlain of our time and you the Churchill.' It was a goodish letter and I put it in an envelope marked 'Personal' to be opened only by him and sent it across at lunch-time to Marcia.

At three o'clock I was due at a Privy Council to admit two new P.C.s—the Judge Advocate for Scotland and an Australian judge. What do I say to the Queen this time in my private audience? I talked to her about the Queen's Speech and her delivery and told her how excited I was by that instant tiny pause she made before she told the Lords about the diminution of their powers. Then we discussed the terrible stuff the Government normally gives her to read aloud, and I said what I would really like would be to compose a speech for her one day which could be delivered properly. We were really having a very cosy little chat when she pressed the button and brought the others in.

I had spare time today and spent it all preparing my speech for the procedure debate which is bound to be very complicated since we've put down more than twenty resolutions.

After drinks at the Privy Council Office I took John and his wife and Anne out to dinner at the Garrick. John had just been made a member and we were celebrating. The Garrick is a lovely club with the candles burning, the dark black carved wood, the portraits of the actors all round, these nice ladies who look after us, and the excellent claret—it really is a splendid place. Rosamund, John's wife, is jolly nice. John and I kept off politics and I knew I'd got to get back to the House by 10 p.m. because Janet Newman and Vera were waiting to finish my speech with me.

However it was a thoroughly nice evening and a great relief to me. When I put John's name down and got Dingle Foot to second him there was a very poor response and I was quietly warned that he was being blackballed. Some said it was because he was a Jew but I'm afraid it was because he was another politician like me and I've not been at all a good club member because I never go there alone and sit at the centre table and mix with the other members. However, thanks to Rosie, who is an actress, he got Donald Wolfit and other actors to sign and everything became O.K.

Back at the Privy Council I got most of the speech done and went home to Anne, who was waiting for me at Vincent Square.

Tuesday, November 14th
I found, reading the papers, that Harold had been at the Guildhall the night before and made a great speech about the European technical revolution— a cover-up of course of the utterly disastrous trade figures which are to appear tomorrow.[1] He'd obviously done the job well and hadn't mentioned the pound except indirectly.

[1] There was a trade gap of £107 million.

At Cabinet this morning Roy asked quite briefly when there would be a Statement.* He was told by the Chancellor that it would come in a few days.

When he'd said this, Callaghan, who sits by me, muttered to me in a loud whisper, 'I hope this isn't regarded as too disingenuous. Is it too disingenuous, Dick?' He was almost telling me that we were going to devalue in a few days. I hadn't known it before but I knew it after that.

Then we had George Thomson talking about his visit to Rhodesia. It was clear beforehand that it was going to be a flop and a flop it was. There was no disagreement between him and Smith except that they attacked each other and then when George returned to London airport Smith put on an extremely offensive radio talk which he'd even taped before the talks. Nothing could show his humiliating contempt for us more than that. But Harold was the same as ever, talking about Smith as a schizophrenic, a mad little man, and once again I had the uneasy feeling that though he may be a mad little man he's holding us up to ransom pretty successfully. However I gather there's going to be yet another last attempt at agreement. It may come a bit easier after devaluation.

My mind was all on the procedure debate which I had to open and manage. Freddy Ward, Janet, Vera, the whole Private Office were mobilized to help to prepare for what had to be a very big and complicated Statement. On these occasions I don't get much help from John Silkin or Freddie Warren, who regard making speeches as my job, not theirs. By three o'clock we had a speech and I knew it was much too long, but as I say, I had twenty resolutions on the Order Paper and I was determined to get at least the first twelve adopted this evening to redeem my failure last time. Before I could start there were three Statements. First George Brown on Aden, where he got away with it pretty easily, then George Thomson on Rhodesia—very depressing—and then, not a Statement strictly, but a protest from Leo Abse and other Welsh M.P.s about the Fuel White Paper which was published today and on which our back-benchers felt that Dick Marsh should have made a Statement and answered Questions.[1] I felt very much caught out. I should have had the gumption to realize that in view of the row which had broken out over the weekend about Robens and pit closures a Statement by the Minister was essential. But the truth is that Dick has been terribly upset by the miners' attacks. They have been lobbying Dick, Robens has been bullying him, and he's beginning to realize that the extraordinary rapid and ruthless closure of the pits which he's forced through Whitehall and Cabinet is going to be pretty unacceptable outside. Certainly this afternoon the whole House was

* This, by the way, is recorded in the Cabinet minutes, which is extremely unusual.
[1] Lord Robens had forecast, on November 9th, that the forthcoming White Paper would lead to a loss of 300,000 jobs in the coalmines by 1980 and an end to coalmining in traditional areas in Scotland, Wales and Northern England. While it did not bear out these predictions, the White Paper *Fuel Policy* (Cmnd. 3438) forecast a drop in coal production of some 100 million tons by 1970.

against him and we're going to have a lot of trouble in dealing with that White Paper in the near future.

All this took forty minutes and then I got up and spoke for fifty minutes — far too long, though there were a lot of interruptions at the end. But I think I built it up as part of our big reform and made people realize the relevance of the resolutions we were asking them to adopt. Not that the House shows the slightest interest in the reform of its procedure. There were some fifty people there during my speech and for Selwyn Lloyd's reply but the numbers then went down to twenty, and when Michael Stewart wound up for us it got up to twenty-five but not more. Not many of the reformers, or of the anti-reformers either, on our side bothered to turn up and the Tories were mainly represented by Selwyn and John Boyd-Carpenter. Yet what I was introducing was a major package of reforms—putting the Finance Bill upstairs, voluntary timetabling, etc., and it was really staggering how quietly it went through. This was slightly helped on our side by Michael Stewart's brilliant wind-up. Nigel Birch, one of the finest demolition men on the Tory side, tried to demolish me as he once demolished Macmillan.[1] But it flopped entirely and Michael then quietly demolished him. Birch made the mistake of quoting from Marlowe without checking the reference too carefully.[2] Michael took full advantage of this, and it's worth looking it up in Hansard.

Once again during this long debate I couldn't help feeling peeved at seeing so little of John Silkin. I know that he was busy talking to the Prime Minister and trying to sort out the problem of the Fuel White Paper as well as dealing with the economic situation. On the other hand, some of the resolutions I was dealing with affected his side of the House—the method of taking votes, for example—and I was completely floored at one point because Brian O'Malley, his new Deputy, knew nothing about the arrangements the Chief and Willie Whitelaw had entered into. I thought they had agreed that after ten we would take the non-controversial resolutions and though there would be no vote we would go on as long as necessary throughout the night. Apparently John had really guaranteed to Willie that under no circumstances would there be a vote and this gave him and Selwyn the veto on the resolutions to be passed that night, an opportunity they seized to make me drop the resolution about the Clerks' wigs, which I'd inserted purely as a personal favour to Barnett Cocks.

In any case, when I'm alone all day on the front bench I get peevish and nervy and I suppose I was unnecessarily peevish about his absence at this particular moment, whereas he felt he was right and that I was being unreason-

---

[1] Accusing him of laying down his friends for his life in the 1962 Cabinet reshuffle.

[2] He said that the new Financial Secretary and his predecessor reminded him 'of the characters in Marlowe's *Tamburlaine* Usumcasane and Theridamas. They were walking-on parts. If they opened their mouths, it was always nonsense which came out, and no one told them anything.' Michael Stewart reminded him that Theridamas 'produces some of the most beautiful and memorable lines in the whole play'. *House of Commons Debates*, Vol. 754, cols. 304 and 365.

able. Part of the difficulty is that the Chief Whip is debarred from speaking—a ridiculous rule by the way—and this makes him even less inclined to sit on the bench beside the Lord President who gets all the speeches about the Chief's work. I can understand his feelings. Nevertheless we achieved infinitely more than in the procedure debate last December, and in a quiet way I felt quite pleased though I knew we should get no kind of press tomorrow morning. But I also knew that John and I had strengthened our hold on Parliament and on the Parliamentary Party.

Wednesday, November 15th

The press, of course, was full of the fuel policy row, the economic crisis, and the ghastly trade figures, and the populars had no room for poor little procedure. However, there were quite good reports in the parliamentary columns of *The Times*, *Guardian* and *Telegraph*, and Alastair Hetherington[1] gave me a very nice leader on the quiet revolution in Parliament. There's no doubt I'm making ground. But meanwhile the left wing has put down a vote of censure for the Party meeting next Tuesday on Callaghan's remark on unemployment. This remark is still reverberating, and so is the contradiction between that and what the P.M. had previously said. After the P.M.'s attempt to reconcile the two, Harold is being accused of deceit and trickery.

When we went into O.P.D. and I passed his chair the P.M. said *sotto voce*, 'I've got your letter and want to reply to it,' and I said, 'Don't worry.'

The two items on the agenda were arms sales to Israel and the Arab states and the Defence Treaty for Mauritius, the same old tag-ends of a tattered defence policy of posture.

At 11 o'clock I had to be at the Party meeting to explain the reference in the Gracious Speech to Lords reform and, in particular, to ask the Party to give the Government the guidelines for the consultations which will now take place with the other Party leaders. Charlie Pannell got up and made a very offensive personal attack before moving a motion that we must come back to the Party before irrevocable decisions are taken. Of course I can't accept it straightaway. But it was an untidy meeting, attended by only twenty-two peers and fifty members of the Parliamentary Party out of 350. This is a relief to me since it shows there's no major discontent in the Party about the proposal. Of course Michael Foot and Jack Mendelson got up to urge the abolition of the House of Lords. Michael said he'd never heard the reasons explained so clearly for acting at once and he's convinced by them but worried that we shall finally come to a wrong agreement with the Tories. An amusing moment came when one of the left-wingers, who object to any extension of patronage, had urged that instead of life peers we should have peers created only for the life of each Parliament. Roy was able to show there could be

---

[1] Editor of the *Guardian* from 1956 until 1975. In 1976 he became Controller, B.B.C. Scotland.

nothing so utterly dependent on patronage as a peer whose reappointment depended on his political reliability.

I lunched with Shackleton because the first consultations were going to take place this very evening. It's a good thing we met because he had to tell me that George Brown had once again gone off his rocker and was sending Eddie off again to head the delegation for the last Aden negotiations. Eddie is the Deputy Leader of the Lords and head of the working party doing all our detailed work and yet he's now been hauled off for this fortnight in Geneva. But nothing can be done about it. He also told me that the Lord Chancellor had gone personally into Lords Committee Room 3 and arranged the tables in a triangle with himself at the point of the triangle and Macleod on his left and me on his right and then everybody else higglety-pigglety around. Asked why he'd done it, he said, 'This isn't going to be a confrontation. We all want agreement and it will be easier to get together if we don't sit as delegations.' Eddie and I agreed that this is a crazy argument and we must get the tables rearranged. I left it to Wheeler-Booth because I had to take the chair at the Cabinet Pensions Committee which as usual plunged into details. I have had to ask for a timetable because we are not getting on at all.

Then I had my meeting with the Chief Whip about next week's business and the fuel crisis which is blowing up. Dick Kelley[1] has already denounced the Minister of Fuel, and our friend Joe Gormley, who's a miner member of the N.E.C. and chairman of the Org. Sub, has stated that he's prepared to start a new Miners' Party because the Labour Party is betraying them. John and I agreed that we'll try to give two separate days to coal — one on the Coal Industry Bill and the other on the White Paper — but that we'll put it off for a week in the hope that the storm will subside.

Now it was time for the all-party consultations to start and I rushed in to the Lord Chancellor's room. Roy Jenkins had blown his top about the arrangement of the tables and I had to say that I agreed. The Lord Chancellor said painfully, 'Nobody here seems to agree,' and one minute before the agreed talks started the tables were rearranged into a square. The Lord Chancellor sat on one side of the square with his civil servants round him. Our delegation sat on his right, the Tory delegation on his left and the Liberals facing us, a sensible arrangement which makes all the delegations feel comfortable.

The Lord Chancellor started the proceedings with a long and very untidy speech picking up one or two points, and then he was interrupted by, thank heavens, the Conservatives. He stopped and asked for the Conservative view. No progress. It's clear that having got himself into the chair in a strictly non-political capacity he can't keep things moving. That is a great relief because it means that as leader of the Labour delegation I can move the discussion on. This I at once did and I was relieved to hear afterwards from Wheeler-Booth that the Tories and Liberals were well content with the way I

[1] Labour M.P. for Don Valley since October 1959.

was handling it. We really got an astonishing amount of agreement in a very short time. It is clear that the Tories and the Liberals really believe in a House of life peers, though of course they insist that hereditary peers who want to take an active part can be made life peers. But the vital thing is that they are willing to abandon the hereditary principle as a reason for membership of the reformed House of Lords. At this meeting we were certainly more enthusiastic than the Tories about the importance of the cross-bench peers and the removal of the hereditaries. But we agreed on the basic structure and a committee of three has been appointed to report back in a fortnight on the two models—a one-tier and a two-tier system.

Late this evening I was sitting quietly in my room when in comes David Marquand[1] with a group of followers saying, 'My God, Dick, it's on the tape that we're negotiating a loan with the French.' I was completely flabbergasted but, my God, they were right.[2] My first feeling was that this was just what I had feared—Harold had double-crossed me and was negotiating behind my back. But it was too late to ring him that evening.

Thursday, November 16th
I rang Harold up at breakfast time. He was still in bed and had had nine hours' sleep for the first time for days and he hadn't seen the papers. When I told him my news he was baffled.[3] After half an hour he rang me back and said, 'Come round here at once.' When I got there I discovered that he had no idea how this story had broken but he didn't deny that it was true. What he added was the information that devaluation is going to take place this week so I was then able to discuss how the business of the House would have to be rearranged before Jim Callaghan arrived to see him.

As soon as Cabinet assembled this morning the Chancellor started reading aloud the details of his package—so much on hire purchase, bank rate, etc., £75 million cuts in public expenditure, abolition of domestic rate-payers' de-rating with a saving of £30 million and the postponement of the raising of the school-leaving age. There was no Cabinet paper. Everything was announced verbally and so fast that there was only just time to write it down. When he'd finished I blew up. I said I'd never seen business done in such a deplorable incompetent way. Roy Jenkins backed me up. 'Why do we have to pre-announce a winter budget?' he asked. 'This will give us the worst of both worlds. And anyway, why do it on education? We can't have these decisions

---

[1] Labour M.P. for Ashfield since 1966.

[2] On November 11th the Governor of the Bank of England had discussed the state of the pound with the central bankers in Basle. On November 13th it was reported that Britain was seeking a £90 million loan from the central bankers, meeting in Paris, and, on November 15th, that the Government was making arrangements to borrow $1,000 million from the I.M.F.

[3] See *Wilson*, pp. 455–6. 'I was wakened ... with a telephone call from Dick Crossman, in a great state and demanding to know what was going on. He was told that all would be revealed when Cabinet met ... but this did not satisfy him ... I opened my morning papers and realized why he had been so upset.'

taken in a split second.' This interjection held things up. Until this point no one in Cabinet seemed to object either to devaluation or to the Chancellor's package. Tony Crosland had obviously been nobbled in advance. He said that the size of the package was roughly right and so did Peter Shore for the same reason. Barbara didn't take much part because her mind was still on her transport plans which were to come later on the agenda.

But the great problem facing us was Robert Sheldon's Private Notice Question which had been put down for the Chancellor this afternoon about the $1,000 million loan. There was a long discussion about how we could prevent it being answered. At last John Silkin was sent across to ask the Speaker not to allow it to be called and at least not to permit an emergency debate under Standing Order 9. This, I knew at the time, was a great mistake. The Speaker is a man who considers his status and undoubtedly if we wanted to please him they should have sent the Lord President across, not the Chief Whip. However, John left the room and I turned to Callaghan and said ,'Well, if necessary, will you be able to deny that devaluation is taking place?' 'Yes, if necessary,' he replied, 'I certainly should have to.' I thought that was firm enough. I was utterly appalled by this meeting. Instead of having an inner Cabinet working things out carefully, the Treasury have been allowed to throw together a collection of items which made no political sense. They and the Governor of the Bank seem to have been dictating the whole policy.

I didn't have much time to feel depressed. I had to get out of No. 10 and back to my office to work out the business Statement and then to go down to the House before the Private Notice Question. Instead of the blank denial required of him, Callaghan merely said he knew nothing about it and made confusion worse confounded.[1] Soon afterwards when I went into the P.M.'s room I said, 'What the hell was Jim up to? He promised to deny devaluation and stop the rumours.' 'You could hardly blame him for that,' he said. 'He could hardly have been asked to make a blank denial. That would be too much to ask him.' The interesting thing is that though Callaghan had promised Cabinet that he would make the denial, clearly after Cabinet Harold had agreed that this was too much to ask and had let him off. This kind of softness is pretty expensive. I must say that if you ask soldiers to die in battle the politicians should be prepared to die politically in battle. Harold's softness probably lost us £200 million that day. It certainly precipitated the appalling sterling crisis. I could say absolutely nothing either to the Questions after my business Statement or to the journalists in my press conference upstairs. But meanwhile the sense of crisis was working itself up in the lobbies. Upstairs in the Party meeting this evening we sat on the platform listening to shouts of 'We mustn't surrender' from all and sundry. Afterwards I ran into Joel Barnett and Sheldon and was so angry that I said, 'What the hell do you think? Do you think you can't trust any of us for one moment?' little knowing

---

[1] 'I did not start the rumours and I do not propose to comment on them.' *House of Commons Debates*, Vol. 754, cols. 632–5.

that this would provoke a major story in every newspaper next morning that there was a split in Cabinet and some members were standing out against the conditions of the loan.

Throughout the evening the feeling of crisis mounted. Finally the Chief and I sat down and had our dinner at our usual table in the dining-room while Roy Jenkins was coolly and capably defending himself about the Court Lees approved school where he has quite rightly sacked the staff and had been bitterly attacked in the press.[1] After him came a miserable defence of the British Museum decision by poor Patrick Gordon Walker. God, it was a depressing day.

Friday, November 17th

First I rang up Harold and told him I must have a proper talk after our weekly meeting since I couldn't take this any more. Next I rang up Thomas and blew my top to him and then I rang Roy and told him I found all this utterly chaotic. We had to have an inner group and we had to have a package with a social philosophy. I would try to raise these issues with Harold that morning. After this there was one more person to call—Peter Shore. He, of course, was one of the people who *had* been consulted and I tried to get a little sense into him.

Then off to my haircut, which did me a power of good. After that I strolled down from Duke Street, St James's, and across the park to No. 10. I found Harold with George and Burke—Burke utterly exhausted—and said straight-away, 'We're going to lose a lot of money through Jim's answer yesterday—the whole operation is going as badly as it could.' It was obvious from the newspapers that Callaghan had utterly destroyed any confidence left in the pound. We finally arranged that George and I should come in this evening to discuss the draft press statement produced by the Treasury with the P.M. What I didn't fully realize yesterday was that, though we discussed the winter budget in some detail, the timetable and the method of carrying out the devaluation had not been mentioned at all. That is another reason why George and I now insisted that we must see the Treasury statement and approve it before it was issued. I also got Harold to agree that Callaghan's Statement on Monday must be submitted to a meeting of S.E.P. that morning and there must then be a Cabinet on Tuesday, which of course would be a formality because it would come after the event.

Outside it was a lovely autumn day and Harold suddenly announced he was popping off to Liverpool, whereat I said, 'Right, I will pop off to Prescote for our annual shoot.' Gosh, what a splendid idea—all our farmer neighbours

---

[1] The Home Office had appointed a barrister to inquire into allegations of excessive punishment at Court Lees approved school and, on August 7th, the Home Secretary closed the school. An Opposition motion debated on November 16th accused Mr Jenkins of being precipitate and treating the staff unfairly, but he refused to modify his decision. There was a strong demand that control of approved schools should be the responsibility of the D.E.S.

were there and they managed to get thirty-five birds and a goodly number of wild duck and hares. I walked the farm with them until the hunter's moon began to rise—a lemon curve over the trees—while the sun was still setting. I just had time to give them a drink and express my hope that Anne would give them a good dinner before Molly took me back. But I was two hours early because Harold, I discovered, wouldn't be there till ten. So I went over to the Athenaeum and dined with Dick Mitchison.[1] Back at ten I found Harold with his inner family. Marcia and Gerald were sitting about, and he was drinking whisky. We had a long discussion on whether he should make his broadcast to the people on Saturday or Sunday.[2] I favoured Sunday but he said that if the devaluation could be announced at three on Saturday and he could make his Statement at ten, it would give an interval before the press could start attacking him. This discussion went on until George Brown arrived.

George had had dinner at Prunier but was in good form. Like me he realized we must have lost most of our reserves in the course of that disastrous day. We got down to discussing the dry hopeless text provided by the Treasury. George and I are expansionists and wanted to give some feeling that devaluation, though a defeat, can be used as a springboard. We wondered why in the first Statement about devaluation the Chancellor intended to announce increases in fuel tax and corporation tax. (The Chancellor, by the way, was in Cardiff. He is due back on Saturday and will redraft the Statement all over again—as far as George and I know. This is the way the Prime Minister still works.) George finally left by the front door through a battery of photographers—which he loves. I was left behind with Harold and the No. 10 family for an hour and a half to talk about his speech and Harold read aloud to us the notes he had made in the train on the way back from Liverpool. I found them ghastly—all about the wicked speculators who have been disloyal and made life intolerable and have driven us off the pound. I said we must get rid of the apologies and the excuses. 'Put it like this,' I went on, ' "I fought for three years as you wanted me to. We fought a gallant fight but we had too heavy a price to pay and I've decided we can't go on paying it and we can't be held enthralled. I don't deny we've been defeated but there are certain possibilities now." Take that line,' I said, 'admit the defeat.' 'Ah,' he said, 'Dick, you like admitting defeats. You admitted you'd failed with morning sittings but I never do that kind of thing.' I could feel him twisting and turning and trying to wriggle out of it. On the whole I had Peter on my side but at 1.15 when we two went home, I felt profoundly depressed because, though I've done my best, I doubt if I've changed him.

[1] Labour M.P. for Kettering, Northants., from 1945 to 1964, when he became a life peer. He died in 1975.
[2] It was to be Sunday. See p. 580.

Saturday, November 18th

Before I caught the train back to Banbury I talked to Harold once again on the phone and tried to drive home the lesson that he must admit the defeat and then look forward to the chances of success when the country really gets together. Be Churchillian, not Chamberlainite was the slogan I again used.

Then I was off to Warwick to address the annual meeting of the Warwickshire Parish Councils Association. I found them gathered together in the splendid but modern shire hall and they gave me an excellent lunch and reminded me of old times when I was Minister of Housing. I gave them a rousing talk about local-government reform and democracy and answered questions at length. In the middle of the questions Anne came in; she was wearing trousers and a thick leather coat, and looked lovely and fresh. We motored home for another exquisite day with the children. And then I had a lovely moonlight walk over the farm and came home to play gramophone records and prepare myself for the devaluation Statement.[1]

Sunday, November 19th

Devaluation Sunday. I've been arranging my transport by phone with Freddy Ward. First I motor over to Hinton, where I lunch with Nicholas Davenport to meet a Jewish textile millionaire. From there I motor on to Windsor, where I have to be well before six o'clock when the Privy Council will be held and the Queen will approve the Orders in Council. From there I motor on to Hampstead to talk to Thomas.

By the way, the Prime Minister will also be doing his broadcast exactly at six o'clock and I've just been talking to him on the phone. He's in tremendous form, thank God. Though I thought today's papers pretty hot, he finds them fairly good and he especially enjoyed Nora Beloff's detailed story in the *Observer* of a Cabinet split, including the names of the people who were for and against. Of course, as I've recorded, there was no split and Cabinet was unanimous. Harold told me that his broadcast is now a great deal better than when I saw him last Friday evening and he has now adopted my central advice that the theme should be 'Yes we fought this for three years and failed but now we have certain advantages.' He was also full of optimism because of the wonderful response he'd had from all over the world to his courageous decision. The $1,000 million standby, he told me, is now available and we must now try to be nice to the central banks who have proved such loyal friends. We've also been fortunate that the right people have devalued with us—Denmark, Ireland, New Zealand and probably Australia. He was in a mood of real euphoria.

I was able with a good conscience to add my own and John's assessment that in Party terms devaluation will, in the short run, be a considerable

---

[1] The Statement was made by the Chancellor on Saturday, November 18th at 9.30 p.m. He announced that sterling had been devalued by 14·3 per cent, from $2·80 to $2·40 to the pound.

advantage. It will diminish opposition and rally support provided we can get the package with the right social mix and prove that unemployment will go down and that we are not going to impose further prices and incomes legislation.

So far I could join in Harold's optimism but I also have to consider the events of last week in terms of central Government control and here the picture is pitiable and almost unbelievable. Having summoned me to London specially last Sunday and agreed enthusiastically about the need for an inner Cabinet, he slapped the package on the table four days later in the worst presidential style after consulting, quite separately, Callaghan, Crosland, Peter Shore and one or two others. Thomas and Peter, for example, were both briefed by him on Monday but with the express condition that they mustn't talk to each other, and I suspect George and Jim were given the same instruction. The handling of this crisis has been just as bad as the handling of the 1966 crisis and we haven't advanced one inch towards any central strategic control. So we've got devaluation I've been wanting for three years but we've got it under very bad conditions with an empty till and with a disastrous public display of incompetence by the Chancellor which has cost us hundreds of millions of pounds from the reserves.

We went over to Hinton to lunch with the Davenports. There I met a great Jewish businessman called Joe Hyman.[1] Apparently he's the boss of Viyella and within minutes he'd told me how he employed 40,000 people and what a driving forceful man he was. I couldn't get much out of it but I think I ought to see him again. Anne drove me on from there to Windsor and got me there in just nice time for the Privy Council. The Lord Chancellor, Patrick Gordon Walker and Peter Shore were waiting for me and we had arranged that we would hold the Council a little early so as to be able to see Harold's television broadcast, which began at six o'clock. This, the Court told us, would be agreeable to the Queen. We got our business done in record time and she immediately said to me, 'Well, we must get along the passage to the television room,' and we practically ran along that great long corridor which I think George III constructed and which the royal children bicycle up and down. Then suddenly she turned sharp left into a little sitting-room and there by a great big coal-fire and a great big television set we watched Harold performing on the screen. He'd already got started about two minutes before. She sat us on her sofa and summoned me to sit beside her while the others got down into comfortable chairs and it wasn't until some minutes after we had started watching that I realized that she and I were in some difficulty. What on earth were we to say to each other when the broadcast finished? I saw her wrapping her fingers round each other and I too felt more and more uncomfortable because I realized that any comment she made would be political and indeed any non-political comment might itself be a political criticism. Sure enough when it stopped there was a long, long silence

[1] Chairman of Viyella International 1962–9 and of the John Crowther Group since 1971.

and then she said *sotto voce,* 'Of course it's extraordinarily difficult to make that kind of speech.' I made some sort of polite noise but before I had replied Patrick Gordon Walker had boomed in—he's the most tactless man in the world—'Oh a wonderful performance.' She couldn't say 'yes'; then I got her on to foot-and-mouth disease.[1] (By the way, foot-and-mouth, that's really something. It's been raging all this week and we're having now sixty, seventy, eighty new cases every day. Already half a per cent of the national herd has been slaughtered.) But though we talked about foot-and-mouth disease both of us felt that this was an uneasy evening and after I'd had a quick drink I slipped out quickly and went up to Hampstead, where I'd arranged to see Tommy. Michael Posner had promised that after he'd finished helping Callaghan draft the Treasury Statement he'd go up to Tommy's house. Well, Posner never turned up because he was busy redrafting till midnight and Tommy and I had a desultory evening waiting for him. About the only cheerful thing we had to discuss was the discomfiture of the Sunday papers. Most of the early editions had come out—including Nora Beloff's story— with stories of a great Cabinet split. By the second edition they had got the Cabinet almost unanimous.

The Government's package included further restrictions on bank loans and the raising of bank rate from 6½ to 8 per cent. Hire purchase restrictions were renewed and corporation tax was increased from 40 to 42½ per cent. From April 1st, 1968, the export rebate was to be abolished and for all firms save those in development areas the manufacturing industry premium received from S.E.T. was abolished. Ministers had now to consider how to implement the cuts of some £200 million in Government spending which the Chancellor envisaged.

Monday, November 20th
First S.E.P., where we spent hours working over Callaghan's Statement for this afternoon. I suppose we got about a fifth out of it and enormously improved it because in the first draft there was a clearly masochistic tinge of laboured apologia. As usual he sat next to me and we had our odd spasms of mutual confidences. Today he told me *sotto voce* about how he had come to make that terrible answer in the House last Thursday. 'Well, you know,' he said, 'if it hadn't been for the back-benchers I would have brazened it out and said negotiations *were* going on. But I didn't want a second row with the back-benchers after that vote of censure.' That reveals Jim's special weakness. When he got up to give his answer he was concerned not about the pound but about the back-benchers. His failure to keep his promise and say the negotiations were going on and to deny devaluation cost us £1,000 million

---

[1] By now some 350,000 animals had been slaughtered and, on December 4th, the Minister of Agriculture was to announce a ban on imports of meat from countries where the disease was endemic, a measure that was particularly resented by the Argentinians, who supplied about 12 per cent of British beef imports. Horse racing was also banned.

that day, I gather, and perhaps after a few days a net £200 million out of the reserves.

Now I come to the Statement itself. It was a brilliant success. Callaghan put on one of the best parliamentary performances I've ever heard. The only new twist which he put in just at the end was less than a whole sentence suggesting he wouldn't be Chancellor for ever. In fact he gave the hint that he was resigning the Chancellorship, which provided the newspapers with their headlines the next day.

I very boldly decided to invite six of the leading right-wing devaluers and also Michael Foot and John Mendelson to come and see me. Poor Sheldon was feeling terribly damaged because Ministers were going round saying he'd lost the country hundreds of millions of pounds when he felt he couldn't possibly be blamed. He said that if the Chancellor had felt so he should have asked for the Private Notice Question to be removed from the paper. Apparently it hadn't occurred to Sheldon that no one who knew about the devaluation could go near him before the answer was given in view of the line he'd been taking about devaluation. Anything one said to him would have provided a hint of our intention to a very hostile critic. Nevertheless I had no difficulty in smoothing them all down and making them realize that this was the moment for all good men to rally to the cause of the Party. Indeed, long before they left I realized that despite all that today's papers were saying about Harold Wilson facing his greatest agony in the Party meeting the Party would respond positively tomorrow morning.

Meanwhile there had been a tremendous lot of bother in the Prime Minister's anteroom about television this evening. Efforts were being made to get a Minister to appear on either *24 Hours* or *Panorama* and when it was finally clear that we had lost *Panorama* Harold decided that I should appear —although I'm not exactly an economic expert—and that I should be briefed by him on the line I should take.

When I went in to see him I found him looking at Ted Heath on the box replying to his Sunday broadcast with an astonishing ten minutes of neurotic attack.[1] He was telling the viewers that devaluation was in principle morally wicked and that Harold was a twister. I couldn't help comparing the two broadcasts. Harold's wasn't bad and it had quite a decent press but it was mushy. Heath's was the exact opposite—too doctrinaire and dogmatic. When I got to Wood Lane I had a chat with Tony Barber (he and a Liberal, Christopher Layton,[2] were with me on the programme). When I asked Barber about the Heath broadcast he said, 'He didn't do it with my advice. He sat

---

[1] In his broadcast explaining the implications of devaluation, the Prime Minister referred to the fact that it did not mean that the pound in our pockets would be worth 14 per cent less than twenty-four hours before. This was attacked as misleadingly suggesting that there would be no rise in prices. See *Wilson*, pp. 463–6.

[2] A former Liberal candidate who subsequently joined the Office of S. Spinelli in Brussels and has since been Director of the Directorate of Electronics, Telecommunications, Air and Inland Transport of the E.E.C.

down and wrote it in the white heat of anger and I wondered myself whether it was wise.'

As for our show, Barber and I were equally surprised to hear from the producer, John Grist, that its purpose was not to have a dog-fight between us but to give us a chance of looking ahead without recrimination and discussing what was to happen. I was the first Minister to appear on the box apart from Harold and I answered the questions quietly and non-sensationally —indeed, Anne thought I sounded a bit sleepy and not terribly interested. But I was determined to keep the temperature low, and though Harold was, I'm sure, not pleased at all, Callaghan felt I had put up a satisfactory defence of his position. As for Barber, he took a very similar quiet attitude. Harold no doubt would have liked a slam-banging response to the press. Most of the Sunday papers had had a great deal of a personal attack on Harold as unprincipled, wicked and twisting, and to some extent today's papers followed this up. It was tempting to slam back but I'm sure I was right to play it cool and say that this is a serious crisis but it gives us a chance to make good if we only seize it.

Tuesday, November 21st

The papers clearly showed that Jim had been successful with his hint of resignation.[1] It had indeed scored headlines. Cabinet had to start early because of the Party meeting at eleven and, of course, it was a mere formality since S.E.P. had already approved Jim's Statement.

We started with a word of congratulation by Harold on 'a perfectly managed operation'. I was so horrified that I still haven't asked myself whether he was congratulating Cabinet, the Civil Service or himself. By that morning Tommy had been able to confirm to me that the Friday loss was something like £1,000 million and the net loss between £150 million and £200 million from our foreign reserves due to the incompetence of Callaghan last Thursday. I suppose Harold must have been congratulating the experts. None of us said anything in reply and then Fred Peart made a statement on foot-and-mouth disease and asked for an immediate ban on meat imports from all countries with foot-and-mouth and Argentina in particular. It is very striking that Australia, New Zealand, the U.S.A. and Ireland, which ban all imports from countries with foot-and-mouth, don't have the disease whereas we do. But nobody thought we could do it. Cabinet didn't feel capable of making any great decisions.

I then had to report on the very ugly parliamentary situation which had developed as a result of the Fuel White Paper. Thinking everything was easy I had announced in the business Statement a debate on the White Paper

[1] On November 18th the Chancellor had offered his resignation to the Prime Minister but the announcement was delayed until November 29th in order, it was said, to permit the Chancellor to deal with the immediate consequences of devaluation and for the Prime Minister to persuade him to stay in the Government in some other office. See *Wilson*, pp. 451 and 467.

and assumed we would put down a motion of approval. But having put it down I found that the Miners' Group were raging round saying they bloody well weren't going to approve and soon I had to receive Manny Shinwell threatening me with every kind of disaster if I tried to force this through. All this I reported to Cabinet and warned them that if we went on with the debate and the vote up to sixty or seventy people would refuse to support us and we should only win by the help of Tory votes.

The discussion at Cabinet was more difficult because of another division— this time between the P.M. and the Minister of Power. Harold and Peter Shore now feel that the whole closure programme over the next eighteen months should be rephased and slowed down. Dick Marsh mutinously replied, 'You can't rephase it because you can't sell any more coal and we've already got some 30 million tons of stocks piled up and there's no more room to pile coal.' All Cabinet could agree was that we should postpone the debate and that Harold would see the miners along with the Chief Whip this afternoon.

The next Minister in difficulty was poor Barbara, who had sacked Stanley Raymond but had not found a definite successor. She had planned to replace him with Peter Parker of Booker Brothers—a socialist businessman.[1] But when she offered Peter the £12,500 which was her maximum he said that having studied the salaries Marsh was paying the Steel Board £17,500 was his minimum. She asked Cabinet whether she could follow Marsh and pay £17,500. Cabinet was by no means sympathetic, partly I think because they felt that she'd unnecessarily botched up her relations with Stanley Raymond. Only Wedgy was on her side, and Harold finally told her she could find somebody else.

At last we came to the devaluation package and the more we looked at it the thinner and more inadequate it seemed. The defence cuts were mere postponements and even the decision to drop Aldabra wasn't a genuine cut because anyway no money was going to be spent this year. And most important, all the heaviest cuts have been levelled on industry and exports by dropping the export rebate and cutting the S.E.T. premium. The only good feature of the package was that Callaghan had dropped the increases in fuel tax—yet another imposition on industry.

In the course of the discussion John Silkin had come round the table and whispered in my ear to ask me whether I could persuade Callaghan not to apologize for the past but to make a forward-looking speech. I put this to Callaghan, who was sitting next to me, and he then said, 'Do you think it would be a good thing for me to apologize for my Statement about unemployment a fortnight ago?' 'Well,' I said, 'if you really want to sweeten relations

---

[1] Director of, among other companies, Booker Bros., McConnell & Co., Ltd 1960–70 and, in 1970, chairman-designate of the National Ports Authority. He was a member of the British Steel Corporation 1962–70 and, since 1971, of the British Airways Board. In 1976 he was chairman-designate of British Rail.

with the Party that kind of apology would do a lot of good.' But I didn't believe that he would do it. However, when we went across to the Party meeting at 11 o'clock and he opened proceedings he made a most ingratiating speech and apologized for what he had said. He got a tremendous ovation and then immediately Michael Foot rose to make a great speech saying he suspended his censure motion and that the Left would not now vote against the Government because there was a possibility of getting it on to the right lines.

Indeed, the only real criticism came from Maurice Edelman and Austen Albu, who both made sensible and critical speeches. But Austen is known as the man who got the sack from D.E.A. and Maurice is known as the man who thinks he ought to have had Austen's job in D.E.A. Maurice entirely discredited himself at one point by remarking, 'Some months ago, when I was in my constituency ...' A gale of laughter interrupted him and prevented him from ever recovering.

It was an amazingly pro-Government meeting and completely contradicted all the press predictions. For instance, in the *Sunday Times* Jimmy Margach (who perhaps for the first time hadn't been briefed by an insider as no one had time) had written a piece saying that the P.M. would have his biggest crisis inside the Party. Well, there was no crisis at all. Heath has been working up a certain amount of anxiety about devaluation and maybe his people won't like it, but in the Labour Party we have no difficulty at all. It was obvious from this morning on that Harold is going to have a swelling atmosphere of goodwill.

The debate this afternoon in the House was just as good for us. Tony Crosland made an extremely able speech and was followed by Macleod, who took what is obviously the official Tory line—attacking the P.M.'s personal honour and making the sharpest distinction between that little twister Wilson and poor honest Jim. I had to go out to the P.M.'s room, where he had the miners protesting about the Fuel White Paper. He had, of course, conceded that the debate should be postponed and told me to make the arrangements. I said to them that I hoped this time they wouldn't leak it all to the press and would let me announce my decision on Thursday. But I had no expectation that they would keep quiet and of course by this evening the Lobby knew that the miners had had their way and that the Government had climbed down and would have to revise their policy. Well, it may reach that point but I hope it doesn't.

After that I went back to hear Keith Joseph give quite a good wind-up for the Tories, saying that devaluation was all right provided you make sure of it, and then Peter Shore made his second wind-up, once again totally ineffectively. He carries no guns, partly because he just hasn't got the feel of the House, but mainly because he's regarded as the P.M.'s henchman at the D.E.A. and not as a full Cabinet Minister.

I went back from there to the P.M.'s room to discuss his speech for the

19*

second day of the debate tomorrow. I had a tremendous go with him, once again saying that he *must* make a personal Statement on how he had struggled and why he didn't adopt devaluation in 1964 and why he had decided to devalue last week. He said what I was doing was superb, but I didn't have any great confidence that it would make very much difference. I had had this confidence when we talked over the broadcast but very little had got through! So, when I came away from No. 10 at 11.30 leaving Harold with his gang— Marcia, Gerald Kaufman, Tommy Balogh and Peter Shore—I wasn't very hopeful.

Wednesday, November 22nd
The morning papers were all dominated by Lord Cromer's speech attacking the Government's economic policies.[1] Outrageous behaviour for a civil servant but why any of us expected any better from Cromer I never understood.

This morning we had another Party meeting—this time on fuel and power—and I had to sit it through. Marsh's speech was tactless, unattractive but powerful—an answer to the miners which they just couldn't take. Frankly I think he was right when he said in Cabinet that these miners' M.P.s are frightened and fairly gutless. But it was a great mistake to make his view of them so clear at the Party meeting and then for him to sit there looking aloof and superior. He had outlined this new closure policy—a modernization plan which I think is absolutely right—in the all-night debate last July, which I described in this diary.[2] I remember how surprised I was at the way the miners' M.P.s swallowed it. I remember also how doubtful I was whether, having got their consent last July, it was wise to publish a Fuel White Paper with a mass of statistics which would only provoke discussion. As it happened, the timing of the publication was disastrous and was made far worse by Alf Robens, who used the White Paper to attack the Minister. We've now got the whole thing fantastically out of perspective. Under the Tories, closures were going on nearly as fast as under us. The only difference is they went on quietly without fuss whereas we are making an enormous bother about them and also giving enormous concessions (£130 million will be spent on redundant miners) and getting nothing but abuse for doing so. What a mess.

At lunch I had asked my farm manager, Mr P. and his wife, to meet the Lord Chancellor. This is an amusing story. Months ago Mr Pritchett had said he would like to be a J.P. I'd been hearing from Gerald how anxious he was for a new type of J.P.—not all from the top drawer but able vigorous people from all walks of life. However, I made the mistake of telling him that Mr P. wasn't a Labour voter but a Tory, not knowing that there are enough

---

[1] Lord Cromer, who had succeeded to his father's earldom in 1953, had been the Governor of the Bank of England from 1961 to 1966 (see Vol. I). He was British Ambassador in Washington 1971–4.
[2] See pp. 431–2.

Tories in North Oxfordshire and that what he wanted was a person who said he was Labour. I'm sure that if Mr P. had said he was Labour he'd have got through without the faintest difficulty but the Chancellor wrote to the chairman of the J.P.s and got back an astonishing letter saying that Mr P. was a difficult fellow with matrimonial troubles. The matrimonial troubles are a piece of pure local scandalous fiction. It's true that he's a difficult man but he's also absolutely sincere and conscientious. I told Gerald that it was intolerable that such scandal should be passed on by the County Clerk. He agreed, therefore, that he personally would vet the Pritchetts, who were at their best.

After lunch I had a quick meeting of our Home Publicity Committee and got my first big decision—that we should have a series of standard statements on the progress made by Labour in the various Departments and that these should be distributed and kept up to date. Meanwhile we should work out a situation paper with proposals for handling the winter months.

I was back in the Chamber for the debate on the economic situation and what we hoped would be the big clash between Heath and Harold. (By the way, Harold was extremely dull in the Party meeting, where he made a short wind-up speech which lasted twenty-five minutes and greatly contrasted with Callaghan's contribution.) Neither Heath nor Harold were much good. Both made long thoroughly partisan attacking speeches and Harold never got near to admitting the defeat he had suffered until right towards the end.

After that as chairman of the Pensions Committee I just had to get down to thinking what to do about social security payments after devaluation. We had been in the middle of revising our social security package for introduction in the spring when devaluation hit us and in his speech Harold had firmly pledged that we would protect the worst off from the effects of the rise in the cost of living. This should certainly help us to extract from the Chancellor a 3 per cent increase in supplementary benefit and family allowances, though there will be tremendous resistance from the Treasury. So I went to Callaghan and tried to get him to see sense. To soften his resistance I said that I didn't propose to increase the seven-shillings improvement in the rate included in the present text of the Bill. What I did suggest was a new clause enabling us to change the rate of family allowances by Order in Council. He listened patiently and then said, 'Sorry, old boy, the I.M.F. won't allow it.' So we're back under the control of the bankers. I knew that the I.M.F. had been in London examining our accounts and telling us public expenditure was high and the package wrong. But I didn't realize until he said this what direct control they exert. Poor Michael Foot thinks that the bankers' control was ended by devaluation. It is, I fear, a pure illusion.

After dinner I went in to hear the wind-up—Barber versus Callaghan. Barber made the Harry Crookshank kind of wind-up—clever, brilliant and dynamic. Callaghan had been supplied with an enormous brief on how to annihilate the case Heath had mounted this afternoon. He scrapped it and I noticed he had a few odd bits of paper on the dispatch box. Instead he gave an informal chat followed by a kind of appeal from a retiring Cincinnatus. It was a deliberate consensus speech, modelled very much on the style of Anthony Eden, and he managed to make everyone in the House feel he was being appealed to individually. Up till then it had been a slap-bang party political debate. Jim put party aside and spoke as though he was above the dust of battle. He showed himself superior to the rough-and-tumble of the party knockabout of the previous two days. I had wanted Harold to do this but in his speech he had remained the party politician. Jim had then seized his opportunity.

When I came back from the division[1] I found Jim sitting on the front bench and said to him, 'That was a marvellous speech, Jim, but it won't do much good in the Cabinet.' 'I know,' he said, 'but it won't be for long.' And I took him to mean that he was going to resign fairly quickly. Knowing how Harold would be feeling I slipped along to his room and found him there with Gerald and Marcia and then, along with Tommy who came a little later, for a very long time we discussed the meaning of Jim's speech. They all thought Jim was intriguing with the Tories and the City. I told them he was planning to retire to the back benches and sit there for four or five months and come back with restored vitality. I've never been in one of these discussions with Harold and his kitchen Cabinet and I felt that his suspicions of conspiracy were unduly strengthened by it.

Thursday, November 23rd

In the morning papers Callaghan had certainly come out on top and Harold had staged no real recovery. His only chance of achieving that was to be in the I.T.N. programme *This Week* which he had to do himself this evening.

As far as Callaghan's speech is concerned, *The Times* has an astonishing article in which Peter Jay (Douglas Jay's son, who was up till quite recently a Treasury official)[2] gives a completely detailed and, as far as I know, truthful inside story of all the previous occasions on which the Treasury and Harold's advisers had pressed devaluation and he had turned them down. The point of the article is perfectly clear—to show that it was Jim who was flexible and Harold who was adamant—and it's all the more sinister because I'm told there's a very similar article by Sam Brittan in the *Financial Times*.[3] It's clear that in the briefing of the press Jim has come out number one and Harold number two. This was clear enough when Harold spoke to me on the

---

[1] Ayes 335; Noes 258.

[2] Economics editor of *The Times* since 1967 and, since 1969, assistant editor of *The Times* Business News. He was private secretary to the Joint Parliamentary Secretary of the Treasury in 1964 and a Principal at the Treasury 1964–7. His wife, Margaret, is the daughter of James Callaghan.

[3] Economics editor of the *Financial Times* since 1966. In 1965 he was an Adviser at the D.E.A., an experience which infuses his book *Steering the Economy* (London: Secker & Warburg, 1971).

telephone and asked me to do a certain amount of briefing about the Jay article, something I tried to do throughout the day.

At Cabinet this morning I had to report once again on the fuel crisis and get it recorded perfectly clearly that the P.M. and Peter Shore accept Dick Marsh's view that it's too late to revise the fuel policy, and that we are only postponing the Order. Next we had George Brown intoxicated by his success at the United Nations. The British resolution, drafted by Lord Caradon, has been accepted by the United Nations and acquiesced in by Israel. This is what pleases George. He doesn't seem to notice that the resolution (No. 272) demands a total Israeli withdrawal.

At the end of Cabinet we had a most miserable discussion of family allowances. The First Secretary and Judith merely were asking for Cabinet consent to a clause in Judith's Bill which will permit her to raise the level of family allowances by Order in Council. I had tried this out on Callaghan and got his reply about the I.M.F. so I was not surprised by his opposition. What shocked me was that the P.M. now supported him and that round the Cabinet table he had won more people over from our side than ever before. The Cabinet decided quite clearly that the Bill could not be amended as Judith wanted.

At my business Statement this afternoon I had thought I might be in difficulties. But I'm in a very secure position at the moment and the miners were amused and the House was amused about the Government giving way on the Fuel White Paper. What could have been a humiliation was actually quite good for me.

After that a strange little incident when Bob Mellish came to ask my support for something Herbert Bowden had always opposed. Bob wants a bust of Sir Thomas More and so to make him the first Catholic politician to have his bust in the House of Commons. In view of the popularity of the film *A Man For All Seasons* I thought this a first-rate idea and said I wouldn't oppose it. In return, he said, he would try to get the bust of Attlee put in the Chief Whip's room.

This evening, in a private room in the Café Royal, Frank Longford was giving a dinner for Carrington, Jellicoe, Shackleton and myself. As an exercise in personal relations this was very successful indeed. I found Carrington able and I think I convinced him that I really want functional reform and to make an effective second Chamber. Indeed, when the evening had ended I was certain I could settle with Carrington and Jellicoe. Next Tuesday we have the second meeting of the inter-party consultations and there's an agreed paper coming up from Eddie Shackleton's working party.

Indeed there are only two snags. Carrington told me that Ted Heath, Macleod and Maudling don't so far show the slightest interest in Lords reform. It's all right, Carrington says, if they really will leave it all to him, but he's not quite sure about the Tory back-benchers. The second snag is that this isn't the time for consensus politics. This crisis has a kind of Suez atmosphere and he thinks it's the wrong climate in which to get Tory Party agreement to proposals which are only possible if fully supported by the usual channels on both sides. He hoped that I wouldn't try and rush them through until the crisis had eased off. I said I didn't want to rush negotiations and we'd wait till well after Christmas before moving. After all, we have to sell it to our party as well.

Friday, November 24th

The morning papers were full of the Wilson I.T.N. interview. Apparently he has at last talked about a set-back, a defeat and mistakes. But the bloody fool should have done this on Sunday and captured the initiative from Callaghan. He has said it nearly a week too late.

I was over with him for my weekly meeting at ten this morning and found that he was not in a hurrying mood. I asked when S.E.P. would be taking our strategy decisions before submitting them to Cabinet and he replied that officials were preparing papers for a fortnight's time and that meanwhile the Treasury was consolidating our position. So it looks as though this Labour government is settling down to a routine which will dissipate our chances for a breakthrough.

At Home Affairs theatre censorship came up again. Roy had been asked by Cabinet to look into the practical problems and he returned to Home Affairs to say that Harold's suggestions were quite impossible and that though Arnold Goodman had been given five months to find a solution he had offered nothing that could appease the Palace. Roy pushed this right through Home Affairs and there wasn't any serious statement, partly because I had to get on to the front bench to move that the Committee on Privilege should deal with some Welsh nationalist who's been threatening to blow us up.

At my press lunch at the Garrick I had among others George Clark, the number two at *The Times*, and found myself discussing devolution; the possibility, for example, of a Stormont-type Parliament in Cardiff and in Scotland. Since I'd been wanting to launch a trial balloon on this subject, I aired my views at length and won't be surprised if Clark's story gets on to the front page.*

Foot-and-mouth had caused the N.F.U. to cancel the dinner in Hampshire at which I was to speak so I decided to go to Coventry instead, where the G.M.C. of the Coventry East Party was holding an emergency meeting to discuss devaluation. David Young, the chairman, has been good and loyal to me but I gather that Peter Lister is once again going round breathing fire and slaughter. When the meeting started there were some thirty people there out of the total G.M.C. membership of 120—a very moderate turnout. I gave them a very sober survey showing what a defeat it had been but indicating how we can now have a forward policy. After that every speaker got up

---

* It did, and stimulated questions next morning from all the Sunday papers.

and said how hopeless things were and asked how they could go on working in the factories to defend a Government which had betrayed every principle of socialism. Peter Lister then broke in to complain about the M.P.s who sit up in Parliament not doing any work and never visiting their constituencies. He compared the indiscipline of the M.P.s with the discipline of a good council group. George Park—he's the chief convener at Rootes and chairman of the Labour Group—was much soberer and more sensible in his criticisms. But it was a demoralizing meeting and we ended with a standing row between Peter Lister and me. I told him he didn't do much good going round Coventry saying that M.P.s did no work. I pointed out that for the last three years I'd offered them a regular monthly meeting and they'd never taken it up simply and solely because they weren't prepared to waste any of their time at the weekend on me. I rely on the Party as my grass-roots organization but the Party is actually an obstacle between me and ordinary people.

Perhaps I was wrong in narrowing the issue down to our own relationships in East Coventry but it does remain true that if there were an election tomorrow Maurice Edelman and Bill Wilson would lose their seats and I would now come near losing Coventry East. And the reason for this is simply the absence of any full-time agent in Coundon Road to replace George Hodgkinson. I came home thoroughly dejected.

Saturday, November 25th
Luckily I was due to go to the fiftieth jubilee dinner of the Mid-Bucks Labour Party, where Bob Maxwell is Member. I went there with some forebodings but found 300 people sitting down to dinner and Bob's wife, who is French, known by everybody and knowing everybody there. Of course they have done badly in their county council elections and they are deeply depressed by devaluation. But the difference from Coventry is that this was a fighting organization—an army with discipline and morale—whereas Coventry Labour Party has no discipline, no centre, no authority.

This weekend's experience reminds one of how patchy things are in the Labour Party. There must be scores of constituencies as bad as Coventry. But there are also scores which are as vigorous as Mid-Bucks.

Sunday, November 26th
So this is the end of the second devaluation week and we're still completely without any central control or central decision-taking in this Labour Government. And the chances of getting this as a result of the devaluation are very small indeed. It's a fortnight now since I went up to London to plead with Harold for an inner Cabinet of six and he agreed entirely. Yet when devaluation came he carried it out not with an inner team but by playing each of us off separately one against another. And now the Whitehall routine is being put into operation. The officials are preparing a huge paper under the direction

of the Chancellor and the President of the Board of Trade for presentation in a fortnight's time, and the tremendous possibilities of this crisis and of the fine morale in the Parliamentary Labour Party are being totally wasted.

I've seen a great deal of Harold during this fortnight and I've watched him gradually settling down after the shock and feeling that everything is O.K. and he's on top of the world. His resilience, his bounce, his india-rubber quality which are a tremendous strength but also a drawback! But his worst drawback is that he apparently can't trust more than one person at one time. This is why he has difficulty in accepting an inner Cabinet. If it is to have four or five people in it who shall they be? When I first talked to him Roy Jenkins was to be in, now Roy Jenkins is out. On the second occasion George Brown was to be excluded, now George Brown must be included as long as he's Foreign Secretary. On both the first two occasions Jim was an essential pillar of the inner Cabinet, now he's regarded as a menace and a threat. This is why Harold never has a solid group of collaborators round him. He's always distrusting somebody and manoeuvring the rest of us against him. I dare say this is the most pessimistic assessment of his leadership that I've made since I started writing this diary, but it's my considered view now and I feel very depressed indeed.

I feel it all the more because the lower the Government plummets the stronger my position grows in my own little corner. Suppose the impossible happened and as a result of the crisis Jim replaced Harold. That's not inconceivable when you remember Macmillan replacing Eden after Suez. But it's something I wouldn't tolerate because I know the qualities of Mr Callaghan. He's not an adventurous bold forward-looking Macmillan who would rejuvenate the Party. Right inside he's a coward with a wonderful outside image and a very likeable personality. And that's why at present he's the only alternative to Harold. But if Callaghan were to be promoted there would be a strong anti-Callaghan movement and the question comes: who would be the anti-Callaghan candidate? At the moment, curiously enough, the answer might well be me. I think I'm the only person who could keep Callaghan out. Eighteen months ago this would have been utterly impossible nonsense. But now inside Cabinet, where these decisions are taken, it isn't. In certain ways I am the Macmillan who could take over from Harold having been very close to him, but the chances of my doing so, thank God, are utterly remote. For one thing I wouldn't last long physically. And yet I'm the only Cabinet Minister who has consistently stood up to Harold and argued my policy of England the offshore island against his futile attempts to keep Great Britain great. Having said this, however, I don't see the remotest chance of Harold going. It's much more likely that he will drag us further down until, in two or three years' time, there is a landslide of 1931 dimensions.

Monday, November 27th
I started with a long confab with Willie Whitelaw and John Silkin. We

discussed the so-called *aide-mémoire*, the agreement under which Ministerial broadcasts take place. We were pleased by what had happened recently. Harold had had a Ministerial broadcast on devaluation on the Sunday. This had been followed by Heath's reply the next day and then the third day there'd been a *24 Hours* programme with the Liberal having his go. We all agreed this was the kind of sensible practical solution of allowing Ministers the advantage of this special kind of broadcast and yet giving the Opposition spokesmen some right of reply. After that I raised with Willie the second question which has been worrying me for some time – Liberal supply days. For a long time Eric Lubbock, the Liberal Chief Whip, has been pressing me for at least one supply day and there's no doubt that a third Party with ten or twelve members has the right to that much time each Session. Of course, the two big parties don't like it because it upsets the usual channels. In British politics you can only have two usual channels and when a third one comes in the whole elaborate system for managing the House breaks down. Willie was very mutinous. I agreed with him that we couldn't allow the rather abstract right of the Liberals to upset the normal management of the House through the usual channels. Nevertheless, I felt he ought to consider it seriously.

When he'd left John stayed behind and I began to pour out my heart to him about my sense of helplessness in the post-devaluation situation and suddenly he said to me, 'Don't you think we ought to insist on Jenkins being made Chancellor instead of Callaghan?' The moment he said it I thought it would work and give us the kind of lift we need. I told the Chief it would fit with my ideas because I'd been in touch with Jenkins during the crisis and I knew that a short time ago Harold wanted him in the inner group. Moreover a straight switch is the minimum change and that would be a great advantage for Harold. But obviously what attracted me about the proposal was that the removal of Callaghan left me the nucleus of a proper inner group. The Prime Minister, Jenkins, Crosland, Peter Shore, Tony Benn – that is the kind of group that might possibly work.

On their supply day, this afternoon the Tories had chosen to discuss Healey's £100 million defence cuts. I thought there might be a big row from our back-benchers, but unless there's a vote at the end of the debate the House of Commons doesn't turn up on a Monday. There were very few people there. Healey spoke at inordinate length and despite all Tam Dalyell's efforts there was no guts in the back-benchers' contributions.

I got a message that the P.M. wanted to see me straightaway in his room. I found John Silkin there and guessed we were to discuss the Chancellorship. The P.M. filled us in as rapidly as possible. On the day of devaluation Jim had handed him a letter resigning not from Cabinet but from being Chancellor. Secondly, on Thursday of last week Jim had been to see George and told him he didn't want to be Foreign Secretary and he therefore got George's strong support for his getting whatever he wanted. He began to talk to George about going on the back benches, though he also mentioned the

Ministry of Education. By the way, he made it clear he didn't want to be Leader of the House. Harold explained that at last he now had to make a quick decision because either Jim went to the I.M.F. conference this week or his successor went. Should we bring matters to a head and get a new Chancellor or should we let Jim go to the I.M.F. first and resign afterwards? Above all, who should we have? At this point Harold looked at me and said 'What's your idea?' I said I'd no doubt in my mind that I wanted Roy Jenkins. The Chief said the same thing and I think Marcia and Gerald, who were also there, were impressed. I said that a straight swap had obvious advantages and that Jim was the right man in the sense that in Opposition he'd earned his living as the parliamentary spokesman for the Police Federation. The Home Secretary is a senior job, he is the senior Secretary of State but there was just the question of whether he would take it. I concluded that I rather thought he wouldn't but I felt it was essential to offer him the job as soon as possible to find out.

At this point I had to rush off, first to an initial Labour Party consultation before the House of Lords meeting which was taking place that evening and then to chair the Committee of Privileges, which was meeting for the second time to consider the idiotic complaint of young Hooson,[1] the Liberal M.P., about an article in a silly little magazine on the training of the Welsh nationalist army. Once it was brought to the notice of the Speaker I knew he would have to declare it a *prima facie* case and give us the difficulty of deciding what to do. If on the other hand the D.P.P. was going to take action outside the House of Commons we wouldn't have to bother. In fact the Committee of Privileges, as usual, was busy trying to avoid doing anything about an obvious *prima facie* case. So we left it to the Attorney-General and the D.P.P. to give us a report.

After that I dined with John Mackintosh, David Marquand and David Owen to discuss devolution.[2] I've mentioned already that on the previous Friday I'd had a long talk to George Clark of *The Times* and that the story I'd given him had appeared unattributed on the front page. But it had caused very great interest and the *Glasgow Herald* man and a good many others wanted me to talk a lot more about it. Since most of the Scottish M.P.s, with the Secretary of State at their head, detest the idea of devolution, John Mackintosh had been terribly pleased by the article and arranged the dinner. All this suited me because for a year now (ever since I found Welsh local government being reorganized in such an insane way) I have thought there is a lot to be said for devolution to Welsh and Scottish Parliaments. The whole thing has got to be looked at as a problem not merely of appeasing the Scottish Nationalists and the Welsh Nationalists but as sensible regional

---

[1] Emlyn Hooson, Liberal M.P. for Montgomeryshire since 1962.

[2] Dr David Owen, Labour M.P. for Plymouth since 1966, was Parliamentary Under-Secretary of State for Defence (R.N.) 1968–70, and since 1974 has been Minister of State at the Department of Health and Social Security.

devolution and I've been popping off minutes to the Prime Minister for the past six weeks. He's very cautious and holding his options open.

This evening's dinner was very pleasant indeed. Mackintosh is nice and nasty, bitchy and enormously gifted, clever and yet in certain ways stupid. He's a kind of radical right-winger. David Marquand is academically extremely able and in certain ways writes rather like me but he has inherited from his father, Hilary Marquand (who used to be one of Cripps's lieutenants),[1] sulkiness and selfishness. David Owen, the member who scraped in for a Plymouth constituency, is a doctor, a scientist and I suspect at home a mother's darling. They're three of our ablest right-wingers. After dinner I returned to the front bench to hear Gerry Reynolds winding up a singularly flat debate.

During a press conference in Paris on November 27th President de Gaulle stated that he was not prepared to begin negotiations with Britain which 'would destroy the partnership' of the E.E.C. Subsequently, at a meeting of the Common Market Council of Ministers on December 18th and 19th, M. Couve de Murville, the French Foreign Minister, announced that because Britain's economy was not sufficiently strong and the effects of devaluation unpredictable her application to negotiate for entry was rejected by the French. Although the other five Common Market countries unanimously supported the British application and although on December 20th George Brown was to announce his intention to have further discussions with the French, it was clear that the second British attempt to join the E.E.C. had foundered, as in 1962, on the hostility of General de Gaulle.

Tuesday, November 28th

Another meeting of my new Home Publicity Committee. This time it was honoured by the attendance of the Permanent Secretary to the D.E.A., Douglas Allen. The reason for his attendance was that we had before us a draft directive on post-devaluation propaganda. This is a good example of the problems one faces in Whitehall. D.E.A., of course, says that we must tell people that they're to face a real cut in their standard of living in order to reduce consumption and make room for exports. Yet I know and every politician (except possibly Michael Stewart) knows that there won't in fact be a real cut and we shall do very well if we fritter away only half the advantage of devaluation by increased prices and increased wages. Now what line should our propaganda take? There is a huge gap between the theory on which our representatives had to negotiate in prices and incomes talks and the kind of words which make sense to our audiences at public meetings. At least we got our minds clear enough to make sure a directive will be available to Ministers for their speeches next weekend.

I went along to the new *Economist* building in St James's Street for lunch.

[1] Labour M.P. for East Cardiff 1945–50 and for Middlesbrough 1950–61. A former Minister, he was, from 1965 to 1968, deputy chairman of the P.I.B. He died in 1973.

I found them all full of rumours about Callaghan's successor and as there wasn't a word I could say I tried to divert the conversation to foot-and-mouth disease. This is now spreading around us at Prescote. There are cases at Stratford-on-Avon on one side and not far away in Northamptonshire on the other. I tried to get *The Economist* staff to realize that we ought to make up our mind between two policies. We could go over to the vaccine policy and become in that sense part of the Common Market. Alternatively, I felt, we should go over to the policy of a total ban on meat imports from countries with foot-and-mouth disease. Our present position is an indefensible compromise. Of course the economists round me were full of the view that if we forbid the import of Argentine beef then the only limitation on soaring meat prices will be removed.

From there I had to go straight to a Privy Council at Buckingham Palace for the approval of the final wind-up orders in Aden while George Brown was simultaneously making a Statement in the House. Of course all the papers today have been dominated by yesterday's statement that General de Gaulle had finally vetoed our entry to the Common Market. The P.M.'s Questions dealt entirely with this subject, and he handled it extremely adroitly. However I missed it, and when I got back from the Privy Council I was at once called away from Question Time to the P.M.'s room. He told me he had an urgent decision to make because Callaghan was coming at 4.15 that afternoon and the P.M. had to be clear in his mind what he wanted. He certainly didn't want Callaghan at the Foreign Office. He certainly wanted to offer Callaghan the Home Office but if Jim refused it he would have put himself in a thoroughly bad position because he'd turned down an office for which he was well qualified and would go on to the back benches in a sulk. 'But he may well refuse,' I said. 'Who should have it then?' 'Who do you think?' asked the P.M. 'Well,' I said, 'there's always Michael Stewart.' 'But I've only got one Home Secretary,' he replied. 'That is you. Like Chuter Ede[1] and Butler you should combine it with being the Leader of the House. I know it would be a strain but you've been complaining about not having a big Department. Here's your chance.' 'That's the last thing I want,' I said. 'The Chief and I have important things to do. For instance, the House of Lords consultations. Still, if you insist I'll think about it,' and that afternoon for four or five hours I had the unpleasant burden of thinking I might be Home Secretary *and* Leader of the House if Callaghan turned it down. I had to leave him and go down the corridor to the inter-party consultations on the House of Lords, where Roy would be sitting beside me. Harold said that if Callaghan accepted he would summon Roy out of the consultations.

On November 30th James Callaghan was appointed Home Secretary and Roy Jenkins Chancellor of the Exchequer, in a straight exchange of the two offices.

[1] M.P. for Mitcham March–November 1923 and for South Shields 1929–31 and 1935–64. He was Home Secretary 1945–51 and Leader of the House in 1951. He died in 1964.

On December 8th the issue of the Government's ban on the sale of arms to South Africa, put into effect on November 17th, 1964, had been raised at a meeting of O.P.D. and some members of the Committee had suggested that the time had come to review the matter. Crossman proposed that discussion be deferred until there had been a complete review of Government expenditure and economic policy. According to Harold Wilson's own account (Wilson, pp. 470–76), while the Prime Minister was himself opposed to the sale of arms to South Africa, other embargoes had to be considered as well. At a meeting of younger Labour M.P.s, James Callaghan, apparently unaware of the O.P.D. discussions and perhaps lightly, questioned the policy of the South African arms embargo, and, alarmed by leaks, some 140 Labour M.P.s signed a motion, published on December 12th, demanding the retention of the embargo. The Chief Whip, it appears, approved of the motion as being in accordance with Government policy and, so the diaries suggest, encouraged back-benchers to sign it.

Cabinet considered the subject on December 14th but, in the absence of the Foreign Secretary, delayed by fog, the item was postponed. In the House that afternoon, the Prime Minister answered a Question put down by Dingle Foot and affirmed that the embargo policy still continued but that a fuller Statement would be made in the following week. When Cabinet met again, on the morning of Friday the 15th, the decision taken at O.P.D. was confirmed. Matters relating to defence and economic policy would be considered in the forthcoming review of defence expenditure. There were many accounts in the press at the time, some of which held that the Prime Minister faced defeat from his Cabinet on this issue and had sought to make a delaying Statement to the House until the matter was fought through Cabinet.[1] An emergency Cabinet was called on Monday, December 18th, and in Parliament that afternoon a Statement was issued repudiating the stories in the press. The policy of an embargo was to continue. The Prime Minister's own lengthy account shows that there was undoubtedly a group of 'possibly like-minded colleagues' in the Government who did not entirely agree with the policy of embargo (Wilson, pp. 596–603).

Tuesday, December 12th
Then back to the Services Committee, which as usual went like clockwork with the two Chief Whips working in complete harmony. The change in the structure of the Committee has been an enormous improvement. We've knocked out no less than five independent Select Committees and now we have a single Services Committee comprising some twelve Members of Parliament, with the relevant sub-committees. The Catering Sub-Committee under Bob Maxwell is making a profit. My particular pleasure is that for the first time for seventeen years I've managed to make a concession to the press gallery, who've been begging to be allowed access to part, at least, of the

[1] There are no transcripts of the passages recording these discussions. It appears that they were accidentally erased from Crossman's original tape-recordings.

terrace. I'm also getting a restoration of 'Annie's Bar' in its original place just behind the entrance to the terrace and there they can at last meet and drink with M.P.s on equal terms.

Harold wanted to see me before I went in to the debate. There he was in his room, full of the wickedness of Denis Healey and how he must get rid of him. I said that it was time for him to consider Healey's successor and that I was the only person who could really do the job of cutting our military commitments. 'You shouldn't talk of getting rid of Healey,' I said. 'You should treat him like Callaghan and move him to another job where he'll be safe.'

I had to be on the front bench punctually at seven o'clock because that was the moment when we were to resume discussion of my procedure package, which the Tories had agreed should be completed, sealed, signed and delivered at 11.30 p.m. I still had three quite controversial reforms to get through: (1) the Standing Order under which we can suspend a sitting and resume it next morning at 10 a.m.; (2) the new Standing Order which forbids counts after 10 p.m.; and (3) another Order limiting debates on affirmative resolutions to ninety minutes. Each of these changes is greatly to the convenience of the Executive and indeed greatly enlarges its control of the House. Taken together they seem to me to balance pretty fairly the great extensions of the powers we conceded to the Commons in the first part of the package—such as the new rules for debates on Standing Order No. 9 and the new Specialist Committees. Of course there was some protest from the Tory backbenches but it hadn't much fire, and it certainly won't cause any interest outside.* While I sat on the front bench the Chief was busy getting his motion on South Africa around the House and ensuring that a really large number of back-benchers signed it.[1]

Wednesday, December 13th
In the papers this morning the South African arms crisis has really hit the front pages with full stories of the split in the Party. At morning prayers I had a row with the P.M. about the Rent Act. I had found to my fury that when he went to the Greater London Group and found them attacking the Act he gave instructions to Tony Greenwood not to appoint a new President of the London Rent Tribunal because the P.M. himself was now going to consider amending the Act. Harold doesn't realize that there is nothing wrong with the Act. It is the tenants who have let us down. If as many tenants and tenants' associations could be induced to apply to the Rent Officers for rent reductions as landlords apply for rent increases everything would work. I was annoyed that Harold should have done this behind my back without a word to me but he soon promised to put things right at the Cabinet Housing Committee which happened to be meeting in No. 10 this afternoon. He was

* It was only mentioned next morning in two papers—the *Sun* and the *Telegraph*.
[1] The motion was signed by 136 M.P.s.

as good as his word and I had the pleasure of hearing the Committee unanimously reaffirm its belief in the Rent Act.

I also told him about the scandalous slowness of the Cabinet Pensions Committee, of which I am chairman, and how the official committee was deliberately making it grind to a halt. By then he was in an affable mood and told me that I could give instructions that all official papers should go direct from the Ministry to my Committee without being first processed by the official committee. So out of No. 10 I went across to the Cabinet Office and took the chair at the Pensions Committee which was assembling. 'I've just been talking to the P.M.,' I said, 'and he's given instructions for a speed-up. All papers must come direct to this Committee in future.' Oh, there was consternation! 'But, Minister, we can't possibly do that. The officials spend hours together and only one per cent of our time is spent with you.' 'All right,' I said, 'you needn't waste your one per cent with me any more. The Ministerial Committee will sit without officials and you can all do your job outside but the papers will come direct to me from the Ministry. I'm not going to have any more of the joint meetings we've been having only to discover that what is presented to me is material pounded into small pieces by secret meetings of the officials where the Treasury can make difficulties for me.' As the discussion went on it was revealed that there are only four people in the whole Ministry of Social Security whose whole-time job it is to prepare the biggest piece of legislation they have ever undertaken. What is worse, the Ministry has never asked for any more staff. It isn't that the Treasury has turned them down. So I gave instructions that they should at once put on the job all the staff required to do the work at reasonable speed. It was also agreed by the Treasury people present that they would allocate more staff on their side to hot the job up.

This was a real blow-up. While I did the demolition work Michael Stewart sat on one side of me and Judith on the other. What scared the officials was that I'd obviously come straight from the Prime Minister's room and was giving them his personal instructions.

After the meeting was over I took Judith back to my room to find out what was going on about the social security items in the devaluation package. Nothing, absolutely nothing—the result, no doubt, of Michael being in charge. While we were in the middle of our conversation the telephone rang. It was our surgeon, Lenton, from Banbury saying that he was worried about Anne. The little operation on her breast had been completed without the faintest difficulty but part of the tissue had been sent to Oxford because he wasn't quite sure about it and would be back by bus on Friday, when he could tell me what the report was. Oh God, that upset me!

We went over together to Room 14 in the Commons where the Party were discussing Rhodesia with storms of indignation about the arms-for-South-Africa proposal. I was able to slip out to the Treasury where I had to see Roy Jenkins about the terms of reference of the Select Committee on the Nationalized Industries which wants to investigate the Bank of England.[1] What we really discussed however were our current political problems. Roy was very indignant with Jim Callaghan for his performance on South African arms, and he and I agreed that the P.M. must be backed up on this occasion. We would do it reluctantly and indeed (I had forgotten to mention this) yesterday evening I had gone in late to see the P.M. and he told me that he had seen Roy, who had agreed to back him to that extent. He still took very much the same view as I do about the whole row.

I had lunch with my old friend Sydney Jacobson of the *Daily Mirror*, who is now on the *Sun*, and Harold Hutchinson.[2] They gave me a splendid meal at the Écu de France and were, of course, full of questions about the Cabinet struggle. I got back to the House in time to show Willie Whitelaw a letter Maxwell had sent me which he had received from Sir Eric Bullus—an unattractive bulky Tory M.P.[3] Apparently some of Sir Eric's correspondence had been taken down to the Manager's office by mistake and when the Manager found it wasn't his he had locked it up in his briefcase whereupon Sir Eric came down, found it locked up, ordered crowbars to be brought, broke open the briefcase and took back his letters. I handed Bob's letter over to Willie and said, 'For God's sake get an apology or we'll be in trouble.' The apology arrived all right that day.

Next week is the last before the Christmas recess and this means that the business of the House is terribly difficult to fit together. We have to find one or two days for the Report Stage of the Transport Bill, we've got to find room for the debate on the adjournment for the recess, we have to get a full day on foreign affairs to please the Opposition, and we're buggered on Monday because Private Members have got the time from 3.30 to 7 p.m. John and his Whips wanted to solve the problem by giving only one day for the Transport Bill and letting the Tories roar themselves silly in protest. I said, 'That's all very well for you but it means that next Thursday at business questions I shall be massacred and with good reason.' We had a thoroughly bad-tempered meeting before John and I went down to the liaison committee where there was another exhibition. Last week when I had been on the front bench dealing with the procedure debate both Willie Hamilton and Douglas Houghton had exploded about the rebellion of the eighteen who voted against the terms of the Letter of Intent to the I.M.F. The row began again.[4]

[1] In 1969 the Committee was empowered to investigate certain aspects only of the Bank of England.

[2] Sydney Jacobson was political editor of the *Daily Mirror* 1952–62, editor of the *Daily Herald* 1963–4, editor of the *Sun* 1964–5, editorial editor of I.P.C. 1968–74 and deputy chairman 1973–4. He became a life peer in 1975. Harold Hutchinson was political correspondent of the *Sun*.

[3] Wing-Commander Sir Eric Bullus, Conservative M.P. for Wembley 1950–74.

[4] On November 23rd the Chancellor had sent the I.M.F. a Letter of Intent outlining the Government's proposals to restore a healthy balance of payments. The new Chancellor, Roy Jenkins, published this on November 30th, and to left-wing Labour M.P.s it offered support for the suspicion that the Government had accepted stringent conditions set out by

Both Douglas and Willie insisted that there must be sanctions against the rebels and that we must introduce the Party's new Standing Orders at once and set an example by disciplining them. Just to make a perfect evening, Willie Hamilton added that this should be the first step to throwing these eighteen out of the Party.

Of course the row in the liaison committee is a reflection of the row which is now tearing the Party to pieces. I left John to stick it out and went up to the Small Committee where I found the Transport House people in a mood of absolute hopelessness. How, I was asked, can we arrange any effective publicity for this Government when this kind of row is going on about South African arms? In a sense I don't blame them because they are sitting on the outside looking at the ghastly spectacle. Nevertheless their sheer inertia drove me frantic and I said, 'Of course there are lots of things you can do. For example, you could launch a "Can I Help You" campaign. Throughout this winter Party members could go out and canvass the general public saying "Do you have the rent rebate to which you are entitled? Do you have your rate rebate? Is yours a house entitled to leasehold enfranchisement?" There are at least a dozen things this Government has done to help ordinary people which ordinary people need to know about.' Everybody else thought this a lousy idea. I still like it.

From there I went up to the Lobby journalists' Christmas party and found the Prime Minister. The whole South African arms crisis was steaming up around him. I persuaded him to come back to No. 10 and sit there quietly. He gave me a long briefing on his intentions: how he would go to the Queen if necessary and hand in his resignation and how he had made arrangements that if he had to resign the Queen wouldn't send for anybody else. There'd be a day or two to organize the election of a new leader and he would get himself re-elected by the Party. He told me he was letting this all be known through the *Manchester Guardian* and said, 'I'm taking on the briefing of the press myself. This time I'm damn well going to get the result I want.' I was a bit taken aback and I thought, 'I suppose he will get what he wants at Cabinet but he's piling it on a bit thick.' And, by God, he was!

Thursday December 14th
The morning papers looked terrible. A £158 million record deficit on the balance of trade in November and the worst N.O.P. poll we have ever had. To make things perfect there was further news of our own British Museum mess. Lord Radcliffe had made an annihilating attack on Gordon Walker in the House of Lords. But all the attention was on South African arms and all the stories made it clear that there was a major parliamentary revolt in

---

the foreign bankers who had given Britain credit. The Chancellor defended his predecessor in a debate on December 5th in which eighteen Labour M.P.s voted against the Government and sixteen abstained.

progress, that the Prime Minister strongly supported the back-benchers and that he was going to get his way in the Cabinet that morning.

I went round to the Chief Whip's office to see what had finally been agreed about business for next week. John was with the Prime Minister preparing for the Cabinet row. But Freddie Warren told me that I would have to take the debate on the Christmas adjournment next Thursday afternoon and that there would only be one day's debate on transport. At first I blew up and said I refused to have this imposed upon me. But I knew very well I would have to accept it and actually I did rather an ingenious job. I accepted the one day before Christmas and then decided to bring Parliament back a week early with a two-day debate on foreign affairs and a second day on transport.*

As soon as we got into Cabinet I cleared the business of next week and then a general attack was launched on Harold about press briefing, partly against John Silkin for his work with the Party and partly against me, since it was assumed that I had done all last week's briefing. Denis Healey explained how terribly upset he had been when a journalist had come to him to say that the Lord President was briefing people against the F-111. I immediately intervened to say I was grateful to hear this because he could now give me the name of the pressman. (Of course I didn't get it, and he didn't know it.) At Cabinet the atmosphere got more and more unpleasant and the air was loaded with charges and countercharges. At first we waited for George Brown, who was late in getting back from Brussels, but when it finally became clear that he was fog-bound for the day it was obvious that Cabinet couldn't come to any decisions. So we proceeded to the only other item on the agenda apart from South African arms, which was whether B.E.A. should buy the Trident or the 211. We decided on the Trident because it cost less.

In the House this afternoon Harold was answering Questions and had told the Speaker he wanted to deal with No. 18 on the export of arms to South Africa. When the P.M. did so he said formally that Cabinet was waiting for the Foreign Secretary but in all kinds of ways Harold implied that he's standing firm by his decision of November 1964. Then came my business Statement. I was prepared for a tremendous row about the one day on transport, but there was no row at all. Just before going in I'd run into Peter Walker in the lobby and told him that I had arranged to give him two days but it wouldn't be in the Statement. 'You get one before Christmas and if you press me I'll arrange to come back a week early and give you the second then,' I said. It was a clever tactic but I hadn't really appreciated its cleverness. The offer scared him stiff—everybody in the House really wants the full month's holiday at Christmas. So I never had to make him the offer and one day on transport sufficed.

At my Lobby conference I gave a very full and careful briefing on the background to the South African arms controversy as well as on the Industrial

* As we shall see, the trick worked.

Expansion Bill. Quite deliberately and carefully I treated the journalists very well.

Then the Party meeting, which was absolutely formal because nobody was worried any more. They think the thing is fixed and not a single question was asked.

There was the same feeling over in No. 10, where I went for my business meeting. Burke is still away, Bill Nield is standing in for him and the Prime Minister wanted the meeting over as soon as possible because he was completely confident he's going to get his way tomorrow.

I dined with Bob Maxwell and found that my fellow guests were Roy Thomson and on the other side of me the general manager of the National Provincial Bank. We had quite an evening. They said everything which makes me feel sick—the British people aren't working hard, there ought to be more unemployment, the best cure would be to cut the social services. And no doubt I said everything which they think utterly futile. The lack of contact between this Labour Government and the world of the City and finance is terrifying.

After dinner I went with Maxwell to Harold Lever's house for yet another talk and to wait for tomorrow morning's Cabinet.

Friday, December 15th
Cabinet. What happened this morning must have come as a shock to Harold. Yesterday he'd been completely confident that he'd worked it all out and was going to get his way. I don't know where he got this confidence from and I didn't share it. We started with an hour and a half of mutual abuse which was nothing more than a repetition of yesterday's meeting. George Brown, back from Brussels, complained that he'd been presented as the villain of the piece and said he has never been so victimized and vilified in all his life. Then there was a great moral outburst from Healey and another from Crosland—all of them complaining about the rigging of the press, virtually accusing the Lord President of doing it, and of the rigging of the Party, which they openly attributed to the Chief Whip. Finally we got down to the issue and Harold made his statement. It was clearly intended to split his opponents and if possible to isolate Healey and Brown, whom he was quite determined to get rid of. He had reckoned that they would be devastated by the exposure to which they had been submitted by the press and by the clear evidence that the Party was fully organized against them. But not at all. They came back at him one after the other. George Brown, Denis Healey, Tony Crosland. The three of them stood together and it was clear that an alliance had been formed in the last twenty-four hours—an alliance of Ministers infuriated by the Prime Minister's campaign against them in the Party and in the press and also, I think, really scared because they realized that they might be for the high-jump if Harold had his way. I'm sure the fact that they stood together saved them and saved us from a real Cabinet split.

They hit back extremely effectively and in concert. They made their points as a united front. At one point Crosland observed, 'If we have to tolerate this South African arms policy I must insist on the postponement of the Industrial Expansion Bill,' and that in itself was a sinister revelation of how carefully their operation had been planned.

After some time it became clear that Harold Wilson's attack had failed to split them and that the Cabinet line-up was almost the same as last week. On the Prime Minister's side was first Michael Stewart, the clearest and most logical of his supporters throughout the crisis, and Gerald Gardiner plus Barbara Castle, Tony Greenwood, Peter Shore and Wedgy Benn who were really satellites. In addition there was Cledwyn Hughes, who finally rallied to the Prime Minister and should perhaps be reckoned as his eighth un-qualified supporter. Against them were ranged the seven implacables — George Brown, James Callaghan, Denis Healey, Gordon Walker, George Thomson, Ray Gunter, Tony Crosland. In the middle were the moderates — Roy Jenkins, Dick Crossman, Fred Peart, Dick Marsh, Frank Longford. We wanted the compromise we had suggested at O.P.D. It was a terrible meeting for me be-cause as it went on it became clearer and clearer that the P.M. had miscalcu-lated and that instead of splitting the opposition he was uniting it into a phalanx. Instead of isolating Brown and Healey so that he could get rid of them and keep the rest the Prime Minister had consolidated the opposition. So right towards the end I put forward my mediating proposal. I proposed that instead of deciding today the decision should be postponed and South African arms considered along with all the other items in the post-devaluation package. 'Why pick this one item out and make the policy decision in isolation?' I asked. 'Denis Healey has been complaining that people were campaigning against the F-111. But there's been no decision on it yet. George Brown has been complaining that people had been campaigning for postponing the raising of the school-leaving age. But the decision has still to be taken, like the decision on prescription charges. I propose that everything, including South African arms, should be decided in one single package decision.' That, I said, was the line the P.M. should take because it would keep the Cabinet together. As soon as I put this forward Harold's unqualified supporters burst into shouts of fury and said it would be fatal. At this point James Callaghan observed, 'That's far worse than anything.' But, apart from Callaghan, George's supporters came out in favour and so did Frank Longford. At this point Harold also accepted it, adding, 'If that is really wanted by Cabinet I'll accept it, but is it really wanted?' I said, 'Please, Prime Minister, don't count the votes again, make up your own mind, decide for yourself.' He said, 'Well, as for what I want personally I would rather not accept your mediating proposal.' 'Very well,' I said, 'don't accept it,' and he replied, 'No, if it's the wish of Cabinet I will.' So he got himself into this curious situation of forcing Cabinet to decide for him. But I wouldn't take it and said, 'No, I can't accept that. This mediating proposal will be useless unless the Prime Minister really believes in it himself.' So he was forced to say that he did but that it would all depend on the closest possible secrecy. The original O.P.D. decision, he reminded us, had depended on secrecy and there had been no leaks. So, this time, there must be no leak from Cabinet before Monday, when he would make a Statement on the lines of the mediating proposal.

While this ghastly debate was going on a message had been sent in to me from my Private Office saying that the report from Oxford had arrived and Mr Lenton said that my wife was O.K. I'd had to bottle up my relief but the moment Cabinet was over I rushed round to Cowley Street to lunch with Pam Berry and couldn't help pouring my heart out to the American Ambassadress. I talked to her and to Pam about nothing except my Anne and I fear I disappointed them in denying them any news of the Cabinet crisis.

When I was back in my office Roy Jenkins rang me up. He had just seen the P.M. and told me an inner Cabinet meeting was fixed for the Wednesday after Christmas. Roy added that he is sure he and I were completely right to keep to our mediating proposal in Cabinet. Then Harold was on the line. He said that in the light of the last thing he'd said to Cabinet any kind of communication with the press from our side is forbidden. So from this afternoon John and I prevented any form of briefing and left the opposition free to do what they could.

Just when I was packing up Michael Halls, the Prime Minister's Private Secretary, came in to tell me about the inner Cabinet on the Wednesday after Christmas and added that there would be a full Cabinet on January 4th and January 11th when the whole post-devaluation package has got to be signed, sealed and delivered. Would I, Michael Stewart and Judith get on with the social security aspects of it as fast as possible? And with those words ringing in my ears I caught the train to Banbury to have my birthday dinner with Anne. I found her in bed looking beautiful but a bit pale. We dined together and cut my cake. What a day, what a day!

Saturday, December 16th
I was wooding on my island all the morning until the Prime Minister rang me up in fury about the morning newspapers. The front pages were all full of stories which had obviously been provided by George Brown and Bill Grieg, his Press Officer.[1] I had thought things over and was aware that this fury was partly synthetic. Harold had allowed the opposition the weekend in which to destroy themselves. His plan was that we should say nothing and they should be allowed to fight back and tell the story of their brave resistance. Since I knew they were delivering themselves into our hands by doing this I wasn't shocked though I doubt whether there's any precedent for a Cabinet opposition publishing their dissent in the press so flagrantly and openly as has happened on this occasion.

Tommy Balogh came over today. It was a beautiful afternoon and I was

[1] Former political correspondent of the *Daily Mirror* and George Brown's Press Office.

back at my wooding but I couldn't get him interested so we came into the house. He was terribly upset because he hadn't received a copy of the paper that Roy Jenkins had circulated about the package. I couldn't tell him that I hadn't seen it myself. Though I'd found it in my office marked 'Top Secret' I'd left it unopened to be dealt with on Monday. I explained to Tommy that he probably hadn't received it from Roy because he was on the list as an economic adviser but without membership of the Cabinet. But he went on bleating and he was terribly upset because he felt the P.M. wasn't talking to him these days. It was no good trying to explain to him that the P.M. had been busy and so had I. I'm afraid I said, 'Oh, for God's sake, Thomas, you always feel persecuted. You've been too long in No. 10. Just stay with the P.M. up to January 15th and leave as soon afterwards as possible.' And away he went with that.

This evening I went over to Coventry for the opening of an extension of the Community Association rooms at Stoke Aldermoor and got back to Prescote to find the P.M. ringing me up again even more angry, even more upset, breathing blood and fire and telling me to read the press tomorrow and ring him back.

Sunday, December 17th

Well, I read the papers and the accounts were at about the same level as before and I reflected on this. Soon I was rung by Wedgy Benn, still white with anger at my mediating proposal. 'No,' he said, 'we must force these buggers to eat dirt, make them accept unconditional surrender. The P.M. must reassert himself and this is the only way he can do it.' 'If you ask them to do that after the last two days,' I said, 'some of them are bound to resign and there'll be a crisis. I don't recommend it.' So I rang Roy, who agreed that on balance we must continue with the mediating proposal and that it would be extremely dangerous to have a Cabinet tomorrow. Then Peter Shore was on the phone to ask me what I would do if the Prime Minister recalls Cabinet. I thought for a moment and said, 'If he recalls the Cabinet tomorrow Roy and I won't have changed our minds; he shouldn't have changed his mind and we shouldn't have changed ours. I talked to Roy and we're going to stand by the mediating proposal.' I knew that Peter would talk to the P.M. straightaway and I'm sure he did. Within two hours Harold had asked me to come up to London and added that in the meanwhile he must call a Cabinet for tomorrow. I said that was his decision and O.K. by me and arranged to go up by the 8.58 p.m. Just before I left Roy called me and I told him what had happened. He too had been down in the country and had been sitting in his Berkshire home waiting all day for the call from No. 10. But the P.M. hadn't spoken to him at all. I had spoken to Roy, I had spoken to the P.M. but the P.M. hadn't bothered to consult his Chancellor and had simply had a message sent telling him to attend at ten o'clock tomorrow morning.

So in the evening I came up to London and went into that little, horrid, stuffy room and there were Tommy, Gerald and Peter Shore—the same gang all busy on his Statement. The P.M. took me into his room. He had kept his word, he hadn't gone back on the mediating position, he was drafting his Statement on that basis and he was going to put it to Cabinet tomorrow.

I had assumed that his anger about the press leaks was a bit synthetic but I was wrong. He raged on and on and he was mostly concerned about the separate resolution he was drafting, which was due to be given to the press, in which Cabinet would repudiate the lies of George Brown. Once again he was insistent that he would never work with George Brown or Denis Healey. I remarked that he should be careful since Denis could surely be given another job. Harold replied that at least he would never work with George Brown after such an act of deliberate treachery. George had put his assistant, Bill Grieg, to work on the press and he, Harold, had hard evidence of it. No one knew the burden he had borne and this was the final bloody limit.

But I'd heard all that so often from Harold that I still didn't take it seriously. I was more struck by his bitterness against Denis for his ruthlessness, for his behaviour as the stooge of McNamara. He wasn't so harsh about Crosland or Gunter or the rest but he was sure he had them on the run. Finally he remarked that he was now certain that he would get the big defence cuts he'd always wanted. Then we went back into the other room and I stayed there for another hour and in the atmosphere of the clique I felt very depressed. Why hadn't he called Roy? Why hadn't he spoken a word to George Brown? Why did he sit there with his coterie? He certainly didn't make things easy for himself.

Monday, December 18th

I rang up Roy from my bed, told him about my meeting with the P.M. and about Harold's mood. Roy was due to go in from ten till eleven with the P.M. before Cabinet. I spent most of my time on the phone since all the Haroldites were ringing me once again—Wedgy Benn, Peter Shore, both furious with me, and Barbara as well. I didn't think I was doing very much good by talking to them.

At Cabinet the P.M. kept his word to me. He didn't abandon the mediating proposal—on the contrary he demanded unanimous support for it from Cabinet and was overridden by Cabinet itself. It was a tactical manoeuvre which worked out extremely well. As was only to be expected, the discussion began with a tremendous personal attack delivered from the chair against all the people who had leaked to the press over the weekend. I had had a word with Tony Crosland while we were waiting to go in and realized that it was no good appealing to his conscience since he felt that George was perfectly entitled to hit back after the treatment he'd received. Nevertheless, I can't help feeling that George was abashed by the castigation he received. I've never heard anybody publicly scourged as George Brown was scourged by

Harold this morning. The P.M. didn't mention his name—he just looked across the table and said everything that could be said and when he had finished there was total silence. George Brown never said a word in reply, nor did any of the others. The whole issue of the weekend leaks dropped dead at that moment.

After about half an hour it was clear that Cabinet had swung in favour of the P.M. and was prepared to make no change in our policy of November 1964. I passed a message to Roy saying that if George Brown was instructed by Cabinet to announce that we'd made up our minds against selling arms to South Africa it would be a first-rate result and we shouldn't oppose it. Roy seemed to agree. Nevertheless we both continued to support the mediating proposal which of course now found a great deal of favour with Brown, Healey and Crosland, all of whom said this is the only thing which could possibly be done. But they were clearly in a small minority. The Cabinet switched, led by James Callaghan (who, to do him justice, was merely repeating what he'd said on the previous occasion) and now by Patrick Gordon Walker. We soon reached agreement that Harold's draft Statement should be modified to include a Statement that we had completed our consideration of the sale of arms to South Africa and that none would be sold. At this point I said that, as the proposer of the mediating plan, I recognized that as a result of the weekend events my suggestion was no longer valid. The P.M. ought to decide whether it should be dropped, to which he again replied that he wasn't going to decide anything and he would leave it to Cabinet, otherwise he would be accused of dictating to it. And so he got exactly the conclusion he wanted. Cabinet conscripted the Prime Minister to write into his draft Statement the sentences he had always intended should be there. It was a complete and total victory.

Directly Cabinet was over I had to deal with the problem of Standing Order No. 9. I knew there were three of our people anxious to move it and one Tory wanted us to move it too. At two o'clock I rushed across to tell the Speaker that the expected change of Government policy, which would have required him to concede a debate, would not take place. 'Anyway,' I added, 'if you feel you must give it, don't postpone it till Tuesday at 3.30. Today is a perfect day since we have three hours for Private Members' business—let's have it from 3.30 to 7 tonight.' He told me he'd been talking to Barney Cocks who had assured him that a debate would only be given on the same day if it was a matter of the very highest urgency—otherwise he would be setting a precedent. I said there wasn't a word of that in the Select Committee's report and that he was not bound by anything at all and begged him to give it today or never, otherwise the whole business of the House would have to be reorganized. So he said he would and then he rang up Barney and of course he insisted on Tuesday. That's what happens to you when a weak Speaker has no precedents to go on.

This afternoon at 3.30 Harold made his Statement—and made it extremely well. It was greatly improved by the work he'd done on it over lunch. All the Tories were certain that he was going to offer the mediating proposal as all the papers had predicted. So in the early part of his Statement they were laughing and jeering and even when he said there would be no change of policy they couldn't believe it. Heath rose to challenge him and said that the Statement was like a piece of wet blancmange, thereby putting off the whole House. In his supplementaries Harold made his unexpected decision more and more explicit and the complete transformation of the atmosphere he achieved was one of the most remarkable parliamentary *bouleversements* I've ever seen. The Opposition were completely flabbergasted by the Prime Minister, who like Houdini had escaped from his bonds. The scene was all the more dramatic because George Brown was sitting on one side of him scowling and gloomy and the Chief and I on the other happy and confident.

After that I had to start reorganizing the business of the week, once again. With the Standing Order 9 debate down for Tuesday, the Transport Bill had to be moved. The negotiations with Willie Whitelaw went to and fro. Finally John Silkin got the Tories' agreement—Tuesday for the S.O.9 plus the Christmas adjournment debate and then two days on foreign affairs. This requires us to come back a week early but that suits the Government quite well because by then we will have post-devaluation package Statements to make. I made the business Statement at seven o'clock and then went across to No. 10, where the P.M. was entertaining the Lobby. I could only stay for half an hour because I was dining with George Weidenfeld but I must mention this episode because it provided a piece of hard evidence about Harold's attitude to the press. This morning he had made a really tremendous fuss about the leaks to the press from the Cabinet. Yet I watched him come up to a group of journalists with whom I was talking and within seconds he was saying, 'On my best calculation there were sixteen members of the Cabinet who explicitly wanted me to make the Statement I made this afternoon.' Then he told them it was a lie that there ever was any majority in favour of selling arms and that he had deliberately sent George Brown to Brussels. After this he went on to describe what had happened in Cabinet this morning. I heard him with my own ears talking in this way and I record it here just because he really and sincerely believes that as far as he is concerned he only briefs the press and never leaks. No doubt his behaviour at this party was a reaction from the enormous tension he'd been under. After all he'd first been broken, battered and nearly knocked out and then he'd made a sensational come-back, and there he was telling his friends among the press in tremendous detail what actually happened.

At George Weidenfeld's I found a great assembly including Hugh and Antonia Fraser,[1] the Chalfonts, Pam Berry and Blankenhorn. We sat at a

---

[1] Hugh Fraser, Conservative M.P. for Stone 1945–50 and for Stafford and Stone since 1950, was Secretary of State for Air 1962–4. His wife, a daughter of the Earl of Longford, is, like her mother, a well-known biographer.

20

table together with Pam and the Ambassador leant towards me across Pam and said, 'You should be the next Foreign Secretary, Mr Crossman, because you would run a really Gaullist policy for Britain. Now that we've turned you down you shouldn't linger on the doorstep but busy yourself with your own affairs. Yes, we shall want you in Europe ultimately because of your drive and originality. But you'd be the man to give your country the Gaullist policy.' I admit I think this is true. If I were Foreign Secretary I would know how to conduct a British Gaullist policy but I don't think there's the remotest chance of my being Foreign Secretary or even Minister of Defence. I think I shall stay on in my present job because it's a very difficult job which I'm doing quite well.

Tuesday, December 19th

The press is so passionately anti-Wilson that instead of reporting straight his sensational and unexpected triumph in the House they announced that there had been a compromise between the Prime Minister and his critics by which, in exchange for announcing that no arms would be sold to South Africa, he had been compelled to commit himself to cuts on the home front. This of course is utterly untrue. On the economic package Harold and Roy are working closely together and no pressure was needed from their critics to make them impose cuts on Cabinet. Yet there were columns of well-informed accounts of a powerful opposition which Wilson still faces inside his Cabinet.

My first job this morning was to chair the Legislation Committee. I got Wedgy Benn's Industrial Expansion Bill through quite easily despite all the rumours. Then came Bill Wilson's Private Member's Divorce Bill, where I expected trouble from Frank Longford. Of course the Government is really giving a great deal of help to this Bill, but on this occasion I had to pretend to be absolutely neutral because otherwise Frank Longford, Willie Ross, Cledwyn Hughes and co. would threaten to resign. Since this Bill has been entirely drafted by the law officers and the Lord Chancellor on the lines of the Archbishop's report, there was nothing much that Frank could do to oppose it. Next came another Private Bill to promote a Parliament for Wales, which Harold Wilson had wanted me to oppose. I frankly refused to do so because in my view devolution – i.e. home rule for Wales and Scotland – is absolutely necessary if we want to win any seats in Scotland (Wales is not quite so serious) in the next election. That's my personal view but I have to recall that it's twelve months since I urged this on the Prime Minister and he has done nothing whatsoever about it. However, Cledwyn Hughes, the Welsh Secretary of State, is working on it and I've got John Mackintosh in charge of a Scottish working party. What's more, the trial balloon I let off at my press dinner at the Garrick has been a great success and all the Scottish M.P.s are now asking why the Lord President has been talking in this way if there's nothing in the wind. Even Willie Ross has had to concede that devolution is now in the air. Of course, even if I get the P.M. to agree it will be a year too late. Nevertheless, better late than never in this instance.

From Legislation I went straight into S.E.P. This was the great S.E.P. meeting to which we'd been looking forward. Actually the officials had provided a miserable report and we all knew that the P.M. and the Chancellor had taken things in hand and were getting on with the job quite independently. As an effective inner Cabinet for economic control the Committee I invented had been entirely sidetracked. Nevertheless we did discuss the balance of trade in the light of the November £158 million deficit. Looking ahead we coolly decided that we must aim at a £500 million surplus next year. Easier said than done.

Last night, the Prices and Incomes Committee had met to consider poor Peter Shore's proposed policy for prices and incomes. It's a fraud. The Government has no effective power since the T.U.C. isn't going to be willing to control wages in any way now that Scanlon's in charge of the A.E.U.[1] and Jack Jones of the dockers. These two are competing for power and there is no real chance that the T.U.C. can do anything at all except to mildly discourage the unions. Yet this poor Minister has to struggle along. Peter Shore boldly suggested that he would work for selective control permitting those price rises that ought to soar and only keeping down prices which needed to be kept down. To this Tony and I replied that no British Government has the capacity for that kind of selective policy and to announce such an attempt would be to submit ourselves to a gratuitous defeat.

I lunched at the Epicure with Alan Watkins. He had come in last night to talk to John and me and we had given him a very detailed account of our side of the crisis. John and I have had a tremendously bad press and we've been presented as the villainous henchmen doing Harold Wilson's filthy work. Poor John, he looks tired and puffy and has a spot on his lip. He doesn't like unpopularity and he now faces a complete transformation of the situation at Westminster. Suddenly a whole segment of the Parliamentary Party has turned against him and accused him of being a creature of the Left. We did our best with Alan Watkins.*

At 3.30 this afternoon we had the postponed S.O.9 debate on South African arms.[2] I didn't hear much of it at the beginning because I had to go to the consultations on Lords reform. The discussions had reached one of the most delicate points—how long the Lords' period of delay should last and from what precise point should it start. To our amazement, Carrington gave us almost everything we asked for. There would, in his view, be a formal period of delay after which legislation would automatically be enacted. Let's

---

* Actually, his article was as near the truth as I saw it as anything can be.

[1] Hugh Scanlon, from 1963 to 1967 a member of the Executive Council and from 1968 the President of the Amalgamated Union of Engineering Workers and a member of the T.U.C. General Council.

[2] In the debate on Southern Africa (British Military Equipment) the motion to adjourn received 241 votes in favour and 331 against

take an example. The Lords veto a Commons' Bill in June. But if Carrington is right, we shall automatically have it on the statute book by December. That's an enormous concession by the Opposition and it makes me rather fancy we shall reach an agreed solution.

We broke off the consultations in time for Maudling and me to get back to the House to hear the wind-up. Ted Heath was in quite good form and raised the level of the debate. But then came Michael Stewart, the hero of the hour. He made an enormously impressive speech based on moral principle and after he had spoken the Tories must have seen that this was not merely a matter of Party manoeuvre and in-fighting. Thank God I got him to speak, but it was only because neither George Brown nor George Thomson wanted to do it.

After that I had to stay on the front bench to deal with the Christmas adjournment debate. I've said all I have to say about this debate in this diary already. This time it started just before seven and ended with my formal reply just before ten. After it was over Alasdair Milne, my old B.B.C. friend who ran our party politicals in 1959, came in to talk about Scottish nationalism. We argued at great length and then Tam and I walked home to bed.

I was so busy during the afternoon that I've forgotten to mention one quite important thing. Suddenly the news came through that Harold Holt, the Prime Minister of Australia, had been drowned and that someone from London would have to represent us at the funeral.[1] It was assumed that George Thomson would go. But suddenly it occurred to us all, should not Harold himself go? The Chief Whip was against it because he said the P.M. was too tired. I said, 'Nonsense. This is a big chance. Get him away, for God's sake. Let him be a Prime Minister outside the country. Let him have his talk with L.B.J. and display a bit of confidence.' I'm glad to say that Burke Trend thoroughly agreed and so in the course of the evening it was announced that the Prime Minister was going to Canberra to be present at the funeral.

Wednesday, December 20th

I woke to a fairly good press. The Tories in Fleet Street had been flabbergasted because they had assumed Cabinet was split and Harold Wilson couldn't get his way. Now they must admit that he had extricated himself from this particular locked safe and is still quite a man. There's also no doubt that Michael Stewart's speech at the end of the three-hour debate has done us a power of good. He's given some dignity and sincerity to what has otherwise been a fairly tawdry affair of party politics. Another thing I noticed was that the decision of the E.E.C. to accept the French veto on our exclusion took second place in today's papers to South African arms. It hadn't been made to look so depressingly important as I had expected.

---

[1] He was drowned while swimming near Portsea, Victoria, on December 17th; on December 18th the Deputy Prime Minister, John McEwen, took up the office. On January 10th, 1968, John Grey Gorton became Prime Minister.

Our black marks this morning were the fact that six Labour M.P.s had abstained because they were in favour of arms to Africa and there was one sinister little piece saying that now there would have to be a reimposition of old-fashioned discipline. This of course had been put in by Douglas Houghton who, after being so tremendously pro-Silkin, has now as a result of the events of the last day or two turned against the Chief Whip and is demanding the reimposition of the P.L.P.'s Standing Orders. This will make things much more difficult.

I spent the morning at the Special Committee the P.M. had set up to decide how we should protect the poorest in the country against the effects of devaluation. I had hoped that we should be able to use my new rate rebates but this was not possible. On the other hand it seemed that more and more Cabinet members were being driven to accept some form of claw-back such as Peter Townsend and Brian Abel-Smith are proposing. Right at the end of the meeting Cledwyn Hughes suddenly said, 'We ought to abolish family allowances altogether.' I didn't take this seriously but it sounded odd when he said it.

Back in my office I found Paisner and Stimpson, my solicitor and accountant, waiting for me. We'd had to postpone our meeting the previous week because of Anne's illness and because we weren't quite sure whether she had cancer. But the problems of Prescote had to be dealt with. There was one remark which I found interesting. After we'd decided what to do to keep the Prescote estate from being split up on Anne's death I said I was still anxious to save every year and put aside something into her account. Well, they said, the only safe way to do that is to insure your life, to which I had to reply that my life is uninsurable. I still insisted that I'd like to help her. Well, they said, the best thing to do is spend money, spend money on things for her. Now, it so happens that months ago we'd asked our neighbour John Makepeace to design us a huge coffee-table to go in the middle of our panelled drawing-room. The table is a huge square frame of polished walnut about a foot and a half high—perhaps two foot high—with inset panels of reddish Welsh slate. The sides underneath look solid enough until you touch them—whereat four beautiful square boxes slip out on silent castors and there we store our drinks, our gramophone records, etc. At enormous cost (we're paying some £230 for this table) we've completely transformed this lovely room. Now I learn from my accountant that I've done a good thing for the estate by buying this expensive table instead of giving Anne highly taxed income-earning equities. So the only way I can save on her behalf is to enjoy myself by giving her jewellery or expensive things for the house.

Then it was time for Harold's last Cabinet before he left for Australia. The first item was the paper marked 'Top Secret' which Jenkins sent round to us ten days ago, revealing the fact that so far devaluation has been completely unsuccessful since none of the money we'd lost in those terrible days has come back and we are losing even more day by day. Even at its new reduced level the pound is having to be sustained. Jenkins used this as his justi-fication for demanding that we now need public sector cuts of some £800 million. The paper also revealed that next year's estimates are 12 per cent above this year's estimates. Why is that? Nobody seemed to know and it's obvious that when such estimates are published in February there will be another parity crisis unless we announce a real austerity budget. As we obviously couldn't discuss this for very long because there were no detailed proposals for the cuts, the Prime Minister explained his timetable. There is to be an inner Cabinet meeting on the Wednesday after Christmas, though he admitted to me afterwards that this so-called inner Cabinet now consists of half the Cabinet. And then at the next full Cabinet we shall try to reach a big decision on the package.

The only interesting point in the discussion was that two Ministers—Denis Healey and Tony Crosland—both observed in passing that we must have much sharper Party discipline. Denis said that some of these fellows who were tabling motions against cuts in the social services should be thrown out and Tony agreed that's what they really deserve. When they said this I slapped back that one could hardly expect the Party to be very well disciplined when certain Ministers had been using the press for attacks on the Prime Minister and had nearly split the Cabinet last week. At this point the P.M. intervened and said, 'There's going to be no discussion of Party discipline here this morning,' and stopped it short. Nevertheless, it was a significant episode. Healey and Crosland represent a lot of people in the Parliamentary Party who want to clean things up and of course people who talk in this style are those who have least control of the back-benchers. I don't suppose there's any man who is more disliked and out of touch with the Parliamentary Party than Denis Healey unless it's Tony Crosland. Both of them are arrogant and despise their colleagues in the Party and they've both been staunch right-wingers who have always regarded the Left as a conspiracy against them. It is they who have been busy going round the lobbies and using their P.P.S.s to stir up dis-satisfaction against the P.M. and against John Silkin, who's still tired and very aware of his new unpopularity.

We then had a short report from George Brown on Europe. He and the Prime Minister want to stand on the doorstep and try and get in at all costs. There was a great deal of talk of working with the five members of the E.E.C. who are on our side to put pressure on the French by warning them that if they keep Britain out then there will be no progress in the E.E.C. I find this policy extremely unattractive since I take Blankenhorn's advice and would like to launch a British Gaullism as the best method of selling ourselves to Europe. But that's entirely out of tune with Harold and George and, I suspect, with Roy and it's no good having a dispute with Roy at this particular time.

The discussion on the Industrial Expansion Bill should have been a for-mality since it came as an agreed proposal from the Cabinet Committee.

But in today's new mood of ill will both Crosland and Callaghan raised the issue of whether the present economic crisis meant it should not be dropped. I noticed that Jim, now he's just another Minister like me, feels as free as I do to say what he bloody well likes.

At this point I had to rush to the Palace for a Privy Council winding up the Session. By the time I got back Cabinet was over so I knew that Roy had kept his word and enabled Harold to bulldoze the Industrial Expansion Bill through. It's my candid view that it should have been dropped because it is a nuisance. Yet, on the other hand, as Leader of the House I know that it saves me four other Bills.

This afternoon was Barbara Castle's big day since the Second Reading Stage of the Transport Bill was taken on the Floor of the House with the votes at eleven and midnight.[1] But all the heat had been taken out of the controversy. Barbara has done amazingly well: she obtained a very good press for her excellent White Papers, and has put the Bill over skilfully. So while it was going on I went down to the Prices and Incomes Policy Committee for an extremely depressing meeting on pay for Scottish teachers and London dockers. Peter Shore said that we must stand up to the dockers who wanted a £17 guaranteed wage. He was smacked down by Ray Gunter, who said quite brutally that we couldn't afford a dock strike in January nor could we bring the soldiers in. 'If you don't want trouble,' he ended, 'you must give way because the T & G is going to give official backing to this strike in an effort to reassert its authority against the dissidents.' I watched the Committee's reactions with interest. On balance Roy Jenkins agreed with Ray Gunter. And so did the rest of us because it's true we can't afford a dock strike in January. But Peter Shore is right in saying that in that case the prices and incomes policy is a mere statement of pious exhortation.

Having conceded to the dockers, the Committee felt it necessary to smack down poor Willie Ross when he tried to offer the Scottish teachers a decent wage. He hadn't a single person on his side and we all knew that the two cases had not been decided on their merits.

I just had time to see the P.M. before the liaison committee. He obviously wanted to tell me that John is too weak a Chief Whip and that there must be more discipline. I told him the best thing to do would be to let the Party discuss the revised Standing Orders and then, if possible, suspend them and keep them in the background. On the other hand I warned him it was perfectly clear that the new code would not be available for weeks.

At the liaison committee things were pretty tense. Douglas Houghton is now really steamed up about the way the Chief organized the South African arms lobby and he is supported by Willie Hamilton. But on the other hand Joyce Butler[2] and Eddie Milne are loyally on Harold's side and there was

[1] The vote on the Second Reading was 325 to 251 and on the Ways and Means motion 314 to 246.
[2] Labour M.P. for Wood Green since 1955.

therefore a majority against Douglas. In so far as anyone got his way at that meeting it was John Silkin—but with greatly reduced prestige and with an ill-omened reputation for colluding with the Left.

Meanwhile in my Privy Council office Sir Barnett Cocks and Sir Burke Trend had been sitting together waiting for me. It's weeks now since I decided to call the meeting of what I call the Patriarch and the Pope to discuss the problem of the confidential papers and memoranda which Ministers are asked to supply Select Committees. Barney insists that the Select Committee must always have the last word about what they publish. I pointed out that if they insisted on this last word then the Departments would have an excuse for refusing to cough up the material. I had not been too sorry that they would be able to have a talk in my absence and when I got there they both assured me that they had agreed on absolutely everything. But when I pressed them I found that Cocks hadn't moved even an inch and that Burke Trend had made it clear that he wasn't going to have a row with the House but equally that he would advise Departments to be very careful before they showed any confidential papers to Select Committees. So in fact the two of them had achieved nothing whatsoever. They had just agreed to be sensible and not to bring the issue up, which of course means that Whitehall will be more and more reluctant to let any Select Committee see papers.

This afternoon I just had time to brief two of the best journalists, David Watt of the *Financial Times* and Jimmy Margach of the *Sunday Times*. They had both just been to a special press conference the P.M. had held because he had been so upset at reading the accusations that he had been forced to compromise in Cabinet and to accept harsh cuts in social services in exchange for getting his way about Africa. Of course this is untrue. It is Harold and Roy who are insisting on imposing the prescription charges and postponing the raising of the school-leaving age. I can't see why the P.M. wanted to give this conference and both Watt and Margach made it clear to me that he had made a very bad impression on the press.

Thursday, December 21st
With Harold off to Australia O.P.D. was chaired by George Brown. The first item was information services and for once we got somewhere. We were able to defeat the Treasury and make it clear that as our military power declines the money we spend on information services and on psychological warfare must increase. Also the balance between services to various countries must be completely rethought. After that we were back as usual on the problem of the economic aid for Malaya and Singapore during and after our withdrawal. I found myself supporting Healey and Crosland in saying that what mattered now we had decided to get out was not saving money on aid but giving enough to be able to get out really quickly. However, they were opposed by Jack Diamond for the Treasury and it was soon clear the problem would have to go to Cabinet.

At business Questions I had the problem of Sachsenhausen. This very after-noon the Parliamentary Commissioner has finally published his report to Airey Neave's complaint and given the back-bench Tory M.P. a tremendous vindication against the Foreign Office. I'd had a frantic message from the F.O. to say that I was on no account to concede a debate but of course I hadn't dreamt of doing that. Instead I sent for Airey Neave, congratulated him and asked him to put a Question to me after the business Statement. When I answered him, George Brown sat beside me looking quite cheerful though he and the P.M. have been responsible for their own defeat. After that one of our rather nuisancy back-benchers, Marcus Lipton,[1] got up to ask me why I wasn't announcing next Monday's business and I said to him sharply that I only gave Monday's business as a matter of convenience and it wasn't convenient for me today. As I sat down I felt a twinge at the fact that I'd been rather insulting and then a warmth of surprise at a round of applause from the House. I suddenly felt 'I'm home and dry as Leader of the House'. Heaven knows it's a trivial job and should be easy to do and I'm getting bored with it already. Nevertheless, it was nice to feel I was home and dry.

Then I had a party for a huge gang of children—our children and Oscar Hahn's. They were all off to the Robinson Crusoe panto but I first gave them lunch in the Strangers' dining-room and then took them up the Big Ben tower. The lunch-room was empty. There's quite a quick service and I dashed them up the tower and dashed them down again in time for Cabinet with its huge wind-up agenda.

We started by ratifying the surrender to the dockers. No wonder Peter Shore is gloomy. In the weeks immediately after devaluation the prices and incomes policy, one of the few things in which we differ from the Tories, has come to pieces in his hands. Next on the agenda was Roy Jenkins's Race Relations Bill, which Callaghan brought back to discuss the problem of owner-occupiers. I can't say anything about this because I was sound asleep. I do sometimes sleep in Cabinet but I've never failed to wake up before we reach my item on the agenda. This time I woke up in time for theatre censor-ship. This was round three of the row between Roy Jenkins and the Prime Minister about the Select Committee report recommending that the whole of the Lord Chamberlain's censorship of the theatre should be abolished.

Harold Wilson had held this up last July on the grounds that he and the Queen were worried about the presentation of live personages in the theatre, because there might be a play put on about the Duke of Edinburgh, and Harold Wilson doesn't much like *Mrs Wilson's Diary*, which has been run-ning at the theatre in Stratford East. Last July Harold was in a powerful enough position to threaten Roy and say he just couldn't do it. Roy played it cool, he did nothing about it. I have been asking him pretty often to go back and talk to Harold but he hasn't done so. I often asked him to go back

---

[1] Labour M.P. for Lambeth since 1945.

20*

and talk to Harold but he was too proud to and now he has ceased to be Home Secretary. James Callaghan presented exactly the same Bill and in Harold's absence the Queen's objections lapsed. In a small way this shows what a decline there has been in Prime Ministerial government.

Next came the Singapore issue, referred from O.P.D. I was surprised that Roy tried to push the Jack Diamond line. I thought he would accept the view that the negotiators knew best and that we should offer more aid. But no, he felt duty bound by the Treasury to have a go but Cabinet was as firmly against withholding the offer as O.P.D. and finally Roy said that he would admit defeat. The Prime Minister will be able to brief Harry Lee in Singapore on his way back from Australia.

Finally came poor Willie Ross with his Scottish teachers' salaries. Of course the Civil Service had put this at the other end of the agenda from the item on dockers' pay because if they had been taken together Willie might have won. But now we all wanted to go off and he was left blasting, bleating and then suddenly threatening to resign. There was an ominous silence because he's not too popular a Secretary of State for Scotland and his resignation would be willingly accepted by a great many of us, including the Prime Minister. By then Cabinet had lasted from a quarter to four until twenty past five and I got away in time to give the children a jolly good high tea at the Great Western Hotel at Paddington before getting into my reserved compartment on the 7.15.

Friday, December 22nd

I went up to London in the morning to do my Christmas shopping and also to give my own Private Office a lunch-time Christmas drink. Then back to Vincent Square where I lunched with Jennie and at long last we did the Christmas orders for the wine which is my standard present for Gilbert and Venice. This year I haven't really dealt with them properly because of Anne's illness. I caught the 4.55 back and at last found myself relaxing.

Sunday, December 24th

The Sunday papers are pretty good. Apparently Harold had his forty minutes with L.B.J. in Australia but unfortunately L.B.J.'s main concern was to talk to the Pope about mediation in Vietnam. This completely confirms my view that there will never be a role for Harold and George as mediators in that dispute. At this point I might as well read into this diary something which Tam Dalyell told me about the meeting of the Foreign Affairs Group on Vietnam last week. Jack Mendelson had made a speech asking why we didn't back U Thant and the United Nations instead of backing the U.S.A. In the reply, which Tam took down virtually verbatim, George Brown said, 'I have an understanding in Moscow so that at any moment when we can get a breakthrough I can act as intermediary. The only basis on which I can stay in play is if the communists in Pekin and Hanoi believe that I can deliver the Americans. The U.S. trusts me not to deliver them unless they can get something suitable in return. I could deliver Johnson in two minutes flat from here if I could get something from Hanoi. I am the one chap who has influence with the Americans. The communists do not ask me to cut myself off from the Americans: the Russians ask me to keep in contact with the United States and keep our association. It is only nice chaps like you who want us to dissociate.' I had always imagined that George Brown spread it on pretty thick when he was speaking safely off the record. But I never imagined that he would talk quite such tripe as that.

Wednesday, December 27th

I was off on the 12.34, arriving at Paddington at 1.55 to be met by a car and Thomas Balogh. He took me to my office for a talk but there were no papers waiting there for our meeting of ten or eleven members of the inner Cabinet at 4.30 this afternoon. Over Christmas I had been brooding more than I should, I suppose, while I had been wooding on my island or lying in bed, and I have been doing a lot of this in my sleep too, as I remember from my dreams. I know, because both of them have told me so, that Harold and Roy are now firmly committed to the view that we have to slaughter some sacred cows in order to appease the bankers and that two of the sacrifices are the raising of the school-leaving age (to be postponed for three years) and the restoration of prescription charges. When I challenged Roy about this the other night he said that £40 million saved on prescription charges is worth £140 million anywhere else because of the impression it makes on the bankers. Well, I've been thinking a lot about this slaughter of the sacred cows and I've come to the conclusion that if we are going to hold the Party together it is essential that we must have some major cuts in defence, i.e. some slaughter of right-wing sacred cows. When I gave Roy dinner at Lockets before Christmas the idea of balance which I sold him was withdrawal from East of Suez and cancellation of the purchase of the F-111 in exchange for two domestic cows. The trouble is that this is weighted in favour of the right. My new bright idea was that to make it fair we should add to the right-wing sacred cows the abandonment of the nuclear deterrent. Recently Harold has talked to me about this, though on the last occasion he said, 'That's not for this package.' On another occasion he remarked that this is the kind of campaign Tam ought to be prosecuting, demanding the abandonment not only of the next generation but of this generation of nuclear weapons. Several times he's mentioned the notion that the Americans might buy *Polaris* back.

Yesterday I went to Nicholas Davenport's for dinner and there was my cousin Michael Howard, now a Fellow of All Souls.[1] I seized the opportunity

---

[1] Professor of War Studies, King's College, London, 1963–8, when he became a Fellow of All Souls College, Oxford. He became Chichele Professor of Military History in 1976.

and though it was rude he and I sat together all evening after dinner discussing this problem. 'If you weigh up *Polaris* against Singapore and Malaya,' he told me, 'we're doing far more good in the Far East than we are in keeping nuclear weapons. *Polaris* is a pure status symbol, or alternatively you can call it a weapon essential to national survival, but in circumstances so unique that they are not worth preparing for.' Michael's view has enormously strengthened my determination to get the idea of abandoning *Polaris* into the discussions today.

I shall fight for this defence package not as a future Defence Minister but as Party Manager, pointing out that with this programme I think I could persuade the Parliamentary Party that we shall still be socialists even if we accept the return of prescription charges and the postponement of the raising of the school-leaving age. In fact it would give us the basis of a socialist foreign policy. The announcement of the end of the British independent deterrent, the end of our presence East of Suez and the end of the F-111 would be the virtual winding-up of our whole present defence posture. For this, as Michael Howard said to me, we need a new Minister of Defence who will think out British defence in a completely novel way. And Michael looked at me and said, 'You are the only person who could do it.' That may be true, but it won't happen.

And so the famous inner Cabinet has come and gone. It wasn't much of an inner Cabinet because as I expected there were ten of us there apart from the P.M. — Roy Jenkins, myself, John Silkin, Peter Shore, Fred Peart, Tony Crosland, Denis Healey, George Brown, Michael Stewart, Jim Callaghan. The proceedings were pretty futile because in the end all we had was an informal pow-wow about the Chancellor's package of cuts. We all suspected it would be a fair waste of time as we stood about outside the Cabinet door. Tony Crosland came in his sports clothes and took off his waistcoat and said it was very stuffy and it was a cursed nuisance coming back from his cottage. Next came Roy back from his cottage in the Hendreds and we all stood apart from each other, eyeing each other rather suspiciously. And then out of the room came the Chiefs of Staff and I knew the P.M. and Roy had been having a meeting of the defence chiefs first to which his own Defence Committee had not been invited.

Roy gave us nothing on paper but said that £850 million had to be taken out of the economy and then began to go through the major areas and show what cuts the Treasury required. 'Before we go through this package in detail,' I said, 'let's get a picture of how the home cuts relate to the defence cuts.' Roy replied that he had reached the conclusion that whatever economies we made on paper there could be no economies in the 1967–8 budget and only £100 million in the 1968–9 budget. But that didn't mean that he failed to see their importance. Indeed it made it all the more important to have strategic decisions taken firmly and decisively now and this is what he hoped to get. I said that I found this intolerable because we were being asked today to agree to specific cuts on the home side while there was nothing specific or hard on the foreign side. To this George Brown replied that the defence chiefs were doing all they possibly could but that we had to consider the security of our allies and the needs of our soldiers and he added the words, 'We simply can't guarantee anything firm by January 15th.' I replied that in that case no announcement could be made on January 15th, because it would be impossible to announce home cuts without an equally fair announcement on foreign cuts. Denis Healey said, 'If we're going to have our policies decided by the number of people who vote for us in the House that's a poor way to consider the national future.' I couldn't help replying that if one could not achieve the credibility of the pound without a return to prescription charges and the postponement of the school-leaving age, it's equally true that one can't achieve the survival of this Government without firm corresponding defence cuts abroad. Roy passed me a note telling me that the defence people had only had one meeting and had agreed nothing and urging me to go on being as tough as I could in my demands about commitments on defence abroad.

After a time we did turn to the home side but with an understanding that no firm decisions could be taken. I insisted on this although it made the meeting completely futile. Indeed, somebody asked what the point was of our coming to London today if this group was to take no kind of group decision. There was no answer because of course this group was to be the inner Cabinet but the inner Cabinet idea once again has been shattered. It's profoundly depressing because this is the third time all this has happened.

There was an interesting episode when Roy turned to housing. He said that there must be a saving of some 10,000 to 15,000 houses approved for construction between 1968 and 1969, although this might well mean bringing the total built down from the 500,000 we promised to 470,000 in 1970 — our planned election year. Harold pleaded that this was a terrible thing and I'm afraid, that though I shouldn't have, I said, 'Well, if you're going to haul down the flag on free prescriptions and on the school-leaving age, hauling down the flag on the 500,000 housing target fits in quite well.' Then we came to Concorde and Roy said he wants quite definitely to stop its production. He saw that we might be in a dangerous situation, compelled to carry on the R and D while stopping production, but before he got any further I said to him, 'You can't possibly cut Concorde and leave the F-111. The two would have to be cut together,' to which Denis Healey remarked, 'What on earth relationship is there between the two?' I retorted, 'Politically, Denis, there's a very close relationship as you may sometime discover.'

The whole meeting lasted a good many hours and my impression was that Roy behaved in a rather ingenuous fashion. Here he was coming along with almost the identical package of cuts that we had heard from Callaghan when he was Chancellor. Nor was Roy particularly well briefed. Even worse, he doesn't yet exert any authority or have any real weight against the men who face him on the other side of the table—Callaghan, Brown and Healey, who have formed a kind of anti-Wilson/Jenkins phalanx. I must add, however, that throughout he was completely loyal to Harold and correct in putting forward the agreed package.

At last the others drifted out and the Prime Minister asked John Silkin and me to stay behind. John had warned me of what our talk would be about. The P.M. has learnt from Hugh Cudlipp that on January 1st the *Daily Mirror* is going to start a tremendous 'Wilson Must Go' campaign and Harold's entourage believe that Healey has something to do with it. Harold told me what he'd heard and then said, 'It's being run by Callaghan and Healey and I believe they're going for a national government.' Then he turned to me and said, 'Isn't that a story that should be given to Ian Aitken for Monday morning or perhaps Jimmy Margach for Sunday—the story of the Callaghan/Healey plot?' I said, 'I'll see what I can do about it.' I have no doubt that an anti-Wilson campaign is being worked up and that one of the forces is the Minister of Defence who is determined to defeat the proposal to cut the F-111. But as for giving the story of the plot to the Sunday papers I very much doubt its wisdom. The P.M. is off for a whole week's holiday leaving Roy Jenkins to work out the package here. I think we should stay quiet for this week at least and see how things go. One thing we've achieved is that the next paper which is prepared will have put together the defence and the home package and treated them as a whole.

What about my idea of scrapping the British deterrent? Well, I hardly managed to bring it in because I'd assumed that the cancellation of the F-111 had been conceded already by Healey along with the withdrawal from Singapore. But since nothing had been conceded on the defence side, all I could say was that there were other cuts we had to consider and one was the deterrent. Healey laughed at me and said that would only save £20 million a year and that there is no real cut there. At this I jumped. 'Well, if it costs nothing that's all the better. Roy Jenkins remarked that though prescription charges would only actually raise £40 million they are worth £140 million in terms of banker mythology. I can tell you that though the abolition of the independent British deterrent would only raise £20 million it would be worth £120 million in terms of the morale of the Parliamentary Party and the radical image we want to present to the country.' But having made this point I had to drop the project for the time being.

Meanwhile Harold is off to the Scillies and I think that for the first time there is something like a threat brewing behind his back. In the short run of course the *Daily Mirror* attack would do him a power of good. That's why I think it would be a great mistake to give Margach or Aitken any kind of story about a Healey/Callaghan plot. But what the *Daily Mirror* campaign will prove is that Cecil King is deliberately working up agitation against the P.M. and that there's a link between that and the defence Ministries. If this is, as I believe, the only danger, Harold's position is secure in the short run.

What I don't know—and I have to reflect on this very carefully—is whether in the long run our government can continue under the kind of leadership he's giving at present. If we keep him it must be as a chairman with under him a small, powerful, central controlling group which should not include Mr Healey.

Friday, December 29th

With virtually no boxes this week I've been completely unemployed and therefore I've been writing more in my diary. I was reading somewhere that Churchill said diaries were bad for writers because they force you to make a judgment before you have had time to reflect. Certainly doing mine once a week has the opposite effect. The longer I do my diary, dictating once a week, the more it becomes considered reflection on what is happening around me. Indeed, since I started I've steadily increased the amount of preparatory work I do each weekend before dictating on to the tape. When I started, I used to dictate slabs without any real preparation. Then I took to jotting down a few notes. Fairly soon I gave instructions to my Private Office that each weekend they should send home with me all the Cabinet Committee minutes, all the Cabinet minutes, the diary of my appointments and all the important departmental papers. Now I find that on Saturday evening I spend several hours reading through these papers and reflecting on them and preparing very full notes for the diary for dictation on Sunday morning. I suspect the diary is getting longer but if so it is certainly more carefully prepared. And the effect is that I'm telescoping the actual picture of what has gone on. When I report on Cabinet meetings and Cabinet Committee meetings I have the minutes there to remind me of what was said. But by the end of the week all my other conversations and talks and impressions are mushed up into a general impression with a great deal of the flesh and blood—the whispered remark on the front bench, the chats over lunch—boiled up together. For example, even with the Prime Minister, with whom I spend a lot of time, I tend to remember only the impression which was left after each meeting, the residue which resulted in action. Nevertheless, I think it is probably a better diary in the sense of having a more balanced picture, though much less good in terms of colour, as there are far fewer actual titbits of conversation.

Last night Peter Shore rang me back and I asked him his impressions of the inner Cabinet. He said he was staggered at having the same old package provided by the Treasury. 'Roy disappointed me,' he said, 'because it's the same list. He disappointed me by reading aloud the same Treasury brief.' Then he said that in his view it was the absence of any attempt to discuss our central strategy which was so depressing. And then finally he remarked on the illiterate character of most of the observations made by our colleagues round the table on the road programme, or on pensions or on housing. I replied, 'You just have to get used to that.' But it was interesting to find his general impressions so close to mine.

An hour later Roy rang me, quiet and confident. He told me he had interviewed three more Ministers and things are going fairly well, and then he emphasized at some length the importance of making sure that the withdrawal from the Far East should be completed within the period of our Parliament—that's to say 1969–70. We must be out of Singapore, he feels, by the next election and that's the battle he wants me to fight against the Chiefs of Staff.

We then discussed the balance of the package again and he told me he'd almost felt like giving up the attempt to postpone the raising of the school-leaving age. I told him that he couldn't because if he did that Denis would keep the F-111.

That's the kind of detail which would occur every day if I made a daily and not a weekly diary. It would certainly become impossibly long. But during this quiet holiday I can reflect on the past week.

At business time on the Thursday before Christmas I felt I was safely home as a successful Leader of the House. But I don't feel any sense of permanency in the office. If I felt permanent I would insist on having a Parliamentary Secretary to hold the fort for me when I'm away. The big difference between the Chief Whip and myself is that he has the whole machinery of the Whips behind him and I have no number two. If Harold stays on and remains Prime Minister I'm pretty sure he's going to move me somewhere else where I shall be needed. But if Harold isn't Prime Minister I don't think I shall stay in the Government very long. Either way my impression is that I shan't be in this office beyond next April. So I'm going to do nothing whatsoever either to make my Private Office more efficient or to get more staff. Of course that's the difficulty of the Leader of the House—it's a wholly personal office without any kind of Department. If I stayed a few months longer I might set down to abolish the whole ridiculous Privy Council mumbo-jumbo which keeps the Queen having to meet five busy Ministers and stand there and say 'Approved' as I read the list of Orders in Council aloud. The sensible thing would be for her signature to be obtainable without this formal meeting altogether. Or, if people like to retain the meeting as a pure formality, we could have it once or twice a year just as I've made Black Rod's interruption of the House of Commons an annual event. Such reforms would be thoroughly sensible and I should like to do them but they would involve me in a battle royal with our two Privy Council civil servants—Godfrey Agnew and Leigh —and I'm not prepared to start it.

I suspect that I sound as though I'm complaining about the work of my civil servants. But I'm not. My Private Office is hopeless because only a small part of my work is done with their knowledge. Most of my work is confidential and involves secret talks with the Prime Minister or it is party politics, which the civil servants don't want to engage in. An efficient Private Office, such as John Delafons built for me at Housing, knew absolutely everything I did and kept tabs on me, read all my letters, heard all my telephone conversations, and could keep me up to scratch and make sure that every suggestion I made was followed up. But my present Private Office knows less than half of what I'm up to. They don't know the talks I have with M.P.s, they don't know officially of the existence of my talks with the journalists, they don't know when I go to see the Prime Minister and nor do they know what happens when I'm with John Silkin in his office. And that's why they find it so difficult to plan my diary, because they don't know how long any interview is likely to last or how late I'm going to return to my own office. Of course if Freddy Ward were John Delafons he would have far greater control and I think he would know more about my party work. But he is very much a civil servant who keeps himself outside politics and as a result I've had to bring Tam Dalyell right in so that I've got a real P.P.S. who acts as my Private Secretary. He not only cooks my breakfast at 9 Vincent Square, he's a confidant, a Sancho Panza, listening to his Don Quixote talking, talking, talking, saying everything aloud in his presence and knowing nothing will be passed on. He also does a great deal of contact work in the smoking-room and makes notes of all my conversations and reminds me of the promises I've made. So he really is doing the work of a civil servant now.

On the other side, how is the Lord President getting on with the Whips' Office? Freddie Warren is still in control of the parliamentary timetable. The more I see of him the more astonishing I find the influence he exerts. He really is the bridge between the Opposition and the Government. It's as though there had been one staff sergeant-major running the British and the German staffs in World War I and it's this which really keeps the House of Commons running and enables us to have so few misunderstandings between the two Chief Whips on either side. Of course John and Willie get on uncommonly well personally and I think Willie trusts me too. It's a great relief that Heath and Anthony Barber have virtually opted out of the business side of the House so that Willie, John and I can work together in the closest possible way. But I strongly suspect that even if there were two quite different Chief Whips and a very different Lord President the one Office in No. 12 would continue to keep the parliamentary machine running extraordinarily quietly. The other day when I was lunching with the Foreign Press Association I said that Freddie Warren was one of the most important persons in British politics and they ought to study him at first hand. One or two of them rang him up and there'd been a couple of good articles — one in a Swiss and the other in a French paper. His is a job which certainly needs studying at length by anybody who wants to describe the process of government in this country.

Sunday, December 31st
New Year's Eve. Today's papers are fairly gloomy but Jimmy Margach has written the kind of story I hoped he would write and I think it will help Harold Wilson a bit. One can't deny that the South African crisis has left a great deal of ill will and distrust of Harold among over half the Cabinet.

This Government has failed more abysmally than any Government since 1931. In Macmillan's case, after all, it was after six years of fantastic success as Supermac. But in Harold's case the failure consists in tearing away the magic and revealing that he's really been failing ever since he entered No. 10. We have simply not succeeded and this feeling has been getting into my bones.

The other day my sister Bridget Bardsley came over to lunch and I mentioned Harold Wilson. Though she's the wife of a Tory clergyman Bridget is a very strong Labour supporter and she said, 'There's someone whose spell has been broken this year. I doubt whether anybody will believe in him again.' And that was said by somebody who has been for years a deep supporter of the Left as well as of her brother on the Left. These days it's almost a disgrace to be a member of the Wilson Government. How gay it was in the early days when I used to travel up from Banbury and the station master was proud to be seen carrying my red box along the platform and finding my reserved compartment. Now it's not quite like that. Now the deputy station master comes along. He's a nice chap, he's a friend of mine, but the station master has long since opted out and his deputy, who is a socialist, meets me and pops me quickly into my compartment. And as I walk there past the row of passengers waiting for the train one or two of them smile at me pleasantly, but even with them there's a sense of embarrassment that their Mr Crossman is one of the members of this devaluation Government. Am I being hypersensitive about this? I don't think so. Nor have I any conviction that things will get better. I very much doubt that Roy, who is young and inexperienced, will be able to restore the credibility of the Government. Credibility is now the modish word—it started about the pound and now it has spread to the Government too, and the more people talk about the credibility of the Government the more they undermine it. I now feel the same kind of dread about going back to London which I felt about going back to school and seeing all the boys again and trying to work things out.

This Christmas I made the mistake of reading a book about politics— Claud Cockburn's autobiography—which I thought would be light and amusing.[1] It turned out to be much more serious. There's one chapter where he describes how he had to come back to Britain from America to cover the election of 1945 for the *Daily Worker*. At that time it was supporting the Labour Party, though Claud didn't really believe in a Labour Government— and he goes on to say why. His kind of communism, he said, was conservatism. He wanted to conserve the civilization of the whole western world and he saw this could only be done by a communist revolution. In fact he wasn't a liberal or a progressive. He didn't believe in introducing abortion or permitting divorce. That wasn't his kind of Left. Claud was a revolutionary conservative and that's why he particularly hated radical leftists with their belief that if the ordinary people are given the chance of running things they will take the right decisions and run things well. On reading that passage I

[1] *I, Claud* — (Harmondsworth: Penguin, 1967).

realized that the whole of my life I've been in this sense a radical leftist. Ever since I was a young don I've believed in the W.E.A., in training the mass of the people for responsibility for self-government and I've been convinced that if we could use education for that purpose we would be able to substitute genuine social democracy for oligarchy. Now, after this experience of a social democratic government, I have seriously begun to doubt. Of course I've known for a long time that the belief in the rationality of man is a *credo quia impossibile*. But this experience has really shaken that ultimate faith in the political educability of man or, more deeply even, in the possibility of a government where decisions are taken by ordinary people. Reading Macmillan's second volume — *The Blast of War* — made me realize that in wartime our democracy functioned far better because the interaction of the two party machines through the usual channels was working permanently and perfectly so that the House of Commons was merely criticizing a permanent central government. I now can't help wondering whether the House of Commons may not be better when there's an all-party government and a kind of consensus of criticism as a background.

Not that this excuses our failures. When I look back over these three years I realize how much better we could have done and how everything we've done has been too little and too late. The main disasters are our own fault, but one has to look deeper and seek the cause for our inadequacy. Why was it, for example, that when the Labour Government came in after thirteen years the men who took charge of foreign policy and defence — Wilson, Brown, Callaghan, Stewart — all believed that it was their role to prove that Labour could run Great Britain as well as the Conservatives? Not one of them admitted that the job of a socialist was to scale Britain down to an off-shore island, to accept devaluation, to accept the winding-up of the sterling area and to do these things voluntarily and not under compulsion. The reason why these men were in charge is because under our system of two-party politics they were bound to get to the top of the Labour Party and we wouldn't have been elected if they hadn't. And, moreover, it is bad luck for us that with all his brilliant powers of opportunism and resilience Harold Wilson has failed at the Prime Minister's essential task of creating a centre of power which imposes a central strategy on the Government. That is what we shall need if we are to reassert over our civil servants the authority we have lost as a result of our catastrophes. When I read *The Blast of War* during my holiday I was enormously struck by the disastrous nature of the instructions Macmillan usually received from the Foreign Office and I agree with Tommy Balogh about the rigidity and cocksureness of the Whitehall machine, its opposition to new ideas and its clannishness. And we also have to overcome something else — the stream of anti-government propaganda, smearing, snarky, derisive, which comes out of Fleet Street. This press propaganda undoubtedly undermines public morale and in particular the morale of the Labour Party that has been the chief casualty in this ghastly year of 1967.

In bed this morning I said to Anne, 'Somehow you seem unhappy,' and she said, 'Well, I'm getting a bit older.' Then under pressure she added, 'Maybe it's you who are unhappy, not me, and I'm merely infected by you?' That was a good remark. My morale certainly has been affected. I hate being a member of such a catastrophically unsuccessful Government and this hatred affects my attitude to Anne and to the children. That's why it's so vital that this new Statement should be a Statement of strategic intention—a new start in Government policy and not merely the announcement of an economy package. There are certain factors working in our favour. Prime Ministerial government is out for the moment. Harold is very much *primus inter pares*. He's working very closely now with his new Chancellor and supporting him he's got a powerful left-wing group—Barbara Castle, Wedgy Benn, Peter Shore, John Silkin and me. Against him there is now clearly ranged a rival group consisting of Crosland, Healey and George Thomson and, to some extent, George Brown. This isn't necessarily a bad thing as we may get a more coherent series of decisions out of an overt struggle.

1968

Monday, January 1st

The day of the New Year's Honours list and my first job was to ring up Pam Berry and congratulate her on her husband, Michael's, becoming a newspaper peer.[1] That won't make the P.M. any more loved at the *Daily Mirror*, where the first of the three great anti-Wilson articles appeared today. It looks as though someone made a last-minute change of policy because instead of attacking Wilson they now chiefly build up Jenkins. In terms of psychological warfare this is far more damaging since it will at once raise Harold's suspicions that Roy and his press agent, John Harris, have been at work.

I did my telephoning from Prescote because I had taken the day off. When I rang up Roy I found that he was going to spend it at his cottage in the Hendreds and so I only went up that evening to see him at 10.30 p.m. I had forgotten the number of his London house and it was a slushy evening with a lot of wet snow. I traipsed around Ladbroke Square from No. 9, where I tried first, until at last I found him at No. 34. He duly gave me a tot of whisky and we sat down to discuss the central strategy that we both know we require. When I said to him that the Statement must not be merely a package of cuts but a new start based on a new strategy he straightaway agreed and said that he felt it was essential for him to make it in the House. I said he was certainly the dominant person who should be responsible for the new thinking and that I would do all I could to see that Burke Trend and Harold both took the same view.

After he'd told me something of his bilateral talks with various Ministers I told him we should give up the idea of an inner Cabinet and go for an effective dyarchy shared between him and Harold. He told me that it was essential to get Denis out of his present job because he finds him dangerous. On the other hand he values him highly and I think he would like to see him in Education and me at Defence, remoulding our policy on the new European basis.

When, after two hours' talk, I went home this evening I felt I'd been doing my main job of cementing the relationship between Roy and Harold, which should be the dominant fact of this Cabinet. My impression of Roy was that he is quickly growing in strength, though I admit I find it a little strange that on a Monday he can sit in his cottage and that he always finds time to dine out and take life easy. Moreover, he doesn't know his Treasury briefs as well as Callaghan did. This is because he is an ambitious man with a wonderful policy mind — the power to think in terms of political strategy and to concentrate on certain narrow goals, precisely what we've lacked up to now.

Tuesday, January 2nd

I spent the whole day on preparations for the all-party consultations on Lords reform. Eddie Shackleton came to see me in the Privy Council early this morning. We first discussed strategy and I suggested that in my view to

[1] As Lord Hartwell.

put forward an all-Party agreed solution now would have great advantages. This is not what I thought just after devaluation when I wondered whether in the abrasive new party political atmosphere an agreed White Paper would look inadequate. I was glad to find that Eddie too had shifted back to believing in an agreed solution and a Bill in the next Session. He showed me the huge new official paper he'd had prepared on the working of the two-tier system as well as his invaluable check list. He really is a tremendous worker and his Cabinet papers are some of the best I've ever seen.

Then we had to go round to continue our discussion with the Lord Chancellor and there we found Callaghan sitting in a big armchair well away from the rest, with an appalling cold. This morning we had another example of the new relaxed Callaghan with his corsets off and his Chancellor's dewlaps flopping about his neck. He's certainly been aged by three years at the Treasury and he's now feeling relaxed and irresponsible; I must admit that his comments as a relaxed and decorseted Home Secretary are not nearly as sensible as his corseted Treasury comments used to be. It's now too obvious that he is an ordinary ambitious politician who was promoted well beyond his station when he served as Chancellor. Nevertheless he had a very special value on this occasion. We could try everything out on him and we could also work hard to win him to our side so that we should leave George Brown isolated in Cabinet. Our object then, before lunch and at 2.30, when we started again, was to try to humour Callaghan and get him out of his oppositional mood.

In the course of the day we had our usual difficulties with Frank Pakenham, who I hear has threatened to resign about the postponement of the school-leaving age.[1] (If only Willie Ross would do the same. If we could replace him with George Thomson and Frank with Eddie Shackleton the Cabinet would be greatly improved.)

But the only major row we had today was about the Whips. I wanted John Silkin and Willie Whitelaw to join the consultations and Frank said that would be impossible unless Beswick and St Aldwyn[2] were also included as the Chief Whips of the House of Lords. From our point of view that would be ridiculous. We need John and Willie because they are responsible for delivering the crucial vote in the Commons and they can advise us on what is acceptable and what isn't. However, we finally had to agree that we would first ask them to give evidence to us before thinking about the problem again. I must speak to Maudling about it this week.

Late this afternoon there was the first meeting of a new Special Committee on Rhodesia for which Lord Caradon had flown back from New York. The idea was that this Committee should discuss with Caradon and all the other

---

[1] He did, on January 16th.

[2] Michael Hicks Beach who succeeded to his grandfather's title of Earl St Aldwyn in 1916. He was Opposition Chief Whip in the House of Lords 1964–70 and Chief Whip 1958–64 and 1970–74.

top officials the practicability of 'getting off the hook' in Rhodesia or alternatively of handing Rhodesia over to the U.N. on a plate. Of course this has
been my pet project ever since I became Lord President and I at once took
over the cross-examination of Caradon while the Lord Chancellor looked on
patiently from the chair. (He is a Caradon supporter.) Caradon started by
saying there must be no question of giving way and that we must intensify
sanctions. I said that it was not the job of this Committee to discuss tactics
but to look at the special problem of unilaterally abrogating our Rhodesian
responsibilities. Was that possible? For instance, could we transfer the problem to the U.N. Trusteeship Council? When I asked the question I didn't
know about Article 77, which makes it quite clear that it is perfectly constitutional to hand over a trust territory to the Trusteeship Council. But
when I put this to Caradon I've never seen such resistance. He said it was
quite impractical because we would be held in scorn and derision. It would in
the first instance go not to the Trusteeship Council but to the General
Assembly, where we would be bombarded with criticism. We had an hour of
really fierce debate during which I discovered that George Thomas was siding
with me. There are to be two more meetings before Lord Caradon, who
obviously hates the whole affair, is to be allowed off the hook.

When I got home I found that the children had arrived for their winter
excursion to London and we all went out to dinner.

Wednesday, January 3rd
I strode across to No. 10 to see how the Prime Minister would react to the
idea that Roy should make the great Statement. I first tried it out on Burke
and he was fiercely against it. Then I went in to the P.M. and he was just as
strong. I'm pretty sure his resistance was partly due to the build-up of Roy in
the *Daily Mirror*. Harold had rung me earlier this morning to say that he had
heard that Jenkins had persuaded Cudlipp to build up the Chancellor instead
of attacking the P.M. Harold had said, 'With this build-up of Roy I can't
possibly afford not to make the Statement myself. I don't see why Roy
shouldn't make the Ministerial broadcast.' I rang Roy back and told him that
it was a good idea provided that he opened the debate with a longer Statement. He said, 'Well, would the P.M. take that?' I then tried *that* out on the
P.M. and he said that Roy would of course do the Ministerial broadcast
and then open the debate on Wednesday.

I didn't have much time for gossip with Harold because he was off to
N.E.D.C., where he was taking the chair to reassert his authority. I went to
Duke Street in St James's to have my hair cut and then went on to an admirable American charade at the Royal Court Theatre called *The Paperhangers*,
which Helga Greene had selected as suitable for children. Together we
collected nine children to see it and she had them to lunch and we to tea.

This evening I had my long-arranged dinner for Wedgy Benn, Peter
Shore, Barbara Castle and Tommy Balogh. I soon discovered they were all

highly suspicious of me. Wedgy Benn and Barbara in particular were both convinced that I was right on the inside, operating in a dangerous top-level policy group which was committing Cabinet to terrible things. It took at least an hour to explain there is no inner Cabinet, that no decisions are taken on the inside and that Harold is up to his old bilateral tricks as before. But if only for this it was an important evening and Anne gave us lovely food and drink which made us feel good and even cheered up Barbara, who was just recovering from flu and being heroic. It was a thoroughly useful preliminary to tomorrow's Cabinet.

Thursday, January 4th
The inner Cabinet started at ten and went on most of the afternoon. It achieved nothing except to reveal how the balance of power lay. We started with foreign policy and defence and never got away from it because such a welter of papers had been put in from the F.O., from Defence and from the Commonwealth Office, all arguing that it was utterly impractical to complete the Far Eastern withdrawal by March 1970 and adding that anyway no mention could be made of any withdrawal from the Persian Gulf.

The opponents were all lined up on the other side of the table, this time with Michael Stewart added to the old gang. There they were, Brown, Healey, Callaghan, Stewart, the four who for three months with their Departments behind them had advised that any withdrawal would produce insurrection in Singapore and in the Persian Gulf. Now they were arguing with the same ferocity that our presence must continue to 1972 in order to avoid these disasters. When we turned to the F-111 the line-up was very much the same.

I took the Chief out to lunch at the Garrick where, greatly venturing, we sat at the centre table where ordinary members sit and chat. On the way back to Cabinet an extraordinary little interview with George Brown occurred. A week or two ago Alec Spearman, who used to be my pair but who has retired now and whose only political function is to run the Anglo-American group which meets in Bermuda each year, had suggested to me that I should lead the British delegation this spring. I had jumped at the idea of such a pleasant holiday in pleasant surroundings. So Alec had talked to John Silkin, who fixes the membership of such things, and John had at once concurred. Yesterday Alec came to tell me that on Monday night he had been hauled out of the theatre by an irate George Brown who said that he had just learnt that the Lord President was to lead the British delegation and that this was an outrage he couldn't permit. To this the Chief had replied that the selecting of the members was entirely his job and it was an outrage of George to behave in this way. Of course the whole row is utterly absurd since there are many precedents for the Leader of the House or the Home Secretary or any other leading member of the Government taking on this job before formal approval of the Foreign Secretary has been obtained. Throughout the whole interview John stood behind Spearman and expressed his outrage without speaking a word. I had to sit down and write a minute to Harold straightaway saying that George had no right to intervene on this. I could understand his forbidding me to go to Palestine during a Middle Eastern crisis but to say that I would be *persona non grata* with American senators was a bit tough.

By three o'clock John and I were through the doors and into No. 10 for Cabinet again. At the beginning Crosland quite rightly tried to get some appreciation of the general situation and of the reasoning behind the decision that nearly £1,000 million should be taken out of the economy by taxation. But at this point Roy was not interested. He pushed ahead because he wanted to deal with the specific proposals in his paper. We started once again with withdrawal from the Middle East and whether it should terminate in 1970–71 or in 1971–2. George Brown, Denis Healey, George Thomson and Michael Stewart between them all made long speeches for more than an hour. Denis made his central point that in future Europe would be the basis of our strategy but that even so the timing of our withdrawal was all-important. From our side we urged that it was essential to have fully withdrawn from the Far East before we went to the country so that we could take full credit for a big decision and for a positive and constructive new policy. What we were asking for in fact was a vote of no confidence in the four pygmies on the other side of the table — Michael Stewart, George Brown, James Callaghan and Denis Healey — who had been running our foreign policy for the last three years. To my amazement we got it with a large majority. Apart from Willie Ross and Fred Peart every other member of Cabinet voted with Harold and Roy.

There was a far stronger case for the F-111. The Exchequer will pay $80 million in compensation, there are no savings in year one and there will be a lot of cancellations of contracts for offset purchases. Healey also strengthened his case by saying there could be no question of cutting down the numbers in the order. There must be either outright cancellation or we must purchase the lot. Once again Harold put this carefully to the vote and the result was a tie, with the P.M. giving his casting vote against the F-111. Not unnaturally Healey pleaded for a second chance and was given it. If he can find another way of saving £400 million he will be entitled to present it to Cabinet.

That was all Cabinet achieved before we broke off at seven. I went off to take Anne to *Heartbreak House*, which to my great disappointment I found rather flat. Was it the production or the overacting of the leading lady? It certainly wasn't Shotover, who was wonderfully played by John Clements. Every time I'd seen it before I'd thought it a brilliant play but this time I couldn't help being reminded of the intellectual pirouetting which makes *Getting Married* so boring. Clever talk for ever and ever. I went home wondering if Shaw is going to last as well as we thought he would.

Friday, January 5th
My poor Private Office had to rearrange all my plans. I had been due to go to Coventry in the morning for a conference on social problems organized by

the Provost but I had to cancel this and go by the 6.30 in order to have my surgery. All this had to be arranged to give room for the second Cabinet meeting this afternoon.

In the morning we had a Home Affairs meeting where Callaghan presented a paper on certain aspects of the Race Relations Bill which he's inherited from Roy. Once again he was his new breezy irresponsible self. In yesterday's Cabinet he had opposed with all his old-fashioned Great Britain jingoism the cuts he had been trying to impose as Chancellor. Now as he sat down beside me at the Committee he said *sotto voce*, 'I haven't got a liberal image to maintain like my predecessor; I'm going to be a simple Home Secretary.' He was so breezy that he made it a good-tempered meeting and we got through it fairly well.

On Harold's suggestion I gave lunch to John Harris. He was Hugh Gaitskell's press man in the 1959 general election and then became Head of Publicity at Transport House. When he took office he was sent first to the Foreign Office to improve Gordon Walker's image and when Patrick got the sack transferred his attentions to Patrick's successor, Michael Stewart. Then it was decided to share him between Michael Stewart at the Foreign Office and Roy Jenkins at the Home Office. Roy took to him very strongly and he has taken him to the Treasury. Harold has always detested the idea that Ministers should have their own private public relations officers but somehow he's reconciled himself to the fact that he can't have Roy without John Harris. So there he was lunching with me at the Garrick and I shall see him at Chequers next Friday to plan the publicity for the great new Statement on the largest possible scale. He's the one man about this place whom I recognize as a professional propagandist and I think we shall be able to get along fine. I had been disconcerted by the *Daily Mirror* build-up of Roy in the New Year and then by a very unpleasant story of the *Daily Mail* describing Roy's great victory in the Cabinet on foreign policy. These are typical Harris leaks. But now that we have a dyarchy John is working on our side not against us.

We re-started Cabinet by considering the £35 million Roy wants to save on social security. I managed to make it clear that he shouldn't say exactly where he's going to manage to impose cuts and that he shouldn't altogether exclude either the principle of a claw-back or the abolition of universal family allowances and personal tax allowances. Cabinet had no objection to this so we have plenty of time to work out a solution.

Next came education and George Brown, who'd obviously hotted himself up a bit at lunch-time, came out with an attack before the feeble Gordon Walker could say anything. It was an unpleasantly class-conscious speech, strongly implying that no one except the middle-class socialist who had never felt the pinch or never had a child at a state school could dare to suggest postponement of the raising of the school-leaving age. Ray Gunter and Jim Callaghan followed much the same working-class line while Tony Crosland and Gerald Gardiner spoke as socialist ideologists. Fred Peart and George

Thomson provided the professional trade-union case as represented by the N.U.T. Gordon Walker sat through this debate speechless and obviously trembling. He had been off the day before to a great meeting in Newcastle where he had talked about heartbreak decisions. Damn him! What an idiotic thing to say—heartbreak decisions! Either you take the decision and don't resign or you resign with heartbreak, but you don't stay put with heartbreak. Roy Jenkins put our case very moderately. He pointed out that no one had suggested another way of getting £40 million out of education without irreparable damage. Then he quietly added that there were really quite a number of teachers and parents of children at comprehensive schools who would welcome postponement. Denis Healey then bashed in saying that if he was going to have cuts of far more than £40 million he wanted to see adequate cuts in home policy. Dick Marsh, the youngest member of the Cabinet and also a trade unionist, clearly didn't feel a crisis of conscience any more than Peter Shore. They both sided with Roy. Barbara, of course, was in a difficulty. Her left-wingism would make her naturally opposed to postponement but on the other hand she wanted to preserve her road programme and to support Harold. It was obvious that we were getting terribly close in numbers and that if there was a majority on Roy's side it was very small. At this point Harold said that Gordon Walker should tell Cabinet what his view was. 'It's an agonizing decision,' he replied, 'but in the last resort I must accept two years' postponement.' I don't know which I disliked more—the pathetic weakness of Gordon Walker or the outrageous cynicism of Callaghan, who as Chancellor of the Exchequer had urged the postponement and was now joining the working-class battle against it.

I was ready for a tremendous fight on prescription charges but Harold very neatly avoided it by announcing, as soon as Roy had made his statement, that he had offered Kenneth Robinson and Judith Hart £15 million of the £40 million to be saved for exemptions to people over sixty-five, nursing mothers and children and possibly for the chronic sick. He informed us that a reply had come from Kenneth Robinson that no formal exemption was administratively possible. Of course I recognized at once that this was a political tactic which probably Michael Stewart had advised the two to adopt in order to prevent any increase of prescription charges. Presumably they hoped that Jennie Lee's passionate plea in this week's *Tribune* would scare Roy into surrender. What it has done is to persuade him to accept a compromise which Peter Shore and I were trying to work out last night. We proposed that 6d. of the total cost of exemption should be paid for out of the National Insurance contribution and that there should be absolute exemption for the old and for children. Kenneth replied that he would like to pay for the whole thing by a ninepenny increase in the N.I. contribution but Roy said he couldn't accept this because the issue had become a matter of confidence with the bankers—just as the F-111 was to be an issue of confidence with the parliamentary parties. So Cabinet agreed that prescription charges and the

F-111 should be brought back to Cabinet next week and only three people, I think, including Barbara Castle, voted against any kind of prescription charge at all.

The last item I heard discussed was housing with Denis Healey, Tony Crosland and Barbara Castle complaining that Roy's proposal to cut the annual approval rate by 15,000 a year was far too small. At this point I had to catch my train to Coventry.[1]

After I left I gather that Concorde was discussed and it was decided that we could not abandon it. Economically, of course, the saving would be enormously worthwhile but I don't think this Labour Government can in the same package cut the F-111, withdraw from East of Suez and scrap the Concorde without demoralizing people absolutely. If we virtually abolish military aircraft we still have to believe in civil aircraft, particularly if we're concerned about jobs in the aircraft industry.

At Coventry I was due to address a delegate meeting in the Elastic Inn, which is down in a corner of Pool Meadow, and I wondered how many people would turn up. There were actually thirty or forty there and I talked to them far more carefully and far more successfully than last time. A lot of the councillors were full of narks because they forget that they are the opposition in the council, not the council group. They've still got to make up their minds whether their aim is to get rid of the Tories from the council majority or whether they are fighting the Government alongside the Tories. It's ironical for example that now the Tories in Coventry have put up rents by 50 per cent the whole attack is on the Labour Government, not only from Tories but also from our own councillors. Apart from council affairs a lot of them were in a very reactionary mood. It was seriously proposed that there should be no family allowances but only selective assistance for proven poverty. This is one effect of our prices and incomes policy. The trade unionists want to see us spending much less on social services so that there'll be more for wage packets. This is what they really value. If this meeting is anything to go by, when the economy package is announced the opposition will not be very serious outside the Parliamentary Party.

Sunday, January 7th

Yesterday we had a pleasant day at Prescote. Indoors we've been enjoying our huge new drawing-room table more and more and John Makepeace came over to polish the slate. Albert Rose stayed for the morning and then George and Carrie Hodgkinson came to lunch and we had an easy day doing nothing much but looking at the brilliant sunshine outside the windows without feeling the frost blown by the wind. Once again I'm not fully extended. I've a lot of spare time but on the other hand in this crisis I really have made myself the lynchpin of the Cabinet and my job of cementing the alliance between Roy and Harold is extremely important.

[1] The programme was eventually reduced by 16,500 houses a year.

Looking back on the week the first thing I must record is an astonishing improvement in public opinion. This is the result of something none of us expected—an excitement among ordinary people of seeing the Government in almost daily session and of reading endless stories in the press about the struggle we are having in Cabinet to work out a fair and just policy. People in the country seem to have had a sense that they were participating in our discussion and even influencing our decisions. Traditionally in our parliamentary system the Government decides first and afterwards expounds its decision to the people. This time, almost by accident—because of the complete disaster of devaluation and the collapse of the old Chancellor, we are doing things in series and in full sight of the public. First we had the actual devaluation plus its immediate measures. Then time has to be given for the new Chancellor to settle in and plan his expenditure cuts, which will be announced in January, and then in April will come his budget and a new prices and incomes policy. Three quite separate stages. We thought it was a tremendous disadvantage but at least in terms of public opinion it has some real advantages. I'm told that even the pound has responded well since the New Year despite the awful December trade figures that were published last week.[1]

Another political windfall has come from five ladies of Surbiton who decided to help Britain by working harder and who thereby launched the 'Backing Britain' campaign, which is now expanding vigorously. It's something we should have nothing to do with but it's certainly been a useful antidote to such black spots as Jennie Lee's threatened resignation this week.

Inside Cabinet, as I've reported, our discussions have confirmed the impression that there is now a powerful right-wing junta of George Brown, Denis Healey and Michael Stewart reinforced by Jim Callaghan. I've listed the four members of the junta who for three years refused either to devalue the pound or to withdraw from our untenable positions in the Far East. But of course the fifth member was formerly Harold Wilson, who stood for precisely the same policy and is now working with Roy and me and insisting on the new policy. Roy's attitude is not resented because everyone in Cabinet knows that he was a critic of the Great Britain addicts and that like me he was in favour of devaluation and of breaking through the status barrier. The status barrier is as difficult to break through as the sound barrier: it splits your ears and it's terribly painful when it happens. And so it's really not surprising that when this sudden about-turn takes place the four are resentful that Harold is siding so quietly with the Little Englanders. Since Harold has scrapped Prime Ministerial government for the time being and is operating Cabinet government the battle has been to shift round the tiddlers in the Cabinet. The top seven or eight members in a Cabinet tend to have serious

[1] There was a £65 million deficit in December 1967. In January 1968 it was to be £35 million rising to £70 million in February.

views and seldom change their minds—they're permanently lined up against each other—but the tiddlers are always sensitive to changes in the wind. When I asked Harold the other day why he is now regularly counting votes he said that if he didn't insist on doing so his position would be challenged by the junta. That is perfectly true. Six months ago he could take the voices and interpret the voices as he liked. But if he had interpreted the 11–10 majority he got to axe the F-111 the other side would have said that he had falsified the vote and insisted on a recount. It's interesting to see how the tiddlers gave Harold his majority of one on education. Against him were ranged Michael Stewart, George Brown, Wedgy Benn, Tony Crosland, Lord Longford, Ray Gunter, Jim Callaghan, Fred Peart and George Thomson. On our side apart from Harold, Roy, myself and Gerald Gardiner and Barbara Castle we had to rely on Tony Greenwood, Cledwyn Hughes, Willie Ross and Patrick Gordon Walker.

As a result of this I feel that John and I have been given the right to demand a vote of confidence from the Parliamentary Party. We can now tell the left wing that we have got them foreign and defence policy changes we never dreamt we could obtain from this Government—changes that may even be a shock to the nation. In exchange for this they've got to give a vote of confidence in a Government which has also swallowed prescription charges and the postponement of an educational ideal. This is the line John and I have got to sell to the Parliamentary Party next week.

Monday, January 8th
I spent the whole day on Lords reform. Last Monday our Labour group agreed on the offer we should make to the Tories. We knew that we could not concede anything on the abolition of the hereditary principle. They must agree: (1) that in future no person there because he had inherited his seat would have a vote in the House of Lords; (2) that existing hereditary peers would become either life peers and thereby acquire a vote or alternatively retain speaking rights only; and (3) even these speaking rights would not descend to their sons. If the Tories were prepared to accept this genuine and total abolition of the hereditary principle, we thought in return we ought to give them an extension of the period of delay. What they care about more than anything else is to retain the appearance of a second Chamber with effective delaying powers and to be able to argue that they have obtained this concession in exchange for the abolition of the inbuilt Conservative majority. We had already decided of our own accord to concede only six months' delay from the Third Reading of a Bill in the Commons whereas they demanded nine months' delay from the moment of disagreement in the Lords, which might well mean a year from Third Reading in the Commons. Wheeler-Booth, who is in the confidence of both sides and behaves in the Lords as Freddie Warren behaves in the Commons, let me know that the minimum the Conservatives would settle for was six months' from disagree-

14 Leaving an emergency
   Cabinet meeting called to
   discuss the 'gold fever'
   hitting the world's financial
   centres, Richard Crossman
   looks cheerful, March 1968

15 Talking to Gladwyn Jebb
   (Lord Gladwyn) at a *Time-
   Life* party, February 1968

16 The official Cabinet photograph, October 1968
Left to right (standing): Judith Hart, George Thomas, Cledwyn Hughes,
Richard Marsh, Edward Short, William Ross, George Thomson, Anthony
Wedgwood Benn, Anthony Greenwood, Lord Shackleton, Roy Mason, John
Diamond, Sir Burke Trend

Left to right (seated): Peter Shore, Denis Healey, Barbara Castle, Lord Gardiner,
Michael Stewart, Harold Wilson, Roy Jenkins, Richard Crossman, James
Callaghan, Fred Peart, Anthony Crosland
(There is no official photograph for the period covered by this volume. When it
was taken Roy Mason had replaced Ray Gunter.)

17 Talking to Stephen Potter at Hinton Manor, the home of Mr and Mrs Nicholas Davenport, 1968

18 Working at home, April 1968

ment and I said to my colleagues, 'I'll fight for six months from introduction to the Lords and then we can settle the difference if necessary.' This was the tactic we had agreed for the consultations this afternoon.

This morning I went through the whole of Eddie's elaborate papers and briefed myself and then I talked to Roy and got him to agree on the basis of the discussions. We started the talks at 2.30 and went on for three hours during the afternoon. They were followed by dinner in the evening at Lord Carrington's house. Frank Pakenham had already given a similar dinner at the Café Royal. When I had found my way there Carrington, Maudling and Jellicoe were waiting for me and on our side there was Eddie, myself and Frank. It was an extremely pleasant evening and by the end we had all virtually agreed what the terms had to be. Of course there were scores of detailed points on which there will be long interesting discussion—whether the Anglican bishops should sit but no other clerics, for example, and whether the speaking peers (this was constitutionally much more important) should have the right to vote on committees since otherwise there won't be enough people to man the committees and take decisions. But these are all points which can be settled after the basic agreement and we agreed that we should try for this tomorrow morning. We should proceed to do the swap—they waiving their objections on the hereditary principle and we conceding somewhat longer delaying powers.

Tuesday, January 9th
This morning we were due to make our deal but last night there had been a tremendously heavy fall of snow—nearly a foot at Prescote—which cut the children off from school and gave them their hearts' desire. Even in London it was very difficult to move about and Iain Macleod never got in to Parliament Square from his house in the suburbs. Callaghan also came in late with a very bad cold and he therefore missed the tactical discussion which the members of the Labour delegation had before the meeting. We had all agreed that Jim, who has kept silent up to now, should state his view on the powers of the Lords and then we would clinch the agreement.

Up to a point everything went according to plan. I waited for the Lord Chancellor to offer the bargain and when he failed to do so I offered it myself in concise terms and soon each side was in agreement that we must go back and report to our colleagues in the Cabinet and the Shadow Cabinet and in both the parliamentary Parties as well. Suddenly Callaghan looked up and said, 'I couldn't agree to any of this. I think it's intolerable. We can't allow delaying powers of that sort to any House of Lords. What they ought to have is much more effective powers as a complementary part of the House of Commons.' So at the last moment he refused to give his consent. This is typical of the post-Treasury Callaghan. As ex-Chancellor of the Exchequer he has given no help whatsoever to Roy Jenkins through the ten days of discussion of the economic crisis. Now, as Home Secretary, he's leaving the

21

responsibility to the rest of us while he acts irresponsibly and then bangs his way out.

We spent the rest of the morning at Cabinet, wading through some more items in Jenkins's package paper on civil cuts. Harold Wilson was snowed up in Manchester and the First Secretary was in the chair because George Brown had already flown out, like George Thomson, to the Far East and was somewhere in Japan. What an idiot he is. He was due to visit Japan in the period before devaluation and unwisely postponed the journey. Now he has to do it and in order to get back quickly he will cut short his stay in Tokyo from four days to two, fly on from there to America to see L.B.J. and Rusk[1] and arrive back totally exhausted. It's a kind of mania which doesn't make any sense at all.

By the time we reached the Home Office cuts Harold had arrived. Callaghan boomed in. He and Roy had come to an unseemly private deal that only £6 million should be cut from £400 million expenditure. Since the Home Office cuts of last July had failed to materialize this now scandalized other spending Ministers, but Callaghan was about as insolent to Harold as anybody could be and refused to accept more than this particular cut. So the day drooled on while we dealt with our old friends, ELDO and *Black Arrow*, which Wedgy Benn saved again, and intrinsically dreary items of lesser local government expenditure. At 7.15 we ran out of steam and halted. By then Tony Crosland had made a very dignified and sensible complaint that we were going into all these detailed cuts without any agreed appreciation of the overall economic situation they were intended to meet or of the total amount of demand which needed to be taken out of the economy, or of the proper division between public expenditure and saving. I had a great deal of sympathy with him because I was worried whether we weren't going to lose altogether the new-look presentation of the strategy which we desperately require. Nevertheless there was something to be thankful for. Cabinet was getting along all right. There are obviously going to be no resignations apart from Frank Longford's. And we are getting into quite a routine.

Wednesday, January 10th

Looking at the papers I saw that the snow and the great freeze-up were dominating the news along with the announcement of the recall of Parliament which Harold and I had agreed we should make after yesterday's Cabinet. There was also some attention to reactions in Singapore to George Thomson's arrival, in particular the hostile reactions of Harry Lee.[2] He has already threatened to withdraw Singapore's sterling balances and announced that

[1] Dean Rusk, U.S. Secretary of State 1961–9. He was President of the Rockefeller Foundation 1952–61, and since 1971 has been Professor of International Law at the University of Georgia.

[2] The defence cuts which the Government was about to implement were not accepted without protest by foreign governments, particularly those of Australia and Singapore.

he's coming to London to say what he thinks of us. This, of course, will strengthen the Government's hand.

I spent most of today on home publicity, attempting to prepare for the launching of the Statement. We had a formal meeting of our publicity committee this morning. I had said that Roy and Peter needn't come provided their officials attended and with John Harris's help I think I got a feeling among the officials that at last we are going to run an efficient centralized information service. We have got a standardized letter out to all Ministries about the kind of brief we want them to bring to us and we also got the librarian of the House of Commons over and saw to it that he was mobilized to produce a complete series of official statements by Government Ministers and Shadow Ministers on all the controversial issues like prescription charges and the raising of the school-leaving age. I am not asking the library for any favour for the Government because this information will be as useful to ordinary Members as to me, and the librarians were delighted to help. I did the same with Terry Pitt, who will collect the material that can only be found at Party headquarters. Conservative Party headquarters have a far better library but it is impossible to use it!

Late this afternoon I asked Kenneth Robinson to come and see me because he seems to be feeling left out and sulky. I wanted to ask him to give us his help. I suspected that he was reckoning that he would get away without any prescription charges. He thought he could prove that there could be no exemptions and that Cabinet wouldn't dare to have a scheme of charges without exemptions. This suspicion was confirmed when he asked me directly whether he would have to accept the charges and whether I was quite sure of this. I said I was sure. He asked how I knew and I said that I didn't like prescription charges any more than he did but I'd seen a great deal of Harold and Roy and they have based their whole package on a fair balance between defence cuts abroad and the slaughter of sacred cows at home. We then had a long discussion about the practical difficulties of a scheme with exemptions and I hope I sent him away knowing that his fate was sealed, and he would have to work out a practicable scheme.

I had another free evening and had to spend it alone because poor Anne couldn't get up to London as the snow was blocking the roads out of Prescote.

Thursday, January 11th
Another free morning with Cabinet postponed until the afternoon so that we could hear George Brown's report on the U.S.A.

I strode across to John Silkin's office at No. 12 where we had a great deal of news from our back benches. Jennie is still on the edge of resignation and the resistance to prescription charges is strengthening.

Then back to my own room for a long personal talk with Peter Shore about his position. Quite rightly he's unhappy about his status as Secretary of State in charge of D.E.A. with the Prime Minister hovering on top of him. He's also unhappy about his failures on the front bench. But inside he's courageous and self-confident and I believe he will come through though it'll take some time to get him through. In came Tommy and we sat down to discuss Europe. They are now staunch anti-Europeans and deeply concerned by George Brown's machinations, his futile rush round Europe trying to persuade the five to start intriguing for us against France. I said it was no use talking to me about this because I could do nothing about it and the conversation turned to prices and incomes, where Peter is supposed to be in charge. He complained that he wanted to make a Statement on the new policy during the two-day debate last week and I had stopped it. I said I must make sure there was something in the Statement and if there is it can take place next Thursday afternoon. He showed me the draft and it was really absolutely empty. He didn't deny this but claimed it was better to have a Statement about nothing than no Statement at all. I told him bluntly I didn't agree that was the way to restore his reputation in Parliament.

Cabinet this afternoon started with more than an hour and a half on the Race Relations Bill.[1] We had the interminable problem of how to apply it, if at all, to the police. The answer is that we won't. This Bill is a purely invocatory Bill and I doubt if it's good to put Bills of that kind on the statute book. Nevertheless I kept my ears half awake while the dispute was going on and soon became aware that Harold's aim was to relax the atmosphere and reduce the temperature because in this way he would get the package through more easily later on when we turned back to our main business.

The first item was a proposal I myself had made that we should do the revolutionary thing and axe the rate-support grant. I expected Tony Greenwood as Minister of Housing to be against me and I'd expected Barbara to back me up but I was sad when Roy read aloud the Treasury brief. This decision would have shown that we are prepared to *make* the local authorities economize whereas the so-called cuts we're now imposing aren't real cuts at all and most of them will get put back in estimates of later years.

Next came overseas aid. Here is an area where public opinion is certainly overwhelmingly in favour of large-scale cuts. However, the proposal was that we should only cut it by the cost of the devaluation—roughly 10 per cent. I was the only person who said we ought to do more. But Harold's feeling about this particular sacred cow is too strong to make any serious cut.

So we came back to prescription charges and despite all my efforts Kenneth Robinson had produced a lamentably inadequate paper. It was clear that he was trying to make as many difficulties as he possibly could. Should the exemptions be for retirement pensioners or for people over sixty-five? If for

---

[1] The Bill, published on April 9th, sought to make it unlawful to discriminate in the provisions of goods, facilities, or services, in the fields of employment, housing and advertisement. A Race Relations Board would be established to administer the legislation.

men over sixty-five should it be for women over sixty? Could it be administered through the doctors just as dentists already give exemptions for payments of dental fees to old people and children? On all these things he was as difficult as he could be. However we forced it through slowly.

After dealing with pensions and housing we had another extraordinary exhibition by Gordon Walker. In one of our first meetings he'd suddenly given way to an attack by George Brown and volunteered a cut of one-third in starts for all university buildings. Since then I'd spoken to Tony Crosland and rung up Roy to say that this cut was absolutely ruinous and far too big to be acceptable. So on the protest of some of Patrick's colleagues it's been suitably watered down from $33\frac{1}{3}$ to 10 per cent. By this time it was 7 o'clock and we stopped.

Friday, January 12th
Cabinet was again postponed until the afternoon and I was regaled with a visit from Cecil King. Some time ago I'd said in answer to a Question by a Labour back-bencher that the newspapers had nothing to fear and indeed that something was going to happen during the recess which would help them. I meant quite obviously that their decision to raise their prices would not be referred to the Prices and Incomes Board. But Cecil King had insisted at a meeting of the N.P.A. that I must have meant something more. After I'd patiently explained that I meant exactly what I'd said and nothing more I had to sit there and listen to another lecture on the badness of our present Government and how good big businessmen alone could save the situation.

Before Cabinet I just had time to see Kenneth Robinson again. He sat down in front of me and said, 'I've sent a paper into Roy in which I have analysed the possible exemptions and said at the bottom "Recommendations —up to you".' That's quite a paper for a Minister of Health to write to his colleague at the Treasury. If I'd been Roy I'd have sent it back with 'Bloody Fool' scrawled across 'You do your job or get out'. Kenneth of course should either have resigned or he should have made the best possible scheme out of the system of exemptions. He's still doing neither. His state of mind is a good example of what happens to a so-called minister of Cabinet rank outside the Cabinet. Even when he attends he usually finds a place at the back and can only speak when he's spoken to and can take no part in general discussion. It's a truly exasperating status. Moreover, in fairness to him, I have to remember that it's not only Jennie Lee and the Left of the Labour Party who are against prescription charges. The officials in his Department are opposed to them; the medical profession is opposed to them and, above all, the chemists are passionately opposed to them. And so the whole world in which he lives is against the return of prescription charges and as a departmental Minister it's very easy for him to feel he's fighting for a great cause when he stands up for the Department against the Cabinet. In the course of our talk this morning Kenneth told me that what had particularly infuriated him was when Harold

Wilson had said yesterday afternoon that only he and the Chancellor of the Exchequer were against abolishing the prescription charges in 1964. 'On the contrary,' said Kenneth, 'I was Minister of Health and I was against it and I spoke up against it.' 'So was I,' I said, and he said, 'Of course, so you were.' His point is sound. It's quite untrue to suggest there was mass Cabinet approval which forced Jim to act. On the contrary the decision was taken by Harold Wilson, who argued that we'd made the pledge in the election manifesto and we couldn't let the electors down.

This afternoon we had our last Cabinet meeting on the package – the general discussion of the economic situation which Tony Crosland had asked for and which should really have begun the whole proceeding. He made a very able speech, as he always does, suggesting that not more than £400 million should be cut back on the public sector. Roy's reply was fairly devastating. Even with £800 million cuts, he said, he would have to impose more than half the necessary cut in demand by increasing taxation in the coming budget. And it was at this point that he revealed that the trade deficits in the last three months of 1967 had come to over £300 million,[1] the same as in the autumn of 1964 when Maudling was having his election spending spree. So we were not merely back to square one but back to square zero. We had lost everything we had won during these three years. I could not help recalling how in October and November Harold talked to me week by week about recovery being in the air and persuaded himself that no drastic measures were really necessary. For those of us who knew about the autumn behaviour of Harold and Jim this was a deadly rehearsal of the facts and Roy brought it out with deadly effect. Cabinet just had to accept the size of his public-sector cuts.

By now George Brown had bustled into the room and we decided he should give us a special report on his interview with Dean Rusk and on the message from L.B.J. which had arrived at the F.O. this morning. Now in considering his behaviour one must realize that he'd travelled round the world in a week and was obviously psychologically and physically upset by this jolting of the passage of time. So, not unexpectedly, he sat down and gave us in his most dramatic and most incoherent way a half-hour description of the appalling onslaught to which he had been submitted, first by Dean Rusk and then by a State Department official whose theme had been, 'Be British, George, be British – how can you betray us?' He told us that he had faithfully reported the decision to leave Singapore by 1970–71 and to scrap the F-111 as unalterable Cabinet decisions. They had expressed nothing but horror and consternation. 'I put the Cabinet case – the case for the new strategy – as well as possible. I put it as well as the Lord President of the Council himself could put it and one can't ask more than that,' he remarked at one point sarcastically. Despite all his rhetoric and confusion one point stood out from his report. The main American complaint was not about the

[1] In October £111 million, in November £158 million and in December £65 million.

withdrawal from the Far East but about the decision to leave the Persian Gulf. When the Americans made this clear George Brown had explained that it didn't cost us much more to hold the Gulf if we were in Singapore and Malaya but that as we had to abandon Singapore and Malaya we couldn't hold the Gulf without incurring colossal expense. His contention was that irreparable damage had been done by his having to make this statement at all and having to tell the Americans of our decisions. And yet something could be done by going back on the decision and giving ourselves an extra year to get out, and by abandoning the decision to cancel the F-111.

So far Roy Jenkins had remained silent. Now in his usual terse way he summed up in a very few sentences. I can't quote him verbally but what he said came to this. Just because there can't be genuine savings in the next two years on defence there has to be a major change of foreign and defence policy from that of the last three years. He said it in a way which destroyed the credibility not only of George but of all the other people who have been running the Great Britain policy since 1964. It was the challenge to the authority of the old Government which he managed to bring out and that was about as far as we got by lunch-time.

After lunch came Healey's last-ditch effort to save the F-111. I had gathered before the meeting that he was now pretty confident that he could win the extra vote required to defeat us. After all there had been a tie before and Harold had given his casting vote. Now Denis knew he had got Longford secretly over to his side and he reckoned he had a safe 11–9 decision. He also hoped that the impact of George's catastrophic news from Washington would switch some timid votes to his side. Denis is not a very successful speaker either in Cabinet or in the House. He plays the role of the young McNamara —the man who is briefed on all the top-level secrets and who can mock and deride any ideas put forward by his amateur colleagues. The supercilious sneering expert is always in danger in a British Cabinet but Denis has a further difficulty. After all, he had already presented us with no less than four successive defence reviews and he had defended each as it came out with new facts, new figures, new statistical demonstrations. Moreover I remembered that he had sold the F-111 to us as an aeroplane essential for defence East of Suez which would in fact be based East of Suez and not used in Europe. Now he was defending it as essential to European defence. I got the impression that he could defend it just as brilliantly as essential to southern Irish defence. When he'd finished the P.M. asked him four questions very unsuccessfully, since he was scored off by Denis in a fairly rude and devastating way. But when Roy began his interrogation things went very differently. He did far better than the Prime Minister in fencing with Denis, undermining him first on the economic side and above all on the political side, showing the essential need to match the cut in commitment by a cut in hardware, and challenging him as to what hardware should be cut, challenging him on *Polaris* as well. Denis was no match for Roy. Indeed, his only convincing case was for *Polaris*, which I had wanted to see scrapped or given away. He was able to demon-strate that it now costs only £20 million a year and that all the enormous capital costs are paid already. If we're to have an enormously expensive top-level weapon system we should keep *Polaris*, he argued. To this I was able to reply, 'Yes, I'm prepared to agree that *Polaris* at £20 million a year main-tenance is worth keeping provided we scrap the F-111.' At this point Long-ford suddenly interjected and revealed the great secret of his switch, which most of us knew already. As soon as he'd done it Cledwyn Hughes intervened to switch his vote our way. Finally Patrick Gordon Walker hummed and hawed and said that in view of the remarks on education he felt he must now vote for dropping the F-111. And so we were 11-9 without the Prime Minister —safely home. Healey looked really shattered, and as he got up George Brown said, 'Well, I shall be resigning.' But he was obviously too tired for anyone to take him seriously.

As soon as we tottered out of Cabinet I had to go upstairs to the reception rooms in No. 10 where Harold was already waiting with three publicity men for a dinner-party to discuss the launching of the great Statement. Roy Jenkins had been asked to come but had sent John Harris. Peter Shore was there, I was there and so were Gerald Kaufman, Marcia and Michael Stewart, as well as Percy Clark from Transport House. So it was quite a competent gang and we had a very good slap-up dinner before we got down to business. It was all perfectly sensible. The publicity men had a string of suggestions about how to exploit the fund of popular goodwill revealed by those five ladies of Surbiton. Then there was the idea that the P.M. should do a regular quarterly Ministerial television show on B.B.C. and I.T.N. It wouldn't matter if Heath wanted to reply since he would sound narky. We also had a longish discussion on whether the national savings campaign should be reactivated and how we could popularize exports. It was a quite sensible practical meeting and the time didn't go so slowly as usual. Indeed it was midnight by the time we finished and I was dropped home by Mark Abrams, who was there repre-senting market research.[1] I couldn't help noticing Harold's resilience through-out that day. He lasted to the end remarkably well. Of course, in Cabinet he had to hand over a great deal of the argument to Roy but he had still been the complete chairman and he had then conducted this long meeting late at night with admirable charm.

Saturday, January 13th
This was the day I'd offered to Douglas Garnett who is regional organizer for East Anglia. I was off by the 8.30 train to Cambridge through heavy snow and bitter cold. But thank God by the end of the day the big thaw had set in and rain was pouring down.

---

[1] Managing director and then chairman of Research Services Ltd 1964–70, director of the Survey Research Unit of the S.S.R.C. since 1970 and, since 1969, a member of the Metrica-tion Board.

At Cambridge I started with a morning coffee-party to which some sixty or seventy people turned up and I found them (but then it's a good Party) in amazingly good heart when I explained to them my ideas for a 'What can I do to help you?' campaign in order to retain grass-roots contact with the electors. Douglas then motored me forty miles out of Cambridge to Halstead in Essex where four constituencies—Ipswich, Saffron Walden, Harwich and Sudbury—were having a big get-together. They had sold two hundred tickets and 240 people turned up in this appalling snow and ice, and here again I had to sit and be photographed with the candidates. They had a forty-minute address from me and then one and a quarter hours of discussion, and though some of them were sharp the atmosphere was amazingly *not* what I found in Coventry on that lamentable night before Christmas. These are people who desperately want to help, and one of them said to me, 'What propaganda can you give us to fight the Tories?' and I replied, 'The only propaganda I can give you is success; you will never be able to fight the Tories except with success, and until we get it you have just got to believe in us because the test of a soldier is his morale in a period of defeat. We need supporters of that kind and I have to say it to you honestly.'

It made an immense effect on them, that they were honestly told that success was the only counter to the present mood of public opinion, and that during this time we just rely on them to fight it through and to have faith in us. It was a pretty good meeting of enormous value for a Minister. After all these hours and hours in Downing Street it is important to get out there to meet the ordinary rank and file, to have the job of giving them encouragement and to give them some leadership. These two meetings did me a power of good, though they left me extremely tired.

Sunday, January 14th
At last a day off. We had my stepdaughter, Venice, and her husband, Christopher, over from Stokenchurch with their three children and all the children were out with me when the floods were seeping up from the river into the fields. It's been a splendid day from that point of view.

There was only one bit of politics to record. I rang up Roy at some grand country house where he is staying in Bedfordshire, and talked to him again about the idea of Denis going to the Foreign Office. 'We have got to keep him in the Government,' I said to Roy. 'We can't have both Denis and George retiring in a mass.' Taking something of a risk, I went on, 'Roy, you and I must give the impression to Denis that if he stays in the Government we can get him into the Foreign Office when George goes. That's a big claim to make, but we've got to make it to him because we can't afford to lose him. I think Harold is beginning to see this.' What's instructive here is that if Roy and Harold are willing even to consider having Denis at the Foreign Office then their enthusiasm for trying to get into Europe must have cooled off. This is where they differ from George Brown who wants to go on kicking at the door which is closed. I believe they may now be beginning to see that as there's no chance of getting in they must have a more Gaullist independent policy for Britain. If that's so, it's good news indeed.

Monday, January 15th

I had to go up to London last night to be in time for the final Cabinet this morning. I knew that yesterday Tommy had been working away drafting the Prime Minister's Statement and that it was all being put together out of bits and pieces. I also knew that this morning George Thomson would have got back from the Far East to report on his visits to Malaya, Singapore, New Zealand and Australia. And then there was also a report in all the papers today on what had taken place in that five-hour meeting between Harry Lee, the Prime Minister of Singapore, and Harold Wilson, Roy Jenkins and George Brown.

Cabinet started with George Thomson's report and then with the P.M.'s account of his five hours and his dinner with Harry Lee. After that there was a tremendous effort to get Cabinet to reverse the decision on East of Suez withdrawal we had taken by such a large majority only ten days ago. It was clear after an hour that the weaker brethren of the Cabinet were swinging back. L.B.J. had certainly stepped up his threats to George, particularly in the economic sphere, which will be a terrible blow to British foreign trade in the U.S.A. It was Gunter, I think, who swung first, then Cledwyn Hughes, then Dick Marsh, and then Gordon Walker. They were all swinging towards the position of the old junta and when the score was about 8–6 I knew that the P.M. would have to act. What he did was to nip in very neatly and offer as a compromise that the terminal date for withdrawal from Malaya should be the end of the calendar year 1971. What he conceded was nine months' further occupation and instead of withdrawing by March 1971 we were now to withdraw by December 1971. That was something for Harry Lee to take back with him to his Cabinet and that was something to satisfy my anxious colleagues. Afterwards Roy said to me, 'I always had that compromise up my sleeve.' Harold delivered it in the nick of time this morning.

But once Cabinet had begun to swing it was clear that given the chance it would swing on every other decision it had reached. The next effort was to change the cancellation of the F-111 and after a lot of discussion we finally decided that later in the day Healey would have the right to propose that Cabinet should consider the issue over again. Victory number two for the junta. And of course the Prime Minister was being hoist on his own petard by having to count the votes each time. This meant, as he put to me dryly, that the final decisions are being taken by the floaters—the Cledwyn Hughes, the Frank Longfords, the Patrick Gordon Walkers. They would decide each issue by whether they had been panicked or not and there would be nothing left of the package.

Late in the morning we reached education and here I reckon that no less than nine people announced their reconversion to the raising of the school-leaving age. But there was one other theme in this last Third Reading debate this morning. Several days ago some of us had begun to realize that it was most extraordinary for the Government to publish a Statement of economic cuts in the public sector without any Statement on exchange controls or hire purchase or any other methods of reducing consumer demand. Clearly, if this Statement is launched in its present form with an announcement that there will be a budget in eight weeks' time it will precipitate an enormous spending spree. This was something Thomas had seen, Anne had seen, and I had seen, and even the vulgarest economic journalists had been complaining about it. This morning I had telephoned Roy and Tony Crosland and when I got to No. 10 I found that Richard Marsh was as concerned as I was. So now I made my plea to stand by the package and bolster the Statement with a big batch of restrictions on consumer demand and a set of exchange controls, which are absolutely essential in view of the attitude of Singapore and Malaya. Of course by the time I said this today it was too late for anything to be done before tomorrow afternoon. But if he'd wished Roy could plan to make the announcement in his opening speech on Wednesday. Instead there has been a curious inactivity. His Treasury advisers, he told me, hadn't given him any advice on this subject. And he certainly hadn't approached either of his two economic advisers—Ken Berrill (the Bursar at King's),[1] or Michael Posner, not to mention Tommy or Nicky.

So all Harold did was to say that the time had come for Cabinet to vote on whether the education issue should be re-raised and re-discussed and on that vote we just won. The same thing happened on the F-111. If the future of the plane had been reconsidered on its merits we couldn't possibly have won but all Cabinet was asked to decide was whether we should re-open the discussions and everybody realized that if we re-opened the discussion on the F-111 we would re-open everything else. So Harold saved the situation by this tactical device.

Perhaps the dreariest moment in this desultory Third Reading was George Brown's intervention. He had sat there brooding and silent the whole afternoon and when asked by Harold to comment said that the whole package was wrong, not only the defence side but the home side—everything was wrong. And I'm afraid that by then there was hardly anybody else round the table with a word to say for the package.

We still had the problem of the draft, which was now presented to us by the Cabinet staff and once again we had the incredible folly of twenty people sitting round a table redrafting a Statement. It was entirely the Prime Minister's fault because he insisted that every word of the Statement should be

[1] Sir Kenneth Berrill, Fellow and First Bursar, King's College, Cambridge, 1962-9. He was Special Adviser to the Treasury 1967-9, chairman of the University Grants Committee 1969-73 and Head of the Government Economic Service and Chief Economic Adviser from 1973 to 1974, when he became Head of the Central Policy Review Staff.

given the Cabinet's O.K. and therefore every Minister felt himself responsible for the wording of the section which related to his Ministry. As we studied the draft it became clear how little initial work had been done during the last ten days, how little thorough appreciation or analysis there had been of particular problems. Moreover, as we talked we began to realize the number of interesting proposals which we have not considered. Shouldn't we announce the deferment of the rebuilding of Whitehall? Shouldn't we save money on social security by transferring from the state to the employer the responsibility for paying the first three days of sickness benefit? These were the sort of ideas which kept dropping out on to the table and since there was no time to take them up, all they did was to expose the inadequacy of the whole process we had so laboriously gone through.

I have remarked that after devaluation we replaced Prime Ministerial by Cabinet government. But it's worth noticing that after thirty hours of Cabinet government the package presented by Roy (indeed the package inherited by Roy from James Callaghan) has been retained almost intact. True, an important concession of nine extra months has been given on withdrawal from the Far East, and there have been useful minor concessions on education and local government. But by and large the package at the end of the process was identical with that at the beginning and yet we have spent thirty hours getting Cabinet to agree it.

I think myself that this was necessary and that the sight of us sitting working so hard impressed the public. Now that Parliament is back and the Parties are sparring and getting ready to fight each other I can only hope that the goodwill we built up during the weeks when Cabinet was confronting the public alone will not be entirely destroyed by a picture of rowing and splits in the Parliamentary Party.

Despite his limitations, Roy has remained the dominating force in Cabinet with a far better image than he has had so far on television or in the House. And Cabinet's the right place to start, by the way. He can learn about television and improve his House of Commons manner but what is essential is to have the authority to assert your will in Cabinet and this, I think, he has succeeded in doing. He faced the junta on the other side of the table and he beat back all its assaults. One thing I've noticed during these thirty hours is the slap John Silkin's reputation has received. Whenever the Prime Minister tried to get John in to make a comment Callaghan or someone else would slap him down. He's detested by the right and centre and regarded as a henchman of the P.M. who has discredited himself as Chief Whip. The row which is boiling up as the Parliamentary Party slowly comes back clearly emanates from the Cabinet. John has been poisoned by shafts emitted from our meetings in No. 10.

After this I had to try to make something of the 'Buy British' campaign which has sprung up as a result of the five ladies of Surbiton. My publicity committee suggested that I should get hold of Joe Hyman, the big Viyella businessman, but I found today that he is engaged in a public quarrel with Bob Maxwell who has already set himself up as chairman of the committee. What was I to do—because in the meantime I'd arranged to go to dinner with Hyman at his house in Hyde Park Square? At 8.30 that's where I found myself along with Nicholas Davenport. Hyman gave me a nice dinner. If the Lord President comes to see you late in the evening a businessman feels gratified and anxious to oblige. I got nothing out of him, though I left impressed by his idea for a national savings campaign. Then I went on to Maxwell's great house in Fitzroy Square and tried to jolly him along. I suppose I do some good by these activities in the cause of Government publicity! Anyhow that's how I spent five hours this evening after a seven-hour Cabinet.

In his Statement to the Commons on January 16th the Prime Minister announced reductions of some £716 million in Government expenditure. The road-building programme was to be cut and 165,000 fewer houses built each year. The raising of the school-leaving age from fifteen to sixteen was deferred from 1971 to 1973. Free milk for secondary-school pupils would no longer be available. National Health Service prescriptions were to carry a charge of 2s. 6d. per item, with exemptions for children, pensioners, expectant mothers and the chronic sick, and dental charges were to rise from £1 to £1 10s. Weekly national insurance contributions were increased by a shilling for employees and sixpence for employers. The proposed family allowance increases would remain, but taxpayers would carry the cost, and the civil defence service was to be drastically reduced.

As far as defence spending was concerned savings of some £110 million for 1969–70 and £210 million to £260 million by 1972–3 were envisaged. All British forces in the Far East save for Hong Kong and the Persian Gulf would be withdrawn by the end of 1971, and the previously announced withdrawals of service personnel and civilians accelerated. By 1971 aircraft carriers were to be phased out of the Royal Navy, and another £400 million was to be saved by cancelling the order for 50 F-111 strike aircraft from America.

Tuesday, January 16th
This was the day when I had to show that in some sense I was the Minister in charge of co-ordinating departmental publicity. Harold was to make his Statement at 2.30 this afternoon and early in the morning I got together Raphael from the Treasury, Groves from the D.E.A.[1] and Freddie Warren for a briefing at which I gave them the line I had worked out with Harold during several discussions. It was a line which I thought could go over well about the big foreign policy decision and about Attlee; though it was not

[1] Chaim Raphael was Head of the Information Division at the Treasury 1959–68 and at C.S.D. from 1968 to 1969, when he became Research Fellow at the University of Sussex. John Groves was Head of the Press Section of the Treasury 1958–62, Deputy Public Relations Adviser to the P.M. 1962–4 and Chief Information Officer at the D.E.A. 1964–8. Since 1968 he has been Chief of Public Relations at the Ministry of Defence.

something which Harold could say himself we could put it in our background briefing, and Harold used it in his own background and press briefing
this afternoon. I think the officials, who had all wanted a Minister of Information, had one for the first time today.

By the time I had dealt with them, the Social Security Ministers—Michael
Stewart, Tony Greenwood, Kenneth Robinson and Judith Hart—were here
to discuss how to put their Statements over, and I found them in a ghastly
mood. Patrick Gordon Walker had the most frightful guidance notes, utterly
defeatist in tone, and I found he had got a press conference this evening. I
wasn't able to prevent him from being pretty awful, but I managed to put the
others into a better frame of mind, and we began to draft right away. For
instance, the obvious point for Kenneth Robinson to make was that he had
saved the hospital-building programme, but that as something had to go he
had preferred to accept prescription charges in part. This was the positive
line to take. Judith was also being difficult, but I got her to see that she
mustn't just talk as though she had had a staggering defeat when in fact she
had had this big step forward on family allowance claw-back. Tony Greenwood had failed to notice that this year he has already achieved the 400,000
annual target for the first time in housing history and the cutback of grants
is a small loss compared with this concrete achievement. I think as the result
of my encouragement each of them did hold his or her own press conference
and though Judith's was a bit of a mess-up they were thoroughly worthwhile.
Ironically, I discovered right at the end that there was only one subject in
Harold's brief about which there was to be no publicity—the decision to
refuse to cut economic aid to the developing world. It's characteristic of
Harold that he should feel the best way of dealing with this embarrassing
issue was to suppress it as far as he could. But I rang him up and insisted that
it must go into his or Roy's speech.

When the publicity bosses left the Chief stayed to discuss the business
statement with me and also to lament his own position. Ever since the South
African arms crisis our relations have been very delicate because he has been
completely determined to regain the goodwill he lost by that manoeuvre
and to do so without my aid. However, by today I felt I could not stand on
the sidelines any longer because it was now clear that despite all his efforts the
Left of the Party was going to vote *en masse* against the Government. I finally
decided to ask Michael Foot, Eric Heffer, John Mendelson and James
Dickens to see me before they went in to hear the P.M.'s Statement. I put
the position quite briefly to Michael. I claimed that I had got far more than
I thought possible out of the others on defence and foreign affairs: that the
great breakthrough had occurred and it must surely be impossible for a
conscientious left-winger who looked at this package as a whole not to give
it support from the Left. Prescription charges were unpleasant, but, good
heavens, they were minor things compared to the decision to withdraw from
East of Suez and Persian Gulf and to cancel the F-111. Michael hummed and

hawed and said that the Government's policy was misunderstood outside, and then he looked at me and said, 'I can see that you've got a lot on the foreign policy but why did you have to give in to them on domestic issues?' I said, 'Life's like that in politics. One has to pay a price for what one gets.' John Mendelson was not unreasonable but Eric Heffer was in an extremely bad temper. Both of them made it clear that what they had to consider was not their relations with the Government but their relations with the people in the Party and movement outside.

In talking to them I discovered an acute difficulty. I couldn't honestly and frankly admit that I had struck a bargain with the junta. A bargain of this kind is regarded as indecent and already by today people like Callaghan were making it one of their main complaints that there should be any suggestion that a bargain had been struck, because in that case the world outside would know that foreign policy had been sacrificed for the sake of Party expediency. But what should be done when we came to the vote? Without telling me, John had sent out a letter to each member of the Parliamentary Party saying that the vote was a vote of confidence like the one we had on Europe. (On that occasion we had insisted that people really must vote with the Government and couldn't even abstain.) The Chief, Harold and I had discussed all this at length and for some time John had tried to wriggle out of the vote of confidence. For hours the other evening I had to hear him arguing that the main resolution was really the Tory reasoned amendment and that this was the resolution which we must compel the Party to vote against. But if the Liberals called a division on the substantial motion on our Public Expenditure White Paper then the Tory amendment couldn't be called the main resolution. When I heard him twisting and writhing in this way Tam and I both said that this would cut no ice whatsoever in the Party and that he had to steel himself to the fact that anybody who abstained on either of these two resolutions would have to be treated as someone who had violated his duty on a vote of confidence. 'Why not announce that?' I said, to which he replied that whether he could announce it would depend on the numbers he could get. I wish he wasn't so determined to reassert himself without my help because in some things he's still too young and he's still a bit egotistical — seeing himself at the centre of every problem and in a sense trying to do too much and to take too big a burden on his shoulders with the excuse that he mustn't burden his friends. But his friends are perfectly willing to be burdened and I'm not sure it wouldn't have looked better to the Party if he and I had gone to war together. Perhaps the reason why he hasn't is because he's determined to assert himself as a Chief Whip in a position which Ted Short never achieved under Herbert Bowden. Herbert Bowden who was an old Chief Whip never allowed a friendly collaboration and was still a Chief Whip when he was Lord President. John wants to be a Chief Whip with that degree of power.

I had to make a business Statement this afternoon and everything went quietly with the minimum of protest. I'm living now in a quiet world. Throughout this week I haven't been mentioned and nobody has attacked me in Cabinet or outside it. Moreover I'm not treated as though I was anything to do with Party discipline. So no wonder I have it easy.

After the business statement we started a highly contentious little Transport Holding Company Bill which we want to get through with the minimum of attention. Barbara is now away with pneumonia and the competent, efficient Stephen Swingler does her job admirably for her. So I was able to go off to the Prime Minister's Lobby at 5.30 and found it only half full partly because Frank Longford was staging his resignation Lobby at the same time. I hear, by the way, from the P.M. that Harold has seen Jennie Lee and because there has been no cut in the Arts Council programme nor in the Open University funds we have kept Jennie safely in the Government. She says she has conscientiously read the package and doesn't feel any need to resign in view of the major importance of the defence cuts. So that leaves Frank as the only resigning Minister. He made his attitude clear some days ago and I think he's quite sincere, but it's also true that he knew some time ago that Harold wanted to replace him as Leader in the Lords by Eddie Shackleton. Nor has he been very enthusiastic about taking part in the Lords reform consultations; I suppose because I have taken them over and he feels pushed aside.

Finally this evening I had one of my parties at the Privy Council. It was due to be a junior Ministers' party but I turned it round a bit and thought we would have it not at the Privy Council but at my room in the House so we could watch Roy Jenkins on television. I also asked Percy Clark and Terry Pitt and some of the Ministers chiefly affected—Judith, Shirley, Kenneth—a sort of party of junior Ministerial activists. The idea was to discuss the new post-devaluation policy and the meeting turned out to be the worst I'd ever held. This was predominantly due to the bloody-mindedness of Percy Clark and Terry Pitt, who instead of trying to help the Government through their difficulties are preparing a document on the social services which is nothing but a scurrilous attack on our complete failure to deal with the problem of poverty and the social services. It was a document which the C.P.A.G. could have published, and that's saying a lot.

Sunday, January 21st[1]

I'm alone at Prescote for once. Anne has taken Virginia to Stratford to see the Covent Garden ballet and Patrick is off to a British Legion party in the village hall. We had a fine walk together with Suki across the farm and then he put on his new jacket and his green tie and brushed his hair and got on his bicycle looking like a grown-up schoolboy. So here I am in the drawing-room with Suki growling there waiting for everybody else to come back and

---

[1] There is no transcript for Wednesday, January 17th to Saturday, January 20th or for Monday, January 22nd to Thursday, February 1st inclusive.

I am just enjoying being at Prescote. I'm also a bit dismal. But heaven knows it's been a dismal week in London. A dismal week for Harold, who hasn't really come off and who's off to Moscow with a record of failure behind him. Not too cheerful a week for Roy, who made a very disappointing start in the House and was not much good on television either. Sad also for John and myself because we are faced with a major disciplinary row on the back benches with the Chief being directly challenged and hitting back left and right. My favourite quotation, 'Things fall apart; the centre cannot hold', does make you realize what's wrong with this Government, the danger that it will disintegrate because it can't move forward and it can't move forward because it can't get itself led. There's no substitute for Harold yet Harold fails to give the leadership we need and so the credibility—that famous word —of the Government is undermined despite the quite sensible policy which we have put forward in the package of cuts in the public sector. This is a policy which could have been sold positively and dynamically. Cabinet worked on it for thirty hours and now it has been largely thrown away by Harold's failure to provide the strategic framework within which the economic cuts should be seen and partly also by the re-emergence of an open cleavage between left and right in the Party. So no wonder I feel a bit depressed as I sit here alone today.

Friday, February 2nd
I went over to the Home Affairs Committee where the census was being discussed. Edmund Dell[1] had brought with him Claus Moser,[2] who is now in charge of the next census and says this time it's essential to have questions on income and race.[3] To get people ready for this innovation there should be a pre-test of the questions next year on some 40,000 people. The proposal provoked a tremendously long discussion. At the end of it both the Home Secretary, Callaghan (who sat on one side of me), and the Minister of Housing, Greenwood (who sat on the other), voted against the questions being asked though they admitted that their offices said that from a departmental point of view it is absolutely essential to have the information. However, like the Secretary of State for Wales, they said politically that it would be too dangerous. The people who voted for taking the risk were the Lord Chancellor and myself, Jennie Lee, rather surprisingly, Michael Stewart as chairman of the Committee and Mallalieu who spoke to the Board of Trade brief but said that personally he was against it. Three years ago I doubt if we

---

[1] Labour M.P. for Birkenhead since 1964. He was Joint Parliamentary Secretary at the Ministry of Technology 1966–7 and at the D.E.A. 1967–8, and Minister of State at the Board of Trade 1968–9 and at the Department of Employment 1969–70. Since 1974 he has been Paymaster-General.

[2] Sir Claus Moser, Professor of Social Statistics at L.S.E. 1961–70 and, since 1967, Director of the Central Statistical Office and Head of the Government Statistical Service. Since 1974 he has been chairman of the Royal Opera House, Covent Garden.

[3] The census is conducted every ten years; the next was to be held in 1971.

would have had a single vote in this Cabinet Committee opposing this but now people are so battered by unpopularity and terrified by the risk of doing anything unpopular that they won't vote for collecting information which is a prerequisite for sound socialist planning. Though we got our majority Michael Stewart, the chairman, will have to take it to Cabinet.

Ian Waller came to see me in my office and asked me to do an article for next Sunday's *Sunday Telegraph* based on the notorious speech I made at Birmingham.[1] Jimmy Margach also came and I briefed him, and Nora Beloff too, though in the latter case I took the precaution of having Tam Dalyell in the room to take a note. My briefing job is now very largely with the Sunday press and I leave the daily press more and more to No. 10 and Harold himself.

I went over to the House to vote for James Tinn's National Lottery Bill and found I was the only Minister there.[2] Then off to Coventry for a meeting on the crisis with my Coventry East G.M.C. A fortnight ago I'd said I would meet them when a delegation came to see me at the Lanchester. So we had an official meeting and out of the 140-odd members some twenty turned up at Coundon Road. At their request I agreed that they should have an hour to put their complaints and then we should have forty minutes' discussion and my reply. George Park and Peter Lister were sitting silent at the front. Everybody else spoke and said almost the same thing, that the reimposition of prescription charges has made life impossible for the Party because the Government is now betraying its socialist principles; that anyway winning an election—either municipal or parliamentary—was now out of the question. Others attacked me for lowering the standard of council housing and for letting the American Chrysler Company into Coventry. None of those who spoke had the faintest sense of loyalty or readiness to stand by the Government in its difficulties. On the way down in the train I had thought a great deal about the kind of reply I should give them. David Young gave me my opening. He asked me why there had been no devaluation in 1964. I told them that we hadn't devalued earlier because it meant a cut in the real standard of living of the workers and we weren't going to rush into something which the Labour movement hated. But now we had been forced into it I asked for their loyalty in carrying it through. I then explained to them how the cuts in public expenditure were meant to reduce demand and how in order to have fair shares in misery the cuts had to be shared out equally round the Ministries. That was why Health had taken its whack. It was either the hospital building programme or prescription charges and I thought Robinson had rightly preferred prescription charges.

One thing I learnt from this meeting is that no one in Coventry worries

[1] On January 20th Crossman had made a speech about defence policy and the cuts following devaluation.
[2] James Tinn, Labour M.P. for Cleveland since 1964, was P.P.S. to the Secretary of State for Commonwealth Relations 1965–6 and to the Minister of Overseas Development 1966–7. His Bill was given a Second Reading by 69 to 17 votes.

about the postponement of the school-leaving age. All they care about is the personal problem they have in the factories because of the promises they made about prescription charges and the way those promises have been broken. Nothing else really matters to them at the moment. I felt fairly gloomy, but Albert Rose and Betty Healey came up and told me that they thought we had made some advance. So Anne brought me home this evening fairly well satisfied.

Sunday, February 4th
Yesterday was a lovely frosty clear day and we went off in the late afternoon to see the *Taming of the Shrew* at the Banbury cinema. Patrick particularly enjoyed it. I've never read the Shakespeare play and before we went I read for the first time the chapter of Lamb's *Tales*. The film wasn't so untrue to Shakespeare and it certainly has wonderful colouring and delicious pictures of Siena.

Today we woke up to a tremendous white frost but by lunch-time it had clouded over and in the afternoon the rain set in and I snoozed over my newspapers until Richard Hartree came in to talk about the Alcan aluminium smelter. Richard is one of our oldest friends here in Oxfordshire and is high up on the management side of the Alcan factory on the main Southam Road. I was anxious to hear what he had to say because I was aware that we were getting into great difficulties with this smelter which was first conceived as a method of import saving—home-smelted aluminium would combine a huge steady market for nuclear electrical power with a lot of dollars saved. That at least was the idea with which we started. But from the beginning there was a good deal of difficulty in getting the import saving because the two chief producers—British Aluminium and Alcan—will insist on continuing some of their imports. Then came the Fuel White Paper, the decision to close down scores of collieries, and the miners' revolt. Just before Conference last year a letter was written to Alf Robens at the Coal Board inviting him to bid in terms of coal for one of the smelters. A joint scheme was cooked up under which the Coal Board would sign a contract to produce coal at an incredibly cheap price for the next twenty-five years in the Northumbrian coalfields and ship it to Invergordon, where Alcan would build the smelter. So much I knew before Richard arrived today. His new point was that we'd better face the fact that if Alcan doesn't get the Invergordon contract and aren't allowed to smelt in Britain they will import the aluminium for all their own needs and will leave us to look elsewhere for a market for the product of the Rio Tinto Zinc and British Aluminium smelters. This is a threat we can't disregard since Alcan is one of our biggest aluminium users in the country. I shall be interested to see how this argument works when I employ it at S.E.P.[1]

Well that's my diary—a fairly gloomy record and today's papers are

---

[1] The Canadian company eventually failed to get the contract and, on July 24th, it was announced that the plant at Invergordon was to be built by British Aluminium.

pretty gloomy too. It may be a good sign that the Gallup Poll published today once more shows that an overwhelming majority of people are in favour of a wage freeze. But then our trouble has never been that people don't like our policies. They like the prices and incomes policy—they also like the prescription charges and the postponement of the school-leaving age. Our difficulty is the opposition in the Parliamentary Party and in the Party in the country. There people are fanatically opposed and are prepared to create another crisis. A second difficulty is that despite all my efforts (which may have caused only extra difficulties) we are unable to sell our post-devaluation economic strategy as new and as a breakthrough without repudiating the members of the Government who opposed devaluation for three years and who supported our presence East of Suez. The only people who are free of this taint are Roy and myself. George, Jim, and Michael were all fully and personally committed and so was Harold. When I say in public that we've made a giant stride forward to socialism by getting rid of our East of Suez commitments and by freeing the pound I know very well that I can't expect any kind of public support from most of my colleagues.

Monday, February 5th

I started off with a big meeting entirely concerned with making the physical conditions tolerable for the members of the Committee which will for the first time in history consider the Finance Bill upstairs in a committee room this year. I thought at first we should take Room No. 10 and one of the rooms adjoining but those who were with me this morning disagreed. Bob Mellish and his officials from the Ministry of Works and the Chief Whip and his officials all thought the right thing was to take Room 14 which is the largest of all the committee rooms as well as Room 13 next door, which should be turned into a lounge-bar/tea-room and so on. As with every innovation at Westminster, there'll be a great deal of scepticism among the members of the Committee and a readiness to find things wrong. It's essential that we should minister to their creature comforts.

My next job was to take the chair at the Cabinet Committee on Procedure which had been urgently assembled when I heard that procedure is to be on the agenda tomorrow. This time there was a special reason for sourness as the Minister of Agriculture is in high dudgeon. He has been worked on by his officials and the whole of Whitehall to make a protest because once again the Select Committee on Agriculture has made an ass of itself. As a background to their work on agriculture they have asked the Ministry for a paper on the national economic plan for the next five years, including the advanced estimates and appreciations of economic developments. Peart said this was a ludicrous demand and that I should be instructed to tell the Select Committee how to do its business. I said I certainly wouldn't and advised the Minister himself to write back politely saying that the information they need will take a very long time to collect and will involve collaboration with many other

Ministries. 'Don't pick a quarrel with these new Committees,' I said, 'play them along.'

The next problem was Sachsenhausen. The ombudsman's report had of course created a great sensation and great anxiety in the Foreign Office lest the case would now be retried all over again not by the ombudsman but by the Select Committee which looks after him in Parliament. Bill Rodgers asked for an explicit assurance that the Committee will not do this. I had to point out this was not excluded by the Committee's terms of reference, which had been drafted after consultation with the Foreign Office. However, in this particular case I would try to persuade the Committee not to undertake a retrial because I didn't want to see an atmosphere of McCarthyism in which back-bench Members of Parliament were persecuting unknown or humble civil servants for the crimes of their superiors. It was a very long meeting and by the end a tremendous atmosphere had been blown up and people like Tony Greenwood were beginning to say that the Ministries were overburdened and couldn't accept any work imposed upon them by the Select Committees. To this my sole ally, Tony Benn, replied that some of this investigation does us all a lot of good and that we shouldn't regard the work of answering all these questions as bad. I was then able to point out that nothing the Agricultural Committee was asking for was unreasonable. Indeed, all that they were asking for should be readily available to the Government in presentable form because it's the kind of information we should be using in our own speeches to the country and indeed in the policy papers we write. 'The truth is,' I added, 'that if this pressure were constantly applied it would force us to present our case much better than we are doing at present.'

At this point I had to go back to see Bob Maxwell, who had come to see me about his Buy British campaign. What a miraculous man that fellow is. However much people hate him, laugh at him, boo him and call him a vulgarian he gets things done. If it wasn't for Bob Maxwell we would have got nowhere with this campaign. He was rebuked and he got a terrible snub from the C.B.I. – who said this was an anti-export campaign – but then he modified it to a Help Britain campaign and persuaded the C.B.I. to support him. Today he was bringing me the drafts of his advertisements. And though these adverts will be big and vulgar at least they'll show people wanting to help Britain, and wanting not to be anti-Wilson and supporting us in the post-devaluation climate.

I spent the whole afternoon on the Sachsenhausen case. First the Labour members of the Select Committee on the ombudsman came to see me – and a pretty prickly, angry, antagonized lot they were. I managed to cool them off a bit and get an assurance that they weren't going to have a McCarthyite attack on civil servants. In return I told them that if George Brown laid himself open I wasn't going to interfere with their right to a further investigation.

By now it was time for the debate itself. I had been discussing the text of George Brown's speech for a couple of days and when I saw it at the last minute it was very good indeed. A bit grudging in not admitting anything,

nevertheless in no way attacking the ombudsman. To my amazement, however, within ten minutes of starting George had launched into a tremendous
personal statement about his sense that he must behave honourably to his
civil servants. Very soon he was attacking the ombudsman and observing that
about this case, 'I know as much as he does. Indeed I think we ought to have an
ombudsman to examine ombudsmen.' Getting down to the ombudsman's
conclusion he rebutted it by claiming that he as Foreign Secretary had personally supervised the whole case, interviewing the people concerned, reading
all the papers with the greatest care, and studying all its complexities. Of course
this was a lot of nonsense. So far from interviewing the officers concerned, he
had merely sent for them to tell them the compensation money was exhausted
and had never asked a single question. Nor had he bothered to understand an
extremely complex problem. I saw the officials in the box looking more and
more appalled. They realized he had left his flank wide open to a counter-
attack and made it almost inevitable that the Select Committee would re-inves-
tigate his case. I don't think he was drunk when he said all this. He was just
himself. As soon as he'd finished he went out and I had to sit there alone on
the front bench listening to a number of very powerful attacks. Douglas
Houghton, for example, who had originally persuaded the Labour Cabinet
to make the ombudsman part of its election policy, indicted George Brown,
who duly came back half way through a little bit drunk and made another
laboured intervention. By the end it was clear the debate was not on Sachsenhausen but on the Foreign Secretary's astonishing attitude to the new institution of the ombudsman. When I got up at 9.40 I still didn't know what line
I should take. Usually in the Commons it's fatal to be doubtful but I took
refuge in a kind of candid good-humoured defence of George Brown. I
pointed out that a Minister can't be expected by the ombudsman to stand
on his head and I emphasized the complete innovation we had introduced
into our system from the point of view of the Government. Here was Sir
Edmund Compton with his unrivalled powers of investigation entitled to
know more than anybody else about this case and to interpret it in any way
he thinks. I suggested we should have to get used to this new relation and
said that I wasn't surprised that the Foreign Secretary hadn't swallowed it at
first sight, without criticism. As I went out past the Serjeant-at-Arms three
or four of the Committee gathered round me to congratulate me on saving
George Brown. I said nothing. I hadn't saved the Foreign Secretary—I'd
saved the Government from an awkward scene by managing to be loyal to
the idea of the ombudsman while standing up for the Foreign Secretary and
making the best of the terrible things he had said.

Tuesday, February 6th
The morning papers were surprisingly favourable to George Brown. My
speech at the end of the debate was only mentioned in passing by one paper.
George had made the news by tearing up his brief and being so outrageous

and as usual the press had at first forgiven him. Indeed the only embarrassing story this morning was about Will Howie. The Chief had told me on Monday that he had decided to sack him from the Whips' Office at 12.15 in order to demonstrate his strength. Since I'd been urging this for months I was delighted. But he didn't do it with tremendous professional skill because he forgot that Howie would go to his local Party last night and tell them he was being sacked for being too tough about Party discipline. So the first impact of his sacking in the press was wholly hostile to us. John will get things right during the week. Undoubtedly here at Westminster he's in a far stronger position now that he's got rid of a Whip who's always going round the tea-rooms criticizing his Chief and criticizing me.

At Legislation Committee my first job was George Strauss's Theatres Bill on censorship.[1] I am still somewhat uneasy about a measure which will deny any protection to living persons except what they can achieve by an *ex post facto* civil action. Perhaps this made me spot very quickly in the paper introducing the draft Bill a paragraph which said that whereas licensees of theatres had been liable under the previous law they should be no longer liable under the new law. I asked why on earth the licensees should not be liable just as the proprietors of newspapers and the printers of newspapers are liable? The Lord Chancellor immediately replied that this would involve having pre-censorship all over again because if the licensees could be sued for libel then they would start controlling the plays. Very soon the usual tension between the Lord Chancellor and me was in the air. We differ on most things. He is a tight-lipped quaker liberal and I am a rather slapdash unliberal conservative socialist. However on the next item we were in full accord. This was a little Private Member's Bill from the Lords about kerb-crawling.[2] Reading aloud the Home Office brief Victor Stonham advised us to vote it down.[3] Under my questioning he admitted that personally he thought it an admirable and progressive measure but had been ordered to oppose it by Jim Callaghan. There followed a long discussion and when I wound up I said, 'Well, let's give it a free vote and see what happens.'*

Next, Cabinet. This was the meeting for which Harold had said at our business meeting there was no business and all he could think of as a fill-in was the Defence White Paper on the Territorials. This turned out to be a fascinating discussion. In the January 22nd package the P.M. had announced the disbandment of the Territorials along with other civil defence organizations. This had produced a storm in the House of Lords, or rather two powerful speeches—one from the Duke of Norfolk and the other from George Wigg—protesting against the disbandment of the Territorials. Apparently

---

* It so happens that it was voted down overwhelmingly. The Callaghan view had prevailed against the liberal views of his number two.

[1] The Theatres Bill received the Royal Assent on July 26th, 1968.

[2] The Street Offences Bill, which aimed to make soliciting from cars illegal.

[3] Victor Stonham became a life peer in 1958. He was Joint Parliamentary Under-Secretary of State at the Home Office 1964–7 and Minister of State 1967–9. He died in 1973.

these protests have been so effective in Whitehall that a formula has been evolved for replying to the Questions in the Commons in which it was said that the proposal to disband the Territorials would now naturally be discussed with the Territorial Association. So the implication was that we hadn't decided to disband them but were only proposing to do so and listening after consultations. When this was put to Denis Healey he didn't deny it but said that there were reasons why he would like to postpone the disbandment for two or three years. He wanted, for example, to stimulate recruiting, which was falling desperately. The moment he'd finished Jim Callaghan from the Home Office said that if we were going to talk about the use of these organizations in peace time it is fairly obvious that the civil defence organizations are far more useful than the Territorials. Look at what had happened in Glasgow during the recent tornado. The civil defence organizations had been invaluable whereas the Territorials had done nothing. This seemed common sense to me. Territorials have no value socially. Politically they're wholly against us. Their only function is as a nucleus for recruiting the armed forces, whereas civil defence or auxiliary fire-fighting, etc., could be useful if we keep it on. Gradually the discussion petered out. Denis Healey obviously wasn't very keen. Callaghan was obviously enjoying himself and Harold remained inscrutable throughout, though I knew through private sources that he had been prompted by George Wigg, who had arrived at No. 10, had visited him at Chequers, and put him up to the whole plan. Quite unwittingly, I think, Callaghan had scotched it.

Next we turned to the ombudsman and Harold politely thanked me for what I had done in the debate to save George Brown from embarrassment. I replied that he's put us in some difficulty by such an outright attack on the whole principle of the ombudsman. Then Harold made a very sensible ruling that in future the civil servants who attend a Select Committee and give evidence shall be nominated by the Permanent Secretary. I accepted this straightaway.

The third item was the census questionnaire, which Michael Stewart had brought to Cabinet as a result of the controversy on the Home Affairs Committee. Once again, though the Departments considered the new questions on incomes and race vital, both Callaghan and Greenwood said they were politically too dangerous and this time they were backed by Barbara Castle simply because of her passions about the race questions. She just assumed that any questionnaire asked of the population would have implications of discrimination. When they'd finished Michael Stewart quietly said that really it was one of the basic principles of socialism that one should base one's policies on reliable information. The collection of the truth and the knowing of the truth was an essential element in socialist planning. At last Harold counted the heads and we had a comfortable majority for courage and common sense.

Curiously enough, since the P.M. started this odious practice I can't remember a major case where Cabinet has been wrong—which suggests that our disastrous decisions were not those into which Harold was driven by Cabinet but those which he took without consulting Cabinet.

At dinner with Pam tonight I found William Clark (the author of *Number 10*, the play I saw the other night), who is now off to Washington to be the publicity officer for the World Bank,[1] Perry Worsthorne and Virginia Crawley,[2] who used to rival Elizabeth Longford as a writer. I sat between Pam and Virginia and got into a tremendous argument about my Birmingham speech. It had completely amazed them that anybody should really believe that what had happened since devaluation was good for Britain and a step towards socialism. The fact that devaluation was demanded by practically every economic expert and that any constructive socialist must have wanted a complete withdrawal from the Far East is forgotten now that we are creating the impression of acting against our principles and against our desires because we've been forced to do so.

This evening I had a long-delayed talk with Roy. I went over to see him installed in his residence at No. 11—it seemed exactly the same as it was under Callaghan, heavily-furnished over-brocaded rooms which Chancellors inherit from one another. How ghastly it must be to live there. However, there he was and he gave me a gin and bitter lemon and himself a whisky and we settled down. He had an agenda but I started by asking how he was getting on with the P.M. He replied that yesterday Harold's mood had changed and he'd become quite cordial and co-operative. 'What happened before that?' I asked. And Roy admitted that he'd hardly seen the P.M. in the previous ten days. One would think that was impossible. In the critical days when the P.M. and the Chancellor were supposed to be preparing for the Government's greatest test they just weren't on speaking terms. He then told me that recently Denis Healey has been very difficult and bloody-minded, 'Because he hasn't got my job,' he added, and yet Denis doesn't want to be thrown out of Defence. So he's throwing his weight about in an erratic way. Then Roy asked me about John Silkin's position and said that he thought the sacking of Will Howie had done the Chief a great deal of damage. Roy is obviously staunchly right-wing in his views on discipline and dislikes John Silkin, seeing him as somebody who should be shifted. I then asked him about the inner Cabinet and he said,

---

[1] He was Public Relations Adviser to the Prime Minister 1955–6, editor of 'The Week' in the *Observer* 1958–60, director of the Overseas Development Institute 1960–68, director of Information and Public Affairs at the International Bank of Reconstruction and Development 1968–73 and, since 1973, its director of External Relations. *Number 10* (London: Heinemann, 1966) was to be followed by his political novel *Special Relationship* (London: Heinemann, 1968).

[2] Virginia Cowles had been Special Assistant to the American Ambassador in London 1942–3 and was author of, among other books, *1913* (London: Weidenfeld & Nicolson, 1967). She was married to Aidan Crawley, Labour M.P. for Buckingham from 1945 to 1951, when he joined the Conservative Party, sitting for West Derbyshire 1962–7. Since 1971 he has been President of London Weekend Television.

'We won't get it yet because there isn't the right kind of confidence between the P.M. and his colleagues. For instance, Harold can't make up his mind about Callaghan,' he remarked, 'he doesn't know whether he wants him in or out.' 'Which would you want?' I asked, adding, 'I would rather have Denis in and Callaghan out.' I think Roy would like the same but he doesn't think Harold is ready to act and he wanted to talk to me more about Callaghan. 'I should tell you,' he said, 'that the Home Office regards him as the most reactionary Home Secretary they've had for some time. He's certainly making his mark. He made it quite clearly at the Legislation Committee the other day on the kerb-crawling Bill and the liberal image is going by the board. It's true that he's had to carry on with my Gaming Bill but that has nothing to do with the liberal image. He'll also have to do my Race Relations Bill, but he'll do most of it with a heavy heart. What'll make him really happy is if he has to introduce the Bill to ban Kenya Asians with British citizenship from entering this country.'[1] (On this, by the way, I myself would be nearer Callaghan than Jenkins.) There's certainly tension enough between the ex-Home Secretary (now Chancellor) and the new Home Secretary (an ex-Chancellor).

But what did he want to talk to me about? Mostly parliamentary business —how we should handle the Vote on Account, how we should handle the Bristol-Siddeley scandal. And finally he turned to the Bank of England, where he's obviously very worried. For months the papers have been full of a row between John Silkin and Ian Mikardo about the reconstitution of the Select Committee on the Nationalized Industries which Ian wants to have new terms of reference to cover the Bank of England. John wouldn't grant them and as a result, months after the Session has begun, there is still no Nationalized Industries Committee and no work is being done. This is mostly Mikardo's own fault since last September he came along to me in the recess and said the investigation of the Bank of England wasn't particularly urgent. At this point I said, 'O.K. Why not reconstitute your Committee with the old terms of reference for this Session? Then next summer I'll get the terms of reference to cover the Bank of England before we recess.' That's how I left it with Ian and he then went off to Israel. But meanwhile the Tories on the Committee have been spoiling for a bit of a row and, quite rightly, regarding the failure to reconstitute the Committee as a minor scandal. They had begun to complain publicly, and we had to do something. I am in some difficulty myself because though it's my job to

[1] The Kenya Government already imposed strict controls on the number of work permits it would issue to Asians, and in February 1968, they were to refuse work permits altogether to some 100,000 people of Indian and Pakistani origin. Under the 1963 Kenyan Independence Agreement, non-citizens of Kenya had been allowed to choose either Kenyan citizenship or to retain their citizenship of the United Kingdom and Colonies, so that while the entry of citizens of the Colonies and of other independent Commonwealth countries was controlled, the Kenya Asians were unhampered by immigration restrictions. Some 7,000 came to Britain in 1966; by 1968 about 2,300 a month were coming.

discuss the terms of reference of these committees, the Chief keeps the nomination of the members in his own hands. Because he's jealous of his patronage he doesn't want to hand over anything to me and find himself a stooge of Crossman as Ted Short was a stooge of Herbert Bowden. I don't blame him but it does make things a bit difficult.

I explained all this to Roy and then asked him what he wanted himself. 'Well, you will be surprised to hear,' he said, 'that I'm not against an inquiry because I've discovered that the Bank of England is a closed book to us all. In a sense it's a part of the Treasury but actually it's absolutely separate. We don't know nearly enough of what's going on because they don't let us into their secrets. So I wouldn't mind them being investigated.' So I said, 'But you won't want a word of this to get out, I mean, if you want to investigate the Bank yourself what do you want Ian Mikardo in for? I am not at all clear what you are getting at, Roy,' and he replied, 'Well, if you can do it for me and relieve me of the bother of it this Session, of course I should be delighted.'

After that he settled down to what he at last said was his main subject—the budget—and for half an hour told me how his thoughts were developing. Mostly he discussed possible ways of increasing taxation and it soon became clear that his real trouble is with the Inland Revenue. He has plenty of ideas himself but he's constantly being told that it's too late to put them into this budget and they've all got to wait for twelve months because the Inland Revenue are overloaded with all the changes Callaghan and Kaldor heaped upon them.

As I was getting up to go we had another little talk about relations with the P.M., and I warned him of the bitterness Harold had felt against him for not consulting Peter Shore when the Treasury liberalized the restrictions on the export of capital. Roy said, 'Yes, I think there was some criticism of me.' Then I said, 'Don't you think it's time we had some social life?' and I told him a little story. 'You know,' I said, 'Harold Wilson found time to dine with my P.P.S., Tam Dalyell, and some back-benchers called the No-Group Group last week. If he could have dinner with them, couldn't he have one dinner in three years with a few Cabinet Ministers? If he can't organize an informal meeting, can't we?' and I left him with that thought.

I got home in time to have a nice drink with Anne before we went out to see the old Galsworthy play *Justice*, which Winston Churchill went to see in 1907 when he was Home Secretary. He was so moved by it that he began to modify the brutality of solitary confinement. I feared it would be completely old-fashioned but it's actually much better written and has much better characters than I expected. The real trouble, as Anne pointed out, was in the third act, the drama on Dartmoor, which should be the climax and which modern cinema technique has made far less riveting for the stage since its first production. But the first two acts were beautifully written and I must say it compared very favourably with *Heartbreak House*.

Wednesday, February 7th

A special meeting of the Social Services Committee had been summoned by Michael Stewart, who wanted to propose a new review of the social services. At first sight this is puzzling because for nearly three years we've been talking about the great review which was being conducted by Douglas Houghton. Endless detailed papers have been written and I'd read many of them, but under Houghton there'd been no overall review of how the services were working—whether the priorities were right, what reorganization was required, what rethinking of basic principles. Nothing of this had been done until Michael Stewart took over.

So here he was saying he wanted to have a really serious review and when we had all made our little speeches from our briefs he recommended that the officials' committee should now be asked to prepare papers for us. Thank God this didn't happen. Both Judith Hart and Kenneth Robinson spoke up about the need to break out of the strait waistcoat of PESC and think more boldly, and then someone fortunately said that we couldn't overburden officials in the present crisis and we wondered whether we really could ask them to take on all this extra work. That gave me my chance. First of all I was able to suggest that here we should rely far more on our economic advisers and if necessary expand their staffs in order to do this work quickly. Secondly, I thought that we Ministers could do a lot more ourselves and, before we knew it, the idea had emerged that the Ministers concerned should come together for a day after the budget to exchange views at a Ministerial Policy Conference. Apart from Harold's Chequers conferences on defence and Europe such a meeting hasn't taken place since 1964. As we were going out some Ministers observed that this had been a wonderful meeting. I only thought 'High time!' Reading the Churchill biography now, especially the second volume when he's Home Secretary, I've noticed that the marvellous thing then was how much Ministers normally thought out their own policy, talked things out among themselves and wrote their own state papers. Now we just haven't the time because we're so overweighted with departmental responsibilities and with reading aloud drafts prepared for us by our civil servants. As a result our policy-making functions are virtually eliminated.

On to the Party meeting, where I was to wind up the Second Reading debate on John Silkin's new code of conduct. Some forty or fifty members were present and the discussion was started by Douglas Houghton in an excellent speech full of humour and emotion, explosiveness and charm. He's a very shrewd old operator and did extremely well. On the whole the speeches were against imposing severer discipline. True, there was one Lancashire M.P. who thought the new code far too soft, but John Mackintosh, a right-winger, and Paul Rose,[1] a left-winger, both said, 'For God's sake don't let's tear each other to pieces.' And then came a

[1] Labour M.P. for Blackley since 1964.

remarkable speech from Alex Lyon who has been for some months a hatchet man and who now got up to confess that he'd been wrong and to admit the terrible damage he'd done. Now he swung to the other extreme and suggested we should have no discipline at all but trust to our sense of personal responsibility. He was followed by Charlie Pannell, who said the code was about right and we should give it a chance. I made a short reply reminding them that though this may have been a splendid meeting it had only been a fortnight ago, when we'd had a jolly good week in the House, relatively speaking, and got the Government Statement over, all the goodwill we had won in the country had been destroyed by three days of inter-Party rowing on the television about discipline until Harold had intervened and saved the situation. That, I said, was mass madness and we couldn't let it happen again. That is why I wanted a code of discipline—not for daily use but in reserve for a crisis. The British two-party system requires far more discipline than any other democratic system in the western world and this is a burden we impose upon ourselves by our particular method of running Parliament.

This afternoon I was in my room behind the Speaker's Chair when I was told that a Coventry industrialist, Arnold Hall, wanted to see me urgently.[1] I had quite a queue outside but I let him in straightaway and he told me that tomorrow there is to be an announcement that the missile factory in my constituency is closing down, making 2,400 men redundant. He assumed that I had been told already. Well, I hadn't been told, although the Minister of Technology knew ten days ago. I was grateful to him for coming. He's a civilized man and obviously the decision is part of a rationalization plan which has nothing to do with defence costs or devaluation. I just had time to give a brief statement to the *Coventry Evening Telegraph*, to prepare a Question which Maurice Edelman could use after the business Statement tomorrow and to ring up Wedgy Benn's Office and ask what the hell all this was about.

This evening I dined with Hugh Cudlipp in a private room at Kettner's. There was a wonderful Château Latour which kept me going and I enjoyed myself a great deal, mainly because I like being wolfed and nagged and beaten and bullied by Hugh while giving nothing away, and that's what happened to me the whole evening. Hugh made it clear that Cecil King, who of course is a Governor of the Bank of England, is now convinced that by the summer there will be a second devaluation which will be the end of the Labour Government and out of which a national government will emerge. A few weeks ago the *Mirror* was a great supporter of Jenkins but during this evening Hugh Cudlipp was saying that Jenkins was rapidly losing the *Mirror*'s goodwill because he was not doing enough. I told him that the talk about a devaluation crisis in three or four months is absurd,

[1] Sir Arnold Hall, vice-chairman of the Hawker-Siddeley Group from 1963 to 1967, when he became chairman and managing director.

but as long as people like Cecil King go round the City and talk in this way the position of the Government remains extremely dicey and everything depends on Roy's budget on March 19th.

I knew that one of Hugh's aims this evening was to detach me from Harold Wilson. However, I made it perfectly clear that, even supposing there were a second devaluation crisis and a national government, which meant the end of Harold Wilson, I would go with him because I am one of his henchmen and I have no ambitions. So if he goes I would like to get out and write my books. It was vital to make it absolutely clear that there was no centre of disloyalty anywhere near Harold because I knew that anything I said would be reported back to Cecil King and might provide ammunition to his implacable anti-Wilson campaign.

Thursday, February 8th

Quite a good press for the Party meeting and, thank heavens, for Bob Maxwell's advertisements, which have provoked Quintin Hogg into a wild attack on the Government.

In the morning I worked away at the article which the *Sunday Telegraph* (perhaps inspired by Pam and Michael Berry) have decided to ask me to write explaining the attitude I first revealed in my Birmingham speech. Precisely because I felt entitled to express the views about devaluation and East of Suez which I've secretly held for three years, the speech has made a great sensation and may well cause Harold some trouble in the House, where I notice he's already got six or seven Questions next Tuesday afternoon. I imagine they will all make hilarious fun of my claim that there have been great strides towards socialism since devaluation. Well, I mustn't make things worse on Sunday so in this article I've deliberately tried to spell out carefully and sensibly why a moderate left-wing socialist can feel that after devaluation and the withdrawal from Suez a new start is possible.

This afternoon while I was waiting for the business Statement the Chief told me he wouldn't be able to stay on the front bench because he had to talk to George Brown about the Anglo-American Group in Bermuda. I said that was fine and that I hoped he would fix it all up. I am really beginning to get quite keen on the idea of four days in the sunshine with the afternoons off for bathing, with plenty of pleasant discussion with good Americans in the company of David Harlech[1] and Selwyn Lloyd. After what Harold had said to me I took it absolutely for granted that the Chief was just going to have a formal talk with George and get the whole thing cleared up in a matter of minutes.

This afternoon Questions on the business Statement went on for more than half an hour quite simply because there was nothing very interesting

---

[1] Lord Harlech, Conservative M.P. for Coventry from 1950 to 1961, when he went to Washington for four years as British Ambassador. In 1964 he succeeded to his father's title and, from 1966 to 1967, he was deputy leader of the Opposition in the House of Lords.

coming up afterwards. It's only a matter of patience and confidence, provided you know all the Bills coming up, every detail about the next month's business and have looked through the hundreds of Early Day Motions. You can mix it a bit with your colleagues as Leader of the House, but you must know all the business and you must be confident. So because there wasn't anything much else to do the Questions to me went on and on and on—good humoured and easy.

As we went upstairs to my Lobby conference I noticed the Chief wasn't with me and that was very queer because I'd emphasized the importance of his attending the conference to answer the questions on discipline. Yet neither he nor his Deputy was there and so I diverted the journalists' attention to the subject of the missile factory in Coventry and gave them a very full briefing on the need for an early warning system: something I'd discussed with Wedgy Benn on the phone this morning. I also pointed out that the Government shouldn't be against these mergers or even against the consequent redundancies because this is part of the necessary re-organization of British industry. What we had to make sure was that we weren't overdoing the movement from the Midlands into the development areas and creating areas of unemployment in Coventry and Birmingham, where only this week the Ministry of Labour has sent out a letter saying that a higher level of unemployment must be expected, rising to 2,500 over the next six months. I took my chance and spelt all this out to the Lobby correspondents, on a strictly non-attributable basis, of course. I hoped that tomorrow I would find that half a dozen of them, short of anything else to write about, had written stories along the lines I suggested.*

Straight down to the Party meeting—John Silkin was not there either. He had gone off to a dinner in Lincoln's Inn. Now I began to suspect that something had gone wrong in his meeting with George Brown. But I was able to handle the only important item—the over-eighties' pensions Bill next Friday[1]—what I call Airey Neave Mark Two because it was the Airey Neave Bill that caused us to have the all-night sitting when George Wigg's inspiration boomeranged on us so badly.[2] At this Party meeting we decided to oppose the Bill outright and to give the reasons simply and tersely and without qualification. I'd asked Judith Hart to come but she made much too lengthy a speech and got people against her. Judith is a strange girl. I like her personally and she's extremely able, but she's an English woman in a Scottish constituency which doesn't like her much, and even south of the border she's regarded as a henchman of the Prime Minister. She has

---

* They had.

[1] The National Insurance (Further Provisions) Bill.

[2] In March 1965, Airey Neave, Conservative M.P. for Abingdon since 1953, had introduced a Private Member's Bill seeking to compensate people who for a variety of reasons were not entitled to receive a contributory old-age pension. George Wigg suggested a procedural device by which the business was deferred, but the Government got a bad press for the manoeuvre. See Vol. I, p. 188.

got to earn her spurs and get the Party to like her. She angered Charlie Pannell and he got up to say that kind of speech would be quite wrong. All we needed to say is that we haven't got the £51 million which this Bill would cost. 'It's much better,' he added, 'to be blank and negative and vote against it than to have a long expression of conscience.' Then in John's absence Brian O'Malley smoothed the meeting down and we wound it up without too much difficulty.

All the week the Lords have been having a television experiment and there'll be one or two quite interesting accounts in the press. Since this was its last day I thought I would go and look and I watched it right up to the adjournment. First I went to the Grand Committee Room in Westminster Hall and there the officials told me that there had only been four people in that day and never more than ten on the previous two days. I watched alone. I then moved into the House of Lords to see how the experiment was faring. Again I was the only person there and nobody had been there for an hour before I came. Finally I claimed my right to sit on the steps of the Throne and spent half an hour in the Lords seeing how it felt to be televised with these unconcealed cameras under the appalling lights. The Lords themselves have made quite a study of their experiment, but according to my inquiries not more than twenty or thirty M.P.s have bothered to see either of the screenings and of those who did many only glanced in for a moment or two. The House of Lords is a very introverted place. It's made up its mind about television and it doesn't want to change its mind.

Dinner with Pat Llewelyn-Davies in Hampstead to talk to Victor Rothschild. I was very depressed and the more they asked me how things were going the more I revealed my depression. I couldn't help describing the lack of a hard-core leadership at the centre and saying that if there is a second devaluation, there will be a national government with Harold out and me out at the same time. I can't conceal the feeling that's growing in my own mind that maybe the economic problem is beyond the capacity of any Party. The Tories are bound to oppose any kind of prices freeze, and any legislative changes to give statutory backing to it. And so they will provide a basis on which our own back-benchers will be able to vote against it. Yet without an effective prices and incomes policy Roy's budget, however good, is not going to work. Richard, Pat and Victor are very nice people— too nice for me this evening—and I got away as soon as possible and went on up to Thomas Balogh, who wanted to brief me for S.E.P. about prices and incomes. His great idea is that we have to introduce a social programme to help the lower-paid worker so that the package will be acceptable to the T.U.C. I was tough and said that there is no evidence at all that better family allowances for lower-paid workers have the faintest effect in keeping down the wages of the higher-paid worker. 'Well,' he said, 'it removes their excuse.' And I said, 'Excuse or no excuse, they put their wages up to keep their differentials.' In this I'm on the same side as Gunter, and I had to say to

Thomas, 'This is just theory—a frightfully expensive theory. The last Chancellor spent hundreds of millions of pounds on expanding the social services in order to get your prices and incomes policy through without any evidence that it will make it any better.' Just when I was going Thomas said to me, 'Be careful, Dick. Your relations with Harold are being poisoned by Roy.' 'Nonsense,' I said, 'my relations with Harold have been poisoned by my independence and by the situation. I don't agree with him, for instance, about the Territorials and his surrender to George Wigg. On all these issues I'm fighting my own battle.' Thomas remains very uneasy about my future. He knows that before Harold left for Washington there was quite a period when the P.M. didn't see me. That week he cancelled morning prayers and we haven't, for a fortnight, had any frank discussion with each other. I agreed with Thomas that this was a fact and that I'm now at a loose end. I'm not being consulted by Harold on the key issues because there's no inner Cabinet or strategy board and so I'm back again in my old role as rogue elephant—a powerful force which isn't harnessed to a useful purpose. Instead of getting on better with Harold I'm getting on worse and disagreeing with him on more and more issues while I'm driven to adopt a so-called Gaitskellite position, which makes him think I am disloyal. This is something I shall have to deal with very carefully when he gets back on Sunday morning.

Friday, February 9th

I woke up at 6.30 and suddenly felt totally discontented with the draft article for the *Sunday Telegraph*. I began to think I'd have to call it off for a week but I then sat up in bed and started to write and as often happens in the early morning in bed it all suddenly came out correctly. I knew I should be able to dictate the article straight off this morning.

At the Cabinet Committee meeting on Lords reform which started my morning I at last saw John Silkin and asked him what had happened with George Brown. 'Nothing very much,' he said and at once I knew that something had gone wrong. So I walked out with him and got into his car and told him to explain. 'Did you clear me with George?' I asked him. 'No I didn't,' he said, 'because George put me on to a new line of thought as to whether we really needed a high-powered Minister this year.' 'You never raised that with George?' I said. I was white with anger. 'But you've put me in a completely impossible position because I've told Alec Spearman that the P.M. has cleared it and Alec's coming to lunch with me today to tidy up the details.' 'I was in an appalling position,' John said. 'What was I to do? I had no authority. George just said he was cabling Washington about the level of the American delegation.' I don't know why I got so angry. Partly because I'd suspected that this was what was happening behind the scenes and partly because I felt you can't treat the Lord President of the Council and the Leader of the House in this insulting way. I don't think

22

I've ever felt so hurt—hurt by John Silkin letting me down with George, hurt that the Prime Minister had once again palmed me off with an assurance that he didn't mean, deeply hurt that I'd let myself be deceived. I also felt that a Leader of the House who is treated as a dear old buffer isn't a serious member of the Government. After all, I had been invited months ago and the Opposition knew I'd been invited and George and Harold had spent weeks considering whether I am fit to head this quite important delegation or whether I mustn't be removed and Michael Stewart put in my place. That I think impossible.

The Second Reading of Bill Wilson's Divorce Reform Bill was going on in the House. Since as Leader I have to remain impartial till after the Second Reading, I told Bill Wilson that with his safe majority I would not cancel my trip to Nottingham in order to remain in the House. But when I looked in our side were very gloomy and beginning to wonder whether they were going to get the hundred that they required at the end of the afternoon. (Actually they got 165.)[1] However, I was off to Nottingham and had a lovely time snoozing in the train and preparing a speech for the University Labour Club. The Vice-Chancellor was being very civilized and asked me to see him, and so did the head of the Politics Faculty, and then I was brought into a big room with about 200 people—which they think a huge meeting in Nottingham—silent and cold, with a very nervous chairman. I made my Birmingham speech but much better than in its first phase. I've made it in between at Coventry and Manchester and it's quite a powerful piece of exposition now. Then I answered questions for an hour and a quarter and I was winning the audience all the time except on two issues—prices and incomes, and Vietnam. I learnt that people have become impossibly committed on Vietnam and I suspect that though Harold was quite brave during this visit to Washington and did warn the President about escalation, the fact that he stood by the Americans will give us a very rough time in the House next week when the Statement is made and a debate takes place. I myself think our attitude to Vietnam morally indefensible. The Americans have been proved as utterly wrong there as Bevin was in Palestine. And as the American Government didn't feel they should support Bevin's Palestine policy out of loyalty to us so frankly I don't see why we should support the Americans in Vietnam now.

Sunday, February 11th
I read the *Sunday Telegraph* article and found it an absolutely first-rate interview—constructive and a jolly sensible statement of the left-of-centre socialist view. All this needs to be said because the country's almost forgotten that there is such a thing as a sensible constructive socialist view which welcomes devaluation and withdrawal from East of Suez as the beginning of a new deal.

[1] The vote was 165 to 64.

This has been another week of Government indecision. The latest instance is in the Home Office. Months ago we decided that if the situation got urgent and there was a threat of a mass expulsion of Asians with British citizenship from Kenya and therefore of a mass entry of these same citizens into this country we would have to clap on a quick special Immigration Bill. But then we changed Home Secretaries and we waited and waited and now we've missed the right moment because Duncan Sandys is up in arms and Enoch Powell too is demanding urgent action.[1] If the Government makes its decision now it will seem to be surrendering to the most reactionary forces in the country.

But does Callaghan want to look as though his hand is being forced? I'm not sure: anyway it's another issue where drift is creating the very impression we want to destroy that nothing has really changed since devaluation.

Monday, February 12th
Sydney Silverman died on Saturday and several papers had asked me to do obituaries. I refused partly because I was busy on the *Sunday Telegraph* article and partly because I could admire him but only with my head. I shall remember him mainly in the battle against Bevin between 1945 and Israeli independence in 1948. Then he was really magnificent—the Lion of Juda, determined, tenacious and tremendously courageous in standing up to the House of Commons when it was baying its hatred of the Jewish terrorists and baying its approval of Bevin's decision to send the *Exodus* back to Hamburg. All that baying frightened me: it didn't frighten Sydney. He led us into battle. Nevertheless, he was vain, difficult and uncooperative. No one could get him to work in any kind of a group. All his life he remained an individualist back-bencher, rather like my friend Tam Dalyell. You have to have a tremendous individual egotism driving you along and concentrating your energies on a few objectives, if you are really going to be a great back-bencher. If you can work in a team (for instance, in one of our new Specialist Committees or for that matter in the Cabinet) you want to be in Government, not to succeed on the back benches. The only people who can really live the back-bench life must have the unattractive characteristics of a Sydney Silverman or a George Wigg.

Coming into S.E.P. I noticed there were some Ministers there already with the Prime Minister—Tony Crosland and Roy Jenkins, for example— and I knew they'd been having some pre-budget talks. But I also guessed that they'd been talking about the front-page story in the *Financial Times* this morning. This was a piece by John Bourne referring to the new law and to Jenkins and Gunter, obviously based on knowledge of the paper we

[1] In forthcoming months, Enoch Powell was to warn that Britons were being made 'strangers in their own country' by increasing waves of immigrants.

were due to discuss this morning. It wasn't a very full leak, not nearly as well informed as usual and it didn't seem to me to have the characteristics of a Gunter leak from the Ministry of Labour. Indeed, it was rather anti-Ministry of Labour and pro Roy Jenkins, and I had a suspicion that it was a John Harris leak, but the extraordinary thing was the P.M.'s behaviour. He said, 'We shan't discuss this paper at all now. Take it off the agenda while we make inquiries about this leak.' So this vital question of prices and incomes legislation disappeared! If it was known that no decision was being taken it would be dreadful for Jenkins, since his budget must be prepared on firm assumptions about our prices and incomes policy. And the whole point of this meeting had been to give Roy a firm basis for his budget. If he could be sure that Cabinet would introduce an intensified prices and incomes policy and make a real effort to hold increases to 5 or 6 per cent at the cost of further legislation—then he could afford a less heavy budget. If there is to be no effective prices and incomes policy then all the burden must be imposed by heavier taxes. Of course Harold knows this and I'm sure he decided to take the item off the agenda because he wanted to fix it quietly with Roy behind the scenes.

After this little episode we turned to the old problem of the aluminium smelter. It was soon clear that practically all the other Ministries concerned had briefed their Minister to oppose the plan put forward by the Minister of Power for a coal deal with Alcan. Of course the Robens proposition for a coal-fired smelter at Invergordon with the coal being shipped from Northumberland was economically ruinous in the sense that the price would have to be subsidized by the rest of the coalfields. It was also clear that it violated the agreement the Minister had reached with the P.M. to link any deal with the vast surplus stocks of coal. Tony Crosland wanted to have the deal forbidden flat. But legally this was not so easy as the Minister was able to point out—the Coal Board and Alcan are perfectly entitled to come to an agreement and Alf Robens can fix his prices without interference from the Government. On the other hand the company had made it clear that they expected the Government to decide and Robens knew perfectly well that as the Coal Board is bankrupt and needs Government help it must have a decision too.

Finally, we agreed that since a veto was illegal the Minister should go to Robens and ask him to cook up another scheme with Alcan based on getting rid of surplus stocks the N.C.B. had agreed at the Prime Minister's Scarborough meeting. And then the P.M. characteristically, 'And we might throw in the coal-fired station at Seaton Carew.' That was a subtle tactical move. The decision to build a nuclear-fired station right in the middle of the Durham coalfield had driven the N.U.M. mad. They weren't in the least impressed by the figures showing that a coal-fired station would load us up for thirty years with inefficient plant and cost far more. Now Dick Marsh was being offered the possibility of going back to the N.U.M. and saying, 'I've got a coal-fired station at Seaton Carew in return for the Coal Board dropping the Alcan scheme.'

Of course in economic terms this proposal was a scandal. The Seaton Carew scheme is far bigger and more ambitious and will cost us far more money than the Alcan scheme. But the Prime Minister is great at thinking up a new tactical manoeuvre on the spur of the moment. Alas, these smelters are not our happiest piece of Government intervention and yet they're the only concrete example we have to excuse our introducing the Industrial Expansion Bill.

In the afternoon we had a meeting of the Prices and Incomes Committee —this time about railway wages. As usual the Chancellor was in the chair and I sat beside him with beyond me the two key men concerned—D.E.A.'s Peter Shore and Ray Gunter. Of all Cabinet Committees this is the one I hate most because I know perfectly well that the statutory prices and incomes policy is one of the few things which makes the difference between a socialist and a Tory Government and I can see that without it we shall have to rely on a rising level of unemployment. And yet whenever I sit at this Committee I come to the conclusion that a statutory policy is unworkable. When I listen to the mumbo-jumbo of nil norms and the rest of it, and criteria, I feel they're infuriatingly bogus and I'm inspired by an Enoch Powellite desire to tear the whole thing to pieces. Yet in the end I have to vote for one of these legalistic formulae.

After that I went up to my room where Callaghan and his whole staff of officials came in to discuss with Freddie Warren and the Chief and me how we could deal with the matter of the Kenya Asians. Now we weren't dealing with the substance of the issue but with what was to happen if the need for a Bill was actually agreed. We decided that if such a Bill was agreed we should try to get it in the shortest possible time. But what was the shortest possible time? After some discussion we agreed that we would conceivably put to the Opposition through the usual channels the proposal to get the Bill through in one day and one night, sitting right through twenty-four hours. The justification for this would simply be that once such legislation had been announced there would be a rush of immigrants coming in on charter flights, with thousands of Indians sitting on the doorstep.

Well, I thought about this and about my own role, and I did give the warning that this would be a Bill that would be infringing the freedom of British nationals, and that we must have a certain decency in dealing with it in the House of Commons. Would it be respectable to take the whole thing through in one day? I felt that Willie Whitelaw and Ted Heath would agree to our doing it in this particular way but should the Leader of the House misuse the Government's big majority and the usual channels to make life easy for the Executive in a matter which would be dismissed as unconstitutional in any country with a written constitution? By the evening I came to the conclusion that I'd been too easy this afternoon. I was surprised to find the Chief going along with me in the quick solution because he has tremendously strong feelings about Black Africa. But perhaps he too was enraptured by the skills of party management.

Back in my room I had to discuss with Barbara Castle the tactical point at which it would pay us to guillotine her enormous Transport Bill. While she was there a letter came from George Brown in which he said that he'd now decided that if I felt it worth while he would let me head the delegation to Bermuda although the Americans wouldn't be worthy of me. This was followed by a telephone message saying the same thing.

I had not spoken to him or to Harold either at the weekend or today. I'd simply sent the P.M. a stinking minute on Friday saying that this behaviour was intolerable. So George had caved in to Harold's pressure over the weekend and the two of them had decided to let me have my way. It's a miserable thing to win on—but somehow I was driven to fight. I saw Harold for a moment this afternoon and he said, 'You've got to go now, Dick, you know. You have really got to behave faultlessly because the Foreign Office will be watching you and hoping you fail.' So I said, 'Right,' and I was committed. But I suddenly realized that as a result I would leave to Michael Stewart the job of announcing the Transport guillotine and perhaps the problem of the Kenya Asians as well.

In the evening I went off to a party given for the new London editor of *Time*.[1] The Time-Life building in Bond Street is a splendid place for a big party and as always 'everybody' was there. I had a long talk to Paul and Marigold Johnson about the future of the *New Statesman* and around the place I found that a good many people had read my *Sunday Telegraph* article and been surprised at how persuasive it was. I believe they were surprised because none of the other party leaders was attempting to write or to say anything so sensible and so convincing.

Tuesday, February 13th
The big news in the morning press was Duncan Sandys's call for action against the Kenya Asians. This of course is despite the fact that it was Duncan Sandys who signed the Kenya Independence Treaty in 1954 and gave special assurances to the Kenya Indians that they would remain British nationals. Our first Cabinet Committee was that on Commonwealth Immigration with our friend Jim Callaghan in the chair. Here's an interesting point about Prime Ministerial government. In normal circumstances the line we should take on Commonwealth immigration would be considered by the Home Affairs Committee but this Kenya Asian problem had been sent to a special committee appointed for the purpose with Jim Callaghan —not Michael Stewart—in the chair. As a matter of fact if it had been considered under the chairmanship of Michael Stewart, things would have been much better. Jim arrived with the air of a man whose mind was made

[1] James Bell.

up. He wasn't going to tolerate this bloody liberalism. He was going to stop this nonsense as the public was demanding and as the Party was demanding. He would do it come what may and anybody who opposed him was a sentimental jackass. This was the tone in which he conducted this Cabinet Committee and it was extremely interesting to see the attitude of the members round the table. Whitehall had lined up the D.E.A., the Ministry of Labour, the Ministry of Education, all the Departments concerned, including even the Foreign Office, behind the Home Office demand that the law must be changed. Only the Commonwealth Department stood out against this pressure and George Thomas, the Minister of State, made a most passionate objection to the Bill in strictly rational form, saying this was being railroaded through and Jim was getting backing from all the Departments. A few years ago everyone there would have regarded the denial of entry to British nationals with British passports as the most appalling violation of our deepest principles. Now they were quite happily reading aloud their departmental briefs in favour of doing just that. Mainly because I'm an M.P. for a constituency in the Midlands, where racialism is a powerful force, I was on the side of Jim Callaghan and said that we had a sharp choice. We had either to take the risk of announcing in advance that there would be no ban on immigration in the hope that this would stem a panic rush, or we had to announce the Bill. The one thing not to do was to hesitate and be indecisive. Between these two courses I felt that a country such as France might possibly choose in favour of the first but the British people wouldn't. There was virtually no opposition to this view except from George Thomas and Elwyn Jones.

In the House this afternoon the P.M. was once again right on top of his form. First of all he answered a number of detailed Questions about incomes policy and showed an extraordinary mastery of precise figures. He loves this kind of thing and, strangely enough, so does Heath. Then Harold came to the account of his American trip and managed to convince the House that it had been a great personal success.[1] He had gone there expecting nothing and he found the Americans expecting nothing and he told me afterwards that when he decided to make the little speech which had won the headlines everybody in the Embassy said he was mad to do it. He didn't clear it with Johnson in any but the most general terms. And yet that speech and Johnson's reply were the apex of his trip. What exactly did he achieve? Did he show that Britain matters and that despite our withdrawal from the Far East and our cancellation of the F-111 we're still a world power? Apparently Johnson never referred to either of these issues despite the thundering telegrams of protest he had sent. It is clear that we have got

[1] Mr Wilson had visited Washington from February 4th to 11th and had made a speech in which he emphasized that there could be no purely military solution to the problem of Vietnam. The President had received these remarks warmly and had told the Prime Minister that he was determined to promote 'a diplomatic offensive'. See *Wilson*, pp. 496–503.

away with it. No doubt it is partly that we have been so weak and feeble that the Americans felt it was a good thing for us to face reality. So Harold really got the best of both worlds—his courageous attitude won him a good deal of respect from L.B.J., and at the same time he stood by the alliance, and he really had a great success in the House of Commons.

I went back to my room to try to resolve the deadlock with the Nationalized Industries Committee about their demand to investigate the Bank of England. Mikardo and his Tory number two, Colonel Lancaster,[1] were both there and I was able to explain to them how the interminable months of delay had occurred, and Ian at once took his full share of blame. When they seemed ready I made my offer that I would get them the right terms of reference for their Committee in the next session. 'I won't commit myself to the new terms of reference being exactly what you want,' I said, 'because I want to study the possibility of a new Select Committee on Finance which might possibly cover this topic. But apart from this I give you my guarantee.' It took only two minutes to clear up the row which had worried Roy so much.

At the Services Committee Bob Mellish and Stephen Swingler turned up for their Ministries and once again we discussed the proposed new parliamentary building on the other side of Bridge Street. I asked for clarification on two points. First, was there a possibility of a brand new Parliament building on that side? They made it clear that this would mean postponing any hope for twenty or thirty years. But then, when I turned to the other point of the difficulty of communication between the old building and the new, a brilliant idea occurred to Leslie Martin. He pointed out that the level of the road where Westminster Bridge starts is some fifteen feet higher than the point where it enters Parliament Square and it occurred to him that he could alter the level of Bridge Street in such a way as to make a kind of colonnade under the road so that one could walk through from Parliament Square to the new building. This would remove the main psychological objection to the extension on the other side of the road. This was well worth looking at and I felt we'd made a real advance.

I was also able to fix the physical arrangements for the Finance Committee in the upstairs corridor. John Silkin and I had recommended that the Committee take Room 14 and use Room 13 next door as a bar and restaurant. At once Willie Whitelaw and Selwyn Lloyd had come to see me privately and said, 'Room 14 is the traditional meeting place for the 1922 Committee and we can't possibly break that tradition.' This was enough for me and I decided we would have to try Room 10. It would be too small for perfection but on the other hand it would satisfy the Tories because they would know that they were responsible for choosing it. I also found that they didn't like the idea of a next-door lounge and restaurant. They wanted to be able to go downstairs and to be sure that the tea-room would be open whenever

[1] Colonel Claude Lancaster, Conservative M.P. for Fylde 1938–70.

the Committee was sitting. And they also wanted vending machines along the committee-room corridor. I was able to oblige them on all these points and I think we bought some solid goodwill from the Opposition by agreeing to move from Room 14 to Room 10.

I had spent a lot of the day looking after a 'Procedural Delegation' which had come over from the Canadian Legislature to study our procedure. In the evening I gave them an official dinner. We had two Ministers of the Canadian Parliament there—from New Brunswick—and what I discovered was the appalling plight they were in as the result of having no 'usual channels' operating. They haven't even got an arrangement under which business can be planned a single week in advance. Indeed they are in the same position as the British Parliament before the 1880s when the Irish members compelled Gladstone to introduce the guillotine and most of our modern methods of organizing business. I'd arranged that Barnett Cocks, Freddie Warren and the two Chief Whips should help to entertain the delegation and as soon as we got through a quick dinner and had a quick toast to the Queen I persuaded them to sit on round the table and have a serious discussion. Willie Whitelaw started it and I thought it was a first-rate meeting which taught me a lot more about modern procedure. I'm sure I learnt as much as the Canadians did from that evening.

Wednesday, February 14th
Shirley Williams had rung me last night to say she wanted to see me. Since I was with the Canadians this was impossible and I told her to ring me at Vincent Square as early as she liked this morning. She didn't ring and just when I was due to leave for morning prayers at 9.45 a girl's voice came on the phone and said, 'I'm Mrs Williams's secretary. I've been put off the train and I'm in a call-box to find out what the Lord President wants.' I remembered that this was the day when the Opposition were moving a vote of censure on our education cuts and here was Shirley Williams going off to open an institute of education in Birmingham. I soon found out from John Silkin that though this took place at midday she had arranged not to appear at all this evening. When I got to Number 10 I told Harold and John and they were as outraged as I was. John ordered her to come back and after long negotiations she said she would be in my room at eight. She came in looking very disturbed but before she could make a speech I said, 'You ought to be here for the big censure debate.' 'This debate has nothing to do with me,' she said. 'I deal with universities.' Of course there is an impossible relationship between Shirley on the one hand and Gordon Walker and Alice Bacon on the other. I don't blame her for finding Patrick pretty miserable and Alice Bacon's voice unbearable but I do blame her for the kind of disloyalty which makes her absent herself during a vote of censure. She's trying to avoid responsibility for the education cut of which she doesn't approve.

22*

The debate itself went quite quietly partly because as usual Edward Boyle couldn't move a vote of censure very convincingly.[1] But really everybody knows that the public has accepted the postponement of the raising of the school-leaving age and that the only people who are opposed to it are the educational élite of both Parties.

I seem to have run ahead from my subject, about the P.M.'s reaction to Shirley Williams at morning prayers. After that we had a discussion of prescription charges and I warned the P.M. again that Kenneth Robinson, who is not exactly enthusiastic about this, has no effective supervision. 'The whole thing,' I said, 'is going along in a very routine way and no one has made it clear to Kenneth that he has got to get a practical working exemption scheme because otherwise the Party won't take the prescription charges.' 'I've had 163 signatures to the letter on prescription charges which I have to circulate to the Cabinet,' said the P.M. He too has lost his enthusiasm.

O.P.D. followed this and it was full of interest. First we had the nuclear non-proliferation treaty. Last week we'd had a very curious scene with Denis saying that in our new relationship with Europe we should defend our allies and not merely be the minor spokesman of the super-powers in giving them orders about nuclear non-proliferation. This was an interesting idea but I'm afraid that when it had been looked into he hadn't really got a leg to stand on. The reply made by the Foreign Office was annihilating, even though poor old Fred Mulley had to deliver it. The second point of interest arose out of a minute I had circulated on the timetable of the Defence White Paper. On reading the draft I had jumped to the conclusion that our announcement of the phased withdrawal was carefully planned to run right up to the last day—December 31st, 1971—whereas all we were committed to was a withdrawal by the last day of 1971 and we *might* be out two or three years earlier if we wanted it. I saw here a trick under which the defence Departments were transforming a last possible day into the only day for withdrawal. George Brown was on my side and said he wanted to be quite sure that he could be out of the Gulf much earlier. Denis Healey said that he had to make his plans and phase them over a definite period. Then the P.M. said that we must draw a distinction about the timetable for our withdrawal and the plans for the run-down of the forces consequent on our withdrawal. This sounded better than it worked out. But I was satisfied because I achieved an absolutely clear statement in the minutes: 'On the timing of our withdrawal we should not go beyond what has already been announced since this gave us the flexibility to withdraw earlier should the opportunity arise.' This is the kind of small difference a non-departmental Minister can occasionally make.

Next, the Nigerian civil war. The Commonwealth Department put in a

[1] The vote was 244 to 323.

demand for an unqualified acceptance in principle of our contribution to any peace-making force for Nigeria if war should break out between Biafra and the Federal forces. Apparently Arnold Smith[1] has said he wanted a force one thousand strong but our Chiefs of Staff said it would have to be at least four times that strength within six months. Here again the Committee really made a difference because we prevented the Commonwealth Office committing us in principle far too early. The more we looked at it the clearer it became that once a force was there we should never get it out. It could become a permanent British peace-keeping commitment inside Nigeria. Second, it was clear that it would be far larger than we had thought possible in which case it wouldn't be a token force but an effective military force and that would be an appalling liability. So we forced the Commonwealth Department to withdraw from the commitment until we had studied the logistics. At least we are not going to drift into it.

Meanwhile in the House the Parliamentary Party was having its pre-budget meeting with the Chancellor. There were never more than forty-seven people there and I came in just as Douglas Jay was lecturing and the rest were giving their views quite sensibly. The Party wants to be consulted before the budget and there's a deep feeling of *fait accompli*. To reduce this even by a fraction helps us a great deal as Party managers.

Before it finished I had to go off to a Privy Council. As usual I had difficulty in knowing what to talk about to the Queen beforehand, so I told her that Lords reform had been getting on very well. She said, 'Oh, yes,' and I said, 'Yes, we are just waiting for Peter Carrington to come back from Australia to complete the negotiations, and I am hoping that we will be successful.' She said, 'By agreement?' and I said, 'Yes.' 'Well, that will be a surprise,' she said. 'It's not something one expected of you,' in a rather tart way with a rather nice little smile, and I thought, 'That's interesting.' No, I suppose they don't expect it of me; they think I'm a dangerous, left-wing republican, a man who is anti-royalty and won't turn up at a Palace banquet.

This evening I had dinner with Peter Shore before hearing the end of the debate. He tells me curtains are down and drawn between the D.E.A. and the Treasury. The old sense of suspicion has been recreated though Tony Crosland is much more humane and open-minded than Roy. Even so this division is very bad since it splits the Prime Minister and his men—Peter Shore and Wedgy Benn on the one hand—and Roy and his team on the other. Peter thinks I've weakened my position a great deal by assuming the role of mediator between Harold and Roy. 'You've got no gratitude from either side,' he said. 'Oh dear, why can't we get back to the old days when

[1] Secretary-General to the Commonwealth 1965–75. He had been Canadian Ambassador to the U.S.S.R. 1961–3 and Assistant Under-Secretary of State for External Affairs, Ottawa, 1963–5, and since 1975 has been Professor of International Affairs at Carleton University, Ottawa.

you and I were members of the same left-wing group?' It was a sad dinner and I sensed that the whole future of the D.E.A. is now in danger.

Thursday, February 15th

We started with our business meeting at No. 10, a day early because tomorrow Harold's off to South Wales for two days. At George Brown's excellent suggestion, John Silkin was invited. I had to raise the awkward issue of Stansted. I had just had a talk with the two Ministers and they had asked me to send a note to Harold, which I had duly done. The P.M. sat there looking very uncomfortable and I had to force him to see that we must have Stansted on the Cabinet agenda next Thursday and that if we were to avoid a catastrophic defeat in the House of Lords—which would also, incidentally, jeopardize Lords reform—we had to volunteer to have another inquiry. He finally agreed to put it on the agenda. What a tremendous lot I'm going to miss in Bermuda—one S.E.P. and at least two Cabinets. I'm not sure I shan't have to fly back on the Wednesday in time for the Thursday Cabinet.

Once again I felt that Harold was carefully keeping his distance from me. I haven't really spoken to him or phoned him since he came back from America and I feel a terrible sense of sitting near the centre and losing his confidence.

At Cabinet this morning the main issue was the Commonwealth Immigrants Bill. The Home Secretary wanted sanction for an immediate Bill. We turned him down because we considered it was ill thought out. Michael Stewart explained that though it might be necessary to impose a quota on Kenya Asians with British passports the controls on their entry to Britain must be quite different from the controls for people who are not British nationals. At the very least there must be a separate quota. 'Moreover,' said Michael, 'before we're driven to this we must make every kind of effort to reach an agreement with Kenyatta.'[1] So the week's delay which we proposed was a pretty good achievement. It was an interesting debate. Barbara was away because she is busy and, like the Lord Chancellor, had been against any Bill on principle. But the key thing to notice was that Roy Jenkins switched at the critical moment. After all, he had come to me last September to warn me that we might have to have this Bill early in the New Year and he had wanted me to slot it into the list and I had slotted it in. Yet on this occasion he showed himself, to put it mildly, unenthusiastic. He didn't give his support to Callaghan, partly because he hates him and partly because Roy was convinced that if we plunged into this in the kind of spirit Callaghan showed we would have offended every decent instinct.

[1] Jomo Kenyatta, a former Mau-Mau terrorist, was President of the Kenya Nationalist Union 1947–52, and is now Prime Minister (since 1963) and First President (since December 1964) of the Republic of Kenya.

Roy pleaded for delay whereas Harold was ready to impose the quota that very day.

In the afternoon my business Statement was routine. I had a lot of questions on Vietnam but the sting has gone out of the discussion that follows and I'm getting away with it more and more easily. Anyway I cleared it with Heath that I'll be away next week in Bermuda. This means missing the Tuesday Cabinet on Europe and foreign policy but not the Thursday Cabinet since I'll fly back on Wednesday.

I was able to use the Lobby conference that day for an off-the-record explanation of the Kenya problem. I tried to follow Harold's technique of adult education and explained all the difficult problems involved and how careful we must always be to make it clear that the Kenya Asians are British nationals unlike other restricted immigrants. I think the Lobby regards me as a well-informed Minister who can really help them and when a story becomes topical, as this did today, the Lobby can provide invaluable inspired news next morning. On the other hand, I know perfectly well that my colleagues are extremely jealous of me. In particular they dislike the feeling that I handle most of the Sunday press each week. This they hate and detest and Harold also detests and distrusts me, even though he's instructed me to brief these journalists. He's always looking out for leaks from Dick, taking the place of briefs from Dick. My position comes very badly out of this.*

Friday, February 16th
I was so worried about the exemption plan for prescription charges that I had asked Kenneth Robinson to look in this morning. There was no reason why the Lord President or the Leader of the House should summon him. Nevertheless he was glad to come and I found that he hadn't talked to a single Cabinet Minister since the last Cabinet on the subject. So far he had had one meeting with the doctors immediately after January 23rd and he had set his next meeting for February 16th, nearly a month later. In between his Permanent Secretary had been negotiating with the other interested parties. He told me that at the very first meeting the doctors had put forward an ingenious and superficially attractive scheme for a kind of Barclaycard —an embossed stamped card—which people would take to the chemist as evidence that they were genuinely exempted. I said, 'That sounds good,' and he said that the Ministry didn't like it. It seems to me strange that the

* My record in the diary was more prescient than I knew at the time. In his personal record Harold Wilson devotes a whole paragraph to the disastrous results of my press briefing on Thursday 15th and describes how next morning the whole press headlined a split in Cabinet over Kenya immigrants (see *Wilson*, p. 505). Fortunately I preserved the press cuttings which were supplied to Harold Wilson and which I also obtained as Lord President. On Friday 16th they show no news story of this kind at all. Indeed there was absolutely no evidence of any Cabinet division on this issue. I suspect that Mr Wilson got his impression from the fertile imagination of Mr Trevor Lloyd-Hughes.

Ministry should turn down a proposal put forward by the B.M.A. and I get the impression that there are some officials who still hope that the prescription charges will not be imposed. I finally told him that he must make his alternatives clear in a short paper and present it on Monday morning at 10.30, when we shall be grappling with the problem under Michael Stewart's chairmanship in the Cabinet Committee. Kenneth was friendly and easy and added, 'We'll get the exemptions in the end,' as though there was no hurry at all. He then explained to me how his constituency G.M.C. had voted by thirteen to five against prescription charges and ordered him to oppose them. Apparently the whole affair had been organized by a girl who works in the Research Department at Transport House. I hope I sent him away a little happier. I felt a good deal clearer myself and was able to report to the Chancellor through John Harris on how the exemption plan was going.

My next visitors were the two officials from the Commonwealth Department who were doing the latest paper on Rhodesia. As I've reported in this diary, a sub-committee with the Lord Chancellor in the chair had been persuaded by me to present to the O.P.D. not a consensus paper drafted by officials but an alternative paper showing what will happen if we make sanctions work and go even further, and what will happen if we try to get off the hook with as little damage as possible, two policies I've called activism and quietism. I found it fascinating to see what these two men had made of the paper. They had turned quietism into something covert and improper that would involve saying one thing in public and another in private. Indeed, the whole paper reeked with prejudice. So when they turned up to see me today I tried to make them realize what kind of paper I wanted and also what I meant by quietism. I suggested that it meant a 'non-enthusiastic execution'—working to rule, shall we say? And I added that working to rule is a perfectly acceptable thing which civil servants sometimes find it easy enough to do. But these civil servants were extremely difficult.

They were followed by John Harris who came with a message from Roy about the Kenya Asians. He told me that though Roy didn't feel as strongly as he did a few days ago, he felt there would be a major crisis in the Party unless this problem was handled carefully by the Home Secretary. I thoroughly agreed.

I had to be in the House just before four o'clock for the division on Airey Neave Mark II—the Private Member's Bill which promises to give pensions by statute to the over-eighties.[1] This time we're in a much stronger position since we haven't experimented with another George Wigg filibuster. Our administrative reasons for opposing this Bill are extremely strong: the abolition of National Assistance and the great widening of Supplementary Benefit has meant that four-fifths of the people affected are getting their

[1] The vote was 150 to 208 on the National Insurance (Further Provisions) Bill.

money already from the Supplementary Benefit Commission. The only issue is whether they should get it as of right in the form of a separate pension or from Supplementary Benefit. I'm convinced by my officials that if we concede it to the over-eighties as of right we break down the insurance principle. We got our majority of fifty-eight, thanks to hard work by the Whips.

This evening I went down to Oxford to stay with William and Iris Hayter and had a long talk with them in their cosy room in the Warden's Lodgings before going out to an undergraduate dinner to which he'd arranged for me to be invited. They both expressed the absolute contempt which Gordon Walker has aroused in the educational world, particularly among people friendly to Labour. Again it isn't the policy of postponing the raising of the school-leaving age which they object to. Many of them wholly approve. It's his combination of cuts and indecision and obvious weakness which upsets our supporters.

I was struck by this very much at dinner, where I found myself talking mostly to four or five senior grammar-school boys with long manes of hair and a beatlish manner and rather nice views. I saw a lot of two of them — one whose father is a clerk in the A.A., the other whose father is a congregational minister from New Zealand, a sort of David Frost type. Both told me how enormously excited their fathers had been about the election of the Labour Government and in particular about Harold Wilson going into No. 10. It was the great hope of their class that a man of their class would do something and so a sense of betrayal has bitten deep into the mind of the intelligentsia and it's going to be a tremendous task to rebuild Harold's reputation.

Sunday, February 18th
Last week's Gallup Poll showed a 22½ per cent Tory lead — an absolute record — and that is sustained by the monthly analysis which the N.O.P. does and which we also got today. It too rubs in the sensational decline in the Government's standing. The sad thing is that devaluation didn't do it. We had a real chance afterwards and our stock rallied a bit but in January came the announcement of the public expenditure cuts which sharply reduced Harold Wilson's prestige and the confidence in the Government. What I think is even more important is another figure revealed in the monthly analysis. 'Question: Do you think the Conservative leaders would have done any better or the same or worse?' The replies are, among Labour voters, 3 per cent think better, 61 per cent they would have done the same, 36 per cent think they would have done worse. This is the point on which we have to concentrate that for an ever-increasing number of Labour voters there is no difference between our Government and a Tory Government and the effect of the reimposition of prescription charges has greatly increased this feeling.

Though Ted Heath is still not popular, the decline in Harold's prestige is a blow to us. For the first couple of years he was such a brilliant personality that his personality carried the public even when the Government was doing unpopular things. Now there's a deep distrust of Harold by the public even when the Government is doing something of which it approves. What used to be our biggest positive asset has now become a negative quantity. It's also going to be a big task to rebuild the Party's reputation as long as Harold Wilson is leader. Yet I'm absolutely certain he'll remain leader unless there's a second devaluation and a national government, from which he is thrown out. All this means is that at the end of this week we're still slithering down-hill. We're faced with a catastrophic series of six by-elections[1] ahead of us and the knowledge that whether we have them in March or in May or in the autumn Meriden is bound to be lost, Dudley with a 10,000 majority is very unsafe, and even if Coventry East were fought today it would be unsafe, whereas the other two parts of Coventry would be certain losers.

Monday, March 4th[2]

This evening Roy had asked me to look in and I knew he wanted to talk to me again about the budget. He could hardly have been gloomier. He repeated that very few of the ghastly losses of the reserves we had suffered in devaluation week have come back to London since then and if they are ever to come back it will be in the two months after the budget. If confidence in the pound is not restored there could be a second devaluation within three months and in that case the Government won't survive. I replied that this was nonsense and that the Government could survive though maybe the Prime Minister could not. And I told Roy pretty clearly that if Harold had to go the Chancellor of the Exchequer was the only person who could take his place. 'After all,' I reminded him, 'Churchill was Minister of Defence when he took Chamberlain's place in 1940.' So he brushed this aside and repeated that the Government couldn't survive a second devalua-tion and that is why we had to have a tremendously effective budget.

I went on from No. 11 to George Weidenfeld's dinner where I met Natasha Spender, a most interesting woman with whom I got on fine.[3] But after dinner I found myself engaged in a furious discussion about immigration. On this issue the whole of the London intelligentsia—well-educated public opinion, people who read the weeklies, the *Guardian* and *The Times*, every virtuous person and of course the Churches—are united in denouncing the Immigration Act as the most shameful and disgraceful Act of any Govern-ment.[4] I know it's nothing of the kind. I feel deeply what Perry Worsthorne

---

[1] Dudley, Meriden, Acton, Oldham West, Sheffield Brightside, and Nelson and Colne.
[2] Apparently Crossman kept no record of events while he was away in Bermuda.
[3] Wife of Stephen Spender, the poet and critic. He was co-editor of *Encounter* 1953–67, and Professor of English at University College, London, 1970–75.
[4] On February 22nd the Home Secretary announced that emergency legislation would be introduced to restrict the entry of Kenya Asians to Britain, just as other Common-

said in the *Sunday Telegraph*—namely that we were right to push the Act through Parliament. We may have done it clumsily but we had to do this job and there is no public opposition to it. On the contrary, there's over-whelming public approval and the intellectuals who were denouncing it this evening are a small minority.

I was almost alone among the intellectuals and I found myself listening in particular to Pat Llewelyn-Davies and Anthony Lewis of the *New York Times*, while they assaulted and attacked me. I answered them back pretty effectively and they all rounded on me and complained that mine wasn't the case put forward in the debate. I'm afraid that's true. Once again our communications failed completely largely because of Jim Callaghan.

But this evening at George Weidenfeld's was a wonderful experience for me because I was on the top of my form in arguing an unpopular case and showing that our whole immigration policy had been right ever since 1964. We had had the courage to publish the Immigration White Paper in 1965,[1] which was bitterly attacked by every level. But it had worked—it had taken the poison out of politics so that in the 1966 election immigration was no longer a political issue—we were getting the social problem in the Midlands under control by severely limiting the incoming stream of immigrants and taking trouble in the schools. The intake was now at about the maximum. We could digest 50,000 at the very most. If that were doubled the whole of the good work we'd done in the last three years would break down and Powellism would become the philosophy of the Birmingham area. We were right to stop that. We were right to keep to a bipartisan policy. The Chief Whip and I were right to work through the usual channels in the Commons and get the Bill on the statute book in a very short time. Of course I admitted it was true that we should have taken infinitely more care. We should have got the tribunal's machinery established first. We should have taken the advice of the Archbishop's Advisory Committee on Immigration. We should perhaps have had even more preliminary negotiations with Commonwealth countries than we did. Yes, there were all kinds of things we could have done better but nevertheless the basic decision was right. I enjoyed waging my lonely defensive battle at Weidenfeld's party that evening.

Tuesday, March 5th
I had to go to No. 10 for a special Cabinet Committee on gas prices. There'd been a thoroughly boring meeting on this topic last week with the P.M. repeating endlessly that no big private business would finance an enormous

wealth citizens were restricted. There was to be a new category of vouchers for up to 1,500 Kenya Asians a year, allowing, with dependants, some 7,000 immigrants. The Bill was introduced on February 27th and all its stages were swiftly pushed through the Commons and Lords so that it received the Royal Assent on March 1st.
[1] The White Paper (Cmnd. 2739) of August 1965 had announced a reduction in the provision of entry vouchers for Commonwealth immigrants from 208,000 per annum to 8,500.

improvement of technique leading to cheaper prices (natural gas was what he meant) by putting the burden on the consumer. We must look again at the chances for the Gas Board to raise the capital for the switch to natural gas in other ways. All this talk from Harold was devastated by a report from the Economic Advisers which showed that the load was *not* being put on the consumer and that the Gas Board was raising most of the money by borrowing. So we'd just have to face the increased prices which the Prices and Incomes Board had now finally agreed.

Of course this will make it even more difficult to have an effective prices and incomes policy and this was what had alarmed the P.M.[1] So we next discussed how to sell the increases and here the Prime Minister began to have second thoughts about the dates of the by-elections. He had tentatively decided to put them just after the budget but now he realized this would be when these new increases of gas, electricity and transport charges would be just announced. Nobody at the meeting thought there was any chance of winning Meriden, Dudley and Acton, but we should be in real trouble with our constituency parties if we announced these price increases just when they were beginning the election campaign.

Cabinet followed immediately afterwards and we began with a great attack against Harold and Roy for their prices and incomes policy by George Brown and James Callaghan. George Brown had resigned in 1966 on the issue of statutory sanctions and he repeated once again that the trade unions wouldn't take this and it really wouldn't work. Callaghan went very much further. He said he thought that it would be difficult to get any legislation through Parliament and anyway would new legislative sanctions in fact keep wage levels down? Wasn't it true, he asked, that despite our prices and incomes policy wages had probably gone up by roughly the same amount as if we'd had no prices and incomes policy at all? So the battle went on and on and a decision was postponed till next Tuesday.

We just had time to turn to family allowances which has been for so long the bitterest cause of disagreement in Cabinet. Now we were able to hear that a quite reasonable arrangement had been agreed between the Chancellor and Judith Hart.

On the way back to my office it suddenly occurred to me that to break the prices and incomes deadlock we must get hold of Aubrey Jones and collect some better evidence than we'd had in the previous discussion. So I asked myself to lunch with him tomorrow.

[1] The 1967 Prices and Incomes Act was due to expire on August 11th, 1968, and the Government were considering new powers to replace the old legislation, with the hope, once again, that both employers and unions would exercise voluntary restraint so that compulsory powers need only be used as a last resort. In the White Paper (Cmnd. 3590) provisions of a new Bill were set out. There was to be a 3½ per cent ceiling on wage increases except in cases of genuine productivity deals. The Government were to be empowered to delay price and wage increases for a further twelve months, to limit increases in rents and dividends and to order price reductions on the recommendation of the P.I.B. These powers would continue until December 3rd, 1969.

I had to be on the front bench in time for the Prime Minister's Questions that afternoon because there was one on my Birmingham speech from Freddie Bennett.[1] Fortunately he's one of the most unpopular M.P.s on his own side and he didn't get much support when he started calling the Prime Minister 'devious'. Finally, after about five or six minutes Harold got up to defend me and used a phrase I knew he would use which punctured the whole balloon. When he sat down he said to me he'd had a much more difficult time when I was in Bermuda and he had to answer Questions about the remarks I had made on Scottish and Welsh devolution. He seemed pleasant and in good form at that particular moment and he had certainly finally dealt with the after-effects of my Birmingham speech. I had fretted and worried about this a good deal and it was a relief to feel that it was over.

This was the second day of the debate on the Defence White Paper[2] and we were due to hear a big speech by Heath. But I couldn't wait because I was chairing the Cabinet Committee on devolution. On the way out I ran into Roy Jenkins and told him I was going to ask Aubrey Jones about the practicability of the scheme outlined in the Prices and Incomes White Paper. 'Are you irrevocably committed to this ridiculous scheme?' I said, to which he replied that he didn't see how they could drop it now without terrible effects. This of course is what Tony Crosland has also been saying. The difficulty is all owing to leaks in the papers saying that the Government is now firmly committed to a 3½ per cent ceiling and statutory control of decisions at plant level, whatever that means. I said, 'Honestly, Roy, it's impossible and I'm afraid you'll have to drop it,' and he replied firmly, 'Well, there will be very big consequential changes if I drop it.' So we left each other, he looking very unhappy and twisted, and I went back to my room to get ready for the meeting on devolution. It was quite successful. I was tactful enough merely to take the chair and to leave the running to our friend Cledwyn Hughes from Wales and Norman Buchan from Scotland. Several of the younger Ministers were here—Shirley Williams, Dick Taverne,[3] Eirene White—all talking freely. They all seemed to enjoy a meeting where there was something new to discuss for a change.

In the evening I'd asked Karl Miller to have dinner with me.[4] For a short time he was the distinguished literary editor of the New Statesman but

[1] Sir Frederick Bennett, Conservative M.P. for Reading North 1951–5 and for Torbay since December 1955.

[2] The Statement on Defence 1968 (Cmnd. 3540).

[3] Dick Taverne, Q.C., Labour M.P. for Lincoln from March 1962 to 1974. He resigned the Labour whip in October 1972. He was elected Democratic Labour M.P. for that constituency in February 1974 but was defeated in October 1974. He was Parliamentary Under-Secretary of State at the Home Office 1968–9 and Financial Secretary to the Treasury 1969–70.

[4] Literary editor of the Spectator 1958–61 and of the New Statesman 1961–7. He was then editor of the Listener until 1974, when he became Northcliffe Professor of Modern English Literature at University College, London.

apparently he quarrelled with Paul Johnson and went straight over to the
Listener, which he has transformed into the liveliest weekly of our time,
much to the fury of the *Spectator* and the *New Statesman* because they think
it's unfair for a subsidized B.B.C. weekly to compete directly for their
readers. He's a sly Scot and I had an enjoyable evening discussing the *New
Statesman* with him, discussing the editorship of John Freeman,[1] who of
course is now going to be our Ambassador in the U.S.A., chatting about
the purpose of a weekly in the modern world and whether I really would
have been happy as editor of the *New Statesman*. I enjoyed myself so much
that I missed Denis Healey's wind-up. The defence debate was a complete
flop because our left-wing back-benchers had held their own meeting in a
committee room and decided not to vote against it. Healey made the kind
of insulting wind-up which makes people walk out. Apart from that today's
proceedings petered out—satisfactorily for the Party managers.

Wednesday, March 6th
This was the day of the execution of three African resistance leaders in
Rhodesia sentenced over three years ago.[2] It was announced on the B.B.C.
in the morning and I knew we would be in for trouble from our back-
benchers.

But my first job was to chair the Cabinet Committee on Electoral
Representation which is going through all the recommendations of the
Speaker's Conference and of the Home Secretary's Electoral Committee.
I sit in the chair, Callaghan has the brief. This was an extremely interesting
example of the new relaxed Callaghan, liberated from the burdens of
Chancellorship. He came along, sat down and said breezily, 'Well I have
an 85-page memorandum from my officials and I've boiled it down to six
pages since I didn't think you people wanted to waste time on all the details.'
I said mildly that we would have to go through all the proposals one by one,
and as we went through it was clear that the Home Secretary hadn't bothered
to read his brief very carefully and I had to have half a dozen points referred
back before the Committee could reach a reasonable decision. For example,
the Speaker's Conference has recommended that if a postal voter spoils his
ballot paper he can get a new one. It's true that if you spoil your ballot
paper in the polling booth you can get a new one so there's logic in this
recommendation. Callaghan simply told the Committee that administratively

---

[1] Labour M.P. for Watford, and a Bevanite, from 1945 to 1951, when he resigned his
post at the Ministry of Supply on the rearmament issue. Like Crossman, he was a *New
Statesman* journalist and in 1951 he became assistant editor, succeeding Kingsley Martin
as editor in 1961. He served as High Commissioner in India 1965–8 and as Ambassador
in Washington 1969–71. Since 1971 he has been chairman and chief executive of London
Weekend Television.

[2] The Rhodesian regime ignored the Royal Prerogative of Mercy, by which the Queen,
acting on the advice of the Commonwealth Secretary, had on March 2nd commuted the
sentence to life imprisonment. On March 4th the Rhodesian Appeal Court ruled that the
British Government had no right to give the monarch such advice.

it was too much nuisance. I told the Committee that in principle we should be in favour of implementing whatever the Speaker's Conference recommended.

As soon as possible I went across to the Parliamentary Party which was discussing the prices and incomes policy. While I was in Bermuda Harold had decided to make the first speech with George Brown winding up. But George Brown had a cold and Harold decided to do both speeches himself. When I heard this I thought it was a thoroughly bad thing but actually it turned out very well indeed. Harold had written out every word of his first speech and it was perfectly sensible. The central theme was that if we're going to save the money wage in a devaluation we must cut the social wage. The one irresponsible thing is to pretend that we can afford to have no cuts in public expenditure and no cuts in wages either. He made his point very well but it was a dull pedestrian speech, and I fear the Party paid no very close attention. Yet right at the end when he wound up informally and was talking *ad lib* everybody attended to what he said. He was getting *en rapport* with the comrades and the difference was amazing. Nevertheless, what stuck in my mind (and also got into the press) was a tiff between the P.M. and Maurice Edelman. Maurice made a very good speech about how we must make the prices and incomes policy work at the grass-roots level and listen to ordinary people in the factories when we're drafting legislation. But after that Maurice had become rather more offensive in his references to the Government and in his *ex tempore* reply Harold remarked tartly, 'I wish that those who have the opportunity to write for the press and get more columns of press for themselves than any Minister can would sometimes put the Government's case.' Up jumps Maurice Edelman to reply, 'My job is an independent conscientious job. I must not put the Government's case but my own opinion.' That gave Harold his chance and he snapped back, 'Well, of course, you must put your own opinion. If you put the Government's case you wouldn't be working very long for your firm, the *Daily Express*.' Wild atmosphere, up stood Maurice, points of order, and Douglas Houghton smacked him down and ordered him to leave the room. I think Maurice enjoyed it but Harold several times sent for him this afternoon to settle it with him. It shows how sensitive Harold is.

My lunch with Aubrey Jones took place at the Stafford Hotel, in the little room in which our wedding breakfast took place fourteen years ago. As soon as he bustled in I asked him whether he'd seen Peter Shore's new scheme. He said that he hadn't got it officially but his officials read all the papers and therefore he had access to it. 'What did you think of it?' I asked. 'Wholly impractical, absolutely impractical to have any control at plant level. It means taking on the responsibility for the whole economic climate and taking the blame for every shower. Anyway,' he added, 'it would mean bypassing the Prices and Incomes Board.' It was clear that in the preparation of this plan Peter had not consulted Aubrey Jones. Though Aubrey had been permitted to submit a paper to Peter and Roy he hadn't received acknowledgment. Our whole interview was very cool and detached and I learnt all I needed from him. Then he asked me to fill him in on the future of the House of Lords, which is obviously something which interests him vitally. So that I did before I went away.

At the last moment I'd had to arrange for three Statements after Questions that afternoon—first George Thomson on Rhodesia, then Fred Peart on the Farm Price Review[1] and finally Dick Marsh on North Sea gas. I thought George Thomson did his job absolutely magnificently. He's extremely skilled at this kind of representational Statement and obviously felt deeply about the issue. What was odious was the row from behind with Andrew Faulds asking for the hanging of the hangman and working up an agitation for military sanctions to destroy the White Rhodesians. This issue has now become a hysterical crusade in the hearts of some of our back-benchers and unfortunately Harold half shares the hysteria. But Thomson damped it down and was very shrewd in his own particular way. After that Fred Peart was lucky because his Farm Price Review came as an anticlimax, and when he said that the N.F.U. were neutral in their opinion there was nothing more to discuss. Actually we hadn't conceded nearly as much to the farmers as we'd thought necessary to keep them quiet. After this the House was too tired to react to the Statement on gas.

At four o'clock I was due for a talk with the P.M., the first I've had with him since our blow-up before I went to Bermuda. I wouldn't say the situation has been festering since then but we've been settling down into a new rather distant relationship. We started by discussing the Party meeting and I emphasized the contrast between the effect of his written speech and his informal remarks at the end. Next, I vainly tried to cool his excitement about Edelman and to persuade the P.M. not to summon him. Then we came to prices and incomes and I told him about my lunch with Aubrey Jones and how he had told me that he hadn't been consulted on the Shore scheme and that he thought it completely impractical. The P.M. promised to see Aubrey Jones at seven o'clock this evening and Peter at 7.15; here I felt I might really have achieved something quite important.

The terrifying thing is that this hare-brained scheme was approved by the Prime Minister, Roy Jenkins, Tony Crosland, Ray Gunter and Peter Shore without any attempt to test it out upon anybody who could calculate its practical consequences.

This evening I was off with Anne. We decided not to go to the cinema, not to go to the opera, just to have dinner at home with each other. And that's exactly what we did on the one day she'd been able to come up to London. When we'd just got into bed I was rung by the Whips because they only had a majority of twenty-one at the end of the Territorial Army debate and Brian O'Malley was ringing round to make sure people were

[1] In which agriculture was to receive, overall, £52½ million in subsidies.

paired.[1] I said everything was in order, I'd been paired—and we went to sleep.

Thursday, March 7th

Lying in bed listening to the eight o'clock news I suddenly heard a long item about how Barbara Castle wanted to guillotine the Transport Bill and that the Leader of the House had refused to concede this to her because he couldn't spare time for the debate. I twigged straightaway. We have an understanding between the usual channels that we allow the Shadow Cabinet to see the proposed business of the following week each Wednesday, and so as soon as it's ready we send it over to them on the clear understanding that they leak nothing to the press. This week after it had gone to the Shadow Cabinet Peter Walker had given it to the press. This infuriated Willie Whitelaw, who immediately informed Heath and protested to his colleagues. Nevertheless, the damage had been done. I rang up the Chief and said I must announce a guillotine this afternoon instead of keeping the news secret until Monday and then suddenly releasing it, which would have been of assistance to Barbara. So the Chief and I had to do a lot of running around before Cabinet this morning.

As a result of the Rhodesian executions we were bound to have a speech from Barbara Castle in Cabinet demanding that we should think again about military sanctions. But nobody else was prepared to listen. George Brown, Denis Healey, George Thomson, Tony Crosland and Roy Jenkins all want to damp this down because they see the danger of committing ourselves any further. If only Harold Wilson shared Barbara's mood of excitement. His new idea was an all-party resolution to be drafted by the Lord Chancellor. We discussed this and agreed it.

Then we turned back to prices and incomes, which was on the agenda because of the powerful resistance to Peter Shore's plan that had been registered at last week's Cabinet. The counter-attack was delivered by the Chancellor of the Exchequer and was so terrifying that it was not recorded in Cabinet minutes. What he said was roughly what he had said to me on Monday evening. He described the terrible dangers we were now in and the pressure on the pound in the markets and also the pressure of the I.M.F. He put it to the Cabinet even more strongly than he put it to me that a second devaluation would occur within the next three months if the budget didn't restore confidence in sterling. This is exactly what Cecil King had said to me in January. At that time it had been indignantly repudiated by everyone. But he had been proved right and Roy was now drawing the conclusion that in such a case the Government couldn't survive. This was the big stick with which he decided to beat Cabinet into accepting a tremendous budget and also accepting the prices and incomes policy.

Everyone listened dutifully but very soon all the doubts and queries were

[1] In the debate on the Territorial Army the vote was in fact 177 to 200.

raised all over again quite simply because no member of Cabinet could understand the proposal that wage decisions at plant level should be checked. When he was put under cross-examination Peter Shore collapsed. He was asked whether there would be five, ten or fifteen thousand of these decisions to be settled in a month or a year and it was clear that he had no idea. He was told to produce an alternative scheme for next Tuesday.

At his Question Time this afternoon the P.M. was in fine form. In an answer on Rhodesia he made it practically impossible to resume talks with Smith by describing him and his government as wicked and evil men, thereby pretty well scuppering the proposals Alec Douglas-Home has just brought back from Salisbury.[1] I doubt if Alec feels sore about it because he knows how very remote they were. It's already clear that the Tories feel that a final burning of the bridges would be a terrible thing and they don't want to see us delivered to the United Nations, who will only hoist us on a wave of further sanctions which might roll us nearer and nearer to the confrontation with South Africa which we must avoid at almost all costs. But the P.M. is on his Rhodesian high horse and nothing can stop him talking in this style.

When I got up to make my business Statement I announced the guillotine and a howl of indignation rose from the Opposition. This is the kind of thing which really rouses Ted Heath and this evening after the 1922 Committee he slammed down a vote of censure on the Leader of the House. Well, it's all routine parliamentary stuff and all it means is that I've got to prepare a good well-reasoned speech for the guillotine motion. True, Barbara's Bill is a monstrous Bill and if we were in opposition we'd be just as angry as they are today.

At my press conference I told the Lobby, as Harold had said I could, that a meeting of the three Party leaders was to take place to discuss the possibility of an all-party motion on Rhodesia. Then Harold sent for me. I guessed before I got there that he was worried about the P.A. account of an all-party motion but I hadn't foreseen how furious he would be. This is the kind of thing which really infuriates him. He walked about the room chewing his lips with anger and then he gradually recovered his temper and became quite decent to me. But I had already deeply upset him. I said, 'Well, you told me to say that talks were going on.' 'But not about an all-party motion and now Heath will probably turn it down. He will think your remarks were a trick to catch him so he'd have to agree.' I replied that Heath would think no such thing. Either he would accept the motion

---

[1] Sir Alec Douglas-Home had been in South Africa to discuss whether a future Conservative Government could resume the supply of arms, and on his return journey he had seen Ian Smith in Salisbury and emphasized the need to agree to the five principles before legal independence could be granted. Sir Alec and Mr Smith had detailed talks on two principles (those dealing with unimpeded progress towards African majority rule) but the mathematics of the voting arrangements Mr Smith suggested turned out to be to the Africans' electoral disadvantage.

or he would reject it and state his reasons why. In neither case would Heath think that I had been instructed to set a trap for him.

Before our weekly meeting at No. 10 in the evening George Brown told me he wanted to stay behind and talk to the P.M. about the Shore plan for prices and incomes. Fortunately the weekly meeting didn't take too long and as soon as Burke Trend had withdrawn George started off by proposing a deal to Harold. 'I'll take Parts I and II,' he said, 'if you will drop Parts III and IV.' All these numbers refer to a paper cooked up by Burke Trend at the last moment outlining the three possibilities: (1) maintaining the existing state of prices and incomes; (2) implementing Part II of the 1966 Act; and (3) taking new powers required to implement the Shore plan. Despite Burke Trend's paper every member of Cabinet knows there has got to be a new Bill which we fight through Parliament and put on the statute book. In terms of the parliamentary situation, we also know that it doesn't make much difference whether the Bill is a good one or a bad one, workable or unworkable. However it is written the minority left-wing militants will oppose it and the moderates will support it. But this evening George emphasized that outside the House of Commons the actual terms of the Bill may make all the difference. He believes we ought to extend the period of retrospective control from two to three months and in exchange give up this whole idea of wage control at plant level. The P.M. listened carefully but was very cagey. Of course he was, because he has agreed the Shore plan with Roy and Tony Crosland. Then suddenly George Brown switched his line and said, 'But what about the inner Cabinet, Harold? Why should we always discuss things like this at the last moment? Why don't we get together as a group?' For twenty minutes he kept urging the P.M. to form the inner group and said that he had promised this before devaluation. 'Ah,' said the P.M., 'but of the seven or eight names we mentioned then, two are hopelessly unsuitable now.' 'That may be so,' said George, 'but we must have an inner group. Pull yourself together, Harold, and get on with forming it.' All this was music in my ears. I stayed quiet and supported George mildly but as the two of us went out of the door I turned and said, 'George, there isn't a chance. He can't do it. It's not in his nature.' George replied, 'But you heard what he said just now, that it can only happen after the reshuffle and that won't be very long.' It's true, he had actually used these words, 'The shuffle won't be very long now.' My God, I wish I could be moved in the shuffle but I don't think he'll do it and I've got no faith in the formation of an inner group. At present we've got a Harold/Roy dyarchy—two extremely uncommunicative suspicious men who are working together tolerably well, who know the budget secrets and are keeping them to themselves. That's not the situation in which an inner group develops.

Friday, March 8th
We started with a big O.P.D. meeting on Rhodesia. I've described in this

diary the goings-on in the Lord Chancellor's Committee where Caradon and I have been fighting the battle between activism, which means intensifying sanctions, and quietism, which I describe as working to rule. This morning Harold started by saying that in the new situation the paper we drafted describing these two alternatives is out of date. No one can now say that after the executions we ought to consider quietism. We have got to think how we can handle the situation vigorously and suddenly Harold was plunging in on ideas about further sanctions, cutting off television programmes, jamming radio broadcasts. Thank heavens Denis Healey held firm and told the P.M. that we ought to have a look at the situation. 'Do you want to intensify sanctions and expose the European nations who are letting their goods go through, Prime Minister?' he asked. 'Haven't we got to bear in mind the cost to our European policy of another plunge forward in Rhodesia?' George Brown supported him, Tony Crosland supported him and I said, 'I think we ought to look at this again, Harold. It's no good saying the long-term strategy is outdated by the new situation, it's made more relevant.' And then came a long discussion in which it was clear that he had the full support of the Lord Chancellor and the Attorney-General. Against him were ranged the Defence Secretary, the Foreign Secretary, the Commonwealth Secretary, Tony Crosland and me. Nevertheless I predict that in the end Harold will get his way because we can't stop him. We shall go on plunging ever deeper into the morass.

After Cabinet the P.M. talked to me again about the press and the Rhodesian all-party motion. As a matter of fact we'd got an excellent press this morning. I'd been an honest broker and told the truth and done nobody any harm. Nevertheless Trevor Lloyd-Hughes had been put up to issue a denial saying the P.A.'s statement was a mistake and I had been told to offer to come to Heath's room and apologize to him. The offer was made but Heath hadn't even bothered to see me. I don't blame him in the least because he was frankly bewildered at what on earth I had to apologize to him for. If only Harold could concentrate his mind not on leaks and technical press problems but on the quality of leadership shown by Ministers in their Departments and on central strategy, how much better off we should be. And here he was this morning still fussing about this and even about Maurice Edelman.

I got back to my room in the Privy Council to find Richard Titmuss waiting to see me. I was deeply touched because all he wanted was to make it clear that he hadn't broken with the Labour Party as had been stated in the press while I was in Bermuda. 'I had to make all those statements about the Kenya Asian Bill,' he said, 'in order to keep the coloured members of the Archbishop's Advisory Committee on Immigration from resigning. I didn't want them to break up the Committee. I now see that there's been no real racialism displayed by the Cabinet but only a terrible administrative muck-up. Callaghan has been extraordinarily incompetent and it really was almost inconceivable that he should make such a decision without consulting the Archbishop's Immigration Committee. But I don't believe his failure to do so had an evil intent and I've come to tell you I haven't broken off from the Labour Party and I still want to help.' 'Right,' I said, 'the best help you can give is to tell the P.M. what your wishes are on this matter and insist on getting your way.' And with his help I wrote an urgent minute to Harold telling him that the Archbishop's Immigration Committee insists that the conciliation tribunals be established by Act of Parliament before the end of Human Rights Year.

At my press lunch at the Garrick this week we had five number two men plus Henry James. Apart from my Thursday Lobby conference this is the only regular press contact I've kept. Otherwise I've scrapped every contact with individual pressmen as well as all my evening meetings with junior Ministers in order to teach Harold Wilson that I'm not going to tolerate accusations of leaking. I've been able to keep the press lunch because I always have Henry James there as well as at the Lobby so that he can report exactly what I say to Trevor Lloyd-Hughes and Harold. On this occasion I briefed them as fully as I possibly could on prices and incomes.

I had my routine meeting of the Home Publicity Committee and at the end we just touched for a moment on preparations for the budget and I remarked that we've this year got two things to do. We've got to sell the budget as a budget and we've got to sell the prices and incomes policy as an integral part of one single strategy alongside the budget linking this up with the public expenditure cuts of last January, so that the package is seen as a whole. This seemed obvious enough to me but immediately I was in a host of difficulties. It was explained to me that the Chancellor would be making his budget Statement on Tuesday and Peter Shore would not be speaking till Thursday. So Peter wanted to reserve all he had to say about prices and incomes for his Thursday speech and he didn't want to see anything put out in the Tuesday brief along with the budget and the Chancellor's Statement. 'You can't expect me to have the best part of my speech anticipated in the Tuesday handout,' he said to me sharply. This shows how quickly really intelligent socialists can become departmental Ministers rather than members of a team. Peter Shore's speech on Thursday won't have much effect since he's a bad speaker anyway and his speeches don't count. What matters to the future of the pound sterling and the existence of this Government is the impact we make in the first forty-eight hours after the budget. What's to do? Can I arrange for Shore to speak a day earlier, or find any other way of avoiding a terrible situation where colleagues begin to think entirely of their own speeches and their own personal success and not of the general appeal of what the Government is doing?

After this I caught a train to Derby for the annual dinner of the highly marginal South-East Derbyshire constituency. It's a fairly hopeless constituency which Trevor Park has held in this Parliament and is most unlikely to hold in the next.[1] But the evening was a tremendous success. They had excellent tap-dancing, a first-rate band and in the middle they jammed my speech. It's the fairly standard speech which I make now about communication between Government and Party and how the Party must put over the things the Government is doing for ordinary people. Nevertheless they were in the mood to cheer me and they sang 'For he's a jolly good fellow'. But when that was over, one after another they came and took me aside to tell me how hopeless the prospects are and how the Government must do better. Anne motored me back down the motorway and in less than two hours we were home and in bed in time for the full quiet weekend on which I now insist.

Sunday, March 10th

Yesterday's papers were dominated by the success of the Cambridge Left in nearly breaking up Denis Healey's meeting as effectively as they'd broken up the Prime Minister's meeting a few weeks ago. Nevertheless, once he got inside he seems to have had quite a success.

On the wireless today I heard one of the Cambridge Proctors[2] talking about the students' attitude and not mentioning undergraduates. I think that at the old universities part of the trouble comes because everybody is a student now, not an undergraduate. We have vastly inflated the student population and brought into our universities hundreds of people who haven't got middle-class backgrounds or bookish backgrounds and who really don't know how to spend three years studying. We have, in fact, enlarged our universities too rapidly with the result that we're getting a number of students who can't become undergraduates or assimilate into university life.

Last night I was reading the monthly report of the National Opinion Poll. There hasn't been much further decline in our popularity. But then it couldn't go down much further than it went last month. What the analysis shows in great detail is the declining confidence not only in the Government but in all politicians. But this works out mainly in huge abstentions of Labour voters. We can get no kind of vote in any election at present and we're looking forward to disastrous local elections and disastrous by-elections because of this almost universal sense that the Government has failed the country and that it's not worth voting for a Cabinet who aren't in control of the situation. Well, that's the end of the week. Not a cheerful week for the Government or the country but for me and my personal relations with Harold perhaps a little less bleak than it was before.

---

[1] Labour M.P. for South-East Derbyshire 1964–70 and, since 1971, lecturer in Industrial Relations, University of Leeds.

[2] Dons with responsibility for the order and discipline of undergraduates in the university.

Monday, March 11th

I started with an interesting and unusual Cabinet Committee which had to decide whether departmental Ministers should be allowed to express their personal views on Private Members' Bills for which the Government provides time while remaining neutral. The row started with the Sunday Entertainments Bill where, as usual, we had decided to declare neutrality but wanted to give time for a House of Commons decision. Now here we had a really formidable small pressure group—the non-conformist Welsh teetotallers—who strongly objected to our giving even neutral support to the Bill. So George Thomas came to Cabinet and demanded the right to speak against Sunday opening even though he has nothing to do with the Home Office and just wants to express his views as a lay preacher. Thomas was surprisingly but strongly supported by Jim Callaghan who asked why, if on the Abortion Bill Roy Jenkins is allowed to give positive arguments in favour of abortion, George Thomas shouldn't speak against this? The difficulty of course is that in the case of the Abortion Bill and the Sexual Offences Bill, and now Sunday Entertainments, the Government hasn't really been behaving neutrally. Quite deliberately as Leader of the House I've made sure that we're getting the best of both worlds. We're using Private Members' Bills to get through a number of controversial social measures which the public overwhelmingly wants but which had previously been blocked by the obstruction of small well-organized pressure groups. Roy made no attempt to disguise the fact that as a liberal Home Secretary he was supporting the Abortion Bill and the Sexual Offences Bill. And Callaghan has a reasonable case for saying that if the agnostic liberals of the Cabinet are permitted to peddle their views in these debates why shouldn't the religious reactionaries do the same? There is really no answer to this objection and Michael Stewart and I both tried to evolve a sensible middle position which laid down that no Minister should express his strong personal opinions when intervening from the front bench on a Private Member's Bill. A Minister should merely intervene in a helpful way to get the Bill tidied up. We couldn't get anything like unanimity for what was regarded as a washy position but I know very well as Leader of the House that I at least must maintain the principle of neutrality. The Divorce Reform Bill, for example, has just got its Second Reading. We must now wait and see how it fares in Committee and if it isn't getting on fast enough I must then be able to say that the House wants a decision one way or the other and I am going to allocate more time. My neutrality is therefore important.

I had a rather delayed lunch with Alec Spearman, who is still anxious to talk about the lessons of the Bermuda talks. His conclusion this year is that Bermuda has become an unsatisfactory and, from the British point of view, extremely expensive compromise. It costs a fortune to get us there and pay our hotel bills while we are there but unfortunately so long as we live in hotels in the main town we see very little of the Americans apart from the formal hours spent in conference. His idea is to invite them next time to a conference in Ditchley Park where there will be a standard of comfort they will admire but also a chance of talking to them out of school as well as in school. I think the simplest solution is to keep the talks in Bermuda, which is now the established meeting place, but to have them at one of the magnificent golf clubs well out of the town (the Mid-Ocean course, for example, where the Churchill–Eisenhower conference took place) where we could really be alone with the Americans and see much more of them.

My next visitor was John Boyd-Carpenter, who is now quite an important person in my parliamentary life. He is the chairman of the informal committee I have established to consider the common problems of all Select and Specialist Committees: problems of travel, for example, the hiring of research investigators and other such matters. He told me that they are having some difficulty in controlling the amount of money the Select and Specialist Committees allot for research expenditure. It sounds ludicrous that a Specialist Committee can hire as many research workers as it wants without any exterior control but that seems to be the existing situation. Barlas,[1] one of the ablest of the Clerks and Secretary of the informal committee, told me the other day that the Services Committee had not reached any firm agreement that his committee should deal with research grants as well as with foreign travel. Perhaps unwisely I was rather sharp to Barlas and said we damn well had decided and he wasn't to tell me that we hadn't. Whereupon he had gone back, talked to John Boyd-Carpenter and made sure that his chairman decided against me. One can very rarely defeat a civil servant or a Clerk when he's really determined and on strong ground.

Aubrey Jones had asked to see me this afternoon. I had a very difficult interview with him because, though I like him and he's extremely able, he's also extremely slippery and you can never discover exactly where he is standing. At the lunch we had together he claimed he knew what was in Shore's paper and thought it completely unworkable. This afternoon he claimed that he didn't know the scheme in detail and only had access to it after he had seen the P.M. Certainly he's now much more moderate about its total impracticality. I suppose when he gave me lunch he was playing the oldest trick in the world and pretending to knowledge in order to obtain it. Anyway, now he has obviously been interviewed by Roy Jenkins and is convinced that we must have at least the appearance of a strong incomes policy for the next three months in order to avoid a second devaluation. This time he almost said to me that whether the Shore scheme was workable or not it had to be supported. On the other hand he detests the idea that all

[1] Richard Barlas was Second Clerk-Assistant 1962–75, Clerk-Assistant 1975–6, and became Clerk of the House in July 1976.

the references should go through the Prices and Incomes Board since there might be thousands of plant decisions and he would be turned into a kind of passport office for the Government. Nevertheless, he sees that the Government can't possibly take on this responsibility directly and so he wants to see the Ministry of Labour doing a good deal of screening before any references come to him. As for the 3½ per cent ceiling, he told me it was quite unrealistic since wage drift by itself probably comes to 3½ per cent. But he realizes that after the leaks we shall probably have to stick to it.

Next I had to go downstairs to the liaison committee with John Silkin for the special meeting which had been called to consider whether under the new code of conduct the Chief Whip should be given the right to fix and to extend the period during which he can suspend a member. Oh dear, this damned code of conduct. During my absence in Bermuda the Chief and Douglas Houghton have been at loggerheads over its interpretation. How right Manny Shinwell was when he warned us right at the beginning that with so many lawyers in the Party one could spend infinite time on introducing a new code of conduct. Anyway this liaison committee is not an ideal body to consider such esoteric matters. We have little Eddie Milne, a miner who represents Blyth, who wobbles to and fro. He opposed John last time and, rebuked by his colleagues, had come over to our side this time. There is Joyce thingummy[1] from Wood Green—dry, tight-lipped, uncooperative—and Willie Hamilton. Willie is a schoolteacher by profession —an anti-royalist by repute. In addition to these three there is Douglas Houghton in the chair, Joe Champion harmlessly representing the House of Lords,[2] John Silkin and myself and the Secretary, Frank Barlow. It was an interminable meeting because Houghton had come along with his own new draft of the Silkin document to which he wanted to add notes and commentaries as well before presenting it to the Party meeting. We did not get very far.

Tuesday, March 12th
As soon as we sat down around the Cabinet table the Chief Whip threw a note across to me saying that if we had a Rhodesia debate on Thursday this week we could get out of the guillotine motion. I was absolutely bewildered and I still don't know quite what he meant. He told me afterwards that he thought Barbara didn't want the guillotine on Thursday because she had persuaded Roy Jenkins to take a large section of her Transport Bill into the Finance Bill and that would mean less pressure on her timetable. But that won't do. I suspected that John had got cold feet about Thursday's guillotine and wanted to get out of it. I threw a note across to him saying,

---

[1] Joyce Butler.

[2] Lord Champion, a former railway signalman, who was Labour M.P. for Derbyshire South-East from 1945 to September 1959. He became a life peer in 1962 and was Deputy Leader of the House of Lords 1964–7. The Labour peers elect one of their number as a back-bench representative at the liaison committee.

'Nonsense, we must get on with it.' So back we were again on a third paper from Peter Shore about prices and incomes. This is the new scheme which Harold made him produce as a result of George Brown's pressure at our meeting with Harold ten days ago. No longer was the Government to take responsibility for all wage settlements at plant level. Now it was merely to control those which exceeded the limit and these are going to be screened through the Prices and Incomes Board. In addition it isn't going to be the individual agreements but totality of the wages given out by the firm which will be under review. In fact Peter's scheme has been enormously watered down and in this new paper even retrospection was treated as a dubious experiment.

For once the discussion was useful. As it went on it became clearer and clearer that whether we should have another dose of retrospection depended on whether we were going to continue the policy for twelve months or keep it as a virtual permanency. If we just meant to go on forbidding retrospective agreements for the next twelve months, people would simply postpone wage agreements for that time and pay up at the end. But if we gave the impression that we might have an annual renewal of our legislation, then the principle of retrospective payments could become less attractive. Suddenly there dawned a collective realization in Cabinet that if we were going to make this thing stick the simplest way was to show that we recognized P.I. as a permanency and that there must be some statutory backing to watch it develop into a voluntary scheme and that we were going to submit whatever statutory backing we had to annual review. Harold had the brilliant idea that we could include the legislation in the Expiring Laws Continuance Bill. What seemed to come out of the meeting was a general agreement that we needed (1) a $3\frac{1}{2}$ per cent ceiling; (2) a 12-month period of statutory renewal; and (3) no retrospection.

We just had time to consider the proposal for a national lottery which had caused such a row in Home Affairs the week before. I expected the Welsh and the Scottish non-conformists to hold up their hands in horror but a surprising lot of people that morning woke up to say that a national lottery would be either improper or frivolous or unworthy of a great country such as ours. Yet it's not denied that it would raise at least £50 million a year of extra money without any increase of taxation. The situation looked desperate and even Eddie Shackleton, our new Leader of the Lords, as sensible and solid a man as you'll find anywhere, turned against it and began to find constitutional difficulties about tacking a clause into the Finance Bill. Nevertheless Cabinet was once again right—we just got it through.

This afternoon Barbara came for a long talk about the guillotine debate on Thursday. I couldn't offer her very much help. Freddy Ward—my one competent civil servant—has been out of action for five or six weeks. My Private Office consists of two very junior Assistant Principals and a couple of girls. So when it comes to a big day when I'm really in charge instead of being a Minister carried by his Private Office I have nothing to sustain me and I feel a bit weak. I had to rely on Barbara's people to prepare a brief for me and they did the job jolly well and I have no complaints.

When Barbara had finished I went along to the Home Affairs Committee where there was an interesting item about dog licensing. When I was Minister of Local Government I included in one of my Bills a clause which enabled each separate Ministry by Order in Council to raise by reasonable levels all the licences relating to its activities. I discovered, by the way, that they were all about one hundred years out of date. The dog licence was the only one where Harold Wilson, I remember, said he thought I had a very strong case. I entirely agree. I had read all the arguments of the dog-breeding societies which say unanimously that if dogs are to be taken seriously licences should be raised and that this would decrease the number of stray dogs and dogs kept by families who neglect them. Against this I discovered that most of my colleagues on the Committee thought it completely mad to increase dog licences, since this would be the most unpopular move in the world. This had been the reaction of nearly all the Welsh and the Scots and Tam Dalyell, for example, had assured me that there would be absolute hell in his constituency if we raised the dog licence as I proposed from 7s. 6d. a year to £1 a year. There's quite a tidy sum of money in it since once we increased it to £1 we could, if we took Harold Wilson's advice, put it at £2 and raise £5 million a year. But this really is a minority idea. At Home Affairs it was overwhelmingly voted down as a wildly dangerous piece of revolutionary change.

I went straight from here to our consultations about the House of Lords where we settled down after a week's absence only to find Peter Carrington away ill and Maudling leading the Tories in his place. The Tories had come back from their party consultations to say that they were in complete agreement with the reform we proposed but that they still stood by the requirement formulated by Macleod that the legislation could not apply in this Parliament but only in the next Parliament. This is the only opposition the Shadow Cabinet have raised against our proposals.

I suggested we should not discuss this straightaway and that we should go back and study the details of our Government paper. Thanks to the wonderful enterprise of Eddie Shackleton's working party, we got through the paper with extraordinary speed. For example, the working party had done a superb piece of research on which to base the proposals for the size of the voting house, and we soon reached agreement on this. There was a tricky problem about the size of the majorities. We had agreed that there should always be a Government majority. If the Government were to have a majority of ten over the main Opposition Party what size should its majority be over the so-called subsidiary Parties? The working party had suggested allocating fifteen to twenty places to these Parties. Now the Liberals in the House of Commons are only twelve in number and the

23

number of Liberal peers will be more merely because the Liberal peers want more. After a long discussion we agreed on this and we managed to limit the total membership of subsidiary opposition Parties—i.e. Liberals, Scot Nats., Welsh Nats.—to twenty and then to add to them a group of thirty to forty cross-benchers. But what about these cross-benchers? At first we stuck for a long time on the question of who should select them. Finally we came to the conclusion that the inter-party consultations should continue and become a permanent committee to advise the Prime Minister on the composition of the House.

We really did make fast progress and when we meet in a fortnight's time we shall probably be able to start drafting the agreed White Paper. Of course this House of Lords reform won't be popular. It will be regarded as prosaic and cautious and obvious just because we are attempting not to create an exciting brand-new house but to reform the existing House of Lords by turning it into something sensible and workable. I know there are people who would like a brand new Second Chamber but frankly you can't create one without making it stronger than the present House of Lords. What we have done is to make the present House of Lords even weaker because the Tories will pay a lot for the continuity of tradition. If we are prepared to keep the present House of Lords in existence and knock out the hereditary element the Tories are prepared to see some of its powers taken away. So in terms of sheer common sense and left-wing political advantage the solution we are achieving is a good one. It should last for at least ten years and provide the proper transition from the present hereditary House of Lords to a House consisting wholly of life peers—a scrutinizing revising Second Chamber which within severe limits can tell the House of Commons not to be a bloody fool about Stansted, for example, or the British Museum. So it's a good reform but I shall have nothing but un-popularity in the Labour Party as its author.

This evening I had to speak in the Kensington by-election. It's a hopeless seat with a huge Tory majority. What I didn't know was that the same evening Quintin Hogg was speaking in the town hall and that he had collected an audience of 1,000. I was taken to a modest secondary school where some fifty or sixty people—mostly middle-class socialists—were gathered together to hear Dick Taverne, the candidate Clive Bradley (who used to be in the B.B.C. and then at Transport House) and me. It was a cosy little meeting and it was obvious from the atmosphere that we were going to do disastrously badly on Thursday.[1] After the meeting Anne took me out into Chelsea and we had an excellent meal at a nearby restaurant called 'The Ark'.

---

[1] The by-election on March 15th at Kensington South had been caused by the death of Sir William Rootes. The Conservative candidate, Sir Brandon Rhys-Williams, won the seat; Clive Bradley was beaten into third place and lost his deposit.

Wednesday, March 13th

I started the day with the second meeting of the Cabinet Committee on Electoral Reform. This time the Home Secretary arrived eight minutes late and totally unbriefed. It's astonishing to see the change in Jim Callaghan. Now he's a great lollopy rather crafty bad-tempered mastiff—never doing any work at all. We waded through the detailed proposals and it should take us only one more meeting to get together our recommendations for Cabinet. But what is really astonishing is that in the third year of a Labour Government there's no kind of a feeling that Labour should have a policy for electoral reform and that this is an important job for Labour's Home Secretary, Jim Callaghan.

Across at No. 10 I find the P.M. friendlier to me at morning prayers than he's been for some time. 'I've had a terrible time,' he said. 'All Friday and Saturday Jim Margach and Nora Beloff were ringing and saying that they have had no information from me. Can't you start feeding them again?' 'No, Prime Minister,' I said. 'I've cut off relations with individual pressmen altogether. I'm a happier man for it and I don't feel inclined to go into that business again.' As long as I did the press briefing for the Prime Minister it destroyed his confidence in me and he suspected me of leaks. Since I've stopped doing it the leaks have been worse than ever but are no longer attributed to me. Incidentally I don't suffer from *Angst* because I don't miss that hopeless anxiety doing a job the P.M. doesn't trust you to do but which demands the greatest confidence from him. So on this occasion I was jolly and friendly and pushed him off.

On the way to the Party meeting I had to go to Westminster Great Hall to attend the ceremony of the unveiling of a tablet to Sir Thomas More who was executed there. The tablet is in the floor alongside that of other people condemned to death in Westminster Hall. I thought it was going to be a nice little House of Commons affair but I found the place full of cardinals and archbishops with the House of Commons pushed aside. There was a formal speech by the Lord Chancellor and an elegant, rather vulgar speech by the Speaker of the House. But the Leader of the House and the Whips who had come along were pushed to one side by the horrible Norman St John Stevas and Bob Mellish, catholics who were really exploiting the chance of catholic propaganda. My hackles rose.

The Party meeting on prescription charges was the worst we have ever had. It started with a feeble and ineffective report by Kenneth Robinson. He made no effort whatsoever to make the best of his case or to argue that he had saved the hospital service by sacrificing prescription charges. Indeed he apologized throughout and gave the impression successfully that he'd struggled against the decision. Then up rose Laurie Pavitt, who used to work in the Health Service, and made a high-minded speech in moving the anti-Government motion, so high-minded that Eric Ogden[1] who moved a

[1] Labour M.P. for Liverpool since 1950.

pro-Government motion lost his nerve, ratted and sat down. That was pretty disastrous. After this no one spoke for the Government except Woodrow Wyatt, who told us that we could no longer afford a decent National Health Service and it's departed from its high standards and we shan't be able to improve it unless we have charges on prescriptions. He was duly howled down. He was followed by the dear old Bristol Whip, William Wilkins,[1] who told us that this was the most awful day in his life — to impose prescription charges meant abandoning the very principles of socialism and betraying everything the Party held dear.

The fact that we've had charges for teeth and spectacles and surgical appliances is nothing to the Parliamentary Party. All it cares about is the sacred cow. Roy Jenkins found things so terrible that he went out for forty minutes and when he came back he could instantly feel the gloom on the platform. I sat next to the P.M. and half way through began to doubt if we'd get a majority. I discussed with him what we should do. 'We'll have to carry on,' I told him, 'and have Cabinet reinforce us tomorrow. Of course we shan't be able to bind our people with a three-line whip and we must simply rely on the Tory votes to win.' He agreed and then he added, 'Make sure, Dick, that the press are briefed. I don't want to do any briefings.' 'Nor do I,' I said. 'Now be serious, Dick. You've got to make sure the press knows tonight so that we can carry Cabinet safely tomorrow.' However, when the vote came at the end of the Party meeting we had a two to one majority, partly due to Michael Stewart's quiet emphatic wind-up: just a reminder that everybody there knew that the Government was firmly committed to prescription charges and couldn't possibly reverse their decision and that all that was taking place was a demonstration of conscience after the conscience had already been raped.

After the second meeting of my Devolution Committee I went to see Roy at No. 11 about the publicity for the budget. I told him how important it was to get all the Ministers making platform speeches next weekend, indeed for the next three weekends, and that I was preparing a full brief for them. All he said to me was that things were going very badly and that the drain on sterling had got worse. Then he added that he was going to have a dividend freeze and he hoped that would make things easier for me. We didn't say very much to each other but at least there was a feeling that we were getting on and that's unusual in this Government.

By then the brief from the Ministry of Transport had arrived safely and I spent the rest of the evening preparing my speech for Thursday's guillotine motion.

On March 8th sterling fell to its lowest point since devaluation as some hundred tons of gold were sold in London. Simultaneously the U.S. Treasury announced that since the beginning of the year America's gold reserves had fallen by

[1] Labour M.P. for Bristol South 1945–70.

$100 millions. On March 9th the Governors of the Central Banks of Britain, the U.S.A. and five Western European countries met in Basle and announced their determination to maintain the price of gold at $35 an ounce. But the speculators were not to be reassured. On March 13th a hundred tons of gold were sold in London, and on March 14th two hundred tons. The price of silver soared. The British Government was asked to close the London gold market and on March 14th at midnight, to a hastily summoned meeting of Privy Councillors at Buckingham Palace, the Queen declared March 15th a Bank Holiday. The financial outcome was to give the governors of the central banks a breathing space, and at a meeting in Washington on March 17th they and the British Government agreed to close the London gold market until April 1st, while, in the meantime, stand-by credits to the U.K. to safeguard sterling against speculation were increased to $4,000 million.

There was however a more immediate political result. The Foreign Secretary and Deputy Prime Minister, George Brown, offered his resignation to the Prime Minister, ostensibly because he had not been consulted on March 14th or summoned to the meeting of the Privy Council.

Thursday, March 14th

I expected this to be my big day but it turned out to be George Brown's. At Cabinet the first item as usual was leaks. The Prime Minister complained that the story of Alcan and the Coal Board had been leaked to the *Sun*, which had also got a big scoop about all the price increases in gas, post office, electricity, coal, etc. Cabinet sat back completely bored because it's clear that nothing can be done about these leaks.

At last we got back to prices and incomes and this time we had yet another paper from Peter Shore on methods and timing. His main argument is that the T.U.C. and the C.B.I. would be driven to make a common front against us if we made any suggestion that the prices and incomes policy was a permanency. Both would fight any permanent system tooth and nail. So Peter came down for eighteen months and the use of the Expiring Laws Continuance Bill. I thought that he had a point in suggesting eighteen months because this takes the discussion of prices and incomes out of July, which is at the end of the Parliamentary session, into autumn, when it's much easier to get things through. The whole discussion was perfectly amicable and George Brown obviously felt that he had had a tremendous triumph and was friendly and positive. When he and I met the Prime Minister last Friday George had suggested the 12-month period, a 3½ per cent ceiling and retrospection. Now we were being offered eighteen months, a 3½ per cent ceiling and no retrospection—a jolly good bargain.[1] So Cabinet also settled down to accepting it.

Over lunch I had to get ready for the business Statement, to take a last

[1] The period was eventually from August 11th, 1968, to December 31st, 1969.

look at the text of my speech which was fairly satisfactory and to rush into Barbara's committee to clear it with her.

At 3.30 there were a tremendous lot of Ministerial Statements in addition to mine and I only got to my feet for my speech about five o'clock because there were endless points of order before I could get started. We'd planned the first part of the guillotine debate as a sort of Second Reading discussion which would end with a vote just before ten. The speeches were very long. I set a bad example by letting mine drag out for nearly forty-five minutes owing to interruptions and there was a brilliant and fantastically funny intervention by Michael Foot. But the only remarkable feature of this first debate was when Clifford Kenyon,[1] our aged 70-year-old chairman of the Selection Committee, suddenly came down to the House for the first time in years to denounce the Government and denounce the guillotine as unfair and improper. On a normal day his speech would have been a major sensation. Fortunately it was submerged by the news which followed later that night.

At 10 p.m. there was an odd little scene when the Speaker forgot to ask for the motion to exempt business. Our Whip was doing his duty. He was on the lookout, he tugged at the gown of the Clerk sitting at the table but the Clerk was not paying attention but talking to Curly Mallalieu about procedure and he missed the precise moment at 10 p.m. At two minutes past Heath got up to ask why we were going on with the debate when the motion had fallen. This was a valid question. If you don't pass the motion for exempted business at ten all business automatically falls. But if that had happened we would have got nothing at all—not even our Second Reading vote. So there was pandemonium with the Tories shouting at the Speaker and our front bench in a terrible jam because we knew that Heath was quite right. However, after ten minutes Heath conceded the point in a very sportsmanlike correct way and we were able to continue our business. The Second Reading vote was taken and we moved on to the first amendment. It was while we were dealing with this at 11 p.m. that I got the first message from Michael Halls saying that the P.M. wanted to talk to me. I went up to my room and over the phone he told me there was a major international crisis: the whole liquidity system was in suspense and the Americans had asked us to close the gold market. He had decided that we must have a Bank Holiday and for that we needed a Privy Council. Would I want to go to the Palace? I said straightaway that I didn't want to go. I'd prefer to stay on the front bench and see the guillotine debate through. I'd be delighted if the Prime Minister would represent me and take anybody else he liked. Strictly speaking, of course, the Lord President, if he's in the House, should automatically go to the Palace for an emergency Privy Council but there was no reason on this occasion to keep to tradition.

It was a typical post-prandial guillotine debate. The Tories were making

[1] Labour M.P. for Chorley, Lancashire, 1945–70. He was born in 1896.

long and amusing speeches to each other and celebrating the Kensington by-election result which had just been announced. As there is never anything new to be said such a debate is always wholly artificial and it usually degenerates into violent personal abuse of the Leader of the House and the Minister in charge of the Bill. Somewhere near midnight George Brown came wandering in, sat down on the front bench and leant across to me and said, 'What's all this I hear?' And I said, 'I've known for some time that something is up because I am Lord President.' He got very angry at this and when we got to the first division on the first amendment there he was getting Ministers—like Tony Wedgwood Benn—and saying he must go over to No. 10 and raise hell with the P.M. for not consulting us. There was obviously trouble in the offing. But I was determined to get that guillotine motion through and at last we got on to the second amendment. This was due to take another couple of hours and in the course of it the Tories tried to move progress, i.e. to abandon the debate. It was actually while one of them was moving progress that the news appeared on the tape of the Privy Council meeting at Buckingham Palace. At this Parliament began to get out of control. The Tories all jumped to the conclusion that this meant that the pound had been devalued and most of our people feared the same thing and began to feel that it was no good sitting all through the night on a guillotine motion when a crisis of this sort was occurring outside. Why should we waste time on this motion, they felt? Why not stop and abandon the debate? During the vote on the second motion Heath and Willie Whitelaw got hold of me and said, 'We can't control our people here unless you get Roy Jenkins over tonight.' I had previously announced that he would speak at eleven tomorrow morning and this had only aggravated the trouble. I had to think quickly and immediately I rang up the Prime Minister, who was sitting in No. 10 with his semi-Cabinet, to tell him the House of Commons was collapsing into complete disorder and that I was going to announce that in forty-five minutes he and Roy Jenkins would be in their places ready to make a Statement. Somewhat to my surprise he agreed at once over the phone and I went back into the House, which immediately became quiet once I made this announcement. In due course Harold and Roy arrived and the Statement was made and Harold answered Questions admirably. The House was quiet. Then they left and the difficulty was to get the guillotine debate started again. Even John Silkin was saying to me that he didn't think we could really carry the motion through that night. I replied, 'Balls. We'll get it through. We've got nothing so far and I'm going to see that we get something.' I had been in the tea-room and heard Douglas Hamilton complaining that it was intolerable for our people to be kept there full of alarm and despondency. Nevertheless we did keep them there, we did rally them and, though I say it myself, I had to do most of the job because there was nobody else to do it. I had no Parliamentary Secretary. Barbara's two assistants had disappeared and she was all the time rushing out to smoke cigarettes. We faced three Tory amendments, then three specialist amendments and then the vote on the Third Reading. We got the second amendment with quite a good majority and then I had to steer the three specialist ones through. I'd done the first and Barbara had done the second rather badly and when we came to the third I had a good idea and gave it away. That did the trick. Suddenly the whole Opposition packed in and the debate was finished by 6.15 in the morning. There I was walking home with Tam and the job finished. I had my bath, got into bed and read the morning papers, and I was back in Downing Street for a meeting before Cabinet.

Friday, March 15th
After we'd finished our business meeting at 9.30 Burke remarked that we can't possibly afford to have George out of the Government now and in fact Harold and John didn't want him sacked and nor did I. I hadn't had time to discuss George with anyone except Tam Dalyell, who had said to me that I ought to make a bid for the Foreign Secretaryship. But I knew that wasn't serious and I didn't play any great part in that discussion with Burke or for that matter in the morning Cabinet. I'd been up all night and I slept most of the time. Afterwards I went back to my office in the Privy Council and signed the final documents to make the arrangements for keeping Prescote Manor Farm in operation in the event of my death or Anne's.

After that I caught the train to Rugby where every three or four years I talk to the sixth form of the school about politics. Last time just before I began President Kennedy was assassinated. This time it went more quietly but I was so tired that I may really have been too hardboiled for their tender consciences. Over dinner with the dons I began to feel really tired and began to develop the most splitting headache—a real hangover. I'd forgotten that on top of real exhaustion even a couple of glasses of white wine can be devastating.

Sunday, March 17th
At last I've had time over this lovely weekend first to think things out and to reflect on the events of this remarkable week. As I've mentioned in this diary, I slept through most of Cabinet just as Barbara Castle did a week or two ago when the Immigration Bill was being discussed on the morning after her all-night sitting on the Transport Bill. So I missed hearing Roy's exposition of the crisis which nearly brought us into catastrophe. Since then I've been filled in by Tommy Balogh. It looks as though the threat of another devaluation within four months had suddenly become a threat of devaluation within four days—just before the post-devaluation budget. We could have lost £500 million or £600 million a day of reserves and we haven't got them to lose because we've already pledged them against the stand-by loan from

the I.M.F. So on this occasion we'd have been really busted and the pound would have floated down and down and down. I gather all this was pretty frankly admitted by Roy Jenkins on Friday morning and it wasn't a tremendous shock because he'd already given us his earlier warning a week ago.

One of the things I asked myself is whether we mightn't have been better able to resist the strain of this crisis if last January Roy Jenkins had overruled the Treasury and taken the advice of most of the economic experts to clap on hire-purchase controls at the same time as his cuts in government expenditure. It looks to me as though the way the post-devaluation package has been divided into three parts—though it may have had its domestic political conveniences—has been thoroughly bad for the presentation of the policy to which we are now committed. I know that when Jenkins got to the Treasury he was told that it was impossible to get a budget ready in time to publish a single package. But once again if he'd been strong-minded he could have overruled his advisers. If he'd been strong-minded. But that's something I certainly failed to do on a critical issue at the Ministry of Housing.

Now the whole internal crisis was of course aggravated by George Brown's resignation on Friday night.[1] I've had a word with Bill Rodgers about it and he confirms my impression that George resigned reluctantly. If there had come a word from No. 10 George would have withdrawn it, but all through Friday he'd hung on in his flat waiting for the word. When the word didn't come he was compelled to write his resignation letter. It was immediately accepted and Michael Stewart was slipped in straightaway. Harold had made up his mind that this time he wasn't going to have George back. And the very next day George Brown hammered a nail into his own coffin by succumbing to the temptation to write an article for the *Sunday Times* for £5,000. This letter of George Brown's reads strangely because it says that he couldn't stay in Cabinet owing to the way things are being run. This has been interpreted as a mere expression of petty opposition.

[1] In the first week of March there had been heavy sales of sterling and increasing speculation that there would be a rise in the price of gold. Although currency revaluations were expected, the Prime Minister hoped to keep the parity of the pound with the dollar, and on March 14th he and the Chancellor of the Exchequer met to discuss the rapidly-worsening situation. To this, and subsequent emergency meetings that evening, George Brown was invited, but he could not be found. The Chancellor and the Prime Minister, with the advice of the Governor of the Bank of England, decided to follow the American proposal to close the gold pool, which meant that the London foreign exchange must be closed and a Bank Holiday declared, by Order in Council. As well as the Prime Minister and the Chancellor, the Lord President of the Council was told of the immediate need for a Privy Council, and so was Peter Shore, who had telephoned the Prime Minister for news, and who was summoned to the Privy Council, at 12.15 a.m., to make up a quorum. At 1 a.m. George Brown telephoned the Prime Minister, incensed that he had been excluded, and Peter Shore included, from the proceedings. On March 16th he resigned from the Foreign Office, complaining of 'dictatorial' methods of government. See *Wilson*, op. cit., pp. 505–15.

23*

But it isn't. There's a great deal in it. If I was ever to resign it would be precisely because I can't stand the way Cabinet is run. It's because of Harold's inability to create a firm inner group with whom to work consistently and his determination to keep bilateral relationships with each one of us and arbitrarily to leave us out of absolutely vital conversations just because we don't happen to be in No. 10 or because we're out of favour that afternoon.

There was no earthly reason why on Thursday evening Harold shouldn't have quietly permitted Burke Trend to organize a meeting of all available members of S.E.P. or of Cabinet, including the Deputy Leader.

Nevertheless the real cause as distinct from reason for George's resignation is his schizophrenia. He's always been a Jekyll and Hyde and the good part has always been extraordinarily nice and talented and, by the way, has been very much in evidence in the last seven or eight weeks when I have found him as helpful as possible in working out a compromise on prices and incomes. But on Thursday night he suddenly blew up and Hyde appeared shouting and screaming round the lobbies like a hysterical barrow-boy. There's only one politician to compare with George Brown and that is Quintin Hogg. He is also something of a schizophrenic. He can be wise, magnanimous and charming, as he was the other day to our Home Secretary when Jim Callaghan made his bloomer of calling someone a murderer before he'd been tried. Quintin doesn't reveal himself quite so often as a caterwauling vulgar creature. After all, he has been to a proper school and taught to control his passions. But their temperaments are similar and just as Quintin has been denied the highest office in the Conservative Party because of his temperament so George has suffered the same fate. But though denied the highest office owing to their deficiencies, they yet achieve the highest celebrity because both these schizophrenics appeal to public opinion. They pull the crowds. When Quintin spoke last week in the town hall at South Kensington he had a thousand people to hear him while I was speaking in a little back-street school to forty. If the Labour Party had had the town hall I would have been lucky to get 400. Quintin is a politician in the big appealing sense of the word and George also has this extraordinary public appeal which time after time earns him public forgiveness for gross misbehaviours and deficiencies which would have been found intolerable in anybody else.

I found George the most attractive member of Cabinet, certainly the most gifted, certainly the most imaginative, possessing a mind which has a sense for the evidence buried in the documents or in a speech and which can smell it out. Here he resembles the other non-university—I was going to say illiterates—Aneurin Bevan and Ernest Bevin. But above all he resembles Aneurin Bevan—an intellectual who if ever there was one could transmogrify the really intelligent analyses provided by Tommy and myself into the gold of political policy thinking. George shared something of this power. Yes, I think that's a fair comparison—with Quintin Hogg on one side and Aneurin on the other. Where George differed from Aneurin was that, like most working-class politicians, he had a huge chip on his shoulder. For years George detested me because I was an intellectual from the universities. He openly detested such people. He sloshed them, he smashed them, he sneered at them and he grew famous as the Party's hatchet man to deal with left-wing intellectuals.

When Gaitskell died George failed to become Leader because the Parliamentary Party had seen him very close for years on end and knew about his feet of clay. So he had to serve as number two to Harold and there was a complete incompatibility of temperament. Harold can be tender-hearted but he's also cool, careful, prim, non-conformist, intellectual, bookish: George is none of these things. He's tough and crude and yet brilliant and imaginative. There's something of Palmerston in George and of Lord John Russell in Harold (I've been reading my Greville of that year over Christmas). Long before the 1964 election Harold Wilson had told me that he was bound to make George his deputy leader and to create D.E.A. as his new vital Ministry. But in those days Harold used to add, 'He won't last long. He'll trip over himself sooner or later and destroy himself.' The only thing wrong with this judgment was that the final trip came so much later than anyone thought possible. George must have survived nearly seventeen or eighteen resignations and so many appalling misbehaviours, in nearly all of which he'd been tenderly spared by the press. So it has taken over three years before he finally got rid of himself. I believe Harold would never have got rid of him. Harold feared him partly because of his immense strength inside the Parliamentary Party. When he threatened to resign in the 1966 crisis a hundred names went down the same night below a motion asking him to come back.[1] However, his position is not nearly as strong today. He certainly horrified many of our back-benchers as well as Cabinet by his exhibition last Thursday night, which only confirmed the suspicion and fears that have been growing for a good many months. The rumours about his increasing drunkenness and rudeness to his officials, and his gross misbehaviours at important banquets have piled up to a point where Members found him pretty unbearable.

One always found George pretty unbearable as long as one merely heard about these misbehaviours. But next time one sat opposite him in Cabinet he was so sensible and practical that one forgot all about it. In fact during the last seven weeks I've found him easier to work with than ever before and the press was beginning to wonder what the hell George Brown was up to. He's been so quiet and good, they commented, that there must be something new blowing up. But will his resignation make him a great menace either in the Parliamentary Party or in the Party outside? Our people don't easily forgive Ministers who in a moment of international

[1] See Vol. I, pp. 578–9.

crisis suddenly pull out in a pet. He will find it difficult to restore his position either inside or outside Parliament and I shall be interested to see whether there's any serious support for the idea he is now promoting that he should remain deputy leader of the Party concerned with restoring Party morale in the constituencies. I don't yet see how a man outside the Cabinet can do this job effectively. On the other hand if he is refused the deputy leadership and defeated by another candidate he will undoubtedly become a centre of disaffection. One has only to think about Nye and Harold and John Freeman in 1951 to realize that the reason for a political resignation is only worked out after it has taken place. Will George Brown now come out full blast against a statutory prices and incomes policy? I don't exclude the possibility and I think it's extremely fortunate that he had agreed on the compromise last Thursday. I think he'll also launch out against our withdrawal from the Far East and his attitude to America will be that of an ultra-right-wing loyalist supporter of Vietnam.

Now let's turn from George Brown to Michael Stewart—Minister of Education, then Foreign Secretary when Gordon Walker went, then at D.E.A. when George went and now back to the Foreign Office when George went again. To be the man who's always put in when somebody resigns is not very attractive and the press practically disregard Michael's appointment today. It will be deeply disappointing to the Parliamentary Party because of his doctrinaire support for the Americans in Vietnam and his opposition to our withdrawal from the Far East and indeed to all the main radical decisions this Cabinet has taken. Harold Wilson told me yesterday that he's a little less doctrinaire about Vietnam now and I hope this is true, but in Cabinet and in the Foreign Office Michael Stewart will be a force for consolidation—a strengthener of the establishment without any of the liveliness and imaginativeness of George. Was there any alternative to him? The newspapers say that Denis was the alternative but to move Denis from Defence would have caused a reshuffle. Certainly I would have staked a very strong claim to replace Denis not because I particularly want Defence but because with Denis in the Foreign Office I would have been determined to get a position where I too could influence foreign and defence policy, which frankly has been left almost unchanged for three years. But the Chiefs of Staff know me far too well and Harold would have had a hell of a job to get me made Minister of Defence in one Friday afternoon in the middle of a world liquidity crisis. But could I have succeeded George Brown? Frankly I'd have liked to and I think I would have been an imaginative Foreign Secretary and a pretty confident administrator in the office as well. Nevertheless, I have to admit to myself that Harold Wilson never even conceived the possibility of making me Foreign Secretary and nobody round him suggested it—neither Burke Trend on the one side nor Gerald Kaufman and Marcia on the other. Partly this is because I'm doing a useful job, as my record on Thursday night in the House showed, but it's also because in foreign affairs from their point of view I'm not trustworthy since I'm a fanatical Little Englander who wants to see us settling down as an offshore island and dropping our special relationship with the U.S.A. So for quite different reasons both Denis Healey and Dick Crossman were excluded from serious consideration and Michael Stewart went in. It's a dumpy dull substitute which gets us through the short-term crisis but intensifies the need for a drastic Cabinet reshuffle as soon as possible.

Finally, just a word about this famous world crisis into which we've been plunged. I've never felt a greater sense of this Government's impotence than I do now. The question whether we devalue again or not is entirely determined by whether the Americans will let us have the cash to sustain the policy they want without forcing devaluation on us. That's our situation two days ahead of a budget in which Roy will ask for immense sacrifices in order that this Labour Government can at last get a firm control of the economy. The truth is that we shan't get control of the economy.

In this kind of crisis I feel personally out of touch. International finance for me was like the problem of India—a subject I had refused to look at altogether—and so I'm treated as the ignoramus of the inner group and my advice is regarded as of no value. It's funny how our reputations go up and down. Thomas Balogh rang me up today blissfully happy because he's now right at the centre of things, invaluable to the Prime Minister, advising him on every point, while here I am sitting in Prescote on a lovely day and I shall go out and do my wooding and be on my own and be a bit lonely. I shan't be unhappy but only a bit autumnal in my feelings. My tummy's getting too big, I move less well, I play games less, I do more wooding, I'm moving into old age in this my sixtieth year. Is it because of the strain of the jobs I've been doing since 1964? Will I get younger if I get out and relax completely? I suspect it might make me get a great deal older to resign. Though I'm not quite as vigorous or as young as I was three years ago, I have a feeling that if I got into Education or some other Department I really liked I would get a new lease of life and regain all the drive and energy which I felt in 1964. But at the moment I feel outside and I'm thinking more about my diary than ever before.

I had to come up to London tonight because I got a message from Downing Street that every member of Cabinet must sleep near enough to attend an emergency Cabinet if it is called. However, only the Chief and I were compelled not only to sleep in or near London but to clock in. The Chief, by the way, duly clocked in at No. 12 and sat there for two and a half hours before they remembered and brought him round. I insisted on coming into the building and I was once again warned to enter through the Cabinet office and not through the door of No. 10 so that the press wouldn't think there was anything going on. I got all those doors unlocked and came down the passages and down the stairs into the anteroom and finally opened the door into the Cabinet Office, and found Harold sitting in his chair at the middle of the big table with the Chancellor and a number of other Ministers round him. One peep and I went round the back into the little room where the old gang always sits. There were Marcia and Gerald Kaufman and Tommy and myself and, a little later, John Silkin. So I was back in the Wilson coterie after my big pre-Bermuda row and we settled down and Thomas started briefing me a bit. Then Harold looked in and said that he'd have got rid of them all in a minute and that the crisis is over. The details, he told me, were now being worked out in New York by the British delegation headed by Harold Lever and Leslie O'Brien, the Governor of the Bank of England.[1] When the Ministers had finally gone off Harold came right into the room and said, 'What about some supper and sandwiches?' and Marcia said, 'Why shouldn't we all go upstairs?' and she rang up Mary and asked her to give supper to the family, so to speak. So I found myself at an old-style supper in No. 10 with Mary looking after us. I hadn't talked to her for some time and she said to me rather awkwardly, 'I remember the only time you came to see us at our home in Hampstead, I offered you Nescafé and you said you'd rather not and we went out to a restaurant and there you got some ordinary coffee. So I suppose you don't like tinned salmon but that's all we've got tonight apart from a bit of cold ham.' We were sitting in that miserable little dining-room and there on the table-cloth was a bit of mutton wrapped up in cellophane, a bit of butter on a plate, a couple of tomatoes and some lettuce, and beside them a very large tin of salmon which had by now been emptied out into a potato dish. 'But I like tinned salmon,' I said to Mary, 'especially in fish cakes.' 'Oh, you do like it in fish cakes?' she replied. 'So do I.' And somehow a part of a terrible barrier had been broken down between us. I'd been made to realize how snobbish the Wilsons regard the Crossmans' attitude to Nescafé and tinned salmon and a thousand other things. So we settled down to supper, and I ate my tinned salmon and my slices of bread and butter and Gerald Kaufman was served with his fried Jewish eggs, and then we all had hot-buttered toast, which came in late, and Marcia provided us with some apricot jam.

After supper Harold disappeared downstairs and Tommy disappeared too, wandering round in attendance on his boss waiting to be useful. I stayed with the rest in the living-room helping to take things out to the kitchen next door and pretending to help to wash up, and in the course of this Mary explained to me that they had intended to spend that evening at Chequers giving dinner to John Fulton and two other guests. But they'd had to cancel the dinner and come back to London for the meetings. They had meant to bring the dinner back with them but they hadn't been allowed to because Government hospitality said they would be charged for the dinner if it was taken from Chequers to No. 10 and not given to the guests for whom it was

[1] He was Deputy Governor 1964–6 and Governor 1966–73. He became a life peer in 1973.

arranged. I said, 'What? Does Government hospitality treat you in that way?' I was thinking how Winston Churchill would have reacted to officials who tried to order him about. But this is the position Harold and Mary are in at Chequers and No. 10. They are very modest people and tremendously correct; they adore being at No. 10 and even more they adore being at Chequers so Chequers is being used exactly as it ought to be used by a Prime Minister who hasn't got a country house and needs an escape in the country. They love every moment there and just because they love it in a very nice way they are bullied and chivvied by Government hospitality and closed and hemmed in by the Ministry of Works and made to feel they are interlopers in a way quite different from what would happen to Alec Douglas-Home, I'm pretty sure.

I had got there at 8.30 and left just after midnight with Tommy just as the Chief arrived, looking very ill, and stayed chatting alone with Harold until 1.30. Nothing happened up there except gossip. There was one moment when the P.M. went down to see Denis Healey, who had looked in. When Harold came back he said, 'Well, he is a cool customer. He asked me about my intentions. I said Michael is there for keeps and he said he didn't believe it.' Denis had replied, 'Michael is only there temporarily, and you will be having me in the F.O. next autumn and I want you to make George Thomson Minister of Defence in my place.' Of course this is only Harold's account of the conversation, but it is an example of Denis's bloody-mindedness and uncooperativeness, refusing to help himself. To behave like that with the Prime Minister means that in the next reshuffle the P.M. will keep him where he is and give him hell.

After this Harold sat down and at extraordinary length rehearsed his version of exactly what happened on Thursday night. He told me that the moment when George's letter had finally come on Friday afternoon he had sent for Michael and he said, 'Actually I warned him just after devaluation that if George were to resign again, he would get the job. Well, that made it easier for me.' I had had those vague feelings about the kind of job I could do as Foreign Secretary and I wondered whether it was possible to bring such a dull man as Michael Stewart in instead of me. But in fact it is clear that Harold never conceived any other possibility. Michael is the man he can trust and the fact that he was a disastrous First Secretary and Minister of D.E.A. makes no difference to that. By the way, Harold was very careful this evening to remind me that though as the result of Michael going to the Foreign Office I was to take over the chairmanship of the Social Services Committee and run Michael's conference next Saturday on the social services, this was all purely temporary and would just be a holding operation while he was making his ultimate decisions.

Monday, March 18th
Budget Cabinet, and really the only point of interest was how complacently

the Chancellor's paper was taken once it was clear that there was going to be a dividend ceiling of 3½ per cent corresponding to the wages ceiling of 3½ per cent. That closed one area of complaint. Roy was very skilful in the presentation of his main proposal—a new tax on investment income of over £3,000 a year. This was his new tax and it impressed us. After he'd finished we had a little discussion and the only thing on which there was any pressure at all was on the subject of hotels, where Roy announced the increase of 50 per cent in S.E.T. for which Nicky Kaldor had been pressing. I took the lead in urging that as well as the special grants for building hotel rooms in the development areas he should have investment grants for hotels in general and no S.E.T. for those in development areas. I kicked Willie Ross, my neighbour, into action and kicked Cledwyn Hughes, and as there was a feebleness in Cabinet this morning I got into the budget speech a reference to the possibility that there might be concessions to hotels in the rural parts of development areas, and that was the best we got. Otherwise there were no changes and we turned to prices and incomes. As the discussion went on it became clearer and clearer that since the cost of living was going to be put up by 6 per cent, the 3½ per cent wages ceiling would be unrealistic. Tony Crosland wanted it raised to 4 per cent, which was neither here nor there, but when somebody else said 4½ per cent Roy said that was an increase he simply couldn't take. Then once again he repeated his story of the second devaluation, this time reminding us that it might have occurred last Friday night if it hadn't been that the President of the United States had rung up and asked to have the gold market stopped and given us an excuse for a Bank Holiday. Without that Bank Holiday we could have had a catastrophic run on the pound leading to a second devaluation. 'That,' he said, 'is how near we were.' But having lost so much in the first devaluation and got very little back since then we now had to have a budget speech which at all costs will bring back the reserves to London—and that means it has to include a prices and incomes policy. It's always been a puzzle why bankers in Zürich and New York should insist that the British economy is subjected to a degree of Government intervention in the area of wages that they wouldn't tolerate in their own countries. This, I think, is something we have to thank Mr Callaghan for, because it was he who sold the prices and incomes policy to Mr Fowler, the American Secretary of the Treasury. Certainly Roy now feels that for the next three months he has to have a tough incomes policy. So I put the precise question to him. 'I can see that if you have a tough policy it will help you with the bankers for these critical next three months, but it may make the economy unworkable later on and it may precipitate a strike which ruins the Labour Government. Which is the greater risk to you—the break-down of the incomes policy in the next twelve months or a run on the pound in the next three?' 'No question,' he said. 'A run on the pound in the next three.' 'In that case,' I said, 'go ahead because we can modify the policy later.' I found Roy's admission important because it's clear that personally he doesn't believe in a prices and incomes policy and he'd rather have a free-for-all, like the strongish group in the Cabinet headed by Dick Marsh who've been routing against a statutory policy week in and week out. But so grave is the immediate threat to sterling that he has to have a strong prices and incomes policy even if it causes catastrophe in a year's time.

In the House this afternoon George Brown got up to make the traditional resignation speech from the corner three rows back below the gangway. There was no need for him to make it and in so doing he merely confirmed that he was out. I didn't hear it because I had to go to a brief meeting of the Home Publicity Committee and by the time I'd got back his speech was over and I heard it had had not the faintest influence.

This evening our ombudsman, Edmund Compton, had a little dinner for the New Zealand ombudsman, who turned out to be a pleasant elderly civil servant who'd been in the job for many years. I found myself sitting opposite Matt Stevenson, who at once reminded me of how appallingly rude I had been in that informal speech I made at the R.I.B.A. We had the whole evening to sit it out there and in the course of it I found that I still liked him and he had begun to like me again, and it was a pleasant evening.

Mr Jenkins's 'stiff budget followed by two years of hard slog' set out tax increases of £923 million, largely drawn from indirect taxation except for a severe levy on personal incomes of £3,000 or more per annum drawn from investments. The tax on cigarettes was increased by 2d. for a packet of twenty, on spirits by 2s. 6d. a bottle and on petrol by 4d. a gallon, purchase tax was increased, betting and gaming taxes raised and the motor-car licence fee was increased by £7 10s. to £25. With these measures the Chancellor hoped to take advantage of the November devaluation and to achieve a balance-of-payments surplus of £500 million a year.

Tuesday, March 19th
I strolled across St James's Park to get my hair cut and when I got back to the office with very little to do I was suddenly told the P.M. wanted to talk to me. At once I felt that this was a talk about the future and, sure enough, when I got down there it was the most relaxed conversation I've had with Harold for a very long time. I don't think it's an accident that this sense of relaxation followed the bleeding row which took place before I flew to Bermuda. I've been very tough to him and completely aloof and now suddenly he wants to make me an offer in a major reshuffle. He started by saying he was talking in the closest personal confidence and I wasn't to tell anybody what he said. What he intended was to make me First Secretary and Minister of Social Services, which would mean combining in a single Ministry the Ministries of Social Security and Health. I paused and said I would like to think it over but my first reaction was that I ought to be

Minister of Defence. 'No future there,' he said abruptly. 'Maybe two years ago you could have gone there when the decisions still had to be taken. It's too late now. You would find that a dead end. You won't leave anything memorable if you go to Defence, but you could be as memorable as Beveridge[1] if you go to the other job and make a go of the two years of reorganization there. You can have something for your memoirs,' he said, looking at me, and I was clearly aware that these are the last two years of my political life, and he was offering me a really big chance to be right at the top with a key job and a genuine promotion.

By now I'd had time to gather my thoughts and I said a good deal would depend on who succeeded me as Leader of the House and what happened to John Silkin. 'John Silkin is not a healthy man now,' he said. 'I'll have to move him and I've got ideas about that. Have you any ideas for your successor?' And before I could answer he said 'I have an idea. Fred Peart.' Since then I've thought of Fred Peart and it's quite a good idea. He's a very different type from me—working-class, a non-intellectual, and so on. Moreover, I've started all the big parliamentary reforms and he may do extremely well in getting people to settle down with them.

'There's one thing,' I added, 'you will have to face, Prime Minister. It is quite impossible to have Peter Shore as head of D.E.A. with you purporting to run it. He's despised by his fellow members of Cabinet, he's hopeless in the House of Commons and he can't put your policy to the T.U.C. and the C.B.I.' 'I know all that,' he said, 'and I see my way through but I agree he has to go.' Then I asked him cautiously about Michael Stewart and he made it clear once more that Michael is a permanency until the election: there's no chance of George Thomson taking his place. As for Denis Healey, Denis is so bloody-minded he will have to stay at the Ministry of Defence. Harold had been talking to him about Technology and Power and he'd shown the same snooty disdain.

I returned to the problems of my own job and he said, 'If you don't take it, Dick, I'll give it to Barbara.' 'If I take it,' I said, 'why not make Barbara head of D.E.A. as you nearly did last summer? She's due for promotion too.' He concluded by saying that he was determined to get the final Cabinet for the run-up to the election—one good enough to last two years. It must be a really new Cabinet with a new look and he added, 'For the first time I can get rid of the people I took over in the Shadow Cabinet. When I became Leader I only had one person in the Parliamentary Committee who had voted for me and when I formed my first Cabinet in 1964 it contained only two or three of you who were my supporters. The rest were opponents. Now I shall be strong and need not worry about any debt I owe to my enemies.' This fierce vindictive tone alarmed me a bit but at least it's interesting that he wants to make some drastic changes. Then we discussed

[1] In February 1943 the Commons gave blessing to Sir William Beveridge's Report setting out a plan for universal social security. It was substantially enacted after the war.

George Brown's future and I suggested that he should become head of Transport House. 'I wouldn't object to that,' said Harold. 'Let me try that out.'

I went back to my office and brooded over all that Harold had said. Then I took Anne and her friend Celia Gimpel out to the Farmers' Club for lunch and told them what I'd been offered. Anne said, 'It's tailor-made for you and it would be silly not to take it—it's an ideal job for you.'

Before the budget speech we had one of those ridiculous Ten-Minute Rule Bills because the Welsh M.P. for Bedfordshire South insisted on his back-bench rights.[1] Then Roy rose for his budget and sitting next to him I felt he was trembling like a leaf. His speech was very long. The Chief Whip was ill and away so I was able to sit in his corner, which is much more comfortable and where unfortunately one can lean one's head. I must have closed my eyes and slept a good deal at the beginning but I heard with the greatest attention all the end of the speech and I watched its effect on both sides of the House. I noticed how nearly Roy lost the House when he said something, expected a laugh, and waited too long for it, and I didn't find the actual delivery very good. It was the content and construction which impressed me. Above all it was genuinely based on socialist principle, fair in the fullest sense by really helping people at the bottom of the scale and by really taxing the wealthy. It was a tremendous performance and for once deserved the back-benchers rising behind him and waving their order papers. Our people were as hysterical this afternoon as they were at the announcement of devaluation. But, thank God, there was much more content in Roy's speech to justify their support and I knew he'd succeeded in his first objective when he sat down.

However, I went out and had a blazing little row with Tony Benn. One of my jobs as Leader of the House is to arrange for the dozens of Ministerial Statements which are put out at 3.30 and of which none can be made without my consent. Last week his Private Office told my Private Office that he must have one on Thursday afternoon and that Wednesday wouldn't work because it would immediately precede Iain Macleod's speech. When I thought about this it was pretty good nonsense and so I said he'd have to be on Wednesday, whereupon I was told that this was impossible because they had already begun printing the Order Paper for Thursday. Of course I knew that Wedgy himself had ordered the printing and so forced my hand. 'You're a twister to behave like that,' I said to him and walked out. I left him in great dismay, anger and fury, and went round to congratulate Roy, whom I found relaxing with his two Treasury officials and his P.P.S., Tom Bradley.

Anne had been listening to the speech in the ladies' gallery with Jennifer Jenkins and Pam Hartwell and I went and had a chat with them before going off to a charming dinner with Jennie and Chris Hall. They have taken

[1] Gwilym Roberts (on an amendment to the Nationalized Industries Act, 1965).

a new house just round the corner from their old house in Hampstead. In modern style they've let off the two top floors to lodgers and they keep the ground floor and the basement and a lovely garden for their own home, which they're gradually going to furnish. Jennie, who of course knows all about No. 10 after her period in my Private Office, was fascinated to hear about the astonishing supper-party last Sunday evening. Talking to her was like old times. I love my Jennie and I'm very fond of her Chris, and for Anne and me it was an ideal end to the budget anxiety. We were even able to see Roy on the box, where he made his first appearance as Chancellor—first-rate. Watching him I felt that it's possible that we've now scraped the bottom and are at last moving upward. That's a sensation I haven't had since Annual Conference.

Wednesday, March 20th
First the third meeting of my own Committee on Devolution. Once again my eager collection of young Ministers are saying to me that it's the most exciting committee on which they serve. In addition to Dick Taverne and Shirley Williams, Dick Mabon turns up as well.[1] At present we're working on Welsh devolution. Cledwyn had put forward another paper of what he thinks home rule for Wales would mean based on the Stormont parallel. But he doesn't want anything like the power of Stormont. He wants to leave social security, judiciary, Civil Service, and central government all at Westminster. I wasn't at all clear what the devil his Welsh Parliament *would* do.

Indeed I began to wonder after this meeting whether Wales was ready for a Stormont solution or whether what they really want is a new regional structure which could parallel the English regional structure we will have in the local government reorganization.

At the Party meeting Roy was explaining his budget and already I felt morale was better. People were laughing and talking in a natural way and two-thirds of the speeches were favourable. The only opposition was that of the Left to the prices and incomes policy. Harold chose to wind up, unwisely, I think. He made one of his threats to the Party about how he must force the prices and incomes policy through. He would have been wiser to let Roy finish the day off himself because there were many people who felt their questions hadn't been answered and they expected Roy to answer them instead of hearing Harold making one of his carefully written speeches.

My next job was to O.K. the big Ministerial brief which is to round off the three facets of our new economic policy and enable every Minister to make speeches on every aspect of it. This week I've had at last a new

[1] Labour M.P. for Greenock December 1955–74 and for Greenock and Port Glasgow since 1974. He was Joint Parliamentary Under-Secretary of State for Scotland 1964–7 and Minister of State at the Scottish Office 1967–70, and has been Minister of State at the Department of Energy since April 1976.

assistant, Paul Odgers, because I've finally been able to mobilize Michael Stewart's staff now that he's gone to the F.O. Odgers is from the Ministry of Education and has the rank of Assistant Under-Secretary and so is quite a senior man. He looked very white and old when he came in and then proceeded to say, looking up at me with his enormous blue eyes, 'I've sat at your feet. I was your worst pupil.' I looked into those eyes and suddenly I did see the undergraduate Odgers, my worst philosophy pupil, and had to admit he was right to call himself hopeless. But now he's quite a senior and quite a successful civil servant and extremely dedicated to the job he was doing for Michael and which Ward was failing to do for me. Of course he made mistakes this week and I could have written a better brief myself, but it was a brief and I went through most of it with him this afternoon before going off to Coventry.

Many weeks before, I'd promised my constituency that I would come down on the evening of the budget and discuss it with them. Of course I overlooked the fact that this particular Wednesday was the day for our absolutely crucial meeting of the liaison committee and that poor John Silkin would be ill and I would be away. And so I missed all the preparations for the business Statement and all the talk at the liaison committee about the future of George Brown and I just rushed off to the Midlands, where Tam had been spending the whole day at the Meriden by-election. As usual only some thirty people bothered to turn up to my G.M.C. but they were wonderfully different in mood from the previous two meetings—friendly and constructive and impressed by Roy as Chancellor and even impressed a little by me. Towards the end Tam came in and Anne drove us both back to Prescote.

Thursday, March 21st
We had to catch the very first train at 7.30 a.m. because I had to be at O.P.D. at 9.30. Glancing at the papers I saw that a big Israeli attack has been launched across the Jordan. At O.P.D. we managed to spend a lot of time worrying about a hodge-podge of problems. With George Brown out of the way Crosland is no longer content to accept the severe strategic embargo which Comecon imposes on trade between America's allies and Russia and China. He wants to go for a much more generous list. But Michael Stewart would have none of it and smacked him down, saying that this would be diplomatically damaging to us. Crosland is a strange man. He's extremely able, his contributions in Cabinet are always relevant and usually wise, and yet he's constantly putting up proposals which get defeated and fighting losing battles. And here I saw a difference. Tony Crosland is fifteen times the man Fred Mulley is but dim little Mulley boring away at his departmental brief gets the Department's way even though he's a bore, whereas despite his brilliance Tony often doesn't even succeed in helping his Department.

Next, a typical Stewart reaction on South African arms. The question was whether we should sell three Rolls Royce engines to South Africa after we'd discovered that we'd already sold nine of them to the French who, in turn, were going to sell them to the South Africans. The Departments wanted to get quietly rid of the last three and it seemed to me pretty obvious that if we didn't want a fuss we ought quite quietly to sell them off so that it shouldn't be known that we'd made the mistake of selling the nine. Everyone was agreeing with this when Michael jumped on his highest horse. 'That wouldn't be right,' he said, 'because we were already bound by the United Nations and therefore how could we sell three Rolls Royce engines?' After a long discussion he got the matter reserved but I'm pretty sure, knowing Michael, that having demonstrated moral principle he will give way quietly to the practical men in the Foreign Office who are going to run him.

Our last item was an interesting problem about UNCTAD, where there's a resolution which most members of the Cabinet want us to vote for committing us to contributing one per cent of our national income to overseas aid. But it is not committing us until 1980. This time Roy was the puritan saying we can't take on obligations which we can't and don't intend to sustain in a few years' time. Somebody remarked that the trouble about the British is that they're always determined to avoid making promises we can't fulfil when others are cheerfully making them and breaking them. Surely like others we should be freer and easier?

I didn't find this convincing because we were hardly very clever about the promise we made to the Kenya Asians, and indeed we've been constantly making promises we can't fulfil and that's one of the problems with this Government. All the promises we've made to Commonwealth Governments about defence during the last three years have come unstuck. I don't blame Roy for trying to build up the Government's credibility by avoiding commitments we can't keep.

I had hoped to slip back to my office after O.P.D. to have ten minutes preparing the business Statement before Cabinet started. But I hadn't time for it and as a result I found myself reading aloud the business of next week and finding I didn't understand next Thursday's business. When I read aloud four civil defence regulations Jim Callaghan broke in and said, 'We've had a debate on that. Why do we want another?' Now if I'd been properly briefed I should have explained that these were affirmative resolutions which the Home Secretary had asked for because he has to get them through the House before the end of March and each affirmative resolution has to be taken after ten and lasts usually an hour and a half to two hours. However, I was not convincing and then Willie Ross jumped in and said, 'What's all this about my Sewerage Bill being started at seven? The amendments aren't ready. I can't have that.' Of course this had been checked by Freddie Warren with Dick Mabon, who said everything was all right. But Willie Ross wouldn't have it and this morning my stock was low. It really was the first time I'd been in trouble in Cabinet as Leader of the House and challenged on my business Statement. If I'd just had ten minutes to look at my business Statement I could have understood it. But without those ten minutes I was incompetent, and the absence of John, who's been ill for three days, made my incompetence stick out even more prominently.

Next we came to Rhodesia and, as I guessed, we're going to support compulsory mandatory sanctions and go the whole hog at U.N.O. There's no checking Harold and now there's no checking Callaghan on this moral crusade. I've done my best and so has George Brown and Michael Stewart but on Rhodesia it's Harold's policy and Harold will always win. Even Michael toed the Harold line though he obviously didn't like it. On the other hand, with regard to the Israeli attack on Jordan he quietly explained that this was a response to guerilla activity and he was far more pro-Israel than George would have been.

The next thing was prices and incomes. We were still worrying about what on earth we can do about lower-paid workers, and once again a completely negative report had come from Peter Shore. We had another outbreak from Dick Marsh about the futility of the whole policy and the uneasy feeling that it has got out of control.

The last item was Post Office telegrams. A magnificent decision by the Postmaster-General to announce that the telegraph service will be completely closed down by 1971. To be fair to Harold he'd spotted this in the papers of Peter Shore's Industrial Committee and had himself put it on the Cabinet agenda. Peter made his case for no more telegrams and there was dead silence in Cabinet. No departmental Minister had been provided with a brief. So I had to come in though I talk far too much and I said, 'Is it really sensible with an image as bad as we've got to announce five years ahead the closure of the telegram service? I notice in these papers that the Postmaster-General admits that whereas 45 per cent of the people have telephones, 55 per cent mainly in agricultural areas don't have them at all in their houses and the telegram is still regarded as an essential service in times of stress. You can't just close the telegram service down unless you want to announce that this Government is failing.' We had a long discussion which led to a typically bad decision. The conclusion was that Cabinet had decided to close it down in 1971 but to postpone the announcement until a more favourable date.

In the House this afternoon the P.M. and I were both in good competent form. After us came Tony Benn's Statement on computers and I went out to talk to the P.M. 'I've been thinking it over,' I said, 'and I certainly shouldn't look a gift horse in the mouth. I accept the offer. I would like to be First Secretary with these responsibilities. But I thought that since I wouldn't have a Ministry to sit in I'd have to stay somewhere in the Cabinet Office. So I might as well stay in my present Lord President's Office for the time being.' He seemed a little puzzled that I was interested in this and couldn't conceive that I really cared about it. But quite honestly the only thing I do mind about is moving from the office where I've collected my pictures and where at last the silver is properly presented and the chairs are properly placed. I want to stay there for as long as I can and let Fred Peart go to Michael Stewart's rooms in the Cabinet Office. Ideally I'd like to be First Secretary and Lord President simultaneously, but I doubt if that is possible.

I then discussed the whole issue of George Brown retaining the deputy leadership; Harold said he wouldn't touch the idea with a barge-pole. Already on Sunday at supper he had suggested that Douglas Houghton should take George Brown's place as deputy leader but that of course is entirely for the liaison committee and the Party to decide. What George Brown should do is to resign from the deputy leadership and accept the general secretaryship or something like it at Transport House. After all the deputy leadership is quite a modern invention. It was created to give Herbert Morrison a place on the N.E.C. when I knocked him off. He had been Deputy Prime Minister but that hadn't given him a place on the N.E.C. and so the constitution was changed and he was elected to the N.E.C. as deputy leader and as a second representative of the parliamentary leadership. But no one expected that the Deputy Prime Minister would walk out of the Government and on his resignation make an attack on the Prime Minister and then try to stay on as deputy leader. If George tries to fight this issue there'll be a big struggle because I think Jim Callaghan will go for the deputy leadership and so will Barbara and Michael Stewart and almost certainly Roy. Nevertheless, there is quite a problem on the N.E.C. As a result of a series of accidents the Foreign Secretary won't be at the meeting, the Chancellor won't be there and I won't be there because I've resigned, so if Harold isn't there the parliamentary leadership is extremely weak.[1]

This evening Peter Shore made another of his languid disastrous speeches[2] and I got a message that Roy wanted to see me. I went in and before he could speak I said that I wanted to fill him in. 'I've seen the Prime Minister and told him that Peter will have to go,' and went on to say that Harold had told me he knew that already and had made up his own mind. I got all that out quick and Roy said, 'Well, I really sent for you to say the same thing to you. It's a relief we all agree.' Then I went on, 'I'd better tell you now that Harold has talked to me about the future and offered me a new job,' and I described roughly what the job was. He at once said that I was right to accept and that it was far better than Defence.

By this time I had to go upstairs to the Party meeting, where poor John Silkin had been trying to get authority as Chief Whip to suspend a member and then to continue the period of suspension. Alas, the Chief Whip's authority has been sadly undermined by Douglas Houghton's ridiculous code of conduct which has transferred more and more authority from the Whips to the liaison committee. John's having a very tough time combined with a

[1] George Brown retained the deputy leadership until 1970.
[2] Forty-two minutes.

physical illness. I gather it's kidney trouble and he's looking extremely ill. He had to sit there quietly while Douglas Houghton explained in his tortuous way that the liaison committee wanted the meeting to approve the Silkin amendment. When he sat down there was dead silence and nobody got up until Hugh Jenkins moved against with a three-minute speech and the thing went through on the nod. Poor John, he was sick to death of it because he knew that tomorrow's papers will describe yet another humiliating defeat for the Chief Whip.

This afternoon I had a most encouraging meeting about the future of the Hansard Society. I want it taken over by the Services Committee and given £5,000 or £6,000 a year to run our public relations, the lectures to schools on the one side and the receiving of foreign visitors on the other as well as maintaining a good journal. And here was Mr Biggs—an excellent business-man who's now the chairman of the Society—really keen on a practical job of reform.[1]

I had a jolly nice end to Thursday because that morning Harold sent me a message that he didn't want to go to Tommy Balogh's party in Hampstead. Would I take Mary? Of course I would, so at 9 p.m. the car drove up to No. 10 and I stepped out and there was Mary coming down the stairs looking elegant and soignée. We had a delicious time chattering away in the back of the car on the way because we'd broken the ice last Sunday and we were able to discuss old times and what it felt like to be a Prime Minister's wife, what it felt like to sit next to L.B.J., not understanding a word of his Texan lingo, what it felt like to read 'Mrs Wilson's Diary' in *Private Eye*—the diary is even coming out as a play quite soon. She has become totally different from the woman I remember when Harold was made Leader and she sat in No. 9 Vincent Square feeling embittered and unhappy and not wanting to go to No. 10. Now she is one of the great successes of the Government and she's created her own completely independent personal image. Every interview she's given has been a success and she's hardly put a foot wrong. As a result she has built up her self confidence and behaves more like a widow than a wife. She is alive and she plays a bigger role in his life than ever and he's not jealous of her success because she's so cool, collected and determined not to go beyond herself.

On the way up to Hampstead we agreed that we would leave at a certain hour and sure enough when an hour and a quarter was finished she came across and we got away. By the time we left there were still very few people there but I had a word with Paul Johnson and I saw Jock Campbell come in and I expect it was three in the morning before this London party reached its climax. Thank God I wasn't there. I was driving back with Mary, chatting again in the back of the car and she was saying what a lovely evening she'd had and I had to admit it was a lovely evening too. After this evening I like

[1] Norman P. Biggs was chairman from 1967 to 1968. Despite this encouraging meeting the Society preferred to retain their independence.

her as much as I like Pam. It's nice having as a friend a remarkable woman whom one can like without any jealousy or feeling of disloyalty and it was a splendid evening which I shall remember.

Friday, March 22nd

At our weekly business meeting Burke, Harold, the Chief and I were there and also Michael Stewart taking the place of George Brown. Was Michael there as Deputy Prime Minister? I have no idea. Anyhow we planned the business for next week and decided to give ourselves a few more days to get the Prices and Incomes White Paper ready and to present it to Cabinet not on Tuesday but on Thursday. The P.M. will have to have a lot of negotiations with the T.U.C. and with the trade-union M.P.s and he's obviously alarmed about the conflict and has the feeling that we must leave room for manoeuvre and not commit ourselves to a White Paper we can't support later on.

Our next meeting was the Home Affairs Committee under the chairmanship of the Lord Chancellor with that splendid topic, the future of Aintree, on which I spent so much time along with George Wigg when I was Minister of Housing.[1] Everybody knows that the racecourse is owned by an extraordinary old lady of eighty-four who has to be kept going each year and the difficulty is that if she dies before a sensible agreement is made the land will be sold to the highest bidder. From the start I'd supported the Lancashire County Council, which wanted to get a compulsory purchase order and establish a sports centre there as the permanent activity with a fortnight of racing a year. But that wasn't exactly the mood of my successor at Housing. The debate started with Tony Greenwood who for the first time in my experience was speaking to Cabinet with something like fervour. He thought it was wicked for socialists to put our money into horse-racing. Many people objected to the Grand National and one just couldn't justify spending the huge sums required for compulsory purchase and rebuilding. He just wasn't going to permit the money normally allocated for planning and development and parks and recreation grounds to be spent on such activity. Up against him was Denis Howell—a tough little Birmingham M.P. who deals with sport in the Ministry of Education.[2] He and I had worked on the subject before and we weighed in jointly against Tony. We said the Grand National was unique and to lose Aintree would be like losing Epsom Downs. Anyway there's a tremendous lot of money in racing and gambling and we have the Totalisator Board, chaired by Lord Wigg, who are all profoundly concerned. Indeed, Denis said, the Liverpool Corporation would only be the ground landlords and the Totalisator Board would run the show. Unfortunately, however, Denis Howell is a great fiction writer. There really was no reason to believe that

[1] See Vol. I, p. 507.
[2] Labour M.P. for Birmingham All Saints 1955–9 and Small Heath since 1961. He was Parliamentary Under-Secretary of State at the D.E.S. 1964–9 and at the M.H.L.G. 1969–70. Since 1974 he has been Minister of State at the D.O.E.

his statements of fact were true and I had to insist that the Committee must have a full written statement from the official committee and postpone a decision. It was a great morning. Against us were ranged the anti-blood sports league, the Lord Chancellor, thin-lipped and implacable, and of course the Welsh and the Scots. But on our side we had Harold Lever, Denis Howell and even—I'm glad to say—Charlie Grey, the Labour Deputy Chief Whip from Durham, who was against Aintree for moral reasons but knew we had to save it. I know I'm right in saying the country wouldn't forgive us if we let Mrs Topham sell it for building development.

Then I was off to one of my press lunches at the Garrick where I was again airing the subject of devolution because of the Prime Minister's speech at Ayr. They thought it meant he had decided against devolution but I told them they were wrong. We also discussed the radio experiment in the Commons which is to take place between Easter and Whitsun. Some interesting problems have come up. We shall have to change the law of defamation and we shall have to consider what will happen when for the first time the B.B.C. gets total coverage of every word spoken in the House. Should they be permitted to sell these tapes to other people? What would be the B.B.C.'s rights to the actual voices of M.P.s and to select the sentences they would use? The more I think about this the more difficult I find it.

I went back to the Privy Council Office to give Jimmy Margach a briefing. Very reluctantly I had agreed with Harold to see him again but nobody else.*

After he'd gone Bob Maxwell blew in at my urgent summons because in the tea-room this morning I discovered that instructions have been given by the fellow who runs the Catering Department to serve powdered milk in tea. We'd already had foreign cheese forbidden in our own restaurant but powdered milk was going a long way. I asked Bob how he could allow this to happen and he explained, 'I've given the chap a commission of £200 a year for any savings he got and he made a saving of £100 a week on powdered milk.' 'Well, you can't make that saving,' I said. 'Off with it this afternoon,' and I'm glad to say it went.

I caught a train to Nuneaton for the by-election at Meriden and then produced an extremely good press release out of the vast brief which I had prepared for my colleagues. I delivered the speech to a small meeting of thirty to thirty-five people in a remote village. By our standards it was quite a decent meeting but of course though all the press were there not a line of it will be published tomorrow. I always remember what Harold Macmillan said about a good speech. 'When you've written one,' he said, 'repeat it again and again until the press print it.' So I shall go on with my first-rate comments on the budget.

* And anybody who works at the two Sunday papers—the *Observer* and the *Sunday Times*—will see the difference. The *Observer* is arguing that No. 10 is trying to ditch Roy Jenkins whereas Jimmy Margach is saying there's a solid relationship between the Chancellor and the Prime Minister. Of course Margach had been briefed by me.

Anne brought the car to Nuneaton to pick me up and so we got home reasonably early tonight and I have a solid two days of holiday weekend in front of me. I'm ruthless now at hogging weekends for myself. Of course I shan't be able to have anything like this number when I become First Secretary with a vast Department to manage and any number of outside engagements. Still, that's a reason for getting the holiday now while I have the chance.

Sunday, March 24th
Last night I went to dinner with Harry and Mary Judge. He is the headmaster of our comprehensive school and I found with them the headmaster of the Bicester comprehensive school with his wife, who is a hospital nurse and now has four children. In addition there was a splendid character called Terry Frost—a very modern artist who teaches art at Reading University—and lastly there were our oldest and best friends here—Anne and Richard Hartree. In the course of the conversation Harry, who doesn't often talk politics to me now, asked me whether big decisions worried a politician more than small decisions. My first answer was that they don't—anyway in my case. Before I became a Minister I used to worry and worry and worry because on the *New Statesman* Kingsley frustrated all my decisions, and I'm a person who loves responsibility. But I found it too easy to answer Harry's question at a superficial level and so I began quietly to think out what were the feelings of the member of this Government, which got in with a big majority and which is now almost universally despised and condemned. Then I began to describe what happens to me on Monday morning at Banbury station (as I once mentioned in this diary).

Life is really pretty humiliating and painful, I said, for a member of a very unsuccessful Government. At which of course they all asked why on earth we stayed on. Long before devaluation we must have passed the point of no return and we are now marching towards almost certain defeat in the next election. Why don't we pack it in? Of course the answer is to be found in the central dynamic of our two-party system. The whole impetus and drive makes a Government which is unsuccessful struggle on and on and on right up to the election rather than admitting defeat. A modern political Party can't go to the country saying we failed and others should take over. The only way this could happen is if the Party's split right down the middle, as John Mackintosh pointed out in a very perceptive article the other day. An election now would be absolutely disastrous for us and we might have a landslide against us of 1931 dimensions. But in two years' time things may look a great deal better and each individual member of the Parliamentary Party will be feeling there's a reasonable chance of our getting back. I think that's the explanation for the present curious mood at Westminster. Nobody talks about the Government being defeated next time but deep down everybody assumes that we're not going to come back as a Government though we may well recover our position to some extent and improve the composition of the Party. Of course things are different for me and for Gerald Gardiner and quite a number of others who haven't any future after 1970. I can expect, if I want it, a position in the House of Lords but for me these years ahead till the election of 1970 are my last three years of political power. I've spent my life trying to climb to the top and to exert political power and now I'm there these two years are what I have to live for and the only issue is whether, when they're over, I shall get right out of Parliament and start writing my book.

Today was particularly pleasant because Jock Campbell and Phyllis, his wife, motored over from Nettlebed, where they have a lovely big house and where Thomas is to be provided with a cottage in their garden. We have met them more than once at political parties and found them both extremely nice. Between them, because they've both been married more than once, they've got seven children and he's a big businessman, but he's also one of those idealistic businessmen socialists who are a little bit of an embarrassment to me. I suppose the only businessman with a business equal to Jock's is Bob Maxwell, that adventurous erratic creature. But within his lights Jock remains a correct high-minded socialist who enjoys having long talks about the morality of possession and the taxation of wealth. When we began to discuss Roy's attitude, Jock was clear that his budget was against the wealthy socialists and welcomed it warmly. Then he turned to the House of Lords and I gave him a description of our two-tier system and he was relieved to hear that although he couldn't be there all the time he would be able to be a voting peer and do his job since we wouldn't ask for more than one-third attendance. Finally we took him over to Farnborough Hall, the place where John Makepeace and Ann Sutton create their furniture and fabrics, and we sent them home with some lovely tables packed in the back of their little Volkswagen. It was a very enjoyable afternoon.

This evening, before I start out for London, I want to put down here a little bit of research I've been doing about the question of how the appalling balls-ups take place in the Cabinet. The one I selected was Callaghan's Immigration Bill—the lack of preparation and the incompetence of the last-minute rush. I've gone through all the Cabinet documents and will just note them down here. July 6th, 1965, C(65)93. Paper from Soskice. This little paper came forward on the same day as the main paper about Commonwealth immigration. See C(65), 35th meeting. Cabinet conclusions page 111. See C(65), 42nd meeting. White Paper. Cabinet discussion. Then we have a great big jump to H(67)119. That's Jenkins's paper to the Home Affairs Committee. Then we go H(67)29, CI(68)1, CI(68)3, C(68)34, C(68)35, C(68)36, CC(68) 13th meeting, C(68)39 21st meeting, CC(68) 15th meeting, February 27th. Those I think are the relevant Cabinet papers. Apart from a few notes at the end about the exact meetings and my own private papers, I haven't got any record of my private meeting with Roy in October 1967 but I have some notes of my meetings with Callaghan in February 1968.

The conclusion from these papers is absolutely clear. Already in 1965 we

should have known all about the Kenya Asians because a paper was put up
to Cabinet raising all the problems. This paper was considered in connection
with the main paper on immigration and the subject of the Kenya Asians was
excluded. But (and this is the important thing) there was a specific Cabinet
injunction that the Commonwealth Immigration Committee should study
the subject of Kenya Asians and make recommendations about it. This 1965
instruction to the Commonwealth Immigration Committee was completely
disregarded. The next event is the meeting of the Home Affairs Committee in
October 1967, when Jenkins presented his conclusions. So for two years,
between 1965 and 1967, although the problem was known to exist nothing was
done about it until it suddenly became acute. Why was there not at least
some contingency planning for a crisis between 1965 and 1967? Presumably
because the Home Office didn't want to touch the subject. The responsibility
rested with the Cabinet Secretariat, which is supposed to be a kind of super
progress-chaser and to keep a look-out for all Cabinet decisions and watch
that they're adequately carried out.

So we come to the second stage. Jenkins suddenly sees the problem as a
potential crisis in the autumn and comes to me privately asking me to slot a
Bill in secretly. In October he puts the problem to Home Affairs. And then
what happens? Apparently absolutely nothing at all until suddenly in
February Callaghan says he must have a Bill in a matter of weeks. So there
are two intervals to explain—the two-year interval in which no contingency
planning is done, and even more urgent the interval between the Home
Affairs Committee's decisions of October 1967 and the moment in February
when Callaghan suddenly feels that action must be taken although no
international work, no preparation for a Bill, no contingency planning has
been undertaken. What wants looking at pretty carefully is the competence
of the Cabinet Secretariat to provide the central dynamic and follow-up for
all decisions taken by Cabinet and Cabinet Committees.

Monday, March 25th
I was up in Vincent Square and had plenty of time to read the morning papers.
They all carried inspired stories about the battle between Roy Jenkins and
the Prime Minister on the future of the D.E.A. The reason why they all
have this is quite illuminating. In the *Sunday Telegraph* Ian Waller—who
hasn't been doing too well for some time since his chief source of information,
George Wigg, resigned—had a huge front-page story describing how Jenkins
wanted to close the D.E.A. down. I found it extremely unlikely, because I
knew the Prime Minister wouldn't agree and I didn't think it was probable
that Jenkins would try a direct assault and that if he did he would give the
story to Ian Waller. So I looked at it with interest but grave suspicion. Yet
today—and this is characteristic of the British press—John Bourne of the
Financial Times and Ian Aitken of the *Guardian* and the rest of them all had
stories along the same line. If you read them carefully there's no more

information in them. What they've done is to lift Waller's story from the *Telegraph* and rewrite it with mild variations giving the impression that they have new facts where there are no new facts. In the old days one paper had a scoop and the others just were angry. Now there are never individual scoops because as soon as a story appears in the early edition of one paper it is rapidly written out in another version and published in all the rest. So there's a tendency for every *canard* to be rapidly magnified by sheer repetition into something which looks like truth. I rang up the P.M. and we tracked the story down. It was given to Ian Waller as an anti-Shore item and he dolled it up as an important news story. The sober fact is that so far from closing down D.E.A. the P.M. is going to strengthen it. He's sending Bill Nield to be the Permanent Secretary and Alex Jarratt,[1] one of the best men at the Ministry of Labour, is managing prices and incomes and I still think it's possible he may put Barbara Castle there as well.

When I got to the office this morning I had nothing whatsoever to do. Actually poor old Freddy Ward, who'd been away sick for seven or eight weeks, looked in—well, cheerful and relaxed—and we had a long pleasant talk. Freddy has come back to find me actively doing the work of the First Secretary with the help of Odgers, who of course is a rank above him. He knows very well that my Private Office is a terribly easy job. There are moments of rush but normally we're greatly over-staffed and one of these days I'm going to work out for myself the manpower cost of keeping me as Lord President and ask whether it's worth it. Well, it was one of those easy mornings in the office and in due course I rang up Burke Trend about the Prices and Incomes White Paper. I had time to read the draft over the weekend and discuss it with the Chancellor and I told Burke that it was in a desperately bad form and that he should put the conclusions at the beginning and then completely rewrite it and I gave him a number of ideas. But the main thing was that it shouldn't be deliberately obscure. We might have to go back on it or modify it but it ought to tell people clearly what we were going to do and provide marching orders for the officials. He said he would give instructions along these lines.

At lunch-time I went along to the House of Lords' bar to pick up Alma Birk, who is a new peeress. Alma is nice but is an enormously ambitious and talkative woman and she wanted to talk to me about the relative standing of the peers in the Parliamentary Party. I explained to her that at the present moment the Labour peers are all automatically members of the Parliamentary Labour Party. They come to the meetings and they vote on any policy issue which is going to be discussed in the Lords as well as in the Commons. So on prescription charges or prices and incomes they are perfectly entitled to swell the Government vote or indeed—as they did on prescription charges—to swell

[1] Alex Jarratt was Secretary to the P.I.B. 1965–8, Deputy Under-Secretary of State at the D.E.P. 1968–70, managing director of I.P.C. 1970–73 and, since 1973, its chairman. Since 1974 he has been chairman of Reed International Ltd.

the opposition vote. I told her there'd always been questioning among Labour back-benchers in the Commons as to whether we should allow Labour peers to swamp our meetings in that way. Certainly when we have reformed the House of Lords there'll be quite a strong case for having two separate Parliamentary Labour Parties meeting separately which then can work out joint policies and joint decisions. But that's some way ahead.

After the memorial service for Sydney Silverman I walked back to the House with Emrys Hughes and we discussed Scottish nationalism. Today's papers had contained a surprising report of the annual Scottish Labour Party Conference at Ayr. It was clear that when Harold had tried to stage a comeback there he had made a rather dull speech. But, even more significant, the Scottish Labour Party under Willie Ross's leadership had crushingly rebutted John Mackintosh and the young turks who were trying to get a motion put forward in favour of early consideration of Scottish self-government. This was obviously the work of Willie Ross, and I said to Emrys that I thought it was time he was moved. 'Who are you going to have?' he asked me, and I said I didn't know whether we should have Dick Mabon or George Thomson. 'George Thomson,' he said, 'would be worse than Willie Ross. A whited sepulchre. He's only a fraud of a man. He won't impress Scotland.' 'If you feel so strongly,' I said, 'you ought to tell the Prime Minister about that.' 'Do you think he'd like it?' And I said, 'He certainly would.'

I went into the Chamber this evening to hear the wind-up of the last day of the budget debate. Budget debates are always quiet, orderly affairs and on this occasion there was even less excitement because we were working according to the new procedure by which we were to have just one vote at the end of the budget speech, with people coming in to vote at ten in the normal way.[1] I watched Roy with some interest because he was deliberately trying to pick a quarrel with Ted Heath who wasn't there. Ted had sent a letter apologizing for his absence because he had a previous engagement. This previous engagement was to receive a watch from Manny Shinwell at a dinner of the National Sporting Club at the Dorchester. I can only conceive that this was a calculated insult by Ted Heath since the apology didn't arrive till 6.30 p.m. Nevertheless it was interesting how deliberately Roy worked up the quarrel with the leader of the Opposition. No doubt he was angry at his absence because after all Heath had made the major speech on the other side and Roy's speech was a careful answer to it. Not that with the Labour Members in the House in that mood, Heath's absence made much difference. Roy was able to stir the budget debate out of its lethargy and keep the row going throughout his wind-up.

Tuesday, March 26th
I had to be at the House of Lords at 10 a.m. because we were resuming our conversations after a fortnight's interval. We had chosen 10 a.m. in order to

[1] The vote was 332 to 248.

get a solid day's work in which to discuss Mr Macleod. From the start he had said that even if we agreed a scheme of reform its implementation must be postponed until the next Parliament. Last Monday we'd had a long talk with Eddie Shackleton, who provided an excellent paper showing what a fatal thing this three-year delay would be. Of course we all knew that if the momentum of the agreement were dropped and if for example a Tory Government were elected, reform in this form would simply never take place. But there was a further powerful argument, the effect of delay on the composition of the House. If we delay reform until the next Parliament we will have to create a hundred new peers. Instead of starting with people who know the tradition and are able to evolve a new House out of the old we will have a complete break. After all, that is something no Tory will accept. Under our scheme we intend to introduce a retiring age first of seventy-five and then, fairly soon, to reduce it to seventy-two, but the old boys are needed to initiate the new House and cushion it for the change.

Eddie's excellent paper provided me with the unexpected arguments I needed to rebut Macleod. So I got to the committee room and settled myself in at 9.55, at 10.05 Frank Byers[1] from the Liberals slouched in and at 10.10 Jellicoe and Maudling came along and said that Carrington was ill again. Our people line up punctually but the slackness and informality of the Tories is remarkable. And at 10.15 (I had to go to the P and I Committee at 11) Macleod was still not there and we had a message that he had forgotten the meeting was in the morning and thought it was in the afternoon. So once again we agreed to drop consideration of his objection. But as a result we got one advantage because we clipped our way through a whole series of secondary points—the problem of the bishops, the problems of affirmative orders, and the law lords—three of the most important and difficult secondary issues were settled.

When we deal with this kind of detail Jellicoe clearly understands because he's on Shackleton's working party, but Maudling is completely out of his depth. The contrast between the enthusiasm of the Tory peers and the lack of interest of the Tories from the lower House is striking and alarming. As for Macleod, he shows no interest except a mild desire to sabotage, while Maudling is amiable, conscientious and willing to go along with almost anything we propose. I haven't ever been able to decide why the Tories have taken this acquiescent co-operative line in these talks. I suspect the reason is that they regard House of Lords reform as very much their own subject and the kind of thing they would do as a Government on the basis of official papers provided from Whitehall. Since we have all the Whitehall official papers they by and large accept our proposals.

At 10.45 I was able to go off to the meeting of the Prices and Incomes Committee with Roy in the chair and settle down to deal with this ghastly

---

[1] Lord Byers, Liberal M.P. for North Dorset 1945–50. He became a life peer in 1964 and, since 1967, had been Liberal Leader in the House of Lords.

White Paper. It had been slightly reorganized since I read it over the weekend but was still unbearably bad. Its sloppiness did not surprise me. What did surprise me was that Peter Shore, who is a brilliant draftsman when he wants to be, seems to have done nothing himself. The remarkable fact about Barbara Castle is that she drafts her own White Papers and that's why she gets her way, but here is Peter, promoted far beyond his station by the P.M., and he is too grand now to do the drafting which would make his paper tolerable.

As we moved through its clauses we came to a whole section where the officials informed us that the text as we saw it was now invalid because masses of amendments had been drafted into it by the official committee the day before but there hadn't been time to incorporate them in our text. Apparently the officials assumed we would approve them unread. Even worse, Peter then said that he wanted to have the White Paper presented to Cabinet in printed form so that it couldn't be changed.[1] At this I blew my top. 'I won't consent to that either here in committee or far less in Cabinet,' I said and insisted on another meeting tomorrow morning, for which all of us had to cancel meetings. It was a tough moment.

After this I went down to No. 10 and found Thomas Balogh hanging about outside the Cabinet room. One of my advantages is that I can go in now whenever I like. I don't use the ordinary door but go through Burke Trend's room and the Secretaries' room and so in with Michael Halls. And that's how I slipped in this time and found myself, as I always do, chatting with Harold about devolution and how we were doing on the Committee. I don't think he was very interested but he sometimes likes chatting for its own sake.

In the afternoon, on a lovely warm spring day, I rushed along the passage to see the Labour peers. Eddie had said he wanted to make the first speech and, my God, he spoke for twenty-five minutes and outlined the scheme in a rather boring way. I then spoke and took questions on which I had answers ready before I had to go. Eddie is an old friend of mine, a reliable, decent friend, a very nice man, but a congenital conservative, an amasser of influence and power. Now that he has become Leader of the House of Lords he isn't going to let me take over the leadership or take all the credit for the reform, and God knows he and his working party have worked hard at it and he is entitled to do so.

I gather the first impact of this meeting was surprisingly good. Edith Summerskill was the only person who really objected and she's a cantankerous bitch who would do so anyway.[2] To everybody's surprise old Dick Mitchison, who is the most difficult of our peers, gave his blessing and young people like Alma Birk and Patricia Llewelyn-Davies seemed quite enthusiastic. It's also

[1] The White Paper, Productivity, Prices and Incomes Policy in 1968 and 1969 (Cmnd. 3590) was published on April 3rd.

[2] Lady Summerskill, Labour M.P. for West Fulham 1938–55 and for Warrington 1955–61, was Minister of National Insurance 1950–51. She became a life peer in 1961.

interesting that though one hundred peers were present there was not a trace of a leak to the press after they'd been asked to keep it confidential. That's more than could ever be said for the Parliamentary Labour Party. And one asks oneself why the Labour peers are so much more discreet than the Labour M.P.s when they meet. I find the House of Lords an infinitely nicer place than the House of Commons, an infinitely better club and I shan't be sorry when I join it in due course. As a member of the Lords in Opposition in the reformed House I have created my position will be infinitely better than if I were a member of the Opposition in the House of Commons.

Back in my Committee on devolution I have Dick Mabon (a careful calculating man), who, after the defeat of the Mackintoshites at Ayr, put forward the proposals of the Secretary of State himself. What Willie Ross wants is a regional Select Committee, a U.K. one with English members as well but sitting in Edinburgh. That's to be the big new thing. He's also willing to consider the expansion of the work of the Scottish Grand Committee, possibly meeting in Edinburgh as well as in London.[1] That's about the total of their package apart from some minor devolution of items like historic buildings and transport. Having heard both sides I said I had to weigh it up and Dick said, 'Why don't you do a paper?' and so I had to. I am getting very lazy but I have knocked off a paper summing up the situation in Scotland.

Next the Services Committee. I was very busy this afternoon with Barnett Cocks in his most characteristic mood. The problem was that we'd reckoned that the Clerks' establishment should be forty-two and we all considered that we must now bring them up to full strength, i.e. appoint three more, since there are only thirty-nine. At this point Barnett Cocks drew himself up and said that he could do nothing of this sort. He's a tall willowy creature with pale sandy hair and pale blue eyes, just like a don at Oxford, but after years in his present position he has all the obstinacy and weakness of a Persian shah. As Accounting Officer, he told me, he had already told the Treasury he would keep the number down to thirty-nine in view of the financial emergency. 'But the last time I saw you,' I said, 'you weren't just a Treasury official, you emphasized to me that you were totally independent as Clerk of the House of Commons and you even put it to me last summer that you couldn't negotiate the salaries of your staff: all you could do was to lay them down because Clerks were too superior to negotiate. Yet today you're saying to me that you're not only a civil servant but you're absolutely the slave of the Treasury and you can't authorize an increase of your establishment from thirty-nine to forty-two.' 'Ah,' he said, 'that's my two hats. As Accounting Officer I wear one hat and then I have to help the Treasury in carrying their policy out, but as

[1] Since 1957 the committee stages of Bills on Scottish matters may be taken in a smaller Scottish Standing Committee. A larger body, the Scottish Grand Committee, contains Members from all Scottish constituencies and may debate not just the estimates and principle of Bills but also matters of general concern to Scotland. There is also a Welsh Grand Committee.

Chief Clerk I have another hat and then I have to say how many Clerks I really need.' 'Well, take off your Treasury hat,' I said, 'and put on your Clerk's hat.' 'I can't do that,' he said. 'I have written my annual report. All I want you to do is to overrule me.' So we solemnly overruled Sir Barnett Cocks and it was decided that I should write to the Chancellor saying that in the next Session we shall need three extra Clerks and we must prepare for that by recruiting them in this Session.

Anne was up this evening and we had to go to a dinner given in my honour by the Dutch Ambassador. Months ago he'd asked if he could give this dinner and I could hardly refuse. We went to Millionaires' Row and there was a grand house and inside it was panelled and comfortable and very wealthy-looking. To receive me there was a very big strapping woman and a little tiny man beside her. I suppose they had gathered together a normal Ambassador's dinner for us. There was Sir Dingle and Lady Foot, Peter Thorneycroft and his Italian countess painter wife,[1] Charles Villiers (who is now head of the new Industrial Reorganization Corporation at £20,000 a year and who was my pupil at New College),[2] Lord St Aldwyn (the Chief Tory Whip in the Lords) and his wife, and also John Foot,[3] who sat next to Anne and gave her a splendid evening. I only go to these things once in a blue moon—and how wise I am.

In the House this evening we had the Consolidated Fund Bill. Under our new reforms neither the Chief Whip nor I have to be there because no count is possible after ten p.m. and only the people who really want to stay for it. Michael Stewart had to be there at eight in the morning for the debate on the Falkland Islands, one of the last before the adjournment.

Wednesday, March 27th

The big news in the papers was George Brown's decision to stay on as deputy leader. I had missed the liaison committee last week when they had discussed the idea that Douglas Houghton might take his place. But it had become clear that there would be a contested election and that is something we have to avoid even if it means leaving him in the office. There's also a considerable advantage in his staying deputy leader as it prevents him from attacking the Government in any way whatsoever, either in his newspaper articles or in speeches.

The other big news was the result of an N.O.P. poll which says there's a

---

[1] Conservative M.P. for Stafford 1938–45 and for Monmouth 1945–66. A former Conservative Minister, he became a life peer in 1967. His wife was Countess Carla Roberti.

[2] A managing director of J. Henry Schroder Wagg 1960–68, and managing director of the I.R.C. 1968–71. Since 1971 he has been chairman of Guinness Mahon and Co. Ltd, and, from 1973 to 1976, executive deputy chairman of the Guinness Peat Group. He received a knighthood in 1976 and, some weeks later, his appointment was announced as Chairman of the British Steel Corporation.

[3] John Foot (a brother of Michael Foot) became a life peer in 1967 and sat on the Liberal benches. Since 1970 he has been chairman of the United Kingdom Immigrants Advisory Service.

24 per cent swing to the Tories in Dudley. I also noticed that the P.M.'s briefing of the press about the future of the D.E.A. has had its effect. The papers were now asserting officially that the P.M. was going to build up the D.E.A. and not to destroy it.

This morning we resumed our P and I Cabinet Committee. The redraft had been knocked together in reasonable form and we didn't have to spend an interminable time on it. Roy was in the chair as usual. He doesn't do a great deal of work beforehand—indeed he hardly reads a draft. He's also inexperienced and quite deferential to me. In fact he prefers me to do his homework on this kind of occasion and I'm quite prepared to do it although I don't know anything about the subject either. Ray Gunter, the Minister of Labour who could help, refuses to do so. It's horrifying to think that this is the way major policies have to be evolved.

One big thing we had to do this afternoon was to deal with the nurses' wage claim. The Prices and Incomes Board having reported on it, we were told it was due to be announced on Thursday. We all soon agreed that the nurses should be given their full 9 per cent. I remembered how in 1962 Selwyn Lloyd gave the surtax payers their tax concession and cut the nurses' pay. Here we can prove that Roy does the opposite. He gives the nurses their pay claim and the surtax payers a new tax on capital. But the main thing we had to ensure was that the concession to the nurses fitted with the rest of the White Paper. We had to sit down and rewrite a lot of the draft giving far more emphasis to the reconstruction of wages where productivity plans have led to greater efficiency. In this way we have managed to drive a coach and four through the $3\frac{1}{2}$ per cent ceiling. But that's something I can't admit publicly.

I was asked to lunch with David Astor and was puzzled about what on earth he wanted to discuss since we lunched alone. We started by discussing Adam von Trott, who was as old a friend of his as he was of mine. He mentioned to me that Christopher Sykes was publishing a new biography of von Trott which was hopelessly unsympathetic because he treated him as a traitor.[1] I said I would certainly try to review the book and give my opinion.

This afternoon was the big debate on Rhodesia, which was preceded by an extraordinary muddle and in-fighting behind the scenes. Harold Wilson, who is always jumpy about Rhodesia, couldn't make up his mind on the tactics he wanted to pursue. Should the debate be on the adjournment or should it be on a positive Government motion? All yesterday he'd been jumping to and fro and then suddenly I had been informed that it was to be on a motion which had been placed on the Order Paper for today. This had been done by Harold and the Chief without bothering to tell me. At once the Tories had begun to make a great fuss and to ask for a business Statement to announce the change of business. I had received a brief note from Freddie Warren saying that there was no need for a business Statement.

[1] *Troubled Loyalty* (London: Collins, 1968).

Well, a Lord President must get used to this kind of behaviour by Chief Whips who are much more experienced than he is. But it did nettle me that before today's debate started there was a great deal of booing on the Tory side and public and quite legitimate complaints about the absence of the business Statement. What was behind it all was Harold's uncertainty whether he should speak before Heath (on a positive motion) or after Heath on the adjournment.

When the speech itself finally came it wasn't bad though it was a bit heavy going and Harold was constantly interrupted from below the gangway. There's nothing more difficult for a front-bench man than to make a speech when the Opposition are deliberately creating an atmosphere of disrespect. On Harold's last big occasion they talked to each other quietly but quite loudly throughout his speech and succeeded in putting him off. On this occasion they didn't talk but selected the device of constant interruptions on points of order. As I said to the Chief afterwards, 'I didn't want Harold to make a good speech because he would then try to repeat his triumph. We want to keep him out of the limelight now and prevent him speaking too often.' That's the treatment our Prime Minister really needs for the next two or three months while he's so unpopular.

This evening after the liaison committee I raised the whole issue of devolution with Freddie Warren. It is clear that neither the Welsh nor the Scots are ready for full self-government but what they would like and what would go down well is devolution plus the visible signs of M.P.s being interested in regional affairs. So I wanted to see special Scottish and Welsh Select Committees sitting in Cardiff and Edinburgh. I want a Monday each fortnight perhaps when Members are in their own regions and I want a host of other devices which would present the image of Parliament in the regions.

This evening I had a word with Percy Clark and Terry Pitt about Government publicity and Transport House. Days ago I sent a text of the brief across to Terry and yet I learnt that no one in Transport House knew anything about it. Sometimes I weep at how we run this Government. We produce an absolutely first-rate brief on Roy's new economic policy which only goes to individual Ministers because it's my job to service them. But where it's most needed is of course Transport House and for back-benchers, to whom we're not allowed to hand out copies. So I had arranged that I would send copies to Transport House for them to process there and provide a version for everybody who required it. Well, they've done absolutely nothing at all. I must say I feel glad that I'm going to move to a job where I shall have no relations with Transport House. Of course it's true that as a result of my resigning from the Executive I've lost a tremendous lot of influence. I've done exactly what Barbara predicted. I've removed myself in the year when it was most important to be on it. However, that can't be helped. I am semi-retired. The edge of my ambition is off and that's a fact.

I had accepted an invitation to a farewell dinner for Philip Hendy, who was leaving the National Gallery to become adviser to the Israeli Art Gallery in Jerusalem. When I got there in my dinner jacket I ran into Harold Lever and his beautiful wife who were sitting at the top table but when I looked at the plan I noticed that I myself was at table 12 along with Anthony Lousada and John and Lady Witt.[1] Anthony and John were both at New College with me. It was pretty interesting to sit down and see what impact the speeches make when one is not at the top table. There were Jennie Lee and Philip Hendy with probably the most distinguished collection of the Jewish intelligentsia to address that I had ever seen, and one thing Jennie and Philip don't know is how to talk to Jews. I do—and they were a ghastly flop. There was a great row next day in the Zionist Federation when they found the mistake in the seating plan; I had been mistaken for a *Guardian* journalist called Crossland and shoved down to table 12.

I had to rush back for the 10 p.m. division and at the end we had boos and cheers, but on a three-line whip we were through the Rhodesia debate! But that was Wednesday night, and tomorrow we face the day of the by-elections.

Thursday, March 28th
The big political news was Desmond Donnelly's expulsion from the Labour Party.[2] This was one of our problems—how to expel Donnelly without providing a great deal of damaging publicity for ourselves. I went through the morning press and saw what a hostile Conservative newspaper can do by playing up a man of Donnelly's type who knows how to be played up and how to use publicity. In certain ways it's not incorrect to call him a fascist. He's a great big thick-set lumbering fellow but with a quiet almost retiring manner who on a platform is transformed into a tremendous demagogue. He's obviously also got a great deal of business drive and administrative skill as well as sexual passion—he's a card and he'll probably hold Pembroke-shire successfully once at least.

We started with a very long and very solid O.P.D. With the Security Council mandatory sanctions now in operation we had to consider the question of passports. Should we deny Rhodesian passports? Should we ban them and declare them invalid if they're issued in Rhodesia? If we do, that will only affect one-third of the Rhodesians since two-thirds travel on British passports. Should we try to invalidate British passports held by Rhodesians? If so, we have to catch any Rhodesian with a British passport and that will mean holding up everybody else at Heathrow. Can we add to our stop list which already includes 600 Rhodesians who have to be banned? These are the questions we argued round, with Harold urging that our main objective

[1] Anthony Lousada was chairman of the Trustees of the Tate Gallery 1967–9 and Sir John Witt chairman of the Trustees of the National Gallery 1967–72.
[2] Desmond Donnelly, Labour M.P. for Pembroke 1950–70, resigned the Labour Whip on the East of Suez issue and from 1968 to 1970 acted as an Independent. In 1971 he joined the Conservative Party but was unable to find a seat. He died in 1974.

is to make life impossible for Rhodesians. Finally Dick Marsh and I exploded. The Rhodesians you want to stop travelling, we pointed out, aren't those coming to England but those going to Germany and America. That's where the harm is being done. Nothing was settled.

Next we had forty minutes on Mozambique oil where Harold is still convinced that we can strike a deadly blow. His usual friends remained silent and embarrassed — the Attorney-General, the Lord Chancellor. When Harold pleaded that we must now turn the heat on the French oil company which was putting oil into Rhodesia through Mozambique, we painfully pointed out that this would only antagonize South Africa, that anyway only a drop of oil would be prevented that way, and, if they really want, oil can be pushed in through other routes. We must have rehearsed this argument six or seven times, but Harold just batters away wanting to believe it's possible, though committee after committee has reported fifteen times that the idea of using pressure through Portugal without involving South Africa is out of the question. So even now we are going to have yet another special study before the Commonwealth Conference.

I had to go away to do the business Statement before we came to the most interesting item — the peace force for Nigeria. I left a message with the Chancellor, 'I rely on you to stop it.' He stopped it successfully by putting down impossible conditions, for example, that Canada should pay equal shares with us and that India should be a member.

Cabinet followed straight on. I had to make a report that time is running short and we can have no new legislation at all. If we run till August 1st and have a fortnight's overspill session in October we can just about pack everything in. Cabinet was told that there's no more time for them, whatever happens. For once they didn't argue: they took it.

The main item was the Prices and Incomes White Paper, which had now been much better written and reasonably well worked out. Richard Marsh, with whom I have a great deal of fellow feeling, repeated that the whole thing is absolute nonsense and that we shall be putting ourselves once again into confrontation both with the trade unions and with the Parliamentary Party for a policy which may have no real influence on the economy at all. Yet we have to do it because of the bankers, because Callaghan first tied us up with the American Secretary to the Treasury and Roy Jenkins has been compelled to tie us up again. The Chancellor himself doesn't believe in a prices and incomes policy. He believes that wages should find their own level. And yet as a Government we are in this situation and can't get out of it.

I stayed on afterwards with the P.M. and he asked me to be very careful in what I said about the arrangements for social services in Michael's absence. Then Burke, he and I talked about the priorities. He wanted to start preparing for the creation of the single Ministry of the Social Services and asked whether it was in order to discuss this with the two Permanent Secretaries without telling the Ministers, who might leak. I said I thought it was.

This afternoon I had a Professor of Politics from the Mormon University in Utah who wanted to discuss the role of the back-bencher. He told me he'd been in the House during the business Statement and had been fascinated by what he called 'your command of the House'. 'Obviously,' he said, 'you could do whatever you wanted.' I thought, 'My God, he should have been there a year ago when I was having my row with Manny. He'd have seen the difference between me now and then.' In this job you are either in trouble or it's a bore. But it's interesting that he had sat there and noticed this particular thing.

At the Party meeting this evening something remarkable happened. George Brown came in a few minutes late and nobody stirred. The meeting went on absolutely quietly. Indeed, it was too quiet for my taste. The members accepted Michael Stewart's Vietnam discussion without a vote and then accepted my explanation about the three-waiting-day period for sickness benefit which was the main thing for which they had come. And so George slips out again disappointed.

I may as well deal with the three waiting days now. There was a point in the January discussions on public expenditure when Judith wanted to get the extra three-shillings increase of family allowance and she wasn't going to get it unless she paid for it out of her estimates. So she tried to do a deal with the Chancellor. She found that the cost of the three waiting days that occur at the beginning of sickness is £15 million. This sickness insurance provides that if you are sick for ten days or more you are paid at the end of the tenth day and the three waiting days at the beginning are included, whereas they don't count if you haven't had ten days' sickness. She told Cabinet she would abolish this benefit, save £15 million and so finance the £3 million extra for family allowances. I doubt whether Roy knew anything more about the waiting days than Judith Hart. The swap was approved twice in Cabinet and the Chancellor thought it was very clever and was well satisfied. Only much later did Judith discover that this was causing her appalling trouble with the trade unions. Apparently when Jim Griffiths,[1] as Minister of National Insurance, tried to abolish the three waiting days in the 1945 Government he had to withdraw under pressure and there's a tremendous history of rank-and-file opposition to this economy. It was obvious from the way she was treated in the Party meeting today that she's in for very serious trouble when she meets the Social Services Group on Monday.

I'd eaten a bit too much at dinner and got indigestion so I didn't stay downstairs and watch television but went up to bed and put the radio on by the bedside. Already the Dudley result had been declared and there was an 18 per cent swing against the Government. So we knew what we were in for

---

[1] Labour M.P. for Llanelly 1936–70. He was Minister of National Insurance 1945–50, Secretary of State for the Colonies 1950–51 and Secretary of State for Wales 1964–6.

24*

at Meriden and Acton. I heard the rejoicing over the disasters in a kind of doze.[1]

Friday, March 29th

I woke up quite suddenly at five in the morning and thought that I must make a big speech at Basildon in which I would call for a Mark II Wilson Government. Since we can't change the measures, we've got to change the men. And I thought out this speech: we can't have a general election now— it's unconstitutional and it's also our duty to carry on and do our unpopular job. We can't have a national government. Right, what can we have? Wilson Mark II. There's a speech there, I realized, and I worked on it till breakfast time.

It so happened that I had my weekly business meeting with Harold. When I got there Burke and Michael were already in attendance, as well as the Chief Whip. We planned the meetings for next week and then I said to Harold, 'I must talk to you about the speech I'm making this evening.' 'All right,' he said. 'We shan't have time at the end of this. Stay on after O.P.D. and I'll get it through quickly.' This was cutting it a bit thin since there was only half an hour for O.P.D. before Harold had to leave for Euston to catch a train to his constituency. Even though the business meeting had finished twelve minutes early, nobody dared to talk about the by-elections. Harold puffed his pipe, Michael Stewart and John were discreet, I'd got my time booked. We just filled in until O.P.D., which we got through in a quarter of an hour; it was merely about the treaties in the Persian Gulf.

So I had a full eighteen minutes to tell him the shape of the speech. 'No,' he says, 'I don't like men not measures. You mustn't separate it as sharply as that. You must deal with the measures as well. But I like Mark I and Mark II. Wilson Government Mark I and Mark II. Yes, I like that and it will be a great help to Harold Wilson.' I saw what he meant because, of course, in the reporting on the election catastrophes the Wilson-must-go campaign had been very prominent. A speech which diverted attention from Wilson Must Go to Wilson's New Team would do the public good and also put the fear of God into Cabinet.

Then he revealed to me what the Mark II Cabinet was. There was going to be an inner Cabinet of six or seven—Harold Wilson, Michael Stewart, Roy Jenkins, Dick Crossman, Barbara Castle, and Fred Peart, the new Leader of the House. Should Denis be in or out? I said, 'Out, he must earn his passage home.' I said that it's important to get much better connections with the Trade Union Group and he mentioned two names so incredibly dismal that I've forgotten them and then he added four names of the most

---

[1] In the by-elections on March 28th there was an average swing of 18 per cent against the Government. At Dudley a 10,000 majority was turned into an 11,000 majority for the Conservatives, at Meriden a 4,581 Labour majority was turned into a 3,720 majority for the Conservatives, and at Acton 4,941 was turned into 15,263.

boring back-benchers whose promotion he thought would enliven our constituency party. But it's clear that Patrick Gordon Walker at least is to go and that Barbara is to be the economic boss while I'm to be the Social Services boss and have Education and part of the Home Office as well. Then there's Michael Stewart, who's the foreign boss, uniting the Foreign Office with Defence and Commonwealth, and Fred Peart as chairman of all the special Cabinet Committees. 'Barbara,' he said, 'is to be the new inspiration: she'll spark the new model. Tell her that today when you see her at lunch but don't tell her any more. She's to make the whole difference by taking over relations with the trade unions.'

This was the closest meeting I've had with Harold and I don't think any-body else—including Michael Stewart, Burke or the Chief Whip—had been told as much about his intentions.

Then I had two fascinating meetings, the first with Judith Hart and Kenneth Robinson on the scheme for exemptions that Kenneth had finally agreed with the doctors. I had been warned by Judith Hart that it was quite im-practical, and she wasn't exaggerating. It requires every single person to fill in a form of thirty questions every time they get a half-crown prescription. Kenneth Robinson has dragged out his arrangements until it's too late to revise the scheme and get the printing done if it's to be in force on June 1st. So I have to make new arrangements, costing an extra half million pounds, to postpone the scheme until June 10th. I authorized Jack Diamond to take charge of it. This is pure bloody-mindedness by Robinson and his officials because he could have co-ordinated with Judith at any time in the last three weeks and discovered that his proposal was intolerable.

Judith stayed behind to talk about her miserable three waiting days with Jack Diamond from the Treasury, and very soon we discovered a ludicrous situation. Diamond was prepared to see the clause disappear because in his view the £15 million it's supposed to save is not a genuine saving. Since it comes from the national insurance fund and not from public expenditure and since a corresponding sum is deducted from the employer's contribution, he can't regard the deal as making any sense. This is a perfect example of the abracadabra which evolves in a PESC exercise.

Still, as Jack Diamond made clear, Judith has yet to find her £15 million and suddenly she proposed that we should insert a clause in the Bill making the employer responsible for the first week. Jack said he didn't mind and I said I'd rather hear an official from Judith's Ministry. But when one arrived he looked very bleak indeed and I suggested that we postpone the Bill till after Easter in order to give plenty of time for consultations with the C.B.I. and the T.U.C. and for working out a practical plan.

I struggled away and got my speech done and then cancelled a lunch with Independent Television to be able to have lunch with Barbara and I told her Harold's news. She was thrilled and excited. Could she tell her husband? I said she could tell Ted she has a big job coming and perhaps I told her more

than I should have done. but she is very discreet. We went through my speech
and she said the end was too flat—'You must put in a piece about partnership
with the Party.' She absolutely made the speech and it is now first-rate, all five
pages of it.

Peter Shore was to see me this afternoon. As usual he was utterly miserable,
more than ever convinced that Roy Jenkins and John Harris are running a
campaign against him as part of their attack on Harold. Now the awkward
thing is that I know Roy wants to get rid of Peter because he's incompetent.
The attacks on Peter are not attacks on Harold but on his henchman, but
I can't tell Peter this or explain to him what he should really be doing in his
Department. So instead I turned to my own speech and told him about it
and then I showed it to him. 'You can't mean that Harold wants you to
deliver this tonight?' he said. 'Yes he does,' but Peter didn't believe it.
However he got to work, took out a sentence which Harold had particularly
liked (suggesting that maybe the best service each member of the Cabinet
could make is resignation). Peter said, 'That won't improve their morale.
If you say that you will be thought to be polishing your axe for cutting off
the heads of all your rivals and that isn't a seemly job for a Leader of the
House to do.' I didn't reply that anyway, when a Leader of the House
suddenly calls for a brand new Cabinet it's usually interpreted as an attack
on the P.M. However, I wisely took most of Peter's suggestions and caught
the train to Basildon.

I had warned the B.B.C. and the I.T.V. that I was going to say something
important that evening and I had also told David Wood of *The Times*. The
press releases were got out just in the nick of time as I set off to Fenchurch
Street. I found a decent little meeting of a hundred or so people in a church
hall. Old Jim Morgan, head of the Basildon Council Group who tried to
bully me when I was Minister of Housing, was there to bully me once again.
He wouldn't sit on the platform with me and was determined to attack me
from the floor. On the platform we only had Eric Moonman, a dark young
man from the Printers' Union, who is certainly an intellectual and whom I
haven't really fathomed.[1] He started the meeting off with a mass of statistics
meant to defend the Government but he was so half-hearted and apologetic
that the audience can hardly have been convinced. So I got up and of course
my speech was hearty and bright and they even listened to the piece I had
to read aloud with very close attention. There were lots of journalists there
and I knew it had got across to them and so I got back home as soon as
possible and was just settling down when Arthur Butler of the *Express* rang
up. He was worried at the difference between the press release with its last
sentence about the Mark II Wilson Government and the P.A. report which
omitted it. 'Did you omit that last sentence from your press release?' he
asked. 'No, I said it and I answered two questions about it.' An hour later,
after I'd gone to bed, it was John Bourne of the *Financial Times* saying he'd

[1] Labour M.P. for Billericay 1966–70.

been hauled out of bed by his office with the identical question. Did I or did I not say that sentence? I repeated to him that I said it and answered questions about it. Since I didn't want to be rung up all night I next took the initiative, got on to the P.A. and told the night editor what had happened. He replied that they had sent a man specially down to Basildon and that his report didn't include the last sentence, but when they checked with the local journalists they found it was in the speech. I asked him whether he could put out a correction as soon as possible.*

Saturday, March 30th
It was certainly the sensation of the morning papers, though David Wood chose to assume that I made the speech without consulting the Prime Minister and called it tactless. This is pretty silly since I tipped him off. On the other hand the *Financial Times* and the *Guardian* have seen its importance. Jimmy Margach rang up this morning and I said that I had nothing to add and I gave the same reply to the B.B.C. and the I.T.V. I didn't want to give any interviews on the speech because I knew that many of my colleagues were either shaking in their shoes or green with envy. They knew very well that when I announced the Mark II Government their days were numbered and that they'd better behave properly if they want to stay in the new Cabinet.

This was the day of our great conference on the social services in Whitehall. I had wanted to make it very small with each Minister bringing only his Permanent Secretary or one other official and broadly speaking this is what the Ministers did. Callaghan was there with Philip Allen, Greenwood with Matthew Stevenson, Judith Hart with Clifford Jarrett, and so on, but alas there were no less than nine Economic Advisers. Tommy had brought along his pair, Judith had brought along her John Nicholson[1] and then there was Donald MacDougall, Economic Adviser to the Treasury, and Nicky Kaldor. As a result there were some twenty-nine or thirty people round the table and we should have had fifteen or sixteen. This made it almost impossible to chair and I dread what would have happened if Michael Stewart had been there. As it was I was forced to scrap discussion on a number of interesting papers which have been produced and get the results I wanted by starting with confessions. I began by saying we were going to be off the record and completely unrecorded. Secondly, we would start by looking back on the lessons of the last three years. Then we would move along to see what we could do between now and this year's PESC exercise, and then look forward from there till 1970 and even to 1975. To set a good example of confessional spirit I admitted that the 500,000 housing target had been announced light-heartedly without any adequate information. I thought it would be better

---

* As a result the B.B.C., which hadn't mentioned the speech in the eleven o'clock news this evening, made it top of the news at seven, eight and nine next morning.
[1] John Nicholson has been Chief Economic Adviser to the D.H.S.S. since 1968.

in future to have a target not of new houses only but of new houses plus improved houses. This example set other people off. Judith Hart tried to grapple with the problem of whether it was a mistake to implement the pension plan in parts and to start with the earnings related unemployment and sickness benefit instead of with the big scheme. She was followed by Kenneth Robinson, very characteristically saying that he has only made two mistakes in his career—one was to take the prescription charges off and the other was to put them on. But the most interesting part of the confessional came when I turned to James Callaghan and said that he was now in a double capacity as an ex-Chancellor and as Home Secretary. He launched into a fascinating defence of himself and an equally fascinating attack on the spending Ministries. First of all he dealt with the 500,000 housing target. He said that the Prime Minister had insisted on making housing an absolute priority and so he had set up a special Cabinet Housing Committee in which the Ministers who wanted to build houses would have a majority and the Chancellor would always be defeated. And all the way through at the beginning he said, looking at me, the Prime Minister had a vigorous Minister at his side determined to get things done. 'That,' he said, 'is how the 500,000 figure got fixed,' although time after time the Chancellor had warned the Committee that the houses mightn't be necessary, and we might do better with a lower figure and much more of an intention to improve old housing. So far he'd been perfectly fair but then he began to talk about the fudging of the figures in the national plan—the deliberate insertion of a far higher figure for growth than was compatible with the action necessary to deal with the balance-of-payments deficit. This point was taken up a good deal later by Donald MacDougall who said that as an objective observer of the Tories and ourselves he could give a detached history of how housing had gone wrong. For eight years the Tories had run the economy very quietly with a slow rate of growth and a modest increase in public expenditure and with favourable terms of trade. Then when they were coming up towards the election they suddenly began to talk about Neddy[1] and planning and the expanding of public expenditure and the new Macmillan policy was to steal the socialist clothes by announcing a policy of planned expansion for growth. Already in the new plans, he observed, the growth figures were far too big for the balance of payments. But then unfortunately the Profumo case came along and the election had to be delayed for ten months.[2] That was fatal because during those ten months the programmes of economic expansion all got out of control and the deficit grew bigger and bigger. If they could have won the election when they planned it they could have cut back much

[1] National Economic Development Council.

[2] The Macmillan Government had been embarrassed by the revelation in June 1963 that John Profumo, Secretary of State for War, had been closely involved with a call-girl, Christine Keeler, who was also associated with a Soviet official. There seemed to be a security risk, Profumo had not told the truth when making a statement to the Commons, and he resigned.

earlier. As it was, the Labour Party inherited growth plans far too big for the balance of payments. The immediate need in the autumn of 1964 was to cut back growth and deal with the balance of payments but the Labour Government wasn't prepared to do this, he said. And so he too came back to the fudging of figures and said that we ought to have cut the growth programme back and that this had not been done because of the political implications.

Then came a very bitter and passionate description of life as it appears to the Financial Secretary to the Treasury, who has to try to keep control of public expenditure. He said this was a hopeless thing to do because the Treasury is under pressure from two forces—the democratic pressure for housing, for example, and Ministerial pressure inside Cabinet, and when these two press in the same direction public expenditure can only get out of control.

All this was interesting but I had to steer the conference back to its real topic, which was the fixing of priorities within the world of social services and within the social service Ministries. I put this idea forward whereupon somebody said that you can't fix social service priorities without a Minister and a super Department. This was a little awkward because I'm going to try to be that Social Services Minister in a few weeks. In a way my speech was a kind of John the Baptist speech, a preaching of the gospel before the announcement of the actual birth.

At lunch-time I had an urgent message from the office that the B.B.C. wanted me to go on the air and I said no. Then I had a message from Tommy saying the P.M. was very pleased with the effect of the speech. Now this was interesting because everybody there including Callaghan and Gordon Walker was anxious about the meaning of the speech. I said that I had of course done it with Harold's approval and that it may well mean that many of us have to face resignation. 'Does that mean,' says Patrick Gordon Walker, 'that you and Michael want to resign?' and I said, 'Well, we've got to face the possibility.' Poor Patrick, he's for it and he knows I'm not for it. Callaghan also felt the situation ominous, that I was much too like an executioner polishing the axe. Certainly the speech was having the effect inside the Cabinet which we had intended.

Back at the conference after lunch we got down to the practical problem and agreed that before our next meeting we would undertake an exercise in which each Minister would look at his programme on the assumption that it was increased by 3 per cent and, alternatively, decreased by 3 per cent—and ask himself what changes he would make. This wasn't a very adventurous step but it's a tremendous job to try to lever our Party away from its attachment to the Tory spending programme it inherited in 1964.

Right at the end we had one frightful row—about prescription charges. I said I would like to see an objective paper prepared by officials about charges in the social services. Should we charge, for example, for nursery schools as we do for so many of the local government services? Kenneth Robinson and his official put up a hundred per cent opposition. They were not even prepared to consider conducting such an inquiry.

I broke off the conference at four o'clock when it was just beginning to fall to pieces. I don't think we shall ever repeat it because there were far too many people there. Anyway if I become First Secretary and Minister of Social Services I shan't have to have a conference of this kind because these people will be directly responsible to me.

Monday, April 1st

On the wireless this morning I heard the news of President Johnson's astonishing broadcast announcing that he isn't going to stand for re-election and is going to dedicate his time to trying to get peace in Vietnam.[1] It sounded momentous but I must say my own assumption is that he's planning a tremendous comeback and this is a typical Johnson trick.

This morning I had to take the chair for the first time of the Agricultural Policy Cabinet Committee which also covers the fish industry. On Friday night in my box I found an enormous document which I worked through over the weekend—the report of a working party which has been sitting for two years. Attached to it were draft recommendations by Fred Peart, Minister of Agriculture, John Diamond, Chief Secretary of the Treasury, and Peter Shore at D.E.A. The other minor Ministries with fishing interests —Scotland, Wales and Home Office representing Northern Ireland— apparently back Fred. Of course there is a mass of detailed recommendations which are accepted by everyone, but the difference arises about money. Agriculture recommends an annual fisheries subsidy of £3·5 million. The Treasury recommends that the level to which the subsidy had been allowed to sink (after the Select Committee had reported that there should be a sinking subsidy) should be temporarily retained in order to give some backbone to the industry. This would mean a subsidy of £1·4 million. And thirdly, the D.E.A., true to its mediating position in Whitehall, has put in a recommendation of £2·2 million. Since, as I say, Fred was backed by Scotland, Wales and Northern Ireland he has four votes on his side and the Treasury only one with between the two sides D.E.A., the honest broker, and the chairman with a vote as well. This is the standard pattern of committee we've evolved for the annual Farm Price Review and all other agricultural negotiations. I'd been profoundly shocked by the draft report, which seemed to me to be completely thoughtless. Britain used to be a major exporter of fish and is now becoming an importer. Everybody agrees we must try to save imports by boosting our own fish industry and improving its marketing and sales abroad. All sound generalities yet when one comes to recommendations one faces a choice between three open-ended subsidies.

[1] The President also declared a partial end to the bombing and, on April 3rd, the North Vietnamese announced their conditional agreement to negotiate for an end to the war.

As soon as we got down to the meeting Fred Peart started reading his brief aloud—his argument for £3·5 million. (He wasn't expecting to get £3·5 million but somewhere between £2 million and £2·5 million as a result of the usual haggle.) After five or six minutes I interrupted with a question and he replied happily that he would answer that when he'd finished what he had to say. I knew then that he had to read aloud his brief because that was all he knew, so I let him read to the end. Then I asked Scotland—no comment there; Wales—no comment there; Home Office—no comment there; all of them taking Fred Peart's lead and waiting. So I started cross-examining Fred on why it is that the deep-sea industry had been losing money while the home-based industry had been gaining profits. And why he thought that if we gave this huge subsidy it would make the industry recover and reorganize itself. Jack Diamond from the Treasury suddenly brightened up when he heard me talk and then he weighed in and asserted that there's no relation between the subsidy and the catch. I said, 'Surely that must be untrue? Clearly there's some relation because if you knocked the subsidy out altogether there wouldn't be a catch at all: they would all stop fishing and the trawlers would be sold up.' At this point Edmund Dell, who represents D.E.A. in the absence of Peter Shore who's always busy on prices and incomes, chipped in to say that he shared my view of the big official report and was disregarding his official brief making the case for the £2·2 million subsidy. He thought the whole idea of an open-ended subsidy wrong and the report itself totally inadequate. Surely we should have learnt after these three years that open-ended subsidies should never be given—indeed, that no financial assistance should be given to private enterprise unless it is linked with express conditions for reorganization? No industry should get money unless it is pledged to reorganize itself. 'This,' he said, 'is what we did in shipbuilding with tremendous success and it's something we must apply to the trawler industry as well.' Fred Peart was dumbfounded and looked across the table at Edmund Dell and said, 'But your officials have agreed the report and the recommendations with my officials.' 'Yes,' said Edmund Dell, 'my officials may have agreed but I have just given the view I am representing at this Ministerial meeting today.' I came in to say that clearly we couldn't accept any of these proposals without a great deal of further study because the working party's report is so hopelessly unsatisfactory. I proposed therefore we should send it back. Consternation round the table! Send the report back after more than two years' work? And Fred Peart said, 'But I'm due to make a Statement next week. They're expecting a Statement from me.' To this I replied that what always goes wrong with this Government is that we accept dud reports because we are due to make Statements and we then make the Statements and get committed to the dud reports. Fred said, 'But we can't possibly ask these hard-working civil servants to do their homework all over again,' and I replied that we should give them two months to start doing some serious thinking about the reorganization of the trawler industry. Anyway, this report was too bad to be accepted.

I strolled back to my room feeling pretty self-satisfied and rang up Thomas Balogh to tell him about this astonishing discovery. 'Were you in the chair of that Committee?' he said. 'I didn't know. I'd already written a note to Fred Peart warning him how bad the report was and I gave a much longer note to D.E.A.' Then I knew where Edmund Dell had got some of his ideas from. It really shows old Thomas at his very best and Edmund Dell too, for he was in fact decisive.

This afternoon I had to chair my own Home Publicity Committee, which now has the job of presenting to the public the Prices and Incomes White Paper due to be published on Wednesday. A great deal of trouble has been taken about this and the brief will not simply be on prices and incomes but will include dividends, rents and public expenditure. The real difficulty is the philosophy behind the brief. Should this measure be presented as a major extension of Government powers or should all the emphasis be on the reduction of prices, or should we mainly concentrate on the details and get people to understand the possibilities of getting something above the $3\frac{1}{2}$ per cent ceiling? There were some jolly good officials present, including Alex Jarratt, but I didn't feel we were able to get any clear answer because, quite simply, Cabinet doesn't want one.

In the House meanwhile there had been a string of Statements culminating in Wedgy Benn's announcement that Rolls had got the contract for the new American engine. It's amusing to remember that we were warned by Healey that if we cancelled the F-111 we should prejudice Rolls's chance of getting the contract. Well, we've cancelled the F-111 and haven't prejudiced the chances and two of these F-111s have crashed on the way to Vietnam. So this contract really is immensely encouraging and let's hope it's a turn in the tide of fortune for British industry.

This evening, though the Prime Minister wasn't very keen, I decided to appear on *24 Hours* because I've been pressured pretty often by the B.B.C. since my Basildon speech and I thought I'd better go on the air and wind the whole thing up. I went down to Lime Grove and there at 5 p.m. I found Bob Mackenzie, who's a clever bastard. Every question he asked me was designed to get me to betray myself more than I intended. His final one was, 'Why doesn't the Prime Minister do the same here as President Johnson did and quit?' To this I made a rather laboured reply about the difference between Presidential and Prime Ministerial government and when I got launched on it I began to feel that this would mean nothing to the ordinary Englishman. He doesn't appreciate the difference between the personal government of the U.S.A. and the group government of Britain, where the Prime Minister is part of a team. And that's the point I was emphasizing. However, to my amazement I found later on that evening that it had been very well received by the Party at Westminster and I realized that I'd once again talked about the need for collective government which the rank and file can't hear too often.

So then I rushed back home to change for the opera, a wonderful performance of *Aida*, tremendous and invigorating. Huw Wheldon of the B.B.C. was there,[1] Robbins,[2] and Claus Moser and Lady Moser. Everybody was wanting to know when the Mark II Government was going to be announced and when I was going to take over my new job, and I couldn't tell them anything. But I told Claus Moser his side was going to be all right and that I think he'll be pleased when he sees it.

Tuesday, April 2nd

I celebrated my last Legislation Committee by having a blazing row about the Hovercraft. This is one of the Bills which I've demoted from the main programme and I'd given instructions that it may only be taken if it can be got through as a completely non-contentious measure taken before a Second Reading Committee. Whereupon that idiotic Board of Trade drafted a Bill which simply said that Hovercraft would be regulated by Order in Council. The argument of the draftsman was that as we don't know how Hovercraft behave we can't give instructions about them. But we must have some instructions because the first Hovercraft is going into service across the Channel this summer and nobody yet knows whether it is to be treated according to the laws applying to sea vessels or as a land vehicle or as an aeroplane. So some real thinking has to be done about the safety and security measures which will apply to Hovercraft. Yet here was the Ministry simply saying, 'We won't bother to think about it. We'll simply have an enabling Bill and leave the thinking to our convenience.' I said this was a gross abuse of the Second Reading procedure and though I was certain the Tories would have refused it, I wouldn't let them even try and gave instructions that the Bill should be withdrawn. There will be chaos and a terrible upset in the Board of Trade. But this is what a Lord President can do when he's got a little standing and feels a pang of regret at the knowledge that he's giving up.

At Cabinet we started with Michael Stewart's report on Vietnam. Things looked pretty bad and all he could say was that we must try to keep things open and use our new hot line to Moscow to see whether we and the Russians as co-chairmen had any role to play in mediation. Alas, this gambit doesn't work any more in Cabinet. Dick Marsh was speaking for a good many of us when he said that as our policy has been a complete failure shouldn't we

[1] Head of B.B.C. Music and Documentary Programmes 1963–5 and Controller of Programmes 1965–8. Since 1969 he has been managing director of Television at the B.B.C.
[2] Lionel Robbins, formerly Professor of Economics at the L.S.E. and chairman of its Court of Governors 1968–74, became first Chancellor of the University of Stirling in 1968. He was a director of the Royal Opera House at Covent Garden. He was made a life peer in 1959.

dissociate from the American Vietnam policy altogether. Barbara backed him but of course Harold Wilson advised that we must watch whether the American initiative comes to anything.

The main item this morning was Judith Hart's famous three waiting days. I'd spent some hours on my own Pensions Committee trying to sort this out without any success and realizing more and more that the kind of change she wants will take months to negotiate and can't possibly be jammed into this Bill. However to my amazement I had read a paper prepared by the Treasury which backed her proposal for an announcement that employers would pay the cost of social insurance for their employees for a period of a month or a fortnight. For once I was in agreement with Gunter, who blew up and said this was totally impractical. With Treasury backing there was a real danger that she would get us out of the frying-pan into the fire by plunging us into an absolutely half-baked scheme. However, we finally got out of it by allowing her to make a statement that she was reconsidering the clause for two months and would start negotiations.

In the House we had the P.M.'s Questions and then the admission of new Members. The P.M. was really quite angry with me because I'd arranged for lots of Statements on Monday and no Statements today so that he would have to sit there, he said, and watch the Tory victors of Meriden, Dudley and Warwick and Leamington all come past him with storms of cheering. Actually it was quite a good thing he did sit there beside me because it was most curiously formal and the cheering wasn't all that loud. Certainly these victories haven't given them all the confidence they needed, and instead of depressing Harold it cheered him up.

Afterwards we went out and had a talk when he told me about the difficulties of Mark II. He had planned that Barbara should go to D.E.A. while Peter might move to Mintech and Wedgy to Education. But when that plan was put to Roy he had turned it down flat and said he wouldn't have it because he didn't want Barbara in a key position in the economic sector reproducing the tension which had caused such appalling damage when George Brown was head of D.E.A. and Callaghan head of the Treasury. Roy made it clear that he was going to jolly well run the show on the economic side without a rival. Certainly he liked Barbara but he wasn't going to have her at D.E.A.

What then was to be done? The P.M. told me that he was now thinking of making Barbara Minister of Labour and also Leader of the House to raise her status. I said I found this difficult to believe but when Barbara came to see me this afternoon with the same story that she was being pressured by the P.M. to take Ray Gunter's place and add to it the Leader of the House I said to her, 'God forbid, Barbara. How could you be Leader of the House and Minister of Labour? Supposing you're busy with a gas workers' strike and there's turmoil in the House of Commons and they complain the Leader isn't there because she's dealing with the gas workers! No, you can't run those two jobs together and anyway if I was the most unsuitable person to be Leader of the House, you're the second most unsuitable. You don't care about procedure and if you take this it's just for status, which is a thoroughly bad reason.'

Meanwhile I'd also been trying to see Roy since I discovered that he is off on Wednesday to America for five days. It seems to me appalling that this major Cabinet reconstruction should take place with Roy on the other side of the Atlantic when his presence and influence should really be felt, from top to bottom. And I felt most terribly depressed. However I had to rush off to the House of Lords where we had a meeting of our negotiating committee.

Here at last the famous Macleod objection was properly presented to us, postponed from last week when he'd forgotten to turn up. Macleod said that this shattered Government with its disastrous by-election record couldn't possibly launch a new House of Lords. This was received with proper gravity and then he was asked whether this Government, despite the poor opinion he had of it, was fit to produce a White Paper. He said yes, he was even prepared to see a Bill. Indeed, the Bill could go through all its stages provided the new House of Lords started in the new Parliament. We were all able to puncture that and Lord Jellicoe was compelled to say that he found it wholly wrong and the Tory peers would find it wholly wrong to postpone the reformed House of Lords to the new Parliament. We would forfeit the help of forty to fifty of the older peers in seeing us through the transition. They thought we ought to get the Bill through next Session and have at least one Session of the reformed House of Lords in this Parliament. Reg Maudling, rather sheepishly, tried to give some support to Iain Macleod but our people and the Liberals began to get angry and I finally said, 'We'd better, each of us, report back to our own sides.' Meanwhile the working party will carry on with the production of the White Paper since the only point of difference now is whether the appointed day for the creation of the new House should be in this Parliament or in the next.

Then I had one of those top-level broadcasting meetings. At the last one Heath had proposed the idea of regional party political broadcasts, much shorter than at present and many more of them. Moreover he'd said they needn't be simultaneously shown on B.B.C. and I.T.V. Now as a matter of fact this is an extraordinarily difficult scheme to work out and I don't blame the B.B.C. for resisting it. But the idea of shorter broadcasts was a good one and I supported the leader of the Opposition in putting it forward and suggested that we might do a deal by which we cut down the total number of minutes allocated to our party political broadcasts in exchange for having one or two extra short ones. Once again Hugh Greene behaved to type. He simply said this could not be considered and wouldn't budge. So as the result of two long meetings we were back at square one. Heath blew his top as he went out and I too found it outrageous. 'Will you promise to write to the chairman of the Governors?' he asked me. And I said, 'Yes,' and it's one of the last things I shall do in this job.

Later this evening I at last went across to No. 11 and found Roy and John Harris. Roy has had three long talks with the P.M. and is quite content with the reconstruction. 'Is it true that you won't take Barbara?' I said, and he said, 'Yes. I don't want to recreate D.E.A. as a centre of power and therefore she can't be there. . . .' But it was hopeless to have her simply as Leader of the House unless we got rid of Callaghan and popped her into the Home Office too. But he wasn't so sure about her being Home Secretary and rather fancied her as Minister of Labour. Then we began to discuss the need to cut the dead wood out of the rest of the Government. He agreed the excision should be drastic and I then said, 'Well, who in your view should replace them? If all this is done while you're away, it will greatly reduce your influence. Shouldn't you, if it's humanly possible, have at least the second part of the shuffle delayed for five days?' He then agreed to let me have a list of the twelve to fourteen young people he thought due for promotion and promised he would try to have the appointments delayed.

After that I went back to the House and saw Anthony Sampson, author of the *Anatomy of Britain* and who is now doing a book on Europe.[1] We had an amiable chat and then in came David Watt of the *Financial Times* and I gave him dinner and thorough inside briefing on the real situation of the Wilson regime without revealing anything about the Cabinet reshuffle. I might mention here that I have very faithfully kept my word to Harold that I wouldn't have any private briefings with the press. The only exceptions have been Jimmy Margach the other day when the P.M. wanted it, and now David Watt. In a curious way I think I've put the heat on Harold by doing this.

Wednesday, April 3rd

My first meeting was Callaghan's Electoral Reform Committee and I had a tiff with the old boy because there really are only two big questions remaining. The first is Party labels. Should we, as in other countries, allow candidates to put Lab or Conservative or Lib after their names on the ballot paper? The second is whether we should have votes at eighteen, twenty or twenty-one. The Speaker's Conference has voted for the miserable compromise of twenty and has also turned down Party labels. I said that my own view is that we should accept the Party labels and either keep to twenty-one or go to eighteen but in both cases reject the recommendations of the Speaker's Conference. Callaghan tried to argue that this had already been decided but I managed to make the Committee realize that all we've decided is that Cabinet should postpone its decision till after the Speaker's Conference had recommended and the matter has been debated in the House. What we now have to do as a Cabinet is to give the House advice

[1] *The New Europeans* (London: Hodder & Stoughton, 1968).

on the possibilities for the voting age and I would like them carefully spelt out.

I only just got the Electoral Reform Committee finished in time to get back to the Privy Council to do a five-minute recording for Irish television. I wish to God I could remember what it was but it seemed at the time quite straightforward. Then I had to see Callaghan about the legislative programme of the Home Office. After the business was over he took me aside and said, 'I gather you're to co-ordinate social services and the proper position to do this from would be the Home Office. Isn't that a good strategic position to operate?' It wasn't until after he'd left the room that I realized he was offering me a swap. If you become Home Secretary why should I not take your place as Leader of the House and Lord President?

I'd already had an urgent message from Roy that he would telephone me at 12.30 so I got back to my room and there he was on the airport phone. He'd had his meeting with Harold this morning and pleaded with him to postpone the shuffle, but Harold was on the warpath and gave him, as Roy put it, a fly in his ear. 'I got nothing out of it,' he said to me, and all he had been able to do was to send his list of names round to me. 'You and Barbara must try and do the best you can in my absence.' So Roy went off to America and I was left feeling profoundly depressed at the prospect of Mark II falling to pieces.

At the meeting of my Devolution Committee in the afternoon I submitted my paper. This shows that there's a sharp choice between moving on to genuine self-government or devolving a certain number of obvious regional activities while strengthening the office of the regional Secretary of State. The only effective answer we could make to the nationalists if we refuse to concede self-government would be to make our present regional system work infinitely better, for instance, by having Grand Committees moved to Cardiff and Edinburgh and new Scottish and Welsh Select Committees of Investigation. The obstacle to all this is that the Welsh want the best of both worlds and may get the worst of both worlds by trying to have both a Secretary of State and an effective Regional Council.

I had to go to the Lords to continue our conversation with the Labour peers about our scheme of reform. It was disconcerting to discover that in addition to Edith Summerskill, Patricia Llewelyn-Davies, for example, has become very critical and cantankerous. So I took her aside and really talked to her seriously. She said there's no political advantage in the reform and that I was adopting a functional pragmatic approach by trying to improve parliamentary procedure to the advantage of the House of Commons. Now this is true. If we reform the Lords and are able to use them in Select Committees and any number of other useful tasks, then Parliament is a more efficient place. But Patricia made me realize that it looks different depending on the place from which you survey the reform. I couldn't tell her that I was ceasing to be Lord President but her talk reminded me that I must make sure that when I change my job I carry on with Lords reform because otherwise it will flounder.

With the Industrial Expansion Bill going on until 2 a.m. I at last had a chance for a long talk with John Silkin. He was mainly concerned about his own fate. His great ambition is to be Deputy Leader of the Commons—a new job which he has thought up which would enable him to have the right to speak in the House and to help Fred Peart. I was a bit dubious whether it will pay a Chief Whip to be a Deputy Leader of the Commons and to speak in the House. But John wants it passionately and if he wants it he should get it.

My main interest this evening was the junior appointments in the big shuffle and I took out of my pocket Roy's list and read it aloud to the meeting. Here it is: Richard Mitchell, Alex Lyon, David Watkins, Brian Walden, Eric Heffer, Joan Lestor, Paul Rose, David Owen, David Marquand, Ivor Richard, Donald Dewar, Michael Barnes, Bob Brown, Bob Cant, Arthur Davidson.[1] I'd been studying this list before and it was clear that Roy had tried to be broad-minded and include as well as his own Jenkinsites and right-wingers a number of people who are by no means right-wing intellectuals such as Eric Heffer, Joan Lestor, Paul Rose and the trade unionists like Bob Brown. But before I started arguing I asked John to give me his list and he reeled off Tom Urwin, whom Harold has been pressing on Barbara as her number two at D.E.A., Garrett, Parkyn, Eadie and Joel Barnett.[1] There are one or two more but I don't remember them. But I do remember that the only name which occurred on both lists was Paul Rose. Directly he heard Roy's list John said, 'Oh, he's got all the intellectuals. We don't want all those names. We want plain practical men like Tom Urwin.' Now I happen to have seen quite a lot of Tom Urwin because I had a whole weekend in his constituency when he made me come up for May Day. He's ultra-anti-intellectual, a building-trade operative, a solid dull trade unionist and I was sad when the Chief said he couldn't have David Marquand

[1] Richard Mitchell was Labour M.P. for Southampton Test 1966–70 and, since 1971, for Itchen. David Watkins has been Labour M.P. for Durham Consett since 1966. Brian Walden, Labour M.P. for Birmingham All Saints 1964–74 and, since 1974, for Ladywood, was Parliamentary Secretary to the Financial Secretary to the Treasury 1964–6. Ivor Richard, Labour M.P. for Barons Court 1964–74, was Parliamentary Under-Secretary (Army) at the Ministry of Defence 1969–70 and, since 1974, has been British Ambassador to the U.N. Donald Dewar was Labour M.P. for Aberdeen South 1966–70. Michael Barnes was Labour M.P. for Brentford and Chiswick 1966–74. Arthur Davidson has been Labour M.P. for Accrington since 1966.

[2] Tom Urwin, Labour M.P. for Houghton-le-Spring since 1964, was Minister of State at the D.E.A. 1968–9 and had special responsibility for regional policy and for the Northern Region 1969–70. William Garrett has been Labour M.P. for Wallsend since 1964 and Brian Parkyn Labour M.P. for Bedfordshire since 1966. Alex Eadie, Labour M.P. for Midlothian since 1966, has been Parliamentary Under-Secretary of State for Energy since 1974.

and David Owen because they were disloyal, Joan Lestor and Eric Heffer because they were impossible, and Brian Walden because he was far too dangerous. But, he added graciously, he would consider Bob Brown.

'But if you're going to turn down all Roy's list,' I said, 'won't you undermine the unity we're trying to build up between him and Harold? When Roy provided that list, wasn't he making it clear that he thinks we must cut out a lot of the old wood? Julian Snow, for instance, has served his time, or Norman Pentland or Charlie Loughlin[1]—they're old things like Harold Davies. People who should be given three years of fat Ministerial life as reward for services rendered but whom one shouldn't keep longer than that.' Well, the Chief was in a conservative mood. He confirmed to me that he was against getting rid of Callaghan or Willie Ross or Tony Greenwood or, indeed, any of the old gang. So on Wednesday evening I saw my Mark II Cabinet in full disintegration. I saw Harold appointing a lot of staid people with none of the intellectual energy and the dynamism we require to renovate the Party. I really went to bed depressed. Indeed, I was so depressed that I refused to worry when I heard on the last two divisions our majority fell to twenty.[2] However, while I was walking home I suddenly wondered why I should be so defeatist, changed my mind and walked across the park to No. 10. Harold was in and I went in there and had what was a not-unimportant talk. I told him that I'd been talking to Barbara and that it was a hopeless idea to make her combine the Ministry of Labour with the Leadership of the House. 'If Barbara isn't content just to be an important Minister,' I said, 'why shouldn't she be First Secretary as well? I know I've been given the job and the promotion it implies but I'm not fussed about promotion and I'm perfectly happy just to remain Lord President, in which case,' I said laughing, 'I'll keep my lovely room in the Privy Council. No, let Barbara be First Secretary.' At first he wasn't interested. 'She doesn't care about titles,' he said. 'It will make no difference to her.' 'Yes it will,' I said. 'It'll make all the difference. She's down at Windsor tonight at a royal banquet and she'll be ringing me up tomorrow morning. I'll try the idea out on her over breakfast.'

Thursday, April 4th
I was still lying in bed looking at the papers when Barbara rang up from Windsor and asked how things were going. I said, 'I think there is a chance and I've got an idea for you.' Then I put it to her direct. 'What about your

[1] Julian Snow, Labour M.P. for Portsmouth Central 1945–50 and for Lichfield 1950–70, was Parliamentary Under-Secretary of State at the Ministry of Aviation 1966–7, at the Ministry of Health 1967–8 and in 1968 became Crossman's Parliamentary Under-Secretary at the D.H.S.S.; on becoming a life peer in 1970 he took the title of Lord Burntwood. Norman Pentland, Labour M.P. for Chester-le-Street 1956–70, was Parliamentary Under-Secretary at the Ministry of Posts 1969–70. Charles Loughlin, Labour M.P. for Gloucestershire West since 1959, was Parliamentary Secretary at the Ministry of Health 1965–7, Joint Parliamentary Secretary at the D.H.S.S. 1967–8 and at M.P.B.W. 1968–70.
[2] The divisions were 146 to 125 and 145 to 124.

being First Secretary instead of me? Why don't you become First Secretary while I stay Lord President and keep my lovely room in the Privy Council. I don't really mind. It's only stuff and titles to me.' She leapt at it with tremendous energy as though it made all the difference to her.

Having got that done I went over to No. 11 to see the Chief. I told him I was desperately upset and had hardly slept as a result of our talk. 'If there were a Cabinet reshuffle now with no major expulsions, with Callaghan and Ross and Greenwood still there and the same old dead wood and the promotions of the same routine kind, within six months there will be a most dangerous conspiracy against Harold.' The Chief replied quite reasonably that patronage was his affair and he must be allowed to put the names forward. 'No,' I replied, 'your job, like mine, is not to put forward your personal choice but to get the right balance in the Cabinet and in the Government.' I then told John the story about Barbara and the First Secretaryship since I knew he was going straight to Harold to discuss the reshuffle. It was the last word I had with the Chief before I went off to my meeting on Europe.

This was under the chairmanship of Michael Stewart who, as Foreign Secretary, was pleading that we should not reveal to the Europeans the fact that we had cancelled participation in all their space projects—ELDO, ESRO, etc.—as part of our economy package. Tony Wedgwood Benn would not stand for this kind of nonsense. The Europeans have these grandiose projects which provide them with no advantage but they think they are grand and a way to compete with the Americans. We, on the other hand, know that the only way to compete with the Americans is on the basis of technological projects launched for sound commercial economic reasons. In this respect our thinking is well in advance of the Europeans and we can't afford to pander to them. So there on the one side we had Stewart backed by Chalfont and on the other side every single one of the Ministers present.

I'd arranged to see Barbara at one o'clock before she went to No. 10. She had to come to my room in the Privy Council because the press are watching No. 10 so carefully. When she strolled in I was talking at the time to my Private Office about my very last business Statement and my very last Lobby conference. She listened for two or three minutes and then she went down the corridor into No. 10 and after two or three minutes, as Harold had carefully arranged with me, I followed after her. I found them both looking extremely happy. She had confirmed to Harold that I'd made the whole difference to her by yielding to her the First Secretaryship and Harold was delighted that she is as happy as she is. Barbara Castle is going to be First Secretary and Minister of the Economy and of Production. But then comes the question of whom she should have as number two. Harold of course wants her to take the terrible Tom Urwin but I said that she ought to keep Roy Hattersley. 'That's impossible,' said Marcia, who had just come in. 'Roy belongs to the other side. He's a Gaitskellite, a conspirator.' 'Look here, Marcia,' I said, 'I've seen a lot of that boy. He's not a Gaitskellite or any other kind of ite. He's a very ambitious young politician. And the only thing Barbara will find embarrassing is that he may become too fond of her and too closely tied to her coat-strings.'

I shall be interested to hear what Harold finally decides. Meanwhile he turned to me and said, 'You don't have much self-interest, Dick, in this affair, do you? I think it's very generous what you've done.' And I replied, 'Well, it's much more important to get Barbara in a good humour as First Secretary and Minister of Labour or Labour and Production or whatever she'll be called. That makes sense. We can build her up in that particular way and I don't need the title anyway.' As we sat there talking and drinking it was clear that Harold had backpedalled a long way from the idea of the Mark II Government. The only major change in this reshuffle will be Barbara's promotion, with mine coming a very poor second. Roy will be upset that by keeping Barbara out of D.E.A. he hasn't kept her out of power. Harold likes this as well and he is doing it in Roy's absence. This may be the saving of the prices and incomes policy because Barbara has already told me that she intends to look at this positively, to go to the trade unions and offer them an 8 per cent increase if they give her some production. If what Barbara said is correct we're going to have a return to the philosophy of George Brown's prices and incomes policy far back in 1964 when it was an expression of expansionism. This shouldn't upset Roy too much because he isn't really a restrictionist and he wants productivity and an export drive.

So we sat and chatted, Barbara and I and the boss and Marcia until I had to go down to the House for my business Statement after Harold's Questions. Once again it went swimmingly, tossing the balls in the air and catching them—there is nothing in this job of Leader of the House except procedure, posture, performance. I can do it easily, effortlessly and successfully, and I have got the House in the hollow of my hand.

But this Thursday evening I begin to get a sense of let-down. I saw a news flash on the tape saying that the one certainty is a really big promotion for me, and I began to wonder whether I haven't given my future away and been too generous. I've given the First Secretaryship to Barbara and for myself I've got the hire of a beautiful office. So I got hold of Tam and talked to him sadly.

Friday, April 5th

All the papers were speculating about the reconstruction but Walter Terry in the *Mail* had an inside story, which though it was not complete was correct in every detail it printed. I was still feeling so unhappy that I rang up Harold and said that I just wanted to make sure what my own position was after the shuffle. He said, 'Well, you certainly haven't been looking after yourself, Dick, these days.' But he gave me the kind of assurance of his goodwill that I needed. I couldn't be really demoted after all this so I slouched over to my last weekly meeting. I think I'm really the only Minister who has been

consulted by Harold throughout all this. Probably this is the last time I shall
be really close to Harold because there are sharp choices in this world. You
can either have a job like the Leader of the House with no effective work to
do but a lot of intimate contact with Harold and the Chief Whip or you can
have a real departmental job which cuts you off from internal leadership
politics. I've taken my choice to go out of the centre into a huge Department.
In the short run I may find that I've fallen between two stools because there
are going to be six months in which I neither have the Leadership of the
House nor any Ministry of my own at all. I shan't really be able to run the
Ministry of Social Security and the Ministry of Health through Judith Hart
and Kenneth Robinson. This has been made very clear to me at a meeting
I had with Odgers and Burke Trend when they came in to discuss my accommodation. For the present I'm staying in my Privy Council room because
there's no room for anybody else, but in the end Fred Peart will have to take
it over and I suspect that he will take over Freddy Ward at the same time
while I keep my two Secretaries.

*On April 6th the Prime Minister announced a major Cabinet reshuffle. Barbara
Castle became First Secretary of State and head of the new Department of
Employment and Productivity. Ray Gunter, hitherto Minister of Labour,
became Minister of Power. Richard Crossman was given overall responsibility
for the Department of Health and Social Security, with Kenneth Robinson and
Judith Hart as Ministers for the two respective wings of the Department.
Patrick Gordon Walker resigned from his office as Secretary of State for
Education and Science, and George Darling from the Board of Trade. Richard
Crossman remained Lord President of the Council but Fred Peart became
Leader of the House of Commons and Cledwyn Hughes took his place as
Minister for Agriculture.*

Sunday, April 7th
This weekend we've had Harold Lever and his Lebanese princess, Diane,
staying with us. The object of the visit was to show them Williamscote, the
house about three quarters of a mile away from ours, looking down over
the Cherwell valley on a perfect wooded site. Williamscote was in the Love-
day family for hundreds of years until young Tom—who came back from
America—decided to sell it up. It was a perfect day for seeing it but of
course it looked utterly dilapidated inside and a lot of it was medieval.
What they wanted was an eighteenth-century palace and so we took them
across to see Farnborough Hall, which they certainly would have bought if
they could. But I think they're probably more likely to buy a huge modern
house with swimming pools near Windsor. They're the most charming
guests and Harold Lever gave me a most interesting account of the recent
devaluation crisis. All that week the Bank of England had known that gold
had been pouring out of the country and done nothing about it. Then

suddenly the country was faced with the threat of devaluation and the Governor proposed to take no action at all, so that we had to be saved by American intervention. The American request for the closing of the gold market enabled us to have our Bank Holiday and save our gold standard. Harold had another horrifying story, which I couldn't quite follow, about the trip he and the Governor took across the Atlantic to try and settle our difficulties, all about the way the Bank of England was in favour of loyalty to the old rules of banking and for doubling the price of gold, even though we had none, rather than supporting American policy.

There's nothing much to add today when I reflect on last week. Indeed I have a sense of anticlimax and am delighted that Harold Lever and his wife are here to make me forget my own position and all the experiences I've been through.

Nevertheless, I suppose I can say that this was the first Cabinet reshuffle in which I was a Minister who worked right on the inside, and I finally persuaded Harold to accept Barbara as Minister of Labour and showed him how to make that job attractive enough. On the other hand there's a great deal which I failed to get through. None of the dead wood has been cut away except poor old Patrick Gordon Walker. Even Gunter has shuffled into Power. So the Sunday papers are already beginning to say this is a characteristic Wilson shuffle. Once again he started off with really big ideas but in the end he just shuffled the pack. I think this is roughly true and from Roy's point of view it's a good thing that it is true since he was away in America during the crucial days and had to rely on Barbara and myself. As for my new job, it's no good talking about that yet.

Monday, April 8th
I didn't write in my diary yesterday and so I didn't record the most dramatic event of the week—the murder of Martin Luther King and the riots all over America.[1] After the President's announcement that he wouldn't stand again and would try to get peace in Vietnam America is now the centre of world news and we are able to watch day by day, almost hour by hour, on television the development of a great internal American crisis. From our narrow political point in England this has been a godsend for Harold Wilson. Jimmy Margach said to me, 'Thank God, if Martin Luther King hadn't been murdered the Sunday papers would have concentrated on tearing Wilson to pieces for failing to carry out the Mark II Cabinet as he said he was going to.'

From George Brown we had the second of his articles—this time on the Foreign Office—and again it was a merciful deliverance. By remaining deputy leader he has completely castrated himself as a writer and these two articles were simply and quite brightly written but not very informative accounts—with a few names thrown in—of what he tried to do in the two Ministries. From the point of view of the Government Brown has become

[1] The American Negro leader was assassinated on April 4th.

much less of a menace than Desmond Donnelly, who yesterday managed to catch the headlines by knocking his chairman off the platform of a meeting at Haverford West.

The Privy Council this morning had to be at 10.15 and at Windsor because the Queen is going to Reading to see a computer station. This meant I could have a very beautiful drive right across Oxfordshire past Thame and Stokenchurch through Marlow and down through Maidenhead and on to Windsor. All the Cabinet Ministers concerned in the reshuffle were there (poor little Mason as Postmaster-General has his swearing in in my office this afternoon). Here was Fred Peart, now Lord Privy Seal and Leader of the House; next to him George Thomas, very bright and bustling as the new Secretary of State for Wales; poor Eddie Shackleton, down-graded from Lord Privy Seal to Paymaster-General; and alongside him Ray Gunter, who was equally depressed because he's switched from Labour to Power. But of course the most important person there was our first lady, Barbara Castle, the new First Secretary and Secretary of State for Employment.

My main job was to get Fred Peart to come into my car on the way to London for an hour's briefing. The actual briefing didn't take very long but what I really wanted to talk about was the division of staff in my Private Office, which had caused me a lot of worry over the weekend. Finally I decided to suggest that he should retain Freddy Ward and the Assistant Principal, Michael Townley, with one secretary while I should take with me the two new men from Michael Stewart's office, Paul Odgers and Oglesby, plus my two favourite girls, Anne Ridoutt and Janet. He seemed quite pleased with the deal and I sold it to Paul and Oglesby. When we got to London and looked over the office it seemed sensible to swap so that he kept his suite and I kept my beautiful room. There was one other delicate thing I had to put to Fred before we went along to the Lord Chancellor's room to discuss Lords reform. Everybody feels very strongly that I should continue to lead the Government delegation to the inter-party conference and that Fred should add his name to our list. Fortunately he complied. No doubt this was because he is very much opposed to the reform we are now making and he will need a great deal of converting. So that leaves the Home Secretary and me still in charge of the reform.

What all this really means is that now Michael Stewart has gone to the Foreign Office I have switched to his job and taken over his chairmanship of committees and retained the chairmanship of the Home Publicity Committee, the leadership of the House of Lords delegation and the chairmanship of my own pet Devolution Committee.

In the Lord Chancellor's room we had a very tough meeting on an extremely interesting issue. We have laid it down that there are to be voting peers who form the new House and speaking peers, who are of course the present hereditary peers permitted to carry on until death but excluded from voting. Now the question we had to decide is whether excluding them from voting means that they are also excluded from voting in committee. Eddie, Jellicoe and Byers and their working party have all been urging me to assume that for practical reasons speaking peers must have the right to vote in committee. If there's going to be an effective committee system in the Lords, they argued, which can take over much of the work of the House of Commons, then all the members of the Committee must be entitled to vote upstairs. I replied that once we concede this we have given way on our central principle that the power of the hereditary peerage must be totally eliminated. After all, voting in committee upstairs can be a very important exercise of power and just because it would be extremely convenient to have our present excellent hereditary peers continuing to form the nucleus of our committees, it doesn't seem possible to me that we can concede this amount of power to them. Fortunately the Lord Chancellor was as adamant as I am on this point. But Eddie warned me after the meeting that this might be a breaking point with the Tories.

This afternoon Fred Peart had to be blooded in the House. He was answering a few Questions and replying to the Easter debate. I was still in my old room in the Commons, No. 4, trying to clear up before he took over. As I walked along the lobby I realized I was no longer Leader, no longer a person people wanted to talk to about the future of the House, no longer a person the P.M. wanted to talk to about prices and incomes or whatever may be. I am clean out of all that consultative work with No. 10 and out of those relationships with John Silkin and the Whips, with the back-benchers and with the Tory Party. I've forfeited it all and chucked it away and now I am just the Lord President with a collection of unknown jobs in Whitehall which count for nothing outside. I've lost them all and no one really minds. I got one or two little laments—a note from the Lord Chancellor saying it was a disaster that there'd be no more reform in the Commons, and a note, strangely enough, from Barnett Cocks but nothing in the press except a couple of bare paragraphs saying I'd been a good Leader. I'm afraid I felt sad this evening because I was beginning to see the emptiness of the desert into which I was entering in my new job.

I gave Judith Hart dinner with Tam Dalyell and as time passed it became clearer and clearer that the so-called clear understanding the P.M. had given me that I was to take over control of these two Departments was something Judith and Kenneth Robinson had not been told themselves. She had the impression that I had accepted the position of a Michael Stewart co-ordinator with the creation of the new Department a very long way ahead, probably in March of next year. As I went to bed I realized that I'd opted myself out of a job in which I was succeeding and jumped myself into another where its very basis is insecure and unestablished.

Tuesday, April 9th
At Cabinet Harold started with a harangue about the new organization.

More and more work must be devolved on the Cabinet Committees and Cabinet itself should meet less frequently than before. In addition to O.P.D. and S.E.P. there will now be a Parliamentary Committee dealing with political questions. He halted at this point and Tony Crosland, who always asks the awkward question, said, 'May we take it that the names of the Parliamentary Committee are those we find in the press?' It looks to me that with ten people on it it will still be far too big for an effective inner Cabinet.

Next, to my surprise, Harold raised the issue of publications—relating to George Brown. This, he said, had been discussed at a previous meeting and he added that it was interesting that one of those who attacked the Lord President most fiercely on that occasion was already in contract with a publisher for a book of memoirs. Consternation round the table—until he added that he is no longer a member of the Cabinet and everyone knew it was George.

George Thomson was back from New Zealand and reported his conversations about our withdrawal from the Far East. Once again it's clear that all the forebodings of ghastly shock and consternation were completely unjustified. Britain is now so ineffective that no one is shocked by the news. Moreover, in this case what he was saying was completely overwhelmed by the news of the American activities in Vietnam. He told us that before the decisions were taken there was even less consultation with Australia and New Zealand, whose troops are taking part in the war, than with us, whose troops are not. That's how the Americans treat their minor allies.

After that the Home Secretary raised the question of the Aldermaston C.N.D. march this year.[1] He had information that dangerous elements—anarchists and communists—were going to infiltrate the march in order to assault Burghfield, which is a home security store full of ammunition and which will have to be defended in order to prevent the ammunition being blown up. From this he went on to tell us about the development of professional techniques of inciting riots. This question of the anarchists and the Trots is getting quite interesting. It all started from the Grosvenor Square demonstration the other Sunday when a relatively peaceful procession was deliberately turned into a riot by a number of anarchists some of whom, the police claim, are German students expressly brought in because they've had professional training at causing riots. I've no idea how much truth there is in this story but it's certainly true that student rioting is becoming prominent throughout the western world, particularly in the U.S.A., West Germany and France. Over here we've had comparatively little of it apart from the bashing of Harold Wilson's and Denis Healey's cars in Oxford and Cambridge.

[1] A march by members of the Campaign for Nuclear Disarmament that took place annually from the atomic weapons research establishment at Aldermaston in Berkshire to London.

As soon as Cabinet was over I had to get Harold and nail him down about my powers as Minister. 'I'll have a letter drafted,' he said. 'I must have it,' I replied, 'in the hands of Judith Hart by five o'clock because I'm seeing her then with her Permanent Secretary and they must both know exactly what the position is.' Harold said that was perfectly all right but I'm only too aware that I'm going to have some very awkward trouble with Judith and with Kenneth, who certainly have not been informed of the fate which is hanging over them.

That afternoon I briefed two press men—Ian Trethowan and David Watt.*

The time had now come for my confrontation with Judith Hart. I took Paul Odgers with me and went round to her Ministry—a nice cosy little office in the Adelphi. I started by suggesting that we should base our discussion on the Prime Minister's paper. She pulled herself together (I saw that she was nearly in tears) and she whispered, 'I'd rather discuss that with you alone.' This nonplussed me for the moment but to fill in time I explained what I want to do in the next three months, both in getting to know the Ministry and also in hurrying up the work on the pension plan. Directly I broke off the meeting and was alone with Judith over a drink, she said, 'I only got that minute from the P.M. five minutes before you arrived. It was the greatest blow in the world to me. I went to see him personally and he assured me that you would just be co-ordinating until the new Ministry was formed and that it couldn't take place before January at the earliest. I feel terribly let down since you will be taking all the credit from me and it's the third time this has happened. At the Scottish Office I got no chance to shine. Then I went to Commonwealth and there I had some achievements but only in obscure areas like Mauritius and Gibraltar. Third, I took over a really unpopular job when I replaced Peggy Herbison and just at the point when I'm winning a little popularity and a bit of position in my career you barge in and take all the credit from me.' I think I managed to make her see that I wasn't going to behave in this way and that if she had new ideas she would get full credit for them. I told her she would of course answer all Questions in the House of Commons but it was an impossible meeting and I crawled out of that building thinking, 'My God, Harold's kindly indecision certainly creates problems.' First he gives me an absolutely clear-cut guarantee that I would take effective control of these two Ministries in the period before amalgamation, and at the same time gives fair assurances to the two Ministers that there will be no effective change in their standing before amalgamation. That's not an easy position for me.

* Their articles both came out on Thursday and provide a good example of the problem of briefing in politics. I told them my own views and of course they added their own opinions. If Harold had known that they wrote the articles after talking to me he would have held me responsible for all their criticism of him. But it's my calculation that the articles would have been 50 per cent more bitter and vindictive and unfair if I hadn't primed David and Ian in the way I did.

25

I rushed back home to find Anne because we'd agreed to go to the *Newsweek* cocktail party. My Office had got things wrong. I went to the big *Newsweek* office at the bottom of the Haymarket, to the penthouse of New Zealand House—all empty. They told us it was Selfridges, I guessed Claridges and we got there on time. I notice that now the press all crowd around me because just at the moment I'm something of a political figure among these journalists. They were all curious about the Mark II Government and trying to get me to admit that it isn't a genuine Mark II. Then we were off to a delicious Danish film—a remote romantic film about a lieutenant in the guards who falls in love with a tightrope walker and they go off into the forest and have their idyll and then they shoot themselves and that's the happy end. A lovely film. We decided to have dinner at Locket's round the corner in Marsham Court and when I walked in what did I find? Mr Elystan Morgan,[1] the successor to Dick Taverne at the Home Office, celebrating his appointment with the Scottish Nationalist, Mrs Ewing. Both of us looked a bit embarrassed.

Wednesday, April 10th

This was the day on which I began to discover the Party reaction to the reshuffle—largely thanks to the intelligence work of Tam Dalyell and Tom Bradley, who is Roy's P.P.S. They say that people approve of what happened right at the top, particularly Barbara's appointment. But at the lower level there's horror at the minor appointments. As I warned the Prime Minister, Tom Urwin, who has been upped to Minister of State at the D.E.A., has infuriated the Parliamentary Secretaries and amazed the Trade Union Group. Then there was Elystan Morgan, a young lawyer with no background in the Party, suddenly promoted to Dick Taverne's place at the Home Office. Dick Taverne's appointment as a Minister of State at the Treasury is an excellent appointment, but there is consternation and fury among the young aspirants outside and the junior Ministers inside the Government at Morgan's appointment.

The Parliamentary Party had been looking forward to a Mark II Cabinet; they had been expecting two or three of the incompetents to be out, Greenwood for certain along with Gordon Walker and Willie Ross. They had expected that at least half a dozen of the able young men—David Marquand, Brian Walden, Paul Rose, Eric Heffer—would be appointed, and that a whole group of men who had been given jobs in 1964 and had earned their keep and their retirement—Julian Snow, Charlie Loughlin, Norman Pentland—would have been knocked out. None of this has happened, and what has made it even worse is the promotion of John Silkin to be Deputy Leader of the House. I had never shown great enthusiasm for this idea of John's. He wanted to be Deputy Leader and thereby enabled to speak, but as a

[1] Labour M.P. for Cardiganshire 1966–74. He was Parliamentary Under-Secretary of State at the Home Office 1968–70.

matter of fact it's a tremendous advantage that the Chief Whip doesn't speak. A hundred years' wisdom is not to be sniffed at. By tradition Whips are silent. They have spoken at the Party meeting but never on the Floor, and this is an important tradition. Whips have all the patronage, all the unpleasant decisions about voting, three-line whips and expulsions, and they have never had to defend them in public on the Floor of the House. Moreover, there's a constitutional issue. The Leader of the House has to combine both Party management and House management: he has to have the confidence of both. The Chief Whip is a pure Party official, who doesn't have to work to win the support of the House. I hear that Willie Whitelaw is unhappy at John's decision. Moreover, the last thing Tam told me was that the fury of the back-benchers was concentrated on three people—Harold, John Silkin and Dick Crossman, who was thought to have had a lot to do with the shuffle.

Early this morning Louis Petch, the Treasury man in charge of the machinery of government, was due to see me.[1] He made a very good impression and within a matter of minutes he and Odgers and I were sitting there deciding how to carry out the Prime Minister's brief. Now that we've seen it we find it is a very precise directive. It says that while the Ministers shall continue to run their Departments they must consult me on matters of major policy and I shall have access to their officials, and it then goes on to describe the terms of the amalgamation. Petch began to discuss the two Ministries and remarked that Social Security are far too lengthy and verbose in their papers because they're an inferior Ministry and they're not quite up to all the work they have to do. An interesting comment.

My meeting on devolution was at 9.30 and I found an atmosphere of complete chaos as a result of Harold's reshuffle. First of all George Thomas, who comes from South Wales and regards Cledwyn Hughes's views as sheer treason, has taken Cledwyn's place. Secondly I have Victor Stonham, who is anti-devolution, instead of Dick Taverne, who had a very open mind. Change of representation on a Cabinet Committee is often a nuisance but doesn't matter much more than that. In this instance, however, I'd hand-picked the Committee to get a fair balance and to get people of independent mind who wouldn't work on a departmental brief and we had been achieving a common mind, or something near it. But within a few minutes I knew we were right back at square one. I don't suppose Harold meant to wreck the Committee but he certainly has.

I had planned to go across to Kenneth Robinson's Ministry and do the same for him as I'd done for Judith Hart. I'd known that Judith would be much easier to deal with because she's ambitious, a close friend of the Prime Minister, and knows she will work herself out of her Ministry into a job in

[1] Sir Louis Petch was Second Secretary at the Treasury 1966–8, Second Permanent Secretary in the Civil Service Department 1968–9, and chairman of the Board of Customs and Excise 1969–73. Since 1974 he has been chairman of the Parole Board.

the Cabinet. Moreover, she also knows that I am the expert on pensions and she can't get on without me. So in her case it was only a psychological affront that I had to deal with. It was a very different situation with Robinson. He's a dry little man with a dry little moustache and neatly brushed hair in whom I first got interested when I heard that he, as a Labour candidate, had published a book on Wilkie Collins[1] and I then came across him again when we met once or twice at Covent Garden. There aren't so many Labour M.P.s who go to the opera. The real difference between Kenneth and Judith is that Kenneth is a genuine expert. He's worked for years inside the hospital service and he's proved himself a skilled and competent Minister, dedicated to his Ministry, knowing it from A to Z and handling the doctors with conspicuous success. What he's hated is being outside the Cabinet with people like Patrick Gordon Walker and Michael Stewart and myself stuck on top of him when he thinks he ought to be at the Cabinet table. All this being so I knew that I'd have far more bloody-mindedness from Robinson than I would from Judith Hart and he'd make things as difficult for me as possible. So I wasn't surprised to hear that instead of going down to Elephant and Castle I was to see the Prime Minister at No. 10. I looked in at 4.30 and he told me he'd had Kenneth there already, cold, furious and threatening resignation. The P.M. had told him that'd he'd make a pretty good fool of himself if, having failed to resign on prescription charges, he resigned now about some personal affront. 'Nevertheless,' Harold added, 'I think he might do it in his present mood and we don't want that at all in view of the problems we shall soon be facing with the doctors. Are you prepared, Dick, to work out a letter to him which clarifies his situation?' I said of course I was and there was nothing I wanted less than to interfere in Kenneth Robinson's affairs during these next six months. All I need are the reserve powers and an ultimate veto if he were to do something I didn't want—on exemption charges, for example. So Harold and I sat down at the big table and began to draft out in longhand the kind of letter which one should leave civil servants to write. I finally persuaded him to let me take it across to my Mr Odgers.

That gave me a moment to discuss the reshuffle. I told him the Party hadn't been very happy about the junior appointments and I mentioned Elystan Morgan, who after all was a nationalist candidate in 1964. 'I was only given three people to choose from,' he replied, 'and Callaghan chose this one among the three.'

I then got on to the subject of the Parliamentary Committee which now consists of ten members, with Peter Shore in as the tenth and Tony Crosland out as the eleventh. 'He has to be punished for what he has done. What he did was very wrong.' 'What on earth has he been doing?' I asked. 'He's been negotiating, talking, intriguing in the Foreign Office with George Brown and George Brown has got a tape of what he said, I can tell you that.' This

[1] *Wilkie Collins, a biography* (London: Davis-Poynter).

absolutely bewildered me and bewilders me still but I'll let it lie at the back of my mind until I can find something which makes sense of it. Finally I told him that we'd been lucky to get away with it that weekend since there wasn't a great deal of satisfaction with the new Government, though Barbara's move had been put across well. Everything now depended on her success.

By now it was 5.30—time for the first meeting of a new Cabinet Committee on Immigration under Jim's chairmanship. It was not only a new Committee but a new kind of committee. The Home officials had produced a paper which really tried to provide a philosophical background for our attitude to race and colour and which argued the case for a nationally agreed consensus policy. Jim characteristically started by saying that it wasn't his own paper and he was just putting it forward as an official paper so that we could all give our reflections upon it. Sure enough, there was a very interesting discussion. The first thing I noticed was that the paper discussed colour and race and left out the whole problem of white immigrants as though coloured immigration was our sole problem. I pointed out that this was based on an astonishing assumption. If a million Jews had entered England from Russia instead of a million coloured people from India and the West Indies then we would have had an anti-semitic problem. We mustn't assume uncritically that colour is an essentially different problem from the differences of culture between peoples of the same colour. For instance, there's the case of the Protestants and the Catholics in Northern Ireland. When I said this the whole Committee united to turn me down. They all agreed with the official paper that colour is a basic problem, totally different from cultural differences. Some of them quoted what was happening in America. I said that that goes back to a long cultural history of slavery and the slaves aren't necessarily coloured persons. You can have white slaves perfectly well. But the Committee was united against me and that was that. Then Harold Lever said he wanted to look at the problem from the point of view of the immigrant, rather than that of the receiving end. 'What immigrants need,' he said, 'is not psychological kindness or anything except a sense of fair justice and equality of treatment.' If we gave them that we would avoid all the problems of America, he said. What an old-fashioned Jewish assimilationist Harold Lever is! If only it were true that provided the immigrant felt happy and secure in his new country everything would be all right. But in sober fact it is the psychology of the home population of the original inhabitants which is the chief problem. By making immigrants comfortable you may placate them but at the same time infuriate the older population, who see immigrants getting what they regard as unfair advantages.

I have put all this down because a discussion of this kind is such a rare event in our Labour Government. We deal pragmatically with problems as they come up without any consideration of the theoretical or rational issues involved. I found the afternoon excellent and we came to a sensible practical decision that we should now discuss the principles upon which the quota should be fixed, and see whether we have the right proportion, for example between Europeans and non-Europeans. The main difference between the Ministers on the Committee is already clear. We're divided into those who want to allow the coloured communities to remain foreign—the Jews to be Jews, the Sikhs to be Sikhs—and don't want to try to turn them into little Englishmen, and those who want full integration or assimilation according to the American pattern.

I had asked Brian Abel-Smith and Richard Titmuss to dinner at the Garrick to meet Paul Odgers. Brian had written me a formal letter of congratulations on my new job but it was soon clear that he and Titmuss are both ardent supporters of the Ministry of Health and considerable sceptics about the whole idea of integrating the two Departments. As the meal went on the reason was revealed. They were nervous of a merger working right the way through from the top to the bottom of both Ministries with transferability from section to section and from job to job. They dislike this whole notion because they believe that the jobs in the Ministry of Social Security—the special work of the Supplementary Benefits Commission, for example—are totally different from the work of the Ministry of Health, and the kind of person who is being trained in the old bureaucratic tradition of the National Assistance Board and the National Insurance Office would not be suitable for work with the doctors in most sections of the Ministry of Health. Of course, as I pointed out to them, what they were revealing was a very strong social feeling—that the officials of the Ministry of Health feel superior in every way to the officials of the Ministry of Social Security. Richard Titmuss did not deny this but he tried to prove his point by emphasizing the terribly low standards of the Ministry of Social Security. Apparently they're testing the accuracy of assessments now and they found that a quarter of the claimants are getting less than their entitlement because of the incompetence of the staff. There is a huge turnover of this unskilled low-paid staff and Titmuss himself is deeply dissatisfied with the section he's responsible for. So, very tactfully, both he and Brian led me to see that whatever I do I mustn't ruin their splendid Ministry of Health by just mixing it up with the vulgar Ministry of Social Security.

Naturally we had a bit of a row about prescription charges but I felt this evening that I'd moved them along and got them to a point where once again they will form a nucleus of the mixed planning group I'm determined to establish as soon as possible to co-ordinate the whole of the social services.

Thursday, April 11th
Thursday was a black day since it was the day of the Gallup Poll. This week the N.O.P. showed a 24 per cent Tory lead which is a reflection of the by-election results and, if anything, slightly worse. There are two interesting features: the decline of Ted Heath's popularity, though his party's still goes

up, and that among Labour supporters the overwhelming number still have confidence in Harold Wilson and don't want any change.

With Easter coming we had a whole series of wind-up meetings. S.E.P. had been slightly reconstituted with all the economic Ministers on it, and we dealt first with a very grandiose proposal by Leylands to build a major motor-bus assembly plant in West Cumberland in order to mop up the unemployment created by the decline of Maryport and Whitehaven. By giving the assurance that he would build this huge plant, Lord Stokes had persuaded the Government to work out a total of some £4·5 million of subsidy in the early stages. But since then the size of the plant has got whittled down so that today only 500 jobs will be created by the erection of the factory and yet Stokes insists that he needs not less money but more. Here, of course, was Peter Shore as the regional Minister saying we must do it and build a major West Cumberland road as well. We heard the same from Fred Peart, who's not only Leader of the House but Member for Maryport and Whitehaven. Tony Crosland from the Board of Trade had the sense to point out that when half the number of jobs are being produced we can't offer even bigger subsidies. As a west midlands M.P. I get more and more worried by the vast sums of money going out in discriminatory allowances, in R.E.P., in local government grants. The cost to the community is getting out of all control and I was relieved that we persuaded the Committee to take another look at the Leyland project.

We passed on to a consideration of the new trade and unemployment figures. Both were deplorable, though Tony Crosland was busy telling us that the trade figures weren't nearly as bad as we might imagine. Although the trade gap had actually increased, although our imports had gone up enormously and our exports had not risen enough, although the figures for the first quarter showed we already had three-quarters of the adverse figures for the whole year he was trying to explain it all away. Next, it was Barbara's job to give the unemployment figures. They too are very alarming since, seasonally adjusted, they seem to show that unemployment is not declining at all in the present period and indeed the best possible test, the figure for vacancies, has been going the wrong way for the last three months. Does this mean that we're getting a rate of unemployment which Jenkins really wants but hasn't dared to confess to us? I fancy not. I fancy we may be suffering from budget overkill.

Immediately after S.E.P. we moved to Cabinet, which we had to have in the House of Commons because it was Thursday morning and the House started at eleven with Questions to the P.M. as well as a business Statement. It's always uncomfortable working in the P.M.'s room in the House of Commons. It's uncomfortable for the officials because it's not security-proof and people can listen in. It's uncomfortable for Ministers because there aren't enough chairs round the table and late-comers have to sit on sofas or out-sticking knobs. The general atmosphere is not that of the

Cabinet Room. The Cabinet Room is light—the light pours in through the big windows looking out on to Horse Guards Parade, it is long, it is the right shape for our discussion, whereas the Prime Minister's room is huddled and crowded and we never have a good discussion there.

Proceedings started with a complaint by the Chief Whip, who pointed out that he'd been rebuked in this morning's *Guardian* 'for his clumsy intervention on prices and incomes'. I myself had a pretty good suspicion where this leak came from but held my tongue. What would Fred Peart do? He was very much on his dignity and told his colleagues that they shouldn't behave in this way, dressing them down on behalf of the Chief Whip. This is the new term of our new Leader of the House.

We then came to our main item—space. I don't know how many times we have turned the Foreign Secretary down about these expensive European establishments—ELDO and ESRO—but he was back again appealing to the Prime Minister as a European. The arguments were repeated absolutely verbatim from both sides—only this time Wedgy Benn was reinforced by the work of my Publicity Committee, which had worked out the timetable, and at the end the P.M. and his Foreign Secretary were completely routed. I doubt if the P.M. was surprised.

At Questions I sat beside the P.M. and listened to Fred Peart answering his first business Questions. Ted Heath and John Boyd-Carpenter rang the changes on an outpouring of Questions about their request for three days' debate on the Finance Bill. It was interesting to see the Tories trying to get a new man down, treating him exactly as they treated me, roughing him up, insulting him, attacking him, and he stood his ground pretty well. This is the kind of job he will do admirably and I sat there and encouraged him.

Our last meeting was O.P.D. on a single subject—assistance to Zambia. There came an awkward moment when the P.M. said, 'Well, it's quite clear what we've decided and we agree therefore that we should answer in terms of the draft.' Now this draft he had in front of him and none of the rest of us had seen it, and it was embarrassing to say, 'Read it aloud,' because that would imply that nobody trusted him. Still, we were determined to hear the draft before we agreed and that is what finally happened.

I had made careful arrangements to be the first member of the Cabinet who saw Roy on his return from the States so I had arranged to give him lunch immediately after Cabinet. He had left on Wednesday of last week, had his talks in Washington, made a speech to the Pilgrim Society in New York and stayed in Boston and then stayed on a day for the funeral of Martin Luther King in Atlanta, Georgia. So he'd only returned last night and he sat through Cabinet looking rather sleepy. I took him off to the Garrick, and there in the back room I found the Chief sitting with Brian O'Malley at a table very close to the one reserved for me, which was slightly awkward, and it must have been obvious because another member noticed it and said, 'Ah, ha, awkward to discuss Mark III in that company!' I thought it illuminating and interesting that he sensed we belonged to different parts of the Cabinet.

I reported on all that had happened and filled Roy in on the minor appointments. I was anxious lest he would feel I had failed in my trust to him and allowed Barbara to be built up in opposition to him. No, he was quite cool and said, 'I don't want her as another economic Minister with her own economic advisers arguing against me: but I have no objection to her being Minister of Labour up-graded and made First Secretary.' That was something of a relief.

He was also interested in the failure of the Mark II Government, particularly the failure to sack anybody except Patrick, and the appointment of Cledwyn Hughes as Minister of Agriculture. He told me he was due to see the P.M. that afternoon and that one of the points he would have to make was Harold's failure to fulfil his promise to find Jack Diamond a place in Cabinet. Roy had asked Harold about this already on the phone and found the explanation unintelligible. He told me he was also worried about the rumours that Tony Crosland was being excluded from the Parliamentary Committee and would raise this as well. He was worried, he said, about 'the little deviousnesses' of the Prime Minister and the lack of a sense of candour in what he said. 'I can feel a sense of candour in my conversations with Barbara which I never feel when I'm talking to the Prime Minister.' Then he spent a long time talking about John Silkin, telling me how unsatisfactory he was and protesting his bewilderment at John's appointment as Deputy Leader of the House.

Just as I was settling down to give an interview to a Mrs Lapping—a representative of *New Society*, who'd been waiting for ages—an urgent message came that the P.M. wanted to see me. When I got there he said that Kenneth Robinson had rejected the redraft of the terms of my appointment and submitted another which was utterly fantastic. He had demanded that a new statement be prepared and issued to the press saying that he was in absolutely full charge of his Department and that the only matter I was entitled to interest myself in was amalgamation. 'That's impossible,' I said and Harold replied, 'I leave it to you. I give you full power and I will support any draft you get him to sign. Let me know if you fail to reach agreement.' I knew I was in for it. He came at 3.30 and from 3.30 to 6.30 he sat in my room and argued. After an hour I thought it was hopeless. 'Did you ever imagine,' he said to me, 'how I would react? The least I can demand is a public statement that I am in complete control and that you have nothing to do with it.' I told him that would be very difficult because I had agreed a draft with Judith and I couldn't give him specially-favoured treatment which I hadn't given her. However, I could give him personal assurances. He said he had not the faintest interest in personal assurances. What he required was a press statement to repair the terrible damage done by the Prime Minister's minute. Finally, I said it was a waste of time to go on and

25*

rang through to Michael Halls to tell him that I must come over and report to Harold that I couldn't reach agreement. 'You can't come at the moment,' he said, 'because Roy is in the room. Come after he's finished.' Maybe it was fortunate that Roy stayed for a full hour because during that hour I got what I wanted. Robinson had typed out his draft himself and after half an hour I took hold of it, knocked out one or two words, threw it across to him and said, 'Will these sentences do?' With the word 'full' omitted, the sentence said that while the Minister was in control of the Department he would submit all major policy decisions to the Secretary of State. This negotiation came off, I suppose, because we started so rough and finally settled down into reasonableness as we became more and more tired. Finally he agreed on a form of words which would be kept secret, not issued to the press and with no question of any further press comment. Only he and I and the Prime Minister and his Permanent Secretary would see the document. It would not go to the Ministry of Social Security. On these conditions I agreed that this *aide-mémoire* should clarify the Prime Minister's minute, but not, as Robinson wanted, be a substitute for it.

Harold seemed to think I had done all right. It would have been a great mistake to let Robinson resign because the whole problem of the doctors is hanging over us and anyway it's most unlikely I shall want to intervene in his Ministry in the next six months. I shall be busy inside the Ministry of Social Security, where I must get on with the pensions plan and also on the planning of the superstructure which will unite the two Ministries into one Department.

I had intended to travel on the 5.35 but owing to Robinson I only caught the 7.35 and as a result got down in the dark, carrying two huge cakes, one for Easter and one for Anne's birthday on Monday, and also my present— a magnificent garnet necklace which I've bought on the sound principle that if you earn money the way to spend it is to buy good things and not merely national saving certificates.

Friday, April 12th
In the evening Anne and I went over to dinner with Roy at his cottage in East Hendred. It's quite a long way, the village nearest to Harwell, where I haven't been for many many years. But it's a lovely place and I remembered it straightaway as a spot from which I had walked out of the cold of the Downs into the warmth of the valley. We drew up ten minutes early in the back courtyard of a rather ramshackle old vicarage with a croquet lawn somewhere about us. Inside we found a very family party: Jennifer's father, who used to be Town Clerk of Birmingham, and her mother; then a tall willowy young man at New College, who is the eldest son, Charles, with his girlfriend; next Cynthia, who is at St Paul's; and finally young Edward, who is at the City of London School and the spitting image of our Patrick, only three years older. It was, as I say, a family evening with Jennifer coping

in a rather ramshackle house. I hadn't at all expected this family atmosphere. It shows how little one knows about one's colleagues. So Roy has got a real family to cope with at home, I thought. Charles is certainly a difficult son and as for the rumbustious boy he's an object lesson of what Patrick may be if we let him talk all the time, busting and crashing into the conversation. Roy gave us some excellent claret and we managed to sit down by the fire and in the noise of the family talk he told me about his conversation with the Prime Minister, which had been long, he said, and unsatisfactory.

In the course of his narrative he repeated the story about Tony Crosland's 'crimes' and the tape-recording George had made. I said to him that since Roy knew Tony so well he can surely talk to him about it. But I don't think that he can and it looks as though Tony isn't as close to Roy now as some people believe. But certainly the impression Roy gave me is that Crosland and Healey are right out on a limb as the men whom Harold sees as the chief conspirators against him. Roy had asked Harold about the inner Cabinet and heard the dreary story of how he had to include Willie Ross and George Thomas and that would make twelve. Roy had pleaded for a smaller group, possibly meeting informally once a week and spelt out the names of the five he would like—the Prime Minister, Barbara, Dick, Denis Healey, Roy Jenkins. I think that's as good an inner group as you can select, though I doubt whether Harold will ever keep to it. Indeed, I tentatively put to Roy this evening that he and Barbara and I might meet regularly together and cover the home front. I told him how worried I was that we were just slithering down the slope and never getting together to discuss the strategy of recovery. And that's about as far as we got before we broke off.

Sunday, April 14th
Easter Sunday. We've had a fortnight now of this dry sunny April with its very cold winds and our cattle having to eat concentrates because we've got no new grass and very little hay. Meanwhile the news on the wireless seems to consist entirely of rioting. For the third night running the German students have been running wild after the shooting of the anarchist leader, Rudi Dütschke.[1] Violence is the new factor we have to face and it lies not far underneath the crust of convention and of parliamentary democracy. It's breaking out in the West just as it's breaking out in Czechoslovakia and Poland, just underneath the crust and the rigidity of Communist totalitarianism. All over the world this revolt against the establishment is like a volcanic eruption destroying the structure of the countryside over which it pours. It's made my main philosophy of life appallingly out of date. I've always worked on the assumption that you can make democracy work by

[1] A German student, Rudi Dütschke, had been shot in West Berlin on April 11th and student movements in Germany accused the Springer newspaper group of incitement. There were riots supported by students in other countries. Dütschke sought asylum in Britain, but the Home Secretary refused to extend his permit to stay here, a decision that attracted some resentment.

education and communication: by enabling people to be not merely formal voters but active participants, settling their own fortunes, taking part in collective decisions. But in this country people don't want to take part in collective decisions. In the W.E.A. we failed completely, just as we failed completely in the *Daily Mirror*, to get anything approaching mass participation. Indeed, throughout my adult life I've seen participation decline. There's less interest in local government now than there was thirty years ago and public opinion is less well-informed despite the radio, the television and the press. What we now have is mass-indifference and mass-alienation —a greater gap between government and people than there was in the time of Disraeli and Gladstone. I have spent my whole life trying to give people a chance to narrow that gap through education. Yet it's been widening all the time. This is something George Hodgkinson, who came over with Carrie on Good Friday and walked over the farm with me looking at the loveliness of it and the comfort of it, reflected on in a long conversation. We agreed that our part of the world has less physical suffering and a much higher material standard of living and indeed much more creative possibilities than it had when George was a boy. But the thing which we two care about most —the creation of a living social democracy—is the one thing which has not come with affluence and mass-education and television. Instead of civilized participation we're getting violence and riot. And all this is reflected through the television into our homes and no doubt this actually weakens the structure of democracy still further. I can't help wondering if the whole of my life has been lived in vain and if that is not the reason why I'm so glad to have given up adult education and journalism and taken on a spell as a professional politician—a member of the ruling establishment. How ironically suitable our position here at Prescote is to this task. Here are Anne and I, people of affluence, running a big farm and therefore just suitable for being members of the establishment. Is it hypocrisy to say this? No, because I've abandoned the aims in which I believed in the W.E.A. and I now accept that the settled and just management of society by a progressive oligarchy is probably the best we can hope for.

Tuesday, April 16th

Now we're in the middle of my holiday and I feel inclined to put down a few thoughts about the Cabinet. Obviously the first fact about our new Cabinet is that it has a completely new balance thanks to the absence of George Brown and the decline of Jim Callaghan. Right up to devaluation the Cabinet was dominated by the troika—Harold along with George and Jim really dominated the Government and the responsibility for its policies was centred in the hands of these three, either in tension with each other or working more or less closely together. It was they who made the basic decision in 1964 not to devalue, who repeated that decision after the 1969 election. It was they who decided to maintain a military presence East of

Suez and fought to maintain that position against the opposition in the Party. And though of course there were disagreements between them, particularly about the July measures of 1966, this didn't basically upset the fact that they dominated the show, with Michael Stewart hanging about on the sidelines and people like Denis Healey and myself as departmental Ministers completely out of the central flow of things. Now George has disappeared, totally discredited, and is just making money by his writings. Now Jim has retired into a thorough old man's unsuccessful decline as Home Secretary. And instead of these two we now have on either side of the Prime Minister Roy Jenkins and Barbara Castle as the dominating personalities in the new Cabinet.

I would add one comment on the shuffle which is less obvious. The removal of Gunter from the Ministry of Labour to Power has done an enormous lot of good. Of course I would have liked to have seen him chucked out of the Cabinet. I wish to God Harold had had the strength to do it. But at least he did remove him from the Ministry of Labour and put Barbara Castle in his place. With a new boss at the Treasury and a new boss at Productivity and Labour we have the chance of a new economic policy for the first time. In the same way we should have the chance of a new foreign policy now that George Brown has gone, but this will not happen under Michael Stewart. If anyone is more European-minded than George Brown it's Michael. He may be slightly more pro-Israel but on the basic issue of Anglo-American relations and entry into Europe he will simply carry on Harold's policy as before. Indeed the only chance of a new policy would have been to have made me Foreign Secretary. I was interested when Roy looked at me last week and said, 'I believe you ought to be made Foreign Secretary. That would make all the difference.' There wasn't the remotest chance of it. But with Roy at the Treasury, Barbara at Labour and me in the Foreign Office we could have given this Government a new look and a new start. Now we can only hope to do so on the home side.

Our other problem is that though this is potentially a new Government it doesn't look like a new Government to the electorate. It can't do so because Harold is still Prime Minister and no man has been associated more with the refusal to devalue and with the East of Suez policy. As long as he is Prime Minister, outside Westminster and Whitehall there will be no sense of a new start. There's a remarkable difference here between the image of the Government which the electorate sees and the image the Government presents to Whitehall and Westminster. In Westminster, however violent the prejudices of the Tories, they know very well that with the appointment of Roy and Barbara there is a new Government running the country which may be much stronger and better than its predecessor. And Whitehall knows it too and is prepared to give the new Government a real chance. I am confident that if Roy, Barbara and I can keep Harold's confidence we could get the confidence of the Parliamentary Party, we could hold the House of

Commons and we could hold Whitehall. But there is one place we can't hold and that's with the public outside. These by-elections have been catastrophic, we are coming up to another round of by-elections[1] and of municipal elections and there will be the same tale of disaster. The public will turn away from us not so much because of our policies but because of the reaction against the Wilson leadership; just as Super-Mac produced a counter-reaction against Macmillan so super-Wilson has produced a reaction and made his presence in No. 10 a liability in the revival of Party morale.

Harold is still our only possible leader—but he's a tarnished leader. Of course he still retains the qualities which brought him to the top, above all his resilience, his power to take punishment and to come up fresh each morning fighting fit. His india-rubber resilience is linked of course with self-deception. No man can be the kind of boy scout Harold is and read aloud Kipling's 'If' as often as he reads it to me without a great deal of self-deception in his make-up. It's because he is unreflective and unphilosophical that he's such a tremendous self-deceiver. I suppose that self-deception reached its zenith when he appointed himself head of the D.E.A. last autumn with Peter Shore as his henchman and from last October until devaluation day lived in a mood of continuous self-deception, week after week believing in recovery when we were running a £600 million trade deficit. Of course he can say now that he wasn't able to consider devaluation because Jim had become the symbol of the pound and wouldn't let him devalue and he couldn't get rid of Jim for fear of the effect on the pound. All these excuses are true enough. But the point I'm making is that whereas other people in that situation would have worked on gloomily facing the disaster ahead, he carried on blithely, not seeing the disaster until the very last moment.

What's new is that his self-confidence and self-deception have been dented by the most appalling personal smear campaign since devaluation. He's been turned into a figure of fun and object of derision by every comic on the B.B.C. and in the press. In the House of Commons he can still hold his own but outside he's booed and we don't dare to put him on show for fear of the derision he will cause. Yet according to the Gallup Poll it's also true that among Labour voters his position is still much stronger than that of the Party. They see him as our only possible leader.

Apart from this dint in his self-esteem I see no change in his personality. In his personal relations he still has a strong preference for the second-rate and the undistinguished. He's managed to collect round him in No. 10 the most undistinguished group of civil servants—Michael Halls, for example, who's been brought in from the Board of Trade to run his Private Office. There couldn't be a nicer man or one more third-rate. He replaced Derek Mitchell, whom Harold condemned as a gossip but whose real fault was that he was far too clever. Apart from Tommy and myself, he allows no one of ability in his entourage—Gerald Kaufman, Trevor Lloyd-Hughes, Peter de

[1] Oldham West, and Nelson and Colne.

Cheminant, incredibly dim people. The other great failure of personality which will never change is his sheer inability to make contact. In one sense Harold Wilson is the easiest person to talk to in the whole world. He's completely unassuming, natural, humble in the proper sense of the word, a perfectly ordinary man who can converse and chat in a perfectly ordinary way. When you come in he puts you at your ease and though he may be a bit of a bore and a bit of a proser and sometimes a little bit conceited, still nothing can be easier than personal relations with Harold—unless of course you want to say something important to him. Roy Jenkins said to me when we dined together on Saturday night that if you go to see Harold at first you get something out of him very easily. But you're made to pay a tremendous price for getting that one thing since for the rest of the time he sedulously and skilfully blocks the approaches to all the things you want. Indeed, his greatest art is preventing his colleagues communicating with him on subjects where he doesn't want communication. And that is why he does not hear what it is most necessary for him to hear. Those who come to tell him are fenced off and pushed aside from saying what is required.

If there's one thing I can claim in the last three years it is that to a small extent I have broken through this communications blockade and talked to him straight. But having said that I must remind myself how often I am still defeated and I must also not forget that I have to a very great extent forfeited Harold's confidence in the last month or two.

Why does he want to avoid these subjects? I think it is timidity. He certainly doesn't like scenes and he's always anxious to avoid having to say anything unpleasant. I've often heard him say that he's going to give so-and-so hell but I know very well that he won't give him hell though he will believe that he has. Take Gunter as an example. I've often heard him talk about Gunter's outrageous leaks and how he was going to send for Gunter and really put him on the mat. I don't believe he ever sent for Gunter and when it came to the shuffle he didn't sack him but promoted him to the Ministry of Power.

Because of his timidity about scenes he will always prefer a whole series of empty meetings to one unpleasant row. He will always postpone a decision until forced to accept the inevitable and then, when he does accept it, he will congratulate himself on the brilliant execution of a well-laid plan. Self-deception in this way turns indecision into great decisions.

I have no doubt that Barbara and Roy and I have an infinitely greater capacity for pulling this Party up by the scruff of its neck but we don't have the emollient qualities. Harold is as resilient as rubber but he is as smooth and round as a ballbearing—and his real function is that of a ballbearing committing great levers to work without friction. If only we could make his Prime Ministership Attleean. Attlee, as a matter of fact, was resourceful and cunning and ruthless and tough but he did let other people thrive and provide the leadership of which he was not capable. Somehow we need to have people who stand out above Harold Wilson and they are Roy and Barbara. Perhaps there are others in the Party too, but I don't see them at present.

That brings me to my thoughts about Roy. I backed him for the Chancellorship although I knew very little about him. My impressions now are these. Undoubtedly he has powers of political decision and when he's taken a decision he sticks to it through thick and thin. I watched him take major decisions on the withdrawal from the Far East, the cancellation of the F-111, the reimposition of prescription charges and the postponement of the raising of the school-leaving age. He knew they were all extremely unpleasant and he much disliked their unpopularity, but he kept to them and he felt for them. So political willpower he possesses. What he lacks are industriousness, physical energy, and resilience—all the qualities Harold has in such abundance. Roy will always be a reserved, aloof man with no great resources of physical vitality, a man who tires easily and needs to be away from London if possible for three days a week in the country. For No. 10 this is a grave disadvantage. When I sit beside him I feel that he has a patrician air—a little like Balfour, disdainful, detached—plus a delicious boyish humour. He also likes his tennis and his croquet and is much more of a family man than I realized. But throughout his political career he has always succeeded in remaining to some extent uncommitted. If he became Prime Minister I'm sure he could live up to the big hours—the big broadcasts, the big speeches. But could he show the energy to do the endless fixing and arranging which is Harold's daily life? I don't know two more sharply contrasted men.

And now for Barbara. She is probably the biggest personality in the Government today. Already she's a natural number two and if she weren't a woman she would be a natural number one; she could quite conceivably be the first lady Prime Minister. Of course she's appallingly highly-strung and she's older than she should be for leadership. Moreover she overstrains herself. Nevertheless, success freshens her vitality in an amazing way. She has the personality to control any Ministry not only by sheer willpower but also by intellectual domination. What distinguishes her from Harold as well as from Roy is that she's still a real socialist as well as a woman of immense gusto and courage in negotiations. If two human beings can make this new economic policy work it's Roy and Barbara getting on well together.

Friday, April 19th
I went up to London to address the regional organizers at Transport House but spent the morning at my Private Office. I found Odgers away on holiday and the two girls deliciously ticking over with no real work to do.

Meanwhile I had a message that Harold wanted me to see him at 12.15. I found that he'd been composing a big speech on prices and incomes for the Scottish T.U.C. His face was very brown and his hair quite white against it and he told me that they'd had nothing but strong winds all the time on the Scillies. We didn't spend much time on his speech because a subject I really wanted to talk to him about was race. There's been a great sensation because after a meeting of the Shadow Cabinet the Conservatives have decided to put down a reasoned amendment to our Race Relations Bill instead of supporting it as was expected. This is very ominous news for any Labour Member in the Midlands, where we've already got a tremendous problem in winning back working-class voters who detest the Prices and Incomes Bill. If, in addition, we're going to have the Conservatives opposing our race relations proposals it will make it a great deal more difficult to win our own people back. What we need is a real bipartisan policy. And this is what we've had since 1966 but the difficulty of trying to deal with the social problems of Coventry and the Black Country will be enormously increased if the Conservatives now abandon it. I suggested to Harold that it would be a good idea for one of our leading ministers to plead the case for bipartisan-ship on race and religion, in which I've always passionately believed. Harold agreed enthusiastically and then disconcerted me by adding that he wondered if we couldn't get Heath on the hop on this subject. I said, 'For heaven's sake, keep party politics out of it. One has to play fair and appeal to the Tories to join in a genuine national campaign and that's what I'd like to say in a speech I'm making in Coventry this evening.' If I remember rightly I drafted a similar speech long ago in 1965 at the Ministry of Housing, but at that time it was suppressed as being undesirable. I think it's become essential now. Harold was quite enthusiastic and in discussing the debate remarked that Ted Heath would try to get out of the difficulty by abstentions. I said, 'We can defeat that by having a three-line whip,' and he at once pressed his button and summoned an official. 'Remind me when the Chief Whip comes in today to tell him we need a three-line whip for the Race Relations Bill,' he said. Poor John is still very much the P.M.'s lieutenant.

We then had a desultory conversation about the Parliamentary Committee and then about my idea of an inner committee of five. I got the impression that despite his holiday he was a bit down. He was facing the formidable list of trade-union conferences and the defeats we are likely to have on the issue of prices and incomes. He was facing the threat of strikes and the danger of another devaluation. All this was in his mind as he sat there and I said to myself, 'He's come back too early from the Scillies. He's not really relaxed or rested though he couldn't be nicer or more friendly.'

Saturday, April 20th
Yesterday evening Anne and I went over to Coventry to a meeting in the Binley ward for Peter Lister, the deputy leader of the Council Group (and I think by far its ablest member), and Betty Healey, the ward secretary of what is the best organized of the wards in my constituency—indeed the only one with any serious organization at all. Peter is not a normal Coventry character. He was a soldier who had a foot blown off in Palestine when his motorcycle ran over a landmine in 1946, and then he joined the staff of

G.E.C. and he might have got to the top but for his politics. Recently he's shot up, as people do in the Coventry Labour movement, not only on the council but also as a parliamentary candidate where he's extremely effective as well. He's outstandingly able, inordinately ambitious and intriguing and, like all Coventry politicians, neglects his poor wife, who is a hospital nurse and who is now trained as a teacher. He characterizes the best in the Coventry Labour movement: self-assertiveness, ambition, a bit of ruthlessness and a great deal of dogmatism. Betty Healey, who works very closely with him, is one of those ugly girls who's nearly a beauty and she's dedicated herself to looking after Peter's ward and they intrigue together. Indeed, they're the counterpart of my Albert Rose and Winnie Lakin, who are the Coventry East party in so far as I am concerned. Albert and Winnie look after me while Peter and Betty claim to represent the rank and file and say that Albert and Winnie are sheltering me from the realities of life. So whenever they ask me I always go. This was a little meeting for party workers in what should be an absolutely safe ward though we lost it last year. With Peter up this year we might lose it again if we don't work really hard.

I turned up at eight o'clock for a meeting timed at 7.30 to find three or four people there and one constituent who wanted to talk to me about the problem of her wages. By the time we'd finished there were some fifteen or sixteen people in the room, the result of a tremendous drive last Friday evening at their social. This shows how demoralized the party is. Nevertheless, there was one Anglican parson, one Methodist parson, the organizer of the youth club and two doctors, so the middle-class element was standing by us loyally in our distress. It's the working-class element who keeps on saying they're too scared to go canvassing. The woman who'd come to see me about her wages remarked that you can't stand up now in the factories because they wallop you. Yet, as Peter and Betty both pointed out to the meeting, anyone who actually goes out canvassing finds no difficulties. It's easy to recruit new members provided you have the courage to go and talk on the doorstep. It's the demoralization of the party we suffer from today rather than the hostility of the general public.

The Coventry people couldn't have cared less about my giving up the Leadership of the House but after I got back I started wondering what others would think about it, in particular people like Selwyn Lloyd and Willie Whitelaw, who'd worked so loyally with me on the Services Committee. I think they're disconcerted by my suddenly giving up just when I was settling in. I myself would have much preferred to stay on until the summer so as to complete the White Paper on the House of Lords reform and be able to announce it as Leader of the House. I would have quite definitely preferred things to go that way but I think this diary has made it clear why I went for the Mark II Government and for my new job in the Mark II Government, and though the Mark II didn't come off I had to accept the change of job I had demanded at the time. Of course the reason for that demand was not that I didn't like being Leader of the House (I liked it a lot) but that I wanted to change because of my personal relations with the Prime Minister and the distrust which was growing between us. For all those months I've been very close to Harold as one of his courtiers, one of the kitchen Cabinet on whom he so much relies. No man could be as close to Harold as this sort of personal courtier without suffering and without wanting to get away from a position of mere influence to a position of real power. My trust in him and his trust in me were both being undermined. John Silkin resented me and wasn't helping me, I think, in the advice he gave to Harold. On the other hand I insisted on having very intimate relations with Roy Jenkins which were beginning to imperil my relations with Harold. I think it was this which basically made me insist on a change of job. To anyone outside it must look terrible. I don't blame Jim for being thoroughly shocked at me and talking about my walking out of one important job long before I'd finished it, and saying, 'That's just the kind of thing one expects of Dick. Before anything is really completed, before he's finished his job, he's out and away to the next bright idea.' On the other hand there's something to be said for Harold's view that I'm at my best starting things, giving things their first impetus. Others can carry on better without me. Basically I got out of being Leader of the House because in that job I had to be Harold's henchman—I had been selected because he thought I would be absolutely loyal to him and in order to remain there I had to remain absolutely loyal. Towards the end I found there were far too many things on which the requirement of absolute loyalty strained my conscience and indeed my whole inner being. I was seeing much too much of Harold and as a result I was liking him less. Now I've deliberately chosen a position outside the inner circle where I shall build up as much power as I can. My new position is one in which I'm entitled not to be absolutely loyal to Harold, in which I can talk to Barbara and to Roy freely and independently without Harold suspecting me. And this is what I intend to do. I've already arranged a dinner, the first of what I hope will be regular meetings between the three of us, at which we can talk uninhibitedly about how to handle Harold. It was this I couldn't do so long as I was Leader of the House without telling Harold about it and making him suspect me of being disloyal to him. And it was this which made me want to get out from the inner circle. We're heading for some pretty awkward times in which I don't want to find myself a henchman of the Prime Minister but a power in the Party in my own right.

Members of the Cabinet 1966–68

When Volume II of the Diaries opens, August 24th, 1966

Prime Minister	Harold Wilson
First Secretary at D.E.A.	Michael Stewart
Lord President of the Council and Leader of the House of Commons	Richard Crossman
Lord Chancellor	Gerald Gardiner
Lord Privy Seal and Leader of the House of Lords	Frank Longford
Chancellor of the Exchequer	James Callaghan
Foreign Secretary	George Brown
Home Secretary	Roy Jenkins
Agriculture, Fisheries and Food	Fred Peart
Commonwealth Relations Office	Herbert Bowden
Defence	Denis Healey
Education and Science	Anthony Crosland
Housing and Local Government	Anthony Greenwood
Labour	Ray Gunter
Minister without Portfolio	Douglas Houghton
Overseas Development	Arthur Bottomley
Power	Richard Marsh
Scottish Office	William Ross
Technology	Anthony Wedgwood Benn
Board of Trade	Douglas Jay
Transport	Barbara Castle
Welsh Office	Cledwyn Hughes

Changes on January 7th, 1967

Minister without Portfolio	Patrick Gordon Walker

Douglas Houghton left the Government

Changes on August 29th, 1967

First Secretary at D.E.A.	Peter Shore
Education and Science	Patrick Gordon Walker

Changes on August 29th, 1967—continued

Board of Trade	Anthony Crosland
Commonwealth Relations Office	George Thomson

Douglas Jay, Frank Longford, Herbert Bowden and Arthur Bottomley left the Cabinet. Michael Stewart remained First Secretary of State. The Ministry of Overseas Development became a non-Cabinet post.

Changes on November 30th, 1967

Chancellor of the Exchequer	Roy Jenkins
Home Secretary	James Callaghan

Changes on January 16th, 1968

Lord Privy Seal and Leader of the House of Lords	Edward Shackleton

Changes on March 16th, 1968

First Secretary of State at the Foreign Office	Michael Stewart

George Brown left the Government.

Changes on April 6th, 1968

First Secretary of State at the Department of Employment and Productivity	Barbara Castle
Agriculture, Fisheries and Food	Cledwyn Hughes
Power	Ray Gunter
Transport	Richard Marsh
Wales	George Thomas
Education and Science	Edward Short

Patrick Gordon Walker left the Cabinet. The Ministry of Labour was reorganized as the Ministry of Employment and Productivity.

Changes on July 1st, 1968

Power	Roy Mason

Ray Gunter resigned as Minister of Power and left the Government.

Changes on October 17th, 1968

The Foreign Office and the Commonwealth Relations Office were merged.

Biographical Notes

AGNEW, Sir Godfrey. A senior Clerk in the Privy Council Office 1946–51, he became Clerk of the Privy Council in 1953, and, in 1972, a Deputy Secretary in the Cabinet Office. He retired in 1974.

BALOGH, Thomas. A Fellow of Balliol College, Oxford, 1945–73 (now an Emeritus Fellow) and 1960–73, Reader in Economics at Oxford University. From 1964 to 1967 he acted as Economic Adviser to the Cabinet and, in 1968, as the Prime Minister's own consultant. He became a Life Peer on leaving No. 10 in 1968. From 1974–5 he served as Minister of State at the Department of Energy and in 1975 he became Deputy Chairman-Designate of the British National Oil Corporation.

BARKER, Sara. Dame Sara Barker (DBE 1970) was Women's Organizer of the Yorkshire Labour Party 1942–52, when she became Assistant National Agent to the Labour Party. She was National Agent 1962–9, with her headquarters in Transport House. She died in September 1973.

BENN, Anthony Wedgwood. Labour M.P. for Bristol South-East 1950–60 and since August 1963, after a successful battle to disclaim the title inherited from his father, Viscount Stansgate. He was Postmaster-General 1964–6 and Minister of Technology from 1966 until Labour's defeat in 1970. In 1974 he became Secretary of State for Industry and in 1975 Secretary of State for Energy.

BERRY, Pamela. Daughter of the Earl of Birkenhead, and wife of Michael Berry, now Lord Hartwell, chairman and editor-in-chief of the *Daily Telegraph* and the *Sunday Telegraph*. She has been President of the Incorporated Society of Fashion Designers since 1954.

BOTTOMLEY, Arthur. Labour M.P. for Rochester and Chatham 1945–59 and for Middlesbrough since 1962. He had been a Parliamentary Under-Secretary for the Dominions 1946–7 and Secretary for Overseas Trade 1947–51. He was Secretary of State for Commonwealth Affairs 1964–6 and Minister of Overseas Development 1966–7.

BOWDEN, Herbert. Labour M.P. for Leicester from 1945 until 1967, when he entered the House of Lords as Lord Aylestone. He had served as P.P.S. to the Postmaster-General 1947–9 and in the Whips' Office 1949–51 in the post-war Labour Government; and as an Opposition Whip and eventually as Opposition Chief Whip, between 1951 and 1964. He was Lord President and Leader of the House 1964–6 and Secretary of State for Commonwealth Affairs 1966–70. From 1967 until 1975 he was Chairman of the Independent Television Authority.

BROWN, George. Labour M.P. for Belper 1945–70; in 1970 he became a Life Peer, taking the title of Lord George-Brown. He had served as P.P.S. to the Minister of Labour, and then to the Chancellor of the Exchequer in 1947, and as Parliamentary Secretary at the Ministry of Agriculture 1947–51 and at the Ministry of Works in 1951. In 1963 he was an unsuccessful candidate for the leadership of the Labour Party. In 1964 he became First Secretary of State at the D.E.A., in 1966 he became Foreign Secretary. He remained deputy leader of the Labour Party after his resignation in 1968 until 1970 and his elevation to the Upper House. He resigned his membership of the Labour Party in 1976.

CALLAGHAN, James. Labour M.P. for Cardiff since 1945, and a member of the Labour Party N.E.C. 1957–67; in 1967 he became Treasurer of the Party. From 1955 to 1964 he was consultant to the Police Federation. He had been Parliamentary Secretary at the Ministry of Transport 1947–50 and at the Admiralty 1950–51, in the post-war Labour Government. In 1964 he became Chancellor of the Exchequer and in 1967 Home Secretary, holding that office until 1970. In 1974 he became Foreign Secretary, succeeding Harold Wilson as Prime Minister in April 1976.

CARRINGTON, Peter. Lord Carrington succeeded to his father's title in 1938 and held various offices in post-war Conservative Governments. He was High Commissioner in Australia 1956–9, First Lord of the Admiralty 1959–63 and Leader of the House of Lords 1963–4. He was Opposition Leader in the Lords 1964–70, Secretary of State for Defence 1970–74 and Secretary for Energy 1974. From 1972–4 he was Chairman of the Conservative Party Organization and since 1974 he has been Opposition Leader in the Lords.

CASTLE, Mrs Barbara. Labour M.P. for Blackburn since 1945 and a member of the Labour Party N.E.C. since 1950. She was chairman of the Labour Party 1958–9. In 1964 she became Minister of Overseas Development, and in 1965 Minister of Transport, an office she held until 1968, when she became First Secretary of State and Secretary of State at the newly created Department of Employment and Productivity, holding that office until Labour's defeat in 1970. From 1974 to 1976 she was Secretary of State for Social Services. Her husband, a former journalist and G.L.C. alderman, became a Life Peer in 1974.

CHALFONT, Alun. Lord Chalfont (before he received a Life Peerage in 1964, Alun Gwynne-Jones) had been a defence correspondent of *The Times* since 1961. He served as Minister of State at the Foreign Office, with special responsibility for Disarmament, from 1964 to 1970.

CLARK, Percy. He became Publications Officer of the Labour Party in 1947, and in 1957 Regional Publicity Director. He was Deputy Director of Information 1960–64 and since 1964 has been Director of Information.

COMPTON, Edmund. Sir Edmund Compton (K.C.B. 1965) joined the Civil Service in 1929 and spent the greater part of his career in the Treasury, becoming Third Secretary in 1949. From 1958 until 1966 he served as Comptroller and Auditor-General, the senior official with responsibility for auditing all departmental accounts. In 1967 he became the first Parliamentary Commissioner for Administration (Ombudsman), serving until 1971. From 1969 to 1971 he was also Parliamentary Commissioner for Northern Ireland. Since 1971 he has been Chairman of the Local Government Boundary Commission.

COUSINS, Frank. A member of the General Council of the T.U.C., and General Secretary of the T.G.W.U. 1956–69, he obtained leave of absence from his union to become M.P. for Nuneaton in January 1965, in order to serve in the Cabinet as Minister of Technology. He returned to the T.G.W.U. in December 1966. He served as Chairman of the Community Relations Commission from 1968 to 1970.

CROSLAND, Anthony. Labour M.P. for South Gloucestershire 1950–55 and for Grimsby since 1959. He was Minister of State for Economic Affairs 1964–5, Secretary of State for Education and Science 1965–7, President of the Board of Trade 1967–9 and then Secretary of State for Local Government and Regional Planning until 1970. In 1974 he became Secretary of State for the Environment and in 1976 Foreign Secretary. He is the author of various books on the theory of socialism, notably *The Future of Socialism* (London: Cape, 1956) and *Socialism Now* (London: Cape, 1974). His wife, Susan Barnes, a journalist and author, gives her picture of Crossman in *Behind the Image: Profiles* (London: Cape, 1974).

DALYELL, Tam. Labour M.P. for West Lothian since 1962. He was a lodger in Crossman's London house and one of the diarist's closest and most loyal friends, serving as his P.P.S. from 1964–70, with only one short interval. He was a member of the House of Commons Public Accounts Committee 1962–6 and of the Select Committee on Science and Technology 1967–9.

DAVENPORT, Nicholas. A civil servant during the war, he then went into the City and worked with J. M. Keynes, becoming deputy chairman of the Mutual Life Assurance Society in 1960. Since 1923 he had also acted as financial correspondent of the *Nation* and then of the *New Statesman*, writing the City column from 1930 until 1953, when he became the *Spectator*'s weekly financial correspondent. He served on the National Investment Council from January 1946 until its abolition in October 1947, and, briefly, on the National Film Finance Corporation established by Harold Wilson. His wife, Olga, was a ballet dancer and actress and is a professional painter.

DIAMOND, John. Labour M.P. for Blackley, Manchester, 1945–51 and for

Gloucester from 1957 to 1970, when he was made a Life Peer. He was Chief Secretary to the Treasury from 1964 until 1970. Since 1974 he has been Chairman of the Royal Commission on the Distribution of Income and Wealth.

DOUGLAS-HOME, Alec. Conservative M.P. for Lanark from 1931 to 1951, when he succeeded his father, the 13th Earl of Home. He had held various offices before and after the war, and had been Leader of the House of Lords 1957–60 and Foreign Secretary 1960–63. In October 1963 he disclaimed his peerage and was thus enabled to become Prime Minister (being elected M.P. for Kinross and West Perthshire in November 1963). His ministry was brief, and from October 1964 to July 1965 he was leader of the Opposition. When the Conservatives came back to office in 1970 he returned to the Foreign Office as Secretary of State, serving until his retirement from the Commons and return to the House of Lords as a Life Peer, Baron Home of the Hirsel, in 1974.

EDELMAN, Maurice. Labour M.P. for Coventry North from 1950 until his death in 1975. Author of several political novels, of which the best known are probably *Who Goes Home?* (London: Hamish Hamilton, 1953) and *Disraeli in Love* (London: Collins, 1972).

FOOT, Michael. Labour M.P. for Ebbw Vale since November 1960; he had represented Devonport between 1945 and 1955. A member of the Tribune Group, he was editor of *Tribune* 1948–52 and 1955–60. In 1974 he became Secretary of State for Employment and in 1976 Lord President of the Council and Leader of the House of Commons. Author of the biography *Aneurin Bevan* (Vol. 1, 1897–1945, London: MacGibbon and Kee, 1962; Vol. 2, 1945–69, London: Davis-Poynter, 1973).

GARDINER, Gerald. Lord Gardiner was called to the Bar in 1925 and took silk in 1948. He was an L.C.C. Alderman 1961–3 and a member of the Lord Chancellor's Law Reform Committee 1952–63. In 1963 he became a Life Peer and, from 1964 to 1970, served as Lord Chancellor. Since 1973 he has been Chancellor of the Open University.

GOODMAN, Arnold. Lord Goodman, who became a Life Peer in 1965, is the senior partner of Goodman, Derrick and Co., Solicitors, and since 1967 has been chairman of the Observer Trust. He was chairman of the Arts Council of Great Britain 1965–72 and from 1970 to 1976 he was Chairman of the Newspaper Publishers' Association. Since 1972 he has been a director of the Royal Opera House, Covent Garden, and President of the Theatres Advisory Council and, since 1973, Chairman of the Housing Corporation and of the National Building Agency. Since August 1976 he has been Master of University College, Oxford.

GORDON WALKER, Patrick. Labour M.P. for Smethwick 1945–60 and for Leyton from 1966 to 1974, when he became a Life Peer. He had been Herbert Morrison's P.P.S. in 1946, and had served as Parliamentary Under-Secretary of State at the Commonwealth Relations Office 1947–50 and as Secretary of State 1950–51. In October 1964 he became Foreign Secretary but was obliged to relinquish that office in January 1965, when he failed to win a by-election at Leyton. In 1967 he became Minister without Portfolio and, from 1967–8, Secretary of State for Education and Science.

GREENE, Hugh. Sir Hugh Greene joined the B.B.C. in 1940 as Head of the German Service. He was Director of News and Current Affairs 1958–9, Director-General 1960–69 and a Governor 1969–71. Since 1969 he has been Chairman of the Bodley Head. During the war he and Crossman had worked together on propaganda methods and psychological warfare.

GREENWOOD, Anthony. Labour M.P. for Heywood and Radcliffe 1946–50 and for Rossendale from 1950 until he became a Life Peer in 1970. He was a member of the N.E.C. of the Labour Party 1954–70. He was Secretary of State for Colonial Affairs 1964–5, Minister for Overseas Development 1965–6 and, succeeding Crossman, Minister of Housing and Local Government 1966–70. Since 1970 he has been a member of the Commonwealth Development Corporation.

GUNTER, Ray. Labour M.P. for Essex South-East 1945–50, for Doncaster 1950–51 and for Southwark 1959–72. He was a member of the N.E.C. 1955–66. In 1964 he became Minister of Labour and in 1968 Minister of Power but, after only two months in that office, he resigned.

HARRIS, John. Former Research Officer for the Labour Party and secretary to Hugh Gaitskell. He was the Party's Press Officer 1962–4 and after Labour's victory he became an official adviser to Michael Stewart and Roy Jenkins. In 1974 he became a Life Peer and a Minister of State at the Home Office.

HART, Mrs Judith. Labour M.P. for Lanark since 1959 and a member of the N.E.C. of the Labour Party since 1969. She was Joint Parliamentary Under-Secretary of State for Scotland 1964–6, Minister of State at the Commonwealth Office 1966–7 and Minister of Social Security 1967–8. She became a Cabinet Minister in 1968, as Paymaster-General. From 1969–70 she was Minister of Overseas Development, a post which she took once more after Labour's return to office in February 1974, but resigned in 1976.

HEALEY, Denis. Labour M.P. for Leeds since 1952 and from 1945 to 1952 Secretary of the International Department of the Labour Party. He was Secretary of State for Defence 1964–70 and in 1974 became Chancellor of the Exchequer.

HEATH, Edward. Conservative M.P. for Bexley since 1950. From February 1951 to October 1959 he served in the Whips' Office, becoming Government Chief Whip in December 1955. He was Minister of Labour 1959–60, and Lord Privy Seal with Foreign Office responsibilities, which included the direction of the British attempt to join the E.E.C., 1960–63. He was Secretary of State for Industry and Trade 1963–4. He was elected leader of the Conservative Party in 1965 and led the Opposition until 1970, when he became Prime Minister. From 1974–5 he was Leader of the Opposition until, in 1975, the Conservatives elected a new leader and he returned to the back benches.

HEFFER, Eric. A Liverpool councillor from 1960 to 1966 and Labour M.P. for the Walton Division of Liverpool since 1964. In 1974 he became Minister of State for Industry, resigning in 1975 on the issue of collective responsibility.

HERBISON, Miss Peggy. Labour M.P. for North Lanark 1945–70 and Joint Parliamentary Secretary at the Scottish Office 1950–51. Minister of Pensions and National Insurance 1964–6 and Minister of Social Security 1966–7. From 1970 to 1971 she was Lord High Commissioner to the General Assembly of the Church of Scotland.

HILL, Charles. A doctor and former Secretary of the British Medical Association (1945–50), he was M.P. for Luton from 1950 to 1963. He held various offices in post-war Conservative Administrations, including that of Postmaster-General, 1955–7, Chancellor of the Duchy of Lancaster, 1957–61, and Minister of Housing and Local Government, October 1961 to July 1962. In 1963 he became a Life Peer and from 1963 to 1967 he was Chairman of the Independent Television Authority. In 1967 he was appointed, not without controversy, Chairman of the Board of Governors of the B.B.C., where he remained until 1972.

HOGG, Quintin (now Lord Hailsham of St Marylebone). Conservative M.P. for Oxford City 1938–50, when he succeeded to his father's viscountcy. He was Joint Parliamentary Under-Secretary for Air in 1945, First Lord of the Admiralty 1956–7 and Minister of Education in 1957. From 1960 to 1963 he was Leader of the Opposition in the House of Lords and held various offices, including that of Secretary of State for Education and Science (April–October 1964). From September 1957 to October 1959 he was Chairman of the Conservative Party Organization. In 1963 he disclaimed his peerage and stood, unsuccessfully, as a candidate for the leadership of his party. He was elected M.P. for St Marylebone and represented that constituency from 1963 until he became Lord Chancellor and a Life Peer in 1970. When the Conservatives lost office in 1974 he retired to the Bar.

HOUGHTON, Douglas. Labour M.P. for Sowerby, Yorkshire, from 1949 to 1974. An L.C.C. alderman from 1947 to 1949, he became widely known as a broadcaster in the B.B.C.'s *Can I Help You?* programme, 1941–64. He was chairman of the Public Accounts Committee from 1963 to 1964, when he became Chancellor of the Duchy of Lancaster, moving in 1966 to become Minister without Portfolio, with special oversight of social security matters. In 1967 he left the Cabinet and replaced Emanuel Shinwell as Chairman of the Parliamentary Labour Party, a post he held until the general election of June 1970. He served in the same capacity from November 1970 until 1974, when he became a Life Peer.

HUGHES, Cledwyn. Labour M.P. for Anglesey since 1951. He was Minister of State for Commonwealth Relations 1964-6, Secretary of State for Wales 1966-8 and Minister of Agriculture 1968-70. Since 1974 he has been Chairman of the Parliamentary Labour Party.

JAY, Douglas. A former civil servant (1941-6) he has been Labour M.P. for North Battersea since July 1946. He was Economic Secretary to the Treasury 1947-50 and Financial Secretary to the Treasury 1950-51. He was President of the Board of Trade 1964-7 and, as a staunch anti-Marketeer, since 1970 he has been Chairman of the Common Market Safeguards Committee.

JELLICOE, George. He succeeded to his father's earldom in 1935 and from 1947 to 1961 served in the Foreign Office. He was a Lord-in-Waiting from 1961 to 1962 and Joint Parliamentary Secretary at the Ministry of Housing and Local Government. From 1962 to 1963 he was Minister of State at the Home Office, from 1963 to 1964 First Lord of the Admiralty and from April to October 1964 Minister of Defence for the Royal Navy. After the Conservatives left government in 1964 he became deputy leader of the Opposition in the House of Lords and, from 1968 to 1970, Chairman of the British Advisory Committee on Oil Pollution of the Sea. On the Conservatives' return to office he was appointed Lord Privy Seal and Minister with responsibility for the Civil Service Department. He held this office, together with the Leadership of the House of Lords, until his resignation in 1973. He has since been a director of S. G. Warburg and Co.

JENKINS, Roy. Labour M.P. for Central Southwark 1948-50 and for Stechford, Birmingham 1950-76. He was Minister of Aviation 1964-5, Home Secretary 1965-7, Chancellor of the Exchequer 1967-70 and deputy leader of the Labour Party 1970-72. In 1974 he became Home Secretary, resigning in 1976 to become President of the Commission of the E.E.C. An author and journalist, his biographies include *Sir Charles Dilke* (London: Collins, 1958) and *Asquith* (London: Collins, 1964).

JONES, Elwyn. Labour M.P. for West Ham 1945-74 and a former Recorder of Cardiff, 1960-64, and of Kingston-upon-Thames 1968-71. He was Labour's Attorney-General 1964-70 and, on the return of the Labour Government in 1974, became a Life Peer and, as Lord Elwyn-Jones, Lord Chancellor.

JONES, Jack. Member of the T.U.C. General Council since 1968, since 1967 deputy chairman of the National Ports Council, and since 1969, General Secretary of the T.G.W.U. During his early years in Coventry as an officer of the T.G.W.U. and as a city magistrate he and Crossman had come to know each other well.

KALDOR, Nicholas. Fellow of King's College, Cambridge, since 1949, Reader in Economics, University of Cambridge, 1964-5 and Professor of Economics since 1966. Economic Adviser to many foreign governments and Special Adviser to the Chancellor of the Exchequer from 1964 to 1968 and from 1974 to 1976. He became a Life Peer in 1974.

KAUFMAN, Gerald. Assistant General Secretary of the Fabian Society 1954–5, a member of the political staff of the *Daily Mirror* 1955–64 and from 1964 to 1965 political correspondent of the *New Statesman*. Between 1965 and 1970, as Parliamentary Press Liaison Officer for the Labour Party and a close associate of Harold Wilson, he had worked intimately with the Prime Minister at No. 10. Since 1970 he has been M.P. for Ardwick, Manchester, from 1974 to 1975 a Parliamentary Under-Secretary at the Department of the Environment and, since 1975, at the Department of Industry.

KING, Cecil Harmsworth. Chairman of Daily Mirror Newspapers Ltd and Sunday Pictorial Newspapers Ltd 1951–63, and of the International Publishing Corporation 1963–8. He was Chairman of the N.P.A. 1961–8. For his reflections on the period see *The Cecil King Diaries 1965–70* (London: Cape, 1972).

KING, Horace. Dr King was Labour M.P. for Southampton from 1950 to 1970. He was Chairman of Ways and Means and Deputy Speaker from 1964 to 1965, when he was elected Speaker of the House of Commons. In 1971 he became a Life Peer, with the title of Lord Maybray-King, and he now acts as a Deputy Speaker of the House of Lords.

LEE, Fred. Labour M.P. for Hulme, Manchester, from 1945 to 1950 and from 1950 to 1974 for Newton, Lancashire. He had been P.P.S. to the Chancellor of the Exchequer and from 1950 to 1951, Parliamentary Secretary at the Ministry of Labour. He was Minister of Power 1964–6, Secretary of State for the Colonies 1966–7, and Chancellor of the Duchy of Lancaster 1967–9. He was made a Life Peer in 1974.

LEE, Jennie. Widow of Aneurin Bevan, and herself an M.P., representing North Lanark 1929–31 and Cannock 1945–70. She was a member of the N.E.C. of the Labour Party 1958–70. She was Parliamentary Secretary at the Ministry of Public Building and Works 1964–5 and Parliamentary Under-Secretary at the Department of Education and Science 1965–7. She became Minister of State with special responsibility for the Arts at that department in 1967 and held office until 1970, when she took a Life Peerage and the title of Baroness Lee of Asheridge.

LEVER, Harold. Labour M.P. for Manchester Exchange 1945–50, for Manchester Cheetham 1950–74 and, since 1974, for Manchester Central. He was Parliamentary Under-Secretary at the Department of Economic Affairs in 1967, Financial Secretary to the Treasury 1967–9, and Paymaster-General 1969–70. He has been chairman of the Public Accounts Committee, and in 1974 he became Chancellor of the Duchy of Lancaster.

LLOYD, Selwyn. Conservative M.P. for Wirral, Cheshire, from 1945 to 1976. He was a Minister of State at the Foreign Office 1951–4, Minister of Supply October 1954–April 1955, Minister of Defence April–December

1955, Foreign Secretary 1955–60 and Chancellor of the Exchequer 1960–62. He was Lord Privy Seal and Leader of the House of Commons 1963–4, and was elected Speaker of the House of Commons in 1970. He retired in February 1976 and became a Life Peer, taking the title of Lord Selwyn-Lloyd.

LLOYD-HUGHES, Trevor. Sir Trevor Lloyd-Hughes (K.C.B. 1970) was formerly a journalist on the *Liverpool Daily Post* and the *Liverpool Echo*. He became Press Secretary to the Prime Minister in 1964 and from 1969 to 1970 was Chief Information Adviser to the Government.

LONGFORD, Frank. An unsuccessful Labour candidate for Oxford City in the 1938 by-election, he was created Baron Pakenham in 1945. He was a Parliamentary Under-Secretary of State at the War Office 1946–7, Chancellor of the Duchy of Lancaster 1947–8, Minister of Civil Aviation 1948–51 and First Lord of the Admiralty May–October 1951. In 1964 he became Lord Privy Seal, in 1965 Secretary of State for the Colonies and in 1966 Lord Privy Seal once more, an office he held until 1968. From 1964 to 1968 he was Leader of the House of Lords. On the death of his brother in 1961 he succeeded to the earldom of Longford, as the seventh Earl.

MACDERMOT, Niall. Labour M.P. for Lewisham North from February 1957 to 1959 and for Derby from 1962 to 1970. He was Financial Secretary to the Treasury 1964–7 and Minister of State at the Ministry of Housing and Local Government 1967–8. Since 1970 he has been Secretary-General, International Commission of Jurists.

MACDOUGALL, Sir Donald. Chief Adviser in the Prime Minister's Statistical Branch 1951–3, Economic Director of N.E.D.C. 1962–4, Director-General at the D.E.A. 1964–8, Chief Economic Adviser to the Treasury and Head of the Government Economic Service 1969–73, and since 1973 Chief Economic Adviser to the C.B.I.

MACLEOD, Iain. Conservative M.P. for Enfield from 1950 until his sudden death in July 1970. He joined the Conservative Research Department in 1948. He was Minister of Health 1952–5, Minister of Labour 1955–9, Secretary of State for the Colonies 1959–61 and Chancellor of the Duchy of Lancaster and Leader of the House of Commons 1961–3. From 1961 to 1963 he was Joint Chairman and Chairman of the Conservative Party Organization, and when the Conservatives returned to Government in 1970 he served as Chancellor of the Exchequer for one month.

MARSH, Richard. Labour M.P. for Greenwich 1959–71. He was Parliamentary Secretary at the Ministry of Labour 1964–5 and at the Ministry of Technology 1965–6, Minister of Power 1966–8 and Minister of Transport from 1968 until his resignation in 1969. From 1971 to 1976 he was Chairman of British Rail. He was knighted in 1976. He succeeded Lord Goodman as Chairman of the Newspaper Publishers' Association.

MAUDLING, Reginald. Conservative M.P. for Barnet since 1950. He was Parliamentary Secretary to the Minister of Civil Aviation 1952, Economic

Secretary to the Treasury 1955–7, Paymaster-General 1957–9, President of the Board of Trade 1959–61, Secretary of State for the Colonies 1961–2 and Chancellor of the Exchequer 1962–4. He was an unsuccessful candidate for the leadership of the Conservative Party in 1965. In 1970 he became Home Secretary and resigned that office in 1972.

MAXWELL, Robert. Labour M.P. for Buckingham 1964–70. Founder, publisher, and, since 1946, Chairman of Pergamon Press.

MELLISH, Robert. Labour M.P. for Bermondsey since 1946. He became a Joint Parliamentary Secretary at the Ministry of Housing in 1964 and worked closely with Crossman. In 1967 he became Minister of Public Building and Works and from 1969 to 1970 he served as Government Chief Whip. He was Opposition Chief Whip until 1974, when he became Chief Whip once more, serving until 1976.

MIKARDO, Ian. Labour M.P. for Reading from 1945 to 1959 and for Poplar since 1964. He was Chairman of the Select Committee on the Nationalized Industries 1966–70, from 1950 a member of the N.E.C. and from February to November 1974 Chairman of the Parliamentary Labour Party.

MULLEY, Frederick. Labour M.P. for Sheffield since 1950. He was Minister of State for the Army 1964–5, Minister of Aviation 1965–7, Joint Minister of State at the Foreign and Commonwealth Office 1967–9 (Minister for Disarmament 1967–9) and Minister of Transport 1969–70. In 1974 he again became Minister of Transport and in 1975 Secretary of State at the Department of Education and Science.

ODGERS, Paul. An Under-Secretary at the Ministry of Education 1958–67 and in the Office of the First Secretary of State 1967–8. He joined Crossman in 1968 and moved with him in that year from the Lord President's Office to the D.H.S.S. In 1970 he went to the Cabinet Office, and from 1971 to 1975 he was a Deputy Secretary at the D.E.S.

PANNELL, Charles. A member of the Amalgamated Engineering Union since 1918, and M.P. for Leeds West from 1949 until 1974, when he became a Life Peer. He became Minister of Public Building and Works in 1964 and held that office until 1966.

PEART, Frederick. Labour M.P. for Workington, Cumberland, since 1945. A schoolmaster, he had been P.P.S. to the Minister of Agriculture in the post-war Labour Cabinets and from 1964 to 1968 was himself Minister of Agriculture. From 1968 to 1970 he was Leader of the House of Commons and Lord President of the Council and since 1974 he has been Minister of Agriculture.

PITT, Terry. He joined Transport House in 1962 and worked on the development of Labour's science policy, helping Crossman with the preparation of the document 'Labour and the Science Revolution' which Harold Wilson moved in his famous speech at the 1963 Scarborough Conference. He became Head of the Research Department in January 1965, when Peter

Shore went into Parliament. He left that post in 1974 and became Special Adviser to the Lord President of the Council.

POWELL, Enoch. Conservative M.P. for Wolverhampton from 1950 to February 1974 and United Ulster Unionist Coalition M.P. for South Down since October 1974. He was Parliamentary Secretary at the Ministry of Housing and Local Government 1955–7, Financial Secretary to the Treasury 1957–8 and Minister of Health 1960–63.

ROBINSON, Kenneth. Labour M.P. for St Pancras 1949–70. He served in the Whips' Office 1950–54. He was Minister of Health 1964–8 and Minister for Planning and Land, Ministry of Housing and Local Government 1968–9. On leaving Parliament he joined the British Steel Corporation and in 1975 became Chairman of the London Transport Executive.

RODGERS, William. Labour M.P. for Stockton-on-Tees since 1962. He was Parliamentary Under-Secretary of State at the D.E.A. 1964–7 and at the Foreign Office 1967–8. From 1967 to 1968 he was leader of the U.K. delegation to the Council of Europe. He was Minister of State at the Board of Trade 1968–9 and at the Treasury 1969–70. He has been Chairman of the Trade and Industry sub-committee of the Expenditure Committee since 1971 and since 1974 Minister of State for Defence.

ROSS, William. Labour M.P. for the Kilmarnock Division of Ayr since 1946. He was Secretary of State for Scotland 1964–70 and took up that office again in 1974.

SHACKLETON, Edward. Lord Shackleton, the son of the polar explorer and an explorer himself, was Labour M.P. for Preston from 1946 to 1955. He became a Life Peer in 1958 and in 1964 Minister of Defence for the R.A.F. He was Minister without Portfolio and Deputy Leader of the House of Lords 1967–8, Minister without Portfolio January–April 1968, Paymaster-General April–October 1968, and Leader of the House of Lords April 1968–70. He was Leader of the Opposition in the House of Lords 1970–74. Since 1975 he has been deputy chairman, Rio Tinto Zinc Corporation.

SHEPHERD, Malcolm. Lord Shepherd succeeded to his father's title in 1954. From 1964 to 1967 he served as Government Chief Whip in the House of Lords, from 1967 to 1970 as Minister of State at the Foreign and Commonwealth Office and from 1968 to 1970 as deputy leader of the House of Lords. He became Opposition Leader in 1970, and, in 1974, Leader of the House and Lord Privy Seal.

SHINWELL, Emanuel. Labour M.P. for Linlithgow 1922–4 and 1928–31, and for Durham (Seaham, and later, Easington Divisions) 1935–70. He had held various offices in earlier Labour Governments, including those of Minister of Fuel and Power (1945–7) and Minister of Defence (1950–51). He was Chairman of the Parliamentary Labour Party from October 1964 until his resignation in 1967. In 1970 he became a Life Peer.

SHORE, Peter. Labour M.P. for Stepney since 1964. He had been Head of the Research Department of the Labour Party from 1959 until 1964 and was

26

influential in Party councils. He was P.P.S. to the Prime Minister 1965–6, Joint Parliamentary Secretary at the Ministry of Technology 1966–7 and at the Department of Economic Affairs 1967. He was Secretary of State for Economic Affairs 1967–9, Minister without Portfolio 1969–70, and, in 1969, deputy leader of the House of Commons. In 1974 he became Secretary of State for Trade and in 1976 Secretary of State for the Environment.

SHORT, Edward. Labour M.P. for Newcastle-upon-Tyne Central since 1951. He served in the Opposition Whips' Office 1955–64. He was Government Chief Whip 1964–6, Paymaster-General 1966–8 and Secretary of State for Education and Science 1968–70. Since 1972 he has been deputy leader of the Labour Party and, from 1974 to 1976, Lord President of the Council.

SILKIN, John. Labour M.P. for Deptford since 1963. He was a Government Whip 1964–6, Deputy Chief Whip April–July 1966, Chief Whip 1966–9 and Deputy Leader of the House of Commons 1968–9. From 1969 to 1970 he was Minister of Public Building and Works and in 1974 he became Minister for Planning and Local Government.

SMITH, Ian. Prime Minister of Rhodesia from April 1964 until November 1965, when the unilateral declaration of independence was made and he became Leader of the rebel Rhodesia Front regime.

STEWART, Michael. Labour M.P. for Fulham since 1945. He had held various offices in the post-war Labour Governments, and was Shadow Minister of Housing while Labour was in Opposition. He was Secretary of State for Education and Science 1964–5, Foreign Secretary 1965–6, First Secretary at the D.E.A. 1966–7. He returned to the Foreign Secretaryship in 1968 and held that office until the 1970 general election.

STONEHOUSE, John. Labour and Co-operative M.P. for Wednesbury 1957–74, and for Walsall North since 1974. Director of the London Co-operative Society 1956–62, and its President 1962–4. He was Parliamentary Secretary at the Ministry of Aviation 1964–6, Parliamentary Under-Secretary of State for the Colonies 1966–7 and Minister of State at the Ministry of Technology 1967–8. He became Postmaster-General in 1968 and Minister of Posts and Telecommunications in 1969. In December 1974 he disappeared, mysteriously, and was found in Australia. On his reappearance in 1975 he returned to the House of Commons, but in 1976, resigned the Labour whip and joined the English Nationalist Party.

THOMSON, George. Labour M.P. for Dundee 1952–72. He was a Minister of State at the Foreign Office 1964–7, Secretary of State at the Commonwealth Office 1967–8, Minister without Portfolio 1968–9 and Chancellor of the Duchy of Lancaster, with responsibility for negotiations with the E.E.C., 1969–70. He was Shadow Minister of Defence after the 1970 general election until in 1973 he accepted Edward Heath's offer of appointment as one of Britain's two Commissioners to the E.E.C. in Brussels.

THORPE, Jeremy. Liberal M.P. for North Devon since 1959. He succeeded

Jo Grimond as Leader of the Liberal Party in 1967, and resigned in May 1976.

TREND, Burke. Sir Burke Trend (K.C.B. 1962) joined the civil service in 1936 and spent the greater part of his career in the Treasury, becoming Second Secretary in 1960. He was Deputy Secretary of the Cabinet 1956–9 and Secretary of the Cabinet 1963–73. He became Rector of Lincoln College, Oxford, in 1973, and a Life Peer in 1974.

TREVELYAN, Dennis. He joined the civil service in 1950 and in 1973 moved from the Home Office to the Treasury, where he remained for a year before becoming Secretary to the Parliamentary Under-Secretary of State at the Home Office. From 1964 to 1967 he was Principal Private Secretary to the Lord President, serving both Herbert Bowden and Richard Crossman. In 1973 he became Assistant Under-Secretary of State at the Northern Ireland Office.

WARREN, Freddie. Private Secretary to successive Chief Whips since 1961, and, as such, indispensable adviser to the Lord President on the subtleties of legislative timetabling and procedural arrangement. He was knighted in 1976.

WHITELAW, William. Conservative M.P. for Penrith, Cumberland, since 1955. He was P.P.S. to the Chancellor of the Exchequer 1957–8 and served in the Whips' Office 1959–62 and as Parliamentary Secretary at the Ministry of Labour 1962–4. He was Opposition Chief Whip 1964–70. He was Lord President of the Council and Leader of the House of Commons 1970–72 and Secretary of State for Northern Ireland 1972–3. In 1974 he was made a Companion of Honour for his services in Northern Ireland. From 1973–4 he was Secretary of State for Employment.

WIGG, George. Labour M.P. for Dudley 1945–67. He was Shinwell's P.P.S. in the post-war Labour Government and an Opposition Whip 1951–4. He was Paymaster-General 1964–7. He took a Life Peerage in 1967 and became Chairman of the Horserace Betting Levy Board (1967–72). His account of the 1964–70 Labour Government is to be found in *George Wigg* (London: Michael Joseph, 1972).

WILLIAMS, Leonard. An official of the National Union of Railwaymen and of the Labour Party since 1920. He was the Party's National Agent 1951–9 and its General Secretary 1962–8. Knighted in 1968, he became Governor-General of Mauritius in the same year. He died in December 1972.

WILLIAMS, Mrs Marcia. Mrs Williams worked for Morgan Phillips, the General Secretary of the Labour Party, at Transport House from 1955 to 1956, when she became Harold Wilson's secretary. She continued to serve him when he became Leader of the Labour Party in 1963 and, after the 1964 general election, she worked at No. 10 as his personal and political secretary, an experience she has described in *Inside No. 10* (London: Weidenfeld and Nicolson, 1972). In Opposition, from 1970 to 1974, and, after the 1974 general election, in Government, she remained one of Harold

Wilson's closest advisers. In 1974 she became a Life Peer, taking the title of Lady Falkender.

WILLIAMS, Mrs Shirley. Labour M.P. for Hitchin since 1964. She was P.P.S. to the Minister of Health 1964–6, and Parliamentary Secretary at the Ministry of Labour 1966–7, Minister of State at the Department of Education and Science 1967–9 and at the Home Office 1969–70. She was Opposition spokesman on Social Services 1970–71 and on Home Affairs from 1971 to 1974, when, on Labour's return to office, she became Secretary of State for Prices and Consumer Protection. In 1976 she was given the additional office of Paymaster-General.

WILSON, Harold. Labour M.P. for the Ormskirk Division of Lancashire 1945–50 and for Huyton since 1950. He joined the civil service in 1943 as an economist and statistician. From October 1947 until his resignation in April 1951 he was President of the Board of Trade. From 1959 to 1963 he was chairman of the Public Accounts Committee. He was Chairman of the N.E.C. of the Labour Party 1961–2 and in 1963 he succeeded Hugh Gaitskell as Leader of the Party. When Labour won the 1964 general election he became Prime Minister and First Lord of the Treasury; after 1970 he continued to lead the party in Opposition, becoming Prime Minister once more in February 1974. He held that office until his resignation and return to the back benches, as Sir Harold Wilson, in April 1976. He published *The Labour Government 1964–1970, A Personal Record* (London: Michael Joseph and Weidenfeld and Nicolson, 1971).